MasteringBIOLOGY

Your gateway to the most widely-used online biology self-study materials and more...

With your purchase of a new copy of Campbell/Reece *Biology*, Eighth Edition, you should have received a **Student Access Kit for MasteringBiology™**. This kit contains instructions and a code for accessing this dynamic website. Your Student Access Kit looks like this →

DON'T THROW YOUR ACCESS KIT AWAY!

If you did not purchase a new textbook or cannot locate the Student Access Kit, you can purchase your subscription to MasteringBiology™ online with a major credit card by selecting Buy Now. To do so, go to www.masteringbio.com. Identify the exact title and edition of your textbook when prompted.

INSTRUCTORS:

Look for your "Instructor Access Kit" that you received with your book. Contact your Pearson Benjamin Cummings sales representative if you need assistance.

What is MasteringBiology™?

MasteringBiology™ offers two valuable learning systems:

1. The **Study Area** for studying on your own or in a study group
2. **MasteringBiology™ Assignments** that your instructor may require

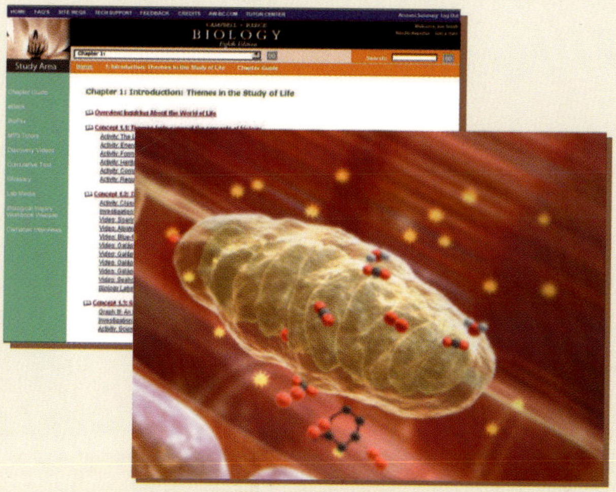

The **Study Area** provides state-of-the-art BioFlix 3-D Animations and student tools plus MP3 Tutors, Discovery Videos, Activities, Investigations, Practice Tests, an eBook, and much more (see other side).

MasteringBiology™ Assignments may include Tutorials, Multiple Choice Chapter Quizzes, and other Multiple Choice Questions required by your instructor. MasteringBiology™ tutorials coach you with feedback specific to your needs and offer hints when you get stuck, optimizing your study time and maximizing your learning.

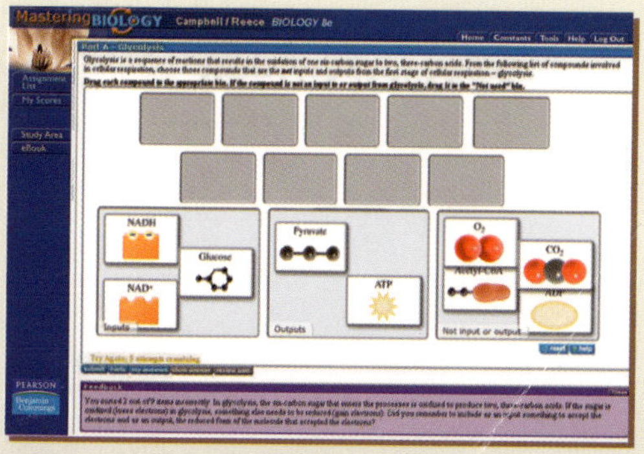

Features of the MasteringBiology™ Study Area for Campbell/Reece *Biology*, Eighth Edition

CHAPTER GUIDE

Review each chapter efficiently and effectively through a focus on Key Concepts. BioFlix 3-D Animations and student tools, MP3 Tutors, Discovery Videos, Videos, Activities, Investigations, GraphIt!, and the eBook are linked directly to each numbered Key Concept in the chapter. The Chapter Guide also includes Quizzes, Practice Tests, Word Study Tools, and Art.

BIOFLIX 3-D ANIMATIONS AND STUDENT TOOLS

BioFlix cover the most challenging biology topics with 3-D, movie-quality animations and carefully constructed student tutorials, labeled slide shows, study sheets, and quizzes. Topics include tour of an animal cell, tour of a plant cell, cellular respiration, photosynthesis, mitosis, meiosis, protein synthesis, water transport in plants, how neurons work, and muscle contraction.

MP3 TUTORS

These MP3 Tutor sessions carefully walk you through "audio tours" of 22 key biological topics.

VIDEOS

29 video clips from the Discovery Channel™ cover topics such as fighting cancer, antibiotic resistance, and introduced species. An additional 153 videos bring biology to life, including 65 Cell Biology Videos.

ACTIVITIES

Explore 212 interactive activities, including animations, virtual labs, and review exercises.

INVESTIGATIONS

Experiment, investigate, and analyze 55 case studies that develop scientific thinking skills.

GRAPHIT!

Learn how to build and interpret graphs with 11 graphing exercises.

PRACTICE TESTS AND QUIZZES

Assess your understanding with three different multiple-choice quizzes for each chapter: an online version of the Self-Quiz from the book, an Activities Quiz with graphics that tests your understanding of the media Activities, and a Practice Test that covers the entire chapter. You may also take Practice Tests on several chapters at once by using the Cumulative Test feature. Tests and Quizzes are graded automatically, and most questions have hints and feedback for right and wrong answers.

ART

View and print art from the textbook, available with and without labels.

WORD STUDY TOOLS AND AUDIO GLOSSARY

Flashcards, Word Roots, Key Terms, and an Audio Glossary will help you improve your biology vocabulary. Includes new audio pronunciations for every term.

E-BOOK

Refer to a convenient online version of the book while you study.

CAMPBELL INTERVIEWS

Learn how scientists think and why they love what they do. Access 64 in-depth interviews with eminent biologists from all eight editions of Campbell/Reece, *Biology*.

BIOLOGY BIO 102

Neil A. Campbell • Jane B. Reece
Lisa A. Urry • Michael L. Cain
Steven A. Wasserman • Peter V. Minorsky
Robert B. Jackson

Northern Virginia Community College
Annandale Campus

Taken from:
Biology, Eighth Edition
by Neil A. Campbell, Jane B. Reece, Lisa A. Urry, Michael L. Cain,
Steven A. Wasserman, Peter V. Minorsky, and Robert B. Jackson

Custom Publishing

New York Boston San Francisco
London Toronto Sydney Tokyo Singapore Madrid
Mexico City Munich Paris Cape Town Hong Kong Montreal

Taken from:

Biology, Eighth Edition
by Neil A. Campbell, Jane B. Reece, Lisa A. Urry, Michael L. Cain, Steven A. Wasserman, Peter V. Minorsky, and Robert B. Jackson

Boston, Massachusetts 02116

This special edition published in cooperation with Pearson Custom Publishing.

Printed in the United States of America

10 9 8 7 6 5 4 3 2 1

2008140250

DM

Pearson
Custom Publishing
is a division of

PEARSON

www.pearsonhighered.com

ISBN 10: 0-555-00298-5
ISBN 13: 978-0-555-00298-8

Brief Contents

About the Authors

Neil A. Campbell

Neil Campbell combined the investigative nature of a research scientist with the soul of an experienced and caring teacher. He earned his M.A. in Zoology from UCLA and his Ph.D. in Plant Biology from the University of California, Riverside, where he received the Distinguished Alumnus Award in 2001. Neil published numerous research articles on desert and coastal plants and how the sensitive plant (*Mimosa*) and other legumes move their leaves. His 30 years of teaching in diverse environments included general biology courses at Cornell University, Pomona College, and San Bernardino Valley College, where he received the college's first Outstanding Professor Award in 1986. Neil was a visiting scholar in the Department of Botany and Plant Sciences at the University of California, Riverside. In addition to his authorship of this book, he coauthored *Biology: Concepts & Connections* and *Essential Biology* with Jane Reece. Neil died shortly after the initial planning of this revision, but his legacy continues in *BIOLOGY*, Eighth Edition.

Jane B. Reece

Lead author Jane Reece, Neil Campbell's longtime collaborator, has participated in every edition of *BIOLOGY*—first as an editor and contributor, then as an author. Her education includes an A.B. in Biology from Harvard University, an M.S. in Microbiology from Rutgers University, and a Ph.D. in Bacteriology from the University of California, Berkeley. Before migrating to California from the Northeast, she taught biology at Middlesex County College and Queensborough Community College. At UC Berkeley, and later as a postdoctoral fellow in genetics at Stanford University, her research focused on genetic recombination in bacteria. Besides her work on *BIOLOGY*, she has been a coauthor on *Biology: Concepts & Connections*, *Essential Biology*, and *The World of the Cell*.

For the Eighth Edition, Jane Reece is joined by five coauthors whose contributions reflect their biological expertise as scientific researchers and their teaching sensibilities gained from years of experience as instructors.

Lisa A. Urry

Units 1–3 (Chapters 2–21) and Chapter 47

Lisa Urry is a professor at Mills College in Oakland, California, and was a major contributor to the Seventh Edition of *BIOLOGY*. After graduating from Tufts University with a double major in Biology and French, Lisa completed her Ph.D. in Molecular and Developmental Biology at MIT. Following postdoctoral appointments at Harvard Medical School, Tufts University, and UC Berkeley, she began teaching at Mills College, where she currently holds the Letts-Villard Professorship and serves as Chair of the Biology Department. She has published research articles on various topics involving gene expression during embryonic development. Her current research interest is in sea urchin development. Lisa is also deeply committed to promoting opportunities for women in science education and research.

Michael L. Cain

Units 4 and 5 (Chapters 22–34)

Michael Cain is an ecologist and evolutionary biologist currently at Bowdoin College. Michael earned a joint degree in Biology and Math from Bowdoin College, an M.Sc. from Brown University, and a Ph.D. in Ecology and Evolutionary Biology from Cornell University. After postdoctoral work in plant ecology at the University of Connecticut and molecular genetics at Washington University in St. Louis, Michael went on to teach general biology, ecology, and evolution in a diverse range of settings, including Carleton College, New Mexico State University, and Rose-Hulman Institute of Technology in Indiana. Michael is the author of dozens of scientific papers on topics that include foraging behavior in insects and plants, long-distance seed dispersal, and speciation in crickets.

Steven A. Wasserman

Unit 7 (Chapters 40–46, 48–51)

Steve Wasserman is a professor at the University of California, San Diego. He earned his A.B. in Biology from Harvard University and his Ph.D. in Biological Sciences from MIT. Since a postdoctoral sojourn at UC Berkeley, where he investigated topological transformations of DNA, he has focused on regulatory pathway mechanisms. Working with the fruit fly *Drosophila*, he has contributed to the fields of embryogenesis, reproduction, and immunity. As a faculty member at the University of Texas Southwestern Medical Center and UC San Diego, he has taught genetics, development, and physiology to undergraduate, graduate, and medical students. He has also served as the research mentor for more than a dozen doctoral students and nearly 40 aspiring scientists at the undergraduate and high school level. Steve has been the recipient of distinguished scholar awards from both the Markey Charitable Trust and the David and Lucille Packard Foundation. He recently received the 2007 Academic Senate Distinguished Teaching Award for undergraduate teaching at UC San Diego.

Peter V. Minorsky

Unit 6 (Chapters 35–39)

Peter Minorsky revised Unit 6 for the Sixth and Seventh Editions of *BIOLOGY* and is a professor at Mercy College in New York, where he teaches evolution, ecology, botany, and introductory biology. He is also the science writer for the journal *Plant Physiology.* He received his B.A. in Biology from Vassar College and his Ph.D. in Plant Physiology from Cornell University. After a postdoctoral fellowship at the University of Wisconsin at Madison, Peter taught at Kenyon College, Union College, Western Connecticut State University, and Vassar College. He is an electrophysiologist who studies plant responses to stress and is currently exploring the possible effects of geomagnetism on plant growth.

Robert B. Jackson

Unit 8 (Chapters 52–56)

Rob Jackson is a professor of biology and Nicholas Chair of Environmental Sciences at Duke University. He directed Duke's Program in Ecology for many years and is currently the Vice President of Science for the Ecological Society of America. Rob holds a B.S. in Chemical Engineering from Rice University, as well as M.S. degrees in Ecology and Statistics and a Ph.D. in Ecology from Utah State University. He was a postdoctoral scientist in Stanford University's Biology Department and an Assistant Professor at the University of Texas, Austin. Rob has received numerous awards, including being honored at the White House with a Presidential Early Career Award in Science and Engineering from the National Science Foundation. He has published a trade book about the environment, *The Earth Remains Forever*, and a children's book of poetry about biology and animals called *Animal Mischief.* His second children's book, *Not Again*, will be published in 2008.

Preface

by Jane Reece

Much has changed in the world since the completion of the previous edition of *BIOLOGY*. In the realm of the biological sciences, the sequencing of the genomes of many more species has had deep ramifications in diverse areas of research, providing new insights, for example, into the evolutionary histories of numerous species. There has been an explosion of discovery about small RNA molecules and their roles in gene regulation and, at the other end of the size spectrum, our knowledge of Earth's biodiversity has expanded to encompass hundreds of new species, including parrots, monkeys, and orchids. And during the same period, biology has become more prominent than ever in our daily lives. The news is filled with stories about the promise of personalized medicine, novel cancer treatments, the possibility of producing biofuels with the help of genetic engineering, and the use of genetic profiling in solving crimes. Other news stories report climate change and ecological disasters, new drug-resistant strains of the pathogens that cause tuberculosis and parasitic infections, and famine—crises in the world around us that are posing new challenges for biologists and their allies in the other sciences. On a personal level, many colleagues and I have missed our inspiring friend, the late Neil Campbell, even as our commitment to leadership in biological education has grown. Our changing world needs biologists and a scientifically literate citizenry as never before, and we are committed to working toward that goal.

The New Coauthors

The Seventh Edition of *BIOLOGY* has been used by more students and instructors than any previous edition, remaining the most widely used college textbook in the sciences. With the privilege of sharing biology with so many students comes the responsibility of improving the book to serve the biology community even better. For that reason, Neil would have been delighted to see that this Eighth Edition fulfills our decade-long goal of expanding the author team. As biological discoveries proliferated, Neil and I realized that it was becoming harder than ever to make judicious decisions about which biological concepts are most important to develop in depth in an introductory textbook. We needed an author team with first-hand expertise across the biological spectrum, and we wanted coauthors who had honed their teaching values in the classroom. Our new coauthors—Lisa Urry, Michael Cain, Steve Wasserman, Peter Minorsky, and Rob Jackson—represent the highest standards of scientific scholarship across a broad range of disciplines and a deep commitment to undergraduate teaching. As described on pages iv–v, their scientific expertise ranges from molecules to ecosystems, and the schools where they teach range from small liberal arts colleges to large universities. In addition, both Lisa and Peter, as major contributors to earlier editions, had prior experience working on the book. The six of us have collaborated unusually closely, starting with book-wide planning meetings and continuing with frequent exchanges of questions and advice as we worked on our chapters. For each chapter, the revising author, editors, and I together formulated a detailed plan; subsequently, my own role involved commenting on early drafts and polishing the final version. Together, we have strived to extend the book's effectiveness for today's students and instructors, while maintaining its core values.

Our Core Values

What are the core values of this book? They start with getting the science right but then focus on helping students make sense of the science. Below I highlight our longtime values and describe how they've been put into practice in the Eighth Edition. You can see examples of many of the book's features in "To the Student: How to Use This Book" (pp. xiv-xix).

Accuracy and Currency

Getting the science right goes beyond making sure that the facts are accurate and up-to-date. Equally important is ensuring that our chapters reflect how scientists in the various subdisciplines of biology, from cell biology to ecology, currently view their area. Changes in the basic paradigms in various biological fields may call for us to reorganize some chapters and even create new ones in a new edition. For example, a new Chapter 21 discusses genomes and their evolution, and neurobiology is now covered in two chapters (Chapters 48 and 49), one focused on the cellular level and one at the organ system level. On pages ix–x, you can read more about new content and organizational improvements in the Eighth Edition.

A Framework of Key Concepts

The explosion of discoveries that makes biology so exciting today also threatens to suffocate students under an avalanche of information. Our primary pedagogical goal is to help students build a framework for learning biology by organizing each chapter around a small number of "Key Concepts," typically three to six. Each chapter begins with a list of its Key Concepts, a photograph that raises an intriguing question, and an Overview section that addresses the question and introduces the chapter. In the body of the chapter, each Key Concept serves as a numbered heading for a major section, in which the prose and pictures tell a more detailed story. At the end of each concept section, Concept Check questions enable students to assess their understanding of that concept before going on to the next concept. Students encounter the Key Concepts one last time when they reach the Chapter Review at the end of the chapter; the Summary of Key Concepts restates them and offers succinct explanatory support in both words and summary diagrams—new to this edition.

Active Learning

Increasingly, instructors tell us that they want their students to take a more active role in learning biology and to think about biological questions at a higher level. In the Eighth Edition, we provide several new ways for students to engage in active learning. First, the Concept Check questions in this edition build in difficulty, and each set now ends with a new "What if?" question that challenges students to integrate what they have learned and to think analytically. There are also questions accompanying selected figures within the text; each of these questions encourages students to delve into the figure and assess their understanding of its underlying ideas. And new "Draw It" exercises in every chapter ask students to put pencil to paper and draw a structure, annotate a figure, or graph experimental data. In addition to appearing regularly in the Chapter Review, a "Draw It" question may show up in a Concept Check or figure legend. Finally, the website that accompanies the book features two especially exciting new student tools, both of which focus on biology's toughest topics: MasteringBiology tutorials and BioFlix 3-D animations and tutorials. These are described on page xx.

Evolution and Other Unifying Themes

Together with *BIOLOGY*'s emphasis on key concepts, a thematic approach has always distinguished our book from an encyclopedia of biology. In the Eighth Edition, as previously, the central theme is evolution. Evolution unifies all of biology by accounting for both the unity and diversity of life and for the remarkable adaptations of organisms to their environments. The evolutionary theme is woven into every chapter of *BIOLOGY*, and Unit Four, Mechanisms of Evolution, has undergone a major revision. In Chapter 1, the other unifying themes have been streamlined from ten to six. And throughout the book, these themes are now referenced more explicitly in Key Concepts and subheadings. The former themes of "scientific inquiry" and "science, technology, and society" continue to be highlighted throughout the book, not as biological themes but as aspects of how science is done and the role of science in our lives.

Integration of Text and Illustrations

We regard text and illustrations as equal in importance, and starting with the First Edition, have always developed them simultaneously. The Eighth Edition has a number of new and improved figures, with the increased use of a more three-dimensional art style where it can enhance understanding of biological structure. At the same time, we avoid excess detail, which can obscure the main point of the figure. We have also improved our popular "Exploring" Figures and have added more (see the list on p. xii). Each of these large figures is a learning unit that brings together a set of related illustrations and the text that describes them. The Exploring Figures enable students to access dozens of complex topics very efficiently. They are core chapter content, not to be confused with some textbooks' "boxes," which have content peripheral to the flow of a chapter. Modern biology is challenging enough without diverting students' attention from a chapter's conceptual storyline.

Telling the Story at the Right Level

Whether in pictures or prose, we are committed to explaining biology at just the right level, and we've continued to use Neil's "quantum theory of teaching biology" as a touchstone. According to this idea, there are discrete levels at which a concept can be successfully explained, and a successful explanation must avoid getting "stuck between levels." Of course, most seasoned instructors have independently recognized this issue, also known as the "too much–too little" problem. The author team has drawn upon both scientific expertise and teaching experience to tell the story of biology at an appropriate level.

The Importance of Scientific Inquiry

Another of our core values is our belief in the importance of introducing students to the scientific way of thinking. In both lecture hall and laboratory, the authors and many of our colleagues are experimenting with diverse approaches for involving students in scientific inquiry, the process by which questions about nature are posed and explored. Special features in the textbook and in inquiry-based supplements make this edition of *BIOLOGY* more effective than ever in helping instructors convey the process of science in their courses.

Modeling Inquiry by Example

Every edition of *BIOLOGY* has traced the history of many research questions and scientific debates to help students appreciate not just "what we know," but "how we know," and "what we do not yet know." In *BIOLOGY*, Seventh Edition, we strengthened this aspect of the book by introducing "Inquiry" Figures, which showcase examples of experiments and field studies in a format that is consistent throughout the book. Each of these inquiry cases begins with a research question, followed by sections describing the experiment, results, and conclusion. Complementing the Inquiry Figures are "Research Method" Figures, which walk students through the techniques and tools of modern biology.

In the Eighth Edition, we have added many more Inquiry Figures; there is now at least one in every chapter and often more (see the list of Inquiry Figures on pp. xii–xiii). Each

Inquiry Figure now ends with a "What if?" question that requires students to demonstrate their understanding of the experiment described. We have also expanded the usefulness of the Inquiry Figures in another important way: In response to feedback from many instructors, we now cite the journal article that is the source of the research, providing a gateway to the primary literature. And the full papers for nine of the Inquiry Figures are reprinted in *Inquiry in Action: Interpreting Scientific Papers*, by Ruth Buskirk and Christopher Gillen. This new supplement, which can be ordered with the book for no additional charge, provides background information on how to read scientific papers plus specific questions that guide students through the nine featured articles.

Learning Inquiry by Practice

BIOLOGY, Eighth Edition, encourages students to practice thinking as scientists by tackling the "What if?" questions in the Concept Checks and Inquiry Figures (and occasional figure legends), as well as the "Scientific Inquiry" questions in the Chapter Review. Many of those in the Chapter Reviews ask students to analyze data or to design an experiment.

The supplements for the Eighth Edition build on the textbook to provide diverse opportunities for students to practice scientific inquiry in more depth. In addition to *Inquiry in Action: Interpreting Scientific Papers*, these include new editions of several other supplements that can be made available without cost. One is *Biological Inquiry: A Workbook of Investigative Cases*, Second Edition, by Margaret Waterman and Ethel Stanley; another is *Practicing Biology: A Student Workbook*, Third Edition, by Jean Heitz and Cynthia Giffen. You can find out more about these and other student supplements, both print and electronic, on pages xx–xxiii.

The BIOLOGY *Interviews: A Continuing Tradition*

Scientific inquiry is a social process catalyzed by communication among people who share a curiosity about nature. One of the many joys of authoring *BIOLOGY* is the privilege of interviewing some of the world's most influential biologists. Eight new interviews, one opening each unit of the textbook, introduce students to eight of the fascinating individuals who are driving progress in biology and connecting science to society. And in this edition, each unit of the text includes an Inquiry Figure based upon the research of the unit's interviewee; for example, see Inquiry Figure 2.2, on page 31. The interviewees for this edition are listed on page xi.

A Versatile Book

Our book is intended to serve students as a textbook in their general biology course and also later as a useful tool for review and reference. *BIOLOGY's* breadth, depth, and versatile organization enable the book to meet these dual goals. Even by limiting our scope to a few Key Concepts per chapter, *BIOLOGY* spans more biological territory than most introductory courses could or should attempt to cover. But given the great diversity of course syllabi, we have opted for a survey broad enough and deep enough to support each instructor's particular emphases. Students also seem to appreciate *BIOLOGY's* breadth and depth; in this era when students sell many of their textbooks back to the bookstore, more than 75% of students who have used *BIOLOGY* have kept it after their introductory course. In fact, we are delighted to receive mail from upper division students and graduate students, including medical students, expressing their appreciation for the long-term value of *BIOLOGY* as a general resource for their continuing education.

Just as we recognize that few courses will cover all 56 chapters of the textbook, we also understand that there is no single correct sequence of topics for a general biology course. Though a biology textbook's table of contents must be linear, biology itself is more like a web of related concepts without a fixed starting point or a prescribed path. Diverse courses can navigate this network of concepts starting with molecules and cells, or with evolution and the diversity of organisms, or with the big-picture ideas of ecology. We have built *BIOLOGY* to be versatile enough to support these different syllabi. The eight units of the book are largely self-contained, and, for most of the units, the chapters can be assigned in a different sequence without substantial loss of coherence. For example, instructors who integrate plant and animal physiology can merge chapters from Unit Six (Plant Form and Function) and Unit Seven (Animal Form and Function) to fit their courses. As another option, instructors who begin their course with ecology and continue with this top-down approach can assign Unit Eight (Ecology) right after Chapter 1, which introduces the unifying themes that provide students with a panoramic view of biology no matter what the topic order of the course syllabus.

Our Partnership with Instructors

A core value underlying all our work as authors is our belief in the importance of our partnership with instructors. Our primary way of serving instructors, of course, is providing a textbook that serves their students well. In addition, Benjamin Cummings makes available a wealth of instructor resources, in both print and electronic form (see pp. xx–xxiii). However, our relationship with instructors is not a one-way street. In our continuing efforts to improve the book and its supplements, we benefit tremendously from instructor feedback, not only in formal reviews from hundreds of scientists, but also via informal communication in person and by phone and e-mail. Neil Campbell built a vast network of colleagues throughout the world, and my new coauthors and I are fully committed to continuing that tradition.

The real test of any textbook is how well it helps instructors teach and students learn. We welcome comments from the students and professors who use *BIOLOGY*. Please address your suggestions to me:

Jane Reece, Pearson Benjamin Cummings
1301 Sansome Street, San Francisco, CA 94111
E-mail address: JaneReece@cal.berkeley.edu

New to the Eighth Edition

This section provides just a few highlights of new content and organizational improvements in *BIOLOGY*, Eighth Edition.

UNIT ONE The Chemistry of Life

New examples make basic chemistry more engaging for students, including an explanation of why steam can burn your skin in Chapter 3, the structures of the enantiomeric medications ibuprofen and albuterol in Chapter 4, and information on trans fats in Chapter 5. A new Inquiry Figure in Chapter 3 relates acidity to the emerging global problem of ocean acidification and its effects on coral reefs. The new Inquiry Figure in Chapter 5 shows Roger Kornberg's 3-D model of the RNA polymerase–DNA–RNA complex, work for which he won the 2006 Nobel Prize in Chemistry.

UNIT TWO The Cell

The judicious addition of recent research includes updated coverage of the sensory roles of primary cilia in Chapter 6, new developments regarding the membrane model in Chapter 7, and Paul Nurse's Nobel Prize–winning work on the cell cycle in Chapter 12. Chapter 11 now ends with a section on apoptosis, formerly in Chapter 21. New Inquiry Figures in this unit describe research on the role of microtubules in orienting cellulose in cell walls (Chapter 6), allosteric regulators of enzymes (Chapter 8), ATP synthase (Chapter 9), yeast cell signaling (Chapter 11), and a cell cycle regulator (Chapter 12).

UNIT THREE Genetics

Chapter 14 now includes "Tips for Genetics Problems." In Chapter 15, sex linkage is discussed directly after the discussion of the white-eye trait in Morgan's fruit flies. Chapter 16 covers replication of the bacterial chromosome and the structure of the eukaryotic chromosome (including a new Exploring Figure), formerly in Chapters 18 and 19, respectively.

We have reorganized Chapters 18–21 with the dual aims of telling a more coherent story and facilitating instructors' coverage of molecular genetics. Regulation of gene expression for both bacteria and eukaryotes is now consolidated in Chapter 18, which also includes a concept section on the crucial role of small RNAs in eukaryotes. We have streamlined material on the genetic basis of development (formerly in Chapter 21), and included it in Chapter 18, where it provides the ultimate example of gene regulation. Chapter 18 ends with a section on the molecular basis of cancer (previously in Chapter 19), to demonstrate what happens when gene regulation goes awry. Material on bacterial genetics in Seventh Edition Chapter 18 has been moved to other chapters within the genetics unit and to Chapter 27 on prokaryotes.

Chapter 19 now covers only viruses (from Seventh Edition Chapter 18), giving this chapter the flexibility to be assigned at any point in the course. Chapter 20 continues to cover biotechnology, but genome sequencing and analysis have been moved to Chapter 21. Cloning and stem cell production are now in Chapter 20. Newly explained techniques include the screening of an arrayed library, BAC clones, Northern blotting, RT-PCR, and *in situ* hybridization. The explosion of discoveries about genomes and their evolution led us to develop a chapter devoted to this subject, the new Chapter 21. This chapter consolidates new material with topics from Chapters 19–21 of the Seventh Edition.

UNIT FOUR Mechanisms of Evolution

Our revision emphasizes the centrality of evolution to biology and the breadth and depth of evidence for evolution. New examples and Inquiry Figures present data from field and laboratory studies and reveal how scientists study evolution.

Chapter 22 discusses how evolution can be viewed as both a pattern and a process, and introduces three key observations about life that are explained by evolution: the match between organisms and their environments (adaptation); the shared characteristics (unity) of life; and the diversity of life. This discussion serves as a conceptual anchor throughout Units Four and Five.

Chapters 24 and 25 have been significantly reorganized. Chapter 24 is now more tightly focused on speciation, enabling better pacing of this highly conceptual material. A new concept section explores hybrid zones as natural laboratories for studying speciation. Chapter 25 focuses on macroevolution, incorporating topics formerly in Chapters 24 and 26, such as the correlations between Earth's geologic and biological history. But the primary storyline concerns what we can learn from the fossil record about the evolutionary history of life. New text and figures explore how the rise and fall of dominant groups of organisms are linked to large-scale processes such as continental drift, mass extinctions, and adaptive radiations. Coverage of evo-devo has been expanded.

Phylogenetic trees are introduced earlier, in a new section on "tree-thinking" in Chapter 22. This material supports students in interpreting diagrams before studying phylogenetics more fully in Chapter 26.

UNIT FIVE The Evolutionary History of Biological Diversity

A new Chapter 26, Phylogeny and the Tree of Life, introduces the unit. Extending material formerly in Chapter 25, it describes how evolutionary trees are constructed and underscores their role as tools for understanding relationships, rather than facts to be memorized. New sections address common misconceptions in interpreting trees and help motivate students with practical applications.

Chapter 27 has a new concept section on prokaryotic reproduction, mutation, and recombination (formerly in Chapter 18). This unifies the coverage of prokaryote biology and supports students in developing a fuller understanding of these microorganisms.

Throughout Unit Five, along with updating the phylogenies of various groups of organisms—introducing, for example, the "supergroup" hypothesis of eukaryotic phylogeny (in Chapter 28) —we have found new opportunities to use the study of phylogeny as an opportunity to illustrate the iterative nature of the scientific process. We aim to help students stay focused on the big picture of why biologists study evolutionary relationships. Each chapter also now includes an Inquiry figure that models how researchers study organisms and their relationships. At the same time, in each chapter we highlight the key roles that various organisms play in the biosphere as well as their applied importance for humans.

UNIT SIX Plant Form and Function

Revisions to this unit draw more attention to the experimental basis of our understanding of plant biology. New examples include recent progress toward identifying the flowering "hormone" (Chapter 39). Featured in new Inquiry Figures are experiments demonstrating, for example, that trichomes affect insect feeding (Chapter 35) and that informational molecules transported through the symplast affect plant development (Chapter 36).

In Chapter 36, now titled Resource Acquisition and Transport in Vascular Plants, a new first concept section explores how architectural features of plants facilitate resource acquisition, helping students relate the transport of water and nutrients to what they learned in Chapter 35 about plant structure and growth. Another new concept section, on symplastic transport, discusses recent insights into changes in plasmodesmata shape and number and the transmission of electrical and molecular signals throughout the plant.

This unit now has more examples of practical applications of plant biotechnology. For instance, Chapter 37 discusses how genetic modification has increased the resistance of some plants to aluminum toxicity and has improved the flood tolerance of rice crops. Chapter 38 elaborates on the principles of plant breeding and incorporates a new section on genetic engineering of biofuels.

UNIT SEVEN Animal Form and Function

An evolutionary perspective more strongly pervades this unit, underscoring how environment and physical laws shape adaptations across animal groups. Each chapter now includes at least one Inquiry Figure; together, these figures highlight the wide range of methodologies used to study animal physiology, including several experiments using molecular biology techniques students studied earlier in the book.

Chapter 40 has been revised and reorganized to highlight functional relationships at all levels of organization in animal bodies; thermoregulation serves as an extended example throughout the chapter. Chapter 43, The Immune System, has been extensively revised. For instance, we now contrast recognition of pathogen class in innate immunity with antigen-specific recognition in adaptive immunity, helping overcome the common misconception that recognition is absent in innate immunity.

We have divided the former nervous system chapter into two, enabling us to better pace difficult material and highlight dynamic current research by focusing first on cellular processes in Chapter 48, and then on nervous system organization and function in Chapter 49. Chapter 50 rounds out the discussion of nervous system function by examining sensory and motor mechanisms. This sequence leads naturally into Chapter 51 on animal behavior (formerly in Unit Eight), which ties together aspects of genetics, natural selection, and physiology, and provides a bridge to the ecology unit.

UNIT EIGHT Ecology

This unit, which now includes Chapters 52-56, incorporates many new examples that demonstrate a range of methods and scales of study. For example, a new figure in Chapter 52 describes a large-scale field experiment in which researchers manipulated precipitation levels in forest plots, while new Research Method figures describe determining population size using the mark-recapture method (Chapter 53), using molecular tools to measure diversity of soil microorganisms (Chapter 54), and determining primary production with satellite data (Chapter 55). By building on earlier units, we hope to demonstrate how ecology represents a fitting capstone to the book.

We provide more microbial examples and more aquatic ones, from diverse locations around the globe. For instance, Chapter 52 now discusses the importance of salinity in determining the distribution of aquatic organisms, and Chapter 54's coverage of the intermediate disturbance hypothesis includes a new figure on a quantitative test of the hypothesis in New Zealand streams. The unit highlights the great relevance of ecology to society and to students' lives. A new concept section in Chapter 54, for example, discusses how community ecology helps us understand pathogen life cycles and control disease.

Interviews

Interview 28
Inquiry Figure 31

UNIT ONE

The Chemistry of Life

Deborah M. Gordon

Stanford University

Interview 92
Inquiry Figure 240

UNIT TWO

The Cell

Paul Nurse

Rockefeller University

Interview 246
Inquiry Figure 322

UNIT THREE

Genetics

Terry L. Orr-Weaver

Massachusetts Institute of Technology

Interview 450
Inquiry Figure 489

UNIT FOUR

Mechanisms of Evolution

Scott V. Edwards

Harvard University

Interview 534
Inquiry Figure 684

UNIT FIVE

The Evolutionary History of Biological Diversity

Sean B. Carroll

University of Wisconsin-Madison

Interview 736
Inquiry Figure 782

UNIT SIX

Plant Form and Function

Patricia Zambryski

University of California, Berkeley

Interview 850
Inquiry Figure 908

UNIT SEVEN

Animal Form and Function

Masashi Yanagisawa

University of Texas Southwestern Medical Center

Interview 1146
Inquiry Figure 1210

UNIT EIGHT

Ecology

Diana H. Wall

Colorado State University

Featured Figures

Exploring Figures

Inquiry Figures

*The original research paper and study questions are provided in *Inquiry in Action: Interpreting Scientific Papers.*

Research Method Figures

Focus on the Key Concepts

Each chapter is organized around a framework of 3 to 6 **Key Concepts** that will help you stay focused on the big picture and give you a context for the supporting details.

Before you begin reading the chapter, get oriented by reading the **list of Key Concepts**, which introduces the big ideas covered in the chapter.

Each **Key Concept** serves as the heading for a major section of the chapter.

25 The History of Life on Earth

▲ **Figure 25.1** **What does fossil evidence say about where these dinosaurs lived?**

KEY CONCEPTS

25.1 **Conditions on early Earth made the origin of life possible**
25.2 **The fossil record documents the history of life**
25.3 **Key events in life's history include the origins of single-celled and multicelled organisms and the colonization of land**
25.4 **The rise and fall of dominant groups reflect continental drift, mass extinctions, and adaptive radiations**
25.5 **Major changes in body form can result from changes in the sequences and regulation of developmental genes**
25.6 **Evolution is not goal oriented**

OVERVIEW

Lost Worlds

Visitors to Antarctica today encounter one of Earth's harshest, most barren environments. In this land of extreme cold where there is almost no liquid water, life is sparse and small—the largest fully terrestrial animal is a fly 5 mm long. But even as early antarctic explorers struggled to survive, some of them made an astonishing discovery: fossil evidence that life once thrived where it now barely exists. Fossils reveal that 500 million years ago, the ocean waters surrounding Antarctica were warm and teeming with tropical invertebrates. Later, the continent was covered in forests for hundreds of millions of years. At various times, a wide range of animals stalked through these forests, including 3-meter-tall predatory "terror birds" and giant dinosaurs such as the voracious *Cryolophosaurus* **(Figure 25.1)**, a 7-meter-long relative of *Tyrannosaurus rex*.

Fossils discovered in other parts of the world tell a similar, if not quite as surprising, story: Past organisms were very different from those now alive. The sweeping changes in life on Earth revealed by fossils illustrate **macroevolution**, the pattern of evolution over large time scales. Specific examples of macroevolutionary change include the origin of key biochemical processes such as photosynthesis, the emergence of the first terrestrial vertebrates, and the long-term impact of a mass extinction on the diversity of life.

▲ ***Cryolophosaurus* skull**

Taken together, such changes provide a grand view of the evolutionary history of life on Earth. We'll examine that history in this chapter, beginning with hypotheses regarding the origin of life. The origin of life is the most speculative topic of the entire unit, for no fossil evidence of that seminal episode exists. We will then turn to the fossil record and what it tells us about major events in the history of life, paying particular attention to factors that have helped to shape the rise and fall of different groups of organisms over time.

CONCEPT 25.1

Conditions on early Earth made the origin of life possible

The earliest evidence of life on Earth comes from fossils of microorganisms that are about 3.5 billion years old. But when and how did the first living cells appear? Observations and experiments in chemistry, geology, and physics have led scientists to propose one scenario that we'll examine here. They hypothesize that chemical and physical processes on early Earth, aided by the emerging force of

When you finish reading a concept section, check your understanding using the **Concept Check questions** at the end of the section. If you can answer them (see Appendix A to check your work), you're ready to move on.

Each set of Concept Check questions builds in difficulty, ending with a **"What if?" question** that asks you to apply what you've learned. Work through these questions on your own or in a study group—they're good practice for the kinds of questions you might be asked on an exam.

CONCEPT CHECK 53.1

1. One species of forest bird is highly territorial, while a second lives in flocks. Predict each species' likely pattern of dispersion, and explain.
2. **DRAW IT** Each female of a particular fish species produces millions of eggs per year. Draw and label the most likely survivorship curve for this species, and explain your choice.
3. **WHAT IF?** As noted in Figure 53.2, an important assumption of the mark-recapture method is that marked individuals have the same probability of being recaptured as unmarked individuals. Describe a situation where this assumption might not be valid, and explain how the estimate of population size would be affected.

For suggested answers, see Appendix A.

Practice thinking like a scientist

To succeed in biology, you need to do more than just memorize facts—you need to understand how scientists go about asking and investigating questions. In each chapter, you'll find one or more **Inquiry Figures** that highlight how researchers designed an experiment, interpreted their results, and drew conclusions.

Scientific Inquiry questions in the Chapter Review provide more opportunities to practice inquiry skills, including developing hypotheses, designing experiments, and analyzing real research data.

SCIENTIFIC INQUIRY

8. **DRAW IT** The nitrogen-fixing bacterium *Rhizobium* infects the roots of some plant species, forming a mutualism in which the bacterium provides the plant with nitrogen, and the plant provides the bacterium with carbohydrates. Scientists measured how well one such plant species (*Acacia irrorata*) grew when its roots were infected by six different *Rhizobium* strains.

(a) Graph the data. (b) Interpret your graph.

Rhizobium strain	Plant mass (g) after 12 weeks of growth
1	0.91
2	0.06
3	1.56
4	1.72
5	0.14
6	1.03

Source: J. J. Burdon, et al., Variation in the effectiveness of symbiotic associations between native rhizobia and temperate Australian *Acacia*: within species interactions, *Journal of Applied Ecology*, 36:398-408 (1999).

Note: In the absence of *Rhizobium*, after 12 weeks of growth, *Acacia* plants have a mass of about 0.1 g.

Some Inquiry Figures invite you to read and analyze the original research paper in its complete form. You can find the journal article, along with a worksheet guiding you through it, in the separate book ***Inquiry in Action: Interpreting Scientific Papers*** **(ISBN 978-0-321-53659-4 | 0-321-53659-2).**

After exploring the featured experiment, test your analytical skills by answering the **"What if?" question**. Suggested answers are provided in Appendix A to help you gauge your understanding.

▼ Figure 2.2 Inquiry

What creates "devil's gardens" in the rain forest?

EXPERIMENT Working under Deborah Gordon and with Michael Greene, graduate student Megan Frederickson sought the cause of "devil's gardens," stands of a single species of tree, *Duroia hirsuta*. One hypothesis was that ants living in these trees, *Myrmelachista schumanni*, produce a poisonous chemical that kills trees of other species; another was that the *Duroia* trees themselves kill competing trees, perhaps by means of a chemical.

To test these hypotheses, Frederickson did field experiments in Peru. Two saplings of a local nonhost tree species, *Cedrela odorata*, were planted inside each of ten devil's gardens. At the base of one, a sticky insect barrier was applied; the other was unprotected. Two more *Cedrela* saplings, with and without barriers, were planted about 50 meters outside each garden.

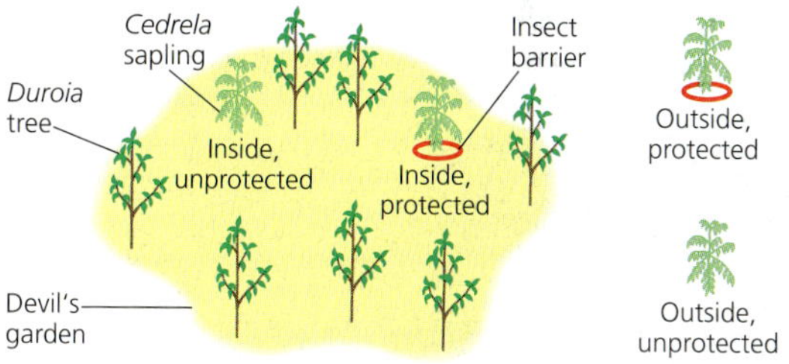

The researchers observed ant activity on the *Cedrela* leaves and measured areas of dead leaf tissue after one day. They also chemically analyzed contents of the ants' poison glands.

RESULTS The ants made injections from the tips of their abdomens into leaves of unprotected saplings in their gardens (see photo). Within one day, these leaves developed dead areas (see graph). The protected saplings were uninjured, as were the saplings planted outside the gardens. Formic acid was the only chemical detected in the poison glands of the ants.

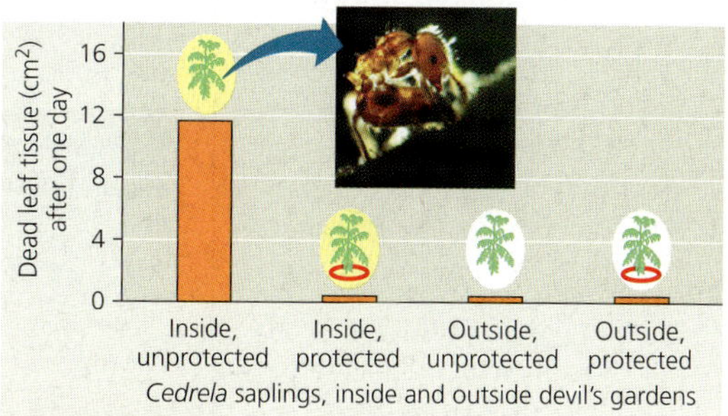

CONCLUSION Ants of the species *Myrmelachista schumanni* kill nonhost trees by injecting the leaves with formic acid, thus creating hospitable habitats (devil's gardens) for the ant colony.

SOURCE M. E. Frederickson, M. J. Greene, and D. M. Gordon, "Devil's gardens" bedevilled by ants, *Nature* 437:495–496 (2005).

Inquiry in Action Read and analyze the original paper in *Inquiry in Action: Interpreting Scientific Papers.*

WHAT IF? What would be the results if the unprotected saplings' inability to grow in the devil's gardens was caused by a chemical released by the *Duroia* trees rather than by the ants?

As you read the text, study the art and photos

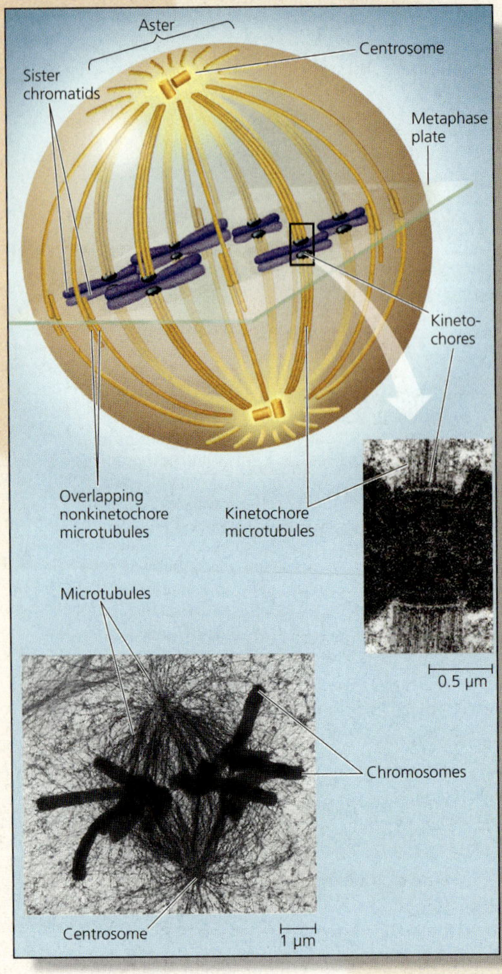

In selected illustrations, a **three-dimensional art style** helps you visualize biological structures.

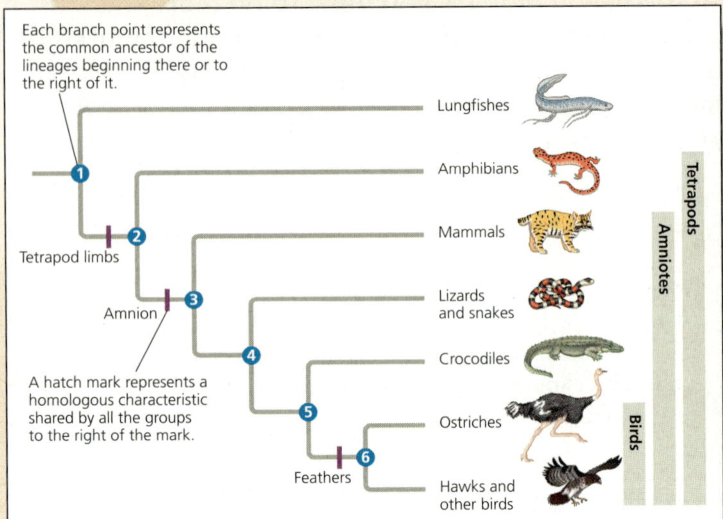

▲ **Figure 22.19 Tree thinking: information provided in an evolutionary tree.** This evolutionary tree for tetrapods and their closest living relatives, the lungfishes, is based on anatomical and DNA sequence data. The purple bars indicate the origin of three important homologies, each of which evolved only once. Birds are nested within and evolved from reptiles; hence, the group of organisms called "reptiles" technically includes birds.

? *Are crocodiles more closely related to lizards or birds? Explain your answer.*

The book's **phylogenetic trees** will prepare you to analyze the evolutionary tree diagrams you may encounter in the scientific literature. This figure walks you through some of the conventions of the phylogenetic trees you will see throughout the evolution and diversity units.

"Guided Tour" figures include concise explanations that walk you through complicated diagrams.

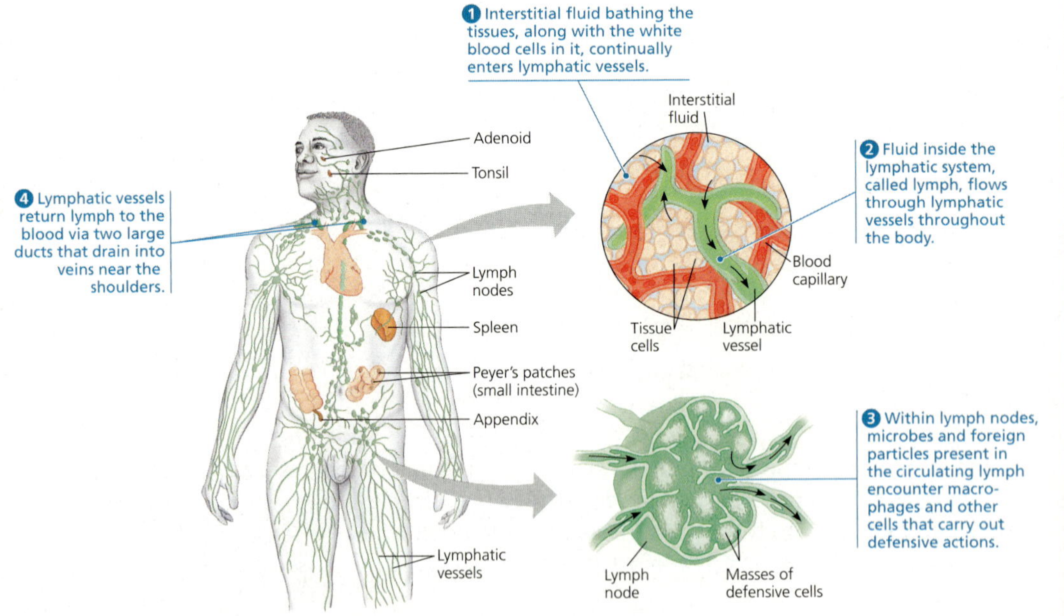

▲ **Figure 43.7 The human lymphatic system.** The lymphatic system consists of lymphatic vessels, through which lymph travels, and various structures that trap "foreign" molecules and particles. These structures include the adenoids, tonsils, lymph nodes, spleen, Peyer's patches, and appendix. Steps 1–4 trace the flow of lymph.

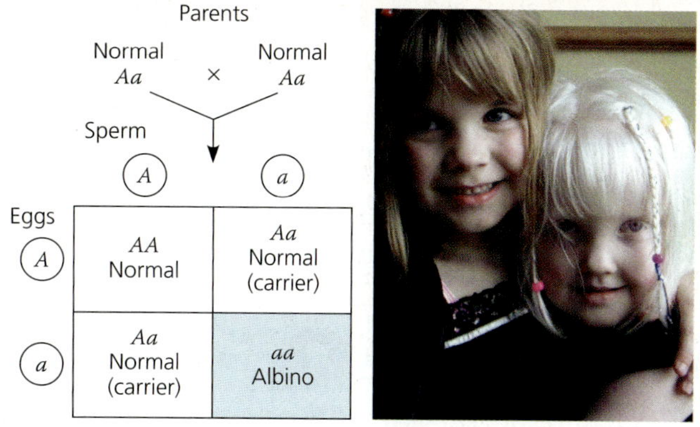

▲ **Figure 14.16 Albinism: a recessive trait.** One of the two sisters shown here has normal coloration; the other is albino. Most recessive homozygotes are born to parents who are carriers of the disorder but themselves have a normal phenotype, the case shown in the Punnett square.

? *What is the probability that the sister with normal coloration is a carrier of the albinism allele?*

Figure Legend questions prompt you to delve into a figure's content to make sure you understand it.

By integrating text and visuals, **Exploring Figures** help you learn more efficiently.

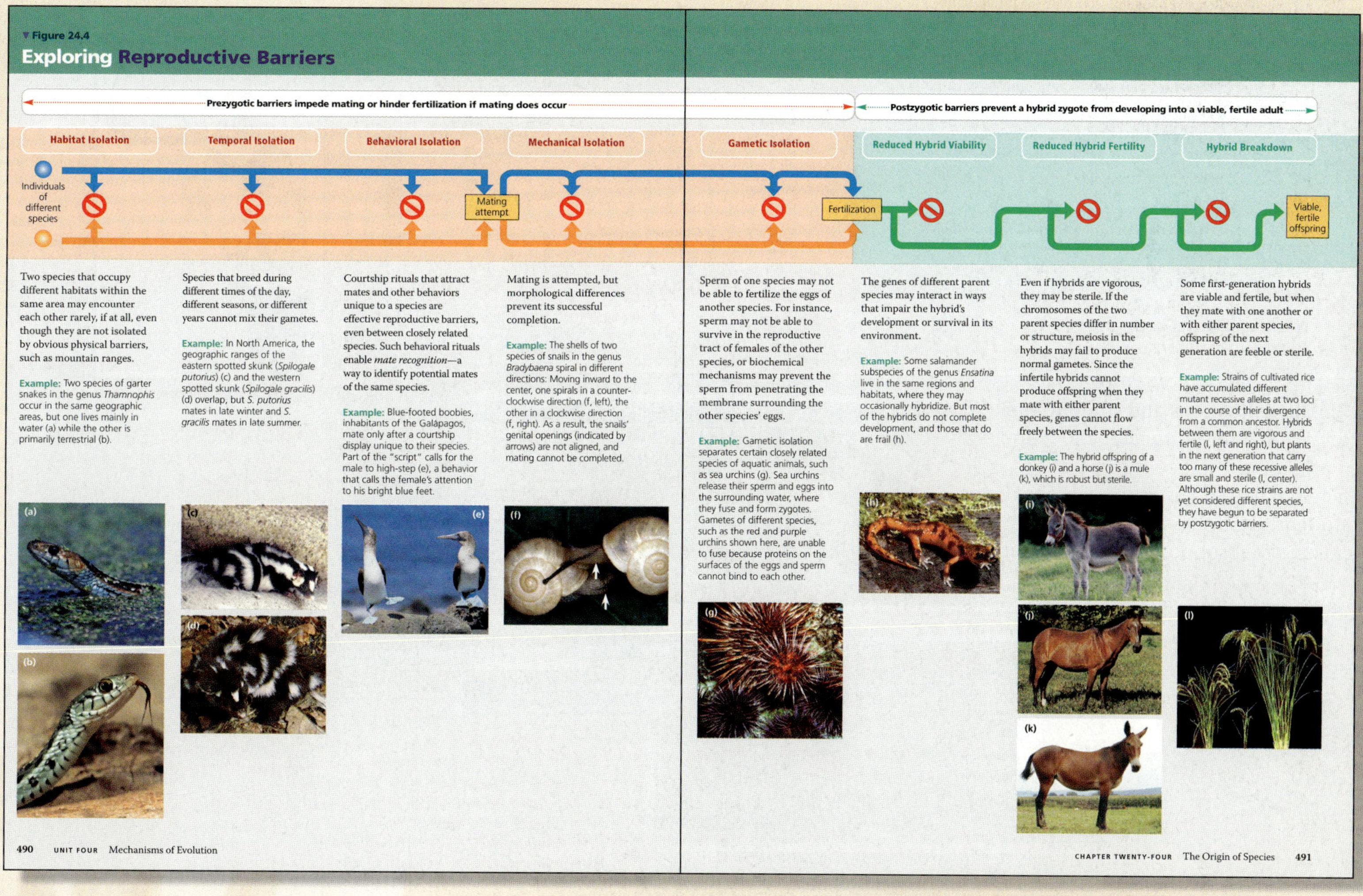
▼ Figure 24.4

Exploring Reproductive Barriers

Two species that occupy different habitats within the same area may encounter each other rarely, if at all, even though they are not isolated by obvious physical barriers, such as mountain ranges.

Example: Two species of garter snakes in the genus *Thamnophis* occur in the same geographic areas, but one lives mainly in water (a) while the other is primarily terrestrial (b).

Species that breed during different times of the day, different seasons, or different years cannot mix their gametes.

Example: In North America, the geographic ranges of the eastern spotted skunk (*Spilogale putorius*) (c) and the western spotted skunk (*Spilogale gracilis*) (d) overlap, but *S. putorius* mates in late winter and *S. gracilis* mates in late summer.

Courtship rituals that attract mates and other behaviors unique to a species are effective reproductive barriers, even between closely related species. Such behavioral rituals enable *mate recognition*—a way to identify potential mates of the same species.

Example: Blue-footed boobies, inhabitants of the Galápagos, mate only after a courtship display unique to their species. Part of the "script" calls for the male to high-step (e), a behavior that calls the female's attention to his bright blue feet.

Mating is attempted, but morphological differences prevent its successful completion.

Example: The shells of two species of snails in the genus *Bradybaena* spiral in different directions: Moving inward to the center, one spirals in a counter-clockwise direction (f, left), the other in a clockwise direction (f, right). As a result, the snails' genital openings (indicated by arrows) are not aligned, and mating cannot be completed.

Sperm of one species may not be able to fertilize the eggs of another species. For instance, sperm may not be able to survive in the reproductive tract of females of the other species, or biochemical mechanisms may prevent the sperm from penetrating the membrane surrounding the other species' eggs.

Example: Gametic isolation separates certain closely related species of aquatic animals, such as sea urchins (g). Sea urchins release their sperm and eggs into the surrounding water, where they fuse and form zygotes. Gametes of different species, such as the red and purple urchins shown here, are unable to fuse because proteins on the surfaces of the eggs and sperm cannot bind to each other.

The genes of different parent species may interact in ways that impair the hybrid's development or survival in its environment.

Example: Some salamander subspecies of the genus *Ensatina* live in the same regions and habitats, where they may occasionally hybridize. But most of the hybrids do not complete development, and those that do are frail (h).

Even if hybrids are vigorous, they may be sterile. If the chromosomes of the two parent species differ in number or structure, meiosis in the hybrids may fail to produce normal gametes. Since the infertile hybrids cannot produce offspring when they mate with either parent species, genes cannot flow freely between the species.

Example: The hybrid offspring of a donkey (i) and a horse (j) is a mule (k), which is robust but sterile.

Some first-generation hybrids are viable and fertile, but when they mate with one another or with either parent species, offspring of the next generation are feeble or sterile.

Example: Strains of cultivated rice have accumulated different mutant recessive alleles at two loci in the course of their divergence from a common ancestor. Hybrids between them are vigorous and fertile (l, left and right), but plants in the next generation that carry too many of these recessive alleles are small and sterile (l, center). Although these rice strains are not yet considered different species, they have begun to be separated by postzygotic barriers.

(a) (b) (c) (d) (e) (f) (g) (h) (i) (j) (k) (l)

490 UNIT FOUR Mechanisms of Evolution

CHAPTER TWENTY-FOUR The Origin of Species 491

Review what you've learned

At the end of the chapter, the **Chapter Review** focuses you again on the main points of the chapter, with a Summary of Key Concepts, practice questions, and references to other study tools.

Go to the **Study Area** at **www.masteringbio.com** for BioFlix 3-D animations and student tools plus MP3 Tutors, Discovery Channel Videos, Practice Tests, Activities, Investigations, an eBook, and more.

Chapter 9 Review

MB **MEDIA** Go to the Study Area at **www.masteringbio.com** for BioFlix 3-D Animations, MP3 Tutors, Videos, Practice Tests, an eBook, and more.

SUMMARY OF KEY CONCEPTS

CONCEPT 9.1

Catabolic pathways yield energy by oxidizing organic fuels (pp. 162–167)

- **Catabolic Pathways and Production of ATP** To keep working, a cell must regenerate the ATP it uses. The breakdown of glucose and other organic fuels is exergonic. Starting with glucose or another organic molecule and using O_2, aerobic respiration yields H_2O, CO_2, and energy in the form of ATP and heat. Cellular respiration includes both aerobic and anaerobic respiration; the latter uses another electron acceptor instead of O_2, but also yields ATP.
- **Redox Reactions: Oxidation and Reduction** The cell taps the energy stored in food molecules through redox reactions, in which one substance partially or totally shifts electrons to another. The substance receiving electrons is reduced; the substance losing electrons is oxidized. During cellular respiration, glucose ($C_6H_{12}O_6$) is oxidized to CO_2, and O_2 is reduced to H_2O. Electrons lose potential energy during their transfer from organic compounds to oxygen. Electrons from organic compounds are usually passed first to NAD^+, reducing it to NADH. NADH passes the electrons to an electron transport chain, which conducts them to O_2 in energy-releasing steps. The energy released is used to make ATP.
- **The Stages of Cellular Respiration: *A Preview*** Glycolysis and the citric acid cycle supply electrons (via NADH or $FADH_2$) to the electron transport chain, which drives oxidative phosphorylation. Oxidative phosphorylation generates ATP.

MEDIA
BioFlix 3-D Animation Cellular Respiration
Activity Build a Chemical Cycling System
Activity Overview of Cellular Respiration

CONCEPT 9.2

Glycolysis harvests chemical energy by oxidizing glucose to pyruvate (pp. 167–169)

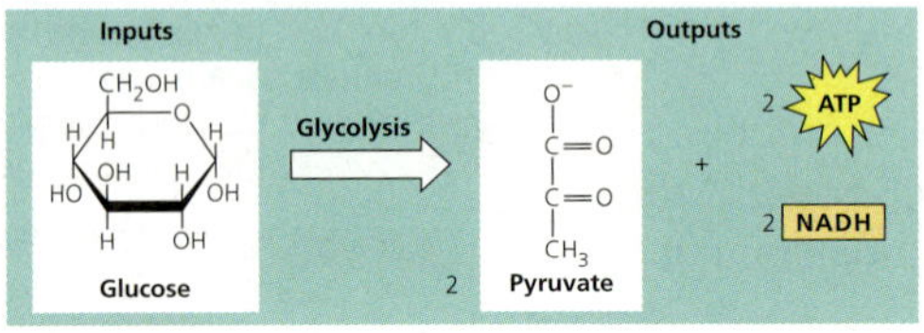

MEDIA
MP3 Tutor Cellular Respiration Part 1—Glycolysis
Activity Glycolysis

CONCEPT 9.3

The citric acid cycle completes the energy-yielding oxidation of organic molecules (pp. 170–172)

- In eukaryotic cells, the import of pyruvate into the mitochondrion and its conversion to acetyl CoA links glycolysis to the citric acid cycle. (In prokaryotic cells, the citric acid cycle occurs in the cytosol.)

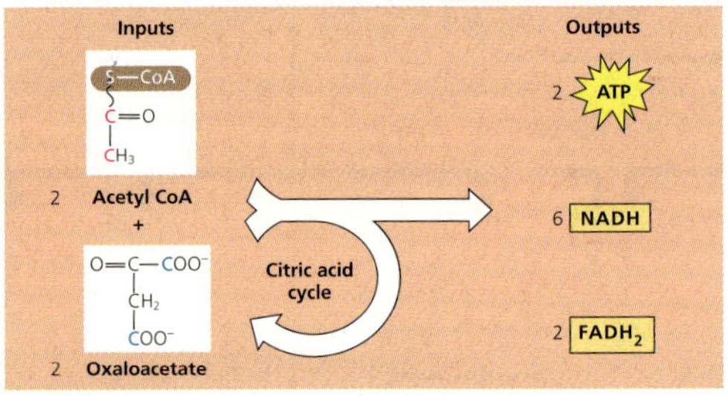

MEDIA
Activity The Citric Acid Cycle

Summary Figures present key information in a visual way, serving as "one-stop shopping" study tools.

MP3 Tutors explain some of the most difficult biological concepts in simple terms. A tutor that goes anywhere you go, anytime.

BioFlix animations and student tools review the most difficult biology topics with 3-D, movie-quality animations, labeled slide shows, carefully constructed student tutorials, study sheets, and quizzes that support all types of learners.

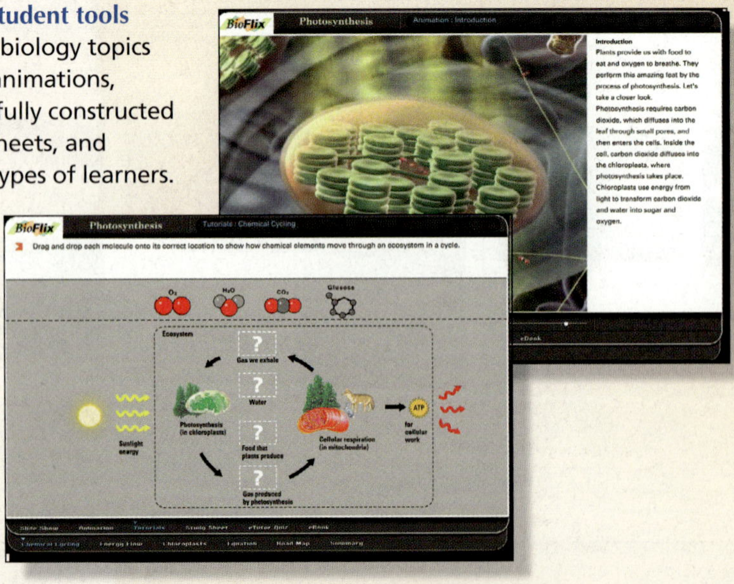

TESTING YOUR KNOWLEDGE

SELF-QUIZ

1. What is the reducing agent in the following reaction?

Pyruvate + NADH + H^+ → Lactate + NAD^+

a. oxygen
b. NADH
c. NAD^+
d. lactate
e. pyruvate

2. The *immediate* energy source that drives ATP synthesis by ATP synthase during oxidative phosphorylation is
a. the oxidation of glucose and other organic compounds.
b. the flow of electrons down the electron transport chain.
c. the affinity of oxygen for electrons.
d. the H^+ concentration gradient across the inner mitochondrial membrane.
e. the transfer of phosphate to ADP.

3. Which metabolic pathway is common to both fermentation and cellular respiration of a glucose molecule?
a. the citric acid cycle
b. the electron transport chain
c. glycolysis
d. synthesis of acetyl CoA from pyruvate
e. reduction of pyruvate to lactate

4. In mitochondria, exergonic redox reactions
a. are the source of energy driving prokaryotic ATP synthesis.
b. are directly coupled to substrate-level phosphorylation.
c. provide the energy that establishes the proton gradient.
d. reduce carbon atoms to carbon dioxide.
e. are coupled via phosphorylated intermediates to endergonic processes.

To start preparing for a test, take the **end-of-chapter Self-Quiz**.

"Draw It" exercises ask you to put pencil to paper and draw a structure, annotate a figure, or graph experimental data. Check your work by turning to the suggested answers in Appendix A.

11. DRAW IT Trace the uptake of water and minerals from root hairs to the vessels in a root, following a symplastic route and an apoplastic route. Label the routes.

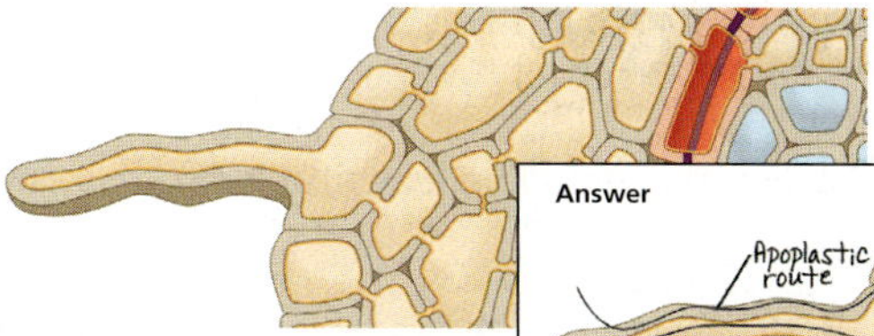

Answer

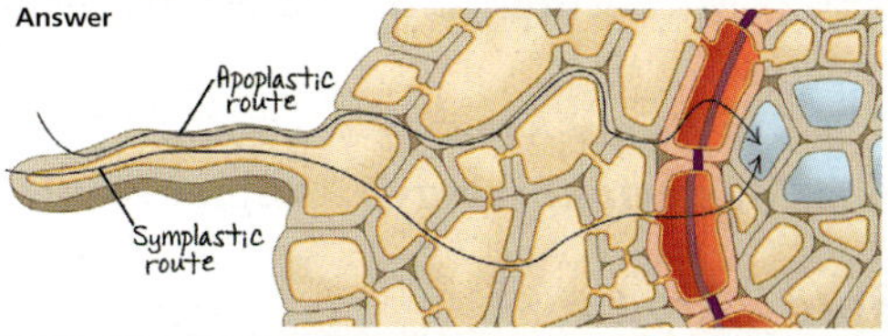

10. DRAW IT The graph here shows the pH difference across the inner mitochondrial membrane over time in an actively respiring cell. At the time indicated by the vertical arrow, a metabolic poison is added that specifically and completely inhibits all function of mitochondrial ATP synthase. Draw what you would expect to see for the rest of the graphed line.

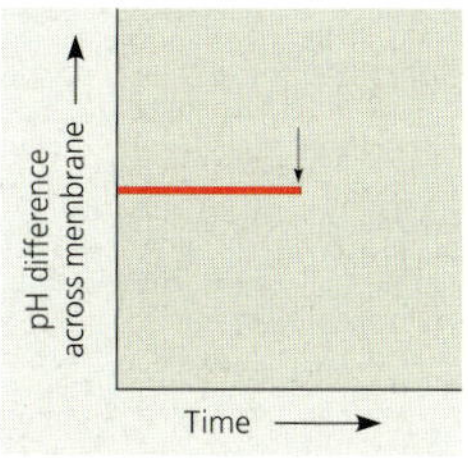

For Self-Quiz answers, see Appendix A.

MEDIA Visit the Study Area at **www.masteringbio.com** for a Practice Test.

For more **practice test questions** visit the Study Area at **www.masteringbio.com**

EVOLUTION CONNECTION

11. ATP synthases are found in the prokaryotic plasma membrane and in mitochondria and chloroplasts. What does this suggest about the evolutionary relationship of these eukaryotic organelles to prokaryotes? How might the amino acid sequences of the ATP synthases from the different sources support or refute your hypothesis?

SCIENTIFIC INQUIRY

12. In the 1940s, some physicians prescribed low doses of a drug called dinitrophenol (DNP) to help patients lose weight. This unsafe method was abandoned after a few patients died. DNP uncouples the chemiosmotic machinery by making the lipid bilayer of the inner mitochondrial membrane leaky to H^+. Explain how this causes weight loss.

SCIENCE, TECHNOLOGY, AND SOCIETY

13. Nearly all human societies use fermentation to produce alcoholic drinks such as beer and wine. The practice dates back to the earliest days of agriculture. How do you suppose this use of fermentation was first discovered? Why did wine prove to be a more useful beverage, especially to a preindustrial culture, than the grape juice from which it was made?

Biological Inquiry: A Workbook of Investigative Cases Explore fermentation further in the case "Bean Brew."

The **essay questions** in the Chapter Review give you practice writing about biological topics and making connections between the content of different chapters, as you may be asked to do in class discussions or on exams.

Supplements

Supplements for the Student

MasteringBIOLOGY
www.masteringbio.com

NEW! MasteringBiology™ offers two valuable learning systems:

1. The **Study Area**
2. **MasteringBiology™ Assignments**

Study Area

Media assets in the Study Area include BioFlix, MP3 Tutors, Discovery Videos, Cell Biology Videos, Activities, Investigations, Graph It!, Quizzes, Practice Tests, Cumulative Test, Word Roots, Key Terms, Flashcards, Audio Glossary, Art, an eBook, and the Campbell/Reece Interviews.

In the **Study Area,** a convenient **Chapter Guide** correlates the student media to the Key Concepts of each textbook chapter.

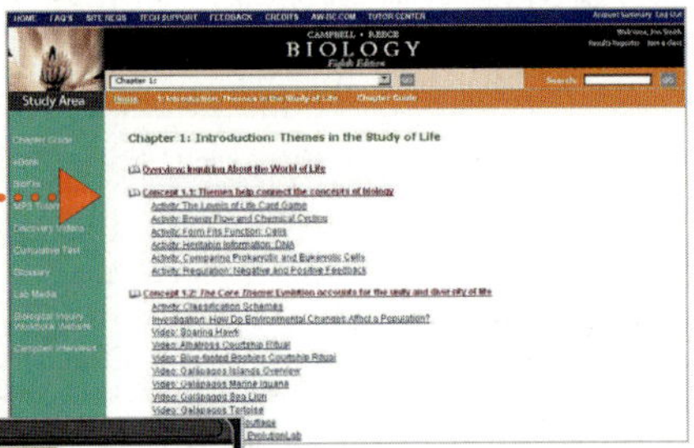

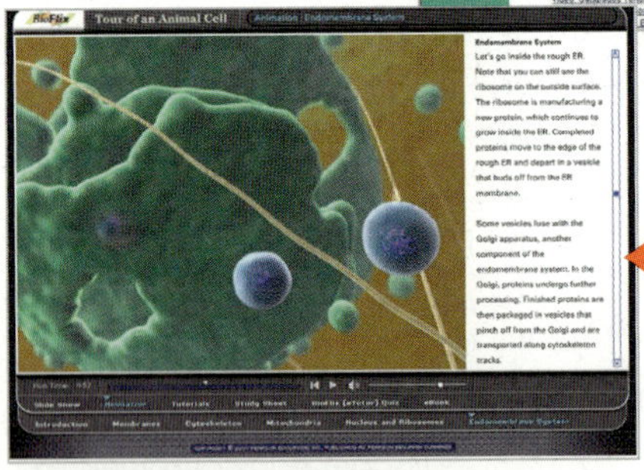

NEW! BioFlix
The student versions of **BioFlix** offer engaging 3-D animations plus labeled slide shows, basic tutorials, study sheets, and quizzes.

Discovery Channel™ Videos bring biology to life.

- **MP3 Tutors** can be played from the website or downloaded onto personal MP3 players for studying anytime.
- **NEW! Audio pronunciations** are included for every term in the Audio Glossary, Key Terms, and Flashcards.

MasteringBiology™ Assignments

MasteringBiology™ offers assignable in-depth Tutorials, Chapter Quizzes with ten questions per chapter, and thousands of additional Multiple Choice Test Bank Questions.

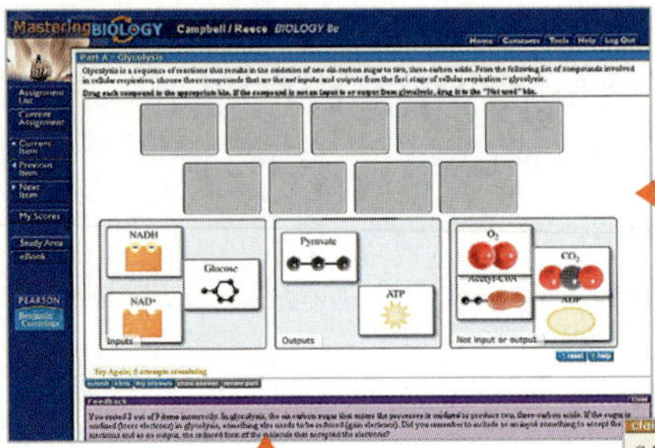

The MasteringBiology™ **Tutorials** guide students through difficult concepts with a series of interactive questions that build on each other.

If a student answers incorrectly, the student is given specific **feedback** that addresses the student's misconceptions.

Students can view **hints** for background information, including animations, and additional assistance.

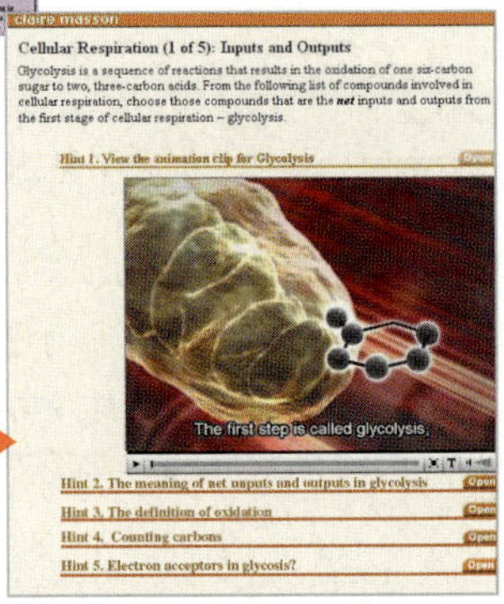

A powerful **Gradebook** automatically records student scores. Shades of red instantly reveal students in trouble or areas of difficulty for the class. Instructors can assign questions to encourage students to read the chapter before class and then adjust their lectures to address student misconceptions. Grades can be exported to another course management system or Excel™, or grades can be imported into the MasteringBiology Gradebook.

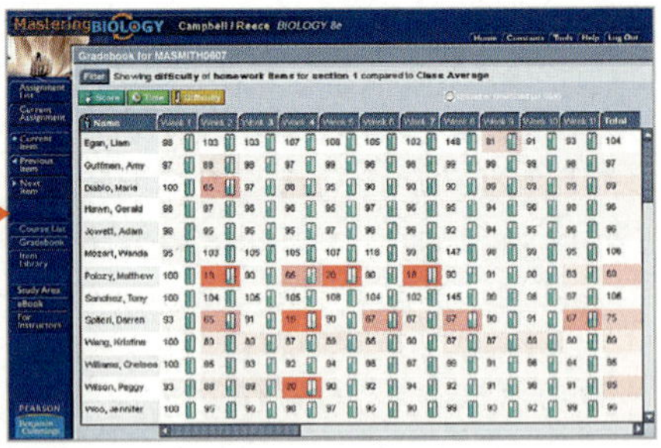

For more information about media for students, see the card inserted at the beginning of this book and the **Access Kit for MasteringBiology™**, which is included with every new copy of *BIOLOGY*, Eighth Edition.

NEW! Inquiry in Action: Interpreting Scientific Papers
(978-0-321-53659-4/0-321-53659-2)
Ruth Buskirk, University of Texas, Austin, and Christopher M. Gillen, Kenyan College
Selected Inquiry Figures in the Eighth Edition direct students to read and analyze the complete original research paper. In this new supplement, those articles are reprinted and accompanied by questions that help students analyze the article.

Student Study Guide for *Biology,* Eighth Edition
(978-0-321-50156-1/0-321-50156-X)
Martha R. Taylor, Cornell University
This popular study guide helps students extract key ideas from the textbook and organize their knowledge of biology. Exercises include concept maps for each chapter, chapter summaries, word roots, chapter tests, and a variety of interactive questions in various formats.

Practicing Biology: A Student Workbook, Third Edition
(978-0-321-52293-1/0-321-52293-1)
Jean Heitz and Cynthia Giffen, University of Wisconsin, Madison
This workbook offers a variety of activities to suit different learning styles. Activities such as modeling and mapping allow students to visualize and understand biological processes. New activities focus on basic skills, such as reading and developing graphs.

Biological Inquiry: A Workbook of Investigative Cases, Second Edition (978-0-321-51320-5/0-321-51320-7)
Margaret Waterman, Southeast Missouri State University, and Ethel Stanley, Beloit College and BioQUEST Curriculum Consortium
This workbook offers ten investigative cases, including new cases on avian influenza and hedgehog developmental pathways. Students pose questions, analyze data, think critically, examine the relationship between evidence and conclusions, construct hypotheses, investigate options, graph data, interpret results, and communicate scientific arguments. A student website is at **www.masteringbio.com**.

Study Card for *Biology,* Eighth Edition
(978-0-321-49436-8/0-321-49436-9)
This quick reference card provides an overview of the entire field of biology and helps students quickly review before a test.

Kaplan MCAT®/GRE® Biology Test Preparation Guide for *Biology,* Eighth Edition
(978-0-321-53463-7/0-321-53463-8)
This exclusive supplement includes sample questions from the Kaplan test preparation guides with page references to *Biology*, Eighth Edition.

Spanish Glossary (978-0-321-49434-4/0-321-49434-2)
Laura P. Zanello, University of California, Riverside

NEW! Into the Jungle: Great Adventures in the Search for Evolution
(978-0-321-55671-4/0-321-55671-2)
Sean B. Carroll, University of Wisconsin, Madison
This book of nine short tales vividly depicts key discoveries in evolutionary biology and the excitement of the scientific process.

NEW! Get Ready for Biology
(978-0-321-50057-1/0-321-50057-1)
This engaging workbook helps students brush up on important math and study skills and get up to speed on biological terminology and the basics of chemistry and cell biology.

A Short Guide to Writing About Biology, Sixth Edition
(978-0-321-51716-6/0-321-51716-4)
Jan A. Pechenik, Tufts University
This best-selling writing guide teaches students to think as biologists and to express ideas clearly and concisely through their writing.

An Introduction to Chemistry for Biology Students, Ninth Edition (978-0-8053-9571-6/0-8053-9571-7)
George I. Sackheim, University of Illinois, Chicago
This text/workbook helps students review and master all the basic facts, concepts, and terminology of chemistry that they need for their life science course.

NEW! Pearson Tutor Services
www.masteringbio.com
Access to MasteringBiology™ includes complimentary access to highly interactive one-on-one biology coaching by qualified instructors seven nights per week during peak study hours. Students can "drop-in" for live online help, submit questions to an e-structor anytime, or pre-schedule a tutoring session with an e-structor. (For college students only.)

Special Topics in Biology Series (booklets)
- Alzheimer's Disease (978-0-1318-3834-5/0-1318-3834-2)
- Biological Terrorism (978-0-8053-4868-2/0-8053-4868-9)
- Biology of Cancer (978-0-8053-4867-5/0-8053-4867-0)
- Emerging Infectious Diseases (978-0-8053-3955-0/0-8053-3955-8)
- Gene Therapy (978-0-8053-3819-5/0-8053-3819-5)
- Genetic Testimony: A Guide to Forensic DNA Profiling (978-0-1314-2338-1/0-1314-2338-X)
- HIV and AIDS (978-0-8053-3956-7/0-8053-3956-6)
- Mad Cows and Cannibals: A Guide to the Transmissible Spongiform Encephalopathies (978-0-1314-2339-8/0-1314-2339-8)
- Stem Cells and Cloning (978-0-8053-4864-4/0-8053-4864-6)
- Understanding the Human Genome Project, Second Edition (978-0-8053-4877-4/0-8053-4877-8)

Supplements for the Instructor

Instructor Resource CD/DVD-ROM Set

(978-0-321-52292-4/0-321-52292-3)

The instructor media for Campbell/Reece *Biology*, Eighth Edition, is combined into one chapter-by-chapter resource along with a **Quick Reference Guide**. **DVDs** provide convenient one-stop access to all the visual media for each chapter. Assets are now organized by chapter folders, making it easy to access files. The **Test Bank CD-ROM** includes test bank questions in Word and TestGen. Assets on the DVDs include:

NEW! *BioFlix*

BioFlix™ 3-D Animations invigorate lectures with movie-quality 3-D animations. Topics include: Tour of an Animal Cell, Tour of a Plant Cell, Cellular Respiration, Photosynthesis, Mitosis, Meiosis, Protein Synthesis, Water Transport in Plants, How Neurons Work, and Muscle Contraction. An additional 123 Animations based on student Activities are also included.

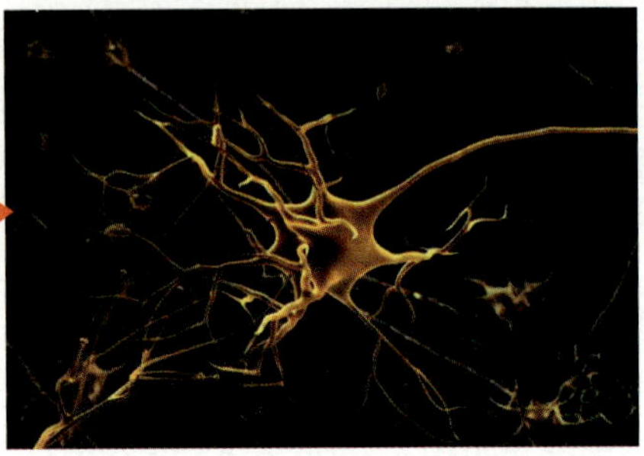

NEW! 29 Discovery Channel™ Videos bring biology to life and show students the process of science. Plus, 65 new **Cell Biology Videos** have been added to the video collection, for a total of 182 videos.

PowerPoint® Label Edit Images include all the art, photos, and tables from the book embedded in PowerPoint® plus **Step Edit Art** broken down into steps. These PowerPoint® files are on the DVDs plus the **Quick Start CD-ROM** for easy access. **PowerPoint® Lecture Presentations** include all of the above plus lecture outlines and links to animations and selected videos. In all PowerPoint files, the text and labels can be edited directly in PowerPoint® and have been enlarged for optimal viewing in large lecture halls. Multiple versions of figures are provided to choose from.

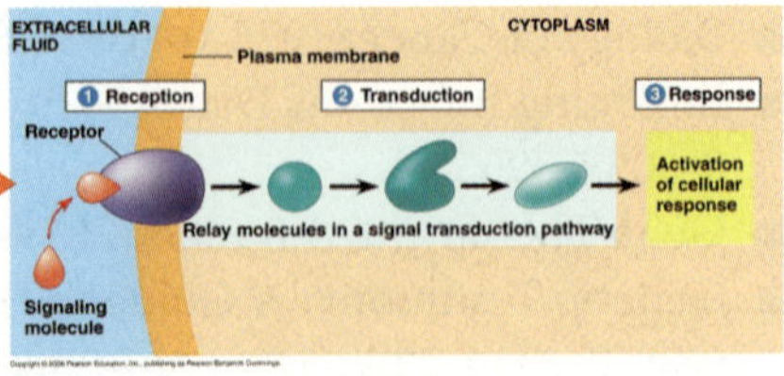

JPEG Images include all the art, photos, and tables from the book with and without labels, selected art layered for step-by-step presentation, and hundreds of extra photos in JPEG format, for a total of more than 1600 photos.

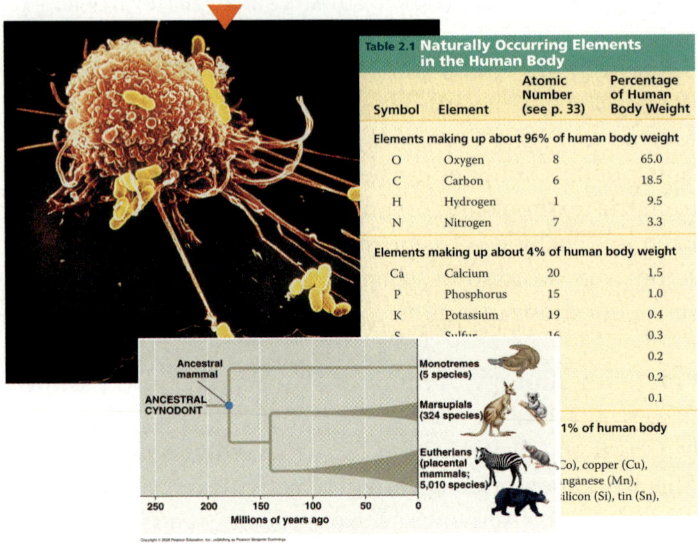

MasteringBIOLOGY
www.masteringbio.com

NEW! The **MasteringBiology™ For Instructors** area includes all the media from the Instructor Resource DVDs:

- PowerPoint® Label Edit Images
- PowerPoint® Lecture Presentations
- Extra Photos (jpegs) plus captions
- Labeled Images (jpegs)
- Unlabeled Images (jpegs)
- BioFlix™ Animations
- Animations
- Discovery Channel™ Videos plus scripts
- Videos plus descriptions

Additional Online Resources:

- PowerPoint® Active Lecture Questions
- Lecture Outlines
- Student Misconceptions with Pre-Tests and Post-Tests
- Quick Reference Guide
- *Practicing Biology* Instructor Guide
- *Inquiry in Action* Instructor Guide
- Answers to selected textbook essay questions
- Lab Media for Instructors

Many instructor assets are also available at the Instructor Resource Center for *Biology*, Eighth Edition, at www.pearsonhighered.com.

Transparency Acetates

(978-0-321-52328-0/0-321-52328-8)

This transparency package provides all the illustrations and tables from the text, many of which incorporate photos. In addition, key figures are broken down into steps.

Electronic Test Bank

Printed Test Bank (978-0-321-49431-3/0-321-49431-8)

More than 4,500 test questions are available in print, Test-Gen®, Microsoft® Word, and from within CourseCompass, Blackboard, and WebCT Course Management Systems. Test Bank questions can also be assigned through MasteringBiology™. The questions have been refined through class testing, and over 30% of the questions are new for the Eighth Edition, including three new question types that encourage critical thinking: interpreting art questions, interpreting graphs and data questions focused on quantitative skills, and scenario-based questions.

Instructor Guide for Biological Inquiry: A Workbook of Investigative Cases, Second Edition

(978-0-321-49435-1/0-321-49435-0)

Margaret Waterman, Southeast Missouri State University, and Ethel Stanley, Beloit College and BioQUEST Curriculum Consortium

This Instructor Guide provides insightful coaching for instructors on how to teach using a case-based problem-solving approach, as well as suggested answers.

Course Management Systems

Test Bank questions, quizzes, and selected content from the Study Area of MasteringBiology™ are available in these popular course management systems:

- **CourseCompass™** (www.aw-bc.com/coursecompass)
- **Blackboard** (www.aw-bc.com/blackboard)
- **WebCT** (www.aw-bc.com/webct)

Supplements for the Lab

NEW! Lab Media at www.masteringbio.com

A new section in the Study Area of MasteringBiology™ brings together all the media assets that can be used to teach scientific inquiry, including Investigating Biology Lab Data Tables in Excel®, Biology Labs On-Line, Investigations, GraphIt!, and LabBench. In the For Instructors area, the Lab Media section includes Investigating Biology Lab Preparation Guide, Answers to Investigations, GraphIt! Instructor Versions, Answers to the LabBench Quizzes, and the *Bio-Explorations* Instructor Guide.

Investigating Biology, Sixth Edition

(978-0-321-53660-0/0-321-53660-6)

Annotated Instructor Edition for Investigating Biology

(978-0-321-54194-9/0-321-54194-4)

Preparation Guide for Investigating Biology

(978-0-321-54166-6/0-321-54166-9)

Judith Giles Morgan, Emory University, and M. Eloise Brown Carter, Oxford College of Emory University

This best-selling laboratory manual encourages students to participate in the process of science and develop creative and critical reasoning skills by posing hypotheses, making predictions, conducting open-ended experiments, collecting data, and applying results to new problems. The Sixth Edition includes a new Bioinformatics Lab and features references to online resources available at www.masteringbio.com, including Lab Data Tables in Excel® for recording data. The Annotated Instructor Edition provides teaching information and marginal notes. A Preparation Guide is also available for instructors in print and online.

New Designs for Bio-Explorations

(978-0-8053-7229-8/0-8053-7229-6)

Instructor Guide for Bio-Explorations

(978-0-8053-7228-1/0-8053-7228-8)

Janet Lanza, University of Arkansas at Little Rock

Eight inquiry-based laboratory exercises offer students creative control over the projects they undertake. Each lab exercise provides students with background information and materials that can be used in the lab projects. The Instructor Guide is provided in the For Instructors area of www.masteringbio.com under Lab Media.

Symbiosis: The Benjamin Cummings Custom Laboratory Program for Biological Sciences

www.pearsoncustom.com/database/symbiosis/bc.html

With Symbiosis, instructors can build a customized lab manual that includes selections from the Benjamin Cummings database along with their own original material.

Biology Labs On-Line

www.biologylabsonline.com

Twelve on-line labs enable students to expand their scientific horizons beyond the traditional wet lab setting and perform potentially dangerous, lengthy, or expensive experiments in an electronic environment. Each experiment can be repeated as often as necessary, employing a unique set of variables each time. The labs are available for purchase individually or in a 12-pack with the printed Student Lab Manual (978-0-8053-7017-1/0-8053-7017-X). An Instructor Lab Manual is also available (978-0-8053-7018-8/0-8053-7018-8).

Reviewers

Eighth Edition Reviewers

Dominique Adriaens, Ghent University
George R. Aliaga, Tarrant County College
J. David Archibald, San Diego State University
David M. Armstrong, University of Colorado-Boulder
Angela S. Aspbury, Texas State University
Ellen Baker, Santa Monica College
Rebecca A. Bartow, Western Kentucky University
Tim Beagley, Salt Lake Community College
Kenneth Birnbaum, New York University
Michael W. Black, California Polytechnic State University, San Luis Obispo
Edward Blumenthal, Marquette University
Jason E. Bond, East Carolina University
Cornelius Bondzi, Hampton University
Oliver Bossdorf, State University of New York, Stony Book
Edward Braun, Iowa State University
Chad Brommer, Emory University
Judith L. Bronstein, University of Arizona
Robb T. Brumfield, Louisiana State University
Richard C. Brusca, University of Arizona, Arizona-Sonora Desert Museum
Jorge Busciglio, University of California, Irvine
Guy A. Caldwell, University of Alabama
Jane Caldwell, West Virginia University
Kim A. Caldwell, University of Alabama
R. Andrew Cameron, California Institute of Technology
W. Zacheus Cande, University of California, Berkeley
Frank R. Cantelmo, St. John's University
Jeffrey Carmichael, University of North Dakota
Laura L. Carruth, Georgia State University
J. Aaron Cassill, University of Texas at San Antonio
P. Bryant Chase, Florida State University
Jung H. Choi, Georgia Institute of Technology
Geoffrey Church, Fairfield University
Patricia J. Clark, Indiana University-Purdue University, Indianapolis
Janice J. Clymer, San Diego Mesa College
Jan Colpaert, Hasselt University
Jay Comeaux, McNeese State University
Gregory Copenhaver, University of North Carolina, Chapel Hill
Karen Curto, University of Pittsburgh
Marymegan Daly, The Ohio State University
Cynthia Dassler, The Ohio State University
Michael A. Davis, Central Connecticut State University
Maria E. de Bellard, California State University, Northridge
Patricia A. DeLeon, University of Delaware
Charles F. Delwiche, University of Maryland
William L. Dentler, University of Kansas
Jean DeSaix, University of North Carolina
Michael Dini, Texas Tech University
Douglas J. Eernisse, California State University, Fullerton
Brad Elder, Doane College
Michelle Elekonich, University of Nevada, Las Vegas
Mary Ellard-Ivey, Pacific Lutheran University
Johnny El-Rady, University of South Florida
John A. Endler, University of California, Santa Barbara
Frederick B. Essig, University of South Florida
Olukemi Fadayomi, Ferris State University
Ellen H. Fanning, Vanderbilt University
Lewis Feldman, University of California, Berkeley
Rebecca Ferrell, Metropolitan State College of Denver
Jonathan S. Fisher, St. Louis University
Kirk Fitzhugh, Natural History Museum of Los Angeles County
Norma Fowler, University of Texas, Austin
Robert Gilbert Fowler, San Jose State University
Jed Fuhrman, University of Southern California
Zofia E. Gagnon, Marist College
Michael Gaines, University of Miami
Stephen Gammie, University of Wisconsin, Madison
Andrea Gargas, University of Wisconsin, Madison
Lauren Garner, California Polytechnic State University, San Luis Obispo
Simon Gilroy, Pennsylvania State University
Alan D. Gishlick, Gustavus Adolphus College
Jessica Gleffe, University of California, Irvine
Tricia Glidewell, Marist School
Elizabeth Godrick, Boston University
Ken Halanych, Auburn University
E. William Hamilton, Washington and Lee University
William F. Hanna, Massasoit Community College
Laszlo Hanzely, Northern Illinois University
Lisa Harper, University of California, Berkeley
Bernard A. Hauser, University of Florida
Evan B. Hazard, Bemidji State University (Emeritus)
S. Blair Hedges, Pennsylvania State University
Brian Hedlund, University of Nevada, Las Vegas
Jean Heitz, University of Wisconsin, Madison
Susan Hengeveld, Indiana University
Albert Herrera, University of Southern California
Kenneth Hillers, California Polytechnic State University, San Luis Obispo
A. Scott Holaday, Texas Tech University
N. Michele Holbrook, Harvard University
Alan R. Holyoak, Brigham Young University, Idaho
Sandra M. Horikami, Daytona Beach Community College
Becky Houck, University of Portland
Daniel J. Howard, New Mexico State University
Cristin Hulslander, University of Oregon
Linda L. Hyde, Gordon College
Jeffrey Ihara, Mira Costa College
Lee Johnson, The Ohio State University
Chad Jordan, North Carolina State University
Walter S. Judd, University of Florida
Thomas W. Jurik, Iowa State University
Caroline M. Kane, University of California, Berkeley
Jennifer Katcher, Pima Community College
Laura A. Katz, Smith College
Maureen Kearney, Field Museum of Natural History
Patrick Keeling, University of British Columbia
Elizabeth A. Kellogg, University of Missouri-St. Louis
Chris Kennedy, Simon Fraser University
Rebecca T. Kimball, University of Florida
Jennifer Knight, University of Colorado
Margareta Krabbe, Uppsala University
Anselm Kratochwil, Universität Osnabrück
Deborah M. Kristan, California State University at San Marcos
William Kroll, Loyola University, Chicago
Justin P. Kumar, Indiana University
Marc-André Lachance, University of Western Ontario
Mohamed Lakrim, Kingsborough Community College
John Latto, University of California, Santa Barbara
Daewoo Lee, Ohio University

Michael R. Leonardo, Coe College
John J. Lepri, University of North Carolina at Greensboro
Graeme Lindbeck, Valencia Community College
Diana Lipscomb, George Washington University
Christopher Little, The University of Texas-Pan American
Kevin D. Livingstone, Trinity University
Andrea Lloyd, Middlebury College
Christopher A. Loretz, State University of New York at Buffalo
Douglas B. Luckie, Michigan State University
Christine R. Maher, University of Southern Maine
Keith Malmos, Valencia Community College – East Campus
Cindy Malone, California State University, Northridge
Carol Mapes, Kutztown University of Pennsylvania
Kathleen A. Marrs, Indiana University-Purdue University, Indianapolis
Diane L. Marshall, University of New Mexico
Andrew McCubbin, Washington State University
Lisa Marie Meffert, Rice University
Scott Meissner, Cornell University
John Merrill, Michigan State University
Michael J. Misamore, Texas Christian University
Alan Molumby, University of Illinois, Chicago
Joseph P. Montoya, Georgia Institute of Technology
Janice Moore, Colorado State University
Jeanette Mowery, Madison Area Technical College
Tom Neils, Grand Rapids Community College
Ray Neubauer, University of Texas, Austin
James Newcomb, New England College
Anders Nilsson, University of Umeå
Mohamed A. F. Noor, Duke University
Shawn Nordell, St. Louis University
Richard S. Norman, University of Michigan, Dearborn (Emeritus)
Gretchen North, Occidental College
Mark P. Oemke, Alma College
Nathan O. Okia, Auburn University, Montgomery
John Oross, University of California, Riverside
Charissa Osborne, Butler University
Thomas G. Owens, Cornell University
Kevin Padian, University of California, Berkeley
Anthony T. Paganini, Michigan State University
Michael A. Palladino, Monmouth University
Imara Y. Perera, North Carolina State University
David S. Pilliod, California Polytechnic State University, San Luis Obispo
J. Chris Pires, University of Missouri-Columbia
Angela R. Porta, Kean University
Daniel Potter, University of California, Davis
Mary V. Price, University of California, Riverside
Mitch Price, Pennsylvania State University
Peter Quinby, University of Pittsburgh
Robert H. Reaves, Glendale Community College
Erin Rempala, San Diego Mesa College
Eric Ribbens, Western Illinois University
Christina Richards, New York University
Loren Rieseberg, University of British Columbia
Bruce B. Riley, Texas A&M University
Laurel Roberts, University of Pittsburgh
Mike Rosenzweig, Virginia Polytechnic Institute and State University
Tyson Sacco, Cornell University
Rowan F. Sage, University of Toronto
Tammy Lynn Sage, University of Toronto
Thomas R. Sawicki, Spartanburg Community College
Inder Saxena, University of Texas, Austin
Maynard H. Schaus, Virginia Wesleyan College
Renate Scheibe, University of Osnabrück
Mark Schlissel, University of California, Berkeley
Christopher J. Schneider, Boston University
Thomas W. Schoener, University of California, Davis
Patricia M. Schulte, University of British Columbia
Karen S. Schumaker, University of Arizona
David J. Schwartz, Houston Community College
Robert W. Seagull, Hofstra University
Duane Sears, University of California, Santa Barbara
Joan Sharp, Simon Fraser University
Timothy E. Shannon, Francis Marion University
Richard M. Showman, University of South Carolina
Rebecca Simmons, University of North Dakota
Anne Simon, University of Maryland, College Park
Robert Simons, University of California, Los Angeles
Julio G. Soto, San Jose State University
John Stachowicz, University of California, Davis
Gail A. Stewart, Camden County College
Michael A. Sypes, Pennsylvania State University
Emily Taylor, California Polytechnic State University, San Luis Obispo
John W. Taylor, University of California, Berkeley
William Thwaites, Tillamook Bay Community College
Eric Toolson, University of New Mexico
Paul Q. Trombley, Florida State University
Nancy J. Trun, Duquesne University
Claudia Uhde-Stone, California State University, East Bay
Saba Valadkhan, Case Western Reserve University School of Medicine
Steven D. Verhey, Central Washington University
Kathleen Verville, Washington College
Sara Via, University of Maryland
Leif Asbjørn Vøllestad, University of Oslo
Linda Walters, University of Central Florida
Nickolas M. Waser, University of California, Riverside
Andrea Weeks, George Mason University
Richard Wetts, University of California, Irvine
Susan Whittemore, Keene State College
Ernest H. Williams, Hamilton College
Kathy Williams, San Diego State University
Paul Wilson, California State University, Northridge
Peter Wimberger, University of Puget Sound
Robert Winning, Eastern Michigan University
E. William Wischusen, Louisiana State University
Vickie L. Wolfe, Marshall University
Denise Woodward, Pennsylvania State University
Sarah E. Wyatt, Ohio University
Ramin Yadegari, University of Arizona
Paul Yancey, Whitman College
Gina M. Zainelli, Loyola University, Chicago
Miriam Zolan, Indiana University

BioFlix Reviewers

Mitch Albers, Minneapolis Community and Technical College
Kirk Bartholomew, Sacred Heart University
Gretchen Bernard, Moraine Valley Community College
Peggy Brickman, University of Georgia
Uriel Buitrago-Suarez, Harper College
Nancy Butler, Kutztown University of Pennsylvania
Guy A. Caldwell, University of Alabama
Kim A. Caldwell, University of Alabama
Jose L. Egremy, Northwest Vista College
Kurt J. Elliott, Northwest Vista College
Gerald G. Farr, Texas State University
Lewis Feldman, University of California, Berkeley
Sandra Gibbons, Moraine Valley Community College
Douglas A. Hamilton, Hartwick College
W. Wyatt Hoback, University of Nebraska at Kearney
Elizabeth Hodgson, York College of Pennsylvania
Kelly Hogan, University of North Carolina at Chapel Hill
Mary Rose Lamb, University of Puget Sound
Cody Locke, University of Alabama
Marvin Brandon Lowery, Sam Houston State University
David Mirman, Mt. San Antonio College
James Newcomb, New England College

Thomas G. Owens, Cornell University
Deb Pires, University of California, Los Angeles
Mitch Price, Pennsylvania State University
David A. Rintoul, Kansas State University
Renee Rivas, University of Alabama
Laurel Roberts, University of Pittsburgh
Chris Romero, Front Range Community College
Juliet Spencer, University of San Francisco
Linda Brooke Stabler, University of Central Oklahoma
Beth Stall, El Centro College
Brian Stout, Northwest Vista College
Diane Sweeney, Crystal Springs Uplands School
Jamey Thompson, Hudson Valley Community College
Paul Q. Trombley, Florida State University
Robert S. Wallace, Iowa State University
Susan Whittemore, Keene State College
Miriam Zolan, Indiana University
Michelle Zurawski, Moraine Valley Community College

MasteringBiology Class-Testers and Reviewers

Peter B. Berget, Carnegie Mellon University
Michael W. Black, California Polytechnic State University, San Luis Obispo
Scott Bowling, Auburn University
Suzanne Butler, Miami Dade College
Alejandro Calderon-Urrea, California State University, Fresno
Kim A. Caldwell, University of Alabama
Jeffrey Carmichael, University of North Dakota
Jung H. Choi, Georgia Institute of Technology
Karen Curto, University of Pittsburgh
Lydia Daniels, University of Pittsburgh
Jill Feinstein, Richland Community College
Donald Glassman, Des Moines Area Community College
Joyce Gordon, University of British Columbia
David Grise, Texas A&M University, Corpus Christi
Douglas A. Hamilton, Hartwick College
Mark Hens, University of North Carolina at Greensboro
John C. Kay, Iolani School
Tracy Kickox, University of Illinois at Urbana-Champaign
Mary Rose Lamb, University of Puget Sound
Deb Maddalena, University of Vermont
C. Smoot Major, University of South Alabama
Nilo Marin, Broward Community College
John Merrill, Michigan State University
Melissa Michael, University of Illinois at Urbana-Champaign
Nancy Rice, Western Kentucky University
Chris Romero, Front Range Community College, Larimer
John Salerno, Kennesaw State University
Brian Stout, Northwest Vista College
Sukanya Subramanian, Collin County Community College
Elizabeth Willott, University of Arizona
Lauren Yaich, University of Pittsburgh at Bradford

Reviewers of Previous Editions

Kenneth Able (State University of New York, Albany), Thomas Adams (Michigan State University), Martin Adamson (University of British Columbia), Shylaja Akkaraju (Bronx Community College of CUNY), John Alcock (Arizona State University), Richard Almon (State University of New York, Buffalo), Bonnie Amos (Angelo State University), Katherine Anderson (University of California, Berkeley), Richard J. Andren (Montgomery County Community College), Estry Ang (University of Pittsburgh at Greensburg), Jeff Appling (Clemson University), J. David Archibald (San Diego State University), David Armstrong (University of Colorado at Boulder), Howard J. Arnott (University of Texas at Arlington), Mary Ashley (University of Illinois at Chicago), Robert Atherton (University of Wyoming), Karl Aufderheide (Texas A&M University), Leigh Auleb (San Francisco State University), P. Stephen Baenziger (University of Nebraska), Ellen Baker (Santa Monica College), Katherine Baker (Millersville University), William Barklow (Framingham State College), Susan Barman (Michigan State University), Steven Barnhart (Santa Rosa Junior College), Andrew Barton (University of Maine Farmington), Ron Basmajian (Merced College), David Bass (University of Central Oklahoma), Bonnie Baxter (Hobart & William Smith), Tim Beagley (Salt Lake Community College), Margaret E. Beard (College of the Holy Cross), Tom Beatty (University of British Columbia), Chris Beck (Emory University), Wayne Becker (University of Wisconsin, Madison), Patricia Bedinger (Colorado State University), Jane Beiswenger (University of Wyoming), Anne Bekoff (University of Colorado, Boulder), Marc Bekoff (University of Colorado, Boulder), Tania Beliz (College of San Mateo), Adrianne Bendich (Hoffman-La Roche, Inc.), Barbara Bentley (State University of New York, Stony Brook), Darwin Berg (University of California, San Diego), Werner Bergen (Michigan State University), Gerald Bergstrom (University of Wisconsin, Milwaukee), Anna W. Berkovitz (Purdue University), Dorothy Berner (Temple University), Annalisa Berta (San Diego State University), Paulette Bierzychudek (Pomona College), Charles Biggers (Memphis State University), Robert Blanchard (University of New Hampshire), Andrew R. Blaustein (Oregon State University), Judy Bluemer (Morton College), Robert Blystone (Trinity University), Robert Boley (University of Texas, Arlington), Eric Bonde (University of Colorado, Boulder), Richard Boohar (University of Nebraska, Omaha), Carey L. Booth (Reed College), Allan Bornstein (Southeast Missouri State University), James L. Botsford (New Mexico State University), Lisa Boucher (University of Nebraska-Omaha), J. Michael Bowes (Humboldt State University), Richard Bowker (Alma College), Robert Bowker (Glendale Community College - Arizona), Barbara Bowman (Mills College), Barry Bowman (University of California, Santa Cruz), Deric Bownds (University of Wisconsin, Madison), Robert Boyd (Auburn University), Sunny Boyd (University of Notre Dame), Jerry Brand (University of Texas, Austin), Theodore A. Bremner (Howard University), James Brenneman (University of Evansville), Charles H. Brenner (Berkeley, California), Lawrence Brewer (University of Kentucky), Donald P. Briskin (University of Illinois, Urbana), Paul Broady (University of Canterbury), Danny Brower (University of Arizona), Carole Browne (Wake Forest University), Mark Browning (Purdue University), David Bruck (San Jose State University), Herbert Bruneau (Oklahoma State University), Gary Brusca (Humboldt State University), Richard C. Brusca (University of Arizona, Arizona-Sonora Desert Museum), Alan H. Brush (University of Connecticut, Storrs), Howard Buhse (University of Illinois at Chicago), Arthur Buikema (Virginia Tech), Al Burchsted (College of Staten Island), Meg Burke (University of North Dakota), Edwin Burling (De Anza College), William Busa (Johns Hopkins University), John Bushnell (University of Colorado), Linda Butler (University of Texas, Austin), David Byres (Florida Community College, Jacksonville), Alison Campbell (University of Waikato), Iain Campbell (University of Pittsburgh), Robert E. Cannon (University of North Carolina at Greensboro), Deborah Canington (University of California, Davis), Frank Cantelmo (St John's University), John Capeheart (University of Houston-Downtown), Gregory Capelli (College of William and Mary), Richard Cardullo (University of California, Riverside), Nina Caris (Texas A&M University), Robert Carroll (East Carolina University), David Champlin (University of Southern Maine), Bruce Chase (University of Nebraska, Omaha), Doug Cheeseman (De Anza College), Shepley Chen (University of Illinois, Chicago), Giovina Chinchar (Tougaloo College), Joseph P.

Chinnici (Virginia Commonwealth University), Henry Claman (University of Colorado Health Science Center), Anne Clark (Binghamton University), Greg Clark (University of Texas), Ross C. Clark (Eastern Kentucky University), Lynwood Clemens (Michigan State University), William P. Coffman (University of Pittsburgh), Austin Randy Cohen (California State University, Northridge), J. John Cohen (University of Colorado Health Science Center), Jim Colbert (Iowa State University), Robert Colvin (Ohio University), David Cone (Saint Mary's University), Elizabeth Connor (University of Massachusetts), Joanne Conover (University of Connecticut), John Corliss (University of Maryland), James T. Costa (Western Carolina University), Stuart J. Coward (University of Georgia), Charles Creutz (University of Toledo), Bruce Criley (Illinois Wesleyan University), Norma Criley (Illinois Wesleyan University), Joe W. Crim (University of Georgia), Greg Crowther (University of Washington), Karen Curto (University of Pittsburgh), Anne Cusic (University of Alabama at Birmingham), Richard Cyr (Pennsylvania State University), W. Marshall Darley (University of Georgia), Marianne Dauwalder (University of Texas, Austin), Larry Davenport (Samford University), Bonnie J. Davis (San Francisco State University), Jerry Davis (University of Wisconsin, La Crosse), Thomas Davis (University of New Hampshire), John Dearn (University of Canberra), Teresa DeGolier (Bethel College), James Dekloe (University of California, Santa Cruz), Veronique Delesalle (Gettysburg College), T. Delevoryas (University of Texas, Austin), Roger Del Moral (University of Washington), Diane C. DeNagel (Northwestern University), Daniel Dervartanian (University of Georgia), Jean DeSaix (University of North Carolina at Chapel Hill), Michael Dini (Texas Tech University), Biao Ding (Ohio State University), Andrew Dobson (Princeton University), Stanley Dodson (University of Wisconsin-Madison), Mark Drapeau (University of California, Irvine), John Drees (Temple University School of Medicine), Charles Drewes (Iowa State University), Marvin Druger (Syracuse University), Gary Dudley (University of Georgia), Susan Dunford (University of Cincinnati), Betsey Dyer (Wheaton College), Robert Eaton (University of Colorado), Robert S. Edgar (University of California, Santa Cruz), Douglas Eernisse (California State University, Fullerton), Betty J. Eidemiller (Lamar University), Brad Elder (University of Oklahoma), William D. Eldred (Boston University), Norman Ellstrand (University of California, Riverside), Dennis Emery (Iowa State University), John Endler (University of California, Santa Barbara), Margaret T. Erskine (Lansing Community College), Gerald Esch (Wake Forest University), Frederick B. Essig (University of South Florida), Mary Eubanks (Duke University), David Evans (University of Florida), Robert C. Evans (Rutgers University, Camden), Sharon Eversman (Montana State University), Lincoln Fairchild (Ohio State University), Peter Fajer (Florida State University), Bruce Fall (University of Minnesota), Lynn Fancher (College of DuPage), Paul Farnsworth (University of Texas at San Antonio), Larry Farrell (Idaho State University), Jerry F. Feldman (University of California, Santa Cruz), Eugene Fenster (Longview Community College), Russell Fernald (University of Oregon), Kim Finer (Kent State University), Milton Fingerman (Tulane University), Barbara Finney (Regis College), Frank Fish (West Chester University), David Fisher (University of Hawaii, Manoa), Steven Fisher (University of California, Santa Barbara), Lloyd Fitzpatrick (University of North Texas), William Fixsen (Harvard University), Abraham Flexer (Manuscript Consultant, Boulder, Colorado), Kerry Foresman (University of Montana), Norma Fowler (University of Texas, Austin), Robert G. Fowler (San Jose State University), David Fox (University of Tennessee, Knoxville), Carl Frankel (Pennsylvania State University, Hazleton), James Franzen (University of Pittsburgh), Bill Freedman (Dalhousie University), Otto Friesen (University of Virginia), Frank Frisch (Chapman University), Virginia Fry (Monterey Peninsula College), Bernard Frye (University of Texas at Arlington), Alice Fulton (University of Iowa), Chandler Fulton (Brandeis University), Sara Fultz (Stanford University), Berdell Funke (North Dakota State University), Anne Funkhouser (University of the Pacific), Michael Gaines (University of Miami), Arthur W. Galston (Yale University), Carl Gans (University of Michigan), John Gapter (University of Northern Colorado), Reginald Garrett (University of Virginia), Patricia Gensel (University of North Carolina), Chris George (California Polytechnic State University, San Luis Obispo), Robert George (University of Wyoming), J. Whitfield Gibbons (University of Georgia), J. Phil Gibson (Agnes Scott College), Frank Gilliam (Marshall University), Simon Gilroy (Pennsylvania State University), Alan Gishlick (National Center for Science Education), Todd Gleeson (University of Colorado), John Glendinning (Barnard College), David Glenn-Lewin (Wichita State University), William Glider (University of Nebraska), Elizabeth A. Godrick (Boston University), Lynda Goff (University of California, Santa Cruz), Elliott Goldstein (Arizona State University), Paul Goldstein (University of Texas, El Paso), Sandra Gollnick (State University of New York at Buffalo) Anne Good (University of California, Berkeley), Judith Goodenough (University of Massachusetts, Amherst), Wayne Goodey (University of British Columbia), Robert Goodman (University of Wisconsin-Madison), Ester Goudsmit (Oakland University), Linda Graham (University of Wisconsin, Madison), Robert Grammer (Belmont University), Joseph Graves (Arizona State University), Phyllis Griffard (University of Houston-Downtown), A. J. F. Griffiths (University of British Columbia), William Grimes (University of Arizona), Mark Gromko (Bowling Green State University), Serine Gropper (Auburn University), Katherine L. Gross (Ohio State University), Gary Gussin (University of Iowa), Mark Guyer (National Human Genome Research Institute), Ruth Levy Guyer (Bethesda, Maryland), R. Wayne Habermehl (Montgomery County Community College), Mac Hadley (University of Arizona), Joel Hagen (Radford University), Jack P. Hailman (University of Wisconsin), Leah Haimo (University of California, Riverside), Jody Hall (Brown University), Douglas Hallett, (Northern Arizona University), Rebecca Halyard (Clayton State College), Sam Hammer (Boston University), Penny Hanchey-Bauer (Colorado State University), Laszlo Hanzely (Northern Illinois University), Jeff Hardin (University of Wisconsin, Madison), Richard Harrison (Cornell University), Carla Hass (Pennsylvania State University), Chris Haufler (University of Kansas), Chris Haynes (Shelton State Community College), H. D. Heath (California State University, Hayward), George Hechtel (State University of New York, Stony Brook), Blair Hedges (Pennsylvania State), David Heins (Tulane University), Jean Heitz (University of Wisconsin, Madison), John D. Helmann (Cornell University), Colin Henderson (University of Montana), Michelle Henricks (University of California, Los Angeles), Caroll Henry (Chicago State University), Frank Heppner (University of Rhode Island), Scott Herrick (Missouri Western State College), Ira Herskowitz (University of California, San Francisco), Paul E. Hertz (Barnard College), David Hibbett (Clark University), R. James Hickey (Miami University), William Hillenius (College of Charleston), Ralph Hinegardner (University of California, Santa Cruz), William Hines (Foothill College), Robert Hinrichsen (Indiana University of Pennsylvania), Helmut Hirsch (State University of New York, Albany), Tuan-hua David Ho (Washington University), Carl Hoagstrom (Ohio Northern University), James Hoffman (University of Vermont), A. Scott Holaday (Texas Tech), James Holland (Indiana State University, Bloomington), Charles Holliday (Lafayette College), Lubbock Karl Holte (Idaho State University), Laura Hoopes (Occidental College), Nancy Hopkins (Massachusetts Institute of Technology), Sandra Horikami (Daytona Beach Community College), Kathy Hornberger (Widener University), Pius F. Horner (San Bernardino Valley College), Margaret Houk (Ripon College), Ronald R. Hoy (Cornell University), Donald Humphrey (Emory University School of Medicine), Robert J. Huskey (University of Virginia), Steven Hutcheson (University of Maryland, College Park), Sandra Hsu (Skyline College), Bradley Hyman (University of California, Riverside), Mark Iked (San Bernardino Valley College), Cheryl Ingram-Smith (Clemson University), Alice Jacklet (State University of New York, Albany), John Jackson (North Hennepin

Community College), John C. Jahoda (Bridgewater State College), Dan Johnson (East Tennessee State University), Randall Johnson (University of California, San Diego), Stephen Johnson (William Penn University), Wayne Johnson (Ohio State University), Kenneth C. Jones (California State University, Northridge), Russell Jones (University of California, Berkeley), Alan Journet (Southeast Missouri State University), Walter Judd (University of Florida), Thomas C. Kane (University of Cincinnati), Tamos Kapros (University of Missouri), E. L. Karlstrom (University of Puget Sound), Jennifer Katcher (Pima Community College), Norm Kenkel (University of Manitoba), George Khoury (National Cancer Institute), Mark Kirk (University of Missouri-Columbia), Robert Kitchin (University of Wyoming), Attila O. Klein (Brandeis University), Daniel Klionsky (University of Michigan), Ned Knight (Linfield College), David Kohl (University of California, Santa Barbara), Greg Kopf (University of Pennsylvania School of Medicine), Thomas Koppenheffer (Trinity University), Janis Kuby (San Francisco State University), David Kurijaka (Ohio University), J. A. Lackey (State University of New York, Oswego), Elaine Lai (Brandeis University), Lynn Lamoreux (Texas A&M University), William L'Amoreaux (College of Staten Island), Carmine A. Lanciani (University of Florida), Kenneth Lang (Humboldt State University), Dominic Lannutti (El Paso Community College), Allan Larson (Washington University), Diane K. Lavett (State University of New York, Cortland, and Emory University), Charles Leavell (Fullerton College), C. S. Lee (University of Texas), Robert Leonard (University of California, Riverside), John Lepri (University of North Carolina at Greensboro), Donald Levin (University of Texas), Austin Mike Levine (University of California, Berkeley), Joseph Levine (Boston College), Bill Lewis (Shoreline Community College), John Lewis (Loma Linda University), Lorraine Lica (California State University, Hayward), Harvey Liftin (Broward Community College), Harvey Lillywhite (University of Florida, Gainesville), Clark Lindgren (Grinnell College), Sam Loker (University of New Mexico), Jane Lubchenco (Oregon State University), Margaret A. Lynch (Tufts University), Steven Lynch (Louisiana State University at Shreveport), Richard Machemer Jr. (St. John Fisher College), Elizabeth Machunis-Masuoka (University of Virginia), James MacMahon (Utah State University), Linda Maier (University of Alabama in Huntsville), Jose Maldonado (El Paso Community College), Richard Malkin (University of California, Berkeley), Charles Mallery (University of Miami), William Margolin (University of Texas Medical School), Lynn Margulis (Boston University), Edith Marsh (Angelo State University), Diane Marshall (University of New Mexico), Linda Martin Morris (University of Washington), Karl Mattox (Miami University of Ohio), Joyce Maxwell (California State University, Northridge), Jeffrey D. May (Marshall University), Lee McClenaghan (San Diego State University), Richard McCracken (Purdue University), Kerry McDonald (University of Missouri-Columbia), Jacqueline McLaughlin (Pennsylvania State University, Lehigh Valley), Neal McReynolds (Texas A&M International), Lisa Meffert (Rice University), Michael Meighan (University of California, Berkeley), Scott Meissner (Cornell University), Paul Melchior (North Hennepin Community College), Phillip Meneely (Haverford College), John Merrill (Michigan State University), Brian Metscher (University of California, Irvine), Ralph Meyer (University of Cincinnati), James Mickle (North Carolina State University), Roger Milkman (University of Iowa), Helen Miller (Oklahoma State University), John Miller (University of California, Berkeley), Kenneth R. Miller (Brown University), John E. Minnich (University of Wisconsin, Milwaukee), Michael Misamore (Louisiana State University), Kenneth Mitchell (Tulane University School of Medicine), Alan Molumby (University of Illinois at Chicago), Nicholas Money (Miami University), Russell Monson (University of Colorado, Boulder), Frank Moore (Oregon State University), Randy Moore (Wright State University), William Moore (Wayne State University), Carl Moos (Veterans Administration Hospital, Albany, New York), Michael Mote (Temple University), Alex Motten (Duke University), Deborah Mowshowitz (Columbia University), Rita Moyes (Texas A&M College Station), Darrel L. Murray (University of Illinois at Chicago), John Mutchmor (Iowa State University), Elliot Myerowitz (California Institute of Technology), Gavin Naylor (Iowa State University), John Neess (University of Wisconsin, Madison), Raymond Neubauer (University of Texas, Austin), Todd Newbury (University of California, Santa Cruz), Harvey Nichols (University of Colorado, Boulder), Deborah Nickerson (University of South Florida), Bette Nicotri (University of Washington), Caroline Niederman (Tomball College), Maria Nieto (California State University, Hayward), Greg Nishiyama (College of the Canyons), Charles R. Noback (College of Physicians and Surgeons, Columbia University), Jane Noble-Harvey (Delaware University), Mary C. Nolan (Irvine Valley College), Peter Nonacs (University of California, Los Angeles), Richard Norman (University of Michigan-Dearborn), David O. Norris (University of Colorado, Boulder), Steven Norris (California State, Channel Islands), Cynthia Norton (University of Maine, Augusta), Steve Norton (East Carolina University), Steve Nowicki (Duke University), Bette H. Nybakken (Hartnell College), Brian O'Conner (University of Massachusetts, Amherst), Gerard O'Donovan (University of North Texas), Eugene Odum (University of Georgia), Linda Ogren (University of California, Santa Cruz), Patricia O'Hern (Emory University), Jeanette Oliver (St. Louis Community College Florissant Valley), Gary P. Olivetti (University of Vermont), John Olsen (Rhodes College), Laura J. Olsen (University of Michigan), Sharman O'Neill (University of California, Davis), Wan Ooi (Houston Community College), Gay Ostarello (Diablo Valley College), Catherine Ortega (Fort Lewis College), Charissa Osborne (Butler University), Thomas G. Owens (Cornell University), Penny Padgett (University of North Carolina at Chapel Hill), Kevin Padian (University of California, Berkeley), Dianna Padilla (State University of New York, Stony Brook), Barry Palevitz (University of Georgia), Daniel Papaj (University of Arizona), Peter Pappas (County College of Morris), Bulah Parker (North Carolina State University), Stanton Parmeter (Chemeketa Community College), Robert Patterson (San Francisco State University), Ronald Patterson (Michigan State University), Crellin Pauling (San Francisco State University), Kay Pauling (Foothill Community College), Daniel Pavuk (Bowling Green State University), Debra Pearce (Northern Kentucky University), Patricia Pearson (Western Kentucky University), Shelley Penrod (North Harris College), Beverly Perry (Houston Community College), David Pfennig (University of North Carolina at Chapel Hill), Bob Pittman (Michigan State University), James Platt (University of Denver), Martin Poenie (University of Texas, Austin), Scott Poethig (University of Pennsylvania), Jeffrey Pommerville (Texas A&M University), Warren Porter (University of Wisconsin), Daniel Potter (University of California, Davis), Donald Potts (University of California, Santa Cruz), Andy Pratt (University of Canterbury), David Pratt (University of California, Davis), Halina Presley (University of Illinois, Chicago), Mitch Price (Pennsylvania State University), Rong Sun Pu (Kean University), Rebecca Pyles (East Tennessee State University), Scott Quackenbush (Florida International University), Ralph Quatrano (Oregon State University), Val Raghavan (Ohio State University), Deanna Raineri (University of Illinois, Champaign-Urbana), Talitha Rajah (Indiana University Southeast), Charles Ralph (Colorado State University), Thomas Rand (Saint Mary's University), Kurt Redborg (Coe College), Ahnya Redman (Pennsylvania State), Brian Reeder (Morehead State University), Bruce Reid (Kean University), David Reid (Blackburn College), C. Gary Reiness (Lewis & Clark College), Charles Remington (Yale University), David Reznick (University of California, Riverside), Douglas Rhoads (University of Arkansas), Fred Rhoades (Western Washington State University), Christopher Riegle (Irvine Valley College), Donna Ritch (Pennsylvania State University), Carol Rivin (Oregon State University East), Laurel Roberts (University of Pittsburgh), Thomas Rodella (Merced College), Rodney Rogers (Drake University), William Roosenburg

(Ohio University), Wayne Rosing (Middle Tennessee State University), Thomas Rost (University of California, Davis), Stephen I. Rothstein (University of California, Santa Barbara), John Ruben (Oregon State University), Albert Ruesink (Indiana University), Neil Sabine (Indiana University), Tyson Sacco (Cornell University), Rowan Sage (University of Toronto), Don Sakaguchi (Iowa State University), Walter Sakai (Santa Monica College), Mark F. Sanders (University of California, Davis), Ted Sargent (University of Massachusetts, Amherst), K. Sathasivan (University of Texas, Austin), Gary Saunders (University of New Brunswick), Carl Schaefer (University of Connecticut), David Schimpf (University of Minnesota, Duluth), William H. Schlesinger (Duke University), Robert Schorr (Colorado State University), David Schwartz (Houston Community College), Christa Schwintzer (University of Maine), Erik P. Scully (Towson State University), Edna Seaman (Northeastern University), Orono Shukdeb Sen (Bethune-Cookman College), Wendy Sera (Seton Hill University), Timothy Shannon (Francis Marion University), Joan Sharp (Simon Fraser University), Victoria C. Sharpe (Blinn College), Elaine Shea (Loyola College, Maryland), Stephen Sheckler (Virginia Polytechnic Institute and State University), Richard Sherwin (University of Pittsburgh), Lisa Shimeld (Crafton Hills College), James Shinkle (Trinity University), Barbara Shipes (Hampton University), Richard Showman (University of South Carolina), Peter Shugarman (University of Southern California), Alice Shuttey (DeKalb Community College), James Sidie (Ursinus College), Daniel Simberloff (Florida State University), Anne Simon (University of Maryland), Alastair Simpson (Dalhousie University), Susan Singer (Carleton College), Roger Sloboda (Dartmouth University), John Smarrelli (Le Moyne College), Andrew T. Smith (Arizona State University), Kelly Smith (University of North Florida), Nancy Smith-Huerta (Miami Ohio University), John Smol (Queen's University), Andrew J. Snope (Essex Community College), Mitchell Sogin (Woods Hole Marine Biological Laboratory), Susan Sovonick-Dunford (University of Cincinnati), Frederick W. Spiegel (University of Arkansas), Amanda Starnes (Emory University), Karen Steudel (University of Wisconsin), Barbara Stewart (Swarthmore College), Cecil Still (Rutgers University, New Brunswick), Margery Stinson (Southwestern College), James Stockand (University of Texas Health Science Center, San Antonio), John Stolz (California Institute of Technology), Richard D. Storey (Colorado College), Stephen Strand (University of California, Los Angeles), Eric Strauss (University of Massachusetts, Boston), Antony Stretton (University of Wisconsin-Madison), Russell Stullken (Augusta College), Mark Sturtevant (University of Michigan-Flint), John Sullivan (Southern Oregon State University), Gerald Summers (University of Missouri), Judith Sumner (Assumption College), Marshall D. Sundberg (Emporia State University), Lucinda Swatzell (Southeast Missouri State University), Daryl Sweeney (University of Illinois, Champaign-Urbana), Samuel S. Sweet (University of California, Santa Barbara), Janice Swenson (University of North Florida), Lincoln Taiz (University of California, Santa Cruz), Samuel Tarsitano (Southwest Texas State University), David Tauck (Santa Clara University), James Taylor (University of New Hampshire), John Taylor (University of California, Berkeley), Martha R. Taylor (Cornell University), Thomas Terry (University of Connecticut), Roger Thibault (Bowling Green State University), William Thomas (Colby-Sawyer College), Cyril Thong (Simon Fraser University), John Thornton (Oklahoma State University), Robert Thornton (University of California, Davis), Stephen Timme (Pittsburg State University), Leslie Towill (Arizona State University), James Traniello (Boston University), Constantine Tsoukas (San Diego State University), Marsha Turell (Houston Community College), Robert Tuveson (University of Illinois, Urbana), Maura G. Tyrrell (Stonehill College), Catherine Uekert (Northern Arizona University), Gordon Uno (University of Oklahoma), Lisa A. Urry (Mills College), James W. Valentine (University of California, Santa Barbara), Joseph Vanable (Purdue University), Theodore Van Bruggen (University of South Dakota), Kathryn VandenBosch (Texas A&M University), Gerald Van Dyke (North Carolina State University), Brandi Van Roo (Framingham State College), Moira Van Staaden (Bowling Green State), Frank Visco (Orange Coast College), Laurie Vitt (University of California, Los Angeles), Neal Voelz (St. Cloud State University), Thomas J. Volk (University of Wisconsin, La Crosse), Susan D. Waaland (University of Washington), William Wade (Dartmouth Medical College), D. Alexander Wait (Southwest Missouri State University), John Waggoner (Loyola Marymount University), Jyoti Wagle (Houston Community College), Edward Wagner (University of California, Irvine), Dan Walker (San Jose State University), Robert L. Wallace (Ripon College), Jeffrey Walters (North Carolina State University), Margaret Waterman (University of Pittsburgh), Charles Webber (Loyola University of Chicago), Peter Webster (University of Massachusetts, Amherst), Terry Webster (University of Connecticut, Storrs), Beth Wee (Tulane University), Peter Wejksnora (University of Wisconsin, Milwaukee), Kentwood Wells (University of Connecticut), David J. Westenberg, (University of Missouri, Rolla), Matt White (Ohio University), Stephen Williams (Glendale Community College), Elizabeth Willott (University of Arizona), Christopher Wills (University of California, San Diego), Fred Wilt (University of California, Berkeley), E. William Wischusen (Louisiana State University), Clarence Wolfe (Northern Virginia Community College), Robert T. Woodland (University of Massachusetts Medical School), Joseph Woodring (Louisiana State University), Patrick Woolley (East Central College), Philip Yant (University of Michigan), Linda Yasui (Northern Illinois University), Hideo Yonenaka (San Francisco State University), Edward Zalisko (Blackburn College), Zai Ming Zhao (University of Texas, Austin), John Zimmerman (Kansas State University), Uko Zylstra (Calvin College)

Acknowledgments

The authors wish to express their gratitude to the global community of instructors, researchers, students, and publishing professionals who have contributed to this edition.

As authors of this text, we are mindful of the daunting challenge of keeping up to date in all areas of our rapidly expanding subject. We are grateful to the numerous scientists who helped shape this edition by discussing their research fields with us, answering specific questions in their areas of expertise, and, often, sharing their ideas about biology education.

For advice in updating the phylogeny of Galápagos finches in Chapter 1, we are indebted to Kevin Burns and Peter Grant. For assistance with the chapters of Units 1 through 3 (chemistry, cell biology, and genetics), we first wish to thank the members of the Mills College Biology and Chemistry/Physics Department, notably Barbara Bowman and Elisabeth Wade. We are also grateful to Tom Owens and Mimi Zolan, who were each exceptionally generous with their time and knowledge, and to Michael Black, Laurie Heyer, and Ed Blake, for noteworthy contributions to figures. And we thank the individuals who took the time to share their expertise on early atmospheric conditions (Laura Schaefer), cell biology (Pat Zambryski, Steve King, Jeremy Reiter, and Jeff Hardin), gene regulation (Phil Zamore, Dave Bartel, Tom Gingeras, Steve Bell, Saba Valadkhan, Joe Heilig, Lorraine Pillus, and Mike Levine), current cloning approaches (Caroline Kane and Andy Cameron), genomics (Nikos Krypides, Emir Khatipov, and Rebekah Rasooly), and homeobox genes (Bill McGinnis). In addition, we thank Lisa Weasel for her feedback on the new "Tips for Genetics Problems."

For the chapters of Units 4 and 5, on evolution and the diversity of life, researchers who generously shared their expertise with us included Richard Anthony, Nick Barton, Toby Bradshaw, Keith Clay, Kevin de Queiroz, Peter and Rosemary Grant, Daniel J. Howard, Patrick Keeling, Andrew H. Knoll, Jon Mallatt, Amy McCune, Axel Meyer, Kevin J. Peterson, Loren Rieseberg, Ole Seehausen, and Mark Webster.

For Units 6 through 8, the units on plant and animal form and function, and ecology, we benefited greatly from the expertise of Charles Michel, Eric Britt, Don Boyer, and Alan French. In addition, Tom Deerinck, Peter Gillespie, Mark Chappell, and Doug DeSimone provided important assistance with figures. We also thank Eric Simon, a coauthor of the Campbell nonmajors texts, for helping us think through some terminology and presentation dilemmas in Unit 7.

And finally, for her many contributions throughout the book, we sincerely thank Marty Taylor, the author of the *Student Study Guide* and a coauthor of *Biology: Concepts & Connections.*

A total of 228 biologists, listed on pages xxiv–xxix, provided detailed reviews of one or more chapters for this edition, helping us ensure the book's scientific accuracy and improve its pedagogical effectiveness. Special thanks for exceptional contributions go to Johnny El-Rady, Graeme Lindbeck, Bruce Riley, Robert Fowler, Alan Gishlick, Alastair Simpson, Ken Halanych, Kevin Padian, John Taylor, Jay Comeaux, Grace Wyngaard, Lauren Garner, Missy Holbrook, Toby Kellogg, Eduardo Zeiger, Richard Norman, Albert Herrera, and Patricia Schulte. Thanks also to the numerous other professors and students, from all over the world, who offered suggestions directly to the authors. Of course, we alone bear the responsibility for any errors that remain in the text, but the dedication of our consultants, reviewers, and other correspondents makes us especially confident in the accuracy and effectiveness of this edition.

Conducting the unit-opening interviews was again one of the great pleasures of revising *BIOLOGY*. For the Eighth Edition, we are proud to include interviews with Deborah Gordon, Paul Nurse, Terry Orr-Weaver, Scott Edwards, Sean Carroll, Pat Zambryski, Masashi Yanagisawa, and Diana Wall (see p. xi). We thank these busy people for generously sharing their experiences with us.

The value of *BIOLOGY* as a learning tool is greatly enhanced by the supplementary materials that have been created for instructors and students. We recognize that the dedicated authors of these materials are essentially writing mini (and not so mini) books. We much appreciate the hard work and creativity of the following: Ruth Buskirk and Christopher Gillen (authors of the new *Inquiry in Action: Interpreting Scientific Papers*); Judith Morgan and Eloise Brown Carter (*Investigating Biology*, 6th Edition); Jean Heitz and Cynthia Giffen (*Practicing Biology*, 3rd Edition); Margaret Waterman and Ethel Stanley (*Biological Inquiry: A Workbook of Investigative Cases*, 2nd Edition); Bill Barstow, Louise Paquin, Michael Dini, John Lepri, John Zarnetske, C. O. Patterson, and Jean DeSaix (*Test Bank*); Ed Zalisko, Margaret Ricci, Lauren Garner, Jung Choi, and Virginia White (*Media Quizzes*); Joan Sharp (*Lecture Outlines, PowerPoint Lectures,* and *Student Misconceptions*); Erin Barley (*PowerPoint Lectures*); Bill Wischusen, Ruth Buskirk, Jung Choi, John Merrill, Melissa Michael, Randy Phillis, Mark Lyford, and Chris Gregg (*Active Learning Questions*); and Laura Zanello (*Spanish Glossary*). Once again, we thank our long-time colleague Marty Taylor for her excellent work on the *Student Study Guide*; she has now completed eight editions of this popular student aid. Special thanks go to Tom Owens for his visionary work on the *BioFlix* animations and his creative, collaborative work as lead author on our new *MasteringBiology* tutorials. We also thank Brad Williamson, Jennifer Yeh, Dawn Keller, and Scott Bowling for their excellent work on the *BioFlix* animations and the accompanying student tools. In addition, we are grateful to the many other people—biology instructors, editors, artists, production experts, and narrators—who are listed in the credits for these and other elements of the electronic media that accompany the book. Finally, we thank the class testers and reviewers of *BioFlix* and *MasteringBiology* who are listed on pages xxv–xxvi.

BIOLOGY, Eighth Edition, results from an unusually strong synergy between a team of scientists and a team of publishing professionals. The expansion of the author team and major revision of many chapters, the creation of new pedagogical features and the improvement of old ones, and the exceptionally rich package of supplements created unprecedented challenges for the publishing team.

The members of our core editorial team at Benjamin Cummings—our Fab Five—brought unmatched talents, commitment, and pedagogical insights to this revision, and working with this team over the past three years has been a great pleasure. Our Editor-in-Chief, Beth Wilbur, continues to be a full colleague in the book's ongoing evolution and a respected advocate for biology education in the academic community. Our extraordinary Supervising Editors, Pat Burner and Beth Winickoff, once again had the awesome responsibility of overseeing in detail the work of all the authors, developmental editors, and developmental artists. Together, Beth and Pat ensured that every page of every chapter has the text, figures, and pedagogy to make this edition the most effective biology textbook ever. Deborah Gale, Executive Director of Development, and our Senior Editorial Manager, the incomparable Ginnie Simione Jutson, oversaw the entire project on a day-by-day basis, a feat equivalent to running a three-ring circus. Ginnie's patience and resourcefulness and Deborah's oversight of the project as a whole have enabled the entire book team to operate at a level of sanity that would not have been possible without their guidance.

We were fortunate to have on our team some of college publishing's top developmental editors. In addition to Beth Winickoff and Pat Burner (who did important hands-on editing themselves, as well as their many other tasks), the primary developmental editors for this edition were John Burner and Matt Lee, joined as the project progressed by Alice Fugate and Suzanne Olivier. We are deeply grateful to all our editors for making us better writers, teachers, and biologists.

Biology is a visual subject, and we are indebted to our developmental artists Hilair Chism, Carla Simmons, Andrew Recher, Connie Balek, and Kelly Murphy for helping us make all our figures better tools for teaching and learning—as well as visually appealing. In addition, the support of our bright, efficient, and good-natured Editorial Assistants—Julia Khait, Ben Pearson, and Logan Triglia—is much appreciated. We couldn't have finished the book without them! We also want to thank Robin Heyden for organizing the annual Benjamin Cummings Biology Leadership Conferences, which always bring us closer to the teaching community and offer a fresh supply of creative teaching ideas from outstanding biology educators.

You would not have a book in your hands today if not for the herculean efforts of the book production team, which has the crucial responsibility of converting the text manuscript and illustrations to pages ready for the printer. For the Eighth Edition, these efforts were headed up by Managing Editor Mike Early. We thank him, as well as our longtime copyeditor Janet Greenblatt, proofreaders Joanna Dinsmore and Marie Dartman, Permissions Editors Sue Ewing and Marcy Lunetta, and indexers Lynn Armstrong and Charlotte Shane. Handling the illustrations were Art Editors Laura Murray and Kelly Murphy; the final rendering of the new and revised illustrations was carried out by the artists of Precision Graphics, working under Kristina Seymour. Senior Photo Editor Donna Kalal and photo researcher Maureen Spuhler obtained a large number of handsome and informative photos for this edition. We are indebted to the entire art and photo team. For the beautiful design of the book's interior, we want to thank Art and Design Director Mark Ong and Design Manager Marilyn Perry for their design of text and art styles that show off the words and pictures in a way that will appeal to readers and help them learn. (And thanks to both of them for their endless patience with all our concerns!) For the user-friendly page layouts, we are grateful to Jennifer Dunn and Jana Anderson. And many thanks to Yvo Riezebos for designing the striking cover. Putting together all the pieces of this complicated book were the staff at S4Carlisle Publishing Services, led by Production Manager Lori Dalberg and Composition Supervisor Holly Paige. Thank you, Lori and Holly!

We are pleased to thank the topnotch publishing professionals who worked on the book's printed supplements: Senior Supplements Project Editor Susan Berge, who coordinated the entire print supplements package; Production Supervisor Jane Brundage; Developmental Editor Susan Weisberg; and Project Editors Mary Douglas, Kim Wimpsett, Elizabeth Campbell, and Melanie Field.

With regard to the wonderful package of electronic media that accompanies the book, we offer special thanks to Senior Media Producer Jon Ballard, Project Editors Nora Lally-Graves and Brienn Buchanan, media correlators Nina Lewallen Hufford and Sarah Kaminker, and proofreader Pete Shanks for their work on the website. We also are grateful to Associate Web Developer Linda Young and Web Technologies Manager Steve Wright. For their work on the *Instructor Resource CD/DVD-ROM*, we thank Project Manager James Bruce; Developmental Artist Hilair Chism; Developmental Editors John Burner, Pat Burner, Matt Lee, and Beth Winickoff; copyeditor John Hammett (*PPT Lectures*); proofreader Pete Shanks (*PPT Lectures*); and Donna King, Production Project Manager at Progressive Information Technologies.

We are especially grateful to the team of publishing professionals whose combined talents are evident in the *BioFlix* animations and student tools: Pat Burner, Russell Chun (storyboard artist extraordinaire), Ginnie Simione Jutson, Jon Ballard, Karen Gulliver (developmental editor), Animated Biomedical Productions (animation production); and Groove 11 (tutorial production). For their work on *MasteringBiology*, we thank the aforementioned Pat Burner, Ginnie Simione Jutson, and Jon Ballard, plus Tania Mlawer, Director of Content Development and Project Management; Mary Catherine Hager, Developmental Editor; Deb Greco, Media Producer; Kristen Sutton, Content Lead; and Developmental Artist Jay McElroy and the artists at Pearson Production Solutions. For their hard work and support, our appreciation goes to the MasteringX Team (in alphabetical order): Ruth Berry, Lewis Costas, Katherine Foley, Julia Henderson, Joseph Ignazi, Jeff King, David Kokorowski, Mary Lee, Claire Masson, Nissi Mathews, Adam Morton, Fred Mueller, Ian Nordby, Maria Panos, Andrea Pascarella, Mary Ann Perry, Caroline Power, Sarah Smith, Margaret Trombley, and Rasil Warnakulasooriya. Last, but not least, we thank Lauren Fogel, Director of Media Development at Benjamin Cummings, for her continued leadership on all things media.

For their important roles in marketing the book, we are very grateful to Director of Marketing Christy Lawrence, Executive Marketing Manager Lauren Harp, and Market Development Manager Josh Frost. For the creation of visually stunning print and electronic promotional materials, we thank Creative Director Lillian Carr; Marketing Communication Specialists Jane Campbell, Kristi Hlaing, and Jessica Perry; Designer Laurie Campbell; Web Designer Mansour Bethoney, who led the creation of the e-brochure; and Webmaster Anna Molodtsova.

Linda Davis, President of Pearson Math, Economics, and Science, has shared our commitment to excellence and provided strong support for four editions now, and we are happy to thank her once again. We also want to thank Paul Corey, now President of Pearson Science, for his enthusiasm, encouragement, and support.

The Pearson Science sales team, which represents *BIOLOGY* on campus, is our living link to the students and professors who use the text. The field representatives tell us what you like and don't like about the book, and they provide prompt service to biology departments. They are strong allies in biology education, and we thank them for their professionalism in communicating the features of our book. For representing our book and its teaching values to our wider international audience, we thank the sustained work of our sales and marketing partners throughout the world, including (but by no means only) Marlene Olsavsky, Ann Oravetz, and Pablo Rendina.

Finally, we wish to thank our families and friends for their encouragement and patience throughout this long project. Our special thanks to: Paul, Dan, Maria, Armelle, and Sean (J.R.); Lily, Grant, Ross, Lily-too, and Alex (L.U.); Debra and Hannah (M.C.); Harry, Elga, Aaron, Sophie, Noah, and Gabriele (S.W.); Natalie (P.M.); and Sally, Robert, David, and Will (R.J.). And as always, Rochelle and Allison.

Jane Reece, Lisa Urry, Michael Cain,
Steve Wasserman, Peter Minorsky, and Rob Jackson

Detailed Contents

CONCEPT **34.8**

Humans are mammals that have a large brain and bipedal locomotion (pp. 728–733)

- **Derived Characters of Humans** Humans are bipedal and have a larger brain and reduced jaw compared to other apes.
- **The Earliest Hominins** Hominins—humans and species that are more closely related to humans than to chimpanzees—originated in Africa at least 6–7 million years ago. Early hominins had a small brain but probably walked upright.
- **Australopiths** Australopiths lived 4–2 million years ago. Some species walked upright and had human-like hands and teeth.
- **Bipedalism** Hominins began to walk long distances on two legs about 1.9 million years ago.
- **Tool Use** The oldest evidence of tool use—cut marks on animal bones—is 2.5 million years old.
- **Early *Homo*** *Homo ergaster* was the first fully bipedal, large-brained hominin. *Homo erectus* was the first hominin to leave Africa.
- **Neanderthals** Neanderthals lived in Europe and the Near East about 200,000—28,000 years ago.
- ***Homo Sapiens*** *Homo sapiens* appeared in Africa by about 195,000 years ago. Its spread to other continents about 115,000 years ago may have been preceded by genetic changes that enabled language and other aspects of cognition. Research into the origins and contemporaries of *Homo sapiens* is a lively area.

MEDIA
Activity Human Evolution

TESTING YOUR KNOWLEDGE

SELF-QUIZ

1. Vertebrates and tunicates share
a. jaws adapted for feeding.
b. a high degree of cephalization.
c. the formation of structures from the neural crest.
d. an endoskeleton that includes a skull.
e. a notochord and a dorsal, hollow nerve cord.

2. Some animals that lived 530 million years ago resembled lancelets but had a brain and a skull. These animals may represent
a. the first chordates.
b. a "missing link" between urochordates and cephalochordates.
c. early craniates.
d. marsupials.
e. nontetrapod gnathostomes.

3. Which of the following could be considered the most recent common ancestor of living tetrapods?
a. a sturdy-finned, shallow-water lobe-fin whose appendages had skeletal supports similar to those of terrestrial vertebrates
b. an armored, jawed placoderm with two pairs of appendages
c. an early ray-finned fish that developed bony skeletal supports in its paired fins
d. a salamander that had legs supported by a bony skeleton but moved with the side-to-side bending typical of fishes
e. an early terrestrial caecilian whose legless condition had evolved secondarily

4. Mammals and living birds share all of the following characteristics *except*
a. endothermy.
b. descent from a common amniotic ancestor.
c. a dorsal, hollow nerve cord.
d. an archosaur common ancestor.
e. an amniotic egg.

5. Unlike eutherians, *both* monotremes and marsupials
a. lack nipples.
b. have some embryonic development outside the mother's uterus.
c. lay eggs.
d. are found in Australia and Africa.
e. include only insectivores and herbivores.

6. Which clade does *not* include humans?
a. synapsids
b. lobe-fins
c. diapsids
d. craniates
e. osteichthyans

7. As hominins diverged from other primates, which of the following appeared first?
a. reduced jawbones
b. language
c. bipedal locomotion
d. the making of stone tools
e. an enlarged brain

For Self-Quiz answers, see Appendix A.

MEDIA Visit the Study Area at **www.masteringbio.com** for a Practice Test.

EVOLUTION CONNECTION

8. Identify one characteristic that qualifies humans for membership in each of the following clades: eukaryotes, animals, deuterostomes, chordates, vertebrates, gnathostomes, amniotes, mammals, primates.

SCIENTIFIC INQUIRY

9. **DRAW IT** As a consequence of size alone, organisms that are large tend to have larger brains than organisms that are small. However, some organisms have brains that are considerably larger than expected for an animal of their size. There are high costs associated with the development and maintenance of brains that are large relative to body size.

(a) The fossil record documents trends in which brains that are large relative to body size evolved in certain lineages, including hominins. In such lineages, what can you infer about the relative magnitude of the costs and benefits of large brains?

(b) Hypothesize how natural selection might favor the evolution of large brains despite the high maintenance costs of such brains.

(c) Data for 14 bird species are listed below. Graph the data, placing deviation from expected brain size on the *x*-axis and mortality rate on the *y*-axis. What can you conclude about the relationship between brain size and mortality?

Deviation from Expected Brain Size*	-2.4	-2.1	2.0	-1.8	-1.0	0.0	0.3	0.7	1.2	1.3	2.0	2.3	3.0	3.2
Mortality Rate	0.9	0.7	0.5	0.9	0.4	0.7	0.8	0.4	0.8	0.3	0.6	0.6	0.3	0.6

*Negative values indicate brain sizes smaller than expected; positive values indicate brain sizes larger than expected.
Source: D. Sol et al., Big-brained birds survive better in nature, *Proceedings of the Royal Society B* 274:763–769 (2007).

UNIT 6

Plant Form and Function

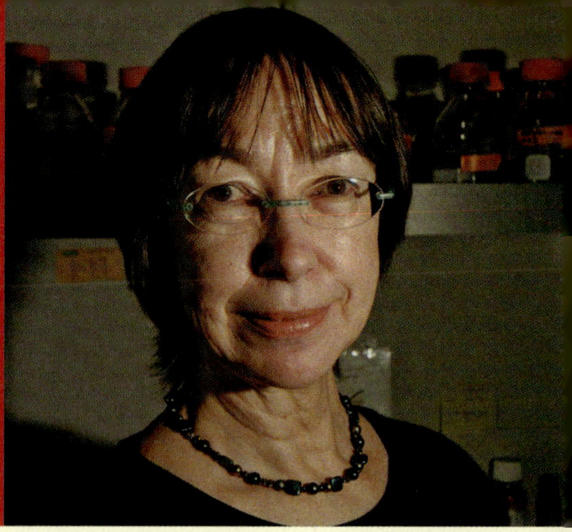

AN INTERVIEW WITH

Patricia C. Zambryski

Pat Zambryski opened the door to genetic engineering in plants by discovering how the bacterium *Agrobacterium tumefaciens* transfers DNA into the plants it infects, and her lab continues to provide insights into this process. She also has a second major research area: plasmodesmata, the channels through plant cell walls. Her work in this area is shedding light on cell-to-cell communication, plant development, and defenses against pathogens. Dr. Zambryski grew up in Montreal, Canada, where she graduated from McGill University, and she earned her Ph.D. from the University of Colorado. After postdoctoral research at the University of California, San Francisco (UCSF), she spent five years as a senior investigator at Ghent University in Belgium. A member of the National Academy of Sciences, Dr. Zambryski is currently a professor of plant and microbial biology at the University of California, Berkeley.

What were the subjects of your early research, leading up to your work with *Agrobacterium*?

In grad school at the University of Colorado, I worked on bacteriophage T4. To learn how to evaluate data and pose new questions in biology, it's good to work with a simple system like a phage or bacterium because you can do an experiment in one day and get the answer quickly. Especially in those days, before genetic engineering, if you were working with a multicellular eukaryote, a research project could take a long, long time. I used gel electrophoresis to separate and identify all the different proteins that this phage made, and I determined that specific groups of proteins were made at different times during infection.

Then I went to UCSF to do a post-doc. I was interested in working with animal tumor viruses. But after a few years I realized that there were thousands of people in that field—all working on the same small viruses, with tiny genomes that encoded just a few proteins! And I didn't feel like I could contribute something novel with so many people working on the same thing.

At the time, there was a powerful new method for using two-dimensional electrophoresis to separate all the proteins from cell extracts, and I was looking at the proteins made in a number of different biological systems. I was invited to visit a lab at Ghent University to use these 2-D gels to try to figure out what might be the gene product that enabled *Agrobacterium tumefaciens* to cause tumors in plants. While I was there, it occurred to me that this would be a very good biological system to study. Little was known about it, and it was a fascinating system of genetic transfer from a prokaryote to a eukaryote. So I got involved with tumors after all—but tumors in plants rather than animals!

It had already been discovered that there was a piece of DNA that *Agrobacterium* transferred into the plant it infected, but we didn't know the exact composition of that DNA, the nature of its borders with surrounding DNA, or how the transfer happened. Meanwhile, back at UCSF, people were just starting to do DNA cloning using phage lambda. When I returned there, my project was to clone the piece of *Agrobacterium* DNA that was inserted into the plant genome—the T DNA—and find out what the ends of the T DNA were.

I would spend summers in Ghent learning the biology of *Agrobacterium* and then return to UCSF to work on cloning the T DNA. Finally, after one summer, I decided to stay, and I spent the next five years at Ghent University. That's where a really big thing happened. I had figured out what the T-DNA ends were, and in Ghent I discovered that *any* DNA inserted between these ends (by recombinant DNA technology) would be transferred to plant cells and stably integrated into their genomes. It was the birth of genetic engineering in plants. [See Figure 20.25 to review how T DNA is used.]

For the genetic engineering of plants, how does the *Agrobacterium* system compare with a "gene gun"?

People generally prefer to use the *Agrobacterium* system because all the DNA carried between the ends of the T element is precisely integrated into the plant cell's DNA. *Agrobacterium* DNA transfer is more precise and significantly more efficient than shooting foreign DNA into plant cells using a gene gun, which fires tiny pellets coated with DNA. But for plants that are not susceptible to *Agrobacterium* infection, you have to use a gene gun.

What have you been studying recently in *Agrobacterium*?

Bacteria have various molecular systems that allow them to transport things out of the cell (secretion) or take things up. A major focus of our current research is one specific bacterial secretion system, called type IV, which is used by *Agrobacterium*. This system is used for translocating both DNA, as in bacterial conjugation, and proteins. In *Agrobacterium*, generation of a transferable T-DNA segment and expression of the type IV secretion system have evolved to occur only in the presence of a wounded plant cell. The wounded cell then is the recipient for DNA and protein transport. It turns out that type IV secretion systems are also used to secrete toxins into host cells by bacteria that are pathogenic for humans, such as those that cause whooping cough, stomach ulcers, and Legionnaires' disease. The system probably evolved first as a bacterial conjugation system and later developed the ability to transfer DNA and proteins to eukaryotic hosts, causing disease. Recall that in nature *Agrobacterium* causes disease—tumorous growths on plants.

How did you become interested in plasmodesmata, your other major area of research?

Although my background was mostly in microbiology, I was hired by a plant biology department, here at Berkeley. So I said to myself, this is cool—maybe I should do some experiments with plants! But knowing almost nothing about plants, I decided to work on something about which little was known. So I started to work on plasmodesmata because I thought I could contribute to the field of plant intercellular communication. I didn't want to start with a well-studied system like photosynthesis!

What are plasmodesmata, and what is currently known about their function?

When adjacent plant cells need to communicate, information must be transferred across the thick cell walls that lie outside the plasma membrane. Plasmodesmata are plant-specific communication channels that span the cell walls and link the cytoplasm of adjacent cells; the plasma membrane of the two cells is continuous in these places. At first, it was thought that plasmodesmata were a fixed size, with apertures so narrow that only ions and small molecules such as sugars and hormones could pass through. However, it was also known that plant viruses could commandeer plasmodesmata, and it was discovered that these viruses encode proteins that open the channels enough to allow passage of the virus.

The big breakthrough in recent years has been the discovery that, even in plants not infected with a virus, the apertures of plasmodesmata are dynamic. And the apertures can open wide enough to allow the transport not only of small molecules but also of macromolecules such as RNA or protein. Also, the aperture size can change during development, both during embryonic development and during the development of new tissues and organs from regions of mature plants called meristems. This discovery has tremendous implications for how plant development proceeds. Immature tissues such as those found in embryos and meristems have very dilated plasmodesmata, suggesting that plasmodesma-mediated communication between cells is likely to be involved in the initiation and coordination of developmental processes.

What do you want to find out about plasmodesmata now?

We want to understand how the structure and function of plasmodesmata are regulated, both during embryonic development and in the life of the mature plant. To get at this, we have been searching for the genes that are responsible for this regulation. We've collected mutants that are deficient in regulating transport between cells of the embryo. We reasoned that we could not screen for mutants in mature plants because plasmodesmata are so important that any mutant would be a dead plant. Thus, we assay plasmodesmata function in so-called embryo defective lines that can be propagated as heterozygotes. The seedpods of heterozygote plants contain both wild-type and homozygous mutant embryos that develop enough to allow us to assay for plasmodesma-mediated transport. Once we identify the gene products affected by the mutations, we can study how these proteins affect the regulation of plasmodesmata in older plants, as well.

Fluorescent tracers are key tools in our research. Tracers of small molecular weight can move from cell to cell during all embryonic stages. However, larger tracers move freely only during the earlier stages. That means there is "down regulation" of plasmodesma apertures during embryonic development. So we used the large fluorescent tracers in a genetic screen for mutants that continued to traffic it at late embryonic stages. We screened 5,000 mutants in this way to find about 10 embryo-defective mutants of the sort we were looking for! Now we're cloning the genes affected, trying to identify their products, and seeing how they affect plasmodesmata.

I want the students to realize that plants are absolutely critical to our lives and also interesting in their own right.

How does the regulation of plasmodesma size benefit the plant?

In a tiny embryo, it makes sense for all the cells to be in communication with each other so that development is properly coordinated. Then, as cells differentiate and tissues and organs develop, groups of cells with related functions need to be in communication. Later, as cells and tissues develop unique functions, they may lose communication with adjacent regions. Cell differentiation occurs by regulation of gene expression, but development requires another layer of control on top of that—the control of what gene products can move cell to cell via plasmodesmata, which in turn coordinates development throughout the plant body.

Why do you and most other plant molecular biologists use *Arabidopsis thaliana* as a research organism?

You can grow thousands of these small plants in a small space, and they go from seed to seed in six weeks. *Arabidopsis* has a small genome, less than one twentieth the size of the corn or human genomes, making it easy to clone its genes. Its genome has been sequenced. The genetics are fabulous. Almost every gene has been tagged by T-DNA insertions to make mutants with particular phenotypes and to facilitate cloning of their affected genes. This plant is very convenient to work with for those reasons and more.

Along with laboratory research, do you enjoy teaching?

When I started teaching, I taught only graduate students, but I've found that I really enjoy teaching undergraduates, too. I teach a class with no prerequisites called "The Secret Life of Plants." I want the students to realize that plants are absolutely critical to our lives and also interesting in their own right. I want students to have enough understanding of science to read the popular press and form decisions about important issues such as global warming and genetically modified organisms (GMOs). We talk about basic biology that is unique to plants, but also about global warming, GMOs, biofuels, and medicinal plants, among other applied topics. Teaching that course is one of the most rewarding things I do.

Inquiry in Action

Learn about an experiment by Pat Zambryski and colleagues in Inquiry Figure 36.22 on page 782.

Jane Reece (left) and Pat Zambryski

35 Plant Structure, Growth, and Development

▲ **Figure 35.1 Why does this plant have two types of leaves?**

KEY CONCEPTS

35.1 The plant body has a hierarchy of organs, tissues, and cells
35.2 Meristems generate cells for new organs
35.3 Primary growth lengthens roots and shoots
35.4 Secondary growth adds girth to stems and roots in woody plants
35.5 Growth, morphogenesis, and differentiation produce the plant body

OVERVIEW

Plastic Plants?

Although the graceful fanwort (*Cabomba caroliniana*) **(Figure 35.1)** is an attractive addition to many aquariums, its most striking feature is its extreme *developmental plasticity*—its ability to alter its form in response to local environmental conditions. The underwater leaves are feathery, an adaptation that protects them from damage by lessening their resistance to moving water. In contrast, the surface leaves are pads that aid in flotation. Both leaf types have genetically identical cells, but dissimilar environments result in the turning on or off of different genes during leaf development. Such extreme developmental plasticity is much more common in plants than in animals and may help compensate for plants' inability to escape adverse conditions by moving.

In addition to structural responses by an individual plant to a specific environment, entire species have by natural selection accumulated adaptations in **morphology**, or external form, that vary little among plants within the species. For example, most cactus species, regardless of local environment, have leaves that are so highly reduced—to spines—that the stems are the primary photosynthetic organs. This adaptation in leaf morphology enhances the survival and reproductive success of cacti because with reduced leaf surface areas, these desert plants lose less water.

Both genetic and environmental factors influence form in plants and animals, but the effect of environment is greater in plants. Consequently, plants typically vary much more within a species than do animals. All lions, for example, have four legs and are roughly the same size at maturity. In contrast, ginkgo trees vary greatly in the numbers, sizes, and positions of their roots, branches, and leaves. Lacking mobility, plants must be adapted to their environment in other ways. Thus, plant form is central to understanding how plants compete in nature.

This chapter focuses on how the body of a plant is formed, setting the stage for the rest of this unit on plant biology. Chapters 29 and 30 described the evolution and characteristics of nonvascular plants, seedless vascular plants, gymnosperms, and angiosperms (flowering plants). Here, in Unit Six, we'll focus primarily on vascular plants—especially angiosperms, because they account for about 90% of plant species and are of great importance to humans. As the world's population increases, the need for plants to supply food, fuel, fiber, medicine, lumber, and paper has never been greater, heightening the importance of understanding how plants grow and develop.

CONCEPT **35.1**

The plant body has a hierarchy of organs, tissues, and cells

Plants, like most animals, have organs composed of different tissues, which in turn are composed of cells of different types. A **tissue** is a group of cells with a common function, structure, or both. An **organ** consists of several types of tissues that together carry out particular functions. In looking at the hierarchy of plant organs, tissues, and cells, we begin with organs because they are the most familiar and easily observed plant structures. As you learn about the hierarchy of plant structure, keep in mind how natural selection has produced plant forms, at all levels of organization, that fit plant function.

The Three Basic Plant Organs: Roots, Stems, and Leaves

The basic morphology of most vascular plants reflects their evolutionary history as terrestrial organisms that inhabit and draw resources from two very different environments—below ground and above ground. They must absorb water and minerals from below the ground surface and CO_2 and light from above the ground surface. The ability to acquire these resources arose from the evolution of three basic organs—roots, stems, and leaves. These organs form a **root system** and a **shoot system**, the latter consisting of stems and leaves **(Figure 35.2)**. With few exceptions, angiosperms and other vascular plants rely completely on both systems for survival. Roots are typically nonphotosynthetic and starve unless *photosynthates*, the sugars and other carbohydrates produced during photosynthesis, are imported from the shoot system. Conversely, the shoot system depends on the water and minerals that roots absorb from the soil.

Vegetative growth—production of nonreproductive leaves, stems, and roots—is only one stage in a plant's life. Many plants also undergo reproductive growth. In angiosperms, reproductive shoots bear flowers, which are composed of leaves that are highly modified for sexual reproduction. Later in this chapter, we'll discuss the transition from vegetative shoot formation to reproductive shoot formation.

In describing plant organs, we'll draw examples mainly from the two major groups of angiosperms: monocots and eudicots (see Figure 30.13).

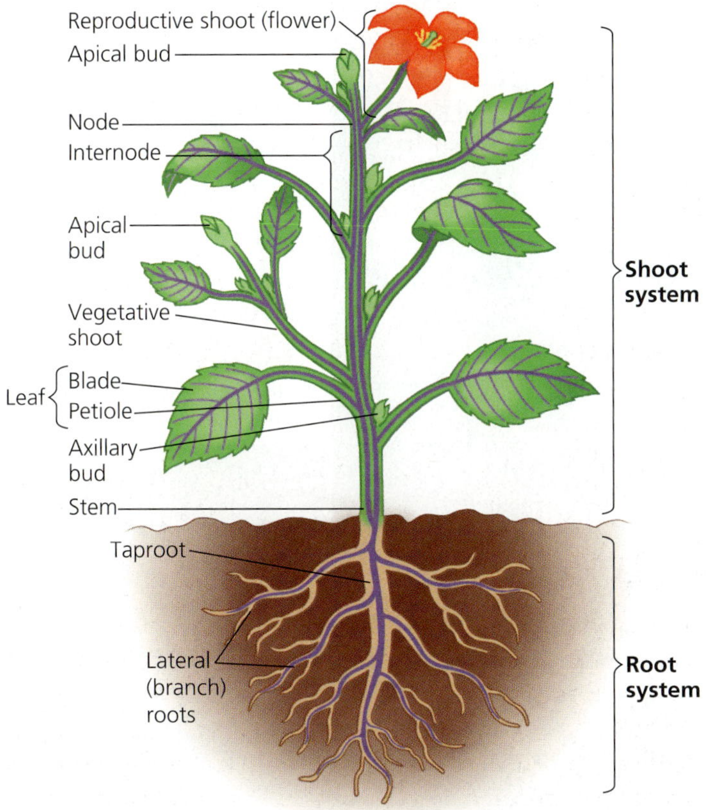

▲ **Figure 35.2 An overview of a flowering plant.** The plant body is divided into a root system and a shoot system, connected by vascular tissue (purple strands in this diagram) that is continuous throughout the plant. The plant shown is an idealized eudicot.

Roots

A **root** is a multicellular organ that anchors a vascular plant in the soil, absorbs minerals and water, and often stores carbohydrates. Most eudicots and gymnosperms have a *taproot system*, consisting of one main vertical root, the **taproot**, that develops from an embryonic root. The taproot gives rise to **lateral roots**, also called branch roots (see Figure 35.2). In many angiosperms, the taproot stores sugars and starches that the plant will consume during flowering and fruit production. For this reason, root crops such as carrots, turnips, and beets are harvested before they flower. Taproot systems generally penetrate deeply and are therefore well adapted to deep soils where the groundwater is not close to the surface.

In seedless vascular plants and in most monocots, such as grasses, the embryonic root dies and does not give rise to a main root. Instead, many small roots grow from the stem. Such roots are said to be *adventitious* (from the Latin *adventicus*, extraneous), a term describing a plant organ that grows in an unusual location, such as roots arising from stems or leaves. Each small root forms its own lateral roots. The result is a *fibrous root system*—a mat of generally thin roots spreading out below the soil surface, with no root functioning as the main one (see Figure 30.13). Fibrous root systems usually do not penetrate deeply and are therefore best adapted to shallow soils or regions where rainfall is light and does not moisten the soil much below the surface layer. Most grasses have shallow roots, concentrated in the upper few centimeters of the soil. Because these shallow roots hold the topsoil in place, grass makes excellent ground cover for preventing erosion.

Although the entire root system helps anchor a plant, in most plants the absorption of water and minerals occurs primarily near the tips of roots, where vast numbers of tiny **root hairs** increase the surface area of the root enormously **(Figure 35.3)**.

◀ **Figure 35.3 Root hairs of a radish seedling.** Root hairs grow by the thousands just behind the tip of each root. By increasing the root's surface area, they greatly enhance the absorption of water and minerals from the soil.

Root hairs are short-lived and constantly replaced. A root hair is a thin, tubular extension of a root epidermal cell. It should not be confused with a lateral root, which is a multicellular organ. Despite their great surface area, root hairs, unlike lateral roots, contribute little to plant anchorage. Their main function is absorption.

Many plants have modified roots **(Figure 35.4)**. Some of these arise from roots, and others are adventitious, developing from stems or, in rare cases, leaves. Some modified roots provide more support and anchorage, whereas others store water and nutrients or absorb oxygen from the air.

Stems

A **stem** is an organ consisting of an alternating system of **nodes**, the points at which leaves are attached, and **internodes**, the stem segments between nodes (see Figure 35.2). In the upper angle (axil) formed by each leaf and the stem is an **axillary bud**, a structure that can form a lateral shoot, commonly called a branch. Most axillary buds of a young shoot are dormant (not growing). Thus, elongation of a young shoot is usually concentrated near the shoot tip, which consists of an **apical bud**, or terminal bud, with developing leaves and a compact series of nodes and internodes.

The proximity of the axillary buds to the apical bud is partly responsible for their dormancy. The inhibition of axillary buds by an apical bud is called **apical dominance**. By concentrating resources on elongation, the evolutionary adaptation of

▼ **Figure 35.4 Modified roots.**

◀ **Prop roots.** The aerial roots of maize (corn) are examples of prop roots, so named because they support tall, top-heavy plants. All roots of a mature maize plant are adventitious after the original roots die. The emerging roots shown here will eventually penetrate the soil.

▶ **Storage roots.** Many plants, such as the common beet, store food and water in their roots.

◀ **"Strangling" aerial roots.** The seeds of this strangler fig germinate in the branches of tall trees of other species and send numerous aerial roots to the ground. These snake-like roots gradually wrap around the host tree and objects such as this Cambodian temple ruin. Eventually, the host tree dies of shading by the fig leaves.

▼ **Buttress roots.** Aerial roots that look like buttresses support the tall trunks of some tropical trees, such as this ceiba tree in Central America.

▲ **Pneumatophores.** Also known as air roots, pneumatophores are produced by trees such as mangroves that inhabit tidal swamps. By projecting above the water's surface, they enable the root system to obtain oxygen, which is lacking in the thick, waterlogged mud.

apical dominance increases the plant's exposure to light. If an animal eats the end of the shoot, or if shading results in the light being more intense to the side of a plant than directly above, axillary buds break dormancy; that is, they start growing. A growing axillary bud gives rise to a lateral shoot, complete with its own apical bud, leaves, and axillary buds. Removing the apical bud usually stimulates the growth of axillary buds, resulting in more lateral shoots. That is why pruning trees and shrubs and pinching back houseplants will make them bushier.

Some plants have stems with additional functions such as food storage and asexual reproduction. These modified stems, which include rhizomes, bulbs, stolons, and tubers, are often mistaken for roots **(Figure 35.5)**.

▼ **Figure 35.5 Modified stems.**

▼ **Rhizomes.** The base of this iris plant is an example of a rhizome, a horizontal shoot that grows just below the surface. Vertical shoots emerge from axillary buds on the rhizome.

▶ **Bulbs.** Bulbs are vertical underground shoots consisting mostly of the enlarged bases of leaves that store food. You can see the many layers of modified leaves attached to the short stem by slicing an onion bulb lengthwise.

▶ **Stolons.** Shown here on a strawberry plant, stolons are horizontal shoots that grow along the surface. These "runners" enable a plant to reproduce asexually, as plantlets form at nodes along each runner.

◀ **Tubers.** Tubers, such as these red potatoes, are enlarged ends of rhizomes or stolons specialized for storing food. The "eyes" of a potato are clusters of axillary buds that mark the nodes.

Leaves

In most vascular plants, the **leaf** is the main photosynthetic organ, although green stems also perform photosynthesis. Leaves vary extensively in form but generally consist of a flattened **blade** and a stalk, the **petiole**, which joins the leaf to the stem at a node (see Figure 35.2). Grasses and many other monocots lack petioles; instead, the base of the leaf forms a sheath that envelops the stem.

Monocots and eudicots differ in the arrangement of **veins**, the vascular tissue of leaves. Most monocots have parallel major veins that run the length of the blade. Eudicots generally have a branched network of major veins (see Figure 30.13).

In identifying angiosperms according to structure, taxonomists rely mainly on floral morphology, but they also use variations in leaf morphology, such as leaf shape, the branching pattern of veins, and the spatial arrangement of leaves. **Figure 35.6** illustrates a difference in leaf shape: simple versus compound. Many

(a) Simple leaf. A simple leaf has a single, undivided blade. Some simple leaves are deeply lobed.

(b) Compound leaf. In a compound leaf, the blade consists of multiple leaflets. Notice that a leaflet has no axillary bud at its base.

(c) Doubly compound leaf. In a doubly compound leaf, each leaflet is divided into smaller leaflets.

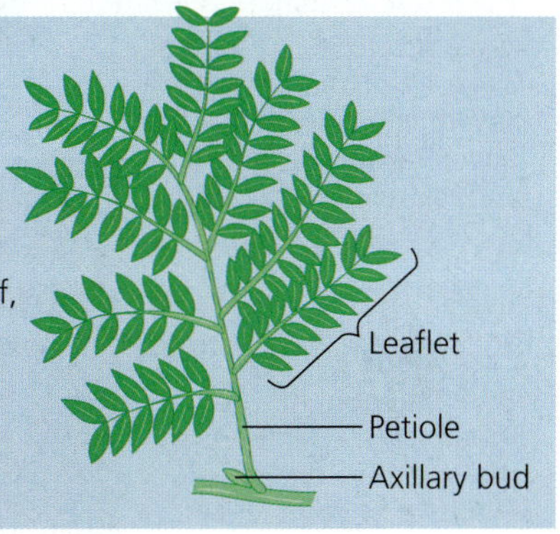

▲ **Figure 35.6 Simple versus compound leaves.** One can distinguish simple leaves from compound leaves by looking for axillary buds. Leaves have axillary buds; leaflets do not.

very large leaves are compound or doubly compound. This structural adaptation may enable large leaves to withstand strong wind with less tearing. It may also confine some pathogens (disease-causing organisms and viruses) that invade the leaf to a single leaflet, rather than allowing them to spread to the entire leaf.

Almost all leaves are specialized for photosynthesis. However, some species have leaves with adaptations that enable them to perform additional functions, such as support, protection, storage, or reproduction **(Figure 35.7)**.

▼ **Figure 35.7 Modified leaves.**

► **Tendrils.** The tendrils by which this pea plant clings to a support are modified leaves. After it has "lassoed" a support, a tendril forms a coil that brings the plant closer to the support. Tendrils are typically modified leaves, but some tendrils are modified stems, as in grapevines.

◄ **Spines.** The spines of cacti, such as this prickly pear, are actually leaves; photosynthesis is carried out by the fleshy green stems.

◄ **Storage leaves.** Most succulents, such as this ice plant, have leaves modified for storing water.

► **Reproductive leaves.** The leaves of some succulents, such as *Kalanchoë daigremontiana*, produce adventitious plantlets, which fall off the leaf and take root in the soil.

► **Bracts.** Often mistaken for petals, the red parts of the poinsettia are actually modified leaves called bracts that surround a group of flowers. Such brightly colored leaves attract pollinators.

Dermal, Vascular, and Ground Tissues

Each plant organ—root, stem, or leaf—has dermal, vascular, and ground tissues. Each of these three categories forms a **tissue system**, a functional unit connecting all of the plant's organs. Although each tissue system is continuous throughout the plant, specific characteristics of the tissues and their spatial relationships to one another vary in different organs **(Figure 35.8)**.

The **dermal tissue system** is the plant's outer protective covering. Like our skin, it forms the first line of defense against physical damage and pathogens. In nonwoody plants, it is usually a single tissue called the **epidermis**, a layer of tightly packed cells. In leaves and most stems, the **cuticle**, a waxy coating on the epidermal surface, helps prevent water loss. In woody plants, protective tissues called **periderm** replace the epidermis in older regions of stems and roots. In addition to protecting the plant from water loss and disease, the epidermis has specialized characteristics in each organ. For example, a root hair is an extension of an epidermal cell near the tip of a root. *Trichomes*, hairlike outgrowths of the shoot epidermis, reduce water loss and reflect excess light. They can also provide defense against insects by forming a barrier or by secreting sticky fluids and toxic

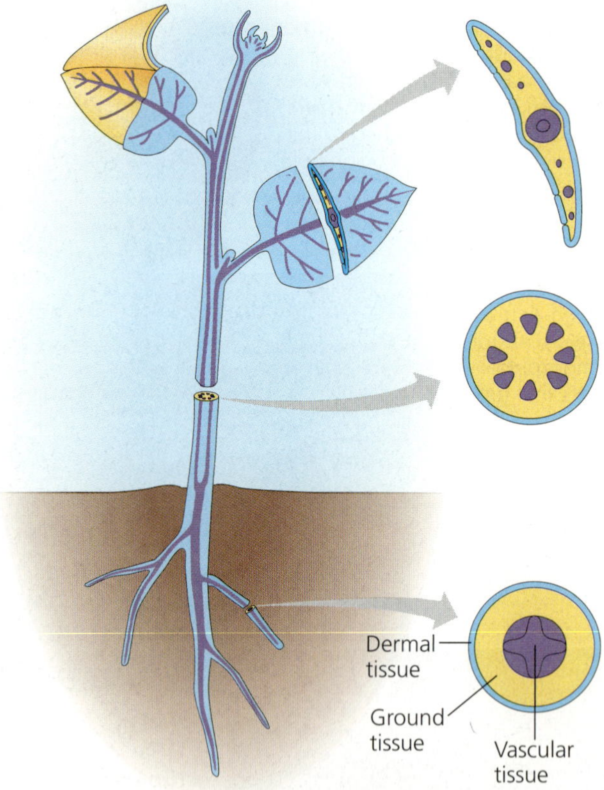

▲ **Figure 35.8 The three tissue systems.** The dermal tissue system (blue) provides a protective cover for the entire body of a plant. The vascular tissue system (purple), which transports materials between the root and shoot systems, is also continuous throughout the plant, but is arranged differently in each organ. The ground tissue system (yellow), which is responsible for most of the plant's metabolic functions, is located between the dermal tissue and the vascular tissue in each organ.

compounds. For instance, the trichomes on aromatic leaves such as mint secrete oils that protect the plants from herbivores and disease. **Figure 35.9** describes an investigation of the relationship between trichome density on soybean pods and damage by beetles.

▼ **Figure 35.9 Inquiry**

Do soybean pod trichomes deter herbivores?

EXPERIMENT Bean leaf beetles (*Cerotoma trifurcata*) feed on developing legume pods, causing pod scarring and decreased seed quality. W. K. Lam and L. P. Pedigo, of Purdue University, investigated whether the stiff trichomes on soybean pods (*Glycine max*) physically deter these beetles. The researchers placed hungry beetles in muslin bags and sealed the bags around the pods of adjacent plants expressing different pod hairiness. The amount of damage to the pods was assessed after 24 hours.

RESULTS Beetle damage to very hairy soybean pods was much lower compared with the other pod types.

CONCLUSION Soybean pod trichomes protect against beetle damage.

SOURCE W. F. Lam and L. P. Pedigo, Effect of trichome density on soybean pod feeding by adult bean leaf beetles (Coleoptera: Chrysomelidae), *Journal of Economic Entomology* 94(6):1459–1463 (2001).

WHAT IF? The pod trichomes of most soybean varieties are white, but some varieties have tawny-colored trichomes. Suppose that the effects of trichome density on beetle feeding were observed only in tawny-haired varieties. What might this finding suggest about how these trichomes deter beetles?

The **vascular tissue system** carries out long-distance transport of materials between the root and shoot systems. The two types of vascular tissues are xylem and phloem. **Xylem** conducts water and dissolved minerals upward from roots into the shoots. **Phloem** transports sugars, the products of photosynthesis, from where they are made (usually the leaves) to where they are needed—usually roots and sites of growth, such as developing leaves and fruits. The vascular tissue of a root or stem is collectively called the **stele** (the Greek word for "pillar"). The arrangement of the stele varies, depending on the species and organ. In angiosperms, for example, the root stele is a solid central *vascular cylinder* of xylem and phloem, whereas the stele of stems and leaves consists of *vascular bundles*, separate strands containing xylem and phloem (see Figure 35.8). Both xylem and phloem are composed of a variety of cell types, including cells that are highly specialized for transport or support.

Tissues that are neither dermal nor vascular are part of the **ground tissue system**. Ground tissue that is internal to the vascular tissue is known as **pith**, and ground tissue that is external to the vascular tissue is called **cortex**. The ground tissue system is not just filler. It includes various cells specialized for functions such as storage, photosynthesis, and support.

Common Types of Plant Cells

Like any multicellular organism, a plant is characterized by cellular differentiation, the specialization of cells in structure and function. Cellular differentiation may involve changes both in the cytoplasm and its organelles and in the cell wall. **Figure 35.10**, on the next two pages, focuses on the major types of plant cells: parenchyma cells, collenchyma cells, sclerenchyma cells, the water-conducting cells of the xylem, and the sugar-conducting cells of the phloem. Notice the structural adaptations in the different cells that make their specific functions possible. You may also wish to review Figures 6.9 and 6.28, which show basic plant cell structure.

CONCEPT CHECK 35.1

1. How does the vascular tissue system enable leaves and roots to function together in supporting growth and development of the whole plant?
2. When you eat the following, what plant structure are you consuming? (a) brussels sprouts; (b) celery sticks; (c) onions; (d) carrot sticks
3. Characterize the role of each of the three tissue systems in a leaf.
4. Describe at least three specializations in plant organs and plant cells that are adaptations to life on land.
5. **WHAT IF?** If humans were photoautotrophs, making food by capturing light energy for photosynthesis, how might our anatomy be different?

For suggested answers, see Appendix A.

▼ Figure 35.10

Exploring Examples of Differentiated Plant Cells

Parenchyma Cells

Parenchyma cells in *Elodea* leaf, with chloroplasts (LM)

Mature **parenchyma cells** have primary walls that are relatively thin and flexible, and most lack secondary walls. (See Figure 6.28 to review primary and secondary cell walls.) When mature, parenchyma cells generally have a large central vacuole. Diagrams of "typical" plant cells often depict parenchyma cells because they are the least specialized structurally. Parenchyma cells perform most of the metabolic functions of the plant, synthesizing and storing various organic products. For example, photosynthesis occurs within the chloroplasts of parenchyma cells in the leaf. Some parenchyma cells in stems and roots have colorless plastids that store starch. The fleshy tissue of many fruits is composed mainly of parenchyma cells. Most parenchyma cells retain the ability to divide and differentiate into other types of plant cells under particular conditions—during wound repair, for example. It is even possible for scientists to grow an entire plant from a single parenchyma cell.

Collenchyma Cells

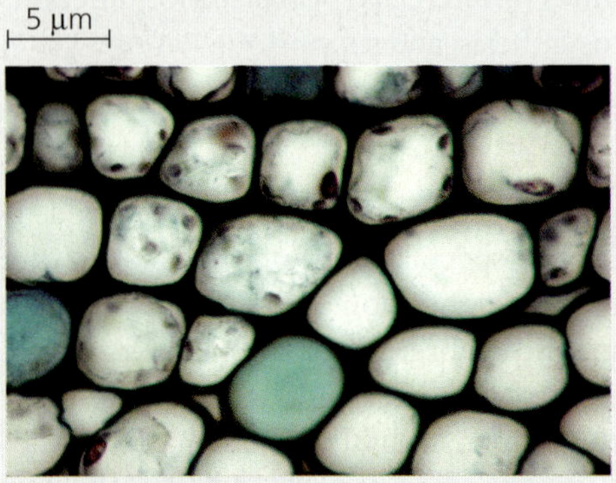

Collenchyma cells (in *Helianthus* stem) (LM)

Grouped in strands or cylinders, **collenchyma cells** help support young parts of the plant shoot. Collenchyma cells have thicker primary walls than parenchyma cells, though the walls are unevenly thickened. Young stems and petioles often have strands of collenchyma cells just below their epidermis (for example, the "strings" of a celery stalk, which is a petiole). Collenchyma cells lack secondary walls, and the hardening agent lignin is absent from their primary walls. Therefore, these cells provide flexible support without restraining growth. At maturity, collenchyma cells are living and flexible, elongating with the stems and leaves they support—unlike sclerenchyma cells, which we discuss next.

Sclerenchyma Cells

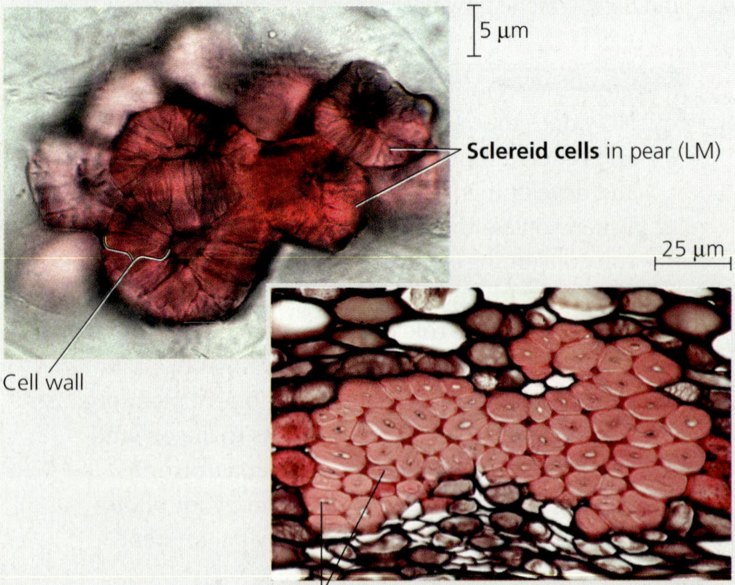

Fiber cells (cross section from ash tree) (LM)

Also functioning as supporting elements in the plant, but with thick secondary walls that are usually strengthened by lignin, **sclerenchyma cells** are much more rigid than collenchyma cells. Mature sclerenchyma cells cannot elongate, and they occur in regions of the plant that have stopped growing in length. Sclerenchyma cells are so specialized for support that many are dead at functional maturity, but they produce secondary walls before the protoplast (the living part of the cell) dies. The rigid walls remain as a "skeleton" that supports the plant, in some cases for hundreds of years.

Two types of sclerenchyma cells, known as **sclereids** and **fibers**, are specialized entirely for support and strengthening. Sclereids, which are shorter than fibers and irregular in shape, have very thick, lignified secondary walls. Sclereids impart the hardness to nutshells and seed coats and the gritty texture to pear fruits. Fibers, which are usually arranged in threads, are long, slender, and tapered. Some are used commercially, such as hemp fibers for making rope and flax fibers for weaving into linen.

Water-Conducting Cells of the Xylem

The two types of water-conducting cells, **tracheids** and **vessel elements**, are tubular, elongated cells that are dead at functional maturity. Tracheids are found in the xylem of nearly all vascular plants. In addition to tracheids, most angiosperms, as well as a few gymnosperms and a few seedless vascular plants, have vessel elements. When the living cellular contents of a tracheid or vessel element disintegrate, the cell's thickened walls remain behind, forming a nonliving conduit through which water can flow. The secondary walls of tracheids and vessel elements are often interrupted by pits, thinner regions where only primary walls are present (see Figure 6.28 to review primary and secondary walls). Water can migrate laterally between neighboring cells through pits.

Tracheids are long, thin cells with tapered ends. Water moves from cell to cell mainly through the pits, where it does not have to cross thick secondary walls. The secondary walls of tracheids are hardened with lignin, which prevents collapse under the tensions of water transport and also provides support.

Vessel elements are generally wider, shorter, thinner walled, and less tapered than the tracheids. They are aligned end to end, forming long micropipes known as **vessels**. The end walls of the vessel elements have perforation plates that enable water to flow freely through the vessels.

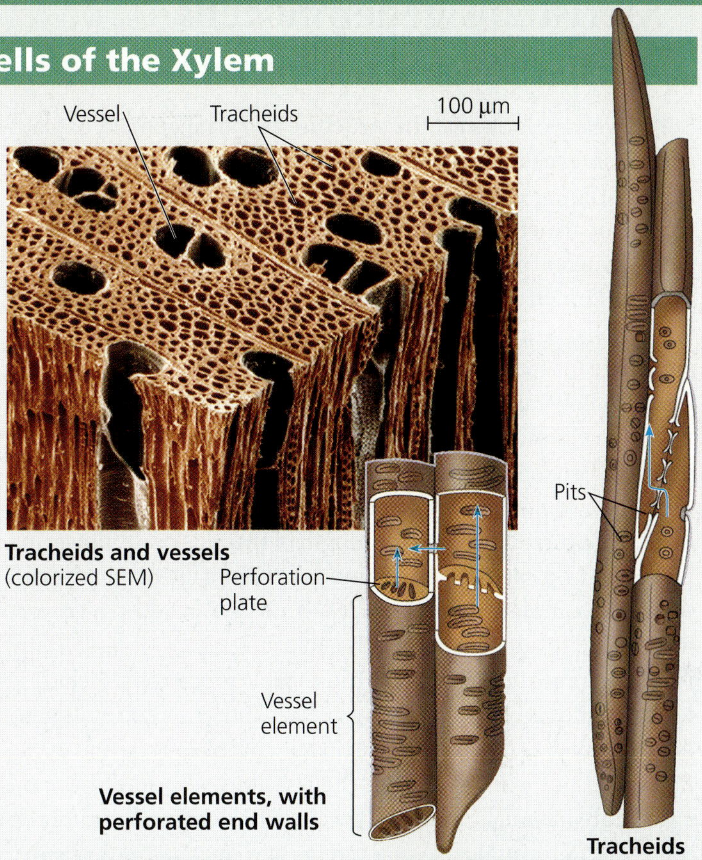

Tracheids and vessels (colorized SEM)

Vessel elements, with perforated end walls

Tracheids

Sugar-Conducting Cells of the Phloem

Unlike the water-conducting cells of the xylem, the sugar-conducting cells of the phloem are alive at functional maturity. In seedless vascular plants and gymnosperms, sugars and other organic nutrients are transported through long, narrow cells called sieve cells. In the phloem of angiosperms, these nutrients are transported through sieve tubes, which consist of chains of cells called **sieve-tube elements**, or sieve-tube members.

Though alive, sieve-tube elements lack a nucleus, ribosomes, a distinct vacuole, and cytoskeletal elements. This reduction in cell contents enables nutrients to pass more easily through the cell. The end walls between sieve-tube elements, called **sieve plates**, have pores that facilitate the flow of fluid from cell to cell along the sieve tube. Alongside each sieve-tube element is a nonconducting cell called a **companion cell**, which is connected to the sieve-tube element by numerous channels, plasmodesmata (see Figure 6.28). The nucleus and ribosomes of the companion cell serve not only that cell itself but also the adjacent sieve-tube element. In some plants, companion cells in leaves also help load sugars into the sieve-tube elements, which then transport the sugars to other parts of the plant.

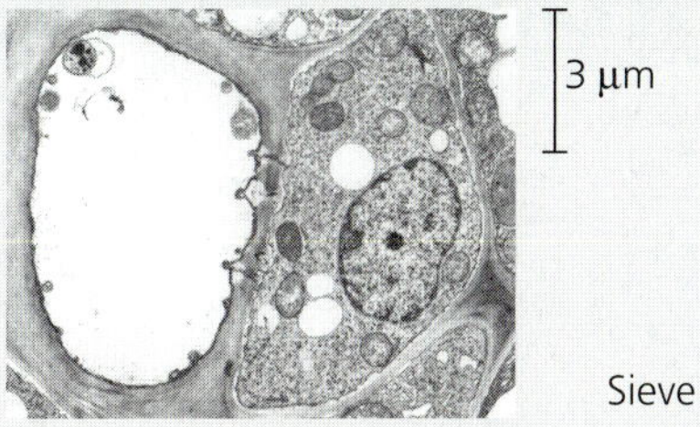

Sieve-tube element (left) and companion cell: cross section (TEM)

Sieve-tube elements: longitudinal view (LM)

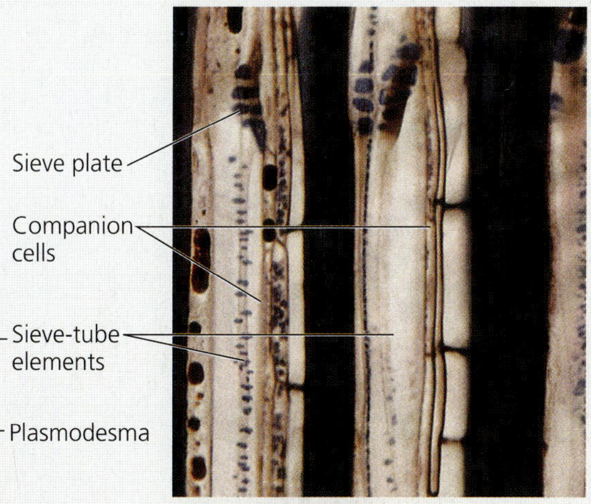

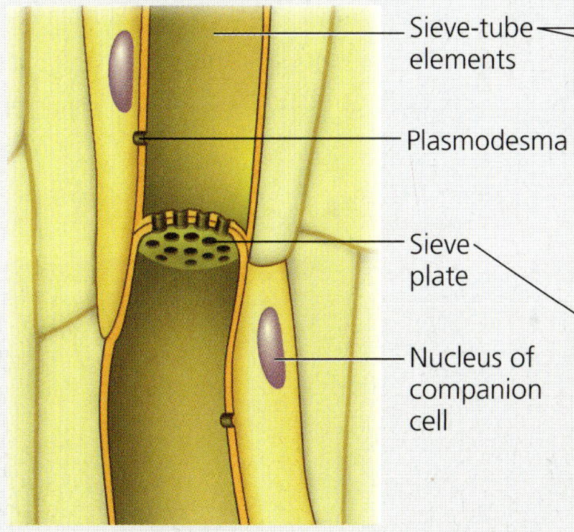

Sieve-tube elements: longitudinal view

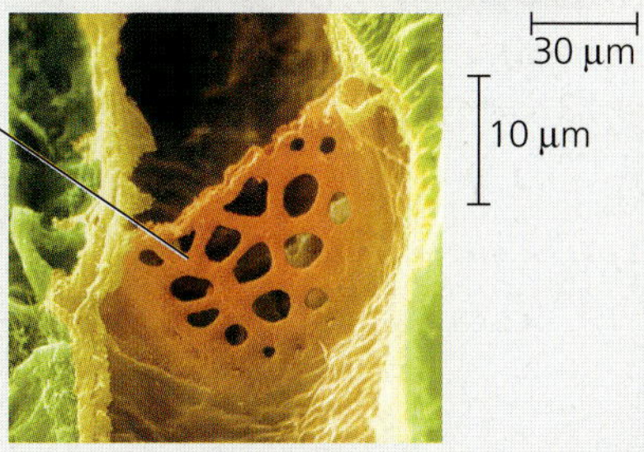

Sieve plate with pores (SEM)

BioFlix Visit the Study Area at **www.masteringbio.com** for the BioFlix 3-D Animation called Tour of a Plant Cell.

CONCEPT 35.2

Meristems generate cells for new organs

So far, we have looked at the structure and arrangement of plant tissues and cells in mature organs. How does this organization arise? A major difference between plants and most animals is that plant growth is not limited to an embryonic or juvenile period. Instead, growth occurs throughout the plant's life, a process known as **indeterminate growth**. At any given time, a typical plant consists of embryonic, developing, and mature organs. Except for dormant periods, most plants grow continuously. In contrast, most animals and some plant organs—such as most leaves, thorns, and flowers—undergo **determinate growth**; that is, they stop growing after reaching a certain size.

Although plants continue to grow throughout their lives, they do die, of course. Based on the length of their life cycle, flowering plants can be categorized as annuals, biennials, or perennials. **Annuals** complete their life cycle—from germination to flowering to seed production to death—in a single year or less. Many wildflowers are annuals, as are most staple food crops, including legumes and cereal grains such as wheat and rice. **Biennials** generally require two growing seasons to complete their life cycle, flowering and fruiting only in their second year. Radishes and carrots are biennials, though they are usually harvested after the first year. **Perennials** live many years and include trees, shrubs, and some grasses. Some buffalo grass of the North American plains is thought to have been growing for 10,000 years from seeds that sprouted at the close of the last ice age. When a perennial dies, it is usually not from old age but from an infection or some environmental trauma, such as fire or severe drought.

Plants are capable of indeterminate growth because they have perpetually embryonic tissues called **meristems**. There are two main types: apical meristems and lateral meristems **(Figure 35.11)**. **Apical meristems**, located at the tips of roots and shoots and in the axillary buds of shoots, provide additional cells that enable the plant to grow in length, a process known as **primary growth**. Primary growth allows roots to extend throughout the soil and shoots to increase their exposure to light. In herbaceous (nonwoody) plants, primary growth produces all, or almost all, of the plant body. Woody plants, however, also grow in girth in the parts of stems and roots that no longer grow in length. This growth in thickness, known as **secondary growth**, is caused by the activity of **lateral meristems** called the vascular cambium and cork cambium. These cylinders of dividing cells extend along the length of roots and stems. The **vascular cambium** adds layers of vascular tissue called secondary xylem (wood) and secondary phloem. The **cork cambium** replaces the epidermis with the thicker, tougher periderm.

The cells within meristems divide relatively frequently, generating additional cells. Some of these new cells remain in the meristem and produce more cells, while others differentiate and are incorporated into tissues and organs of the growing plant. Cells that remain as sources of new cells are called *initials*. The new cells displaced from the meristem, called *derivatives*, continue to divide until the cells they produce become specialized within developing tissues.

The relationship between primary and secondary growth is clearly seen in the winter twig of a deciduous tree. At the shoot

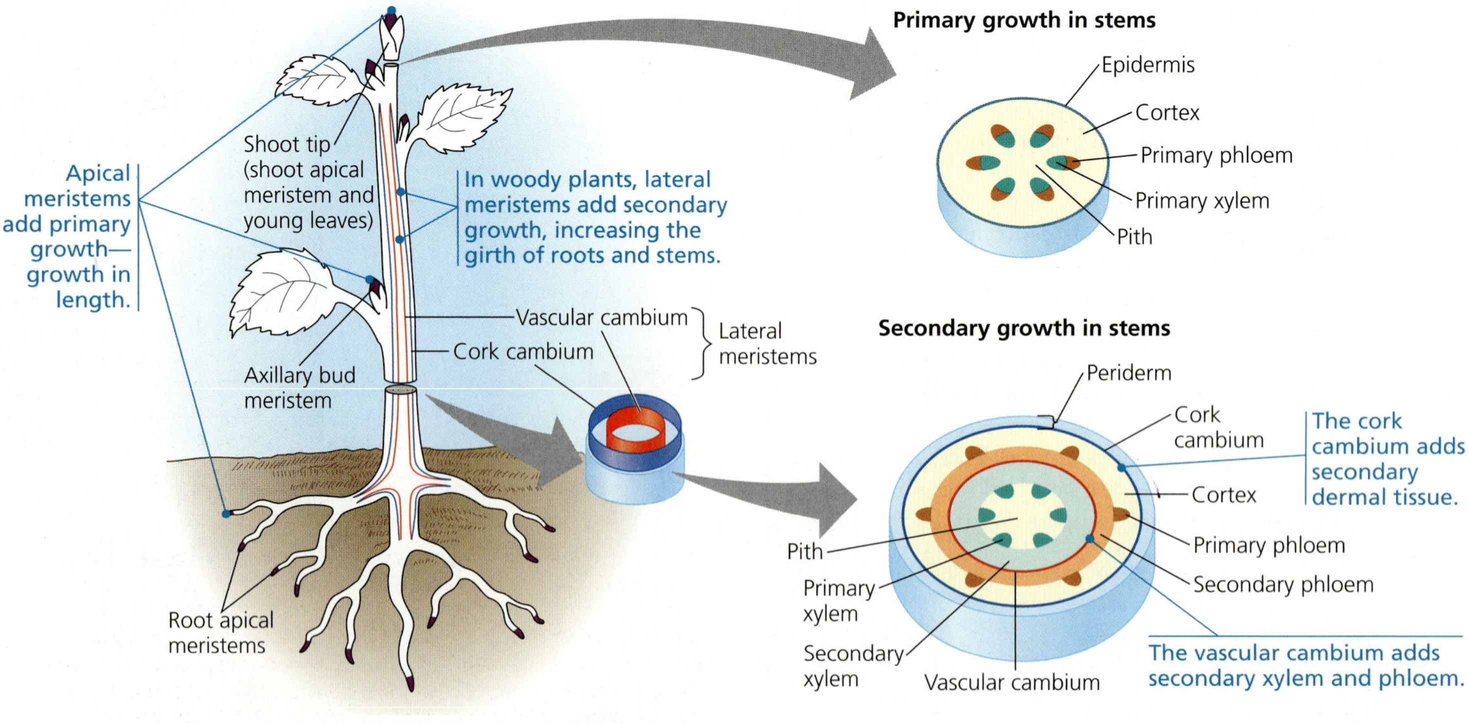

▲ **Figure 35.11 An overview of primary and secondary growth.**

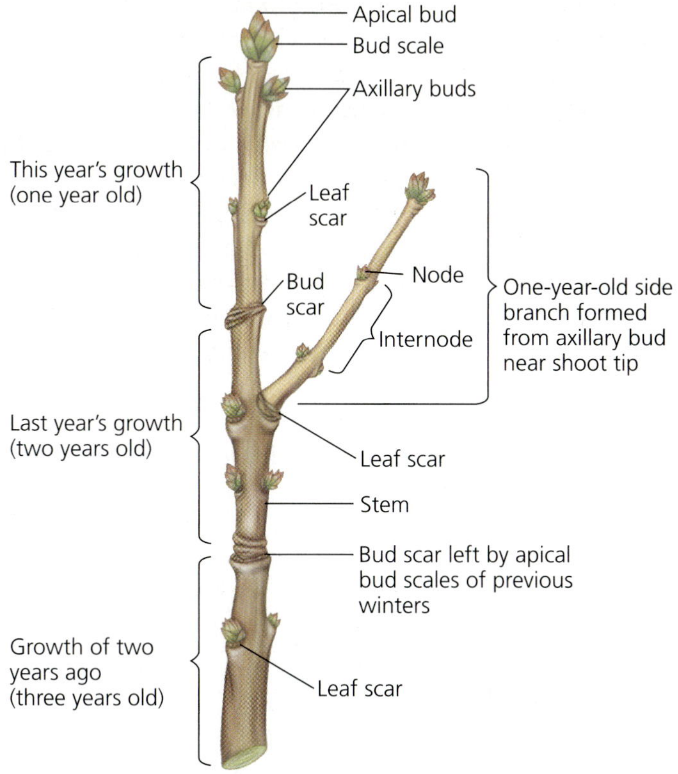

▲ **Figure 35.12 Three years' growth in a winter twig.**

tip is the dormant apical bud, enclosed by scales that protect its apical meristem **(Figure 35.12)**. In spring, the bud sheds its scales and begins a new spurt of primary growth, producing a series of nodes and internodes. Along each growth segment, nodes are marked by scars that were left when leaves fell. Above each leaf scar is an axillary bud or a branch formed by an axillary bud. Farther down the twig are bud scars from the whorls of scales that enclosed the apical bud during the previous winter. During each growing season, primary growth extends the shoots, and secondary growth thickens the parts that formed in previous years.

CONCEPT CHECK 35.2

1. Distinguish between primary and secondary growth.
2. Cells in lower layers of your skin divide and replace dead cells sloughed from the surface. Why is it inaccurate to compare such regions of cell division to a plant meristem?
3. Roots and stems grow indeterminately, but leaves do not. How might this benefit the plant?
4. **WHAT IF?** Suppose a gardener picks some radishes and finds that they are too small. Since radishes are biennials, the gardener leaves the remaining plants in the ground, thinking that they will grow larger during their second year. Is this a good idea? Explain.

For suggested answers, see Appendix A.

CONCEPT **35.3**

Primary growth lengthens roots and shoots

As you have learned, primary growth is growth in length, produced by apical meristems. Collectively, the results of this growth are called the **primary plant body**. In herbaceous plants, it is usually the entire plant. In woody plants, it consists only of the youngest parts, which are not yet woody. Although apical meristems lengthen both roots and shoots, there are differences in the primary growth of these two systems.

Primary Growth of Roots

The tip of a root is covered by a thimble-like **root cap**, which protects the delicate apical meristem as the root pushes through the abrasive soil during primary growth. The root cap also secretes a polysaccharide slime that lubricates the soil around the tip of the root. Growth occurs just behind the tip in three zones of cells at successive stages of primary growth. Moving away from the tip, they are the zones of cell division, elongation, and differentiation **(Figure 35.13)**.

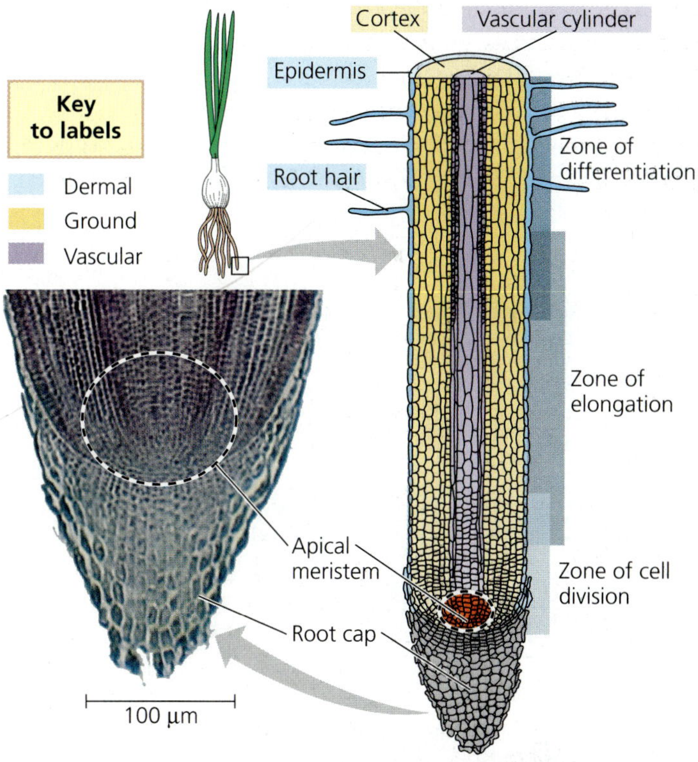

▲ **Figure 35.13 Primary growth of a root.** The light micrograph and diagram reveal the anatomical features of the tip of an onion root. Mitosis is concentrated in the zone of cell division, where the apical meristem and its immediate growth products are located. The apical meristem also maintains the root cap by generating new cells that replace those that are sloughed off. Most lengthening of the root occurs in the zone of elongation. Cells become functionally mature in the zone of differentiation. The zones grade into one another without sharp boundaries.

The three zones grade together, with no sharp boundaries. The *zone of cell division* includes the root apical meristem and its derivatives. New root cells are produced in this region, including the root cap. Typically, about a millimeter behind the tip of the root is the *zone of elongation*, where root cells elongate, sometimes to more than ten times their original length. Cell elongation in this zone pushes the tip farther into the soil. Meanwhile, the root apical meristem keeps adding cells to the younger end of the zone of elongation. Even before the root cells finish lengthening, many begin specializing in structure and function. In the *zone of differentiation*, or zone of maturation, cells complete their differentiation and become distinct cell types.

The primary growth of a root produces its epidermis, ground tissue, and vascular tissue. **Figure 35.14** shows in cross section the three primary tissue systems in the young roots of a eudicot (*Ranunculus*, buttercup) and a monocot (*Zea*, maize). Water and minerals absorbed from the soil must enter through the root's epidermis. Root hairs, which account for much of this absorption, enhance this process by greatly increasing the surface area of epidermal cells.

In most roots, the stele is a vascular cylinder, a solid core of xylem and phloem **(Figure 35.14a)**. In most eudicot roots, the xylem has a starlike appearance and the phloem occupies the indentations between the arms of the xylem "star." In many monocot roots, the vascular tissue consists of a central core of parenchyma cells surrounded by a ring of xylem and a ring of phloem **(Figure 35.14b)**. The central region is often called pith but should not be confused with stem pith, which is ground tissue.

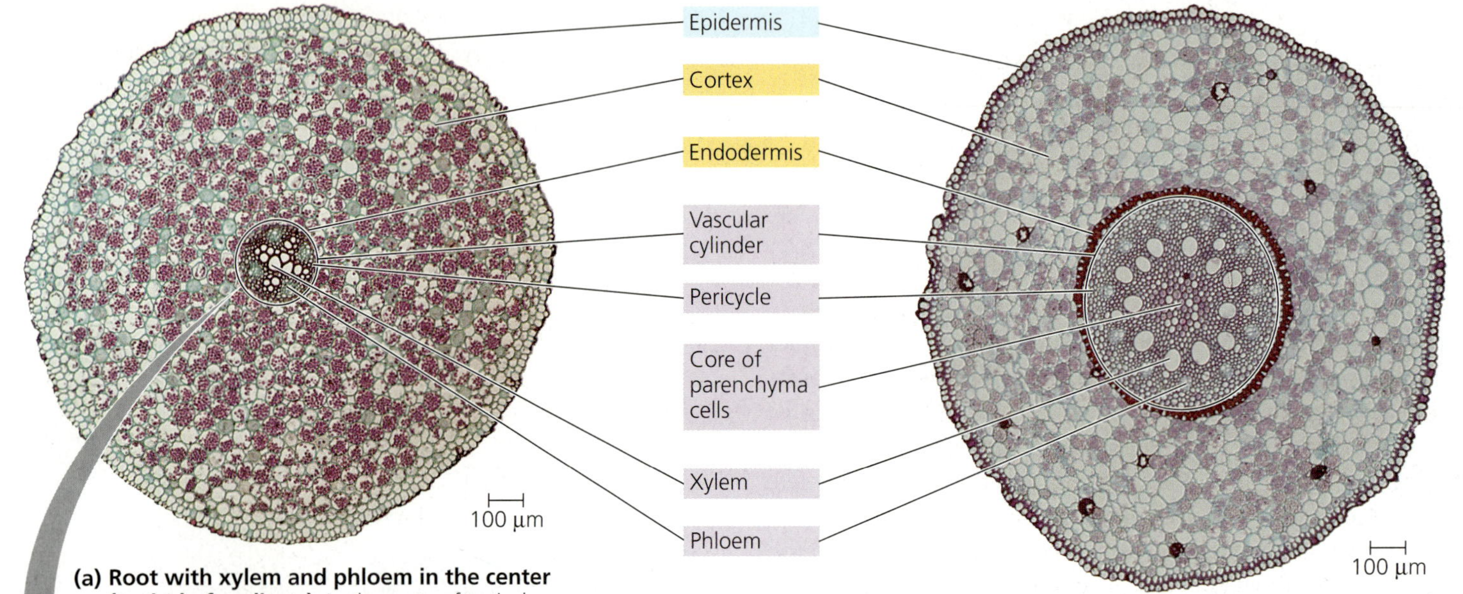

(a) Root with xylem and phloem in the center (typical of eudicots). In the roots of typical gymnosperms and eudicots, as well as some monocots, the stele is a vascular cylinder consisting of a lobed core of xylem with phloem between the lobes.

(b) Root with parenchyma in the center (typical of monocots). The stele of many monocot roots is a vascular cylinder with a core of parenchyma surrounded by a ring of xylem and a ring of phloem.

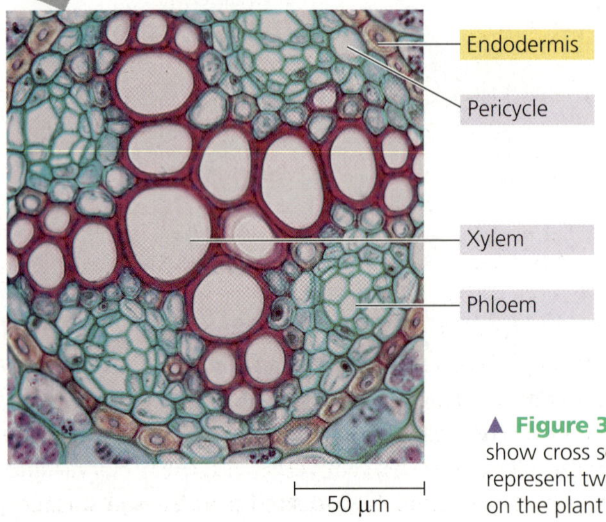

▲ **Figure 35.14 Organization of primary tissues in young roots.** Parts **(a)** and **(b)** show cross sections of the roots of *Ranunculus* (buttercup) and *Zea* (maize), respectively. These represent two basic patterns of root organization, of which there are many variations, depending on the plant species (all LMs).

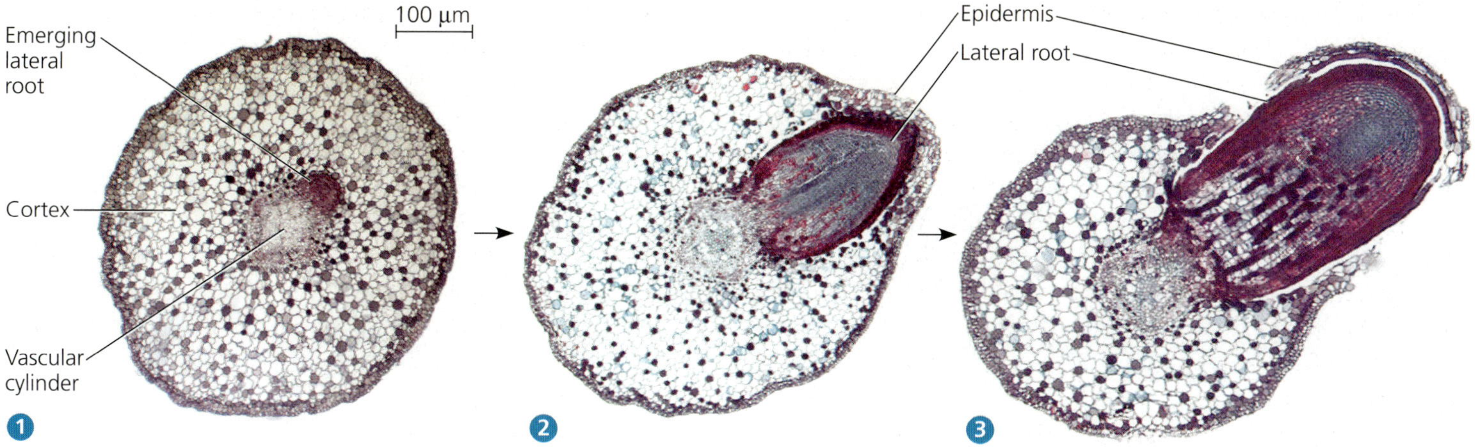

▲ **Figure 35.15 The formation of a lateral root.** A lateral root originates in the pericycle, the outermost layer of the vascular cylinder of a root, and grows out through the cortex and epidermis. In this series of light micrographs, the view of the original root is a cross section, while the view of the lateral root is a longitudinal section.

The ground tissue of roots, consisting mostly of parenchyma cells, fills the cortex, the region between the vascular cylinder and epidermis. Cells within the ground tissue store carbohydrates, and their plasma membranes absorb water and minerals from the soil. The innermost layer of the cortex is called the **endodermis**, a cylinder one cell thick that forms the boundary with the vascular cylinder. As you will see in Chapter 36, the endodermis is a selective barrier that regulates passage of substances from the soil into the vascular cylinder.

Lateral roots arise from the **pericycle**, the outermost cell layer in the vascular cylinder, which is adjacent to and just inside the endodermis (see Figure 35.14). A lateral root pushes through the cortex and epidermis until it emerges from the established root **(Figure 35.15)**. A lateral root cannot originate near the root's surface because its vascular system must be continuous with the vascular cylinder at the center of the established root.

Primary Growth of Shoots

A shoot apical meristem is a dome-shaped mass of dividing cells at the shoot tip **(Figure 35.16)**. Leaves develop from **leaf primordia** (singular, *primordium*), finger-like projections along the sides of the apical meristem. Axillary buds develop from islands of meristematic cells left by the apical meristem at the bases of the leaf primordia. Axillary buds can form lateral shoots at some later time (see Figure 35.12).

Within a bud, leaf primordia are spaced close together because the internodes are very short. Most shoot elongation is due to the lengthening of internode cells below the shoot tip. In some plants, including grasses, a few leaf cells are produced by areas of meristematic tissue separated from the apical meristem. These areas, called *intercalary meristems*, remain at the base of leaf blades and stem internodes. This morphological feature helps grasses tolerate grazing because the elevated part of the leaf blade can be removed without stopping growth.

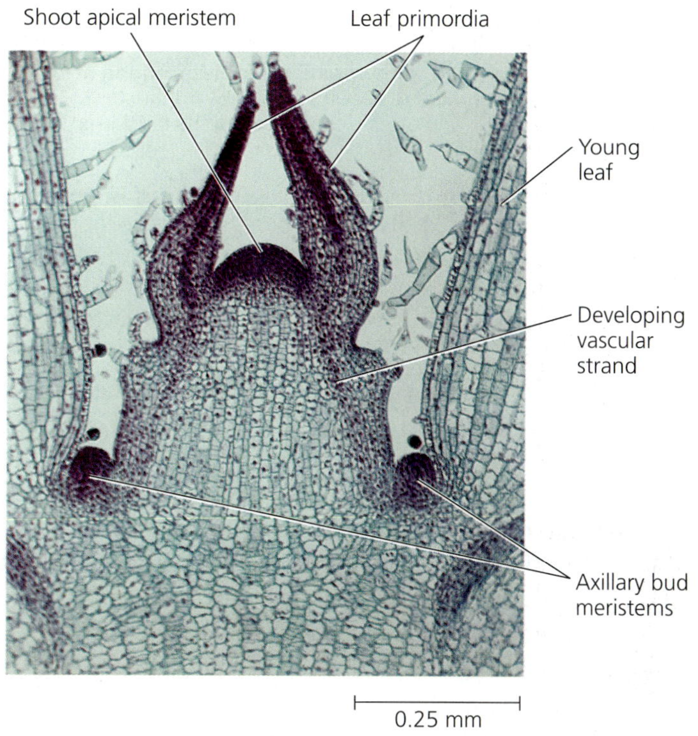

▲ **Figure 35.16 The shoot tip.** Leaf primordia arise from the flanks of the dome of the apical meristem. This is a longitudinal section of the shoot tip of *Coleus* (LM).

Tissue Organization of Stems

The epidermis covers stems as part of the continuous dermal tissue system. Vascular tissue runs the length of a stem in vascular bundles. Unlike lateral roots, which arise from vascular tissue deep within a root and disrupt the vascular cambium, cortex, and epidermis as they emerge (see Figure 35.15), lateral shoots develop from axillary bud meristems on the stem's surface and disrupt no other tissues (see Figure 35.16). The vascular bundles of the stem converge with the root's vascular cylinder in a zone of transition located near the soil surface.

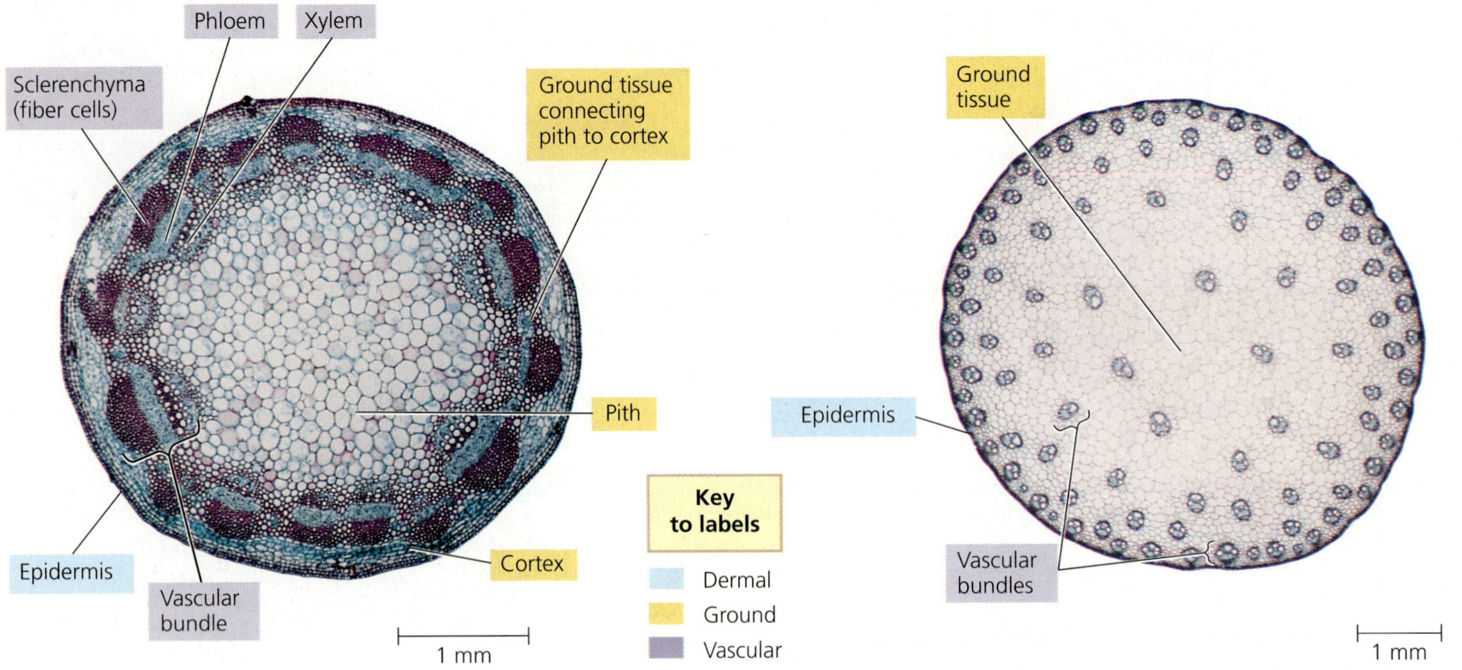

(a) Cross section of stem with vascular bundles forming a ring (typical of eudicots). Ground tissue toward the inside is called pith, and ground tissue toward the outside is called cortex (LM).

(b) Cross section of stem with scattered vascular bundles (typical of monocots). In such an arrangement, ground tissue is not partitioned into pith and cortex (LM).

▲ **Figure 35.17 Organization of primary tissues in young stems.**

? *Why aren't the terms* pith *and* cortex *used to describe the ground tissue of monocot stems?*

In most eudicot species, the vascular tissue consists of vascular bundles arranged in a ring **(Figure 35.17a)**. The xylem in each vascular bundle is adjacent to the pith, and the phloem in each bundle is adjacent to the cortex. In most monocot stems, the vascular bundles are scattered throughout the ground tissue, rather than forming a ring **(Figure 35.17b)**. In the stems of both monocots and eudicots, the ground tissue consists mostly of parenchyma cells. However, collenchyma cells just beneath the epidermis strengthen many stems. Sclerenchyma cells, especially fiber cells, also provide support in those parts of the stems that are no longer elongating.

Tissue Organization of Leaves

Figure 35.18 provides an overview of leaf structure. The epidermal barrier is interrupted by **stomata** (singular, *stoma*), which allow gas exchange between the surrounding air and the photosynthetic cells inside the leaf. In addition to regulating CO_2 uptake for photosynthesis, stomata are major avenues for the evaporative loss of water. The term *stoma* can refer to the stomatal pore or to the entire stomatal complex consisting of a pore flanked by two **guard cells**, which regulate the opening and closing of the pore. We'll discuss stomata in detail in Chapter 36.

The ground tissue of a leaf, a region called the **mesophyll** (from the Greek *mesos*, middle, and *phyll*, leaf), is sandwiched between the upper and lower epidermal layers. Mesophyll consists mainly of parenchyma cells specialized for photosynthesis. The leaves of many eudicots have two distinct areas: palisade mesophyll and spongy mesophyll. The *palisade mesophyll* consists of one or more layers of elongated parenchyma cells on the upper part of the leaf. The *spongy mesophyll* is below the palisade mesophyll. These parenchyma cells are more loosely arranged, with a labyrinth of air spaces through which CO_2 and oxygen circulate around the cells and up to the palisade region. The air spaces are particularly large in the vicinity of stomata, where gas exchange with the outside air occurs.

The vascular tissue of each leaf is continuous with the vascular tissue of the stem. *Leaf traces*, connections from vascular bundles in the stem, pass through petioles and into leaves. Veins are the leaf's vascular bundles, which subdivide repeatedly and branch throughout the mesophyll. This network brings xylem and phloem into close contact with the photosynthetic tissue, which obtains water and minerals from the xylem and loads its sugars and other organic products into the phloem for transport to other parts of the plant. The vascular structure also functions as a skeleton that reinforces the shape of the leaf. Each vein is enclosed by a protective *bundle sheath*, consisting of one or more layers of cells, usually parenchyma cells. Bundle sheath cells are particularly prominent in leaves of plants that undergo C_4 photosynthesis (see Chapter 10). Unlike stems and roots, leaves rarely undergo secondary growth, which is the topic of the next section.

▼ **Figure 35.18 Leaf anatomy.**

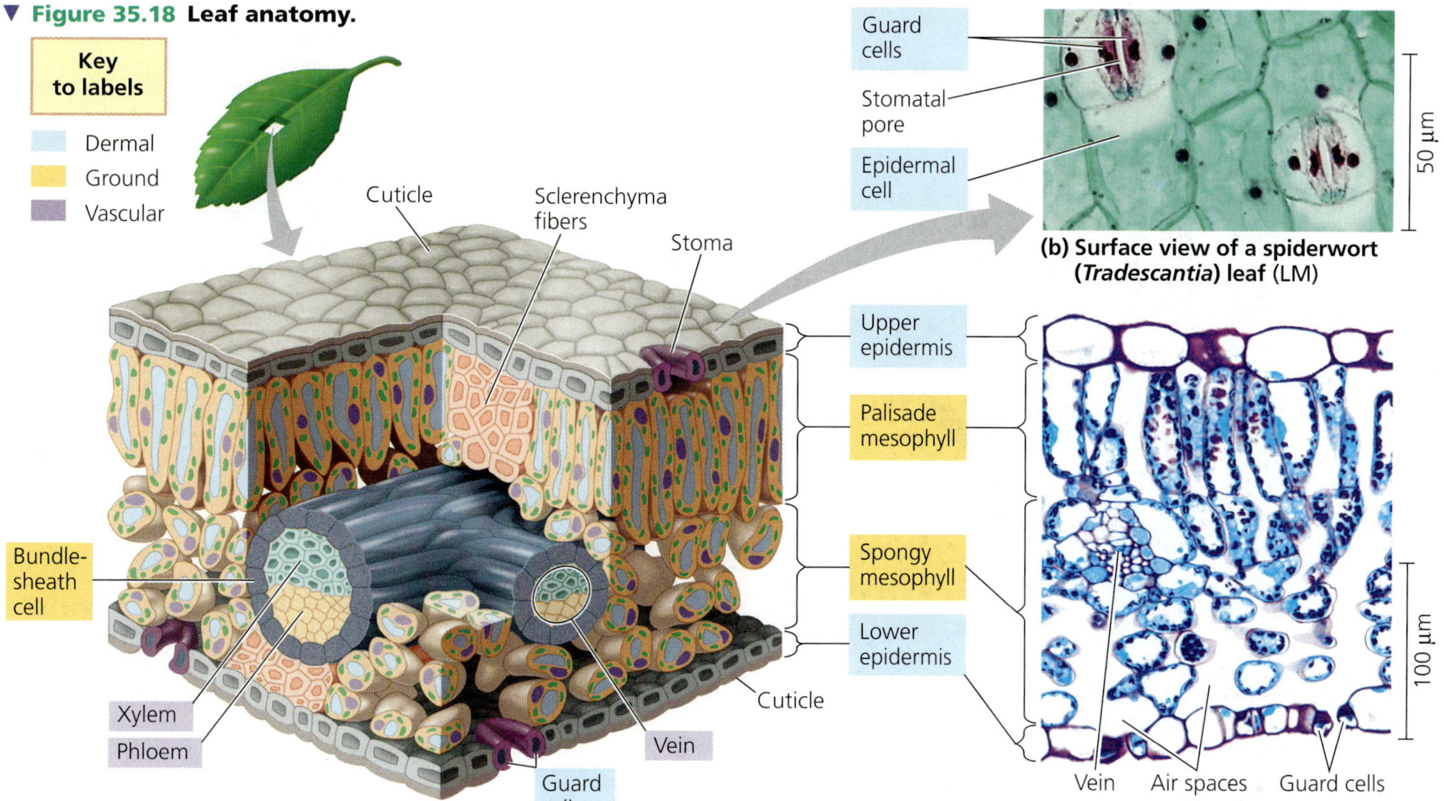

(a) Cutaway drawing of leaf tissues

(b) Surface view of a spiderwort (*Tradescantia*) leaf (LM)

(c) Cross section of a lilac (*Syringa*) leaf (LM)

CONCEPT CHECK 35.3

1. Describe how roots and shoots differ in branching.
2. Contrast primary growth in roots and shoots.
3. When grazing animals are removed from grasslands, eudicots often replace grasses. Suggest a reason why.
4. **WHAT IF?** If a leaf is vertically oriented, would you expect its mesophyll to be divided into spongy and palisade layers? Explain.

For suggested answers, see Appendix A.

CONCEPT **35.4**

Secondary growth adds girth to stems and roots in woody plants

As you have seen, primary growth arises from apical meristems and involves the production and elongation of roots, stems, and leaves. In contrast, secondary growth, the growth in thickness produced by lateral meristems, occurs in stems and roots of woody plants, but rarely in leaves. The **secondary plant body** consists of the tissues produced by the vascular cambium and cork cambium. The vascular cambium adds secondary xylem (wood) and secondary phloem, increasing vascular flow and support for the shoot system. The cork cambium produces a tough, thick covering consisting mainly of wax-impregnated cells that protect the stem from water loss and from invasion by insects, bacteria, and fungi. All gymnosperm species and many eudicot species have secondary growth, but it is rare in monocots.

Primary growth and secondary growth occur simultaneously. As primary growth adds leaves and lengthens stems and roots in the younger regions of a plant, secondary growth thickens stems and roots in older regions where primary growth has stopped. The process is similar in shoots and roots. **Figure 35.19**, on the next page, provides an overview of growth in a woody stem.

The Vascular Cambium and Secondary Vascular Tissue

The vascular cambium is a cylinder of meristematic cells, often only one cell thick. It increases in circumference and also adds layers of secondary xylem to its interior and secondary phloem to its exterior. Each layer has a larger diameter than the previous layer (see Figure 35.19). In this way, the vascular cambium thickens roots and stems.

In a typical woody stem, the vascular cambium consists of a continuous cylinder of undifferentiated parenchyma cells, located outside the pith and primary xylem and to the inside of the cortex and primary phloem. In a typical woody root, the vascular cambium forms to the exterior of the primary xylem and interior to the primary phloem and pericycle.

(a) Primary and secondary growth in a two-year-old stem

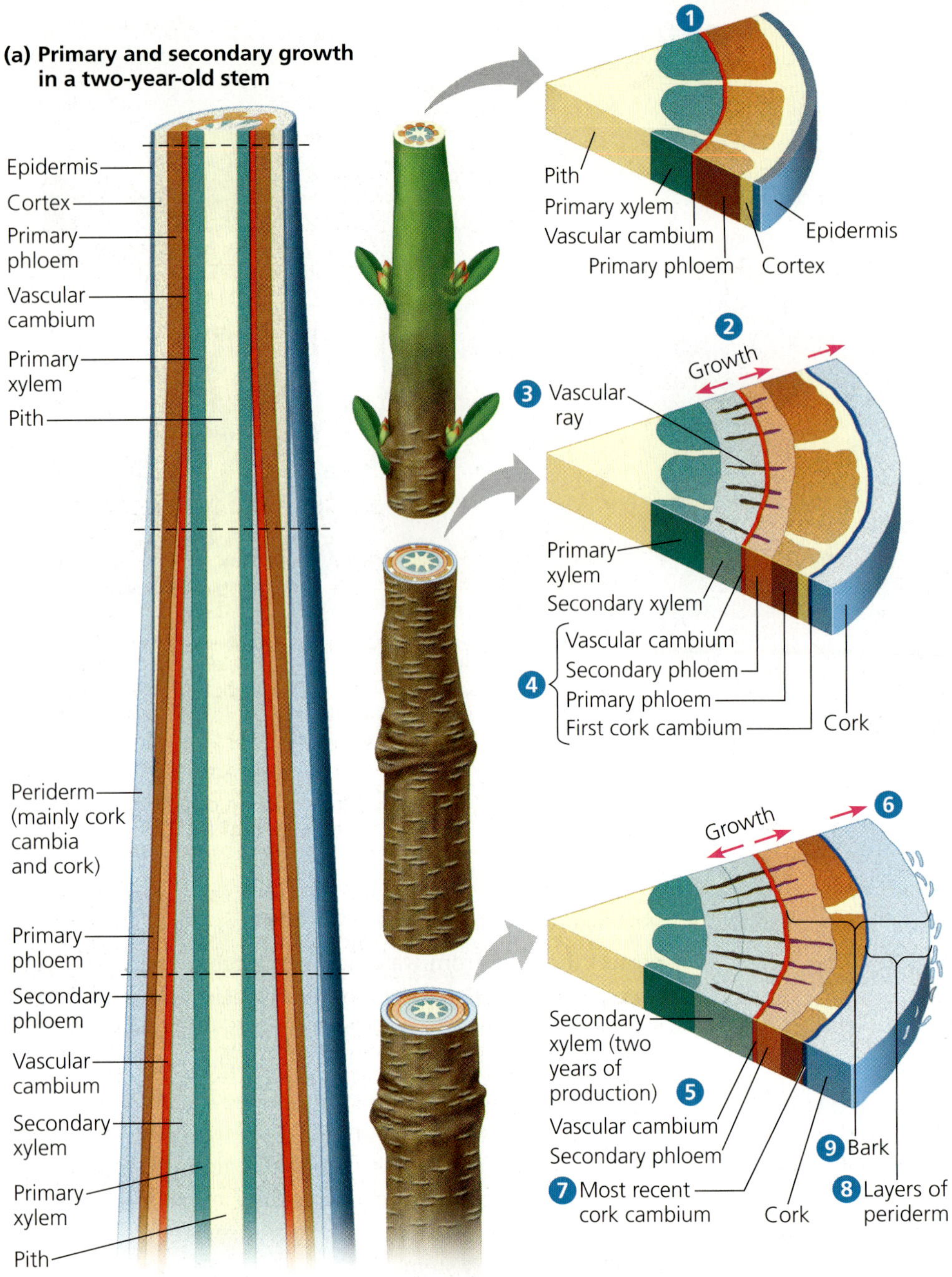

1 Primary growth from the activity of the apical meristem is nearing completion. The vascular cambium has just formed.

2 Although primary growth continues in the apical bud, only secondary growth occurs in this section. The stem thickens as the vascular cambium forms secondary xylem to the inside and secondary phloem to the outside.

3 Some initials of the vascular cambium give rise to vascular rays (see next page).

4 As the vascular cambium's diameter increases, the secondary phloem and other tissues external to the cambium can't keep pace because their cells no longer divide. As a result, these tissues, including the epidermis, will eventually rupture. A second lateral meristem, the cork cambium, develops from parenchyma cells in the cortex. The cork cambium produces cork cells, which replace the epidermis.

5 In year 2 of secondary growth, the vascular cambium produces more secondary xylem and phloem, and the cork cambium produces more cork.

6 As the stem's diameter increases, the outermost tissues exterior to the cork cambium rupture and are sloughed off.

7 In many cases, the cork cambium re-forms deeper in the cortex. When none of the cortex is left, the cambium develops from phloem parenchyma cells.

8 Each cork cambium and the tissues it produces form a layer of periderm.

9 Bark consists of all tissues exterior to the vascular cambium.

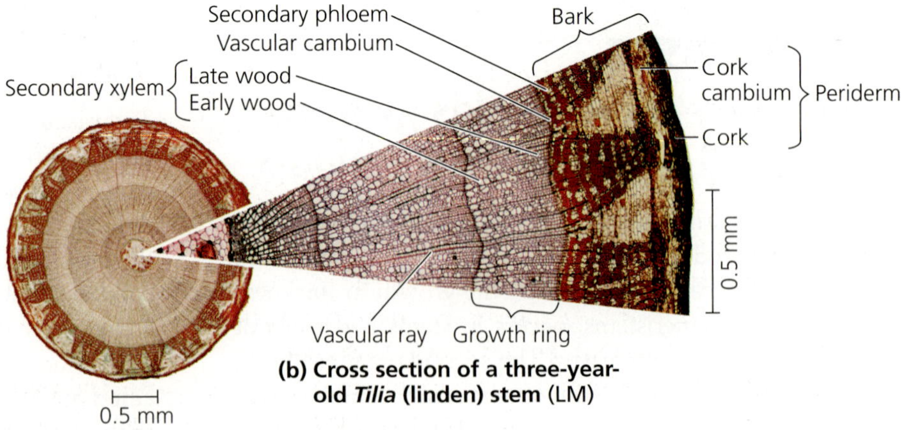

(b) Cross section of a three-year-old *Tilia* (linden) stem (LM)

▲ **Figure 35.19 Primary and secondary growth of a stem.** The progress of secondary growth can be tracked by examining the sections through sequentially older parts of the stem.

? *How does the vascular cambium cause some tissues to rupture?*

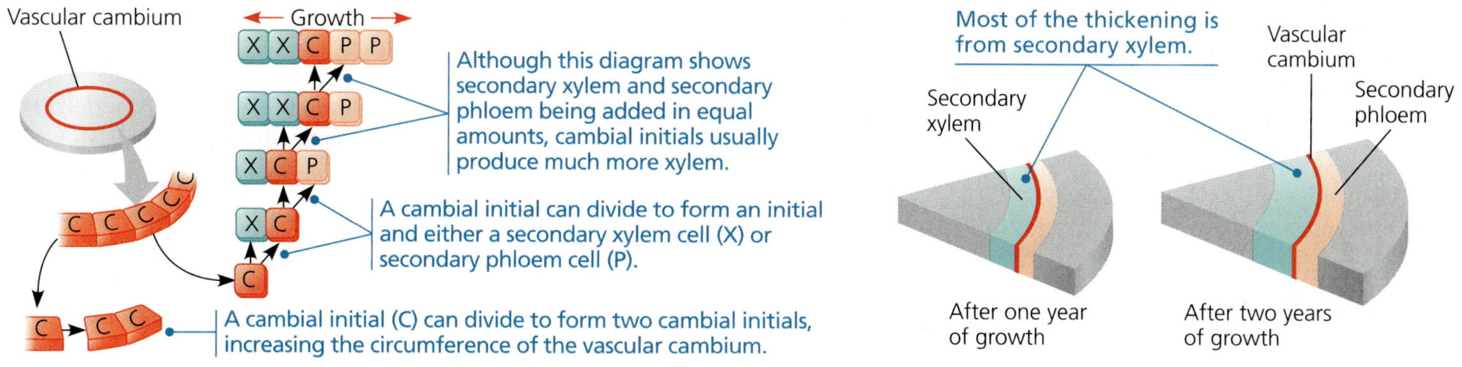

▲ **Figure 35.20 Secondary growth produced by the vascular cambium.**

Lateral

Viewed in cross section, the vascular cambium appears as a ring of initials. As these meristematic cells divide, they increase the circumference of the vascular cambium and also add secondary xylem to the inside of the cambium and secondary phloem to the outside **(Figure 35.20)**. Some initials are elongated and are oriented with their long axis parallel to the axis of the stem or root. They produce cells such as the tracheids, vessel elements, and fibers of the xylem, as well as the sieve-tube elements, companion cells, parenchyma, and fibers of the phloem. The other initials are shorter and are oriented perpendicular to the axis of the stem or root. They produce *vascular rays*—radial files of cells that connect the secondary xylem with the secondary phloem. The cells of a vascular ray move water and nutrients between the secondary xylem and phloem, store carbohydrates, and aid in wound repair.

As secondary growth continues over many years, layers of secondary xylem (wood) accumulate, consisting mainly of tracheids, vessel elements, and fibers (see Figure 35.10). Gymnosperms have only tracheids, whereas almost all angiosperms have both tracheids and vessel elements. The walls of secondary xylem cells are heavily lignified and account for the hardness and strength of wood. In temperate regions, wood that develops early in the spring, known as early wood, usually consists of secondary xylem cells with relatively large diameters and thin cell walls (see Figure 35.19b). This structure maximizes delivery of water to new, growing leaves. Wood produced later in the growing season, during late summer or early fall, is known as late wood. It is composed of thick-walled cells that do not transport as much water but contribute more to stem support.

In temperate regions, the vascular cambium becomes dormant during winter, and after growth resumes in spring, there is a marked contrast between the large cells of the new early wood and the smaller cells of the late wood of the previous growing season. A year's growth appears as a distinct ring in cross sections of most tree trunks and roots. Therefore, researchers can estimate a tree's age by counting its annual rings. *Dendrochronology* (from the Greek *dendron,* trees) is the science of analyzing tree ring growth patterns. Rings can vary in thicknesses, depending on seasonal growth. Trees grow well in wet and warm years but may grow hardly at all in cold or dry years. Because a thick ring indicates a warm year and a thin ring indicates a cold or dry one, scientists can use ring patterns to study climate changes **(Figure 35.21)**.

▼ **Figure 35.21 Research Method**

Using Dendrochronology to Study Climate

APPLICATION Dendrochronology, the science of analyzing tree rings, is useful in studying climate change. Most scientists attribute recent global warming to the burning of fossil fuels and release of CO_2 and other greenhouse gases, whereas a minority think it is a natural variation. Studying climate patterns requires comparing past and present temperatures, but instrumental climate records span only the last two centuries and apply only to some regions. By examining growth rings of Mongolian conifers dating back to the mid-1500s, G. C. Jacoby and Rosanne D'Arrigo, of the Lamont-Doherty Earth Observatory, and colleagues sought to learn whether Mongolia experienced similar warm periods in the past.

TECHNIQUE Researchers can analyze patterns of rings in living and dead trees. They can even study wood used for building long ago by matching samples with those from naturally situated specimens of overlapping age. Core samples, each about the diameter of a pencil, are taken from the bark to the center of the trunk. Each sample is dried and sanded to reveal the rings. By comparing, aligning, and averaging many samples from the Mongolian conifers, the researchers compiled a chronology. In this way, the trees served as a chronicle of environmental change.

RESULTS

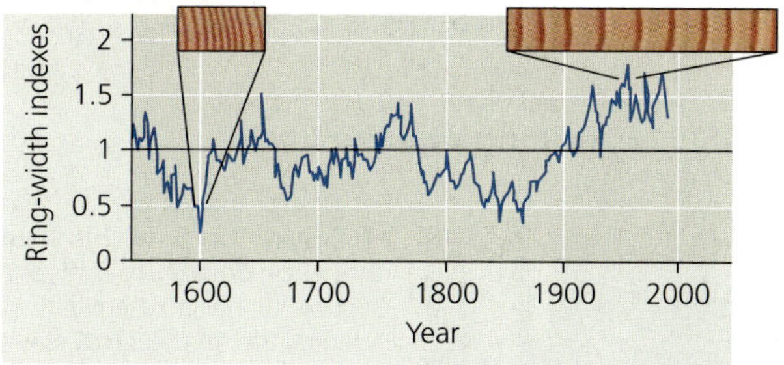

This graph summarizes a composite record of ring-width indexes for the Mongolian conifers from 1550 to 1993. Higher indexes indicate wider rings and warmer temperatures. The highest growth period was from 1974 to 1993, and 17 of the 20 highest-growth years occurred since 1946, suggesting unusual warming during the 1900s.

As a tree or woody shrub ages, the older layers of secondary xylem no longer transport water and minerals (a solution called xylem sap). These layers are called *heartwood* because they are closer to the center of a stem or root **(Figure 35.22)**. The newest, outer layers of secondary xylem still transport xylem sap and are therefore known as *sapwood*. That is why a large tree can survive even if the center of its trunk is hollow **(Figure 35.23)**. Because each new layer of secondary xylem has a larger circumference, secondary growth enables the xylem to transport more sap each year, supplying an increasing number of leaves. Heartwood is generally darker than sapwood because of resins and other compounds that permeate the cell cavities and help protect the core of the tree from fungi and wood-boring insects.

Only the youngest secondary phloem, closest to the vascular cambium, functions in sugar transport. As a stem or root increases in circumference, the older secondary phloem is sloughed off, which is why secondary phloem does not accumulate as extensively as does secondary xylem.

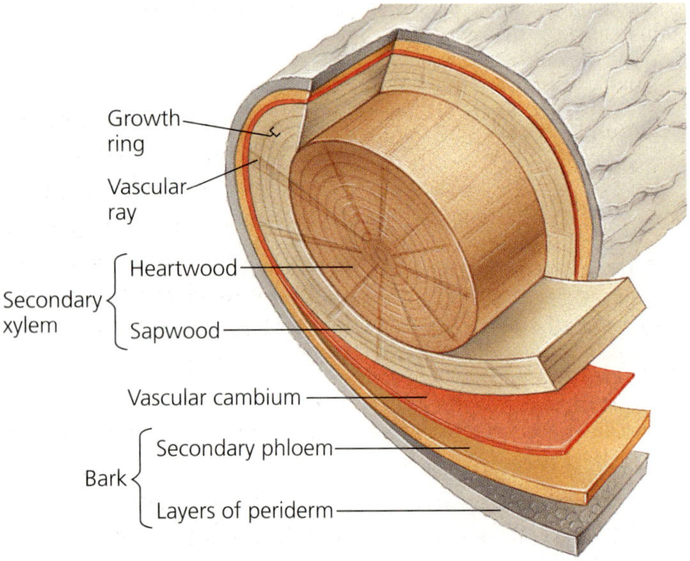

▲ **Figure 35.22 Anatomy of a tree trunk.**

◀ **Figure 35.23 Is this tree living or dead?** The Wawona Sequoia tunnel in Yosemite National Park in California was cut in 1881 as a tourist attraction. This giant sequoia (*Sequoiadendron giganteum*) lived for another 88 years before it fell during a severe winter. It was 71.3 m tall and estimated to be 2,100 years old. Though conservation policies today would forbid the mutilation of such an important specimen, the Wawona Sequoia did teach a valuable botanical lesson: Trees do not need heartwood to survive.

The Cork Cambium and the Production of Periderm

During the early stages of secondary growth, the epidermis is pushed outward, causing it to split, dry, and fall off the stem or root. It is replaced by two tissues produced by the first cork cambium, a cylinder of dividing cells that arises in the outer cortex of stems (see Figure 35.19a) and in the outer layer of the pericycle in roots. One tissue, called *phelloderm*, is a thin layer of parenchyma cells that forms to the interior of the cork cambium. The other tissue consists of cork cells that accumulate to the exterior of the cork cambium. As cork cells mature, they deposit a waxy material called *suberin* in their walls and then die. The cork tissue then functions as a barrier that helps protect the stem or root from water loss, physical damage, and pathogens. Each cork cambium and the tissues it produces comprise a layer of periderm.

Because cork cells have suberin and are usually compacted together, most of the periderm is impermeable to water and gases, unlike the epidermis. In most plants, therefore, water and minerals are absorbed primarily in the youngest parts of roots. The older parts of roots anchor the plant and transport water and solutes between the soil and shoots. Dotting the periderm are small, raised areas called **lenticels**, in which there is more space between cork cells, enabling living cells within a woody stem or root to exchange gases with the outside air. Lenticels often appear as slits, as shown in Figure 35.19a.

The thickening of a stem or root often splits the first cork cambium, which loses its meristematic activity and differentiates into cork cells. A new cork cambium forms to the inside, resulting in another layer of periderm. As this process continues, older layers of periderm are sloughed off, as you can see in the cracked, peeling bark of many tree trunks.

Many people think that bark is only the protective outer covering of a woody stem or root. Actually, **bark** includes all tissues external to the vascular cambium. In an outward direction, its main components are the secondary phloem (produced by the vascular cambium), the most recent periderm, and all the older layers of periderm (see Figure 35.22).

CONCEPT CHECK 35.4

1. A sign is hammered into a tree 2 m from the tree's base. If the tree is 10 m tall and elongates 1 m each year, how high will the sign be after 10 years?
2. Stomata and lenticels are both involved in gas exchange. Why do stomata need to be able to close, but lenticels do not?
3. Would you expect a tropical tree to have distinct growth rings? Why or why not?
4. **WHAT IF?** If a complete ring of bark is removed around a tree trunk (a process called girdling), the tree usually dies. Explain why.

For suggested answers, see Appendix A.

CONCEPT 35.5

Growth, morphogenesis, and differentiation produce the plant body

So far, we have described the development of the plant body from meristems. Here we will move from a description of plant growth and development to the mechanisms that underlie these processes.

Consider that a typical small plant may consist of billions of cells—some large, some small, some highly specialized and others not. The growth that occurs during the life of the plant results from both cell division and cell expansion. But what controls these two processes? Why do leaves stop growing upon reaching a certain size, whereas the cells of apical meristems keep dividing? Also, what controls cell specialization and the development of recognizable tissues and organs? Leaves arise from nodes; roots usually do not. Epidermis forms on the exterior of the leaf, and vascular tissue in the interior—never vice versa.

Each cell in the plant contains the same set of genes. The different patterns of gene expression among various cells cause the cellular differentiation that creates a diversity of cell types (see Chapter 18). Other processes lead to the development of body form and organization, called **morphogenesis**. The three developmental processes of growth, morphogenesis, and cellular differentiation act in concert to produce the body of a plant.

Molecular Biology: Revolutionizing the Study of Plants

Modern molecular techniques are helping plant biologists explore how growth, morphogenesis, and cellular differentiation give rise to a plant. In the current renaissance in plant biology, new laboratory methods and a focus on model organisms have catalyzed a research explosion. A major research focus is *Arabidopsis thaliana*, a weed of the mustard family that is small enough to allow researchers to cultivate thousands of plants in a few square meters of lab space. Its short generation span, about six weeks from germination to flowering, makes *Arabidopsis* an excellent model for genetic studies. It also has among the smallest genomes of all known plants. *Arabidopsis* was the first plant to have its entire genome sequenced—a six-year, multinational effort (**Figure 35.24**). More recently, rice, a species of poplar, the common grape, and maize have had their entire genomes sequenced, too.

Arabidopsis has about 26,700 protein-encoding genes, but many of these are duplicates. There are probably fewer than 15,000 different types of genes, a number similar to that found in the fly *Drosophila*. Determining the function of many *Arabidopsis* genes has greatly expanded our understanding of plant development. To fill the gaps in our knowledge, plant biologists have launched an ambitious quest to determine the function of every one of the plant's genes. Toward this goal, they are attempting to create mutants for every gene in the genome of this species. We will discuss some of these mutants shortly, as we take a closer look at the molecular mechanisms that underlie growth, morphogenesis, and cellular differentiation. By identifying each gene's function and tracking every biochemical pathway, researchers aim to establish a blueprint for how plants develop, a major goal of systems biology. It may one day be possible to create a computer-generated "virtual plant" that enables researchers to visualize which plant genes are activated in different parts of the plant during the entire course of development.

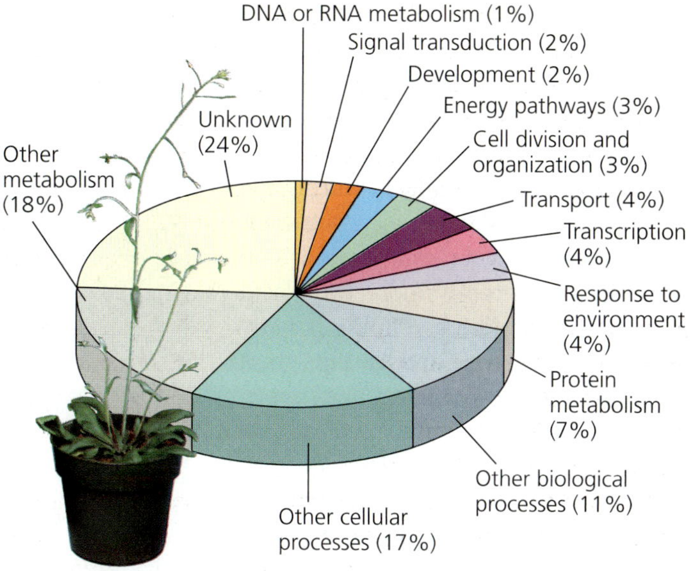

▲ **Figure 35.24** ***Arabidopsis thaliana*** **gene functions.** Due to its small size, rapid life cycle, and small genome, *Arabidopsis* was the first plant to have its entire genome sequenced (containing about 26,700 genes). The pie chart represents the proportion of *Arabidopsis* genes in different functional categories. (Data from TAIR, The *Arabidopsis* Information Resource, 2007.)

Growth: Cell Division and Cell Expansion

By increasing cell number, cell division in meristems increases the potential for growth. However, it is cell expansion, particularly cell elongation, that accounts for increase in size. The process of plant cell division is described more fully in Chapter 12 (see Figure 12.10), and Chapter 39 discusses the process of cell elongation (see Figure 39.8). Here we are more concerned with how these processes contribute to plant form.

The Plane and Symmetry of Cell Division

The plane (direction) and symmetry of cell division are immensely important in determining plant form. Imagine a single cell that is ready to undergo mitosis. If the planes of division of its descendants are parallel to the plane of the first cell division, a single file of cells will be produced (**Figure 35.25a**). At the other extreme, if the planes vary randomly, a disorganized clump of cells results. Meanwhile, even though chromosomes are allocated to daughter cells equally during mitosis, the cytoplasm may divide asymmetrically. *Asymmetrical cell division*, in which one daughter cell receives more cytoplasm than the other during mitosis, is fairly common in plant cells and usually signals a key event in development. For example, the formation of guard cells typically involves both an asymmetrical cell division and a change in the plane of cell division. An epidermal cell divides asymmetrically, forming a large cell that remains an unspecialized epidermal cell and a small cell that becomes the guard cell "mother cell." Guard cells form when this small mother cell divides in a plane perpendicular to the first cell division (**Figure 35.25b**).

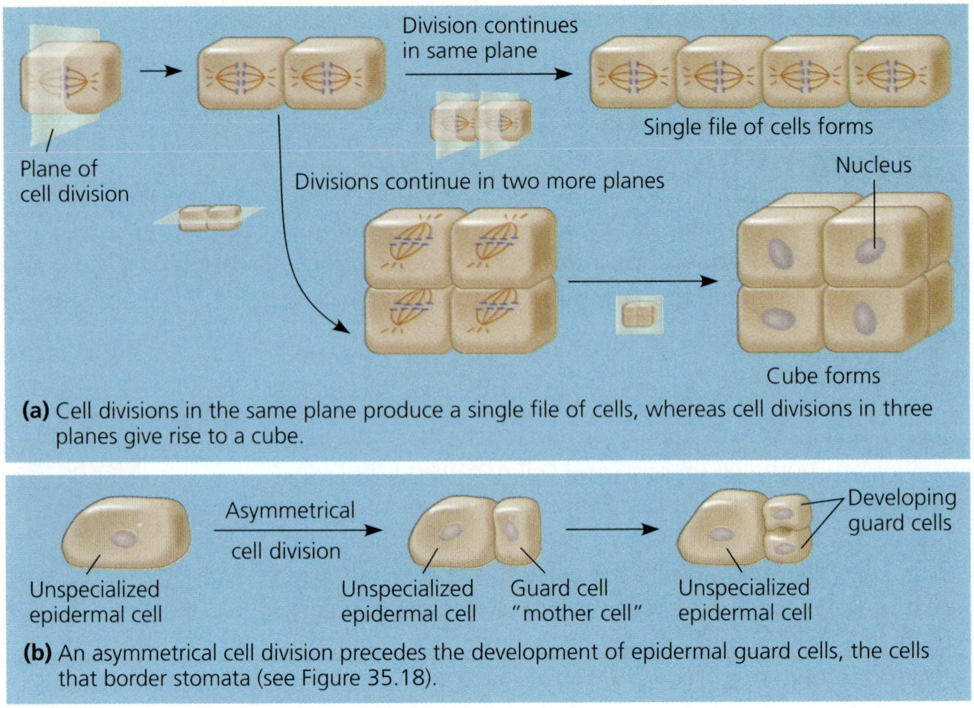

(a) Cell divisions in the same plane produce a single file of cells, whereas cell divisions in three planes give rise to a cube.

(b) An asymmetrical cell division precedes the development of epidermal guard cells, the cells that border stomata (see Figure 35.18).

▲ **Figure 35.25 The plane and symmetry of cell division influence development of form.**

The plane in which a cell divides is determined during late interphase. The first sign of this spatial orientation is a rearrangement of the cytoskeleton. Microtubules in the cytoplasm become concentrated into a ring that is called the **preprophase band** (**Figure 35.26**). The band disappears before metaphase, but it predicts the future plane of cell division. The "imprint" consists of an ordered array of actin microfilaments that remain after the microtubules disperse.

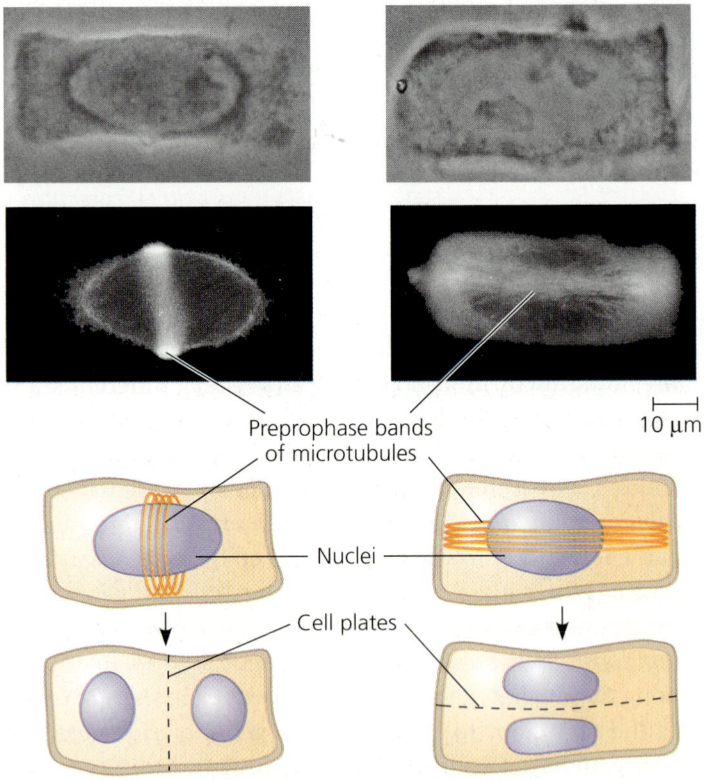

▲ **Figure 35.26 The preprophase band and the plane of cell division.** The location of the preprophase band predicts the plane of cell division. Although the cells shown on the left and right are similar in shape, they will divide in different planes. Each cell is represented by two light micrographs, one (top) unstained and the other (bottom) stained with a fluorescent dye that binds specifically to microtubules. The stained microtubules form a "halo" (preprophase band) around the nucleus in the outer cytoplasm.

Orientation of Cell Expansion

Before discussing how cell expansion contributes to plant form, it is useful to consider the difference in cell expansion between plants and animals. Animal cells grow mainly by synthesizing protein-rich cytoplasm, a metabolically expensive process. Growing plant cells also produce additional protein-rich material in their cytoplasm, but water uptake typically accounts for about 90% of expansion. Most of this water is packaged in the large central vacuole. Vacuolar sap is very dilute and nearly devoid of the energetically expensive macromolecules that are found in great abundance in the rest of the cytoplasm. Large vacuoles are therefore a "cheap" way of filling space, enabling a plant to grow rapidly and economically. Bamboo shoots, for instance, can elongate more than 2 m per week. Rapid extensibility of shoots and roots was an important evolutionary adaptation that increased their exposure to light and soil.

In a growing cell, enzymes weaken the cross-links in the cell wall, allowing it to expand as water diffuses into the vacuole by osmosis. Loosening of the wall occurs when hydrogen ions secreted by the cell activate cell wall enzymes that break the

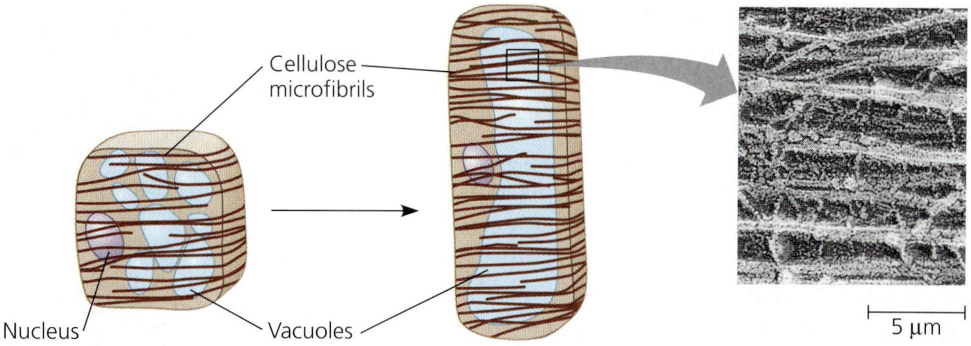

▶ **Figure 35.27 The orientation of plant cell expansion.** Growing plant cells expand mainly through water uptake. In a growing cell, enzymes weaken cross-links in the cell wall, allowing it to expand as water diffuses into the vacuole by osmosis; at the same time, more microfibrils are made. The orientation of cell growth is mainly in the plane perpendicular to the orientation of cellulose microfibrils in the wall. The microfibrils are embedded in a matrix of other (noncellulose) polysaccharides, some of which form the cross-links visible in the micrograph (TEM).

cross-links between polymers in the wall. This reduces constraint on the turgid cell, which can take up more water and expand. Small vacuoles, which accumulate most of this water, coalesce and form the cell's central vacuole.

Plant cells rarely expand equally in all directions. Their greatest expansion is usually oriented along the plant's main axis. For example, cells near the tip of the root may elongate up to 20 times their original length, with relatively little increase in width. The orientation of cellulose microfibrils in the innermost layers of the cell wall causes this differential growth. The microfibrils do not stretch, so the cell expands mainly perpendicular to the "grain" of the microfibrils, as shown in **Figure 35.27**.

As with the plane of cell division, microtubules play a key role in regulating the plane of cell expansion. It is the orientation of microtubules in the cell's outermost cytoplasm that determines the orientation of cellulose microfibrils, the basic structural units of the cell wall.

Microtubules and Plant Growth

Studies of *fass* mutants of *Arabidopsis* have confirmed the importance of cytoplasmic microtubules in cell division and expansion. The *fass* mutants have unusually squat cells with seemingly random planes of cell division. Their roots and stems have no ordered cell files and layers. Despite these abnormalities, *fass* mutants develop into tiny adult plants, but their organs are compressed longitudinally **(Figure 35.28)**.

The stubby form and disorganized tissue arrangement can be traced to the abnormal organization of microtubules. During interphase, the microtubules are randomly positioned, and preprophase bands do not form prior to mitosis (see Figure 35.26). As a result, there is no orderly "grain" of cellulose microfibrils in the cell wall to determine the direction of elongation (see Figure 35.27). This defect gives rise to cells that expand in all directions and divide haphazardly without respect to orientation.

Morphogenesis and Pattern Formation

A plant's body is more than a collection of dividing and expanding cells. Morphogenesis must occur for development to proceed properly; that is, cells must be organized into multicellular arrangements of tissues and organs. The development of specific structures in specific locations is called **pattern formation**.

Many developmental biologists postulate that pattern formation is determined by **positional information** in the form of signals that continuously indicate to each cell its location within a developing structure. According to this hypothesis, each cell within a developing organ responds to positional information from neighboring cells by differentiating into a particular cell type, oriented in a particular way. Biologists have accumulated

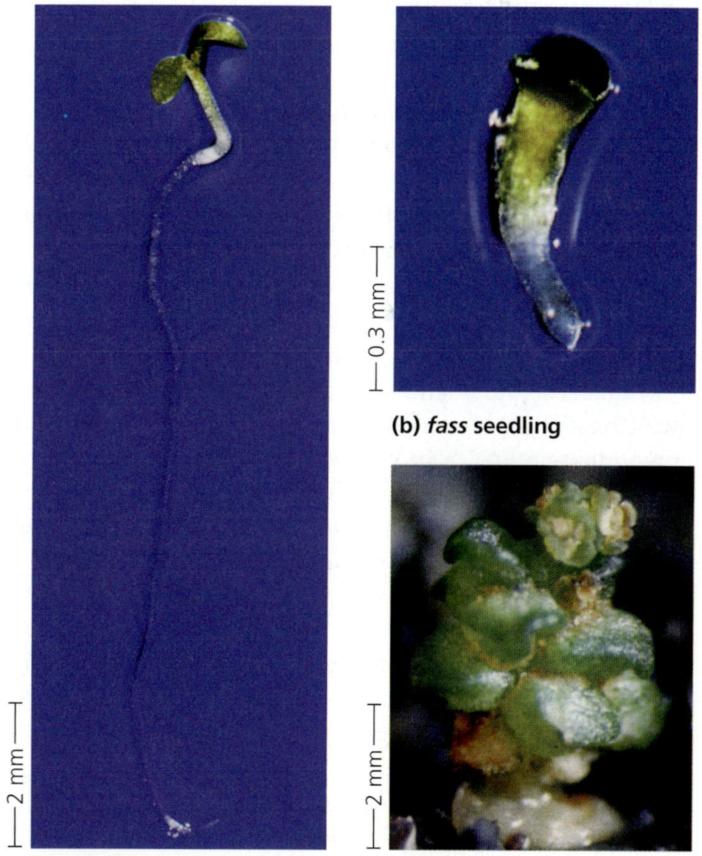

(a) Wild-type seedling

(b) *fass* seedling

(c) Mature *fass* mutant

▲ **Figure 35.28 The *fass* mutant of *Arabidopsis* confirms the importance of cytoplasmic microtubules in plant growth.** The squat body of the *fass* mutant results from cell division and cell elongation being oriented randomly instead of in the direction of the normal plant axis.

evidence that gradients of specific molecules, such as hormones, proteins, or mRNAs, provide positional information. For example, the diffusion of a growth-regulating molecule produced in the shoot apical meristem may "inform" the cells below of their distance from the shoot tip. Cells possibly "gauge" their radial positions within the developing organ by detecting a second chemical signal from the outermost cells. The gradients of these two substances would be sufficient for each cell to "get a fix" on its position relative to the longitudinal and radial axes of the developing organ. This hypothesis of diffusible chemical signals is just one that developmental biologists are testing.

One type of positional information is associated with **polarity**, the condition of having structural or chemical differences at opposite ends of an organism. Plants typically have an axis, with a root end and a shoot end. Such polarity is most obvious in morphological differences, but it is also manifest in physiological properties, including the unidirectional movement of the hormone auxin (see Chapter 39) and the emergence of adventitious roots and shoots from "cuttings." Adventitious roots form within the root end of a stem cutting, and adventitious shoots arise from the shoot end of a root cutting.

The first division of a plant zygote is normally asymmetrical, initiating polarization of the plant body into shoot and root. Once this polarity has been induced, it becomes exceedingly difficult to reverse experimentally. Therefore, the proper establishment of axial polarity is a critical step in a plant's morphogenesis. In the *gnom* mutant of *Arabidopsis,* the establishment of polarity is defective. The first cell division of the zygote is abnormal because it is symmetrical, and the resulting ball-shaped plant has neither roots nor leaves **(Figure 35.29)**.

Morphogenesis in plants, as in other multicellular organisms, is often under the control of homeotic genes, master regulatory genes that mediate many of the major events in an individual's development, such as the initiation of an organ (see Chapter 21). For example, the protein product of the homeotic gene *KNOTTED-1*, found in many plant species, is important in the development of leaf morphology, including the production of compound leaves. If the *KNOTTED-1* gene is expressed in greater quantity in the genome of tomato plants, the normally compound leaves become "super-compound" **(Figure 35.30)**.

◄ **Figure 35.29 Establishment of axial polarity.** The normal *Arabidopsis* seedling (left) has a shoot end and a root end. In the *gnom* mutant (right), the first division of the zygote was not asymmetrical; as a result, the plant is ball-shaped and lacks leaves and roots. The defect in *gnom* mutants has been traced to an inability to transport the hormone auxin in a polar manner.

▲ **Figure 35.30 Overexpression of a homeotic gene in leaf formation.** *KNOTTED-1* is a homeotic gene involved in leaf and leaflet formation. An increase in its expression in tomato plants results in leaves that are "super-compound" (right) compared with normal leaves (left).

Gene Expression and Control of Cellular Differentiation

Cells of a developing organism can synthesize different proteins and diverge in structure and function even though they share a common genome. If a mature cell removed from a root or leaf can dedifferentiate in tissue culture and give rise to the diverse cell types of a plant, then it must possess all the genes necessary to make any kind of plant cell (see Figure 20.16). This means that cellular differentiation depends, to a large extent, on the control of gene expression—the regulation of transcription and translation, resulting in the production of specific proteins. Researchers are beginning to unravel the molecular mechanisms that switch specific genes on and off at critical times during cellular differentiation (see Chapter 18).

The activation or inactivation of specific genes involved in cellular differentiation depends, to a large extent, on positional information—where a particular cell is located relative to other cells. For example, two distinct cell types are formed in the root epidermis of *Arabidopsis*: root hair cells and hairless epidermal cells. Cell fate is associated with the position of the epidermal cells. The immature epidermal cells that are in contact with two underlying cells of the root cortex differentiate into root hair cells, whereas the immature epidermal cells in contact with only one cortical cell differentiate into mature hairless cells. Differential expression of a homeotic gene called *GLABRA-2* (from the Latin *glaber*, bald) is required for appropriate root hair distribution. Researchers have demonstrated this by coupling the *GLABRA-2* gene to a "reporter gene" that causes every cell expressing *GLABRA-2* in the root to turn pale blue following a certain treatment **(Figure 35.31)**. The *GLABRA-2* gene is normally expressed only in epidermal cells that will not develop root hairs.

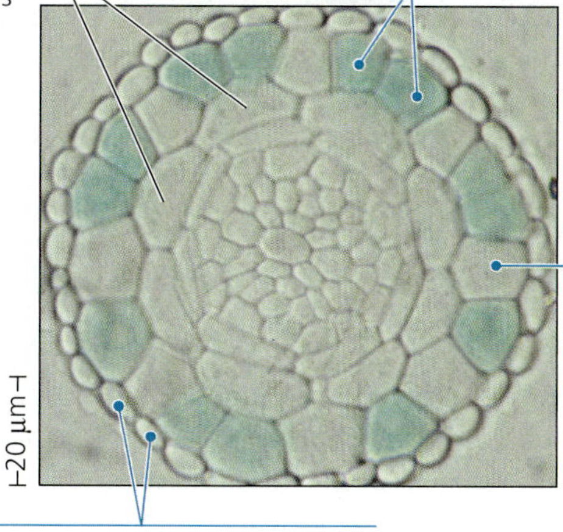

▲ **Figure 35.31 Control of root hair differentiation by a homeotic gene** (LM).

WHAT IF? *What would the roots look like if GLABRA-2 were rendered dysfunctional by a mutation?*

Location and a Cell's Developmental Fate

In the process of shaping an organ, patterns of cell division and cell expansion affect the differentiation of cells by placing them in specific locations relative to other cells. Thus, positional information underlies all the processes of development: growth, morphogenesis, and differentiation. One way to study the relationships among these processes is *clonal analysis*, in which the cell lineages derived from each cell in an apical meristem are mapped during organ development. Researchers use mutations to distinguish a specific meristematic cell from the neighboring cells in the shoot tip. All cells derived from the mutant cell by cell division will thereby be "marked." For example, a single cell in the meristem may have a mutation that prevents chlorophyll synthesis. This cell and all of its descendants will be "albino," and they will appear as a linear file of "albino" cells running down the long axis of the otherwise green shoot.

How early is a cell's developmental fate determined by its position in an embryonic structure? To some extent, the developmental fates of cells in the shoot tip are predictable very early. For example, clonal analysis has shown that almost all the cells derived from the outermost meristematic cells become part of the dermal tissue. However, we cannot pinpoint which meristematic cells will give rise to specific tissues and organs. Apparently random changes in rates and planes of cell division can reorganize the meristem. For example, the outermost cells *usually* divide perpendicularly to the surface of the shoot tip, adding cells to the surface layer. Occasionally, however, one of the outermost cells divides parallel to the surface of the shoot tip, placing one daughter cell beneath the surface, among cells derived from different lineages. Such exceptions indicate that meristematic cells are not dedicated early to forming specific tissues and organs. Instead, the cell's *final* position in an emerging organ determines what kind of cell it will become.

Shifts in Development: Phase Changes

Multicellular organisms generally pass through developmental phases. In humans, these are infancy, childhood, adolescence, and adulthood, with puberty as the dividing line between the nonreproductive and reproductive phases. Plants also pass through phases, developing from a juvenile phase to an adult vegetative phase to an adult reproductive phase. In animals, these developmental changes take place throughout the entire organism, such as when a larva develops into an adult animal. In contrast, plant developmental phases occur within a single region, the shoot apical meristem. The morphological changes that arise from these transitions in shoot apical meristem activity are called **phase changes**. During the transition from a juvenile phase to an adult phase, the most obvious morphological changes typically occur in leaf size and shape **(Figure 35.32)**. Juvenile

▲ **Figure 35.32 Phase change in the shoot system of *Acacia koa*.** This native of Hawaii has compound juvenile leaves, consisting of many small leaflets, and simple mature "leaves" (technically, highly modified petioles). This dual foliage reflects a phase change in the development of the apical meristem of each shoot. Once a node forms, the developmental phase—juvenile or adult—is fixed; that is, compound leaves do not mature into simple leaves.

nodes and internodes retain their juvenile status even after the shoot continues to elongate and the shoot apical meristem has changed to the adult phase. Therefore, any *new* leaves that develop on branches that emerge from axillary buds at juvenile nodes will also be juvenile, even though the apical meristem of the stem's main axis may have been producing mature nodes for years.

Phase changes are examples of developmental plasticity. The transition from juvenile to adult leaves is only one type of phase change. The transition in the fanwort (see Figure 35.1) from feathery underwater leaves to fan-shaped floating leaves is another example. Next we'll examine a common but nevertheless remarkable phase change—the transition of a vegetative shoot apical meristem into a floral meristem.

Genetic Control of Flowering

Flower formation involves a phase change from vegetative growth to reproductive growth. This transition is triggered by a combination of environmental cues, such as day length, and internal signals, such as hormones. (You will learn more about the roles of these signals in flowering in Chapter 39.) Unlike vegetative growth, which is indeterminate, floral growth is determinate: The production of a flower by a shoot apical meristem stops the primary growth of that shoot. The transition from vegetative growth to flowering is associated with the switching on of floral **meristem identity genes**. The protein products of these genes are transcription factors that regulate the genes required for the conversion of the indeterminate vegetative meristems to determinate floral meristems.

When a shoot apical meristem is induced to flower, the relative position of each primordium determines its development into a specific type of floral organ—a sepal, petal, stamen, or carpel (see Figure 30.7 to review basic flower structure). Viewed from above, the floral organs develop in four concentric circles, or whorls: Sepals form the fourth (outermost) whorl; petals form the third; stamens form the second; and carpels form the first (innermost) whorl. Plant biologists have identified several **organ identity genes** that regulate the development of this characteristic floral pattern. Organ identity genes, also called plant homeotic genes, code for transcription factors. Positional information determines which organ identity genes are expressed in a particular floral organ primordium. The result is the development of an emerging floral primordium into a specific floral organ. And just as a mutation in a fruit fly homeotic gene can cause legs to grow in place of antennae (see Figure 18.18), a mutation in a plant organ identity gene can cause abnormal floral development, such as petals growing in place of stamens, as shown in **Figure 35.33**.

By studying mutants with abnormal flowers, researchers have identified and cloned three classes of floral organ identity genes, and their studies are beginning to reveal how these genes function. The **ABC model** of flower formation, diagrammed in **Figure 35.34a**, identifies how these three classes of genes direct the formation of the four types of floral organs. According to the ABC model, each class of organ identity genes is switched on in two specific whorls of the floral meristem. Normally, *A* genes are switched on in the two outer whorls (sepals and petals); *B* genes are switched on in the two middle whorls (petals and stamens); and *C* genes are switched on in the two inner whorls (stamens and carpels). Sepals arise from those parts of the floral meristems in which only *A* genes are active; petals arise where *A* and *B* genes are active; stamens where *B* and *C* genes are active; and carpels where only *C* genes are active. The ABC model can account for the phenotypes of mutants lacking *A*, *B*, or *C* gene activity, with one addition: Where gene *A* activity is present, it inhibits *C*, and vice versa. If either *A* or *C* is missing, the other takes its place. **Figure 35.34b** shows the floral patterns of mutants lacking each of the three classes of organ identity

(a) Normal *Arabidopsis* flower. *Arabidopsis* normally has four whorls of flower parts: sepals (Se), petals (Pe), stamens (St), and carpels (Ca).

(b) Abnormal *Arabidopsis* flower. Researchers have identified several mutations of organ identity genes that cause abnormal flowers to develop. This flower has an extra set of petals in place of stamens and an internal flower where normal plants have carpels.

▶ **Figure 35.33 Organ identity genes and pattern formation in flower development.**

▼ Figure 35.34 The ABC hypothesis for the functioning of organ identity genes in flower development.

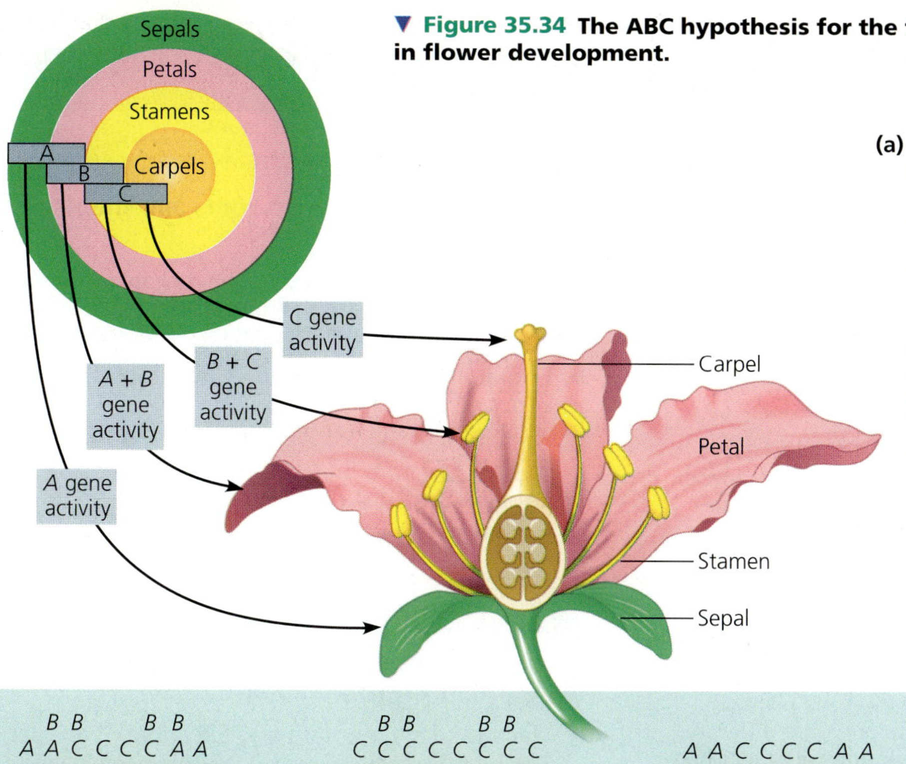

(a) A schematic diagram of the ABC hypothesis. Studies of plant mutations reveal that three classes of organ identity genes are responsible for the spatial pattern of floral parts. These genes, designated *A*, *B*, and *C*, regulate expression of other genes responsible for development of sepals, petals, stamens, and carpels. Sepals develop from the meristematic region where only *A* genes are active. Petals develop where both *A* and *B* genes are expressed. Stamens arise where *B* and *C* genes are active. Carpels arise where only *C* genes are expressed.

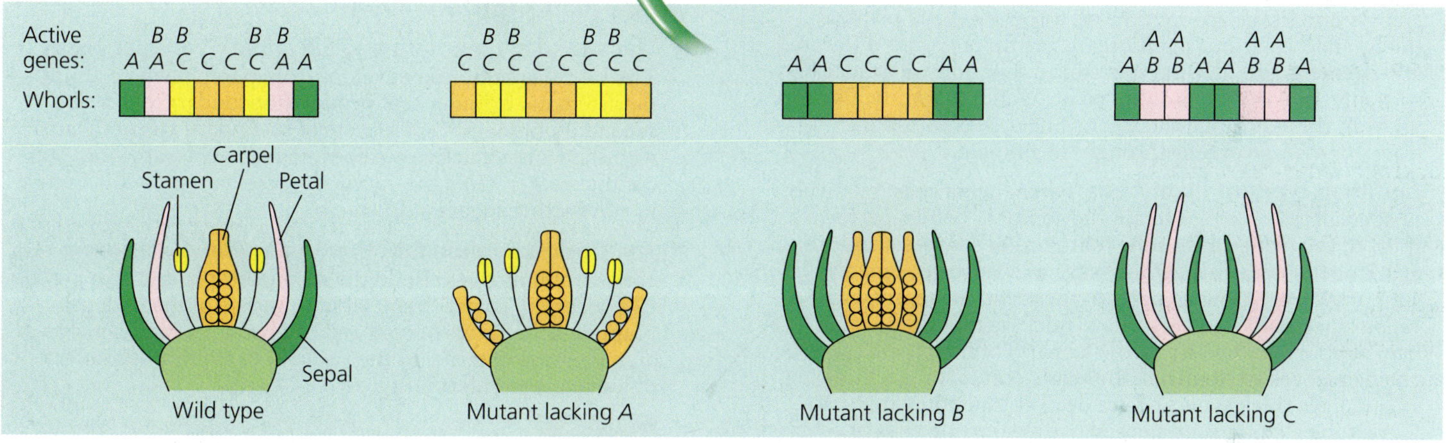

(b) Side view of flowers with organ identity mutations. The phenotype of mutants lacking a functional *A*, *B*, or *C* organ identity gene can be explained by combining the model in part (a) with the rule that if *A* or *C* activity is missing, the other activity occurs through all four whorls.

genes and depicts how the model accounts for the floral phenotypes. By constructing such hypotheses and designing experiments to test them, researchers are tracing the genetic basis of plant development.

In dissecting the plant to examine its parts, as we have done in this chapter, we must remember that the whole plant functions as an integrated organism. In the following chapters, you'll learn more about how materials are transported within vascular plants (Chapter 36), how plants obtain nutrients (Chapter 37), how plants reproduce (Chapter 38, focusing on flowering plants), and how plant functions are coordinated (Chapter 39). Remembering that structure fits function and that plant anatomy and physiology reflect evolutionary adaptations to the challenges of living on land will enhance your understanding of plants.

CONCEPT CHECK 35.5

1. What attributes of the weed *Arabidopsis thaliana* make it such a useful research organism?
2. How can two cells in a plant have vastly different structures even though they have the same genome?
3. Explain how the *fass* mutation in *Arabidopsis* results in a stubby plant rather than a normal elongated one.
4. **WHAT IF?** In some species, such as the magnolia on the cover of this book, sepals look like petals, and both are collectively called "tepals." Suggest an extension to the ABC model that could hypothetically account for the origin of tepals.

For suggested answers, see Appendix A.

Chapter 35 Review

MEDIA Go to the Study Area at **www.masteringbio.com** for BioFlix 3-D Animations, MP3 Tutors, Videos, Practice Tests, an eBook, and more.

SUMMARY OF KEY CONCEPTS

CONCEPT 35.1

The plant body has a hierarchy of organs, tissues, and cells (pp. 738–745)

- **The Three Basic Plant Organs: Roots, Stems, and Leaves** Roots anchor the plant, absorb and conduct water and minerals, and store food. Shoots consist of stems, leaves, and (in angiosperms) flowers. Leaves are attached to the nodes of the stem and are the primary organs of photosynthesis. Axillary buds, located in axils of leaves and stems, give rise to shoot branches. Plant organs may be modified for specialized functions.
- **Dermal, Vascular, and Ground Tissues** Dermal tissue (epidermis and periderm), vascular tissue (xylem and phloem), and ground tissue are continuous throughout the plant, although in the various plant organs the three tissues differ in arrangement and in some specialized functions. Vascular tissues integrate the parts of the plant. Water and minerals move up from roots through the xylem. Sugar is exported from leaves or storage organs through the phloem.
- **Common Types of Plant Cells** Parenchyma cells, relatively unspecialized cells that retain the ability to divide, perform most of the plant's metabolic functions of synthesis and storage. Collenchyma cells, which have unevenly thickened walls, support young, growing parts of the plant. Sclerenchyma cells—fibers and sclereids—have thick, lignified walls that help support mature, nongrowing parts of the plant. Tracheids and vessel elements, the water-conducting cells of xylem, have thick walls and are dead at functional maturity. Sieve-tube elements are the sugar-transporting cells of phloem in angiosperms. Though alive at functional maturity, sieve-tube elements depend on neighboring companion cells.

MEDIA

BioFlix 3-D Animation Tour of a Plant Cell

CONCEPT 35.2

Meristems generate cells for new organs (pp. 746–747)

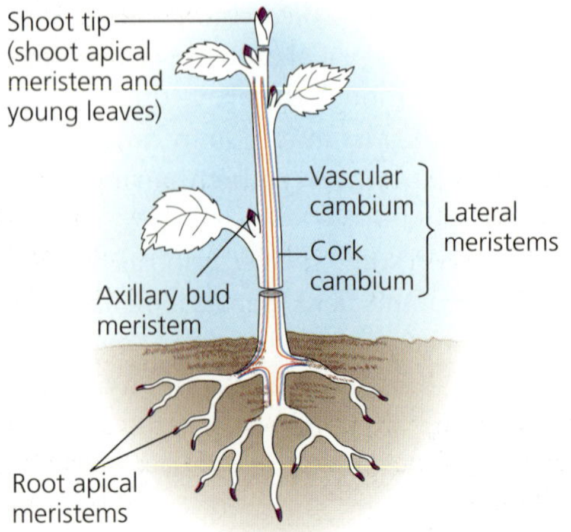

CONCEPT 35.3

Primary growth lengthens roots and shoots (pp. 747–751)

- **Primary Growth of Roots** The root apical meristem is located near the tip of the root, where it generates cells for the growing root axis and the root cap.
- **Primary Growth of Shoots** The apical meristem of a shoot is located in the apical bud, where it gives rise to a repetition of internodes and leaf-bearing nodes.

MEDIA

Activity Root, Stem, and Leaf Sections

Investigation What Are Functions of Monocot Tissues?

CONCEPT 35.4

Secondary growth adds girth to stems and roots in woody plants (pp. 751–754)

- **The Vascular Cambium and Secondary Vascular Tissue** The vascular cambium develops from parenchyma cells into a meristematic cylinder that produces secondary xylem and secondary phloem. Older layers of secondary xylem (heartwood) become inactive, while younger layers (sapwood) still conduct water. Only the youngest secondary phloem is active in conducting sugars.
- **The Cork Cambium and the Production of Periderm** The cork cambium gives rise to the secondary plant body's protective covering, or periderm, which consists of the cork cambium plus the layers of cork cells it produces. Bark consists of all the tissues external to the vascular cambium: secondary phloem and periderm.

MEDIA

Activity Primary and Secondary Growth

CONCEPT 35.5

Growth, morphogenesis, and differentiation produce the plant body (pp. 755–761)

- **Molecular Biology: Revolutionizing the Study of Plants** New techniques and model systems, including *Arabidopsis*, are catalyzing progress in understanding plants. *Arabidopsis* was the first plant to have its genome sequenced.
- **Growth: Cell Division and Cell Expansion** Cell division and cell expansion are the primary determinants of growth and form. A preprophase band determines where a cell plate will form in a dividing cell. Cytoskeleton orientation affects the direction of cell elongation by controlling the orientation of cellulose microfibrils in the cell wall.
- **Morphogenesis and Pattern Formation** Development of tissues and organs in specific locations depends on cells responding to positional information, such as polarity. Homeotic genes often control morphogenesis.
- **Gene Expression and Control of Cellular Differentiation** Despite having identical genomes, plant cells differentiate because of differential gene activation.

- **Location and a Cell's Developmental Fate** The way in which a plant cell differentiates is determined largely by the cell's position in the developing plant body.
- **Shifts in Development: Phase Changes** Internal or environmental cues may cause a plant to switch from one developmental phase to another—for example, from developing juvenile leaves to developing mature leaves. Such morphological changes are called phase changes.
- **Genetic Control of Flowering** Research on organ identity genes in developing flowers provides a model system for studying pattern formation. The ABC model identifies how three classes of organ identity genes control formation of sepals, petals, stamens, and carpels.

TESTING YOUR KNOWLEDGE

SELF-QUIZ

1. Which structure is *incorrectly* paired with its tissue system?
   a. root hair—dermal tissue
   b. palisade mesophyll—ground tissue
   c. guard cell—dermal tissue
   d. companion cell—ground tissue
   e. tracheid—vascular tissue

2. In a root, a vessel element completes its development in which area of growth?
   a. zone of cell division
   b. zone of elongation
   c. zone of differentiation
   d. root cap
   e. apical meristem

3. Heartwood and sapwood consist of
   a. bark.
   b. periderm.
   c. secondary xylem.
   d. secondary phloem.
   e. cork.

4. Which of the following is *not* part of an older tree's bark?
   a. cork
   b. cork cambium
   c. lenticels
   d. secondary xylem
   e. secondary phloem

5. The phase change of an apical meristem from the juvenile to the mature vegetative phase is often revealed by
   a. a change in the morphology of the leaves produced.
   b. the initiation of secondary growth.
   c. the formation of lateral roots.
   d. a change in the orientation of preprophase bands and cytoplasmic microtubules in lateral meristems.
   e. the activation of floral meristem identity genes.

6. Which of the following arise from meristematic activity?
   a. secondary xylem
   b. leaves
   c. dermal tissue
   d. tubers
   e. all of the above

7. Pinching off the tops of snapdragons causes the plants to make many more flowers than they would if left alone. Why does the removal of the top cause more flowers to form?
   a. Removal of an apical meristem causes a phase transition from vegetative to floral development.
   b. Removal of an apical meristem causes cell division to become disorganized, as in the *fass* mutant of *Arabidopsis.*
   c. Removal of an apical meristem allows more nutrients to be delivered to floral meristems.
   d. Removal of an apical meristem causes outgrowth of lateral buds that produce extra branches, which ultimately produce flowers.
   e. Removal of an apical meristem allows the periderm to produce new lateral branches.

8. Which of these are *not* produced by the vascular cambium?
   a. sclerenchyma cells
   b. parenchyma cells
   c. sieve-tube elements
   d. root hairs
   e. vessel elements

9. The type of mature cell that a particular embryonic plant cell will become appears to be determined mainly by
   a. the selective loss of genes.
   b. the cell's final position in a developing organ.
   c. the cell's pattern of migration.
   d. the cell's age.
   e. the cell's particular meristematic lineage.

10. Based on the ABC model, what would be the structure of a flower that had normal expression of genes *A* and *C* and expression of gene *B* in all four whorls?
    a. carpel-petal-petal-carpel
    b. stamen-stamen-petal-petal
    c. sepal-carpel-carpel-sepal
    d. sepal-sepal-carpel-carpel
    e. carpel-carpel-carpel-carpel

11. **DRAW IT** On this cross section from a woody eudicot, label a growth ring, late wood, early wood, and a vessel element. Then draw an arrow in the pith-to-cork direction.

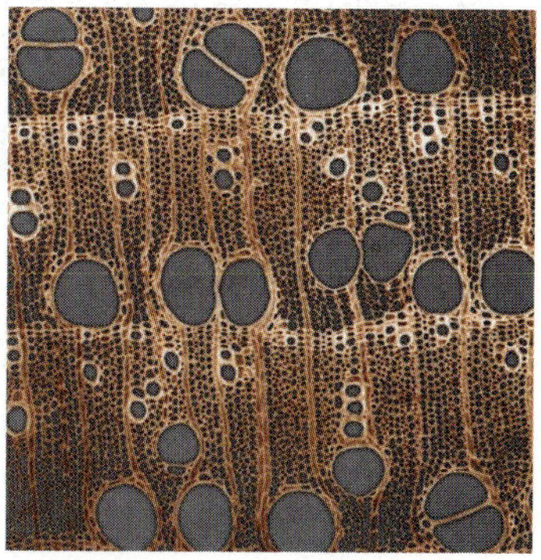

For Self-Quiz answers, see Appendix A.

MEDIA Visit the Study Area at **www.masteringbio.com** for a Practice Test.

EVOLUTION CONNECTION

12. Evolutionary biologists have coined the term *exaptation* to describe a common occurrence in the evolution of life: A limb or organ originally has a particular function but later fulfills a new function. What are some examples of exaptations in plant organs?

SCIENTIFIC INQUIRY

13. Write a paragraph explaining why mutants are useful for investigating the regulation of plant development. Include at least one specific example.

36 Resource Acquisition and Transport in Vascular Plants

▲ **Figure 36.1 Plants or pebbles?**

KEY CONCEPTS

36.1 Land plants acquire resources both above and below ground
36.2 Transport occurs by short-distance diffusion or active transport and by long-distance bulk flow
36.3 Water and minerals are transported from roots to shoots
36.4 Stomata help regulate the rate of transpiration
36.5 Sugars are transported from leaves and other sources to sites of use or storage
36.6 The symplast is highly dynamic

OVERVIEW

Underground Plants

The Kalahari Desert of southern Africa receives only about 20 cm of precipitation a year, almost exclusively during the summer months, when daytime temperatures reach a scorching 35–45°C (95–113°F). Many animals escape the desert heat by seeking shelter underground. A peculiar genus of perennial plants called stone plants (*Lithops*) has a similar, mostly subterranean lifestyle **(Figure 36.1)**. Except for the tips of two succulent leaves that are exposed to the surface, a stone plant lives entirely below ground. Each leaf tip has a region of clear, lens-like cells that allow light to penetrate to the photosynthetic tissues underground. These adaptations enable stone plants to conserve moisture and avoid the potentially harmful temperatures and high light intensities of the desert.

The remarkable growth habit of *Lithops* reminds us that the success of plants depends largely on their ability to gather and conserve resources from their environment. Through natural selection, many plant species have become highly proficient in acquiring resources that are especially limited in their environment, but there are often trade-offs in such specializations. For example, the mostly subterranean lifestyle of stone plants is good for the net acquisition of water but not for photosynthesis. As a result, stone plants grow very slowly.

This chapter begins by examining structural features of shoot and root systems that increase their efficiency in acquiring resources. Resource acquisition, however, is not the end of the story but only the beginning. Once acquired, resources must be transported to those parts of the plant where they are needed. The transport of materials, therefore, is critical for the integrated functioning of the whole plant. A central theme of this chapter is how three basic transport mechanisms—diffusion, active transport, and bulk flow—work together in vascular plants to transfer water, minerals, and the products of photosynthesis (sugars).

CONCEPT **36.1**

Land plants acquire resources both above and below ground

Land plants typically inhabit two worlds—above ground, where their shoot systems acquire sunlight and CO_2, and below ground, where their root systems acquire water and minerals. Without adaptations that allow acquisition and transport of these resources from these dual sites, plants could not have colonized land.

The algal ancestors of land plants absorbed water, minerals, and CO_2 directly from the water in which they lived. Transport in these algae was relatively simple because each cell was close to the source of these substances. The earliest land plants were nonvascular plants that grew photosynthetic shoots above the shallow fresh water in which they lived. These leafless shoots had waxy cuticles and few stomata, which allowed them to avoid excessive water loss while still permitting gas exchange for photosynthesis. The anchoring and absorbing functions of early land plants were assumed by the base of the stem or by threadlike rhizoids (see Figure 29.8).

As land plants evolved and increased in number, competition for light, water, and nutrients intensified. Taller plants with broad, flat appendages had an advantage in absorbing light. This increase in surface area, however, resulted in more evaporation and therefore a greater need for water. Larger shoots also required more anchorage. These needs favored the production of multicellular, branching roots. Meanwhile, as greater shoot heights further separated the top of the photosynthetic shoot from the nonphotosynthetic parts below ground, natural selection favored plants capable of efficient long-distance transport of water, minerals, and products of photosynthesis.

The evolution of vascular tissue consisting of xylem and phloem made possible the development of extensive root and shoot systems that carry out long-distance transport (see Figure 35.10). The xylem transports water and minerals from roots to shoots. The phloem transports products of photosynthesis from where they are made or stored to where they are needed. **Figure 36.2** provides an overview of resource acquisition and transport in a vascular plant.

Because plant success depends on photosynthesis, evolution has resulted in many mechanisms for acquiring light from the sun, CO_2 from the air, and water from the ground. Perhaps just as important, land plants must minimize evaporative loss of water, particularly in environments where water is scarce. The adaptations of each species represent compromises between enhancing photosynthesis and minimizing water loss in the species' particular habitat. Later in the chapter, we'll discuss how plants minimize water loss. Here, we'll examine how the basic architecture of shoots and roots helps plants acquire resources.

Shoot Architecture and Light Capture

In shoot systems, stems serve as supporting structures for leaves and as conduits for the transport of water and nutrients. Variations in shoot systems arise largely from the form and arrangement of leaves, the outgrowth of axillary buds, and the relative growth in stem length and thickness.

Leaf size and structure account for much of the outward diversity we see in plant form. Leaves range in length from the minuscule 1.3-mm leaves of the pygmy weed (*Crassula erecta*), a native weed of dry, sandy regions in the western United States, to the 20-m leaves of the palm *Raphia regalis*, a native of African rain forests. These species represent extreme examples of a general correlation observed between water availability and leaf size. The largest leaves are generally found in tropical rain forests, and the smallest are usually found in dry or very cold environments, where liquid water is scarce and evaporative loss from leaves is potentially more problematic.

The arrangement of leaves on a stem, known as **phyllotaxy**, is an architectural feature of immense importance in light capture.

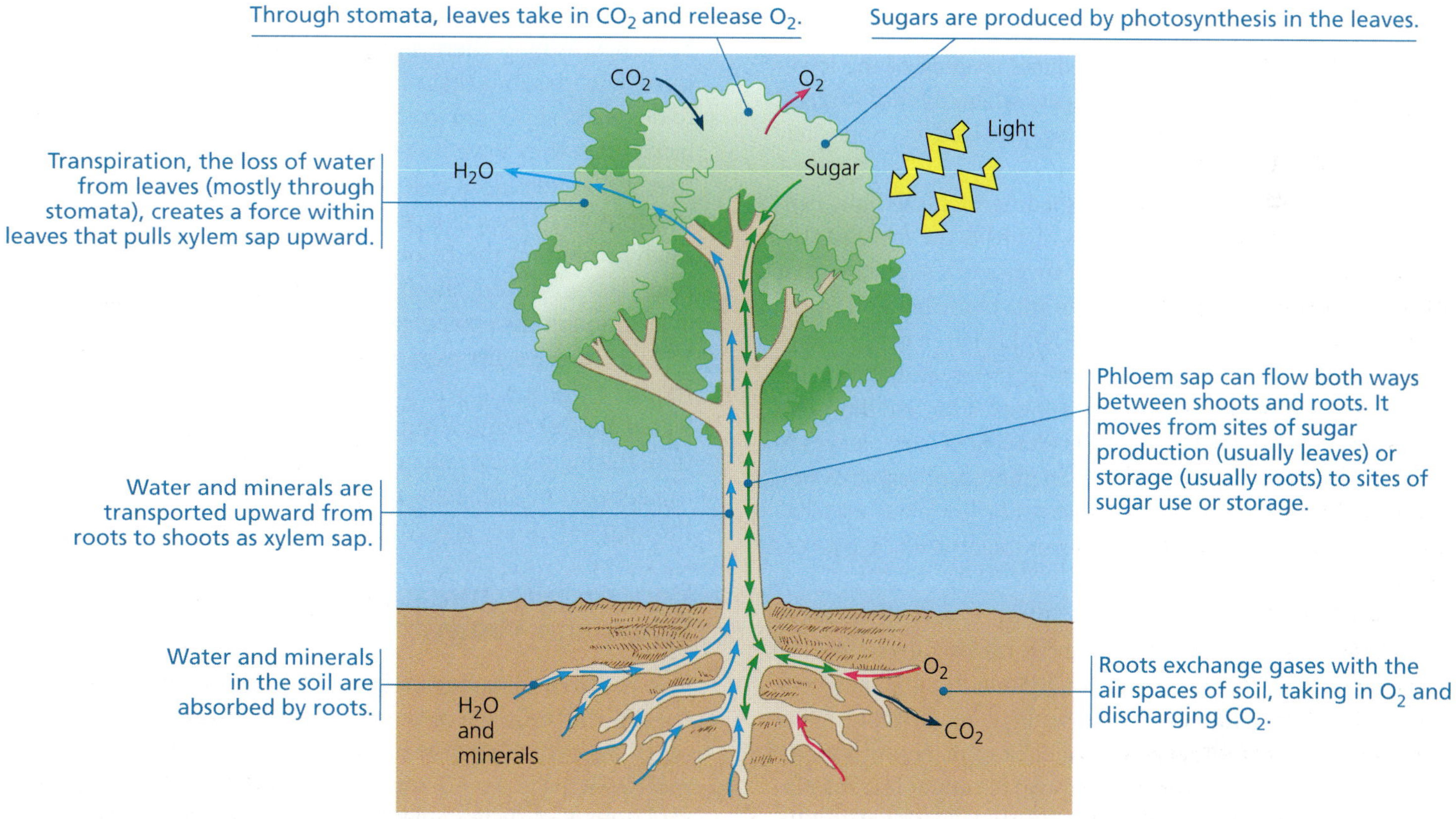

▲ **Figure 36.2 An overview of resource acquisition and transport in a vascular plant.**

▲ **Figure 36.3 Emerging phyllotaxy of Norway spruce.** This SEM, taken from above a shoot tip, shows the pattern of emergence of leaves. The leaves are numbered, with 1 being the youngest. (Some numbered leaves are not visible in the close-up.)

? *With your finger, trace the progression of leaf emergence, starting with leaf number 29. What is the pattern?*

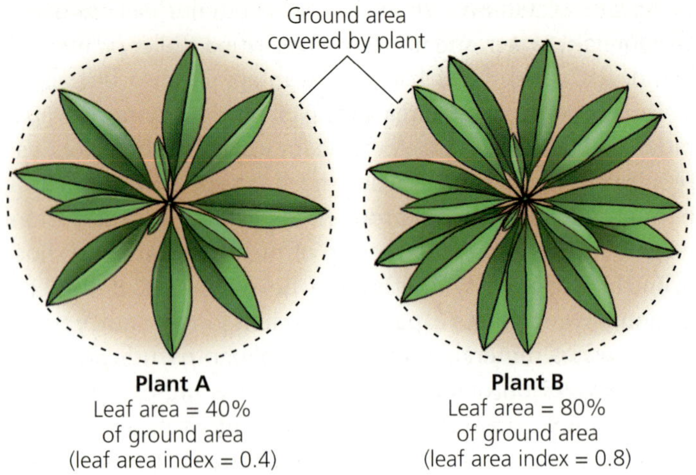

▲ **Figure 36.4 Leaf area index.** The leaf area index of a single plant is the ratio of the total area of the top surfaces of the leaves to the area of ground covered by the plant, as shown in this illustration of two plants viewed from the top.

? *Would a higher leaf area index always increase the amount of photosynthesis? Explain.*

Phyllotaxy is determined by the shoot apical meristem and is specific to each species **(Figure 36.3)**. A species may have one leaf per node (alternate, or spiral, phyllotaxy), two leaves per node (opposite phyllotaxy), or more (whorled phyllotaxy). Most angiosperms have alternate phyllotaxy, with leaves arranged in an ascending spiral around the stem, each successive leaf emerging about 137.5° from the site of the previous one. Why 137.5°? Mathematical analyses suggest that this angle allows each leaf to get the maximum exposure to light and reduces shading of the lower leaves by those above. In environments where intense sunlight can harm leaves, the greater shading provided by oppositely arranged leaves may be advantageous.

Plant features that reduce self-shading increase light capture. A useful measurement in this regard is the *leaf area index*, the ratio of the total upper leaf surface of a single plant or an entire crop divided by the surface area of the land on which the plant or crop grows **(Figure 36.4)**. Leaf area index values of up to 7 are common for many mature crops, and there is little agricultural benefit to leaf area indexes higher than this value. Adding more leaves increases shading of lower leaves to the point that they respire more than photosynthesize. When this happens, the nonproductive leaves or branches undergo programmed cell death and are eventually shed, a process called *self-pruning*.

Another factor affecting light capture is leaf orientation. Some plants have horizontally oriented leaves; others, such as grasses, have leaves that are vertically oriented. In low-light conditions, horizontal leaves capture sunlight much more effectively than vertical leaves. In grasslands or other sunny regions, however, horizontal orientation may expose upper leaves to intense light, injuring leaves and reducing photosynthesis. But if a plant's leaves are nearly vertical, light rays are essentially parallel to the leaf surfaces, so no leaf receives too much light, and light penetrates more deeply to the lower leaves.

Some other factors that contribute greatly to the outward appearance and ecological success of plants are bud outgrowth and stem elongation. Carbon dioxide and sunlight are resources that are more effectively exploited by branching. However, some plants, such as palms, generally do not branch, whereas others, such as grasses, have short stems with many branches. Why is there so much variation in shoot architecture? The reason is that plants have a finite amount of energy to devote to shoot growth. If they put most of that energy into branching, they have less to devote toward growing tall, and they are at increased risk of being shaded by taller plants. If they put all of their energy into being tall, they are not optimally exploiting the resources above ground. Natural selection has produced shoot architectures that optimize light absorption in the ecological niche plants naturally occupy.

Plant species also vary in stem thickness. Most tall plants require thick stems, which enable greater vascular flow to the leaves and mechanical support for them. Vines are an exception, relying on other structures (usually other plants) to raise their leaves higher. In woody plants, stems become thicker through secondary growth (see Figure 35.11).

Root Architecture and Acquisition of Water and Minerals

Just as carbon dioxide and sunlight are resources exploited by the shoot system, soil contains resources mined by the root system. The evolution of root branching enabled land plants to more effectively acquire water and nutrients from the soil, while also providing strong anchorage. The tallest plant species, including gymnosperms and eudicots, are typically anchored by strong taproot systems with numerous branches (see Figure 35.2). Although there are exceptions, such as palms, most monocots do not reach treelike heights because their fibrous root systems do not anchor a tall plant as strongly as a taproot system (see Figure 30.13).

Recent evidence suggests that physiological mechanisms reduce competition within the root system of a plant. Cuttings from the stolons of buffalo grass (*Buchloe dactyloides*) developed fewer and shorter roots in the presence of cuttings from the same plant than they did in the presence of cuttings from another buffalo grass plant. Moreover, when cuttings from the same node were separated, their root systems eventually began competing with each other. Although the mechanism underlying this ability to distinguish self from nonself is unknown, avoiding competition between roots of the same plant for the same limited pool of resources certainly seems beneficial.

Evolution of mutualistic associations between roots and fungi was a critical step in the successful colonization of land by plants, especially given the poorly developed soils available at that time. The very specialized mutualistic associations between roots and fungi are called **mycorrhizae** **(Figure 36.5)**. About 80% of extant land plant species form mycorrhizal associations (discussed in Chapters 31 and 37). Mycorrhizal hyphae endow the fungus and plant roots with an enormous surface area for absorbing water and minerals, particularly phosphate. As much as 3 m of hyphae can extend from each centimeter along a root's length, facilitating access to a far greater volume of soil than the root alone could penetrate.

Once acquired, resources must be transported to other parts of the plant that need them. In the next section, we'll examine the processes that enable resources such as water, minerals, and sugars to be transported throughout the plant.

▲ **Figure 36.5 A mycorrhiza, a mutualistic association of fungi and roots.** The white mycelium of the fungus ensheathes these roots of a pine tree. The branched, club-shaped roots are often characteristic of this association. The fungal hyphae provide an extensive surface area for the absorption of water and minerals.

CONCEPT CHECK 36.1

1. Why is long-distance transport important for vascular plants?
2. What architectural features influence self-shading?
3. Why might a crop develop a mineral deficiency after being treated with a fungicide?
4. Some plants can detect increased levels of light reflected from leaves of encroaching neighbors. This detection elicits stem elongation, production of erect leaves, and reduced lateral branching. How do these responses help the plant compete?
5. **WHAT IF?** If you prune a plant's shoot tips, what will be the short-term effect on the plant's branching and leaf area index?

For suggested answers, see Appendix A.

CONCEPT **36.2**

Transport occurs by short-distance diffusion or active transport and by long-distance bulk flow

Like animals, plants need to transport water and nutrients from one part of their body to another. How do they do this without a pumping mechanism like a heart? To answer this question, we must first look at the basic transport processes of plants.

Transport begins with the absorption of resources by plant cells. As in any organism, the selective permeability of the plasma membrane controls the movement of substances into and out of the cell. We examined the transport of solutes and water across plasma membranes in detail in Chapter 7. Here we'll review diffusion and active transport in the context of short-distance transport in plant cells, and then we'll look at long-distance transport through bulk flow.

Diffusion and Active Transport of Solutes

Recall from Chapter 7 that a solute tends to diffuse down its electrochemical gradient, the combined effect of the solute's concentration gradient and the voltage (charge difference) across the membrane. Diffusion across a membrane is called *passive transport* because it happens without the cell directly using metabolic energy. *Active transport* is the pumping of a solute across a membrane against its electrochemical gradient. It is called "active" because the cell must expend energy, usually in the form of ATP, to transport a solute counter to the net direction in which the solute diffuses.

Most solutes cannot diffuse across the phospholipid bilayer of the membrane directly. Instead, they must pass through **transport proteins** embedded in the membrane. Transport proteins involved in active transport require energy to function,

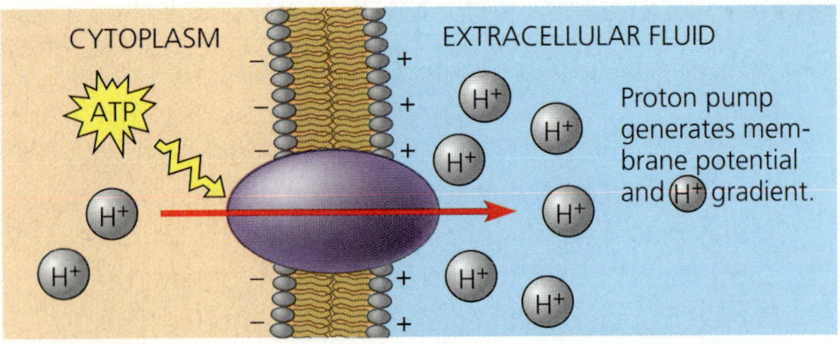

▲ **Figure 36.6 Proton pumps provide energy for solute transport.** By pumping H^+ out of the cell, proton pumps produce an H^+ gradient and a charge separation called a membrane potential. These two forms of potential energy can drive the transport of solutes.

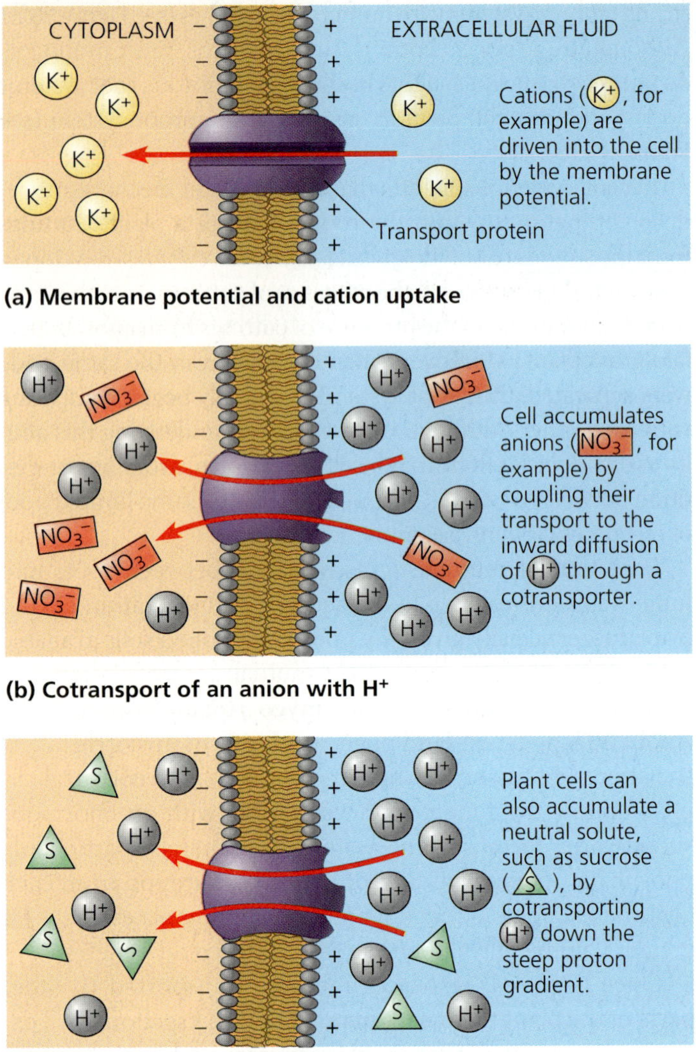

▲ **Figure 36.7 Solute transport in plant cells.**

whereas those engaged in passive transport do not. In some cases, transport proteins bind selectively to a solute on one side of the membrane and then change shape, releasing the solute on the opposite side. Other transport proteins provide selective channels across the membrane. For example, membranes of most plant cells have potassium channels that allow potassium ions (K^+) to pass but not other cations, such as sodium (Na^+). Some channels are gated, opening or closing in response to stimuli such as chemicals, pressure, or voltage. Later in this chapter, we'll discuss how K^+ channels in guard cells function in opening and closing stomata.

In active transport in plant cells, the most important transport proteins are **proton pumps**, which use energy from ATP to pump protons (H^+) out of the cell. This movement results in an H^+ gradient (proton gradient), with a higher H^+ concentration outside the cell than inside **(Figure 36.6)**. The H^+ gradient across the membrane is a form of potential (stored) energy, and the flow of H^+ back into the cell can be harnessed to do work. The movement of H^+ out of the cell also makes the inside of the cell negative in charge relative to the outside. This charge separation across the membrane contributes to a voltage called a **membrane potential**, another form of potential energy that can be harnessed to perform cellular work.

Plant cells use the energy in the H^+ gradient and membrane potential to drive the active transport of many different solutes. For example, the membrane potential generated by proton pumps contributes to the absorption of K^+ by root cells **(Figure 36.7a)**. In the mechanism called **cotransport**, a transport protein couples the diffusion of one solute (H^+) with active transport of another (NO_3^- in **Figure 36.7b**).

The "coattail" effect of cotransport is also responsible for absorption of neutral solutes, such as the sugar sucrose, by plant cells **(Figure 36.7c)**. A sucrose-H^+ cotransporter couples movement of sucrose against its concentration gradient with movement of H^+ down its electrochemical gradient.

Diffusion of Water (Osmosis)

To survive, plants must balance water absorption and loss. The net absorption or loss of water by a cell occurs by **osmosis**, the diffusion of water across a membrane (see Figure 7.12). What determines the direction of water movement? In an animal cell, if the plasma membrane is impermeable to the solutes, water will move from the solution with the lower solute concentration to the solution with the higher solute concentration. But a plant cell has an almost rigid cell wall, which adds another factor that affects osmosis: the physical pressure of the cell wall pushing back against the expanding protoplast (the living part of the cell, consisting of the nucleus, cytoplasm, and plasma membrane). The combined effects of solute concentration and physical pressure are incorporated into a quantity called the **water potential**.

Water potential determines the direction of water movement. The primary idea to keep in mind is that free water—water that is not bound to solutes or surfaces—moves *from regions of higher water potential to regions of lower water potential* if there is no barrier to its flow. For example, if a plant cell is immersed in a solution that has a higher water potential than the cell, water will move into the cell. As it moves, water can perform work, such as cell expansion. The word *potential* in the term *water potential* refers to water's potential energy—water's capacity to perform work when it moves from a region of higher water potential to a region of lower water potential.

Water potential is abbreviated by the Greek letter ψ (psi, pronounced "sigh"). Plant biologists measure ψ in units of pressure called **megapascals** (abbreviated **MPa**). Physicists have assigned the value of zero ($\psi = 0$ MPa) to the water potential of pure water in a container open to the atmosphere under standard conditions (at sea level and at room temperature). One MPa is equal to about 10 atmospheres of pressure. (An atmosphere is the pressure exerted at sea level by the volume of air extending through the entire height of the atmosphere—about 1 kg of pressure per square centimeter.) The internal pressure of a plant cell is approximately 0.5 MPa, about twice the air pressure inside an inflated car tire.

How Solutes and Pressure Affect Water Potential

Both pressure and solute concentration can affect water potential, as expressed in the *water potential equation*:

$$\psi = \psi_S + \psi_P$$

where ψ is the water potential, ψ_S is the solute potential (osmotic potential), and ψ_P is the pressure potential. The **solute potential** (ψ_S) of a solution is proportional to its molarity. Solute potential is also called **osmotic potential** because solutes affect the direction of osmosis. Solutes are dissolved chemicals, which in plants are typically mineral ions and sugars. By definition, the ψ_S of pure water is 0. But what happens when solutes are added? The solutes bind water molecules, reducing the number of free water molecules and lowering the capacity of the water to move and do work. Thus, adding solutes always lowers water potential, and the ψ_S of a solution is always negative. A 0.1 *M* solution of a sugar, for example, has a ψ_S of -0.23 MPa.

Pressure potential (ψ_P) is the physical pressure on a solution. Unlike ψ_S, ψ_P can be positive or negative relative to atmospheric pressure. For example, the water in the nonliving xylem cells (tracheids and vessel elements) of a plant is often under a negative pressure potential (tension) of less than -2 MPa. Conversely, much like the air in a balloon, the water in living cells is usually under positive pressure. Specifically, the cell contents press the plasma membrane against the cell wall, and the cell wall, in turn, presses against the protoplast, producing what is called **turgor pressure**.

Measuring Water Potential

Now let's put the water potential equation to use. We'll apply it to an artificial model and then to a living plant cell.

A U-shaped tube can be used to demonstrate water movement across a selectively permeable membrane **(Figure 36.8)**. As you consider this model, keep in mind the key point: *Water moves from regions of higher water potential to regions of lower water potential.* The two arms of the U-tube are separated by a membrane (shown as a vertical dashed line) that is permeable to water but not to solutes. If the right arm of the tube contains a 0.1 *M* solution ($\psi_S = -0.23$ MPa) and the left arm contains pure water ($\psi_S = 0$), and there is no physical pressure (that is, $\psi_P = 0$), the water potential ψ is equal to ψ_S. Thus, the ψ of the right arm is -0.23 MPa, whereas the ψ of the left arm (pure water) is 0 MPa. Because water moves from regions of higher water potential to regions of lower water potential, the net water movement will be from the left arm of the tube to

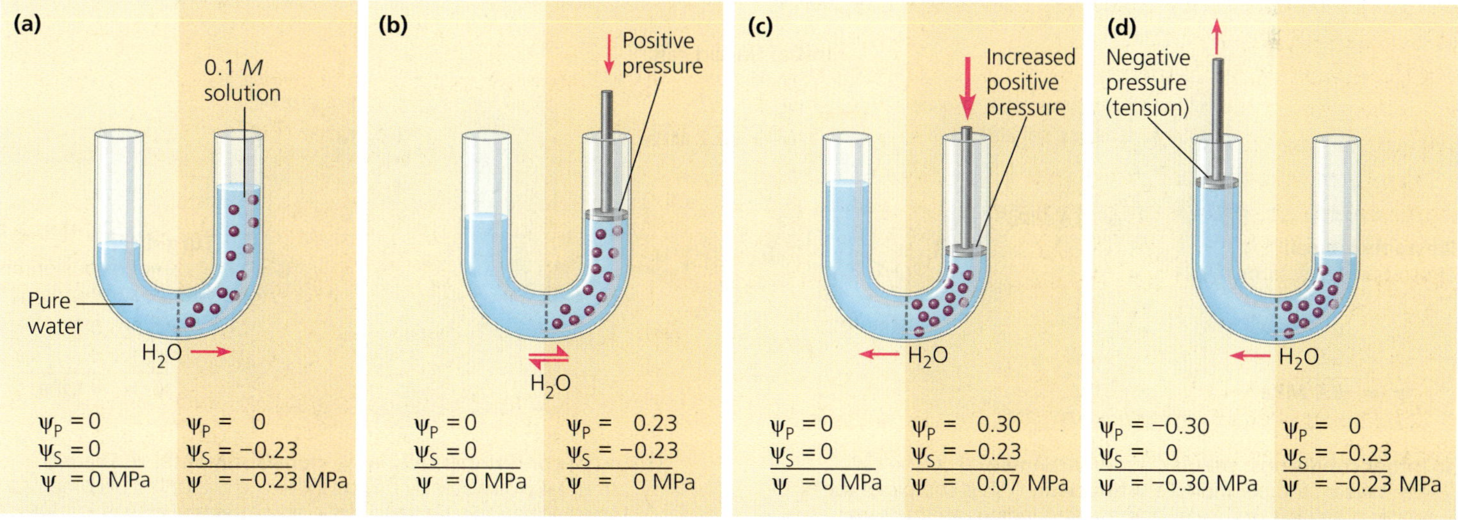

▲ **Figure 36.8 Water potential and water movement: an artificial model.** In this U-shaped apparatus, a membrane separates pure water (left arm) from a 0.1 *M* solution (right arm) containing a solute that cannot pass freely across the membrane. The values for ψ, ψ_S, and ψ_P in the left and right arms of the U-tube are given for *initial* conditions, *before* any net movement of water. **(a)** If no pressure is applied, ψ_S determines net movement of water. **(b)** Positive pressure (increased ψ_P) on the right raises ψ on the right, here making ψ the same in both arms, so eventually there is no net water movement. **(c)** Further increasing positive pressure on the right causes net water movement to the left. **(d)** Negative pressure reduces ψ_P. In this case, negative pressure on the left decreases ψ on the left, causing net water movement to the left.

the right arm, as shown in Figure 36.8a. But applying a positive physical pressure of +0.23 MPa to the solution in the right arm raises its water potential from a negative value to 0 MPa ($\psi = -0.23 + 0.23$). As shown in Figure 36.8b, there is now no net flow of water between this pressurized solution and the compartment of pure water. If we increase ψ_P to +0.30 MPa in the right arm, as in Figure 36.8c, then the solution has a water potential of +0.07 MPa ($\psi = -0.23 + 0.30$), and this solution will actually *lose* water to a compartment containing pure water. Whereas applying positive pressure increases ψ, applying negative pressure (tension) reduces ψ, as shown in Figure 36.8d. In this case, a negative pressure potential of −0.30 MPa reduces the ψ of the water compartment enough so that water is drawn from the solution on the right side.

Now let's consider how water potential affects absorption and loss of water by a living plant cell. First, imagine a cell that is **flaccid** (limp) as a result of losing water. The cell has a ψ_P of 0 MPa. Suppose this flaccid cell is bathed in a solution of higher solute concentration (more negative solute potential) than the cell itself **(Figure 36.9a)**. Since the external solution has the lower (more negative) water potential, water diffuses out of the cell. The cell's protoplast undergoes **plasmolysis**—that is, it shrinks and pulls away from the cell wall. If we place the same flaccid cell in pure water ($\psi = 0$ MPa) **(Figure 36.9b)**, the cell, because it contains solutes, has a lower water potential than the water, and water enters the cell by osmosis. The contents of the cell begin to swell and press the plasma membrane against the cell wall. The partially elastic wall, exerting turgor pressure, pushes back against the pressurized protoplast. When this pressure is enough to offset the tendency for water to enter because of the solutes in the cell, then ψ_P and ψ_S are equal, and $\psi = 0$. This matches the water potential of the extracellular environment: in this example, 0 MPa. A dynamic equilibrium has been reached, and there is no further net movement of water.

In contrast to a flaccid cell, a walled cell with a greater solute concentration than its surroundings is **turgid**, or very firm. When turgid cells in a nonwoody tissue push against each other, the tissue is stiffened. The effects of turgor loss are seen during **wilting**, when leaves and stems droop as a result of cells losing water **(Figure 36.10)**.

▲ **Figure 36.10 A wilted *Impatiens* plant regains its turgor when watered.**

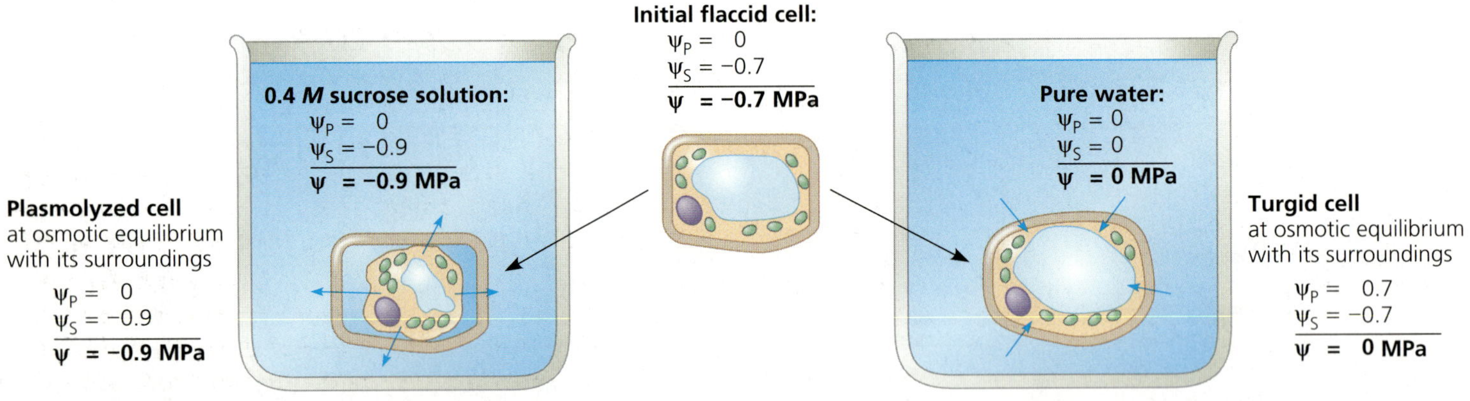

(a) Initial conditions: cellular ψ > environmental ψ. The cell loses water and plasmolyzes. After plasmolysis is complete, the water potentials of the cell and its surroundings are the same.

(b) Initial conditions: cellular ψ < environmental ψ. There is a net uptake of water by osmosis, causing the cell to become turgid. When this tendency for water to enter is offset by the back pressure of the elastic wall, water potentials are equal for the cell and its surroundings. (The volume change of the cell is exaggerated in this diagram.)

▲ **Figure 36.9 Water relations in plant cells.** In these experiments, identical cells, initially flaccid, are placed in two environments. (Protoplasts of flaccid cells are in contact with their walls but lack turgor pressure.) Blue arrows indicate initial net water movement.

Aquaporins: Facilitating Diffusion of Water

A difference in water potential determines the *direction* of water movement across membranes, but how do water molecules actually cross the membranes? Water molecules are small enough to diffuse across the phospholipid bilayer, even though the middle zone is hydrophobic (see Figure 7.2), but their movement is too rapid to be explained by unaided diffusion. Indeed, transport proteins called **aquaporins** facilitate the diffusion (see Chapter 7). These selective channels, which have been found most commonly in plants, affect the *rate* at which water diffuses down its water potential gradient. Evidence is accumulating that the rate of water movement through these proteins is regulated by phosphorylation of the aquaporin proteins, which can be induced by increases in cytoplasmic calcium ions or decreases in cytoplasmic pH. Recent evidence suggests that aquaporins may also facilitate absorption of CO_2 by plant cells.

Three Major Pathways of Transport

Transport within plants is also regulated by the compartmental structure of plant cells **(Figure 36.11a)**. Outside the protoplast is a cell wall (see Figures 6.9 and 6.28), consisting of a mesh of polysaccharides through which mineral ions diffuse readily. Because every plant cell is separated from its neighboring cells by cell walls, ions can diffuse across a tissue (or be carried passively by water flow) entirely through the **apoplast (Figure 36.11b)**, the continuum formed by cell walls, extracellular spaces, and the dead interiors of tracheids and vessels. However, it is the plasma membrane that directly controls the traffic of molecules into and out of the protoplast. Just as the cell walls form a continuum, so does the cytosol of cells, collectively referred to as the **symplast** (see Figure 36.11b). The cytoplasmic channels called **plasmodesmata** connect the cytoplasm of neighboring cells.

The compartmental structure of plant cells provides three routes for short-distance transport within a plant tissue or organ: the apoplastic, symplastic, and transmembrane routes (see Figure 36.11b). In the apoplastic route, water and solutes move along the continuum of cell walls and extracellular spaces. In the symplastic route, water and solutes move along the continuum of cytosol within a plant tissue. This route requires only one crossing of a plasma membrane. After entering one cell, substances can move from cell to cell via plasmodesmata. In the transmembrane route, water and solutes move out of one cell, across the cell wall, and into the neighboring cell, which may pass them to the next cell in the same way. The transmembrane route requires repeated crossings of plasma membranes as water and solutes exit one cell and enter the next. Substances may use more than one route. Scientists are debating which route, if any, is responsible for the most transport.

Bulk Flow in Long-Distance Transport

Diffusion and active transport are fairly efficient for short-distance transport within a cell and between cells. However, these processes are much too slow to function in long-distance transport within a plant. Although diffusion from one end of a cell to the other takes just seconds, diffusion from the roots to the top of a giant redwood would take decades or longer. Instead, long-distance transport occurs through **bulk flow**, the movement of a fluid driven by pressure.

Within tracheids and vessel elements of the xylem and within the sieve-tube elements (also called sieve-tube members) of the phloem, water and dissolved solutes move together in the same direction by bulk flow. The structures of these conducting cells of the xylem and phloem help to make bulk flow possible. If you have ever dealt with a partially clogged drain, you know that the volume of flow depends on the pipe's diameter. Clogs reduce the effective diameter of the drainpipe. Such experiences help us

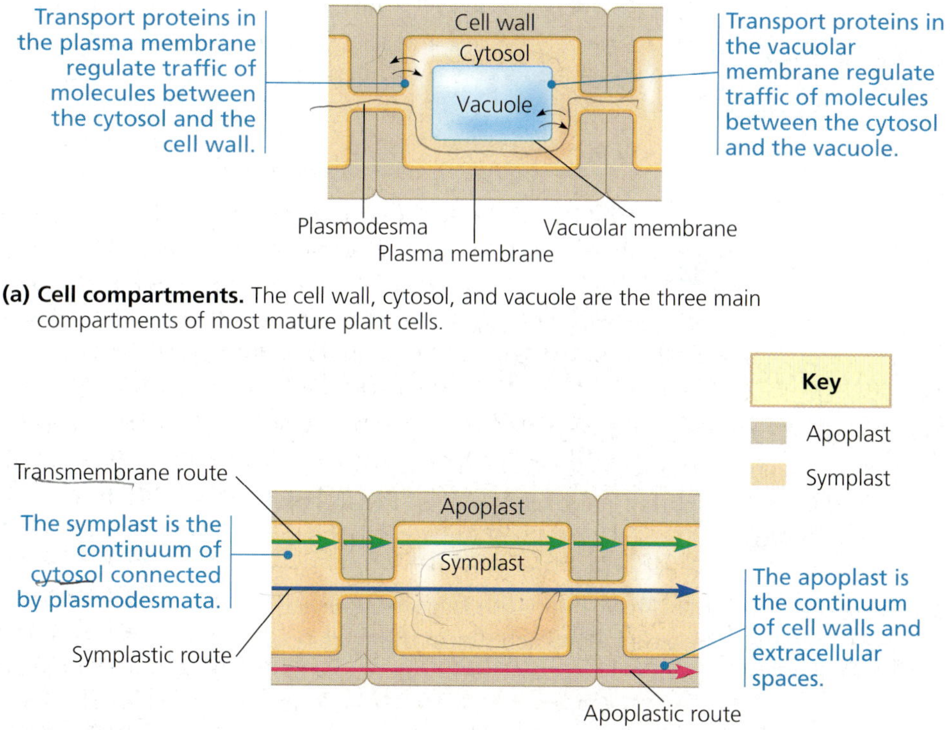

(a) Cell compartments. The cell wall, cytosol, and vacuole are the three main compartments of most mature plant cells.

(b) Transport routes between cells. At the tissue level, there are three pathways: the transmembrane, symplastic, and apoplastic routes. Substances can transfer from one pathway to another.

▲ **Figure 36.11 Cell compartments and routes for short-distance transport.**

understand how the structures of plant cells specialized for bulk flow fit their function. As you learned in Chapter 35, mature tracheids and vessel elements are dead cells and therefore have no cytoplasm, and the cytoplasm of sieve-tube elements is almost devoid of internal organelles (see Figure 35.10). Like unplugging a kitchen drain, loss of cytoplasm in a plant's "plumbing" allows for efficient bulk flow through the xylem and phloem. Bulk flow is also enhanced by the perforation plates at the ends of vessel elements and the porous sieve plates connecting sieve-tube elements.

Diffusion, active transport, and bulk flow act in concert to transport resources throughout the whole plant. For example, bulk flow due to a pressure difference is the mechanism of long-distance transport of sugars in the phloem, but active transport of sugar at the cellular level maintains this pressure difference. In the next three sections, we'll examine in more detail the transport of water and minerals from roots to shoots, the control of evaporation, and the transport of sugars.

CONCEPT CHECK 36.2

1. If a plant cell immersed in distilled water has a ψ_S of -0.7 MPa and a ψ of 0 MPa, what is the cell's ψ_P? If you put it in an open beaker of solution that has a ψ of -0.4 MPa, what would be its ψ_P at equilibrium?
2. How would an aquaporin deficiency affect a plant cell's ability to adjust to new osmotic conditions?
3. How would the long-distance transport of water be affected if vessel elements and tracheids were alive at maturity? Explain.
4. **WHAT IF?** What would happen if you put plant protoplasts in pure water? Explain.

For suggested answers, see Appendix A.

CONCEPT **36.3**

Water and minerals are transported from roots to shoots

Picture yourself struggling to carry a very large container of water up several flights of stairs. Then consider the fact that water within a plant is transported effortlessly against the force of gravity. Up to 800 L (800 kg or 1,760 lb) of water reach the top of an average-sized tree every day. But trees and other plants have no pumping mechanism. So how is this feat accomplished? To answer this question, we'll follow each step in the journey of water and minerals from the tips of roots to the tips of shoots.

Absorption of Water and Minerals by Root Cells

Although all living plant cells absorb nutrients across their plasma membranes, the cells near the tips of roots are particularly important because most of the water and mineral absorption occurs there. In this region, the epidermal cells are permeable to water, and many are differentiated into root hairs, modified cells that account for much of the absorption of water by roots (see Figure 35.3). The root hairs absorb the soil solution, which consists of water molecules and dissolved mineral ions that are not bound tightly to soil particles. The soil solution flows into the hydrophilic walls of epidermal cells and passes freely along the cell walls and the extracellular spaces into the root cortex. This flow enhances the exposure of the cells of the cortex to the soil solution, providing a much greater membrane surface area for absorption than the surface area of the epidermis alone. Although the soil solution usually has a low mineral concentration, active transport enables roots to accumulate essential minerals, such as K^+, to concentrations hundreds of times higher than in the soil.

Transport of Water and Minerals into the Xylem

Water and minerals that pass from the soil into the root cortex cannot be transported to the rest of the plant until they enter the xylem of the stele, or vascular cylinder. The **endodermis**, the innermost layer of cells in the root cortex, surrounds the stele and functions as a last checkpoint for the selective passage of minerals from the cortex into the vascular tissue **(Figure 36.12)**. Minerals already in the symplast when they reach the endodermis continue through the plasmodesmata of endodermal cells and pass into the stele. These minerals were already screened by the plasma membrane they had to cross to enter the symplast in the epidermis or cortex. Those minerals that reach the endodermis via the apoplast encounter a dead end that blocks their passage into the stele. This barrier, located in the transverse and radial walls of each endodermal cell, is the **Casparian strip**, a belt made of suberin, a waxy material impervious to water and dissolved minerals (see Figure 36.12). Thus, water and minerals cannot cross the endodermis and enter the vascular tissue via the apoplast. The Casparian strip forces water and minerals that are passively moving through the apoplast to cross the plasma membrane of an endodermal cell and enter the stele via the symplast.

The endodermis, with its Casparian strip, ensures that no minerals can reach the vascular tissue of the root without crossing a selectively permeable plasma membrane. The endodermis also prevents solutes that have accumulated in the xylem from leaking back into the soil solution. The structure of the endodermis and its strategic location fit its function as an apoplastic barrier between the cortex and the stele. The endodermis helps roots to transport certain minerals preferentially from the soil into the xylem.

The last segment in the soil-to-xylem pathway is the passage of water and minerals into the tracheids and vessel elements of the xylem. These water-conducting cells lack protoplasts when mature and therefore are part of the apoplast. Endodermal cells, as well as living cells within the stele, discharge minerals

▼ Figure 36.12 Transport of water and minerals from root hairs to the xylem.

? *How does the Casparian strip force water and minerals to pass through the plasma membranes of endodermal cells?*

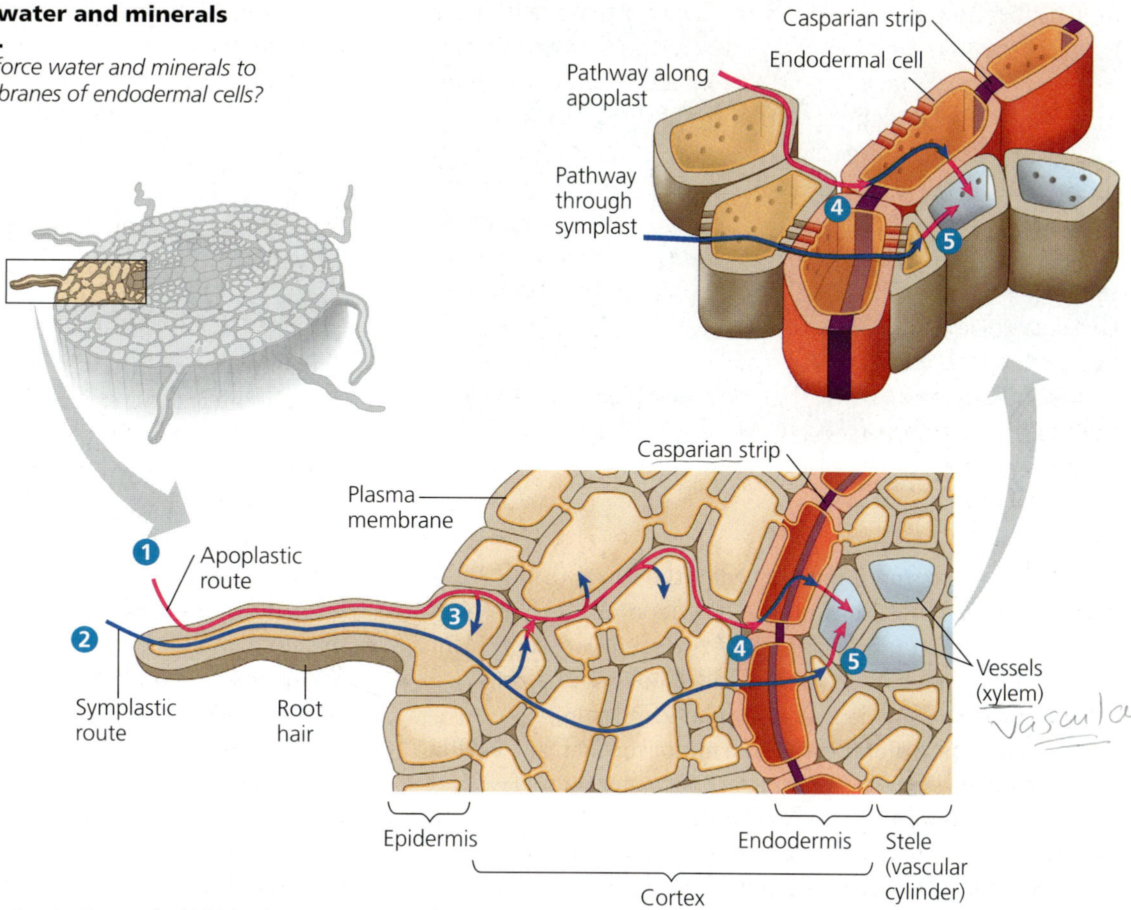

1 Apoplastic route. Uptake of soil solution by the hydrophilic walls of root hairs provides access to the apoplast. Water and minerals can then diffuse into the cortex along this matrix of walls.

2 Symplastic route. Minerals and water that cross the plasma membranes of root hairs can enter the symplast.

3 Transmembrane route. As soil solution moves along the apoplast, some water and minerals are transported into the protoplasts of cells of the epidermis and cortex and then move inward via the symplast.

4 The endodermis: controlled entry to the stele. Within the transverse and radial walls of each endodermal cell is the Casparian strip, a belt of waxy material (purple band) that blocks the passage of water and dissolved minerals. Only minerals already in the symplast or entering that pathway by crossing the plasma membrane of an endodermal cell can detour around the Casparian strip and pass into the stele, the vascular cylinder.

5 Transport in the xylem. Endodermal cells and also living cells within the stele discharge water and minerals into their walls (apoplast). The xylem vessels then transport the water and minerals upward into the shoot system.

from their protoplasts into their own cell walls. Both diffusion and active transport are involved in this transfer of solutes from symplast to apoplast, and the water and minerals are now free to enter the tracheids and vessels, where they are transported to the shoot system by bulk flow.

Bulk Flow Driven by Negative Pressure in the Xylem

Water and minerals from the soil enter the plant through the epidermis of roots, cross the root cortex, and pass into the stele. From there the **xylem sap**, the water and dissolved minerals in the xylem, gets transported long distances by bulk flow to the veins that branch throughout each leaf.

As noted earlier, bulk flow is much faster than diffusion or active transport. Peak velocities in the transport of xylem sap can range from 15 to 45 m/hr for trees with wide vessels. Leaves depend on this efficient delivery system for their supply of water. Plants lose an astonishing amount of water by **transpiration**, the loss of water vapor from leaves and other aerial parts of the plant. Consider the example of maize (commonly called corn in the United States). A single plant transpires 60 L (60 kg) of water during a growing season. A maize crop growing at a typical density of 60,000 plants per hectare transpires almost 4 million L of water per hectare every growing season (about 400,000 gallons of water per acre per growing season). Unless the transpired water is replaced by water transported up from the roots, the leaves will wilt, and the plants will eventually die. The flow of xylem sap also brings mineral nutrients to the shoot system.

Xylem sap rises to heights of more than 100 m in the tallest trees. Is the sap mainly *pushed* upward from the roots, or is it mainly *pulled* upward by the leaves? Let's evaluate the relative contributions of these two mechanisms.

Pushing Xylem Sap: Root Pressure

At night, when there is almost no transpiration, root cells continue pumping mineral ions into the xylem of the stele. Meanwhile, the endodermis helps prevent the ions from leaking out. The resulting accumulation of minerals lowers the water potential within the stele. Water flows in from the root cortex, generating **root pressure**, a push of xylem sap. The root pressure

▲ **Figure 36.13 Guttation.** Root pressure is forcing excess water from this strawberry leaf.

sometimes causes more water to enter the leaves than is transpired, resulting in **guttation**, the exudation of water droplets that can be seen in the morning on the tips or edges of some plant leaves **(Figure 36.13)**. Guttation fluid should not be confused with dew, which is condensed atmospheric moisture.

In most plants, root pressure is a minor mechanism driving the ascent of xylem sap, at most pushing water only a few meters. The positive pressures produced are simply too weak to overcome the gravitational force of the water column in the xylem, particularly in tall plants. Many plants do not generate any root pressure. Even in plants that display guttation, root pressure cannot keep pace with transpiration after sunrise. For the most part, xylem sap is not pushed from below by root pressure but pulled by the leaves themselves.

Pulling Xylem Sap: The Transpiration-Cohesion-Tension Mechanism

Material can be moved upward by positive pressure from below or negative pressure from above. Here we'll focus on how water is pulled by negative pressure potential in the xylem. As we investigate this mechanism of transport, we'll see that transpiration provides the pull and that the cohesion of water due to hydrogen bonding transmits the pull along the entire length of the xylem to the roots.

Transpirational Pull Stomata on a leaf's surface lead to a maze of internal air spaces that expose the mesophyll cells to the CO_2 they need for photosynthesis. The air in these spaces is saturated with water vapor because it is in contact with the moist walls of the cells. On most days, the air outside the leaf is drier; that is, it has a lower water potential than the air inside the leaf. Therefore, water vapor in the air spaces of a leaf diffuses down its water potential gradient and exits the leaf via the stomata. It is this loss of water vapor from the leaf by diffusion and evaporation that we call transpiration.

But how does loss of water vapor from the leaf translate into a pulling force for upward movement of water through a plant? The negative pressure potential that causes water to move up through the xylem develops at the surface of mesophyll cell walls in the leaf **(Figure 36.14)**. The cell wall acts like a very fine capillary network. Water adheres to the cellulose microfibrils and other hydrophilic components of the cell wall. As water evaporates from the water film that covers the cell walls of mesophyll cells, the air-water interface retreats farther into the cell wall. Because of the high surface tension of water, the curvature of the

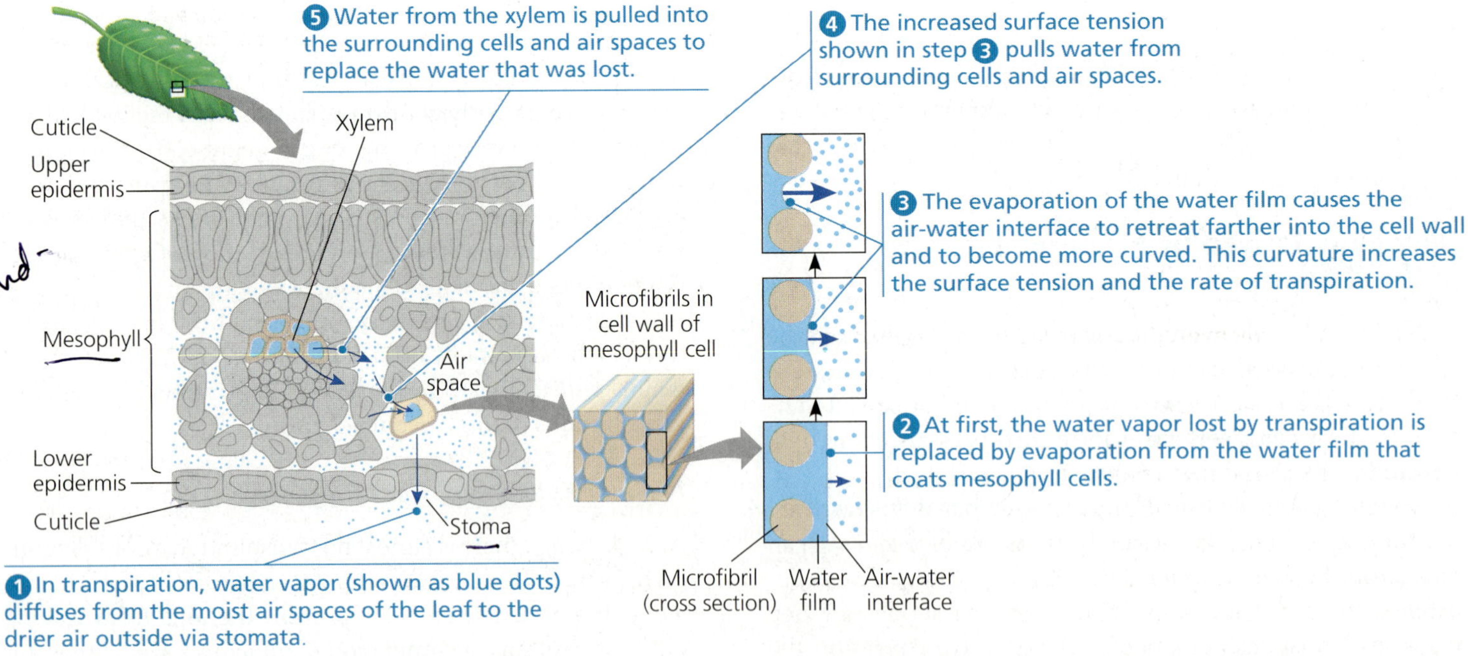

▲ **Figure 36.14 Generation of transpirational pull.** Negative pressure (tension) at the air-water interface in the leaf is the basis of transpirational pull, which draws water out of the xylem.

interface induces a tension, or negative pressure potential, in the water. As more water evaporates from the cell wall, the curvature of the air-water interface increases and the pressure of the water becomes more negative. Water molecules from the more hydrated parts of the leaf are then pulled toward this area to reduce the tension. These pulling forces are transferred to the xylem because each water molecule is cohesively bound to the next by hydrogen bonds. Thus, transpirational pull depends on several of the properties of water discussed in Chapter 3: adhesion, cohesion, and surface tension.

The role of negative pressure potential in transpiration is consistent with the water potential equation because negative pressure potential (tension) *lowers* water potential (see Figure 36.8d). Because water moves from areas of higher water potential to areas of lower water potential, the more negative pressure potential at the air-water interface causes water in xylem cells to be "pulled" into mesophyll cells, which lose water to the air spaces, where it diffuses out through stomata. In this way, the negative water potential of leaves provides the "pull" in transpirational pull.

Cohesion and Adhesion in the Ascent of Xylem Sap The transpirational pull on xylem sap is transmitted all the way from the leaves to the root tips and even into the soil solution **(Figure 36.15)**. Cohesion and adhesion facilitate this long-distance transport by bulk flow. The cohesion of water due to hydrogen bonding makes it possible to pull a column of xylem sap from above without the water molecules separating. Water molecules exiting the xylem in the leaf tug on adjacent water molecules, and this pull is relayed, molecule by molecule, down the entire column of water in the xylem. Meanwhile, the strong adhesion of water molecules (again by hydrogen bonds) to the hydrophilic walls of xylem cells helps offset the downward force of gravity.

The upward pull on the sap creates tension within the xylem vessels and tracheids, which are like elastic pipes. Positive pressure causes an elastic pipe to swell, whereas tension pulls the walls of the pipe inward. On a warm day, a decrease in the diameter of a tree trunk can even be measured. As transpirational pull puts the vessels and tracheids under tension, their thick secondary walls prevent them from collapsing, much as wire rings maintain the shape of a vacuum-cleaner hose. The tension produced by transpirational pull lowers water potential in the root xylem to such an extent that water flows passively from the soil, across the root cortex, and into the stele.

Transpirational pull can extend down to the roots only through an unbroken chain of water molecules. Cavitation, the formation of a water vapor pocket, breaks the chain. It is more common in wide vessels than in tracheids and can occur during drought stress or when xylem sap freezes in winter. The air bubbles resulting from cavitation expand and block water channels of the xylem. The rapid expansion of air bubbles produces

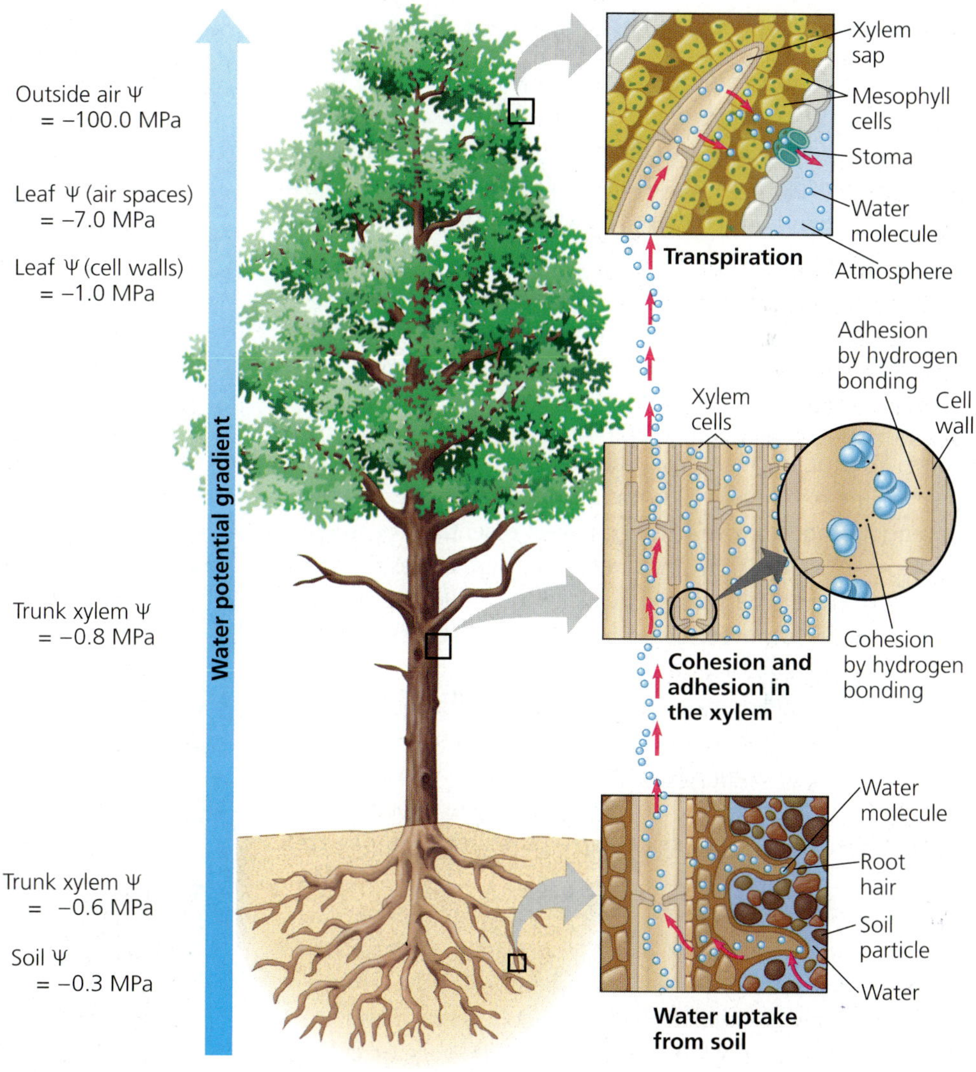

▲ **Figure 36.15 Ascent of xylem sap.** Hydrogen bonding forms an unbroken chain of water molecules extending from leaves to the soil. The force driving the ascent of xylem sap is a gradient of water potential (ψ). For bulk flow over long distance, the ψ gradient is due mainly to a gradient of the pressure potential (ψ_P). Transpiration results in the ψ_P at the leaf end of the xylem being lower than the ψ_P at the root end. The ψ values shown at the left are a "snapshot." During daylight, they may vary, but the direction of the ψ gradient remains the same.

BioFlix Visit the Study Area at **www.masteringbio.com** for the BioFlix 3-D Animation on Water Transport in Plants.

clicking noises that can be heard by placing sensitive microphones at the surface of the stem.

Root pressure enables small plants to refill blocked vessels in spring. In trees, though, root pressure is insufficient to push water to the top, so a vessel with a water vapor pocket usually cannot function in xylem sap transport. However, the chain of molecules can detour around the pocket through pits between adjacent tracheids or vessels. In addition, secondary growth adds a layer of new xylem each year. Only the youngest, outermost secondary xylem transports water. Although the older secondary xylem no longer transports water, it does provide support for the tree (see Figure 35.22).

Xylem Sap Ascent by Bulk Flow: *A Review*

The transpiration-cohesion-tension mechanism that transports xylem sap against gravity is an excellent example of how physical principles apply to biological processes. In the long-distance transport of water from roots to leaves by bulk flow, the movement of fluid is driven by a water potential difference at opposite ends of xylem tissue. The water potential difference is created at the leaf end of the xylem by the evaporation of water from leaf cells. Evaporation lowers the water potential at the air-water interface, thereby generating the negative pressure (tension) that pulls water through the xylem.

Bulk flow in the xylem differs from diffusion in some key ways. First, it is driven by differences in pressure potential (ψ_P); solute potential (ψ_S) is not a factor. Therefore, the water potential gradient within the xylem is essentially a pressure gradient. Also, the flow does not occur across plasma membranes of living cells, but instead within hollow, dead cells. Furthermore, it moves the entire solution together—not just water or solutes—and at much greater speed than diffusion.

The plant expends no energy to lift xylem sap by bulk flow. Instead, the absorption of sunlight drives most of transpiration by causing water to evaporate from the moist walls of mesophyll cells and by lowering the water potential in the air spaces within a leaf. Thus, the ascent of xylem sap is ultimately solar powered.

CONCEPT CHECK 36.3

1. How do xylem cells facilitate long-distance transport?
2. A horticulturalist notices that when *Zinnia* flowers are cut at dawn, a small drop of water collects at the surface of the stump. However, when the flowers are cut at noon, no drop is observed. Suggest an explanation.
3. A scientist adds a water-soluble inhibitor of photosynthesis to a plant's roots, but photosynthesis is not reduced. Why?
4. **WHAT IF?** Suppose an *Arabidopsis* mutant lacking functional aquaporins has a root mass three times greater than that of wild-type plants. Suggest an explanation.

For suggested answers, see Appendix A.

CONCEPT **36.4**

Stomata help regulate the rate of transpiration

Leaves generally have large surface areas and high surface-to-volume ratios. The large surface area enhances light absorption for photosynthesis. The high surface-to-volume ratio aids in CO_2 absorption during photosynthesis as well as in the release of O_2 as a by-product of photosynthesis. Upon diffusing through the stomata, CO_2 enters a honeycomb of air spaces formed by the spongy mesophyll cells (see Figure 35.18). Because of the irregular shapes of these cells, the leaf's internal surface area may be 10 to 30 times greater than the external surface area.

Although large surface areas and high surface-to-volume ratios increase the rate of photosynthesis, they also increase water loss by way of the stomata. Thus, a plant's tremendous requirement for water is largely a negative consequence of the shoot system's need for ample gas exchange for photosynthesis. By opening and closing the stomata, guard cells help balance the plant's requirement to conserve water with its requirement for photosynthesis **(Figure 36.16)**.

Stomata: Major Pathways for Water Loss

About 95% of the water a plant loses escapes through stomata, although these pores account for only 1–2% of the external leaf surface. The waxy cuticle limits water loss through the remaining surface of the leaf. Each stoma is flanked by a pair of guard cells. Guard cells control the diameter of the stoma by changing shape, thereby widening or narrowing the gap between the guard cell pair. Under the same environmental conditions, the amount of water lost by a leaf depends largely on the number of stomata and the average size of their pores.

The stomatal density of a leaf, which may be as high as 20,000 per square centimeter, is under both genetic and environmental control. For example, as a result of evolution by

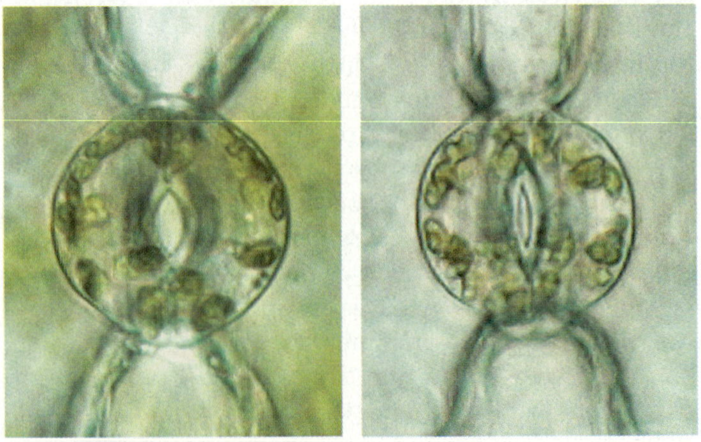

▲ **Figure 36.16 An open stoma (left) and closed stoma (LMs).**

natural selection, desert plants have lower stomatal densities than do marsh plants. Stomatal density, however, is a developmentally plastic feature of many plants. High light exposures and low CO_2 levels during leaf development lead to increased density in many species. By measuring stomatal density of leaf fossils, scientists have gained insight into the levels of atmospheric CO_2 in past climates. A recent British survey found that stomatal density of many woodland species has decreased since 1927, when a similar survey was made. This survey is consistent with other findings that atmospheric CO_2 levels increased dramatically during the 1900s.

Mechanisms of Stomatal Opening and Closing

When guard cells take in water from neighboring cells by osmosis, they become more turgid. In most angiosperm species, the cell walls of guard cells are uneven in thickness, and the cellulose microfibrils are oriented in a direction that causes the guard cells to bow outward when turgid **(Figure 36.17a)**. This bowing outward increases the size of the pore between the guard cells. When the cells lose water and become flaccid, they become less bowed, and the pore closes.

The changes in turgor pressure in guard cells result primarily from the reversible absorption and loss of K^+. Stomata open when guard cells actively accumulate K^+ from neighboring epidermal cells **(Figure 36.17b)**. The flow of K^+ across the plasma membrane of the guard cell is coupled to the generation of a membrane potential by proton pumps. Stomatal opening correlates with active transport of H^+ out of the guard cell. The resulting voltage (membrane potential) drives K^+ into the cell through specific membrane channels (see Figure 36.7a). The absorption of K^+ causes the water potential to become more negative within the guard cells, and the cells become more turgid as water enters by osmosis. Because most of the K^+ and water are stored in the vacuole, the vacuolar membrane also plays a role in regulating guard cell dynamics. Stomatal closing results from a loss of K^+ from guard cells to neighboring cells, which leads to an osmotic loss of water. Aquaporins also help regulate the osmotic swelling and shrinking of guard cells.

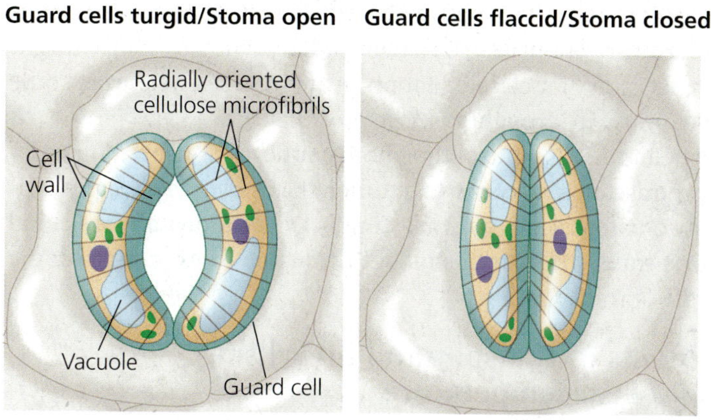

(a) Changes in guard cell shape and stomatal opening and closing (surface view). Guard cells of a typical angiosperm are illustrated in their turgid (stoma open) and flaccid (stoma closed) states. The radial orientation of cellulose microfibrils in the cell walls causes the guard cells to increase more in length than width when turgor increases. Since the two guard cells are tightly joined at their tips, they bow outward when turgid, causing the stomatal pore to open.

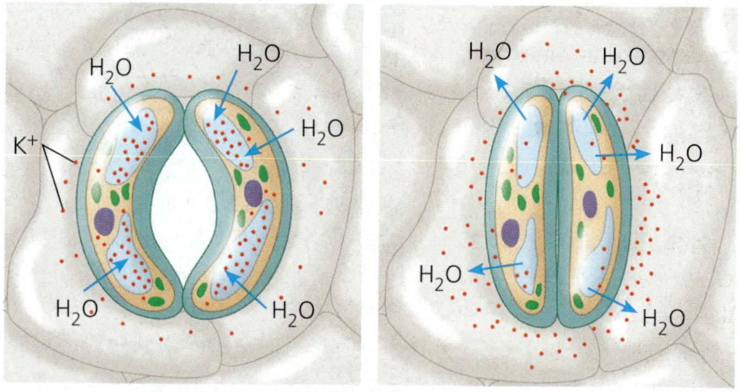

(b) Role of potassium in stomatal opening and closing. The transport of K^+ (potassium ions, symbolized here as red dots) across the plasma membrane and vacuolar membrane causes the turgor changes of guard cells. The uptake of anions, such as malate and chloride ions (not shown), also contributes to guard cell swelling.

▲ **Figure 36.17 Mechanisms of stomatal opening and closing.**

Stimuli for Stomatal Opening and Closing

In general, stomata are open during the day and closed at night, preventing the plant from losing water under conditions when photosynthesis cannot occur. At least three cues contribute to stomatal opening at dawn: light, CO_2 depletion, and an internal "clock" in guard cells.

The light stimulates guard cells to accumulate K^+ and become turgid. This response is triggered by illumination of blue-light receptors in the plasma membrane of guard cells. Activation of these receptors stimulates the activity of proton pumps in the plasma membrane of the guard cells, in turn promoting absorption of K^+.

The stomata also open in response to depletion of CO_2 within the leaf's air spaces as a result of photosynthesis. As CO_2 concentrations decrease during the day, the stomata progressively open if sufficient water is supplied to the leaf.

A third cue, the internal "clock" in the guard cells, ensures that stomata continue their daily rhythm of opening and closing. This rhythm occurs even if a plant is kept in a dark location. All eukaryotic organisms have internal clocks that regulate cyclic processes. Cycles with intervals of approximately 24 hours are called **circadian rhythms**, which you'll learn more about in Chapter 39.

Environmental stresses, such as droughts, can cause stomata to close during the daytime. When the plant has a water deficiency, guard cells may lose turgor and close stomata. In addition, a hormone called abscisic acid, produced in roots and leaves in response to water deficiency, signals guard cells to close stomata. This response reduces wilting but also restricts CO_2 absorption, thereby slowing photosynthesis. Since turgor is necessary for cell elongation, growth ceases. These are some reasons why droughts reduce crop yields.

Guard cells control the photosynthesis-transpiration compromise on a moment-to-moment basis by integrating a variety of internal and external stimuli. Even the passage of a cloud or a transient shaft of sunlight through a forest can affect the rate of transpiration.

Effects of Transpiration on Wilting and Leaf Temperature

As long as most stomata remain open, transpiration is greatest on a day that is sunny, warm, dry, and windy because these environmental factors increase evaporation. If transpiration cannot pull sufficient water to the leaves, the shoot becomes slightly wilted as cells lose turgor pressure (see Figure 36.10). Although plants respond to such mild drought stress by rapidly closing stomata, some evaporative water loss still occurs through the cuticle. Under prolonged drought conditions, leaves can become severely wilted and irreversibly injured.

Transpiration also results in evaporative cooling, which can lower a leaf's temperature by as much as 10°C compared with the surrounding air. This cooling prevents the leaf from reaching temperatures that could denature enzymes involved in photosynthesis and other metabolic processes.

Adaptations That Reduce Evaporative Water Loss

Plants that are adapted to deserts and other regions with little moisture are called **xerophytes** (from the Greek *xero*, dry). The stone plants in Figure 36.1 are an example. **Figure 36.18**

▼ **Figure 36.18 Some xerophytic adaptations.**

► Ocotillo (*Fouquieria splendens*) is common in the southwestern region of the United States and northern Mexico. It is leafless during most of the year, thereby avoiding excessive water loss (right). Immediately after a heavy rainfall, it produces small leaves (below and inset). As the soil dries, the leaves quickly shrivel and die.

▼ Oleander (*Nerium oleander*), shown in the inset, is commonly found in arid climates. Its leaves have a thick cuticle and multiple-layered epidermal tissue that reduce water loss. Stomata are recessed in cavities called "crypts," an adaptation that reduces the rate of transpiration by protecting the stomata from hot, dry wind. Trichomes help minimize transpiration by breaking up the flow of air, allowing the chamber of the crypt to have a higher humidity than the surrounding atmosphere (LM).

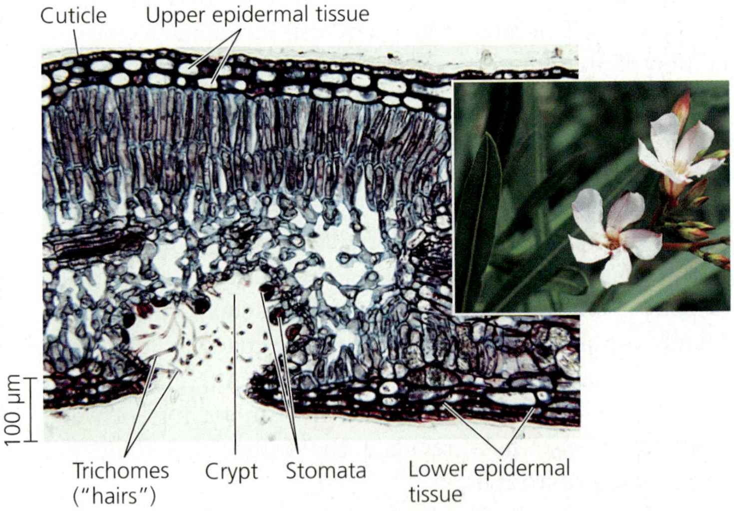

► This is a close-up view of stems of old man cactus (*Cephalocereus senilis*), a Mexican desert plant. The long, white, hairlike bristles help reflect the sun.

shows others. Rain comes infrequently in deserts, but when it arrives the vegetation is transformed. Many species of desert plants avoid drying out by completing their short life cycles during the brief rainy seasons. Longer-lived species have unusual physiological or morphological adaptations that enable them to withstand the harsh desert conditions. Xerophytes are also found in other environments where access to liquid fresh water is problematic, such as frozen regions and seashores. Many xerophytes, such as cacti, have highly reduced leaves that resist excessive water loss; they carry out photosynthesis mainly in their stems. The stems of many xerophytes are fleshy because they store water for use during prolonged dry periods. Another adaptation to arid habitats is crassulacean acid metabolism (CAM), a specialized form of photosynthesis found in succulents of the family Crassulaceae and several other families (see Figure 10.20). Because the leaves of CAM plants take in CO_2 at night, the stomata can remain closed during the day, when evaporative stresses are greater.

As we have seen, plants face a dilemma: how to acquire as much CO_2 from the air as they can and at the same time retain as much water as possible. Stomata are the most important mediators of the conflicting demands of CO_2 acquisition and water retention.

CONCEPT CHECK 36.4

1. What are the stimuli that control the opening and closing of stomata?
2. The pathogenic fungus *Fusicoccum amygdali* secretes a toxin called fusicoccin that activates the plasma membrane proton pumps of plant cells and leads to uncontrolled water loss. Suggest a mechanism by which the activation of proton pumps could lead to severe wilting.
3. **WHAT IF?** If you buy cut flowers, why might the florist recommend cutting the stems underwater and then transferring the flowers to a vase while the cut ends are still wet?

For suggested answers, see Appendix A.

CONCEPT **36.5**

Sugars are transported from leaves and other sources to sites of use or storage

You have read how water and minerals are absorbed by root cells, transported through the endodermis, released into the vessels and tracheids of the xylem, and carried to the tops of plants by the bulk flow driven by transpiration. However, transpiration cannot meet all the long-distance transport needs of the plant. The flow of water and minerals from soil to roots to leaves is largely in a direction opposite to the direction necessary for transporting sugars from mature leaves to lower parts of the plants, such as root tips that require large amounts of sugars for energy and growth. It is another tissue—the phloem—that transports the products of photosynthesis, a process called **translocation**.

Movement from Sugar Sources to Sugar Sinks

In angiosperms, the specialized cells that are conduits for translocation are the sieve-tube elements. Arranged end to end, they form long sieve tubes (see Figure 35.10). Between these cells are sieve plates, structures that allow the flow of sap along the sieve tube.

Phloem sap, the aqueous solution that flows through sieve tubes, differs markedly from xylem sap. By far the most prevalent solute in phloem sap is sugar, typically sucrose in most species. The sucrose concentration may be as high as 30% by weight, giving the sap a syrupy thickness. Phloem sap may also contain amino acids, hormones, and minerals.

In contrast to the unidirectional transport of xylem sap from roots to leaves, phloem sap moves from sites of sugar production to sites of sugar use or storage (see Figure 36.2). A **sugar source** is a plant organ that is a net producer of sugar, by photosynthesis or by breakdown of starch. A **sugar sink** is an organ that is a net consumer or depository of sugar. Growing roots, buds, stems, and fruits are sugar sinks. Although expanding leaves are sugar sinks, fully grown leaves, if well illuminated, are sugar sources. A storage organ, such as a tuber or a bulb, may be a source or a sink, depending on the season. When stockpiling carbohydrates in the summer, it is a sugar sink. After breaking dormancy in the spring, it is a sugar source because its starch is broken down to sugar, which is carried to the growing shoot tips.

Sinks usually receive sugar from the nearest sugar sources. The upper leaves on a branch, for example, may export sugar to the growing shoot tip, whereas the lower leaves may export sugar to the roots. A growing fruit may monopolize the sugar sources that surround it. For each sieve tube, the direction of transport depends on the locations of the sugar source and sugar sink that are connected by that tube. Therefore, neighboring sieve tubes may carry sap in opposite directions if they originate and end in different locations.

Sugar must be transported, or loaded, into sieve-tube elements before being exported to sugar sinks. In some species, it moves from mesophyll cells to sieve-tube elements via the symplast, passing through plasmodesmata. In other species, it moves by symplastic and apoplastic pathways. In maize leaves, for example, sucrose diffuses through the symplast from photosynthetic mesophyll cells into small veins. Much of it then moves into the apoplast and is accumulated by nearby sieve-tube elements, either directly or through companion cells

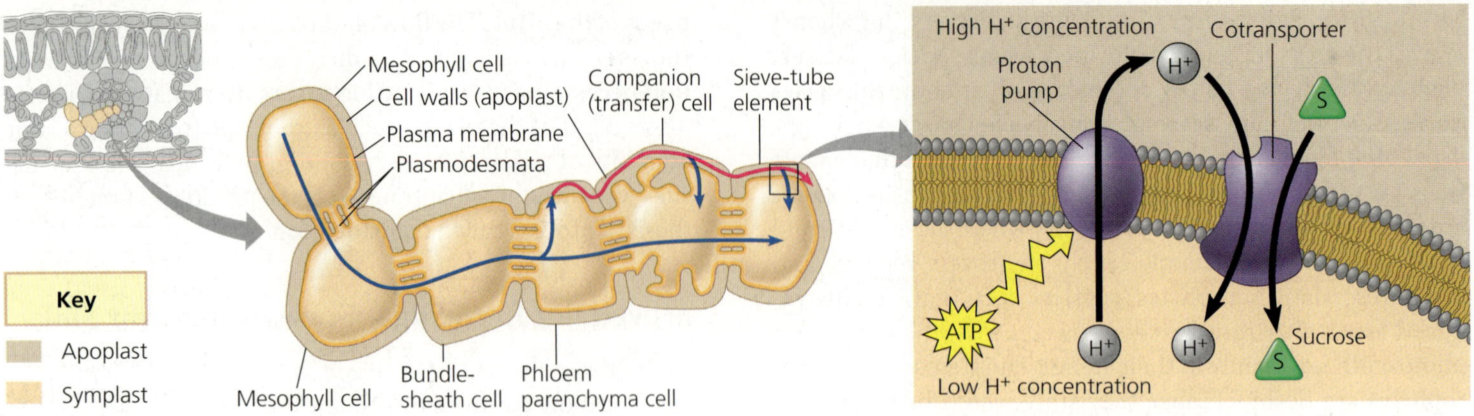

▲ **Figure 36.19** **Loading of sucrose into phloem.**

(a) Sucrose manufactured in mesophyll cells can travel via the symplast (blue arrows) to sieve-tube elements. In some species, sucrose exits the symplast near sieve tubes and travels through the apoplast (red arrow). It is then actively accumulated from the apoplast by sieve-tube elements and their companion cells.

(b) A chemiosmotic mechanism is responsible for the active transport of sucrose into companion cells and sieve-tube elements. Proton pumps generate an H^+ gradient, which drives sucrose accumulation with the help of a cotransport protein that couples sucrose transport to the diffusion of H^+ back into the cell.

(Figure 36.19a). In some plants, the walls of the companion cells feature many ingrowths, enhancing solute transfer between apoplast and symplast. Such modified cells are called **transfer cells** (see Figure 29.5).

In many plants, sugar movement into the phloem requires active transport because sucrose is more concentrated in sieve-tube elements and companion cells than in mesophyll. Proton pumping and cotransport enable sucrose to move from mesophyll cells to sieve-tube elements **(Figure 36.19b)**.

Sucrose is unloaded at the sink end of a sieve tube. The process varies by species and organ. However, the concentration of free sugar in the sink is always lower than in the sieve tube because the unloaded sugar is consumed during growth and metabolism of the cells of the sink or converted to insoluble polymers such as starch. As a result of this sugar concentration gradient, sugar molecules diffuse from the phloem into the sink tissues, and water follows by osmosis.

Bulk Flow by Positive Pressure: The Mechanism of Translocation in Angiosperms

Phloem sap flows from source to sink at rates as great as 1 m/hr, much faster than diffusion or cytoplasmic streaming, the circular flow of cytoplasm within cells. In studying angiosperms, researchers have concluded that phloem sap moves through a sieve tube by bulk flow driven by positive pressure, known as *pressure flow* **(Figure 36.20)**. The building of pressure at the source end and reduction of that pressure at the sink end cause water to flow from source to sink, carrying the sugar along.

The pressure flow hypothesis explains why phloem sap flows from source to sink, and experiments build a strong case for pressure flow as the mechanism of translocation in angiosperms **(Figure 36.21)**. However, studies using electron microscopes suggest that in nonflowering vascular plants, the pores between phloem cells may be too small or obstructed to permit pressure flow. Thus, it is not known if the model applies to all other vascular plants.

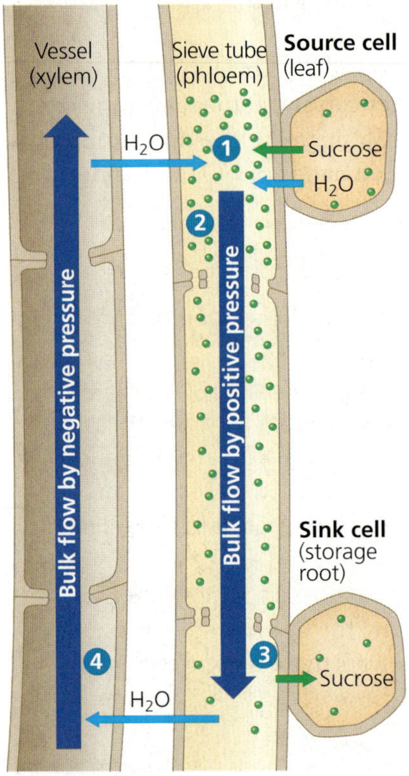

1 Loading of sugar (green dots) into the sieve tube at the source reduces water potential inside the sieve-tube elements. This causes the tube to take up water by osmosis.

2 This uptake of water generates a positive pressure that forces the sap to flow along the tube.

3 The pressure is relieved by the unloading of sugar and the consequent loss of water at the sink.

4 In leaf-to-root translocation, xylem recycles water from sink to source.

▲ **Figure 36.20** **Bulk flow by positive pressure (pressure flow) in a sieve tube.**

Sinks vary in energy demands and capacity to unload sugars. Sometimes there are more sinks than can be supported by sources. In such cases, a plant might abort some flowers, seeds, or fruits—a phenomenon called *self-thinning*. Removing sinks can also be a horticulturally useful practice. For example, since large apples command a much better price than small ones, growers sometimes remove flowers or young fruits so that their trees produce fewer but larger apples.

▼ **Figure 36.21 Inquiry**

Does phloem sap contain more sugar near sources than sinks?

EXPERIMENT The pressure flow hypothesis predicts that phloem sap near sources should have a higher sugar content than phloem sap near sinks. To test this aspect of the hypothesis, S. Rogers and A. J. Peel, at the University of Hull in England, used aphids that feed on phloem sap. An aphid probes with a hypodermic-like mouthpart called a stylet that penetrates a sieve-tube element. As sieve-tube pressure forced out phloem into the stylets, the researchers separated the aphids from the stylets, which then acted as taps exuding sap for hours. Researchers measured the sugar concentration of sap from stylets at different points between a source and sink.

Aphid feeding

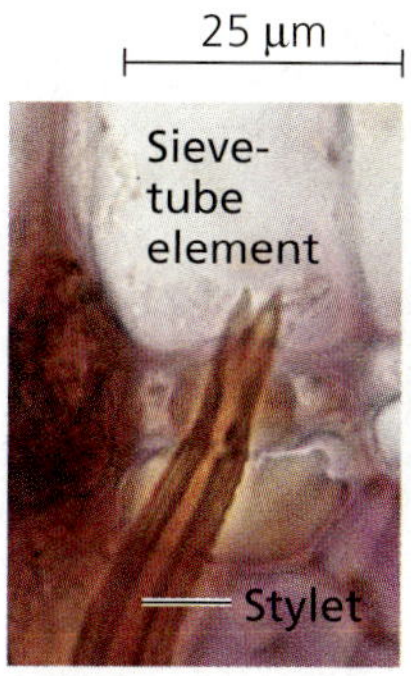

Stylet in sieve-tube element

Separated stylet exuding sap

RESULTS The closer the stylet was to a sugar source, the higher its sugar concentration was.

CONCLUSION The results of such experiments support the pressure flow hypothesis, which predicts that sugar concentrations should be higher in sieve tubes closer to sugar sources.

SOURCE S. Rogers and A. J. Peel, Some evidence for the existence of turgor pressure in the sieve tubes of willow (*Salix*), *Planta* 126, no. 3:259–267 (1975).

WHAT IF? Spittle bugs are xylem sap feeders that use strong muscles to pump xylem sap through their guts. Could you isolate xylem sap from the excised stylets of spittle bugs?

CONCEPT CHECK 36.5

1. Compare and contrast the forces that move phloem sap and xylem sap over long distance.
2. Identify plant organs that are sugar sources, organs that are sugar sinks, and organs that might be either. Explain.
3. Why can xylem transport water and minerals using dead cells, whereas phloem requires living cells?
4. **WHAT IF?** Apple growers in Japan sometimes make a nonlethal spiral slash around the bark of trees destined for removal after the growing season. This practice makes the apples sweeter. Why?

For suggested answers, see Appendix A.

CONCEPT 36.6
The symplast is highly dynamic

Although we have been discussing transport in mostly physical terms, almost like the flow of solutions through pipes, plant transport is a dynamic process. That is, the transport needs of a plant cell typically change during its development. A leaf, for example, may begin as a sugar sink but spend most of its life as a sugar source. Also, environmental changes may trigger marked responses in plant transport processes. Water stress may activate signal transduction pathways that greatly alter the membrane transport proteins governing the overall transport of water and minerals. Because the symplast is living tissue, it is largely responsible for the dynamic changes in plant transport processes.

Plasmodesmata: Continuously Changing Structures

Plasmodesmata provide an example of the dynamic nature of the symplast. Biologists formerly thought of plasmodesmata as unchanging pore-like structures, based mostly on the static images from electron microscopy. Recently, however, new techniques have revealed that plasmodesmata are highly dynamic structures that can change in permeability and number. They can open or close rapidly in response to changes in turgor pressure, cytoplasmic calcium levels, or cytoplasmic pH. Although some form during cytokinesis, they can also form much later. Moreover, loss of function is common during differentiation. For example, as a leaf matures from a sink to a source, its plasmodesmata either close or are eliminated, causing phloem unloading to cease.

Early studies by plant physiologists and pathologists came to differing conclusions regarding pore sizes of plasmodesmata. Physiologists injected fluorescent probes of different molecular sizes into cells and recorded whether the molecules passed into adjacent cells. Based on these observations, they concluded that the pore sizes were approximately 2.5 nm—too small for macromolecules such as proteins to pass. In contrast, pathologists provided electron micrographs showing evidence of passage of viral particles with diameters of 10 nm or greater. One hypothesis to explain these discordant findings was that viruses can greatly dilate plasmodesmata.

Subsequently, it was learned that plant viruses produce *viral movement proteins* that do cause plasmodesmata to dilate, enabling viral RNA to pass between cells. More recent evidence shows that plant cells themselves regulate plasmodesmata as part of a dynamic communication network. Viruses subvert this network by mimicking the cell's regulators of plasmodesmata.

A high degree of cytoplasmic interconnectedness exists only within certain groups of cells and tissues, known as *symplastic domains*. Informational molecules, such as proteins and RNAs, coordinate development between cells within each symplastic domain. If symplastic communication is altered by mutation, development can be grossly affected, as was shown by Patricia Zambryski and colleagues at the University of California, Berkeley **(Figure 36.22)**. (See the interview on pages 736–737.)

Electrical Signaling in the Phloem

Rapid, long-distance electrical signaling through the phloem is another dynamic feature of the symplast. Electrical signaling has been studied extensively in plants that have rapid leaf movements, such as the sensitive plant (*Mimosa pudica*) and Venus flytrap (*Dionaea muscipula*). However, its role in other species is less clear. Some studies have revealed that a stimulus in one part of a plant can trigger an electrical signal in the phloem that affects another part, such as eliciting a change in gene transcription, respiration, photosynthesis, phloem unloading, or hormonal levels. Thus, the phloem can serve a nerve-like function, allowing for swift electrical communication between widely separated organs.

Phloem: An Information Superhighway

In addition to transporting sugars and conducting electrical signals, the phloem is a "superhighway" for the systemic transport of macromolecules and viruses. **Systemic** changes are those that spread throughout the body, affecting many or all of the body's systems or organs. Macromolecules translocated through the phloem include proteins and various types of RNA that enter the sieve tubes through plasmodesmata. Although plasmodesmata are often likened to the gap junctions between animal cells, their ability to traffic proteins and RNA is unique.

Systemic communication through the phloem helps integrate the functions of the whole plant. One classic example is the delivery of a flower-inducing signal from leaves to vegetative meristems. Another is a defensive response to localized infection, in which signals traveling through the phloem activate defense genes in noninfected tissues.

The coordinated transport of materials and information is central to plant survival. Plants acquire only so many resources in the course of their lifetimes. If these resources are not distributed and used in an optimal manner, the plant will not be able to compete well. Ultimately, the successful acquisition and conservation of resources and the integrated functioning of the whole plant are the most critical determinants of whether the plant will compete successfully.

CONCEPT CHECK 36.6

1. What factors influence symplastic communication?
2. How do plasmodesmata differ from gap junctions?
3. **WHAT IF?** If plants were genetically modified to be unresponsive to viral movement proteins, would this be a good way to prevent spread of infection? Explain.

For suggested answers, see Appendix A.

▼ Figure 36.22 Inquiry

Do alterations in symplastic communication affect plant development?

EXPERIMENT Patricia Zambryski and colleagues at the University of California, Berkeley, loaded large and small fluorescent probes at the base of the cotyledon and the root tip of developing *Arabidopsis* embryos. Studies of wild-type embryos had revealed a period in the middle of embryogenesis when symplastic transport of the large probes ceased but transport of small probes continued. The researchers screened for mutants that still transported the large probes during this period and then analyzed their growth into seedlings. The light micrographs below contrast the movement of the large probes (green fluorescence) in a wild-type embryo and mutant embryo.

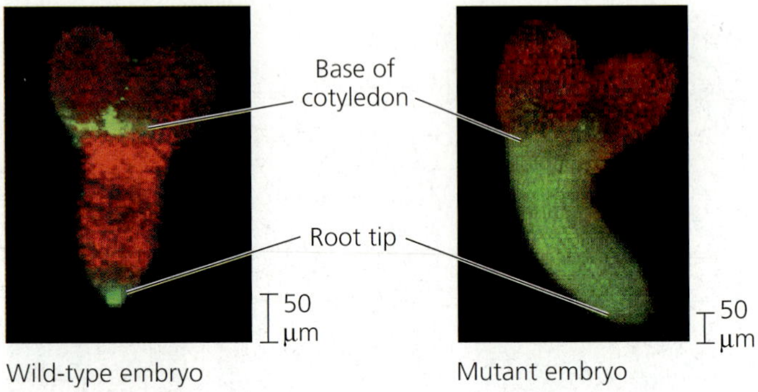

RESULTS As shown in the scanning electron micrograph on the left, about half of the cell files in the wild type consisted of differentiated cells without root hairs (examples marked with yellow Xs). The mutant seedlings were developmentally retarded, with less cell differentiation than the wild-type seedlings. All cell files in a mutant seedling's root epidermis developed root hairs (examples marked with red circles).

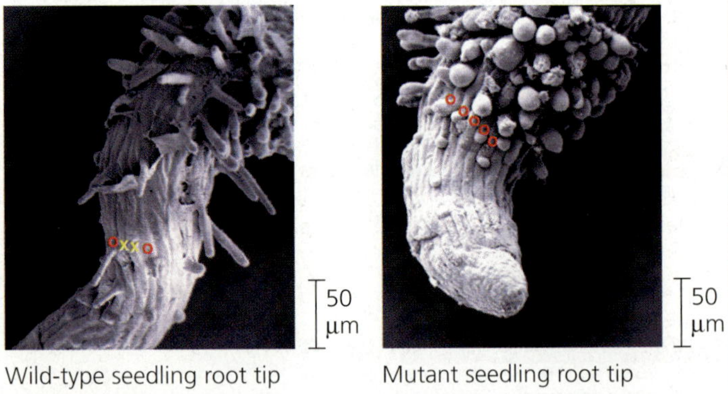

CONCLUSION Isolation of the mutant and demonstration of its altered development support the hypothesis that maintaining symplastic domains is critical for proper plant development.

SOURCE I. Kim, F. Hempel, K. Sha, J. Pfluger, and P. Zambryski, Identification of a developmental transition in plasmodesmatal function during embryogenesis in *Arabidopsis thaliana, Development* 125:1261–1272 (2002).

WHAT IF? Suppose it was found that the mutation caused overproduction of an enzyme that cleaved the fluorescent molecule off the large probe midway through embryogenesis. Would you interpret the results differently?

Chapter 36 Review

MEDIA Go to the Study Area at **www.masteringbio.com** for BioFlix 3-D Animations, MP3 Tutors, Videos, Practice Tests, an eBook, and more.

SUMMARY OF KEY CONCEPTS

CONCEPT 36.1

Land plants acquire resources both above and below ground (pp. 764–767)

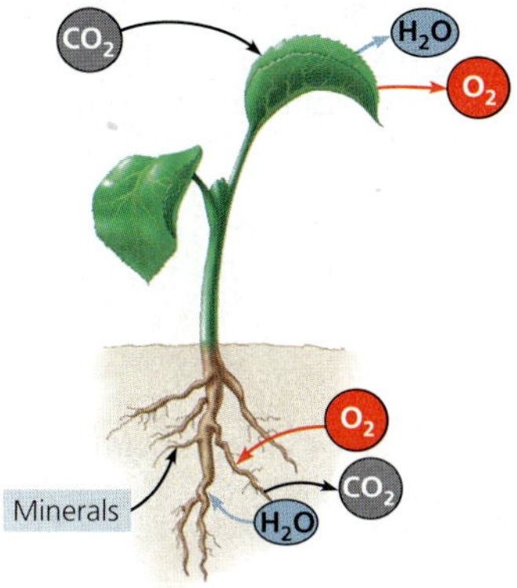

- **Shoot Architecture and Light Capture** Arrangement and size of leaves, branching, and stem thickness help shoots acquire CO_2 and light.
- **Root Architecture and Acquisition of Water and Minerals** Elongation, branching, and mycorrhizae help roots mine the soil for water and minerals.

CONCEPT 36.2

Transport occurs by short-distance diffusion or active transport and by long-distance bulk flow (pp. 767–772)

- **Diffusion and Active Transport of Solutes** Diffusion is the spontaneous movement down concentration gradients. Transport proteins aid diffusion across membranes. Proton pumps generate an H^+ gradient used to transport solutes.
- **Diffusion of Water (Osmosis)** Osmosis is the spontaneous movement of free water down its concentration gradient. Water flows across membranes from regions with higher water potential (ψ) to regions with lower ψ. Solutes decrease ψ. Pressure may increase or decrease ψ.
- **Three Major Pathways of Transport** The symplast is the cytoplasmic continuum linked by plasmodesmata. The apoplast is the continuum of cell walls and extracellular spaces.
- **Bulk Flow in Long-Distance Transport** Bulk flow is due to pressure differences at opposite ends of vessel elements and tracheids (for xylem sap) or sieve tubes (for phloem sap).

CONCEPT 36.3

Water and minerals are transported from roots to shoots (pp. 772–776)

- **Absorption of Water and Minerals by Root Cells** Root hairs and the extensive surface area of cortical cell membranes enhance uptake of water and minerals.
- **Transport of Water and Minerals into the Xylem** Water can cross the cortex via the symplast or apoplast, but minerals moving via the apoplast must finally cross the selective membranes of endodermal cells. The Casparian strip blocks apoplastic transfer of minerals to the stele.
- **Bulk Flow Driven by Negative Pressure in the Xylem** Transpiration lowers ψ in the leaf by producing a negative pressure potential (tension). This low ψ draws water from the xylem. Cohesion and adhesion of water transmit the pulling force to the roots.
- **Xylem Sap Ascent by Bulk Flow: *A Review*** Transpiration maintains movement of xylem sap against gravity.

MEDIA
BioFlix 3-D Animation Water Transport in Plants
MP3 Tutor Transpiration
Activity Transport of Xylem Sap

CONCEPT 36.4

Stomata help regulate the rate of transpiration (pp. 776–779)

- **Stomata: Major Pathways for Water Loss** Guard cells widen or narrow the diameter of stomatal pores. Genetic and environmental factors influence stomatal density.
- **Mechanisms of Stomatal Opening and Closing** When guard cells take up K^+, they bow outward, widening the pore. Stomatal closing involves the loss of K^+.
- **Stimuli for Stomatal Opening and Closing** Stomatal aperture is controlled by light, CO_2, water availability, the hormone abscisic acid, and circadian rhythm.
- **Effects of Transpiration on Wilting and Leaf Temperature** If water lost by transpiration is not replaced by absorption from roots, the plant will wilt. Cooling by transpiration can lower leaf temperature.
- **Adaptations That Reduce Evaporative Water Loss** Reduced leaves and CAM photosynthesis are examples of adaptations to arid environments.

MEDIA
Investigation How Is the Rate of Transpiration Calculated?

CONCEPT 36.5

Sugars are transported from leaves and other sources to sites of use or storage (pp. 779–781)

- **Movement from Sugar Sources to Sugar Sinks** Mature leaves are the main sources, though storage organs can be seasonal sources. Meristems and developing fruits and seeds are examples of sinks. Phloem loading and unloading depend on active transport of sucrose. Sucrose is cotransported with H^+, which diffuses down a gradient generated by proton pumps.
- **Bulk Flow by Positive Pressure: The Mechanism of Translocation in Angiosperms** Loading of sugar at the source and unloading at the sink maintain a pressure difference that keeps sap flowing through a sieve tube.

MEDIA
Activity Translocation of Phloem Sap

CONCEPT 36.6

The symplast is highly dynamic (pp. 781–782)

- **Plasmodesmata: Continuously Changing Structures** Plasmodesmata can change in number. When dilated, they can provide a passageway for macromolecules such as RNA and proteins.

▶ **Electrical Signaling in the Phloem** The phloem can conduct nerve-like electrical signals that propagate through the symplast and help to integrate whole-plant function.

▶ **Phloem: An Information Superhighway** Phloem helps integrate whole-plant function by transporting proteins, RNAs, and other macromolecules over long distances.

TESTING YOUR KNOWLEDGE

SELF-QUIZ

1. Which of the following does *not* affect self-shading?
a. leaf area index
b. phyllotaxy
c. self-pruning
d. stem thickness
e. leaf orientation

2. What would enhance water uptake by a plant cell?
a. decreased ψ of the surrounding solution
b. an increase in pressure exerted by the cell wall
c. the loss of solutes from the cell
d. an increase in ψ of the cytoplasm
e. positive pressure on the surrounding solution

3. A plant cell with a ψ_S of -0.65 MPa maintains a constant volume when bathed in a solution that has a ψ_S of -0.30 MPa and is in an open container. The cell has a
a. ψ_P of $+0.65$ MPa.
b. ψ of -0.65 MPa.
c. ψ_P of $+0.35$ MPa.
d. ψ_P of $+0.30$ MPa.
e. ψ of 0 MPa.

4. Which structure or compartment is *not* part of the apoplast?
a. the lumen of a xylem vessel
b. the lumen of a sieve tube
c. the cell wall of a mesophyll cell
d. an extracellular air space
e. the cell wall of a root hair

5. Which of the following is an adaptation that enhances the uptake of water and minerals by roots?
a. mycorrhizae
b. cavitation
c. active uptake by vessels
d. rhythmic contractions by cortical cells
e. pumping through plasmodesmata

6. Which of the following is *not* part of the transpiration-cohesion-tension mechanism for the ascent of xylem sap?
a. loss of water from the mesophyll cells, which initiates a pull of water molecules from neighboring cells
b. transfer of transpirational pull from one water molecule to the next, due to cohesion by hydrogen bonds
c. hydrophilic walls of tracheids and vessels that help maintain the column of water against gravity
d. active pumping of water into the xylem of roots
e. lowering of ψ in the surface film of mesophyll cells due to transpiration

7. Photosynthesis ceases when leaves wilt, mainly because
a. the chlorophyll of wilting leaves breaks down.
b. flaccid mesophyll cells are incapable of photosynthesis.
c. stomata close, preventing CO_2 from entering the leaf.
d. photolysis, the water-splitting step of photosynthesis, cannot occur when there is a water deficiency.
e. accumulation of CO_2 in the leaf inhibits enzymes.

8. Stomata open when guard cells
a. sense an increase in CO_2 in the air spaces of the leaf.
b. open because of a decrease in turgor pressure.
c. become more turgid because of an addition of K^+, followed by the osmotic entry of water.
d. close aquaporins, preventing uptake of water.
e. accumulate water by active transport.

9. Movement of phloem sap from a source to a sink
a. occurs through the apoplast of sieve-tube elements.
b. may translocate sugars from the breakdown of stored starch in a root up to developing shoots.
c. depends on tension, or negative pressure potential.
d. depends on pumping water into sieve tubes at the source.
e. results mainly from diffusion.

10. Which of these is *not* transported via the symplast?
a. sugars
b. mRNA
c. DNA
d. proteins
e. viruses

11. **DRAW IT** Trace the uptake of water and minerals from root hairs to the vessels in a root, following a symplastic route and an apoplastic route. Label the routes.

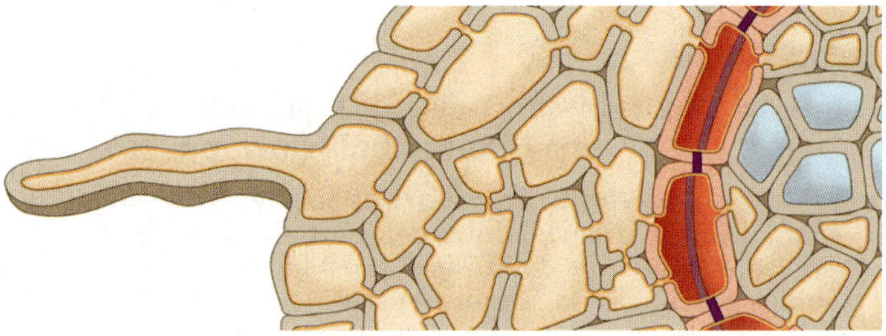

For Self-Quiz answers, see Appendix A.

MEDIA Visit the Study Area at **www.masteringbio.com** for a Practice Test.

EVOLUTION CONNECTION

12. Large brown algae called kelps can grow as tall as 25 m. Kelps consist of a holdfast anchored to the ocean floor, blades that float at the surface and collect light, and a long stalk connecting the blades to the holdfast (see Figure 28.15). Specialized cells in the stalk, although nonvascular, transport sugar. Suggest a reason why these structures analogous to sieve-tube elements might have evolved in kelps.

SCIENTIFIC INQUIRY

13. Tomato and cotton plants wilt within a few hours of flooding their roots. Flooding leads to low oxygen conditions, increases in cytoplasmic calcium, and decreases in cytoplasmic pH. Suggest a hypothesis to explain how it leads to wilting.

SCIENCE, TECHNOLOGY, AND SOCIETY

14. In the arid southwestern United States, there has been growing criticism of water use for lawns and golf courses. Should such use be limited or even banned? Explain.

37 Soil and Plant Nutrition

▲ **Figure 37.1 Could this happen again?**

KEY CONCEPTS

37.1 Soil is a living, finite resource
37.2 Plants require essential elements to complete their life cycle
37.3 Plant nutrition often involves relationships with other organisms

OVERVIEW

"The Nation that Destroys Its Soil Destroys Itself"

President Franklin D. Roosevelt wrote these words in 1937 in referring to an ecological and human disaster that ravaged the southwestern Great Plains, a region that came to be called the Dust Bowl. The series of devastating dust storms was caused by a massive drought and decades of inappropriate farming techniques. Before the arrival of farmers, the Great Plains had been covered by hardy grasses that held the soil in place in spite of recurring droughts and torrential rains. But in the late 1800s and early 1900s, many homesteaders settled in the region, planting wheat and raising cattle. These land uses left the soil exposed to erosion by winds. A few years of drought made the problem worse. During the 1930s, huge quantities of fertile soil were blown away in "black blizzards," rendering millions of hectares of farmland useless **(Figure 37.1)**. In one of the worst dust storms, clouds of dust blew eastward to Chicago, where soil fell like snow, and even reached as far east as New York City and Washington, D.C. Hundreds of thousands of people in the Dust Bowl region were forced to abandon their homes and land, a plight immortalized in John Steinbeck's novel *The Grapes of Wrath*.

Soil mismanagement in various forms has been a recurrent problem throughout human history and continues to this day. More than 30% of the world's farmland has reduced productivity stemming from poor soil conditions, such as chemical contamination, mineral deficiencies, acidity, salinity, and poor drainage. As the world's population continues to grow, the demand for food increases. Because soil quality is a major determinant of crop yield, the need to manage soil resources prudently has never been greater.

Healthy soil improves plant growth by enhancing plant **nutrition**, the process by which an organism takes in and makes use of food substances. As discussed in Chapter 36, plants obtain nutrients from both the atmosphere and the soil. Using sunlight as an energy source, plants produce organic nutrients by reducing carbon dioxide to sugars through the process of photosynthesis. Land plants also take up water and various mineral nutrients from the soil through their root systems. In this chapter, we discuss the basic physical properties of soils and the factors that govern soil quality. We then explore why certain inorganic nutrients are essential for plant function. Finally, we examine some nutritional adaptations that have evolved in plants, often in relationships with other organisms.

CONCEPT 37.1

Soil is a living, finite resource

The upper layers of the soil, from which plants absorb nearly all of the water and minerals they require, contain a wide range of living organisms that interact with each other and with the physical environment. This complex ecosystem may take centuries to form but can be destroyed by human mismanagement in just a few years. To understand why soil must be conserved and why particular plants grow where they do, we must appreciate the basic physical properties of soil: its texture and composition.

Soil Texture

The texture of soil depends on the sizes of its particles. Soil particles can range from coarse sand (0.02–2 mm in diameter) to silt (0.002–0.02 mm) to microscopic clay particles (less than 0.002 mm). These different-sized particles arise ultimately from the weathering of rock. Water freezing in the crevices of rocks causes mechanical fracturing, and weak acids in the soil break rocks down chemically. When organisms penetrate the rock, they accelerate breakdown by chemical and mechanical means. Plant roots, for example, secrete acids that dissolve the rock, and their growth in fissures leads to mechanical fracturing. The mineral particles released by weathering become mixed with living organisms and **humus**, the remains of dead organisms and other organic matter, forming **topsoil**. The topsoil and other distinct soil layers, or **soil horizons**, are often visible where there is a road cut or deep hole **(Figure 37.2)**. The topsoil, or A horizon, can range in depth from millimeters to meters. We focus mostly on the properties of topsoil because it is the most important soil layer for the growth of most plants.

In the topsoil, plants are nourished by the soil solution, the water and dissolved minerals in the pores between soil particles. The pores also contain air pockets. After a heavy rainfall, water drains away from the larger spaces in the soil, but smaller spaces retain water because water molecules are attracted to the negatively charged surfaces of clay and other soil particles.

The topsoils that are the most fertile—supporting the most abundant growth—are **loams**, which are composed of roughly equal amounts of sand, silt, and clay. Loamy soils have enough small silt and clay particles to provide ample surface area for the adhesion and retention of minerals and water. Meanwhile, the large spaces between sand particles enable efficient diffusion of oxygen to the roots. Sandy soils generally don't retain enough water to support vigorous plant growth, and clayey soils tend to retain too much water. When soil does not drain adequately, the air is replaced by water, and the roots suffocate from lack of oxygen. Typically, the most fertile topsoils have pores that are about half water and half air, providing a good balance between aeration, drainage, and water storage capacity. The physical properties of soils can be adjusted by adding soil amendments, such as peat moss, compost, manure, or sand.

Topsoil Composition

A soil's composition encompasses its inorganic (mineral) and organic chemical components. The organic components include the many life-forms that inhabit the soil.

Inorganic Components

The surface charges of soil particles determine their ability to bind many nutrients. Most soil particles are negatively charged. Positively charged ions (cations)—such as potassium (K^+), calcium (Ca^{2+}), and magnesium (Mg^{2+})—adhere to these particles and are therefore not easily lost by *leaching*, the percolation of water through the soil. Roots, however, do not absorb mineral cations directly from soil particles. Instead, they become available in the soil solution, through **cation exchange**. In this process, mineral cations are displaced from soil particles by other cations, particularly H^+, and enter the soil solution, which is then absorbed by root hairs **(Figure 37.3)**. A soil's capacity to exchange cations is determined by the number of

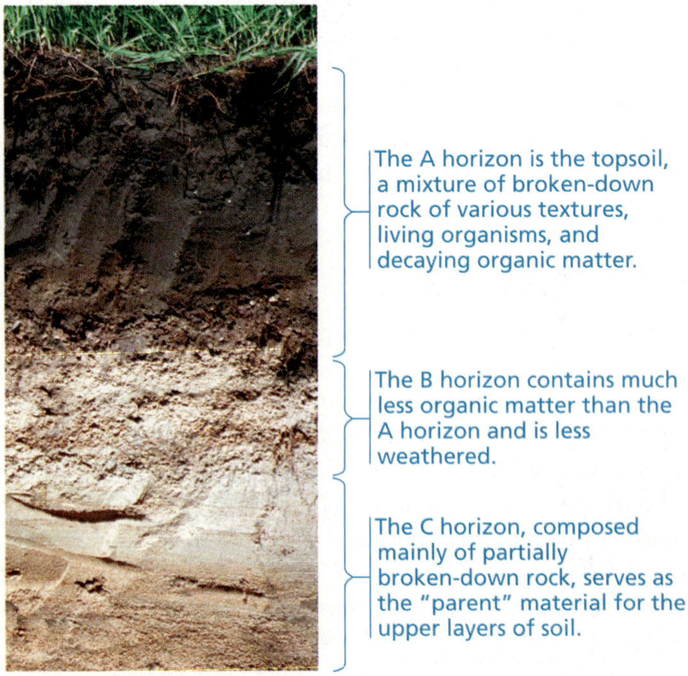

▲ **Figure 37.2 Soil horizons.**

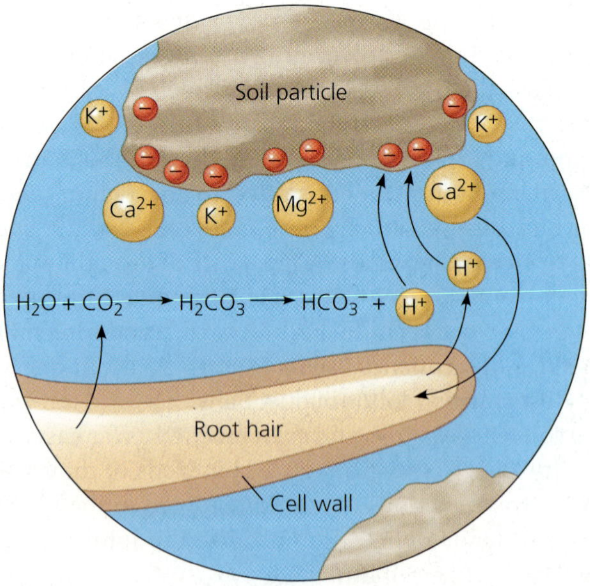

▲ **Figure 37.3 Cation exchange in soil.**

? *Which are more likely to be leached from the soil by heavy rains—cations or anions? Explain.*

cation adhesion sites and by the pH. Soils with higher capacities generally have a larger reserve of mineral nutrients.

Negatively charged ions (anions)—such as the plant nutrients nitrate (NO_3^-), phosphate ($H_2PO_4^-$), and sulfate (SO_4^{2-})—are not bound tightly to the negatively charged soil particles and are therefore easily released. During heavy rain or irrigation, they are leached into the groundwater, making them unavailable for uptake by roots.

Organic Components

Humus is a major organic component of topsoil, consisting of organic material produced by the decomposition of dead organisms, feces, fallen leaves, and other organic matter by bacteria and fungi. Humus prevents clay particles from packing together and forms a crumbly soil that retains water but is still porous enough to aerate roots adequately. Humus also increases the soil's capacity to exchange cations and serves as a reservoir of mineral nutrients that return gradually to the soil as microorganisms decompose the organic matter.

Topsoil is also home to an astonishing number and variety of organisms. A teaspoon of topsoil has about 5 billion bacteria that cohabit with fungi, algae and other protists, insects, earthworms, nematodes, and plant roots. The activities of all these organisms affect the soil's physical and chemical properties. Earthworms, for example, consume organic matter and derive their nutrition from the bacteria and fungi growing on this material. They excrete wastes and move large amounts of material to the soil surface. In addition, they move organic matter into deeper layers of the soil. In effect, earthworms mix and clump the soil particles, allowing for better gaseous diffusion and retention of water. Plant roots also affect soil texture and composition. For example, by binding the soil, they reduce erosion, and by excreting acids, they lower soil pH.

Soil Conservation and Sustainable Agriculture

Ancient farmers recognized that yields on a particular plot of land decreased over the years. Moving to uncultivated areas, they observed the same pattern of reduced yields over time. Eventually, they realized that soil—if fertilized—was a renewable resource that enabled crops to be cultivated season after season at a fixed location. This sedentary agriculture facilitated a new way of life. Humans began to build permanent dwellings—the first villages. They also stored food for use between harvests, and food surpluses enabled some members of these early communities to specialize in nonfarming occupations. In short, soil management, by fertilization and other practices, helped prepare the way for the establishment of modern societies.

In this section, we'll discuss how farmers irrigate and modify soil to maintain good crop yields. The goal is **sustainable agriculture**, a commitment embracing a variety of farming methods that are conservation minded, environmentally safe, and profitable. We will also examine how problems such as erosion, soil compaction, and soil contamination are causing global soil degradation.

Irrigation

Because water is often the limiting factor in plant growth, perhaps no technology has increased crop yield as much as irrigation. However, irrigation is a huge drain on freshwater resources. Globally, about 75% of all freshwater use is devoted to agriculture. Many rivers in the southwestern United States have been reduced to trickles by the diversion of water for irrigation. The primary source of irrigation water, however, is not surface waters, such as rivers and lakes, but underground water reserves called *aquifers*. In some parts of the world, the rate of water removal is exceeding the natural refilling of the aquifers. The result is *land subsidence*, a gradual settling or sudden sinking of Earth's surface **(Figure 37.4)**. Land subsidence alters drainage patterns, causes damage to human-made structures, promotes loss of underground springs, and increases the risk of flooding.

◀ To emphasize the dramatic effects of land subsidence in California's San Joaquin Valley, geologist Joseph F. Poland (shown here in 1977) had signs posted to represent approximate altitudes of the land surface in 1925 and 1955.

▲ Sudden land subsidence resulting from the overuse of groundwater for irrigation triggered the formation of this sinkhole in Florida.

▲ **Figure 37.4 Land subsidence caused by excessive removal of groundwater.**

Irrigation, particularly from groundwater, can also lead to soil *salinization*—formation of soil too salty for cultivating plants. Salts dissolved in irrigation water accumulate in the soil as the water evaporates, making the water potential of the soil solution more negative. The water potential gradient from soil to roots is lowered, reducing water uptake (see Chapter 36).

Many forms of irrigation, such as the flooding of fields, are wasteful because much of the water evaporates. In order to use water efficiently, farmers must understand the water-holding capacity of their soil, the water needs of their crops, and the appropriate irrigation technology. One popular technology is *drip irrigation*, the slow release of water to soil and plants from perforated plastic tubing placed directly at the root zone. Because drip irrigation requires less water and reduces salinization, it is used in many arid agricultural regions.

Fertilization

In natural ecosystems, mineral nutrients are usually recycled by the decomposition of dead organic material and by the excretion of animal wastes. Agriculture, however, is unnatural. The lettuce in your salad, for example, contains minerals extracted from a farmer's field. As you excrete wastes, these minerals are now deposited far from their original source. Over many harvests, the farmer's field will become depleted of nutrients if they are not restored. Nutrient depletion is a major cause of global soil degradation. Farmers must reverse nutrient depletion by **fertilization**, the addition of mineral nutrients to the soil.

Today, most farmers in industrialized nations use fertilizers containing minerals that are either mined or prepared by energy-intensive processes. These fertilizers are usually enriched in nitrogen (N), phosphorus (P), and potassium (K)—the nutrients most commonly deficient in depleted soils. You may have seen fertilizers labeled with a three-number code, called the N-P-K ratio. A fertilizer marked "15-10-5," for instance, is 15% N (as ammonium or nitrate), 10% P (as phosphoric acid), and 5% K (as the mineral potash).

Manure, fishmeal, and compost are called "organic" fertilizers because they are of biological origin and contain decomposing organic material. Before plants can use organic material, however, it must be decomposed into the inorganic nutrients that roots can absorb. Whether from organic fertilizer or a chemical factory, the minerals a plant extracts are in the same form. However, organic fertilizers release them gradually, whereas minerals in commercial fertilizers are immediately available but may not be retained by the soil for long. Minerals not absorbed by roots are often leached from the soil by rainwater or irrigation. To make matters worse, mineral runoff into lakes may lead to explosions in algal populations that can deplete oxygen levels and decimate fish populations.

Adjusting Soil pH

Soil pH is another important factor influencing mineral availability because it affects cation exchange and the chemical form of minerals. Depending on the soil pH, a particular mineral may be bound too tightly to clay particles or may be in a chemical form that the plant cannot absorb. Most plants prefer slightly acidic soil because the high H^+ concentrations can displace positively charged minerals from soil particles, making them more available for absorption. Adjusting soil pH for optimal crop growth is tricky because a change in H^+ concentration may make one mineral more available but another mineral less available. At pH 8, for instance, plants can absorb calcium, but iron is almost completely unavailable. The soil pH should be matched to a crop's mineral needs. If the soil is too alkaline, adding sulfate will lower the pH. Soil that is too acidic can be adjusted by adding lime (calcium carbonate or calcium hydroxide).

When the soil pH dips to 5 or lower, toxic aluminum ions (Al^{3+}) become more soluble and are absorbed by roots, stunting root growth and preventing the uptake of calcium, a needed plant nutrient. Some plants can cope with high Al^{3+} levels by secreting organic anions that bind the Al^{3+} and render it harmless. However, low soil pH and Al^{3+} toxicity continue to pose serious problems, especially in tropical regions, where growing populations and food production pressures are often most acute.

Controlling Erosion

As happened most dramatically in the Dust Bowl, water and wind erosion can remove considerable amounts of topsoil. Erosion is a major cause of soil degradation because soil nutrients are carried far away by wind and streams. To limit erosion, farmers can take precautions such as planting rows of trees as windbreaks, terracing hillside crops, and cultivating in a contour pattern **(Figure 37.5)**. Crops such as alfalfa and wheat provide good ground cover and protect the soil better

▲ **Figure 37.5 Contour tillage.** These crops in Wisconsin are planted in rows that go around, rather than up and down, the hills. Contour tillage helps slow water runoff and topsoil erosion after heavy rains.

than maize and other crops that are usually planted in more widely spaced rows.

Erosion can also be reduced by a plowing technique called **no-till agriculture**. In traditional plowing, the entire field is tilled, or turned over. Although this practice helps control weeds, it also disrupts the meshwork of roots that holds the soil in place, leading to increased surface runoff and erosion. In no-till agriculture, a specialized plow creates narrow furrows for seeds and fertilizer. In this way, the field can be seeded with minimal disturbance of the soil, while also requiring less fertilizer.

Preventing Soil Compaction

Large heavy farm equipment causes a problem called soil compaction: Soil particles are pressed together, reducing pore space between them. Heavily compacted soils contain few large pores and have reduced rates of water absorption and drainage because the small pores that remain are less effective in moving water through the soil. Compaction also slows down gas exchange between roots and the soil. In addition, compaction reduces root growth by making it harder for them to penetrate the soil, thereby decreasing absorption of water and nutrients. The best cure for soil compaction is to avoid it by not farming soil that is too wet and by redesigning agricultural equipment with more and broader tires to redistribute the weight.

Phytoremediation

Some land areas are unfit for cultivation because toxic heavy metals or organic pollutants have contaminated the soil or groundwater. Traditionally, soil remediation, the detoxification of contaminated soils, has focused on nonbiological technologies, such as removing and storing contaminated soil in landfills, but these techniques are very costly and often disrupt the landscape. **Phytoremediation** is a nondestructive biotechnology that harnesses some plants' ability to extract soil pollutants and concentrate them in portions of the plant that can be easily removed for safe disposal. For example, alpine pennycress (*Thlaspi caerulescens*) can accumulate zinc in its shoots at concentrations 300 times higher than most plants can tolerate. The shoots can then be harvested and the contaminating zinc removed. Such plants show promise for cleaning up areas contaminated by smelters, mining operations, or nuclear testing. Phytoremediation is one form of the more general technology of bioremediation, which also includes the use of prokaryotes and protists to detoxify polluted sites (see Chapters 27 and 56).

In this section, we have discussed the importance of soil conservation for sustainable agriculture. Mineral nutrients are major factors contributing to soil fertility, but which minerals are most important, and why do plants need them? These are the topics of the next section.

CONCEPT CHECK 37.1

1. Explain how the phrase "too much of a good thing" can apply to watering and fertilizing plants.
2. Some lawn mowers collect clippings for easy disposal and to prevent clumps from inhibiting photosynthesis. What is a possible drawback of this practice with respect to plant nutrition?
3. **WHAT IF?** How would adding clay to loamy soil affect the soil's capacity to exchange cations and retain water? Explain.

For suggested answers, see Appendix A.

CONCEPT 37.2
Plants require essential elements to complete their life cycle

Watch a large plant grow from a tiny seed, and you cannot help wondering where all the plant mass comes from. Aristotle hypothesized that plants "ate" soil because they were seen to arise from the ground. In the 1640s, the Belgian physiologist Jan Baptista van Helmont tested the hypothesis that plants grow by consuming soil. He planted a small willow in a pot that contained 90.9 kg of soil. After five years, the plant weighed 76.8 kg, but only 0.06 kg of soil had disappeared from the pot. He concluded that the willow had grown mainly from the water he had added. A century later, the English physiologist Stephen Hales, armed with knowledge from recent advances in physics and chemistry that air is a substance with mass, postulated that plants are nourished mostly by air.

There is some truth to all three hypotheses because soil, water, and air all contribute to plant growth. The water content of a plant can be measured by comparing the mass of plant material before and after it is dried. Typically, 80–90% of a plant's fresh mass is water. We can also analyze the chemical composition of the dry residue. Organic substances generally account for about 96% of the dry mass. Thus, the inorganic nutrients from the soil, although essential for plant survival, contribute very little to the plant's total mass. The majority of a plant's dry mass is derived neither from water nor from soil minerals but from the CO_2 that is assimilated from the air during photosynthesis. Water also supplies most of the hydrogen atoms and some of the oxygen atoms incorporated into organic compounds by photosynthesis (see Figure 10.4). Most of the organic material of plants is carbohydrate, including the cellulose of cell walls. Thus, the components of carbohydrates—carbon, oxygen, and hydrogen—are the most abundant elements in a dried plant. Because many macromolecules contain nitrogen, sulfur, or phosphorus, these elements are also relatively abundant in plants.

Macronutrients and Micronutrients

The inorganic substances in plants contain more than 50 chemical elements. In studying the chemical composition of plants, we must distinguish elements that are essential from those that are merely present in the plant. A chemical element is considered an **essential element** only if it is required for a plant to complete its life cycle and produce another generation.

To determine which chemical elements are essential, researchers use **hydroponic culture**, in which plants are grown in mineral solutions instead of soil **(Figure 37.6)**. Such studies have helped identify 17 essential elements needed by all plants **(Table 37.1)**. Hydroponic culture is also used on a small scale to grow some greenhouse crops.

Nine of the essential elements are called **macronutrients** because plants require them in relatively large amounts. Six of these are the major components of organic compounds forming a plant's structure: carbon, oxygen, hydrogen, nitrogen, phosphorus, and sulfur. The other three macronutrients are potassium, calcium, and magnesium. Of all the mineral nutrients, nitrogen contributes the most to plant growth and crop yields. Plants require nitrogen as a component of proteins, nucleic acids, chlorophyll, and other important organic molecules.

The remaining eight essential elements are known as **micronutrients** because plants need them in tiny quantities. They are chlorine, iron, manganese, boron, zinc, copper, nickel, and molybdenum. In some cases, sodium may be a ninth essential micronutrient: Plants that use the C_4 and CAM pathways of photosynthesis (see Chapter 10) require sodium ions to regenerate phosphophenolpyruvate, which is the CO_2 acceptor in these two types of carbon fixation.

Micronutrients function in plants mainly as cofactors, nonprotein helpers in enzymatic reactions (see Chapter 8). Iron, for example, is a metallic component of cytochromes, the proteins in the electron transport chains of chloroplasts and mitochondria. It is because micronutrients generally play catalytic roles that plants need only tiny quantities. The requirement for molybdenum, for instance, is so modest that there is only one atom of this rare element for every 60 million atoms of hydrogen in dried plant material. Yet a deficiency of molybdenum or any other micronutrient can weaken or kill a plant.

Symptoms of Mineral Deficiency

The symptoms of a deficiency depend partly on the mineral's function as a nutrient. For example, a deficiency of magnesium, a component of chlorophyll, causes *chlorosis*, yellowing of the leaves. In some cases, the relationship between a mineral deficiency and its symptoms is less direct. For instance, iron deficiency can cause chlorosis even though chlorophyll contains no iron, because iron ions are required as a cofactor in one of the enzymatic steps of chlorophyll synthesis.

Mineral deficiency symptoms depend not only on the role of the nutrient but also on its mobility within the plant. If a nutrient moves about freely, symptoms appear first in older organs because young, growing tissues have more "drawing power" for nutrients that are in short supply. For example, magnesium is relatively mobile and is shunted preferentially to young leaves. Therefore, a plant deficient in magnesium first shows signs of chlorosis in its older leaves. The mechanism for preferential routing is the source-to-sink translocation in phloem, as minerals move along with sugars to the growing tissues (see Figure 36.20). In contrast, a deficiency of a mineral that is relatively immobile affects young parts of the plant first. Older tissues may have adequate amounts that they retain during periods of short supply. For example, iron does not move freely within a plant, and an iron deficiency causes yellowing of young leaves before any effect on older leaves is visible. The mineral requirements of a plant may also change with the time of the year and the age of the plant. Young seedlings, for example, rarely show mineral deficiency symptoms because their mineral requirements are met largely by minerals released from stored reserves in the seed itself.

▼ Figure 37.6 **Research Method**

Hydroponic Culture

APPLICATION In hydroponic culture, plants are grown in mineral solutions without soil. One use of hydroponic culture is to identify essential elements in plants.

TECHNIQUE Plant roots are bathed in aerated solutions of known mineral composition. Aerating the water provides the roots with oxygen for cellular respiration. (Note: The flasks would normally be opaque to prevent algal growth.) A mineral, such as potassium, can be omitted to test whether it is essential.

Control: Solution containing all minerals

Experimental: Solution without potassium

RESULTS If the omitted mineral is essential, mineral deficiency symptoms occur, such as stunted growth and discolored leaves. By definition, the plant would not be able to complete its life cycle. Deficiencies of different elements may have different symptoms, which can aid in diagnosing mineral deficiencies in soil.

Table 37.1 Essential Elements in Plants

Element	Form Available to Plants	% Mass in Dry Tissue	Major Functions
Macronutrients			
Carbon	CO_2	45%	Major component of plant's organic compounds
Oxygen	CO_2	45%	Major component of plant's organic compounds
Hydrogen	H_2O	6%	Major component of plant's organic compounds
Nitrogen	NO_3^-, NH_4^+	1.5%	Component of nucleic acids, proteins, hormones, chlorophyll, coenzymes
Potassium	K^+	1.0%	Cofactor that functions in protein synthesis; major solute functioning in water balance; operation of stomata
Calcium	Ca^{2+}	0.5%	Important in formation and stability of cell walls and in maintenance of membrane structure and permeability; activates some enzymes; regulates many responses of cells to stimuli
Magnesium	Mg^{2+}	0.2%	Component of chlorophyll; activates many enzymes
Phosphorus	$H_2PO_4^-$, HPO_4^{2-}	0.2%	Component of nucleic acids, phospholipids, ATP, several coenzymes
Sulfur	SO_4^{2-}	0.1%	Component of proteins, coenzymes
Micronutrients			
Chlorine	Cl^-	0.01%	Required for water-splitting step of photosynthesis; functions in water balance
Iron	Fe^{3+}, Fe^{2+}	0.01%	Component of cytochromes; activates some enzymes
Manganese	Mn^{2+}	0.005%	Active in formation of amino acids; activates some enzymes; required for water-splitting step of photosynthesis
Boron	$H_2BO_3^-$	0.002%	Cofactor in chlorophyll synthesis; may be involved in carbohydrate transport and nucleic acid synthesis; role in cell wall function
Zinc	Zn^{2+}	0.002%	Active in formation of chlorophyll; activates some enzymes
Copper	Cu^+, Cu^{2+}	0.001%	Component of many redox and lignin-biosynthetic enzymes
Nickel	Ni^{2+}	0.001%	Cofactor for an enzyme functioning in nitrogen metabolism
Molybdenum	MoO_4^{2-}	0.0001%	Essential for mutualistic relationship with nitrogen-fixing bacteria; cofactor in nitrate reduction

Deficiencies of phosphorus, potassium, and especially nitrogen are most common. Micronutrient shortages are less common and tend to occur in certain geographic regions because of differences in soil composition. The symptoms of a mineral deficiency may vary between species but are often distinctive enough for a plant physiologist or farmer to diagnose the cause **(Figure 37.7)**. One way to confirm a diagnosis is to analyze the mineral content of the plant or soil. The amount of a micronutrient needed to correct a deficiency is usually quite small. For example, a zinc deficiency in fruit trees can usually be cured by hammering a few zinc nails into each tree trunk.

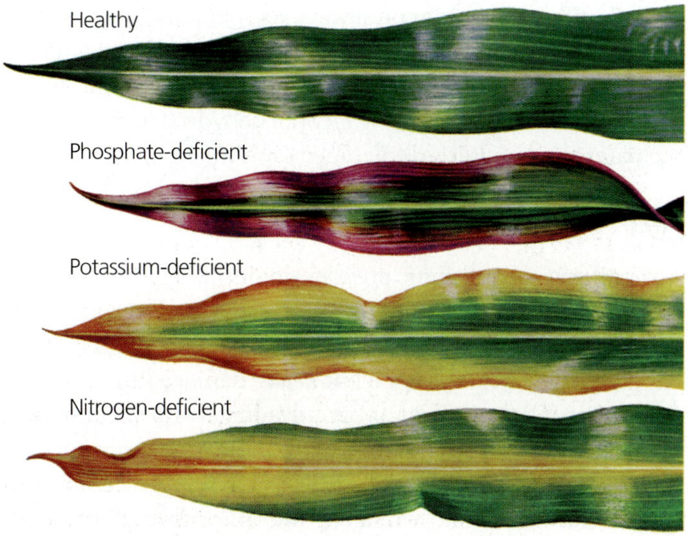

▶ **Figure 37.7 The most common mineral deficiencies, as seen in maize leaves.** Mineral deficiency symptoms may vary in different species. In maize, phosphate-deficient plants have reddish purple margins, particularly in young leaves. Potassium-deficient maize plants exhibit "firing," or drying, along tips and margins of older leaves. Nitrogen deficiency is evident in a yellowing that starts at the tip and moves along the center (midrib) of older leaves.

Moderation is important because overdoses of many nutrients can be detrimental or toxic to plants. Too much nitrogen, for example, can lead to excessive vine growth in tomato plants at the expense of good fruit production.

Improving Plant Nutrition by Genetic Modification: Some Examples

In exploring plant nutrition so far, we have discussed how farmers use irrigation, fertilization, and other means to tailor the soil to fit the needs of a crop. An opposite approach involves tailoring the plant by genetic engineering to better fit the soil. Here we highlight a few examples of how genetic engineering is improving plant nutrition and fertilizer usage.

Resistance to Aluminum Toxicity

As previously discussed, aluminum in acidic soils damages roots and greatly reduces crop yields. The major mechanism of aluminum resistance is the secretion of organic acids (such as malic acid and citric acid) by roots. These acids bind to free aluminum ions and lower aluminum levels in the soil. Luis Herrera-Estrella and colleagues, at the Research and Advanced Studies Center in Mexico, altered tobacco and papaya plants by introducing a citrate synthase gene from a bacterium into the plants' genomes. The resulting overproduction of citric acid increased aluminum resistance in these two crops.

Flood Tolerance

Waterlogged soil not only deprives roots of oxygen but also can injure plants as ethanol and other toxic products of alcoholic fermentation by soil microbes accumulate. In Asian countries, flooding during the monsoon season often destroys rice crops. Although most varieties of rice die after being submerged for a week, some types can survive weeks of flooding. A gene called *Submergence 1A-1* (*Sub1A-1*) is the main source of submergence tolerance in flood-resistant rice. Sub1A-1 proteins regulate the expression of genes that are normally activated under anaerobic conditions, such as those that code for alcohol dehydrogenase, an enzyme that breaks down ethanol. The heightened expression of *Sub1A-1* in flooding-intolerant varieties of rice increased the alcohol dehydrogenase levels of the plants and conferred tolerance to submergence.

Smart Plants

Agricultural researchers are developing ways to maintain crop yields while reducing fertilizer use. One approach is to genetically engineer "smart" plants that signal when a nutrient deficiency is imminent—but *before* damage has occurred. One type of smart plant takes advantage of a promoter (a DNA sequence that indicates where the transcription of a gene starts) that more readily binds RNA polymerase (the transcription enzyme) when the phosphorus content of the plant's tissues begins to decline. This promoter is linked to a "reporter" gene that leads to production of a light blue pigment in the leaf cells **(Figure 37.8)**. When leaves of these smart plants develop a blue tinge, the farmer knows it is time to add phosphate-containing fertilizer.

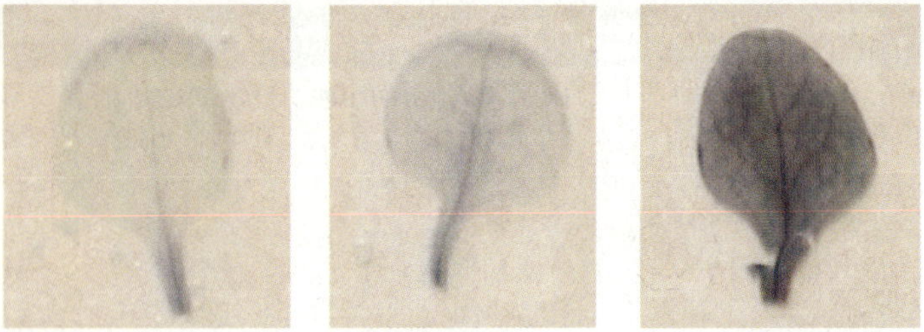

▲ **Figure 37.8 Deficiency warnings from "smart" plants.** Some plants have been genetically modified to signal an impending nutrient deficiency before irreparable damage occurs. For example, after laboratory treatments, the research plant *Arabidopsis* develops a blue color in response to an imminent phosphate deficiency.

So far, you have learned that soil, to support vigorous plant growth, must have an adequate supply of mineral nutrients, sufficient aeration, good water-holding capacity, low salinity, and a pH near neutrality. It must also be free of toxic concentrations of minerals and other chemicals. These physical and chemical features of soil, however, are just half the story. To understand soil fully, we must also consider its living components.

CONCEPT CHECK 37.2

1. Explain how Table 37.1 supports Stephen Hales's hypothesis.
2. Are some essential elements more important than others? Explain.
3. **WHAT IF?** The element silicon (Si) is absorbed by plants and increases the quality and yield of agricultural crops. Would this be sufficient evidence to consider it an essential plant nutrient?

For suggested answers, see Appendix A.

CONCEPT 37.3

Plant nutrition often involves relationships with other organisms

To this point, we have portrayed plants as exploiters of soil resources. But plants and soil have a two-way relationship. Dead plants provide much of the energy needed by soil-dwelling microorganisms, while secretions from living roots support a wide variety of microbes in the near-root environment. Here we'll focus on some mutualistic, or mutually beneficial, relationships between plants and soil bacteria or fungi. Then we'll look at some unusual plants that form nonmutualistic relationships with other plants or, in a few cases, with animals.

Soil Bacteria and Plant Nutrition

Some beneficial bacteria are found predominantly in the **rhizosphere**, the soil layer that is bound to the plant's roots. Others are decomposers, deriving nutrition from decaying organic material (humus) in the topsoil. Yet another class of important nitrogen-providing bacteria grow inside roots.

Rhizobacteria

Rhizobacteria are soil bacteria with especially large populations in the rhizosphere. Different soils vary greatly in the types and number of rhizobacteria they harbor. Microbial activity within a plant's rhizosphere is 10 to 100 times higher than in unbound soil because the roots secrete nutrients such as sugars, amino acids, and organic acids. Up to 20% of a plant's photosynthetic production fuels the organisms in this miniature ecosystem. As a result of diverse plant-microbe interactions, the composition of this microbial population often differs greatly from the surrounding soil and the rhizospheres of other plant species. Each rhizosphere contains a unique and complex cocktail of root secretions and microbial products.

Some rhizobacteria, known as *plant-growth-promoting rhizobacteria,* enhance plant growth by a variety of mechanisms. Some produce chemicals that stimulate plant growth. Others produce antibiotics that protect roots from disease. Still others absorb toxic metals or make nutrients more available to roots. Inoculation of seeds with plant-growth-promoting rhizobacteria can increase crop yield and reduce the need for fertilizers and pesticides. How do the bacteria benefit by interacting with plants? Root secretions supply most of the energy in the rhizosphere, so bacterial adaptations that help a plant thrive and secrete nutrients also help the bacteria.

Bacteria in the Nitrogen Cycle

Plants also have mutualistic relationships with several groups of bacteria that help make nitrogen more available. From a global perspective, no mineral nutrient is more limiting to plant growth than nitrogen, which is required in large amounts as a component of proteins and nucleic acids. The **nitrogen cycle**, discussed in Chapter 55, describes transformations of nitrogen and nitrogenous compounds in nature. Here we focus on processes leading directly to nitrogen assimilation by plants.

Unlike other soil minerals, ammonium ions (NH_4^+) and nitrate ions (NO_3^-) are not derived from the weathering of rocks. Although lightning produces small amounts of NO_3^- that get carried to the soil in rain, most soil nitrogen comes from the activity of bacteria **(Figure 37.9)**. *Ammonifying bacteria,* which are usually decomposers living in humus-rich soil, release ammonia (NH_3) by breaking down proteins and other organic compounds in humus. *Nitrogen-fixing bacteria* convert gaseous nitrogen (N_2) into NH_3, in a process we'll discuss shortly. In either case, the NH_3 produced picks up another H^+ in the soil solution to form NH_4^+, which plants can absorb. However, plants acquire nitrogen mainly in the form of NO_3^-. Soil NO_3^- is largely formed by a two-step process called *nitrification,* which consists of the oxidation of NH_3 to nitrite (NO_2^-), followed by oxidation of nitrite to nitrate (NO_3^-). Different types of *nitrifying bacteria* mediate each step. After the roots absorb NO_3^-, a plant enzyme reduces it back to NH_4^+, which other enzymes incorporate into amino acids and other organic compounds. Most plant species export nitrogen from roots to shoots via the xylem as NO_3^- or organic compounds synthesized in the roots. Some soil nitrogen is lost, particularly in anaerobic soils, when denitrifying bacteria convert NO_3^- to N_2, which diffuses into the atmosphere.

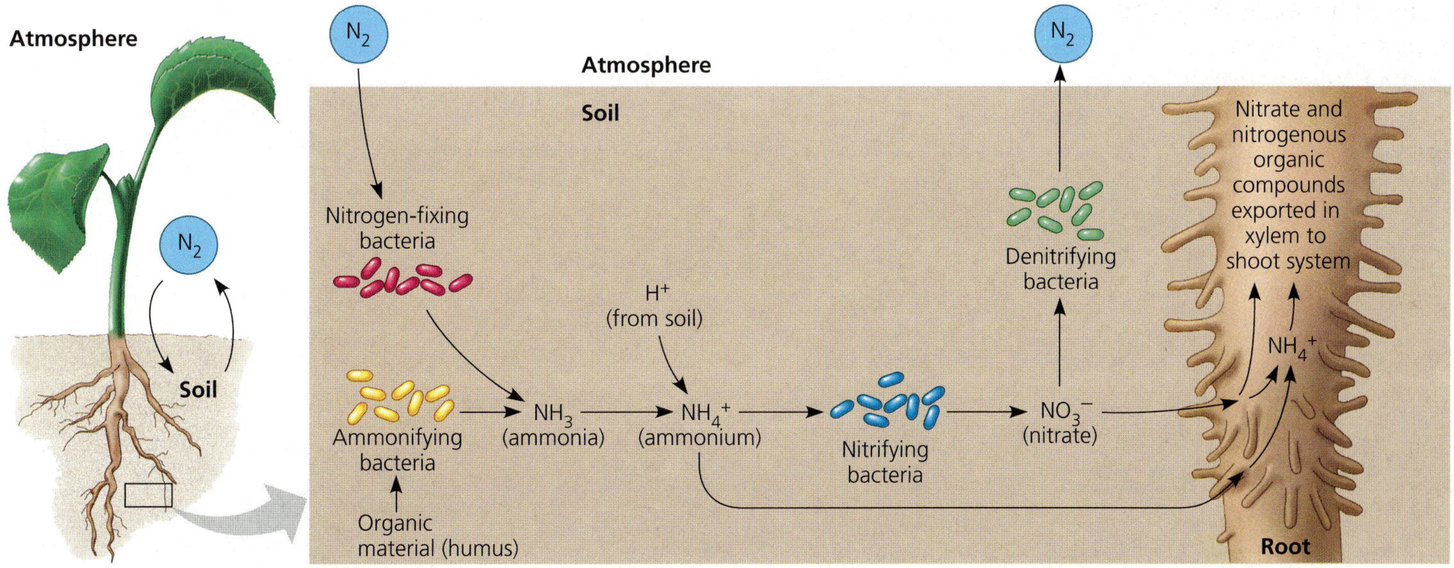

▲ **Figure 37.9 The roles of soil bacteria in the nitrogen nutrition of plants.** Ammonium is made available to plants by two types of soil bacteria: those that fix atmospheric N_2 (nitrogen-fixing bacteria) and those that decompose organic material (ammonifying bacteria). Although plants absorb some ammonium from the soil, they absorb mainly nitrate, which is produced from ammonium by nitrifying bacteria. Plants reduce nitrate back to ammonium before incorporating the nitrogen into organic compounds.

Nitrogen-Fixing Bacteria: A Closer Look

Although Earth's atmosphere is 79% nitrogen, plants cannot use free gaseous nitrogen (N_2) because there is a triple bond between the two nitrogen atoms, making the molecule almost inert. For atmospheric N_2 to be of use to plants, it must be reduced to NH_3 by a process called **nitrogen fixation**. All N_2-fixing organisms are prokaryotes, and some that carry out this process are free living (see Figure 37.9). In the particular case of N_2 fixation by the bacterium *Rhizobium*, the bacteria form an intimate association with the roots of legume plants (such as peas, soybeans, alfalfa, and clover) and markedly alter root structure. Although *Rhizobium* bacteria can be free living in the soil, they cannot fix N_2 in their free state, nor can legume roots fix N_2 without the bacteria.

The conversion of N_2 to NH_3 is a complicated, multistep process, but the reactants and products in nitrogen fixation can be summarized as follows:

$$N_2 + 8\,e^- + 8\,H^+ + 16\,ATP \rightarrow 2\,NH_3 + H_2 + 16\,ADP + 16\,Ⓟ_i$$

The enzyme complex nitrogenase catalyzes the entire reaction sequence, which reduces N_2 to NH_3 by adding electrons and H^+. Because the process of nitrogen fixation requires eight ATP molecules for each NH_3 synthesized, nitrogen-fixing bacteria require a rich supply of carbohydrates from decaying material, root secretions, or (in the case of *Rhizobium*) the vascular tissue of roots.

The specialized mutualism between *Rhizobium* bacteria and legume roots involves dramatic changes in root structure. Along a legume's roots are swellings called **nodules** composed of plant cells that have been "infected" by *Rhizobium* ("root living") bacteria **(Figure 37.10a)**. Inside the nodule, *Rhizobium* bacteria assume a form called **bacteroids**, which are contained within vesicles formed in the root cell **(Figure 37.10b)**. Legume-*Rhizobium* relationships generate more usable nitrogen for plants than all industrial fertilizers used today, and the mutualism provides the right amount of nitrogen at the right time at virtually no cost to the farmer. In addition to supplying the legume with nitrogen, this nitrogen fixation significantly reduces spending on fertilizers for subsequent crops.

The location of the bacteroids inside living, nonphotosynthetic cells is conducive to nitrogen fixation, which requires an anaerobic environment. Lignified external layers of root nodules also limit gas exchange. Some root nodules appear reddish because of a molecule called leghemoglobin (*leg-* for "legume"), an iron-containing protein that binds reversibly to oxygen (it is similar to the hemoglobin in human red blood cells). This protein is an oxygen "buffer," reducing the concentration of free oxygen and thereby providing an anaerobic environment for nitrogen fixation while regulating the oxygen supply for the intense cellular respiration required to produce ATP for nitrogen fixation.

Each legume species is associated with a particular strain of *Rhizobium*. **Figure 37.11** describes how a root nodule develops after bacteria enter through an "infection thread." The symbiotic relationship between a legume and nitrogen-fixing bacteria is mutualistic in that the bacteria supply the host plant with fixed nitrogen while the plant provides the bacteria with carbohydrates and other organic compounds. The root nodules use most of the ammonium produced to make amino

(a) Pea plant root. The bumps on this pea plant root are nodules containing *Rhizobium* bacteria. The bacteria fix nitrogen and obtain photosynthetic products supplied by the plant.

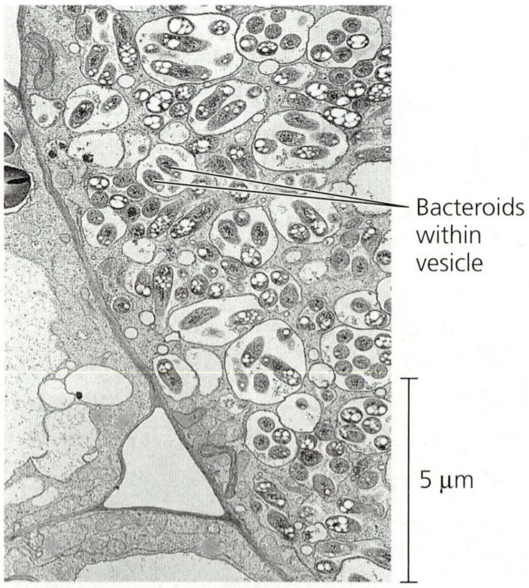

(b) Bacteroids in a soybean root nodule. In this TEM, a cell from a root nodule of soybean is filled with bacteroids in vesicles. The cells on the left are uninfected.

◄ **Figure 37.10 Root nodules on legumes.** The coordinated activities of the legume and the *Rhizobium* bacteria depend on a chemical dialogue between the mutualistic partners.

? *How is the relationship between legume plants and* Rhizobium *bacteria mutualistic?*

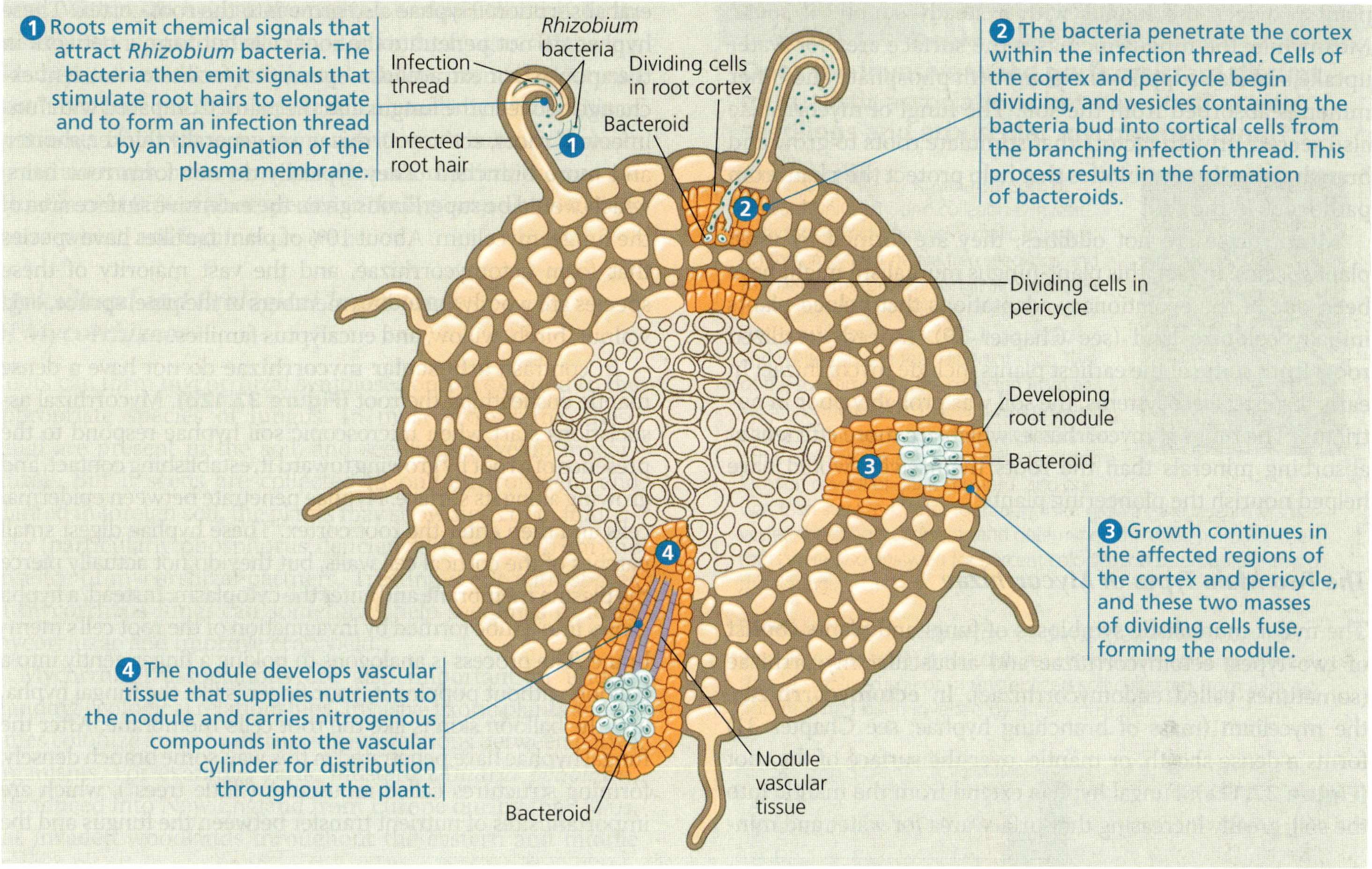

▲ **Figure 37.11 Development of a soybean root nodule.**

? *What plant tissue systems are modified by nodulation?*

acids, which are then transported up to the shoot through the xylem.

How does a legume species recognize a certain strain of *Rhizobium* among the many bacterial strains in the soil? And how does an encounter with that specific *Rhizobium* strain lead to development of a nodule? These two questions have led researchers to uncover a chemical dialogue between the bacteria and the root. Each partner responds to chemical signals from the other by expressing certain genes whose products contribute to nodule formation. By understanding the molecular biology underlying the formation of root nodules, researchers hope to learn how to induce *Rhizobium* uptake and nodule formation in crop plants that do not normally form such nitrogen-fixing mutualistic relationships.

Nitrogen Fixation and Agriculture

The agricultural benefits of mutualistic nitrogen fixation underlie most types of **crop rotation**. In this practice, a nonlegume such as maize is planted one year, and the following year alfalfa or some other legume is planted to restore the concentration of fixed nitrogen in the soil. To ensure that the legume encounters its specific *Rhizobium* strain, the seeds are soaked in a culture of the bacteria or dusted with bacterial spores before sowing. Instead of being harvested, the legume crop is often plowed under so that it will decompose as "green manure," reducing the need for manufactured fertilizers.

Many plant families besides legumes include species that benefit from mutualistic nitrogen fixation. For example, alder trees and certain tropical grasses host gram-positive bacteria of the actinomycete group (see Figure 27.18). Rice, a crop of great commercial importance, benefits indirectly from mutualistic nitrogen fixation. Rice farmers culture a free-floating aquatic fern, *Azolla*, which has mutualistic cyanobacteria that fix nitrogen. The growing rice eventually shades and kills the *Azolla*, and decomposition of this nitrogen-rich organic material increases the paddy's fertility.

Fungi and Plant Nutrition

Certain species of soil fungi also form mutualistic relationships with roots and play a major role in plant nutrition. **Mycorrhizae** ("fungus roots") are mutualistic associations of roots and fungi (see Figures 31.15 and 36.5). The host

▼ Figure 37.14

Exploring Unusual Nutritional Adaptations in Plants

Epiphytes

An **epiphyte** (from the Greek *epi*, upon, and *phyton*, plant) nourishes itself but grows on another plant, usually anchored to branches or trunks of living trees. Epiphytes absorb water and minerals from rain, mostly through leaves rather than roots. Some examples are staghorn ferns, bromeliads, and many orchids.

Staghorn fern, an epiphyte. This tropical fern (genus *Platycerium*) grows on large rocks, cliffs, and trees. It has two types of fronds: branched fronds resembling antlers and circular fronds that form a collar around the base of the fern.

Parasitic Plants

Unlike epiphytes, parasitic plants absorb sugars and minerals from their living hosts, although some parasitic species are photosynthetic.

Many species have roots that function as haustoria, nutrient-absorbing projections that enter the host plant.

Mistletoe, a photosynthetic parasite. Tacked above doorways during the holiday season, mistletoe (genus *Phoradendron*) lives in nature as a parasite on oaks and other trees.

Dodder, a nonphotosynthetic parasite. Dodder (genus *Cuscuta*), the orange "strings" on this pickleweed, draws its nutrients from the host. The cross section shows haustoria tapping the host's phloem (LM).

Indian pipe, a nonphotosynthetic parasite. Also called the ghost flower, this species (*Monotropa uniflora*) absorbs nutrients from the fungal hyphae of mycorrhizae of green plants.

Carnivorous Plants

Carnivorous plants are photosynthetic but obtain some nitrogen and minerals by killing and digesting insects and other small animals.

Carnivorous plants live in acid bogs and other habitats where soils are poor in nitrogen and other minerals. Various insect traps consist of modified leaves, usually equipped with glands that secrete digestive enzymes. Fortunately for animals, such turnabouts are rare!

Venus flytrap. Triggered by electrical impulses from sensory hairs, two leaf lobes close in half a second. Despite its common name, *Dionaea muscipula* usually catches ants and grasshoppers.

Pitcher plants. *Nepenthes*, *Sarracenia*, and other genera have water-filled funnels. The insects drown and are digested by enzymes.

Sundews. Sundews (genus *Drosera*) exude a sticky fluid that glitters like dew. Insects get stuck to the leaf hairs, which enfold the prey.

Chapter 37 Review

MEDIA Go to the Study Area at **www.masteringbio.com** for BioFlix 3-D Animations, MP3 Tutors, Videos, Practice Tests, an eBook, and more.

SUMMARY OF KEY CONCEPTS

CONCEPT 37.1

Soil is a living, finite resource (pp. 785–789)

- **Soil Texture** Particles of various sizes derived from the breakdown of rock are found in soil. Soil particle size affects the availability of water, oxygen, and minerals in the soil.
- **Topsoil Composition** A soil's composition refers to its inorganic and organic components. Topsoil is a complex ecosystem teeming with bacteria, fungi, protists, animals, and the roots of plants.
- **Soil Conservation and Sustainable Agriculture** Some agricultural practices can deplete the mineral content of soil, tax water reserves, and promote erosion. The goal of soil conservation is to minimize this damage.

MEDIA

Activity How Plants Obtain Minerals from Soil
Investigation How Does Acid Precipitation Affect Mineral Deficiency?
GraphIt! Global Soil Degradation

CONCEPT 37.2

Plants require essential elements to complete their life cycle (pp. 789–792)

- **Macronutrients and Micronutrients** Macronutrients, elements required in relatively large amounts, include carbon, oxygen, hydrogen, nitrogen, and other major ingredients of organic compounds. Micronutrients, elements required in very small amounts, typically have catalytic functions as cofactors of enzymes.
- **Symptoms of Mineral Deficiency** Deficiency of a mobile nutrient usually affects older organs more than younger ones; the reverse is true for nutrients that are less mobile within a plant. Macronutrient deficiencies are most common, particularly deficiencies of nitrogen, phosphorus, and potassium.
- **Improving Plant Nutrition by Genetic Modification: Some Examples** Rather than tailoring the soil to match the plant, genetic engineers are tailoring the plant to match the soil.

CONCEPT 37.3

Plant nutrition often involves relationships with other organisms (pp. 792–798)

- **Soil Bacteria and Plant Nutrition** Many soil bacteria are decomposers, living on decaying organic material. Other soil bacteria, called rhizobacteria, derive their energy from the rhizosphere, a microbe-enriched ecosystem intimately associated with roots. Plant secretions support the energy needs of the rhizosphere. Some rhizobacteria produce antibiotics, whereas others make nutrients more available for plants. Most are free-living, but some live inside plants.

Plants satisfy most of their huge needs for nitrogen from the bacterial decomposition of humus and the fixation of gaseous nitrogen.

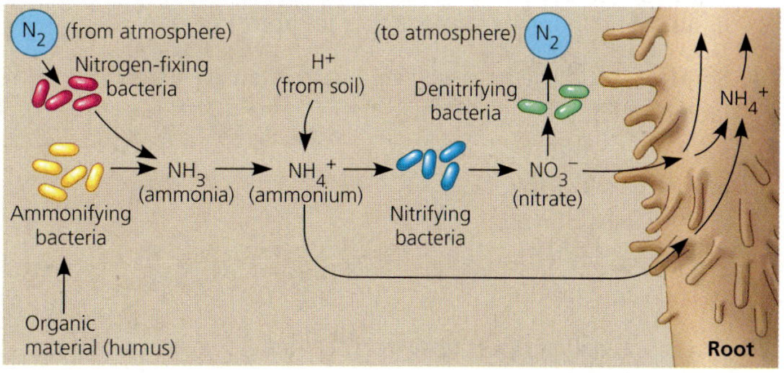

Nitrogen-fixing bacteria convert atmospheric N_2 to nitrogenous minerals that plants can absorb as a nitrogen source for organic synthesis. The most efficient mutualism between plants and nitrogen-fixing bacteria occurs in the nodules formed by *Rhizobium* bacteria growing in the roots of legumes. These bacteria obtain sugar from the plant and supply the plant with fixed nitrogen. In agriculture, legume crops are rotated with other crops to restore nitrogen to the soil.

- **Fungi and Plant Nutrition** Mycorrhizae are mutualistic associations of fungi and roots. The fungal hyphae of both ectomycorrhizae and arbuscular mycorrhizae absorb water and minerals, which they supply to their plant hosts.
- **Epiphytes, Parasitic Plants, and Carnivorous Plants** Epiphytes grow on the surfaces of other plants but acquire water and minerals from rain. Parasitic plants absorb nutrients from host plants. Carnivorous plants supplement their mineral nutrition by digesting animals.

MEDIA

Activity The Nitrogen Cycle

TESTING YOUR KNOWLEDGE

SELF-QUIZ

1. Most of the mass of organic material of a plant comes from
   a. water.
   b. carbon dioxide.
   c. soil minerals.
   d. atmospheric oxygen.
   e. nitrogen.

2. Micronutrients are needed in very small amounts because
   a. most of them are mobile in the plant.
   b. most serve mainly as cofactors of enzymes.
   c. most are supplied in large enough quantities in seeds.
   d. they play only a minor role in the growth and health of the plant.
   e. only the most actively growing regions of the plants require micronutrients.

3. The rhizosphere would best be described as
   a. legume root swellings that are involved in nitrogen fixation.
   b. the part of the topsoil that supplies carbohydrates to plants.
   c. soil that is bound to roots and differs from the surrounding soil in containing many more microbes.
   d. the spherical soil horizon in which roots typically grow.
   e. all of the living organisms that inhabit the soil.

4. Some of the problems associated with intensive irrigation include all but
   a. mineral runoff.
   b. overfertilization.
   c. land subsidence.
   d. aquifer depletion.
   e. soil salinization.

5. A mineral deficiency is likely to affect older leaves more than younger leaves if
   a. the mineral is a micronutrient.
   b. the mineral is very mobile within the plant.
   c. the mineral is required for chlorophyll synthesis.
   d. the mineral is a macronutrient.
   e. the older leaves are in direct sunlight.

6. Two groups of tomatoes were grown under laboratory conditions, one with humus added to the soil and one a control without humus. The leaves of the plants grown without humus were yellowish (less green) compared with those of the plants grown in humus-enriched soil. The best explanation for this difference is that
   a. the healthy plants used the food in the decomposing leaves of the humus for energy to make chlorophyll.
   b. the humus made the soil more loosely packed, so water penetrated more easily to the roots.
   c. the humus contained minerals such as magnesium and iron, needed for the synthesis of chlorophyll.
   d. the heat released by the decomposing leaves of the humus caused more rapid growth and chlorophyll synthesis.
   e. the healthy plants absorbed chlorophyll from the humus.

7. The specific relationship between a legume and its mutualistic *Rhizobium* strain probably depends on
   a. each legume having a chemical dialog with a fungus.
   b. each *Rhizobium* strain having a form of nitrogenase that works only in the appropriate legume host.
   c. each legume being found where the soil has only the *Rhizobium* specific to that legume.
   d. specific recognition between the chemical signals and signal receptors of the *Rhizobium* strain and legume species.
   e. destruction of all incompatible *Rhizobium* strains by enzymes secreted from the legume's roots.

8. Mycorrhizae enhance plant nutrition mainly by
   a. absorbing water and minerals through the fungal hyphae.
   b. providing sugar to the root cells, which have no chloroplasts of their own.
   c. converting atmospheric nitrogen to ammonia.
   d. enabling the roots to parasitize neighboring plants.
   e. stimulating the development of root hairs.

9. We would expect the greatest difference in plant health between two groups of plants of the same species, one group with mycorrhizae and one group without mycorrhizae, in an environment
   a. where nitrogen-fixing bacteria are abundant.
   b. that has soil with poor drainage.
   c. that has hot summers and cold winters.
   d. in which the soil is relatively deficient in mineral nutrients.
   e. that is near a body of water, such as a pond or river.

10. Carnivorous adaptations of plants mainly compensate for soil that has a relatively low content of
   a. potassium.
   b. nitrogen.
   c. calcium.
   d. water.
   e. phosphate.

11. **DRAW IT** Draw a simple sketch of cation exchange, showing a root hair, a soil particle with anions, and a hydrogen ion displacing a mineral cation.

For Self-Quiz answers, see Appendix A.

MEDIA Visit the Study Area at **www.masteringbio.com** for a Practice Test.

EVOLUTION CONNECTION

12. Imagine taking the plant out of the picture in Figure 37.9. Write a paragraph explaining how soil bacteria could sustain the recycling of nitrogen *before* land plants evolved.

SCIENTIFIC INQUIRY

13. Acid precipitation has an abnormally high concentration of hydrogen ions (H^+). One effect of acid precipitation is to deplete the soil of nutrients such as calcium (Ca^{2+}), potassium (K^+), and magnesium (Mg^{2+}). Suggest a hypothesis to explain how acid precipitation washes these nutrients from the soil. How might you test your hypothesis?

SCIENCE, TECHNOLOGY, AND SOCIETY

14. About 10% of U.S. cropland is irrigated. Agriculture is by far the biggest user of water in arid western states, including Colorado, Arizona, and California. As the populations of these states grow, there is ongoing conflict between cities and farm regions over water. To ensure adequate water supplies for urban growth, cities are buying water rights from farmers. This is often the least expensive way to obtain more water, and it is possible for some farmers to make more money by selling water rights than by growing crops. Discuss the possible consequences of this trend. Is this the best way to allocate water? Why or why not?

38 Angiosperm Reproduction and Biotechnology

▲ **Figure 38.1 Why is this wasp trying to mate with this flower?**

KEY CONCEPTS

38.1 Flowers, double fertilization, and fruits are unique features of the angiosperm life cycle

38.2 Flowering plants reproduce sexually, asexually, or both

38.3 Humans modify crops by breeding and genetic engineering

OVERVIEW

Flowers of Deceit

Male wasps of the species *Campsoscolia ciliata* often attempt to copulate with the flowers of the Mediterranean orchid *Ophrys speculum* **(Figure 38.1)**. During this encounter, a sac of pollen becomes glued to the insect's body. Eventually frustrated, the wasp flies off and deposits the pollen onto another *Ophrys* flower that has become the object of his misplaced ardor. *Ophrys* flowers offer no reward such as nectar to the male wasps, only sexual frustration. So what makes the male wasps so enamored of this orchid? The traditional answer has been that the shape of the orchid's largest petal and the frill of orange bristles around it vaguely resemble the female wasp. These visual cues, however, are only part of the deception: *Ophrys* orchids also emit chemicals with a scent similar to that produced by sexually receptive female wasps.

This orchid and its wasp pollinators are one example of the amazing ways in which angiosperms (flowering plants) reproduce sexually with spatially distant members of their own species. Sex, however, is not their only means of reproduction. Many species also reproduce asexually, creating offspring that are genetically identical to the parent.

An unusual aspect of the orchid and wasp example is that the insect does not profit from interacting with the flower. In fact, by wasting time and energy trying to copulate with it, the wasp is probably rendered less fit. More typically, a plant lures an animal pollinator to its flowers not with offers of sex but with rewards of energy-rich nectar or pollen. Thus, both plant and pollinator benefit; that is, the symbiotic relationship is mutualistic. Participating in mutualistic relationships with other organisms is very common in the plant kingdom. In fact, in recent evolutionary times, some flowering plants have formed mutualistic relationships with an animal that not only disperses their seeds but also provides the plants with water and mineral nutrients and vigorously protects them from encroaching competitors, pathogens, and predators. In return for these favors, the animal typically gets to eat a fraction of the plants' seeds and fruits. The plant symbionts involved in these remarkable mutualistic interactions are called crops; the animal symbionts are called humans.

Since the origins of crop domestication over 10,000 years ago, plant breeders have genetically manipulated the traits of a few hundred wild angiosperm species by artificial selection, transforming them into the crops we grow today. Genetic engineering has dramatically increased the variety of ways and the speed with which we can now modify plants.

In Chapters 29 and 30, we approached plant reproduction from an evolutionary perspective, tracing the descent of land plants from algal ancestors. Here, we'll explore the reproductive biology of flowering plants in much greater detail because they are the most important group of plants in most terrestrial ecosystems and in agriculture. After discussing the sexual and asexual reproduction of angiosperms, we'll examine the role of humans in genetically altering crop species, as well as the controversies surrounding modern plant biotechnology.

CONCEPT 38.1

Flowers, double fertilization, and fruits are unique features of the angiosperm life cycle

The life cycles of plants are characterized by an alternation of generations, in which multicellular haploid (n) and diploid ($2n$)

generations take turns producing each other (see Figures 29.5 and 30.10). The diploid plant, the sporophyte, produces haploid spores by meiosis. These spores divide by mitosis, giving rise to the multicellular gametophytes, the male and female haploid plants that produce gametes (sperm and eggs). **Fertilization**, the fusion of gametes, results in diploid zygotes, which divide by mitosis and form new sporophytes. In angiosperms, the sporophyte is the dominant generation: It is larger, more conspicuous, and longer-lived than the gametophyte. Over the course of seed plant evolution, gametophytes became reduced in size and wholly dependent on the sporophyte for nutrients. Angiosperm gametophytes are the most reduced of all plants, consisting of only a few cells. **Figure 38.2** reviews the angiosperm life cycle, which is shown in more detail in Figure 30.10. The key derived traits of the angiosperm life cycle can be remembered as the "three Fs"—*f*lowers, double *f*ertilization, and *f*ruits. Since angiosperms, along with gymnosperms, are seed plants, a knowledge of seed structure and function is also critical to understanding the angiosperm life cycle.

Flower Structure and Function

Flowers, the reproductive shoots of angiosperm sporophytes, are typically composed of four whorls of modified leaves called floral organs, which are separated by short internodes. Unlike vegetative shoots, flowers are determinate shoots. That is, they cease growing after the flower and fruit are formed.

Floral organs—**sepals, petals, stamens**, and **carpels**—are attached to a part of the stem called the **receptacle**. Stamens and carpels are reproductive organs, whereas sepals and petals are sterile. Sepals, which enclose and protect the floral bud before it opens, are usually green and more leaflike in appearance than the other floral organs. In many species, petals are more brightly colored than sepals and advertise the flower to insects and other pollinators.

A stamen consists of a stalk called the *filament* and a terminal structure called the **anther**; within the anther are chambers called microsporangia (pollen sacs) that produce pollen. A carpel has an **ovary** at its base and a long, slender neck called the **style**. At the top of the style is a generally sticky structure called the **stigma** that serves as a landing platform for pollen. Within the ovary are one or more **ovules**; the number of ovules depends on the species. The flower shown in Figure 38.2 has a single carpel, but many species have multiple carpels. In most species, two or more are fused into a single structure; the result is an ovary with two or more chambers, each containing one or more ovules. The term **pistil** is sometimes used to refer to a single carpel or a group of fused carpels.

Complete flowers have all four basic floral organs (see Figure 38.2a). Some species have **incomplete flowers**, lacking sepals, petals, stamens, or carpels. For example, most grass flowers lack petals. Some incomplete flowers are sterile, lacking functional stamens and carpels; others are *unisexual*, lacking either stamens or carpels. Flowers also vary in size, shape, color, odor, organ arrangement, and time of opening. Some are borne singly, while others are arranged in showy clusters called **inflorescences**. For example, a sunflower's central disk consists of hundreds of tiny incomplete flowers, and what look like petals are actually sterile flowers (see Figure 1.3). Much of floral diversity represents adaptation to specific pollinators.

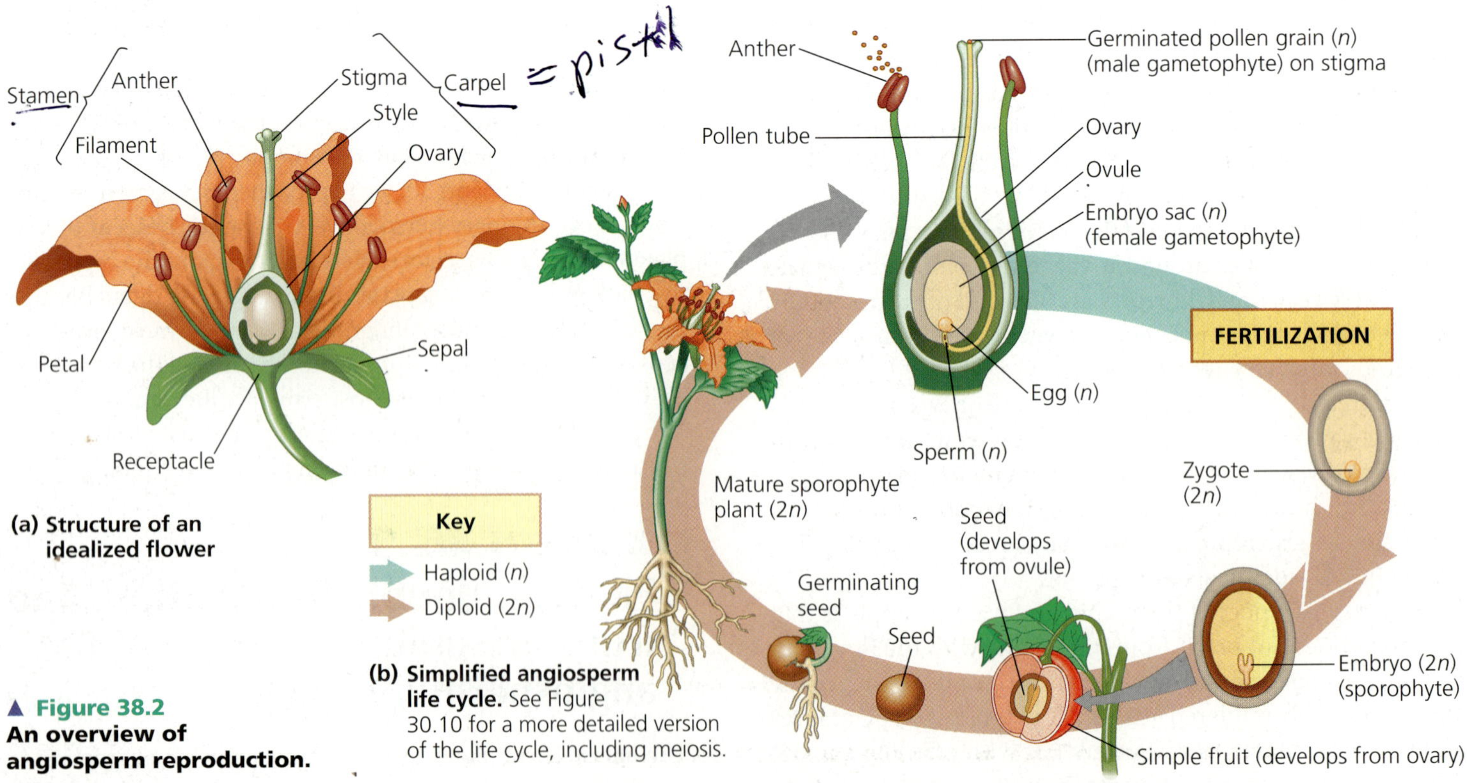

(a) Structure of an idealized flower

(b) Simplified angiosperm life cycle. See Figure 30.10 for a more detailed version of the life cycle, including meiosis.

▲ **Figure 38.2** **An overview of angiosperm reproduction.**

Development of Male Gametophytes in Pollen Grains

Each anther contains four microsporangia, also known as pollen sacs. Within the microsporangia are many diploid cells called microsporocytes, or microspore mother cells **(Figure 38.3a)**. Each microsporocyte undergoes meiosis, forming four haploid **microspores**, each of which eventually gives rise to a haploid male gametophyte. Each microspore then undergoes mitosis, producing a male gametophyte consisting of only two cells: the *generative cell* and the *tube cell*. Together, these two cells and the spore wall constitute a **pollen grain**. The spore wall, which consists of material produced by both the microspore and the anther, usually exhibits an elaborate pattern unique to the species. During maturation of the male gametophyte, the generative cell passes into the tube cell and the spore wall is completed. The tube cell now has a completely free-standing cell inside it. After the microsporangium breaks open and releases the pollen, a pollen grain may be transferred to a receptive surface of a stigma. There, the tube cell produces the **pollen tube**, a long cellular protuberance that delivers sperm to the female gametophyte. Pollen tubes can grow very quickly, at rates of 1 cm/hr or more. As a pollen tube elongates through the style, the generative cell usually divides and produces two sperm cells, which remain inside the tube cell (see Figure 30.10). The pollen tube grows through the style and into the ovary, where it releases the sperm cells in the vicinity of the female gametophyte.

Development of Female Gametophytes (Embryo Sacs)

Among angiosperm species, there are over 15 variations in the development of the female gametophyte, also known as an **embryo sac**. We'll focus on just one. The entire process occurs within the carpel's ovary, in a tissue within each ovule called the megasporangium. Two *integuments* (layers of protective sporophytic tissue that will develop into the seed coat) surround each megasporangium except at a gap called the *micropyle*. Female gametophyte development begins when one cell in the megasporangium of each ovule, the *megasporocyte* (or megaspore mother cell), enlarges and undergoes meiosis, producing four haploid **megaspores (Figure 38.3b)**. Only one megaspore survives; the others disintegrate.

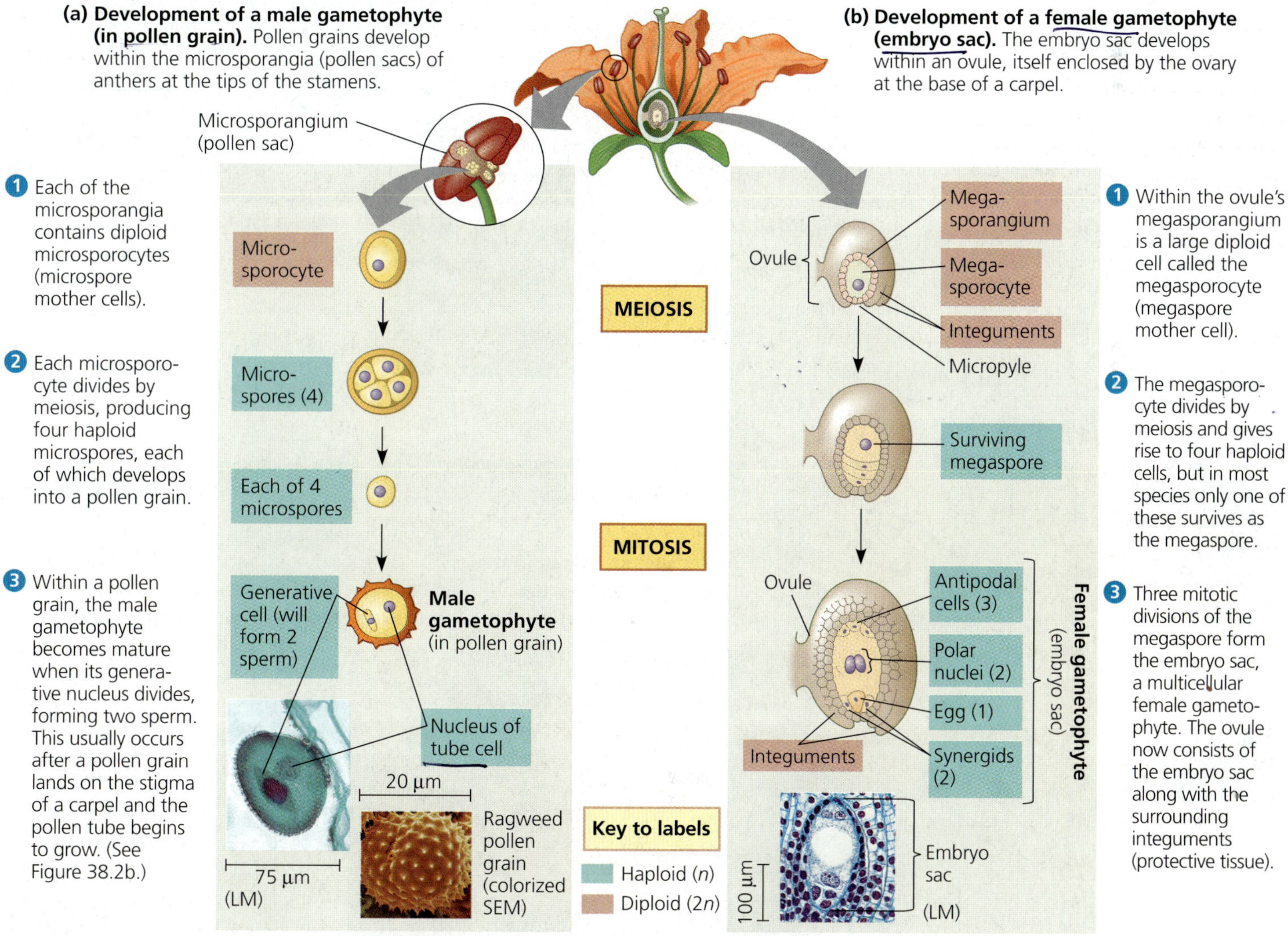

▲ **Figure 38.3 The development of male and female gametophytes in angiosperms.**

The surviving megaspore continues to grow, and its nucleus divides by mitosis three times without cytokinesis, resulting in one large cell with eight haploid nuclei. Membranes then partition this mass into a multicellular female gametophyte—the embryo sac. Three of the cells within the embryo sac are near the micropyle: the egg cell and two cells called synergids. The synergids flank the egg cell and help attract and guide the pollen tube to the embryo sac. At the opposite end of the embryo sac are three antipodal cells of unknown function. The remaining two nuclei, called polar nuclei, are not partitioned into separate cells but instead share the cytoplasm of the large central cell of the embryo sac. The ovule, which will eventually become a seed, now consists of the embryo sac and two surrounding integuments.

▼ **Figure 38.4**

Exploring Flower Pollination

Some angiosperm species can self-pollinate, but such species are limited to inbreeding in nature. Most angiosperm species rely on a living (biotic) or nonliving (abiotic) pollinating agent that can move pollen from the anther of a stamen of a flower on one plant to the stigma of a carpel of a flower on another plant. Approximately 80% of all angiosperm pollination is biotic, employing animal go-betweens. Among abiotically pollinated species, 98% rely on wind and 2% on water.

Abiotic Pollination by Wind

About 20% of all angiosperm species are wind-pollinated. Since their reproductive success does not depend on attracting pollinators, there was no selective pressure favoring colorful or scented flowers. Accordingly, the evolution of wind-pollinated species has resulted in flowers that are often small, green, and inconspicuous, and they produce neither nectar nor scent. Most temperate trees and grasses are wind-pollinated. The flowers of hazel (*Corylus avellana* shown here) and many other temperate, wind-pollinated trees appear in the early spring, when leaves are not present to interfere with pollen movement. The relative inefficiency of wind pollination is compensated for by production of copious amounts of pollen grains. Wind tunnel studies reveal that wind pollination is often more efficient than it appears because floral structures can create eddy currents that aid in pollen capture.

▲ Hazel staminate flowers (stamens only)

◀ Hazel carpellate flower (carpels only)

Pollination by Bees

About 65% of all flowering plants require insects for pollination; the percentage is even greater for major crops. Bees are the most important insect pollinators, and there is great concern in Europe and North America that honeybee populations have shrunk. Pollinating bees depend on nectar and pollen for food. Typically, bee-pollinated flowers have a delicate, sweet fragrance. Bees are attracted to bright colors, primarily yellow and blue. Red appears dull to them, but they can see ultraviolet radiation. Many bee-pollinated flowers, such as the common dandelion (*Taraxacum vulgare*), have markings called "nectar guides" that help insects locate the nectaries but are only visible to human eyes under ultraviolet light.

▲ Common dandelion under normal light

▶ Common dandelion under ultraviolet light

Pollination

In angiosperms, **pollination** is the transfer of pollen from an anther to a stigma. It is accomplished by wind, water, or animals **(Figure 38.4)**. In wind-pollinated species, including grasses and many trees, the release of enormous quantities of pollen compensates for the randomness of dispersal by the wind. At certain times of the year, the air is loaded with pollen grains, as anyone who is plagued with pollen allergies can attest. Some species of aquatic plants rely on water to disperse pollen. Most angiosperm species, however, depend on insects, birds, or other animal pollinators to transfer pollen directly from one flower to another flower. If pollination is successful, a pollen grain produces a pollen tube, which then grows down into the ovary via the style.

Pollination by Moths and Butterflies

Moths and butterflies detect odors, and the flowers they pollinate are often sweetly fragrant. Butterflies perceive many bright colors, but moth-pollinated flowers are usually white or yellow, which stand out in low light (as at night). A yucca plant (shown here) is typically pollinated by a single species of moth with appendages that pack pollen onto the stigma. The moth then deposits eggs directly into the ovary. The larvae eat some developing seeds, but this cost is outweighed by the benefit of an efficient and reliable pollinator. If a moth deposits too many eggs, the flower aborts and drops off, selecting against individuals that overexploit the plant.

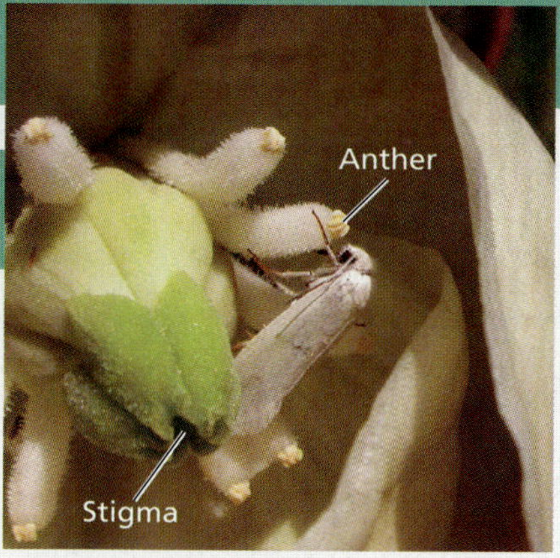

▲ Moth on yucca flower

Pollination by Flies

Fly-pollinated flowers are reddish and fleshy, with an odor like rotten meat. Blowflies visiting carrion flowers (*Stapelia* species) mistake the flower for a rotting corpse and lay their eggs on it. In the process, the blowflies become dusted with pollen that they carry to other flowers. When the eggs hatch, the larvae find no carrion to eat and therefore die.

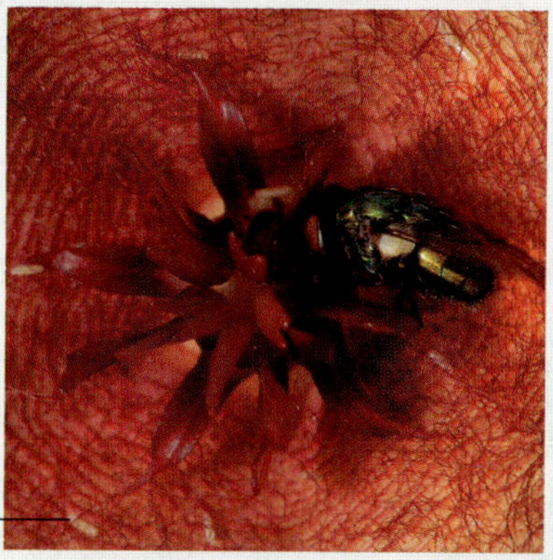
Fly egg

▲ Blowfly on carrion flower

Pollination by Birds

Bird-pollinated flowers, such as poro flowers, are usually large and bright red or yellow, but they have little odor. Since birds often do not have a well-developed sense of smell, there was no selective pressure favoring scent production. However, the flowers produce copious nectar that helps meet the high energy demands of the pollinating birds. Nectar is a sugary solution produced by nectaries at the base of many flowers. Nectar's primary function is to "reward" the pollinator. The petals of such flowers often fuse, forming a bent floral tube that fits the curved beak of the bird.

▲ Hummingbird drinking nectar of poro flower

? *What are the benefits and dangers to a plant of having a highly specific animal pollinator?*

Pollination by Bats

Bat-pollinated flowers, like moth-pollinated flowers, are light-colored and aromatic, attracting their nocturnal pollinators. The lesser long-nosed bat (*Leptonycteris curasoae yerbabuenae*) feeds on the nectar and pollen of agave and cactus flowers in the southwestern United States and Mexico. In feeding, the bats transfer pollen from plant to plant. Long-nosed bats are on the federal list of endangered species.

▲ Long-nosed bat feeding on cactus flower at night

Double Fertilization

At the time of pollination, the living pollen grain typically consists of only the tube cell and the generative cell. After a pollen grain lands on a suitable stigma, it absorbs water and germinates by producing a pollen tube, which grows between the cells of the style toward the ovary **(Figure 38.5)**. The nucleus of the generative cell divides by mitosis and forms two sperm. Directed by a chemical attractant produced by the two synergids flanking the egg, the tip of the pollen tube enters the ovule through the micropyle and discharges its two sperm near or within the female gametophyte (embryo sac). A gradient in gamma-aminobutyric acid (GABA), a chemical that functions as a neurotransmitter in animal cells, may be the critical signal for attracting the pollen tube **(Figure 38.6)**.

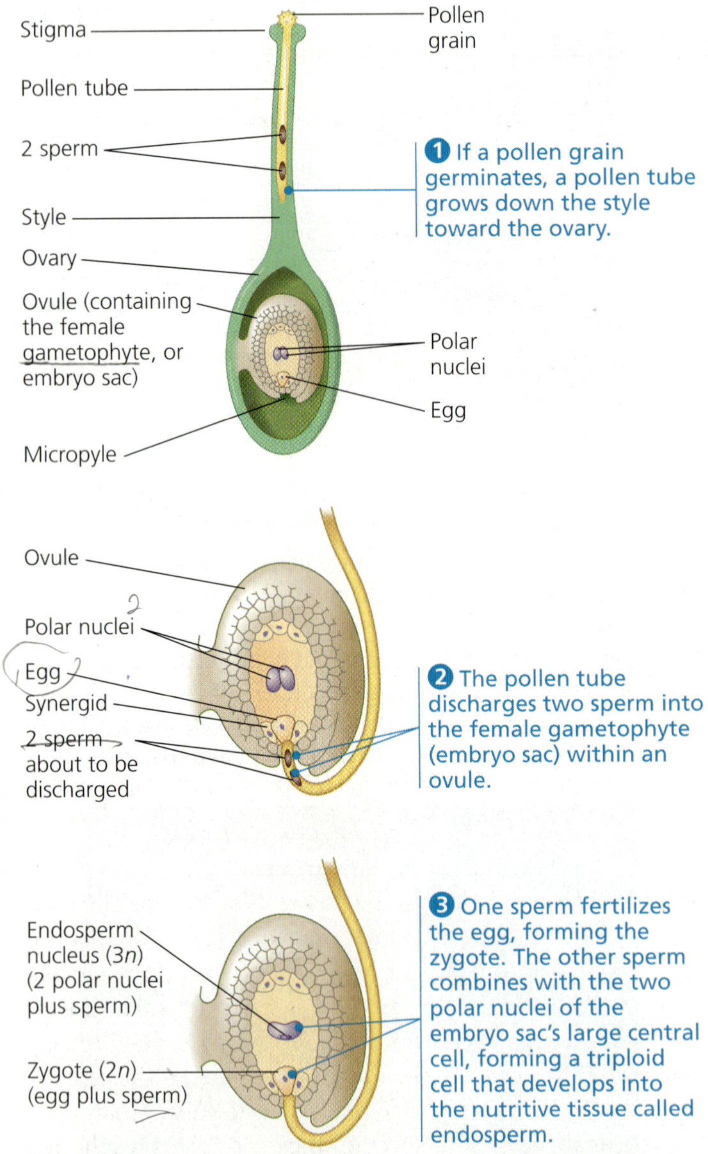

▲ **Figure 38.5 Growth of the pollen tube and double fertilization.**

Upon reaching the female gametophyte, one sperm fertilizes the egg, forming the zygote. The other sperm combines with the two polar nuclei, forming a triploid (3*n*) nucleus in the center of the large central cell of the female gametophyte. This large cell will give rise to the **endosperm**, a food-storing tissue of the seed. The union of two sperm cells with different nuclei of the female gametophyte is called **double fertilization**. Dou-

▼ **Figure 38.6 Inquiry**

Do GABA gradients play a role in directing pollen tubes to the eggs in *Arabidopsis*?

EXPERIMENT Researchers at the University of Chicago found an *Arabidopsis* mutant (carrying a mutation called *pop2*) that failed to produce viable seeds because pollen tubes couldn't seem to "find" the egg. In wild-type *Arabidopsis*, the pollen tubes (thick red lines in the LMs below) have little trouble finding the egg, but in *pop2* mutants none of the numerous pollen tubes turn down the seed stalk toward the micropyle and the egg. The *pop2* mutation was mapped, and the wild-type allele was identified as coding for a protein related to gamma-aminobutyric acid (GABA) transaminase, an enzyme that breaks down GABA. The researchers tested the hypothesis that GABA plays a role in pollen tube guidance by measuring GABA levels in the flowers of *pop2* and wild-type flowers and by examining the effects of GABA on pollen tube growth *in vitro*.

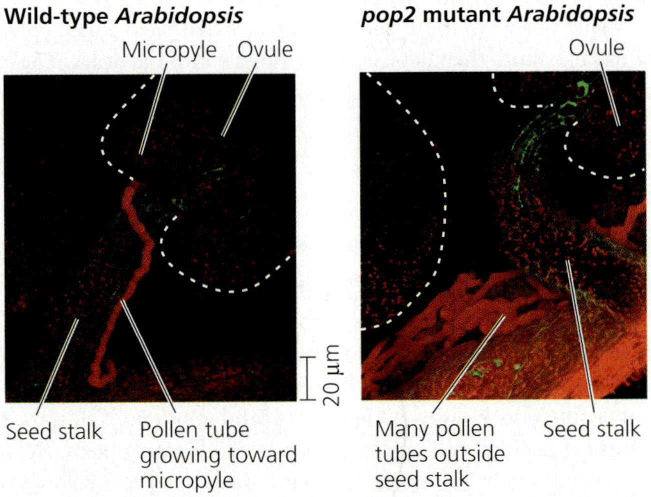

RESULTS GABA levels were 113-fold higher in *pop2* flowers than in wild-type flowers. Other intermediates in the GABA pathway were unaffected by *pop2*. Measurements of GABA content in wild-type flowers revealed a gradient from the stigma (low) to the ovary (high), but this gradient was disrupted in the *pop2* mutant. *In vitro,* GABA stimulated pollen tube growth, although vast excesses were inhibitory.

CONCLUSION A GABA gradient helps guide the pollen tube to the egg in *Arabidopsis* flowers.

SOURCE R. Palinivelu et al., Pollen tube growth and guidance is regulated by *POP2*, an *Arabidopsis* gene that controls GABA levels, *Cell* 114: 47–59 (2003).

WHAT IF? What phenotypic effects would occur in a mutant that could not synthesize any GABA in its flowers?

ble fertilization ensures that the endosperm will develop only in ovules where the egg has been fertilized, thereby preventing angiosperms from squandering nutrients.

The tissues surrounding the female gametophyte have prevented researchers from directly observing fertilization in plants grown under normal conditions. Scientists have, however, isolated sperm from germinated pollen grains and eggs from female gametophytes and have observed the merging of plant gametes *in vitro* (in an artificial environment). The first cellular event that takes place after gamete fusion is an increase in the levels of cytoplasmic calcium ions (Ca^{2+}) in the egg, as also occurs during animal gamete fusion (see Chapter 47). Another similarity to animals is the establishment of a block to *polyspermy,* the fertilization of an egg by multiple sperm. Thus, sperm cannot fuse with zygotes even *in vitro.* In maize (*Zea mays*), for example, this barrier to polyspermy is established as early as 45 seconds after the initial sperm fusion with the egg.

Seed Development, Form, and Function

After double fertilization, each ovule develops into a seed, and the ovary develops into a fruit enclosing the seed(s). As the embryo develops from the zygote, the seed stockpiles proteins, oils, and starch to varying degrees, depending on the species. This is why seeds are such major sugar sinks—sites of sugar use and storage (see Chapter 36). Initially, these nutrients are stored in the seed's endosperm, although later in seed development, the main nutrient-storage sites for most species are the swelling cotyledons, or seed leaves, of the embryo.

Endosperm Development

Endosperm usually develops before the embryo does. After double fertilization, the triploid nucleus of the ovule's central cell divides, forming a multinucleate "supercell" that has a milky consistency. This liquid mass, the endosperm, becomes multicellular when cytokinesis partitions the cytoplasm by forming membranes between the nuclei. Eventually, these "naked" cells produce cell walls, and the endosperm becomes solid. Coconut "milk" and "meat" are examples of liquid and solid endosperm, respectively. The white fluffy part of popcorn is also solid endosperm.

In grains and most other species of monocots, as well as many eudicots, the endosperm stores nutrients that can be used by the seedling after germination. In other eudicot seeds (including those of beans), the food reserves of the endosperm are completely exported to the cotyledons before the seed completes its development; consequently, the mature seed lacks endosperm.

Embryo Development

The first mitotic division of the zygote splits the fertilized egg into a basal cell and a terminal cell **(Figure 38.7)**. The terminal cell eventually gives rise to most of the embryo. The basal cell continues to divide, producing a thread of cells called the *suspensor,* which anchors the embryo to the parent plant. The suspensor helps in transferring nutrients to the embryo from the parent plant and, in some species of plants, from the endosperm. As the suspensor elongates, it pushes the embryo deeper into the nutritive and protective tissues. Meanwhile, the terminal cell divides several times and forms a spherical proembryo (early embryo) attached to the suspensor. The cotyledons begin to form as bumps on the proembryo. A

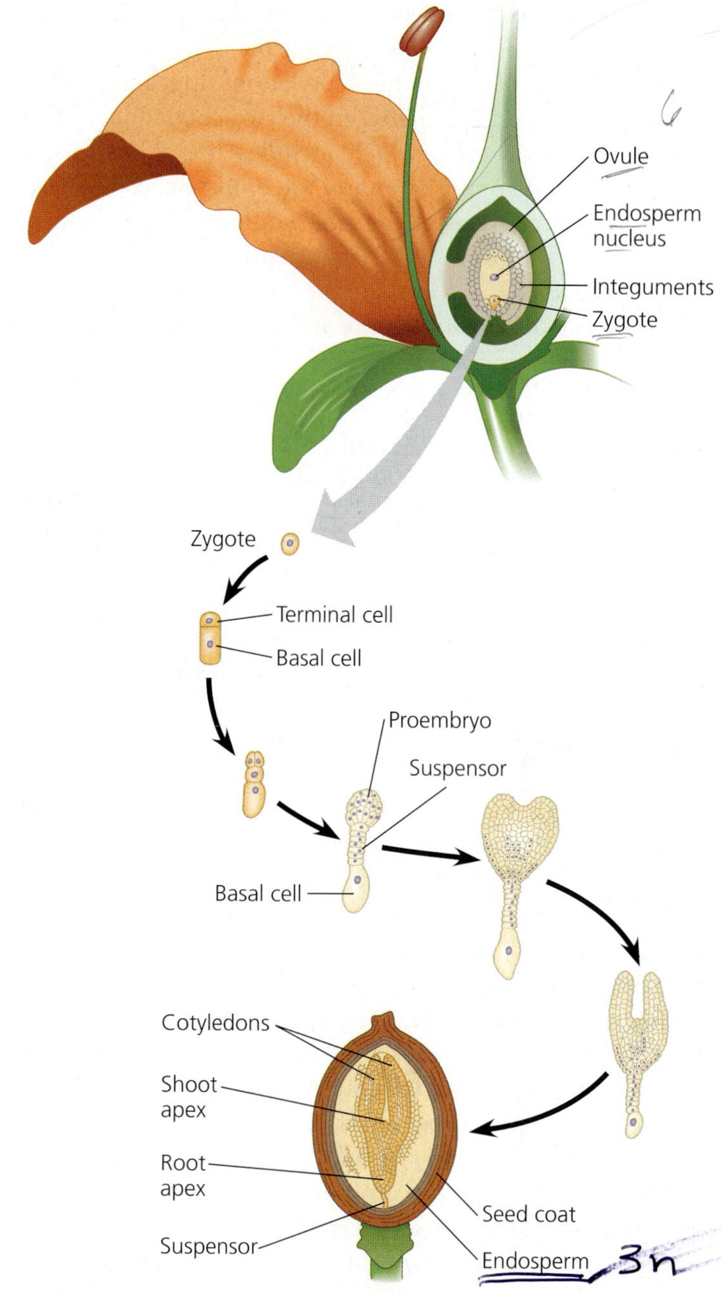

▲ **Figure 38.7 The development of a eudicot plant embryo.** By the time the ovule becomes a mature seed and the integuments harden and thicken into the seed coat, the zygote has given rise to an embryonic plant with rudimentary organs.

eudicot, with its two cotyledons, is heart-shaped at this stage. Only one cotyledon develops in monocots.

Soon after the rudimentary cotyledons appear, the embryo elongates. Cradled between the two cotyledons is the embryonic shoot apex, which includes the shoot apical meristem. At the opposite end of the embryo's axis, where the suspensor attaches, is the embryonic root apex, which includes the root apical meristem. After the seed germinates—indeed, for the rest of the plant's life—the apical meristems at the tips of shoots and roots sustain primary growth (see Figure 35.11).

Structure of the Mature Seed

During the last stages of its maturation, the seed dehydrates until its water content is only about 5–15% of its weight. The embryo, which is surrounded by a food supply (cotyledons, endosperm, or both), enters **dormancy**; that is, it stops growing and its metabolism nearly ceases. The embryo and its food supply are enclosed by a hard, protective **seed coat** formed from the integuments of the ovule. In some species, dormancy is imposed by the presence of an intact seed coat rather than by the embryo itself.

You can take a closer look at one type of eudicot seed by splitting open the seed of a common garden bean. The embryo consists of an elongate structure, the embryonic axis, attached to fleshy cotyledons **(Figure 38.8a)**. Below where the cotyledons are attached, the embryonic axis is called the **hypocotyl** (from the Greek *hypo*, under). The hypocotyl terminates in the **radicle**, or embryonic root. The portion of the embryonic axis above where the cotyledons are attached and below the first pair of miniature leaves is the **epicotyl** (from the Greek *epi*, on, over). The epicotyl, young leaves, and shoot apical meristem are collectively called the *plumule*.

The cotyledons of the common garden bean are packed with starch before the seed germinates because they absorbed carbohydrates from the endosperm when the seed was developing. However, the seeds of some eudicot species, such as castor beans (*Ricinus communis*), retain their food supply in the endosperm and have very thin cotyledons **(Figure 38.8b)**. The cotyledons absorb nutrients from the endosperm and transfer them to the rest of the embryo when the seed germinates.

The embryo of a monocot has a single cotyledon **(Figure 38.8c)**. Members of the grass family, including maize and wheat, have a specialized cotyledon called a *scutellum* (from the Latin *scutella*, small shield, a reference to its shape). The scutellum, which has a large surface area, is pressed against the endosperm, from which it absorbs nutrients during germination. The embryo of a grass seed is enclosed by two protective sheathes: a **coleoptile**, which covers the young shoot, and a **coleorhiza**, which covers the young root.

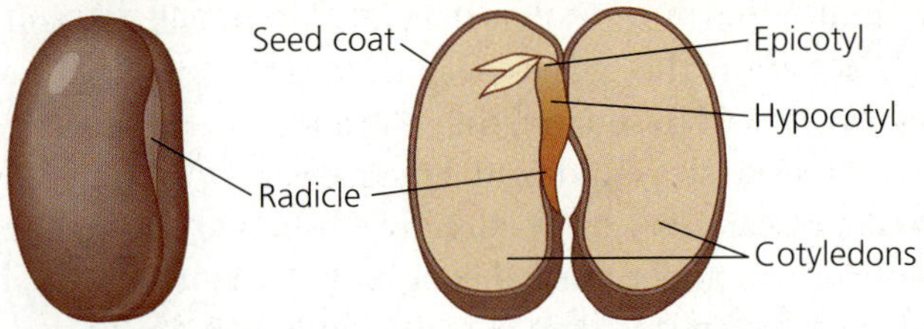

(a) Common garden bean, a eudicot with thick cotyledons. The fleshy cotyledons store food absorbed from the endosperm before the seed germinates.

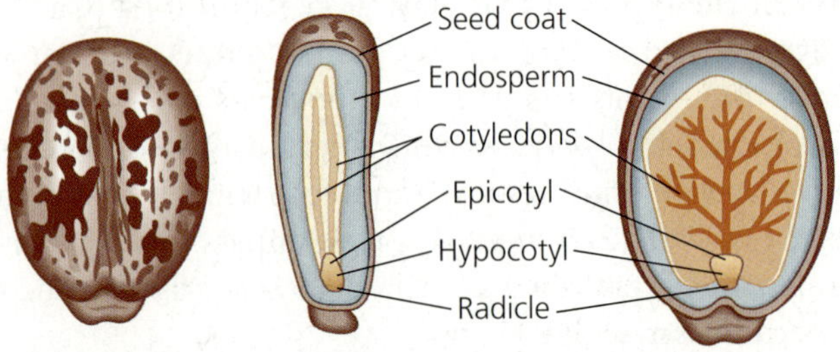

(b) Castor bean, a eudicot with thin cotyledons. The narrow, membranous cotyledons (shown in edge and flat views) absorb food from the endosperm when the seed germinates.

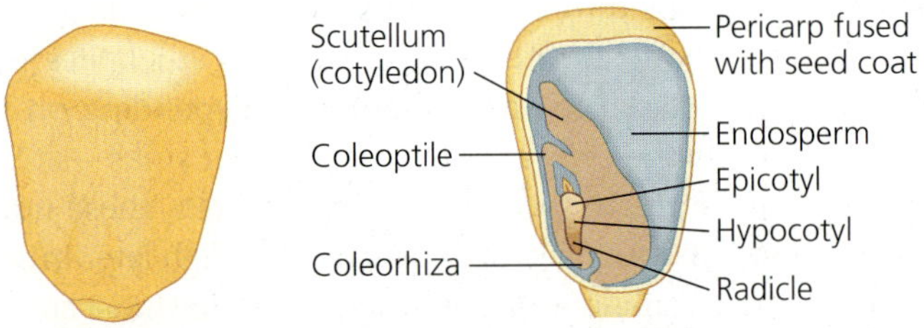

(c) Maize, a monocot. Like all monocots, maize has only one cotyledon. Maize and other grasses have a large cotyledon called a scutellum. The rudimentary shoot is sheathed in a structure called the coleoptile, and the coleorhiza covers the young root.

▲ **Figure 38.8 Seed structure.**

Seed Dormancy: An Adaptation for Tough Times

Dormancy (from the Latin word meaning "to sleep") is a condition of extremely low metabolic rate and suspension of growth and development. Environmental conditions required to break dormancy vary among species. Seeds of some species germinate as soon as they are in a suitable environment. Others remain dormant, even if sown in a favorable place, until an environmental cue causes them to break dormancy.

The requirement for specific cues to break seed dormancy increases the chances that germination will occur at a time and place most advantageous to the seedling. Seeds of many desert plants, for instance, germinate only after a substantial rainfall. If they were to germinate after a mild drizzle, the soil might soon become too dry to support the seedlings. Where natural fires are common, many seeds require intense heat or smoke to break dormancy; seedlings are therefore most abundant after fire has cleared away competing vegetation. Where winters are harsh, seeds may require extended exposure to cold. Seeds sown during summer or fall do not germinate until the following spring, ensuring a long growth season before the next winter. Some small seeds, such as those of some lettuce varieties, require light for germination and will break dormancy only if buried shallow enough for the seedlings to poke through the soil surface. Some seeds have coats that must be weakened by chemical attack as they pass through an animal's digestive tract and thus are usually carried a considerable distance before being defecated.

The length of time a dormant seed remains viable and capable of germinating varies from a few days to decades or even longer, depending on the plant species and environmental conditions. Most seeds are durable enough to last a year or two until conditions are favorable for germinating. Thus, the soil has a bank of ungerminated seeds that may have accumulated for several years. This is one reason vegetation reappears so rapidly after a fire, drought, flood, or other environmental disruption.

Seed Germination and Seedling Development

Germination depends on **imbibition**, the uptake of water due to the low water potential of the dry seed. Imbibing water causes the seed to expand and rupture its coat and also triggers metabolic changes in the embryo that enable it to resume growth. Following hydration, enzymes begin digesting the storage materials of the endosperm or cotyledons, and the nutrients are transferred to the growing regions of the embryo.

The first organ to emerge from the germinating seed is the radicle, the embryonic root. Next, the shoot tip must break through the soil surface. In garden beans and many other eudicots, a hook forms in the hypocotyl, and growth pushes the hook above ground **(Figure 38.9a)**. Stimulated by light, the hypocotyl straightens, raising the cotyledons and epicotyl. Thus, the delicate shoot tip and bulky cotyledons are pulled upward rather than being pushed tip-first through the abrasive soil. The epicotyl now spreads its first foliage leaves, which are true leaves, as distinguished from the cotyledons, or seed leaves. The foliage leaves expand, become green, and begin making food by photosynthesis. The cotyledons shrivel and fall away from the seedling, their food reserves having been exhausted by the germinating embryo.

Some monocots, such as maize and other grasses, use a different method for breaking ground when they germinate **(Figure 38.9b)**. The coleoptile, the sheath enclosing and protecting the embryonic shoot, pushes upward through the soil and into the air. The shoot tip then grows straight up through the tunnel provided by the tubular coleoptile and eventually breaks out through the coleoptile's tip.

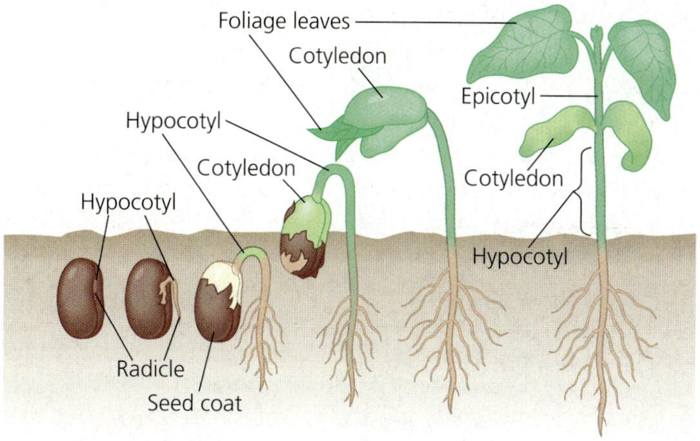

(a) Common garden bean. In common garden beans, straightening of a hook in the hypocotyl pulls the cotyledons from the soil.

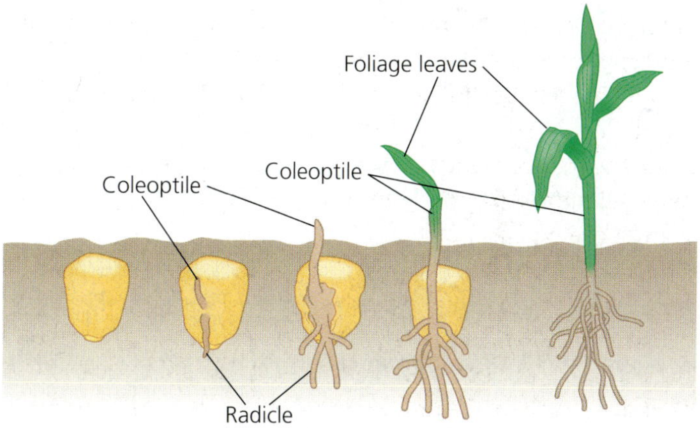

(b) Maize. In maize and other grasses, the shoot grows straight up through the tube of the coleoptile.

▲ **Figure 38.9 Two common types of seed germination.**

? *How do bean and maize seedlings protect their shoot systems as they push through the soil?*

Fruit Form and Function

While the seeds are developing from ovules, the ovary of the flower is developing into a **fruit**, which protects the enclosed seeds and, when mature, aids in their dispersal by wind or animals. Fertilization triggers hormonal changes that cause the ovary to begin its transformation into a fruit. If a flower has not been pollinated, fruit typically does not develop, and the entire flower usually withers and falls away.

During fruit development, the ovary wall becomes the pericarp, the thickened wall of the fruit. As the ovary grows, the other parts of the flower usually wither and are shed. For example, the pointed tip of a pea pod is the withered remains of the pea flower's stigma.

▲ **Figure 38.10 Developmental origin of fruits.**

Fruits are classified into several types, depending on their developmental origin. Most fruits are derived from a single carpel or several fused carpels and are called **simple fruits** **(Figure 38.10a)**. Some simple fruits are dry, such as a pea pod or a nut, whereas others are fleshy, such as a nectarine (see Figure 30.8). An **aggregate fruit** results from a single flower that has more than one separate carpel, each forming a small fruit **(Figure 38.10b)**. These "fruitlets" are clustered together on a single receptacle, as in a raspberry. A **multiple fruit** develops from an inflorescence, a group of flowers tightly clustered together. When the walls of the many ovaries start to thicken, they fuse together and become incorporated into one fruit, as in a pineapple **(Figure 38.10c)**.

In some angiosperms, other floral parts in addition to ovaries contribute to what we commonly call the fruit. Such fruits are called **accessory fruits**. In apple flowers, for example, the ovary is embedded in the receptacle, and the fleshy part of this simple fruit is derived mainly from the enlarged receptacle; only the apple core develops from the ovary **(Figure 38.10d)**. Another example is the strawberry, an aggregate fruit consisting of an enlarged receptacle embedded with tiny one-seeded fruits.

A fruit usually ripens about the same time that its seeds complete their development. Whereas the ripening of a dry fruit, such as a soybean pod, involves the aging and drying out of fruit tissues, the process in a fleshy fruit is more elaborate. Complex interactions of hormones result in an edible fruit that entices animals that help spread the seeds. The fruit's "pulp" becomes softer as a result of enzymes digesting components of the cell walls. The color usually changes from green to another color, such as red, orange, or yellow. The fruit becomes sweeter as organic acids or starch molecules are converted to sugar, which may reach a concentration of as much as 20% in a ripe fruit. **Figure 38.11** examines some mechanisms of fruit dispersal in more detail.

In this section, you have learned about the unique features of sexual reproduction in angiosperms—flowers, fruits, and double fertilization. As you will learn in the next section, many angiosperms also reproduce asexually.

CONCEPT CHECK 38.1

1. Distinguish between pollination and fertilization.
2. What is the advantage of seed dormancy?
3. Explain why the four types of fruits described in Figure 38.10 are not completely separate categories.
4. **WHAT IF?** If flowers had shorter styles, pollen tubes would more easily reach the embryo sac. Suggest an explanation for why very long styles have nevertheless evolved in most flowering plants.

For suggested answers, see Appendix A.

▼ **Figure 38.11**

Exploring Fruit and Seed Dispersal

A plant's life depends on finding fertile ground. But a seed that falls and sprouts beneath the parent plant stands little chance of competing successfully for nutrients. To prosper, seeds must be widely dispersed. Plants use biotic dispersal agents as well as abiotic agents such as water and wind.

Dispersal by Water

▶ Some buoyant seeds and fruits can survive months or years at sea. In coconut, the seed embryo and fleshy white "meat" (endosperm) are within a hard layer (endocarp) surrounded by a thick and buoyant fibrous husk.

Dispersal by Wind

▶ The winged seed of the tropical Asian climbing gourd *Alsomitra macrocarpa* glides through the air of the rain forest in wide circles when released.

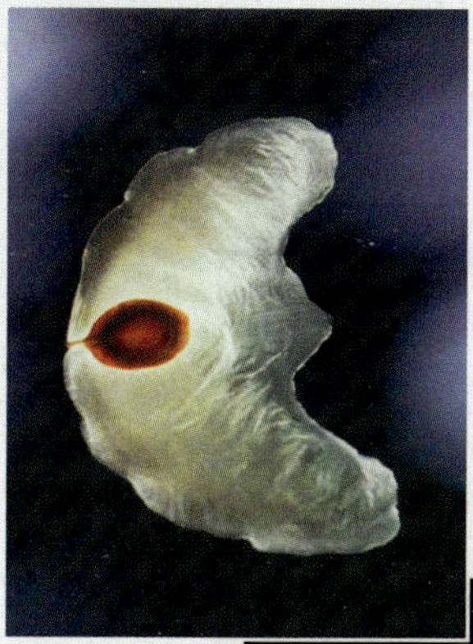

▶ Some seeds and fruits have "parachutes" with an umbrella-like crown of intricately branched hairs, often produced in puffy clusters, such as these dandelion seeds. The slightest gust carries them aloft.

▶ The winged fruits of maples spin like helicopter blades, slowing descent and increasing the chance of being carried farther by horizontal winds.

▶ Some tumbleweeds break off at the ground and tumble across the terrain, scattering their seeds.

Dispersal by Animals

▶ The sharp, tack-like spines on the fruits of puncture vine (*Tribulus terrestris*) can pierce bicycle tires and injure animals, including humans. When these painful "tacks" are removed and discarded, the seeds are dispersed.

◀ Seeds in edible fruits are often dispersed in feces, such as the black bear feces shown here. Such dispersal may carry seeds far from the parent plant.

▶ Ants are chemically attracted to seeds with food bodies rich in fatty acids, amino acids, and sugars. The ants carry the seed to their underground nest, where the food body (the lighter-colored portion shown here) is removed and fed to larvae. Due to the seed's size, unwieldy shape, or hard coating, the remainder is usually left intact in the nest, where it germinates.

▶ Some animals, such as squirrels, hoard seeds or fruits in underground caches. If the animal dies or forgets the cache's location, the seeds may germinate.

CONCEPT 38.2

Flowering plants reproduce sexually, asexually, or both

Imagine chopping off your finger and watching it develop into an exact copy of you. If this could actually occur, it would be an example of **asexual reproduction**, in which offspring are derived from a single parent without genetic recombination. The result would be a clone, an asexually produced, genetically identical organism. Asexual reproduction is common in angiosperms, as well as in other plants, and for some plant species it is the predominant mode of reproduction.

Mechanisms of Asexual Reproduction

Asexual reproduction in plants is typically an extension of the capacity for indeterminate growth. Plants, remember, have meristems, tissues of dividing, undifferentiated cells that can sustain or renew growth indefinitely. In addition, parenchyma cells throughout the plant can divide and differentiate into more specialized types of cells, enabling plants to regenerate lost parts. Detached vegetative fragments of some plants can develop into whole offspring; a severed stem, for instance, may develop adventitious roots and become a whole plant. Such **fragmentation**, the separation of a parent plant into parts that develop into whole plants, is one of the most common modes of asexual reproduction. The adventitious plantlets on *Kalanchoë* leaves exemplify an unusual type of fragmentation (see Figure 35.7). In another form of asexual reproduction in some species, the root system of a single parent gives rise to many adventitious shoots that become separate shoot systems. The result is a clone formed by asexual reproduction from one parent **(Figure 38.12)**. Such asexual propagation has produced the oldest of all known plant clones, a ring of creosote bushes in the Mojave Desert of California, estimated to be at least 12,000 years old.

▲ **Figure 38.12 Asexual reproduction in aspen trees.** Some aspen groves, such as those shown here, actually consist of thousands of trees descended by asexual reproduction. Each grove of trees derives from the root system of one parent. Notice that genetic differences between groves descended from different parents result in different timing for the development of fall color and the loss of leaves.

An entirely different mechanism of asexual reproduction has evolved in dandelions and some other plants. These plants can sometimes produce seeds without pollination or fertilization. This asexual production of seeds is called **apomixis** (from the Greek words meaning "away from the act of mixing") because there is no joining or, indeed, production of sperm and egg. Instead, a diploid cell in the ovule gives rise to the embryo, and the ovules mature into seeds, which in the dandelion are dispersed by windblown fruits. Thus, these plants clone themselves by an asexual process but have the advantage of seed dispersal, usually associated with sexual reproduction. Introducing apomixis into hybrid crops is a goal of great interest to plant breeders because apomixis would allow hybrid plants to pass on their desirable genomes intact to their offspring.

Advantages and Disadvantages of Asexual Versus Sexual Reproduction

An important advantage of asexual reproduction is that there is no need for a pollinator. This may be beneficial in situations where plants of the same species are sparsely distributed and unlikely to be visited by the same pollinator. Asexual reproduction also allows the plant to pass on all of its genetic legacy intact to its progeny. In contrast, when reproducing sexually, a plant passes on only half of its alleles. If a plant is superbly suited to a stable environment, asexual reproduction can be advantageous. A vigorous plant that is well adapted to its environment can clone many copies of itself, and if the environmental circumstances remain stable, these clones will also be genetically well adapted to the same environmental conditions under which the parent flourished.

Generally, the clones produced by asexual reproduction are not as frail as seedlings produced by sexual reproduction. The clones usually arise from mature vegetative fragments from the parent plant, which is why asexual reproduction in plants is also known as **vegetative reproduction**. In contrast, seed germination is a precarious stage in a plant's life. The tough seed gives rise to a fragile seedling that is exposed to predators, parasites, wind, and other hazards. In the wild, only a small fraction of seedlings endure long enough to become parents themselves. Production of enormous numbers of seeds compensates for the odds against individual survival and gives natural selection ample genetic variations to screen. However, this is a very expensive means of reproduction in terms of the resources consumed in flowering and fruiting.

Sexual reproduction generates variation in offspring and populations and can therefore be advantageous in unstable environments where evolving pathogens and fluctuating variables affect survival and reproductive success. In contrast, the genotypic uniformity of asexually produced plants puts them at great risk of local extinction if there is a catastrophic environmental change, such as a new strain of disease. Moreover, seeds (which are almost always produced sexually) facilitate the dispersal of offspring to more distant locations. Finally, seed dormancy allows growth to be suspended until environmental conditions become more favorable.

While the great advantage of sexual reproduction is that it increases the genetic diversity of offspring, some flowers, such as garden peas, self-fertilize. This process, called "selfing," can be a desirable attribute in some crop plants because it ensures that a seed will develop. In many angiosperm species, however, mechanisms have evolved that make it difficult or impossible for a flower to fertilize itself, as we'll discuss next.

Mechanisms That Prevent Self-Fertilization

The various mechanisms that prevent self-fertilization contribute to genetic variety by ensuring that sperm and eggs come from different parents. In the case of **dioecious** species, plants cannot self-fertilize because different individuals have either staminate flowers (lacking carpels) or carpellate flowers (lacking stamens) **(Figure 38.13a)**. Other plants have flowers with functional stamens and carpels that mature at different times or are structurally arranged in such a way that it is unlikely that an animal pollinator could transfer pollen from an anther to a stigma of the same flower **(Figure 38.13b)**. However, the most common anti-selfing mechanism in flowering plants is **self-incompatibility**, the ability of a plant to reject its own pollen and sometimes the pollen of closely related individuals. If a pollen grain lands on a stigma of a flower on the same plant, a biochemical block prevents the pollen from completing its development and fertilizing an egg.

(a) Some species, such as *Sagittaria latifolia* (common arrowhead), are dioecious, having plants that produce only staminate flowers (left) or carpellate flowers (right).

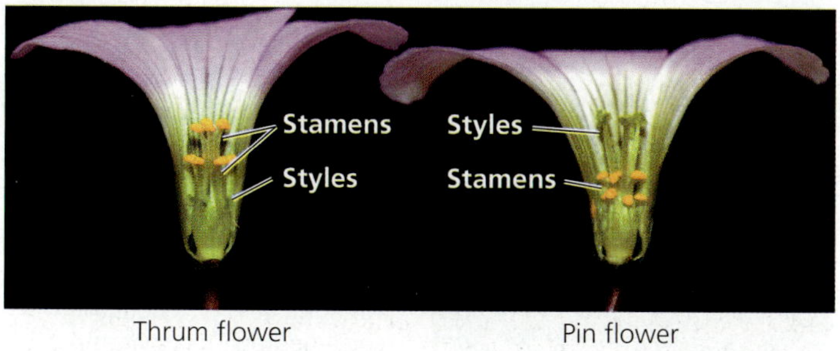

(b) Some species, such as *Oxalis alpina* (alpine woodsorrel), produce two types of flowers on different individuals: "thrums," which have short styles and long stamens, and "pins," which have long styles and short stamens. An insect foraging for nectar would collect pollen on different parts of its body; thrum pollen would be deposited on pin stigmas, and vice versa.

▲ **Figure 38.13 Some floral adaptations that prevent self-fertilization.**

Researchers are unraveling the molecular mechanisms involved in self-incompatibility. This plant response is analogous to the immune response of animals in that both are based on the ability to distinguish the cells of "self" from those of "nonself." The key difference is that the animal immune system rejects nonself, as when the system mounts a defense against a pathogen or rejects a transplanted organ (see Chapter 43). Self-incompatibility in plants, in contrast, is a rejection of self.

Recognition of "self" pollen is based on genes for self-incompatibility, called *S*-genes. In the gene pool of a plant population, there can be dozens of alleles of an *S*-gene. If a pollen grain has an allele that matches an allele of the stigma on which it lands, the pollen tube fails to grow. Depending on the species, self-recognition blocks pollen tube growth by one of two molecular mechanisms: gametophytic self-incompatibility or sporophytic self-incompatibility.

In gametophytic self-incompatibility, the *S*-allele in the pollen genome governs the blocking of fertilization. For example, an S_1 pollen grain from an S_1S_2 parental sporophyte will fail to fertilize eggs of an S_1S_2 flower but will fertilize an S_2S_3 flower. An S_2 pollen grain will not fertilize either flower. Self-recognition of this kind involves the enzymatic destruction of RNA within a pollen tube. RNA-hydrolyzing enzymes are produced by the style and enter the pollen tube. If the pollen tube is a "self" type, these enzymes destroy its RNA.

In sporophytic self-incompatibility, fertilization is blocked by *S*-allele gene products in tissues of the parental sporophyte that adhere to the pollen wall. For example, neither an S_1 nor S_2 pollen grain from an S_1S_2 parental sporophyte will fertilize eggs of an S_1S_2 flower or S_2S_3 flower, due to the S_1S_2 parental tissue attached to the pollen grain wall. Sporophytic incompatibility involves a signal transduction pathway in epidermal cells of the stigma that prevents germination of the pollen grain.

Some crops, such as peas, maize, and tomatoes, routinely self-pollinate with satisfactory results. However, plant breeders frequently hybridize different varieties of a crop plant to combine the best traits of the varieties and counter the loss of vigor that can often result from excessive inbreeding (see Chapter 14). To obtain hybrid seeds, plant breeders today must prevent self-fertilization either by laboriously removing the anthers from the parent plants that provide the seeds or by developing male-sterile plants. The latter option is increasingly common. Eventually, it may also be possible to impose self-incompatibility genetically on crop species that are normally self-compatible. Basic research on mechanisms of self-incompatibility may thus have agricultural applications.

Vegetative Propagation and Agriculture

With the objective of improving crops and ornamental plants, humans have devised various methods for asexual propagation of angiosperms. Most of these methods are based on the ability of plants to form adventitious roots or shoots.

Clones from Cuttings

Most houseplants, woody ornamentals, and orchard trees are asexually reproduced from plant fragments called cuttings. In some cases, shoot cuttings are used. At the cut end of the shoot, a mass of dividing, undifferentiated cells called a **callus** forms, and adventitious roots then develop from the callus. If the shoot fragment includes a node, then adventitious roots form without a callus stage. Some plants, including African violets, can be propagated from single leaves rather than stems. For other plants, cuttings are taken from specialized storage stems. For example, a potato can be cut up into several pieces, each with a vegetative bud, or "eye," that regenerates a whole plant.

Grafting

In a modification of vegetative reproduction from cuttings, a twig or bud from one plant can be grafted onto a plant of a closely related species or a different variety of the same species. Grafting makes it possible to combine the best qualities of different species or varieties into a single plant. The graft is usually done when the plant is young. The plant that provides the root system is called the **stock**; the twig grafted onto the stock is referred to as the **scion**. For example, scions from French varieties of vines that produce superior wine grapes are grafted onto root stocks of American varieties, which are more resistant to certain soil pathogens. The genes of the scion determine the quality of the fruit, so the quality is not diminished by the genetic makeup of the stock. In some cases of grafting, however, the stock can alter the characteristics of the shoot system that develops from the scion. For example, dwarf fruit trees, which allow for easier harvesting of the fruit, are made by grafting normal twigs onto stocks of dwarf varieties that retard the vegetative growth of the shoot system. Because seeds are produced by the part of the plant derived from the scion, they give rise to plants of the scion species when planted.

Test-Tube Cloning and Related Techniques

Plant biologists have adopted *in vitro* methods to create and clone novel plant varieties. It is possible to grow whole plants by culturing small pieces of tissue cut from the parent or even single parenchyma cells on an artificial medium containing nutrients and hormones **(Figure 38.14a)**. The cultured cells divide and form an undifferentiated callus. When the hormonal balance is manipulated in the culture medium, the callus can sprout shoots and roots with fully differentiated cells **(Figure 38.14b)**. The test-tube plantlets can then be transferred to soil, where they continue their growth. A single plant can be cloned into thousands of copies by dividing calluses as they grow. This method is now used for propagating orchids and also a wide variety of horticulturally important trees and shrubs.

(a) Just a few parenchyma cells from a carrot gave rise to this callus, a mass of undifferentiated cells.

(b) The callus differentiates into an entire plant, with leaves, stems, and roots.

▲ **Figure 38.14 Test-tube cloning of carrots.** (See also Figure 20.16.)

Plant tissue culture also facilitates genetic engineering. Most techniques for the introduction of foreign genes into plants require small pieces of plant tissue or single plant cells as the starting material. In plant biology, the term **transgenic** is used to describe genetically modified (GM) organisms that have been engineered to express a gene from another species. Test-tube culture makes it possible to regenerate GM plants from a single plant cell into which the foreign DNA has been incorporated. The techniques of genetic engineering are discussed in more detail in Chapter 20.

Some researchers couple a technique known as **protoplast fusion** with tissue culture methods to invent new plant varieties that can be cloned. Protoplasts are plant cells with their cell walls removed by treatment with enzymes (cellulases and pectinases) isolated from fungi **(Figure 38.15)**. Before protoplasts

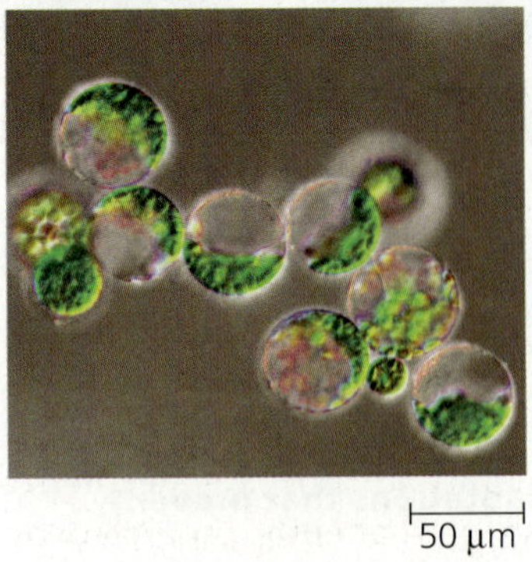

◀ **Figure 38.15 Protoplasts.** These wall-less plant cells are prepared by treating cells or tissues with wall-degrading enzymes isolated from certain types of fungi. Researchers can fuse protoplasts from different species to make hybrids and can also culture the hybrid cells to produce a new plant (LM).

are cultured, they can be screened for mutations that may improve the plant's agricultural value. In some cases, it is possible to fuse two protoplasts from different plant species that would otherwise be reproductively incompatible and then culture the hybrid protoplasts. Each protoplast can regenerate a wall and eventually form a hybrid plantlet. One success of this method is a hybrid between a potato and a wild relative called black nightshade. The nightshade is resistant to an herbicide commonly used to kill weeds. The hybrids are also resistant, making it possible to "weed" a field with the herbicide without killing potato plants.

The *in vitro* culturing of plant cells and tissues is fundamental to most types of plant biotechnology. The other basic process is the production of transgenic plants through various methods of genetic engineering. In the next section, we take a closer look at plant biotechnology.

CONCEPT CHECK 38.2

1. Explain how both asexual and sexual "strategies" contribute to the reproductive success of plants.
2. The seedless banana, the world's most popular fruit, is losing the battle against two fungal epidemics. Why do such epidemics generally pose a greater risk to asexually propagated crops?
3. Given the seeming disadvantages of selfing as a reproductive "strategy" in nature, it is surprising that about 20% of angiosperm species primarily rely on selfing. Although fairly common in nature, self-fertilization has been called an "evolutionary dead end." Suggest a reason why selfing might be selected for in nature and yet still be an evolutionary dead end.
4. **WHAT IF?** Potatoes (*Solanum tuberosum*) and tomatoes (*Solanum lycopersicum*) are fairly closely related species. If you managed to cross the two, would it be possible to have a hybrid that makes potato-like tubers and tomato-like fruits on the same plant?

For suggested answers, see Appendix A.

CONCEPT **38.3**

Humans modify crops by breeding and genetic engineering

Humans have intervened in the reproduction and genetic makeup of plants since the dawn of agriculture. Indeed, it is no exaggeration to say that maize is an unnatural monster created by humans. Left on its own in nature, maize would soon become extinct for the simple reason that it cannot spread its seeds. Maize kernels are not only permanently attached to the central axis (the "cob") but also permanently protected by tough, overlapping leaf sheathes (the "husk") **(Figure 38.16)**. These attributes arose by artificial selection by humans. (See Chapter 22 to review the basic concept of artificial selection.) Despite having no understanding of the scientific principles underlying plant breeding, Neolithic (late Stone Age) humans domesticated most of our crop species over a relatively short period about 10,000 years ago. But genetic modification began long before humans started altering crops by artificial selection. For example, the wheat species we rely on for much of our food evolved by the natural hybridization between different species of grasses. Such hybridization is common in plants and has long been exploited by breeders to introduce genetic variation for artificial selection and crop improvement.

▲ **Figure 38.16 Maize: a product of artificial selection.** Modern maize (bottom) was derived from teosinte (top). Teosinte kernels are tiny, and each row has a husk that must be removed to get at the kernel. The seeds are loose at maturity, allowing dispersal, which probably made harvesting difficult for early farmers. Neolithic farmers selected for larger cob and kernel size as well as the permanent attachment of seeds to the cob and the encasing of the entire cob by a tough husk.

Plant Breeding

The art of recognizing valuable traits is important in plant breeding. Breeders scrutinize their fields carefully and travel to other countries searching for domesticated varieties or wild relatives with desirable traits. Such traits occasionally arise spontaneously through mutation, but the natural rate of mutation is too slow and unreliable to produce all the mutations that breeders would like to study. Breeders sometimes hasten mutations by treating large batches of seeds or seedlings with X-rays, radiation, or chemicals.

When a desirable trait is identified in a wild species, the wild species is crossed with a domesticated variety. Generally, those progeny that have inherited the desirable trait from the wild parent have also inherited many traits that are not desirable for agriculture. The progeny that express the desired trait are again crossed with members of the domesticated species and their progeny examined for the desired trait. This process is continued until the progeny with the desired wild trait resemble the original domesticated parent in their other agricultural attributes.

While most breeders cross-pollinate plants of a single species, some breeding methods rely on hybridization between two distant species of the same genus. For example, a cross between two species of the genus *Musa* produced the familiar Cavendish banana. Distant crosses often result in the abortion of the hybrid seed during development. Very often the embryo begins to develop, but the endosperm does not. Hybrid embryos are sometimes rescued by surgically removing them from the ovule and culturing them *in vitro*.

Less commonly, distant hybridization is carried out between members of two different genera. A cross between wheat (*Triticum aestivum*) and rye (*Secale cereale*), for example, produced a novel grain called triticale, which contains a copy of all the chromosomes from both species. When triticale was first produced in the 1870s, it was considered little more than a botanical oddity. In the mid-1900s, however, plant breeders realized that triticale could potentially be developed into a crop with the yield and quality of bread wheat and with rye's tolerance of cold stress, moisture stress, and acidic soils. The early triticales were plagued with problems. These tall, late-maturing plants tended to fall over, were partially sterile, and were low yielding. They typically produced shriveled seeds that germinated poorly and were of poor quality for milling and baking. But through continued artificial selection, these problems were overcome, and triticale is now grown on more than 1 million hectares worldwide (1 ha = 2.47 acres). Some 600,000 ha are on the sandy, acidic soils of Poland, where the grain is used primarily for animal feed. It is nutritionally superior to rye, and the flour blends better with wheat in the baking of bread. Triticale grows well on *marginal land*, agriculturally inferior land that usually yields a poor return. If we are to feed the burgeoning world population in the 21st century, such marginal lands will have to become increasingly productive.

Plant Biotechnology and Genetic Engineering

Plant biotechnology has two meanings. In the general sense, it refers to innovations in the use of plants (or substances obtained from plants) to make products of use to humans—an endeavor that began in prehistory. In a more specific sense, biotechnology refers to the use of GM organisms in agriculture and industry. Indeed, in the last two decades, genetic engineering has become such a powerful force that the terms *genetic engineering* and *biotechnology* have become synonymous in the media.

Unlike traditional plant breeders, modern plant biotechnologists, using techniques of genetic engineering, are not limited to the transfer of genes between closely related species or varieties of the same species. For example, traditional breeding techniques could not be used to insert a desired gene from daffodil into rice because the many intermediate species between rice and daffodil and their common ancestor are extinct. In theory, if breeders had the intermediate species, over the course of several centuries they could probably introduce a daffodil gene into rice by traditional hybridization and breeding methods. With genetic engineering, however, such gene transfers can be done more quickly and without the need for intermediate species.

In the remainder of this chapter, we expand on discussions in Chapter 20 by examining the prospects and the controversies surrounding the use of genetically modified crops. The advocates of plant biotechnology believe that the genetic engineering of crop plants is the key to overcoming some of the most pressing problems of the 21st century, including world hunger and fossil fuel dependency.

Reducing World Hunger and Malnutrition

Currently, 800 million people on Earth suffer from nutritional deficiencies, with 40,000 dying each day of malnutrition, half of them children. There is much disagreement about the causes of such hunger. Some argue that food shortages arise from inequities in distribution and that the dire poor simply cannot afford food. Others regard food shortages as evidence that the world is overpopulated—that the human species has exceeded the carrying capacity of the planet (see Chapter 53). Whatever the social and demographic causes of malnutrition, increasing food production is a humane objective. Because land and water are the most limiting resources, the best option is to increase yields on the available land. Indeed, there is very little "extra" land that can be farmed, especially if the few remaining pockets of wilderness are to be preserved. Based on conservative estimates of population growth, farmers will have to produce 40% more grain per hectare to feed the human population in 2030. Plant biotechnology can help make these crop yields possible.

The commercial use of transgenic crops has been one of the most dramatic examples of rapid technology adoption in the history of agriculture. These crops include varieties and hybrids of cotton, maize, and potatoes that contain genes from the bacterium *Bacillus thuringiensis.* These "transgenes" encode a protein (*Bt* toxin) that is toxic to insect pests. The use of such plant varieties greatly reduces the need for chemical insecticides. The *Bt* toxin used in crops is produced in the plant as a harmless protoxin that only becomes toxic if activated by alkaline conditions, such as occur in the guts of insects. Because vertebrates have highly acidic stomachs, protoxin consumed by humans or farm animals is destroyed without becoming active.

Considerable progress has also been made in developing transgenic plants of cotton, maize, soybeans, sugar beets, and wheat that tolerate certain herbicides. The cultivation of these plants may reduce production costs by enabling farmers to "weed" crops with herbicides that do not damage the transgenic crop plants instead of by heavy tillage, which can cause soil erosion. Researchers are also engineering plants with enhanced resistance to disease. In one case, a transgenic papaya

◀ **Figure 38.17 Genetically modified papaya.** A ring spot virus has devastated papaya cultivation worldwide. However, a transgenic papaya variety rescued the industry in Hawaii. The genetically engineered papaya on the left is more resistant to ring spot virus than the nontransgenic papaya on the right.

▲ **Figure 38.18 "Golden Rice" and prevention of blindness associated with vitamin A deficiency.** Some 250,000 to 500,000 children go blind each year because of vitamin A deficiencies. The onset of blindness, indicated by a cloudy white spot in the eye, is a sign of severe underlying health problems: More than half of these children die within a year of becoming blind. The golden color and increased nutritional value of Golden Rice are attributable to its ability to make beta-carotene (provitamin A).

resistant to a ring spot virus was introduced into Hawaii, thereby saving its papaya industry **(Figure 38.17)**.

The nutritional quality of plants is also being improved. "Golden Rice," a transgenic variety carrying two daffodil genes, produces grain containing beta-carotene, a precursor of vitamin A. This rice was developed to prevent the blindness that occurs in those of the world's poor whose diet is deficient in vitamin A **(Figure 38.18)**. Recently, scientists have developed a new variety with much more beta-carotene than the original.

Reducing Fossil Fuel Dependency

Global sources of inexpensive fossil fuels, particularly oil, are rapidly being depleted. Moreover, climatologists attribute global warming mostly to the rampant burning of fossil fuels, such as coal and oil, and the resulting release of greenhouse gases. How can the world meet its energy demands in the 21st century in an economical and nonpolluting way? In certain localities, wind or solar power may become economically viable, but such alternative energy sources are unlikely to fill all the energy demands of the planet. Many scientists predict that the biomass from extremely fast-growing plants, such as switchgrass (*Panicum virgatum*) and poplar (*Populus trichocarpa*), could produce a sizable fraction of the world's energy needs in the not-too-distant future.

Under optimal conditions, poplars can grow 3–4 m each year, and switchgrass grows well under a wide variety of conditions found in regions where most types of agriculture are not economically viable. Scientists do not envisage the plant biomass being burned directly. Instead, the polymers in cell walls, such as cellulose and hemicellulose, which constitute the most abundant organic compounds on Earth, would be broken down into sugars by enzymatic reactions. These sugars, in turn, would be fermented into alcohol and distilled to yield **biofuels**.

The use of biofuels from plant biomass would reduce the net emission of the greenhouse gas CO_2. Whereas burning fossil fuels increases atmospheric CO_2 concentrations, biofuel crops reabsorb by photosynthesis the CO_2 emitted when biofuels are burned, creating a cycle that is carbon neutral. Plant breeders are trying to genetically engineer faster-growing poplar trees that produce more readily convertible biomass.

Biofuel technology does have its critics. For example, ecologist David Pimentel, of Cornell University, and geoengineer Tad Patzek, of UC Berkeley, have published estimates that more energy may be required to produce biofuels than would be produced from combustion of these products. Biofuel advocates, in turn, have questioned the accuracy of the data underlying these estimates.

The Debate over Plant Biotechnology

Much of the debate about GM organisms in agriculture is political, social, economic, or ethical and outside the scope of this book. But we *should* consider the biological concerns about GM crops. There are some biologists, particularly ecologists, who are concerned about the unknown risks associated with the release of GM organisms (GMOs) into the environment. The debate centers on the extent to which GMOs could harm human health or the environment. Those who want to proceed more slowly with agricultural biotechnology (or end it) are concerned about the unstoppable nature of the "experiment." If a drug trial produces unanticipated harmful results, the trial is stopped. But we may not be able to stop the "trial" of introducing novel organisms into the biosphere.

Chapter 20 introduced the key concerns regarding biotechnology in general. Here we take a closer look at some issues as they relate to plant biotechnology. Laboratory and field studies continue to examine the possible consequences of using GM crops, including the effects on human health and nontarget organisms and the potential for transgene escape.

Issues of Human Health

Many GMO opponents worry that genetic engineering may inadvertently transfer allergens, molecules to which some humans are allergic, from a species that produces an allergen to a plant used for food. However, biotechnologists are engaged in removing genes that encode allergenic proteins from soybeans and other crops. So far, there is no credible evidence that GM plants specifically designed for human consumption have adverse effects on human health. In fact, some GM foods are potentially healthier than non-GM foods. For example, *Bt* maize (the transgenic variety with the *Bt* toxin) contains 90% less of a cancer-causing and birth defect–causing mycotoxin than non-*Bt* maize. Called fumonisin, this toxin is highly resistant to degradation and has been found in alarmingly high concentrations in some batches of processed maize products, ranging from cornflakes to beer. Fumonisin is produced by a fungus (*Fusarium*) that infects insect-damaged maize. Because *Bt* maize generally suffers less insect damage than non-GM maize, it contains much less fumonisin.

Nevertheless, because of health concerns, GMO opponents lobby for the clear labeling of all foods containing products of GMOs. Some also argue for strict regulations against the mixing of GM foods with non-GM foods during food transport, storage, and processing. Biotechnology advocates, however, note that similar demands were not made when "transgenic" crops produced by traditional plant-breeding techniques were put on the market. There are, for example, some commercially grown varieties of wheat derived by traditional plant-breeding techniques that contain entire chromosomes (and thousands of genes) from rye.

Possible Effects on Nontarget Organisms

Many ecologists are concerned that the growing of GM crops might have unforeseen effects on nontarget organisms. One laboratory study indicated that the larvae (caterpillars) of monarch butterflies responded adversely and even died after eating milkweed leaves (their preferred food) heavily dusted with pollen from transgenic *Bt* maize. This study has since been discredited and affords a good example of the self-correcting nature of science. As it turns out, when the original researchers shook the male maize inflorescences onto the milkweed leaves in the laboratory, the filaments of stamens, opened microsporangia, and other floral parts also rained onto the leaves. Subsequent research found that it was these other floral parts, *not* the pollen, that contained *Bt* toxin in high concentrations. Unlike pollen, these floral parts would not be carried by the wind to neighboring milkweed plants when shed under natural field conditions. Only one *Bt* maize line, accounting for less than 2% of commercial *Bt* maize production (and now discontinued), produced pollen with high *Bt* toxin concentrations.

In considering the negative effects of *Bt* pollen on monarch butterflies, one must also weigh the effects of an alternative to the cultivation of *Bt* maize—the spraying of non-*Bt* maize with chemical pesticides. Recent studies have shown that such spraying was much more harmful to nearby monarch populations than was *Bt* maize production. Although the effects of *Bt* maize pollen on monarch butterfly larvae appear to be minor, the controversy has emphasized the need for accurate field testing of all GM crops and the importance of targeting gene expression to specific tissues to improve safety.

Addressing the Problem of Transgene Escape

Perhaps the most serious concern raised about GM crops is the possibility of the introduced genes escaping from a transgenic crop into related weeds through crop-to-weed hybridization. The fear is that the spontaneous hybridization between a crop engineered for herbicide resistance and a wild relative might give rise to a "superweed" that would have a selective advantage over other weeds in the wild and would be much more difficult to control in the field. Some crops *do* hybridize with weedy relatives, and crop-to-weed transgene escape is a possibility. Its likelihood depends on the ability of the crop and weed to hybridize and on how the transgenes affect the overall fitness of the hybrids. A desirable crop trait—a dwarf phenotype, for example—might be disadvantageous to a weed growing in the wild. In other instances, there are no weedy relatives nearby with which to hybridize; soybean, for example, has no wild relatives in the United States. However, canola, sorghum, and many other crops do hybridize readily with weeds.

Many different strategies are being pursued with the goal of preventing transgene escape. For example, if male sterility could be engineered into plants, these plants would still produce seeds and fruit if pollinated by nearby nontransgenic plants, but they would produce no viable pollen. A second approach involves genetically engineering apomixis into transgenic crops. When a seed is produced by apomixis, the embryo and endosperm develop without fertilization. The transfer of this trait to transgenic crops would therefore minimize the possibility of transgene escape via pollen because plants could be male-sterile without compromising seed or fruit production. A third approach is to engineer the transgene into the chloroplast DNA of the crop. Chloroplast DNA in many plant species is inherited strictly from the egg, so transgenes in the chloroplast cannot be transferred by pollen (see Chapter 15 to review maternal inheritance). A fourth approach for preventing transgene escape is to genetically engineer flowers that develop normally but fail to open. Consequently, self-pollination would occur, but pollen would be unlikely to escape from the flower. This solution would require modifications to flower design. Several floral genes have been identified that could be manipulated to this end.

The continuing debate about GMOs in agriculture exemplifies one of this textbook's recurring ideas: the relationship of science and technology to society. Technological advances almost always involve some risk of unintended outcomes. In plant biotechnology, zero risk is probably unattainable. Therefore, scientists and the public must assess on a case-by-case basis the possible benefits of transgenic products versus the risks that society is willing to take. The best scenario is for these discussions and decisions to be based on sound scientific information and rigorous testing rather than on reflexive fear or blind optimism.

CONCEPT CHECK 38.3

1. Compare traditional plant-breeding methods with genetic engineering.
2. Explain some benefits and risks of GM crops.
3. Why does *Bt* maize have less fumonisin than non-GM maize?
4. WHAT IF? In a few species, chloroplast genes are inherited only from sperm. How might this affect efforts to prevent transgene escape?

For suggested answers, see Appendix A.

Chapter 38 Review

MEDIA Go to the Study Area at **www.masteringbio.com** for BioFlix 3-D Animations, MP3 Tutors, Videos, Practice Tests, an eBook, and more.

SUMMARY OF KEY CONCEPTS

CONCEPT 38.1

Flowers, double fertilization, and fruits are unique features of the angiosperm life cycle (pp. 801–811)

- The sporophyte, the dominant generation, produces spores that develop within flowers into male gametophytes (in pollen grains) and female gametophytes (embryo sacs).
- **Flower Structure and Function** Flowers function in sexual reproduction. The four floral organs are sepals, petals, stamens, and carpels. Pollen develops from microspores within the microsporangia of anthers; female gametophytes develop from megaspores within ovules. Pollination, which precedes fertilization, is the placing of pollen on the stigma of a carpel.
- **Double Fertilization** The pollen tube discharges two sperm into the female gametophyte; one sperm fertilizes the egg, while the other combines with the polar nuclei, giving rise to food-storing endosperm.

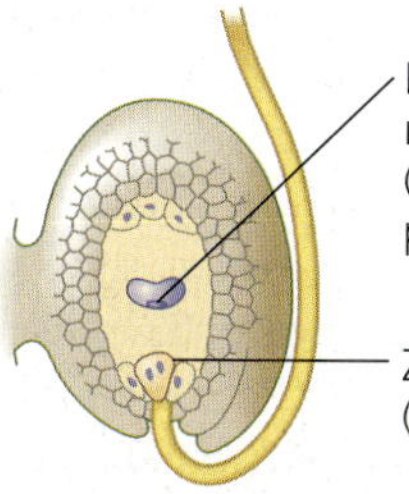

- **Seed Development, Form, and Function** The seed coat encloses the embryo along with a food supply stocked in either the endosperm or the cotyledons. Seed dormancy ensures that seeds germinate only when conditions for seedling survival are optimal. The breaking of dormancy often requires environmental cues, such as temperature or lighting changes.
- **Fruit Form and Function** The fruit protects the enclosed seeds and aids in wind dispersal or in the attraction of seed-dispersing animals.

MEDIA

MP3 Tutor From Flower to Fruit
Activity Angiosperm Life Cycle
Investigation What Tells Desert Seeds When to Germinate?
Activity Seed and Fruit Development

CONCEPT 38.2

Flowering plants reproduce sexually, asexually, or both (pp. 812–815)

- **Mechanisms of Asexual Reproduction** Modes of asexual reproduction include fragmentation and the production of adventitious shoots.
- **Advantages and Disadvantages of Asexual Versus Sexual Reproduction** Asexual reproduction enables successful clones to spread; sexual reproduction generates the genetic variation that makes evolutionary adaptation possible.
- **Mechanisms That Prevent Self-Fertilization** Some plants reject pollen that has an *S*-gene matching an allele in the stigma cells. Recognition of "self" pollen triggers a signal transduction pathway leading to a block in growth of a pollen tube.
- **Vegetative Propagation and Agriculture** Cloning plants from cuttings is an ancient practice. Plants can be cloned from single cells, which can be genetically manipulated before being allowed to develop into a plant.

CONCEPT 38.3

Humans modify crops by breeding and genetic engineering (pp. 815–819)

- **Plant Breeding** Interspecific hybridization of plants is common in nature and has been used by breeders, ancient and modern, to introduce new genes into crops. After two plants are successfully hybridized, plant breeders select those progeny that have the desired traits.
- **Plant Biotechnology and Genetic Engineering** In genetic engineering, genes from unrelated organisms are incorporated into plants. Genetically modified (GM) plants have the potential of increasing the quality and quantity of food worldwide and may also become increasingly important as biofuels.
- **The Debate over Plant Biotechnology** There are concerns about the unknown risks of releasing GM organisms into the environment, but the potential benefits of transgenic crops need to be considered.

MEDIA

Activity Making Decisions About DNA Technology: Golden Rice

TESTING YOUR KNOWLEDGE

SELF-QUIZ

1. A plant that has small, green petals is most likely to be
   a. bee-pollinated.
   b. bird-pollinated.
   c. bat-pollinated.
   d. wind-pollinated.
   e. moth-pollinated.

2. A seed develops from
   a. an ovum.
   b. a pollen grain.
   c. an ovule.
   d. an ovary.
   e. an embryo.

3. A fruit is
   a. a mature ovary.
   b. a mature ovule.
   c. a seed plus its integuments.
   d. a fused carpel.
   e. an enlarged embryo sac.

4. Double fertilization means that
   a. flowers must be pollinated twice to yield fruits and seeds.
   b. every egg must receive two sperm to produce an embryo.
   c. one sperm is needed to fertilize the egg, and a second sperm is needed to fertilize the polar nuclei.
   d. the egg of the embryo sac is diploid.
   e. every sperm has two nuclei.

5. Some dioecious species have the XY genotype for male and XX for female. After double fertilization, what would be the genotypes of the embryos and endosperm nuclei?
   a. embryo X and endosperm XX or embryo Y and endosperm XY
   b. embryo XX and endosperm XX or embryo XY and endosperm XY
   c. embryo XX and endosperm XXX or embryo XY and endosperm XYY
   d. embryo XX and endosperm XXX or embryo XY and endosperm XXY
   e. embryo XY and endosperm XXX or embryo XX and endosperm XXY

6. Which statement concerning grafting is correct?
   a. Stocks and scions refer to twigs of different species.
   b. Stocks come from vines, but scions come from trees.
   c. Stocks provide root systems for grafting.
   d. Grafting creates new species.
   e. Stocks and scions must come from unrelated species.

7. Plant biotechnologists use protoplast fusion mainly to
   a. culture plant cells *in vitro*.
   b. asexually propagate desirable plant varieties.
   c. introduce bacterial genes into a plant genome.
   d. study the early events following fertilization.
   e. produce new hybrid species.

8. The basal cell from the zygote's first division develops into
   a. the suspensor that anchors the embryo and transfers nutrients.
   b. the proembryo.
   c. the endosperm that nourishes the developing embryo.
   d. the root apex of the embryo.
   e. two cotyledons in eudicots, but one in monocots.

9. The development of *Bt* crops raises concerns because
   a. *Bt* crops have been shown to be toxic to humans.
   b. pollen from these crops is harmful to monarch butterfly larvae in the field.
   c. if genes for *Bt* toxin "escape" to related weed species, the hybrid weeds could have harmful ecological effects.
   d. *Bacillus thuringiensis* is a pathogen of humans.
   e. *Bt* toxin reduces the nutritional quality of crops.

10. "Golden Rice" is a transgenic variety that
    a. is resistant to various herbicides, making it practical to weed rice fields with those herbicides.
    b. is resistant to a virus that commonly attacks rice fields.
    c. includes bacterial genes that produce a toxin that reduces damage from insect pests.
    d. produces larger, golden grains that increase crop yields.
    e. contains daffodil genes that increase vitamin A content.

11. **DRAW IT** Draw and label the parts of a flower.

For Self-Quiz answers, see Appendix A.

MEDIA Visit the Study Area at **www.masteringbio.com** for a Practice Test.

EVOLUTION CONNECTION

12. With respect to sexual reproduction, some plant species are fully self-fertile, others are fully self-incompatible, and some exhibit a "mixed strategy" with partial self-incompatibility. These reproductive strategies differ in their implications for evolutionary potential. How, for example, might a self-incompatible species fare as a small founder population or remnant population in a severe population bottleneck (see Chapter 23), as compared with a self-fertile species?

SCIENTIFIC INQUIRY

13. Critics of GM foods have argued that foreign genes may disturb normal cellular functioning, causing unexpected and potentially harmful substances to appear inside cells. Toxic intermediary substances that normally occur in very small amounts may arise in larger amounts, or new substances may appear. The disruption may also lead to loss of substances that help maintain normal metabolism. If you were your nation's chief scientific advisor, how would you respond to these criticisms?

Biological Inquiry: A Workbook of Investigative Cases Explore GM crops further with the case "Corn Under Construction."

SCIENCE, TECHNOLOGY, AND SOCIETY

14. Humans have engaged in genetic manipulation for millennia, producing plant and animal varieties through selective breeding and hybridization processes that significantly modify the genomes of organisms. Why do you think modern genetic engineering, which often entails introducing or modifying only one or a few genes, has met with so much public opposition? Should some forms of genetic engineering be of greater concern than others? Explain.

39

Plant Responses to Internal and External Signals

▲ **Figure 39.1 Can flowers tell you the time of day?**

KEY CONCEPTS

- **39.1 Signal transduction pathways link signal reception to response**
- **39.2 Plant hormones help coordinate growth, development, and responses to stimuli**
- **39.3 Responses to light are critical for plant success**
- **39.4 Plants respond to a wide variety of stimuli other than light**
- **39.5 Plants respond to attacks by herbivores and pathogens**

OVERVIEW

Stimuli and a Stationary Life

Carolus Linnaeus, the father of taxonomy, was a keen naturalist and observer of plants. Linnaeus noted that certain plants opened and closed their flowers at particular times of the day, with these times varying from species to species. Therefore, one could deduce the approximate time of day according to which species had opened or closed its flowers. If the times of opening and closing were arranged in sequence, they could serve as a kind of floral clock, or *horologium florae,* as Linnaeus called it. **Figure 39.1** shows a modern simplified representation as a 12-hour clock face. Why does the timing vary? The time at which flowers open presumably reflects the time when their insect pollinators are most active, just one of many environmental factors that a plant must sense to compete successfully. Contrary to the common notion of plants as being almost inanimate, a plant's morphology and physiology are constantly tuned to its surroundings by complex interactions between environmental stimuli and internal signals.

This chapter focuses on how plants respond to external and internal cues. At the organismal level, plants and animals respond to environmental stimuli by very different means. Animals, being mobile, respond mainly by behavioral mechanisms, moving toward positive stimuli and away from negative stimuli. Being stationary, a plant generally responds to environmental cues by adjusting its individual pattern of growth and development. For this reason, plants of the same species vary in body form much more than do animals of the same species. Before a plant can initiate growth responses to environmental signals, it must first detect the change in its environment. At the cellular level, the processes by which plants perceive environmental changes are as complex as those used by animal cells and are often homologous to them.

CONCEPT 39.1

Signal transduction pathways link signal reception to response

All organisms receive specific signals and respond to them in ways that enhance survival and reproductive success. For example, bees, which have UV-sensitive photoreceptors in their eyes, can discern nectar-guiding patterns on flower petals—patterns that are completely invisible to humans (see Figure 38.4). Plants, too, have cellular receptors that they use to detect important changes in their internal or external environments, whether the change is an increase in the concentration of a growth hormone, an injury from a caterpillar munching on leaves, or a decrease in day length as winter approaches.

For a stimulus to elicit a response, an organism must have cells with an appropriate receptor, a molecule affected by the stimulus. For example, humans' inability to see UV-reflecting floral patterns is due to our eyes lacking UV photoreceptors. Upon receiving a stimulus, a receptor initiates a signal transduction pathway, a series of biochemical steps that couples reception to response (see Chapter 11 to review general concepts of signal transduction). Plants are sensitive to a wide range of stimuli, each initiating a specific signal transduction pathway.

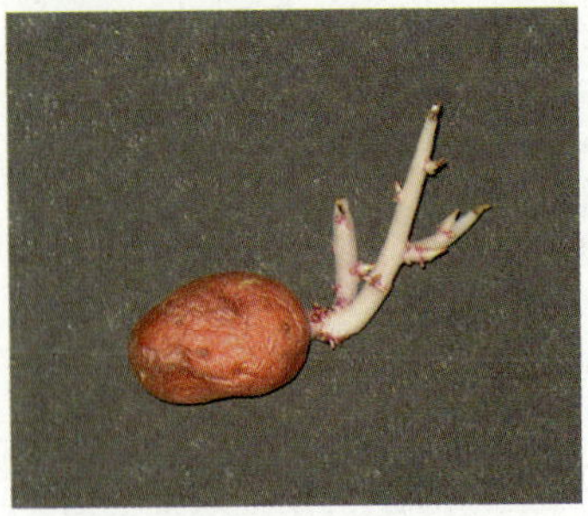

(a) Before exposure to light. A dark-grown potato has tall, spindly stems and nonexpanded leaves—morphological adaptations that enable the shoots to penetrate the soil. The roots are short, but there is little need for water absorption because little water is lost by the shoots.

(b) After a week's exposure to natural daylight. The potato plant begins to resemble a typical plant with broad green leaves, short sturdy stems, and long roots. This transformation begins with the reception of light by a specific pigment, phytochrome.

▲ **Figure 39.2 Light-induced de-etiolation (greening) of dark-grown potatoes.**

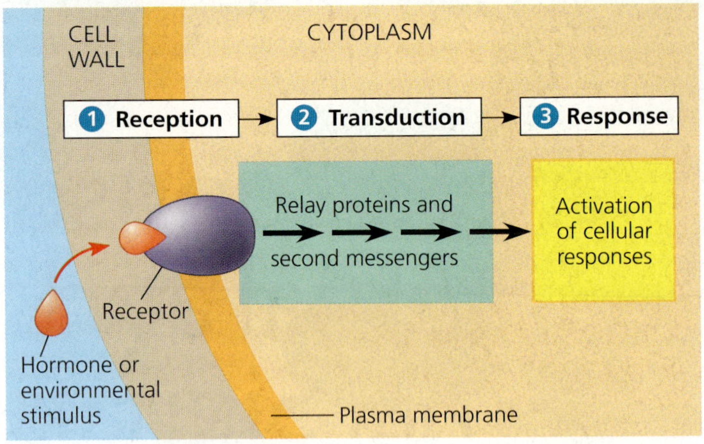

▲ **Figure 39.3 Review of a general model for signal transduction pathways.** As discussed in Chapter 11, a hormone or other kind of stimulus interacting with a specific receptor protein can trigger the sequential activation of relay proteins and also the production of second messengers that participate in the pathway. The signal is passed along, ultimately bringing about cellular responses. In this diagram, the receptor is on the surface of the target cell; in other cases, the stimulus interacts with receptors inside the cell.

Consider a forgotten potato in the back corner of a kitchen cupboard. This modified underground stem, or tuber, has sprouted shoots from its "eyes" (axillary buds). These shoots, however, scarcely resemble those of a typical plant. Instead of sturdy stems and broad green leaves, these plants have ghostly pale stems and unexpanded leaves, as well as short, stubby roots **(Figure 39.2a)**. These morphological adaptations for growing in darkness, collectively referred to as **etiolation**, make sense if we consider that a young potato plant in nature usually encounters continuous darkness when sprouting underground. Under these circumstances, expanded leaves would be a hindrance to soil penetration and would be damaged as the shoots pushed through the soil. Because the leaves are unexpanded and underground, there is little evaporative loss of water and little requirement for an extensive root system to replace the water lost by transpiration. Moreover, the energy expended in producing green chlorophyll would be wasted because there is no light for photosynthesis. Instead, a potato plant growing in the dark allocates as much energy as possible to elongating its stems. This adaptation enables the shoots to break ground before the nutrient reserves in the tuber are exhausted. The etiolation response is one example of how a plant's morphology and physiology are tuned to its surroundings by complex interactions between environmental and internal signals.

When a shoot reaches the sunlight, the plant undergoes profound changes, collectively called **de-etiolation** (informally known as greening). Stem elongation slows; leaves expand; roots elongate; and the shoot produces chlorophyll. In short, it begins to resemble a typical plant **(Figure 39.2b)**. In this section, we will use this de-etiolation response as an example of how a plant cell's reception of a signal—in this case, light—is transduced into a response (greening). Along the way, we will explore how studies of mutants provide insights into the molecular details of the stages of cell-signal processing: reception, transduction, and response **(Figure 39.3)**.

Reception

Signals are first detected by receptors, proteins that undergo changes in shape in response to a specific stimulus. The receptor involved in de-etiolation is a type of *phytochrome*, a photoreceptor that we'll examine more closely later in the chapter. Unlike most receptors, which are built into the plasma membrane, the phytochrome that functions in the de-etiolation response is located in the cytoplasm. Researchers demonstrated the requirement for phytochrome in de-etiolation through studies of the tomato, a close relative of the potato. The *aurea* mutant tomato, which has lower-than-normal levels of phytochrome, greens less than wild-type tomatoes when exposed to light. (The name *aurea* comes from the Latin for "gold-colored." In the absence of chlorophyll, the yellow plant pigments called carotenoids are more obvious.) Researchers produced a normal de-etiolation response in individual *aurea* leaf cells by injecting phytochrome from other plants and then exposing the cells to light. Such experiments indicate that phytochrome functions in light detection during de-etiolation.

Transduction

Receptors can be sensitive to very weak environmental or chemical signals. Some de-etiolation responses are triggered by extremely low levels of light. For example, light levels equivalent to a few seconds of moonlight are sufficient to slow stem elongation in dark-grown oat seedlings. How is the information from these extremely weak signals amplified, and how is their reception transduced into a specific response by the plant? The answer is **second messengers**—small molecules and ions in the cell that amplify the signal and transfer it from the receptor to other proteins that carry out the response. In de-etiolation, for example, each activated phytochrome molecule may give rise to hundreds of molecules of a second messenger, each of which may lead to the activation of hundreds of molecules of a specific enzyme. By such mechanisms, a second messenger in a signal transduction pathway rapidly amplifies the signal. In Chapter 11, we discussed several kinds of second messengers in general (see Figures 11.11 and 11.13). Here, we examine the particular roles of second messengers in de-etiolation. Refer to **Figure 39.4** frequently as you read the following description of this complex process.

Light causes phytochrome to undergo a change in shape that leads to increases in levels of the second messengers cyclic GMP (cGMP) and Ca^{2+}. One function of GMP is the activation of protein kinases, a diverse class of enzymes that influence the activation of other proteins by phosphorylation, a modification in which a phosphate group is attached to the protein at a specific site. Injection of cGMP into *aurea* tomato leaf cells induces a partial de-etiolation response, even without the addition of phytochrome, via the upper pathway in the figure. Changes in cytosolic Ca^{2+} levels also play an important role in phytochrome signal transduction. The concentration of Ca^{2+} is generally very low in the cytosol (about 10^{-7} *M*). But phytochrome activation can open Ca^{2+} channels and lead to a transient 100-fold increase in cytosolic Ca^{2+} levels. In other cases of signal transduction, both cGMP and cytosolic Ca^{2+} can influence the activity of specific ion channels, cytoskeletal proteins, and enzymes, including protein kinases.

Response

Ultimately, a signal transduction pathway leads to regulation of one or more cellular activities. In most cases, these responses involve the increased activity of particular enzymes. There are two main mechanisms by which a signaling pathway can enhance an enzymatic step in a biochemical pathway: transcriptional regulation and post-translational modification. Transcriptional regulation increases or decreases synthesis of the mRNA that codes for the enzyme. Post-translational modification activates existing enzyme molecules.

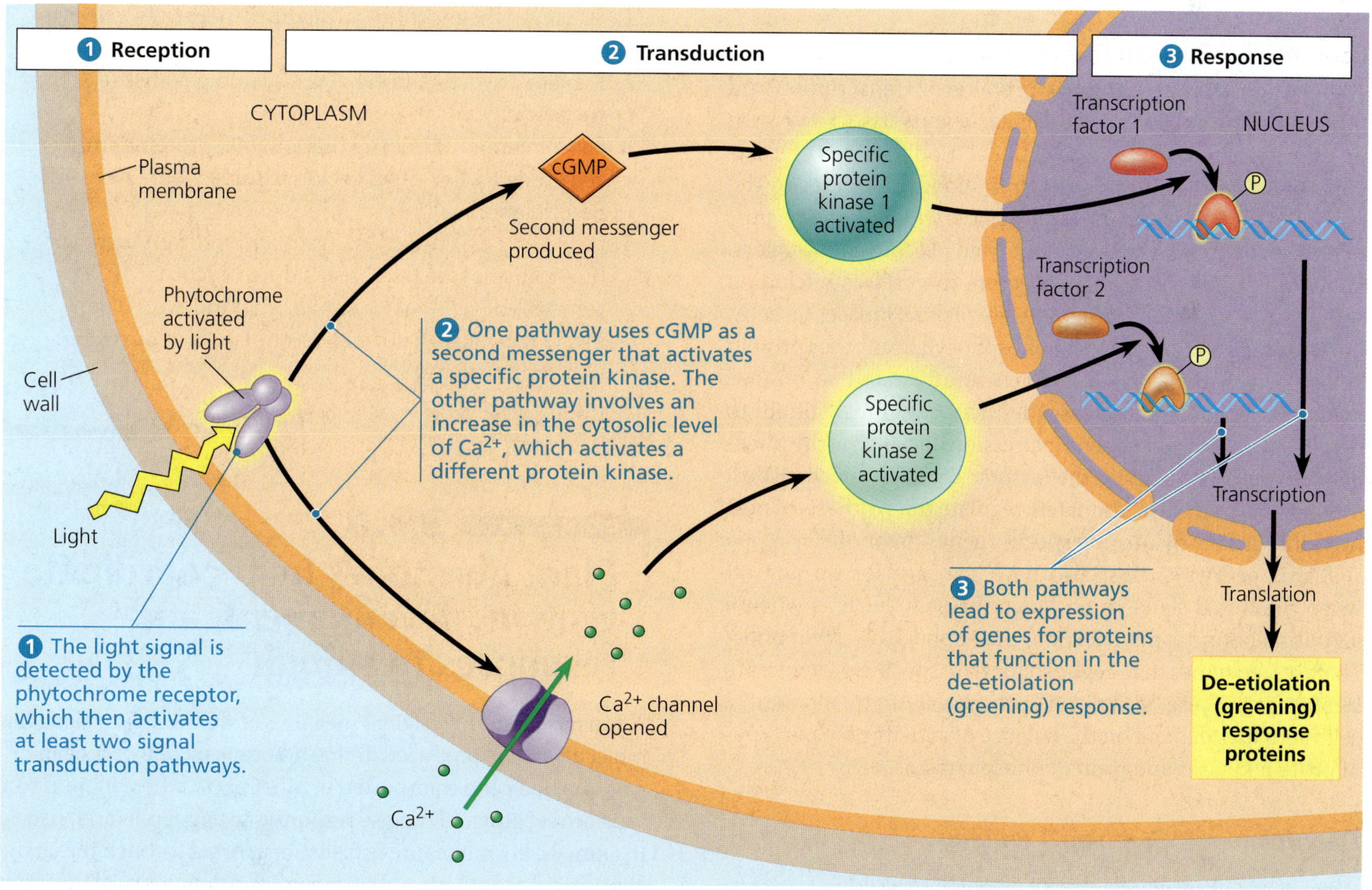

▲ **Figure 39.4 An example of signal transduction in plants: the role of phytochrome in the de-etiolation (greening) response.**

Transcriptional Regulation

As discussed in Chapter 18, the proteins we call *specific transcription factors* bind to specific regions of DNA and control the transcription of specific genes (see Figure 18.9). In the case of phytochrome-induced de-etiolation, several such transcription factors are activated by phosphorylation in response to the appropriate light conditions. The activation of some of these transcription factors depends on cGMP, whereas the activation of others requires Ca^{2+}.

The mechanism by which a signal promotes a new developmental course may depend on transcription factors that are activators (which *increase* transcription of specific genes) or repressors (which *decrease* transcription) or both. For example, consider *Arabidopsis* mutants that, except for their pale color, have a light-grown morphology when grown in the dark; they have expanded leaves and short, sturdy stems but are not green because the final step in chlorophyll production requires light directly. These mutants have defects in a repressor that inhibits the expression of other genes normally activated by light. When the repressor is eliminated by mutation, the pathway that it normally blocks proceeds. Thus, these mutants appear to have been grown in the light, except for their pale color.

Post-Translational Modification of Proteins

Although the syntheses of new proteins by transcription and translation are important molecular events associated with de-etiolation, so are post-translational modifications of existing proteins. Most often, existing proteins are modified by the phosphorylation of specific amino acids, which alters the protein's hydrophobicity and activity. Many second messengers, including cGMP, and some receptors themselves, including some forms of phytochrome, activate protein kinases directly. Often, one protein kinase will phosphorylate another protein kinase, which then phosphorylates another, and so on (see Figure 11.9). Such kinase cascades may link initial stimuli to responses at the level of gene expression, usually via the phosphorylation of transcription factors. By such mechanisms, many signal pathways ultimately regulate the synthesis of new proteins, usually by turning specific genes on or off.

Signal pathways must also have a means for turning off when the initial signal is no longer present, such as when a sprouting potato is put back into the cupboard. Protein phosphatases, enzymes that dephosphorylate specific proteins, are important in these "switch-off" processes. At any moment, a cell's activities depend on the balance of activity of many types of protein kinases and protein phosphatases.

De-Etiolation ("Greening") Proteins

What types of proteins are either newly transcribed or activated by phosphorylation during the de-etiolation process? Many are enzymes that function in photosynthesis directly; others are enzymes involved in supplying the chemical precursors necessary for chlorophyll production; still others affect the levels of plant hormones that regulate growth. For example, the levels of auxin and brassinosteroids, hormones that enhance stem elongation, decrease following phytochrome activation. That decrease explains the slowing of stem elongation that accompanies de-etiolation.

We have discussed the signal transduction involved in the de-etiolation response of a potato plant in some detail to give you a sense of the complexity of biochemical changes that underlie this one process. Every plant hormone and every environmental stimulus triggers one or more signal transduction pathways of comparable complexity. As with the *aurea* mutant tomato, techniques of molecular biology combined with genetic studies of mutants are helping researchers identify these various pathways. But molecular biology builds on a long history of careful physiological and biochemical investigations into how plants work. As you will read in the next section, classical experiments provided the first clues that transported signaling molecules called hormones are internal regulators of plant growth.

CONCEPT CHECK 39.1

1. What are the morphological differences between dark- and light-grown plants?
2. Explain how etiolation helps a seedling compete successfully.
3. Cycloheximide is a drug that inhibits protein synthesis. Predict what effect cycloheximide would have on de-etiolation.
4. **WHAT IF?** The sexual dysfunction drug Viagra inhibits an enzyme that breaks down cyclic GMP. If tomato leaf cells have a similar enzyme, would applying Viagra cause a normal de-etiolation of *aurea* mutant tomato leaves?

For suggested answers, see Appendix A.

CONCEPT 39.2

Plant hormones help coordinate growth, development, and responses to stimuli

A **hormone**, in the original meaning of the term, is a signaling molecule that is produced in tiny amounts by one part of an organism's body and transported to other parts, where it binds to a specific receptor and triggers responses in target cells and tissues. In animals, hormones are usually transported through the circulatory system, a criterion often included in definitions of the term.

The hormone concept originated from studies of animals and was adopted by plant physiologists in the early 1900s. Many modern plant biologists, however, argue that it is too limiting to describe plant physiological processes using the narrow definitions established by animal physiologists. For example, plants don't have blood or a circulatory system to transport hormone-like signaling molecules. Moreover, some signaling molecules that are considered plant hormones act only locally. Finally, there are some signaling molecules in plants, such as sucrose, which typically occur in plants at concentrations that are hundreds of thousands times greater than a typical hormone. Nevertheless, they are transported through plants and activate signal transduction pathways that greatly alter the functioning of plants in a manner similar to a hormone. Thus, many plant biologists prefer the broader term *plant growth regulator* to describe organic compounds, either natural or synthetic, that modify or control one or more specific physiological processes within a plant. At this point in time, the terms *plant hormone* and *plant growth regulator* are used about equally, but for historical continuity we will use the term *plant hormone* and adhere to the criterion that plant hormones are active at very low concentrations.

Virtually every aspect of plant growth and development is under hormonal control to some degree. A single hormone can regulate an amazingly diverse array of cellular and developmental processes. Conversely, multiple hormones can influence a single process.

The Discovery of Plant Hormones

The idea that chemical messengers exist in plants emerged from a series of classic experiments on how stems respond to light. As you know, the shoot of a houseplant on a windowsill grows toward light. If you rotate the plant, it soon reorients its growth until its leaves again face the window. Any growth response that results in plant organs curving toward or away from stimuli is called a **tropism** (from the Greek *tropos*, turn). The growth of a shoot toward light or away from it is called **phototropism**; the former is positive phototropism, the latter negative phototropism.

In a forest or other natural ecosystem where plants may be crowded, phototropism directs growing seedlings toward the sunlight that powers photosynthesis. What is the mechanism for this adaptive response? Much of what is known about phototropism has been learned from studies of grass seedlings, particularly oats. The shoot of a sprouting grass seedling is enclosed in a sheath called the coleoptile (see Figure 38.9b), which grows straight upward if the seedling is kept in the dark or if it is illuminated uniformly from all sides. If the growing coleoptile is illuminated from one side, it grows toward the light. This response results from a differential growth of cells on opposite sides of the coleoptile; the cells on the darker side elongate faster than the cells on the brighter side.

Charles Darwin and his son Francis conducted some of the earliest experiments on phototropism in the late 1800s **(Figure 39.5)**. They observed that a grass seedling could bend toward light only if the tip of the coleoptile was present. If the

▼ Figure 39.5 Inquiry

What part of a grass coleoptile senses light, and how is the signal transmitted?

EXPERIMENT In 1880, Charles and Francis Darwin removed and covered parts of grass coleoptiles to determine what part senses light. In 1913, Peter Boysen-Jensen separated coleoptiles with different materials to determine how the signal for phototropism is transmitted.

RESULTS

Control

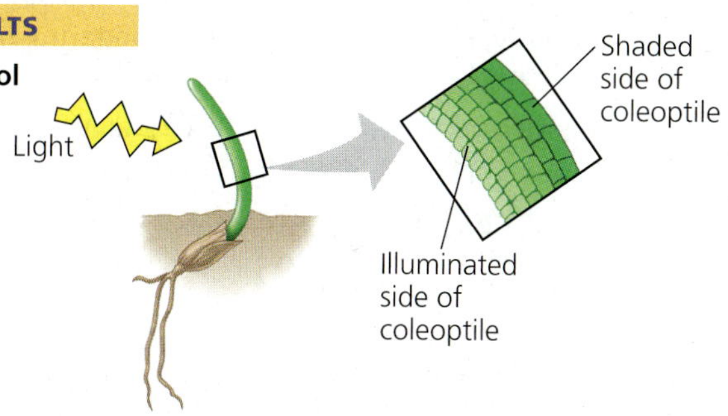

Darwin and Darwin: Phototropism occurs only when the tip is illuminated.

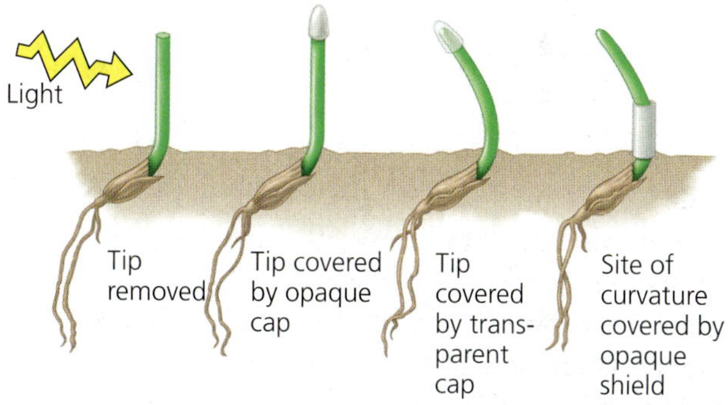

Boysen-Jensen: Phototropism occurs when the tip is separated by a permeable barrier but not an impermeable barrier.

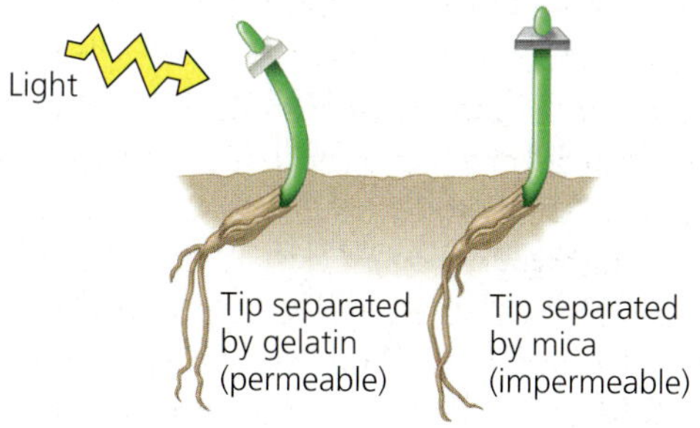

CONCLUSION The Darwins' experiment suggested that only the tip of the coleoptile senses light. The phototropic bending, however, occurred at a distance from the site of light perception (the tip). Boysen-Jensen's results suggested that the signal for the bending is a light-activated mobile chemical.

SOURCE C. R. Darwin, The power of movement in plants, John Murray, London (1880). P. Boysen-Jensen, Concerning the performance of phototropic stimuli on the *Avena* coleoptile, *Berichte der Deutschen Botanischen Gesellschaft* (Reports of the German Botanical Society) 31:559–566 (1913).

WHAT IF? How could you experimentally determine which colors of light cause the most phototropic bending?

tip was removed, the coleoptile did not curve. The seedling also failed to grow toward light if the tip was covered with an opaque cap; but neither a transparent cap over the tip nor an opaque shield placed below the coleoptile tip prevented the phototropic response. It was the tip of the coleoptile, the Darwins concluded, that was responsible for sensing light. However, they noted that the differential growth response that led to curvature of the coleoptile occurred some distance below the tip. The Darwins postulated that some signal was transmitted downward from the tip to the elongating region of the coleoptile. A few decades later, the Danish scientist Peter Boysen-Jensen demonstrated that the signal was a mobile chemical substance. He separated the tip from the remainder of the coleoptile by a cube of gelatin, which prevented cellular contact but allowed chemicals to pass. These seedlings responded normally, bending toward light. However, if the tip was experimentally separated from the lower coleoptile by an impermeable barrier, such as the mineral mica, no phototropic response occurred.

In 1926, Frits Went, a Dutch graduate student, extracted the chemical messenger for phototropism by modifying the experiments of Boysen-Jensen **(Figure 39.6)**. Went removed the coleoptile tip and placed it on a cube of agar, a gelatinous material. The chemical messenger from the tip, Went reasoned, should diffuse into the agar, and the agar block should then be able to substitute for the coleoptile tip. Went placed the agar blocks on decapitated coleoptiles that were kept in the dark. A block that was centered on top of the coleoptile caused the stem to grow straight upward. However, when the block was placed off center, the coleoptile began to bend away from the side with the agar block, as though growing toward light. Went concluded that the agar block contained a chemical produced in the coleoptile tip, that this chemical stimulated growth as it passed down the coleoptile, and that a coleoptile curved toward light because of a higher concentration of the growth-promoting chemical on the darker side of the coleoptile. For this chemical messenger, or hormone, Went chose the name auxin (from the Greek *auxein*, to increase). Auxin was later purified by Kenneth Thimann, at the California Institute of Technology, and its chemical structure found to be indoleacetic acid (IAA).

The classical hypothesis for what causes grass coleoptiles to grow toward light, based on the work of the Darwins, Boysen-Jensen, and Went, is that an asymmetrical distribution of auxin moving down from the coleoptile tip causes cells on the darker side to elongate faster than cells on the brighter side. But studies of phototropism by organs other than grass coleoptiles provide less support for this idea. There is no evidence that illumination from one side causes asymmetrical distribution of auxin in stems of sunflowers or other eudicots. There *is*, however, asymmetrical distribution of certain substances that may act as growth *inhibitors*, and these substances are more concentrated on the lighted side of a stem.

▼ Figure 39.6 Inquiry

Does asymmetrical distribution of a growth-promoting chemical cause a coleoptile to grow toward the light?

EXPERIMENT In 1926, Frits Went's experiment identified how a growth-promoting chemical causes a coleoptile to grow toward light. He placed coleoptiles in the dark and removed their tips, putting some tips on agar cubes that he predicted would absorb the growth-promoting chemical. On a control coleoptile, he placed a cube that lacked the chemical. On others, he placed cubes containing the chemical, either centered on top of the coleoptile to distribute the chemical evenly or offset to increase the concentration on one side.

RESULTS The coleoptile grew straight if the growth-promoting chemical was distributed evenly. If the chemical was distributed unevenly, the coleoptile curved away from the side with the cube, as if growing toward light, even though it was grown in the dark.

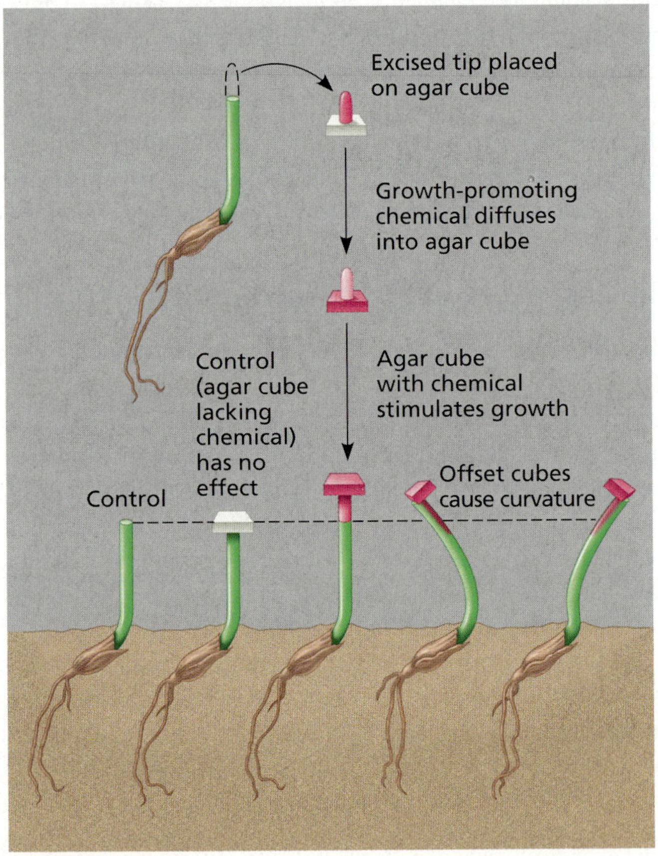

CONCLUSION Went concluded that a coleoptile curved toward light because its dark side had a higher concentration of the growth-promoting chemical, which he named auxin.

SOURCE F. Went, A growth substance and growth, *Recueils des Travaux Botaniques Néerlandais* (Collections of Dutch Botanical Works) 25:1–116 (1928).

WHAT IF? Triiodobenzoic acid (TIBA) inhibits auxin transport. If a tiny agar bead containing TIBA were placed off center on the tip of an intact coleoptile, which way would the coleoptile bend: toward the side with the bead or away from it? Explain.

A Survey of Plant Hormones

The early studies on phototropism that we have just discussed provided the basis for subsequent research on plant hormones. **Table 39.1** previews some major classes of plant hormones: auxin, cytokinins, gibberellins, brassinosteroids, abscisic acid, and ethylene. Many molecules in plants that function in defense against pathogens are probably plant hormones as well. (These molecules will be discussed later in the chapter.)

Plant hormones are produced in very low concentrations, but a tiny amount of hormone can have a profound effect on the growth and development of a plant organ. This implies that the hormonal signal must be amplified in some way. A hormone may act by altering the expression of genes, by affecting the activity of existing enzymes, or by changing properties of membranes. Any of these actions could redirect the metabolism and development of a cell responding to a small number of hormone molecules. Signal transduction pathways amplify the hormonal signal and connect it to a cell's specific responses.

In general, hormones control plant growth and development by affecting the division, elongation, and differentiation of cells. Some hormones also mediate shorter-term physiological responses of plants to environmental stimuli. Each hormone has multiple effects, depending on its site of action, its concentration, and the developmental stage of the plant.

Response to a hormone usually depends not so much on the amount of that hormone as on its relative concentration compared with other hormones. It is hormonal balance, rather than hormones acting in isolation, that may control growth and development. These interactions will become apparent in the following survey of hormone function.

Auxin

The term **auxin** is used for any chemical substance that promotes elongation of coleoptiles, although auxins have multiple

Table 39.1 Overview of Plant Hormones

Hormone	Where Produced or Found in Plant	Major Functions
Auxin (IAA)	Shoot apical meristems and young leaves are the primary sites of auxin synthesis. Root apical meristems also produce auxin, although the root depends on the shoot for much of its auxin. Developing seeds and fruits contain high levels of auxin, but it is unclear whether it is newly synthesized or transported from maternal tissues.	Stimulates stem elongation (low concentration only); promotes the formation of lateral and adventitious roots; regulates development of fruit; enhances apical dominance; functions in phototropism and gravitropism; promotes vascular differentiation; retards leaf abscission.
Cytokinins	These are synthesized primarily in roots and transported to other organs, although there are many minor sites of production as well.	Regulate cell division in shoots and roots; modify apical dominance and promote lateral bud growth; promote movement of nutrients into sink tissues; stimulate seed germination; delay leaf senescence.
Gibberellins	Meristems of apical buds and roots, young leaves, and developing seeds are the primary sites of production.	Stimulate stem elongation, pollen development, pollen tube growth, fruit growth, and seed development and germination; regulate sex determination and the transition from juvenile to adult phases.
Brassinosteroids	These compounds are present in all plant tissues, although different intermediates predominate in different organs. Internally produced brassinosteroids act near the site of synthesis.	Promote cell expansion and cell division in shoots; promote root growth at low concentrations; inhibit root growth at high concentrations; promote xylem differentiation and inhibit phloem differentiation; promote seed germination and pollen tube elongation.
Abscisic acid (ABA)	Almost all plant cells have the ability to synthesize abscisic acid, and its presence has been detected in every major organ and living tissue; may be transported in the phloem or xylem.	Inhibits growth; promotes stomatal closure during drought stress; promotes seed dormancy and inhibits early germination; promotes leaf senescence; promotes desiccation tolerance.
Ethylene	This gaseous hormone can be produced by almost all parts of the plant. It is produced in high concentrations during senescence, leaf abscission, and the ripening of some types of fruits. Synthesis is also stimulated by wounding and stress.	Promotes ripening of many types of fruit, leaf abscission, and the triple response in seedlings (inhibition of stem elongation, promotion of lateral expansion, and horizontal growth); enhances the rate of senescence; promotes root and root hair formation; promotes flowering in the pineapple family.

functions in flowering plants. The natural auxin in plants is indoleacetic acid, or IAA, but several other compounds, including some synthetic ones, have auxin activity. Throughout this chapter, however, the term *auxin* is used specifically to refer to IAA. Although IAA was the first plant hormone to be discovered, much remains to be learned about auxin signal transduction and the regulation of auxin biosynthesis.

Auxin is transported down the stem from the shoot apex at a speed of about 10 mm/hr, much too fast for diffusion, although slower than translocation in phloem. Auxin seems to be transported directly through parenchyma tissue, from one cell to the next. In the shoot, it moves only from tip to base, not in the reverse direction. This unidirectional transport of auxin is called polar transport. Polar transport has nothing to do with gravity; experiments have shown that auxin travels upward when a stem or coleoptile segment is placed upside down. Rather, the polarity of auxin movement is attributable to the polar distribution of auxin transport protein in the cells. Concentrated at the basal end of a cell, the auxin transporters move the hormone out of the cell. The auxin can then enter the apical end of the neighboring cell **(Figure 39.7)**. Auxin has a variety of effects, including stimulating cell elongation and lateral root formation.

The Role of Auxin in Cell Elongation Although auxin affects several aspects of plant development, one of its chief functions is to stimulate elongation of cells within young developing shoots. The apical meristem of a shoot is a major site of auxin synthesis. As auxin from the shoot apex moves down to the region of cell elongation (see Figure 35.16), the hormone stimulates cell growth, probably by binding to a receptor in the plasma membrane. Auxin stimulates growth only over a certain concentration range, from about 10^{-8} to 10^{-4} *M*. At higher concentrations, auxin may inhibit cell elongation, probably by inducing production of ethylene, a hormone that generally inhibits elongation. We will return to this hormonal interaction when we discuss ethylene.

According to a model called the *acid growth hypothesis*, proton pumps play a major role in the growth response of cells to auxin. In a shoot's region of elongation, auxin stimulates the plasma membrane's proton (H^+) pumps. This pumping of H^+ increases the voltage across the membrane (membrane potential) and lowers the pH in the cell wall within minutes **(Figure 39.8)**. Acidification of the wall activates enzymes called **expansins** that break the cross-links (hydrogen bonds) between cellulose microfibrils and other cell wall constituents, loosening the wall's fabric. (Expansins can even weaken the integrity of filter paper made of pure cellulose.) Increasing the membrane potential enhances ion uptake into the cell, which causes osmotic uptake of water and increased turgor. Increased turgor and increased cell wall plasticity enable the cell to elongate.

Auxin also rapidly alters gene expression, causing cells in the region of elongation to produce new proteins within minutes. Some of these proteins are short-lived transcription factors that repress or activate the expression of other genes. For sustained growth after this initial spurt, cells must make more cytoplasm and wall material. Auxin also stimulates this sustained growth response.

Lateral and Adventitious Root Formation Auxins are used commercially in the vegetative propagation of plants by cuttings. Treating a detached leaf or stem with rooting powder containing auxin often causes adventitious roots to form near the cut surface. Auxin is also involved in the branching of roots. Researchers found that an *Arabidopsis* mutant that exhibits extreme proliferation of lateral roots has an auxin concentration 17-fold higher than normal.

▼ **Figure 39.7 Inquiry**

What causes polar movement of auxin from shoot tip to base?

EXPERIMENT To investigate how auxin is transported unidirectionally, Leo Gälweiler and colleagues designed an experiment to identify the location of the auxin transport protein. They used a greenish yellow fluorescent molecule to label antibodies that bind to the auxin transport protein. Then they applied the antibodies to longitudinally sectioned *Arabidopsis* stems.

RESULTS The light micrograph on the left shows that auxin transport proteins are not found in all stem tissues, but only in the xylem parenchyma. In the light micrograph on the right, a higher magnification reveals that these proteins are primarily localized at basal ends of the cells.

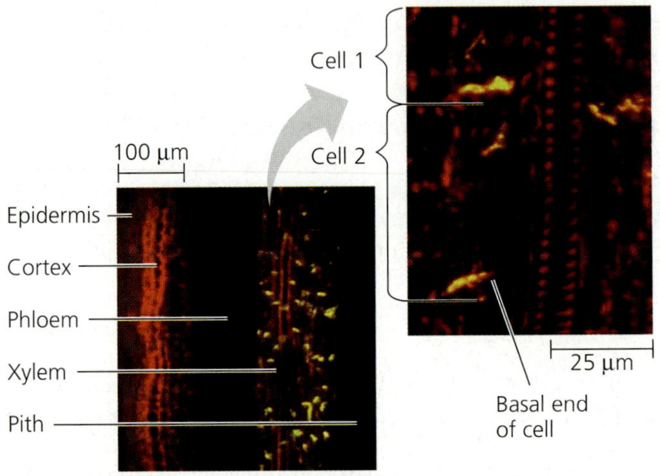

CONCLUSION The results support the hypothesis that concentration of the auxin transport protein at the basal ends of cells mediates the polar transport of auxin.

SOURCE L. Gälweiler et al., Regulation of polar auxin transport by AtPIN1 in *Arabidopsis* vascular tissue, *Science* 282:2226–2230 (1998).

WHAT IF? If auxin transport proteins were equally distributed at both ends of the cells, would polar auxin transport still be possible? Explain.

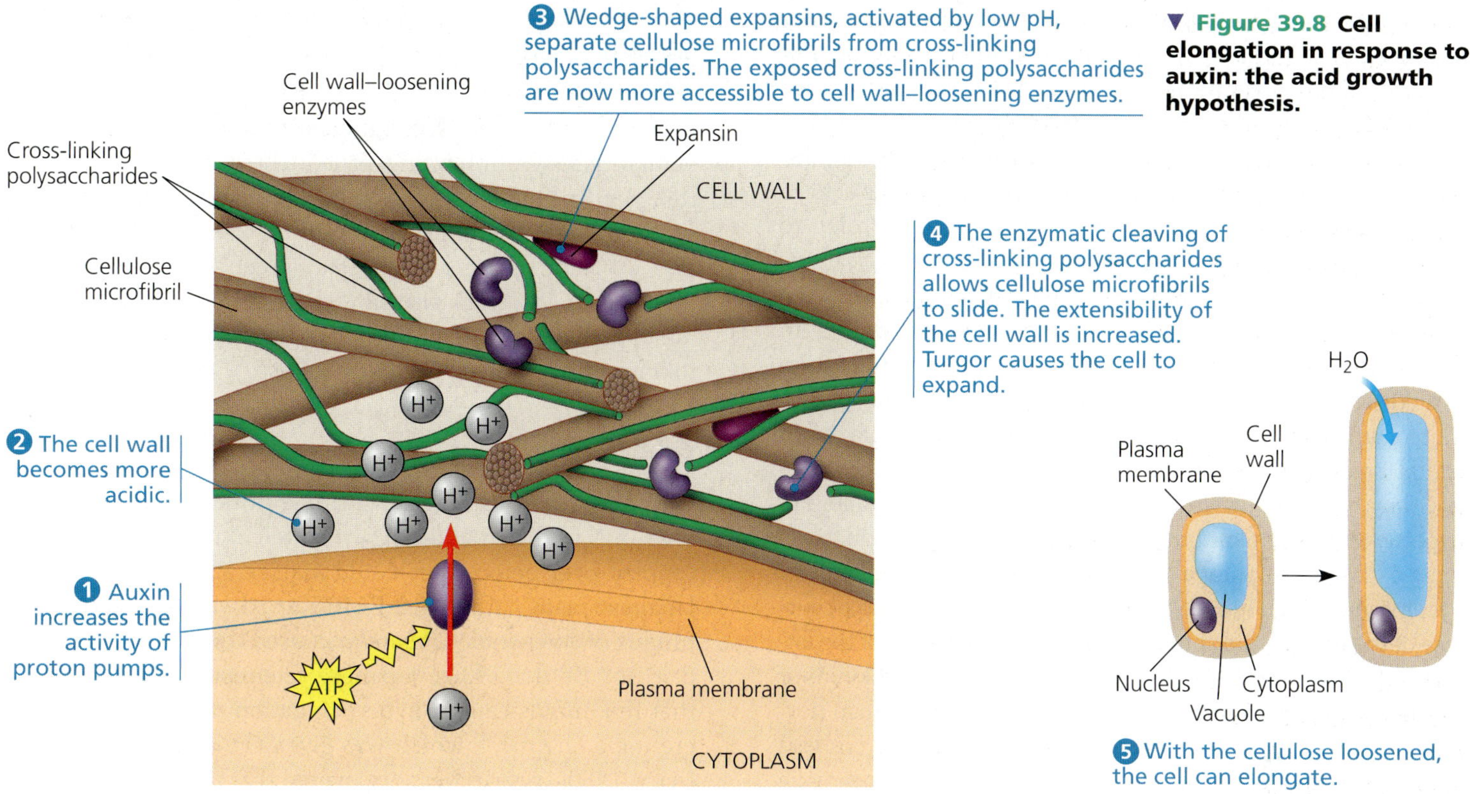

▼ **Figure 39.8 Cell elongation in response to auxin: the acid growth hypothesis.**

Auxins as Herbicides Certain synthetic auxins, including 2,4-dichlorophenoxyacteic acid (2,4-D), are widely used as herbicides. Monocots, such as maize and turfgrass, can rapidly inactivate such synthetic auxins. However, eudicots cannot and therefore die from hormonal overdose. Spraying cereal fields or turf with 2,4-D eliminates eudicot (broadleaf) weeds.

Other Effects of Auxin In addition to stimulating cell elongation during primary growth, auxin affects secondary growth by increasing cambial activity and influencing the differentiation of cambial initials (see Figure 35.20).

Developing seeds produce auxin, which promotes fruit growth. In greenhouses, seed production is often poor because of the lack of insect pollinators, resulting in poorly developed tomato fruits. However, spraying synthetic auxins on greenhouse-grown tomato vines induces normal fruit development without pollination, making the greenhouse-cultivated tomato fruits commercially viable.

Cytokinins

Trial-and-error attempts to find chemical additives that would enhance the growth and development of plant cells in tissue culture led to the discovery of **cytokinins**. In the 1940s, Johannes van Overbeek, working at the Cold Spring Harbor Laboratory in New York, found he could stimulate the growth of plant embryos by adding coconut milk, the liquid endosperm of a coconut's giant seed, to his culture medium. A decade later, Folke Skoog and Carlos O. Miller, at the University of Wisconsin, Madison, induced cultured tobacco cells to divide by adding degraded DNA samples. The active ingredients of both experimental additives turned out to be modified forms of adenine, a component of nucleic acids. These growth regulators were named cytokinins because they stimulate cytokinesis, or cell division. The most common natural cytokinin is zeatin, so named because it was discovered first in maize (*Zea mays*). Although much remains to be learned about cytokinin synthesis and signal transduction, the effects of cytokinins on cell division and differentiation, apical dominance, and aging are well documented.

Control of Cell Division and Differentiation Cytokinins are produced in actively growing tissues, particularly in roots, embryos, and fruits. Cytokinins produced in roots reach their target tissues by moving up the plant in the xylem sap. Acting in concert with auxin, cytokinins stimulate cell division and influence the pathway of differentiation. The effects of cytokinins on cells growing in tissue culture provide clues about how this class of hormones may function in an intact plant. When a piece of parenchyma tissue from a stem is cultured in the absence of cytokinins, the cells grow very large but do not divide. But if cytokinins are added along with auxin, the cells divide. Cytokinins alone have no effect. The ratio of cytokinins to auxin controls cell differentiation. When the concentrations of these two hormones are at certain levels, the mass of cells continues to grow, but it remains a cluster of undifferentiated cells called a callus (see Figure 38.14). If cytokinin levels increase, shoot buds develop from the callus. If auxin levels increase, roots form.

Control of Apical Dominance Cytokinins, auxin, and other factors interact in the control of apical dominance, the ability of the apical bud to suppress the development of axillary buds **(Figure 39.9a)**. Until recently, the leading hypothesis to explain the hormonal regulation of apical dominance—the direct inhibition hypothesis—proposed that auxin and cytokinins act antagonistically in regulating axillary bud growth. According to this view, auxin transported down the shoot from the apical bud directly inhibits axillary buds from growing, causing a shoot to lengthen at the expense of lateral branching. Meanwhile, cytokinins entering the shoot system from roots counter the action of auxin by signaling axillary buds to begin growing. Thus, the ratio of auxin and cytokinins was viewed as the critical factor in controlling axillary bud inhibition.

Many observations are consistent with the direct inhibition hypothesis. If the apical bud, the primary source of auxin, is removed, the inhibition of axillary buds is removed and the plant becomes bushier **(Figure 39.9b)**. Applying auxin to the cut surface of the decapitated shoot resuppresses the growth of the lateral buds **(Figure 39.9c)**. Mutants that overproduce cytokinins or plants treated with cytokinins also tend to be bushier than normal. However, one prediction of the direct inhibition hypothesis *not* supported by experiment is that decapitation, by removing the primary source of auxin, should lead to a decrease in the auxin levels of axillary buds. Biochemical studies have in fact revealed the opposite: Auxin levels actually *increase* in the axillary buds of decapitated plants. The direct inhibition hypothesis, therefore, does not account for all experimental findings. It is likely that plant biologists have not uncovered all the pieces of this puzzle.

(a) Apical bud intact (not shown in photo) **(b) Apical bud removed** **(c) Auxin added to decapitated stem**

▲ **Figure 39.9 Apical dominance. (a)** The inhibition of growth of axillary buds, possibly influenced by auxin from the apical bud, favors elongation of the shoot's main axis. **(b)** Removal of the apical bud from the same plant enables lateral branches to grow. **(c)** Applying a gelatin capsule containing auxin to the stump prevents the lateral branches from growing.

Anti-Aging Effects Cytokinins retard the aging of certain plant organs by inhibiting protein breakdown, stimulating RNA and protein synthesis, and mobilizing nutrients from surrounding tissues. If leaves removed from a plant are dipped in a cytokinin solution, they stay green much longer than otherwise. Cytokinins also slow the deterioration of leaves on intact plants. Because of this anti-aging effect, florists use cytokinin sprays to keep cut flowers fresh.

Gibberellins

In the early 1900s, farmers in Asia noticed that some rice seedlings in their paddies grew so tall and spindly that they toppled over before they could mature and flower. In 1926, Japanese plant pathologist Ewiti Kurosawa discovered that a fungus of the genus *Gibberella* caused this "foolish seedling disease." By the 1930s, Japanese scientists had determined that the fungus caused hyperelongation of rice stems by secreting a chemical, which was given the name **gibberellin**. In the 1950s, researchers discovered that plants also produce gibberellins (GAs). Since that time, scientists have identified more than 100 different gibberellins that occur naturally in plants, although a much smaller number occur in each plant species. "Foolish rice" seedlings, it seems, suffer from an overdose of gibberellins normally found in plants in lower concentrations. Gibberellins have a variety of effects, such as stem elongation, fruit growth, and seed germination.

Stem Elongation The major sites of gibberellin production are roots and young leaves. Gibberellins stimulate stem and leaf growth but have little effect on roots. In stems, they stimulate cell elongation *and* cell division. One hypothesis proposes that they activate enzymes that loosen cell walls, facilitating entry of expansin proteins. Thus, gibberellins act in concert with auxin to promote stem elongation.

The effects of gibberellins in enhancing stem elongation are evident when certain dwarf (mutant) varieties of plants are treated with gibberellins. For instance, some dwarf pea plants (including the variety Mendel studied; see Chapter 14) grow tall if treated with gibberellins. But there is often no response if the gibberellins are applied to wild-type plants. Apparently, these plants already produce an optimal dose of the hormone. The most dramatic example of gibberellin-induced stem elongation is *bolting,* rapid growth of the floral stalk **(Figure 39.10a)**.

Fruit Growth In many plants, both auxin and gibberellins must be present in order for fruit to develop. The most important commercial application of gibberellins is in the spraying of Thompson seedless grapes **(Figure 39.10b)**. The hormone makes the individual grapes grow larger, a trait valued by the consumer. The gibberellin sprays also make the internodes of the grape bunch elongate, allowing more space for the individual grapes. By enhancing air circulation between the grapes, this increase in space also makes it harder for yeasts and other microorganisms to infect the fruits.

(a) Some plants develop in a rosette form, low to the ground with very short internodes, as in the *Arabidopsis* plant shown at the left. As the plant switches to reproductive growth, a surge of gibberellins induces bolting: Internodes elongate rapidly, elevating floral buds that develop at stem tips (right).

(b) The Thompson seedless grape bunch on the left is from an untreated control vine. The bunch on the right is growing from a vine that was sprayed with gibberellin during fruit development.

◄ **Figure 39.10 Effects of gibberellins on stem elongation and fruit growth.**

Germination The embryo of a seed is a rich source of gibberellins. After water is imbibed, the release of gibberellins from the embryo signals the seed to break dormancy and germinate. Some seeds that require particular environmental conditions to germinate, such as exposure to light or low temperatures, break dormancy if they are treated with gibberellins. Gibberellins support the growth of cereal seedlings by stimulating the synthesis of digestive enzymes such as α-amylase that mobilize stored nutrients **(Figure 39.11)**.

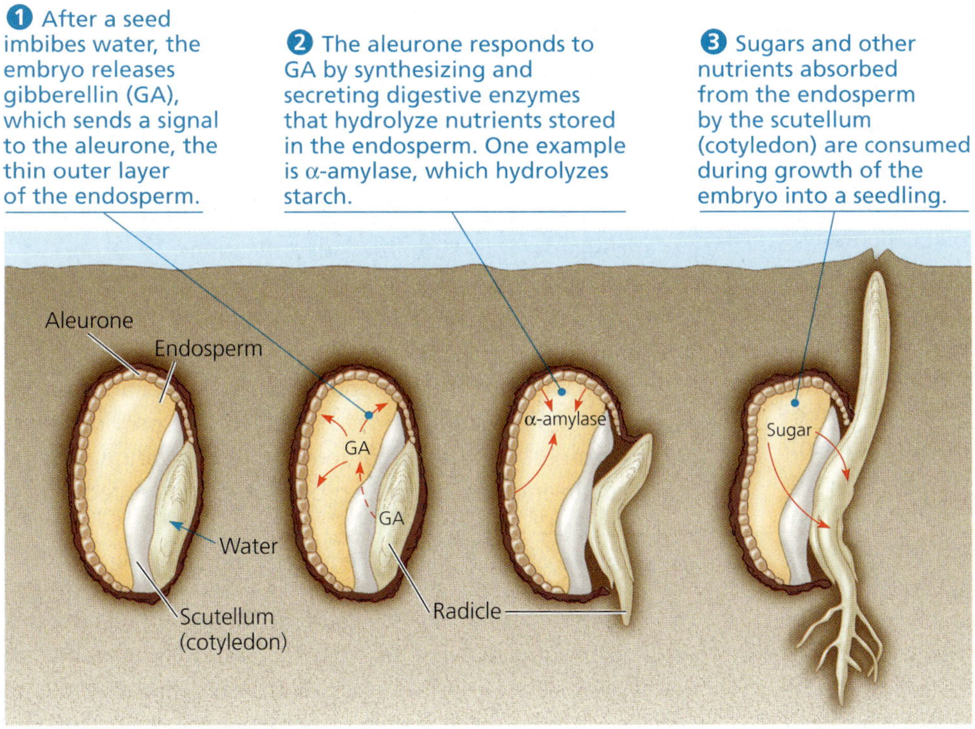

▲ **Figure 39.11 Mobilization of nutrients by gibberellins during the germination of grain seeds such as barley.**

Brassinosteroids

Brassinosteroids are steroids and therefore chemically similar to cholesterol and the sex hormones of animals. They induce cell elongation and division in stem segments and seedlings at concentrations as low as 10^{-12} *M*. They also retard leaf abscission (leaf drop) and promote xylem differentiation. These effects are so qualitatively similar to those of auxin that it took several years for plant physiologists to determine that brassinosteroids were not types of auxins.

Evidence from molecular biology established brassinosteroids as plant hormones. Joanne Chory and colleagues at the Salk Institute in San Diego were interested in mutant *Arabidopsis* with morphological features similar to those of light-grown plants, even though the mutants were grown in the dark. The researchers discovered that the mutation affects a gene that normally codes for an enzyme similar to one involved in steroid synthesis in mammals. They also found that this brassinosteroid-deficient mutant could be restored to the wild-type phenotype by applying brassinosteroids in the lab.

Abscisic Acid

In the 1960s, one research group studying the chemical changes that precede bud dormancy and leaf abscission in deciduous trees and another team investigating chemical changes preceding abscission of cotton fruits isolated the same compound, **abscisic acid (ABA)**.

Ironically, ABA is no longer thought to play a primary role in bud dormancy or leaf abscission, but it is very important in other functions. Unlike the growth-stimulating hormones we have studied so far—auxin, cytokinins, gibberellins, and brassinosteroids—ABA *slows* growth. ABA often antagonizes the actions of growth hormones, and the ratio of ABA to one or more growth hormones determines the final physiological outcome. We will consider here two of ABA's many effects: seed dormancy and drought tolerance.

Seed Dormancy Seed dormancy increases the likelihood that seeds will germinate only when there are sufficient amounts of light, temperature, and moisture for the seedlings to survive (see Chapter 38). What prevents seeds dispersed in autumn from germinating immediately, only to die in the winter? What mechanisms ensure that such seeds do not germinate until spring? For that matter, what prevents seeds from germinating in the dark, moist interior of the fruit? The answer to these questions is ABA. The levels of ABA may increase 100-fold during seed maturation. The high levels of ABA in maturing seeds inhibit germination and induce the production of certain proteins that help the seeds withstand the extreme dehydration that accompanies maturation.

Many types of dormant seeds germinate when ABA is removed or inactivated. The seeds of some desert plants break dormancy only when heavy rains wash ABA out of them. Other seeds require light or prolonged exposure to cold to inactivate ABA. Often, the ratio of ABA to gibberellins determines whether the seed remains dormant or germinates, and adding ABA to seeds that are primed to germinate makes them dormant again. Inactivated ABA or low levels of ABA can lead to precocious (early) germination **(Figure 39.12)**. For example, a maize mutant with grains that germinate while still on the cob lacks a functional transcription factor required for ABA to induce expression of certain genes. Precocious germination of red mangrove seeds, due to low ABA levels, is actually an adaptation that helps the young seedlings to plant themselves in the soft mud below the parent tree.

Drought Tolerance ABA is the primary internal signaling molecule that enables plants to withstand drought. When a plant begins to wilt, ABA accumulates in leaves and causes stomata to close rapidly, reducing transpiration and preventing further water loss. By affecting second messengers such as calcium, ABA causes potassium channels in the plasma membrane of guard cells to open, leading to a massive loss of potassium ions from the cells. The accompanying osmotic loss of water reduces guard cell turgor and leads to closing of the stomatal pores (see Figure 36.17). In some cases, water shortage stresses the root system before the shoot system, and ABA transported from roots to leaves may function as an "early warning system." Many mutants that are especially prone to wilting are deficient in ABA production.

◄ Red mangrove (*Rhizophora mangle*) seeds produce only low levels of ABA, and their seeds germinate while still on the tree. In this case, early germination is a useful adaptation. When released, the radicle of the dart-like seedling deeply penetrates the soft mudflats in which the mangroves grow.

▲ Precocious germination in this maize mutant is caused by lack of a functional transcription factor required for ABA action.

▲ **Figure 39.12 Precocious germination of wild-type mangrove and mutant maize seeds.**

Ethylene

During the 1800s, when coal gas was used as fuel for streetlights, leakage from gas pipes caused nearby trees to drop leaves prematurely. In 1901, the Russian scientist Dimitry Neljubow demonstrated that the gas **ethylene** was the active factor in the coal gas. The idea that ethylene is a plant hormone was not widely accepted, however, until the advent of gas chromatography simplified identification.

Plants produce ethylene in response to stresses such as drought, flooding, mechanical pressure, injury, and infection. Ethylene is also produced during fruit ripening and programmed cell death and in response to high concentrations of externally applied auxin. Indeed, many effects previously ascribed to auxin, such as inhibition of root elongation, may be due to auxin-induced ethylene production. We will focus here on four of ethylene's many effects: response to mechanical stress, senescence, leaf abscission, and fruit ripening.

The Triple Response to Mechanical Stress Imagine a pea seedling pushing upward through the soil, only to come up against a stone. As it pushes against the obstacle, the stress in its delicate tip induces the seedling to produce ethylene. The hormone then instigates a growth maneuver known as the **triple response** that enables the shoot to avoid the obstacle. The three parts of this response are a slowing of stem elongation, a thickening of the stem (which makes it stronger), and a curvature that causes the stem to start growing horizontally. As the effects of the initial ethylene pulse lessen, the stem resumes vertical growth. If it again contacts a barrier, another burst of ethylene is released, and horizontal growth resumes. However, if the upward touch detects no solid object, then ethylene production decreases, and the stem, now clear of the obstacle, resumes its normal upward growth. It is ethylene that induces the stem to grow horizontally rather than the physical obstruction itself; when ethylene is applied to normal seedlings growing free of physical impediments, they still undergo the triple response **(Figure 39.13)**.

Studies of *Arabidopsis* mutants with abnormal triple responses are an example of how biologists identify a signal transduction pathway. Scientists isolated ethylene-insensitive (*ein*) mutants, which fail to undergo the triple response after exposure to ethylene **(Figure 39.14a)**. Some types of *ein* mutants are insensitive to ethylene because they lack a functional ethylene receptor. Mutants of a different sort undergo the triple response even out of soil, in the air, where there are no physical obstacles. Some of these mutants have a regulatory defect that causes them to produce ethylene at rates 20 times normal. The phenotype of such ethylene-overproducing (*eto*) mutants can be restored to wild-type by treating the seedlings with inhibitors of ethylene synthesis. Other mutants, called constitutive triple-response (*ctr*) mutants, undergo the triple response in air but do not respond to inhibitors of ethylene synthesis **(Figure 39.14b)**. (Constitutive genes are genes that are continually expressed in all cells of an organism.) In *ctr mutants*, ethylene signal transduction is permanently turned on, even though ethylene is not present.

The affected gene in *ctr* mutants codes for a protein kinase. The fact that this mutation *activates* the ethylene response suggests that the normal kinase product of the wild-type allele is a *negative* regulator of ethylene signal transduction. Here is one hypothesis for how the pathway works in wild-type plants: Binding of the hormone ethylene to the ethylene receptor leads to inactivation of the kinase; and inactivation of this negative regulator allows synthesis of the proteins required for the triple response.

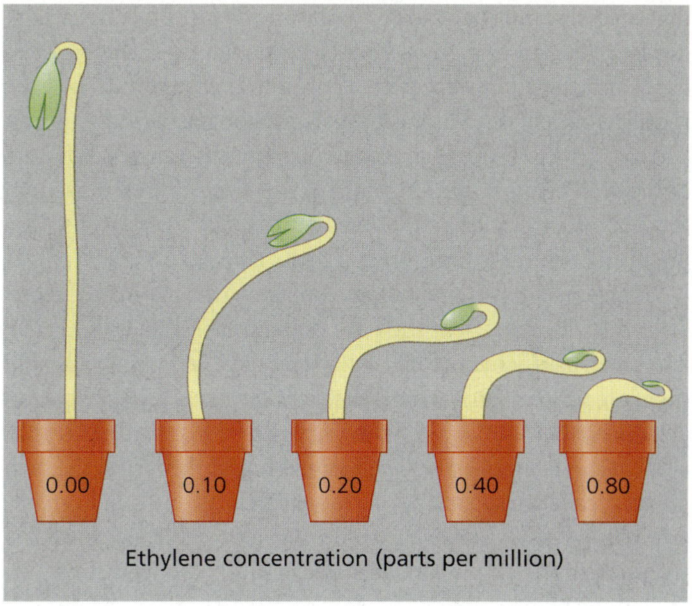

▲ **Figure 39.13 The ethylene-induced triple response.** In response to ethylene, a gaseous plant hormone, germinating pea seedlings grown in the dark undergo the triple response—slowing of stem elongation, stem thickening, and horizontal stem growth. The response is greater with increased ethylene concentration.

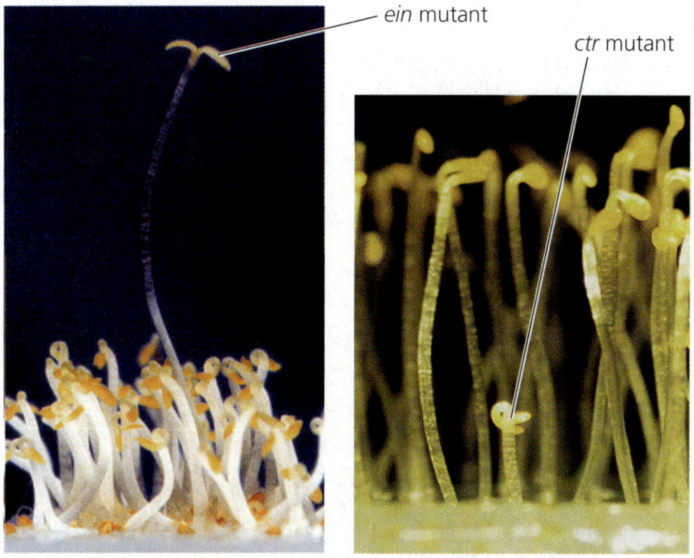

(a) *ein* mutant. An ethylene-insensitive (*ein*) mutant fails to undergo the triple response in the presence of ethylene.

(b) *ctr* mutant. A constitutive triple-response (*ctr*) mutant undergoes the triple response even in the absence of ethylene.

▲ **Figure 39.14 Ethylene triple-response *Arabidopsis* mutants.**

Senescence Consider the shedding of a leaf in autumn or the death of an annual after flowering. Or think about the final step in differentiation of a vessel element, when its living contents are destroyed, leaving a hollow tube behind. Such events involve **senescence**—the programmed death of certain cells or organs or the entire plant. Cells, organs, and plants genetically programmed to die on a schedule do not simply shut down cellular machinery and await death. Instead, at the molecular level, the onset of programmed cell death, called **apoptosis**, is a very busy time in a cell's life, requiring new gene expression (see Figure 11.19). During apoptosis, newly formed enzymes break down many chemical components, including chlorophyll, DNA, RNA, proteins, and membrane lipids. The plant salvages many of the breakdown products. A burst of ethylene is almost always associated with the programmed destruction of cells, organs, or the whole plant.

Leaf Abscission The loss of leaves from deciduous trees helps prevent desiccation during seasonal periods of climatic stress that severely limit the availability of water to the roots. Before dying leaves abscise, many essential elements are salvaged from them and stored in stem parenchyma cells. These nutrients are recycled back to developing leaves the following spring. Autumn leaf color is due to newly made red pigments as well as yellow and orange carotenoids (see Chapter 10) that were already present in the leaf and are rendered visible by the breakdown of the dark green chlorophyll in autumn.

When an autumn leaf falls, the breaking point is an abscission layer that develops near the base of the petiole **(Figure 39.15)**. The small parenchyma cells of this layer have very thin walls, and there are no fiber cells around the vascular tissue. The abscission layer is further weakened when enzymes hydrolyze polysaccharides in the cell walls. Finally, the weight of the leaf, with the help of wind, causes a separation within the abscission layer. Even before the leaf falls, a layer of cork forms a protective scar on the twig side of the abscission layer, preventing pathogens from invading the plant.

A change in the ratio of ethylene to auxin controls abscission. An aging leaf produces less and less auxin, rendering the cells of the abscission layer more sensitive to ethylene. As the influence of ethylene on the abscission layer prevails, the cells produce enzymes that digest the cellulose and other components of cell walls.

▲ **Figure 39.15 Abscission of a maple leaf.** Abscission is controlled by a change in the ratio of ethylene to auxin. The abscission layer is seen in this longitudinal section as a vertical band at the base of the petiole. After the leaf falls, a protective layer of cork becomes the leaf scar that helps prevent pathogens from invading the plant (LM).

Fruit Ripening Immature fleshy fruits are generally tart, hard, and green—features that help protect the developing seeds from herbivores. After ripening, the mature fruits help *attract* animals that disperse the seeds (see Figures 30.8 and 30.9). In many cases, a burst of ethylene production in the fruit triggers the ripening process. The enzymatic breakdown of cell wall components softens the fruit, and the conversion of starches and acids to sugars makes the fruit sweet. The production of new scents and colors helps advertise ripeness to animals, which eat the fruits and disperse the seeds.

A chain reaction occurs during ripening: Ethylene triggers ripening, and ripening triggers more ethylene production—a rare example of positive feedback in physiology (see Figure 1.13). The result is a huge burst in ethylene production. Because ethylene is a gas, the signal to ripen spreads from fruit to fruit. If you pick or buy green fruit, you may be able to speed ripening by storing the fruit in a paper bag, allowing ethylene to accumulate. On a commercial scale, many kinds of fruits are ripened in huge storage containers in which ethylene levels are enhanced. In other cases, fruit producers take measures to slow ripening caused by natural ethylene. Apples, for instance, are stored in bins flushed with carbon dioxide. Circulating the air prevents ethylene from accumulating, and carbon dioxide inhibits synthesis of new ethylene. Stored in this way, apples picked in autumn can still be shipped to grocery stores the following summer.

Given the importance of ethylene in the postharvest physiology of fruits, the genetic engineering of ethylene signal transduction pathways has potential commercial applications. For example, by engineering a way to block the transcription of one of the genes required for ethylene synthesis, molecular biologists have created tomato fruits that ripen on demand. These fruits are picked while green and will not ripen unless ethylene gas is added. As such methods are refined, they will reduce spoilage of fruits and vegetables, a problem that ruins almost half the produce harvested in the United States.

Systems Biology and Hormone Interactions

As we have discussed, plant responses often involve the interactions of many hormones and their signal transduction pathways. The study of hormone interactions can be a complex problem. For example, flooding of deepwater rice leads to a 50-fold increase in internal ethylene levels and rapid stem elongation. But ethylene's role in this response is a small part of the story. Flooding also leads to an increase in sensitivity to gibberellins that is mediated by a decrease in ABA levels. Thus, stem elongation results from an interaction of these three hormones and their signal transduction pathways.

Imagine yourself as a molecular biologist assigned the task of genetically engineering a deepwater rice plant so that it grows even faster when submerged. Would the best molecular target for genetic manipulation be an enzyme that inactivates ABA? An enzyme that produces more gibberellins? An ethylene receptor? It is difficult to predict. And this is by no means an unusual problem. Virtually every plant response discussed in this chapter is of comparable complexity. Because of this pervasive and unavoidable issue of complex interactions, many plant biologists are promoting a new, systems-based approach to plant biology.

Chapter 1 provided a general description of systems biology, which attempts to discover and understand biological properties that emerge from the interactions of many system elements (for example, mRNAs, proteins, hormones, and metabolites). Using genomic techniques, biologists can now identify all the genes in a plant. As of early 2008, the genomes of several plant species have been sequenced, including the research plant *Arabidopsis*, rice (*Oryza sativa*), a species of poplar (*Populus trichocarpa*), grape (*Vitus vinifera*), and maize (*Zea mays*). Moreover, using microarray and proteomic techniques (see Chapters 20 and 21), scientists can determine which genes are activated or inactivated during development or in response to an environmental change. However, simply identifying all the genes and proteins (system elements) in an organism is comparable to listing all the parts of an airplane. Although such a list provides a catalog of components, it is not sufficient for understanding the complexity underlying the integrated system. What plant biologists really need to know is how all these system elements interact.

A systems-based approach may greatly alter how plants are studied. One vision is laboratories equipped with high-throughput robotic scanners that record which genes in a plant's genome are activated in which cells and under what conditions. New hypotheses and avenues of research will emerge from analysis of these comprehensive data sets. Ultimately, one goal of systems biology is to model an entire living plant. Armed with such detailed knowledge, a biologist attempting to genetically engineer faster stem elongation in rice could proceed much more efficiently. The ability to model a living plant could make it possible to predict the result of a genetic manipulation before setting foot in the laboratory.

CONCEPT CHECK 39.2

1. Suggest a physiological reason for the old adage "One bad apple spoils the bunch."
2. Suggest a reason why cut flowers such as carnations are often treated with cytokinins prior to shipping.
3. Fusicoccin is a fungal toxin that stimulates the plasma membrane H^+ pumps of plant cells. How may it affect the growth of isolated stem sections?
4. **WHAT IF?** If a plant has the double mutation *ctr* and *ein*, what would be its triple-response phenotype? Explain your answer.

For suggested answers, see Appendix A.

CONCEPT **39.3**

Responses to light are critical for plant success

Light is an especially important environmental factor in the lives of plants. In addition to being required for photosynthesis, light cues many key events in plant growth and development. Effects of light on plant morphology are what plant biologists call **photomorphogenesis**. Light reception also allows plants to measure the passage of days and seasons.

Plants can detect not only the presence of light but also its direction, intensity, and wavelength (color). A graph called an **action spectrum** depicts the relative effectiveness of different wavelengths of radiation in driving a particular process. For example, the action spectrum for photosynthesis has two peaks, one in red light and one in blue light (see Figure 10.9b). This is because chlorophyll absorbs light primarily in the red and blue portions of the visible spectrum. Action spectra are useful in studying *any* process that depends on light, such as phototropism **(Figure 39.16)**. By

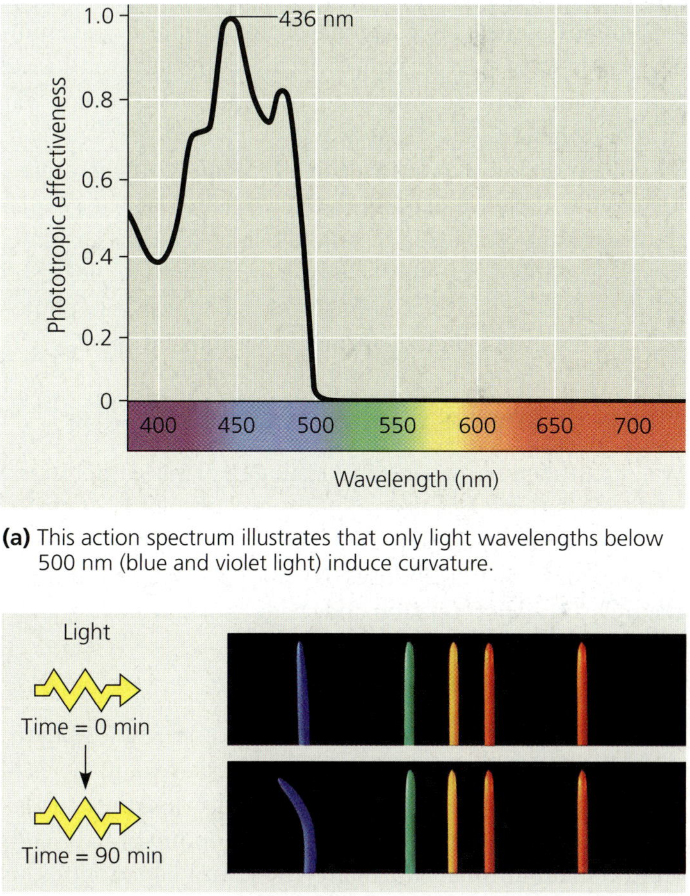

(a) This action spectrum illustrates that only light wavelengths below 500 nm (blue and violet light) induce curvature.

(b) These photographs of coleoptiles were taken before and after 90-minute exposures to light sources of the colors indicated.

▲ **Figure 39.16 Action spectrum for blue-light-stimulated phototropism in maize coleoptiles.** Phototropic bending toward light is controlled by phototropin, a photoreceptor sensitive to blue and violet light, particularly blue light.

comparing action spectra of various plant responses, researchers determine which responses are mediated by the same photoreceptor (pigment). They also compare action spectra with absorption spectra of pigments; a close correspondence for a given pigment suggests that the pigment is the photoreceptor mediating the response. Action spectra reveal that red and blue light are the most important colors in regulating a plant's photomorphogenesis. These observations led researchers to two major classes of light receptors: **blue-light photoreceptors** and **phytochromes**, photoreceptors that absorb mostly red light.

Blue-Light Photoreceptors

Blue light initiates a variety of responses in plants, including phototropism, the light-induced opening of stomata (see Figure 36.16), and the light-induced slowing of hypocotyl elongation that occurs when a seedling breaks ground. The biochemical identity of the blue-light photoreceptor was so elusive that in the 1970s, plant physiologists began to call this putative receptor "cryptochrome" (from the Greek *kryptos*, hidden, and *chrom*, pigment). In the 1990s, molecular biologists analyzing *Arabidopsis* mutants found that plants use at least three different types of pigments to detect blue light. *Cryptochromes*, molecular relatives of DNA repair enzymes, are involved in the blue-light-induced inhibition of stem elongation that occurs, for example, when a seedling first emerges from the soil. *Phototropin* is a protein kinase involved in mediating phototropic curvatures, such as those studied in grass seedlings by the Darwins, and in chloroplast movements in response to light. There is currently much debate about whether phototropin or a carotenoid-based photoreceptor called *zeaxanthin* is the major blue-light photoreceptor involved in blue-light-mediated stomatal opening.

Phytochromes as Photoreceptors

When introducing signal transduction in plants earlier in the chapter, we discussed the role of the plant pigments called phytochromes in the de-etiolation process. Phytochromes regulate many plant responses to light. Let's look at two more examples: seed germination and shade avoidance.

Phytochromes and Seed Germination

Studies of seed germination led to the discovery of phytochromes. Because of limited nutrient reserves, many types of seeds, especially small ones, germinate only when the light environment and other conditions are near optimal. Such seeds often remain dormant for many years until light conditions change. For example, the death of a shading tree or the plowing of a field may create a favorable light environment.

In the 1930s, scientists at the U.S. Department of Agriculture determined the action spectrum for light-induced germination of lettuce seeds. They exposed water-swollen seeds to a few minutes of monochromatic (single-colored) light of various wavelengths and then stored the seeds in the dark. After two days, the researchers counted the number of seeds that had germinated under each light regimen. They found that red light of wavelength 660 nm increased the germination percentage of lettuce seeds maximally, whereas far-red light—that is, light of wavelengths near the upper edge of human visibility (730 nm)—*inhibited* germination compared with dark controls **(Figure 39.17)**. What happens when the lettuce seeds are subjected to a flash of red

▼ **Figure 39.17 Inquiry**

How does the order of red and far-red illumination affect seed germination?

EXPERIMENT Scientists at the U.S. Department of Agriculture briefly exposed batches of lettuce seeds to red light or far-red light to test the effects on germination. After the light exposure, the seeds were placed in the dark, and the results were compared with control seeds that were not exposed to light.

RESULTS The bar below each photo indicates the sequence of red light exposure, far-red light exposure, and darkness. The germination rate increased greatly in groups of seeds that were last exposed to red light (left). Germination was inhibited in groups of seeds that were last exposed to far-red light (right).

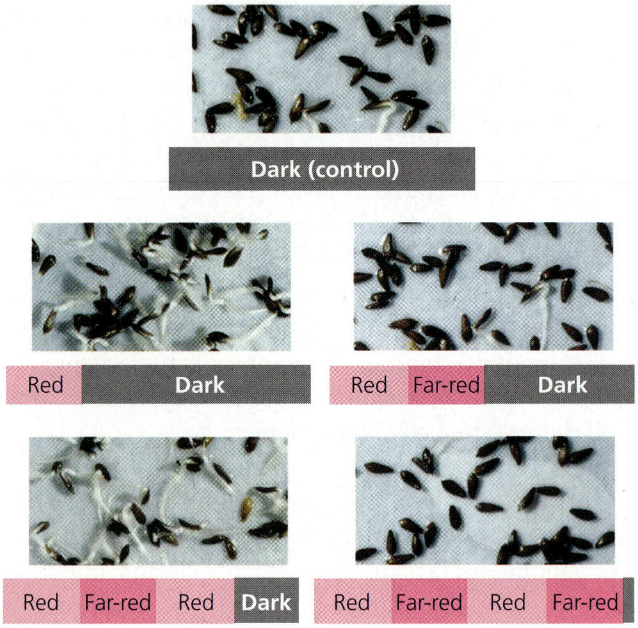

CONCLUSION Red light stimulated germination, and far-red light inhibited germination. The final light exposure was the determining factor. The effects of red and far-red light were reversible.

SOURCE H. Borthwick et al., A reversible photoreaction controlling seed germination, *Proceedings of the National Academy of Sciences, USA* 38:662–666 (1952).

WHAT IF? Phytochrome responds faster to red light than to far-red. If the seeds had been placed in white light instead of the dark after their red and far-red light treatments, would the results have been different?

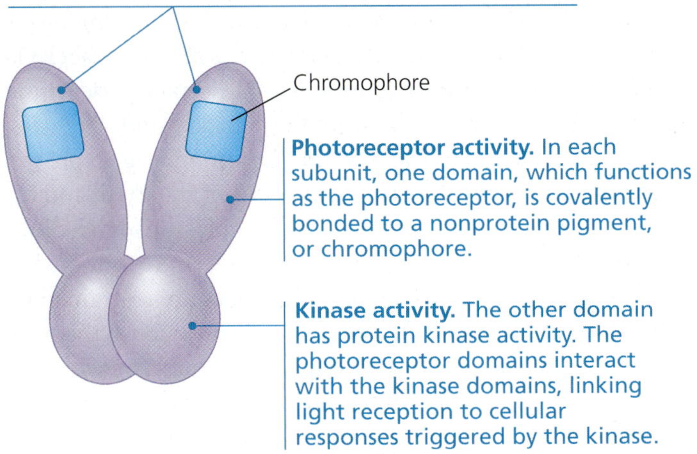

▲ **Figure 39.18 Structure of a phytochrome.**

light followed by a flash of far-red light or, conversely, to far-red light followed by red light? The *last* flash of light determines the seeds' response. In other words, the effects of red and far-red light are reversible.

The photoreceptors responsible for the opposing effects of red and far-red light are phytochromes. A phytochrome has two identical subunits, each consisting of a polypeptide component covalently bonded to a nonpolypeptide *chromophore*, the light-absorbing part of the subunit **(Figure 39.18)**. So far, researchers have identified five phytochromes in *Arabidopsis*, each with a slightly different polypeptide component.

The chromophore of a phytochrome is photoreversible, reverting back and forth between two isomeric forms, depending on the color of light provided (see Figure 4.7 to review isomers). In its P_r isomer form, a phytochrome absorbs red (r) light maximally, whereas in its P_{fr} isomer form, it absorbs far-red (fr) light:

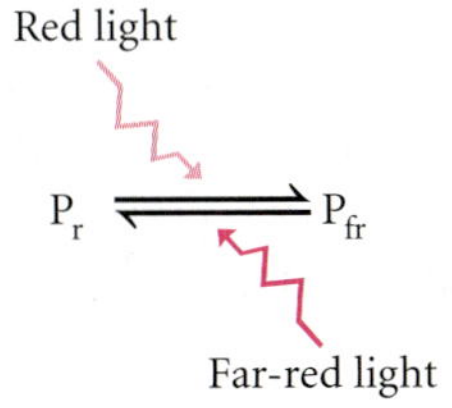

This $P_r \rightleftharpoons P_{fr}$ interconversion is a switching mechanism that controls various light-induced events in the life of the plant **(Figure 39.19)**. P_{fr} is the form of phytochrome that triggers many of a plant's developmental responses to light. For example, P_r in lettuce seeds exposed to red light is converted to P_{fr}, stimulating the cellular responses that lead to germination. When red-illuminated seeds are then exposed to far-red light, the P_{fr} is converted back to P_r, inhibiting the germination response.

How does phytochrome switching explain light-induced germination in nature? Plants synthesize phytochrome as P_r, and if seeds are kept in the dark, the pigment remains almost entirely in the P_r form (see Figure 39.19). Sunlight contains both red light and far-red light, but the conversion to P_{fr} is faster than the conversion to P_r. Therefore, the ratio of P_{fr} to P_r increases in the sunlight. When seeds are exposed to adequate sunlight, the production and accumulation of P_{fr} will trigger their germination.

Phytochromes and Shade Avoidance

The phytochrome system also provides the plant with information about the *quality* of light. Because sunlight includes both red and far-red radiation, during the day the $P_r \rightleftharpoons P_{fr}$ interconversion reaches a dynamic equilibrium, with the ratio of the two phytochrome forms indicating the relative amounts of red and far-red light. This sensing mechanism enables plants to adapt to changes in light conditions. Consider, for example, the "shade avoidance" response of a tree that requires relatively high light intensity. If other trees in a forest shade this tree, the phytochrome ratio shifts in favor of P_r because the forest canopy screens out more red light than far-red light. This is because the chlorophyll pigments in the leaves of the canopy absorb red light and allow far-red light to pass. The shift in the ratio of red to far-red light induces the tree to allocate more of its resources to growing taller. In contrast, direct sunlight increases the proportion of P_{fr}, which stimulates branching and inhibits vertical growth.

In addition to helping plants detect light, phytochrome helps a plant to keep track of the passage of days and seasons. To understand phytochrome's role in these timekeeping processes, we must first examine the nature of the plant's internal clock.

▶ **Figure 39.19 Phytochrome: a molecular switching mechanism.** Absorption of red light causes the P_r to change to the P_{fr}. Far-red light reverses this conversion. In most cases, it is the P_{fr} form of the pigment that switches on physiological and developmental responses in the plant.

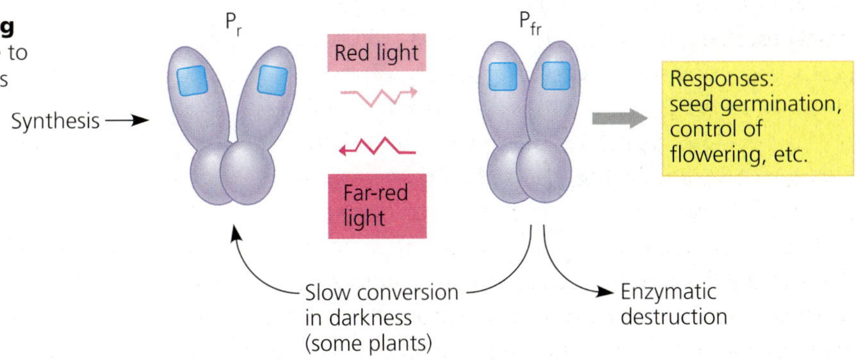

Biological Clocks and Circadian Rhythms

Many plant processes, such as transpiration and the synthesis of certain enzymes, oscillate during the course of a day. Some of these cyclic variations are responses to the changes in light levels, temperature, and relative humidity that accompany the 24-hour cycle of day and night. One can control these external factors by growing plants in growth chambers under rigidly maintained conditions of light, temperature, and humidity. But even under artificially constant conditions, many physiological processes in plants, such as the opening and closing of stomata and the production of photosynthetic enzymes, continue to oscillate with a frequency of about 24 hours. For example, many legumes lower their leaves in the evening and raise them in the morning **(Figure 39.20)**. A bean plant continues these "sleep movements" even if kept in constant light or constant darkness; the leaves are not simply responding to sunrise and sunset. Such cycles, with a frequency of about 24 hours and not directly controlled by any known environmental variable, are called **circadian rhythms** (from the Latin *circa*, approximately, and *dies*, day), and they are common to all eukaryotic life. Your pulse rate, blood pressure, temperature, rate of cell division, blood cell count, alertness, urine composition, metabolic rate, sex drive, and response to medications all fluctuate in a circadian manner.

Current research indicates that the molecular "gears" of the circadian clock are internal, rather than a daily response to some subtle but pervasive environmental cycle, such as geomagnetism or cosmic radiation. Organisms, including plants and humans, continue their rhythms even when placed in deep mine shafts or when orbited in satellites, conditions that alter these subtle geophysical periodicities. However, daily signals from the environment can entrain (set) the circadian clock to a period of precisely 24 hours.

If an organism is kept in a constant environment, its circadian rhythms deviate from a 24-hour period (a period is the duration of one cycle). These free-running periods, as they are called, vary from about 21 to 27 hours, depending on the particular rhythmic response. The sleep movements of bean plants, for instance, have a period of 26 hours when the plants are kept in the free-running condition of constant darkness. Deviation of the free-running period from exactly 24 hours does not mean that biological clocks drift erratically. Free-running clocks are still keeping perfect time, but they are not synchronized with the outside world.

How do biological clocks work? In attempting to answer this question, we must distinguish between the clock and the rhythmic processes it controls. For example, the leaves of the bean plant in Figure 39.20 are the clock's "hands" but are not the essence of the clock itself. If bean leaves are restrained for several hours and then released, they will reestablish the position appropriate for the time of day. We can interfere with a biological rhythm, but the underlying clockwork continues.

Researchers are tracing the clock to a molecular mechanism that may be common to all eukaryotes. A leading hypothesis is that biological timekeeping may depend on the synthesis of a protein that regulates its own production through feedback control. This protein may be a transcription factor that inhibits transcription of the gene that encodes the transcription factor itself. The concentration of this transcription factor may increase during the first half of the circadian cycle and then decline during the second half as a result of inhibiting its own production.

Researchers have recently used a novel technique to identify clock mutants of *Arabidopsis*. One prominent circadian rhythm in plants is the daily production of certain photosynthesis-related proteins. Molecular biologists traced the cause of this rhythm to the promoter that initiates the transcription of the genes for these photosynthesis proteins. To identify clock mutants, scientists spliced the gene for an enzyme responsible for the bioluminescence of fireflies, called luciferase, to the promoter. When the biological clock turned on the promoter in the *Arabidopsis* genome, it also turned on the production of luciferase. The plants began to glow with a circadian periodicity. Clock mutants were then isolated by selecting specimens that glowed for a longer or shorter time than normal. The genes altered in some of these mutants affect proteins that normally bind photoreceptors. Perhaps these particular mutations disrupt a light-dependent mechanism that sets the biological clock.

Noon

Midnight

▲ **Figure 39.20 Sleep movements of a bean plant (*Phaseolus vulgaris*).** The movements are caused by reversible changes in the turgor pressure of cells on opposing sides of the pulvini, motor organs of the leaf.

The Effect of Light on the Biological Clock

As we have discussed, the free-running period of the circadian rhythm of bean leaf movements is 26 hours. Consider a bean plant placed at dawn in a dark cabinet for 72 hours: Its leaves would not rise again until 2 hours after natural dawn on the second day, 4 hours after natural dawn on the third day, and so on. Shut off from environmental cues, the plant becomes desynchronized. Desynchronization happens to humans when we cross several time zones in an airplane; when we reach our destination, the clocks on the wall are not synchronized with our internal clocks. All eukaryotes are probably prone to jet lag.

The factor that entrains the biological clock to precisely 24 hours every day is light. Both phytochrome and blue-light photoreceptors can entrain circadian rhythms in plants, but our understanding of how phytochrome does this is more complete. The mechanism involves turning cellular responses on and off by means of the $P_r \rightleftharpoons P_{fr}$ switch.

Consider again the photoreversible system in Figure 39.19. In darkness, the phytochrome ratio shifts gradually in favor of the P_r form, partly as a result of turnover in the overall phytochrome pool. The pigment is synthesized in the P_r form, and enzymes destroy more P_{fr} than P_r. In some plant species, P_{fr} present at sundown slowly converts to P_r. In darkness, there is no means for the P_r to be reconverted to P_{fr}, but upon illumination, the P_{fr} level suddenly increases again as P_r is rapidly converted. This increase in P_{fr} each day at dawn resets the biological clock: Bean leaves reach their most extreme night position 16 hours after dawn.

In nature, interactions between phytochrome and the biological clock enable plants to measure the passage of night and day. The relative lengths of night and day, however, change over the course of the year (except at the equator). Plants use this change to adjust activities in synchrony with the seasons.

Photoperiodism and Responses to Seasons

Imagine the consequences if a plant produced flowers when pollinators were not present or if a deciduous tree produced leaves in the middle of winter. Seasonal events are of critical importance in the life cycles of most plants. Seed germination, flowering, and the onset and breaking of bud dormancy are all stages that usually occur at specific times of the year. The environmental stimulus that plants use most often to detect the time of year is the photoperiod, the relative lengths of night and day. A physiological response to photoperiod, such as flowering, is called **photoperiodism**.

Photoperiodism and Control of Flowering

An early clue to how plants detect seasons came from a mutant variety of tobacco, Maryland Mammoth, which grew tall but failed to flower during summer. It finally bloomed in a greenhouse in December. After trying to induce earlier flowering by varying temperature, moisture, and mineral nutrition, researchers learned that the shortening days of winter stimulated this variety to flower. If the plants were kept in light-tight boxes so that lamps could manipulate "day" and "night," flowering occurred only if the day length was 14 hours or shorter. It did not flower during summer because at Maryland's latitude, the summer days were too long.

The researchers called Maryland Mammoth a **short-day plant** because it apparently required a light period *shorter* than a critical length to flower. Chrysanthemums, poinsettias, and some soybean varieties are also short-day plants, which generally flower in late summer, fall, or winter. Another group of plants flower only when the light period is *longer* than a certain number of hours. These **long-day plants** generally flower in late spring or early summer. Spinach, for example, flowers when days are 14 hours or longer. Radishes, lettuce, irises, and many cereal varieties are also long-day plants. **Day-neutral plants**, such as tomatoes, rice, and dandelions, are unaffected by photoperiod and flower when they reach a certain stage of maturity, regardless of day length.

Critical Night Length In the 1940s, researchers learned that flowering and other responses to photoperiod are actually controlled by night length, not day length. Many of these scientists worked with cocklebur (*Xanthium strumarium*), a short-day plant that flowers only when days are 16 hours or shorter (and nights are at least 8 hours long). These researchers found that if the daytime portion of the photoperiod is broken by a brief exposure to darkness, there is no effect on flowering. However, if the nighttime part of the photoperiod is interrupted by even a few minutes of dim light, cocklebur will not flower, and this turned out to be true for other short-day plants as well **(Figure 39.21a)**. Cocklebur is unresponsive to day length, but it requires at least 8 hours of continuous darkness to flower. Short-day plants are really long-night plants, but the older term is embedded firmly in the jargon of plant physiology. Similarly, long-day plants are actually short-night plants. A long-day plant grown on photoperiods of long nights that would not normally induce flowering will flower if the period of continuous darkness is interrupted by a few minutes of light **(Figure 39.21b)**. Notice that we distinguish long-day from short-day plants *not* by

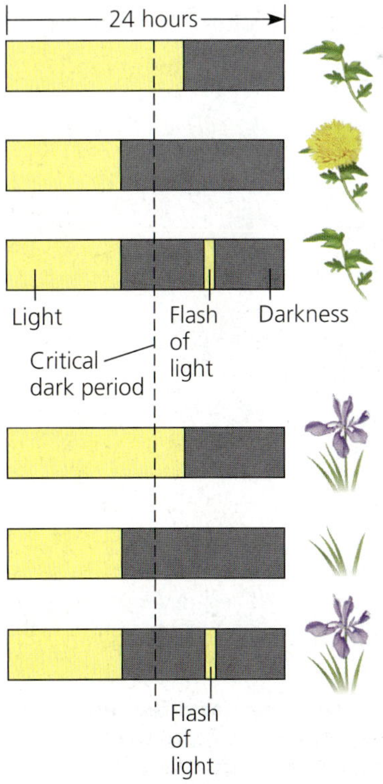

(a) Short-day (long-night) plant. Flowers when night exceeds a critical dark period. A flash of light interrupting the dark period prevents flowering.

(b) Long-day (short-night) plant. Flowers only if the night is shorter than a critical dark period. A brief flash of light artificially interrupts a long dark period, thereby inducing flowering.

▲ **Figure 39.21 Photoperiodic control of flowering.**

an absolute night length but by whether the critical night length sets a maximum (long-day plants) or minimum (short-day plants) number of hours of darkness required for flowering. In both cases, the actual number of hours in the critical night length is specific to each species of plant.

Red light is the most effective color in interrupting the nighttime portion of the photoperiod. Action spectra and photoreversibility experiments show that phytochrome is the pigment that detects the red light **(Figure 39.22)**. For example, if a flash of red (R) light during the dark period is followed by a flash of far-red (FR) light, then the plant detects no interruption of night length. As in the case of phytochrome-mediated seed germination, red/far-red photoreversibility occurs.

Plants detect night length very precisely; some short-day plants will not flower if night is even 1 minute shorter than the critical length. Some plant species always flower on the same day each year. It appears that plants use their biological clock, entrained by night length with the help of phytochrome, to tell the season of the year. The floriculture (flower-growing) industry applies this knowledge to produce flowers out of season. Chrysanthemums, for instance, are short-day plants that normally bloom in fall, but their blooming can be stalled until Mother's Day in May by punctuating each long night with a flash of light, thus turning one long night into two short nights.

Some plants bloom after a single exposure to the photoperiod required for flowering. Other species need several successive days of the appropriate photoperiod. Still other plants respond to a photoperiod only if they have been previously exposed to some other environmental stimulus, such as a period of cold temperatures. Winter wheat, for example, will not flower unless it has been exposed to several weeks of temperatures below 10°C. The use of pretreatment with cold to induce flowering is called **vernalization** (from the Latin for "spring"). Several weeks after winter wheat is vernalized, a photoperiod with long days (short nights) induces flowering.

A Flowering Hormone?

Although flowers form from apical or axillary bud meristems, it is leaves that detect changes in photoperiod and produce signaling molecules that cue buds to develop as flowers. In many short-day and long-day plants, exposing just one leaf to the appropriate photoperiod is enough to induce flowering. Indeed, as long as one leaf is left on the plant, photoperiod is detected and floral buds are induced. If all leaves are removed, the plant is insensitive to photoperiod.

Classic experiments revealed that the floral stimulus could move across a graft from an induced plant to a noninduced plant and trigger flowering in the latter. Moreover, the flowering stimulus appears to be the same for short-day and long-day plants, despite the differing photoperiodic conditions required for leaves to send this signal **(Figure 39.23)**. The hypothetical signaling molecule for flowering, called **florigen**, is still unidentified after 70 years, possibly because plant scientists had focused on small hormone-like molecules. As discussed in Chapter 36, large macromolecules, such as mRNA and proteins, can move by the

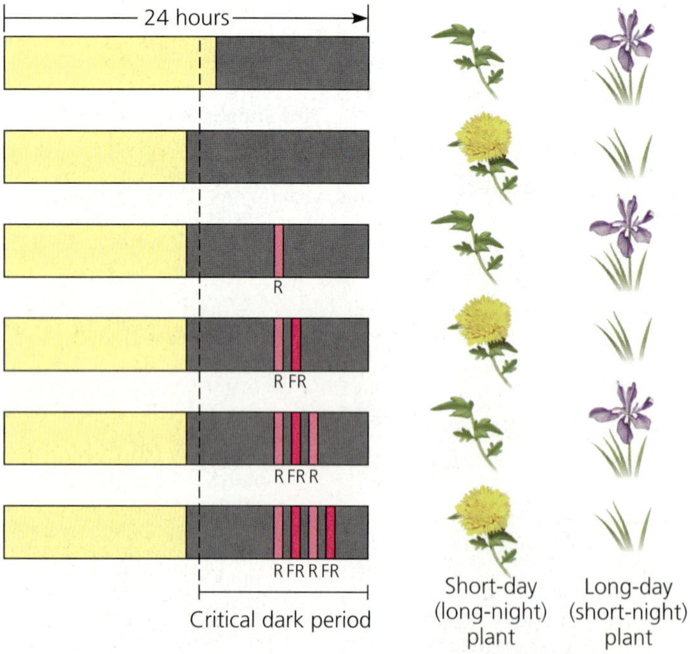

▲ **Figure 39.22 Reversible effects of red and far-red light on photoperiodic response.** A flash of red (R) light shortens the dark period. A subsequent flash of far-red (FR) light cancels the red flash's effect.

? *How would a single flash of full-spectrum light affect each plant?*

▲ **Figure 39.23 Experimental evidence for a flowering hormone.** If grown individually under short-day conditions, a short-day plant will flower and a long-day plant will not. However, both will flower if grafted together and exposed to short days. This result indicates that a flower-inducing substance (florigen) is transmitted across grafts and induces flowering in both short-day and long-day plants.

WHAT IF? *If flowering were inhibited in both parts of the grafted plants, what would you conclude?*

symplastic route via plasmodesmata (see Figure 36.11) and regulate plant development. Could florigen be a macromolecule? Plant biologists are now excited about this possibility. *Arabidopsis* is a long-day plant that requires a functional *CONSTANS* gene to flower under long days. Brian Ayre and Robert Turgeon, of Cornell University, noted that *Arabidopsis* plants flowered only when *CONSTANS* was expressed in the leaf, a finding consistent with the observation that florigen is made only in leaves. They provided further evidence for a role for the CONSTANS protein in floral signaling when they grafted *Arabidopsis* plants that contained no CONSTANS protein onto plants synthesizing CONSTANS in their leaves. This elegant experiment showed that CONSTANS, or another factor that it interacts with, can move through the graft junction to signal flowering in the parts of the plant that formerly were devoid of the protein. More recent evidence suggests that CONSTANS turns on a gene called *FLOWERING LOCUS T* (*FT*) in the leaf and that the FT protein travels to the shoot apical meristem and initiates flowering.

Meristem Transition and Flowering

Whatever combination of environmental cues (such as photoperiod or vernalization) and internal signaling molecules (such as the FT protein) is necessary for flowering, the outcome is the transition of a bud's meristem from a vegetative state to a flowering state. This transition requires changes in the expression of genes that regulate pattern formation. Meristem identity genes that induce the bud to form a flower instead of a vegetative shoot must first be switched on. Then the organ identity genes that specify the spatial organization of the floral organs—sepals, petals, stamens, and carpels—are activated in the appropriate regions of the meristem (see Figure 35.34). Research on flower development is progressing rapidly, and one goal is to identify the signal transduction pathways that link such cues as photoperiod and hormonal changes to the gene expression required for flowering.

CONCEPT CHECK 39.3

1. If an enzyme in field-grown soybean leaves is most active at noon and least active at midnight, is its activity under circadian regulation?
2. A guard absentmindedly turns on the lights in a greenhouse one night, but the plants still flower on schedule. Suggest two reasons why they were not affected by the interruption of darkness.
3. Some vine seedlings grow toward darkness until reaching an upright structure. This adaptation helps them "find" a shaded object to climb. How might you test whether this negative phototropism is mediated by blue-light photoreceptors or by phytochrome?
4. **WHAT IF?** If a plant flowers in a controlled chamber with a daily cycle of 10 hours of light and 14 hours of darkness, is it a short-day plant? Explain.

For suggested answers, see Appendix A.

CONCEPT 39.4

Plants respond to a wide variety of stimuli other than light

Plants can neither migrate to a watering hole when water is scarce nor seek shelter from wind. A seed landing upside down in the soil cannot maneuver itself into an upright position. Because of their immobility, plants must adjust to a wide range of environmental circumstances through developmental and physiological mechanisms, and natural selection has refined these responses. Light is so important in the life of a plant that we devoted the entire previous section to a plant's reception of and response to this one environmental factor. In this section, we examine responses to some of the other environmental stimuli that a plant commonly encounters.

Gravity

Because plants are solar-powered organisms, it is not surprising that mechanisms for growing toward sunlight have evolved. But what environmental cue does the shoot of a young seedling use to grow upward when it is completely underground and there is no light for it to detect? Similarly, what environmental factor prompts the young root to grow downward? The answer to both questions is gravity.

Place a plant on its side, and it adjusts its growth so that the shoot bends upward and the root curves downward. In their responses to gravity, or **gravitropism**, roots display positive gravitropism **(Figure 39.24a)** and shoots exhibit negative

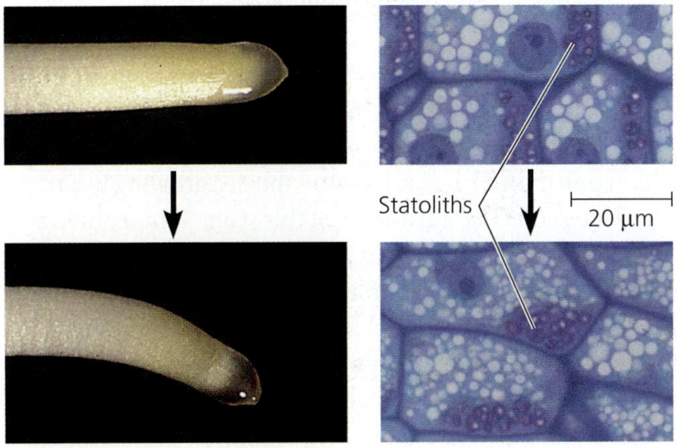

(a) Over the course of hours, a horizontally oriented primary root of maize bends gravitropically until its growing tip becomes vertically oriented (LMs).

(b) Within minutes after the root is placed horizontally, plastids called statoliths begin settling to the lowest sides of root cap cells. This settling may be the gravity-sensing mechanism that leads to redistribution of auxin and differing rates of elongation by cells on opposite sides of the root (LMs).

▲ **Figure 39.24 Positive gravitropism in roots: the statolith hypothesis.**

gravitropism. Gravitropism occurs as soon as a seed germinates, ensuring that the root grows into the soil and the shoot grows toward sunlight, regardless of how the seed is oriented when it lands. Auxin plays a key role in gravitropism.

Plants may detect gravity by the settling of **statoliths**, specialized plastids containing dense starch grains, to the lower portions of cells (**Figure 39.24b**, on the previous page). In roots, statoliths are located in certain cells of the root cap. According to one hypothesis, the aggregation of statoliths at the low points of these cells triggers redistribution of calcium, which causes lateral transport of auxin within the root. The calcium and auxin accumulate on the lower side of the root's zone of elongation. Because these chemicals are dissolved, they do not respond to gravity but must be actively transported to one side of the root. At high concentration, auxin inhibits cell elongation, an effect that slows growth on the root's lower side. The more rapid elongation of cells on the upper side causes the root to curve as it grows. This tropism continues until the root grows straight down.

Plant physiologists are refining the "falling statolith" hypothesis of root gravitropism, based on new experiments. For example, mutants of *Arabidopsis* and tobacco that lack statoliths are still capable of gravitropism, though the response is slower than in wild-type plants. It could be that the entire cell helps the root sense gravity by mechanically pulling on proteins that tether the protoplast to the cell wall, stretching the proteins on the "up" side and compressing the proteins on the "down" side of the root cells. Dense organelles, in addition to starch granules, may also contribute by distorting the cytoskeleton as they are pulled by gravity. Statoliths, because of their density, may enhance gravitational sensing by a mechanism that works more slowly in their absence.

Mechanical Stimuli

A tree growing on a windy mountain ridge usually has a shorter, stockier trunk than a tree of the same species growing in a more sheltered location. The advantage of this stunted morphology is that it enables the plant to hold its ground against strong gusts of wind. The term **thigmomorphogenesis** (from the Greek *thigma*, touch) refers to the changes in form that result from mechanical perturbation. Plants are very sensitive to mechanical stress: Even the act of measuring the length of a leaf with a ruler alters its subsequent growth. Rubbing the stems of a young plant a couple of times daily results in plants that are shorter than controls **(Figure 39.25)**. Mechanical stimulation activates a signal transduction pathway involving an increase in cytosolic Ca^{2+} that mediates the activation of specific genes, some of which code for proteins that affect cell wall properties.

Some plant species have become, over the course of their evolution, "touch specialists." Acute responsiveness to mechanical stimuli is an integral part of these plants' "life strategies."

▲ **Figure 39.25 Altering gene expression by touch in *Arabidopsis*.** The shorter plant on the left was rubbed twice a day. The untouched plant (right) grew much taller.

Most vines and other climbing plants have tendrils that coil rapidly around supports (see Figure 35.7). These grasping organs usually grow straight until they touch something; the contact stimulates a coiling response caused by differential growth of cells on opposite sides of the tendril. This directional growth in response to touch is called **thigmotropism**, and it allows the vine to take advantage of whatever mechanical supports it comes across as it climbs upward toward a forest canopy.

Other examples of touch specialists are plants that undergo rapid leaf movements in response to mechanical stimulation. For example, when the compound leaf of the sensitive plant *Mimosa pudica* is touched, it collapses and its leaflets fold together **(Figure 39.26)**. This response, which takes only a second or two, results from a rapid loss of turgor in cells within pulvini, specialized motor organs located at the joints of the leaf. The motor cells suddenly become flaccid after stimulation because they lose potassium, which causes water to leave the cells by osmosis. It takes about 10 minutes for the cells to regain their turgor and restore the "unstimulated" form of the leaf. The function of the sensitive plant's behavior invites speculation. Perhaps by folding its leaves and reducing its surface area when jostled by strong winds, the plant conserves water. Or perhaps because the collapse of the leaves exposes thorns on the stem, the rapid response of the sensitive plant discourages herbivores.

A remarkable feature of rapid leaf movements is the mode of transmission of the stimulus through the plant. If one leaflet on a sensitive plant is touched, first that leaflet responds, then the adjacent leaflet responds, and so on, until all the leaflet pairs have folded together. From the point of stimulation, the signal that produces this response travels at a speed of about 1 cm/sec. An electrical impulse, traveling at the same rate, can

(a) Unstimulated state (leaflets spread apart) **(b) Stimulated state (leaflets folded)**

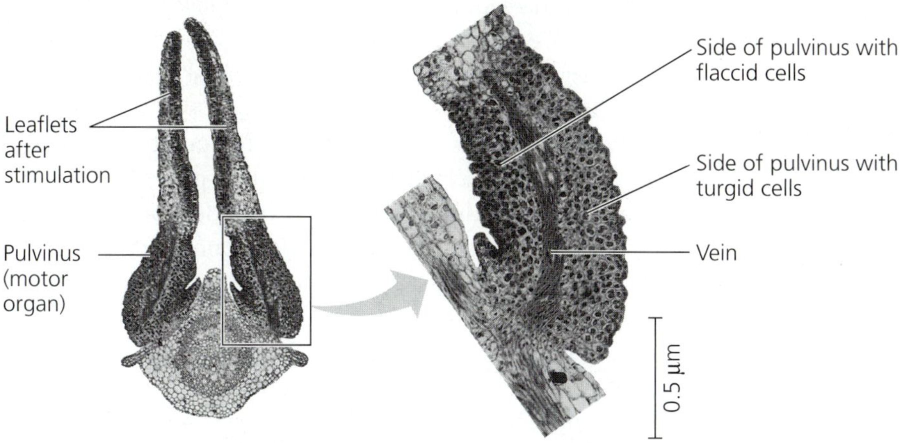

(c) Cross section of a leaflet pair in the stimulated state (LM). The curvature of a pulvinus (motor organ) is caused when motor cells on one side of the pulvinus lose water and become flaccid while cells on the opposite side retain their turgor.

▲ **Figure 39.26 Rapid turgor movements by the sensitive plant (*Mimosa pudica*).**

be detected by attaching electrodes to the leaf. These impulses, called **action potentials**, resemble nerve impulses in animals, though the action potentials of plants are thousands of times slower. Action potentials, which have been discovered in many species of algae and plants, may be widely used as a form of internal communication. For example, in the Venus flytrap (*Dionaea muscipula*), action potentials are transmitted from sensory hairs in the trap to the cells that respond by closing the trap (see Figure 37.14). In the case of *Mimosa pudica*, more violent stimuli, such as touching a leaf with a hot needle, causes *all* the leaves and leaflets on a plant to droop, but this systemic response involves the spread of signaling molecules released from the injured area to other parts of the shoot.

Environmental Stresses

Occasionally, certain factors in the environment change severely enough to have a potentially adverse effect on a plant's survival, growth, and reproduction. Environmental stresses, such as flooding, drought, or extreme temperatures, can have a devastating impact on crop yields in agriculture. In natural ecosystems, plants that cannot tolerate an environmental stress either will succumb or will be outcompeted by other plants, and they will become locally extinct. Thus, environmental stresses are an important factor in determining the geographic ranges of plants. Here, we will consider some of the more common **abiotic** (nonliving) stresses that plants encounter. In the last section of this chapter, we will examine the defensive responses of plants to common **biotic** (living) stresses, such as pathogens and herbivores.

Drought

On a bright, warm, dry day, a plant may be stressed by a water deficiency because it is losing water by transpiration faster than the water can be restored by uptake from the soil. Prolonged drought can stress crops and the plants of natural ecosystems for weeks or months. Severe water deficit, of course, will kill a plant, as you may know from experience with neglected houseplants. But plants have control systems that enable them to cope with less extreme water deficits.

Many of a plant's responses to water deficit help the plant conserve water by reducing the rate of transpiration. Water deficit in a leaf causes guard cells to lose turgor, a simple control mechanism that slows transpiration by closing stomata (see Figure 36.17). Water deficit also stimulates increased synthesis and release of abscisic acid in the leaf; this hormone helps keep stomata closed by acting on guard cell membranes. Leaves respond to water deficit in several other ways. Because cell expansion is a turgor-dependent process, water deficits inhibit the growth of young leaves, as does the accumulation of abscisic acid. This response minimizes the transpirational loss of water by slowing the increase in leaf surface. When the leaves of many grasses and other plants wilt from a water deficit, they roll into a shape that reduces transpiration by exposing less leaf surface to dry air and wind. Although these leaf responses conserve water, they reduce photosynthesis, which is one reason why a drought diminishes crop yield.

Root growth also responds to water deficit. During a drought, the soil usually dries from the surface down. This inhibits the growth of shallow roots, partly because cells cannot maintain the turgor required for elongation. Deeper roots surrounded by soil that is still moist continue to grow. Thus, the root system proliferates in a way that maximizes exposure to soil water.

Flooding

Too much water is also a problem for a plant. An overwatered houseplant may suffocate because the soil lacks the air spaces that provide oxygen for cellular respiration in the roots. Some plants are structurally adapted to very wet habitats. For example, the submerged roots of mangroves, which inhabit coastal marshes, are continuous with aerial roots exposed to oxygen (see Figure 35.4). But how do less specialized plants cope with oxygen deprivation in waterlogged soils? Oxygen deprivation stimulates the production of ethylene, which causes some cells in the root cortex to undergo apoptosis. The destruction of these cells creates air tubes that function as "snorkels," providing oxygen to the submerged roots **(Figure 39.27)**.

Salt Stress

An excess of sodium chloride or other salts in the soil threatens plants for two reasons. First, by lowering the water potential of the soil solution, salt can cause a water deficit in plants even though the soil has plenty of water. As the water potential of the soil solution becomes more negative, the water potential gradient from soil to roots is lowered, thereby reducing water uptake (see Chapter 36). The second problem with saline soil is that sodium and certain other ions are toxic to plants when their concentrations are relatively high. The selectively permeable membranes of root cells impede the uptake of most harmful ions, but this only aggravates the problem of acquiring water from soil that is rich in solutes. Many plants can respond to moderate soil salinity by producing solutes that are well tolerated at high concentrations: These mostly organic compounds keep the water potential of cells more negative than that of the soil solution without admitting toxic quantities of salt. However, most plants cannot survive salt stress for long. The exceptions are halophytes, salt-tolerant plants with adaptations such as salt glands that pump salts out across the leaf epidermis.

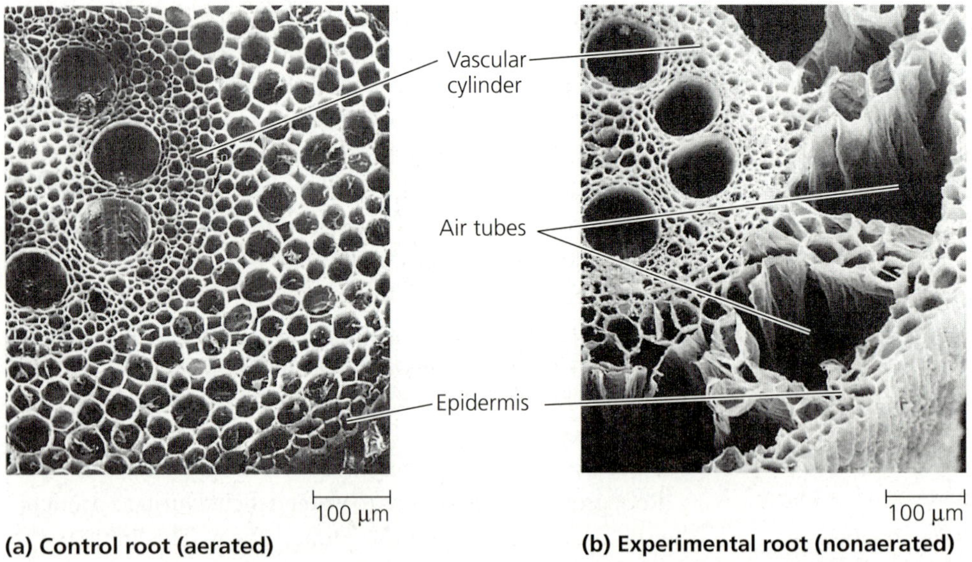

▲ **Figure 39.27 A developmental response of maize roots to flooding and oxygen deprivation. (a)** A cross section of a control root grown in an aerated hydroponic medium. **(b)** A root grown in a nonaerated hydroponic medium. Ethylene-stimulated apoptosis (programmed cell death) creates the air tubes (SEMs).

Heat Stress

As is true for other organisms, excessive heat harms and even kills a plant by denaturing its enzymes and damaging its metabolism. One function of transpiration is evaporative cooling. On a warm day, for example, the temperature of a leaf may be 3–10°C below the ambient air temperature. Hot, dry weather also tends to dehydrate many plants; the closing of stomata in response to this stress conserves water but then sacrifices evaporative cooling. This dilemma is one reason why very hot, dry days take a toll on most plants.

Most plants have a backup response that enables them to survive heat stress. Above a certain temperature—about 40°C for most plants in temperate regions—plant cells begin synthesizing **heat-shock proteins**, which help protect other proteins from heat stress. This response also occurs in heat-stressed animals and microorganisms. Some heat-shock proteins are chaperone proteins (chaperonins), which function in unstressed cells as temporary scaffolds that help other proteins fold into their functional shapes (see Chapter 5). In their roles as heat-shock proteins, perhaps these molecules bind to other proteins and help prevent their denaturation.

Cold Stress

One problem plants face when the temperature of the environment falls is a change in the fluidity of cell membranes. Recall from Chapter 7 that a biological membrane is a fluid mosaic, with proteins and lipids moving laterally in the plane of the membrane. When a membrane cools below a critical point, it loses its fluidity as the lipids become locked into crystalline structures. This alters solute transport across the membrane and also adversely affects the functions of membrane proteins. Plants respond to cold stress by altering the lipid composition of their membranes. For example, membrane lipids increase in their proportion of unsaturated fatty acids, which have shapes that help keep membranes fluid at lower temperatures by impeding crystal formation (see Figure 7.5b). Such membrane modification requires from several hours to days, which is one reason why unseasonably cold temperatures are generally more stressful to plants than the more gradual seasonal drop in air temperature.

Freezing is a more severe version of cold stress. At subfreezing temperatures, ice forms in the cell walls and intercellular spaces of most plants. The cytosol generally does not freeze at the cooling rates encountered in nature because it contains more solutes than the very dilute solution found in the cell wall, and solutes lower the freezing point of a solution. The reduction in liquid water in the cell wall caused by ice formation lowers the extracellular water potential, causing water to leave the cytoplasm. The resulting increase in the concentration of ions in the cytoplasm is harmful and can lead to cell death. Whether the cell survives depends largely on how well it resists dehydration. In regions with cold winters, native plants are adapted to cope with freezing stress. For example, before the onset of winter, the cells of many frost-tolerant species increase cytoplasmic levels of specific solutes, such as sugars, that are well tolerated at high concentrations and that help reduce the loss of water from the cell during extracellular freezing. The unsaturation of membrane lipids also increases, thereby maintaining proper levels of membrane fluidity.

CONCEPT CHECK 39.4

1. Thermal images are photographs of the heat emitted by an object. Researchers have used thermal imaging of plants to isolate mutants that overproduce abscisic acid. Suggest a reason why these mutants are warmer than wild-type plants under conditions that are normally nonstressful.
2. A greenhouse worker finds that potted chrysanthemums nearest to the aisles are often shorter than those in the middle of the bench. Explain this "edge effect," a common problem in horticulture.
3. Plants normally subjected to drought stress are often more resistant to freezing stress than plants that are not drought adapted. Suggest a reason why.
4. **WHAT IF?** If you removed the root cap from a root, would the root still respond to gravity? Explain.

For suggested answers, see Appendix A.

CONCEPT 39.5

Plants respond to attacks by herbivores and pathogens

Plants do not exist in isolation but interact with many other species in their communities. Some interspecific interactions—for example, the associations of plants with fungi in mycorrhizae (see Figure 37.12) or with pollinators (see Figure 38.4)—are mutually beneficial. Most of a plant's interactions with other organisms, however, do not benefit the plant. As primary producers, plants are at the base of most food webs and are subject to attack by a wide range of plant-eating (herbivorous) animals. A plant is also subject to infection by diverse viruses, bacteria, and fungi that can damage tissues or even kill the plant. Plants counter these threats with defense systems that deter herbivory and prevent infection or combat pathogens that infect the plant.

Defenses Against Herbivores

Herbivory—animals eating plants—is a stress that plants face in any ecosystem. Plants prevent excessive herbivory by using both physical defenses, such as thorns, and chemical defenses, such as the production of distasteful or toxic compounds. For example, some plants produce an unusual amino acid called *canavanine*, named for one of its sources, the jackbean (*Canavalia ensiformis*). Canavanine resembles arginine, one of the 20 amino acids that organisms incorporate into their proteins. If an insect eats a plant containing canavanine, the molecule is incorporated into the insect's proteins in place of arginine. Because canavanine is different enough from arginine to adversely affect the shape and hence the function of the proteins, the insect dies.

Some plants even "recruit" predatory animals that help defend the plant against specific herbivores. For example, insects called parasitoid wasps inject their eggs into their prey, including caterpillars feeding on plants (see Figure 54.1). The eggs hatch within the caterpillars, and the larvae eat through their organic containers from the inside out. The plant, which benefits from the destruction of the herbivorous caterpillars, has an active role in this drama. A leaf damaged by caterpillars releases volatile compounds that attract parasitoid wasps. The stimulus for this response is a combination of physical damage to the leaf caused by the munching caterpillar and a specific compound in the caterpillar's saliva **(Figure 39.28)**.

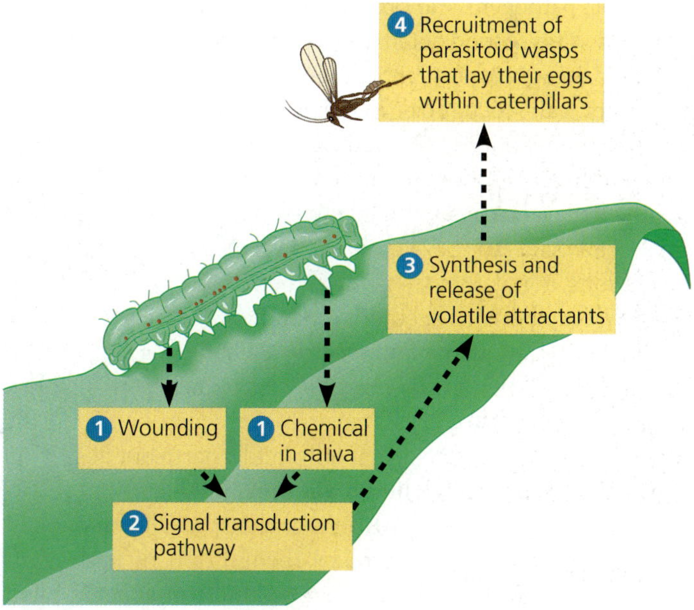

▲ **Figure 39.28 A maize leaf "recruiting" a parasitoid wasp as a defensive response to an armyworm caterpillar, an herbivore.**

The volatile molecules a plant releases in response to herbivore damage can also function as an "early warning system" for nearby plants of the same species. For example, lima bean plants infested with spider mites release a cocktail of volatile chemicals, including methyljasmonic acid, that signal "news" of the attack to neighboring, noninfested lima bean plants. In response to these chemicals, noninfested lima bean leaves express defense genes. Volatile chemicals released from leaves that are mechanically wounded in experiments do not have the same effect. As a result of the activation of specific genes by these released volatile chemicals, noninfested neighbors become less susceptible to spider mites and more attractive to another species of mite that preys on spider mites. Iris Kappers and her colleagues at Wageningen University, in the Netherlands, transgenically engineered *Arabidopsis* plants to produce two volatile chemicals that normally are not made by *Arabidopsis* but which have been found to attract carnivorous predatory mites in other plants. The predatory mites were now also attracted to the genetically modified *Arabidopsis*, a finding that could have implications for the genetic engineering of insect resistance in crop plants.

Defenses Against Pathogens

A plant's first line of defense against infection is the physical barrier presented by the epidermis of the primary plant body and the periderm of the secondary plant body (see Figure 35.19). This first defense system, however, is not impenetrable. Viruses, bacteria, and the spores and hyphae of fungi can still enter the plant through wounds or through the natural openings in the epidermis, such as stomata. Once a pathogen invades, the plant mounts a chemical attack as a second line of defense that destroys the pathogens and prevents their spread from the site of infection. This second defense system is enhanced by the plant's ability to recognize certain pathogens.

Plants can recognize invading pathogens and defend against them. Successful pathogens cause disease because they evade recognition or suppress the host's defense mechanisms. Pathogens against which a plant has little specific defense are said to be **virulent** pathogens. They are the exceptions, for if they were not, then hosts and pathogens would soon perish together. A kind of "compromise" has evolved between plants and most of their pathogens. In such cases, the pathogen gains enough access to its host to enable it to perpetuate itself without severely damaging or killing the plant. Strains of pathogens that only mildly harm but do not kill the host plant are said to be **avirulent** pathogens.

Gene-for-gene recognition is a widespread form of plant disease resistance that involves recognition of pathogen-derived molecules by the protein products of specific plant disease resistance (*R*) genes. There are many pathogens, and plants have many *R* genes—*Arabidopsis* has at least several hundred. An R protein usually recognizes only a single corresponding pathogen molecule that is encoded by one of a pathogen's avirulence (*Avr*) genes. Despite their name, Avr proteins are harmful to the plant; they are thought to redirect the host's metabolism to the advantage of the pathogen. The recognition of pathogen-derived molecules called *elicitors* by R proteins triggers signal transduction pathways leading to the activation of an arsenal of defense responses. These include the **hypersensitive response**—the genetically programmed death of infected cells—as well as tissue reinforcement and antibiotic production at the infection site. Pathogen invasion can also trigger **systemic acquired resistance**, a long-lasting systemic response that primes the plant for resisting a broad spectrum of pathogens. Local and systemic responses to pathogens require extensive genetic reprogramming and commitment of cellular resources. Therefore, a plant activates these defenses only after detecting an invading pathogen.

The Hypersensitive Response

The hypersensitive response is a defense response that causes cell and tissue death near the infection site, thereby restricting the spread of a pathogen. After the cells at the infection site mount a chemical defense and seal off the area, they destroy themselves. The hypersensitive response is initiated when pathogen elicitors bind to R proteins, altering the selective permeability of the plasma membrane and stimulating the production of *phytoalexins*, which are toxic compounds with general fungicidal and bactericidal properties. The hypersensitive response also induces production of *PR proteins* (pathogenesis-related proteins), many of which are enzymes that hydrolyze components in the cell walls of the pathogens. Infection also stimulates the cross-linking of molecules within the cell wall and the deposition of lignin, responses that set up a local barricade that slows the spread of the pathogen to other parts of the plant.

We can see the result of a hypersensitive response as lesions on a leaf. As "sick" as such a leaf appears, it will still survive, and its defensive response will help protect the rest of the plant **(Figure 39.29)**.

Systemic Acquired Resistance

The hypersensitive response is localized and specific, a containment response based on gene-for-gene (*R-Avr*) recognition between host and pathogen. However, as noted previously, pathogen invasions can also produce signaling molecules that "sound the alarm" of infection to the whole plant. The resulting systemic acquired resistance, which is associated with the systemic expression of defense genes, is nonspecific, providing protection against a diversity of pathogens that lasts for days. The search for a signaling molecule that moves from the infection site to elicit the systemic acquired resistance led to the

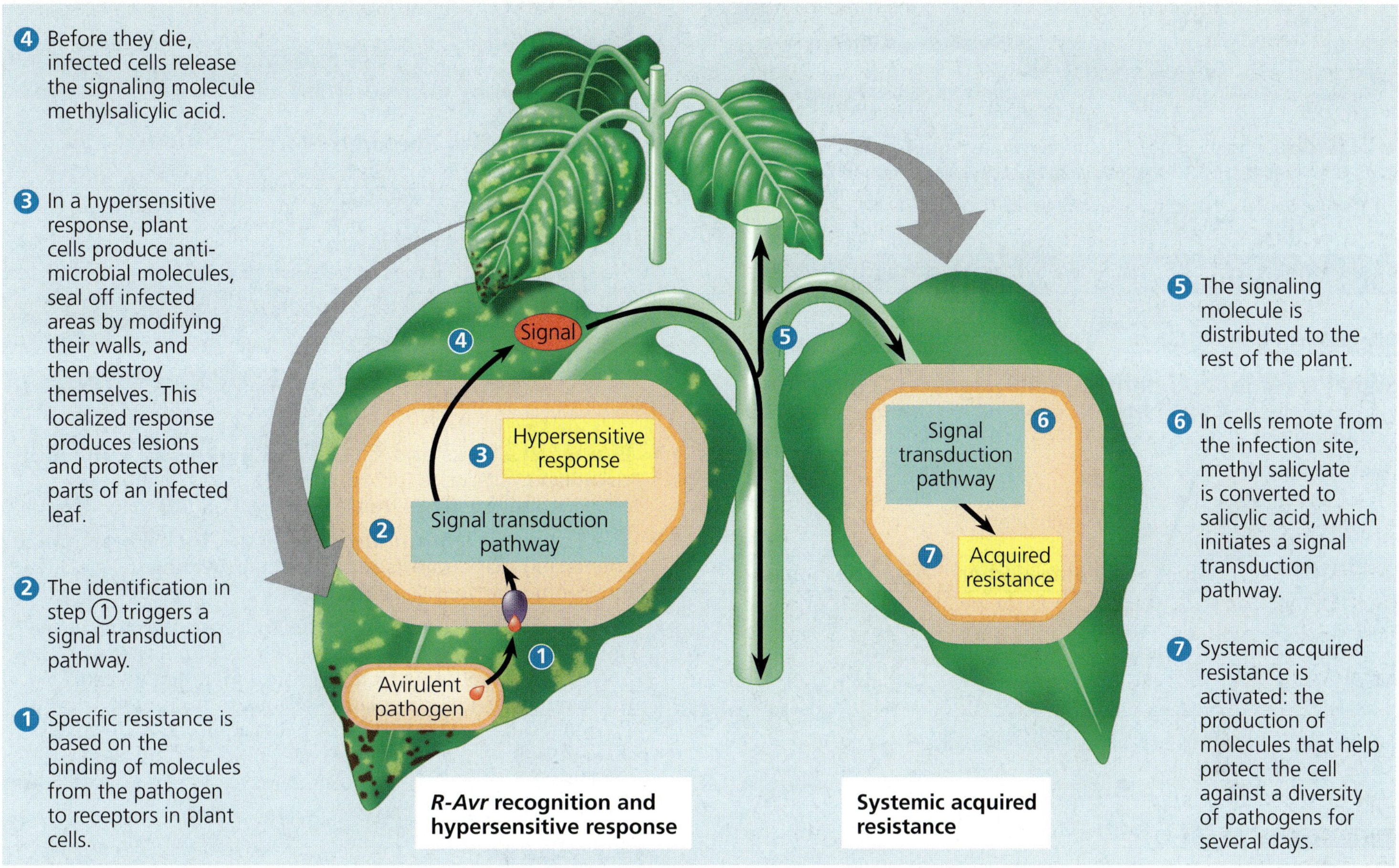

▲ **Figure 39.29 Defense responses against an avirulent pathogen.**

identification of *methylsalicylic acid* as the most likely candidate. Methylsalicylic acid is produced around the infection site and carried by the phloem throughout the plant, where it is converted to **salicylic acid** in areas remote from the sites of infection. Salicylic acid activates a signal transduction pathway that induces the production of PR proteins and resistance to pathogen attack (see Figure 39.29).

A modified form of salicylic acid, acetylsalicylic acid, is the active ingredient in aspirin. Centuries before aspirin was sold as a pain reliever, some cultures had learned that chewing the bark of a willow tree (*Salix*) would lessen the pain of a toothache or headache. With the discovery of systemic acquired resistance, biologists have finally learned one function of salicylic acid in plants. Aspirin is a natural medicine in the plants that produce it, but with effects entirely different from the medicinal action in humans who consume the drug.

Plant biologists investigating disease resistance and other evolutionary adaptations of plants are getting to the heart of how a plant responds to internal and external signals. These scientists, along with thousands of other plant biologists working on other questions and millions of students experimenting with plants in biology courses, are all extending a centuries-old tradition of curiosity about the green organisms that feed the biosphere.

CONCEPT CHECK 39.5

1. What are some drawbacks of spraying fields with general-purpose insecticides?
2. Chewing insects mechanically damage plants and lessen the surface area of leaves for photosynthesis. In addition, these insects make plants more vulnerable to pathogen attack. Suggest a reason why.
3. Many fungal pathogens get their food by causing plant cells to become leaky, thereby releasing nutrients into the intercellular spaces. Would it benefit the fungus to kill the host plant in a way that results in all the nutrients leaking out?
4. **WHAT IF?** Suppose a scientist finds that a population of plants growing in a breezy location is more prone to herbivory by insects than a population of the same species growing in a sheltered area. Suggest a hypothesis to account for this observation.

For suggested answers, see Appendix A.

Chapter 39 Review

MEDIA Go to the Study Area at **www.masteringbio.com** for BioFlix 3-D Animations, MP3 Tutors, Videos, Practice Tests, an eBook, and more.

SUMMARY OF KEY CONCEPTS

CONCEPT 39.1

Signal transduction pathways link signal reception to response (pp. 821–824)

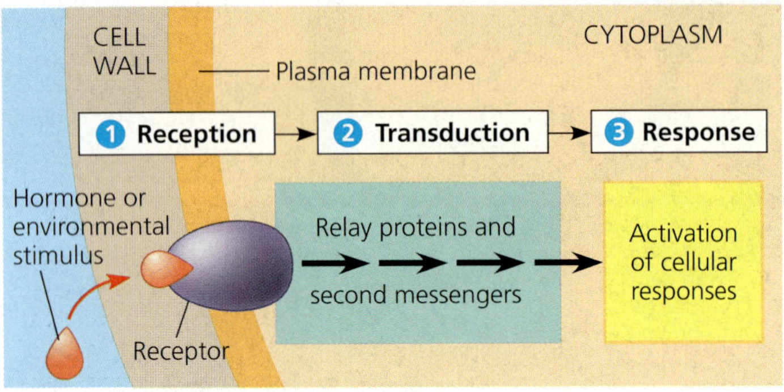

CONCEPT 39.2

Plant hormones help coordinate growth, development, and responses to stimuli (pp. 824–835)

- **The Discovery of Plant Hormones** Researchers discovered auxin by identifying the compound responsible for transmitting a signal downward through coleoptiles, from the tips to the elongating regions, during phototropism.
- **A Survey of Plant Hormones** Auxin, produced primarily in the apical meristem of the shoot, stimulates cell elongation in different target tissues. Cytokinins stimulate cell division. Gibberellins, produced in roots and young leaves, stimulate growth in leaves and stems. Brassinosteroids, chemically similar to the sex hormones of animals, induce cell elongation and division. Abscisic acid maintains dormancy in seeds. Ethylene helps control fruit ripening.
- **Systems Biology and Hormone Interactions** Interactions between hormones and their signal transduction pathways make it difficult to predict what effect a genetic manipulation will have on a plant. Systems biology seeks a comprehensive understanding of plants that will permit successful modeling of plant functions.

MEDIA

Activity Leaf Abscission
Investigation What Plant Hormones Affect Organ Formation?

CONCEPT 39.3

Responses to light are critical for plant success (pp. 835–841)

- **Blue-Light Photoreceptors** Various blue-light photoreceptors control the responses of hypocotyl elongation, stomatal opening, and phototropism.
- **Phytochromes as Photoreceptors**

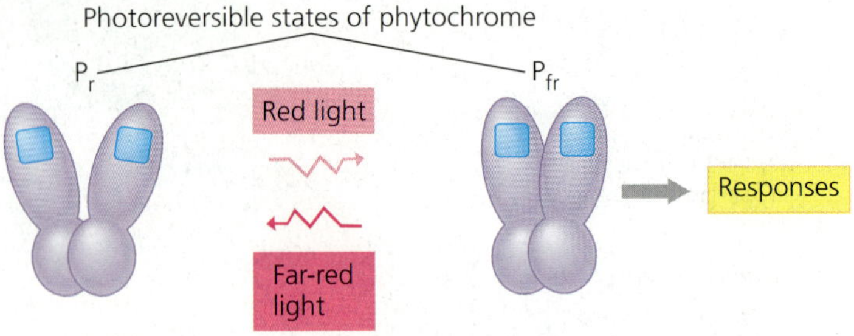

- **Biological Clocks and Circadian Rhythms** Free-running circadian cycles are approximately 24 hours long but are entrained to exactly 24 hours by the day/night cycle.
- **The Effect of Light on the Biological Clock** Phytochrome conversion marks sunrise and sunset, providing the clock with environmental cues.
- **Photoperiodism and Responses to Seasons** Some developmental processes, including flowering in many species, require a certain photoperiod. A critical night length sets a minimum (in short-day plants) or maximum (in long-day plants) number of hours of darkness required for flowering.

MEDIA

Activity Flowering Lab

CONCEPT 39.4

Plants respond to a wide variety of stimuli other than light (pp. 841–845)

- **Gravity** Gravitropism is a growth response to gravity. Roots show positive gravitropism, and stems show negative gravitropism. Plastids called statoliths may enable plant roots to detect gravity.
- **Mechanical Stimuli** Growth in response to touch is called thigmotropism. Rapid leaf movements involve transmission of electrical impulses called action potentials.
- **Environmental Stresses** During drought, plants respond to water deficit by reducing transpiration. Enzymatic destruction of cells creates air tubes that help plants survive oxygen deprivation during flooding. Plants respond to salt stress by producing solutes tolerated at high concentrations, keeping the water potential of cells more negative than the soil solution. Heat-shock proteins help plants survive heat stress. Altering lipid composition of membranes is a response to cold stress.

CONCEPT 39.5

Plants respond to attacks by herbivores and pathogens (pp. 845–847)

- **Defenses Against Herbivores** In addition to physical defenses such as thorns, plants defend themselves chemically by producing distasteful or toxic compounds, as well as airborne attractants that bring animals that destroy herbivores.
- **Defenses Against Pathogens** A pathogen is avirulent if it has a specific *Avr* gene corresponding to a particular *R* allele in the host plant. A hypersensitive response against an avirulent pathogen seals off the infection and destroys both pathogen and host cells in the region of the infection. Systemic acquired resistance is a generalized defense response in organs distant from the infection site.

TESTING YOUR KNOWLEDGE

SELF-QUIZ

1. Which of the following does *not* occur in a signal transduction pathway?
   a. stimulation of the receptor by a relay molecule
   b. production of second messengers such as cGMP
   c. expression of specific genes
   d. activation of protein kinases
   e. phosphorylation of transcription factors

2. Auxin enhances cell elongation in all of these ways *except*
   a. increased uptake of solutes.
   b. gene activation.
   c. acidification of the cell wall, causing denaturation of growth-inhibiting cell wall proteins.
   d. increased activity of plasma membrane proton pumps.
   e. cell wall loosening.

3. Charles and Francis Darwin discovered that
   a. auxin is responsible for phototropic curvature.
   b. auxin can pass through agar.
   c. light destroys auxin.
   d. light is perceived by the tips of coleoptiles.
   e. red light is most effective in causing phototropic curvatures.

4. Which hormone is *incorrectly* paired with its function?
   a. auxin—promotes stem growth through cell elongation
   b. cytokinins—initiate programmed cell death
   c. gibberellins—stimulate seed germination
   d. abscisic acid—promotes seed dormancy
   e. ethylene—inhibits cell elongation

5. The hormone that helps plants respond to drought is
   a. auxin.
   b. gibberellin.
   c. cytokinin.
   d. ethylene.
   e. abscisic acid.

6. The signaling molecule for flowering might be released earlier than normal in a long-day plant exposed to flashes of
   a. far-red light during the night.
   b. red light during the night.
   c. red light followed by far-red light during the night.
   d. far-red light during the day.
   e. red light during the day.

7. If a long-day plant has a critical night length of 9 hours, which 24-hour cycle would prevent flowering?
   a. 16 hours light/8 hours dark
   b. 14 hours light/10 hours dark
   c. 15.5 hours light/8.5 hours dark
   d. 4 hours light/8 hours dark/4 hours light/8 hours dark
   e. 8 hours light/8 hours dark/light flash/8 hours dark

8. If a scientist discovers an *Arabidopsis* mutant that does not store starch in plastids but has normal gravitropic bending, what aspect of our understanding of gravitropism would need to be reevaluated?
   a. the role of auxin in gravitropism
   b. the role of calcium in gravitropism
   c. the role of statoliths in gravitropism
   d. the role of light in gravitropism
   e. the role of differential growth in gravitropic bending

9. How may a plant respond to *severe* heat stress?
   a. by orienting leaves to increase evaporative cooling
   b. by producing ethylene, which kills some cortex cells and creates air tubes for ventilation
   c. by initiating a systemic acquired resistance response
   d. by increasing the proportion of unsaturated fatty acids in cell membranes, reducing their fluidity
   e. by producing heat-shock proteins, which may protect the plant's proteins from denaturing

10. In systemic acquired resistance, salicylic acid probably
    a. destroys pathogens directly.
    b. activates defenses throughout the plant before infection spreads.
    c. closes stomata, thus preventing the entry of pathogens.
    d. activates heat-shock proteins.
    e. sacrifices infected tissues by hydrolyzing cells.

11. **DRAW IT** Indicate the response to each condition by drawing a straight seedling or one with the triple response.

	Control	Ethylene added	Ethylene synthesis inhibitor
Wild-type			
Ethylene insensitive (*ein*)			
Ethylene overproducing (*eto*)			
Constitutive triple response (*ctr*)			

For Self-Quiz answers, see Appendix A.

MEDIA Visit the Study Area at **www.masteringbio.com** for a Practice Test.

EVOLUTION CONNECTION

12. Coevolution is defined as the evolution of reciprocal adaptations in two species, with each species adapting its interaction with the other. In this context, explain the coevolutionary relationship between a plant and an avirulent pathogen.

SCIENTIFIC INQUIRY

13. A plant biologist observed a peculiar pattern when a tropical shrub was attacked by caterpillars. After a caterpillar ate a leaf, it would skip over nearby leaves and attack a leaf some distance away. Simply removing a leaf did not deter caterpillars from eating nearby leaves. The biologist suspected that an insect-damaged leaf sent out a chemical that signaled nearby leaves. How could the researcher test this hypothesis?

SCIENCE, TECHNOLOGY, AND SOCIETY

14. Describe how our knowledge about the control systems of plants is being applied to agriculture or horticulture, giving three examples.

UNIT 7

Animal Form and Function

AN INTERVIEW WITH

Masashi Yanagisawa

While still in graduate school, Masashi Yanagisawa became famous for discovering endothelins, local regulators that are the most potent constrictors of blood vessels known. Later he discovered orexins, which regulate food intake and wakefulness. He received his M.D. and Ph.D. degrees from the University of Tsukuba, Japan. Since 1996, Dr. Yanagisawa has been a professor and Howard Hughes Medical Institute Investigator at the University of Texas Southwestern Medical Center at Dallas, where he holds the Patrick E. Haggerty Distinguished Chair in Basic Biomedical Science. The recipient of many awards, he is also a member of the National Academy of Sciences.

How did you get to be a medical scientist?

Even as a small child, I wanted to be a scientist. And in Japan, you really have to decide what you want to do before college; it's a European-style system. My decision to enter medical school, which is a 6-year undergraduate program there, was influenced by something my father told me. He said—this was the late 1970s—that biology would be very exciting in the coming era and that if I wanted to do biology, going to medical school was not a bad choice. I believed him, and I decided to go to medical school.

Until then, basic biology hadn't genuinely excited me, partly because of a bias at that time in Japan, where biology was regarded as a science discipline for "humanities people." And high-school biology mostly meant traditional taxonomy and lots of memorization. But in medical school, I was exposed to cutting-edge biology and found it very exciting, and I did some informal research internships that confirmed my interest in basic research. Clinical medicine excited me as well—it's impressive to see a patient improve dramatically.

The decision about what to do after medical school was probably the most difficult I've faced in my life. Should I continue with clinical training or go directly into basic research? An experience I had toward the end of medical school helped me make up my mind. When I was on rotation in the OB-GYN department, there was a patient—a young woman—suffering from a terminal case of ovarian cancer. Her abdominal cavity was full of cancer cells; no surgery could help. The doctors were discussing how aggressively to treat her with chemotherapy. At that time in Japan, most terminal cancer patients were not told of their condition. So this patient didn't know about her own condition and certainly didn't know about her options. Immediately after that, I had a chance to go to Australia in an exchange program, and there I was assigned to surgery and oncology. Their philosophy was totally different: The patient was at the center. The young me was very moved. If I had been a more aggressive person, I might have decided to try to change clinical practice in Japan, but I wasn't like that. I just decided not to go through clinical training, but instead to enroll in a Ph.D. program in pharmacology.

Why did you choose pharmacology?

Actually, pharmacology itself didn't matter. I was considering various programs all over Japan, but eventually I realized that I wanted to work under Tomoh Masaki, who happened to be a professor in pharmacology at Tsukuba. It was his open style of running his lab that appealed to me. I felt I could be a semi-independent researcher in his lab. My first research project was in Masaki's lifelong research area, the biochemistry of contractile proteins in muscles. My specific goal was to clone the gene for the large polypeptide subunit of the muscle protein myosin. I was sent off to another institution for almost a year to learn DNA cloning and other molecular techniques.

I finished the myosin project, but I strongly wanted to do something more medically oriented. So I started to look for an interesting topic. Many researchers were talking about a newly identified factor made by the endothelium (lining) of blood vessels that caused the vessel walls to relax. This was clearly a hot topic. I went to the library to browse through the scientific literature. (Remember, this was the pre-Internet era, so browsing meant actually flipping pages—very time-consuming!) I was lucky to find one abstract describing a mysterious vascular constricting factor that was secreted into culture medium when endothelial cells were cultured. This seemed interesting—and a promising research topic for me because the abstract authors hadn't gone on to identify the factor. I thought I could do this. In my lab and neighboring labs, I had all the techniques and teachers I needed for the project.

The great thing about my mentor, Masaki, is that he supported me in this project, even though it was outside his field; he gave me half a year to try it. Amazingly, within a few months I had purified the factor, a 21-amino-acid peptide. When I sequenced the peptide, it turned out to be previously unknown. When we injected the peptide into rats, their blood pressure shot up, because their blood vessels were being constricted. We called the peptide endothelin. It's a local regulator, a signaling molecule that acts on muscle cells lying just outside the blood-vessel endothelium. Endothelin recognizes its target cells by means of specific receptor proteins on the target cell surface. The binding of endothelin, the "ligand," to its receptor triggers a signal-transduction pathway that leads to muscle cell contraction. I stayed on as a post-doc and cloned the gene for the endothelin receptor, which is a G protein-coupled receptor (GPCR). [See Chapter 11 to review cell signaling.]

How did all the publicity arising from your work influence your career path?

My endothelin discoveries had attracted attention to me. I realized that I wanted to be in the United States, which seemed to be the center of the world for biology. I also wanted more independence as a researcher. Unfortunately, to be head of a laboratory in Japan, you had to be a full professor, which meant 37 years old at least. I was then about 27, and 10 years seemed too long to wait! This department offered me a lot of support, and it was an easy decision to come here.

What did you work on once you got here?

I wanted to learn more about how endothelin functioned, so we genetically engineered strains of mice each lacking a component of the endothelin system—"knock-out" mice. We got some surprising results. The effects of endothelin go way beyond the vascular system. We learned that this protein has a fundamental role in certain stages of embryonic development. In the embryo, it's made by cells derived from a structure called the neural crest and is necessary for normal development of the intestine and several other organs. In adults, genes for endothelins (there are actually several) and their receptors are expressed in many, many places, and they seem to be doing a variety of things outside the vascular system.

Let's talk about the orphan receptor project, which led to orexin. Why is your approach called "reverse" pharmacology?

In the past, scientists usually went from the discovery of an intercellular signaling molecule, such as a hormone, to the eventual discovery of its receptor and the pathway leading to the response in target cells. For example, insulin was discovered years ago as a blood sugar-lowering hormone, and it was only later that the insulin receptor and the cellular pathway were identified. But the sequencing of the human genome has made the reverse approach possible. Now we can directly identify the genes for receptor proteins, especially for GPCRs, which all have very similar sequences. The human genome has more than 1,000 such genes. Many encode sensory receptors, especially for smell, but there are probably 400 or so encoding receptors that sense something internally. Out of these receptors, the ligands of more than 100 haven't been identified yet—these are the "orphan" receptors.

The genes encoding the ligands we're interested in—the peptides called neuropeptides because they are often made by neurons—can be extremely hard to find. We decided to search for novel neuropeptides that, like endothelin, had GPCRs. We developed a strategy to screen orphan receptors for peptide ligands—and we had beginners' luck. Orexin was found as the ligand for one of the first receptors we tested.

How did you find out what orexin did in the body?

The first clue was that both the orexin gene and its receptor gene are expressed only in the brain, and orexin is produced by neurons located only in the lateral hypothalamus. This part of the brain was known to play a role in appetite, which was immediately very exciting. Our next experiment was to inject orexin into the brains of mice, which then ate much more than the control mice. Shortly afterwards, we discovered that when you withhold a mouse's food, more orexin mRNA is made in its lateral hypothalamus. So that seemed to be the story: The animal gets hungry, somehow signals to its orexin neurons, more orexin is made, and the animal eats more. We got the name orexin from the Greek word for appetite.

Next, as usual, we engineered mice with the orexin gene or orexin receptor gene knocked out. Our hypothesis was that a mouse without orexin would have less appetite and become leaner. But we were wrong. It turned out that the mice lacking orexin were, if anything, chubbier. Now we know the reason was that orexin knock-out mice had a reduced appetite but also an even more reduced metabolic rate, so the net effect was that they became fatter.

That's when my instinct as a whole-animal physiologist kicked in. The orexin system must be doing something more important than the subtle effect we'd seen, I thought. Then I realized that observing the mice during the day was probably a mistake. Physiological research is usually done in the daytime for human convenience. But mice are nocturnal, so observing them during the day and concluding anything about their behavior is like sneaking into someone's home at night and concluding that humans are a lazy, sleepy species. So to observe the eating behavior of our mice at night, we set up a night-vision camera. And we discovered a weird phenomenon: A mouse would be running around, and all of a sudden it would fall to the side and stop moving for a minute or two and then suddenly get up and behave as if nothing had happened.

This strange behavior and subsequent tests told us that the mice had the sleep disorder called narcolepsy, which until then had been a mystery. People with narcolepsy have normal 24-hour sleep-wake cycles, but their wakeful periods are fragmented, and they go into REM sleep suddenly and inappropriately. My standard joke is this: When I'm giving a boring seminar in a dimly lit room, it's normal for a few in the audience to doze off. But if I start to doze off during my own talk, that's abnormal. That kind of thing can happen to a narcolepsy patient without medication. What's fundamentally abnormal is the regulation of sleep-state transitions. It turns out that people with narcolepsy don't have orexin-secreting neurons; these neurons disappear during adolescence, presumably from an autoimmune attack. Their orexin genes are OK.

So what's the connection between appetite regulation and sleep regulation?

It's well known that when animals are hungry they are more active; that's an important physiological adaptation. When an animal is hungry, it has to go out and hunt or seek for food, while protecting itself from danger. In the lab, if you don't feed a mouse, it becomes more awake and active. But an orexin-deficient animal doesn't do that, suggesting that orexin may be a crucial part of a connection between the brain's roles in regulating feeding and sleep.

What advice do you have for students aspiring to be biologists?

I always say that identifying a good research question is more difficult than solving it. The question should be important and feasible to answer. Something else I tell my students is this: In every class you attend, try to ask at least one meaningful question. If you can't come up with one, then you're not taking the class seriously enough. That's a mode of study very different from just knowledge absorption. To be a scientist, you have to question everything.

Our hypothesis was that a mouse without orexin would have less appetite and become leaner. But we were wrong.

Inquiry in Action

Learn about an experiment by Masashi Yanagisawa and colleagues in Inquiry Figure 42.12 on page 908.

Left to right: Steve Wasserman, Masashi Yanagisawa, Jane Reece

Basic Principles of Animal Form and Function

40

▲ **Figure 40.1 How does a jackrabbit keep from overheating?**

KEY CONCEPTS

40.1 Animal form and function are correlated at all levels of organization
40.2 Feedback control loops maintain the internal environment in many animals
40.3 Homeostatic processes for thermoregulation involve form, function, and behavior
40.4 Energy requirements are related to animal size, activity, and environment

OVERVIEW

Diverse Forms, Common Challenges

The outer ears of the jackrabbit (*Lepus alleni*) in **Figure 40.1** are thin and remarkably large. They provide this hare with an acute sense of hearing, a primary defense against predators. The ears also help the jackrabbit shed excess heat. Blood flowing through each ear's network of vessels transfers heat to the surrounding air. At times, however, blood flow in the ear could be a liability. When the air is hot, blood passing through the ears could absorb heat, raising body temperature to dangerous levels. So how does a big-eared jackrabbit survive in the midday desert heat? To answer this question, we need to look more closely at the biological form, or **anatomy**, of the animal.

Over the course of its life, a jackrabbit faces the same fundamental challenges as any other animal, whether hydra, hawk, or human. All animals must obtain oxygen and nutrients, fight off infection, and produce offspring. Given that they share these basic requirements, why do species vary so enormously in makeup, complexity, organization, and appearance? The answer is that natural selection favors, over many generations, the variations appearing in a population that best meet the animal's needs. The solutions to the challenges of survival vary among environments and species, but for the jackrabbit and other animals, they frequently result in a close match of form to function.

Because form and function are correlated, examining anatomy often provides clues to **physiology**—biological function. In the case of the jackrabbit, researchers noted that its large pink-tinged ears turn pale when the air temperature exceeds 40°C (104°F), the normal temperature of the jackrabbit's body. The color change reflects a temporary narrowing of blood vessels in response to a hot environment. With their blood supply reduced, the ears can absorb heat without overheating the rest of the body. When the air cools, blood flow resumes, and the large ears again help release excess heat.

In this chapter, we will begin our study of animal form and function by examining the levels of organization in the animal body and the systems for coordinating the activities of distinct body parts. Next, we will discuss how animals regulate their internal environment, using body temperature regulation to introduce and illustrate the concept of homeostasis. Finally, we will explore how anatomy and physiology relate to an animal's interactions with the environment and its management of energy use.

CONCEPT **40.1**

Animal form and function are correlated at all levels of organization

An animal's size and shape are fundamental aspects of form that significantly affect the way an animal interacts with its environment. Although we may refer to size and shape as elements of a "body plan" or "design," this does not imply a process of conscious invention. The body plan of an animal is the result of a pattern of development programmed by the genome, itself the product of millions of years of evolution.

Physical Constraints on Animal Size and Shape

Many different body plans have arisen during the course of evolution, but the variations fall within certain bounds. Physical laws that govern strength, diffusion, movement, and heat exchange limit the range of animal forms.

As an example of how physical laws constrain evolution, let's consider how some properties of water limit the possible shapes for animals that are fast swimmers. Water is about a thousand times denser than air and also far more viscous. Thus, any bump on an animal's body surface that causes drag impedes a swimmer more than it would a runner or flyer. Tuna and other fast ray-finned fishes can swim at speeds up to 80 km/hr (50 mph). Sharks, penguins, dolphins, and seals are also fast swimmers. As apparent in the examples in **Figure 40.2**, such animals share a streamlined body contour: a shape that is fusiform, meaning tapered on both ends. The similar shape found in these speedy fishes, birds, and mammals is an example of convergent evolution (see Chapter 22). Natural selection often shapes similar adaptations when diverse organisms face the same environmental challenge, such as the resistance of water to fast travel.

Physical laws also influence animal body plans with regard to maximum size. As body dimensions increase, thicker skeletons are required to maintain adequate strength. This limitation affects internal skeletons, such as those of vertebrates, as well as external skeletons, such as those of insects and other arthropods. In addition, as bodies increase in size, the muscles required for locomotion must represent an ever-larger fraction of the total body mass. At some point, mobility becomes limited. By considering the fraction of body mass in leg muscles and the effective force such muscles generate, scientists can estimate maximum running speed for a wide range of body plans. Such calculations indicate that the dinosaur *Tyrannosaurus rex*, over 6 m tall, probably could reach speeds of 30 km/hr (19 mph), as fast as a professional soccer player but not quite the thunderous sprint depicted in the movie *Jurassic Park*.

▲ **Figure 40.2 Convergent evolution in fast swimmers.**

Exchange with the Environment

Animals need to exchange materials with their environment, and this need imposes limitations on their body plans (as it does for all other multicellular organisms). Exchange occurs as substances dissolved in an aqueous medium move across the plasma membrane of each cell. The rates of exchange for nutrients, waste products, and gases are proportional to membrane surface area. In contrast, the amount of material that must be exchanged to sustain life is proportional to volume.

The opportunity for exchange is strongly influenced by cell number. A single-celled organism, such as the amoeba in **Figure 40.3a**, has a sufficient membrane surface area in contact with its environment to carry out all necessary exchange. In contrast, an animal is composed of many cells, each with its own plasma membrane across which exchange must occur. A multicellular organization therefore works only if every cell has access to a suitable aqueous environment, either inside or outside of the animal's body.

Many animals with a simple internal organization have body plans that enable direct exchange between the external environment and nearly all cells. For example, a pond-dwelling hydra, which has a saclike body plan, has a body wall only two cell layers thick **(Figure 40.3b)**. Because its gastrovascular cavity

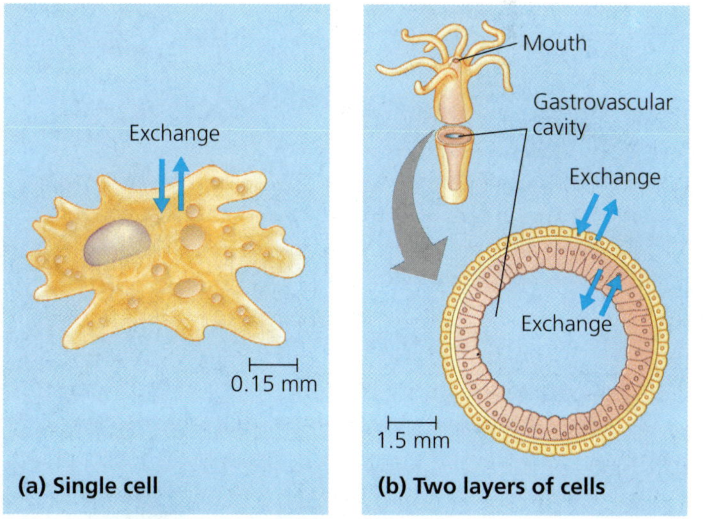

▲ **Figure 40.3 Contact with the environment. (a)** In a single-celled organism, such as an amoeba, the entire surface area contacts the environment. **(b)** Although all animals are multicellular, some have a simple organization in which all or nearly all cells contact the environment. For example, a hydra's body consists of two layers of cells. As fluid moves in and out of the hydra's mouth, every body cell can exchange material directly with the aqueous environment.

opens to the external environment, both the outer and inner layers of cells are constantly bathed by pond water. Another common design that maximizes exposure to the surrounding medium is a flat body shape. Consider, for instance, a parasitic tapeworm, which can reach several meters in length (see Figure 33.12). A thin, flat shape places most cells of the worm in direct contact with its specialized environment—the nutrient-rich intestinal fluid of a vertebrate host.

Most animals have a much more complex internal organization than that of a hydra or a tapeworm. Composed of compact masses of cells, these animals have outer surfaces that are relatively small compared with their volumes. As cell number increases, the ratio of the outer surface area of the animal to its total volume steadily decreases (see Figure 6.8). As an extreme comparison, the ratio of outer surface to volume for a whale is hundreds of thousands of times smaller than that for a water flea (*Daphnia*). Nevertheless, every cell in the whale must be bathed in fluid and have access to oxygen, nutrients, and other resources. How is this accomplished?

In whales and most other animals, extensively branched or folded surfaces are the evolutionary adaptation that enables sufficient exchange with the environment (**Figure 40.4**). In almost all cases, these surfaces lie within the body, protecting delicate exchange tissues from abrasion or dehydration and allowing for streamlined body contours. In humans, the digestive, respiratory, and circulatory systems rely on exchange surfaces within the body that in each system have a total area more than 25 times that of the skin.

Internal body fluids link exchange surfaces to body cells. In all animals, the spaces between cells are filled with fluid, often called **interstitial fluid** (from the Latin for "stand between"). Complex body plans also include a circulatory fluid, such as blood. Exchange between the interstitial fluid and circulatory fluid enables cells throughout the body to obtain nutrients and get rid of wastes (see Figure 40.4).

Despite the greater challenges of exchange with the environment, complex body plans have distinct benefits over simple ones. For example, an external skeleton can protect against

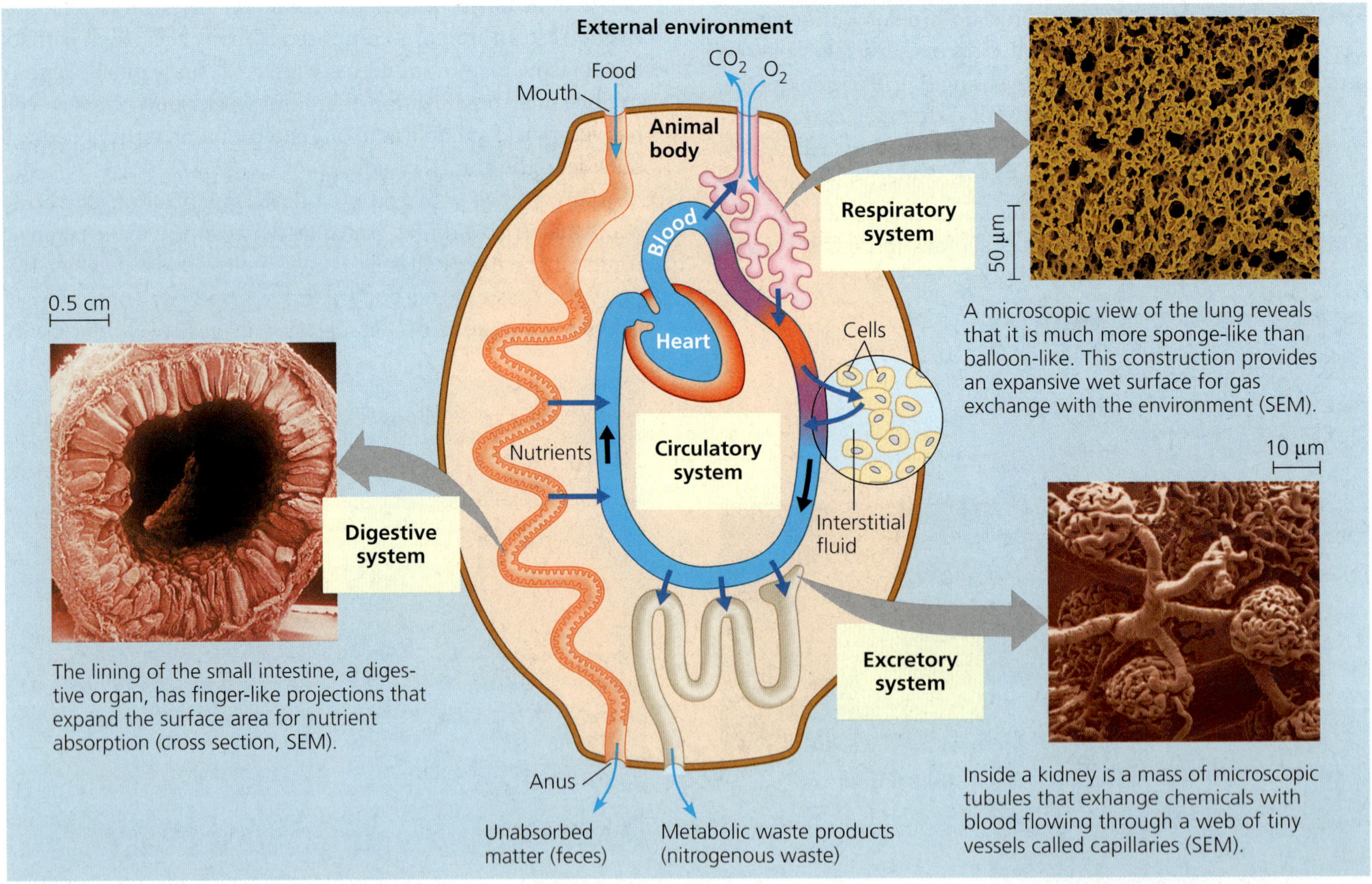

▲ **Figure 40.4 Internal exchange surfaces of complex animals.** This diagram provides an overview of chemical exchange between an animal body and the environment. Most animals have surfaces that are specialized for exchanging chemicals with the surroundings. These exchange surfaces are usually internal but are connected to the environment via openings on the body surface (the mouth, for example). The exchange surfaces are finely branched or folded, giving them a very large area. The digestive, respiratory, and excretory systems all have such exchange surfaces. The circulatory system carries chemicals transported across these surfaces throughout the body.

? *In what sense are exchange surfaces such as the lining of the digestive system both internal and external?*

predators, and sensory organs can provide detailed information on the animal's surroundings. Internal digestive organs can break down food gradually, controlling the release of stored energy. In addition, specialized filtration systems can adjust the composition of the internal fluid that bathes the animal's body cells. In this way, an animal can maintain a relatively stable internal environment while living in a variable external environment. A complex body plan is especially advantageous for animals living on land, where the external environment may be highly variable.

Hierarchical Organization of Body Plans

Cells form an animal's body through their emergent properties. Recall from Chapter 1 that emergent properties arise through successive levels of structural and functional organization. Cells are organized into **tissues**, groups of cells of similar appearance and a common function. In all but the simplest animals (such as sponges), different tissues are further organized into functional units called **organs**. Groups of organs that work together provide an additional level of organization and coordination and make up an **organ system** **(Table 40.1)**. Thus, for example, the skin is an organ of the integumentary system, which protects against infection and helps regulate body temperature.

Organs often contain tissues with distinct physiological roles. In some cases, the roles are different enough that we consider the organ to belong to more than one organ system. The pancreas, for instance, produces enzymes critical to the function of the digestive system and also regulates the level of sugar in the blood as a vital part of the endocrine system.

Just as viewing the hierarchy of the body's organization from the "bottom up" (from cells to organ systems) reveals emergent properties that underlie organ systems, a view of the hierarchy from the "top down" makes clear the multilayered basis of specialization. Consider the digestive system, which in humans consists of the mouth, pharynx, esophagus, stomach, small and large intestines, accessory organs, and anus. Each organ has specific roles in digestion. One important function of the stomach, for example, is to initiate the breakdown of proteins. This process requires a churning powered by stomach muscles, as well as digestive juices secreted by the stomach lining. Production of digestive juices, in turn, requires several highly specialized cell types, one of which generates concentrated hydrochloric acid.

The specialization characteristic of complex body plans is based on varied combinations of a limited set of cell and tissue types. For example, lungs and blood vessels have distinct functions but are lined by tissues that are of the same basic type and therefore share many properties. To introduce these shared properties, we next survey the major tissue types in vertebrates. In later chapters, we'll discuss how the tissues described here contribute to the functions of each organ system.

Tissue Structure and Function

Animal tissues fall into four main categories: epithelial tissue, connective tissue, muscle tissue, and nervous tissue. We explore the structure and function of each type in **Figure 40.5** and in the accompanying text, on the next four pages.

Table 40.1 Organ Systems: Their Main Components and Functions in Mammals

Organ System	Main Components	Main Functions
Digestive	Mouth, pharynx, esophagus, stomach, intestines, liver, pancreas, anus	Food processing (ingestion, digestion, absorption, elimination)
Circulatory	Heart, blood vessels, blood	Internal distribution of materials
Respiratory	Lungs, trachea, other breathing tubes	Gas exchange (uptake of oxygen; disposal of carbon dioxide)
Immune and lymphatic	Bone marrow, lymph nodes, thymus, spleen, lymph vessels, white blood cells	Body defense (fighting infections and cancer)
Excretory	Kidneys, ureters, urinary bladder, urethra	Disposal of metabolic wastes; regulation of osmotic balance of blood
Endocrine	Pituitary, thyroid, pancreas, adrenal, and other hormone-secreting glands	Coordination of body activities (such as digestion and metabolism)
Reproductive	Ovaries or testes, and associated organs	Reproduction
Nervous	Brain, spinal cord, nerves, sensory organs	Coordination of body activities; detection of stimuli and formulation of responses to them
Integumentary	Skin and its derivatives (such as hair, claws, skin glands)	Protection against mechanical injury, infection, drying out; thermoregulation
Skeletal	Skeleton (bones, tendons, ligaments, cartilage)	Body support, protection of internal organs, movement
Muscular	Skeletal muscles	Locomotion and other movement

Epithelial Tissue

Occurring as sheets of cells, **epithelial tissue** covers the outside of the body and lines organs and cavities within the body. The close packing of epithelial cells, often involving tight junctions (see Figure 6.32), enables epithelial tissue to function as a barrier against mechanical injury, pathogens, and fluid loss. The cells of an epithelial tissue, or **epithelium** (plural, *epithelia*), also form active interfaces with the environment. For example, the epithelium that lines the nasal passages has a critical function in olfaction, the sense of smell.

Epithelial cell shape may be *cuboidal* (like dice), *columnar* (like bricks standing on end), or *squamous* (like floor tiles). In addition, cells may be arranged in a *simple epithelium* (single cell layer), a *stratified epithelium* (multiple tiers of cells), or a *pseudostratified epithelium* (a single layer of cells varying in height). As shown in Figure 40.5, different cell shapes and arrangements correlate with distinct functions. For example, columnar epithelia, which have cells with relatively large cytoplasmic volumes, are often located where secretion or active absorption is important.

▼ **Figure 40.5**

Exploring Structure and Function in Animal Tissues

Epithelial Tissue

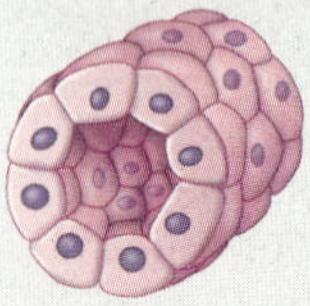

Cuboidal epithelium, with dice-shaped cells specialized for secretion, makes up the epithelium of kidney tubules and many glands, including the thyroid gland and salivary glands.

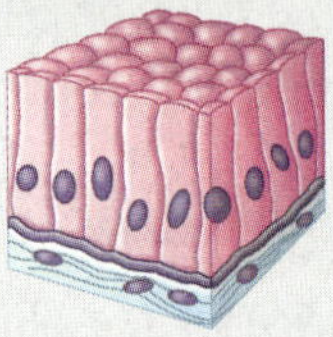

Simple columnar epithelium lines the intestines. This epithelium secretes digestive juices and absorbs nutrients.

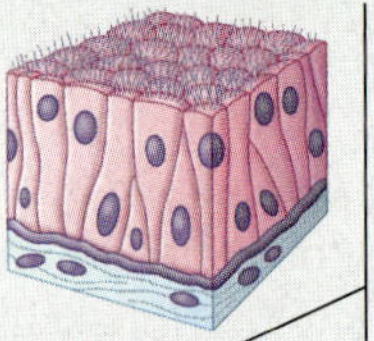

Pseudostratified ciliated columnar epithelium forms a mucous membrane that lines portions of the respiratory tract of many vertebrates. The beating cilia move the film of mucus along the surface.

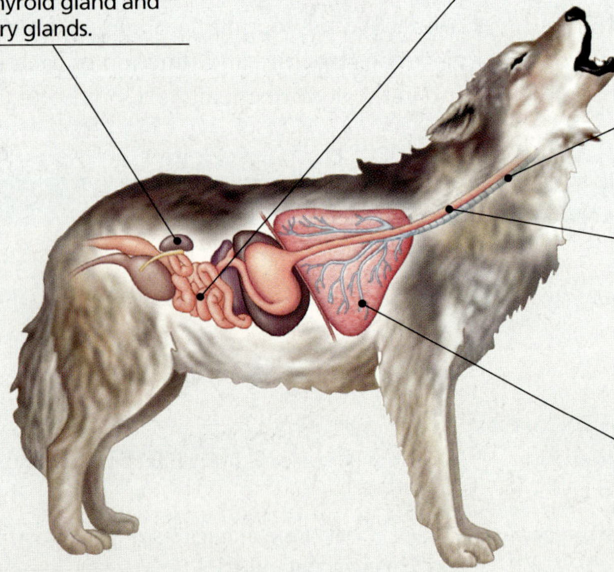

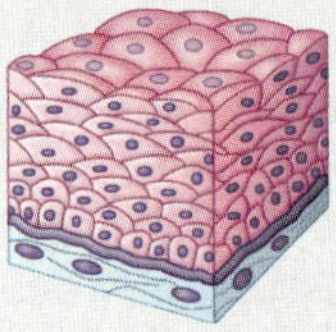

Stratified squamous epithelium regenerates rapidly by cell division near the basal lamina (see below). The new cells are pushed outward, replacing cells that are sloughed off. This epithelium is commonly found on surfaces subject to abrasion, such as the outer skin and linings of the esophagus, anus, and vagina.

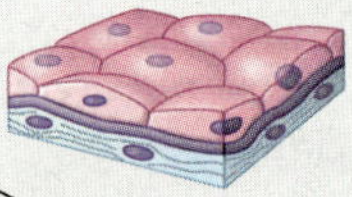

Simple squamous epithelium, which is thin and leaky, functions in the exchange of material by diffusion. This type of epithelium lines blood vessels and the air sacs of the lungs, where diffusion of nutrients and gases is critical.

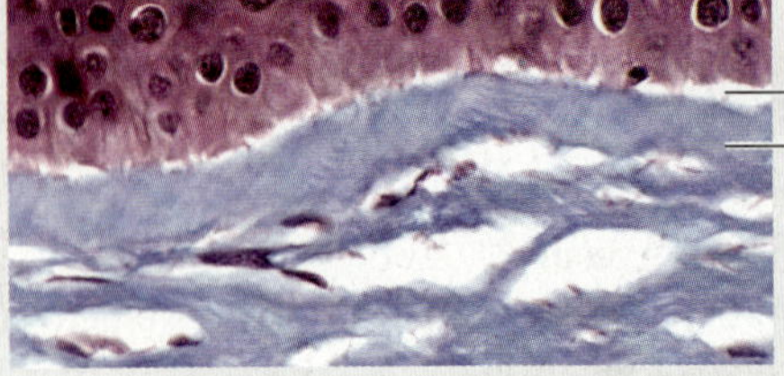

All epithelia are polarized, meaning that they have two different sides. The *apical* surface faces the lumen (cavity) or outside of the organ and is therefore exposed to fluid or air. It is this surface that is often covered with specialized projections. For example, the epithelium of the small intestine is covered with microvilli, projections that increase the surface area available for absorbing nutrients (see Figure 40.4). The opposite side of each epithelium is the *basal* surface. The basal surface is attached to a *basal lamina*, a dense mat of extracellular matrix, which separates the epithelium from the underlying tissue.

(All photos in figure are LMs.)

Connective Tissue

The most common functions of **connective tissues** are to bind and support other tissues in the body (see Figure 40.5). Connective tissue consists of a sparse population of cells scattered through an extracellular matrix. The matrix generally consists of a web of fibers embedded in a uniform foundation that may be liquid, jellylike, or solid. This variation in matrix structure is reflected in the six major types of connective tissue in vertebrates: loose connective tissue, cartilage, fibrous connective tissue, adipose tissue, blood, and bone.

Connective tissue fibers, which are made of protein, are of three kinds: collagenous, elastic, and reticular. *Collagenous fibers* provide strength combined with flexibility. They are made of collagen, probably the most abundant protein in the animal kingdom. Collagenous fibers are nonelastic and do not tear easily when pulled lengthwise. *Elastic fibers* are easily stretched but are also resilient, snapping back to their original length when tension is released. Shaped as long threads, elastic fibers are made of a protein called elastin. *Reticular fibers* are very thin and branched. Composed of collagen and continuous with collagenous fibers,

Connective Tissue

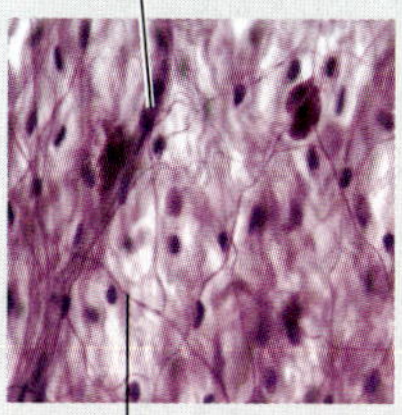

The most widespread connective tissue in the vertebrate body is *loose connective tissue.* Collagenous, elastic, and reticular fibers in this tissue type bind epithelia to underlying tissues and hold organs in place.

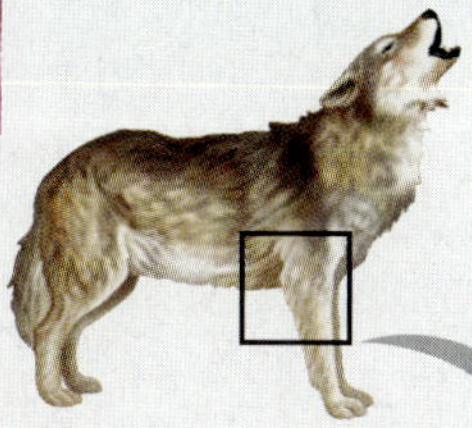

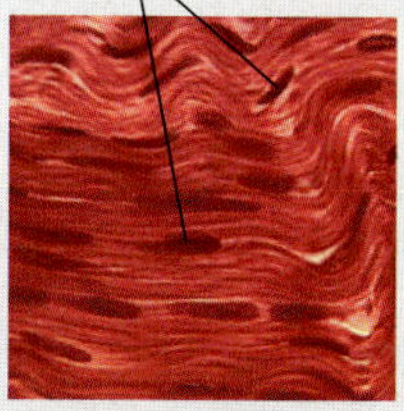

Fibrous connective tissue is dense with collagenous fibers. The fibers form parallel bundles, which maximize nonelastic strength. Fibrous connective tissue is found in **tendons**, which attach muscles to bones, and in **ligaments**, which connect bones at joints.

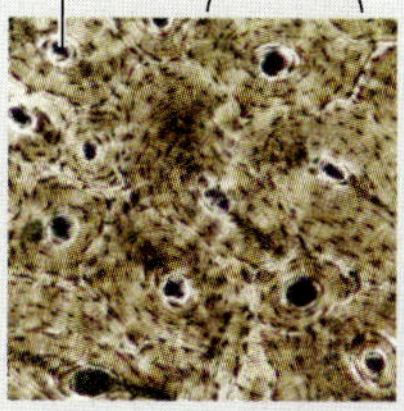

The skeleton of most vertebrates is made of **bone**, a mineralized connective tissue. Bone-forming cells called *osteoblasts* deposit a matrix of collagen. Calcium, magnesium, and phosphate ions combine into a hard mineral within the matrix. The combination of hard mineral and flexible collagen makes bone harder than cartilage without being brittle. The microscopic structure of hard mammalian bone consists of repeating units called *osteons.* Each osteon has concentric layers of the mineralized matrix, which are deposited around a central canal containing blood vessels and nerves.

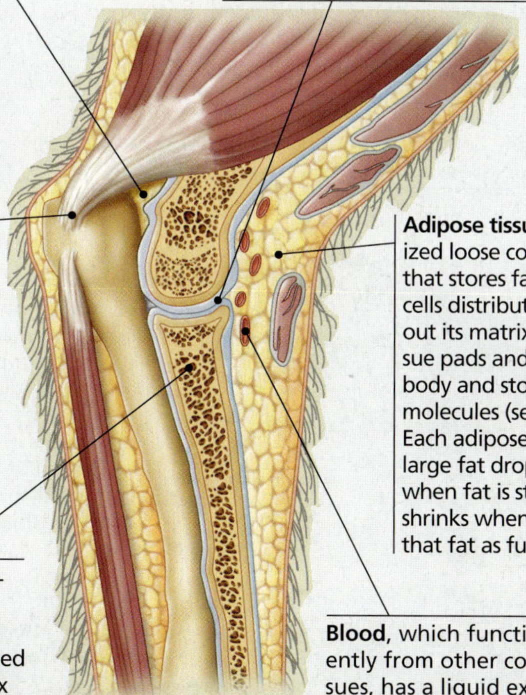

Cartilage has an abundance of collagenous fibers embedded in a rubbery matrix made of a protein-carbohydrate complex called chondroitin sulfate. Cells called *chondrocytes* secrete the collagen and chondroitin sulfate that make cartilage a strong yet flexible support material. Many vertebrate embryos have cartilaginous skeletons, but most of the cartilage is replaced by bone as the embryo matures. Cartilage is retained in some locations, such as the disks that act as cushions between vertebrae.

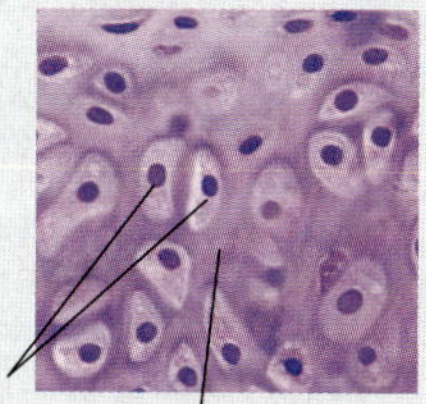

Adipose tissue is a specialized loose connective tissue that stores fat in adipose cells distributed throughout its matrix. Adipose tissue pads and insulates the body and stores fuel as fat molecules (see Figure 4.6). Each adipose cell contains a large fat droplet that swells when fat is stored and shrinks when the body uses that fat as fuel.

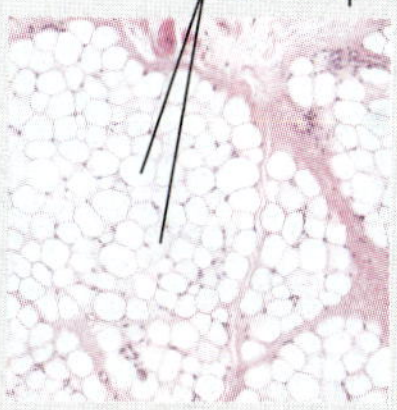

Blood, which functions differently from other connective tissues, has a liquid extracellular matrix called plasma. Consisting of water, salts, and dissolved proteins, plasma contains erythrocytes (red blood cells), leukocytes (white blood cells), and cell fragments called platelets. Red cells carry oxygen; white cells function in defense; and platelets aid in blood clotting.

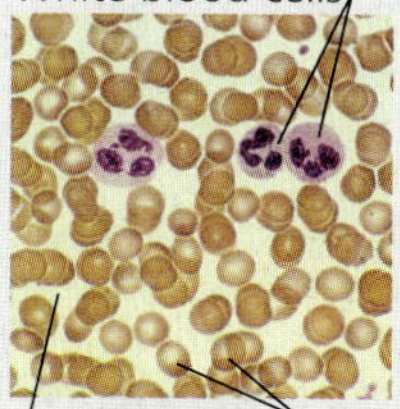

Continued on next page

they form a tightly woven fabric that joins connective tissue to adjacent tissues. If you pinch a fold of skin on the back of your hand, the collagenous and reticular fibers prevent the tissue from being pulled far from the bone; the elastic fibers then restore the skin to its original shape when you release your grip.

The connective tissue that holds many tissues and organs together and in place contains scattered cells of varying function. Of these cells, two types predominate: fibroblasts and macrophages. **Fibroblasts** secrete the protein ingredients of the extracellular fibers. **Macrophages** are cells that roam the maze of fibers, engulfing both foreign particles and the debris of dead cells by phagocytosis (see Chapter 6).

Muscle Tissue

The tissue responsible for nearly all types of body movement is **muscle tissue**. All muscle cells consist of filaments containing the proteins actin and myosin, which together enable muscles to contract. Muscle is the most abundant tissue in many animals, and muscle activity accounts for much of the energy-consuming cellular work in an active animal. Figure 40.5 shows the three types of muscle tissue in the vertebrate body: skeletal, cardiac, and smooth muscle.

Nervous Tissue

The function of **nervous tissue** is to sense stimuli and transmit signals in the form of nerve impulses from one part of the animal to another. Nervous tissue contains **neurons**, or nerve cells, which have extensions called axons that are uniquely specialized to transmit nerve impulses (see Figure 40.5). It also includes different forms of **glial cells**, or **glia**, which help nourish, insulate, and replenish neurons. In many animals, a concentration of nervous tissue forms a brain, an information-processing center. As we will discuss next, neurons have a critical role in managing many of the animal's physiological functions.

▼ Figure 40.5 (continued)

Exploring Structure and Function in Animal Tissues

Muscle Tissue

Attached to bones by tendons, **skeletal muscle** is responsible for voluntary movements. Skeletal muscle consists of bundles of long cells called muscle fibers. The arrangement of contractile units, or sarcomeres, along the length of the fibers gives the cells a striped (striated) appearance under the microscope. For this reason, skeletal muscle is also called *striated muscle*. Adult mammals have a fixed number of muscle cells; building muscle does not increase the number of cells but rather enlarges those already present.

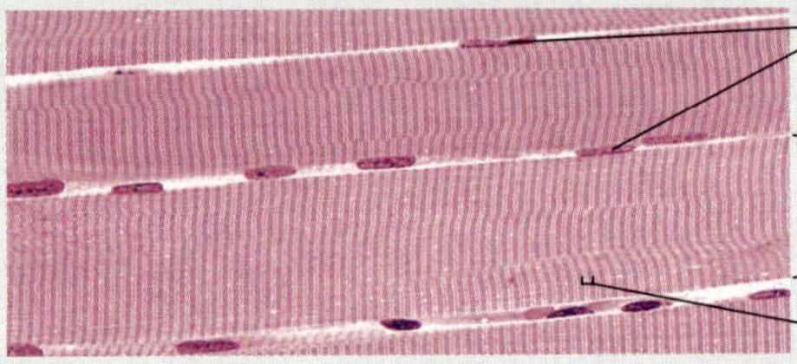

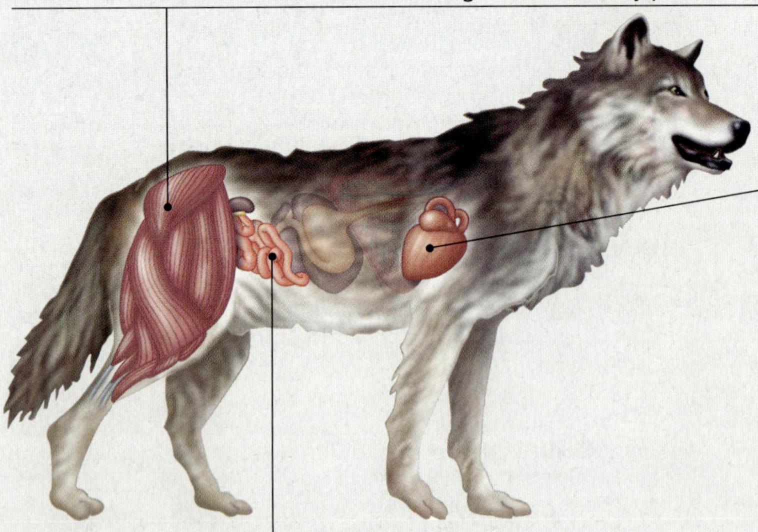

Cardiac muscle forms the contractile wall of the heart. It is striated like skeletal muscle and has contractile properties similar to those of skeletal muscle. Unlike skeletal muscle, however, cardiac muscle carries out an unconscious task: contraction of the heart. Cardiac muscle fibers branch and interconnect via intercalated disks, which relay signals from cell to cell and help synchronize the heartbeat.

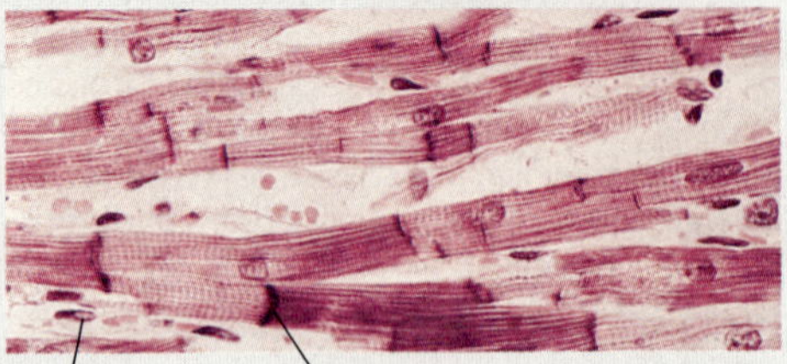

Smooth muscle, so named because it lacks striations, is found in the walls of the digestive tract, urinary bladder, arteries, and other internal organs. The cells are spindle-shaped. Controlled by different kinds of nerves than those controlling skeletal muscles, smooth muscles are responsible for involuntary body activities, such as churning of the stomach or constriction of arteries.

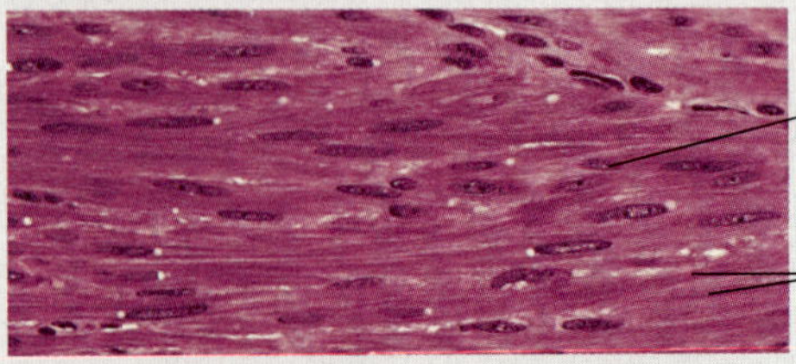

Coordination and Control

An animal's tissues, organs, and organ systems must act in conjunction with one another. For example, during long dives the harbor seal in Figure 40.2 slows its heart rate, collapses its lungs, and lowers its body temperature while propelling itself forward with its hind flippers. Coordinating activity across an animal's body in this way requires communication. What signals are used? How do the signals move within the body? There are two sets of answers to these questions, reflecting the two major systems for control and coordination: the endocrine system and the nervous system **(Figure 40.6)**. In the endocrine system, signaling molecules released into the bloodstream by endocrine cells reach all locations in the body. In the nervous system, neurons transmit information between specific locations.

The signaling molecules broadcast throughout the body by the endocrine system are called **hormones**. Different hormones cause distinct effects, and only cells that have receptors for a particular hormone respond **(Figure 40.6a)**. Depending on which cells have receptors for that hormone, the hormone may have an effect in just a single location or in sites throughout the body. Cells, in turn, can express more than one receptor type. Thus, cells in the ovaries and testes are regulated not only by sex hormones but also by metabolic hormones. Such hormones include insulin, which controls the level of glucose in the blood by binding to and regulating virtually every cell outside of the brain.

Hormones are relatively slow acting. It takes many seconds for insulin and other hormones to be released into the bloodstream and be carried throughout the body. Hormone effects are often long-lasting, however, because hormones remain in the bloodstream and target tissue for seconds, minutes, or even hours.

Nervous Tissue

Nerve cells (neurons) are the basic units of the nervous system. A neuron consists of a cell body and two or more extensions called dendrites and axons. Dendrites transmit signals from their tips toward the rest of the neuron. Axons, which are often bundled together into nerves, transmit signals toward another neuron or toward an effector, a structure such as a muscle cell that carries out a body response. The supporting glial cells help neurons function properly.

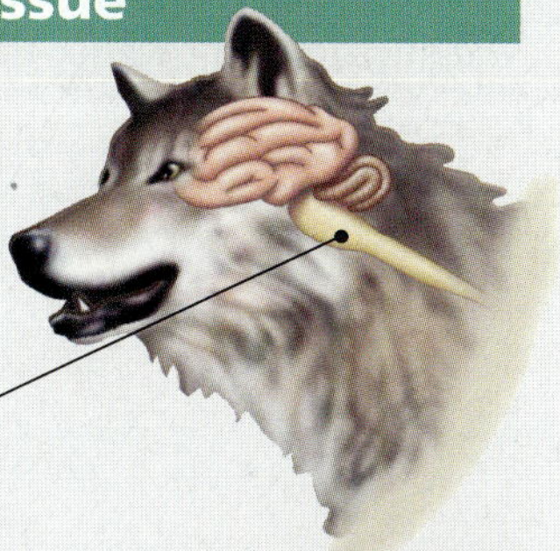

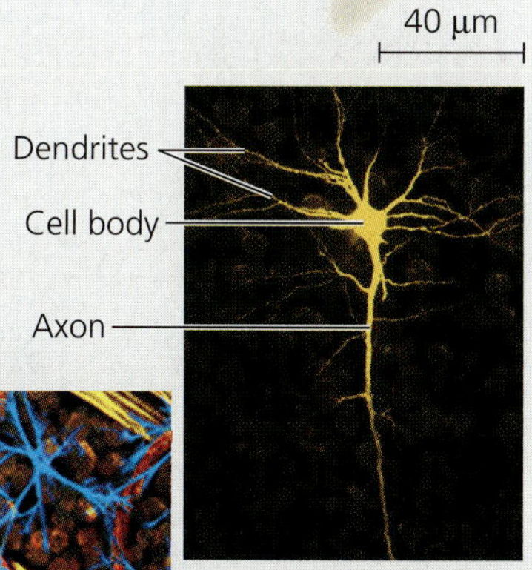

(Fluorescent LM)

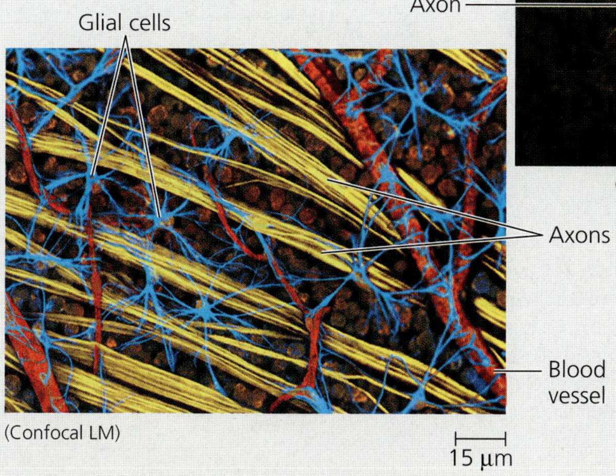

(Confocal LM)

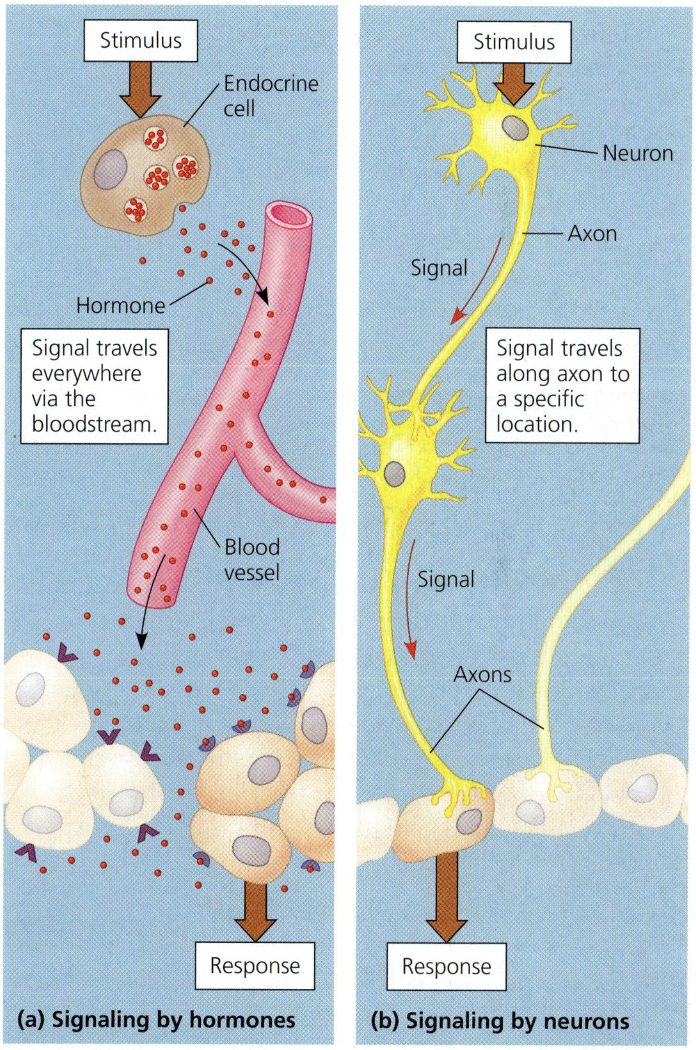

▲ **Figure 40.6 Signaling in the endocrine and nervous systems.** Endocrine cells secrete specific hormones—signaling molecules (shown as red dots)—into the bloodstream. Only cells expressing the corresponding receptor receive and respond to the signal. Nerve cells (neurons) generate signals that travel along axons. Only cells that form a specialized junction with the axon of an activated neuron receive and respond to the signal.

In the nervous system, a signal is not broadcast throughout the entire body. Instead, each signal, called a nerve impulse, travels to a target cell along a dedicated communication line, consisting mainly of the neuron extensions called axons **(Figure 40.6b)**. Four types of cells receive nerve impulses: other neurons, muscle cells, endocrine cells, and exocrine cells. Unlike the endocrine system, the nervous system conveys information by the *pathway* the signal takes. For example, a person can distinguish different musical notes because each note's frequency activates different neurons connecting the ear to the brain.

Signaling in the nervous system usually involves more than one type of signal. Nerve impulses travel within axons, sometimes over long distances, as changes in voltage. But in many cases, passing signals from one neuron to another involves very short-range chemical signals. Overall, transmission is extremely fast; nerve impulses take only a fraction of a second to reach the target and last only a fraction of a second.

Because the two major communication systems of the body differ in signal type, transmission, speed, and duration, they are adapted to different functions. The endocrine system is well suited for coordinating gradual changes that affect the entire body, such as growth and development, reproduction, metabolic processes, and digestion. The nervous system is well suited for directing immediate and rapid responses to the environment, especially in controlling fast locomotion and behavior. Both systems contribute to maintaining a stable internal environment, our next topic of discussion.

CONCEPT CHECK 40.1

1. What properties are shared by all types of epithelia?
2. Under what temperature conditions would it benefit a jackrabbit to flatten its ears against its body? Explain.
3. **WHAT IF?** Suppose you are standing at the edge of a cliff and you suddenly slip—you barely manage to keep your balance to keep from falling. As your heart races, you feel a burst of energy, due in part to a surge of blood into dilated (widened) vessels in your muscles and an upward spike in the level of glucose in your blood. Why might you expect that this "fight-or-flight" response requires both the nervous system and the endocrine system?

For suggested answers, see Appendix A.

CONCEPT **40.2**

Feedback control loops maintain the internal environment in many animals

Imagine that your body temperature soared every time you took a hot shower or drank a freshly brewed cup of coffee. Managing the state of the internal environment is a major challenge for the animal body. Faced with environmental fluctuations, animals manage their internal environment by either regulating or conforming.

Regulating and Conforming

An animal is said to be a **regulator** for a particular environmental variable if it uses internal control mechanisms to regulate internal change in the face of external fluctuation. For example, the river otter in **Figure 40.7** is a regulator for temperature, keeping its body at a temperature that is largely independent of that of the water in which it swims.

An animal is said to be a **conformer** for a particular environmental variable if it allows its internal condition to conform to external changes in the variable. For instance, the largemouth bass in Figure 40.7 conforms to the temperature of the lake in which it lives. As the water warms or cools, so do the cells of the bass. Some animals conform to more constant environments. For example, many marine invertebrates, such as spider crabs of the genus *Libinia*, let their internal solute concentration conform to the relatively stable solute concentration (salinity) of their ocean environment.

Regulating and conforming represent extremes on a continuum. An animal may regulate some internal conditions while allowing others to conform to the environment. For example, even though the bass conforms to the temperature of the surrounding water, the solute concentration in its blood

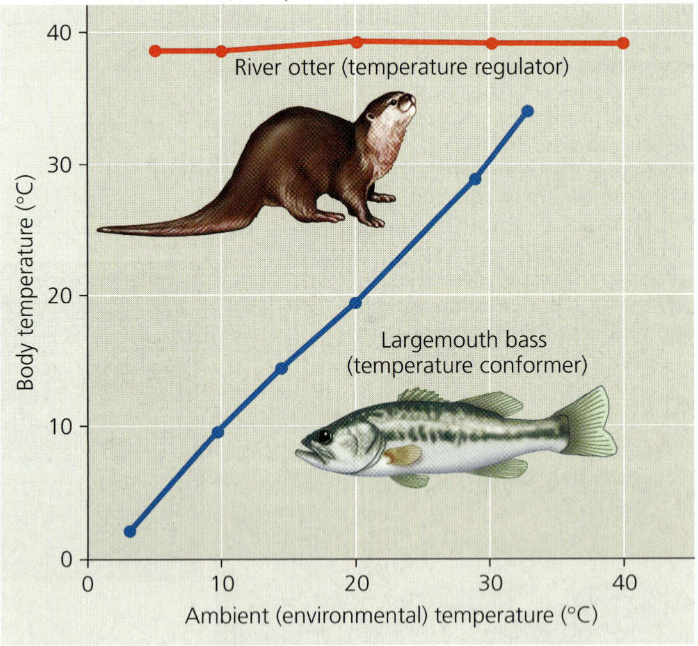

▲ **Figure 40.7 The relationship between body and environmental temperatures in an aquatic temperature regulator and an aquatic temperature conformer.** The river otter regulates its body temperature, keeping it stable across a wide range of environmental temperatures. The largemouth bass, meanwhile, allows its internal environment to conform to the water temperature.

and interstitial fluid differs from the solute concentration of the fresh water in which it lives. This difference occurs because the fish's anatomy and physiology enable it to regulate internal changes in solute concentration. (You will learn more about the mechanisms of this regulation in Chapter 44.)

Homeostasis

The steady body temperature of a river otter and the stable concentration of solutes in a freshwater bass are examples of **homeostasis**, which means "steady state," or internal balance. In achieving homeostasis, animals maintain a relatively constant internal environment even when the external environment changes significantly.

Like many animals, humans exhibit homeostasis for a range of physical and chemical properties. For example, the human body maintains a fairly constant body temperature of about 37°C (98.6°F) and a pH of the blood and interstitial fluid within 0.1 pH unit of 7.4. The body also regulates the solute concentration of glucose in the bloodstream so that it does not fluctuate for long from about 90 mg of glucose per 100 mL of blood.

Mechanisms of Homeostasis

Before exploring homeostasis in animals, let's first consider a nonliving example: the regulation of room temperature (**Figure 40.8**). Let's assume we want to keep a house at 20°C (68°F), a comfortable temperature for normal activity. We adjust a control device—the thermostat—to 20°C and allow a thermometer in the thermostat to monitor temperature. If the room temperature falls below 20°C, the thermostat responds by turning on the heating system. Heat is produced until the room reaches 20°C, at which point the thermostat switches off the heater. Whenever the temperature in the room again drifts below 20°C, the thermostat activates another heating cycle.

Like a home heating system, an animal achieves homeostasis by maintaining a variable, such as body temperature or solute concentration, at or near a particular value, or **set point**. Fluctuations in the variable above or below the set point serve as the **stimulus**. A receptor, or **sensor**, detects the stimulus and triggers a **response**, a physiological activity that helps return the variable to the set point. In the home heating example, a drop in temperature below the set point acts as a stimulus, the thermometer serves as the sensor, and the heater produces the response.

Feedback Loops in Homeostasis

Like the regulatory circuit shown in Figure 40.8, homeostasis in animals relies largely on **negative feedback**, a response that reduces, or "damps," the stimulus. For example, when you exercise vigorously, you produce heat, which increases body temperature. Your nervous system detects this increase and triggers sweating. As you sweat, the evaporation of moisture from your skin cools your body, helping return your body temperature to its set point.

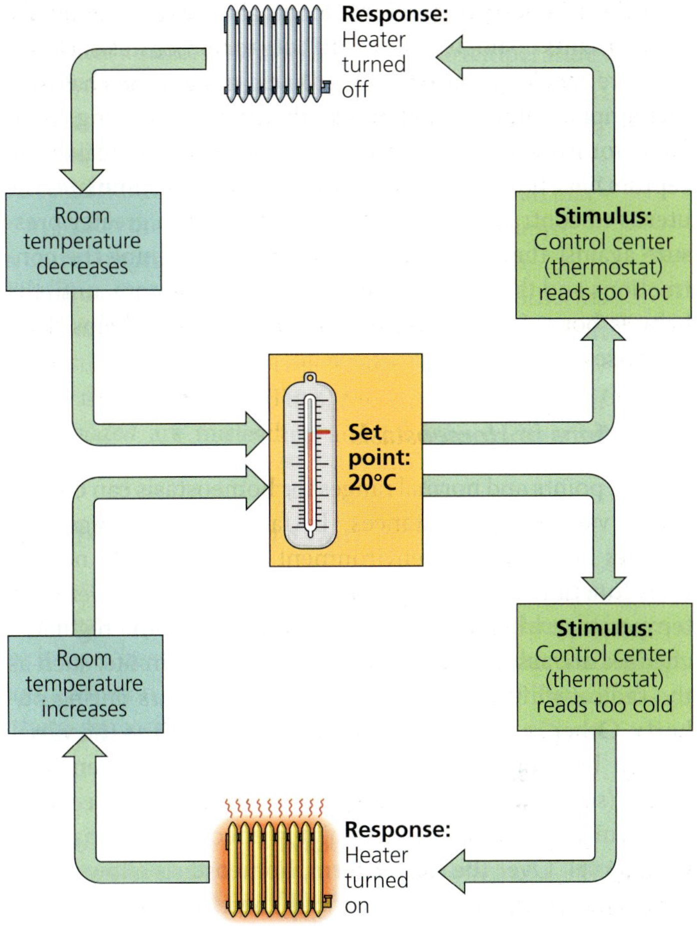

▲ **Figure 40.8 A nonliving example of negative feedback: control of room temperature.** Regulating room temperature depends on a control center (a thermostat) that detects temperature change and activates mechanisms that reverse that change.

? *How would adding an air conditioner to the system contribute to homeostasis?*

Homeostasis is a dynamic equilibrium, the interplay between external factors that tend to change the internal environment and internal control mechanisms that oppose such changes. Note that physiological responses to stimuli are not instantaneous, just as switching on a furnace does not immediately warm a house. As a result, homeostasis reduces but doesn't eliminate changes in the internal environment. Additional fluctuation occurs if a variable has a **normal range**—an upper and lower limit—rather than a single set point. This is equivalent to a heating system that begins producing heat when the room temperature drops to 19°C (66°F) and stops heating when the temperature reaches 21°C (70°F). Regardless of whether there is a set point or a normal range, homeostasis is enhanced by mechanisms that reduce fluctuations, such as insulation in the case of temperature and physiological buffers in the case of pH.

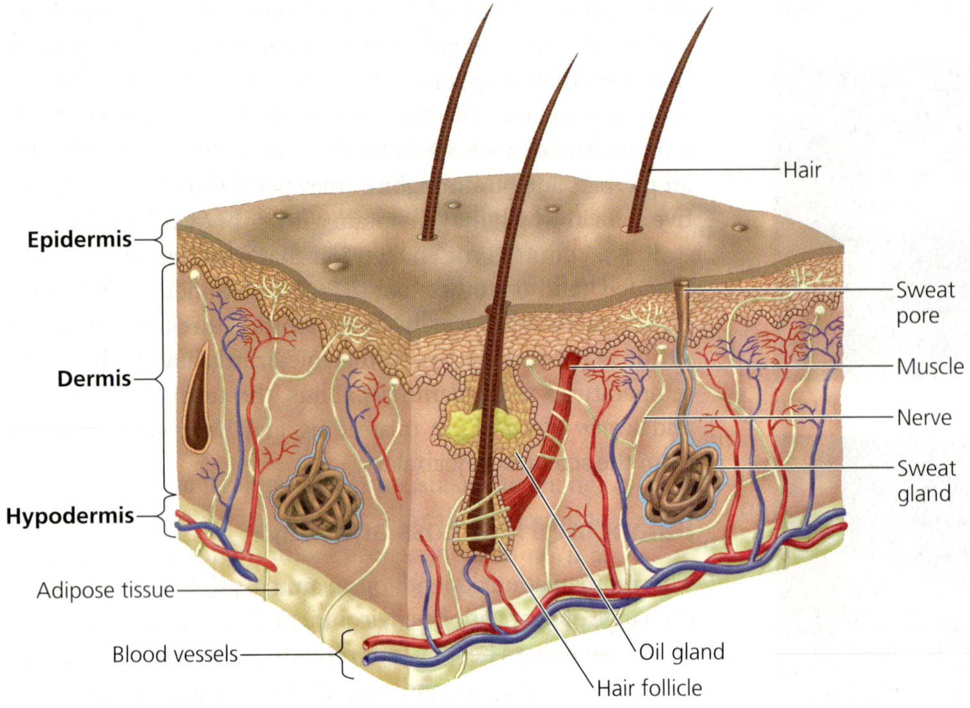

▲ **Figure 40.11 Mammalian integumentary system.** The skin and its derivatives serve important functions in mammals, including protection and thermoregulation.

both within an organism and between an organism and its external environment. Note that heat is always transferred from an object of higher temperature to one of lower temperature.

The essence of thermoregulation is maintaining rates of heat gain that equal rates of heat loss. Animals do this through mechanisms that either reduce heat exchange overall or that favor heat exchange in a particular direction. In mammals, several of these mechanisms involve the **integumentary system**, the outer covering of the body, consisting of the skin, hair, and nails (claws or hooves in some species). A key organ of this system is the skin, which consists of the epidermis and the dermis **(Figure 40.11)**. The epidermis is the outermost layer of skin and is composed mostly of dead epithelial cells that continually flake and fall off. New cells pushing up from lower layers replace the cells that are lost. The inner layer, the dermis, contains hair follicles, oil and sweat glands, muscles, nerves, and blood vessels. Beneath the skin lies the hypodermis, a layer of adipose tissue that includes fat-storing cells as well as blood vessels.

Insulation

A major thermoregulatory adaptation in mammals and birds is insulation, which reduces the flow of heat between an animal and its environment. Sources of insulation include hair, feathers, and layers of fat formed by adipose tissue.

Many animals that rely on insulation to reduce overall heat exchange also adjust their insulating layers to help thermoregulate. Most land mammals and birds, for example, react to cold by raising their fur or feathers. This action traps a thicker layer of air, thereby increasing the insulating power of the fur or feather layer. To repel water that would reduce the insulating capacity of feathers or fur, some animals secrete oily substances, such as the oils that birds apply to their feathers during preening. Lacking feathers or fur, humans must rely primarily on fat for insulation. "Goose bumps" are a vestige of hair raising inherited from our furry ancestors.

Insulation plays a particularly important role in thermoregulation by marine mammals, such as whales and walruses. These animals swim in water colder than their body core temperature, and many species spend at least part of the year in nearly freezing polar seas. The problem of thermoregulation is made worse by the fact that the transfer of heat to water occurs 50 to 100 times more rapidly than heat transfer to air. Just under the skin, marine mammals have a very thick layer of insulating fat called blubber. The insulation blubber provides is so effective that marine mammals maintain body core temperatures of about 36–38°C (97–100°F) without requiring much more food energy than land mammals of similar size.

Circulatory Adaptations

Circulatory systems provide a major route for heat flow between the interior and exterior of the body. Adaptations that regulate the extent of blood flow near the body surface or that trap heat within the body core play a significant role in thermoregulation.

In response to changes in the temperature of their surroundings, many animals alter the amount of blood (and hence heat) flowing between their body core and their skin. Nerve signals that relax the muscles of the vessel walls result in *vasodilation*, an increase in the diameter of superficial blood vessels (those near the body surface). As a consequence of the increase in vessel diameter, blood flow in the skin is elevated. In endotherms, vasodilation usually warms the skin and increases the transfer of body heat to the environment by radiation, conduction, and convection (see Figure 40.10). The reverse process, *vasoconstriction*, reduces blood flow and heat transfer by decreasing the diameter of superficial vessels. It is vasoconstriction in blood vessels of the ear that allows the jackrabbit shown in Figure 40.1 to avoid overheating on hot desert days.

Like endotherms, some ectotherms control heat exchange by regulating blood flow. For example, when the marine iguana of the Galápagos Islands swims in the cold ocean, its superficial blood vessels will undergo vasoconstriction. This process routes more blood to the central core of the body, conserving body heat.

In many birds and mammals, reduction of heat loss relies on **countercurrent exchange**, the flow of adjacent fluids in opposing directions that maximizes transfer rates of heat or solutes. Heat transfer involves an antiparallel arrangement of blood vessels called a *countercurrent heat exchanger*. When tissues are organized this way, arteries and veins are located adjacent to each other. As warm blood passes through arteries, it transfers heat to the colder blood returning from the extremities in the veins. Because the arteries and veins have countercurrent blood flow—blood flowing in opposite directions—heat transfer occurs along the entire length of the exchanger. **Figure 40.12** illustrates countercurrent heat exchange in a goose and dolphin.

Certain sharks, bony fishes, and insects also use countercurrent heat exchange. Although most sharks and fishes are temperature conformers, countercurrent heat exchangers are found in some large, powerful swimmers, including great white sharks, bluefin tuna, and swordfish. By keeping the main swimming muscles several degrees warmer than tissues near the animal's surface, this adaptation enables the vigorous, sustained activity that is characteristic of these animals. Similarly, many endothermic insects (bumblebees, honeybees, and some moths) have a countercurrent exchanger that helps maintain a high temperature in the thorax, where flight muscles are located.

In controlling heat gain and loss, some species regulate the extent of blood flow to the countercurrent exchanger. By allowing blood to pass through the heat exchanger or diverting it to other blood vessels, these animals alter the rate of heat loss as their physiological state or environment changes. For example, insects flying in hot weather run the risk of overheating because of the large amount of heat produced by working flight muscles. In some species, the countercurrent mechanism can be "shut down," allowing muscle-produced heat to be lost from the thorax to the abdomen and then to the environment.

Cooling by Evaporative Heat Loss

Many mammals and birds live in places where thermoregulation requires cooling as well as warming. If environmental temperature is above body temperature, animals gain heat from the environment as well as from metabolism, and evaporation is the only way to keep body temperature from rising rapidly. Terrestrial animals lose water by evaporation across the skin and when they breathe. Water absorbs considerable heat when it evaporates (see Chapter 3); this heat is carried away from the body surface with the water vapor.

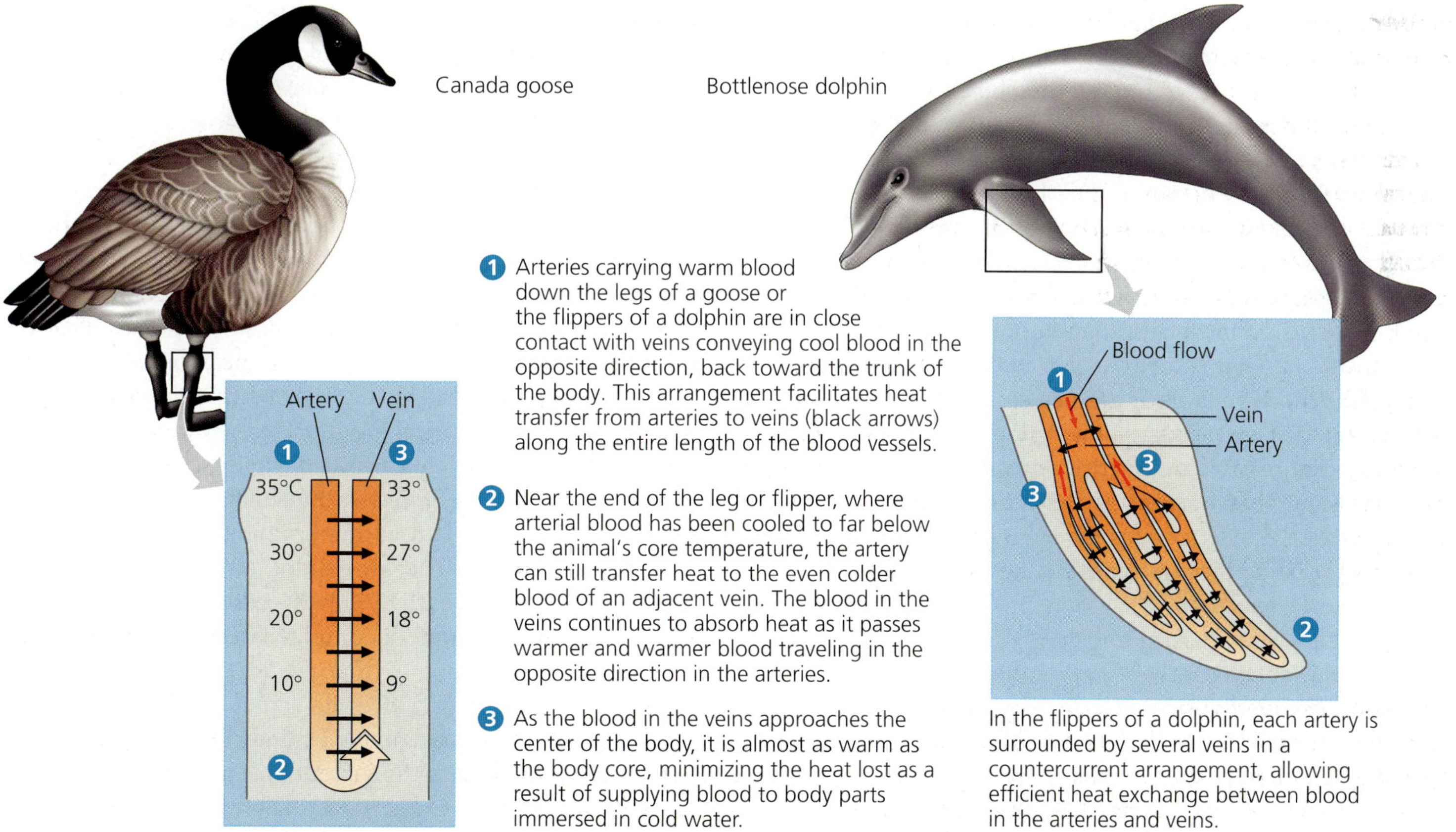

▲ **Figure 40.12 Countercurrent heat exchangers.** A countercurrent exchange system traps heat in the body core, thus reducing heat loss from the extremities, particularly when they are immersed in cold water or in contact with ice or snow. In essence, heat in the arterial blood emerging from the body core is transferred directly to the returning venous blood instead of being lost to the environment.

Thermoregulation in some animals is aided by adaptations that can greatly augment this cooling effect. Panting is important in birds and many mammals. Some birds have a pouch richly supplied with blood vessels in the floor of the mouth; fluttering the pouch increases evaporation. Pigeons, for example, can use evaporative cooling to keep body temperature close to 40°C (104°F) in air temperatures as high as 60°C (140°F), as long as they have sufficient water. Sweating or bathing moistens the skin and enhances evaporative cooling. Many terrestrial mammals have sweat glands controlled by the nervous system (see Figure 40.11).

Behavioral Responses

Both endotherms and ectotherms control body temperature through behavioral responses. Many ectotherms maintain a nearly constant body temperature through relatively simple behaviors. More extreme behavioral adaptations in some animals include hibernation or migration to a more suitable climate.

All amphibians and most reptiles other than birds are ectothermic. Therefore, these organisms control body temperature mainly by behavior. When exposed to air, most amphibians lose heat rapidly by evaporation from their moist body surfaces, making it difficult to keep sufficiently warm. However, an amphibian can maintain a satisfactory body temperature simply by moving to a location where solar heat is available. When the surroundings are too warm, amphibians seek shady spots or other cooler microenvironments.

Like amphibians, reptiles other than birds use behavior as their dominant means of thermoregulation. When cold, they seek warm places, orienting themselves toward heat sources and expanding the portion of their body surface exposed to the heat source (see Figure 40.9b). When hot, they move to cool areas or turn in another direction. Many reptiles keep their body temperatures very stable over the course of a day by shuttling back and forth between warm and cool spots.

Many terrestrial invertebrates can adjust internal temperature by the same behavioral mechanisms used by vertebrate ectotherms. The desert locust, for example, must reach a certain temperature to become active, and on cold days it orients in a direction that maximizes the absorption of sunlight. Other terrestrial invertebrates have certain postures that enable them to maximize or minimize their absorption of heat from the sun **(Figure 40.13)**.

Honeybees use a thermoregulatory mechanism that depends on social behavior. In cold weather, they increase heat production and huddle together, thereby retaining heat. They maintain a relatively constant temperature by changing how densely they huddle. Individuals move between the cooler outer edges of the cluster and the warmer center, thus circulating and distributing the heat. Even when huddling, honeybees must expend considerable energy to keep warm during long periods of cold weather, and this is the main function of storing large quantities of fuel in the hive in the form of honey.

◀ **Figure 40.13** **Thermoregulatory behavior in a dragonfly.** This dragonfly's "obelisk" posture is an adaptation that minimizes the amount of body surface exposed to the sun. This posture helps reduce heat gain by radiation.

Honeybees also control the temperature of their hive by transporting water to the hive in hot weather and fanning with their wings, promoting evaporation and convection. Thus, a colony of honeybees uses many of the mechanisms of thermoregulation seen in individual organisms.

Adjusting Metabolic Heat Production

Because endotherms generally maintain body temperatures considerably higher than that of the environment, they must counteract constant heat loss. Endotherms can vary heat production to match changing rates of heat loss. For example, heat production—*thermogenesis*—is increased by such muscle activity as moving or shivering. In some mammals, certain hormones can cause mitochondria to increase their metabolic activity and produce heat instead of ATP. This *nonshivering thermogenesis* takes place throughout the body, but some mammals also have a tissue called *brown fat* in the neck and between the shoulders that is specialized for rapid heat production. Through shivering and nonshivering thermogenesis, mammals and birds in cold environments can increase their metabolic heat production by as much as five to ten times the levels that occur in warm conditions. For example, chickadees, birds with a body mass of only 20 g, can remain active and hold body temperature nearly constant at 40°C (104°F) in environmental temperatures as low as −40°C (−40°F), as long as they have adequate food.

A few large reptiles become endothermic in particular circumstances. In the early 1960s, Herndon Dowling, at the Bronx Zoo in New York, documented this phenomenon for a female Burmese python (*Python molurus bivittatus*). Placing temperature-recording devices along the snake's coils, Dowling found that the snake maintained a body temperature roughly 6°C (10°F) above that of the surrounding air during the month when she was incubating eggs. Where did the heat come from? To answer this question, Dowling carried out studies together with a graduate student, Allen Vinegar, and his research supervisor, Victor Hutchison **(Figure 40.14)**. What they found was that pythons, like mammals, can generate heat

▼ **Figure 40.14 Inquiry**

How does a Burmese python generate heat while incubating eggs?

EXPERIMENT Herndon Dowling and colleagues at the Bronx Zoo in New York observed that when a female Burmese python incubated eggs by wrapping her body around them, she raised her body temperature and frequently contracted the muscles in her coils. To learn if the contractions were elevating her body temperature, they placed the python and her eggs in a chamber. They varied the chamber's temperature and monitored the python's muscle contractions and her oxygen uptake, a measure of her rate of cellular respiration.

RESULTS The python's oxygen consumption increased when the temperature in the chamber decreased. Her oxygen consumption also changed with the rate of muscle contraction:

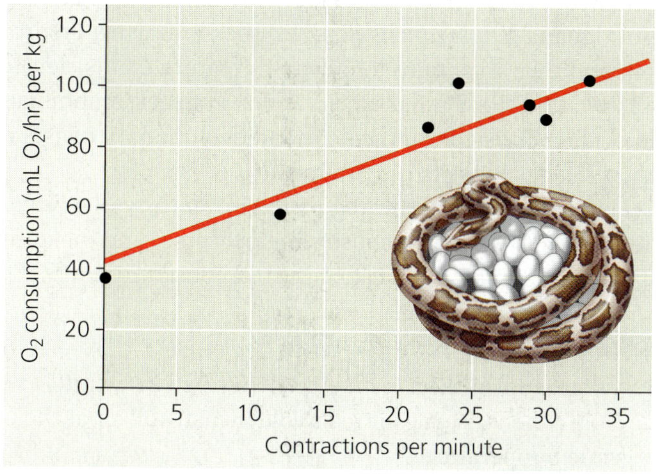

CONCLUSION Because oxygen consumption generates heat through cellular respiration and increases linearly with the rate of muscle contraction, the researchers concluded that the muscle contractions, a form of shivering, were the source of the Burmese python's elevated body temperature.

SOURCE V. H. Hutchison, H.G. Dowling, and A. Vinegar, Thermoregulation in a brooding female Indian python, *Python molurus bivittatus*, *Science* 151:694–696 (1966).

WHAT IF? Suppose you varied air temperature and measured oxygen consumption for a female Burmese python without a clutch of eggs. Since she would not show shivering behavior, how would the snake's oxygen consumption vary with environmental temperature?

through spasmodic muscle contraction—in other words, shivering. These findings and others have led to new insights into thermoregulation in reptiles and contributed to the idea, still under debate, that certain groups of dinosaurs were endothermic (see Chapter 34).

As mentioned earlier, many species of flying insects, such as bees and moths, are endothermic—the smallest of all endotherms. The capacity of such endothermic insects to elevate body temperature depends on powerful flight muscles, which generate large amounts of heat when operating. Many endothermic insects warm up by shivering before taking off. As they contract their flight muscles in synchrony, only slight wing movements occur, but considerable heat is produced. Chemical reactions, and hence cellular respiration, speed up in the warmed-up flight "motors," enabling these insects to fly even on cold days or at night **(Figure 40.15)**.

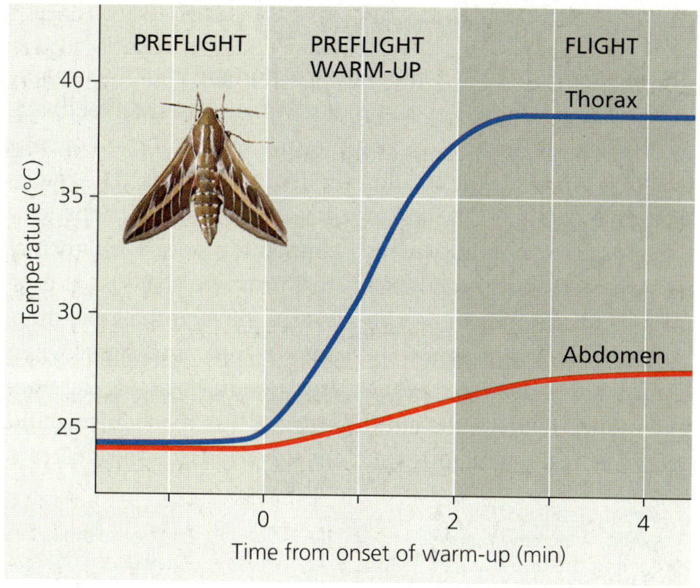

▲ **Figure 40.15 Preflight warm-up in the hawkmoth.** The hawkmoth (*Manduca sexta*) is one of many insect species that use a shivering-like mechanism for preflight warm-up of thoracic flight muscles. Warming up helps these muscles produce enough power to let the animal take off. Once airborne, flight muscle activity maintains a high thoracic temperature.

Acclimatization in Thermoregulation

Acclimatization contributes to thermoregulation across many animal species. In birds and mammals, acclimatization to seasonal temperature changes often includes adjusting the amount of insulation—by growing a thicker coat of fur in the winter and shedding it in the summer, for example. These changes help endotherms keep a constant body temperature throughout the year.

Acclimatization in ectotherms often includes adjustments at the cellular level. Cells may produce variants of enzymes that have the same function but different optimal temperatures. Also, the proportions of saturated and unsaturated lipids in membranes may change; unsaturated lipids help keep membranes fluid at lower temperatures (see Figure 7.5). Some ectotherms that experience subzero body temperatures protect themselves by producing "antifreeze" compounds that prevent ice formation in the cells. In the Arctic and Southern (Antarctic) oceans, these compounds in the body fluids of certain fishes enable survival where water temperatures can be as low as −2°C (28°F), below the freezing point of unprotected body fluids (about −1°C, or 30°F).

Physiological Thermostats and Fever

The regulation of body temperature in humans and other mammals is brought about by a complex system based on feedback mechanisms. The sensors for thermoregulation are concentrated in a brain region called the **hypothalamus**. The hypothalamus contains a group of nerve cells that functions as a thermostat, responding to body temperatures outside a normal range by activating mechanisms that promote heat loss or gain **(Figure 40.16)**. Warm receptors signal the hypothalamic thermostat when temperatures increase; cold receptors signal when temperatures decrease. At body temperatures below the normal range, the thermostat inhibits heat loss mechanisms and activates heat-saving ones such as the constriction of certain

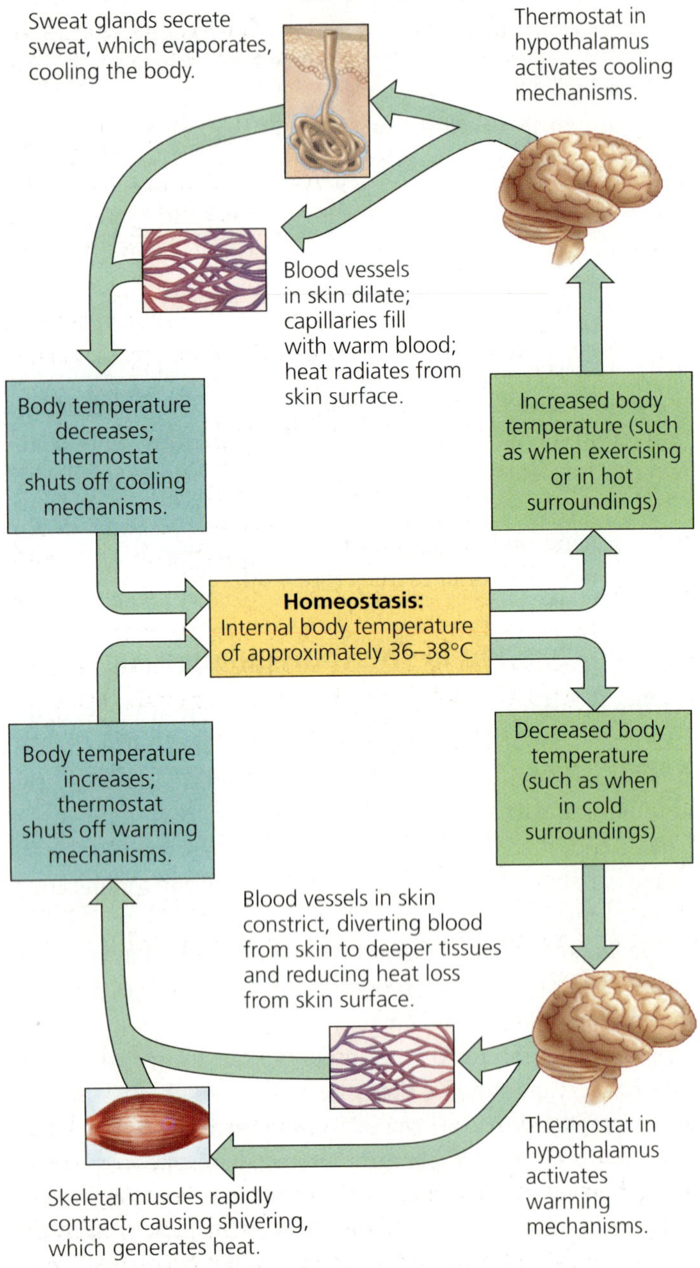

▲ **Figure 40.16 The thermostatic function of the hypothalamus in human thermoregulation.**

blood vessels and the raising of fur, while stimulating heat-generating mechanisms (shivering and nonshivering thermogenesis). In response to elevated body temperature, the thermostat shuts down heat retention mechanisms and promotes body cooling by vasodilation, sweating, or panting. Because the same blood vessel supplies the hypothalamus and ears, an ear thermometer records the temperature detected by the hypothalmic thermostat.

In the course of certain bacterial and viral infections, mammals and birds develop fever, an elevated body temperature. A variety of experiments have shown that fever reflects an increase in the set point for the biological thermostat. For example, artificially raising the temperature of the hypothalamus in an infected animal reduces fever in the rest of the body.

Although only endotherms develop fever, lizards exhibit a related response. When infected with certain bacteria, the desert iguana (*Dipsosaurus dorsalis*) seeks a warmer environment and then maintains a body temperature that is elevated by 2–4°C (4–7°F). Similar observations in fishes, amphibians, and even cockroaches indicate broad evolutionary conservation of this response to certain infections.

Having explored thermoregulation in depth, we'll now consider some other energy-consuming processes and the different ways that animals allocate, use, and conserve energy.

CONCEPT CHECK 40.3

1. What mode of heat exchange is involved in "wind chill," when moving air feels colder than still air at the same temperature?
2. Flowers differ in how much sunlight they absorb. Why might this matter to a hummingbird seeking nectar on a cool morning?
3. **WHAT IF?** Suppose at the end of a hard run on a hot day you find that there are no drinks left in the cooler. If, out of desperation, you dunk your head into the cooler, how might the ice-cold water affect the rate at which your body temperature returns to normal?

For suggested answers, see Appendix A.

CONCEPT **40.4**

Energy requirements are related to animal size, activity, and environment

Like other organisms, animals require chemical energy for growth, repair, activity, and reproduction. The overall flow and transformation of energy in an animal—its **bioenergetics**—determines nutritional needs and is related to an animal's size, activity, and environment.

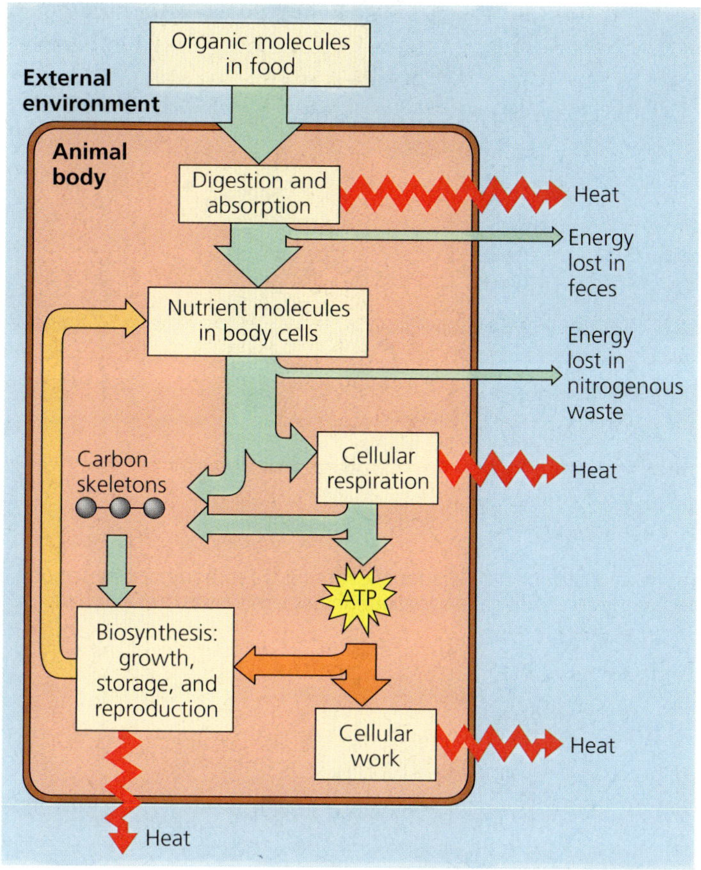

▲ **Figure 40.17 Bioenergetics of an animal: an overview.**

Energy Allocation and Use

As we have discussed in other chapters, organisms can be classified by how they obtain chemical energy. Most autotrophs, such as plants, use light energy to build energy-rich organic molecules and then use those organic molecules for fuel. Heterotrophs, such as animals, must obtain their chemical energy from food, which contains organic molecules synthesized by other organisms.

Animals use chemical energy harvested from the food they eat to fuel metabolism and activity **(Figure 40.17)**. Food is digested by enzymatic hydrolysis (see Figure 5.2b), and nutrients are absorbed by body cells. Most energy-containing molecules are used to generate ATP. ATP produced by cellular respiration and fermentation (see Chapter 9) powers cellular work, enabling cells, organs, and organ systems to perform the functions that keep an animal alive. Energy in the form of ATP is also used in biosynthesis, which is needed for body growth and repair, synthesis of storage material such as fat, and production of gametes. The production and use of ATP generates heat, which the animal eventually gives off to its surroundings.

Quantifying Energy Use

How much of the total energy an animal obtains from food does it need just to stay alive? How much energy must be expended to walk, run, swim, or fly from one place to another? What fraction of the energy intake is used for reproduction? Physiologists answer such questions by measuring the rate at which an animal uses chemical energy and how this rate changes in different circumstances.

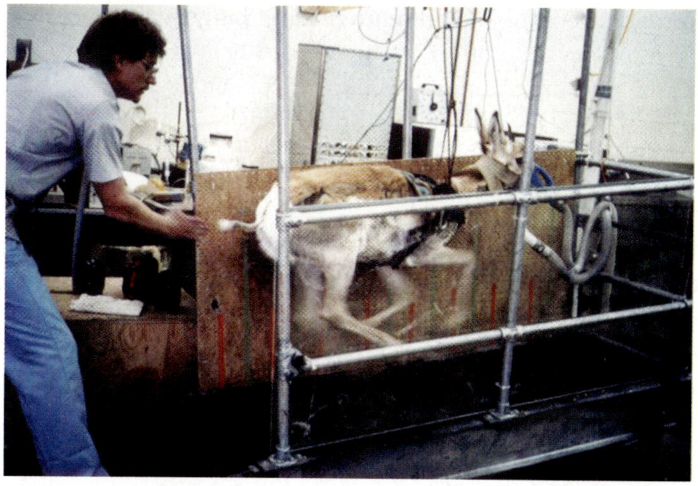

▲ **Figure 40.18 Measuring rate of oxygen consumption in a running pronghorn.** A researcher collects respiratory data from a pronghorn running on a treadmill at 40 km/hr.

The amount of energy an animal uses in a unit of time is called its **metabolic rate**—the sum of all the energy-requiring biochemical reactions over a given time interval. Energy is measured in joules or in calories (cal) and kilocalories (kcal). (A kilocalorie equals 1,000 calories. The unit Calorie, with a capital C, as used by many nutritionists, is actually a kilocalorie.)

Metabolic rate can be determined in several ways. Because nearly all of the chemical energy used in cellular respiration eventually appears as heat, metabolic rate can be measured by monitoring an animal's rate of heat loss. For this approach, researchers use a calorimeter, which is a closed, insulated chamber equipped with a device that records an animal's heat loss. Metabolic rate can also be determined from the amount of oxygen consumed or carbon dioxide produced by an animal's cellular respiration **(Figure 40.18)**. To calculate metabolic rate over longer periods, researchers record the rate of food consumption, the energy content of the food (about 4.5–5 kcal per gram of protein or carbohydrate and about 9 kcal per gram of fat), and the chemical energy lost in waste products (feces and nitrogenous waste).

Minimum Metabolic Rate and Thermoregulation

Animals must maintain a minimum metabolic rate for basic functions such as cell maintenance, breathing, and heartbeat. Researchers measure this minimum metabolic rate differently for endotherms and ectotherms. The minimum metabolic rate of a nongrowing endotherm that is at rest, has an empty stomach, and is not experiencing stress is called the **basal metabolic rate (BMR)**. BMR is measured under a "comfortable" temperature range—a range that requires no generation or shedding of heat above the minimum. The minimum metabolic rate of ectotherms is determined at a specific temperature because changes in the environmental temperature alter body temperature and therefore metabolic rate. The metabolic rate of a fasting, nonstressed ectotherm at rest at a particular temperature is called its **standard metabolic rate (SMR)**.

Comparisons of minimum metabolic rates reveal that endothermy and ectothermy have distinct energy costs. The BMR for humans averages 1,600–1,800 kcal per day for adult males and 1,300–1,500 kcal per day for adult females. These BMRs are about equivalent to the rate of energy use by a 75-watt light bulb. In contrast, SMR calculations reveal that an American alligator at rest consumes only about 60 kcal per day at 20°C (68°F). Since this represents less than 1/20 the energy used by a comparably sized adult human, the lower energetic requirement of ectothermy is readily apparent.

Influences on Metabolic Rate

Metabolic rate is affected by many factors besides whether the animal is an endotherm or an ectotherm. Some key factors are age, sex, size, activity, temperature, and nutrition. Here we'll examine the effects of size and activity.

Size and Metabolic Rate

An intriguing, yet largely unanswered, question in animal biology has to do with the relationship between body size and metabolic rate. Larger animals have more body mass and therefore require more chemical energy. Remarkably, the relationship between overall metabolic rate and body mass is constant across a wide range of sizes and forms, as illustrated for various mammals in **Figure 40.19a**. For creatures ranging in size from bacteria to blue whales, metabolic rate is roughly proportional to body mass to the three-quarter power ($m^{3/4}$).

The relationship of metabolic rate to size profoundly affects energy consumption by body cells and tissues. As shown in **Figure 40.19b**, the energy it takes to maintain each gram of body weight is inversely related to body size. Each gram of a mouse, for instance, requires about 20 times as many calories as a gram of an elephant, even though the whole elephant uses far more calories than the whole mouse. The smaller animal's higher metabolic rate per gram demands a greater rate of oxygen delivery. Correlated with its higher metabolic rate per gram, the smaller animal has a higher breathing rate, blood volume (relative to its size), and heart rate. Also, it must eat much more food per unit of body mass.

The reason for the inverse relationship of metabolic rate per unit of body mass to body size is still a subject of debate. One hypothesis is that for endotherms the smaller the animal, the greater the energy cost of maintaining a stable body temperature. In effect, the smaller an animal is, the greater its surface-to-volume ratio is and thus the faster it loses heat to (or gains heat from) the surroundings. Logical as this hypothesis seems, it does not explain the fact that the inverse relationship between metabolic rate per gram and size is also observed in ectotherms, which do not use metabolic heat to maintain body temperature.

Bioenergetic considerations associated with body size provide a clear example of how trade-offs shape the evolution of body plans. As body size becomes smaller, each gram of tissue increases in energy cost. As body size increases, energy costs per gram of tissue lessen, but an ever-larger fraction of body tissue is required for exchange, support, and locomotion.

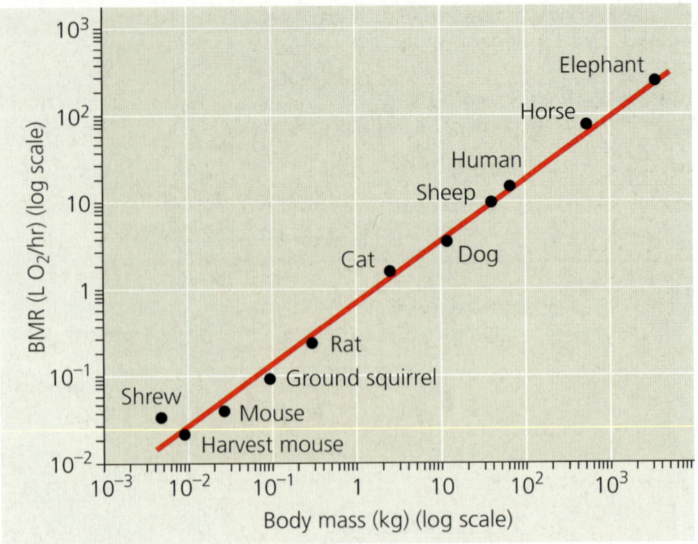

(a) Relationship of basal metabolic rate (BMR) to body size for various mammals. From shrew to elephant, size increases 1 millionfold.

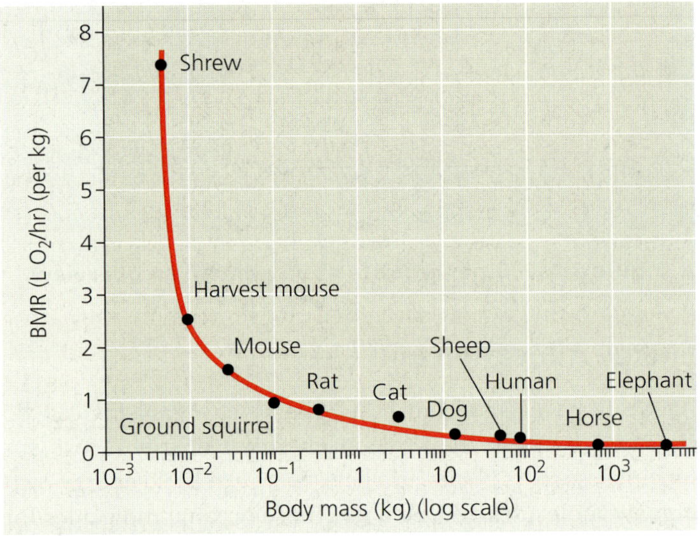

(b) Relationship of BMR per kilogram of body mass to body size for the same mammals as in (a).

▲ **Figure 40.19 The relationship of metabolic rate to body size.**

Activity and Metabolic Rate

For both ectotherms and endotherms, activity greatly affects metabolic rate. Even a person reading quietly at a desk or an insect twitching its wings consumes energy beyond the BMR or SMR. Maximum metabolic rates (the highest rates of ATP use) occur during peak activity, such as lifting heavy weights, sprinting, or high-speed swimming. In general, the maximum metabolic rate an animal can sustain is inversely related to the duration of activity.

For most terrestrial animals, the average daily rate of energy consumption is 2 to 4 times BMR (for endotherms) or SMR (for ectotherms). Humans in most developed countries have an unusually low average daily metabolic rate of about 1.5 times BMR—an indication of their relatively sedentary lifestyles.

Energy Budgets

As we have seen, the ways in which animals use the chemical energy of food depend on environment, behavior, size, and thermoregulation. To understand how these influences affect bioenergetics in animal bodies, let's consider typical annual energy "budgets" of four terrestrial vertebrates varying in size and thermoregulatory strategy: a 60-kg female human, a 4-kg male Adélie penguin, a 25-g (0.025-kg) female deer mouse, and a 4-kg female eastern indigo snake **(Figure 40.20)**. Reproduction is included in these energy budgets because it can greatly influence energy allocation and is critical to species survival.

The female human, an endothermic mammal, spends the largest fraction of her annual energy budget for BMR and relatively little for activity and thermoregulation. The small amount of growth, about 1%, is equivalent to adding about 1 kg of body fat or 5–6 kg of other tissues. (Growth is not shown in the budgets for the penguin and deer mouse because these animals don't typically gain weight year to year after they are adults.) The cost of nine months of pregnancy and several months of breast-feeding is only 5–8% of the mother's annual energy requirements.

A male penguin spends the largest fraction of his energy for activity because he must swim to catch food. Being well insulated and fairly large, he has relatively low costs of thermoregulation in spite of living in the cold Antarctic. His reproductive costs, about 6% of annual energy expenditures, come mainly from incubating eggs (brooding) and bringing food to his chicks. Like most birds, penguins do not grow after they become adults.

Despite living in a temperate climate, the female deer mouse spends a large fraction of her energy budget for temperature regulation. Because of the high surface-to-volume ratio that goes with small size, deer mice lose body heat rapidly and must constantly generate metabolic heat to maintain body temperature.

In contrast with these endothermic animals, the ectothermic snake has no thermoregulation costs. Like most snakes, she grows continuously throughout her life. In the example in Figure 40.20, the snake added about 750 g of new body tissue in a year. She also produced about 650 g of eggs. The snake's economical ectothermic strategy is revealed by her very low energy expenditure, only 1/40 the energy expended by the similarly sized endothermic penguin.

For all the animals in Figure 40.20, locomotion and other activities are a major part of the energy budget. Some animals can conserve energy by temporarily decreasing their activity to a very low level, a process we will consider next.

Torpor and Energy Conservation

Despite their many adaptations for homeostasis, animals may encounter conditions that severely challenge their abilities to balance their heat, energy, and materials budgets. For example, at certain seasons or times of day, temperatures may be extremely high or low, or food may be unavailable. **Torpor**, a physiological

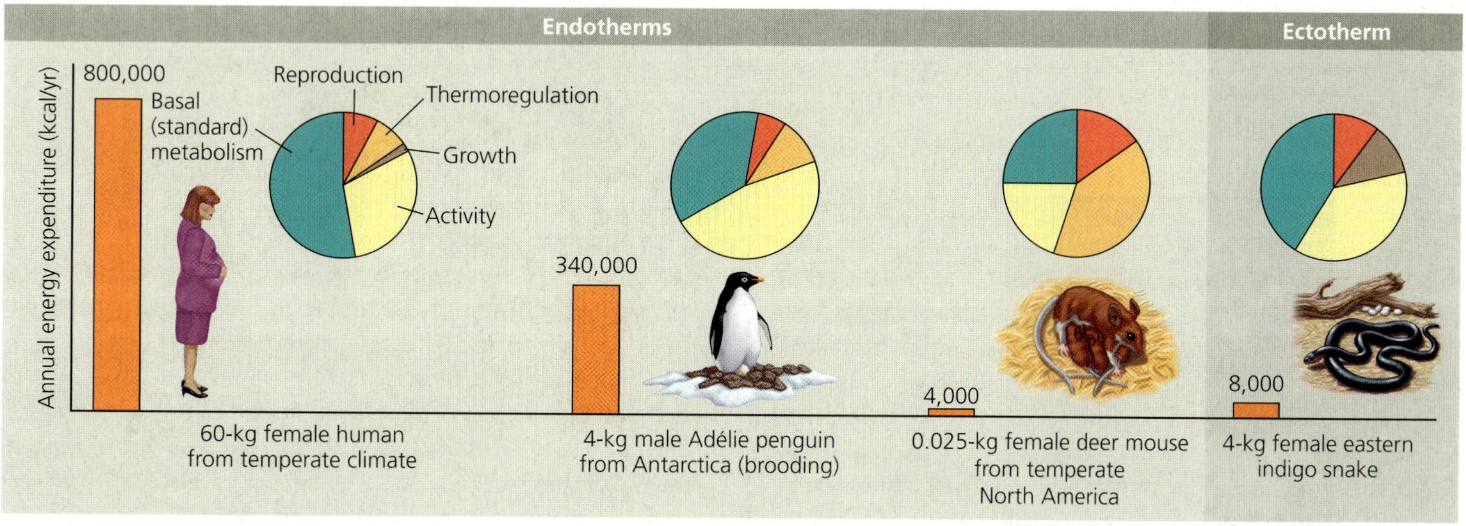

▲ **Figure 40.20 Energy budgets for four animals.** The slices of the pie charts indicate annual energy expenditures for various functions.

state in which activity is low and metabolism decreases, is an adaptation that enables animals to save energy while avoiding difficult and dangerous conditions.

Hibernation is long-term torpor that is an adaptation to winter cold and food scarcity. When vertebrate endotherms (birds and mammals) enter hibernation, their body temperatures decline as their body's thermostat is turned down. The temperature reduction may be dramatic: Some hibernating mammals cool to as low as 1–2°C (34–35°F), and a few even drop slightly below 0°C (32°F) in a supercooled (unfrozen) state. The resulting energy savings are huge; metabolic rates during hibernation can be much lower than if the animal attempted to maintain normal body temperatures of 36–38°C (97–100°F). Consider, for example, a Belding's ground squirrel (*Spermophilus beldingi*) living in the high mountains of California **(Figure 40.21)**. Instead of spending 150 kcal per day to maintain body temperature in winter weather, a hibernating squirrel spends an average of only 5–8 kcal per day. As a result, hibernators such as the ground squirrel can survive through the winter on limited supplies of energy stored in the body tissues or as food cached in a burrow. Similarly, the slow metabolism and inactivity of *estivation*, or summer torpor, enables animals to survive long periods of high temperatures and scarce water supplies.

Many small mammals and birds exhibit a daily torpor that seems to be adapted to feeding patterns. For instance, some bats feed at night and go into torpor in daylight. Chickadees and hummingbirds feed during the day and often go into torpor on cold nights; the body temperature of chickadees drops as much as 10°C (18°F) at night, and the temperature of hummingbirds can fall 25°C (45°F) or more. All endotherms that use daily torpor are relatively small; when active, they have high metabolic rates and thus very high rates of energy consumption.

From discussing body shape to considering energy conservation, this chapter has focused on the whole animal. We explored common tissue types that make up organs and organ systems. We also investigated how body plans provide for exchange, how size affects metabolic rate, and how some animals maintain a constant internal environment. For much of the rest of this unit, we'll see how specialized organs and organ systems enable animals to meet the basic challenges of life.

CONCEPT CHECK 40.4

1. If a mouse and a small lizard of the same mass (both at rest) were placed in experimental chambers under identical environmental conditions, which animal would consume oxygen at a higher rate? Explain.
2. Which animal must eat a larger proportion of its weight in food each day: a house cat or an African lion caged in a zoo? Explain.
3. **WHAT IF?** If you monitored energy allocation in the penguin in Figure 40.20 for just a few months, the "growth" category might now be a significant part of the pie chart, even though adult penguins don't change in size from year to year. What limitation in such energy budget studies does this lead you to consider?

For suggested answers, see Appendix A.

▶ **Figure 40.21 Body temperature and metabolism during hibernation in Belding's ground squirrels.**

WHAT IF? *Propose two different hypotheses about the environmental change that triggers hibernation. Then suppose that, during one year, the outside temperatures dropped steadily a month earlier than normal. For each hypothesis, what effect on the timing of hibernation would you expect?*

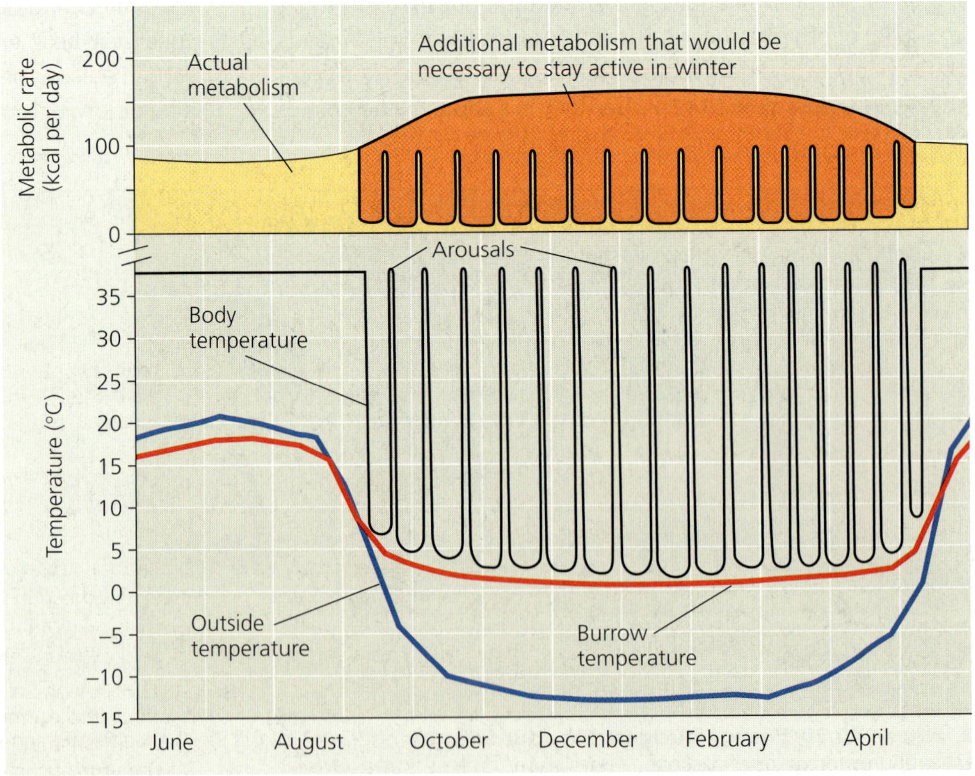

Chapter 40 Review

MEDIA Go to the Study Area at **www.masteringbio.com** for BioFlix 3-D Animations, MP3 Tutors, Videos, Practice Tests, an eBook, and more.

SUMMARY OF KEY CONCEPTS

CONCEPT 40.1

Animal form and function are correlated at all levels of organization (pp. 852–860)

- **Physical Constraints on Animal Size and Shape** The ability to perform certain actions, such as fast swimming, depends on an animal's size and shape. Convergent evolution reflects different species' independent adaptations to a similar environmental challenge.
- **Exchange with the Environment** Each cell of an animal must have access to an aqueous environment. Simple two-layered sacs and flat shapes maximize exposure to the surrounding medium. More complex body plans have highly folded internal surfaces specialized for exchanging materials.
- **Hierarchical Organization of Body Plans** Animals are composed of cells. Groups of cells with a common structure and function make up tissues. Different tissues make up organs, which together make up organ systems.
- **Tissue Structure and Function** Epithelial tissue covers the outside of the body and lines internal organs and cavities. Connective tissues bind and support other tissues. Muscle tissue contracts in response to nerve signals. Nervous tissue transmits nerve signals throughout the animal.
- **Coordination and Control** The endocrine and nervous systems function as the two means of communication between distinct locations in the body. The endocrine system broadcasts signaling molecules called hormones everywhere via the bloodstream, but only certain cells are responsive. The nervous system uses dedicated cellular circuits involving electrical and chemical signals to send information to specific locations.

MEDIA

Activity Overview of Animal Tissues
Activity Epithelial Tissue
Activity Connective Tissue
Activity Muscle Tissue
Activity Nervous Tissue

CONCEPT 40.2

Feedback control loops maintain the internal environment in many animals (pp. 860–862)

- **Regulating and Conforming** Animals cope with environmental fluctuations by regulating certain internal variables while allowing others to conform to external changes.
- **Homeostasis** Homeostasis describes an animal's internal steady state. It is a balance between external changes and the animal's internal control mechanisms that oppose the changes. The interstitial fluid surrounding an animal's cells is usually very different from the external environment. Homeostatic mechanisms moderate changes in the internal environment and usually involve negative feedback. These mechanisms enable regulated change.

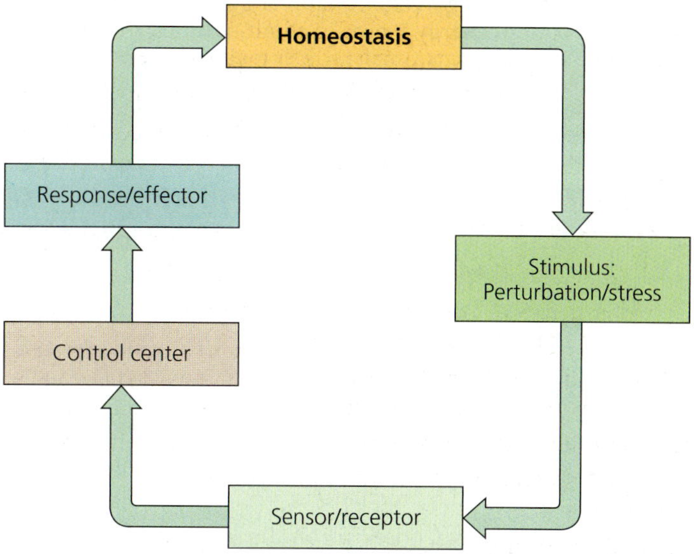

Regulated change in the internal environment is essential to normal body functions. Acclimatization involves temporary changes in homeostasis in response to alterations in the environment.

MEDIA

Activity Regulation: Negative and Positive Feedback

CONCEPT 40.3

Homeostatic processes for thermoregulation involve form, function, and behavior (pp. 862–868)

- An animal maintains its internal temperature within a tolerable range by processes of thermoregulation.
- **Endothermy and Ectothermy** Endotherms are warmed mostly by heat generated by metabolism. Ectotherms get most of their heat from external sources. Endothermy requires an animal to expend more energy.
- **Variation in Body Temperature** Body temperature varies in poikilotherms and is relatively constant in homeotherms.
- **Balancing Heat Loss and Gain** Conduction, convection, radiation, and evaporation account for heat exchange. Thermoregulation involves physiological and behavioral adjustments that balance heat gain and loss. Insulation, vasodilation, vasoconstriction, and countercurrent heat exchange alter the rate of heat exchange. Panting, sweating, and bathing increase evaporation, cooling the body. Both ectotherms and endotherms adjust the rate of heat exchange with their surroundings by behavioral responses. Some animals can even adjust their rate of metabolic heat production.
- **Acclimatization in Thermoregulation** Many mammals and birds adjust the amount of body insulation in response to changes in environmental temperature. Ectotherms undergo a variety of changes at the cellular level to acclimatize to shifts in temperature.
- **Physiological Thermostats and Fever** Mammals regulate their body temperature by complex negative-feedback mechanisms that involve several organ systems, including the nervous, circulatory, and integumentary systems.

CONCEPT 40.4

Energy requirements are related to animal size, activity, and environment (pp. 868–872)

- **Energy Allocation and Use** Animals obtain chemical energy from food, storing it for short-term use in ATP.
- **Quantifying Energy Use** An animal's metabolic rate is the total amount of energy it uses in a unit of time. Metabolic rates for birds and mammals, which maintain a fairly constant body temperature using metabolic heat (endothermy), are generally higher than those for most fishes, nonavian reptiles, amphibians, and invertebrates, which rely mostly on external sources of heat for maintaining body temperature (ectothermy).
- **Minimum Metabolic Rate and Thermoregulation** Under similar conditions and for animals of the same size, BMR, the minimum metabolic rate of endotherms, is substantially higher than SMR, the standard metabolic rate of ectotherms.
- **Influences on Metabolic Rate** Minimum metabolic rate per gram is inversely related to body size among similar animals. Activity increases metabolic rate.
- **Energy Budgets** Animals use energy for basal (or standard) metabolism, activity, homeostasis (such as temperature regulation), growth, and reproduction.
- **Torpor and Energy Conservation** Torpor involves a decrease in metabolic rate, conserving energy during environmental extremes. Animals may enter torpor in winter (hibernation), summer (estivation), or during sleep periods (daily torpor).

MEDIA

Investigation How Does Temperature Affect Metabolic Rate in *Daphnia*?

TESTING YOUR KNOWLEDGE

SELF-QUIZ

1. Compared with a smaller cell, a larger cell of the same shape has
a. less surface area.
b. less surface area per unit of volume.
c. the same surface-to-volume ratio.
d. a smaller average distance between its mitochondria and the external source of oxygen.
e. a smaller cytoplasm-to-nucleus ratio.

2. The epithelium best adapted for a body surface subject to abrasion is
a. simple squamous.
b. simple cuboidal.
c. simple columnar.
d. stratified columnar.
e. stratified squamous.

3. Which of the following is not an adaptation for reducing the rate of heat exchange between an animal and its environment?
a. feathers or fur
b. vasoconstriction
c. nonshivering thermogenesis
d. countercurrent heat exchanger
e. blubber or fat layer

4. Which of the following animals uses the highest percent of its energy budget for homeostatic regulation?
a. a hydra
b. a marine jelly (an invertebrate)
c. a snake in a temperate forest
d. a desert insect
e. a desert bird

5. Consider the energy budgets for a human, an elephant, a penguin, a mouse, and a snake. The ______________ would have the highest total annual energy expenditure, and the ______________ would have the highest energy expenditure per unit mass.
a. elephant; mouse
b. elephant; human
c. human; penguin
d. mouse; snake
e. penguin; mouse

6. An animal's inputs of energy and materials would exceed its outputs
a. if the animal is an endotherm, which must always take in more energy because of its high metabolic rate.
b. if it is actively foraging for food.
c. if it is hibernating.
d. if it is growing and increasing its mass.
e. never; homeostasis makes these energy and material budgets always balance.

7. **DRAW IT** Draw a model of the control loop(s) required for driving an automobile at a fairly constant speed over a hilly road. Assuming that either the driver or a cruise control device is the control center, indicate each feature that represents a sensor, input, or response.

For Self-Quiz answers, see Appendix A.

MEDIA Visit the Study Area at **www.masteringbio.com** for a Practice Test.

EVOLUTION CONNECTION

8. The biologist C. Bergmann noted that mammals and birds living at higher latitudes are on average larger and bulkier than related species found at lower latitudes. Suggest an evolutionary hypothesis for this observation.

SCIENTIFIC INQUIRY

9. Eastern tent caterpillars (*Malacosoma americanum*) live in large groups in silk nests, or tents, which they build in trees. They are among the first insects to be active in early spring, when daily temperature fluctuates from freezing to very hot. Over the course of a day, they display striking differences in behavior: Early in the morning, they rest in a tightly packed group on the tent's east-facing surface. In midafternoon, they are on its undersurface, each caterpillar hanging by a few of its legs. Propose a hypothesis to explain this behavior. How could you test it?

SCIENCE, TECHNOLOGY, AND SOCIETY

10. Medical researchers are investigating artificial substitutes for various human tissues. Why might artificial blood or skin be useful? What characteristics would these substitutes need in order to function well in the body? Why do real tissues work better? Why not use the real tissues if they work better? What other artificial tissues might be useful? What problems do you anticipate in developing and applying them?

41 Animal Nutrition

▲ **Figure 41.1** **How does a lean fish help a bear make fat?**

KEY CONCEPTS

41.1 **An animal's diet must supply chemical energy, organic molecules, and essential nutrients**

41.2 **The main stages of food processing are ingestion, digestion, absorption, and elimination**

41.3 **Organs specialized for sequential stages of food processing form the mammalian digestive system**

41.4 **Evolutionary adaptations of vertebrate digestive systems correlate with diet**

41.5 **Homeostatic mechanisms contribute to an animal's energy balance**

OVERVIEW

The Need to Feed

Dinnertime has arrived for the Kodiak bear in **Figure 41.1** (and for the salmon, though in quite a different sense). The skin, muscles, and other parts of the fish will be chewed into pieces, broken down by acid and enzymes in the bear's digestive system, and finally absorbed as small molecules into the body of the bear. Such a process is what is meant by animal **nutrition**: food being taken in, taken apart, and taken up.

Although a diet of fish plucked from a waterfall is not common, all animals eat other organisms—dead or alive, piecemeal or whole. Unlike plants, animals rely on their food for both the energy and the organic molecules used to assemble new molecules, cells, and tissues. Despite this shared need, animals have diverse diets. **Herbivores**, such as cattle, parrotfish, and termites, dine mainly on plants or algae. **Carnivores**, such as sharks, hawks, and spiders, mostly eat other animals. Bears and other **omnivores** (from the Latin *omni*, all) don't in fact eat everything, but they do regularly consume animals as well as plants or algae. We humans are typically omnivores, as are cockroaches and crows.

The terms *herbivore*, *carnivore*, and *omnivore* represent the kinds of food an animal usually eats. Keep in mind, however, that most animals are opportunistic feeders, eating foods outside their standard diet when their usual foods aren't available. For example, deer are herbivores, but in addition to feeding on grass and other plants, they occasionally eat insects, worms, or bird eggs. Note as well that microorganisms are an unavoidable "supplement" in every animal's diet.

Animals must eat. But to survive and reproduce, they must also balance their consumption, storage, and use of food. Bats, for example, store energy, largely in the form of body fat, for periods of hibernation. Eating too little food, too much food, or the wrong mixture of foods can endanger an animal's health. In this chapter, we will survey the nutritional requirements of animals, explore some of the diverse evolutionary adaptations for obtaining and processing food, and investigate the regulation of energy intake and expenditure.

CONCEPT **41.1**

An animal's diet must supply chemical energy, organic molecules, and essential nutrients

The activities of cells, tissues, organs, and whole animals depend on sources of chemical energy in the diet. This energy, after being converted to ATP, powers processes ranging from DNA replication and cell division to vision and flight. To meet the continuous requirement for ATP, animals ingest and digest nutrients, such as carbohydrates, proteins, and lipids, for use in cellular respiration and energy storage.

In addition to providing fuel for ATP production, an animal's diet must supply the raw materials needed for biosynthesis. To build the complex molecules it needs to grow, maintain itself, and reproduce, an animal must obtain two types of organic precursors from its food. Animals need a source of organic carbon (such as sugar) and a source of organic nitrogen (usually amino acids from the digestion of protein). Starting with these materials, animals can construct a great variety of organic molecules.

The materials that an animal's cells require but cannot synthesize are called **essential nutrients**. Obtained from dietary sources, these nutrients include both minerals and preassembled organic molecules. Some nutrients are essential for all animals, whereas others are needed only by certain species. For instance, ascorbic acid (vitamin C) is an essential nutrient for humans and other primates, guinea pigs, and some birds and snakes, but not for most other animals.

Overall, an adequate diet thus satisfies three nutritional needs: chemical energy for cellular processes, organic building blocks for carbohydrates and other macromolecules, and essential nutrients.

Essential Nutrients

There are four classes of essential nutrients: essential amino acids, essential fatty acids, vitamins, and minerals.

Essential Amino Acids

Animals require 20 amino acids to make proteins. The majority of animal species can synthesize about half of these amino acids, as long as their diet includes organic nitrogen. The remaining amino acids must be obtained from food in prefabricated form and are therefore called **essential amino acids**. Most animals, including adult humans, require eight amino acids in their diet (infants also need a ninth, histidine).

A diet that provides insufficient amounts of one or more essential amino acids causes protein deficiency, the most common type of malnutrition among humans. The victims are usually children, who, if they survive infancy, often have impaired physical and sometimes mental development.

The proteins in animal products such as meat, eggs, and cheese are "complete," which means that they provide all the essential amino acids in their proper proportions. In contrast, most plant proteins are "incomplete," being deficient in one or more essential amino acids. Corn (maize), for example, is deficient in tryptophan and lysine, whereas beans are lacking in methionine. To prevent protein deficiency, vegetarian diets must therefore include combinations of plant products that together provide all of the essential amino acids **(Figure 41.2)**.

Some animals have adaptations that help them through periods when their bodies demand extraordinary amounts of protein. In penguins, for example, muscle protein provides a source of amino acids for making new proteins when feathers are replaced after molting **(Figure 41.3)**.

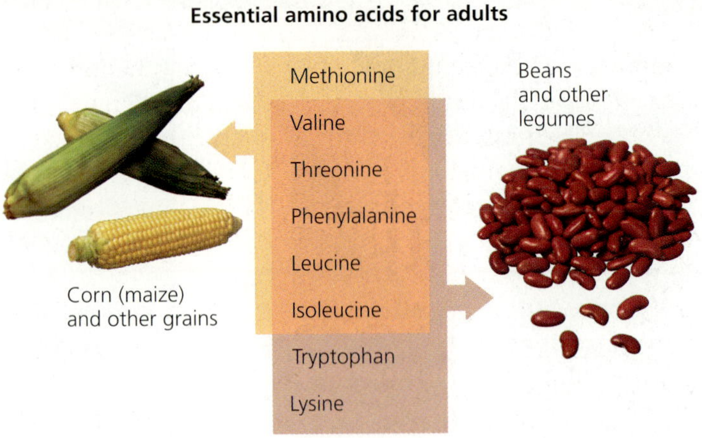

▲ **Figure 41.2 Essential amino acids from a vegetarian diet.** In combination, corn and beans provide an adult human with all essential amino acids.

▲ **Figure 41.3 Storing protein for growth.** Penguins, such as this Adélie from Antarctica, must make an abundance of new protein when they molt (grow new feathers). Because of the temporary loss of their insulating coat of feathers, penguins cannot swim—or feed—when molting. What is the source of amino acids for production of feather protein? Before molting, a penguin greatly increases its muscle mass. The penguin then breaks down the extra muscle protein, which supplies the amino acids for growing new feathers.

Essential Fatty Acids

Animals can synthesize most, but not all, of the fatty acids they need. The **essential fatty acids**, the ones they cannot make, are certain fatty acids that are unsaturated (containing one or more double bonds; see Figure 5.12). For example, humans require linoleic acid to make some membrane phospholipids. Because seeds, grains, and vegetables in the diets of humans and other animals generally furnish ample quantities of essential fatty acids, deficiencies in this class of nutrients are rare.

Vitamins

Vitamins are organic molecules with diverse functions that are required in the diet in very small amounts. Vitamin B_2, for example, is converted in the body to FAD, a coenzyme used in many metabolic processes, including cellular respiration (see Figure 9.12). For humans, 13 essential vitamins have been identified. Depending on the vitamin, the required amount ranges from about 0.01 to 100 mg per day.

Vitamins are classified as water-soluble or fat-soluble **(Table 41.1)**. The water-soluble vitamins include the B complex, which are compounds that generally function as coenzymes, and vitamin C, which is required to produce connective tissue. Among the fat-soluble vitamins are vitamin A, which is incorporated into visual pigments of the eye, and vitamin K, which functions in blood clotting. Another is vitamin D, which aids in calcium absorption and bone formation. Our dietary requirement for vitamin D is variable because we synthesize this vitamin from other molecules when the skin is exposed to sunlight.

For people with poorly balanced diets, taking vitamin supplements that provide recommended daily levels is certainly reasonable. It is much less clear whether massive doses of vitamins confer any health benefits or are, in fact, safe. Moderate overdoses of water-soluble vitamins are probably harmless because excesses of these vitamins are excreted in urine. However, excesses of

Table 41.1 Vitamin Requirements of Humans

Vitamin	Major Dietary Sources	Major Functions in the Body	Symptoms of Deficiency **or Extreme Excess**
Water-Soluble Vitamins			
Vitamin B_1 (thiamine)	Pork, legumes, peanuts, whole grains	Coenzyme used in removing CO_2 from organic compounds	Beriberi (nerve disorders, emaciation, anemia)
Vitamin B_2 (riboflavin)	Dairy products, meats, enriched grains, vegetables	Component of coenzymes FAD and FMN	Skin lesions such as cracks at corners of mouth
Niacin (B_3)	Nuts, meats, grains	Component of coenzymes NAD^+ and $NADP^+$	Skin and gastrointestinal lesions, nervous disorders **Liver damage**
Vitamin B_6 (pyridoxine)	Meats, vegetables, whole grains	Coenzyme used in amino acid metabolism	Irritability, convulsions, muscular twitching, anemia **Unstable gait, numb feet, poor coordination**
Pantothenic acid (B_5)	Most foods: meats, dairy products, whole grains, etc.	Component of coenzyme A	Fatigue, numbness, tingling of hands and feet
Folic acid (folacin) (B_9)	Green vegetables, oranges, nuts, legumes, whole grains	Coenzyme in nucleic acid and amino acid metabolism	Anemia, birth defects **May mask deficiency of vitamin B_{12}**
Vitamin B_{12}	Meats, eggs, dairy products	Coenzyme in nucleic acid metabolism; maturation of red blood cells	Anemia, nervous system disorders
Biotin	Legumes, other vegetables, meats	Coenzyme in synthesis of fat, glycogen, and amino acids	Scaly skin inflammation, neuromuscular disorders
Vitamin C (ascorbic acid)	Fruits and vegetables, especially citrus fruits, broccoli, cabbage, tomatoes, green peppers	Used in collagen synthesis (such as for bone, cartilage, gums); antioxidant; aids in detoxification; improves iron absorption	Scurvy (degeneration of skin, teeth, blood vessels), weakness, delayed wound healing, impaired immunity **Gastrointestinal upset**
Fat-Soluble Vitamins			
Vitamin A (retinol)	Provitamin A (beta-carotene) in deep green and orange vegetables and fruits; retinal in dairy products	Component of visual pigments; maintenance of epithelial tissues; antioxidant; helps prevent damage to cell membranes	Blindness and increased death rate **Headache, irritability, vomiting, hair loss, blurred vision, liver and bone damage**
Vitamin D	Dairy products, egg yolk; also made in human skin in presence of sunlight	Aids in absorption and use of calcium and phosphorus; promotes bone growth	Rickets (bone deformities) in children, bone softening in adults **Brain, cardiovascular, and kidney damage**
Vitamin E (tocopherol)	Vegetable oils, nuts, seeds	Antioxidant; helps prevent damage to cell membranes	Degeneration of the nervous system
Vitamin K (phylloquinone)	Green vegetables, tea; also made by colon bacteria	Important in blood clotting	Defective blood clotting **Liver damage and anemia**

fat-soluble vitamins are deposited in body fat, so overconsumption may result in accumulating toxic levels of these compounds.

Minerals

Dietary **minerals** are inorganic nutrients, such as zinc and potassium, that are usually required in small amounts—from less than 1 mg to about 2,500 mg per day **(Table 41.2)**. Mineral requirements vary among animal species. For example, humans and other vertebrates require relatively large quantities of calcium and phosphorus for building and maintaining bone. In addition, calcium is necessary for the functioning of nerves and muscles, and phosphorus is an ingredient of ATP and nucleic acids. Iron is a component of the cytochromes that function in cellular respiration (see Figure 9.13) and of hemoglobin, the oxygen-binding protein of red blood cells. Many minerals are cofactors built into the structure of enzymes; magnesium, for example, is present in enzymes that split ATP. Vertebrates need iodine to make thyroid hormones, which regulate metabolic rate. Sodium, potassium, and chloride ions are important in the functioning of nerves and in maintaining osmotic balance between cells and the surrounding body fluid.

Table 41.2 Mineral Requirements of Humans

Mineral	Major Dietary Sources	Major Functions in the Body	Symptoms of Deficiency*
Greater than 200 mg per day required:			
Calcium (Ca)	Dairy products, dark green vegetables, legumes	Bone and tooth formation, blood clotting, nerve and muscle function	Retarded growth, possibly loss of bone mass
Phosphorus (P)	Dairy products, meats, grains	Bone and tooth formation, acid-base balance, nucleotide synthesis	Weakness, loss of minerals from bone, calcium loss
Sulfur (S)	Proteins from many sources	Component of certain amino acids	Symptoms of protein deficiency
Potassium (K)	Meats, dairy products, many fruits and vegetables, grains	Acid-base balance, water balance, nerve function	Muscular weakness, paralysis, nausea, heart failure
Chlorine (Cl)	Table salt	Acid-base balance, formation of gastric juice, nerve function, osmotic balance	Muscle cramps, reduced appetite
Sodium (Na)	Table salt	Acid-base balance, water balance, nerve function	Muscle cramps, reduced appetite
Magnesium (Mg)	Whole grains, green leafy vegetables	Cofactor; ATP bioenergetics	Nervous system disturbances
Iron (Fe)	Meats, eggs, legumes, whole grains, green leafy vegetables	Component of hemoglobin and of electron carriers in energy metabolism; enzyme cofactor	Iron-deficiency anemia, weakness, impaired immunity
Fluorine (F)	Drinking water, tea, seafood	Maintenance of tooth (and probably bone) structure	Higher frequency of tooth decay
Zinc (Zn)	Meats, seafood, grains	Component of certain digestive enzymes and other proteins	Growth failure, skin abnormalities, reproductive failure, impaired immunity
Copper (Cu)	Seafood, nuts, legumes, organ meats	Enzyme cofactor in iron metabolism, melanin synthesis, electron transport	Anemia, cardiovascular abnormalities
Manganese (Mn)	Nuts, grains, vegetables, fruits, tea	Enzyme cofactor	Abnormal bone and cartilage
Iodine (I)	Seafood, dairy products, iodized salt	Component of thyroid hormones	Goiter (enlarged thyroid)
Cobalt (Co)	Meats and dairy products	Component of vitamin B_{12}	None, except as B_{12} deficiency
Selenium (Se)	Seafood, meats, whole grains	Enzyme cofactor; antioxidant functioning in close association with vitamin E	Muscle pain, possibly heart muscle deterioration
Chromium (Cr)	Brewer's yeast, liver, seafood, meats, some vegetables	Involved in glucose and energy metabolism	Impaired glucose metabolism
Molybdenum (Mo)	Legumes, grains, some vegetables	Enzyme cofactor	Disorder in excretion of nitrogen-containing compounds

*All of these minerals are also harmful when consumed in excess.

Ingesting large amounts of some minerals can upset homeostatic balance and cause toxic side effects. For example, liver damage due to iron overload affects as much as 10% of the population in some regions of Africa where the water supply is especially iron-rich. Many individuals in these regions have a genetic alteration in mineral metabolism that increases the toxic effects of iron overload. In a different example, excess salt (sodium chloride) is not toxic but can contribute to high blood pressure. This is a particular problem in the United States, where the typical person consumes enough salt to provide about 20 times the required amount of sodium. Packaged (prepared) foods often contain large amounts of sodium chloride, even if they do not taste very salty.

Dietary Deficiencies

Diets that fail to meet basic needs can lead to either undernourishment or malnourishment. **Undernourishment** is the result of a diet that consistently supplies less chemical energy than the body requires. In contrast, **malnourishment** is the long-term absence from the diet of one or more essential nutrients. Both have negative impacts on health and survival.

Undernourishment

When an animal is undernourished, a series of events unfold: The body uses up stored fat and carbohydrates; the body begins breaking down its own proteins for fuel; muscles begin to decrease in size; and the brain may become protein-deficient. If energy intake remains less than energy expenditures, the animal will eventually die. Even if a seriously undernourished animal survives, some of the damage may be irreversible.

Because adequate amounts of just a single staple such as rice or corn can provide sufficient calories, human undernourishment is most common when drought, war, or another crisis severely disrupts the food supply. In sub-Saharan Africa, where the AIDS epidemic has crippled both rural and urban communities, approximately 200 million children and adults cannot obtain enough food.

Sometimes undernourishment occurs within well-fed populations as a result of eating disorders. For example, anorexia nervosa leads individuals, usually female, to starve themselves compulsively.

Malnourishment

The potential effects of malnourishment include deformities, disease, and even death. For example, cattle, deer, and other herbivores may develop fragile bones if they graze on plants growing in soil that lacks phosphorus. Some grazing animals obtain the missing nutrients by consuming concentrated sources of salt or other minerals **(Figure 41.4)**. Among carnivores, recent experiments reveal that spiders can adjust for dietary deficiencies by switching to prey that restores nutritional balance.

▲ **Figure 41.4 Obtaining essential nutrients by eating antlers.** A caribou, an arctic herbivore, chews on discarded antlers from another animal. Because antlers contain calcium phosphate, this behavior is common among herbivores living where soils and plants are deficient in phosphorus. Animals require phosphorus to make ATP, nucleic acids, phospholipids, and components of bones.

Like other animals, humans sometimes suffer from malnourishment. Among populations subsisting on simple rice diets, individuals are often afflicted with vitamin A deficiency, which can cause blindness or death. To overcome this problem, scientists have engineered a strain of rice to synthesize beta-carotene, the orange-colored source of vitamin A that is abundant in carrots. The potential benefit of this "Golden Rice" is enormous because, at present, 1 to 2 million young children worldwide die every year from vitamin A deficiency.

Assessing Nutritional Needs

Determining the ideal diet for the human population is an important but difficult problem for scientists. As objects of study, people present many challenges. Unlike laboratory animals, humans are genetically diverse. They also live in settings far more varied than the stable and uniform environment that scientists use to facilitate comparisons in laboratory experiments. Ethical concerns present an additional barrier. For example, it is not acceptable to investigate the nutritional needs of children in a way that might harm a child's growth or development.

The methods used to study human nutrition have changed dramatically over time. To avoid harming others, several of the researchers who discovered vitamins a century ago used themselves as subject animals. Today, an important approach is the study of genetic defects that disrupt food uptake, storage, or use. For example, a genetic disorder called hemochromatosis causes iron buildup in the absence of any abnormal iron consumption or exposure. Fortunately, this common disorder is remarkably easy to treat: Drawing blood regularly removes enough iron from the body to restore homeostasis. By studying the defective genes that can cause the disease, scientists have learned a great deal about the regulation of iron absorption.

Many insights into human nutrition have come from *epidemiology*, the study of human health and disease at the population level. By tracking the causes and distribution of a disease among many individuals, epidemiologists can identify potential nutritional strategies for preventing and controlling diseases and disorders. For example, researchers discovered that dietary intake of the vitamin folic acid substantially reduces the frequency of neural tube defects, which are a serious and sometimes fatal type of birth defect.

Neural tube defects occur when tissue fails to enclose the developing brain and spinal cord. In the 1970s, studies revealed that these defects were more frequent in children born to women of low socioeconomic status. Richard Smithells, of the University of Leeds, thought that malnutrition among these women might be responsible. As described in **Figure 41.5**, he found that vitamin supplementation greatly reduced the risk of neural tube defects. In other studies, he obtained evidence that folic acid (B_9) was the specific vitamin responsible, a finding confirmed by other researchers. Based on this evidence, the FDA in 1998 began to require that folic acid be added to enriched grain products used to make bread, cereals, and other foods. Follow-up studies have documented the effectiveness of this program in reducing the frequency of neural tube defects. Thus, at a time when microsurgery and sophisticated diagnostic imaging dominate the headlines, simple dietary changes such as folic acid supplements or consumption of Golden Rice may be among the greatest contributors to human health.

▼ Figure 41.5 Inquiry

Can diet influence the frequency of birth defects?

EXPERIMENT Richard Smithells, of the University of Leeds, examined the effect of vitamin supplementation on the risk of neural tube defects. Women who had had one or more babies with such a defect were put into two study groups. The experimental group consisted of those who were planning a pregnancy and began taking a multivitamin at least four weeks before attempting conception. The control group, who were not given vitamins, included women who declined them and women who were already pregnant. The numbers of neural tube defects resulting from the pregnancies were recorded for each group.

RESULTS

Group	Number of infants/fetuses studied	Infants/fetuses with a neural tube defect
Vitamin supplements (experimental group)	141	1 (0.7%)
No vitamin supplements (control group)	204	12 (5.9%)

CONCLUSION This study provided evidence that vitamin supplementation protects against neural tube defects, at least in pregnancies after the first. Follow-up trials demonstrated that folic acid alone provided an equivalent protective effect.

SOURCE R.W. Smithells et al., Possible prevention of neural tube defects by periconceptional vitamin supplementation, *Lancet* 339–340 (1980).

Inquiry in Action Read and analyze the original paper in *Inquiry in Action: Interpreting Scientific Papers.*

WHAT IF? Subsequent studies were designed to learn if folic acid supplements prevent neural tube defects during first-time pregnancies. To determine the required number of subjects, what additional information did the researchers need?

CONCEPT CHECK 41.1

1. All 20 amino acids are needed to make animal proteins. Why aren't they all essential to animal diets?
2. Explain why vitamins are required in much smaller amounts than carbohydrates.
3. **WHAT IF?** If a zoo animal shows signs of malnutrition, how might a researcher determine which nutrient is lacking?

For suggested answers, see Appendix A.

CONCEPT **41.2**

The main stages of food processing are ingestion, digestion, absorption, and elimination

In this section, we turn from nutritional requirements to the mechanisms by which animals process food. Food processing can be divided into four distinct stages: ingestion, digestion, absorption, and elimination. The first stage, **ingestion**, is the act of eating. Food can be ingested in many liquid and solid forms. **Figure 41.6** surveys and classifies the principal feeding mechanisms that have evolved among animals. Given the variation in food sources, it is not surprising that strategies for extracting resources from food also differ widely among animal species. We will focus, however, on the shared processes, pausing periodically to consider some adaptations to particular diets or environments.

In **digestion**, the second stage of food processing, food is broken down into molecules small enough for the body to absorb. This stage is necessary because animals cannot directly use the proteins, carbohydrates, nucleic acids, fats, and phospholipids in food. One problem is that these molecules are too large to pass through membranes and enter the cells of the animal. In addition, the large molecules in food are not all identical to those the animal needs for its particular tissues and functions. When large molecules in food are broken down into their components, however, the animal can use these smaller mol-

▼ Figure 41.6

Exploring Four Main Feeding Mechanisms of Animals

Suspension Feeders

Many aquatic animals are **suspension feeders**, which sift small food particles from the water. For example, attached to the upper jaw of this humpback whale are comb-like plates called baleen, which strain small invertebrates and fish from enormous volumes of water. Clams and oysters are also suspension feeders. They use their gills to trap tiny morsels; cilia then sweep the food particles to the mouth in a film of mucus.

Substrate Feeders

Substrate feeders are animals that live in or on their food source. This leaf miner caterpillar, the larva of a moth, is eating through the soft tissue of an oak leaf, leaving a dark trail of feces in its wake. Some other substrate feeders include maggots (fly larvae), which burrow into animal carcasses.

Fluid Feeders

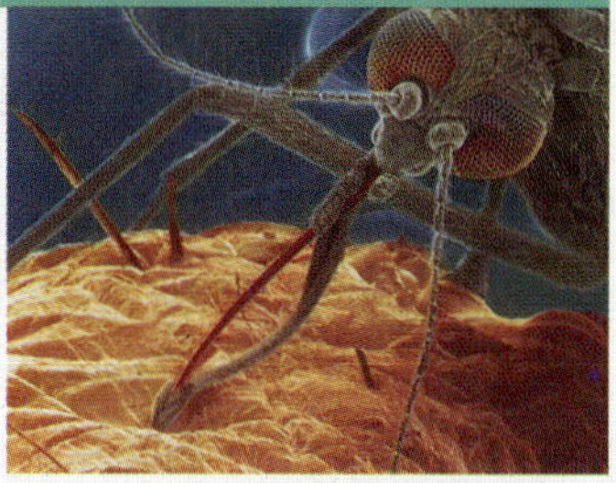

Fluid feeders suck nutrient-rich fluid from a living host. This mosquito has pierced the skin of its human host with hollow, needle-like mouthparts and is consuming a blood meal (colorized SEM). Similarly, aphids are fluid feeders that tap the phloem sap of plants. In contrast to such parasites, some fluid feeders actually benefit their hosts. For example, hummingbirds and bees move pollen between flowers as they fluid-feed on nectar.

Bulk Feeders

Most animals, including humans, are **bulk feeders**, which eat relatively large pieces of food. Their adaptations include tentacles, pincers, claws, poisonous fangs, jaws, and teeth that kill their prey or tear off pieces of meat or vegetation. In this amazing scene, a rock python is beginning to ingest a gazelle it has captured and killed. Snakes cannot chew their food into pieces and must swallow it whole—even if the prey is much bigger than the diameter of the snake. They can do so because the lower jaw is loosely hinged to the skull by an elastic ligament that permits the mouth and throat to open very wide. After swallowing its prey, which may take more than an hour, the python will spend two weeks or more digesting its meal.

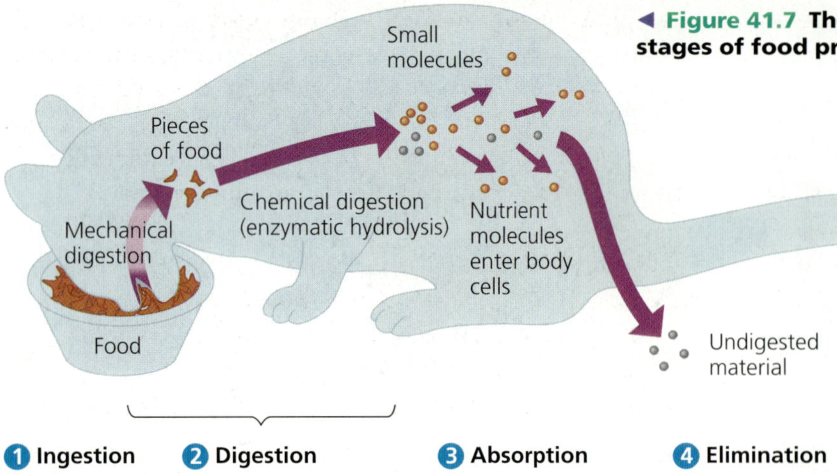

◀ **Figure 41.7 The four stages of food processing.**

ecules to assemble the large molecules it needs. For example, although fruit flies and humans have very different diets, both convert proteins in their food to the same 20 amino acids from which they assemble all of the proteins specific for their species.

Recall from Chapter 5 that a cell makes a macromolecule or fat by linking together smaller components; it does so by removing a molecule of water for each new covalent bond formed. Chemical digestion by enzymes reverses this process by breaking bonds with the addition of water (see Figure 5.2). This splitting process is called **enzymatic hydrolysis**. A variety of enzymes catalyze the digestion of large molecules in food. Polysaccharides and disaccharides are split into simple sugars; proteins are broken down into amino acids; and nucleic acids are cleaved into nucleotides. Enzymatic hydrolysis also releases fatty acids and other components from fats and phospholipids. Such chemical digestion is typically preceded by mechanical digestion—by chewing, for instance. Mechanical digestion breaks food into smaller pieces, increasing the surface area available for chemical processes.

The last two stages of food processing occur after the food is digested. In the third stage, **absorption**, the animal's cells take up (absorb) small molecules such as amino acids and simple sugars. **Elimination** completes the process as undigested material passes out of the digestive system. **Figure 41.7** reviews the four stages of food processing.

Digestive Compartments

In our overview of food processing, we have seen that digestive enzymes hydrolyze the same biological materials (such as proteins, fats, and carbohydrates) that make up the bodies of the animals themselves. How, then, are animals able to digest food without digesting their own cells and tissues? The evolutionary adaptation found across a wide range of animal species is the processing of food within specialized compartments. Such compartments can be intracellular, in the form of food vacuoles, or extracellular, as in digestive organs and systems.

Intracellular Digestion

Food vacuoles—cellular organelles in which hydrolytic enzymes break down food—are the simplest digestive compartments. The hydrolysis of food inside vacuoles, called **intracellular digestion**, begins after a cell engulfs solid food by phagocytosis or liquid food by pinocytosis (see Figure 7.20). Newly formed food vacuoles fuse with lysosomes, organelles containing hydrolytic enzymes. This fusion of organelles brings food together with the enzymes, allowing digestion to occur safely within a compartment enclosed by a protective membrane. A few animals, such as sponges, digest their food entirely by this intracellular mechanism (see Figure 33.4).

Extracellular Digestion

In most animals, at least some hydrolysis occurs by **extracellular digestion**, the breakdown of food in compartments that are continuous with the outside of the animal's body. Having one or more extracellular compartments for digestion enables an animal to devour much larger sources of food than can be ingested by phagocytosis.

Many animals with relatively simple body plans have a digestive compartment with a single opening **(Figure 41.8)**. This pouch, called a **gastrovascular cavity**, functions in digestion as well as in the distribution of nutrients throughout the body (hence the *vascular* part of the term). The carnivorous

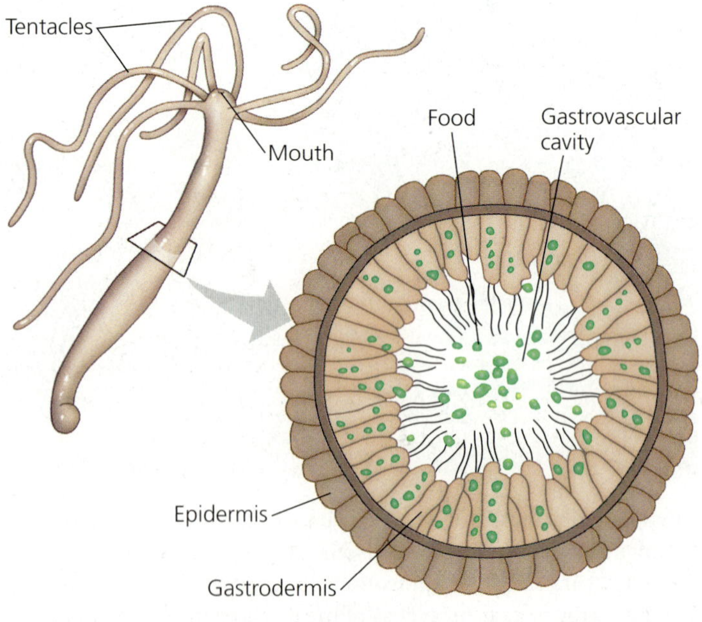

▲ **Figure 41.8 Digestion in a hydra.** Digestion begins in the gastrovascular cavity and is completed intracellularly after small food particles are engulfed by specialized cells of the gastrodermis.

cnidarians called hydras provide a good example of how a gastrovascular cavity works. A hydra uses its tentacles to stuff captured prey through its mouth into its gastrovascular cavity. Specialized gland cells of the hydra's gastrodermis, the tissue layer that lines the cavity, then secrete digestive enzymes that break the soft tissues of the prey into tiny pieces. Other cells of the gastrodermis engulf these food particles, and most of the actual hydrolysis of macromolecules occurs intracellularly, as in sponges. After a hydra has digested its meal, undigested materials that remain in the gastrovascular cavity, such as exoskeletons of small crustaceans, are eliminated through the same opening by which food entered. Many flatworms also have a gastrovascular cavity with a single opening (see Figure 33.10).

In contrast with cnidarians and flatworms, most animals have a digestive tube extending between two openings, a mouth and an anus. Such a tube is called a **complete digestive tract** or, more commonly, an **alimentary canal**. Because food moves along the alimentary canal in a single direction, the tube can be organized into specialized compartments that carry out digestion and nutrient absorption in a stepwise fashion **(Figure 41.9)**. An animal with an alimentary canal can ingest food while earlier meals are still being digested, a feat that is likely to be difficult or inefficient for animals with gastrovascular cavities. In the next section, we'll explore the spatial and functional organization of an alimentary canal.

CONCEPT CHECK 41.2

1. Distinguish the overall structure of a gastrovascular cavity from that of an alimentary canal.
2. In what sense are nutrients from a recently ingested meal not really "inside" your body prior to the absorption stage of food processing?
3. **WHAT IF?** Thinking in broad terms, what similarities can you identify between digestion in an animal body and the breakdown of gasoline in an automobile? (You don't have to know about auto mechanics.)

For suggested answers, see Appendix A.

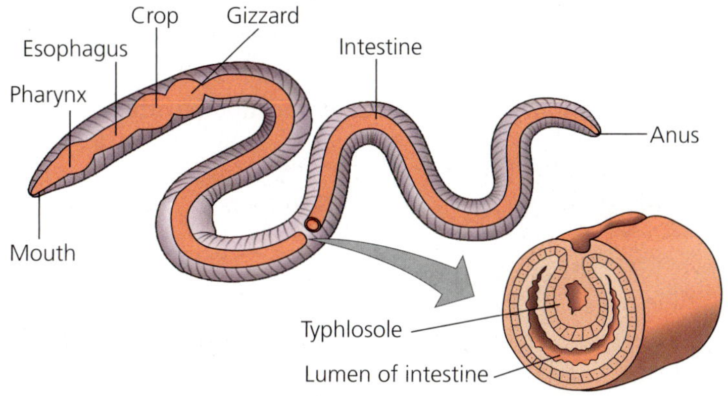

(a) Earthworm. The alimentary canal of an earthworm includes a muscular pharynx that sucks food in through the mouth. Food passes through the esophagus and is stored and moistened in the crop. Mechanical digestion occurs in the muscular gizzard, which pulverizes food with the aid of small bits of sand and gravel. Further digestion and absorption occur in the intestine, which has a dorsal fold, the typhlosole, that increases the surface area for nutrient absorption.

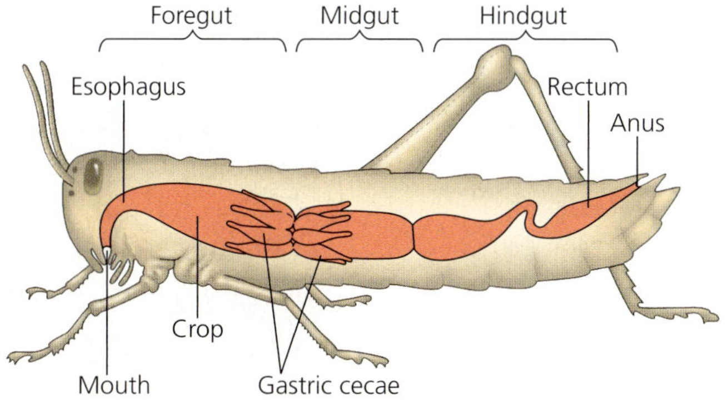

(b) Grasshopper. A grasshopper has several digestive chambers grouped into three main regions: a foregut, with an esophagus and crop; a midgut; and a hindgut. Food is moistened and stored in the crop, but most digestion occurs in the midgut. Gastric cecae, (singular, ceca), pouches extending from the beginning of the midgut, function in digestion and absorption.

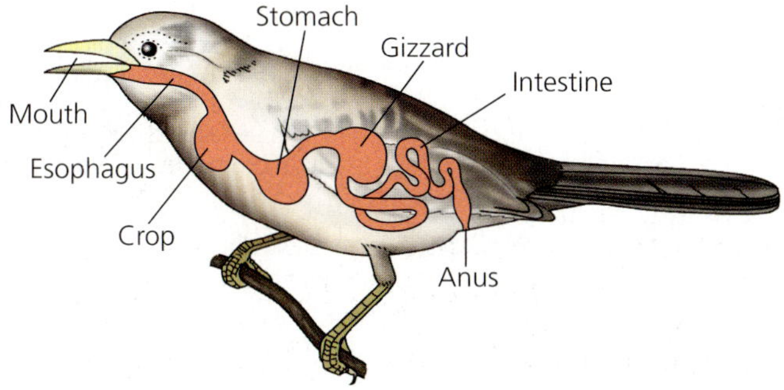

(c) Bird. Many birds have three separate chambers—the crop, stomach, and gizzard—where food is pulverized and churned before passing into the intestine. A bird's crop and gizzard function very much like those of an earthworm. In most birds, chemical digestion and absorption of nutrients occur in the intestine.

▲ **Figure 41.9 Variation in alimentary canals.**

CONCEPT 41.3

Organs specialized for sequential stages of food processing form the mammalian digestive system

Because most animals, including mammals, have an alimentary canal, we can use the mammalian digestive system as a representative example of the general principles of food processing. In mammals, the digestive system consists of the alimentary canal and various accessory glands that secrete digestive juices through ducts into the canal **(Figure 41.10)**. The accessory glands of the mammalian digestive system are three pairs of salivary glands, the pancreas, the liver, and the gallbladder.

Food is pushed along the alimentary canal by **peristalsis**, alternating waves of contraction and relaxation in the smooth muscles lining the canal. It is peristalsis that enables us to process and digest food even while lying down. At some of the junctions between specialized compartments, the muscular layer forms ringlike valves called **sphincters**. Acting like drawstrings to close off the alimentary canal, sphincters regulate the passage of material between compartments.

Using the human digestive system as a model, let's now follow a meal through the alimentary canal. As we do so, we'll examine in more detail what happens to the food in each digestive compartment along the way.

The Oral Cavity, Pharynx, and Esophagus

Ingestion and the initial steps of digestion occur in the mouth, or **oral cavity**. Mechanical digestion begins as teeth of various shapes cut, smash, and grind food, making the food easier to swallow and increasing its surface area. Meanwhile, the presence of food stimulates a nervous reflex that causes the **salivary glands** to deliver saliva through ducts to the oral cavity. Saliva may also be released before food enters the mouth, triggered by a learned association between eating and the time of day, a cooking odor, or another stimulus.

Saliva initiates chemical digestion while also protecting the oral cavity. **Amylase**, an enzyme in saliva, hydrolyzes starch (a glucose polymer from plants) and glycogen (a glucose polymer from animals) into smaller polysaccharides and the disaccharide maltose. Mucin, a slippery glycoprotein (carbohydrate-protein complex) in saliva, protects the lining of the mouth from abrasion. Mucin also lubricates food for easier swallowing. Additional components of saliva include buffers, which help prevent tooth decay by neutralizing acid, and antibacterial agents (such as lysozyme; see Figure 5.19), which protect against microorganisms that enter the mouth with food.

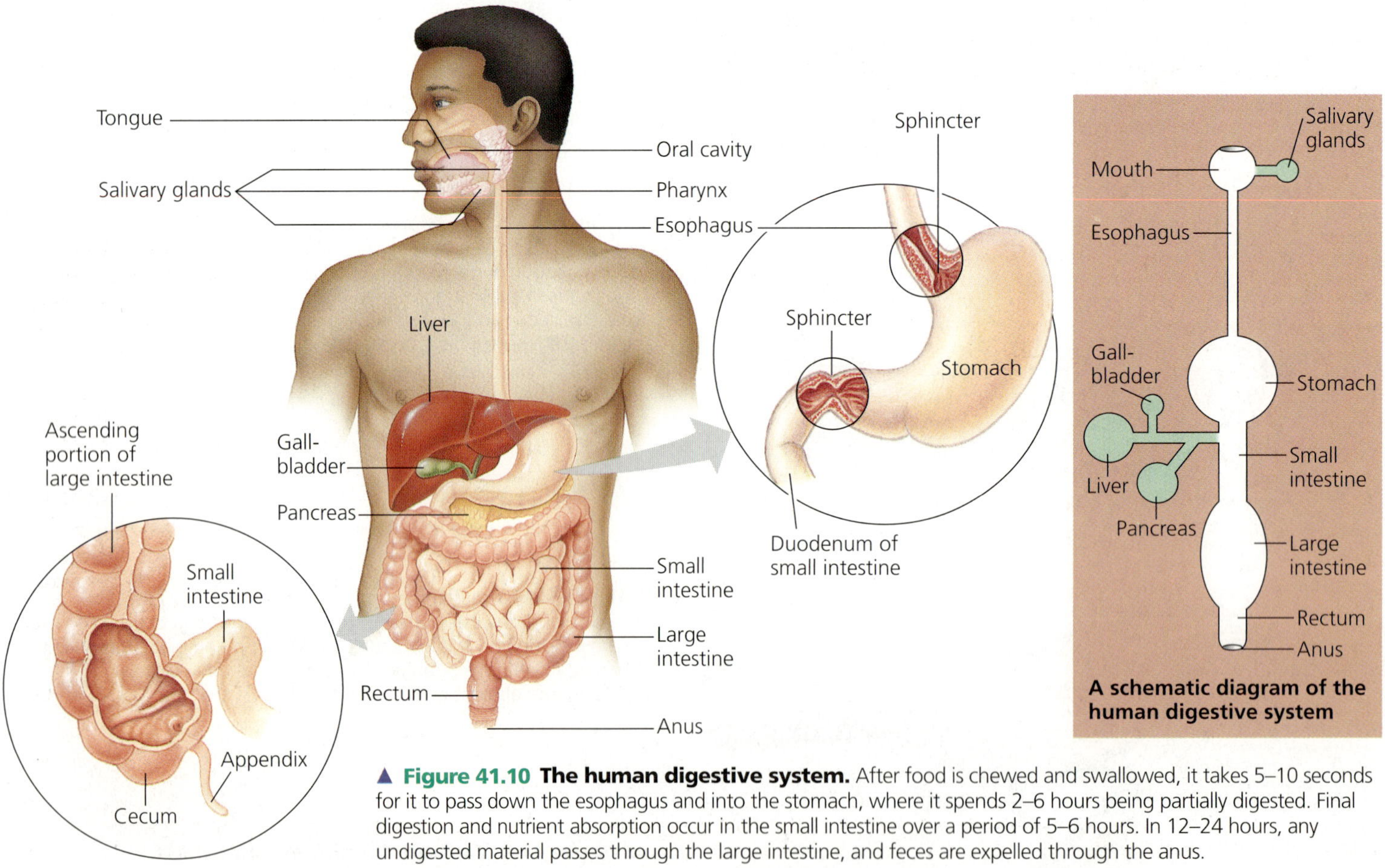

▲ **Figure 41.10 The human digestive system.** After food is chewed and swallowed, it takes 5–10 seconds for it to pass down the esophagus and into the stomach, where it spends 2–6 hours being partially digested. Final digestion and nutrient absorption occur in the small intestine over a period of 5–6 hours. In 12–24 hours, any undigested material passes through the large intestine, and feces are expelled through the anus.

Much as a doorman screens and assists people entering a building, the tongue aids digestive processes by evaluating ingested material and then enabling its further passage. When food arrives at the oral cavity, the tongue plays a critical role in distinguishing which foods should be processed further (see Chapter 50 for a discussion of the sense of taste). After food is deemed acceptable and chewing commences, tongue movements manipulate the food, helping shape it into a ball called a **bolus**. During swallowing, the tongue provides further help, pushing the bolus to the back of the oral cavity and into the pharynx.

The **pharynx**, or throat region, opens to two passageways: the esophagus and the trachea (windpipe). The **esophagus** connects to the stomach, whereas the trachea leads to the lungs. Swallowing must therefore be carefully choreographed to keep food from entering and blocking the airway. When you swallow, a flap of cartilage called the *epiglottis* prevents food from entering the trachea by covering the *glottis*—the vocal cords and the opening between them. Guided by the movements of the *larynx*, the upper part of the respiratory tract, this swallowing mechanism directs each bolus into the entrance of the esophagus (**Figure 41.11**, steps 1–4). If the swallowing reflex fails, food or liquids can reach the windpipe and cause choking, a blockage of the trachea. The resulting lack of airflow into the lungs can be fatal if the material is not dislodged by vigorous coughing or a forced upward thrust of the diaphragm (the Heimlich maneuver).

The esophagus contains both striated and smooth muscle (see Figure 40.5). The striated muscle is situated at the top of the esophagus and is active during swallowing. Throughout the rest of the esophagus, smooth muscle functions in peristalsis. The rhythmic cycles of contraction move each bolus to the stomach (see Figure 41.11, step 6). As with other parts of the digestive system, the form of the esophagus fits its function and varies among species. For example, fishes have no lungs to bypass and therefore have a very short esophagus. And it will come as no surprise that giraffes have a very long esophagus.

Digestion in the Stomach

The **stomach** is located just below the diaphragm in the upper abdominal cavity. A few nutrients are absorbed from the stomach into the bloodstream, but the stomach primarily stores food and continues digestion. With accordion-like folds and a very elastic wall, it can stretch to accommodate about 2 L of food and fluid. The stomach secretes a digestive fluid called **gastric juice** and mixes this secretion with the food through a churning action. This mixture of ingested food and digestive juice is called **chyme**.

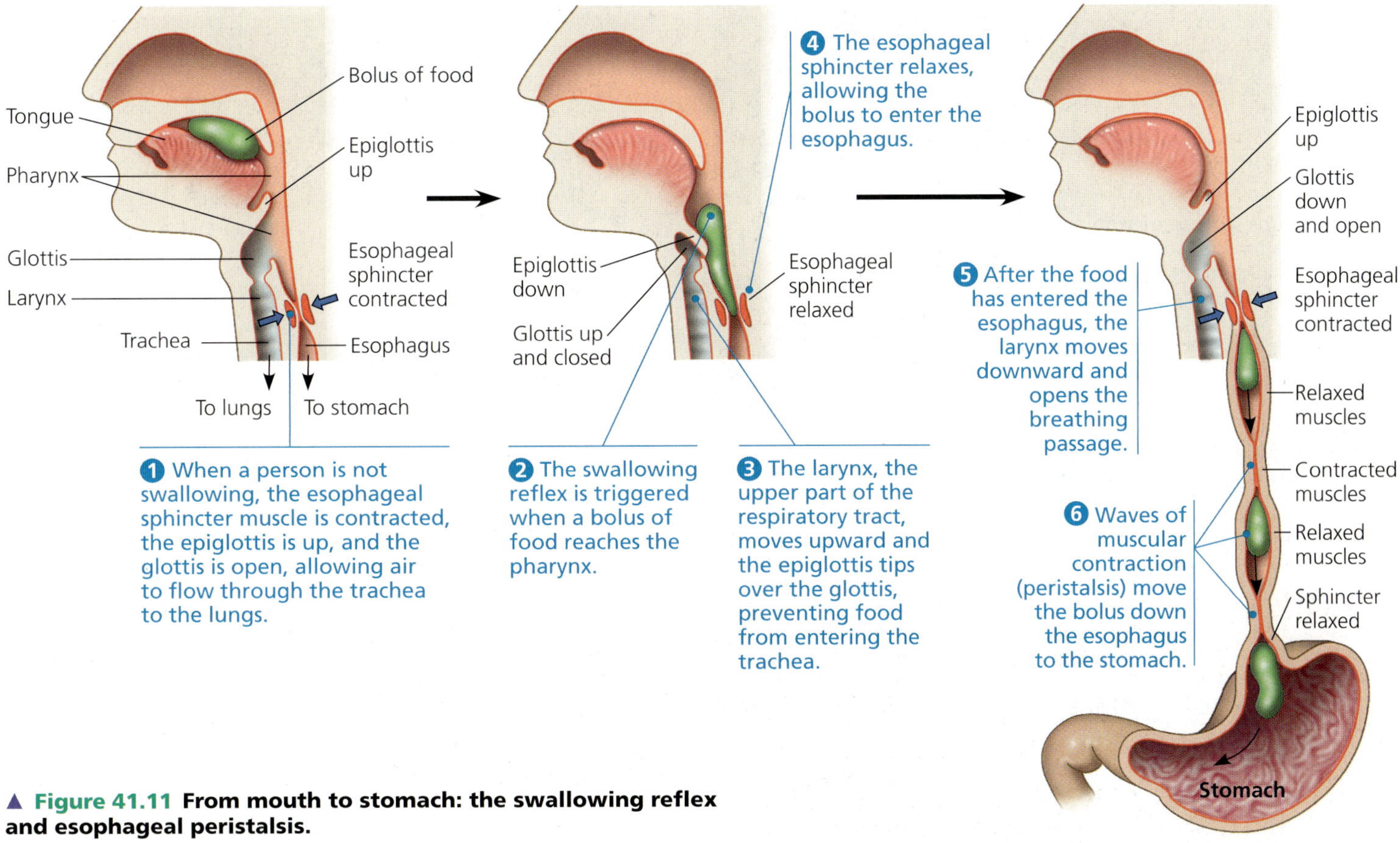

▲ **Figure 41.11 From mouth to stomach: the swallowing reflex and esophageal peristalsis.**

Chemical Digestion in the Stomach

Two components of gastric juice carry out chemical digestion. One is hydrochloric acid (HCl), which disrupts the extracellular matrix that binds cells together in meat and plant material. The concentration of HCl is so high that the pH of gastric juice is about 2, acidic enough to dissolve iron nails. This low pH not only kills most bacteria but also denatures (unfolds) proteins in food, increasing exposure of their peptide bonds. The exposed bonds are attacked by the second component of gastric juice—a **protease**, or protein-digesting enzyme, called **pepsin**. Unlike most enzymes, pepsin works best in a strongly acidic environment. By breaking peptide bonds, it cleaves proteins into smaller polypeptides. Further digestion to individual amino acids occurs in the small intestine.

Why doesn't gastric juice destroy the stomach cells that make it? The answer is that the ingredients of gastric juice are kept inactive until they are released into the lumen (cavity) of the stomach. The components of gastric juice are produced by cells in the gastric glands of the stomach **(Figure 41.12)**. *Parietal cells* secrete hydrogen and chloride ions, which form hydrochloric acid (HCl). Using an ATP-driven pump, the parietal cells expel hydrogen ions into the lumen at very high concentration. There the hydrogen ions combine with chloride ions that diffuse into the lumen through specific membrane channels. Meanwhile, *chief cells* release pepsin into the lumen in an inactive form called **pepsinogen**. HCl converts pepsinogen to active pepsin by clipping off a small portion of the molecule and exposing its active site. Through these processes, both HCl and pepsin form in the lumen of the stomach, not within the cells of the gastric glands.

After hydrochloric acid converts a small amount of pepsinogen to pepsin, a second chemical process helps activate the remaining pepsinogen. Pepsin, like HCl, can clip pepsinogen to expose the enzyme's active site. This generates more pepsin, which activates more pepsinogen, forming more active enzyme. This series of events is an example of positive feedback.

When HCl and pepsin form within the stomach lumen, why aren't the cells that line the stomach damaged? Actually, these cells are vulnerable to gastric juice as well as to acid-tolerant pathogens in food. However, the stomach lining protects against self-digestion by secreting **mucus**, a viscous and slippery mixture of glycoproteins, cells, salts, and water. In addition, cell division adds a new epithelial layer every three days, replacing cells

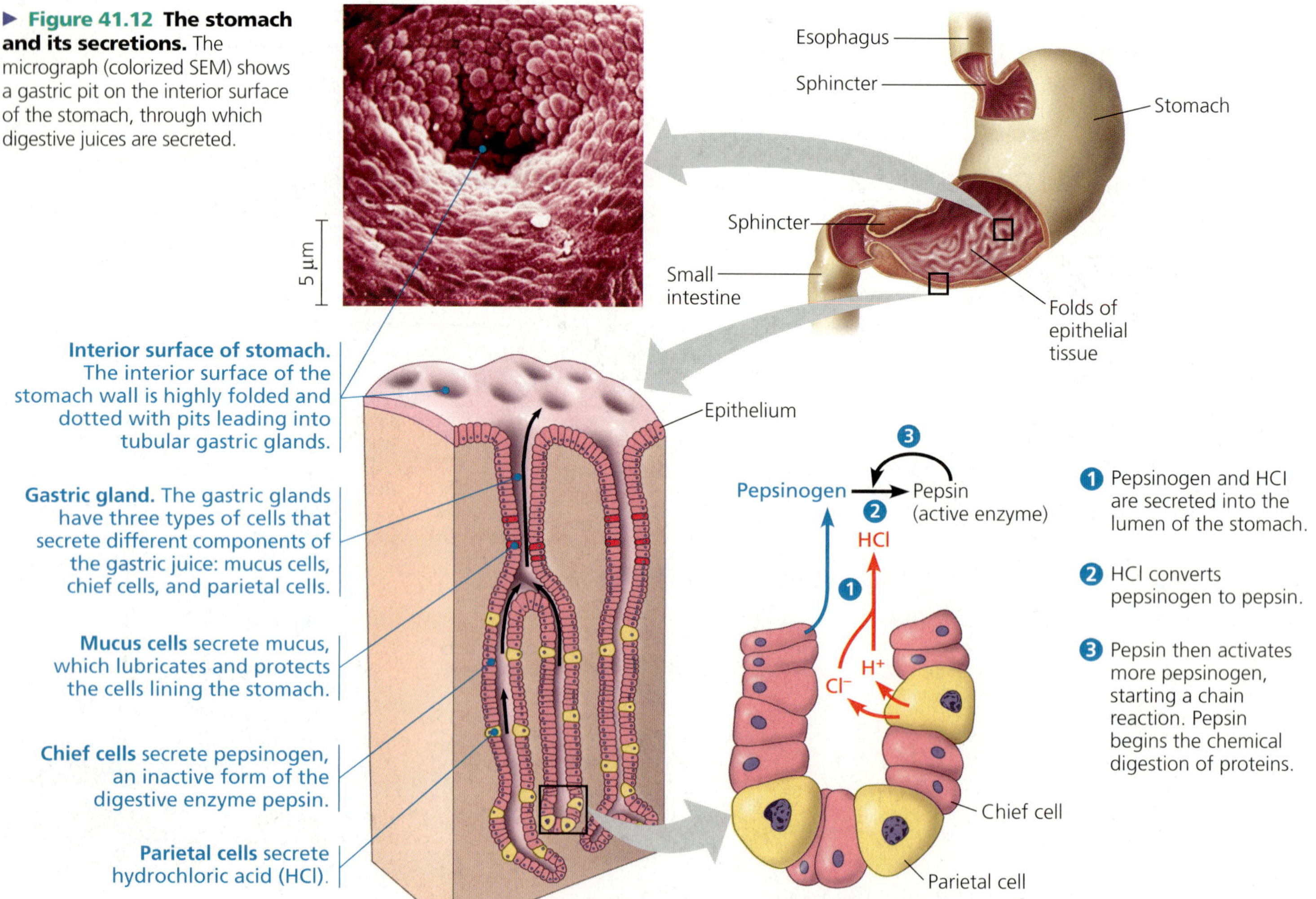

▶ **Figure 41.12 The stomach and its secretions.** The micrograph (colorized SEM) shows a gastric pit on the interior surface of the stomach, through which digestive juices are secreted.

eroded by digestive juices. Despite these defenses, damaged areas of the stomach lining called gastric ulcers may appear. For decades, scientists thought they were caused by psychological stress and resulting excess acid secretion. In 1982, however, researchers Barry Marshall and Robin Warren, at Royal Perth Hospital in Australia, reported that infection by the acid-tolerant bacterium *Helicobacter pylori* causes ulcers. They also demonstrated that an antibiotic treatment could cure most gastric ulcers. For these findings, they were awarded the Nobel Prize in 2005.

Stomach Dynamics

Chemical digestion by gastric juice is accompanied by the churning action of the stomach. This coordinated series of muscle contractions and relaxations mixes the stomach contents about every 20 seconds. As a result of mixing and enzyme action, what begins as a recently swallowed meal becomes the acidic, nutrient-rich broth known as chyme. Most of the time, the stomach is closed off at both ends (see Figure 41.10). The sphincter between the esophagus and the stomach normally opens only when a bolus arrives. Occasionally, however, a person experiences acid reflux, a backflow of chyme from the stomach into the lower end of the esophagus. The resulting irritation of the esophagus is commonly but inaccurately called "heartburn."

The sphincter located where the stomach opens to the small intestine helps regulate the passage of chyme into the small intestine, allowing only one squirt at a time. The mixture of acid, enzyme, and partially digested food typically leaves the stomach 2–6 hours after a meal.

Digestion in the Small Intestine

Most enzymatic hydrolysis of macromolecules from food occurs in the **small intestine** **(Figure 41.13)**. Over 6 m long in

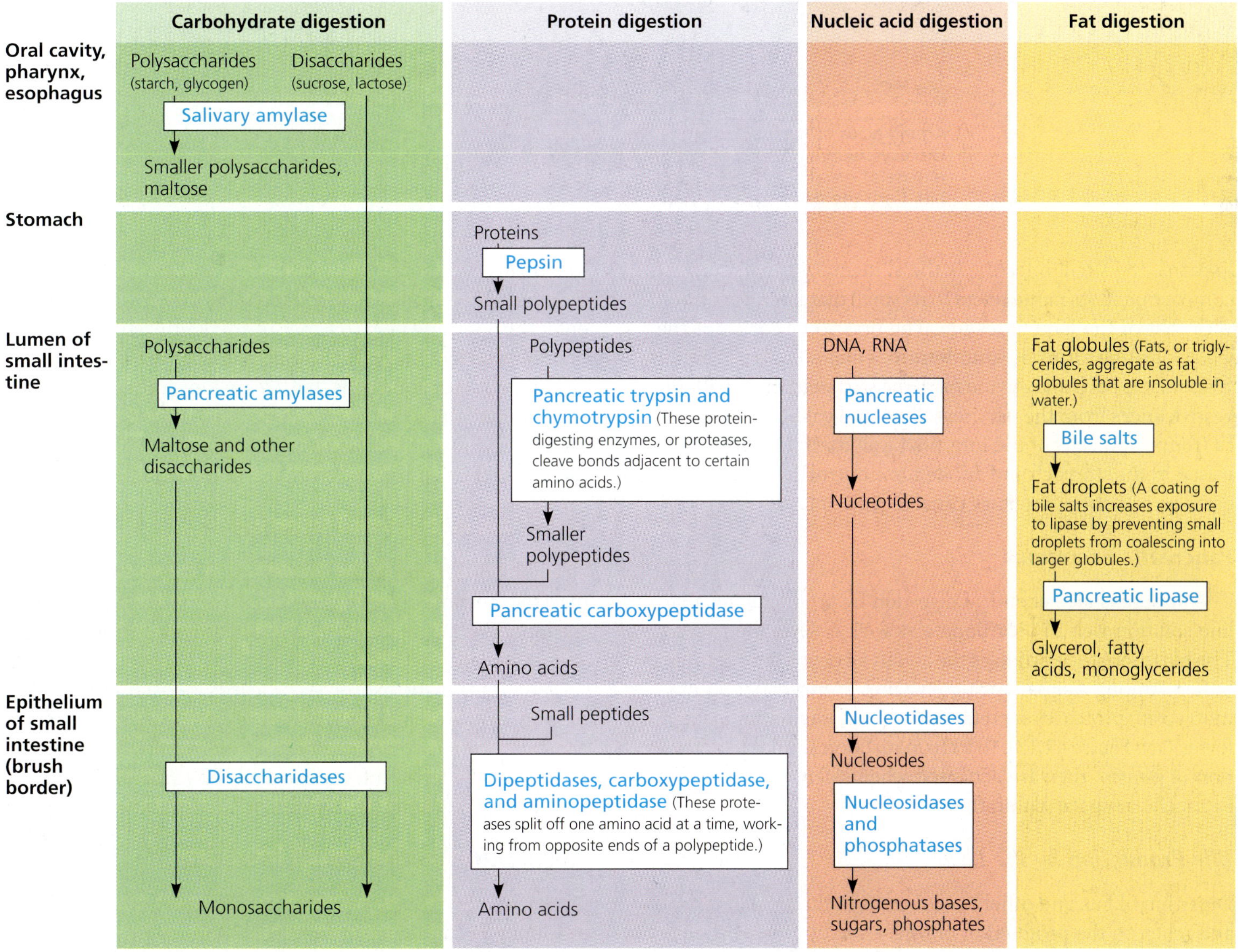

▲ **Figure 41.13 Enzymatic hydrolysis in the human digestive system.**

? *Pepsin is resistant to the denaturing effect of the low pH environment of the stomach. Thinking about the different digestive processes that occur in the small intestine, what adaptation do you think the digestive enzymes in that compartment share?*

▶ **Figure 41.14 Hormonal control of digestion.** Many animals go for long intervals between meals and do not need their digestive systems to be active continuously. Hormones released by the stomach and duodenum help ensure that digestive secretions are present only when needed. Like all hormones, they are transported through the bloodstream. In the case of gastrin, the target is the organ that secretes the hormone.

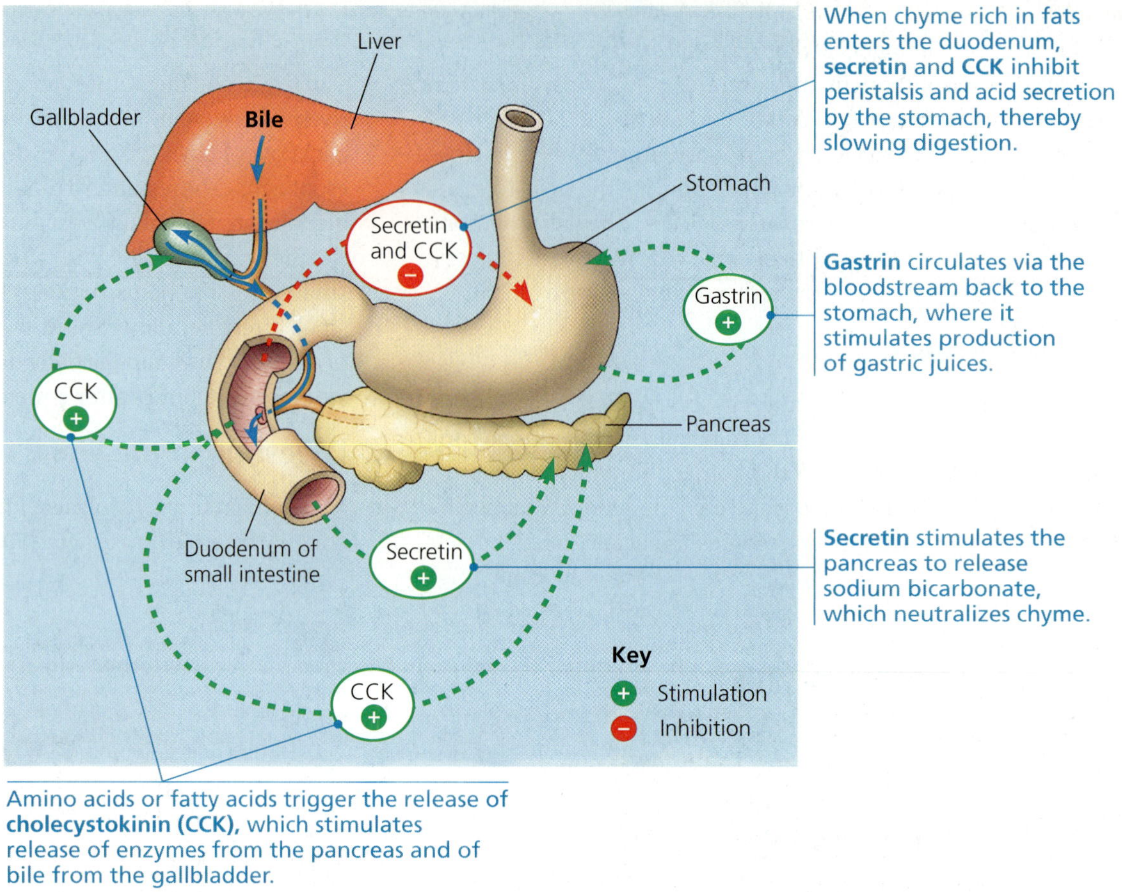

humans, the small intestine is the alimentary canal's longest compartment. Its name refers to its small diameter, compared with that of the large intestine. The first 25 cm or so of the small intestine forms the **duodenum**, a major crossroad in digestion. It is here that chyme from the stomach mixes with digestive juices from the pancreas, liver, and gallbladder, as well as from gland cells of the intestinal wall itself. Hormones released by the stomach and duodenum control the digestive secretions into the alimentary canal **(Figure 41.14)**.

Pancreatic Secretions

The **pancreas** aids chemical digestion by producing an alkaline solution rich in bicarbonate as well as several enzymes. The bicarbonate neutralizes the acidity of chyme and acts as a buffer. Among the pancreatic enzymes are trypsin and chymotrypsin, proteases secreted into the duodenum in inactive forms (see Figure 41.13). In a chain reaction similar to activation of pepsin, they are activated when safely located in the extracellular space within the duodenum.

Bile Production by the Liver

Digestion of fats and other lipids begins in the small intestine and relies on the production of **bile**, a mixture of substances that is made in the **liver**. Bile contains bile salts, which act as detergents (emulsifiers) that aid in digestion and absorption of lipids. Bile is stored and concentrated in the **gallbladder**.

The liver has many vital functions in addition to bile production. As we shall see shortly, it also breaks down toxins that enter the body and helps balance nutrient utilization. Bile production itself is integral to another task of the liver: the destruction of red blood cells that are no longer fully functional. In producing bile, the liver incorporates some pigments that are by-products of red blood cell disassembly. These bile pigments are then eliminated from the body with the feces.

Secretions of the Small Intestine

The epithelial lining of the duodenum is the source of several digestive enzymes (see Figure 41.13). Some are secreted into the lumen of the duodenum, whereas others are bound to the surface of epithelial cells.

While enzymatic hydrolysis proceeds, peristalsis moves the mixture of chyme and digestive juices along the small intestine. Most digestion is completed in the duodenum. The remaining regions of the small intestine, called the *jejunum* and *ileum*, function mainly in the absorption of nutrients and water.

Absorption in the Small Intestine

To reach body tissues, nutrients in the lumen must first cross the lining of the alimentary canal. Most of this absorption occurs in the small intestine. This organ has a huge surface area—300 m^2, roughly the size of a tennis court. Large folds in the lining have finger-like projections called **villi**. In turn, each

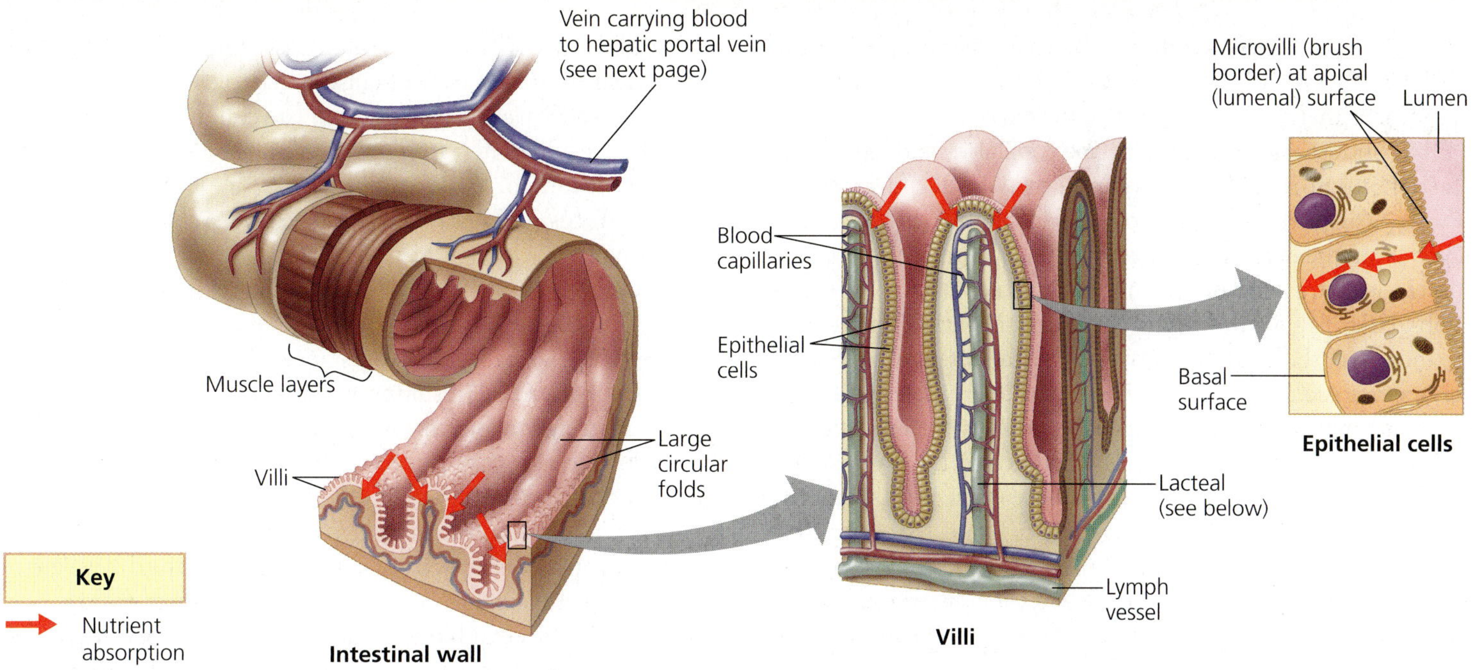

▲ **Figure 41.15 The structure of the small intestine.**

? *Tapeworms sometimes infect humans, anchoring themselves to the wall of the small intestine. Based on how digestion is compartmentalized along the alimentary canal, what digestive functions would you expect these parasites to have?*

epithelial cell of a villus has on its apical surface many microscopic appendages, or **microvilli**, that are exposed to the intestinal lumen **(Figure 41.15)**. The many side-by-side microvilli give the intestinal epithelium a brush-like appearance—reflected in the name *brush border*. The enormous surface area presented by microvilli is an adaptation that greatly increases the total capacity for nutrient absorption.

Depending on the nutrient, transport across the epithelial cells can be passive or active. The sugar fructose, for example, moves by facilitated diffusion down its concentration gradient from the lumen of the small intestine into the epithelial cells. From there, fructose exits the basal surface and is absorbed into microscopic blood vessels, or capillaries, at the core of each villus. Other nutrients, including amino acids, small peptides, vitamins, and most glucose molecules, are pumped against concentration gradients by the epithelial cells of the villus. This active transport allows much more absorption of nutrients than would be possible with passive diffusion alone.

Although many nutrients leave the intestine through the bloodstream, some products of fat (triglyceride) digestion take a different path. After being absorbed by epithelial cells, fatty acids and monoglycerides (glycerol joined to a single fatty acid) are recombined into triglycerides within those cells. These fats are then coated with phospholipids, cholesterol, and proteins, forming water-soluble globules called **chylomicrons (Figure 41.16)**. These globules are too large to pass through the membranes of capillaries. Instead, they are transported into a **lacteal**, a vessel at the core of each villus (see Figures 41.15 and 41.16). Lacteals are part of the vertebrate lymphatic system, which is a network of vessels that are filled with a clear fluid called lymph. Starting

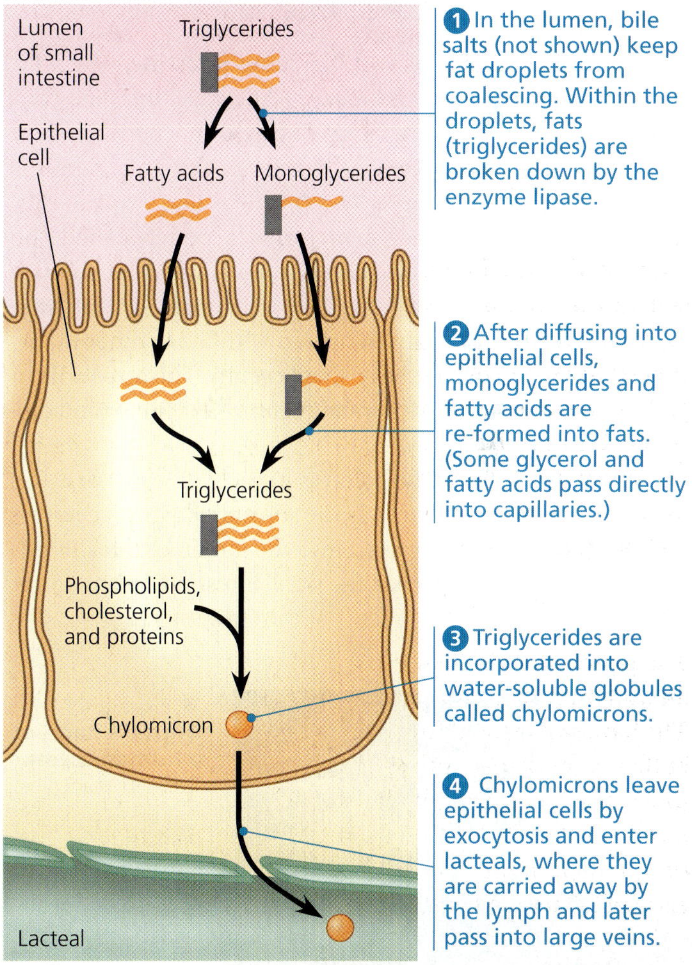

▲ **Figure 41.16 Absorption of fats.** Because fats are insoluble in water, adaptations are needed to digest and absorb them. Bile salts maintain a small droplet size, exposing more surface for enzymatic hydrolysis to fatty acids and monoglycerides. These molecules can diffuse into epithelial cells, where fats are reassembled and incorporated into water-soluble chylomicrons that enter the bloodstream via the lymphatic system.

at the lacteals, lymph containing the chylomicrons passes into the larger vessels of the lymphatic system and eventually into large veins that return the blood to the heart.

In contrast with the lacteals, the capillaries and veins that carry nutrient-rich blood away from the villi all converge into the **hepatic portal vein**, a blood vessel that leads directly to the liver. From the liver, blood travels to the heart and then to other tissues and organs. This arrangement serves two major functions. First, it allows the liver to regulate distribution of nutrients to the rest of the body. Because the liver can interconvert many organic molecules, blood that leaves the liver may have a very different nutrient balance than the blood that entered via the hepatic portal vein. For example, blood exiting the liver usually has a glucose concentration very close to 90 mg per 100 mL, regardless of the carbohydrate content of a meal. Second, the arrangement allows the liver to remove toxic substances before the blood circulates broadly. The liver is the primary site for the detoxification of many organic molecules, including drugs, that are foreign to the body.

Absorption in the Large Intestine

The alimentary canal ends with the **large intestine**, which includes the colon, cecum, and rectum. The small intestine connects to the large intestine at a T-shaped junction, where a sphincter controls the movement of material. One arm of the T is the 1.5-m-long **colon** (**Figure 41.17**), which leads to the rectum and anus. The other arm forms a pouch called the **cecum** (see Figure 41.10). The cecum is important for fermenting ingested material, especially in animals that eat large amounts of plant material. Compared with many other mammals, humans have a relatively small cecum. The **appendix**, a finger-like extension of the human cecum, has a minor and dispensable role in immunity.

A major function of the colon is to recover water that has entered the alimentary canal as the solvent of digestive juices. About 7 L of fluid are secreted into the lumen of the alimentary canal each day. Together, the small intestine and colon reabsorb about 90% of the water that enters the alimentary canal. Since there is no biological mechanism for active transport of water, water absorption in the colon occurs by osmosis that results when ions, particularly sodium, are pumped out of the lumen.

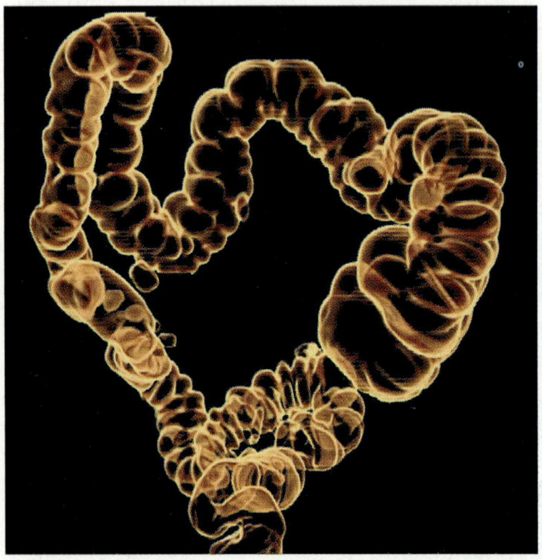

◀ **Figure 41.17 Digital image of a human colon.** This CAT scan image was produced by integrating two-dimensional sectional views of the large intestine.

The **feces**, the wastes of the digestive system, become increasingly solid as they are moved along the colon by peristalsis. It takes approximately 12–24 hours for material to travel the length of the colon. If the lining of the colon is irritated—by a viral or bacterial infection, for instance—less water than normal may be reabsorbed, resulting in diarrhea. The opposite problem, constipation, occurs when the feces move along the colon too slowly. An excess of water is reabsorbed, and therefore the feces become compacted.

A rich flora of mostly harmless bacteria resides in the human colon, contributing approximately one-third of the dry weight of feces. One inhabitant is *Escherichia coli*, a favorite research organism of molecular biologists (see Chapter 18). Because *E. coli* is so common in human digestive systems, its presence in lakes and streams is a useful indicator of contamination by untreated sewage. Within the intestine, *E. coli* and other bacteria live on unabsorbed organic material. As by-products of their metabolism, many colon bacteria generate gases, including methane and hydrogen sulfide, which has an offensive odor. These gases and ingested air are expelled through the anus. Some of the bacteria produce vitamins, such as biotin, vitamin K, and several B vitamins, including folic acid. These vitamins, absorbed into the blood, supplement our dietary intake of vitamins.

Besides bacteria, feces contain undigested material, including cellulose fiber. Although it has no caloric value to humans, fiber helps move food along the alimentary canal.

The terminal portion of the large intestine is the **rectum**, where feces are stored until they can be eliminated. Between the rectum and the anus are two sphincters, the inner one being involuntary and the outer one being voluntary. Periodically (once a day or so in most individuals), strong contractions of the colon create an urge to defecate.

We have followed a meal from one opening (the mouth) of the alimentary canal to the other (the anus). Next we'll see how some digestive adaptations may have evolved.

CONCEPT CHECK 41.3

1. In the zero-gravity environment of space, how does food swallowed by an astronaut reach his or her stomach?
2. What step in food processing occurs more readily for fats than for proteins and carbohydrates?
3. **WHAT IF?** Some early experiments involved obtaining samples of digestive juices and observing digestion outside the body. If you mixed gastric juice with crushed food, how far would the process of digestion proceed?

For suggested answers, see Appendix A.

CONCEPT **41.4**

Evolutionary adaptations of vertebrate digestive systems correlate with diet

The digestive systems of mammals and other vertebrates are variations on a common plan, but there are many intriguing adaptations, often associated with the animal's diet. To highlight how form fits function, we'll examine a few of them.

Some Dental Adaptations

Dentition, an animal's assortment of teeth, is one example of structural variation reflecting diet. Consider the dentition of carnivorous, herbivorous, and omnivorous mammals in **Figure 41.18**. The evolutionary adaptation of teeth for processing different kinds of food is one of the major reasons mammals have been so successful. Nonmammalian vertebrates generally have less specialized dentition, but there are interesting exceptions. For example, poisonous snakes, such as rattlesnakes, have fangs, modified teeth that inject venom into prey. Some fangs are hollow, like syringes, whereas others drip the poison along grooves on the surfaces of the teeth. Other teeth are absent. Combined with an elastic ligament that permits the mouth to open very wide, these anatomical adaptations allow prey to be swallowed whole, as in the astonishing scene in Figure 41.6.

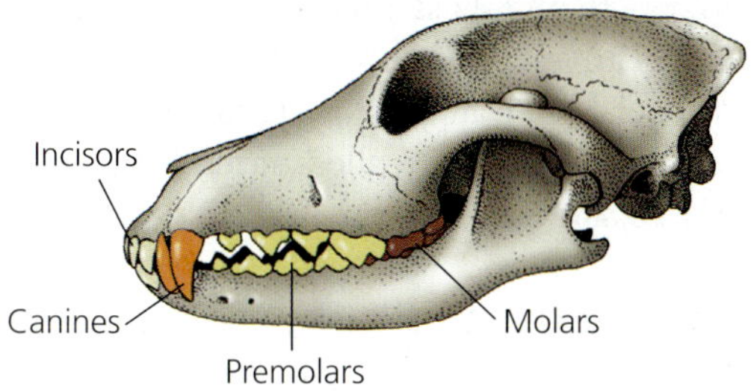

(a) Carnivore. Carnivores, such as members of the dog and cat families, generally have pointed incisors and canines that can be used to kill prey and rip or cut away pieces of flesh. The jagged premolars and molars crush and shred food.

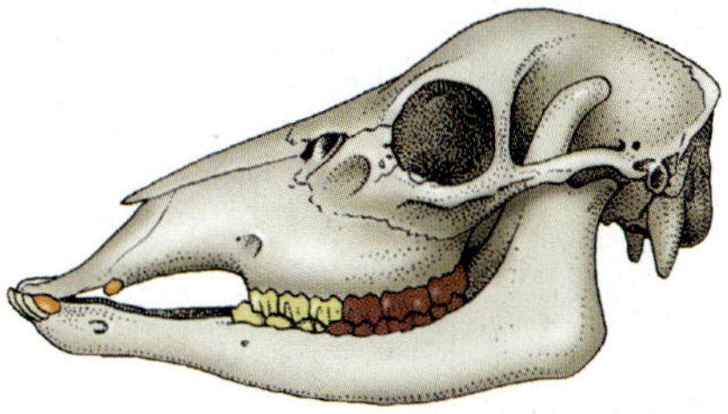

(b) Herbivore. In contrast, herbivorous mammals, such as horses and deer, usually have teeth with broad, ridged surfaces that grind tough plant material. The incisors and canines are generally modified for biting off pieces of vegetation. In some herbivorous mammals, canines are absent.

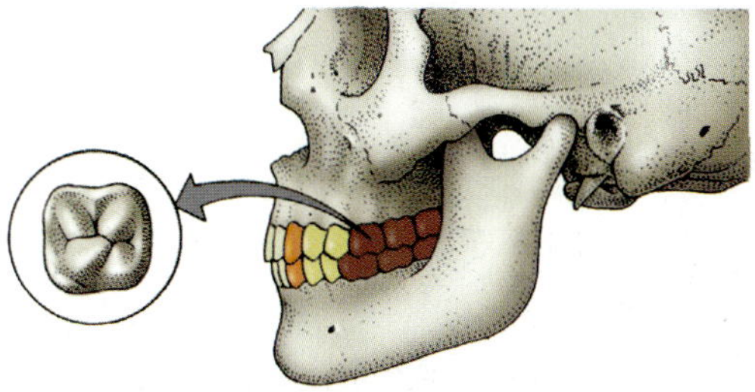

(c) Omnivore. Humans, being omnivores adapted for eating both vegetation and meat, have a relatively unspecialized dentition consisting of 32 permanent (adult) teeth. From the midline to the back along one side of one jaw, there are two bladelike incisors for biting, a pointed canine for tearing, two premolars for grinding, and three molars for crushing.

▲ **Figure 41.18 Dentition and diet.**

Stomach and Intestinal Adaptations

Large, expandable stomachs are common in carnivorous vertebrates, which may go for a long time between meals and must eat as much as they can when they do catch prey. A 200-kg African lion can consume 40 kg of meat in one meal!

The length of the vertebrate digestive system is also correlated with diet. In general, herbivores and omnivores have longer alimentary canals relative to their body size than do carnivores **(Figure 41.19)**. Vegetation is more difficult to digest than meat because it contains cell walls. A longer digestive tract furnishes more time for digestion and more surface area for the absorption of nutrients.

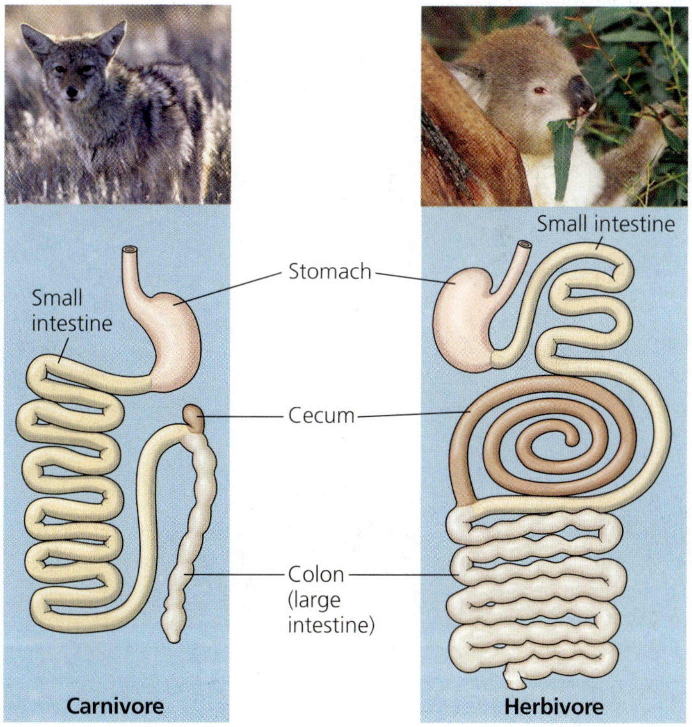

▲ **Figure 41.19 The alimentary canals of a carnivore (coyote) and herbivore (koala).** Although these two mammals are about the same size, the koala's intestines are much longer, enhancing processing of fibrous, protein-poor eucalyptus leaves from which it obtains virtually all its food and water. Extensive chewing chops the leaves into tiny pieces, increasing exposure to digestive juices. In the long cecum, symbiotic bacteria convert the shredded leaves to a more nutritious diet.

Mutualistic Adaptations

Some digestive adaptations involve mutualistic symbiosis, a mutually beneficial interaction between two species (see Chapter 54). For example, microorganisms help herbivores digest plants. Much of the chemical energy in herbivore diets comes from the cellulose of plant cell walls, but animals do not produce enzymes that hydrolyze cellulose. Instead, many vertebrates (as well as termites, whose wood diets are largely cellulose) house large populations of mutualistic bacteria and protists in fermentation chambers in their alimentary canals. These microorganisms have enzymes that can digest cellulose to simple sugars and other compounds that the animal can absorb. In many cases, the microorganisms also use the sugars from digested cellulose to produce a variety of nutrients essential to the animal, such as vitamins and amino acids.

The location of mutualistic microbes in alimentary canals varies, depending on the type of herbivore. For example:

- The hoatzin, an herbivorous bird that lives in the South American rain forests, has a large, muscular crop (an esophageal pouch; see Figure 41.9) that houses mutualistic microorganisms. Hard ridges in the wall of the crop grind plant leaves into small fragments, and the microorganisms break down cellulose.
- Horses and many other herbivorous mammals house mutualistic microorganisms in a large cecum, the pouch where the small and large intestines connect.
- In rabbits and some rodents, mutualistic bacteria live in the large intestine as well as in the cecum. Since most nutrients are absorbed in the small intestine, nourishing by-products of fermentation by bacteria in the large intestine are initially lost with the feces. Rabbits and rodents recover these nutrients by *coprophagy* (from the Greek, meaning "dung eating"), feeding on some of their feces and then passing the food through the alimentary canal a second time. The familiar rabbit "pellets," which are not reingested, are the feces eliminated after food has passed through the digestive tract twice.
- The koala, an Australian marsupial, also has an enlarged cecum, where mutualistic bacteria ferment finely shredded eucalyptus leaves (see Figure 41.19).
- The most elaborate adaptations for an herbivorous diet have evolved in the animals called **ruminants**, which include deer, sheep, and cattle **(Figure 41.20)**.

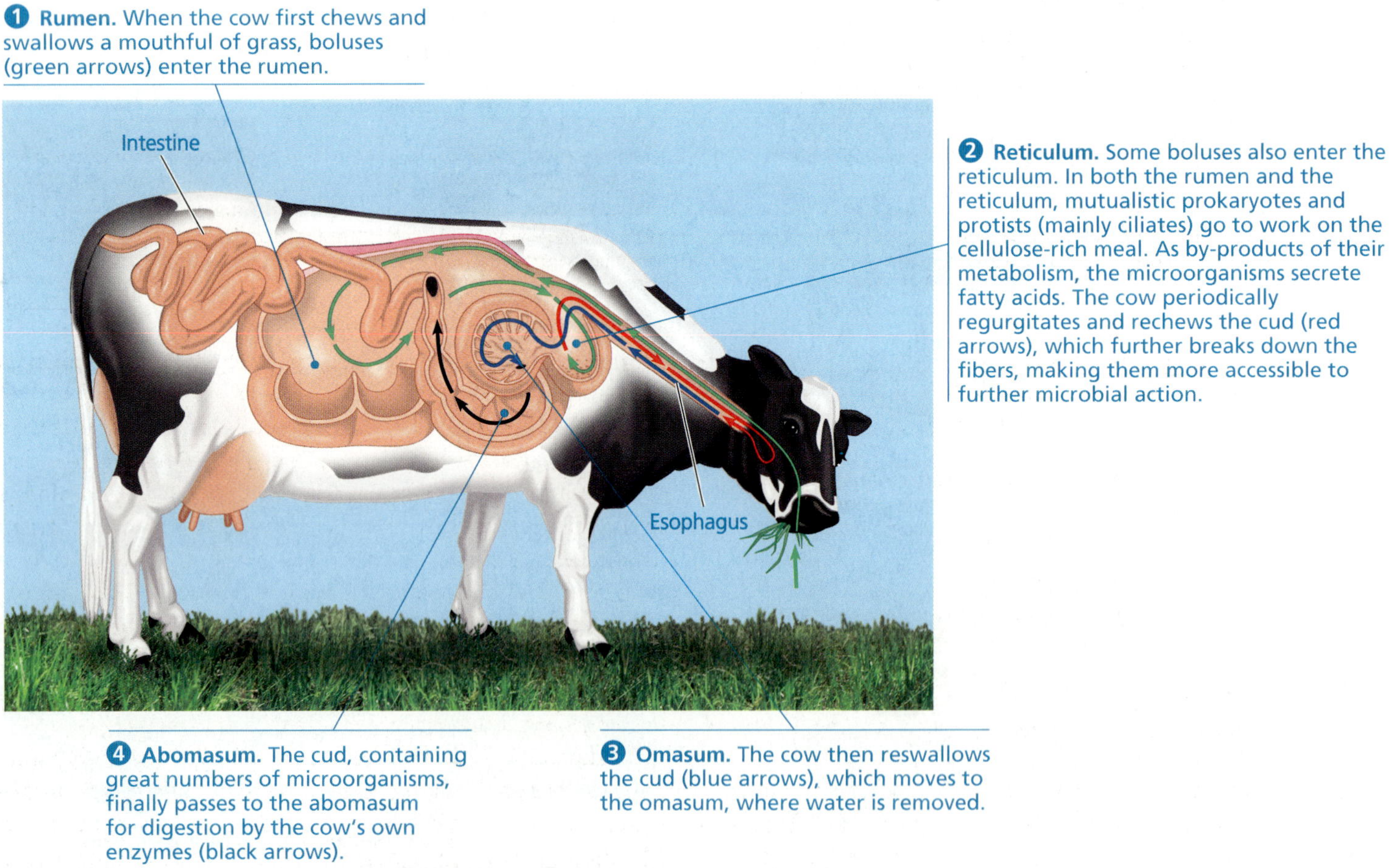

▲ **Figure 41.20 Ruminant digestion.** The stomach of a ruminant has four chambers. Because of the microbial action in the chambers, the diet from which a ruminant actually absorbs its nutrients is much richer than the grass the animal originally eats. In fact, a ruminant eating grass or hay obtains many of its nutrients by digesting the mutualistic microorganisms, which reproduce rapidly enough in the rumen to maintain a stable population.

Although we have focused our discussion on vertebrates, adaptations related to digestion are also widespread among other animals. Some of the most remarkable examples are the giant tubeworms that live at deep-sea hydrothermal vents (see Figure 52.18). These worms, which thrive at pressures as high as 260 atmospheres in water that reaches a remarkable 400°C (752°F), have no mouth or digestive system. Instead, they rely entirely on mutualistic bacteria to generate energy and nutrients from the carbon dioxide, oxygen, hydrogen sulfide, and nitrate available at the vents. Thus, for invertebrates and vertebrates alike, mutualistic symbiosis has evolved as a general strategy for expanding the sources of nutrition available to animals.

Having examined how animals optimize their extraction of nutrients from food, we will next turn to the challenge of balancing the use of these nutrients.

CONCEPT CHECK 41.4

1. What are the two advantages of a longer alimentary canal for processing plant material that is difficult to digest?
2. What features of an animal's digestive system make it an attractive habitat for mutualistic microorganisms?
3. **WHAT IF?** "Lactose-intolerant" people have a shortage of lactase, the enzyme that breaks down lactose in milk. As a result, they sometimes develop cramps, bloating, or diarrhea after consuming dairy products. Suppose such a person ate yogurt, which contains bacteria that produce lactase. Why might you expect that eating yogurt would provide at best only temporary relief of the symptoms?

For suggested answers, see Appendix A.

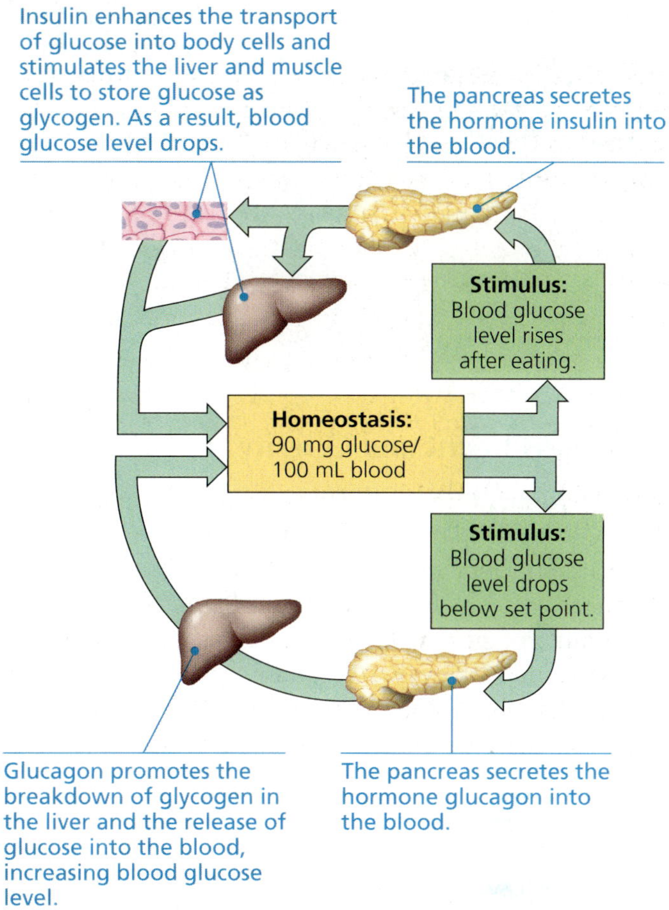

▲ **Figure 41.21 Homeostatic regulation of cellular fuel.** After a meal is digested, glucose and other monomers are absorbed into the blood from the digestive tract. The human body regulates the use and storage of glucose, a major cellular fuel. Notice that these regulatory loops are examples of the negative feedback control described in Chapter 40.

CONCEPT 41.5

Homeostatic mechanisms contribute to an animal's energy balance

As discussed in Chapter 40, the energy obtained from food balances the expenditure of energy for metabolism, activity, and storage. In concluding our overview of nutrition, we'll examine some ways in which animals achieve this balance.

Energy Sources and Stores

In deriving energy from their diet, animals make use of certain fuel sources before others. Nearly all of an animal's ATP generation is based on the oxidation of energy-rich organic molecules—carbohydrates, proteins, and fats—in cellular respiration. Although any of these substances can be used as fuel, most animals "burn" proteins only after exhausting their supply of carbohydrates and fats. Fats are especially rich in energy; oxidizing a gram of fat liberates about twice the energy liberated from a gram of carbohydrate or protein.

When an animal takes in more energy-rich molecules than it breaks down, the excess is converted to storage molecules. In humans, the primary sites of storage are liver and muscle cells. Excess energy from the diet is stored there in the form of glycogen, a polymer made up of many glucose units (see Figure 5.6b). When fewer calories are taken in than are expended—perhaps because of sustained heavy exercise or lack of food—glycogen is oxidized. The hormones insulin and glucagon maintain glucose homeostasis by tightly regulating glycogen synthesis and breakdown **(Figure 41.21)**.

Adipose (fat) cells represent a secondary site of energy storage in the body. If glycogen depots are full and caloric intake exceeds caloric expenditure, the excess is usually stored as fat. When more energy is required than is generated from the diet, the human body generally expends liver glycogen first and then draws on muscle glycogen and fat. Most healthy people have enough stored fat to sustain them through several weeks without food.

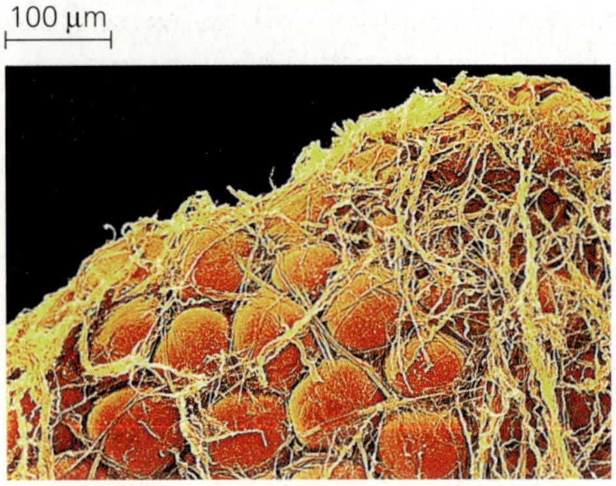

◀ **Figure 41.22 Fat cells from the abdomen of a human.** Strands of connective tissue (yellow) hold the fat-storing adipose cells in place (colorized SEM).

Overnourishment and Obesity

Overnourishment, the consumption of more calories than the body needs for normal metabolism, causes obesity, the excessive accumulation of fat **(Figure 41.22).** Obesity, in turn, contributes to a number of health problems, including the most common type of diabetes (type 2), cancer of the colon and breast, and cardiovascular disease that can lead to heart attacks and strokes. It is estimated that obesity is a factor in about 300,000 deaths per year in the United States alone.

Researchers have discovered several homeostatic mechanisms that help regulate body weight. Operating as feedback circuits, these mechanisms control the storage and metabolism of fat. Several hormones regulate long-term and short-term appetite by affecting a "satiety center" in the brain **(Figure 41.23).** A network of neurons relays and integrates information from the digestive system to regulate hormone release.

Mutations that cause mice to be chronically obese played a key role in advancing our understanding of the satiety pathway. Mice with mutations in the *ob* or *db* gene eat voraciously and become much more massive than normal. Doug Coleman, a researcher at the Jackson Laboratory in Maine, investigated how *ob* and *db* mutations disrupt normal control of appetite **(Figure 41.24).** Based on his experiments, Coleman deduced that the *ob* gene is required to produce the satiety factor, and the *db* gene is required to respond to the factor.

Cloning of the *ob* gene led to the demonstration that it produces a hormone, now known as leptin (from the Greek *lepto*, thin). The *db* gene encodes the leptin receptor. Leptin and the leptin receptor are key components of the circuitry that regulates appetite over the long term. Leptin is a product of adipose cells, so levels rise when body fat increases, cuing the

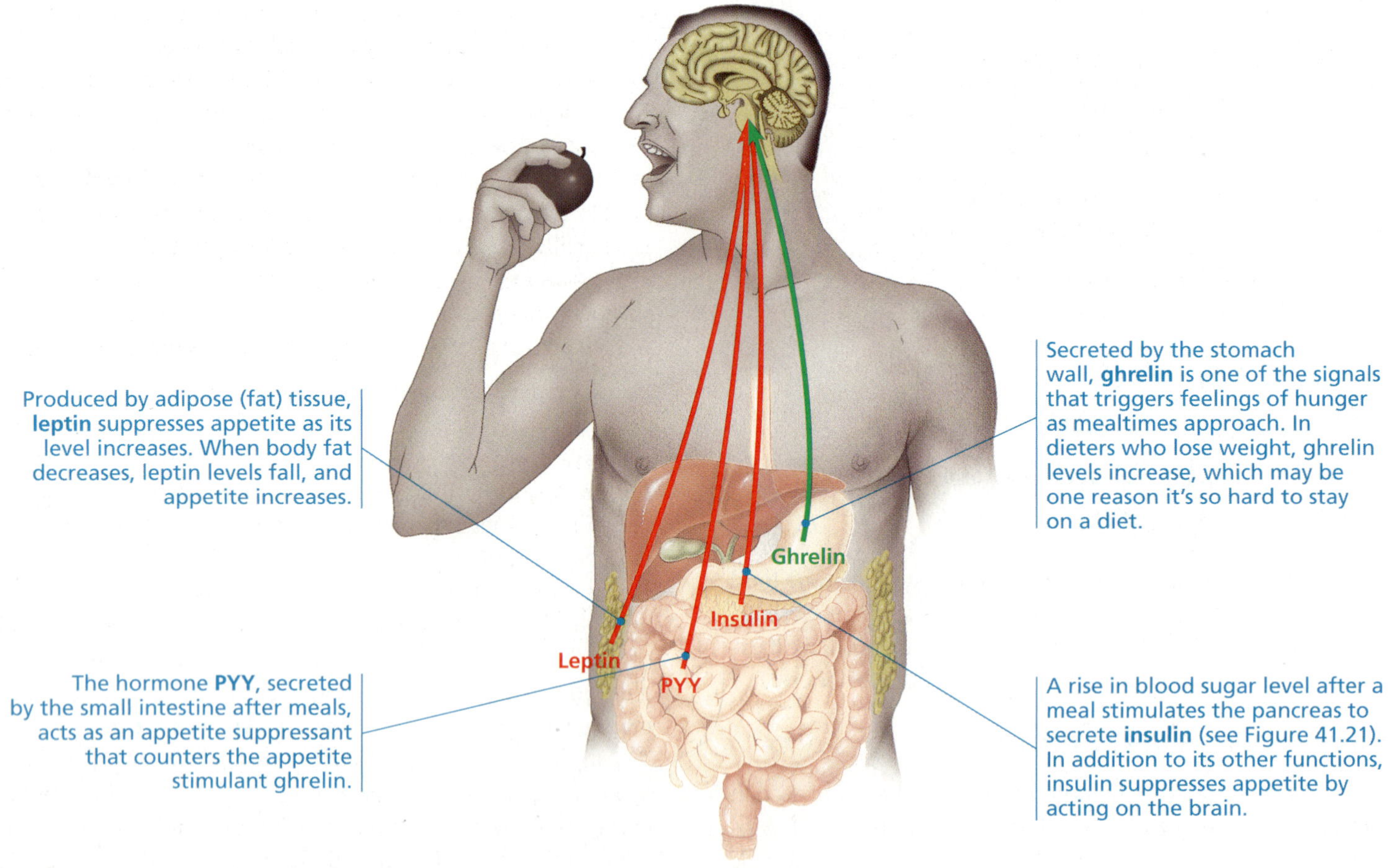

▲ **Figure 41.23 A few of the appetite-regulating hormones.** Secreted by various organs and tissues, the hormones reach the brain via the bloodstream. The hormones act on a region of the brain that in turn controls the "satiety center," which generates the nervous impulses that make us feel either hungry or satiated ("full"). The green arrow indicates an appetite stimulant; red arrows represent appetite suppressants.

▼ **Figure 41.24 Inquiry**

What are the roles of the *ob* and *db* genes in appetite regulation?

EXPERIMENT Margaret Dickie, Katherine Hummel, and Doug Coleman, of the Jackson Laboratory in Bar Harbor, Maine, discovered that mice with a mutant *ob* gene or a mutant *db* gene eat voraciously and grow much more massive than mice with the wild-type (nonmutant) forms of both genes (designated ob^+, db^+).

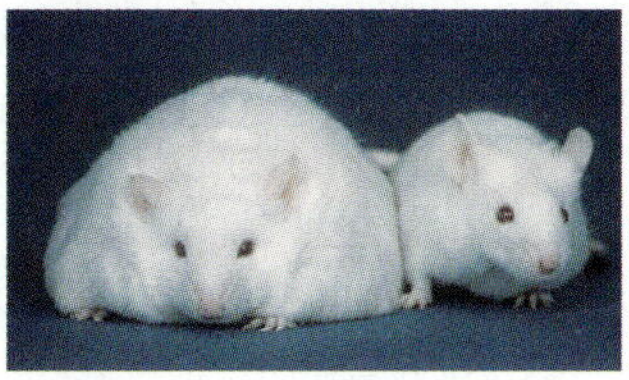

Obese mouse with mutant *ob* gene (left) next to wild-type mouse.

To explore further the roles of the two genes, Coleman measured the body masses of pairs of young mice with various genotypes and then surgically linked the circulatory systems of each pair. This procedure ensured that any factor circulating in the bloodstream of either mouse would be transferred to the other. After several weeks, he again measured the mass of each mouse.

RESULTS

Genotype pairing (red type indicates mutant genes; bar indicates pairing)	Average body mass (g) Starting	Ending
ob^+, db^+	20.3	23.6
ob^+, db^+	20.8	21.4
ob, db^+	27.6	47.0
ob, db^+	26.6	44.0
ob, db^+	29.4	39.8
ob^+, db^+	22.5	25.5
ob, db^+	33.7	18.8
ob^+, *db*	30.3	33.2

CONCLUSION Because an *ob* mouse gains less weight when surgically joined with an ob^+ mouse than when joined with an *ob* mouse, Coleman concluded that the *ob* mouse fails to make a satiety factor but can respond to the factor when it is present. To explain the weight loss in an *ob* mouse that receives circulating factors from a *db* mouse, he reasoned that the *db* mutation blocks the response to the satiety factor but not its production. Subsequent molecular studies demonstrated the validity of both parts of Coleman's conclusion. The ob^+ gene product is leptin, the satiety factor, whereas the db^+ gene product is the leptin receptor. Thus, mice with the *ob* mutation cannot produce leptin, and mice with the *db* mutation produce leptin but cannot respond to it.

SOURCE D. L. Coleman, Effects of parabiosis of obese with diabetes and normal mice. *Diabetologia* 9:294–298 (1973).

WHAT IF? Suppose you collected blood from a wild-type mouse and a *db* mouse. Which would you expect to have a higher concentration of leptin, the satiety factor, and why?

brain to suppress appetite (see Figure 41.23). Conversely, loss of fat decreases leptin levels, signaling the brain to increase appetite. In this way, the feedback signals provided by leptin maintain body fat levels within a set range.

Our understanding of leptin may lead to treatments for obesity, but uncertainties remain. For one thing, leptin has complex functions, including a role in how the nervous system develops. Also, most obese people have an abnormally high leptin level, which somehow fails to elicit a response from the brain's satiety center. Clearly, there is much to learn in this important area of human physiology.

Obesity and Evolution

Though fat hoarding can be a health liability, it may have been an advantage in our evolutionary past. Our ancestors on the African savanna were hunter-gatherers who probably survived mainly on seeds and other plant products, a diet only occasionally supplemented by hunting game or scavenging meat from animals killed by other predators. In such a feast-or-famine existence, natural selection may have favored those individuals with a physiology that induced them to gorge on rich, fatty foods on those rare occasions when such treats were abundantly available. Such individuals with genes promoting the storage of high-energy molecules during feasts may have been more likely than their thinner friends to survive famines. So perhaps our present-day taste for fats is partly an evolutionary vestige of less nutritious times.

The relationship between fat storage and evolutionary adaptation in animals is sometimes complex. Consider the plump offspring of the seabirds called petrels **(Figure 41.25)**. Their parents must fly long distances to find food. Most of the food that they bring to their chicks is very rich in lipids. The fact that fat has twice as many calories per gram as other

▲ **Figure 41.25 A plump petrel.** Too heavy to fly, the petrel chick (right) will have to lose weight before it takes wing. In the meantime, its stored fat provides energy during times when its parent fails to bring enough food.

fuels minimizes the number of foraging trips. However, growing baby petrels need lots of protein for building new tissues, and there is relatively little in their oily diet. To get all the protein they need, young petrels have to consume many more calories than they burn in metabolism and consequently become obese. Their fat depots nevertheless help them survive periods when parents cannot find enough food. When food is not scarce, chicks at the end of the growth period weigh much more than their parents. The youngsters must then fast for several days to lose enough weight to be capable of flight.

In the next chapter, we'll see that obtaining food, digesting it, and absorbing nutrients are parts of a larger story. Provisioning the body also involves distributing nutrients (circulation) and exchanging respiratory gases with the environment.

CONCEPT CHECK **41.5**

1. Explain how people can become obese even if their intake of dietary fat is relatively low compared with carbohydrate intake.
2. After reviewing Figure 41.23, explain how PYY and leptin complement each other in regulating body weight.
3. WHAT IF? Suppose you were studying two groups of obese people with genetic abnormalities in the leptin pathway. In one group, the leptin levels are abnormally high; in the other group, they are abnormally low. How would each group's leptin levels change if both groups were placed on a low-calorie diet for an extended period? Explain.

For suggested answers, see Appendix A.

Chapter 41 Review

MEDIA Go to the Study Area at **www.masteringbio.com** for BioFlix 3-D Animations, MP3 Tutors, Videos, Practice Tests, an eBook, and more.

SUMMARY OF KEY CONCEPTS

- Animals have diverse diets. Herbivores mainly eat plants; carnivores mainly eat other animals; and omnivores eat both. Animals must balance consumption, storage, and use of food.

CONCEPT 41.1

An animal's diet must supply chemical energy, organic molecules, and essential nutrients (pp. 875–880)

- Animals need fuel to produce ATP, carbon skeletons for biosynthesis, and essential nutrients—nutrients that must be supplied in preassembled form.
- **Essential Nutrients** Essential nutrients include essential amino acids, essential fatty acids, vitamins, and minerals. Essential amino acids are those an animal cannot synthesize. Essential fatty acids are unsaturated. Vitamins are organic molecules required in small amounts. Minerals are inorganic nutrients, usually required in small amounts.
- **Dietary Deficiencies** Undernourished animals have diets deficient in calories. Malnourished animals are missing one or more essential nutrients.
- **Assessing Nutritional Needs** Studies of genetic defects and the study of disease at the population level help researchers determine human dietary requirements.

MEDIA

Activity Analyzing Food Labels

CONCEPT 41.2

The main stages of food processing are ingestion, digestion, absorption, and elimination (pp. 880–883)

- Food processing in animals involves ingestion (eating), digestion (enzymatic breakdown of large molecules), absorption (uptake of nutrients by cells), and elimination (passage of undigested materials out of the body in feces).
- Suspension feeders sift small particles from the water. Substrate feeders eat as they tunnel through their food. Fluid feeders suck nutrient-rich fluids from a living host. Most animals are bulk feeders, eating large pieces of food.
- **Digestive Compartments** In intracellular digestion, food particles are engulfed by endocytosis and digested within food vacuoles that have fused with lysosomes. Most animals use extracellular digestion: Enzymatic hydrolysis occurs outside cells in a gastrovascular cavity or alimentary canal.

MEDIA

Activity Feeding Mechanisms of Animals

CONCEPT 41.3

Organs specialized for sequential stages of food processing form the mammalian digestive system (pp. 884–890)

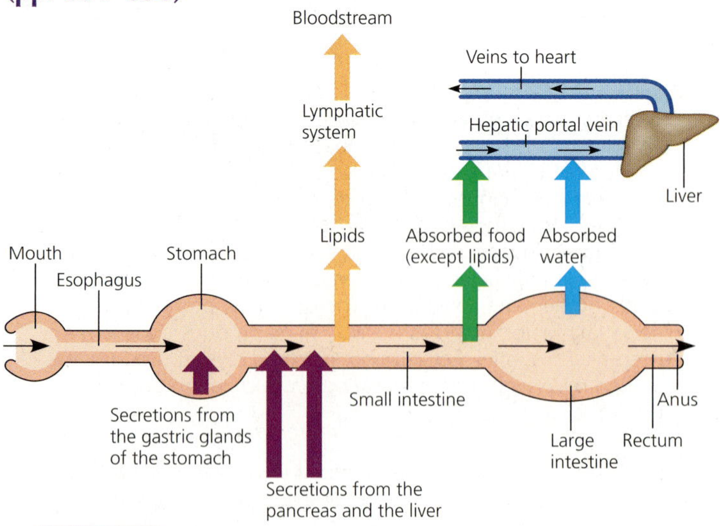

MEDIA

MP3 Tutor The Human Digestive System
Activity Digestive System Function
Investigation What Role Does Amylase Play in Digestion?
Activity Hormonal Control of Digestion

CONCEPT **41.4**

Evolutionary adaptations of vertebrate digestive systems correlate with diet (pp. 891–893)

- **Some Dental Adaptations** Dentition generally correlates with diet.
- **Stomach and Intestinal Adaptations** Herbivores generally have longer alimentary canals than carnivores, reflecting the longer time needed to digest vegetation.
- **Mutualistic Adaptations** Many herbivores have fermentation chambers where microorganisms digest cellulose.

CONCEPT **41.5**

Homeostatic mechanisms contribute to an animal's energy balance (pp. 893–896)

- **Energy Sources and Stores** Vertebrates store excess calories as glycogen in the liver and muscles and as fat. These energy stores can be tapped when an animal expends more calories than it consumes.
- **Overnourishment and Obesity** Overnourishment, the consumption of more calories than the body needs for normal metabolism, can lead to the serious health problem of obesity. Several hormones regulate appetite by affecting the brain's satiety center. Studies of the hormone leptin may lead to treatments for obesity.
- **Obesity and Evolution** The problem of maintaining a healthy weight partly stems from our evolutionary past, when fat hoarding may have been important for survival.

MEDIA

Activity Case Studies of Nutritional Disorders

TESTING YOUR KNOWLEDGE

SELF-QUIZ

1. Individuals whose diet consists primarily of corn would likely become
a. obese.
b. anorexic.
c. overnourished.
d. undernourished.
e. malnourished.

2. Which of the following animals is *incorrectly* paired with its feeding mechanism?
a. lion—substrate feeder
b. baleen whale—suspension feeder
c. aphid—fluid feeder
d. clam—suspension feeder
e. snake—bulk feeder

3. The mammalian trachea and esophagus both connect to the
a. large intestine.
b. stomach.
c. pharynx.
d. rectum.
e. epiglottis.

4. Which of the following enzymes works most effectively at a very low pH?
a. salivary amylase
b. trypsin
c. pepsin
d. pancreatic amylase
e. pancreatic lipase

5. Which of the following organs is *incorrectly* paired with its function?
a. stomach—protein digestion
b. oral cavity—starch digestion
c. large intestine—bile production
d. small intestine—nutrient absorption
e. pancreas—enzyme production

6. After surgical removal of an infected gallbladder, a person must be especially careful to restrict dietary intake of
a. starch.
b. protein.
c. sugar.
d. fat.
e. water.

7. The mutualistic microorganisms that help nourish a ruminant live mainly in specialized regions of the
a. large intestine.
b. liver.
c. small intestine.
d. pharynx.
e. stomach.

8. If you were to jog a mile a few hours after lunch, which stored fuel would you probably tap?
a. muscle proteins
b. muscle and liver glycogen
c. fat stored in the liver
d. fat stored in adipose tissue
e. blood proteins

9. DRAW IT Make a flowchart of the events that occur after partially digested food leaves the stomach. Use the following terms: bicarbonate secretion, circulation, decrease in acid, secretin secretion, increase in acid, signal detection. Next to each term, indicate the compartment(s) involved. You may use a term more than once.

For Self-Quiz answers, see Appendix A.

MEDIA Visit the Study Area at **www.masteringbio.com** for a Practice Test.

EVOLUTION CONNECTION

10. The human esophagus and trachea share a passage leading from the mouth and nasal passages. After reviewing vertebrate evolution in Chapter 34, explain the historical (evolutionary) basis for this "imperfect" anatomy.

SCIENTIFIC INQUIRY

11. In adult populations of northern European origin, the disorder called hemochromatosis causes excess iron uptake from food and affects one in 200 individuals. Men are ten times more likely to suffer symptoms than are women. Given that only women menstruate, devise a hypothesis for the difference in the disease between the two genders.

Biological Inquiry: A Workbook of Investigative Cases Explore several mammalian mechanisms for starch digestion in the case "Galloper's Gut."

42 Circulation and Gas Exchange

▲ **Figure 42.1 How does a feathery fringe help this animal survive?**

KEY CONCEPTS

42.1 Circulatory systems link exchange surfaces with cells throughout the body
42.2 Coordinated cycles of heart contraction drive double circulation in mammals
42.3 Patterns of blood pressure and flow reflect the structure and arrangement of blood vessels
42.4 Blood components function in exchange, transport, and defense
42.5 Gas exchange occurs across specialized respiratory surfaces
42.6 Breathing ventilates the lungs
42.7 Adaptations for gas exchange include pigments that bind and transport gases

OVERVIEW

Trading Places

The animal in **Figure 42.1** may look like a creature from a science fiction film, but it's actually an axolotl, a salamander native to shallow ponds in central Mexico. The feathery red appendages jutting out from the head of this albino adult are gills. Although external gills are uncommon in adult animals, they help satisfy the need shared by all animals to exchange substances with their environment.

Exchange between an axolotl or any other animal and its surroundings ultimately occurs at the cellular level. The resources that animal cells require, such as nutrients and oxygen (O_2), enter the cytoplasm by crossing the plasma membrane. Metabolic by-products, such as carbon dioxide (CO_2), exit the cell by crossing the same membrane. In unicellular organisms, exchange occurs directly with the external environment. For most multicellular organisms, however, direct exchange between every cell and the environment is not possible. Instead, these organisms rely on specialized systems that carry out exchange with the environment and that transport materials between sites of exchange and the rest of the body.

The reddish color and branching structure of the axolotl's gills reflect the intimate association between exchange and transport. Tiny blood vessels lie close to the surface of each filament in the gills. Across this surface, there is a net diffusion of O_2 from the surrounding water into the blood and of CO_2 from the blood into the water. The short distances involved allow diffusion to be rapid. Pumping of the axolotl's heart propels the oxygen-rich blood from the gill filaments to all other tissues of the body. There, more short-range exchange occurs, involving nutrients and O_2 as well as CO_2 and other wastes.

Because internal transport and gas exchange are functionally related in most animals, not just axolotls, we will examine both circulatory and respiratory systems in this chapter. We will explore the remarkable variation in form and organization of these systems by considering examples from a number of species. We will also highlight the roles of circulatory and respiratory systems in maintaining homeostasis under a range of physiological and environmental stresses.

CONCEPT 42.1

Circulatory systems link exchange surfaces with cells throughout the body

The molecular trade that animals carry out with their environment—gaining O_2 and nutrients while shedding CO_2 and other waste products—must ultimately involve every cell in the body. As you learned in Chapter 7, small, nonpolar molecules such as O_2 and CO_2 can move between cells and their immediate surroundings by diffusion. But diffusion is very slow for distances of more than a few millimeters. That's because the time it takes for a substance to diffuse from one place to another is proportional to the *square* of the distance. For example, if it takes 1 second for a given quantity of glucose to diffuse 100 µm, it will take 100 seconds for the same quantity to diffuse 1 mm, and almost 3 hours to diffuse 1 cm. This relationship between diffusion time and distance places a substantial constraint on the body plan of any animal.

Given that diffusion is rapid only over small distances, how does each cell of an animal participate in exchange? Natural selection has resulted in two general solutions to this problem. The first solution is a body size and shape that keep many or all cells in direct contact with the environment. Each cell can thus exchange materials directly with the surrounding medium. This type of body plan is found only in certain invertebrates, including sponges, cnidarians, and flatworms. The second solution, found in all other animals, is a circulatory system that moves fluid between each cell's immediate surroundings and the tissues where exchange with the environment occurs.

Gastrovascular Cavities

Let's begin by looking at animals that lack a distinct circulatory system. In hydras and other cnidarians, a central gastrovascular cavity functions both in digestion and in the distribution of substances throughout the body. As was shown for a hydra in Figure 41.8, a single opening maintains continuity between the fluid inside the cavity and the water outside. As a result, both the inner and outer tissue layers are bathed by fluid. Only the cells of the inner layer have direct access to nutrients, but since the body wall is a mere two cells thick, the nutrients must diffuse only a short distance to reach the cells of the outer layer. Thin branches of a hydra's gastrovascular cavity extend into the animal's tentacles. Some cnidarians, such as jellies, have gastrovascular cavities with a much more elaborate branching pattern **(Figure 42.2a)**.

Planarians and most other flatworms also survive without a circulatory system. Their combination of a gastrovascular cavity and a flat body is well suited for exchange with the environment **(Figure 42.2b)**. A flat body optimizes diffusional exchange by increasing surface area and minimizing diffusion distances.

Open and Closed Circulatory Systems

For animals with many cell layers, diffusion distances are too great for adequate exchange of nutrients and wastes by a gastrovascular cavity. In these organisms, a circulatory system minimizes the distances that substances must diffuse to enter or leave a cell. By transporting fluid throughout the body, the circulatory system functionally connects the aqueous environment of the body cells to the organs that exchange gases, absorb nutrients, and dispose of wastes. In mammals, for example, O_2 from inhaled air diffuses across only two layers of cells in the lungs before reaching the blood. The circulatory system, powered by the heart, then carries the oxygen-rich blood to all parts of the body. As the blood streams throughout the body tissues in tiny blood vessels, O_2 in the blood again diffuses only a short distance before entering the interstitial fluid that directly bathes the cells.

A circulatory system has three basic components: a circulatory fluid, a set of interconnecting tubes, and a muscular pump, the **heart**. The heart powers circulation by using metabolic energy to elevate the hydrostatic pressure of the circulatory fluid, which then flows through a circuit of vessels and back to the heart.

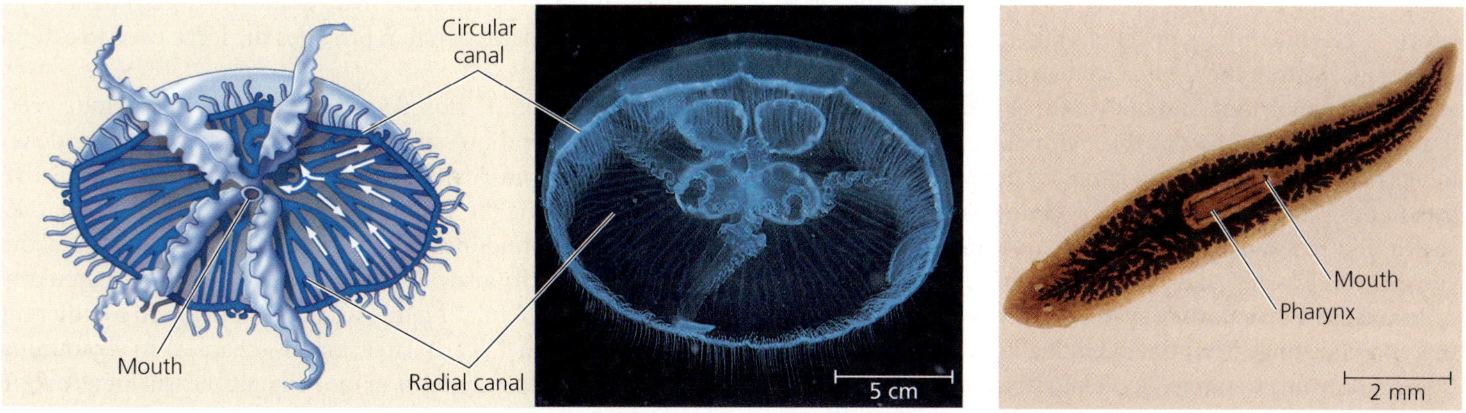

(a) The moon jelly *Aurelia*, a cnidarian. The jelly is viewed here from its underside (oral surface). The mouth leads to an elaborate gastrovascular cavity that consists of radial arms (canals) leading to and from a circular canal. Ciliated cells lining the canals circulate fluid within the cavity as indicated by the arrows.

(b) The planarian *Dugesia*, a flatworm. The mouth and pharynx on the ventral side lead to the highly branched gastrovascular cavity, stained dark brown in this specimen (LM).

▲ **Figure 42.2 Internal transport in gastrovascular cavities.**

WHAT IF? *Suppose a gastrovascular cavity were open at two ends, with fluid entering one end and leaving the other. How would this affect the gastrovascular cavity's function?*

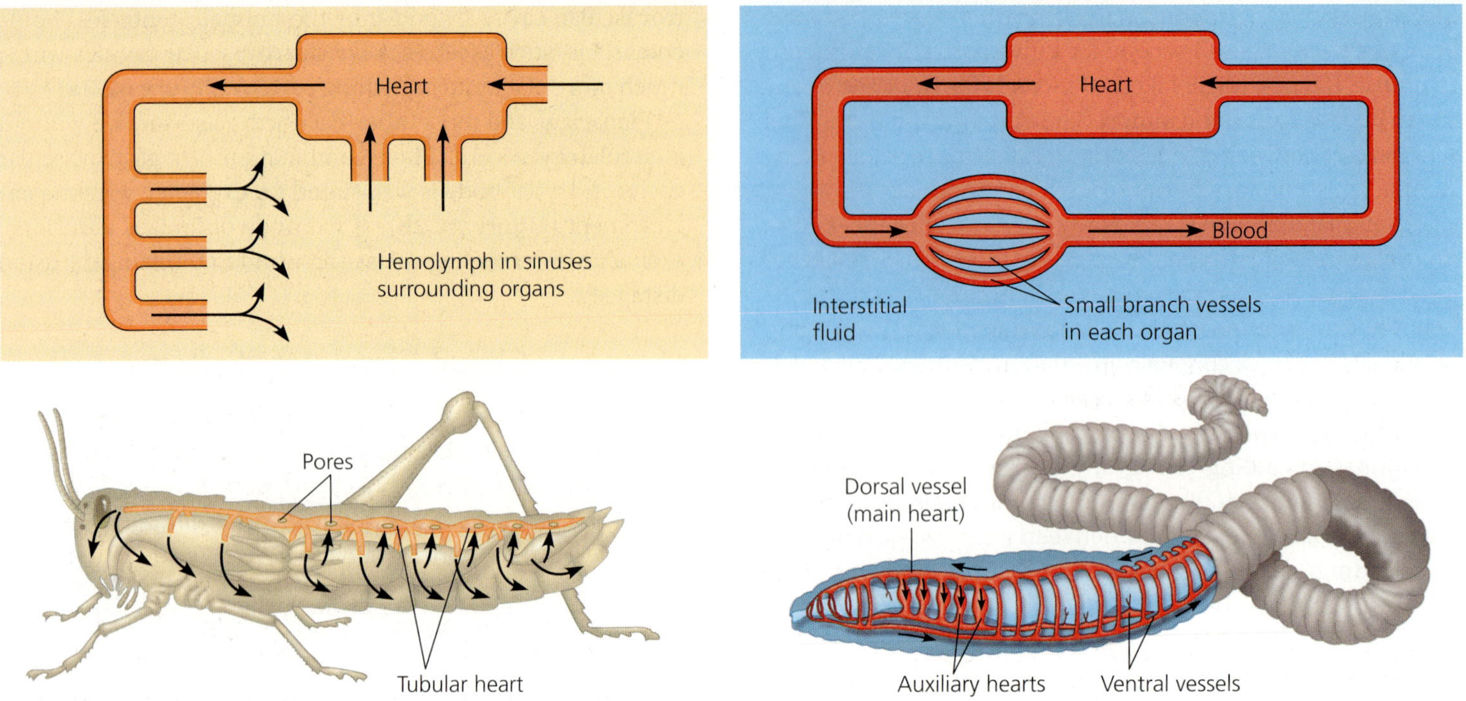

(a) An open circulatory system. In an open circulatory system, such as that of a grasshopper, the circulatory fluid, called hemolymph, is the same as interstitial fluid. The heart pumps hemolymph through vessels into sinuses, fluid-filled spaces where materials are exchanged between the hemolymph and cells. Hemolymph returns to the heart through pores, which are equipped with valves that close when the heart contracts.

(b) A closed circulatory system. Closed circulatory systems circulate blood entirely within vessels, so the blood is distinct from the interstitial fluid. Chemical exchange occurs between the blood and the interstitial fluid, as well as between the interstitial fluid and body cells. In an earthworm, the dorsal vessel functions as the main heart, pumping blood forward by peristalsis. Near the worm's anterior end, five pairs of vessels loop around the digestive tract and function as auxillary hearts.

▲ **Figure 42.3 Open and closed circulatory systems.**

Arthropods and most mollusks have an **open circulatory system**, in which the circulatory fluid bathes the organs directly **(Figure 42.3a)**. In these animals, the circulatory fluid, called **hemolymph**, is also the interstitial fluid. Contraction of one or more hearts pumps the hemolymph through the circulatory vessels into interconnected sinuses, spaces surrounding the organs. Within the sinuses, chemical exchange occurs between the hemolymph and body cells. Relaxation of the heart draws hemolymph back in through pores, and body movements help circulate the hemolymph by periodically squeezing the sinuses. The open circulatory system of larger crustaceans, such as lobsters and crabs, includes a more extensive system of vessels as well as an accessory pump.

In a **closed circulatory system**, blood is confined to vessels and is distinct from the interstitial fluid **(Figure 42.3b)**. One or more hearts pump blood into large vessels that branch into smaller ones coursing through the organs. Materials are exchanged between the smallest vessels and the interstitial fluid bathing the cells. Annelids (including earthworms), cephalopods (including squids and octopuses), and all vertebrates have closed circulatory systems.

The fact that both open and closed circulatory systems are widespread among animals suggests that there are advantages to each system. The lower hydrostatic pressures associated with open circulatory systems make them less costly than closed systems in terms of energy expenditure. In some invertebrates, open circulatory systems serve additional functions. For example, in spiders, the hydrostatic pressure generated by the open circulatory system provides the force used to extend the animal's legs.

The benefits of closed circulatory systems include relatively high blood pressures, which enable the effective delivery of O_2 and nutrients to the cells of larger and more active animals. Among the molluscs, for instance, closed circulatory systems are found in the largest and most active species, the squids and octopuses. Closed systems are also particularly well suited to regulating the distribution of blood to different organs, as you'll learn later in this chapter. In examining closed circulatory systems in more detail, we will focus on the vertebrates.

Organization of Vertebrate Circulatory Systems

The closed circulatory system of humans and other vertebrates is often called the **cardiovascular system**. Blood circulates to and from the heart through an amazingly extensive network of vessels: The total length of blood vessels in an average human adult is twice Earth's circumference at the equator!

Arteries, veins, and capillaries are the three main types of blood vessels. Within each type, blood flows in only one direction. **Arteries** carry blood away from the heart to organs throughout the body. Within organs, arteries branch into **arterioles**, small vessels that convey blood to the capillaries. **Capillaries** are microscopic vessels with very thin, porous walls. Networks of these vessels, called **capillary beds**, infiltrate each tissue, passing within a few cell diameters of every cell in the body. Across the thin walls of capillaries, chemicals, including dissolved gases, are exchanged by diffusion between the blood and the interstitial fluid around the tissue cells. At their "downstream" end, capillaries converge into **venules**, and venules converge into **veins**, the vessels that carry blood back to the heart.

Arteries and veins are distinguished by the *direction* in which they carry blood, not by the O_2 content or other characteristics of the blood they contain. Arteries carry blood from the heart *toward* capillaries, and veins return blood to the heart *from* capillaries. There is one exception: the portal veins, which carry blood between pairs of capillary beds. The hepatic portal vein, for example, carries blood from capillary beds in the digestive system to capillary beds in the liver (see Chapter 41). From the liver, blood passes into the hepatic veins, which conduct blood toward the heart.

Natural selection has modified the cardiovascular systems of different vertebrates in accordance with their level of activity. For example, animals with higher metabolic rates generally have more complex circulatory systems and more powerful hearts than animals with lower metabolic rates. Similarly, within an animal, the complexity and number of blood vessels in a particular organ correlate with that organ's metabolic requirements.

The hearts of all vertebrates contain two or more muscular chambers. The chambers that receive blood entering the heart are called **atria** (singular, *atrium*). The chambers responsible for pumping blood out of the heart are called **ventricles**. The number of chambers and the extent to which they are separated from one another differ substantially among groups of vertebrates, as we will discuss next. These important differences reflect the close fit of form to function.

Single Circulation

In bony fishes, rays, and sharks, the heart consists of two chambers: an atrium and a ventricle. The blood passes through the heart once in each complete circuit, an arrangement called **single circulation** **(Figure 42.4)**. Blood entering the heart collects in the atrium before transfer to the ventricle. Contraction of the ventricle pumps blood to the gills, where there is a net diffusion of O_2 into the blood and of CO_2 out of the blood. As

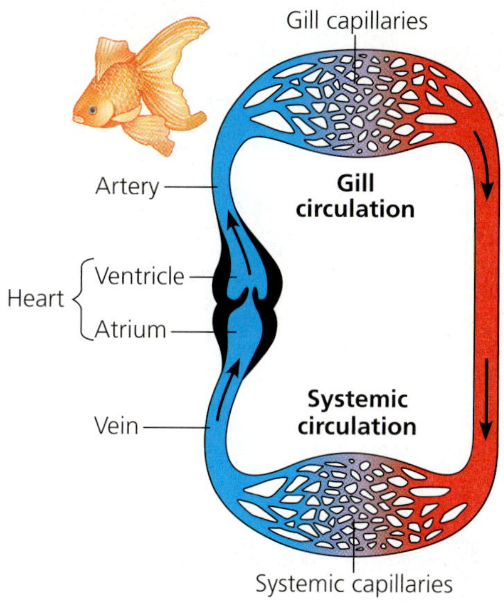

▲ **Figure 42.4 Single circulation in fishes.** Fishes have a two-chambered heart and a single circuit of blood flow.

blood leaves the gills, the capillaries converge into a vessel that carries oxygen-rich blood to capillary beds throughout the body. Blood then returns to the heart.

In single circulation, blood that leaves the heart passes through two capillary beds before returning to the heart. When blood flows through a capillary bed, blood pressure drops substantially, for reasons we will explain shortly. The drop in blood pressure in the gills of a bony fish, ray, or shark limits the rate of blood flow in the rest of the animal's body. As the animal swims, however, the contraction and relaxation of its muscles help accelerate the relatively sluggish pace of circulation.

Double Circulation

As shown in **Figure 42.5**, on the next page, the circulatory systems of amphibians, reptiles, and mammals have two distinct circuits, an arrangement called **double circulation**. The pumps for the two circuits serve different tissues but are combined into a single organ, the heart. Having both pumps within a single heart simplifies coordination of the pumping cycles.

One pump, the right side of the heart, delivers oxygen-poor blood to the capillary beds of the gas exchange tissues, where there is a net movement of O_2 into the blood and of CO_2 out of the blood. This part of the circulation is called a **pulmonary circuit** if the capillary beds involved are all in the lungs, as in reptiles and mammals. It is called a **pulmocutaneous circuit** if it includes capillaries in both the lungs and the skin, as in many amphibians.

After the oxygen-enriched blood leaves the gas exchange tissues, it enters the other pump, the left side of the heart. Contraction of the heart propels this blood to capillary beds in organs and tissues throughout the body. Following the exchange of O_2 and CO_2, as well as nutrients and waste products, the

▼ **Figure 42.5**

Exploring Double Circulation in Vertebrates

Amphibians

Amphibians have a three-chambered heart and two circuits of blood flow: pulmocutaneous and systemic.

Reptiles (Except Birds)

Lizards, snakes, and turtles have a three-chambered heart, with a septum partially dividing the single ventricle. In crocodilians, the septum is complete and the heart is four-chambered.

Mammals and Birds

Mammals and birds have a four-chambered heart. In birds, the major vessels near the heart are slightly different than shown, but the pattern of double circulation is essentially the same.

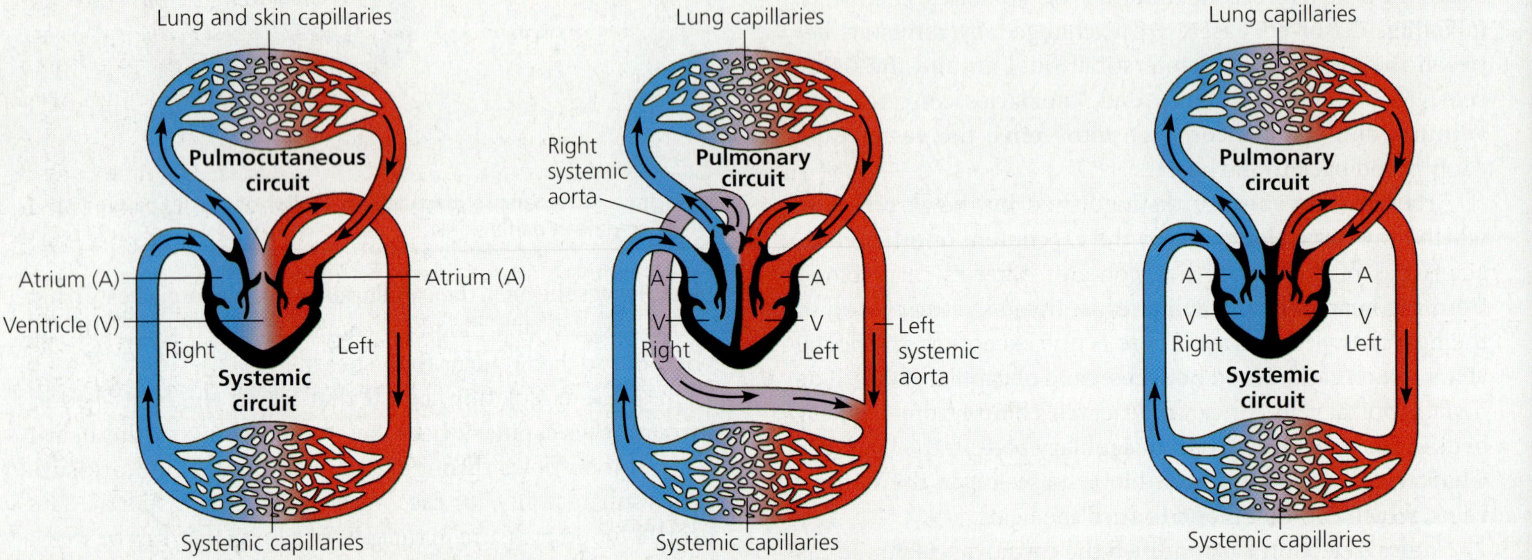

Systemic circuits include all body tissues except the primary gas exchange tissues. Note that circulatory systems are depicted as if the animal is facing you: The right side of the heart is shown on the left, and vice versa.

now oxygen-poor blood returns to the heart, completing the **systemic circuit**.

Double circulation provides a vigorous flow of blood to the brain, muscles, and other organs because the heart repressurizes the blood destined for these tissues after it passes through the capillary beds of the lungs or skin. Indeed, blood pressure is often much higher in the systemic circuit than in the gas exchange circuit. This contrasts sharply with single circulation, in which, as you read earlier, blood flows directly from the respiratory organs to other organs, under reduced pressure.

Adaptations of Double Circulatory Systems

Having considered the general properties of double circulation, let's examine the adaptations found in the hearts of different vertebrate groups that have this type of circulation. As you read, refer to the illustrations in Figure 42.5.

Amphibians Frogs and other amphibians have a heart with three chambers: two atria and one ventricle. A ridge within the ventricle diverts most (about 90%) of the oxygen-poor blood from the right atrium into the pulmocutaneous circuit and most of the oxygen-rich blood from the left atrium into the systemic circuit. When underwater, a frog adjusts its circulation, for the most part shutting off blood flow to its temporarily ineffective lungs. Blood flow continues to the skin, which acts as the sole site of gas exchange while the frog is submerged.

Reptiles (Except Birds) Turtles, snakes, and lizards have a three-chambered heart, with a septum partially dividing the ventricle into separate right and left chambers. In alligators, caimans, and other crocodilians, the septum is complete, but the pulmonary and systemic circuits are connected where the arteries exit the heart. When a crocodilian is underwater, arterial valves divert most of the blood flow from the pulmonary circuit to the systemic circuit through this connection.

Mammals and Birds In all mammals and birds, the ventricle is completely divided, such that there are two atria and two ventricles. The left side of the heart receives and pumps only oxygen-rich blood, while the right side receives and pumps only oxygen-poor blood.

A powerful four-chambered heart is a key adaptation that supports the endothermic way of life characteristic of mammals and birds. Endotherms use about ten times as much energy as equal-sized ectotherms; therefore, their circulatory systems need to deliver about ten times as much fuel and O_2 to their tissues (and remove ten times as much CO_2 and other wastes). This large traffic of substances is made possible by separate and independently powered systemic and pulmonary circuits and by large hearts that pump the necessary volume of blood. As we discussed in Chapter 34, mammals and birds descended from different tetrapod ancestors, and their four-chambered hearts evolved independently—an example of convergent evolution.

CONCEPT CHECK 42.1

1. How is the flow of hemolymph through an open circulatory system similar to the flow of water through an outdoor fountain?
2. Three-chambered hearts with incomplete septa were once viewed as being less adapted to circulatory function than mammalian hearts. What advantage of such hearts did this viewpoint overlook?
3. **WHAT IF?** The heart of a human fetus has a hole between the left and right ventricles. In some cases, this hole does not close completely before birth. If the hole weren't surgically corrected, how would it affect the O_2 content of the blood entering the systemic circuit from the heart?

For suggested answers, see Appendix A.

CONCEPT 42.2

Coordinated cycles of heart contraction drive double circulation in mammals

The timely delivery of O_2 to the body's organs is critical: Brain cells, for example, die within just a few minutes if their O_2 supply is interrupted. How does the mammalian cardiovascular system meet the body's continuous but variable demand for O_2? To answer this question, we need to consider how the parts of the system are arranged and how each part functions.

Mammalian Circulation

Let's first examine the overall organization of the mammalian cardiovascular system, beginning with the pulmonary circuit. (The circled numbers refer to corresponding locations in **Figure 42.6**). (1) Contraction of the right ventricle pumps blood to the lungs via (2) the pulmonary arteries. As the blood flows through (3) capillary beds in the left and right lungs, it loads O_2 and unloads CO_2. Oxygen-rich blood returns from the lungs via the pulmonary veins to (4) the left atrium of the heart. Next, the oxygen-rich blood flows into (5) the left ventricle, which pumps the oxygen-rich blood out to body tissues through the systemic circuit. Blood leaves the left ventricle via (6) the aorta, which conveys blood to arteries leading throughout the body. The first branches from the aorta are the coronary arteries (not shown), which supply blood to the heart muscle itself. Then branches lead to (7) capillary beds in the head and arms (forelimbs). The aorta then descends into the abdomen, supplying oxygen-rich blood to arteries leading to (8) capillary beds in the abdominal organs and legs (hind limbs). Within the capillaries, there is a net diffusion of O_2 from the blood to the tissues and of CO_2 produced by cellular respiration into the blood. Capillaries rejoin, forming venules, which convey blood to veins. Oxygen-poor blood from the head, neck, and forelimbs is channeled into a large vein, (9) the superior vena cava. Another large vein, (10) the inferior vena cava, drains blood from the trunk and hind limbs. The two venae cavae empty their blood into (11) the right atrium, from which the oxygen-poor blood flows into the right ventricle.

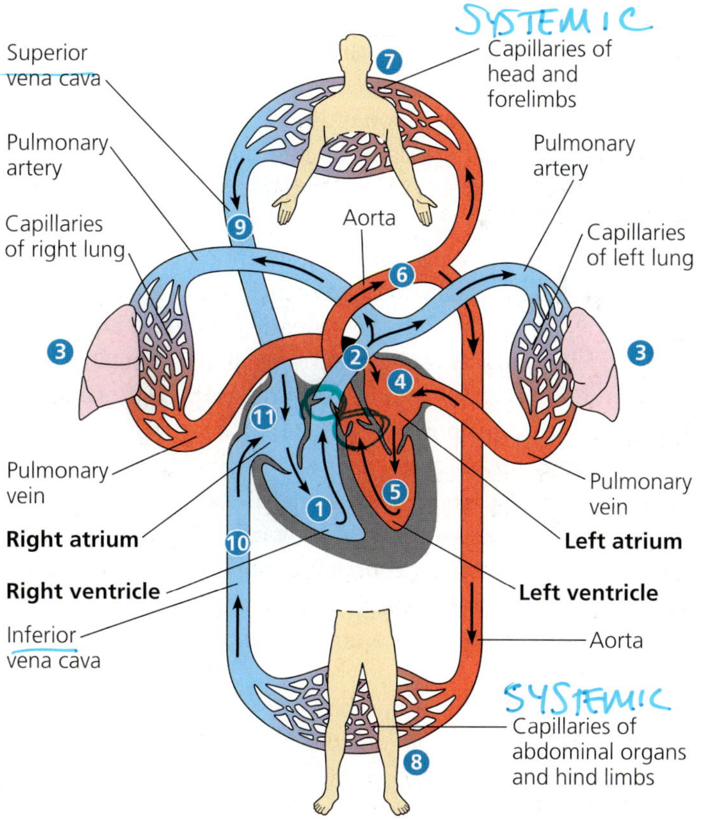

▲ **Figure 42.6 The mammalian cardiovascular system: an overview.** Note that the dual circuits operate simultaneously, not in the serial fashion that the numbering in the diagram suggests. The two ventricles pump almost in unison; while some blood is traveling in the pulmonary circuit, the rest of the blood is flowing in the systemic circuit.

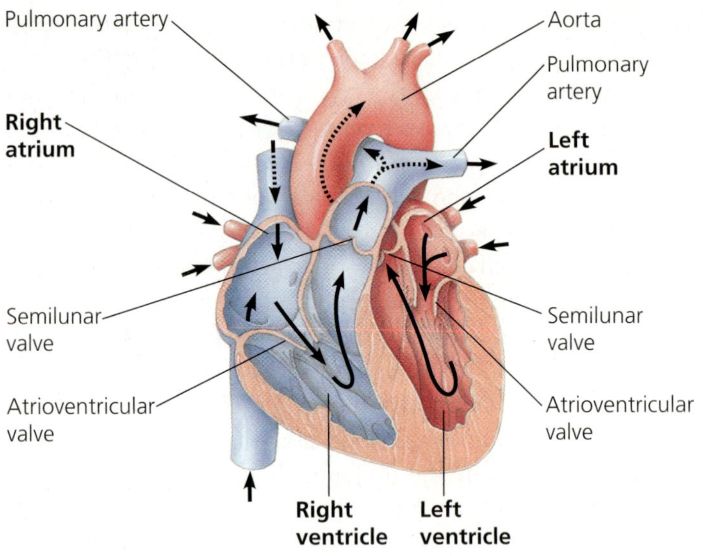

▲ **Figure 42.7 The mammalian heart: a closer look.** Notice the locations of the valves, which prevent backflow of blood within the heart. Also notice how the atria and left and right ventricles differ in the thickness of their muscular walls.

The Mammalian Heart: *A Closer Look*

Using the human heart as an example, let's now take a closer look at how the mammalian heart works **(Figure 42.7)**. Located behind the sternum (breastbone), the human heart is about the size of a clenched fist and consists mostly of cardiac muscle (see Figure 40.5). The two atria have relatively thin walls and serve as collection chambers for blood returning to the heart. Much of the blood entering the atria flows into the ventricles while all heart chambers are relaxed. Contraction of the atria transfers the remainder before the ventricles begin to contract. The ventricles have thicker walls and contract much more forcefully than the atria—especially the left ventricle, which pumps blood to all body organs through the systemic circuit. Although the left ventricle contracts with greater force than the right ventricle, it pumps the same volume of blood as the right ventricle during each contraction.

The heart contracts and relaxes in a rhythmic cycle. When it contracts, it pumps blood; when it relaxes, its chambers fill with blood. One complete sequence of pumping and filling is referred to as the **cardiac cycle**. The contraction phase of the cycle is called **systole**, and the relaxation phase is called **diastole (Figure 42.8)**. The volume of blood each ventricle pumps per minute is the **cardiac output**. Two factors determine cardiac output: the rate of contraction, or **heart rate** (number of beats per minute), and the **stroke volume**, the amount of blood pumped by a ventricle in a single contraction. The average stroke volume in humans is about 70 mL. Multiplying this stroke volume by a resting heart rate of 72 beats per minute yields a cardiac output of 5 L/min—about equal to the total volume of blood in the human body. During heavy exercise, cardiac output increases as much as fivefold.

Four valves in the heart prevent backflow and keep blood moving in the correct direction (see Figures 42.7 and 42.8). Made of flaps of connective tissue, the valves open when pushed from one side and close when pushed from the other. An **atrioventricular (AV) valve** lies between each atrium and ventricle. The AV valves are anchored by strong fibers that prevent them from turning inside out. Pressure generated by the powerful contraction of the ventricles closes the AV valves, keeping blood from flowing back into the atria. **Semilunar valves** are located at the two exits of the heart: where the aorta leaves the left ventricle and where the pulmonary artery leaves the right ventricle. These valves are pushed open by the pressure generated during contraction of the ventricles. When the ventricles relax, pressure built up in the aorta closes the semilunar valves and prevents significant backflow. You can follow these events either with a stethoscope or by pressing your ear tightly against the chest of a friend (or a friendly dog). The sound pattern is "lub-dup, lub-dup, lub-dup." The first heart sound ("lub") is created by the recoil of blood against the closed AV valves. The second sound ("dup") is produced by the recoil of blood against the closed semilunar valves.

If blood squirts backward through a defective valve, it may produce an abnormal sound called a **heart murmur**. Some

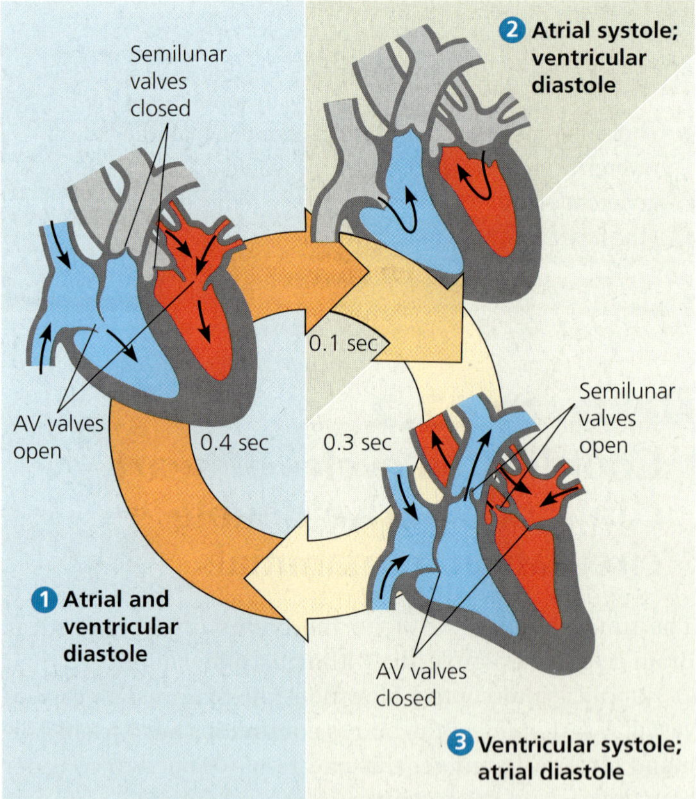

▲ **Figure 42.8 The cardiac cycle.** For an adult human at rest with a heart rate of about 72 beats per minute, one complete cardiac cycle takes about 0.8 second. **1** During a relaxation phase (atria and ventricles in diastole), blood returning from the large veins flows into the atria and ventricles through the AV valves. **2** A brief period of atrial systole then forces all blood remaining in the atria into the ventricles. **3** During the remainder of the cycle, ventricular systole pumps blood into the large arteries through the semilunar valves. Note that during all but 0.1 second of the cardiac cycle, the atria are relaxed and are filling with blood returning via the veins.

people are born with heart murmurs; in others, the valves may be damaged by infection (from rheumatic fever, for instance). When a valve defect is severe enough to endanger health, surgeons may implant a mechanical replacement valve. However, not all heart murmurs are caused by a defect, and most valve defects do not reduce the efficiency of blood flow enough to warrant surgery.

Maintaining the Heart's Rhythmic Beat

In vertebrates, the heartbeat originates in the heart itself. Some cardiac muscle cells are autorhythmic, meaning they contract and relax repeatedly without any signal from the nervous system. You can even see these rhythmic contractions in tissue that has been removed from the heart and placed in a dish in the laboratory! Because each of these cells has its own intrinsic contraction rhythm, how are their contractions coordinated in the intact heart? The answer lies in a group of autorhythmic cells located in the wall of the right atrium, near where the superior vena cava enters the heart. This cluster of cells is called the **sinoatrial (SA) node**, or *pacemaker*, and it sets the rate and timing at which all cardiac muscle cells contract. (In contrast to vertebrates, some arthropods have pacemakers located in the nervous system, outside the heart.)

The SA node generates electrical impulses much like those produced by nerve cells. Because cardiac muscle cells are electrically coupled through gap junctions (see Figure 6.32), impulses from the SA node spread rapidly within heart tissue. In addition, these impulses generate currents that are conducted to the skin via body fluids. The medical test called an **electrocardiogram** (**ECG** or, sometimes, **EKG**) uses electrodes placed on the skin to detect and record these currents. The resulting graph has a characteristic shape that represents the stages in the cardiac cycle **(Figure 42.9)**.

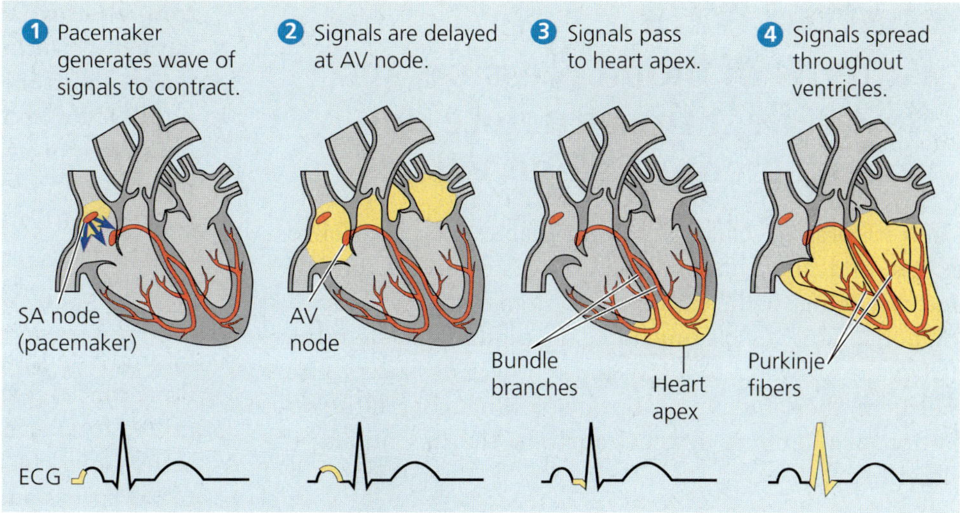

▲ **Figure 42.9 The control of heart rhythm.** The sequence of electrical events in the heart is shown at the top; the corresponding components of an electrocardiogram (ECG) are highlighted below in gold. In step 4, the portion of the ECG to the right of the gold "spike" represents electrical activity that reprimes the ventricles for the next round of contraction.

Impulses from the SA node first spread rapidly through the walls of the atria, causing both atria to contract in unison. During atrial contraction, the impulses originating at the SA node reach other autorhythmic cells that are located in the wall between the left and right atria. These cells form a relay point called the **atrioventricular (AV) node**. Here the impulses are delayed for about 0.1 second before spreading to the walls of the ventricles. This delay allows the atria to empty completely before the ventricles contract. Then, the signals from the AV node are conducted throughout the ventricular walls by specialized muscle fibers called bundle branches and Purkinje fibers.

Physiological cues alter heart tempo by regulating the SA node. Two sets of nerves, the sympathetic and parasympathetic nerves, are largely responsible for this regulation. These nerves function like the spurs and reins used in riding a horse: One set speeds up the pacemaker, and the other set slows it down. For example, when you stand up and start walking, the sympathetic nerves increase your heart rate, an adaptation that enables your circulatory system to provide the additional O_2 needed by the muscles that are powering your activity. If you then sit down and relax, the parasympathetic nerves decrease your heart rate, an adaptation that conserves energy. Hormones secreted into the blood also influence the pacemaker. For instance, epinephrine, the "fight-or-flight" hormone secreted by the adrenal glands, causes the heart rate to increase. A third type of input that affects the pacemaker is body temperature. An increase of only 1°C raises the heart rate by about 10 beats per minute. This is the reason your heart beats faster when you have a fever.

Having examined the operation of the circulatory pump, we turn in the next section to the forces and structures that influence blood flow in the vessels of each circuit.

CONCEPT CHECK 42.2

1. Explain why blood in the pulmonary veins has a higher O_2 concentration than blood in the venae cavae, which are also veins.
2. Why is it important that the AV node delay the electrical impulse moving from the SA node and the atria to the ventricles?
3. **WHAT IF?** After exercising regularly for several months, you find that your resting heart rate has decreased. Given that your body now requires fewer cardiac cycles in a given time, what other change in the function of your heart at rest would you expect to find? Explain.

For suggested answers, see Appendix A.

CONCEPT **42.3**

Patterns of blood pressure and flow reflect the structure and arrangement of blood vessels

The vertebrate circulatory system enables blood to deliver oxygen and nutrients and remove wastes throughout the body. In doing so, the circulatory system relies on a branching network of vessels much like the plumbing system that delivers fresh water to a city and removes its wastes. Furthermore, the same physical principles that govern the operation of plumbing systems apply to the functioning of blood vessels.

Blood Vessel Structure and Function

Blood vessels contain a central lumen (cavity) lined with an **endothelium**, a single layer of flattened epithelial cells. The smooth surface of the endothelium minimizes resistance to the flow of blood. Surrounding the endothelium are layers of tissue that differ among capillaries, arteries, and veins, reflecting the specialized functions of these vessels.

Capillaries are the smallest blood vessels, having a diameter only slightly greater than that of a red blood cell **(Figure 42.10)**. Capillaries also have very thin walls, which consist of just the endothelium and its basal lamina. This structural organization facilitates the exchange of substances between the blood in capillaries and the interstitial fluid.

The walls of arteries and veins have a more complex organization than those of capillaries. Both arteries and veins have two layers of tissue surrounding the endothelium: an outer layer of connective tissue containing elastic fibers, which allow the vessel to stretch and recoil, and a middle layer containing smooth muscle and more elastic fibers. However, arteries and veins differ in important ways. For a given blood vessel diameter, an artery has a wall about three times as thick as that of a vein (see Figure 42.10). The thicker walls of arteries are very strong, accommodating blood pumped at high pressure by the heart, and their elastic recoil helps maintain blood pressure when the heart relaxes between contractions. Signals from the nervous system and hormones circulating in the blood act on the smooth muscles in arteries, controlling blood flow to different parts of the body. The thinner-walled veins convey blood back to the heart at a lower velocity and pressure. Valves in the veins maintain a unidirectional flow of blood in these vessels (see Figure 42.10).

Blood Flow Velocity

To understand how blood vessel diameter influences blood flow, consider how water flows through a thick hose connected to a faucet. When the faucet is turned on, water flows at the same velocity everywhere in the hose. However, if a narrow nozzle is attached to the end of the hose, the water will exit the nozzle at a much greater velocity. Because water doesn't compress under pressure, the volume of water moving through the nozzle in a given time must be the same as the volume moving through the rest of the hose. The cross-sectional area of the nozzle is smaller than that of the hose, so the water speeds up in the nozzle.

▼ Figure 42.10 The structure of blood vessels.

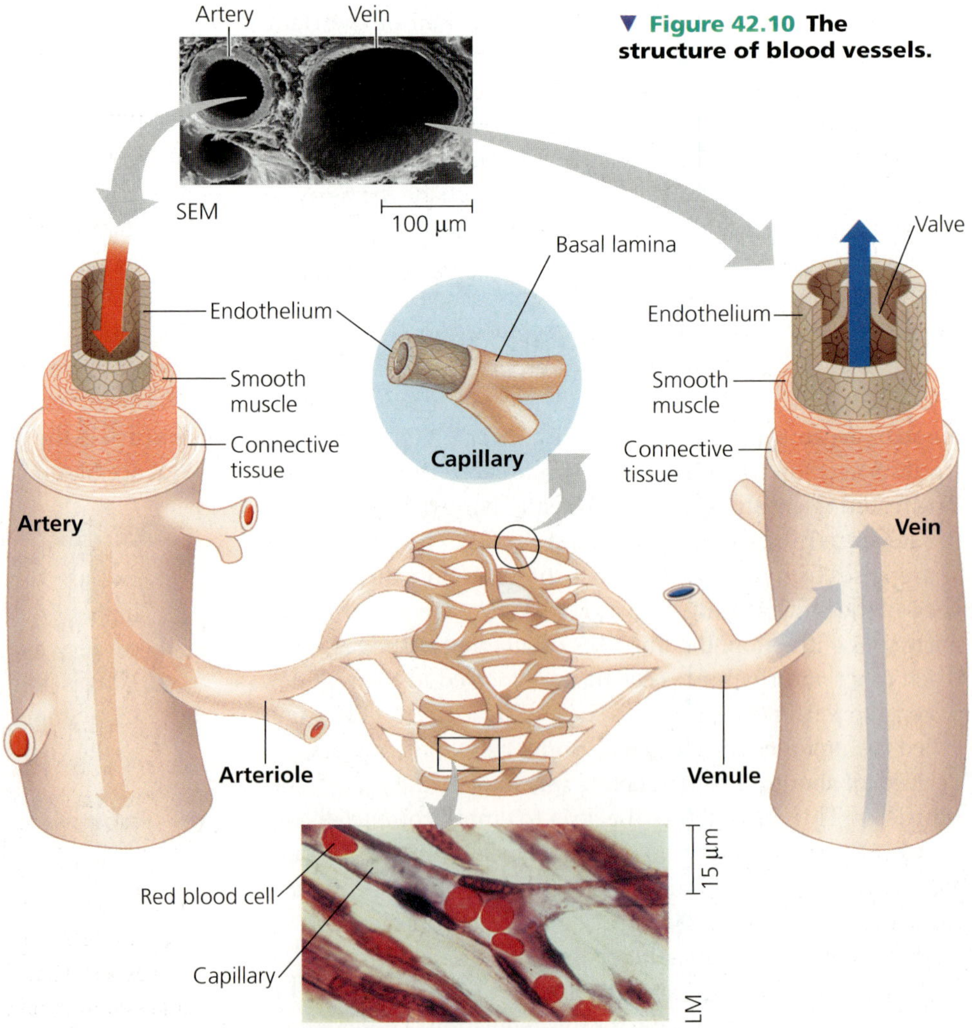

An analogous situation exists in the circulatory system, but blood *slows* as it moves from arteries to arterioles to capillaries. Why? The reason is that the number of capillaries is enormous. Each artery conveys blood to so many capillaries that the *total* cross-sectional area is much greater in capillary beds than in the arteries or any other part of the circulatory system **(Figure 42.11)**. The result is a dramatic decrease in velocity from the arteries to the capillaries: Blood travels 500 times slower in the capillaries (about 0.1 cm/sec) than in the aorta (about 48 cm/sec).

The reduced velocity of blood flow in capillaries is critical to the function of the circulatory system. Capillaries are the only vessels with walls thin enough to permit the transfer of substances between the blood and interstitial fluid. The slower flow of blood through these tiny vessels allows time for exchange to occur. After passing through the capillaries, the blood speeds up as it enters the venules and veins, which have smaller total cross-sectional areas (see Figure 42.11).

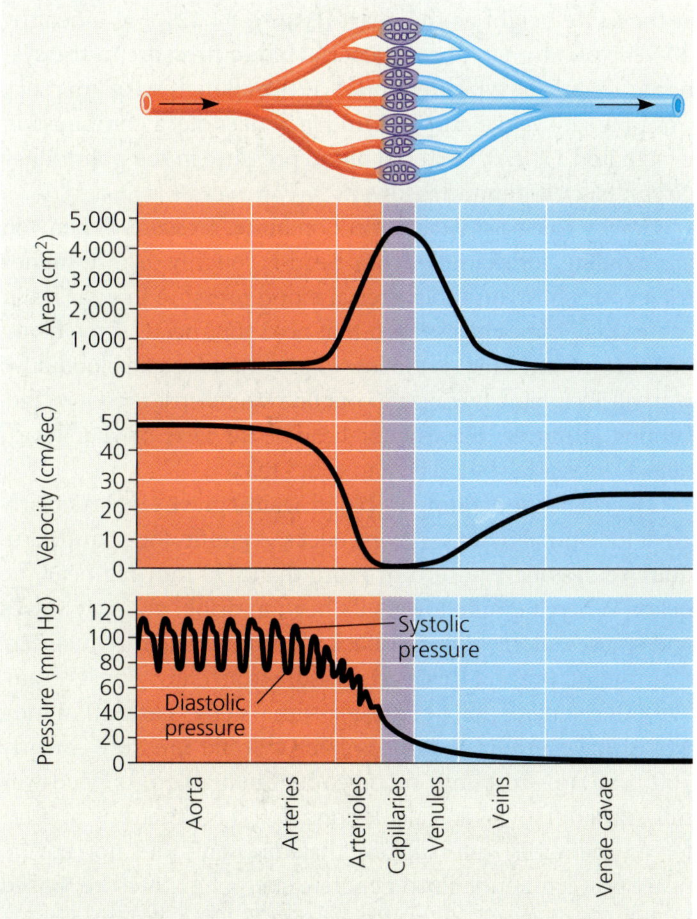

▲ **Figure 42.11 The interrelationship of cross-sectional area of blood vessels, blood flow velocity, and blood pressure.** Owing to an increase in total cross-sectional area, blood flow velocity decreases markedly in the arterioles and is lowest in the capillaries. Blood pressure, the main force driving blood from the heart to the capillaries, is highest in the aorta and other arteries.

Blood Pressure

Blood, like all fluids, flows from areas of higher pressure to areas of lower pressure. Contraction of a heart ventricle generates blood pressure, which exerts a force in all directions. The force directed lengthwise in an artery causes the blood to flow away from the heart, the site of highest pressure. The force exerted against the elastic wall of an artery stretches the wall, and the recoil of arterial walls plays a critical role in maintaining blood pressure, and hence blood flow, throughout the cardiac cycle. Once the blood enters the millions of tiny arterioles and capillaries, the narrow diameter of these vessels generates substantial resistance to flow. This resistance dissipates much of the pressure generated by the pumping heart by the time the blood enters the veins.

Changes in Blood Pressure During the Cardiac Cycle

Arterial blood pressure is highest when the heart contracts during ventricular systole. The pressure at this time is called **systolic pressure** (see Figure 42.11). The spikes in blood pressure caused by the powerful contractions of the ventricles stretch the arteries. By placing your fingers on your wrist, you can feel a **pulse**—the rhythmic bulging of the artery walls with each heartbeat. The surge of pressure is partly due to the narrow openings of arterioles impeding the exit of blood from the arteries. Thus, when the heart contracts, blood enters the arteries faster than it can leave, and the vessels stretch from the rise in pressure. During diastole, the elastic walls of the arteries snap back. As a consequence, there is a lower but still substantial blood pressure when the ventricles are relaxed (**diastolic pressure**). Before enough blood has flowed into the arterioles to completely relieve pressure in the arteries, the heart contracts again. Because the arteries remain pressurized throughout the cardiac cycle (see Figure 42.11), blood continuously flows into arterioles and capillaries.

Regulation of Blood Pressure

Blood pressure fluctuates over two different time scales. The first is the oscillation in arterial blood pressure during each cardiac cycle (see bottom graph in Figure 42.11). Blood pressure also fluctuates on a longer time scale in response to signals that change the state of smooth muscles in arteriole walls. For example, physical or emotional stress can trigger nervous and hormonal responses that cause smooth muscles in arteriole walls to contract, a process called **vasoconstriction**. When that happens, the arterioles narrow, thereby increasing blood pressure upstream in the arteries. When the smooth muscles relax, the arterioles undergo **vasodilation**, an increase in diameter that causes blood pressure in the arteries to fall.

Vasoconstriction and vasodilation are often coupled to changes in cardiac output that also affect blood pressure. This coordination of regulatory mechanisms maintains adequate blood flow as the body's demands on the circulatory system change. During heavy exercise, for example, the arterioles in working muscles dilate, causing a greater flow of oxygen-rich blood to the muscles. By itself, this increased flow to the muscles

▼ **Figure 42.12 Inquiry**

How do endothelial cells control vasoconstriction?

EXPERIMENT In 1988, Masashi Yanagisawa set out to identify the endothelial factor that triggers vasoconstriction in mammals. He isolated endothelial cells from blood vessels and grew them in liquid medium. Then he collected the liquid, which contained substances secreted by the cells. Next, he bathed a small piece of an artery in the liquid. The artery tissue contracted, indicating that the cells grown in culture had secreted a factor that causes vasoconstriction. Using biochemical procedures, Yanagisawa separated the substances in the fluid on the basis of size, charge, and other properties. He then tested each substance for its ability to cause arterial contraction. After several separation steps and many tests, he purified the vasoconstriction factor.

RESULTS The vasoconstriction factor, which Yanagisawa named **endothelin**, is a peptide that contains 21 amino acids. Two disulfide bridges between cysteines stabilize the peptide structure.

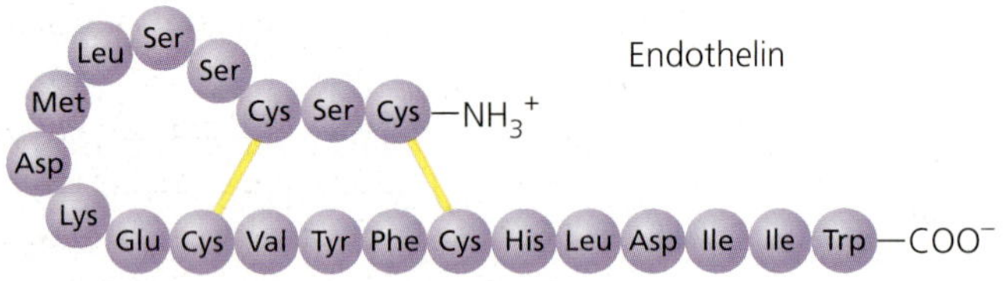

Using the amino acid sequence of the peptide as a guide, Yanagisawa identified the endothelin gene. The polypeptide encoded by the gene is much longer than endothelin, containing 203 amino acids. The amino acids in endothelin extend from position 53 (Cys) to position 73 (Trp) in the longer polypeptide:

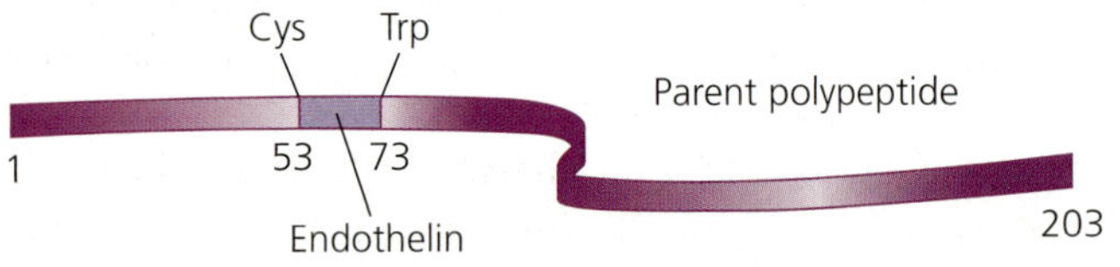

Yanagisawa also showed that treating endothelial cells with other substances already known to promote vasoconstriction, such as the hormone epinephrine, led to increased production of endothelin mRNA.

CONCLUSION Endothelial cells produce and translate endothelin mRNA in response to signals, such as hormones, that circulate in the blood. The resulting polypeptide is cleaved to form active endothelin, the substance that triggers vasoconstriction. Yanagisawa and colleagues subsequently demonstrated that endothelial cells also make the enzyme that catalyzes this cleavage.

SOURCE M. Yanagisawa et al., A novel potent vasoconstrictor peptide produced by vascular endothelial cells, *Nature* 332:411–415 (1988).

WHAT IF? Given what you know about epithelial tissue organization (see Figure 40.5) and the function of endothelin, what would you predict about the location of endothelin secretion with regard to endothelial cell surfaces?

would cause a drop in blood pressure (and therefore blood flow) in the body as a whole. However, cardiac output increases at the same time, maintaining blood pressure and supporting the necessary increase in blood flow.

Recent experiments have identified the molecules that serve as signals for vasodilation and vasoconstriction. Three scientists in the United States—Robert Furchgott, Louis Ignarro, and Ferid Murad—demonstrated that the gas nitric oxide (NO) serves as a major inducer of vasodilation in the cardiovascular system. Their research was honored with a Nobel Prize in 1998. Independent studies by Masashi Yanagisawa, then a graduate student at the University of Tsukuba in Japan, identified a peptide, **endothelin**, as a potent inducer of vasoconstriction **(Figure 42.12)**. As discussed in the interview with Dr. Yanagisawa on pages 850–851, his findings led to fundamental discoveries about signals that regulate not only blood vessel diameter but also the embryonic development of the digestive system.

Blood Pressure and Gravity

Blood pressure is generally measured for an artery in the arm at the same height as the heart **(Figure 42.13)**. For a healthy 20-year-old human at rest, arterial blood pressure in the systemic circuit is typically about 120 millimeters of mercury (mm Hg) at systole and 70 mm Hg at diastole, a combination designated 120/70. (Arterial blood pressure in the pulmonary circuit is six to ten times lower.)

Gravity has a significant effect on blood pressure. When you are standing, for example, your head is roughly 0.35 m higher than your chest, and the arterial blood pressure in your brain is about 27 mm Hg less than that near your heart. If the blood pressure in your brain is too low to provide adequate blood flow, you will likely faint. By causing your body to collapse to the ground, fainting effectively places your head at the level of your heart, quickly increasing blood flow to your brain.

The challenge of pumping blood against gravity is particularly great for animals with very long necks. A giraffe, for example, requires a systolic pressure of more than 250 mm Hg near the heart. When a giraffe lowers its head to drink, one-way valves and sinuses, along with feedback mechanisms that reduce cardiac output, prevent this high pressure from damaging its brain. We can calculate that a dinosaur with a neck nearly 10 m long would have required even greater systolic pressure—nearly 760 mm Hg—to pump blood to its brain when its head was fully raised. However, calculations based on anatomy and inferred metabolic rate suggest that dinosaurs did not have a heart powerful enough to generate such high pressure. Based on this evidence as well as studies of neck bone structure, some biologists have concluded that the long-necked dinosaurs fed close to the ground rather than on high foliage.

Gravity is also a consideration for blood flow in veins, especially those in the legs. Although blood pressure in veins is relatively low, several mechanisms assist the return of venous blood to the heart. First, rhythmic contractions of smooth muscles in the walls of venules and veins aid in the movement of the blood. Second, and more important, the contraction of skeletal muscles during exercise squeezes blood through the veins toward the heart **(Figure 42.14)**. This is why periodically walking up and down the aisle during a long airplane flight helps prevent potentially dangerous blood clots from forming in veins. Third, the change in pressure within the thoracic (chest) cavity during inhalation causes the venae cavae and other large veins near the heart to expand and fill with blood.

In rare instances, runners and other athletes can suffer heart failure if they stop vigorous exercise abruptly. When the leg muscles suddenly cease contracting and relaxing, less blood returns to the heart, which continues to beat rapidly. If the heart is weak or damaged, this inadequate blood flow may cause the heart to malfunction. To reduce the risk of stressing the heart excessively, athletes are encouraged to follow hard exercise with moderate activity, such as walking, to "cool down" until their heart rate approaches its resting level.

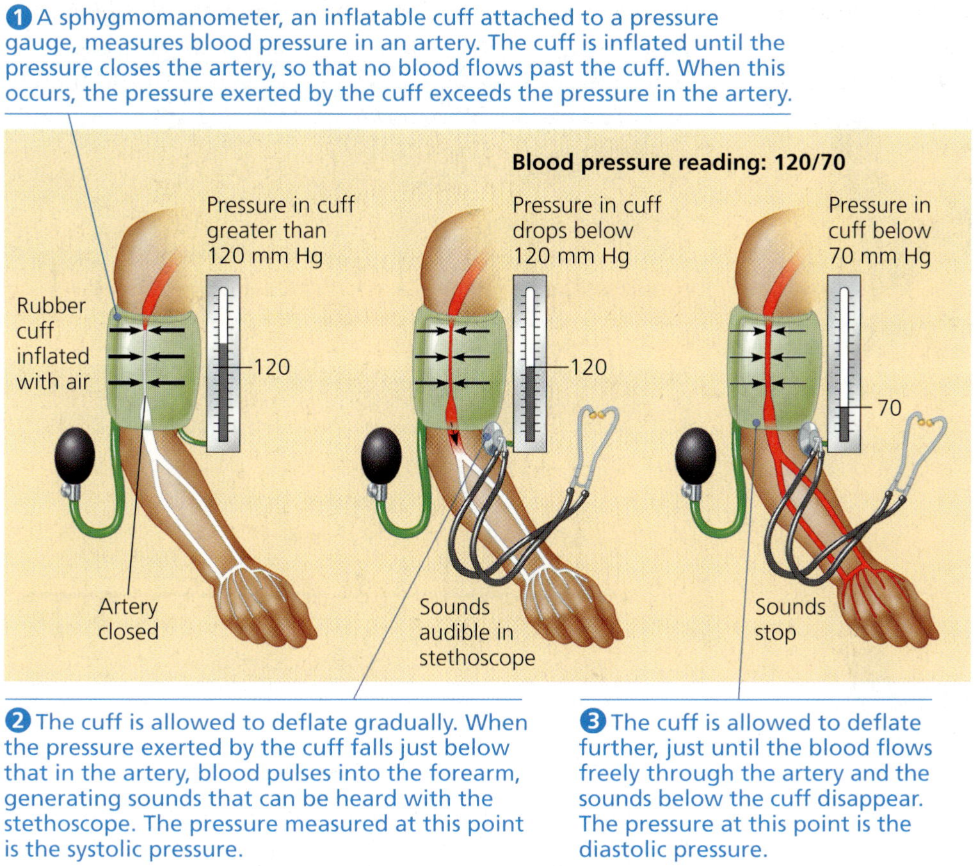

▲ **Figure 42.13 Measurement of blood pressure.** Blood pressure is recorded as two numbers separated by a slash. The first number is the systolic pressure; the second is the diastolic pressure.

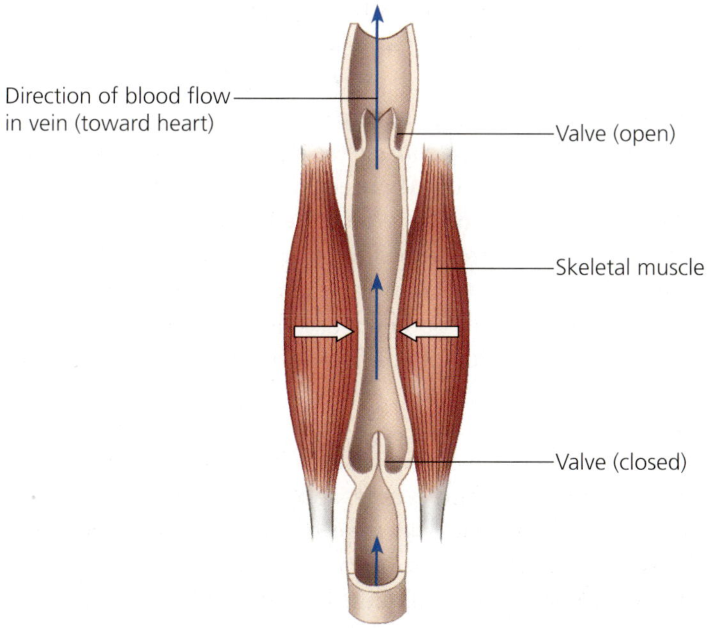

▲ **Figure 42.14 Blood flow in veins.** Skeletal muscle contraction squeezes and constricts veins. Flaps of tissue within the veins act as one-way valves that keep blood moving only toward the heart. If you sit or stand too long, the lack of muscular activity may cause your feet to swell as blood pools in your veins.

Capillary Function

At any given time, only about 5–10% of the body's capillaries have blood flowing through them. However, each tissue has many capillaries, so every part of the body is supplied with blood at all times. Capillaries in the brain, heart, kidneys, and liver are usually filled to capacity, but at many other sites the blood supply varies over time as blood is diverted from one destination to another. For example, blood flow to the skin is regulated to help control body temperature, and blood supply to the digestive tract increases after a meal. During strenuous exercise, blood is diverted from the digestive tract and supplied more generously to skeletal muscles and skin. This is one reason why exercising heavily immediately after eating a big meal may cause indigestion.

Given that capillaries lack smooth muscles, how is blood flow in capillary beds altered? There are two mechanisms, both of which rely on signals that regulate flow into capillaries. One mechanism involves contraction of the smooth muscle in the wall of an arteriole, which reduces the vessel's diameter and decreases blood flow to the adjoining capillary beds. When the smooth muscle relaxes, the arterioles dilate, allowing blood to enter the capillaries. The other mechanism for altering flow,

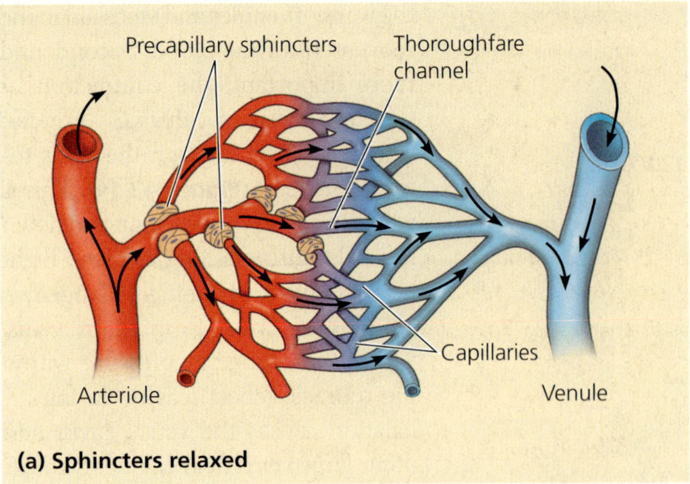

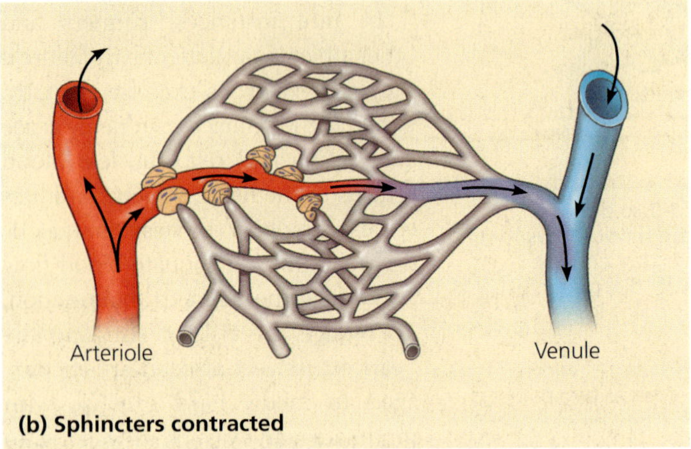

▲ **Figure 42.15 Blood flow in capillary beds.** Precapillary sphincters regulate the passage of blood into capillary beds. Some blood flows directly from arterioles to venules through capillaries called thoroughfare channels, which are always open.

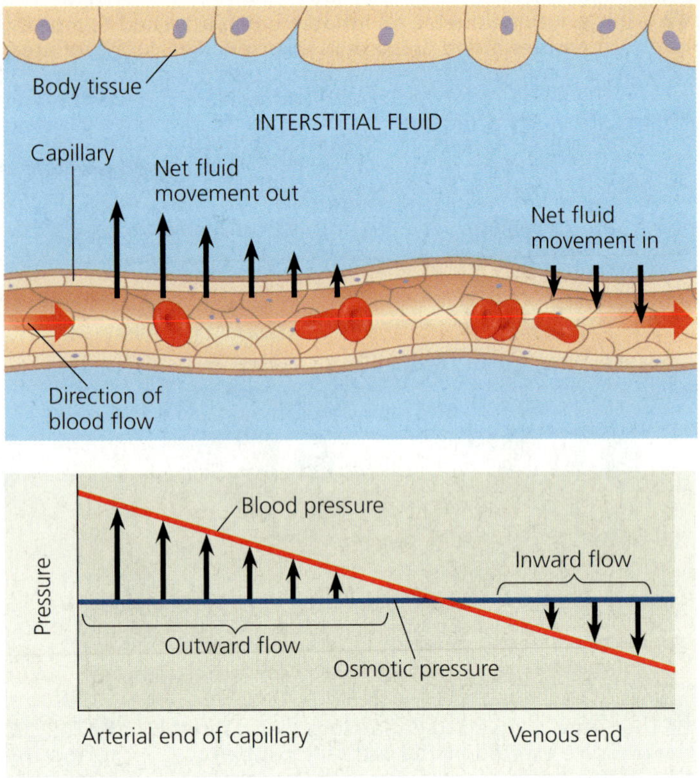

▲ **Figure 42.16 Fluid exchange between capillaries and the interstitial fluid.** This diagram shows a hypothetical capillary in which osmotic pressure is constant along its length. At the arterial end, where blood pressure exceeds osmotic pressure, fluid flows out of the capillary into the interstitial fluid. At the venous end, the blood pressure is less than osmotic pressure, and fluid flows from the interstitial fluid into the capillary. In many capillaries, blood pressure may be higher or lower than osmotic pressure throughout the entire length of the capillary.

shown in **Figure 42.15**, involves the action of *precapillary sphincters*, rings of smooth muscle located at the entrance to capillary beds. The signals that regulate blood flow include nerve impulses, hormones traveling throughout the bloodstream, and chemicals produced locally. For example, the chemical histamine released by cells at a wound site causes smooth muscle relaxation, dilating blood vessels and increasing blood flow. The dilated vessels also provide disease-fighting white blood cells greater access to invading microorganisms.

As you have read, the critical exchange of substances between the blood and interstitial fluid takes place across the thin endothelial walls of the capillaries. Some substances are carried across the endothelium in vesicles that form on one side by endocytosis and release their contents on the opposite side by exocytosis. Small molecules, such as O_2 and CO_2, simply diffuse across the endothelial cells or through the openings within and between adjoining cells. These openings also provide the route for transport of small solutes such as sugars, salts, and urea, as well as for bulk flow of fluid into tissues driven by blood pressure within the capillary.

While blood pressure tends to drive fluid out of the capillaries, the presence of blood proteins tends to pull fluid back into the capillaries. Many blood proteins (and all blood cells) are too large to pass readily through the endothelium, and they remain in the capillaries. The proteins, especially albumin, create an osmotic pressure difference between the capillary interior and the interstitial fluid. In places where the blood pressure is greater than the osmotic pressure difference, there is a net loss of fluid from the capillaries. In contrast, where the osmotic pressure difference exceeds the blood pressure, there is a net movement of fluid from the tissues into the capillaries **(Figure 42.16)**.

Fluid Return by the Lymphatic System

Throughout the body, only about 85% of the fluid that leaves the capillaries because of blood pressure reenters them as a result of osmotic pressure. Each day, this imbalance results in a loss of about 4 L of fluid from capillaries to the surrounding tissues. There is also some leakage of blood proteins, even though the capillary wall is not very permeable to large molecules. The lost fluid and proteins return to the blood via the **lymphatic system**, which includes a network of tiny vessels intermingled among capillaries of the cardiovascular system. After entering the lymphatic system by diffusion, the fluid is called **lymph**; its composition is about the same as that of interstitial fluid. The lymphatic system drains into large veins of the circulatory system at the base of the neck (see Figure 43.7). As you read in Chapter 41, this joining of the lymphatic and circulatory systems functions in the transfer of lipids from the small intestine to the blood.

The movement of lymph from peripheral tissues to the heart relies on much the same mechanisms that assist blood flow in veins. Lymph vessels, like veins, have valves that prevent the backflow of fluid. Rhythmic contractions of the vessel walls help draw fluid into the small lymphatic vessels. In addition, skeletal muscle contractions play a role in moving lymph.

Disorders that interfere with the lymphatic system highlight its role in maintaining proper fluid distribution in the body. Disruptions in the movement of lymph often cause edema, swelling resulting from the excessive accumulation of fluid in tissues. Severe blockage of lymph flow, as occurs when certain parasitic worms lodge in lymph vessels, results in extremely swollen limbs or other body parts, a condition known as elephantiasis.

Along a lymph vessel are organs called **lymph nodes**. By filtering the lymph and by housing cells that attack viruses and bacteria, lymph nodes play an important role in the body's defense. Inside each lymph node is a honeycomb of connective tissue with spaces filled by white blood cells. When the body is fighting an infection, these cells multiply rapidly, and the lymph nodes become swollen and tender (which is why your doctor may check for swollen lymph nodes in your neck, armpits, or groin when you feel sick). Because lymph nodes have filtering and surveillance functions, doctors may examine the lymph nodes of cancer patients to detect the spread of diseased cells.

In recent years, evidence has appeared suggesting that the lymphatic system also has a role in harmful immune responses, such as those responsible for asthma. Because of these and other findings, the lymphatic system, largely ignored until the 1990s, has become a very active and promising area of biomedical research.

CONCEPT CHECK 42.3

1. What is the primary cause of the low velocity of blood flow through capillaries?
2. What short-term changes in cardiovascular function might best enable skeletal muscles to help an animal escape from a dangerous situation?
3. **WHAT IF?** If you had additional hearts distributed throughout your body, what would be one likely advantage and one likely disadvantage?

For suggested answers, see Appendix A.

CONCEPT 42.4

Blood components function in exchange, transport, and defense

As we discussed earlier, the fluid transported by an open circulatory system is continuous with the fluid that surrounds all of the body cells and therefore has the same composition. In contrast, the fluid in a closed circulatory system can be much more highly specialized, as is the case for the blood of vertebrates.

Blood Composition and Function

Vertebrate blood is a connective tissue consisting of cells suspended in a liquid matrix called **plasma**. Dissolved in the plasma are ions and proteins that, together with the blood cells, function in osmotic regulation, transport, and defense. Separating the components of blood using a centrifuge reveals that cellular elements (cells and cell fragments) occupy about 45% of the volume of blood (**Figure 42.17**, on the next page). The remainder is plasma.

Plasma

Among the many solutes in plasma are inorganic salts in the form of dissolved ions, sometimes referred to as blood electrolytes (see Figure 42.17). Although plasma is about 90% water, the dissolved salts are an essential component of the blood. Some of these ions buffer the blood, which in humans normally has a pH of 7.4. Salts are also important in maintaining the osmotic balance of the blood. In addition, the concentration of ions in plasma directly affects the composition of the interstitial fluid, where many of these ions have a vital role in muscle and nerve activity. To serve all of these functions, plasma electrolytes must be kept within narrow concentration ranges, a homeostatic function we will explore in Chapter 44.

Plasma proteins act as buffers against pH changes, help maintain the osmotic balance between blood and interstitial fluid, and contribute to the blood's viscosity (thickness). Particular plasma proteins have additional functions. The immunoglobulins, or antibodies, help combat viruses and other foreign agents that invade the body (see Chapter 43). Others are escorts for lipids, which are insoluble in water and can travel in blood only when bound to proteins. A third group of plasma proteins are clotting factors that help plug leaks when blood vessels are injured. (The term *serum* refers to blood plasma from which these clotting factors have been removed.)

Plasma also contains a wide variety of other substances in transit from one part of the body to another, including nutrients, metabolic wastes, respiratory gases, and hormones. Plasma has a much higher protein concentration than interstitial fluid, although the two fluids are otherwise similar. (Capillary walls, remember, are not very permeable to proteins.)

Plasma 55%	
Constituent	**Major functions**
Water	Solvent for carrying other substances
Ions (blood electrolytes)	
Sodium Potassium Calcium Magnesium Chloride Bicarbonate	Osmotic balance, pH buffering, and regulation of membrane permeability
Plasma proteins	
Albumin	Osmotic balance pH buffering
Fibrinogen	Clotting
Immunoglobulins (antibodies)	Defense
Substances transported by blood	
Nutrients (such as glucose, fatty acids, vitamins) Waste products of metabolism Respiratory gases (O_2 and CO_2) Hormones	

Cellular elements 45%		
Cell type	**Number** per µL (mm^3) of blood	**Functions**
Erythrocytes (red blood cells)	5–6 million	Transport oxygen and help transport carbon dioxide
Leukocytes (white blood cells)	5,000–10,000	Defense and immunity
Platelets	250,000–400,000	Blood clotting

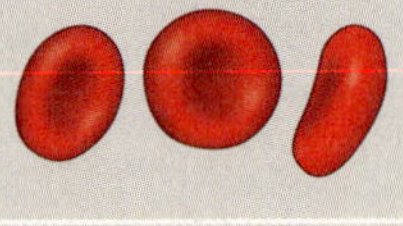

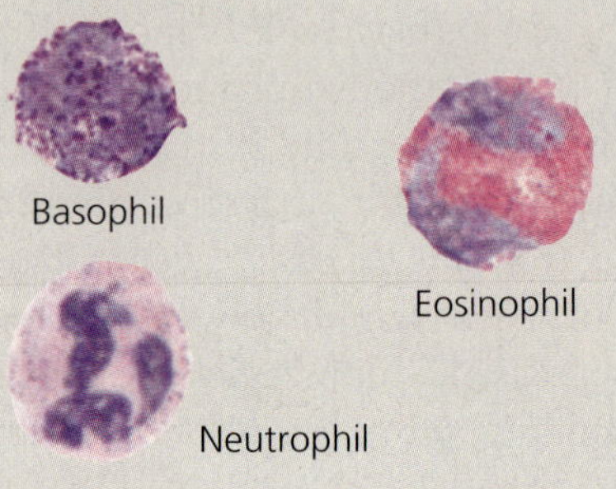

▲ **Figure 42.17 The composition of mammalian blood.**

Cellular Elements

Suspended in blood plasma are two classes of cells: red blood cells, which transport O_2, and white blood cells, which function in defense (see Figure 42.17). Blood also contains **platelets**, fragments of cells that are involved in the clotting process.

Erythrocytes Red blood cells, or **erythrocytes**, are by far the most numerous blood cells. Each microliter (µL, or mm^3) of human blood contains 5–6 million red cells, and there are about 25 trillion of these cells in the body's 5 L of blood. Their main function is O_2 transport, and their structure is closely related to this function. Human erythrocytes are small disks (7–8 µm in diameter) that are biconcave—thinner in the center than at the edges. This shape increases surface area, enhancing the rate of diffusion of O_2 across their plasma membranes. Mature mammalian erythrocytes lack nuclei. This unusual characteristic leaves more space in these tiny cells for **hemoglobin**, the iron-containing protein that transports O_2 (see Figure 5.21). Erythrocytes also lack mitochondria and generate their ATP exclusively by anaerobic metabolism. Oxygen transport would be less efficient if erythrocytes were aerobic and consumed some of the O_2 they carry.

Despite its small size, an erythrocyte contains about 250 million molecules of hemoglobin. Because each molecule of hemoglobin binds up to four molecules of O_2, one erythrocyte can transport about a billion O_2 molecules. As erythrocytes pass through the capillary beds of lungs, gills, or other respiratory organs, O_2 diffuses into the erythrocytes and binds to hemoglobin. In the systemic capillaries, O_2 dissociates from hemoglobin and diffuses into body cells.

Leukocytes The blood contains five major types of white blood cells, or **leukocytes**. Their function is to fight infections. Some are phagocytic, engulfing and digesting microorganisms as well as debris from the body's own dead cells. As we will see in Chapter 43, other leukocytes, called lymphocytes, develop into specialized B cells and T cells that mount immune responses against foreign substances. Normally, 1 µL of human blood contains about 5,000–10,000 leukocytes; their numbers increase temporarily whenever the body is fighting an infection. Unlike erythrocytes, leukocytes are also found outside the circulatory system, patrolling both interstitial fluid and the lymphatic system.

Platelets Platelets are pinched-off cytoplasmic fragments of specialized bone marrow cells. They are about 2–3 µm in diameter and have no nuclei. Platelets serve both structural and molecular functions in blood clotting.

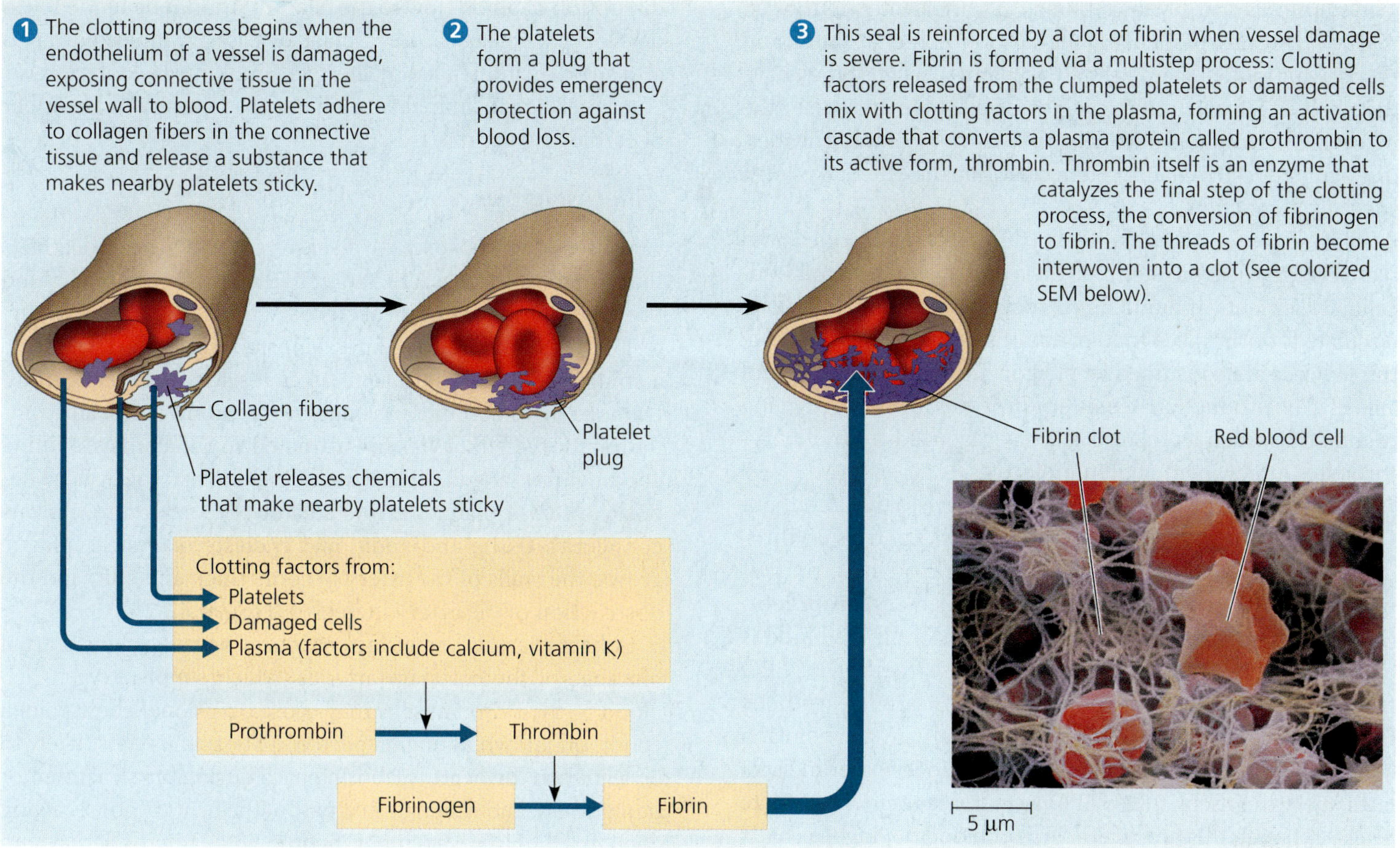

▲ **Figure 42.18 Blood clotting.**

Blood Clotting

The occasional cut or scrape is not life-threatening because blood components seal the broken blood vessels. A break in a blood vessel wall exposes proteins that attract platelets and initiate coagulation, the conversion of liquid components of blood to a solid clot. The coagulant, or sealant, circulates in an inactive form called fibrinogen. Clotting involves the conversion of fibrinogen to its active form, **fibrin**, which aggregates into threads that form the framework of the clot. The formation of fibrin is the last step in a series of reactions triggered by the release of clotting factors from platelets **(Figure 42.18)**. A genetic mutation that affects any step of the clotting process causes hemophilia, a disease characterized by excessive bleeding and bruising from even minor cuts and bumps.

Anticlotting factors in the blood normally prevent spontaneous clotting in the absence of injury. Sometimes, however, clots form within a blood vessel, blocking the flow of blood. Such a clot is called a **thrombus**. We will explore how a thrombus forms and the danger that it poses later in this chapter.

Stem Cells and the Replacement of Cellular Elements

Erythrocytes, leukocytes, and platelets all develop from a common source: multipotent **stem cells** that are dedicated to replenishing the body's blood cell populations **(Figure 42.19)**.

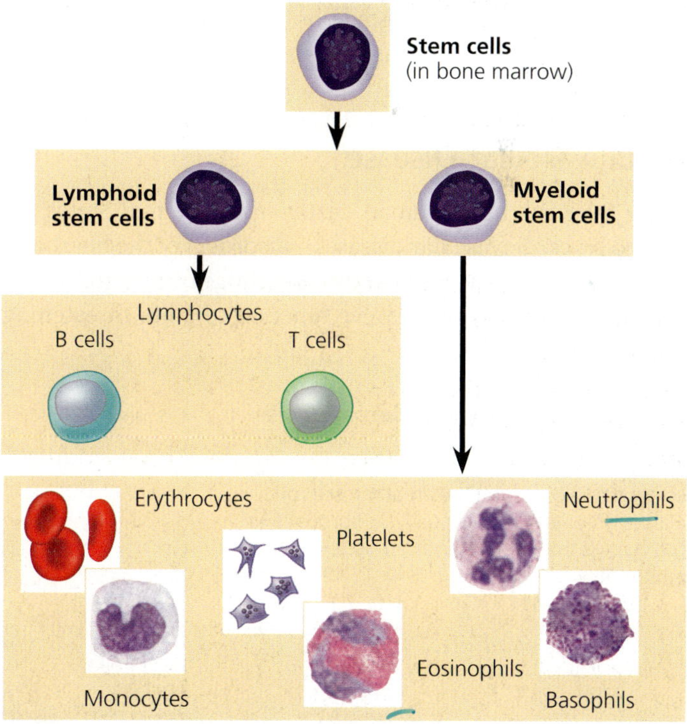

▲ **Figure 42.19 Differentiation of blood cells.** Some of the multipotent stem cells differentiate into lymphoid stem cells, which then develop into B cells and T cells, two types of lymphocytes that function in the immune response (see Chapter 43). All other blood cells differentiate from myeloid stem cells.

The stem cells that produce blood cells are located in the red marrow of bones, particularly the ribs, vertebrae, sternum, and pelvis. Multipotent stem cells are so named because they have the ability to form multiple types of cells—in this case, the myeloid and lymphoid cell lineages. When any stem cell divides, one daughter cell remains a stem cell while the other takes on a specialized function.

Throughout a person's life, erythrocytes, leukocytes, and platelets formed from stem cell divisions replace the worn-out cellular elements of blood. Erythrocytes, for example, usually circulate for only three to four months before being replaced; the old cells are consumed by phagocytic cells in the liver and spleen. The production of new erythrocytes involves recycling of materials, such as the use of iron scavenged from old erythrocytes in new hemoglobin molecules.

A negative-feedback mechanism, sensitive to the amount of O_2 reaching the body's tissues via the blood, controls erythrocyte production. If the tissues do not receive enough O_2, the kidneys synthesize and secrete a hormone called **erythropoietin (EPO)** that stimulates erythrocyte production. If the blood is delivering more O_2 than the tissues can use, the level of EPO falls and erythrocyte production slows. Physicians use synthetic EPO to treat people with health problems such as anemia, a condition of lower-than-normal hemoglobin levels. Some athletes inject themselves with EPO to increase their erythrocyte levels, although this practice, a form of blood doping, has been banned by the International Olympic Committee and other sports organizations. In recent years, a number of well-known runners and cyclists have tested positive for EPO-related drugs and have forfeited both their records and their right to participate in future competitions.

Cardiovascular Disease

More than half of all human deaths in the United States are caused by cardiovascular diseases—disorders of the heart and blood vessels. Cardiovascular diseases range from a minor disturbance of vein or heart valve function to a life-threatening disruption of blood flow to the heart or brain. The tendency to develop particular cardiovascular diseases is inherited but is also strongly influenced by lifestyle. Smoking, lack of exercise, and a diet rich in animal fat each increase the risk of a number of cardiovascular diseases.

Atherosclerosis

One reason cardiovascular diseases cause so many deaths is that they often aren't detected until they disrupt critical blood flow. An example is **atherosclerosis**, the hardening of the arteries by accumulation of fatty deposits. Healthy arteries have a smooth inner lining that reduces resistance to blood flow. Damage or infection can roughen the lining and lead to inflammation. Leukocytes are attracted to the damaged lining and begin to take up lipids, including cholesterol. A fatty deposit, called a plaque, grows steadily, incorporating fibrous connective tissue and additional cholesterol. As the plaque grows, the walls of the artery become thick and stiff, and the obstruction of the artery increases **(Figure 42.20)**.

Atherosclerosis sometimes produces warning signs. Partial blockage of the coronary arteries, which supply oxygen-rich blood to the heart muscle, may cause occasional chest pain, a condition known as angina pectoris. The pain is most likely to be felt when the heart is laboring hard during physical or emotional stress, and it signals that part of the heart is not receiving enough O_2. However, many people with atherosclerosis are completely unaware of their condition until catastrophe strikes.

Heart Attacks and Stroke

If unrecognized and untreated, the result of atherosclerosis is often a heart attack or a stroke. A **heart attack**, also called a *myocardial infarction*, is the damage or death of cardiac muscle tissue resulting from blockage of one or more coronary arteries. Because the coronary arteries are small in diameter, they are especially vulnerable to obstruction. Such blockage can destroy cardiac muscle quickly because the constantly beating heart muscle cannot survive long without O_2. If the

▶ **Figure 42.20 Atherosclerosis.** These light micrographs contrast **(a)** a cross section of a normal (healthy) artery with **(b)** that of an artery partially blocked by an atherosclerotic plaque. Plaques consist mostly of fibrous connective tissue and smooth muscle cells infiltrated with lipids.

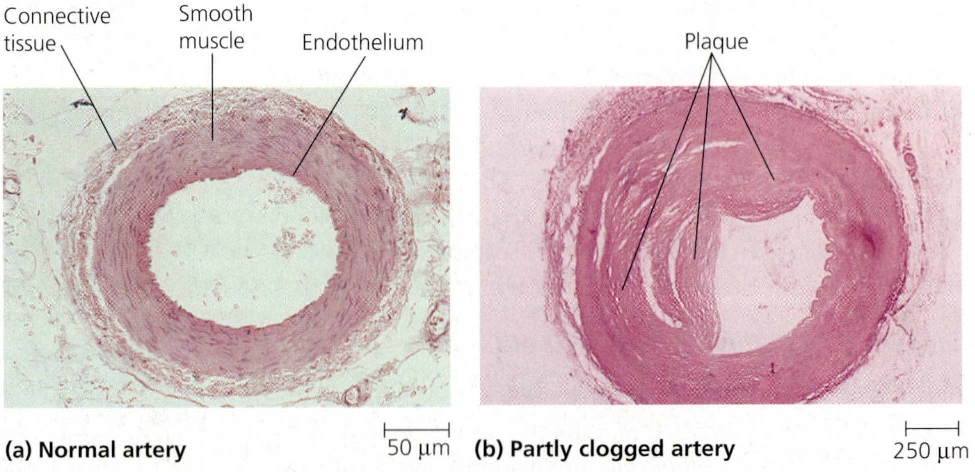

(a) Normal artery **(b) Partly clogged artery**

heart stops beating, the victim may nevertheless survive if a heartbeat is restored by cardiopulmonary resuscitation (CPR) or some other emergency procedure within a few minutes of the attack. A **stroke** is the death of nervous tissue in the brain due to a lack of O_2. Strokes usually result from rupture or blockage of arteries in the head. The effects of a stroke and the individual's chance of survival depend on the extent and location of the damaged brain tissue.

Heart attacks and strokes frequently result from a thrombus that clogs an artery. A key step in thrombus formation is the rupture of plaques by an inflammatory response, analogous to the body's response to a cut infected by bacteria (see Figure 43.8). A fragment released by plaque rupture is swept along in the bloodstream, sometimes lodging in an artery. The thrombus may originate in a coronary artery or an artery in the brain, or it may develop elsewhere in the circulatory system and reach the heart or brain via the bloodstream.

Treatment and Diagnosis of Cardiovascular Disease

One major contributor to atherosclerosis is cholesterol. Cholesterol travels in the blood plasma mainly in the form of particles consisting of thousands of cholesterol molecules and other lipids bound to a protein. One type of particle—**low-density lipoprotein (LDL)**, often called "bad cholesterol"—is associated with the deposition of cholesterol in arterial plaques. Another type—**high-density lipoprotein (HDL)**, or "good cholesterol"—appears to reduce the deposition of cholesterol. Exercise decreases the LDL/HDL ratio. Smoking and consumption of certain processed vegetable oils called *trans fats* (see Chapter 5) have the opposite effect. Many individuals at high risk for cardiovascular disease are treated with drugs called statins, which lower LDL levels and thereby reduce the frequency of heart attacks.

The recent recognition that inflammation has a central role in atherosclerosis and thrombus formation is changing the diagnosis and treatment of cardiovascular disease. For example, aspirin, which blocks the inflammatory response, has been found to help prevent the recurrence of heart attacks and stroke. Researchers have also focused attention on C-reactive protein (CRP), which is produced by the liver and found in the blood during episodes of acute inflammation. Like a high level of LDL cholesterol, the presence of significant amounts of CRP in blood is a useful predictor of cardiovascular disease.

Hypertension (high blood pressure) is yet another contributor to heart attack and stroke as well as other health problems. According to one hypothesis, chronic high blood pressure damages the endothelium that lines the arteries, promoting plaque formation. The usual definition of hypertension in adults is a systolic pressure above 140 mm Hg or a diastolic pressure above 90 mm Hg. Fortunately, hypertension is simple to diagnose and can usually be controlled by dietary changes, exercise, medication, or a combination of these approaches.

CONCEPT CHECK 42.4

1. Explain why a physician might order a white cell count for a patient with symptoms of an infection.
2. Clots in arteries can cause heart attacks and strokes. Why, then, does it make sense to treat hemophiliacs by introducing clotting factors into their blood?
3. **WHAT IF?** Nitroglycerin (the key ingredient in dynamite) is sometimes prescribed for heart disease patients. Within the body, the nitroglycerin is converted to nitric oxide. Why would you expect nitroglycerin to relieve chest pain in these patients?

For suggested answers, see Appendix A.

CONCEPT 42.5
Gas exchange occurs across specialized respiratory surfaces

In the remainder of this chapter, we will focus on the process of **gas exchange**. Although this process is often called respiratory exchange or respiration, it should not be confused with the energy transformations of cellular respiration. Gas exchange is the uptake of molecular O_2 from the environment and the discharge of CO_2 to the environment.

Partial Pressure Gradients in Gas Exchange

To understand the driving forces for gas exchange, we must calculate **partial pressure**, which is simply the pressure exerted by a particular gas in a mixture of gases. To do so, we need to know the pressure that the mixture exerts and the fraction of the mixture represented by a particular gas. Let's consider O_2 as an example. At sea level, the atmosphere exerts a downward force equal to that of a column of mercury (Hg) 760 mm high. Therefore, atmospheric pressure at sea level is 760 mm Hg. Since the atmosphere is 21% O_2 by volume, the partial pressure of O_2 is 0.21×760, or about 160 mm Hg. This value is called the *partial pressure* of O_2 (abbreviated P_{O_2}) because it is the portion of atmospheric pressure contributed by O_2. The partial pressure of CO_2, P_{CO_2}, is much less, only 0.29 mm Hg at sea level.

Calculating partial pressure for a gas dissolved in liquid, such as water, is also straightforward. When water is exposed to air, the amount of a gas that dissolves in the water is proportional to its partial pressure in the air and its solubility in water. Equilibrium is reached when gas molecules enter and leave the solution at the same rate. At equilibrium, the partial pressure of the gas in the solution equals the partial pressure of the gas in the air. Therefore, the P_{O_2} in water exposed to air at sea level must be 160 mm Hg, the same as that in the atmosphere. However, the *concentrations* of O_2 in the air and water differ substantially because O_2 is much less soluble in water than in air.

Once we have calculated partial pressures, we can readily predict the net result of diffusion at gas exchange surfaces: A gas always diffuses from a region of higher partial pressure to a region of lower partial pressure.

Respiratory Media

The conditions for gas exchange vary considerably, depending on whether the respiratory medium—the source of O_2—is air or water. As already noted, O_2 is plentiful in air, making up about 21% of Earth's atmosphere by volume. Compared to water, air is much less dense and less viscous, so it is easier to move and to force through small passageways. As a result, breathing air is relatively easy and need not be particularly efficient. Humans, for example, extract only about 25% of the O_2 in the air we inhale.

Gas exchange with water as the respiratory medium is much more demanding. The amount of O_2 dissolved in a given volume of water varies but is always less than in an equivalent volume of air: Water in many marine and freshwater habitats contains only 4–8 mL of dissolved O_2 per liter, a concentration roughly 40 times less than in air. The warmer and saltier the water is, the less dissolved O_2 it can hold. Water's lower O_2 content, greater density, and greater viscosity mean that aquatic animals such as fishes and lobsters must expend considerable energy to carry out gas exchange. In the context of these challenges, adaptations have evolved that in general enable aquatic animals to be very efficient in gas exchange. Many of these adaptations involve the organization of the surfaces dedicated to exchange.

Respiratory Surfaces

Specialization for gas exchange is apparent in the structure of the respiratory surface, the part of an animal's body where gas exchange occurs. Like all living cells, the cells that carry out gas exchange have a plasma membrane that must be in contact with an aqueous solution. Respiratory surfaces are therefore always moist.

The movement of O_2 and CO_2 across moist respiratory surfaces takes place entirely by diffusion. The rate of diffusion is proportional to the surface area across which it occurs and inversely proportional to the square of the distance through which molecules must move. In other words, gas exchange is fast when the area for diffusion is large and the path for diffusion is short. As a result, respiratory surfaces tend to be large and thin.

The structure of a respiratory surface depends mainly on the size of the animal and whether it lives in water or on land, but it is also influenced by metabolic demands for gas exchange. Thus, an endotherm generally has a larger area of respiratory surface than a similar-sized ectotherm.

In some relatively simple animals, such as sponges, cnidarians, and flatworms, every cell in the body is close enough to the external environment that gases can diffuse quickly between all

(a) Marine worm. Many polychaetes (marine worms of the phylum Annelida) have a pair of flattened appendages called parapodia on each body segment. The parapodia serve as gills and also function in crawling and swimming.

(b) Crayfish. Crayfish and other crustaceans have long, feathery gills covered by the exoskeleton. Specialized body appendages drive water over the gill surfaces.

(c) Sea star. The gills of a sea star are simple tubular projections of the skin. The hollow core of each gill is an extension of the coelom (body cavity). Gas exchange occurs by diffusion across the gill surfaces, and fluid in the coelom circulates in and out of the gills, aiding gas transport. The surfaces of a sea star's tube feet also function in gas exchange.

▲ **Figure 42.21 Diversity in the structure of gills, external body surfaces that function in gas exchange.**

cells and the environment. In many animals, however, the bulk of the body's cells lack immediate access to the environment. The respiratory surface in these animals is a thin, moist epithelium that constitutes a respiratory organ.

The skin serves as a respiratory organ in some animals, including earthworms and some amphibians. Just below the skin, a dense network of capillaries facilitates the exchange of gases between the circulatory system and the environment. Because the respiratory surface must remain moist, earthworms and many other skin-breathers can survive for extended periods only in damp places.

The general body surface of most animals lacks sufficient area to exchange gases for the whole organism. The solution is a respiratory organ that is extensively folded or branched, thereby enlarging the available surface area for gas exchange. Gills, tracheae, and lungs are three such organs.

Gills in Aquatic Animals

Gills are outfoldings of the body surface that are suspended in the water. As illustrated in **Figure 42.21**, on the facing page, the distribution of gills over the body can vary considerably. Regardless of their distribution, gills often have a total surface area much greater than that of the rest of the body.

Movement of the respiratory medium over the respiratory surface, a process called **ventilation**, maintains the partial pressure gradients of O_2 and CO_2 across the gill that are necessary for gas exchange. To promote ventilation, most gill-bearing animals either move their gills through the water or move water over their gills. For example, crayfish and lobsters have paddle-like appendages that drive a current of water over the gills, whereas mussels and clams move water with cilia. Octopuses and squids ventilate their gills by taking in and ejecting water, with the side benefit of locomotion by jet propulsion. Fishes use the motion of swimming or coordinated movements of the mouth and gill covers to ventilate their gills. In both cases, a current of water enters the mouth, passes through slits in the pharynx, flows over the gills, and then exits the body **(Figure 42.22)**.

The arrangement of capillaries in a fish gill allows for **countercurrent exchange**, the exchange of a substance or heat between two fluids flowing in opposite directions. In a fish gill, this process maximizes gas exchange efficiency. Because blood flows in the direction opposite to that of water passing over the gills, at each point in its travel blood is less saturated with O_2 than the water it meets (see Figure 42.22). As blood enters a gill capillary, it encounters water that is completing its passage through the gill. Depleted of much of its dissolved O_2, this water nevertheless has a higher P_{O_2} than the incoming blood, and O_2 transfer takes place. As the blood continues its passage, its P_{O_2} steadily increases, but so does that of the water it encounters, since each successive position in the blood's travel corresponds to an earlier position in the water's passage over the gills. Thus, a partial pressure gradient favoring the diffusion of O_2 from water to blood exists along the entire length of the capillary.

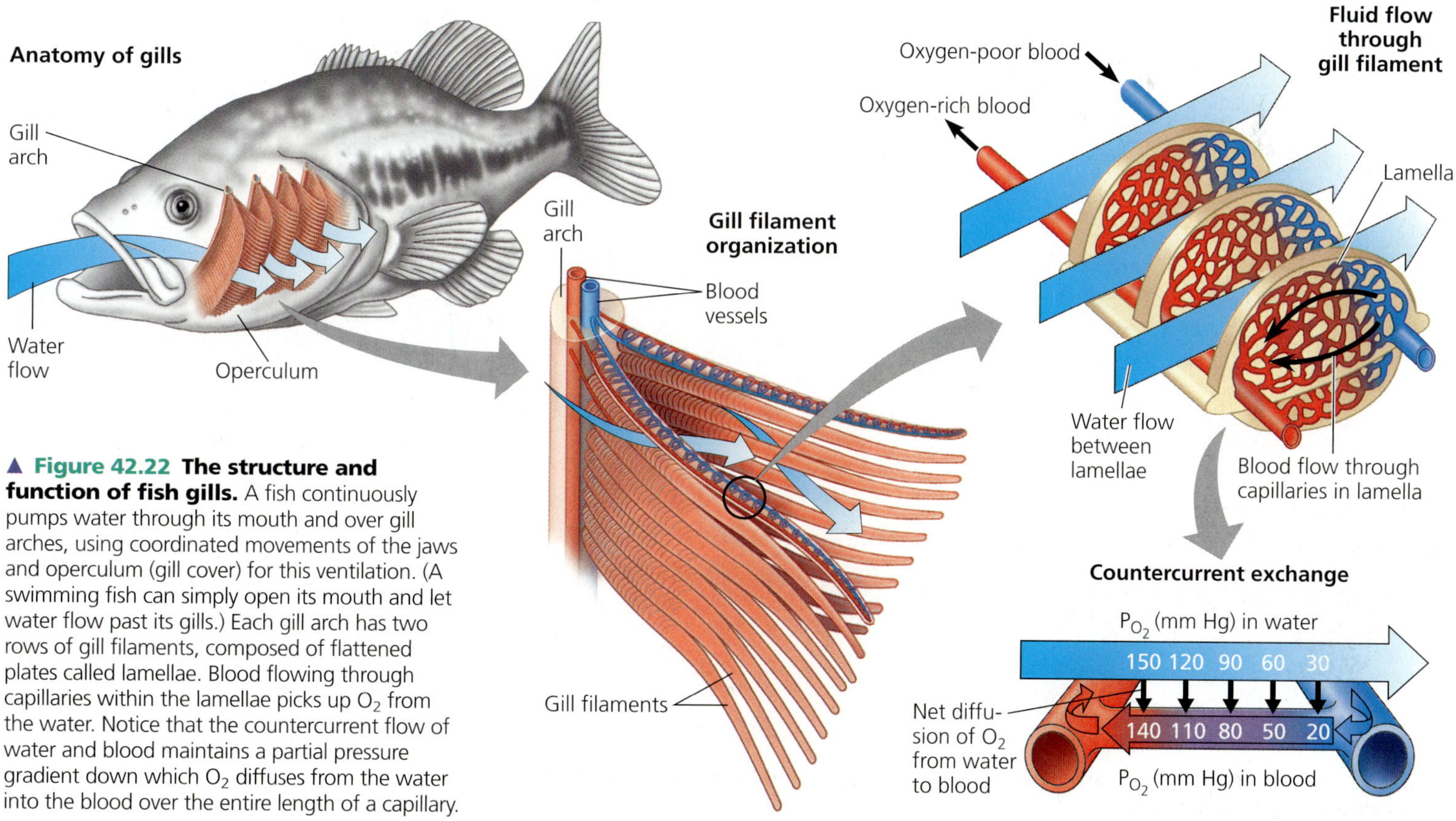

▲ **Figure 42.22 The structure and function of fish gills.** A fish continuously pumps water through its mouth and over gill arches, using coordinated movements of the jaws and operculum (gill cover) for this ventilation. (A swimming fish can simply open its mouth and let water flow past its gills.) Each gill arch has two rows of gill filaments, composed of flattened plates called lamellae. Blood flowing through capillaries within the lamellae picks up O_2 from the water. Notice that the countercurrent flow of water and blood maintains a partial pressure gradient down which O_2 diffuses from the water into the blood over the entire length of a capillary.

Countercurrent exchange mechanisms are remarkably efficient. In the fish gill, more than 80% of the O_2 dissolved in the water is removed as it passes over the respiratory surface. Countercurrent exchange also contributes to temperature regulation (see Chapter 40) and to the functioning of the mammalian kidney, as we will see in Chapter 44.

Gills are generally unsuitable for an animal living on land. An expansive surface of wet membrane exposed directly to air currents in the environment would lose too much water by evaporation. Furthermore, the gills would collapse as their fine filaments, no longer supported by water, would cling together. In most terrestrial animals, respiratory surfaces are enclosed within the body, exposed to the atmosphere through narrow tubes.

Tracheal Systems in Insects

Although the most familiar respiratory structure among terrestrial animals is the lung, the most common is actually the **tracheal system** of insects. Made up of air tubes that branch throughout the body, this system is one variation on the theme of an internal respiratory surface. The largest tubes, called tracheae, open to the outside **(Figure 42.23a)**. The finest branches extend close to the surface of nearly every cell, where gas is exchanged by diffusion across the moist epithelium that lines the tips of the tracheal branches **(Figure 42.23b)**. Because the tracheal system brings air within a very short distance of virtually all body cells in an insect, it can transport O_2 and CO_2 without the participation of the animal's open circulatory system.

For small insects, diffusion through the tracheae brings in enough O_2 and removes enough CO_2 to support cellular respiration. Larger insects meet their higher energy demands by ventilating their tracheal systems with rhythmic body movements that compress and expand the air tubes like bellows. For example, an insect in flight has a very high metabolic rate, consuming 10 to 200 times more O_2 than it does at rest. In many flying insects, alternating contraction and relaxation of the flight muscles pumps air rapidly through the tracheal system. The flight muscle cells are packed with mitochondria that support the high metabolic rate, and the tracheal tubes supply each of these ATP-generating organelles with ample O_2 **(Figure 42.23c)**. Thus, adaptations of tracheal systems are directly related to bioenergetics.

Lungs

Unlike tracheal systems, which branch throughout the insect body, **lungs** are localized respiratory organs. Representing an infolding of the body surface, they are typically subdivided into numerous pockets. Because the respiratory surface of a lung is not in direct contact with all other parts of the body, the gap must be bridged by the circulatory system, which transports gases between the lungs and the rest of the body. Lungs have evolved in organisms with open circulatory systems, such as spiders and land snails, as well as in vertebrates.

Among vertebrates that lack gills, the use of lungs for gas exchange varies. Amphibian lungs, when present, are relatively small and lack an extensive surface for exchange. Amphibians

▼ **Figure 42.23 Tracheal systems.**

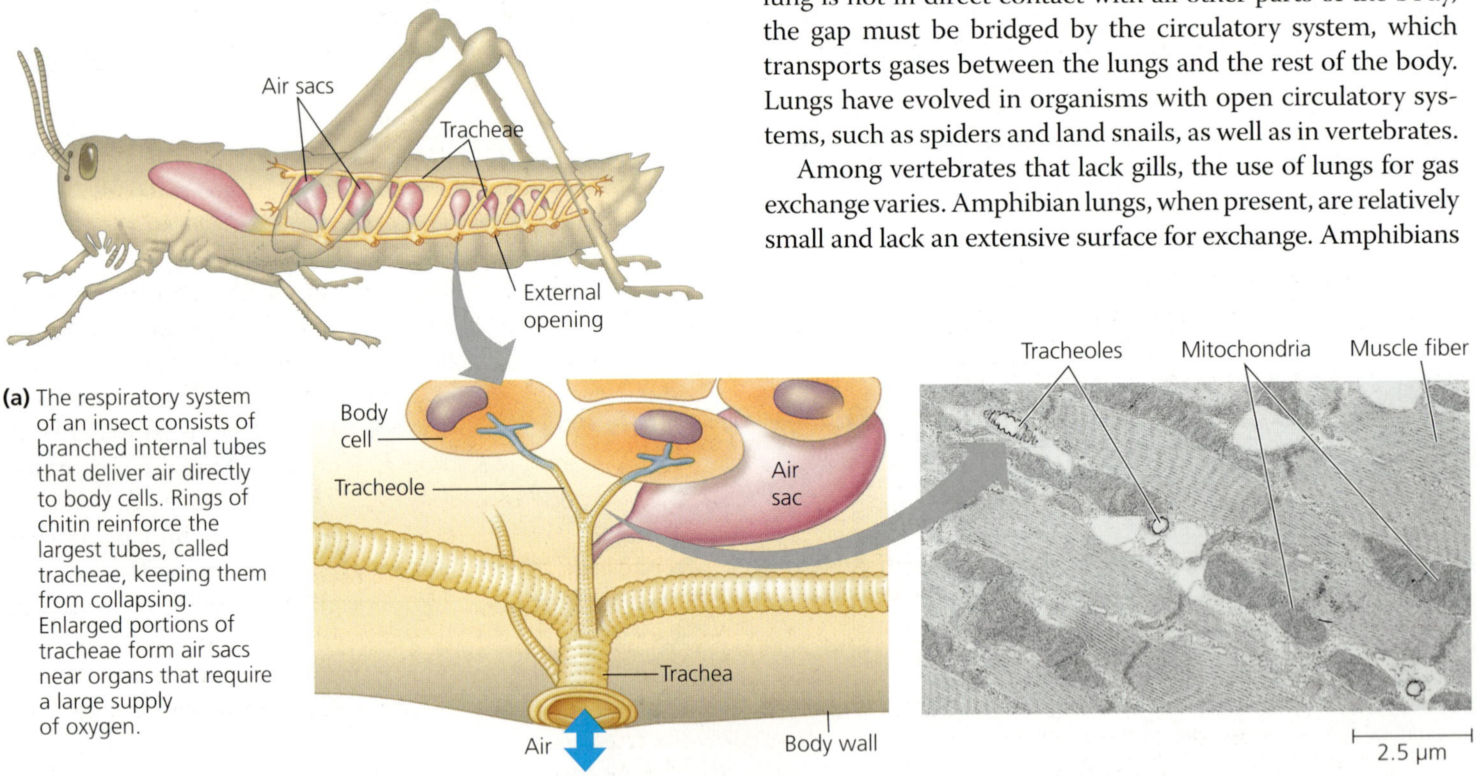

(a) The respiratory system of an insect consists of branched internal tubes that deliver air directly to body cells. Rings of chitin reinforce the largest tubes, called tracheae, keeping them from collapsing. Enlarged portions of tracheae form air sacs near organs that require a large supply of oxygen.

(b) Air enters the tracheae through openings on the insect's body surface and passes into smaller tubes called tracheoles. The tracheoles are closed, and their terminal ends contain fluid (blue-gray). When the animal is active and using more O_2, most of the fluid is withdrawn into the body. This increases the surface area of air-filled tracheoles in contact with cells.

(c) The micrograph above shows cross sections of tracheoles in a tiny piece of insect flight muscle (TEM). Each of the numerous mitochondria in the muscle cells lies within about 5 μm of a tracheole.

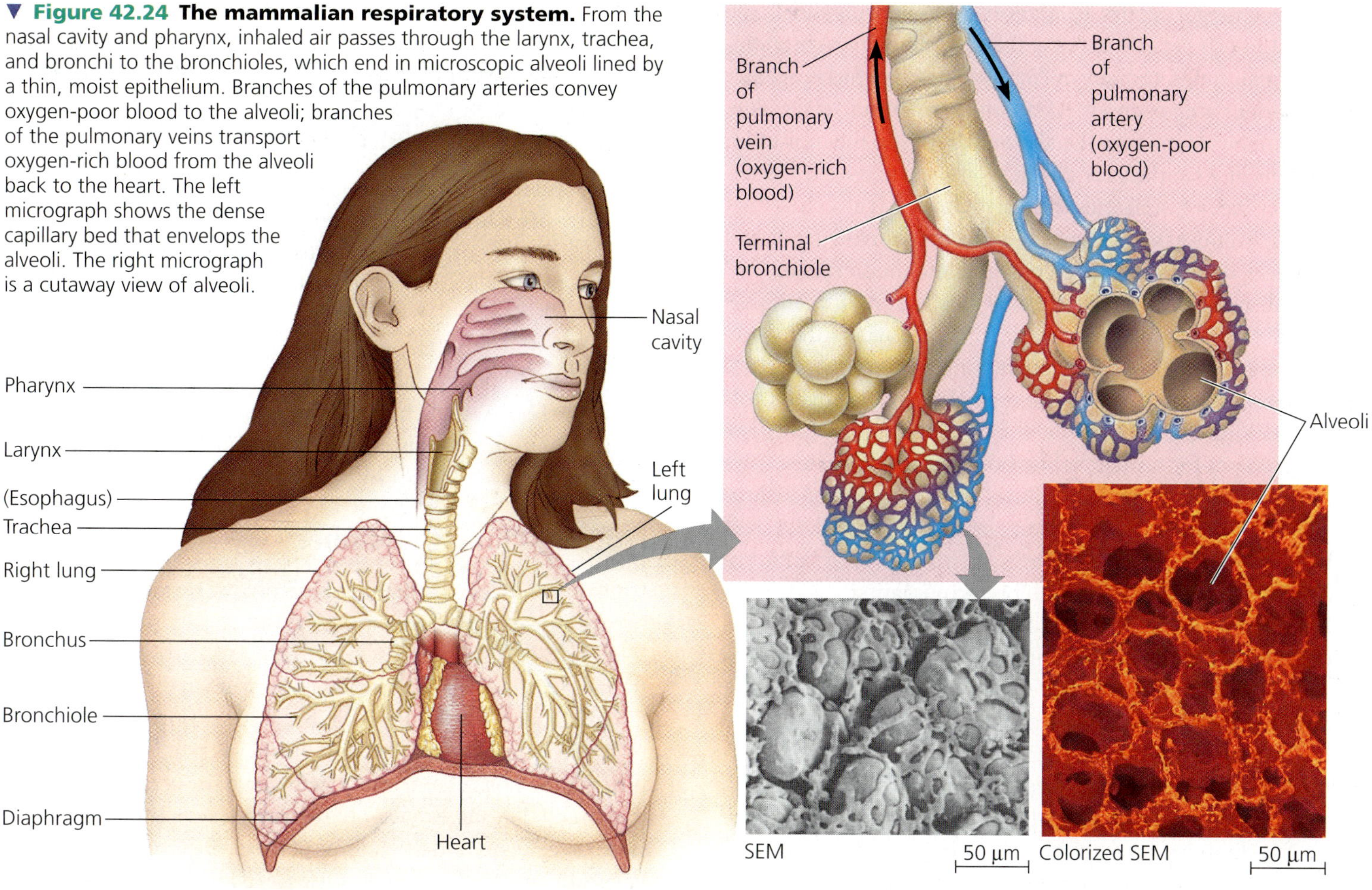

▼ **Figure 42.24 The mammalian respiratory system.** From the nasal cavity and pharynx, inhaled air passes through the larynx, trachea, and bronchi to the bronchioles, which end in microscopic alveoli lined by a thin, moist epithelium. Branches of the pulmonary arteries convey oxygen-poor blood to the alveoli; branches of the pulmonary veins transport oxygen-rich blood from the alveoli back to the heart. The left micrograph shows the dense capillary bed that envelops the alveoli. The right micrograph is a cutaway view of alveoli.

instead rely heavily on diffusion across other body surfaces, such as the skin, to carry out gas exchange. In contrast, most reptiles (including all birds) and all mammals depend entirely on lungs for gas exchange. Turtles are an exception; they supplement lung breathing with gas exchange across moist epithelial surfaces continuous with their mouth or anus. Lungs and air breathing have evolved in a few aquatic vertebrates (including lungfishes) as adaptations to living in oxygen-poor water or to spending part of their time exposed to air (for instance, when the water level of a pond recedes).

In general, the size and complexity of lungs are correlated with an animal's metabolic rate (and hence its rate of gas exchange). For example, the lungs of endotherms have a greater area of exchange surface than those of similar-sized ectotherms.

Mammalian Respiratory Systems: A Closer Look

In mammals, a system of branching ducts conveys air to the lungs, which are located in the thoracic cavity **(Figure 42.24)**. Air enters through the nostrils and is then filtered by hairs, warmed, humidified, and sampled for odors as it flows through a maze of spaces in the nasal cavity. The nasal cavity leads to the pharynx, an intersection where the paths for air and food cross. When food is swallowed, the **larynx** (the upper part of the respiratory tract) moves upward and tips the epiglottis over the glottis (the opening of the **trachea**, or windpipe). This allows food to go down the esophagus to the stomach (see Figure 41.11). The rest of the time, the glottis is open, enabling breathing.

From the larynx, air passes into the trachea. Cartilage reinforcing the walls of both the larynx and the trachea keeps this part of the airway open. In most mammals, the larynx also functions as a voice box. Exhaled air rushes by the **vocal cords**, a pair of elastic bands of muscle in the larynx. Sounds are produced when muscles in the voice box are tensed, stretching the cords so they vibrate. High-pitched sounds result from tightly stretched cords vibrating rapidly; low-pitched sounds come from less tense cords vibrating slowly.

From the trachea fork two **bronchi** (singular, *bronchus*), one leading to each lung. Within the lung, the bronchi branch repeatedly into finer and finer tubes called **bronchioles**. The entire system of air ducts has the appearance of an inverted tree, the trunk being the trachea. The epithelium lining the major branches of this respiratory tree is covered by cilia and a thin film of mucus. The mucus traps dust, pollen, and other particulate contaminants, and the beating cilia move the mucus upward to the pharynx, where it can be swallowed into the esophagus. This process, sometimes referred to as the "mucus escalator," plays a critical role in cleansing the respiratory system.

Gas exchange occurs in **alveoli** (singular, *alveolus*; see Figure 42.24), air sacs clustered at the tips of the tiniest bronchioles. Human lungs contain millions of alveoli, which together have a surface area of about 100 m^2, fifty times that of the skin. Oxygen in the air entering the alveoli dissolves in the moist film lining their inner surfaces and rapidly diffuses across the epithelium into a web of capillaries that surrounds each alveolus. Carbon dioxide diffuses in the opposite direction, from the capillaries across the epithelium of the alveolus and into the air space.

Alveoli are so small that specialized secretions are required to relieve the surface tension in the fluid that coats their surface. These secretions, called **surfactants**, contain a mixture of phospholipids and proteins. In their absence, the alveoli collapse, blocking the entry of air. A lack of lung surfactants is a major problem for human babies born very prematurely. Surfactants typically appear in the lungs after 33 weeks of embryonic development. Among infants born before week 28, half suffer serious respiratory distress. Artificial surfactants are now used routinely to treat such preterm infants.

Lacking cilia or significant air currents to remove particles from their surface, alveoli are highly susceptible to contamination. White blood cells patrol alveoli, engulfing foreign particles. However, if too much particulate matter reaches the alveoli, the defenses can break down, leading to diseases that reduce the efficiency of gas exchange. Coal miners and other workers exposed to large amounts of dust from rock are susceptible to silicosis, a disabling, irreversible, and sometimes fatal lung disease. Cigarette smoke also brings damaging particulates into the alveoli.

Having surveyed the route that air follows when we breathe, we will turn next to the process of breathing itself.

CONCEPT CHECK 42.5

1. Why is the position of lung tissues *within* the body an advantage for terrestrial animals?
2. After a heavy rain, earthworms come to the surface. How would you explain this behavior in terms of an earthworm's requirements for gas exchange?
3. **WHAT IF?** The walls of alveoli contain elastic fibers that allow the alveoli to expand and contract with each breath. If alveoli lost their elasticity, how might gas exchange be affected? Explain.

For suggested answers, see Appendix A.

CONCEPT **42.6**

Breathing ventilates the lungs

Like fishes, terrestrial vertebrates rely on ventilation to maintain high O_2 and low CO_2 concentrations at the gas exchange surface. The process that ventilates lungs is **breathing**, the alternating inhalation and exhalation of air. A variety of mechanisms for moving air in and out of lungs have evolved, as we will see by considering breathing in amphibians, mammals, and birds.

How an Amphibian Breathes

An amphibian such as a frog ventilates its lungs by **positive pressure breathing**, inflating the lungs with forced airflow. During the first stage of inhalation, muscles lower the floor of an amphibian's oral cavity, drawing in air through its nostrils. Next, with the nostrils and mouth closed, the floor of the oral cavity rises, forcing air down the trachea. During exhalation, air is forced back out by the elastic recoil of the lungs and by compression of the muscular body wall. When male frogs puff themselves up in aggressive or courtship displays, they disrupt this breathing cycle, taking in air several times without allowing any release.

How a Mammal Breathes

Unlike amphibians, mammals employ **negative pressure breathing**—pulling, rather than pushing, air into their lungs **(Figure 42.25)**. Using muscle contraction to actively expand the thoracic cavity, mammals lower air pressure in their lungs below that of the air outside their body. Because gas flows from a region of higher pressure to a region of lower pressure, air rushes through the nostrils and mouth and down the breathing tubes to the alveoli. During exhalation, the muscles controlling the thoracic cavity relax, and the volume of the cavity is reduced. The increased air pressure in the alveoli forces air up the breathing tubes and out of the body. Thus, inhalation is always active and requires work, whereas exhalation is usually passive.

Expanding the thoracic cavity during inhalation involves the animal's rib muscles and the **diaphragm**, a sheet of skeletal muscle that forms the bottom wall of the cavity. Contracting the rib muscles expands the rib cage, the front wall of the thoracic cavity, by pulling the ribs upward and the sternum outward. At the same time, the diaphragm contracts, expanding the thoracic cavity downward. The effect of the descending diaphragm is similar to that of a plunger being drawn out of a syringe.

Within the thoracic cavity, a double membrane surrounds the lungs. The inner layer of this membrane adheres to the outside of the lungs, and the outer layer adheres to the wall of the thoracic cavity. A thin space filled with fluid separates the two layers. Surface tension in the fluid causes the two layers to stick together like two plates of glass separated by a film of water: The layers can slide smoothly past each other, but they cannot be pulled apart easily. Consequently, the volume of the thoracic cavity and the volume of the lungs change in unison.

Depending on activity level, additional muscles may be recruited to aid breathing. The rib muscles and diaphragm are sufficient to change lung volume when a mammal is at rest. During exercise, other muscles of the neck, back, and chest increase the volume of the thoracic cavity by raising the rib cage. In kangaroos and some other species, locomotion causes a

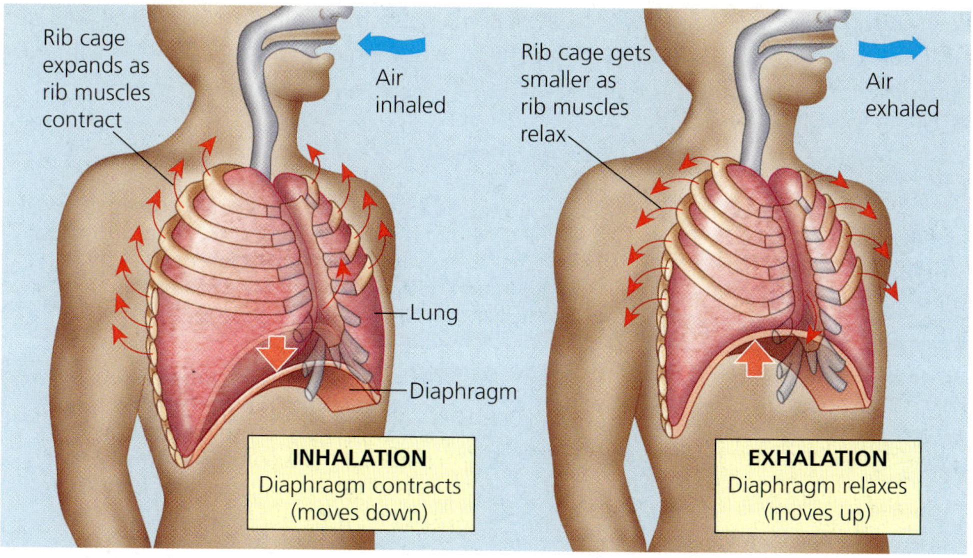

▲ **Figure 42.25 Negative pressure breathing.** A mammal breathes by changing the air pressure within its lungs relative to the pressure of the outside atmosphere.

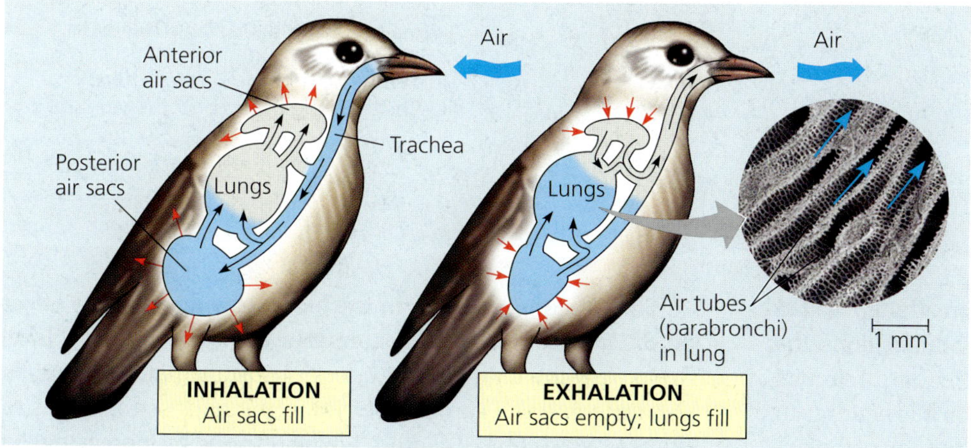

▲ **Figure 42.26 The avian respiratory system.** Inflation and deflation of the air sacs (red arrows) ventilates the lungs, forcing air in one direction through tiny parallel tubes in the lungs called parabronchi (inset, SEM). During inhalation, both sets of air sacs inflate. The posterior sacs fill with fresh air (blue) from the outside, while the anterior sacs fill with stale air (gray) from the lungs. During exhalation, both sets of air sacs deflate, forcing air from the posterior sacs into the lungs, and air from the anterior sacs out of the system via the trachea. Gas exchange occurs across the walls of the parabronchi. Two cycles of inhalation and exhalation are required for the air to pass all the way through the system and out of the bird.

rhythmic movement of organs in the abdomen, including the stomach and liver. The result is a piston-like pumping motion that pushes and pulls on the diaphragm, further increasing the volume of air moved in and out of the lungs.

The volume of air inhaled and exhaled with each breath is called **tidal volume**. It averages about 500 mL in resting humans. The tidal volume during maximal inhalation and exhalation is the **vital capacity**, which is about 3.4 L and 4.8 L for college-age women and men, respectively. The air that remains after a forced exhalation is called the **residual volume**. As we age, our lungs lose their resilience, and residual volume increases at the expense of vital capacity.

Because the lungs in mammals do not completely empty with each breath, and because inhalation occurs through the same airways as exhalation, each inhalation mixes fresh air with oxygen-depleted residual air. As a result, the maximum P_{O_2} in alveoli is always considerably less than in the atmosphere.

How a Bird Breathes

Ventilation is both more efficient and more complex in birds than in mammals. When birds breathe, they pass air over the gas exchange surface in only one direction. Furthermore, incoming, fresh air does not mix with air that has already carried out gas exchange. To bring fresh air to their lungs, birds use eight or nine air sacs situated on either side of the lungs (**Figure 42.26**). The air sacs do not function directly in gas exchange but act as bellows that keep air flowing through the lungs. Instead of alveoli, which are dead ends, the sites of gas exchange in bird lungs are tiny channels called *parabronchi*. Passage of air through the entire system—lungs and air sacs—requires two cycles of inhalation and exhalation. In some passageways, the direction in which air moves alternates (see Figure 42.26). Within the parabronchi, however, air always flows in the same direction.

Because the air in a bird's lungs is renewed with every exhalation, the maximum P_{O_2} in the lungs is higher in birds than in mammals. This is one reason birds function better than mammals at high altitude. For example, humans have great difficulty obtaining enough O_2 when climbing Earth's highest peaks, such as Mount Everest (8,850 m), in the Himalayas. But bar-headed geese and several other bird species easily fly over the Himalayas during migration.

Control of Breathing in Humans

Although you can voluntarily hold your breath or breathe faster and deeper, most of the time your breathing is regulated by involuntary mechanisms. These control mechanisms ensure that gas exchange is coordinated with blood circulation and with metabolic demand.

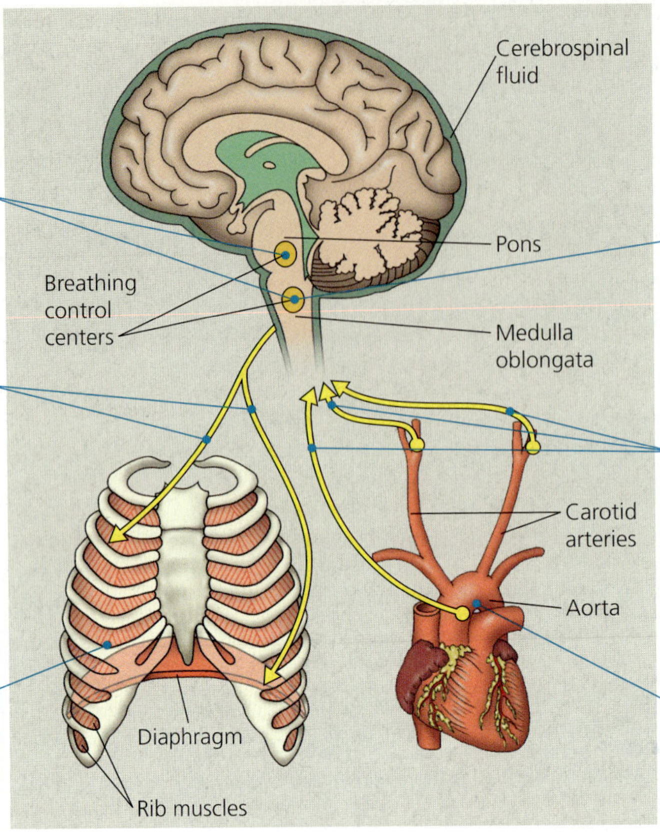

▲ **Figure 42.27 Automatic control of breathing.**

Networks of neurons that regulate breathing, called **breathing control centers**, are located in two brain regions, the medulla oblongata and the pons **(Figure 42.27)**. Control circuits in the medulla establish the breathing rhythm, while neurons in the pons regulate its tempo. (The number and location of the circuits in the medulla is a subject of active research.) When you breathe deeply, a negative-feedback mechanism prevents the lungs from overexpanding: During inhalation, sensors that detect stretching of the lung tissue send nerve impulses to the control circuits in the medulla, inhibiting further inhalation.

In regulating breathing, the medulla uses the pH of the surrounding tissue fluid as an indicator of blood CO_2 concentration. The reason pH can be used in this way is that blood CO_2 is the main determinant of the pH of *cerebrospinal fluid*, the fluid surrounding the brain and spinal cord. Carbon dioxide diffuses from the blood to the cerebrospinal fluid, where it reacts with water and forms carbonic acid (H_2CO_3). The H_2CO_3 can then dissociate into a bicarbonate ion (HCO_3^-) and a hydrogen ion (H^+):

$$CO_2 + H_2O \rightleftharpoons H_2CO_3 \rightleftharpoons HCO_3^- + H^+$$

Increased metabolic activity, such as occurs during exercise, lowers pH by increasing the concentration of CO_2 in the blood. In response, the medulla's control circuits increase the depth and rate of breathing. Both remain high until the excess CO_2 is eliminated in exhaled air and pH returns to a normal value.

The O_2 concentration in the blood usually has little effect on the breathing control centers. However, when the O_2 level drops very low (at high altitudes, for instance), O_2 sensors in the aorta and the carotid arteries in the neck send signals to the breathing control centers, which respond by increasing the breathing rate.

Breathing control is effective only if it is coordinated with control of the cardiovascular system so that ventilation is matched to blood flow through alveolar capillaries. During exercise, for instance, an increased breathing rate, which enhances O_2 uptake and CO_2 removal, is coupled with an increase in cardiac output.

CONCEPT CHECK 42.6

1. How does an increase in the CO_2 concentration in the blood affect the pH of cerebrospinal fluid?
2. A slight decrease in blood pH causes the heart's pacemaker to speed up. What is the function of this control mechanism?
3. **WHAT IF?** Suppose that you broke a rib in a fall. If the broken end of the rib tore a small hole in the membranes surrounding your lungs, what effect on lung function would you expect?

For suggested answers, see Appendix A.

CONCEPT 42.7

Adaptations for gas exchange include pigments that bind and transport gases

The high metabolic demands of many animals necessitate the exchange of large quantities of O_2 and CO_2. Here we'll examine how blood molecules called respiratory pigments facilitate this exchange through their interaction with O_2 and CO_2. We will also investigate physiological adaptations that enable animals to be active under conditions of high metabolic load or very limiting P_{O_2}. As a basis for exploring these topics, let's summarize the basic gas exchange circuit in humans.

Coordination of Circulation and Gas Exchange

The partial pressures of O_2 and CO_2 in the blood vary at different points in the circulatory system, as shown in **Figure 42.28**. Blood arriving at the lungs via the pulmonary arteries has a lower P_{O_2} and a higher P_{CO_2} than the air in the alveoli. As blood enters the alveolar capillaries, CO_2 diffuses from the blood to the air in the alveoli. Meanwhile, O_2 in the air dissolves in the fluid that coats the alveolar epithelium and diffuses into the blood. By the time the blood leaves the lungs in the pulmonary veins, its P_{O_2} has been raised and its P_{CO_2} has been lowered. After returning to the heart, this blood is pumped through the systemic circuit.

In the tissue capillaries, gradients of partial pressure favor the diffusion of O_2 out of the blood and CO_2 into the blood. These gradients exist because cellular respiration in the mitochondria of cells near each capillary removes O_2 from and adds CO_2 to the surrounding interstitial fluid. After the blood unloads O_2 and loads CO_2, it is returned to the heart and pumped to the lungs again.

Although this description faithfully characterizes the driving forces for gas exchange in different tissues, it omits the critical role of the specialized carrier proteins we will discuss next.

Respiratory Pigments

The low solubility of O_2 in water (and thus in blood) poses a problem for animals that rely on the circulatory system to deliver O_2. For example, a person requires almost 2 L of O_2 per minute during intense exercise, and all of it must be carried in the blood from the lungs to the active tissues. At normal body temperature and air pressure, however, only 4.5 mL of O_2 can dissolve into a liter of blood in the lungs. Even if 80% of the dissolved O_2 were delivered to the tissues (an unrealistically high percentage), the heart would still need to pump 555 L of blood per minute!

In fact, animals transport most of their O_2 bound to certain proteins called **respiratory pigments**. Respiratory pigments circulate with the blood or hemolymph and are often contained within specialized cells. The pigments greatly increase the amount of O_2 that can be carried in the circulatory fluid (to about 200 mL of O_2 per liter in mammalian blood). In our

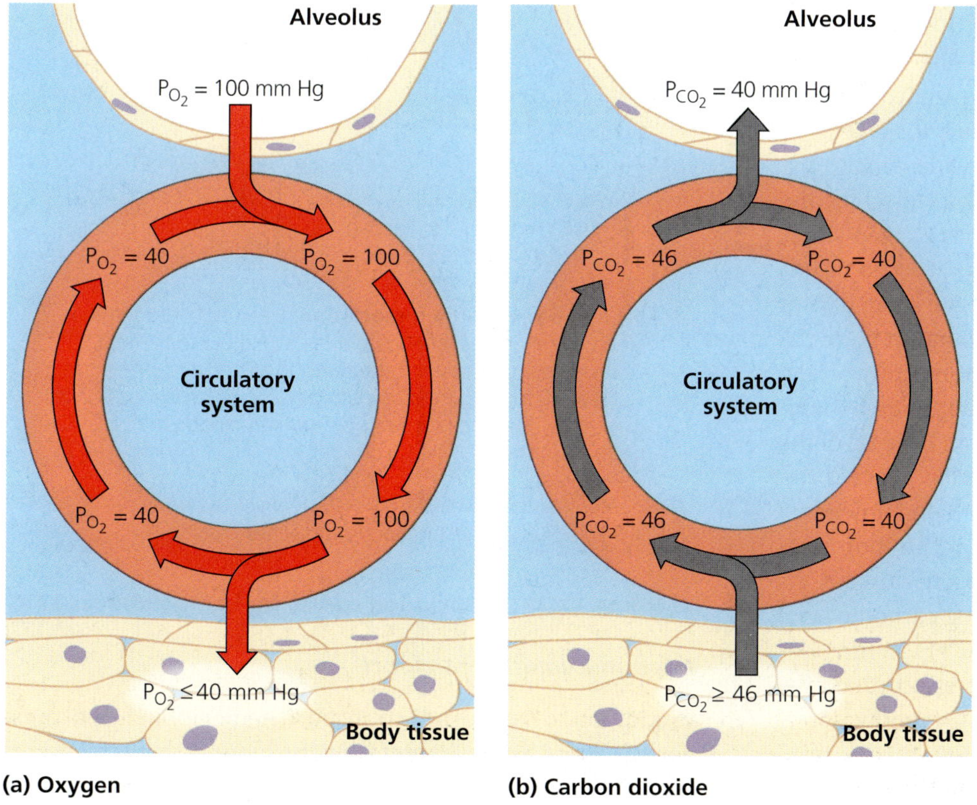

◀ **Figure 42.28 Loading and unloading of respiratory gases.**

WHAT IF? *If you consciously forced more air out of your lungs each time you exhaled, how would that affect the values shown in these diagrams?*

example of an exercising human with an O_2 delivery rate of 80%, the presence of respiratory pigments reduces the cardiac output necessary for O_2 transport to a manageable 12.5 L of blood per minute.

A variety of respiratory pigments have evolved among the animal taxa. With a few exceptions, these molecules have a distinctive color (hence the term *pigment*) and consist of a protein bound to a metal. One example is the blue pigment *hemocyanin*, which has copper as its oxygen-binding component and is found in arthropods and many molluscs. The respiratory pigment of almost all vertebrates and many invertebrates is hemoglobin. In vertebrates, it is contained in the erythrocytes.

Hemoglobin

Vertebrate hemoglobin consists of four subunits (polypeptide chains), each with a cofactor called a heme group that has an iron atom at its center. Each iron atom binds one molecule of O_2; hence, a single hemoglobin molecule can carry four molecules of O_2. Like all respiratory pigments, hemoglobin binds O_2 reversibly, loading O_2 in the lungs or gills and unloading it in other parts of the body. This process depends on cooperativity between the hemoglobin subunits (see Chapter 8). When O_2 binds to one subunit, the others change shape slightly, increasing their affinity for O_2. When four O_2 molecules are bound and one subunit unloads its O_2, the other three subunits more readily unload, as an associated shape change lowers their affinity for O_2.

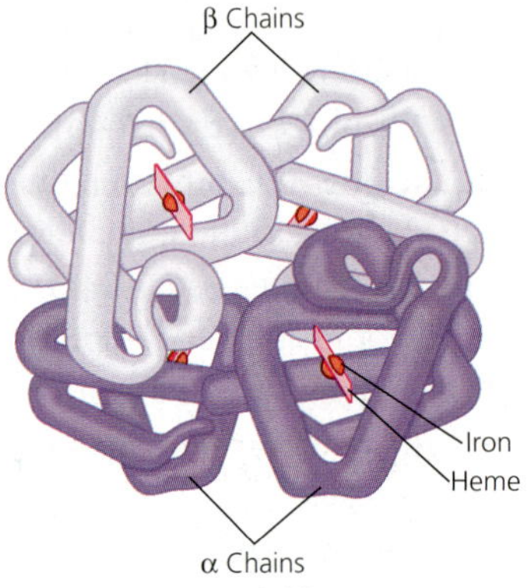

Hemoglobin

Cooperativity in O_2 binding and release is evident in the dissociation curve for hemoglobin **(Figure 42.29a)**. Over the range of P_{O_2} where the dissociation curve has a steep slope, even a slight change in P_{O_2} causes hemoglobin to load or unload a substantial amount of O_2. Notice that the steep part of the curve corresponds to the range of P_{O_2} found in body tissues. When cells in a particular location begin working harder—during exercise, for instance—P_{O_2} dips in their vicinity as the O_2 is consumed in cellular respiration. Because of the effect of subunit cooperativity, a slight drop in P_{O_2} causes a relatively large increase in the amount of O_2 the blood unloads.

The production of CO_2 during cellular respiration promotes the unloading of O_2 by hemoglobin in active tissues. As we have seen, CO_2 reacts with water, forming carbonic acid, which lowers the pH of its surroundings. Low pH, in turn, decreases the affinity of hemoglobin for O_2, an effect called the **Bohr shift (Figure 42.29b)**. Thus, where CO_2 production is greater, hemoglobin releases more O_2, which can then be used to support more cellular respiration.

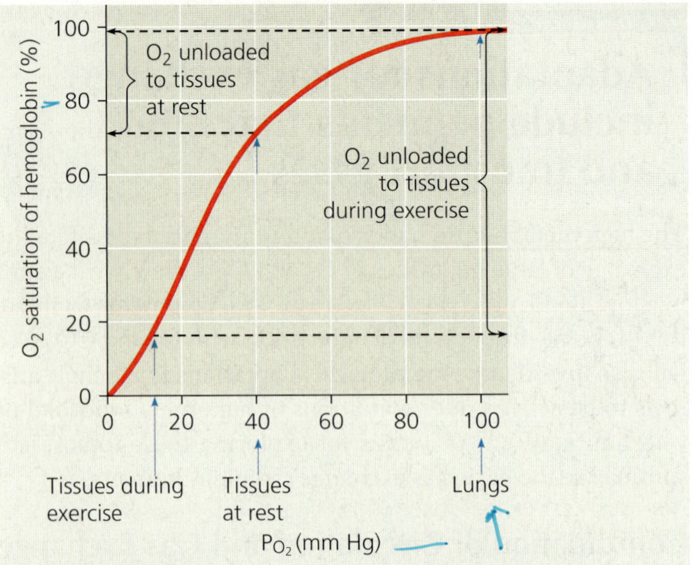

(a) P_{O_2} and hemoglobin dissociation at pH 7.4. The curve shows the relative amounts of O_2 bound to hemoglobin exposed to solutions with different P_{O_2}. At a P_{O_2} of 100 mm Hg, typical in the lungs, hemoglobin is about 98% saturated with O_2. At a P_{O_2} of 40 mm Hg, common in the vicinity of tissues at rest, hemoglobin is about 70% saturated. Hemoglobin can release additional O_2 to metabolically very active tissues, such as muscle tissue during exercise.

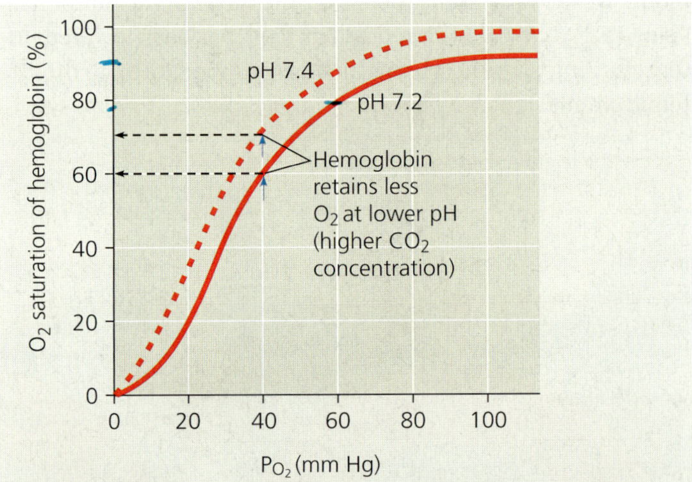

(b) pH and hemoglobin dissociation. Because hydrogen ions affect the shape of hemoglobin, a drop in pH shifts the O_2 dissociation curve toward the right (the Bohr shift). At a given P_{O_2}, say 40 mm Hg, hemoglobin gives up more O_2 at pH 7.2 than at pH 7.4, the normal pH of human blood. The pH decreases in very active tissues because the CO_2 produced by cellular respiration reacts with water, forming carbonic acid. Hemoglobin then releases more O_2, which supports the increased cellular respiration in the active tissues.

▲ **Figure 42.29 Dissociation curves for hemoglobin at 37°C.**

Carbon Dioxide Transport

In addition to its role in O_2 transport, hemoglobin helps transport CO_2 and assists in buffering the blood—that is, preventing harmful changes in pH. Only about 7% of the CO_2 released by respiring cells is transported in solution in blood plasma. Another 23% binds to the amino ends of the hemoglobin polypeptide chains, and about 70% is transported in the blood in the form of bicarbonate ions (HCO_3^-).

As shown in **Figure 42.30**, carbon dioxide from respiring cells diffuses into the blood plasma and then into erythrocytes. There the CO_2 reacts with water (assisted by the enzyme carbonic anhydrase) and forms H_2CO_3, which dissociates into H^+ and HCO_3^-. Most of the H^+ binds to hemoglobin and other proteins, minimizing the change in blood pH. The HCO_3^- diffuses into the plasma.

When blood flows through the lungs, the relative partial pressures of CO_2 favor the diffusion of CO_2 out of the blood. As CO_2 diffuses into alveoli, the amount of CO_2 in the blood decreases. This decrease shifts the chemical equilibrium in favor of the conversion of HCO_3^- to CO_2, enabling further net diffusion of CO_2 into alveoli.

Elite Animal Athletes

For some animals, such as long-distance runners and migratory birds and mammals, the O_2 demands of daily activities would overwhelm the capacity of a typical respiratory system. Other animals, such as diving mammals, are capable of being active underwater for extended periods without breathing. What evolutionary adaptations enable these animals to perform such feats?

The Ultimate Endurance Runner

The elite animal marathon runner may be the pronghorn, an antelope-like mammal native to the grasslands of North America. Second only to the cheetah in top speed for a land vertebrate, pronghorns are capable of running as fast as 100 km/hr and can sustain an average speed of 65 km/hr over long distances.

Stan Lindstedt and his colleagues at the University of Wyoming and the University of Bern were curious about how pronghorns achieve their combination

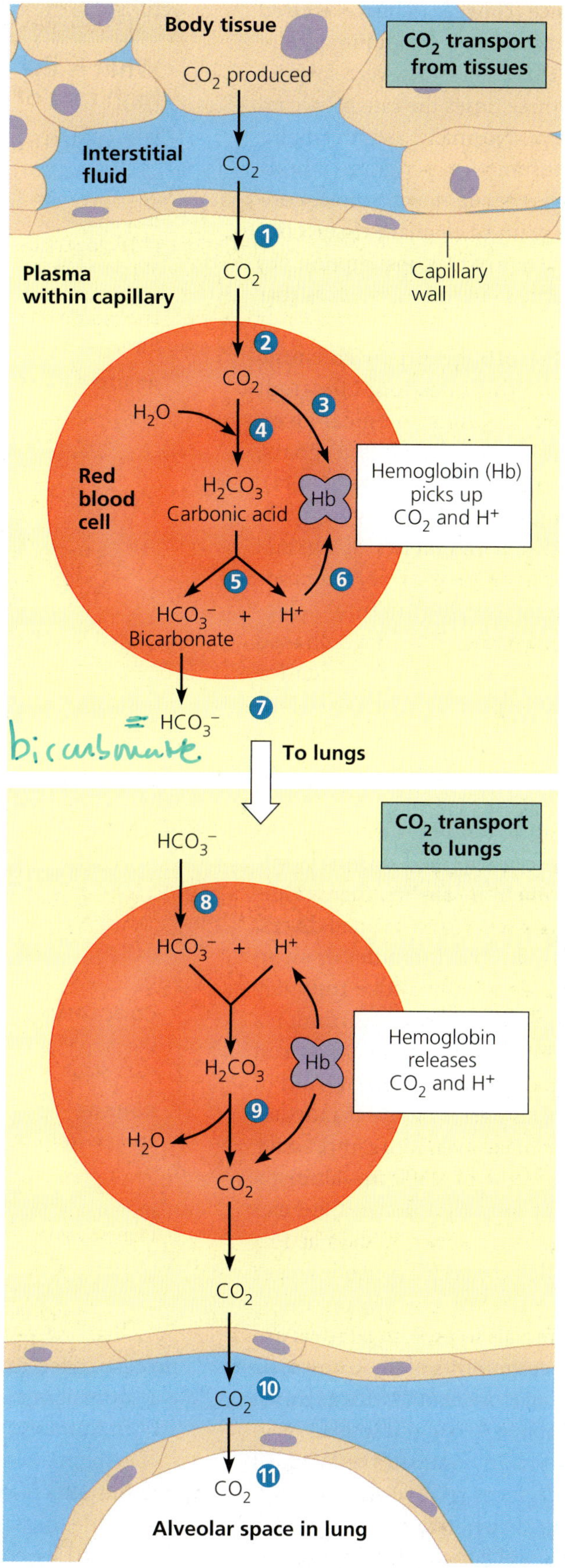

1. Carbon dioxide produced by body tissues diffuses into the interstitial fluid and the plasma.
2. Over 90% of the CO_2 diffuses into red blood cells, leaving only 7% in the plasma as dissolved CO_2.
3. Some CO_2 is picked up and transported by hemoglobin.
4. However, most CO_2 reacts with water in red blood cells, forming carbonic acid (H_2CO_3), a reaction catalyzed by carbonic anhydrase contained within red blood cells.
5. Carbonic acid dissociates into a bicarbonate ion (HCO_3^-) and a hydrogen ion (H^+).
6. Hemoglobin binds most of the H^+ from H_2CO_3, preventing the H^+ from acidifying the blood and thus preventing the Bohr shift.
7. Most of the HCO_3^- diffuses into the plasma, where it is carried in the bloodstream to the lungs.
8. In the lungs, HCO_3^- diffuses from the plasma into red blood cells, combining with H^+ released from hemoglobin and forming H_2CO_3.
9. Carbonic acid is converted back to CO_2 and water. CO_2 is also unloaded from hemoglobin.
10. CO_2 diffuses into the plasma and the interstitial fluid.
11. CO_2 diffuses into the alveolar space, from which it is expelled during exhalation. The reduction of CO_2 concentration in the plasma drives the breakdown of H_2CO_3 into CO_2 and water in the red blood cells (see step 9), a reversal of the reaction that occurs near body tissues (see step 4).

▲ **Figure 42.30 Carbon dioxide transport in the blood.**

? *In what three forms is CO_2 transported in the bloodstream?*

of exceptional speed and endurance. The researchers exercised pronghorns on a treadmill to estimate their maximum rate of O_2 consumption (see Figure 40.18). The results were surprising: Pronghorns consume O_2 at three times the rate predicted for an average animal of their size. Normally, as animals increase in size, their rate of O_2 consumption per gram of body mass declines. One gram of shrew tissue, for example, consumes as much O_2 in a day as a gram of elephant tissue consumes in an entire month. But the rate of O_2 consumption per gram of tissue by a pronghorn turned out to be as high as that of a 10-g mouse!

What adaptations enable the pronghorn to consume O_2 at such a high rate? To answer this question, Lindstedt and his colleagues compared various physiological characteristics of pronghorns with those of domestic goats, which lack great speed and endurance **(Figure 42.31)**. They concluded that the pronghorn's unusually high O_2 consumption rate results from enhancements of normal physiological mechanisms at each stage of O_2 metabolism. These enhancements are the result of natural selection, perhaps exerted by the predators that have chased pronghorns across the open plains of North America for more than 4 million years.

▼ Figure 42.31 Inquiry

What is the basis for the pronghorn's unusually high rate of O_2 consumption?

EXPERIMENT Stan Lindstedt and colleagues had demonstrated that the pronghorn's maximal rate of O_2 consumption (V_{O_2} max) is five times that of a domestic goat, a similar-sized mammal adapted to climbing rather than running. To discover the physiological basis for this difference, they measured the following parameters in both animals: lung capacity (a measure of O_2 uptake), cardiac output (a measure of O_2 delivery), muscle mass, and muscle mitochondrial volume. (The last two parameters are measures of the muscles' potential O_2 use.)

RESULTS

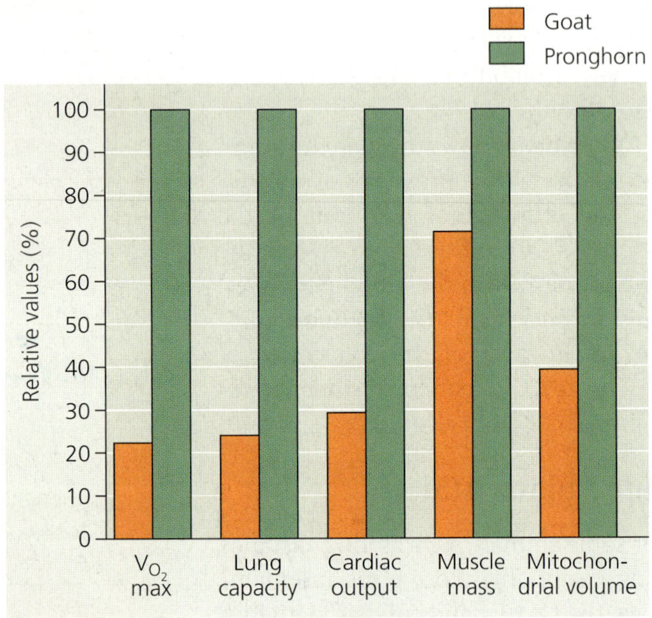

CONCLUSION The dramatic difference in V_{O_2} max between the pronghorn and the goat reflects comparable differences at each stage of O_2 metabolism: uptake, delivery, and use.

SOURCE S. L. Lindstedt et al., Running energetics in the pronghorn antelope, *Nature* 353:748–750 (1991).

WHAT IF? Suppose you measured V_{O_2} max among a large group of humans. To what extent would you expect those with the highest values to be the fastest runners?

Diving Mammals

Animals vary greatly in their ability to temporarily inhabit environments in which there is no access to their normal respiratory medium—for example, when an air-breather swims underwater. Whereas most humans, even well-trained divers, cannot hold their breath longer than 2 or 3 minutes or swim deeper than 20 m, the Weddell seal of Antarctica routinely plunges to 200–500 m and remains there for about 20 minutes (sometimes for more than an hour). (Humans can remain submerged for comparable periods, but only with the aid of specialized gear and compressed air tanks.) Some sea turtles, whales, and other species of seals make even more impressive dives. Elephant seals can reach depths of 1,500 m—almost a mile—and stay submerged for as long as 2 hours! One elephant seal carrying a recording device spent 40 days at sea, diving almost continuously with no surface period longer than 6 minutes.

One adaptation of diving mammals to prolonged stays underwater is an ability to store large amounts of O_2. Compared with humans, the Weddell seal can store about twice as much O_2 per kilogram of body mass. About 36% of our total O_2 is in our lungs, and 51% is in our blood. In contrast, the Weddell seal holds only about 5% of its O_2 in its relatively small lungs (and may exhale before diving, which reduces buoyancy), stockpiling 70% in the blood. The seal has about twice the volume of blood per kilogram of body mass as a human. Diving mammals also have a high concentration of an oxygen-storing protein called **myoglobin** in their muscles. The Weddell seal can store about 25% of its O_2 in muscle, compared with only 13% in humans.

Diving mammals not only have a relatively large O_2 stockpile but also have adaptations that conserve O_2. They swim with little muscular effort and glide passively upward or downward by changing their buoyancy. Their heart rate and O_2 consumption rate decrease during a dive. At the same time, regulatory mechanisms route most blood to the brain, spinal cord, eyes, adrenal glands, and, in pregnant seals, the placenta. Blood supply to the muscles is restricted or, during the longest dives, shut off altogether. During dives of more than about 20 minutes, a Weddell seal's muscles deplete the O_2 stored in myoglobin and then derive their ATP from fermentation instead of respiration (see Chapter 9).

The unusual abilities of the Weddell seal and other air-breathing divers to power their bodies during long dives showcase two related themes in our study of organisms—the response to environmental challenges over the short term by physiological adjustments and over the long term as a result of natural selection.

CONCEPT CHECK 42.7

1. What determines whether O_2 and CO_2 diffuse into or out of the capillaries in the tissues and near the alveoli? Explain.
2. How does the Bohr shift help deliver O_2 to very active tissues?
3. **WHAT IF?** A doctor might use bicarbonate (HCO_3^-) to treat a patient who is breathing very rapidly. What assumption is the doctor making about the blood chemistry of the patient?

For suggested answers, see Appendix A.

Chapter 42 Review

MEDIA Go to the Study Area at **www.masteringbio.com** for BioFlix 3-D Animations, MP3 Tutors, Videos, Practice Tests, an eBook, and more.

SUMMARY OF KEY CONCEPTS

CONCEPT 42.1

Circulatory systems link exchange surfaces with cells throughout the body (pp. 898–903)

- **Gastrovascular Cavities** Gastrovascular cavities in small animals with simple body plans mediate exchange between the environment and cells that can be reached by short-range diffusion.
- **Open and Closed Circulatory Systems** Because diffusion is slow over all but short distances, most complex animals have internal transport systems. These systems circulate fluid between cells and the organs that exchange gases, nutrients, and wastes with the outside environment. In the open circulatory systems of arthropods and most molluscs, the circulating fluid bathes the organs directly. Closed systems circulate fluid in a closed network of pumps and vessels.
- **Organization of Vertebrate Circulatory Systems** In vertebrates, blood flows in a closed cardiovascular system consisting of blood vessels and a two- to four-chambered heart. Arteries convey blood to capillaries, the sites of chemical exchange between blood and interstitial fluid. Veins return blood from capillaries to the heart. Fishes, rays, and sharks have a single pump in their circulation. Air-breathing vertebrates have two pumps combined in a single heart. Variations in ventricle number and separation reflect adaptations to different environments and metabolic needs.

CONCEPT 42.2

Coordinated cycles of heart contraction drive double circulation in mammals (pp. 903–905)

- **Mammalian Circulation** Heart valves dictate a one-way flow of blood through the heart. The right ventricle pumps blood to the lungs, where it loads O_2 and unloads CO_2. Oxygen-rich blood from the lungs enters the heart at the left atrium and is pumped to the body tissues by the left ventricle. Blood returns to the heart through the right atrium.

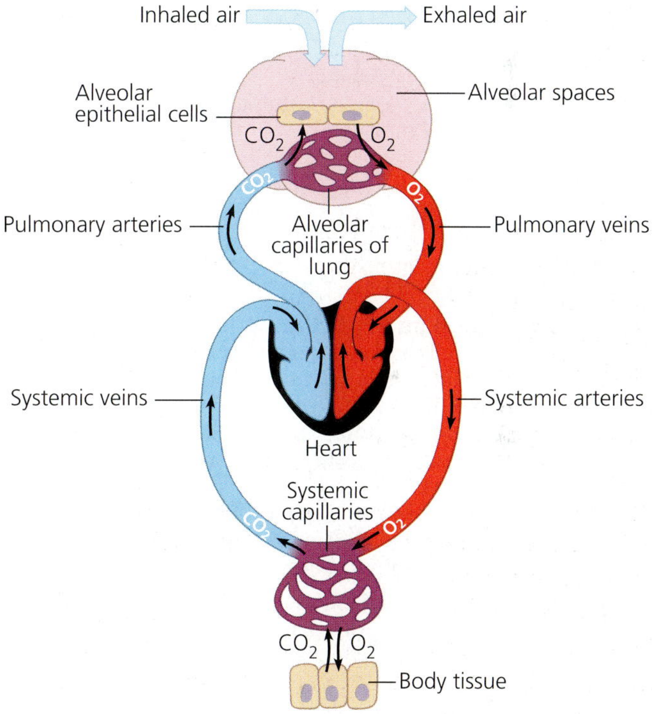

- **The Mammalian Heart: *A Closer Look*** The pulse is a measure of the number of times the heart beats each minute. The cardiac cycle, one complete sequence of the heart's pumping and filling, consists of a period of contraction, called systole, and a period of relaxation, called diastole. Cardiac output is the volume of blood pumped by each ventricle per minute.
- **Maintaining the Heart's Rhythmic Beat** Impulses originating at the sinoatrial (SA) node (pacemaker) of the right atrium pass to the atrioventricular (AV) node. After a delay, they are conducted along the bundle branches and Purkinje fibers. The pacemaker is influenced by nerves, hormones, and body temperature.

MEDIA
Activity Mammalian Cardiovascular System Structure

CONCEPT 42.3

Patterns of blood pressure and flow reflect the structure and arrangement of blood vessels (pp. 906–911)

- **Blood Vessel Structure and Function** Capillaries have narrow diameters and thin walls that facilitate exchange. Arteries contain thick elastic walls that maintain blood pressure. Veins contain one-way valves that contribute to the return of blood to the heart.
- **Blood Flow Velocity** Physical laws governing the movement of fluids through pipes influence blood flow and blood pressure. The velocity of blood flow varies in the circulatory system, being lowest in the capillary beds as a result of their large total cross-sectional area.
- **Blood Pressure** Blood pressure is altered by changes in cardiac output and by variable constriction of arterioles.
- **Capillary Function** Transfer of substances between the blood and the interstitial fluid occurs across the thin walls of capillaries.
- **Fluid Return by the Lymphatic System** The lymphatic system returns fluid to the blood and parallels the circulatory system in its extent and its mechanisms for fluid flow under low hydrostatic pressure. It also plays a vital role in defense against infection.

MEDIA

Activity Path of Blood Flow in Mammals
Activity Mammalian Cardiovascular System Function
Biology Labs On-Line CardioLab

CONCEPT 42.4

Blood components function in exchange, transport, and defense (pp. 911–915)

- **Blood Composition and Function** Whole blood consists of cellular elements (cells and cell fragments called platelets) suspended in a liquid matrix called plasma. Plasma proteins influence blood pH, osmotic pressure, and viscosity and function in lipid transport, immunity (antibodies), and blood clotting (fibrinogen). Red blood cells, or erythrocytes, transport O_2. Five types of white blood cells, or leukocytes, function in defense against microbes and foreign substances in the blood. Platelets function in blood clotting, a cascade of reactions that converts plasma fibrinogen to fibrin.
- **Cardiovascular Disease** The deposition of lipids and tissues on the lining of arteries is a prime contributor to cardiovascular disease that can result in life-threatening damage to the heart or brain.

MEDIA

Investigation How Is Cardiovascular Fitness Measured?

CONCEPT 42.5

Gas exchange occurs across specialized respiratory surfaces (pp. 915–920)

- **Partial Pressure Gradients in Gas Exchange** At all sites of gas exchange, gases diffuse from where their partial pressures are higher to where they are lower.
- **Respiratory Media** Air is more conducive to gas exchange because of its higher O_2 content, lower density, and lower viscosity.
- **Respiratory Surfaces** Animals require large, moist respiratory surfaces for the adequate diffusion of O_2 and CO_2 between their cells and the respiratory medium, either air or water.
- **Gills in Aquatic Animals** Gills are outfoldings of the body surface specialized for gas exchange in water. The effectiveness of gas exchange in some gills, including those of fishes, is increased by ventilation and countercurrent flow of blood and water.
- **Tracheal Systems in Insects** The tracheae of insects are tiny, branching tubes that penetrate the body, bringing O_2 directly to cells.
- **Lungs** Spiders, land snails, and most terrestrial vertebrates have internal lungs. In mammals, air inhaled through the nostrils passes through the pharynx into the trachea, bronchi, bronchioles, and dead-end alveoli, where gas exchange occurs.

MEDIA

Activity The Human Respiratory System

CONCEPT 42.6

Breathing ventilates the lungs (pp. 920–922)

- **How an Amphibian Breathes** An amphibian ventilates its lungs by positive pressure breathing, which forces air down the trachea.
- **How a Mammal Breathes** Mammals ventilate their lungs by negative pressure breathing, which pulls air into the lungs. Lung volume increases as the rib muscles and diaphragm contract.
- **How a Bird Breathes** Besides lungs, birds have eight or nine air sacs that act as bellows, keeping air flowing through the lungs in one direction only. Every exhalation completely renews the air in the lungs.
- **Control of Breathing in Humans** Control centers in the medulla oblongata and pons of the brain regulate the rate and depth of breathing. Sensors detect the pH of cerebrospinal fluid (reflecting CO_2 concentration in the blood), and the medulla adjusts breathing rate and depth to match metabolic demands. Secondary control over breathing is exerted by sensors in the aorta and carotid arteries that monitor blood levels of O_2 and CO_2 and blood pH.

CONCEPT 42.7

Adaptations for gas exchange include pigments that bind and transport gases (pp. 923–927)

- **Coordination of Circulation and Gas Exchange** In the lungs, gradients of partial pressure favor the diffusion of O_2 into the blood and CO_2 out of the blood. The opposite situation exists in the rest of the body.
- **Respiratory Pigments** Respiratory pigments transport O_2, greatly increasing the amount of O_2 that blood or hemolymph can carry. Many arthropods and molluscs have copper-containing hemocyanin; vertebrates and a wide variety of invertebrates have hemoglobin. Hemoglobin also helps transport CO_2 and assists in buffering.
- **Elite Animal Athletes** The pronghorn's high O_2 consumption rate underlies its ability to run at high speeds over long distances. Deep-diving air-breathers stockpile O_2 and deplete it slowly.

MEDIA

Activity Transport of Respiratory Gases
Biology Labs On-Line HemoglobinLab

TESTING YOUR KNOWLEDGE

SELF-QUIZ

1. Which of the following respiratory systems is not closely associated with a blood supply?
a. the lungs of a vertebrate
b. the gills of a fish
c. the tracheal system of an insect
d. the skin of an earthworm
e. the parapodia of a polychaete worm

2. Blood returning to the mammalian heart in a pulmonary vein drains first into the
a. vena cava.
b. left atrium.
c. right atrium.
d. left ventricle.
e. right ventricle.

3. Pulse is a direct measure of
a. blood pressure.
b. stroke volume.
c. cardiac output.
d. heart rate.
e. breathing rate.

4. The conversion of fibrinogen to fibrin
a. occurs when fibrinogen is released from broken platelets.
b. occurs within red blood cells.
c. is linked to hypertension and may damage artery walls.
d. is likely to occur too often in an individual with hemophilia.
e. is the final step of a clotting process that involves multiple clotting factors.

5. In negative pressure breathing, inhalation results from
a. forcing air from the throat down into the lungs.
b. contracting the diaphragm.
c. relaxing the muscles of the rib cage.
d. using muscles of the lungs to expand the alveoli.
e. contracting the abdominal muscles.

6. When you hold your breath, which of the following blood gas changes first leads to the urge to breathe?
a. rising O_2
b. falling O_2
c. rising CO_2
d. falling CO_2
e. rising CO_2 and falling O_2

7. Compared with the interstitial fluid that bathes active muscle cells, blood reaching these cells in arteries has a
a. higher P_{O_2}.
b. higher P_{CO_2}.
c. greater bicarbonate concentration.
d. lower pH.
e. lower osmotic pressure.

8. Which of the following reactions prevails in red blood cells traveling through alveolar capillaries? (Hb = hemoglobin)
a. $Hb + 4\,O_2 \rightarrow Hb(O_2)_4$
b. $Hb(O_2)_4 \rightarrow Hb + 4\,O_2$
c. $CO_2 + H_2O \rightarrow H_2CO_3$
d. $H_2CO_3 \rightarrow H^+ + HCO_3^-$
e. $Hb + 4\,CO_2 \rightarrow Hb(CO_2)_4$

9. **DRAW IT** Draw a pair of simple diagrams comparing the essential features of single and double circulation.

For Self-Quiz answers, see Appendix A.

MEDIA Visit the Study Area at **www.masteringbio.com** for a Practice Test.

EVOLUTION CONNECTION

10. One of the many mutant opponents that the movie monster Godzilla contends with is Mothra, a giant mothlike creature with a wingspan of several dozen feet. Science fiction creatures like these can be critiqued on the grounds of biomechanical and physiological principles. What problems of respiration and gas exchange would Mothra face? The largest insects that have ever lived are Paleozoic dragonflies with half-meter wingspans. Why do you think truly giant insects are improbable?

SCIENTIFIC INQUIRY

11. The hemoglobin of a human fetus differs from adult hemoglobin. Compare the dissociation curves of the two hemoglobins in the graph below. Propose a hypothesis for the *function* of this difference between these two versions of hemoglobin.

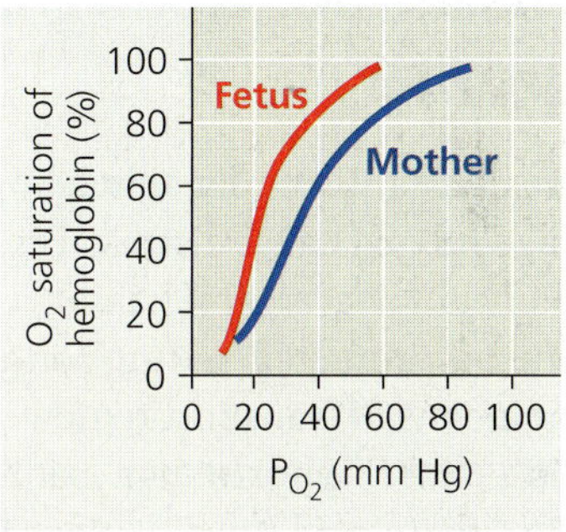

SCIENCE, TECHNOLOGY, AND SOCIETY

12. Hundreds of studies have linked smoking with cardiovascular and lung disease. According to most health authorities, smoking is the leading cause of preventable, premature death in the United States. Antismoking and health groups have proposed that cigarette advertising in all media be banned entirely. What are some arguments in favor of a total ban on cigarette advertising? What are arguments in opposition? Do you favor or oppose such a ban? Defend your position.

43 The Immune System

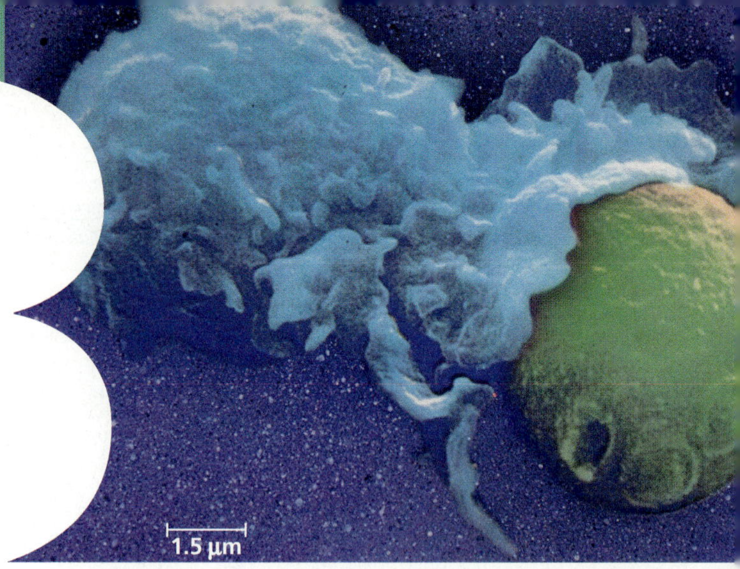

▲ **Figure 43.1 How do immune cells of animals recognize foreign cells?**

KEY CONCEPTS

43.1 In innate immunity, recognition and response rely on shared traits of pathogens

43.2 In acquired immunity, lymphocyte receptors provide pathogen-specific recognition

43.3 Acquired immunity defends against infection of body cells and fluids

43.4 Disruptions in immune system function can elicit or exacerbate disease

OVERVIEW

Reconnaissance, Recognition, and Response

Animals are constantly under attack by **pathogens**, infectious agents that cause disease. For a pathogen, an animal body is a nearly ideal habitat, offering a ready source of nutrients, a protected setting for growth and reproduction, and a means of transport to new hosts and environments. Seizing this opportunity, pathogens—mostly viruses, bacteria, protists, and fungi—infect a wide range of animals, including humans. In response, animals fight back in various ways. Dedicated immune cells patrol the body fluids of most animals, searching out and destroying foreign cells. For example, as shown in the colorized scanning electron micrograph in **Figure 43.1**, an immune cell called a macrophage (blue) engulfs a yeast cell (green). Additional responses to infection take many forms, including proteins that punch holes in bacterial membranes or block viruses from entering body cells. These and other defenses make up an **immune system**, which enables an animal to avoid or limit many infections.

An animal's most basic defense against pathogens is a barrier. An outer covering, such as skin or a shell, provides a significant obstacle to invasion by the microbes that are present on the body. Sealing off the entire body surface is impossible, however, because gas exchange, nutrition, and reproduction require openings to the environment. Additional barrier defenses, such as chemical secretions that trap or kill microbes, guard the body's entrances and exits.

If a pathogen breaches the barrier defenses and enters the animal's body, the problem of how to fend off attack changes substantially. Housed within the body fluids and tissues, the invader is no longer an outsider. To fight pathogens within the body, the animal's immune system must detect foreign particles and cells. In other words, an immune system must carry out recognition, distinguishing nonself from self.

In identifying pathogens, animal immune systems use receptors that specifically bind molecules from foreign cells or viruses. There are two general strategies for such molecular recognition, each forming the basis for a particular system for immunity. One defense system, **innate immunity**, is found in all animals. Innate immune responses are active immediately upon infection and are the same whether or not the pathogen has been encountered previously. Innate immunity includes the barrier defenses (for example, skin), as well as defenses that combat pathogens after they enter the body (see, for example, Figure 43.1). The activation of many of these internal defenses relies on recognition of pathogens. Innate immune cells produce a small preset group of receptor proteins that accomplish this task. Each innate immune receptor binds a molecule or structure that is absent from animal bodies but is common to a large class of microbes. In this way, innate immune systems detect a very broad range of pathogens.

A second defense system, found only in vertebrates, is **acquired immunity**, also known as *adaptive immunity*. Acquired (adaptive) immune responses are activated after innate immune defenses take effect and develop more slowly. The name *acquired* reflects the fact that this immune response is enhanced by previous exposure to the infecting pathogen. Ex-

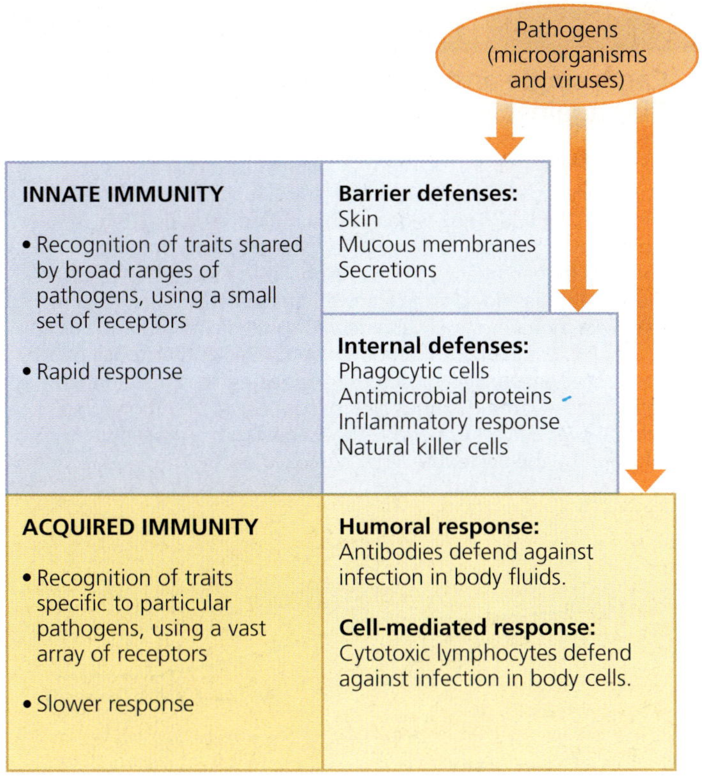

▲ **Figure 43.2 Overview of animal immunity.** Immune responses in animals can be divided into innate and acquired immunity. Some components of innate immunity contribute to activation of acquired immune defenses.

amples of acquired responses include the synthesis of proteins that inactivate a bacterial toxin and the targeted killing of a virally infected body cell. Animals with acquired immunity produce a large arsenal of receptors. Each acquired immune receptor recognizes a feature typically found only on a particular part of a particular molecule in a particular microbe. Accordingly, an acquired immune system detects pathogens with tremendous specificity.

Figure 43.2 provides an overview of the basic properties of innate and acquired immune systems. In this chapter, you will learn how each type of immune system protects animals from disease. You will also examine how pathogens can avoid or overwhelm an immune system and how defects in an immune system can imperil an animal's health.

CONCEPT **43.1**

In innate immunity, recognition and response rely on shared traits of pathogens

Innate immune systems are found among all animals (as well as in plants). In exploring innate immunity, we will begin with invertebrates, which repel and fight infection with only this type of immune system. We will then turn to vertebrates, in which innate immunity serves both as an immediate defense against infection and as the foundation for acquired immune defenses.

Innate Immunity of Invertebrates

The great success of insects in terrestrial and water habitats teeming with diverse assortments of microbes highlights the effectiveness of an innate immune system. In each of these environments, insects rely on their exoskeleton as a first line of defense against infection. Composed largely of the polysaccharide chitin, the exoskeleton provides an effective barrier defense against most pathogens. A chitin-based barrier is also present in the insect intestine, where it blocks infection by many microbes ingested with food. **Lysozyme**, an enzyme that digests microbial cell walls, and a low pH further protect the insect digestive system.

Any pathogen that breaches an insect's barrier defenses encounters a number of internal immune defenses. Immune cells called *hemocytes* circulate within the hemolymph, the insect equivalent of blood. Some hemocytes carry out a cellular defense called **phagocytosis**, the ingestion and digestion of bacteria and other foreign substances **(Figure 43.3)**. Other hemocytes trigger the production of chemicals that kill microbes and help entrap multicellular parasites. Encounters with pathogens in the hemolymph also cause hemocytes and certain other cells to secrete *antimicrobial peptides*. The antimicrobial peptides circulate throughout

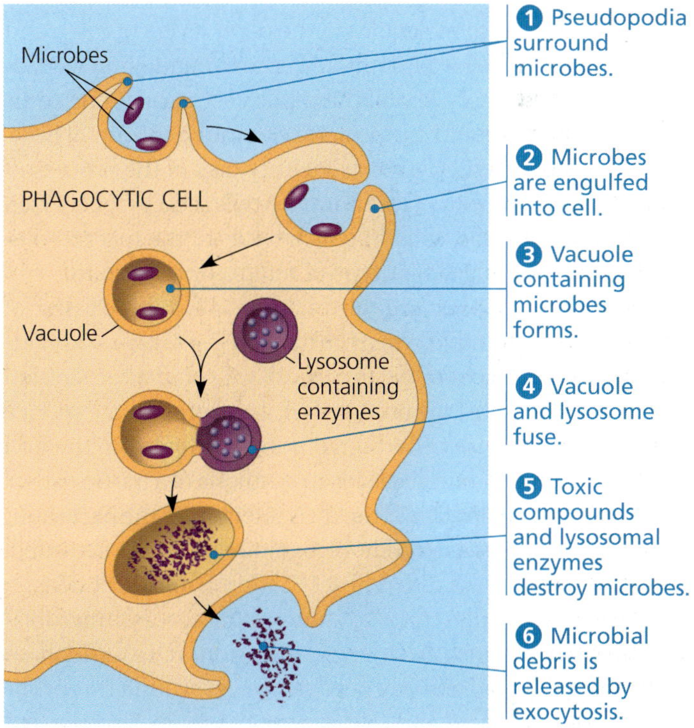

▲ **Figure 43.3 Phagocytosis.** This schematic depicts events in the ingestion and destruction of a microbe by a typical phagocytic cell.

▲ **Figure 43.4 An inducible innate immune response.** These fruit flies were engineered to express the green fluorescent protein (GFP) gene upon activation of the innate immune response. The fly on the top was injected with bacteria; the fly on the bottom was stabbed but not infected. Only the infected fly activates antimicrobial peptide genes, expresses GFP, and glows a bright green under fluorescent light.

the body of the insect **(Figure 43.4)** and inactivate or kill fungi and bacteria by disrupting their plasma membranes.

In recognizing foreign cells, immune response cells of insects rely on unique molecules in the outer layers of fungi and bacteria. Fungal cell walls contain certain unique polysaccharides, while bacterial cell walls have polymers containing combinations of sugars and amino acids not found in animal cells. Such macromolecules serve as identity tags in the process of pathogen recognition. Insect immune cells secrete specialized recognition proteins, each of which binds to the macromolecule specific to a particular type of fungus or bacterium.

Immune responses are distinct for different classes of pathogens. For example, when the fungus *Neurospora crassa* infects a fruit fly, pieces of the fungal cell wall bind a recognition protein that activates the protein Toll, a receptor on the surface of immune response cells. Signal transduction from the Toll receptor to the cell nucleus leads to synthesis of a particular set of antimicrobial peptides. If the fly is infected by the bacterium *Micrococcus luteus,* a different recognition protein is activated, and the fly produces a different set of antimicrobial peptides.

Because fruit flies secrete many different antimicrobial peptides in response to a single infection, it is difficult to study the activity of any one peptide. To get around this problem, Bruno Lemaitre and fellow researchers in France used modern genetic techniques to reprogram the fly immune system **(Figure 43.5)**. They found that the synthesis of a single

▼ **Figure 43.5 Inquiry**

Can a single antimicrobial peptide protect fruit flies against infection?

EXPERIMENT In 2002, Bruno Lemaitre and colleagues in France devised a novel strategy to test the function of a single antimicrobial peptide. They began with a mutant fruit fly strain in which pathogens are recognized but the signaling that would normally trigger innate immune responses is blocked. As a result, the mutant flies do not make any antimicrobial peptides. The researchers then genetically engineered some of the mutant fruit flies to express significant amounts of a single antimicrobial peptide, either drosomycin or defensin. The scientists infected the various flies with the fungus *Neurospora crassa* and monitored survival over a five-day period. They repeated the procedure for infection by the bacterium *Micrococcus luteus.*

RESULTS

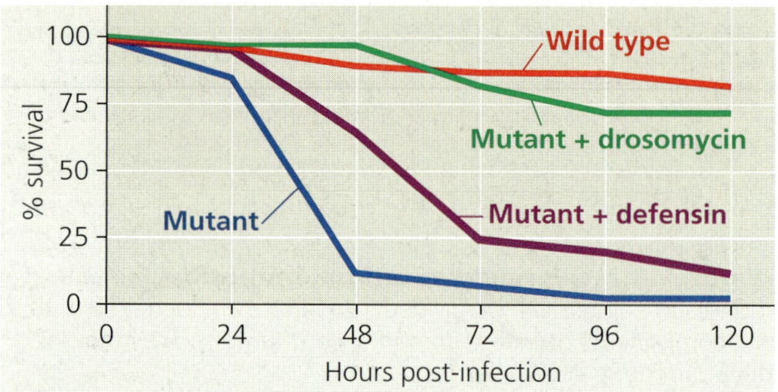

Fruit fly survival after infection by *N. crassa* fungi

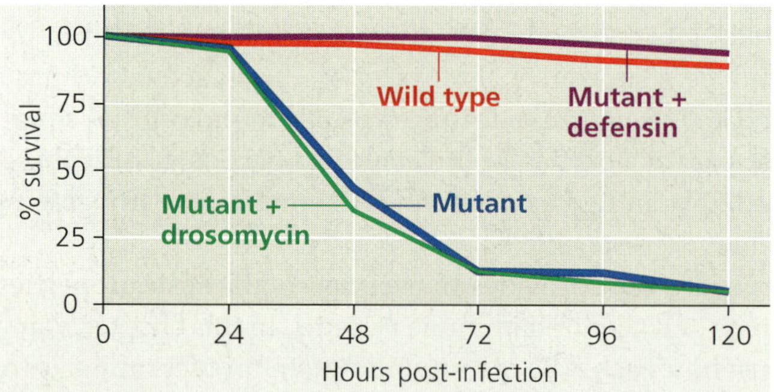

Fruit fly survival after infection by *M. luteus* bacteria

CONCLUSION Each of the two antimicrobial peptides provided a protective immune response. Furthermore, the different peptides defended against different pathogens. Drosomycin was effective against *N. crassa*, and defensin was effective against *M. luteus*.

SOURCE P. Tzou, J. Reichhart, and B. Lemaitre, Constitutive expression of a single antimicrobial peptide can restore wild-type resistance to infection in immunodeficient *Drosophila* mutants, *Proceedings of the National Academy of Sciences, USA* 99:2152 (2002).

WHAT IF? Even if a particular antimicrobial peptide showed no beneficial effect in such an experiment, why might it still be beneficial to flies?

antimicrobial peptide in the fly's body can provide an effective and specific immune defense against a particular pathogen.

Innate Immunity of Vertebrates

In vertebrates, innate immune defenses coexist with the more recently evolved system of acquired immunity. We'll focus here on mammals because most of the recent discoveries regarding vertebrate innate immunity have come from studies of mice and humans. First we'll outline the innate defenses that are similar to those found among invertebrates: barrier defenses, phagocytosis, and antimicrobial peptides. Then we'll examine two unique aspects of vertebrate innate immunity: the inflammatory response and natural killer cells.

Barrier Defenses

In mammals, epithelial tissues block the entry of many pathogens. These barrier defenses include not only the skin but also the mucous membranes lining the digestive, respiratory, urinary, and reproductive tracts. Certain cells of the mucous membranes produce *mucus*, a viscous fluid that enhances defenses by trapping microbes and other particles. In the trachea, ciliated epithelial cells sweep mucus and any entrapped microbes upward, helping prevent infection of the lungs. Saliva, tears, and mucous secretions that bathe various exposed epithelia provide a washing action that also inhibits colonization by microbes.

Beyond their physical role in inhibiting microbe entry, body secretions create an environment that is hostile to many microbes. Lysozyme in saliva, mucous secretions, and tears destroys susceptible bacteria as they enter the upper respiratory tract or the openings around the eyes. Microbes in food or water and those in swallowed mucus must also contend with the acidic environment of the stomach, which kills most microorganisms before they can enter the intestines. Similarly, secretions from sebaceous (oil) glands and sweat glands give human skin a pH ranging from 3 to 5, acidic enough to prevent the growth of many microorganisms.

Cellular Innate Defenses

Pathogens that make their way into the body are subject to detection by phagocytic white blood cells (leukocytes). These cells recognize microbes using receptors that are very similar to the Toll receptor of insects. Each mammalian **Toll-like receptor**, or **TLR**, recognizes fragments of molecules characteristic of a set of pathogens **(Figure 43.6)**. For example, TLR4, located on immune cell plasma membranes, recognizes lipopolysaccharide, a type of molecule found on the surface of many bacteria. Similarly, TLR3, on the inner surface of vesicles formed by endocytosis, is the sensor for double-stranded RNA, a form of nucleic acid characteristic of certain viruses. In each case, the recognized macromolecule is normally absent from the vertebrate body and is an essential component of a class of microbes.

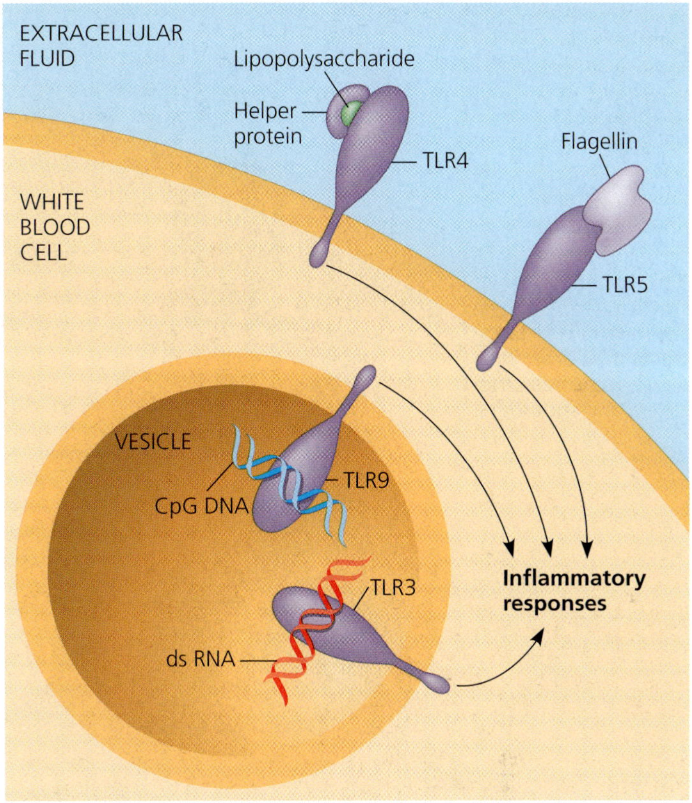

▲ **Figure 43.6 TLR signaling.** Each human Toll-like receptor (TLR) recognizes a molecular pattern characteristic of a group of pathogens. Lipopolysaccharide, flagellin, CpG DNA (DNA containing unmethylated CG sequences), and double-stranded (ds) RNA are all found in microorganisms or viruses, but not in animal cells. Together with other recognition and response factors, TLR proteins trigger internal innate immune defenses.

? *Some TLR proteins are on the cell surface, whereas others are inside vesicles. Suggest a possible benefit of this distribution.*

As in insects, recognition by a TLR triggers a series of internal defenses, beginning with phagocytosis. A white blood cell recognizes and engulfs invading microbes, trapping them in a vacuole. The vacuole then fuses with a lysosome (see Figure 43.3), leading to destruction of the microbes in two ways. First, nitric oxide and other gases produced in the lysosome poison the engulfed microbes. Second, lysozyme and other enzymes degrade microbial components.

The most abundant phagocytic cells in the mammalian body are **neutrophils** (see Figure 42.17). Signals from infected tissues attract neutrophils, which then engulf and destroy microbes. **Macrophages** ("big eaters"), like the one shown in Figure 43.1, provide an even more effective phagocytic defense. Some of these large phagocytic cells migrate throughout the body, while others reside permanently in various organs and tissues. Macrophages in the spleen, lymph nodes, and other tissues of the lymphatic system are particularly well positioned to combat pathogens. Microbes in the blood become trapped in the spleen,

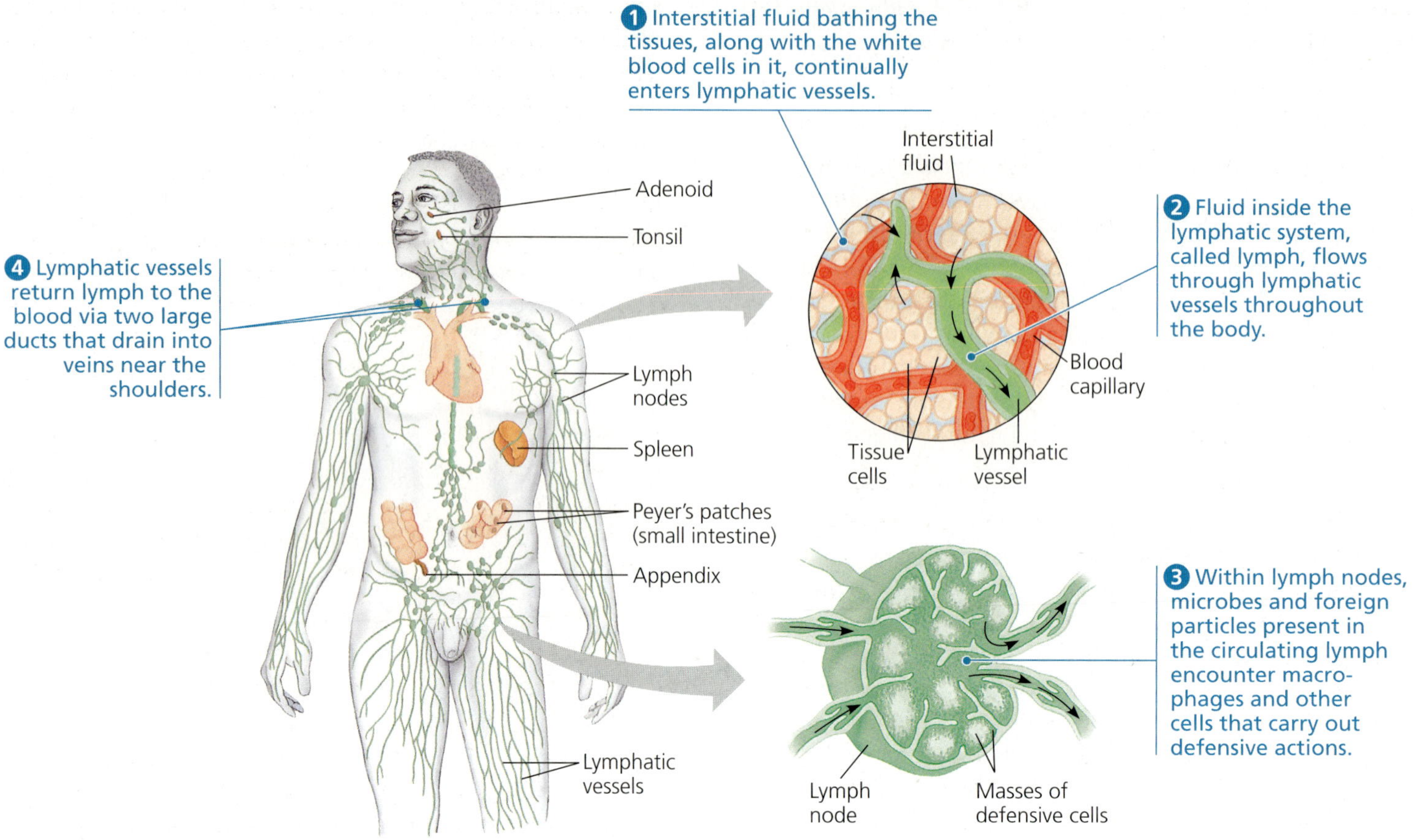

▲ **Figure 43.7 The human lymphatic system.** The lymphatic system consists of lymphatic vessels, through which lymph travels, and various structures that trap "foreign" molecules and particles. These structures include the adenoids, tonsils, lymph nodes, spleen, Peyer's patches, and appendix. Steps 1–4 trace the flow of lymph.

whereas microbes in interstitial fluid flow into lymph and are trapped in lymph nodes. In either location, they encounter resident macrophages. **Figure 43.7** provides an overview of the lymphatic system and its role in the body's defenses.

Two other types of phagocytes—eosinophils and dendritic cells—play more limited roles in innate defense. **Eosinophils** have low phagocytic activity but are important in defending against multicellular invaders, such as parasitic worms. Rather than engulfing such parasites, eosinophils position themselves against the parasite's body and then discharge destructive enzymes that damage the invader. **Dendritic cells** populate tissues that are in contact with the environment. They mainly stimulate development of acquired immunity against microbes they encounter, a function we will explore later in this chapter.

Antimicrobial Peptides and Proteins

Pathogen recognition in mammals triggers the production and release of a variety of peptides and proteins that attack microbes or impede their reproduction. Some of these defense molecules function like the antimicrobial peptides of insects, damaging broad groups of pathogens by disrupting membrane integrity. Others, including the interferons and complement proteins, are unique to vertebrate immune systems.

Interferons are proteins that provide innate defense against viral infections. Virus-infected body cells secrete interferons, inducing nearby uninfected cells to produce substances that inhibit viral reproduction. In this way, interferons limit the cell-to-cell spread of viruses in the body, helping control viral infections such as colds and influenza. Some white blood cells secrete a different type of interferon that helps activate macrophages, enhancing their phagocytic ability. Pharmaceutical companies now mass-produce interferons by recombinant DNA technology for treating certain viral infections, such as hepatitis C.

The **complement system** consists of roughly 30 proteins in blood plasma that function together to fight infections. These proteins circulate in an inactive state and are activated by substances on the surface of many microbes. Activation results in a cascade of biochemical reactions leading to lysis (bursting) of invading cells. The complement system also functions in inflammation, our next topic, as well as in the acquired defenses discussed later in the chapter.

Inflammatory Responses

The pain and swelling that alert you to a splinter under your skin are the result of a local **inflammatory response**, the changes brought about by signaling molecules released upon injury or infection. One important inflammatory signaling molecule is **histamine**, which is stored in **mast cells**, connective tissue cells that store chemicals in granules for secretion. **Figure 43.8** summarizes the progression of events in local inflammation, starting with infection from a splinter. Histamine released by mast cells at sites of tissue damage triggers nearby blood vessels to dilate and become more permeable. Activated macrophages and other cells discharge additional signaling molecules that further promote blood flow to the injured site. The resulting increase in local blood supply causes the redness and heat typical of inflammation (from the Latin *inflammare*, to set on fire). Capillaries engorged with blood leak fluid into neighboring tissues, causing swelling.

During inflammation, cycles of signaling and response transform the infection site. Enhanced blood flow to the injury site helps deliver antimicrobial proteins. Activated complement proteins promote further release of histamine and help attract phagocytes. Nearby endothelial cells secrete signaling molecules that attract neutrophils and macrophages. Taking advantage of increased vessel permeability to enter injured tissues, these cells carry out additional phagocytosis and inactivation of microbes. The result is an accumulation of *pus*, a fluid rich in white blood cells, dead microbes, and cell debris.

A minor injury causes local inflammation, but severe tissue damage or infection may lead to a response that is systemic (throughout the body)—such as an increased production of white blood cells. Cells in injured or infected tissue often secrete molecules that stimulate the release of additional neutrophils from the bone marrow. In a severe infection, such as meningitis or appendicitis, the number of white blood cells in the blood may increase several-fold within a few hours.

Another systemic inflammatory response is fever. Some toxins produced by pathogens, as well as substances called *pyrogens* released by activated macrophages, can reset the body's thermostat to a higher temperature (see Chapter 40). The benefits of the resulting fever are still a subject of debate. One hypothesis is that an elevated body temperature may enhance phagocytosis and, by speeding up chemical reactions, accelerate tissue repair.

Certain bacterial infections can induce an overwhelming systemic inflammatory response, leading to a life-threatening condition called *septic shock*. Characterized by very high fever, low blood flow, and low blood pressure, septic shock occurs most often in the very old and the very young. It is fatal in more than one-third of cases.

Natural Killer Cells

Natural killer (NK) cells help recognize and eliminate certain diseased cells in vertebrates. With the exception of red blood cells, all cells in the body normally have on their surface a protein called a class I MHC molecule (we will say much more about this molecule shortly). Following viral infection or conversion to a cancerous state, cells sometimes stop expressing this protein. The NK cells that patrol the body attach to such stricken cells and release chemicals that lead to cell death, inhibiting further spread of the virus or cancer.

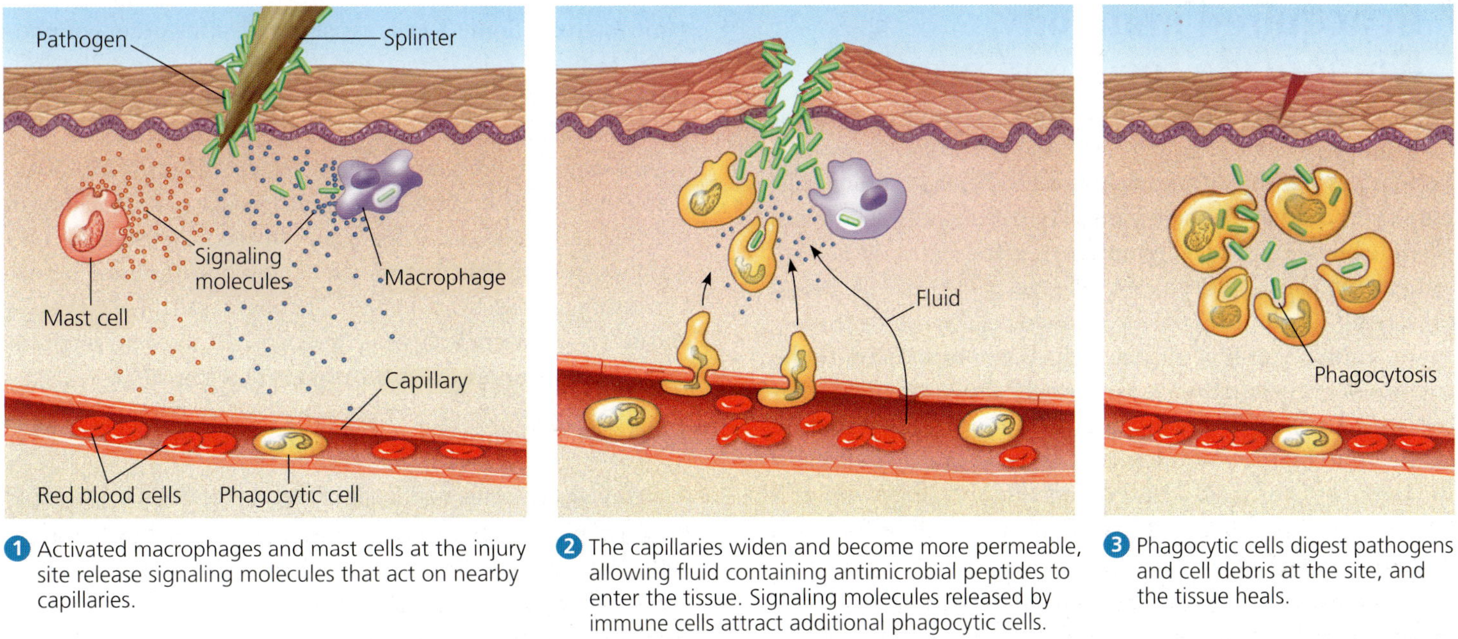

▲ **Figure 43.8 Major events in a local inflammatory response.**

Innate Immune System Evasion by Pathogens

Adaptations have evolved in some pathogens that enable them to avoid destruction by phagocytic cells. For example, the outer capsule that surrounds certain bacteria hides the polysaccharides of their cell walls, preventing recognition. One such bacterium, *Streptococcus pneumoniae*, played a critical role in the discovery that DNA can convey genetic information (see Figure 16.2). Among bacteria that do not avoid recognition, some are resistant to breakdown within lysosomes following phagocytosis. One example is the bacterium that causes tuberculosis (TB). Rather than being destroyed within the host's cells, such microbes grow and reproduce, effectively hidden from the innate immune defenses of the body. These and other mechanisms that prevent destruction by the innate immune system make the microbes that possess them substantial pathogenic threats: TB kills more than a million people a year worldwide.

CONCEPT CHECK 43.1

1. What are the main advantages and disadvantages of relying on a physical barrier against infection?
2. Although pus is often seen simply as a sign of infection, it is also an indicator of immune defenses in action. Explain.
3. **WHAT IF?** If a microbe grew optimally at low pH, how might this affect its ability to act as a human pathogen? Explain.

For suggested answers, see Appendix A.

CONCEPT **43.2**

In acquired immunity, lymphocyte receptors provide pathogen-specific recognition

Vertebrates are unique among animals in having acquired immunity in addition to innate immunity. B cells and T cells, types of white blood cells called **lymphocytes** (see Figure 42.17), are critical for this acquired immune defense. Like all blood cells, lymphocytes originate from stem cells in the bone marrow. Lymphocytes that migrate from the bone marrow to the **thymus**, an organ in the thoracic cavity above the heart, mature into **T cells** ("T" for thymus). Lymphocytes that mature in the bone marrow develop as **B cells**. (The "B" stands for the bursa of Fabricius, a bird organ where B cells were first discovered. But you can think of "B" as standing for bone marrow, where B cells mature in most vertebrates.)

B cells and T cells recognize and inactivate foreign cells and molecules. Both types of cells also contribute to *immunological memory*, an enhanced response to a foreign molecule encountered previously. Immunological memory, which can persist for many decades, is responsible for the protection we obtain against chickenpox and many other diseases from either a prior infection or vaccination. Its existence was apparent to the Greek historian Thucydides almost 2,400 years ago: He noted that individuals who had recovered from the plague could safely care for those who were sick or dying, "for the same man was never attacked twice—never at least fatally."

Although B cells and T cells function only in the acquired immune system, innate immunity and acquired immunity are not independent. At the start of an infection, signaling molecules from phagocytic cells carrying out innate immune responses activate lymphocytes, setting the stage for the slower-developing acquired response. For example, as macrophages and dendritic cells ingest microbes, these phagocytic cells secrete **cytokines**, proteins that help recruit and activate lymphocytes. Macrophages and dendritic cells also have a direct role in pathogen recognition by B cells and T cells, as you will see shortly.

Acquired Immunity: *An Overview*

The basic facts of acquired immunity can be summarized by the following set of statements. Each B cell or T cell has on its surface many receptor proteins that can each bind a particular foreign molecule. The receptor proteins on a single lymphocyte are all the same, but there are millions of lymphocytes in the body that differ in the foreign molecules that their receptors recognize. When an animal is infected, B and T cells with receptors that can recognize the microbe are activated for particular roles in the immune response. In the activation process, the B and T cells interact with fragments of microbes displayed on the surface of cells. Activated lymphocytes undergo cell division, with a set of daughter cells being set aside to fight any future infections of the host by the same microbe. Some T cells assist in activating other lymphocytes. Other T cells detect and kill infected host cells. Specialized B cells secrete soluble receptor proteins that attack foreign molecules and cells circulating in body fluids.

Although the preceding paragraph is a fair summary of acquired immunity, it raises many questions: How are millions of different receptors made? How does infection activate the very lymphocytes that fight that infection? How does the immune system distinguish self from nonself? The answers to these questions and others will become clear as we explore acquired immunity in more detail, beginning with the process of recognition.

Antigen Recognition by Lymphocytes

Any foreign molecule that is specifically recognized by lymphocytes and elicits a response from them is called an **antigen**. Most antigens are large molecules, either proteins or polysaccharides. Some antigens, such as toxins secreted by bacteria, are released into the extracellular fluid. Many other antigens protrude from the surface of pathogens or other foreign cells.

B cells and T cells recognize antigens using the antigen-specific receptors embedded in their plasma membranes **(Figure 43.9)**. A single B or T lymphocyte has about 100,000 of these **antigen receptors** on its surface. B cells sometimes give rise to *plasma cells* that secrete a soluble form of the antigen receptor. This secreted protein is called an **antibody**, or **immunoglobulin (Ig)**.

Antigen receptors and antibodies recognize just a small, accessible portion of an antigen that is called an **epitope**, or *antigenic determinant*. A single antigen usually has several different epitopes, each capable of inducing a response from a lymphocyte that recognizes the epitope **(Figure 43.10)**.

All of the antigen receptors on a single lymphocyte are identical; that is, they recognize the same epitope. Each of the body's lymphocytes thus displays *specificity* for a particular epitope. Consequently, each lymphocyte defends against any pathogen that produces molecules containing that epitope.

The Antigen Receptors of B Cells and T Cells

Each **B cell receptor** for an antigen is a Y-shaped molecule consisting of four polypeptide chains: two identical **heavy chains** and two identical **light chains**, with disulfide bridges linking chains together (Figure 43.9a). A transmembrane region near one end of each heavy chain anchors the receptor in the cell's plasma membrane. A short tail region at the end of the heavy chain extends into the cytoplasm.

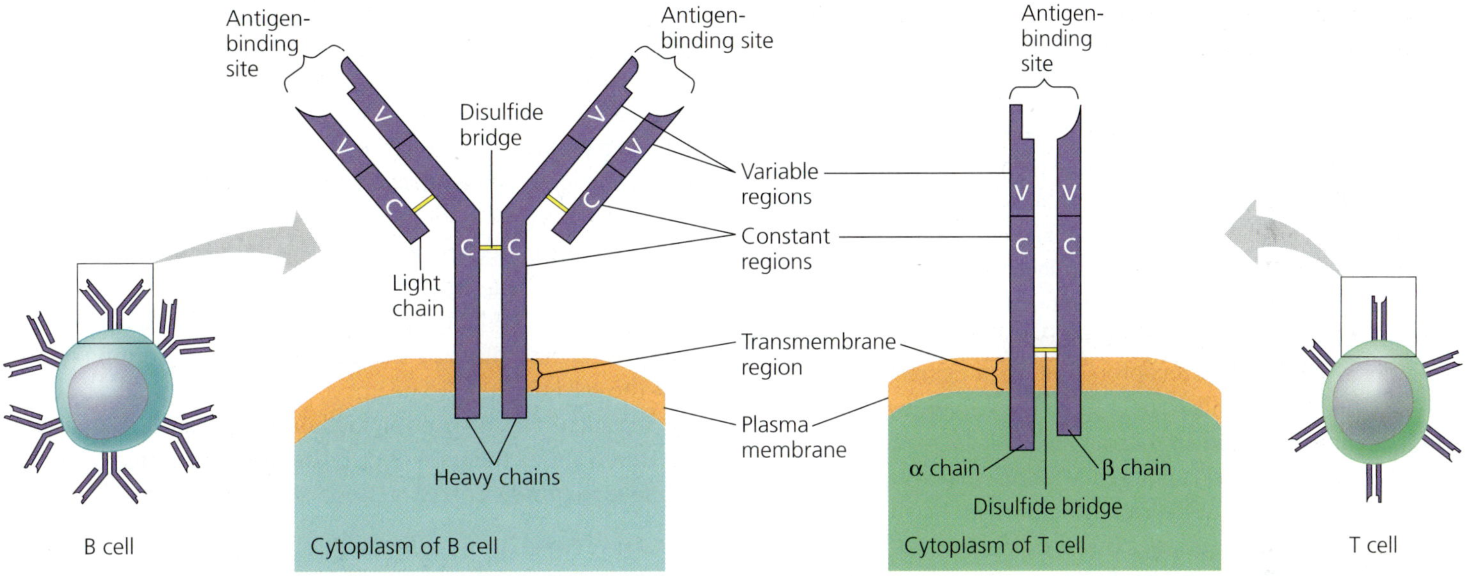

(a) A B cell receptor consists of two identical heavy chains and two identical light chains linked by disulfide bridges.

(b) A T cell receptor consists of one α chain and one β chain linked by a disulfide bridge.

▲ **Figure 43.9 Antigen receptors on lymphocytes.** All the antigen receptors on a particular B cell or T cell are identical and bind identical antigens. The variable (V) regions of receptors vary extensively from cell to cell, accounting for the different binding specificities of individual lymphocytes; the constant (C) regions vary little or not at all.

▶ **Figure 43.10 Epitopes (antigenic determinants).** Only small, specific regions on antigens, called epitopes, are bound by the antigen receptors on lymphocytes and by secreted antibodies. In this example, three different antibody molecules bind to different epitopes on the same large antigen molecule. Note that epitopes and antigen-binding sites are typically irregular in shape, as illustrated for the antibody molecule on the left, but are often represented in a simplified, symmetrical manner, as illustrated for the antibodies on the right.

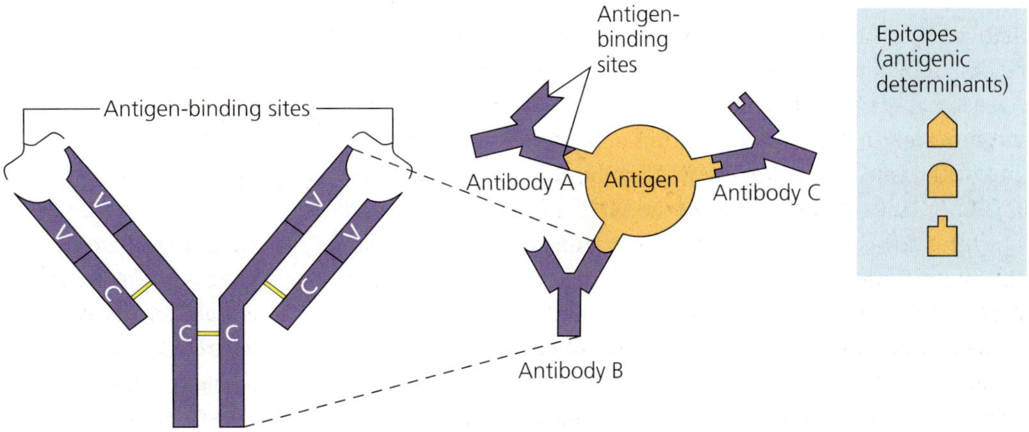

The light and heavy chains each have a *constant (C) region*, where amino acid sequences vary little among the receptors present on different B cells. The C region includes the cytoplasmic tail and transmembrane region of the heavy chain and all of the disulfide bridges. Within the two tips of the Y shape, the light and heavy chains each have a *variable (V) region*, so named because its amino acid sequence varies extensively from one B cell to another. Together, parts of a heavy-chain V region and a light-chain V region form an asymmetrical binding site for an antigen. As shown in Figure 43.9a, each B cell receptor has two identical antigen-binding sites.

Antibodies have the same overall organization as B cell receptors, except that they lack the transmembrane region and cytoplasmic tail (see Figures 43.9 and 43.10). As a result, antibodies are secreted rather than membrane-bound, a difference associated with distinct functions that we will discuss shortly.

Each **T cell receptor** for an antigen consists of two different polypeptide chains, an α *chain* and a β *chain*, linked by a disulfide bridge (Figure 43.9b). Despite having two rather than four chains, T cell receptors have many features in common with B cell receptors. Near the base of the T cell receptor is a transmembrane region that anchors the molecule in the cell's plasma membrane. At the outer tip of the molecule, the α and β chain variable (V) regions form a single antigen-binding site. The remainder of the molecule is made up of the constant (C) regions.

B cell and T cell receptors have closely related but distinct functions. Both types of receptors bind to antigens via noncovalent bonds that stabilize the interaction between an epitope and the binding surface. In this manner, B cell receptors recognize and bind to an intact antigen, whether that antigen is free or on the surface of a pathogen. In contrast, T cell receptors bind only to antigen fragments that are displayed, or *presented*, on the surface of host cells. Each of the genes in a group called the **major histocompatibility complex (MHC)** produces a host cell protein that can present an antigen fragment to T cell receptors in this way. The simultaneous interaction of an antigen fragment, an MHC molecule, and a T cell receptor is a central event in acquired immunity and is our next topic.

The Role of the MHC

Antigen recognition by T cells begins with a pathogen either infecting or being engulfed by a host cell. Once the pathogen is inside a host cell, enzymes in the cell cleave the pathogen proteins into smaller pieces, called peptide antigens or antigen fragments. These antigen fragments then bind to an MHC molecule inside the cell. Movement of the MHC molecule and bound fragment to the cell surface results in **antigen presentation**, the display of the antigen fragment on the cell surface **(Figure 43.11)**. If an antigen-presenting cell encounters a T cell, the receptors on the T cell can bind to the antigen fragment.

Antigen presentation by MHC proteins either activates immune responses against the antigen or targets for destruction

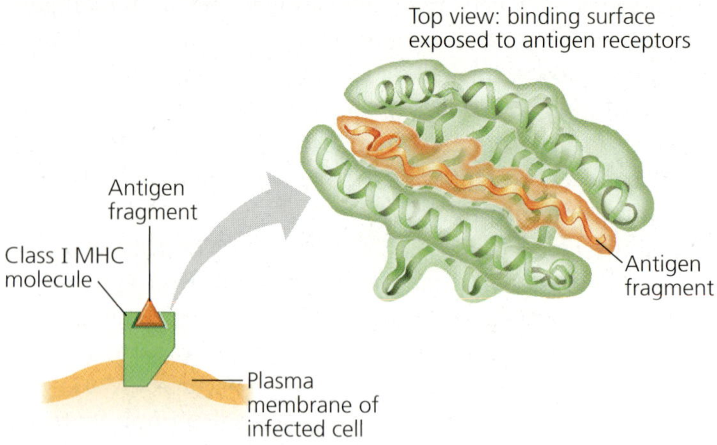

▲ **Figure 43.11 Antigen presentation by an MHC molecule.** A class I MHC molecule extending from the plasma membrane displays a bound antigen fragment for recognition by the antigen receptor of a lymphocyte. The enlarged view is of the MHC surface that binds and presents an antigen fragment.

an infected cell displaying the antigen fragment. The type of cell that presents the antigen determines which kind of response occurs. When a phagocyte or lymphocyte that has engulfed a pathogen displays an antigen, it signals the immune system that an infection is under way. The immune system responds by increasing its response to that antigen and the pathogen that produces it. When a cell that has been invaded by a pathogen displays an antigen, it signals the immune system that the cell is infected. The immune system responds by eliminating such cells, disrupting further spread of the infection.

To recognize the type of cell displaying an antigen, the immune system relies on two classes of MHC molecules:

- **Class I MHC molecules** are found on almost all cells of the body (the notable exceptions being non-nucleated cells, such as red blood cells). Class I MHC molecules bind to peptide fragments of foreign antigens synthesized within the cell. Any body cell that becomes infected or cancerous can synthesize foreign antigens and display antigen fragments by virtue of its class I MHC molecules **(Figure 43.12a)**. Class I MHC molecules displaying bound antigen fragments are recognized by a subgroup of T cells called **cytotoxic T cells**. The term *cytotoxic* refers to their use of toxic gene products to kill infected cells.
- **Class II MHC molecules** are made by just a few cell types, mainly dendritic cells, macrophages, and B cells. In these cells, class II MHC molecules typically bind to antigen fragment derived from foreign materials that have been internalized through phagocytosis or endocytosis **(Figure 43.12b)**. Dendritic cells, macrophages, and B cells are known as **antigen-presenting cells** because of their key role in displaying such internalized antigens. Antigen-presenting cells display antigens for recognition by cytotoxic T cells and **helper T cells**, a group of T cells that assist both B cells and cytotoxic T cells.

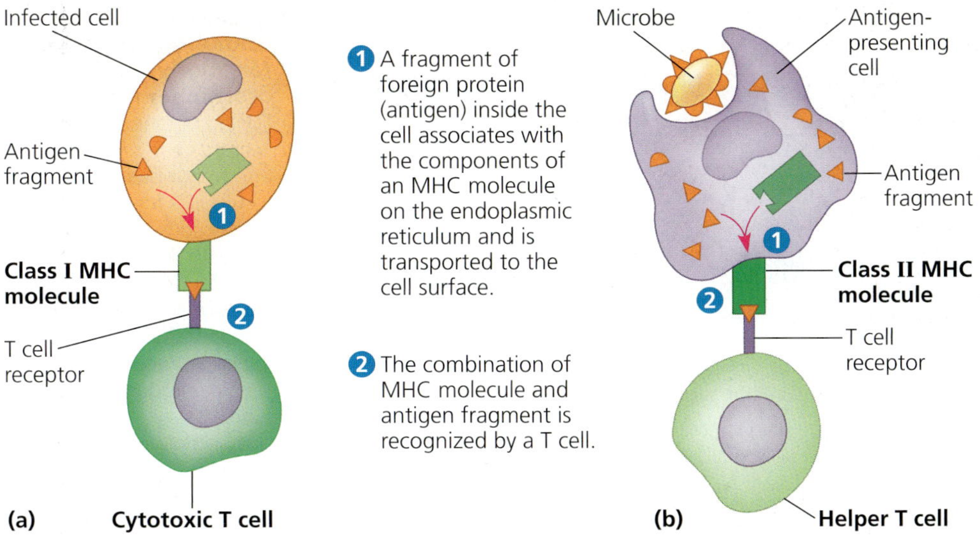

◄ **Figure 43.12 The interaction of T cells with antigen-presenting cells.** **(a)** Class I MHC molecules display fragments of antigens to cytotoxic T cells. **(b)** Class II MHC molecules display fragments of antigens to both cytotoxic T cells and, as shown here, helper T cells.

In both (a) and (b), the T cell receptor binds with an MHC molecule–antigen fragment complex. Class I MHC molecules are made by most nucleated cells, whereas class II MHC molecules are made primarily by antigen-presenting cells (macrophages, dendritic cells, and B cells).

Lymphocyte Development

Now that you know how lymphocytes recognize antigens, let's consider three major properties of the acquired immune system. First, the tremendous diversity of receptors ensures that even pathogens never before encountered will be recognized as foreign. Second, this ability to recognize vast numbers of foreign molecules coexists with a lack of reactivity against the molecules that make up the animal's own cells and tissues. Third, the response to an antigen that has been encountered previously is stronger and more rapid than the initial response—a feature called immunological memory.

Three events in a lymphocyte's life provide the basis for receptor diversity, lack of self-reactivity, and immunological memory. The first two events take place as a lymphocyte matures. The third important event happens when a mature lymphocyte encounters and binds a specific antigen. Let's consider these three events in the order in which they occur.

Generation of Lymphocyte Diversity by Gene Rearrangement

Differences in the amino acid sequence of the variable region account for the specificity of antigen receptors on lymphocytes. Recall that a single B or T cell displays about 100,000 antigen receptors, all identical. If we randomly selected any two B cells or T cells, it is highly unlikely that they would have the same antigen receptor. Instead, the variable regions at the tip of a particular antigen receptor would differ in their amino acid sequence from one cell to the other. Because the variable regions form the antigen-binding site, a particular amino acid sequence generates specificity for a certain epitope.

Each person has more than 1 million different B cells and 10 million different T cells, each with a particular antigen-binding specificity. Yet there are only about 20,500 protein-coding genes in the human genome. How, then, do we generate such remarkable diversity in antigen receptors? The answer lies in a variety of combinations. Think of selecting a car with a choice of three interior colors and six exterior colors. There are 18 (3×6) color combinations to consider. Similarly, by combining variable elements, the immune system assembles many different receptors from a much smaller collection of parts.

To understand the origin of receptor diversity, let's consider an immunoglobulin (Ig) gene that encodes the light chain of secreted antibodies (immunoglobulins) and membrane-bound B cell receptors. Although we'll analyze only a single Ig light-chain gene, all B cell antigen receptor and T cell antigen receptor genes undergo very similar transformations.

The capacity to generate diversity is built into the structure of the Ig light-chain gene. A receptor light chain is encoded by three gene segments: a variable (*V*) segment, a joining (*J*) segment, and a constant (*C*) segment. The *V* and *J* segments together encode the variable region of the receptor chain, while the *C* segment encodes the entire constant region. DNA sequencing reveals that the light-chain gene contains a single *C* segment, 40 different *V* segments, and 5 different *J* segments. These alternative copies of the *V* and *J* segments are arranged within the gene in a series (**Figure 43.13**, on the next page). Because a functional gene is built from one copy of each type of segment, the pieces can be combined in 200 ($40\ V \times 5\ J \times 1\ C$) different ways. (The number of different heavy-chain genes is even greater.)

Assembling a functional light-chain gene requires rearranging the DNA. Early in B cell development, a set of enzymes collectively called recombinase links one *V* gene segment to one *J* gene segment. This recombination event eliminates the long stretch of DNA between the segments, forming a single exon that is part *V* and part *J*. Because there is only an intron between the *J* and *C* DNA segments, no further DNA rearrangement is required. Instead, the *J* and *C* segments will be joined after transcription by splicing out the intervening RNA (see Figure 17.10 to review RNA splicing).

Recombinase acts randomly, linking any one of the 40 *V* gene segments to any one of the 5 *J* gene segments. Heavy-chain genes

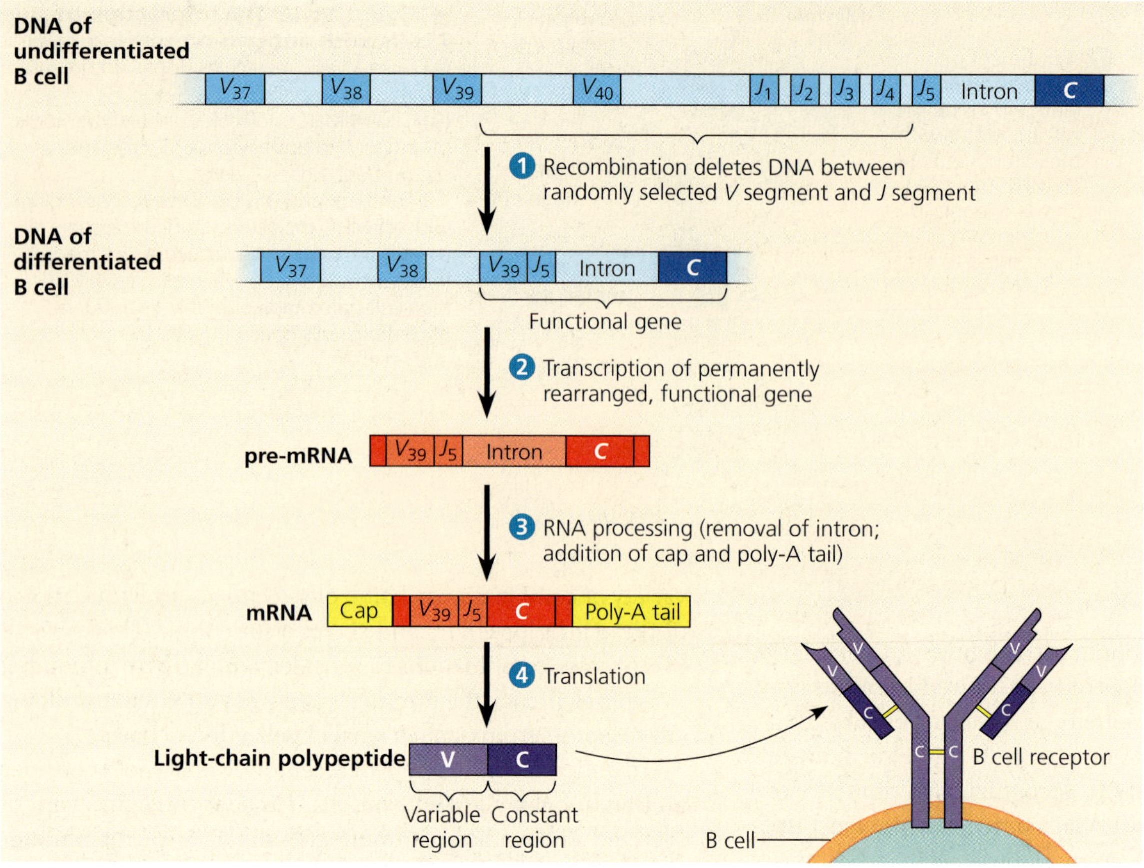

◀ **Figure 43.13 Immunoglobulin (antibody) gene rearrangement.** The joining of randomly selected *V* and *J* gene segments (V_{39} and J_5 in this example) results in a functional gene that encodes the light-chain polypeptide of a B cell receptor. Transcription, splicing, and translation result in a light chain that combines with a polypeptide produced from an independently rearranged heavy-chain gene to form a functional receptor. Mature B cells (and T cells) are exceptions to the generalization that all body cells have exactly the same DNA.

undergo a similar rearrangement. In any given cell, however, only one light-chain gene and one heavy-chain gene are rearranged. Furthermore, the rearrangements are permanent and are passed on to the daughter cells when the lymphocyte divides.

After both the light- and heavy-chain genes have rearranged, antigen receptors can be synthesized. The rearranged genes are transcribed, and the transcripts are processed for translation. Following translation, the light chain and heavy chain assemble together, forming an antigen receptor (see Figure 43.13). Each pair of randomly rearranged heavy and light chains results in a different antigen-binding surface. For the total population of B cells in a human body, the number of such combinations has been calculated as 1.65×10^6. Furthermore, mutations introduced during *VJ* recombination add additional variation, making the number of possible antigen-binding specificities even greater.

Origin of Self-Tolerance

Because antigen receptor genes are randomly rearranged, some immature lymphocytes produce receptors specific for epitopes on the body's own molecules. If these self-reactive lymphocytes were not eliminated or inactivated, the immune system could not distinguish self from nonself and would attack body proteins, cells, and tissues. Instead, as lymphocytes mature in the bone marrow or thymus, their antigen receptors are tested for self-reactivity. Lymphocytes with receptors specific for the body's own molecules are typically either destroyed by apoptosis or rendered nonfunctional, leaving only those that react to foreign molecules. Since the body normally lacks mature lymphocytes that can react against its own components, the immune system is said to exhibit *self-tolerance.* As you will read later, failure of self-tolerance can lead to autoimmune diseases, such as multiple sclerosis.

Amplifying Lymphocytes by Clonal Selection

Because the body contains an enormous variety of antigen receptors, only a tiny fraction are specific for the epitopes on a given antigen. As a result, it is very rare for an antigen to encounter a lymphocyte with a receptor specific for that antigen. How, then, can the acquired immune response be so effective? The answer lies in the changes in cell number and behavior triggered by the binding of antigen to lymphocyte.

The binding of an antigen receptor to its specific antigen initiates events that activate the lymphocyte. Activated B cells or T cells amplify the response by dividing many times, forming two types of clones: effector cells and memory cells. **Effector cells,** which are short-lived, attack the antigen and any pathogens producing that antigen. **Memory cells,** which are long-lived but less numerous, bear receptors specific for the antigen.

The proliferation of a lymphocyte into a clone of cells in response to binding an antigen is called **clonal selection (Figure 43.14).** This concept is so fundamental to understanding acquired immunity that it is worth restating: The presentation of an antigen to specific receptors on a lymphocyte

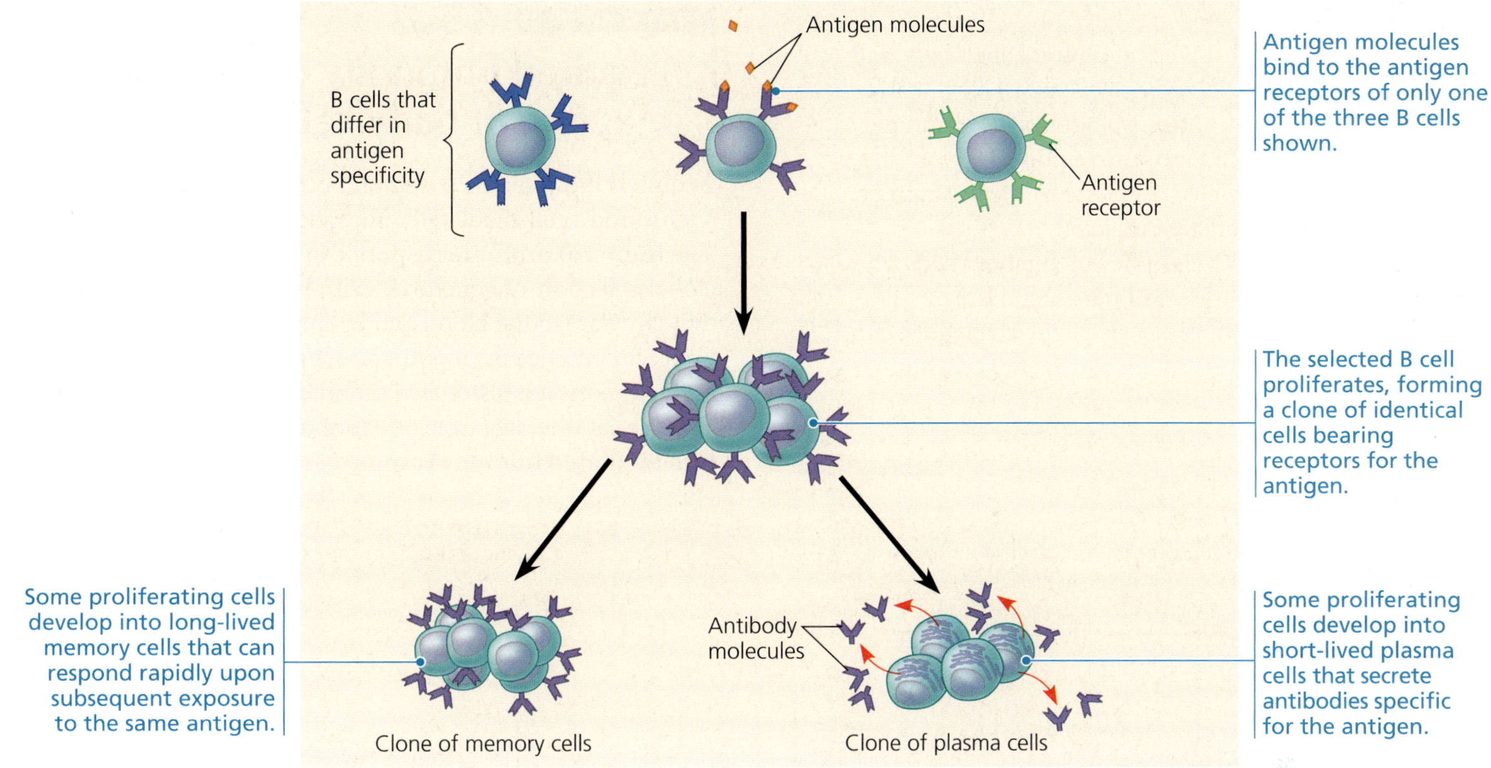

▲ **Figure 43.14 Clonal selection of B cells.** In response to its specific antigen and immune cell signals, a B cell divides and forms a clone of cells. Some of these cells become memory B cells; others become antibody-secreting plasma cells. T cells specific for the antigen undergo a similar process, generating memory T cells and effector T cells. Lymphocytes with a different antigen specificity (represented in this figure by different shapes and colors of the receptors) do not respond.

leads to repeated rounds of cell division. The result is a clonal population of thousands of cells, all specific for that antigen.

Prior exposure to an antigen alters the speed, strength, and duration of the immune response. The production of effector cells from a clone of lymphocytes during the first exposure to an antigen represents the **primary immune response**. The primary response peaks about 10 to 17 days after the initial exposure. During this time, selected B cells generate antibody-secreting effector B cells, called **plasma cells**, and selected T cells are activated to their effector forms, consisting of helper cells and cytotoxic cells. If an individual is exposed again to the same antigen, the response is faster (typically peaking only 2 to 7 days after exposure), of greater magnitude, and more prolonged. This is the **secondary immune response**. Measures of antibody concentrations in blood serum over time clearly show the difference between primary and secondary immune responses **(Figure 43.15)**.

The secondary immune response relies on the reservoir of T and B memory cells generated following initial exposure to an antigen. Because these cells are long-lived, they provide the basis for immunological memory that can span many decades. If and when an antigen is encountered again, memory cells specific for that antigen enable the rapid formation of large clones of effector cells and thus a greatly enhanced immune defense.

Although the processes for antigen recognition, clonal selection, and immunological memory are similar for B cells and T cells, these two classes of lymphocytes fight infection in different ways and in different settings, as we will explore next.

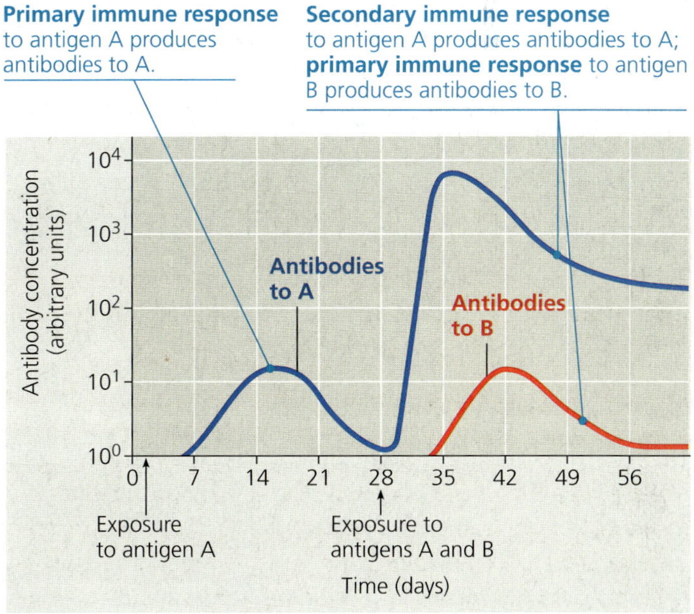

▲ **Figure 43.15 The specificity of immunological memory.** Long-lived memory cells generated in the primary response to antigen A give rise to a heightened secondary response to the same antigen, but do not affect the primary response to a different antigen (B).

CONCEPT CHECK 43.2

1. **DRAW IT** Sketch a B cell receptor. Label the V and C regions of the light and heavy chains. Now mark the positions of the antigen-binding sites, disulfide bridges, and transmembrane regions. How do the positions of these features relate to the location of the variable and constant regions?
2. Explain two advantages of having memory cells when a pathogen is encountered for a second time.
3. **WHAT IF?** If both copies of a light-chain gene and a heavy-chain gene recombined in each B cell, how would this affect B cell development?

For suggested answers, see Appendix A.

CONCEPT 43.3

Acquired immunity defends against infection of body cells and fluids

Acquired immunity is based on both a humoral immune response and a cell-mediated immune response **(Figure 43.16)**. The **humoral immune response** involves the activation and clonal selection of effector B cells, which secrete antibodies that circulate in the blood and lymph. The humoral response is so named because blood and lymph were long ago called body humors. It is also called the antibody-mediated response because of the key role of antibodies. The predominant **cell-mediated immune response** involves the activation and

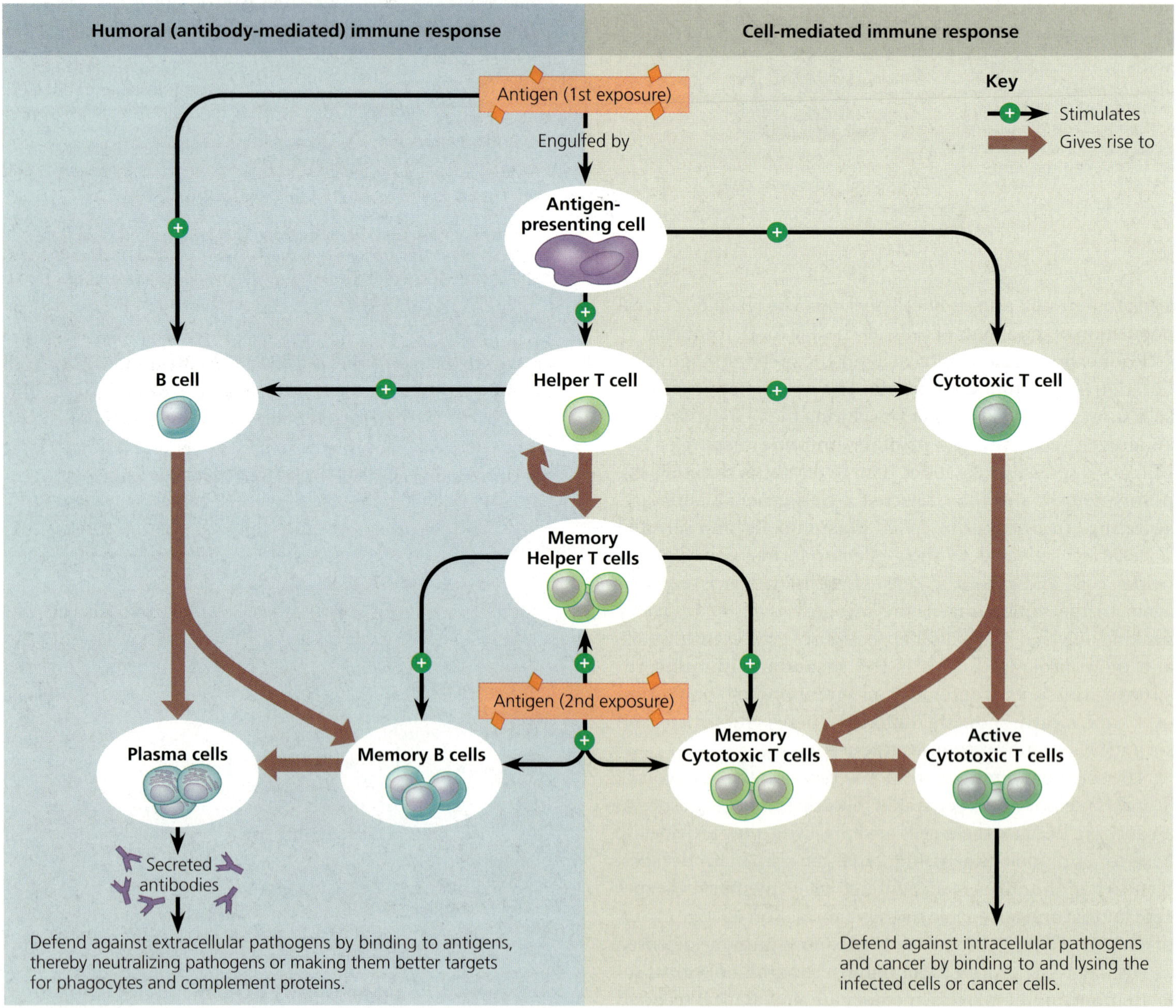

▲ **Figure 43.16 An overview of the acquired immune response.**

? *Identify each black or brown arrow as representing part of the primary or secondary response.*

clonal selection of cytotoxic T cells, which identify and destroy the target cells. A third population of lymphocytes, the helper T cells, aids both responses. As we examine the cellular interactions that underlie the acquired immune response, you can refer to the diagram in Figure 43.16 to appreciate how these interactions work together.

Helper T Cells: A Response to Nearly All Antigens

Activated by encounters with antigen-presenting cells, helper T cells play a central role in enhancing humoral and cell-mediated responses. The helper T cell proliferates after interacting with antigen fragments displayed by antigen-presenting cells (usually dendritic cells). The resulting clone of cells differentiates into activated helper T cells and memory helper T cells. Activated helper T cells secrete cytokines that stimulate the activation of nearby B cells and cytotoxic T cells.

A helper T cell and the antigen-presenting cell displaying its specific epitope have a complex interaction **(Figure 43.17)**. The T cell receptors on the surface of the helper T cell bind to the antigen fragment that is held by a class II MHC molecule on the antigen-presenting cell. At the same time, a protein called **CD4**, found on the surface of most helper T cells, binds to the class II MHC molecule. CD4 helps keep the helper T cell and antigen-presenting cell joined. As the two cells interact, signals in the form of cytokines are exchanged in both directions. For example, cytokines secreted from a dendritic cell act in combination with the antigen to stimulate the helper T cell, causing it to produce its own set of cytokines. The net result is activation of the helper T cell.

The three principal types of antigen-presenting cells—dendritic cells, macrophages, and B cells—interact with helper T cells in different contexts. Dendritic cells are particularly important in triggering a primary immune response. They serve as sentinels in the epidermis and other tissues frequently exposed to foreign antigens. After dendritic cells capture antigens, they migrate from the infection site to lymphoid tissues. There they present antigens, via class II MHC molecules, to helper T cells (see Figure 43.17). Macrophages play the key role in initiating a secondary immune response by presenting antigens to memory helper T cells, while the humoral response relies mainly on B cells to present antigens to helper T cells.

Cytotoxic T Cells: A Response to Infected Cells

Cytotoxic T cells are the effector cells in a cell-mediated immune response. To become active, they require signaling molecules from helper T cells as well as interaction with an antigen-presenting cell. Once activated, they can eliminate cancerous body cells and body cells infected by viruses or other intracellular pathogens. Fragments of nonself proteins synthesized in such target cells associate with class I MHC molecules and are displayed on the cell surface, where they can be recognized by cytotoxic T cells (**Figure 43.18**, on the next page). A surface protein called **CD8**, found on most cytotoxic T cells, enhances the interaction between a target cell and a cytotoxic T cell. Binding of CD8 to a class I MHC molecule helps keep the two cells in contact while the cytotoxic T cell is activated. Thus, the roles of class I MHC molecules and CD8 are similar to those of class II MHC molecules and CD4.

The targeted destruction of an infected cell by a cytotoxic T cell involves the secretion of proteins that cause cell rupture and cell death (see Figure 43.18). The death of the infected cell not only deprives the pathogen of a place to reproduce but also exposes it to circulating antibodies, which mark it for disposal. After destroying an infected cell, the cytotoxic T cell may move on and kill other cells infected with the same pathogen.

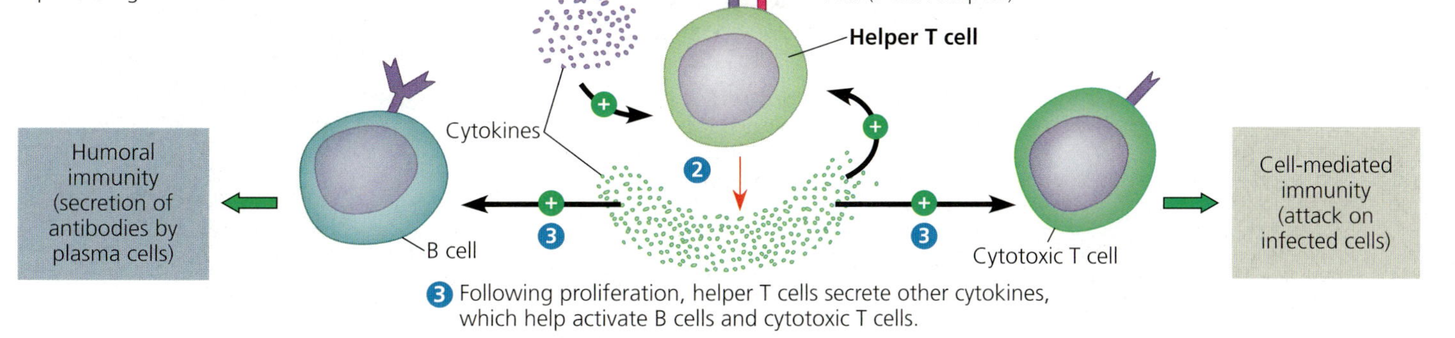

▲ **Figure 43.17 The central role of helper T cells in humoral and cell-mediated immune responses.**

1 An activated cytotoxic T cell binds to a class I MHC–antigen fragment complex on a target cell via its TCR with the aid of the protein CD8.

2 The T cell releases perforin molecules, which form pores in the target cell membrane, and granzymes, enzymes that break down proteins. Granzymes enter the target cell by endocytosis.

3 The granzymes initiate apoptosis within the target cell, leading to fragmentation of the nucleus and cytoplasm and eventual cell death. The released cytotoxic T cell can attack other target cells.

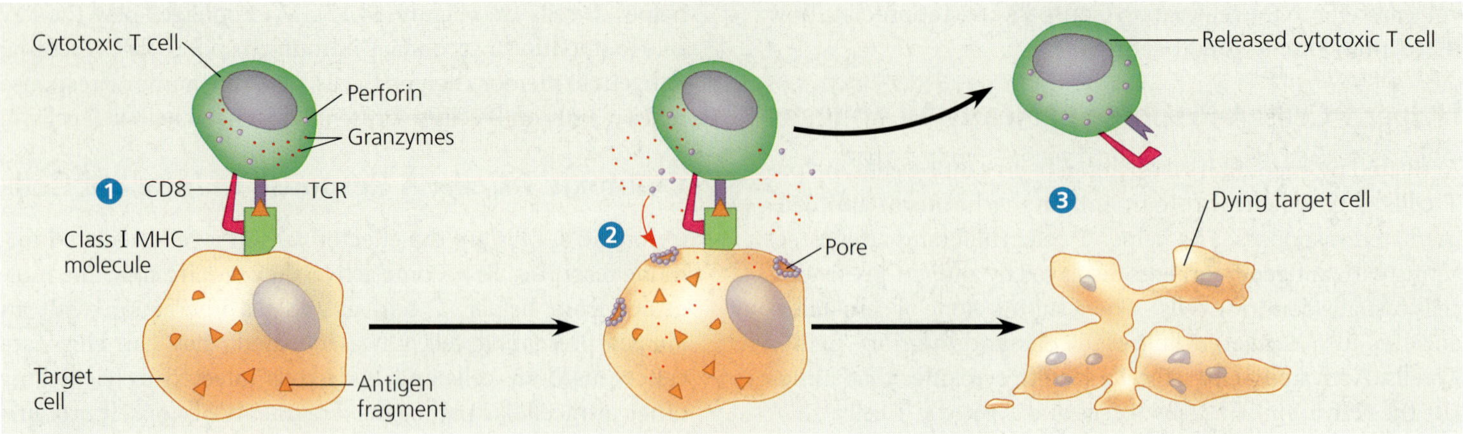

▲ **Figure 43.18 The killing action of cytotoxic T cells.** An activated cytotoxic T cell releases molecules that make pores in a target cell's membrane and enzymes that break down proteins, promoting the cell's death.

1 After an antigen-presenting cell engulfs and degrades a bacterium, it displays an antigen fragment (peptide) complexed with a class II MHC molecule. A helper T cell that recognizes the complex is activated with the aid of cytokines secreted from the antigen-presenting cell, forming a clone of activated helper T cells (not shown).

2 A B cell with receptors for the same peptide internalizes the antigen and displays it on the cell surface in a complex with a class II MHC protein. An activated helper T cell bearing receptors specific for the displayed antigen fragment binds to the B cell. This interaction, with the aid of cytokines from the T cell, activates the B cell.

3 The activated B cell proliferates and differentiates into antibody-secreting plasma cells and memory B cells. The secreted antibodies are specific for the same bacterial antigen that initiated the response.

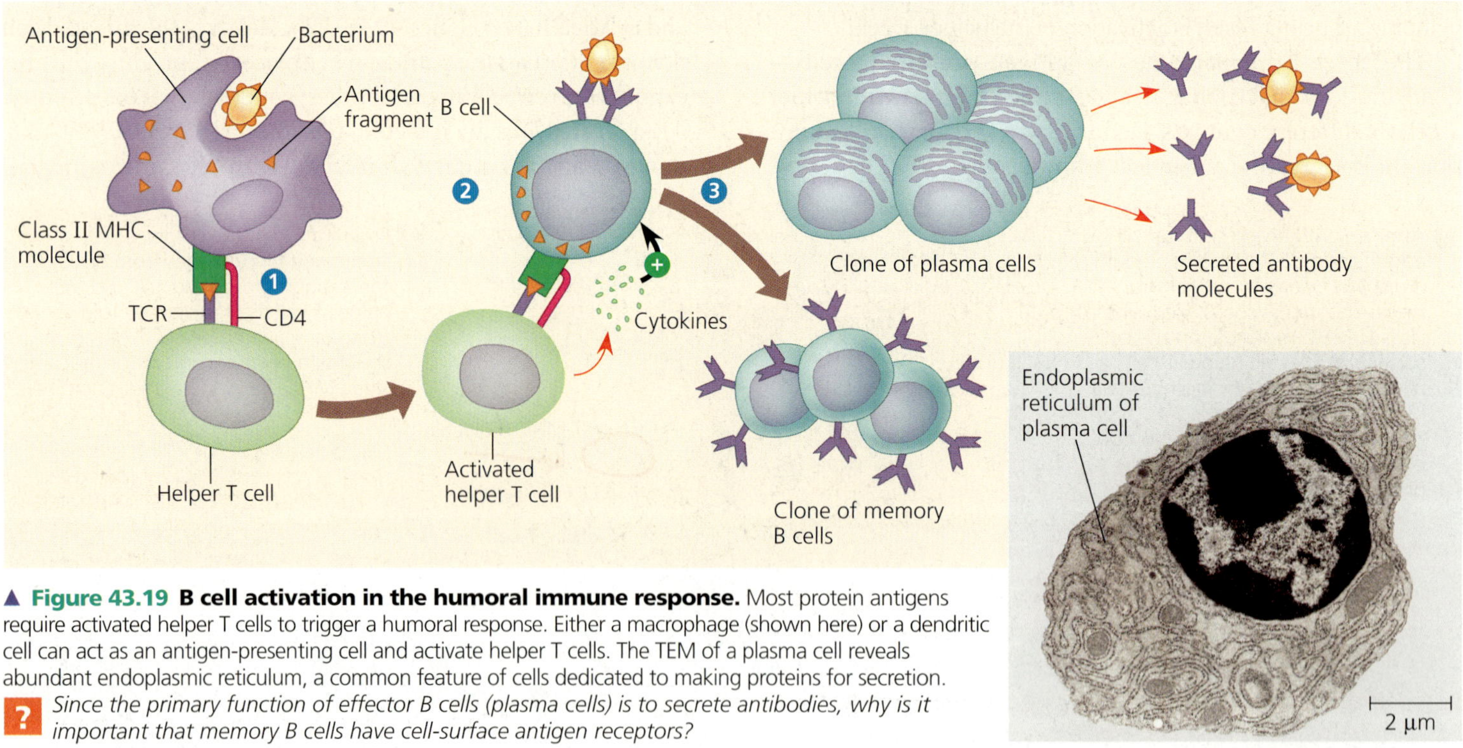

▲ **Figure 43.19 B cell activation in the humoral immune response.** Most protein antigens require activated helper T cells to trigger a humoral response. Either a macrophage (shown here) or a dendritic cell can act as an antigen-presenting cell and activate helper T cells. The TEM of a plasma cell reveals abundant endoplasmic reticulum, a common feature of cells dedicated to making proteins for secretion.

? *Since the primary function of effector B cells (plasma cells) is to secrete antibodies, why is it important that memory B cells have cell-surface antigen receptors?*

B Cells: A Response to Extracellular Pathogens

The secretion of antibodies by clonally selected B cells is the hallmark of the humoral response **(Figure 43.19)**. Activation of this response typically involves B cells and helper T cells, as well as proteins on the surface of bacteria. As depicted in Figure 43.19, B cell activation by an antigen is aided by cytokines secreted from helper T cells that have encountered the same antigen. Stimulated by both an antigen and cytokines, the B cell proliferates and differentiates into a clone of antibody-secreting plasma cells and a clone of memory B cells.

The pathway for antigen processing and display in B cells differs from that in other antigen-presenting cells. A macrophage or dendritic cell can present fragments from a wide variety of protein antigens, whereas a B cell presents only the antigen to which it specifically binds. When an antigen first binds to receptors on the surface of a B cell, the cell takes in a few of the foreign molecules by receptor-mediated endocytosis (see Figure 7.20). The B cell then presents an MHC-antigen fragment complex to a helper T cell. This achieves the direct cell-to-cell contact that is usually critical to B cell activation (see step 2 in Figure 43.19).

B cell activation leads to a robust humoral response: An activated B cell gives rise to a clone of thousands of plasma cells, each of which secretes approximately 2,000 antibody molecules every second of the cell's 4- to 5-day life span. Furthermore, most antigens recognized by B cells contain multiple epitopes. An exposure to a single antigen therefore normally activates a variety of B cells, with different clones of plasma cells directed against different epitopes on the common antigen.

For antigens, including polysaccharides, that contact multiple receptors on a single cell, a B cell response can occur without the involvement of cytokines or helper T cells. Although such responses generate no memory B cells, they play an important role in defending against many bacteria.

Antibody Classes

For a given B cell, the antibodies produced differ from the B cell receptor only in the constant (C) region of the heavy chain. In place of a transmembrane region and cytoplasmic tail, the heavy chain contains sequences that determine where the antibody is distributed and how it mediates antigen disposal.

The five major types of heavy-chain C regions determine five major classes of antibodies. **Figure 43.20** summarizes the structures and functions of these antibody classes. Changes in the heavy-chain gene that switch B cells from production of one antibody class to another occur only in response to antigen stimulation and to specific regulatory signals from T cells.

The power of antibody specificity and antigen-antibody binding has been harnessed in laboratory research and clinical diagnosis. Some antibody tools are *polyclonal*: They are the products of many different clones of B cells, each specific for a different epitope. Antibodies produced following exposure to a microbial antigen are polyclonal. In contrast, other antibody tools are *monoclonal*: They are prepared from a single clone of B cells grown in culture. All the **monoclonal antibodies** produced by such a culture are identical and specific for the same epitope on an antigen. Monoclonal antibodies are particularly

Class of Immunoglobulin (Antibody)	Distribution	Function
IgM (pentamer) 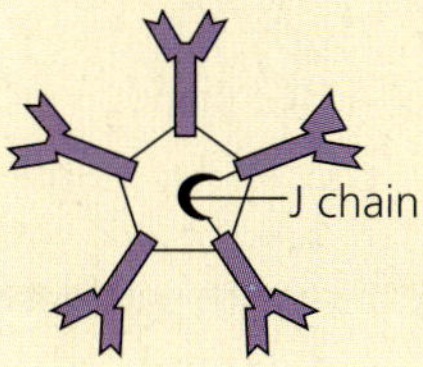	First Ig class produced after initial exposure to antigen; then its concentration in the blood declines	Promotes neutralization and cross-linking of antigens; very effective in complement system activation (see Figure 43.21)
IgG (monomer) 	Most abundant Ig class in blood; also present in tissue fluids	Promotes opsonization, neutralization, and cross-linking of antigens; less effective in activation of complement system than IgM (see Figure 43.21) Only Ig class that crosses placenta, thus conferring passive immunity on fetus
IgA (dimer) 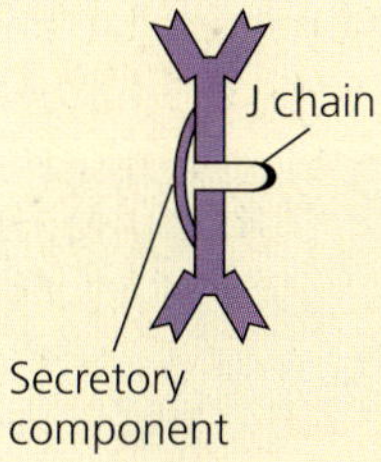	Present in secretions such as tears, saliva, mucus, and breast milk	Provides localized defense of mucous membranes by cross-linking and neutralization of antigens (see Figure 43.21) Presence in breast milk confers passive immunity on nursing infant
IgE (monomer) 	Present in blood at low concentrations	Triggers release from mast cells and basophils of histamine and other chemicals that cause allergic reactions (see Figure 43.23)
IgD (monomer) 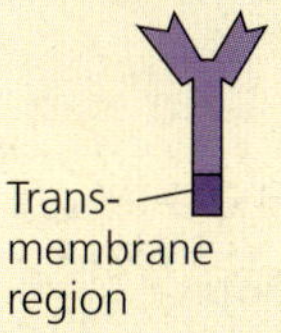	Present primarily on surface of B cells that have not been exposed to antigens	Acts as antigen receptor in the antigen-stimulated proliferation and differentiation of B cells (clonal selection)

▲ **Figure 43.20 The five antibody, or immunoglobulin (Ig), classes.** All antibody classes consist of similar Y-shaped molecules in which the tail region determines the distribution and functions characteristic of each class. IgM and IgA antibodies contain a J chain (unrelated to the *J* gene segment) that helps hold the subunits together. As an IgA antibody is secreted across a mucous membrane, it acquires a secretory component that protects it from cleavage by enzymes.

useful for tagging specific molecules. For example, home pregnancy kits use monoclonal antibodies to detect human chorionic gonadotropin (HCG). Because HCG is produced as soon as an embryo implants in the uterus (see Chapter 46), the presence of this hormone in a woman's urine provides a reliable indicator for a very early stage of pregnancy.

The Role of Antibodies in Immunity

The binding of antibodies to antigens can interfere with pathogen function in many ways, some of which are diagrammed in **Figure 43.21**. In the simplest of these, *neutralization*, antibodies bind to surface proteins of a virus or bacterium, thereby blocking the pathogen's ability to infect a host cell. Similarly, antibodies sometimes bind to and neutralize toxins released in body fluids. In a process called *opsonization*, the antibodies bound to antigens present a readily recognized structure for macrophages and therefore increase phagocytosis. Because each antibody has two antigen-binding sites, antibodies can also facilitate phagocytosis by linking bacterial cells, virus particles, or antigens into aggregates.

Antibodies sometimes work together with the proteins of the complement system to dispose of pathogens. (The name *complement* reflects the fact that these proteins increase the effectiveness of antibody-directed attacks on bacteria.) Binding of antigen-antibody complexes on a microbe or foreign cell to one of the complement proteins triggers a cascade in which each protein of the complement system activates the next. Ultimately, activated complement proteins generate a *membrane attack complex* that forms a pore in the membrane of the foreign cell. Ions and water rush into the cell, causing it to swell and lyse (see Figure 43.21, right). Whether activated as part of innate or acquired defenses, this cascade of complement protein activity results in the lysis of microbes and produces factors that promote inflammation or stimulate phagocytosis.

When antibodies facilitate phagocytosis (see Figure 43.21, middle), they also help fine-tune the humoral immune response. Recall that phagocytosis enables macrophages and dendritic cells to present antigens to and stimulate helper T cells, which in turn stimulate the very B cells whose antibodies contribute to phagocytosis. This positive feedback between the innate and acquired immune systems contributes to a coordinated, effective response to infection.

Although antibodies are the cornerstones of the response in body fluids, there is also a mechanism by which they can bring about the death of infected body cells. When a virus uses a cell's biosynthetic machinery to produce viral proteins, these viral products can appear on the cell surface. If antibodies specific for epitopes on these viral proteins bind the exposed proteins, the presence of bound antibody at the cell surface can recruit a natural killer cell. The NK cell then releases proteins that cause the infected cell to undergo apoptosis.

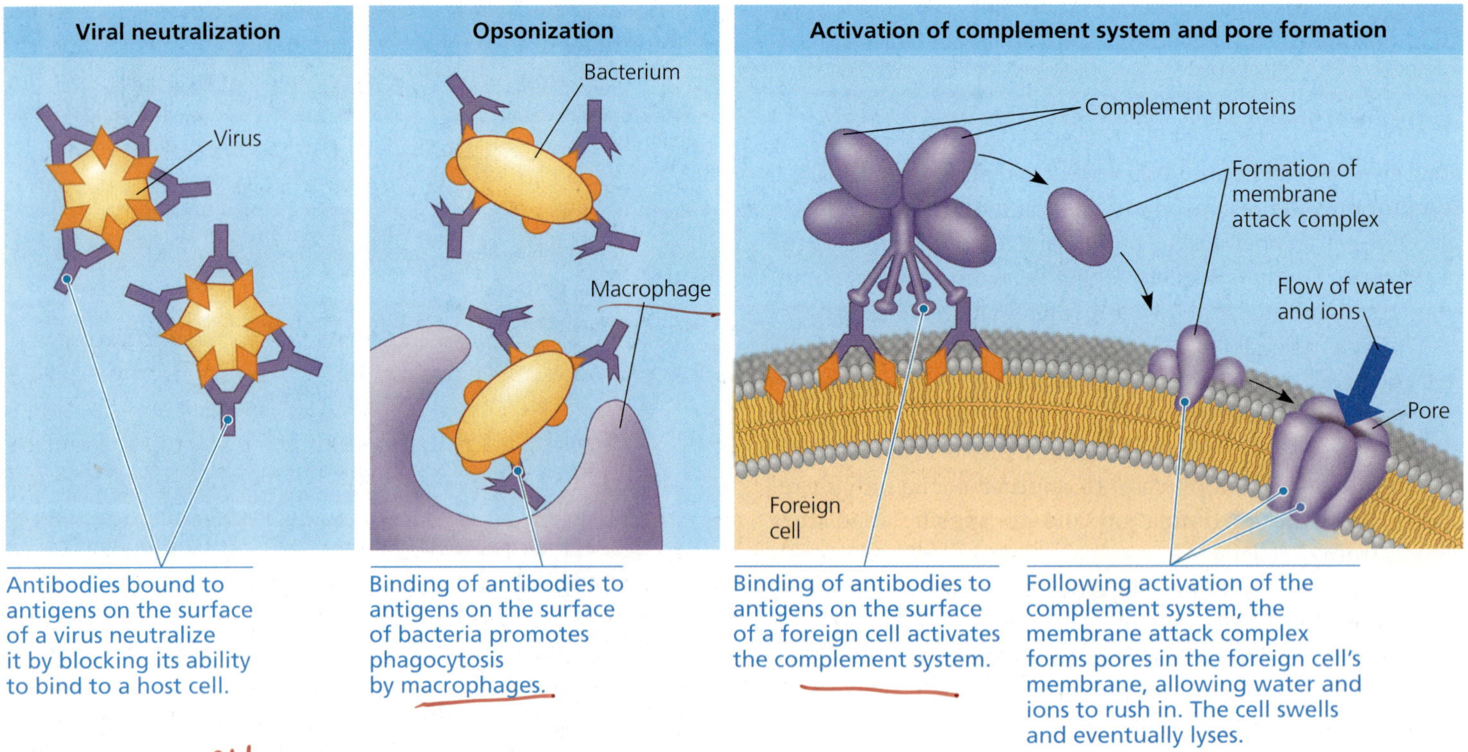

▲ **Figure 43.21 Antibody-mediated mechanisms of antigen disposal.** The binding of antibodies to antigens marks microbes, foreign particles, and soluble antigens for inactivation or destruction.

Active and Passive Immunization

Our discussion of acquired immunity has to this point focused on the defenses that arise when a particular microbe infects the body. In response to infection, clones of memory cells form, providing **active immunity**. In contrast, a distinct type of immunity results when the IgG antibodies of a pregnant woman cross the placenta to her fetus. The transferred antibodies are poised to immediately help destroy any pathogens for which they are specific. This protection is called **passive immunity** because the antibodies provided by the mother guard against microbes that have never infected the newborn. Because passive immunity does not involve the recipient's B and T cells, it persists only as long as the transferred antibodies last (a few weeks to a few months). However, IgA antibodies are passed from a mother to her infant in breast milk **(Figure 43.22)**. These antibodies provide additional protection against infection while the infant's immune system develops.

◀ **Figure 43.22**
Passive immunization of an infant occurs during breast-feeding.

Both active immunity and passive immunity can be induced artificially. Active immunity can develop from the introduction of antigens into the body through **immunization**, often called **vaccination**. The virus causing cowpox, a mild disease usually seen in cows, was used over two centuries ago as the first vaccine (from the Latin *vacca,* cow). Vaccination with cowpox was significant because it enhanced the immune response to the closely related and far more dangerous smallpox virus. Today, many sources of antigen are used to make vaccines, including inactivated bacterial toxins, killed microbes, parts of microbes, weakened microbes that generally do not cause illness, and even genes encoding microbial proteins. Because all of these agents induce a primary immune response and immunological memory, an encounter with the pathogen from which the vaccine was derived triggers a rapid and strong secondary response.

Vaccination programs have been successful against many infectious diseases that once killed, crippled, or incapacitated large numbers of people. A worldwide vaccination campaign led to eradication of smallpox in the late 1970s. In industrialized countries, routine active immunization of infants and children has dramatically reduced the incidence of sometimes devastating diseases, such as polio, measles, and whooping cough. Unfortunately, not all pathogens are easily managed by vaccination. Furthermore, some vaccines are not readily available in impoverished areas of the globe. Even in developed countries, the failure of some parents to immunize children with available vaccines has led to sporadic outbreaks of serious but fully preventable diseases. For example, a decline in vaccination rates within the former Soviet Union led to an outbreak of diphtheria during the mid-1990s that resulted in over 5,000 deaths.

In artificial passive immunization, antibodies from an immune animal are injected into a nonimmune animal. For example, humans bitten by venomous snakes are sometimes treated with antivenin, a serum from sheep or horses that have been immunized against the venom of one or more species of poisonous snakes. When injected immediately after a snakebite, the antibodies in antivenin can neutralize toxins in the venom before the toxins do massive damage.

Immune Rejection

Like pathogens, cells from another person can be recognized and attacked by immune defenses. For example, skin transplanted from one person to a genetically nonidentical person will look healthy for a week or so but will then be destroyed (rejected) by the recipient's immune response. (It remains something of a puzzle why a pregnant woman does not reject her fetus as nonself tissue.) Keep in mind that the body's hostile reaction to a transplant of other tissues or whole organs or to an incompatible blood transfusion is the expected reaction of a healthy immune system exposed to foreign antigens.

Blood Groups

To avoid harmful immune reactions in human blood transfusions, ABO blood groups must be taken into account. As discussed in Chapter 14, red blood cells are designated as type A if they have A antigen molecules on their surface. Similarly, the B antigen is found on type B red blood cells; both A and B antigens are found on type AB red blood cells; and neither antigen is found on type O red blood cells (see Figure 14.11).

To understand how ABO blood groups affect transfusions, let's consider the immune response of someone with type A blood. It turns out that certain bacteria normally present in the body have epitopes very similar to the A and B blood group antigens. By responding to the bacterial epitope similar to B antigen, a person with type A blood makes antibodies that can react with B antigen. No antibodies are made against the bacterial epitope similar to A antigen, since lymphocytes reactive with self antigens are inactivated or eliminated during development. If the person with type A blood receives a transfusion of type B blood, that person's anti-B antibodies cause an immediate and devastating transfusion reaction. The transfused red blood cells undergo lysis, which can lead to chills, fever, shock, and kidney malfunction. By the same token, anti-A antibodies in the donated type B blood can act against the recipient's type A red blood cells.

Tissue and Organ Transplants

In the case of tissue and organ transplants, or grafts, it is MHC molecules that stimulate the immune response that leads to rejection. Each vertebrate species has many different alleles for each class I and class II MHC gene, enabling presentation of antigen fragments that vary in shape and charge. This diversity of MHC molecules almost guarantees that no two people, except identical twins, will have exactly the same set. Thus, in the vast majority of graft and transplant recipients, some MHC molecules on the donated tissue are foreign to the recipient. To minimize rejection, physicians try to use donor tissue bearing MHC molecules that match those of the recipient as closely as possible. In addition, the recipient takes medicines that suppress immune responses. However, these medicines can leave the recipient more susceptible to infections during the course of treatment.

In a bone marrow transplant between individuals, the problem of rejection is reversed: The donor tissue can reject the recipient's body tissues. Bone marrow transplants are used to treat leukemia and other cancers as well as various hematological (blood cell) diseases. Prior to receiving transplanted bone marrow, the recipient is typically treated with radiation to eliminate his or her own bone marrow cells, thus destroying the source of abnormal cells. This treatment effectively obliterates the recipient's immune system, leaving little chance of graft rejection. However, lymphocytes in the donated marrow may react against the recipient. This *graft versus host reaction* is limited if the MHC molecules of the donor and recipient are well matched. Bone marrow donor programs continually seek volunteers because the great variability of MHC molecules makes a diverse pool of donors essential.

CONCEPT CHECK 43.3

1. If a child were born without a thymus, what cells and functions would be deficient? Explain.
2. Treatment of antibodies with a particular protease clips the heavy chains in half, releasing the two arms of the Y-shaped molecule. How might the antibodies continue to function?
3. **WHAT IF?** Suppose that a snake handler bitten by a particular venomous snake species was treated with antivenin. Why might the treatment for a second such bite be different?

For suggested answers, see Appendix A.

CONCEPT **43.4**

Disruptions in immune system function can elicit or exacerbate disease

Although acquired immunity offers significant protection against a wide range of pathogens, it is not fail-safe. In this last section of the chapter, we'll first examine the problems that arise when the acquired immune system is blocked or misregulated. We'll then turn to some of the evolutionary adaptations of pathogens that diminish the effectiveness of host immune responses.

Exaggerated, Self-Directed, and Diminished Immune Responses

The highly regulated interplay among lymphocytes, body cells, and foreign substances generates an immune response that provides extraordinary protection against many pathogens. When allergic, autoimmune, or immunodeficiency disorders disrupt this delicate balance, the effects are frequently severe and sometimes life-threatening.

Allergies

Allergies are exaggerated (hypersensitive) responses to certain antigens called **allergens**. The most common allergies involve antibodies of the IgE class (see Figure 43.20). Hay fever, for instance, occurs when plasma cells secrete IgE antibodies specific for antigens on the surface of pollen grains **(Figure 43.23)**. Some of these antibodies attach by their base to mast cells in connective tissues. Later, when pollen grains again enter the body, they attach to the antigen-binding sites of IgE on the surface of mast cells. Interaction with the large pollen grains cross-links adjacent IgE molecules, inducing the mast cell to release histamine and other inflammatory agents from granules (vesicles), a process called *degranulation*. Recall that histamine causes dilation and increased permeability of small blood vessels. Such vascular changes lead to typical allergy symptoms: sneezing, runny nose, tearing eyes, and smooth muscle contractions that can result in breathing difficulty. Drugs called antihistamines diminish allergy symptoms (and inflammation) by blocking receptors for histamine.

An acute allergic response sometimes leads to *anaphylactic shock*, a whole-body, life-threatening reaction that can occur within seconds of exposure to an allergen. Anaphylactic shock develops when widespread mast cell degranulation triggers abrupt dilation of peripheral blood vessels, causing a precipitous drop in blood pressure. Death may occur within minutes. Allergic responses to bee venom or penicillin can lead to anaphylactic shock in people who are extremely allergic to these substances. Likewise, people very allergic to peanuts, fish, or other foods can die from ingesting only tiny amounts of these

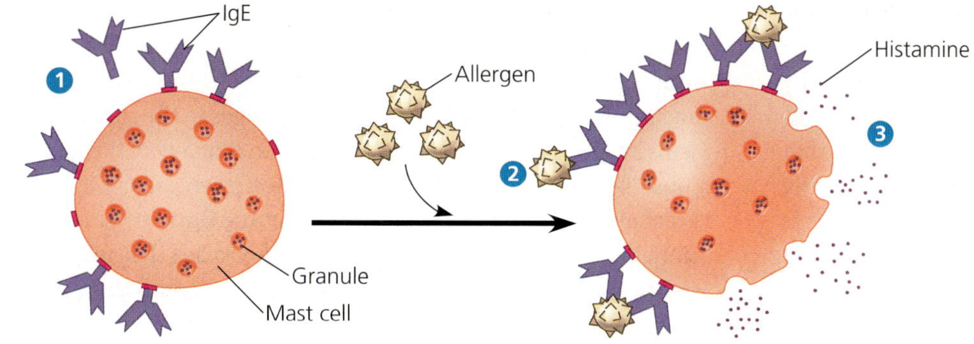

▲ **Figure 43.23 Mast cells, IgE, and the allergic response.**

allergens. People with severe hypersensitivities often carry syringes containing the hormone epinephrine, which counteracts this allergic response.

Autoimmune Diseases

In some people, the immune system turns against particular molecules of the body, causing an **autoimmune disease**. This loss of self-tolerance can take many forms. In *systemic lupus erythematosus*, commonly called *lupus*, the immune system generates antibodies against histones and DNA released by the normal breakdown of body cells. These self-reactive antibodies cause skin rashes, fever, arthritis, and kidney dysfunction. Another antibody-mediated autoimmune disease, *rheumatoid arthritis*, leads to damage and painful inflammation of the cartilage and bone of joints **(Figure 43.24)**. In *Type 1 diabetes mellitus*, the insulin-producing beta cells of the pancreas are the targets of autoimmune cytotoxic T cells. The most common chronic neurological disorder in developed countries is an autoimmune disease—*multiple sclerosis*. In this disease, T cells infiltrate the central nervous system, leading to destruction of the myelin sheath that surrounds parts of many neurons (see Figure 48.12).

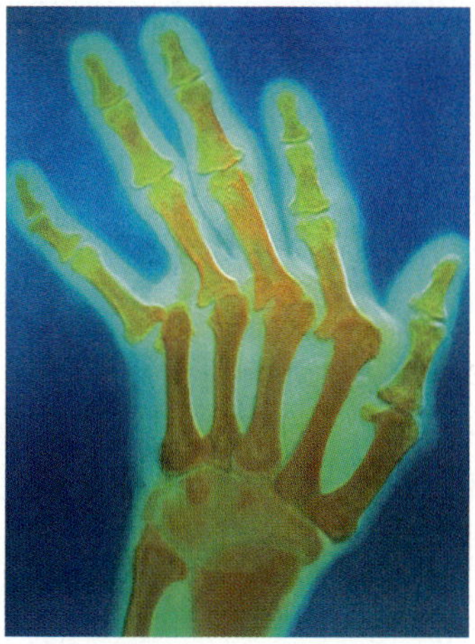

▲ **Figure 43.24 X-ray of a hand deformed by rheumatoid arthritis.**

Gender, genetics, and environment all influence susceptibility to autoimmune disorders. For example, members of certain families show an increased susceptibility to particular autoimmune disorders. In addition, many autoimmune diseases afflict females more often than males. Women are two to three times as likely as men to suffer from multiple sclerosis and rheumatoid arthritis and nine times more likely to develop lupus. There has been substantial progress in the field of autoimmunity. For example, we now know that regulatory T cells ordinarily help prevent attack by any self-reactive lymphocytes that remain functional in adults. Nevertheless, much remains to be learned about these often devastating disorders.

Exertion, Stress, and the Immune System

Many forms of exertion and stress influence immune system function. Consider, for example, susceptibility to the common cold and other infections of the upper respiratory tract. Moderate exercise improves immune system function and significantly reduces the risk of these infections. In contrast, exercise to the point of exhaustion leads to more frequent infections and to more severe symptoms. Studies of marathon runners support the conclusion that exercise intensity is the critical variable. Such runners get sick less often than their more sedentary peers during training, a time of moderate exertion, but have a marked increase in illness in the period immediately following the grueling race itself. Similarly, psychological stress has been shown to disrupt immune system regulation by altering the interplay of the hormonal, nervous, and immune systems.

Immunodeficiency Diseases

A disorder in which the ability of an immune system to protect against pathogens is defective or absent is called an **immunodeficiency**. An *inborn immunodeficiency* results from a genetic or developmental defect in the immune system. An *acquired immunodeficiency* develops later in life following exposure to chemical or biological agents. Whatever its cause and nature, an immunodeficiency can lead to frequent and recurrent infections and increased susceptibility to certain cancers.

Inborn immunodeficiencies result from defects in the development of various immune system cells or defects in the production of specific proteins, such as antibodies or the proteins of the complement system. Depending on the specific genetic defect, either innate or acquired defenses—or both—may be impaired. In severe combined immunodeficiency (SCID), functional lymphocytes are rare or absent. Lacking an acquired immune response, SCID patients are susceptible to recurrent infections, such as pneumonia and meningitis, that can cause death in infancy. Treatments include bone marrow and stem cell transplantation.

Exposure to certain agents can cause immunodeficiencies that develop later in life. Drugs used to fight autoimmune diseases or prevent transplant rejection suppress the immune system, leading to an immunodeficient state. The immune system is also suppressed by certain cancers, especially Hodgkin's disease, which damages the lymphatic system. Acquired immunodeficiencies range from temporary states that may arise from physiological stress to the devastating **acquired immunodeficiency syndrome**, or **AIDS**, which is caused by a virus. We will discuss AIDS further in the next section, which focuses on how pathogens escape the acquired immune response.

Acquired Immune System Evasion by Pathogens

Just as immune systems that ward off pathogens have evolved in animals, mechanisms that thwart immune responses have evolved in pathogens. Using human pathogens as examples, we'll examine some common mechanisms: antigenic variation, latency, and direct attack on the immune system.

Antigenic Variation

One mechanism for escaping the body's defenses is for a pathogen to alter how it appears to the immune system. Immunological memory is a record of the foreign epitopes an animal has encountered. If the pathogen that expressed those epitopes no longer does so, it can reinfect or remain in a host without triggering the rapid and robust response that memory cells provide. Such changes in epitope expression, which are called *antigenic variation*, are regular events for some viruses and parasites. The parasite that causes sleeping sickness (trypanosomiasis) provides one example. By periodically switching at random among 1,000 different versions of the protein found over its entire surface, this pathogen can persist in the body without facing an effective acquired immune response **(Figure 43.25)**.

Antigenic variation is the major reason the influenza, or "flu," virus remains a major public health problem. As it replicates in one human host after another, the human influenza virus mutates. Because any change that lessens recognition by the immune system provides a selective advantage, the virus steadily accumulates such alterations. These changes in the surface proteins of the influenza virus are the reason that a new flu vaccine must be manufactured and distributed each year. Of much greater danger, however, is the fact that the human virus occasionally exchanges genes with influenza viruses that infect domesticated animals, such as pigs or chickens. When this occurs, influenza can take on such a radically different appearance that none of the memory cells in the human population completely recognize the new strain. Such an event caused the influenza outbreak of 1918–1919, which killed more than half a million people in the United States. Worldwide more than 20 million people died, a greater number than had died in World War I. Today, a very potent form of an avian influenza virus poses the threat of another devastating outbreak (see Chapter 54).

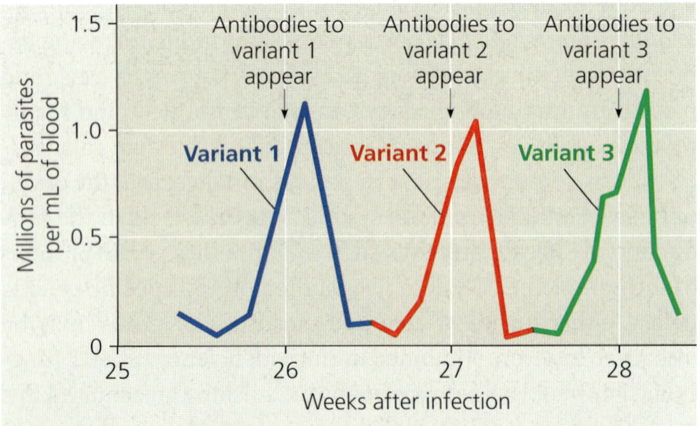

▲ **Figure 43.25 Antigenic variation in the parasite that causes sleeping sickness.** Blood samples taken from a patient during a chronic infection of sleeping sickness reveal cyclic variation in the surface coat protein of the parasite. The infection has become chronic because this weekly variation allows the parasite to evade the acquired immune response.

Latency

Some viruses remain in a host without activating immune defenses, ceasing production of viral products targeted by lymphocytes. In this largely inactive state called *latency*, there are typically no free virus particles. Instead, the viral genome persists in the nuclei of infected cells, either as a separate small DNA molecule or as a copy integrated into the host genome. Latency typically persists until conditions arise that are favorable for viral transmission or unfavorable for host survival. Such circumstances trigger the synthesis and release of particles that can infect new hosts.

Herpes simplex viruses, which establish themselves in human sensory neurons, provide a good example of latency. The type 1 virus causes most oral herpes infections, whereas the type 2 virus is responsible for most cases of genital herpes. Because sensory neurons express relatively few MHC I molecules, the infected cells are inefficient at presenting viral antigens to circulating lymphocytes. Stimuli such as fever, emotional stress, or menstruation reactivate the virus and infection of surrounding epithelial tissues. Activation of the type 1 virus can result in blisters around the mouth that are inaccurately called "cold" sores. The type 2 virus can cause genital sores, but people infected with either type 1 or type 2 virus often lack any apparent symptoms. Infections of the type 2 virus, which is sexually transmitted, pose a serious threat to the babies of infected mothers and can increase transmission of HIV, the virus that causes AIDS.

Attack on the Immune System: HIV

The human immunodeficiency virus (HIV), the pathogen that causes AIDS, both escapes and attacks the acquired immune response. Once introduced into the body, HIV infects helper T cells with high efficiency. To infect these cells, the virus binds specifically to the cell's CD4 molecules. However, HIV also infects some cell types that have low levels of CD4, including macrophages and brain cells. Within the cell, the HIV RNA genome is reverse-transcribed, and the product DNA is integrated into the host cell's genome. In this form, the viral genome can direct production of new virus particles (see Figure 19.8).

Although the body responds to HIV with an aggressive immune response sufficient to eliminate most viral infections, some HIV invariably escapes. One reason HIV persists is antigenic variation. The virus mutates at a very high rate during replication. Altered proteins on the surface of some mutated viruses prevent recognition and elimination by the immune system. Such viruses survive, proliferate, and mutate further. The virus thus evolves within the body. The continued presence of HIV is also helped by latency. When the viral DNA integrates into the chromosome of an infected cell but does not produce new virus proteins or particles, it is shielded from surveillance by the immune system. This inactive, or latent, viral DNA is also protected from antiviral agents currently used against HIV because they attack only actively replicating viruses.

Over time, an untreated HIV infection not only avoids the acquired immune response but also abolishes it **(Figure 43.26)**. The damaging effects of viral reproduction and cell death triggered by the virus leads to loss of T cells, impairing both humoral and cell-mediated immune responses. The result is a susceptibility to infections and cancers that a healthy immune system would most of the time defeat. For example, *Pneumocystis carinii* is a common fungus that does not cause disease in healthy individuals but can result in severe pneumonia in people with AIDS. Likewise, the Kaposi's sarcoma herpes virus causes a cancer among AIDS patients that is extremely rare in individuals not infected with HIV. Such opportunistic diseases, as well as nerve damage and body wasting, are the primary cause of death in AIDS patients.

At present, HIV infection cannot be cured, although certain drugs can slow HIV reproduction and the progression to AIDS. Mutations that occur in each round of viral reproduction can generate strains of HIV that are drug resistant. The impact of such viral drug resistance is reduced by the use of a

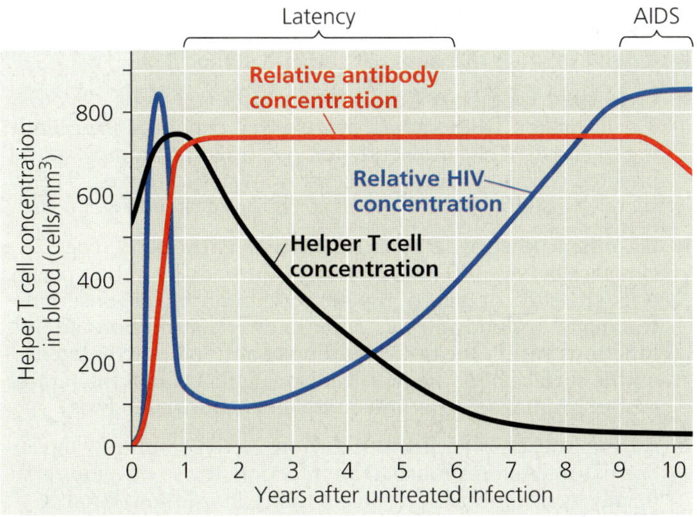

▲ **Figure 43.26 The progress of an untreated HIV infection.**

combination of drugs; viruses newly resistant to one drug can be defeated by another. But the appearance of strains resistant to multiple drugs reduces the effectiveness of multidrug "cocktails" in some patients. Frequent mutations in HIV surface antigen genes also have hampered efforts to develop an effective vaccine. Worldwide, the AIDS epidemic continues to grow. In 2006, more than 2.5 million people died of AIDS, with the disease now being the leading cause of death in Africa.

Transmission of HIV requires the transfer of virus particles or infected cells from person to person via body fluids such as semen or blood. Unprotected sex (that is, without a condom) and transmission via HIV-contaminated needles (typically among intravenous drug users) account for nearly all HIV infections. The virus can enter the body through the mucosal linings of the vagina, vulva, penis, or rectum during intercourse or via the mouth during oral sex. The likelihood of transmission is increased by factors that may damage these linings, especially other sexually transmitted infections that cause ulcers or inflammation. People infected with HIV transmit the disease most readily in the first few weeks of infection, before they express HIV-specific antibodies that can be detected in a blood test.

Cancer and Immunity

The relationship between the immune response and cancer remains only partially understood. It is clear that the frequency of certain cancers increases when the immune response is impaired. This observation has led to the suggestion that the immune system normally attacks body cells that become cancerous. However, there is an alternative explanation. Impairment of the immune response leaves the body open to infection, which causes inflammatory responses. Inflammation, in turn, is now known to be a condition contributing to the development of many cancers. Therefore, it may be that the immune system does not fight cancer effectively, and its impairment leads to increased cancer as the result of increased inflammation. Determining how cancer and immunity are linked and whether passive or active immunization can be used to fight cancer remain active areas of investigation.

CONCEPT CHECK 43.4

1. In myasthenia gravis, antibodies bind to and block acetylcholine receptors at neuromuscular junctions, preventing muscle contraction. Is this disease best classified as an immunodeficiency disease, an autoimmune disease, or an allergic reaction? Explain.
2. People with herpes simplex type 1 viruses often get mouth sores when they have a cold or similar infection. How might this location benefit the virus?
3. **WHAT IF?** How would a macrophage deficiency likely affect a person's innate and acquired defenses?

For suggested answers, see Appendix A.

Chapter 43 Review

MEDIA Go to the Study Area at **www.masteringbio.com** for BioFlix 3-D Animations, MP3 Tutors, Videos, Practice Tests, an eBook, and more.

SUMMARY OF KEY CONCEPTS

CONCEPT 43.1

In innate immunity, recognition and response rely on shared traits of pathogens (pp. 931–936)

- **Innate Immunity of Invertebrates** Invertebrates are protected by physical and chemical barriers as well as cell-based defenses. In insects, microbes that penetrate barrier defenses are ingested by cells in the hemolymph that also release antimicrobial peptides. Activation of innate immune responses to a pathogen class relies on recognition proteins.
- **Innate Immunity of Vertebrates** Intact skin and mucous membranes form barriers to microbes. Mucus produced by membrane cells, the low pH of the skin and stomach, and degradation by lysozyme also deter pathogens. Microbes that penetrate barrier defenses are ingested by phagocytes, which help trigger an inflammatory response. Complement proteins, interferons, and other antimicrobial proteins also act against microbes. In local inflammation, histamine and other chemicals released from injured cells promote changes in blood vessels that allow fluid, more phagocytes, and antimicrobial proteins to enter tissues. Natural killer (NK) cells can induce the death of virus-infected cells.
- **Innate Immune System Evasion by Pathogens** The outer capsule of some bacteria prevents recognition. Some bacteria are resistant to breakdown within lysosomes.

CONCEPT 43.2

In acquired immunity, lymphocyte receptors provide pathogen-specific recognition (pp. 936–942)

- Acquired immunity relies on lymphocytes that arise from stem cells in the bone marrow and complete their maturation in the bone marrow (B cells) or in the thymus (T cells).
- **Acquired Immunity: *An Overview*** Lymphocytes have cell-surface receptors for foreign molecules. All receptor proteins on a single lymphocyte are the same, but there are millions of lymphocytes in the body that differ in the foreign molecules that their receptors recognize. Upon infection, B and T cells specific for the microbe are activated. Some T cells help other lymphocytes; others kill infected host cells. B cells produce soluble receptor proteins that inhibit foreign molecules and cells. Some activated lymphocytes defend against future infections by the same microbe.
- **Antigen Recognition by Lymphocytes** Variable regions of receptors bind to small regions of an antigen (epitopes). B cells recognize epitopes in intact antigens. T cells recognize epitopes in small antigen fragments (peptides) complexed with cell-surface proteins called major histocompatibility (MHC) molecules. Class I MHC molecules, located on all nucleated cells, display antigen fragments to cytotoxic T cells. Class II MHC molecules, located mainly on dendritic cells, macrophages, and B cells (antigen-presenting cells), display antigen fragments to helper T cells and cytotoxic T cells.
- **Lymphocyte Development**

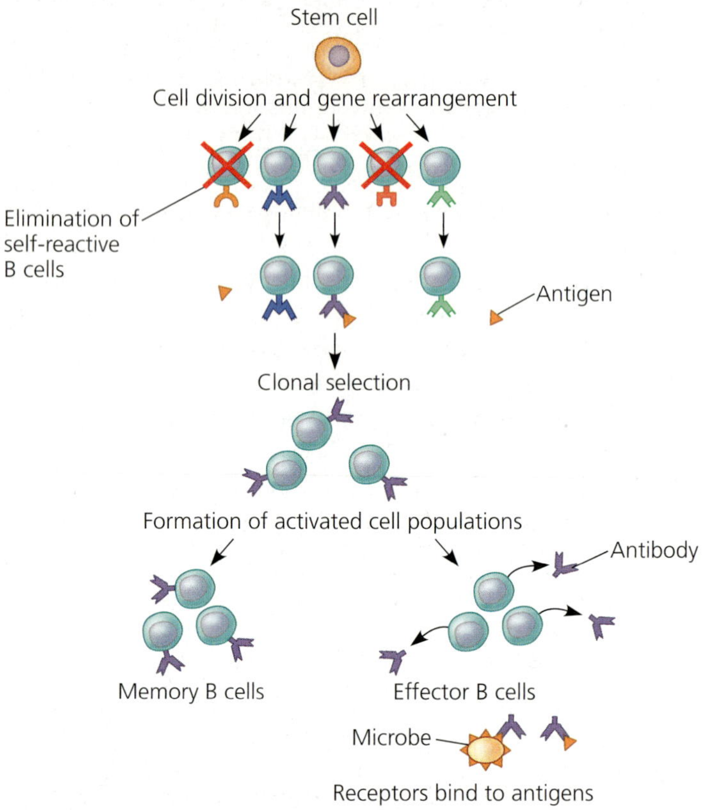

CONCEPT 43.3

Acquired immunity defends against infection of body cells and fluids (pp. 942–948)

- Infection of body fluids and infection of body cells are subject to humoral and cell-mediated responses, respectively.
- **Helper T Cells: A Response to Nearly All Antigens** Helper T cells make CD4, a surface protein that enhances their binding to class II MHC molecule–antigen fragment complexes on antigen-presenting cells. Activated helper T cells secrete different cytokines that stimulate other lymphocytes.
- **Cytotoxic T Cells: A Response to Infected Cells** Cytotoxic T cells make CD8, a surface protein that enhances their binding to class I MHC molecule–antigen fragment complexes on infected cells and cancerous cells. Activated cytotoxic T cells secrete proteins that initiate destruction of their target cells.
- **B Cells: A Response to Extracellular Pathogens** The clonal selection of B cells generates antibody-secreting plasma cells, the effector cells of the humoral immune response. The five major antibody classes differ in their distributions and functions within the body. Binding of antibodies to antigens on the surface of pathogens leads to elimination of the microbes by phagocytosis and complement-mediated lysis.
- **Active and Passive Immunization** Active immunity develops naturally in response to an infection; it also develops artificially by immunization (vaccination). In immunization, a nonpathogenic form of a microbe or part of a microbe elicits an immune response to and immunological memory for that

microbe. Passive immunity, which provides immediate, short-term protection, is conferred naturally when IgG crosses the placenta from mother to fetus or when IgA passes from mother to infant in breast milk. It also can be conferred artificially by injecting antibodies into a nonimmune person.

▶ **Immune Rejection** Certain antigens on red blood cells determine whether a person has type A, B, AB, or O blood. Because antibodies to nonself blood antigens already exist in the body, transfusion with incompatible blood leads to destruction of the transfused cells. MHC molecules are responsible for stimulating the rejection of tissue grafts and organ transplants. The chances of successful transplantation are increased if the donor and recipient MHC tissue types are well matched and if immunosuppressive drugs are given to the recipient. Lymphocytes in bone marrow transplants may cause a graft versus host reaction in recipients.

MEDIA
MP3 Tutor The Human Immune System
Activity Immune Responses

CONCEPT 43.4

Disruptions in immune system function can elicit or exacerbate disease (pp. 948–951)

▶ **Exaggerated, Self-Directed, and Diminished Immune Responses** In localized allergies, IgE attached to receptors on mast cells induces the cells to release histamine and other mediators that cause vascular changes and allergic symptoms. Loss of normal self-tolerance can lead to autoimmune diseases, such as multiple sclerosis. Inborn immunodeficiencies result from hereditary or congenital defects that interfere with innate, humoral, or cell-mediated defenses. AIDS is an acquired immunodeficiency caused by the human immunodeficiency virus (HIV).

▶ **Acquired Immune System Evasion by Pathogens** Pathogens use antigenic variation, latency, and direct assault on the immune system to thwart immune responses. HIV infection destroys helper T cells, leaving the patient prone to disease due to deficient humoral and cell-mediated immunity.

▶ **Cancer and Immunity** Although cancers are more common with immunodeficiencies, it is unclear whether this reflects reduced immune response or an increase in infections that contribute to cancer development through inflammation.

MEDIA
Activity HIV Reproductive Cycle
Investigation What Causes Infections in AIDS Patients?
Investigation Why Do AIDS Rates Differ Across the U.S.?

TESTING YOUR KNOWLEDGE

SELF-QUIZ

1. Which of these is *not* part of insect immunity?
   a. enzyme activation of microbe-killing chemicals
   b. activation of natural killer cells
   c. phagocytosis by hemocytes
   d. production of antimicrobial peptides
   e. a protective exoskeleton

2. What is a characteristic of early stages of local inflammation?
   a. anaphylactic shock
   b. fever
   c. attack by cytotoxic T cells
   d. release of histamine
   e. antibody- and complement-mediated lysis of microbes

3. An epitope associates with which part of an antibody?
   a. the antibody-binding site
   b. the heavy-chain constant regions only
   c. variable regions of a heavy chain and light chain combined
   d. the light-chain constant regions only
   e. the antibody tail

4. Which of the following is *not* true about helper T cells?
   a. They function in cell-mediated and humoral responses.
   b. They are activated by polysaccharide fragments.
   c. They bear surface CD4 molecules.
   d. They are subject to infection by HIV.
   e. When activated, they secrete cytokines.

5. Which statement best describes the difference in responses of effector B cells (plasma cells) and cytotoxic T cells?
   a. B cells confer active immunity; cytotoxic T cells confer passive immunity.
   b. B cells kill viruses directly; cytotoxic T cells kill virus-infected cells.
   c. B cells secrete antibodies against a virus; cytotoxic T cells kill virus-infected cells.
   d. B cells accomplish the cell-mediated response; cytotoxic T cells accomplish the humoral response.
   e. B cells respond the first time the invader is present; cytotoxic T cells respond subsequent times.

6. Which of the following results in long-term immunity?
   a. the passage of maternal antibodies to a developing fetus
   b. the inflammatory response to a splinter
   c. the injection of serum from people immune to rabies
   d. the administration of the chicken pox vaccine
   e. the passage of maternal antibodies to a nursing infant

7. HIV targets include all of the following except
   a. macrophages. b. cytotoxic T cells. c. helper T cells.
   d. cells bearing CD4. e. brain cells.

8. **DRAW IT** Consider a pencil-shaped protein with two epitopes, Y (the "eraser" end) and Z (the "point" end). They are recognized by antibodies A1 and A2, respectively. Draw and label a picture showing the antibodies linking proteins into a complex that could trigger endocytosis by a macrophage.

For Self-Quiz answers, see Appendix A.

MEDIA Visit the Study Area at **www.masteringbio.com** for a Practice Test.

EVOLUTION CONNECTION

9. Describe one invertebrate defense mechanism and discuss how it is an evolutionary adaptation retained in vertebrates.

SCIENTIFIC INQUIRY

10. To test for tuberculosis in AIDS patients, why wouldn't you inject purified bacterial antigen and assess signs of immune system reaction several days later?

Biological Inquiry: A Workbook of Investigative Cases Explore the immune response to flu pathogens with the case "Pandemic Flu (Past and Possible)."

44 Osmoregulation and Excretion

▲ **Figure 44.1 How does an albatross drink saltwater without ill effect?**

KEY CONCEPTS

44.1 Osmoregulation balances the uptake and loss of water and solutes
44.2 An animal's nitrogenous wastes reflect its phylogeny and habitat
44.3 Diverse excretory systems are variations on a tubular theme
44.4 The nephron is organized for stepwise processing of blood filtrate
44.5 Hormonal circuits link kidney function, water balance, and blood pressure

OVERVIEW

A Balancing Act

With a wingspan that can reach 3.5 m, the largest of any living bird, a wandering albatross (*Diomedea exulans*) soaring over the ocean is hard not to notice **(Figure 44.1)**. Yet the albatross commands attention for more than just its size. This massive bird remains at sea day and night throughout the year, returning to land only to reproduce. A human with only seawater to drink would die of dehydration, but under the same conditions the albatross thrives.

In surviving without fresh water, the albatross relies on **osmoregulation**, the general process by which animals control solute concentrations and balance water gain and loss. In the fluid environment of cells, tissues, and organs, osmoregulation is essential. For physiological systems to function properly, the relative concentrations of water and solutes must be kept within fairly narrow limits. In addition, ions such as sodium and calcium must be maintained at concentrations that permit normal activity of muscles, neurons, and other body cells. Osmoregulation is thus a process of homeostasis.

A number of strategies for water and solute control have evolved, reflecting the varied and often severe osmoregulatory challenges presented by an animal's surroundings. Desert animals live in an environment that can quickly deplete their body water. Despite a quite different environment, albatrosses and other marine animals also face the potential problem of dehydration. Success in such circumstances depends critically on conserving water and, for marine birds and bony fishes, eliminating excess salts. In contrast, freshwater animals live in an environment that threatens to flood and dilute their body fluids. These organisms survive by limiting water uptake, conserving solutes, and absorbing salts from their surroundings.

In safeguarding their internal fluid environment, animals must also deal with a hazardous metabolite produced by the dismantling of proteins and nucleic acids. Breakdown of *nitrogenous* (nitrogen-containing) molecules releases ammonia, a very toxic compound. Several different mechanisms have evolved for **excretion**, the process that rids the body of nitrogenous metabolites and other waste products. Because systems for excretion and osmoregulation are structurally and functionally linked in many animals, we will consider both of these processes in this chapter.

CONCEPT **44.1**

Osmoregulation balances the uptake and loss of water and solutes

Just as thermoregulation depends on balancing heat loss and gain (see Chapter 40), regulating the chemical composition of body fluids depends on balancing the uptake and loss of water and solutes. This process of osmoregulation is based largely on controlled movement of solutes between internal fluids and the external environment. Because water follows solutes by osmosis, the net effect is to regulate both solute and water content.

Osmosis and Osmolarity

All animals—regardless of phylogeny, habitat, or type of waste produced—face the same need for osmoregulation. Over time,

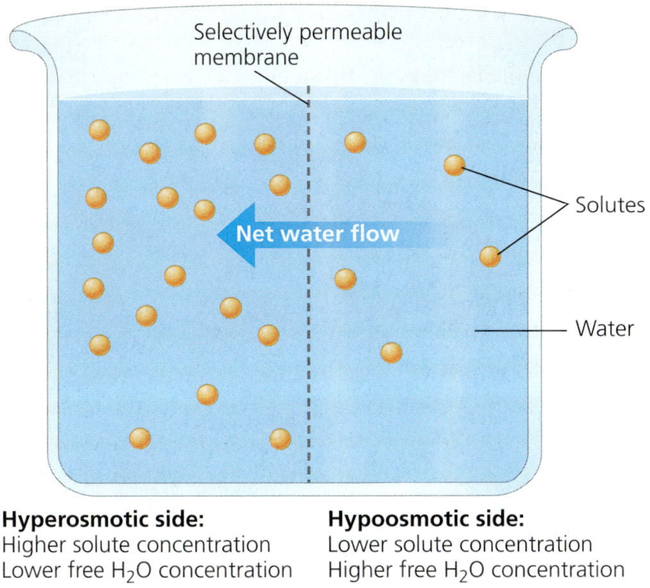

▲ **Figure 44.2 Solute concentration and osmosis.**

water uptake and loss must balance. If water uptake is excessive, animal cells swell and burst; if water loss is substantial, they shrivel and die (see Figure 7.13).

Water enters and leaves cells by osmosis. Recall from Chapter 7 that osmosis, a special case of diffusion, is the movement of water across a selectively permeable membrane. It occurs whenever two solutions separated by the membrane differ in osmotic pressure, or **osmolarity** (total solute concentration expressed as molarity, or moles of solute per liter of solution). The unit of measurement for osmolarity used in this chapter is milliOsmoles per liter (mOsm/L); 1 mOsm/L is equivalent to a total solute concentration of 10^{-3} *M*. The osmolarity of human blood is about 300 mOsm/L, while seawater has an osmolarity of about 1,000 mOsm/L.

If two solutions separated by a selectively permeable membrane have the same osmolarity, they are said to be *isoosmotic*. Under these conditions, water molecules continually cross the membrane, but they do so at equal rates in both directions. In other words, there is no *net* movement of water by osmosis between isoosmotic solutions. When two solutions differ in osmolarity, the one with the greater concentration of solutes is said to be *hyperosmotic*, and the more dilute solution is said to be *hypoosmotic* **(Figure 44.2)**. Water flows by osmosis from a hypoosmotic solution to a hyperosmotic one.*

Osmotic Challenges

An animal can maintain water balance in two ways. One is to be an **osmoconformer**, which is isoosmotic with its surroundings. The second is to be an **osmoregulator**, which controls its internal osmolarity independent of that of its environment.

* In this chapter, we use the terms *isoosmotic*, *hypoosmotic*, and *hyperosmotic*, which refer specifically to osmolarity, instead of the more familiar terms *isotonic*, *hypotonic*, and *hypertonic*. The latter set of terms applies to the response of animal cells—whether they swell or shrink—in solutions of known solute concentrations.

▲ **Figure 44.3 Sockeye salmon (*Oncorhynchus nerka*), euryhaline osmoregulators.**

All osmoconformers are marine animals. Because an osmoconformer's internal osmolarity is the same as that of its environment, there is no tendency to gain or lose water. Many osmoconformers live in water that has a stable composition and hence have a constant internal osmolarity.

Osmoregulation enables animals to live in environments that are uninhabitable for osmoconformers, such as freshwater and terrestrial habitats. It also allows many marine animals to maintain an internal osmolarity different from that of seawater. To survive in a hypoosmotic environment, an osmoregulator must discharge excess water. In a hyperosmotic environment, an osmoregulator must instead take in water to offset osmotic loss.

Most animals, whether osmoconformers or osmoregulators, cannot tolerate substantial changes in external osmolarity and are said to be **stenohaline** (from the Greek *stenos*, narrow, and *halos*, salt). In contrast, **euryhaline** animals (from the Greek *eurys*, broad), which include certain osmoconformers and osmoregulators, can survive large fluctuations in external osmolarity. Many barnacles and mussels covered and uncovered by ocean tides are euryhaline osmoconformers; familiar examples of euryhaline osmoregulators are the striped bass and the various species of salmon **(Figure 44.3)**.

Next we'll examine some adaptations for osmoregulation that have evolved in marine, freshwater, and terrestrial animals.

Marine Animals

Most marine invertebrates are osmoconformers. Their osmolarity (the sum of the concentrations of all dissolved substances) is the same as that of seawater. They therefore face no substantial challenges in water balance. However, because they differ considerably from seawater in the concentrations of *specific* solutes, they must actively transport these solutes to maintain homeostasis.

Many marine vertebrates and some marine invertebrates are osmoregulators. For most of these animals, the ocean is a strongly dehydrating environment. For example, marine bony

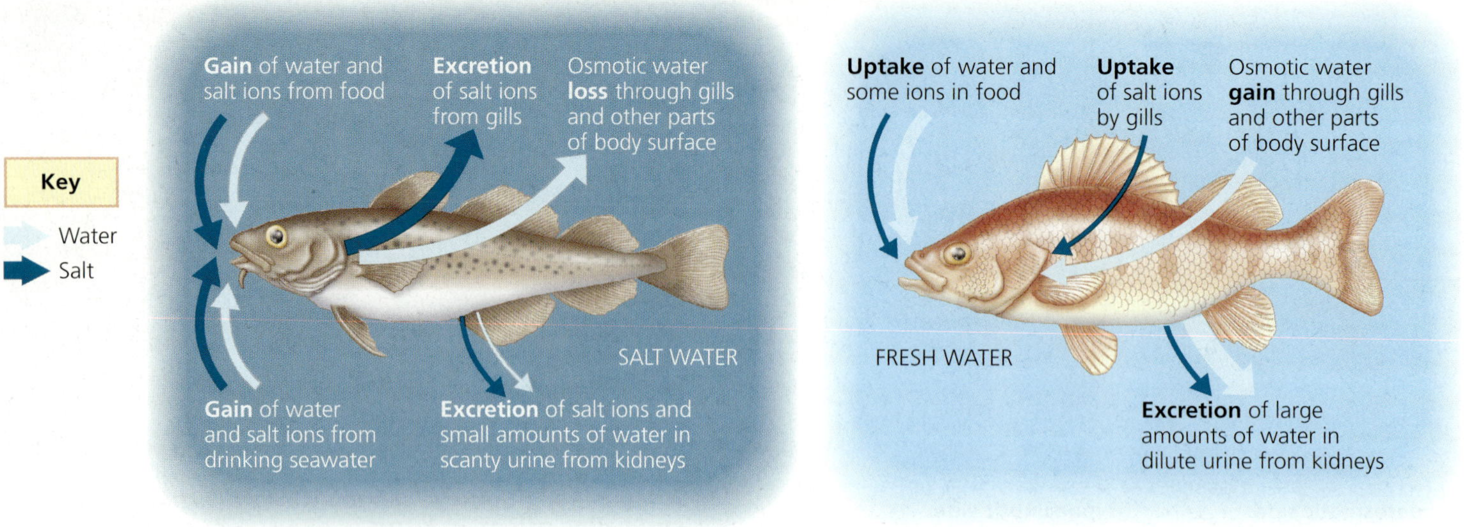

(a) Osmoregulation in a saltwater fish

(b) Osmoregulation in a freshwater fish

▲ **Figure 44.4 Osmoregulation in marine and freshwater bony fishes: a comparison.**

fishes, such as the cod in **Figure 44.4a**, constantly lose water by osmosis. Such fishes balance the water loss by drinking large amounts of seawater. They then make use of both their gills and kidneys to rid themselves of salts. In the gills, specialized *chloride cells* actively transport chloride ions (Cl^-) out, and sodium ions (Na^+) follow passively. In the kidneys, excess calcium, magnesium, and sulfate ions are excreted with the loss of only small amounts of water.

A distinct osmoregulatory strategy evolved in marine sharks and most other chondrichthyans (cartilaginous animals; see Chapter 34). Like bony fishes, sharks have an internal salt concentration much less than that of seawater, so salt tends to diffuse into their bodies from the water, especially across their gills. Unlike bony fishes, however, marine sharks are not hypoosmotic to seawater. The explanation is that shark tissue contains high concentrations of urea, a nitrogenous waste product of protein and nucleic acid metabolism (see Figure 44.9). Their body fluids also contain trimethylamine oxide (TMAO), an organic molecule that protects proteins from damage by urea. Together, the salts, urea, TMAO, and other compounds maintained in the body fluids of sharks result in an osmolarity very close to that of seawater. For this reason, sharks are often considered osmoconformers. However, because the solute concentration in their body fluids is actually somewhat greater than 1,000 mOsm/L, water slowly *enters* the shark's body by osmosis and in food (sharks do not drink). This small influx of water is disposed of in urine produced by the shark's kidneys. The urine also removes some of the salt that diffuses into the shark's body; the rest is lost in feces or is excreted by an organ called the rectal gland.

Freshwater Animals

The osmoregulatory problems of freshwater animals are the opposite of those of marine animals. The body fluids of freshwater animals must be hyperosmotic because animal cells cannot tolerate salt concentrations as low as those of lake or river water. Having internal fluids with an osmolarity higher than that of their surroundings, freshwater animals face the problem of gaining water by osmosis and losing salts by diffusion. Many freshwater animals, including fishes, solve the problem of water balance by drinking almost no water and excreting large amounts of very dilute urine. At the same time, salts lost by diffusion and in the urine are replenished by eating. Freshwater fishes, such as the perch in **Figure 44.4b**, also replenish salts by uptake across the gills. Chloride cells in the gills of the fish actively transport Cl^- into the body, and Na^+ follows.

Salmon and other euryhaline fishes that migrate between seawater and fresh water undergo dramatic changes in osmoregulatory status. While living in the ocean, salmon carry out osmoregulation like other marine fishes by drinking seawater and excreting excess salt from their gills. When they migrate to fresh water, salmon cease drinking and begin to produce large amounts of dilute urine. At the same time, their gills start taking up salt from the dilute environment—just like fishes that spend their entire lives in fresh water.

Animals That Live in Temporary Waters

Extreme dehydration, or *desiccation*, is fatal for most animals. However, a few aquatic invertebrates that live in temporary ponds and in films of water around soil particles can lose almost all their body water and survive. These animals enter a dormant state when their habitats dry up, an adaptation called **anhydrobiosis** ("life without water"). Among the most striking examples are the tardigrades, or water bears **(Figure 44.5)**. Less than 1 mm long, these tiny invertebrates are found in marine, freshwater, and moist terrestrial environments. In their active, hydrated state, they contain about 85% water by weight, but they can dehydrate to less than 2% water and survive in an

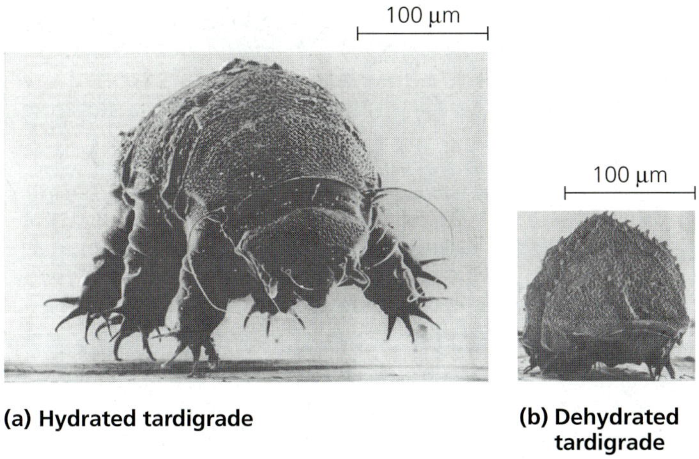

▲ **Figure 44.5 Anhydrobiosis.** Tardigrades (water bears) inhabit temporary ponds and droplets of water in soil and on moist plants (SEMs).

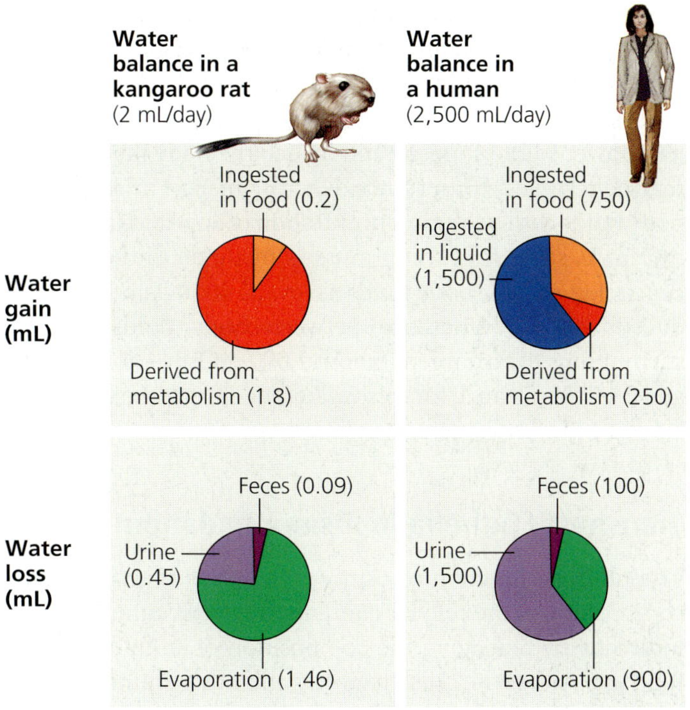

▲ **Figure 44.6 Water balance in two terrestrial mammals.** Kangaroo rats, which live in the American Southwest, eat mostly dry seeds and do not drink water. A kangaroo rat gains water mainly from cellular metabolism and loses water mainly by evaporation during gas exchange. In contrast, a human gains water in food and drink and loses the largest fraction of it in urine.

inactive state, dry as dust, for a decade or more. Just add water, and within hours the rehydrated tardigrades are moving about and feeding.

Anhydrobiosis requires adaptations that keep cell membranes intact. Researchers are just beginning to learn how tardigrades survive drying out, but studies of anhydrobiotic roundworms (phylum Nematoda) show that desiccated individuals contain large amounts of sugars. In particular, a disaccharide called trehalose seems to protect the cells by replacing the water that is normally associated with proteins and membrane lipids. Many insects that survive freezing in the winter also use trehalose as a membrane protectant, as do some plants resistant to desiccation.

Land Animals

The threat of dehydration is a major regulatory problem for terrestrial plants and animals. Humans, for example, die if they lose as little as 12% of their body water (desert camels can withstand approximately twice that level of dehydration). Adaptations that reduce water loss are key to survival on land. Much as a waxy cuticle contributes to the success of land plants, the body coverings of most terrestrial animals help prevent dehydration. Examples are the waxy layers of insect exoskeletons, the shells of land snails, and the layers of dead, keratinized skin cells covering most terrestrial vertebrates, including humans. Many terrestrial animals, especially desert-dwellers, are nocturnal, which reduces evaporative water loss because of the lower temperature and higher relative humidity of night air.

Despite these and other adaptations, most terrestrial animals lose water through many routes: in urine and feces, across their skin, and from moist surfaces in gas exchange organs. Land animals maintain water balance by drinking and eating moist foods and by producing water metabolically through cellular respiration. A number of desert animals, including many insect-eating birds and other reptiles, are well enough adapted for minimizing water loss that they can survive without drinking. A noteworthy example is the kangaroo rat: It loses so little water that 90% is replaced by water generated metabolically **(Figure 44.6)**; the remaining 10% comes from the small amount of water in its diet of seeds.

Energetics of Osmoregulation

When an animal maintains an osmolarity difference between its body and the external environment, there is an energy cost. Because diffusion tends to equalize concentrations in a system, osmoregulators must expend energy to maintain the osmotic gradients that cause water to move in or out. They do so by using active transport to manipulate solute concentrations in their body fluids.

The energy cost of osmoregulation depends on how different an animal's osmolarity is from its surroundings, how easily water and solutes can move across the animal's surface, and how much work is required to pump solutes across the membrane. Osmoregulation accounts for 5% or more of the resting metabolic rate of many freshwater and marine bony fishes. For brine shrimp, small crustaceans that live in Utah's Great Salt Lake and other extremely salty lakes, the gradient between internal and external osmolarity is very large, and the cost of osmoregulation is correspondingly high—as much as 30% of the resting metabolic rate.

The energy cost to an animal of maintaining water and salt balance is minimized by a body fluid composition adapted to the salinity of the animal's habitat. Comparing closely related species reveals that the body fluids of most freshwater animals have lower solute concentrations than the body fluids of their marine relatives. For instance, whereas marine molluscs have body fluids with a solute concentration of approximately 1,000 mOsm/L, some freshwater mussels maintain the solute concentration of their body fluids as low as 40 mOsm/L. The reduced osmotic difference between body fluids and the surrounding environment (about 1,000 mOsm/L for seawater and 0.5–15 mOsm/L for fresh water) decreases the energy the animal expends for osmoregulation.

Transport Epithelia in Osmoregulation

The ultimate function of osmoregulation is to maintain the composition of the cellular contents, but most animals do this indirectly by managing the composition of an internal body fluid that bathes the cells. In insects and other animals with an open circulatory system, this fluid is the hemolymph (see Chapter 42). In vertebrates and other animals with a closed circulatory system, the cells are bathed in an interstitial fluid that contains a mixture of solutes controlled indirectly by the blood. Maintaining the composition of such fluids depends on structures ranging from cells that regulate solute movement to complex organs, such as the vertebrate kidney.

In most animals, osmotic regulation and metabolic waste disposal rely on one or more kinds of **transport epithelium**—one or more layers of specialized epithelial cells that regulate solute movements. Transport epithelia move specific solutes in controlled amounts in specific directions. Transport epithelia are typically arranged into complex tubular networks with extensive surface areas. Some transport epithelia face the outside environment directly, while others line channels connected to the outside by an opening on the body surface.

The transport epithelium that enables the albatross to survive on seawater remained undiscovered for many years. Some scientists suggested that marine birds do not actually drink water, asserting that although the birds take water into their mouths they do not swallow. Questioning this idea, Knut Schmidt-Nielsen and colleagues carried out a simple but informative experiment **(Figure 44.7)**.

As Schmidt-Nielsen demonstrated, the adaptation that enables the albatross and other marine birds to maintain internal salt balance is a specialized nasal gland. In removing excess sodium chloride from the blood, the nasal gland relies on countercurrent exchange **(Figure 44.8)**. Recall from Chapter 40 that countercurrent exchange occurs between two fluids separated by one or more membranes and flowing in opposite directions. In the albatross's nasal gland, the net result is the secretion of fluid much saltier than the ocean. Thus, even though drinking seawater brings in a lot of salt, the bird achieves a net gain of water. By contrast, humans who drink a given volume of seawater must use a greater volume of water to excrete the salt load, with the result that they become dehydrated.

Transport epithelia that function in maintaining water balance also often function in disposal of metabolic wastes. We will see examples of this coordinated function in our upcoming consideration of earthworm and insect excretory systems as well as the vertebrate kidney.

▼ Figure 44.7 Inquiry

How do seabirds eliminate excess salt from their bodies?

EXPERIMENT Knut Schmidt-Nielsen and colleagues, at the Mount Desert Island Laboratory, Maine, gave captive marine birds nothing but seawater to drink. However, only a small amount of the salt the birds consumed appeared in their urine. The remainder was concentrated in a clear fluid dripping from the tip of the birds' beaks. Where did this salty fluid come from? The researchers focused their attention on the nasal glands, a pair of structures found in the heads of all birds. The nasal glands of seabirds are much larger than those of land birds, and Schmidt-Nielsen hypothesized that the nasal glands function in salt elimination. To test this hypothesis, the researchers inserted a thin tube through the duct leading to a nasal gland and withdrew fluid.

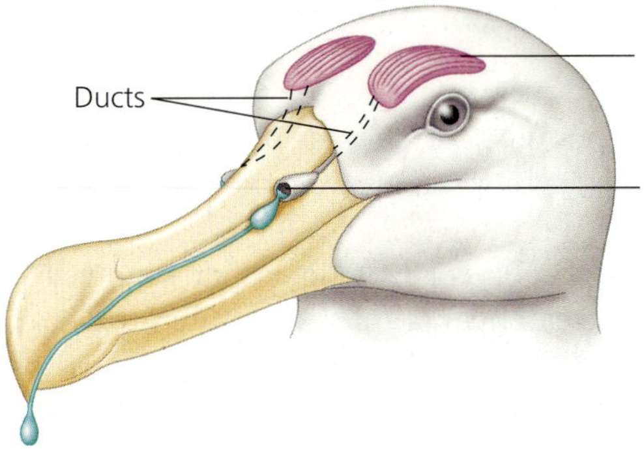

RESULTS The fluid drawn from the nasal glands of the captive marine birds was a nearly pure solution of NaCl. The salt concentration was 5%, nearly twice as salty as seawater (and many times saltier than human tears). Control samples of fluid drawn from other glands in the head revealed no other location of high salt concentration.

CONCLUSION Marine birds utilize their nasal glands to eliminate excess salt from the body. It is these organs that make life at sea possible for species such as gulls and albatrosses. Similar structures, called salt glands, provide the identical function in sea turtles and marine iguanas.

SOURCE K. Schmidt-Nielsen et al., Extrarenal salt excretion in birds, *American Journal of Physiology* 193:101–107 (1958).

WHAT IF? The nasal glands enable marine birds to eliminate excess salt they gain from consuming prey as well as from drinking salt water. How would the type of animal prey that a marine bird eats influence how much salt it needs to eliminate?

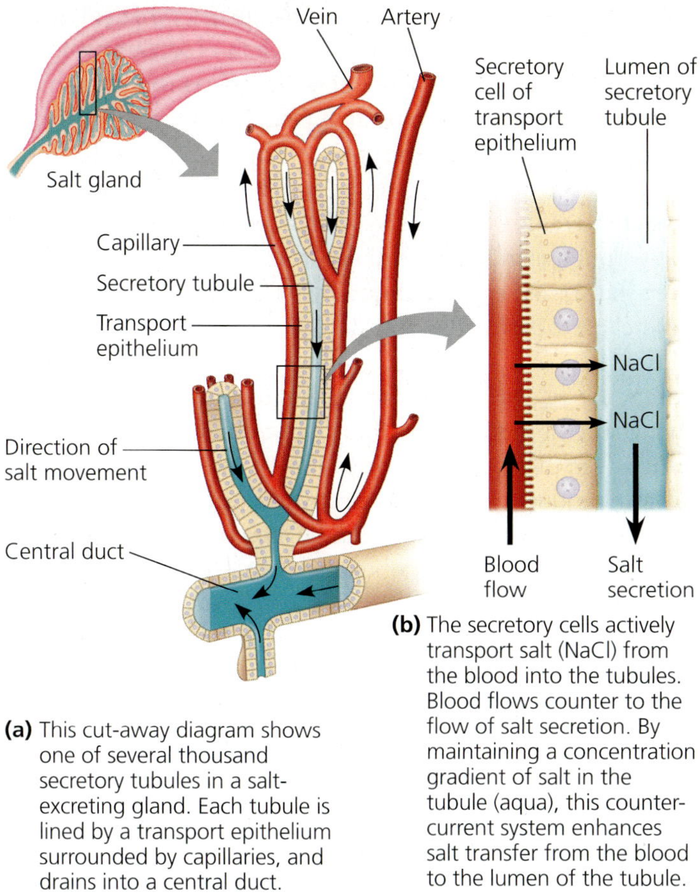

(a) This cut-away diagram shows one of several thousand secretory tubules in a salt-excreting gland. Each tubule is lined by a transport epithelium surrounded by capillaries, and drains into a central duct.

(b) The secretory cells actively transport salt (NaCl) from the blood into the tubules. Blood flows counter to the flow of salt secretion. By maintaining a concentration gradient of salt in the tubule (aqua), this countercurrent system enhances salt transfer from the blood to the lumen of the tubule.

▲ **Figure 44.8 Countercurrent exchange in salt-excreting nasal glands.**

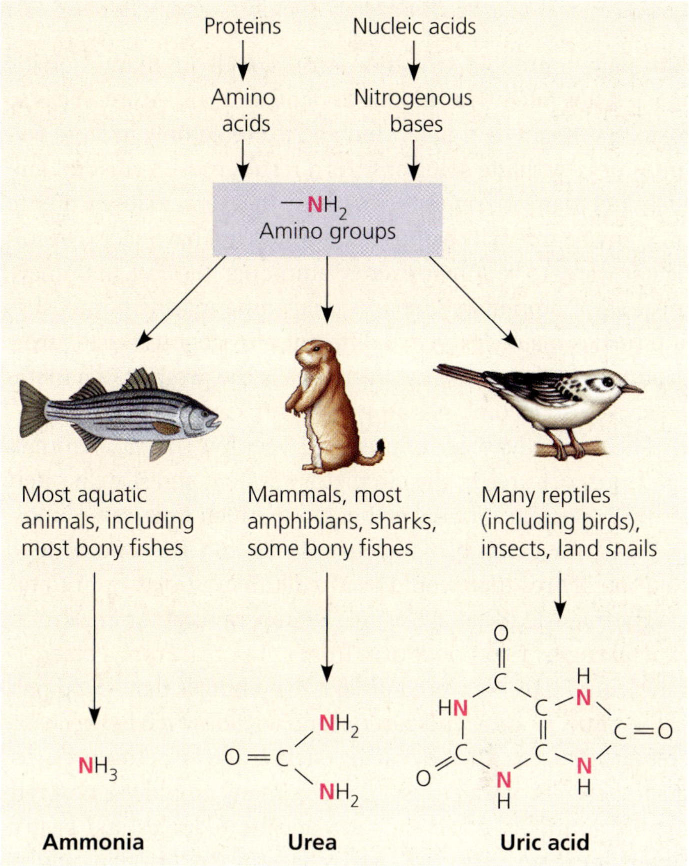

▲ **Figure 44.9 Nitrogenous wastes.**

CONCEPT CHECK 44.1

1. The movement of salt from the surrounding water to the blood of a freshwater fish requires the expenditure of energy in the form of ATP. Why?
2. Why aren't any freshwater animals osmoconformers?
3. **WHAT IF?** Researchers found that a camel standing in the sun required much more water when its fur was shaved off, although its body temperature remained the same. What can you conclude about the relationship between osmoregulation and the insulation provided by fur?

For suggested answers, see Appendix A.

CONCEPT 44.2

An animal's nitrogenous wastes reflect its phylogeny and habitat

Because most metabolic wastes must be dissolved in water to be excreted from the body, the type and quantity of waste products may have a large impact on an animal's water balance. In this regard, some of the most significant waste products are the nitrogenous breakdown products of proteins and nucleic acids **(Figure 44.9)**. When proteins and nucleic acids are broken apart for energy or converted to carbohydrates or fats, enzymes remove nitrogen in the form of **ammonia** (NH_3). Ammonia is very toxic, in part because its ion, ammonium (NH_4^+), interferes with oxidative phosphorylation. Although some animals excrete ammonia directly, many species expend energy to convert it to less toxic compounds prior to excretion.

Forms of Nitrogenous Waste

Animals excrete nitrogenous wastes as ammonia, urea, or uric acid. These different forms vary significantly in their toxicity and the energy costs of producing them.

Ammonia

Because ammonia can be tolerated only at very low concentrations, animals that excrete nitrogenous wastes as ammonia need access to lots of water. Therefore, ammonia excretion is most common in aquatic species. Being highly soluble, ammonia molecules easily pass through membranes and are readily lost by diffusion to the surrounding water. In many invertebrates, ammonia release occurs across the whole body surface. In fishes, most of the ammonia is lost as NH_4^+ across the epithelium of the gills; the kidneys excrete only minor amounts of nitrogenous waste.

Urea

Although ammonia excretion works well in many aquatic species, it is much less suitable for land animals. Ammonia is so toxic that it can be transported and excreted only in large volumes of very dilute solutions. As a result, most terrestrial animals and many marine species (those that tend to lose water to their environment by osmosis) simply do not have access to sufficient water to routinely excrete ammonia. Instead, mammals, most adult amphibians, sharks, and some marine bony fishes and turtles mainly excrete a different nitrogenous waste, **urea**. Produced in the vertebrate liver, urea is the product of a metabolic cycle that combines ammonia with carbon dioxide.

The main advantage of urea is its very low toxicity. Animals can transport urea in the circulatory system and store it safely at high concentrations. Furthermore, much less water is lost when a given quantity of nitrogen is excreted in a concentrated solution of urea than would be in a dilute solution of ammonia.

The main disadvantage of urea is its energy cost: Animals must expend energy to produce urea from ammonia. From a bioenergetic standpoint, we would predict that animals that spend part of their lives in water and part on land would switch between excreting ammonia (thereby saving energy) and excreting urea (reducing excretory water loss). Indeed, many amphibians excrete mainly ammonia when they are aquatic tadpoles and switch largely to urea excretion when they become land-dwelling adults.

Uric Acid

Insects, land snails, and many reptiles, including birds, excrete **uric acid** as their primary nitrogenous waste. Uric acid is relatively nontoxic and does not readily dissolve in water. It therefore can be excreted as a semisolid paste with very little water loss. This is a great advantage for animals with little access to water, but there is a cost: Uric acid is even more energetically expensive to produce than urea, requiring considerable ATP for synthesis from ammonia.

Many animals, including humans, produce a small amount of uric acid as a product of purine breakdown. Diseases that disrupt this process reflect the problems that can arise when a metabolic product is insoluble. For example, a genetic defect in purine metabolism predisposes dalmatian dogs to form uric acid stones in their bladder. Humans may develop *gout*, a painful inflammation of the joints caused by deposits of uric acid crystals. Meals containing purine-rich animal tissues can increase the inflammation. Some dinosaurs appear to have been similarly affected: Fossilized bones of the carnivore *Tyrannosaurus rex* exhibit joint damage characteristic of gout.

The Influence of Evolution and Environment on Nitrogenous Wastes

In general, the kind of nitrogenous wastes excreted depend on an animal's evolutionary history and habitat, especially the availability of water. For example, terrestrial turtles (which often live in dry areas) excrete mainly uric acid, whereas aquatic turtles excrete both urea and ammonia. In addition, reproductive mode seems to have been an important factor in determining which type of nitrogenous waste has become the major form during the evolution of a particular group of animals. For example, soluble wastes can diffuse out of a shell-less amphibian egg or be carried away from a mammalian embryo by the mother's blood. However, the shelled eggs produced by birds and other reptiles are permeable to gases but not to liquids, which means that soluble nitrogenous wastes released by an embryo would be trapped within the egg and could accumulate to dangerous levels. (Although urea is much less harmful than ammonia, it does become toxic at very high concentrations.) The evolution of uric acid as a waste product conveyed a selective advantage because it precipitates out of solution and can be stored within the egg as a harmless solid left behind when the animal hatches.

Regardless of the type of nitrogenous waste, the amount produced by an animal is coupled to the energy budget. Endotherms, which use energy at high rates, eat more food and produce more nitrogenous waste than ectotherms. The amount of nitrogenous waste is also linked to diet. Predators, which derive much of their energy from protein, excrete more nitrogen than animals that rely mainly on lipids or carbohydrates as energy sources.

Having surveyed the forms of nitrogenous waste and their interrelationship with evolutionary lineage, habitat, and energy consumption, we will turn next to the processes and systems animals use to excrete these and other wastes.

CONCEPT CHECK 44.2

1. What advantage does uric acid offer as a nitrogenous waste in arid environments?
2. **WHAT IF?** Suppose a bird and a human are both suffering from gout. Why might reducing the amount of purine in the diet help the human much more than the bird?

For suggested answers, see Appendix A.

CONCEPT 44.3

Diverse excretory systems are variations on a tubular theme

Whether an animal lives on land, in salt water, or in fresh water, water balance depends on the regulation of solute movement between internal fluids and the external environment. Much of this movement is handled by excretory systems. These systems are central to homeostasis because they dispose of metabolic wastes and control body fluid composition. Before we describe particular excretory systems, let's consider the basic process of excretion.

Excretory Processes

Animals across a wide range of species produce a fluid waste called urine through the basic steps shown in **Figure 44.10**. In the first step, body fluid (blood, coelomic fluid, or hemolymph) is brought in contact with the selectively permeable membrane of a transport epithelium. In most cases, hydrostatic pressure (blood pressure in many animals) drives a process of **filtration**. Cells, as well as proteins and other large molecules, cannot cross the epithelial membrane and remain in the body fluid. In contrast, water and small solutes, such as salts, sugars, amino acids, and nitrogenous wastes, cross the membrane, forming a solution called the **filtrate**.

The filtrate is converted into a waste fluid by the specific transport of materials into or out of the filtrate. The process of selective **reabsorption** recovers useful molecules and water from the filtrate and returns them to the body fluids. Valuable solutes—including glucose, certain salts, vitamins, hormones, and amino acids—are reabsorbed by active transport. Nonessential solutes and wastes are left in the filtrate or are added to it by selective **secretion**, which also occurs by active transport. The pumping of various solutes adjusts the osmotic movement of water into or out of the filtrate. In the last step—excretion—the processed filtrate is released from the body as urine.

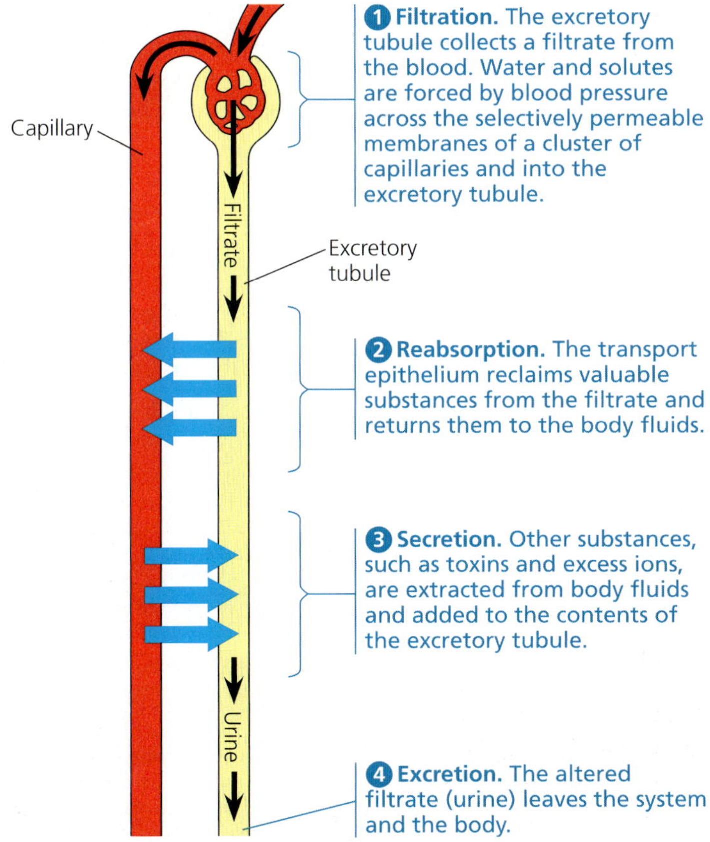

▲ **Figure 44.10 Key functions of excretory systems: an overview.** Most excretory systems produce a filtrate by pressure-filtering body fluids and then modify the filtrate's contents. This diagram is modeled after the vertebrate excretory system.

Survey of Excretory Systems

The systems that perform the basic excretory functions vary widely among animal groups. However, they are generally built on a complex network of tubules that provide a large surface area for the exchange of water and solutes, including nitrogenous wastes. We'll examine the excretory systems of flatworms, earthworms, insects, and vertebrates as examples of evolutionary variations on tubule networks.

Protonephridia

Flatworms (phylum Platyhelminthes), which lack a coelom or body cavity, have excretory systems called protonephridia (singular, *protonephridium*). The **protonephridia** form a network of dead-end tubules connected to external openings. As shown in **Figure 44.11**, the tubules branch throughout the body. Cellular units called flame bulbs cap the branches of each protonephridium. Formed from a tubule cell and a cap cell, each flame bulb has a tuft of cilia projecting into the tubule. During filtration, the beating of the cilia draws water and solutes from the interstitial fluid through the flame bulb, releasing filtrate into the tubule network. (The moving cilia resemble a flickering flame; hence the name *flame bulb*.) The processed filtrate then moves outward through the tubules and empties as urine into the external environment. The urine excreted by freshwater flatworms has a low solute concentration, helping to balance the osmotic uptake of water from the environment.

► **Figure 44.11 Protonephridia: the flame bulb system of a planarian.** Protonephridia are branching internal tubules that function mainly in osmoregulation.

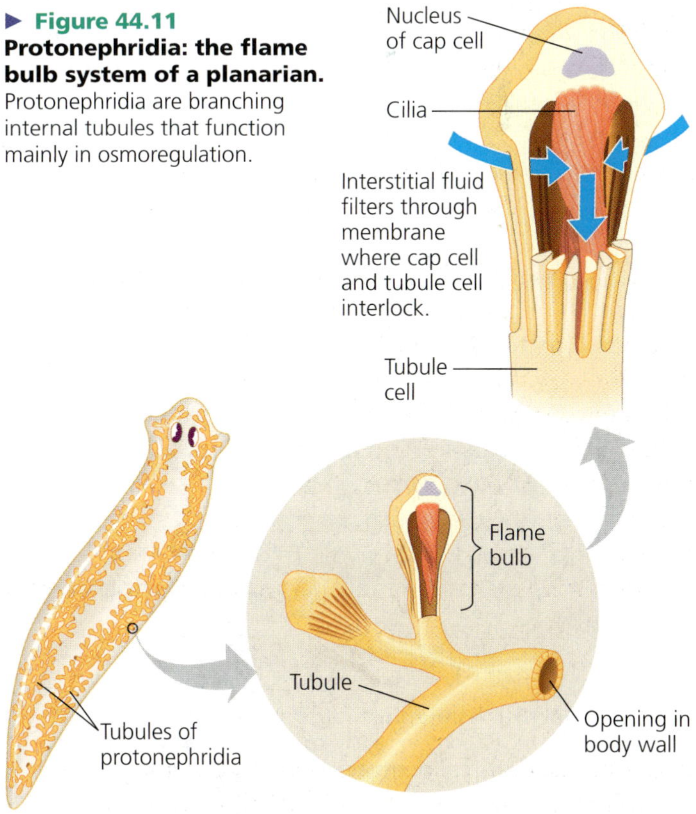

Protonephridia are also found in rotifers, some annelids, mollusc larvae, and lancelets (see Figure 34.4). Among these animals, the function of the protonephridia varies. In the freshwater flatworms, protonephridia serve mainly in osmoregulation. Most metabolic wastes diffuse out of the animal across the body surface or are excreted into the gastrovascular cavity and eliminated through the mouth (see Figure 33.10). However, in some parasitic flatworms, which are isoosmotic to the surrounding fluids of their host organisms, the main function of protonephridia is the disposal of nitrogenous wastes. Natural selection has thus adapted protonephridia to distinct tasks in different environments.

Metanephridia

Most annelids, such as earthworms, have **metanephridia** (singular, *metanephridium*), excretory organs that open internally to the coelom **(Figure 44.12)**. Each segment of a worm has a pair of metanephridia, which are immersed in coelomic fluid and enveloped by a capillary network. A ciliated funnel surrounds the internal opening. As the cilia beat, fluid is drawn into a collecting tubule, which includes a storage bladder that opens to the outside.

The metanephridia of an earthworm have both excretory and osmoregulatory functions. As urine moves along the tubule, the transport epithelium bordering the lumen reabsorbs most solutes and returns them to the blood in the capillaries. Nitrogenous wastes remain in the tubule and are excreted to the outside. Earthworms inhabit damp soil and usually experience a net uptake of water by osmosis through their skin. Their metanephridia balance the water influx by producing urine that is dilute (hypoosmotic to body fluids).

Malpighian Tubules

Insects and other terrestrial arthropods have organs called **Malpighian tubules** that remove nitrogenous wastes and also function in osmoregulation **(Figure 44.13)**. The Malpighian tubules extend from dead-end tips immersed in hemolymph (circulatory fluid) to openings into the digestive tract. The filtration step common to other excretory systems is absent. Instead, the transport epithelium that lines the tubules secretes certain solutes, including nitrogenous wastes, from the hemolymph into the lumen of the tubule. Water follows the solutes into the tubule by osmosis, and the fluid then passes into the rectum. There, most solutes are pumped back into the hemolymph, and water reabsorption by osmosis follows. The nitrogenous wastes—mainly insoluble uric acid—are eliminated as nearly dry matter along with the feces. Capable of conserving water very effectively, the insect excretory system is a key adaptation contributing to these animals' tremendous success on land.

Kidneys

In vertebrates and some other chordates, a specialized organ called the kidney functions in both osmoregulation and excretion. Like the excretory organs of most animal phyla, kidneys consist of tubules. The numerous tubules of these compact organs are arranged in a highly organized manner and closely associated with a network of capillaries. The vertebrate

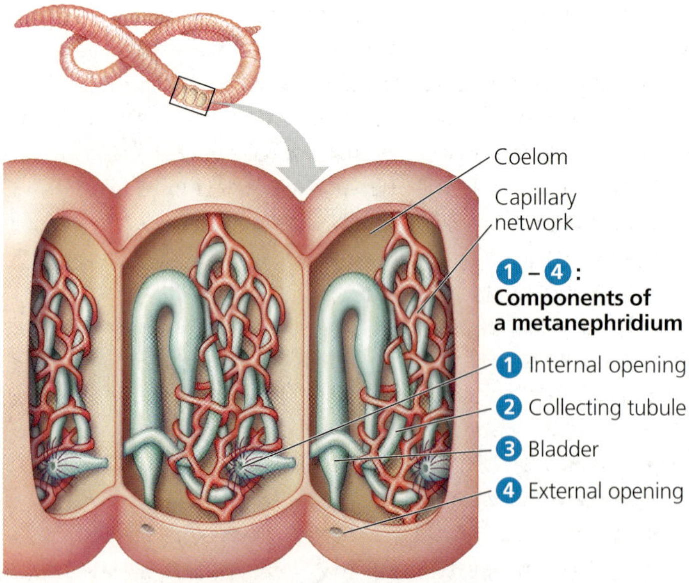

▲ **Figure 44.12 Metanephridia of an earthworm.** Each segment of the worm contains a pair of metanephridia, which collect coelomic fluid from the adjacent anterior segment. (Only one metanephridium of each pair is shown here.)

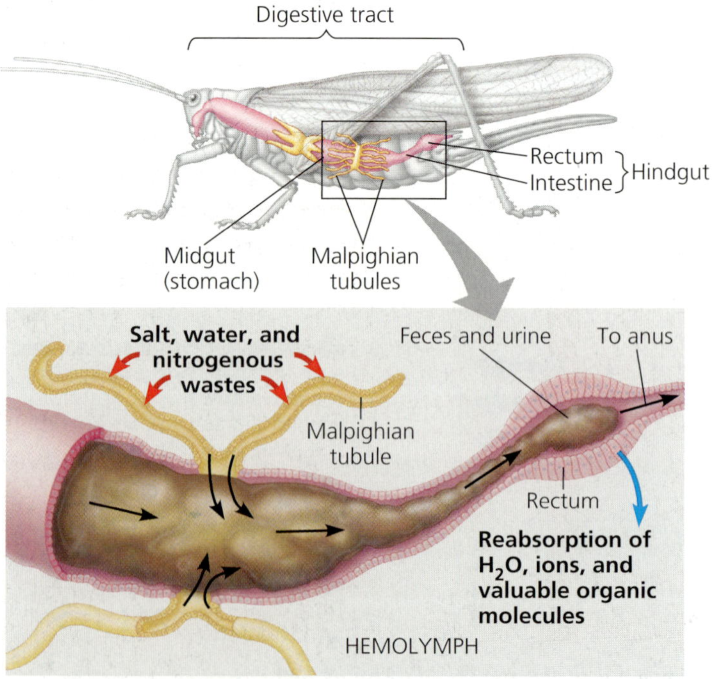

▲ **Figure 44.13 Malpighian tubules of insects.** Malpighian tubules are outpocketings of the digestive tract that remove nitrogenous wastes and function in osmoregulation.

excretory system also includes ducts and other structures that carry urine from the tubules out of the kidney and, eventually, the body.

Vertebrate kidneys are typically nonsegmented. But hagfishes, which are invertebrate chordates, have kidneys with segmentally arranged excretory tubules; so, the excretory structures of vertebrate ancestors may have been segmented.

Structure of the Mammalian Excretory System

As a prelude to exploring kidney function, let's take a closer look at the routes that fluids follow in the mammalian excretory system. The excretory system of mammals centers on a pair of kidneys. In humans, each kidney is about 10 cm long and is supplied with blood by a **renal artery** and drained by a **renal vein** **(Figure 44.14a)**. Blood flow through the kidneys is voluminous. The kidneys account for less than 1% of human body mass but receive roughly 25% of the blood exiting the heart. Urine exits each kidney through a duct called the **ureter**, and both ureters drain into a common **urinary bladder**. During urination, urine is expelled from the bladder through a tube called the **urethra**, which empties to the outside near the vagina in females and through the penis in males. Urination is regulated by sphincter muscles close to the junction of the urethra and the bladder.

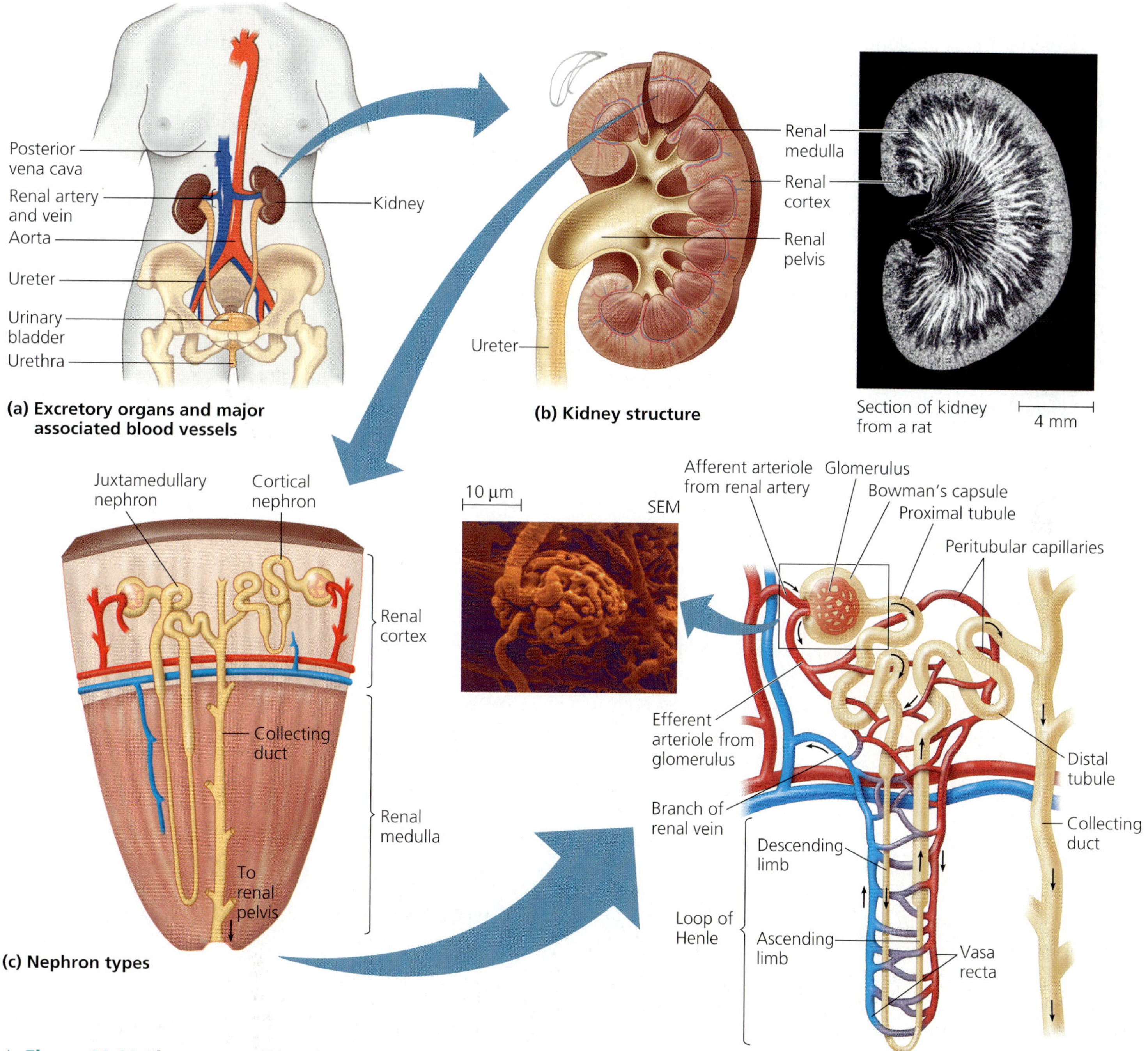

▲ **Figure 44.14 The mammalian excretory system.**

The mammalian kidney has an outer **renal cortex** and an inner **renal medulla** (**Figure 44.14b**). Microscopic excretory tubules and their associated blood vessels pack both regions. Weaving back and forth across the cortex and medulla is the **nephron**, the functional unit of the vertebrate kidney. A nephron consists of a single long tubule as well as a ball of capillaries called the **glomerulus** (**Figure 44.14c** and **d**). The blind end of the tubule forms a cup-shaped swelling, called **Bowman's capsule**, which surrounds the glomerulus. Each human kidney contains about a million nephrons, with a total tubule length of 80 km.

Filtration of the Blood

Filtration occurs as blood pressure forces fluid from the blood in the glomerulus into the lumen of Bowman's capsule (see Figure 44.14d). The porous capillaries and specialized cells of the capsule are permeable to water and small solutes, but not to blood cells or large molecules such as plasma proteins. Thus, the filtrate in Bowman's capsule contains salts, glucose, amino acids, vitamins, nitrogenous wastes, and other small molecules. Because filtration of small molecules is nonselective, the mixture mirrors the concentrations of these substances in blood plasma.

Pathway of the Filtrate

From Bowman's capsule, the filtrate passes into the **proximal tubule**, the first of three major regions of the nephron. Next is the **loop of Henle**, a hairpin turn with a descending limb and an ascending limb. The **distal tubule**, the last region of the nephron, empties into a **collecting duct**, which receives processed filtrate from many nephrons. This filtrate flows from all of the collecting ducts of the kidney into the **renal pelvis**, which is drained by the ureter.

Among the vertebrates, only mammals and some birds have loops of Henle. In the human kidney, 85% of the nephrons are **cortical nephrons**, which have short loops of Henle and are almost entirely confined to the renal cortex. The other 15%, the **juxtamedullary nephrons**, have loops that extend deeply into the renal medulla. It is the juxtamedullary nephrons that enable mammals to produce urine that is hyperosmotic to body fluids, an adaptation that is extremely important for water conservation.

The nephron and the collecting duct are lined by a transport epithelium that processes the filtrate, forming the urine. One of this epithelium's most important tasks is reabsorption of solutes and water. Under normal conditions, approximately 1,600 L of blood flows through a pair of human kidneys each day, a volume about 300 times the total volume of blood in the body. From this enormous traffic of blood, the nephrons and collecting ducts process about 180 L of initial filtrate. Of this, about 99% of the water and nearly all of the sugars, amino acids, vitamins, and other organic nutrients are reabsorbed into the blood, leaving only about 1.5 L of urine to be voided.

Blood Vessels Associated with the Nephrons

Each nephron is supplied with blood by an **afferent arteriole**, an offshoot of the renal artery that branches to form the capillaries of the glomerulus (see Figure 44.14d). The capillaries converge as they leave the glomerulus, forming an **efferent arteriole**. Branches of this vessel form the **peritubular capillaries**, which surround the proximal and distal tubules. A third set of capillaries extend downward and form the **vasa recta**, hairpin-shaped capillaries that serve the long loop of Henle of juxtamedullary nephrons.

The direction of blood flow within the capillaries of the vasa recta is opposite that of the filtrate in the neighboring loop of Henle (see Figure 44.14d). Said another way, each ascending portion of the vasa recta lies next to the descending portion of a loop of Henle, and vice versa. Both the tubules and capillaries are immersed in interstitial fluid, through which various substances diffuse between the plasma within capillaries and the filtrate within the nephron tubule. Although they do not exchange materials directly, the vasa recta and the loop of Henle function together as part of a countercurrent system that enhances nephron efficiency, a topic we will explore further in the next section.

CONCEPT CHECK 44.3

1. Compare and contrast the different ways that metabolic waste products enter the excretory systems of flatworms, earthworms, and insects.
2. What is the function of the filtration step in excretory systems?
3. **WHAT IF?** Kidney failure is often treated by hemodialysis, in which blood diverted out of the body is filtered and then allowed to flow on one side of a semipermeable membrane. Fluid called dialysate flows in the opposite direction on the other side of the membrane. In replacing the reabsorption and secretion of solutes in a functional kidney, the makeup of the starting dialysate is critical. What initial solute composition would work well?

For suggested answers, see Appendix A.

CONCEPT **44.4**

The nephron is organized for stepwise processing of blood filtrate

We'll continue our exploration of the nephron with a discussion of filtrate processing. We will then focus further on how tubules, capillaries, and surrounding tissue function together.

From Blood Filtrate to Urine: *A Closer Look*

In this section, we will follow filtrate along its path in the nephron and collecting duct, examining how each region contributes to the stepwise processing of filtrate into urine. The circled numbers correspond to the numbers in **Figure 44.15**.

1 Proximal tubule. Reabsorption in the proximal tubule is critical for the recapture of ions, water, and valuable nutrients from the huge initial filtrate volume. NaCl (salt) in the filtrate diffuses into the cells of the transport epithelium, where Na^+ is actively transported into the interstitial fluid. This transfer of positive charge out of the tubule drives the passive transport of Cl^-. As salt moves from the filtrate to the interstitial fluid, water follows by osmosis. The salt and water then diffuse from the interstitial fluid into the peritubular capillaries. Glucose, amino acids, potassium ions (K^+), and other essential substances are also actively or passively transported from the filtrate to the interstitial fluid and then into the peritubular capillaries.

Processing of filtrate in the proximal tubule helps maintain a relatively constant pH in body fluids. Cells of the transport epithelium secrete H^+ but also synthesize and secrete ammonia, which acts as a buffer to trap H^+ in the form of ammonium ions (NH_4^+). The more acidic the filtrate, the more ammonia the cells produce and secrete, and a mammal's urine usually contains some ammonia from this source (even though most nitrogenous waste is excreted as urea). The proximal tubules also reabsorb about 90% of the buffer bicarbonate (HCO_3^-) from the filtrate, contributing further to pH balance in body fluids.

As the filtrate passes through the proximal tubule, materials to be excreted become concentrated. Many wastes leave the body fluids during the nonselective filtration process and remain in the filtrate while water and salts are reabsorbed. Urea, for example, is reabsorbed at a much lower rate than are salt and water. Some other toxic materials are actively secreted into filtrate from surrounding tissues. For example, drugs and toxins that have been processed in the liver pass from the peritubular capillaries into the interstitial fluid. These molecules then enter the proximal tubule, where they are actively secreted from the transport epithelium into the lumen.

2 Descending limb of the loop of Henle. Reabsorption of water continues as the filtrate moves into the descending limb of the loop of Henle. Here numerous water channels formed by **aquaporin** proteins make the transport epithelium freely permeable to water. In contrast, there is a near absence of channels for

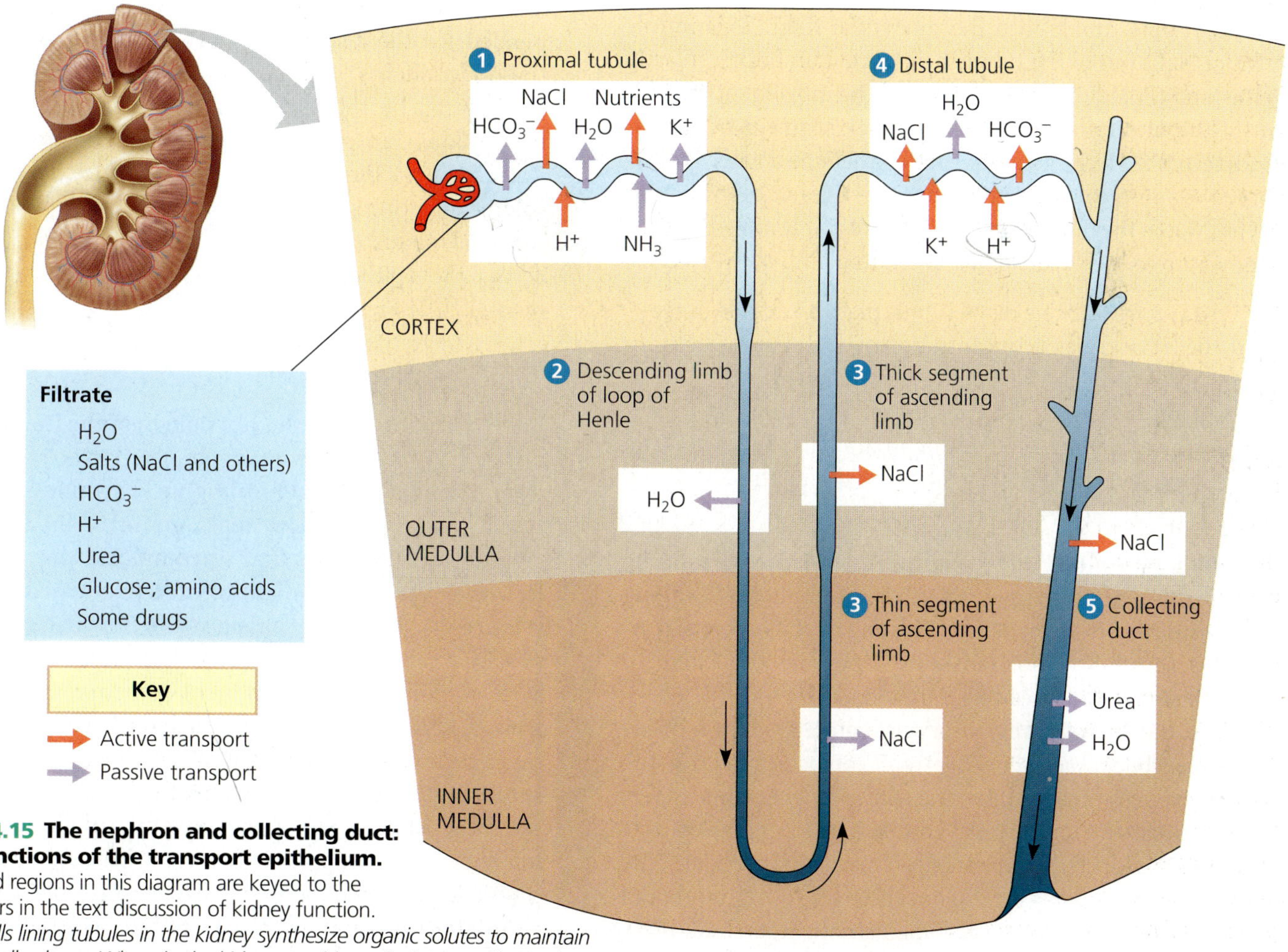

▲ **Figure 44.15 The nephron and collecting duct: regional functions of the transport epithelium.** The numbered regions in this diagram are keyed to the circled numbers in the text discussion of kidney function.

? *Some cells lining tubules in the kidney synthesize organic solutes to maintain normal cell volume. Where in the kidney would you find these cells? Explain.*

salt and other small solutes, resulting in a very low permeability for these substances.

For water to move out of the tubule by osmosis, the interstitial fluid bathing the tubule must be hyperosmotic to the filtrate. This condition is met along the entire length of the descending limb, because the osmolarity of the interstitial fluid increases progressively from the outer cortex to the inner medulla of the kidney. As a result, the filtrate undergoes a loss of water and an accompanying increase in solute concentration at every point in its downward journey along the descending limb.

3 Ascending limb of the loop of Henle. The filtrate reaches the tip of the loop and then travels within the ascending limb as it returns to the cortex. Unlike the descending limb, the ascending limb has a transport epithelium that contains ion channels, but not water channels. Indeed, this membrane is impermeable to water. Lack of permeability to water is very rare among biological membranes and is critical to the function of the ascending limb.

The ascending limb has two specialized regions: a thin segment near the loop tip and a thick segment adjacent to the distal tubule. As filtrate ascends in the thin segment, NaCl, which became concentrated in the descending limb, diffuses out of the permeable tubule into the interstitial fluid. This movement of NaCl out of the tubule helps maintain the osmolarity of the interstitial fluid in the medulla. The movement of NaCl out of the filtrate continues in the thick segment of the ascending limb. Here, however, the epithelium actively transports NaCl into the interstitial fluid. As a result of losing salt but not water, the filtrate becomes progressively more dilute as it moves up to the cortex in the ascending limb of the loop.

4 Distal tubule. The distal tubule plays a key role in regulating the K^+ and NaCl concentration of body fluids. This regulation involves variation in the amount of the K^+ that is secreted into the filtrate, as well as the amount of NaCl reabsorbed from the filtrate. Like the proximal tubule, the distal tubule contributes to pH regulation by the controlled secretion of H^+ and reabsorption of HCO_3^-.

5 Collecting duct. The collecting duct carries the filtrate through the medulla to the renal pelvis. As filtrate passes along the transport epithelium of the collecting duct, hormonal control of permeability and transport determines the extent to which the urine becomes concentrated.

When the kidneys are conserving water, aquaporin channels in the collecting duct allow water molecules to cross the epithelium. At the same time, the epithelium remains impermeable to salt and, in the renal cortex, to urea. As the collecting duct traverses the gradient of osmolarity in the kidney, the filtrate becomes increasingly concentrated, losing more and more water by osmosis to the hyperosmotic interstitial fluid. In the inner medulla, the duct becomes permeable to urea. Because of the high urea concentration in the filtrate at this point, some urea diffuses out of the duct and into the interstitial fluid. Along with NaCl, this urea contributes to the high osmolarity of the interstitial fluid in the medulla. The net result is urine that is hyperosmotic to the general body fluids.

In producing dilute rather than concentrated urine, the kidney actively reabsorbs salts without allowing water to follow by osmosis. At these times, the epithelium lacks water channels, and NaCl is actively transported out of filtrate. As we will see shortly, the state of the collecting duct epithelium is controlled by hormones that together maintain homeostasis for osmolarity, blood pressure, and blood volume.

Solute Gradients and Water Conservation

The mammalian kidney's ability to conserve water is a key terrestrial adaptation. In humans, the osmolarity of blood is about 300 mOsm/L, but the kidney can excrete urine up to four times as concentrated—about 1,200 mOsm/L. Some mammals can do even better: Australian hopping mice, which live in dry desert regions, can produce urine with an osmolarity of 9,300 mOsm/L, 25 times as concentrated as the animal's blood.

In a mammalian kidney, the production of hyperosmotic urine is possible only because considerable energy is expended for the active transport of solutes against concentration gradients. The nephrons—particularly the loops of Henle—can be thought of as energy-consuming machines that produce an osmolarity gradient suitable for extracting water from the filtrate in the collecting duct. The two primary solutes affecting osmolarity are NaCl, which is deposited in the renal medulla by the loop of Henle, and urea, which passes across the epithelium of the collecting duct in the inner medulla (see Figure 44.15).

The Two-Solute Model

To better understand the physiology of the mammalian kidney as a water-conserving organ, let's retrace the flow of filtrate through the excretory tubule. This time, let's focus on how the juxtamedullary nephrons maintain an osmolarity gradient in the tissues that surround the loop of Henle and how they use that gradient to excrete a hyperosmotic urine **(Figure 44.16)**. Filtrate passing from Bowman's capsule to the proximal tubule has an osmolarity of about 300 mOsm/L, the same as blood. A large amount of water *and* salt is reabsorbed from the filtrate as it flows through the proximal tubule in the renal cortex. As a result, the filtrate's volume decreases substantially, but its osmolarity remains about the same.

As the filtrate flows from cortex to medulla in the descending limb of the loop of Henle, water leaves the tubule by osmosis. Solutes, including NaCl, become more concentrated, increasing the osmolarity of the filtrate. The highest osmolarity (about 1,200 mOsm/L) occurs at the elbow of the loop of

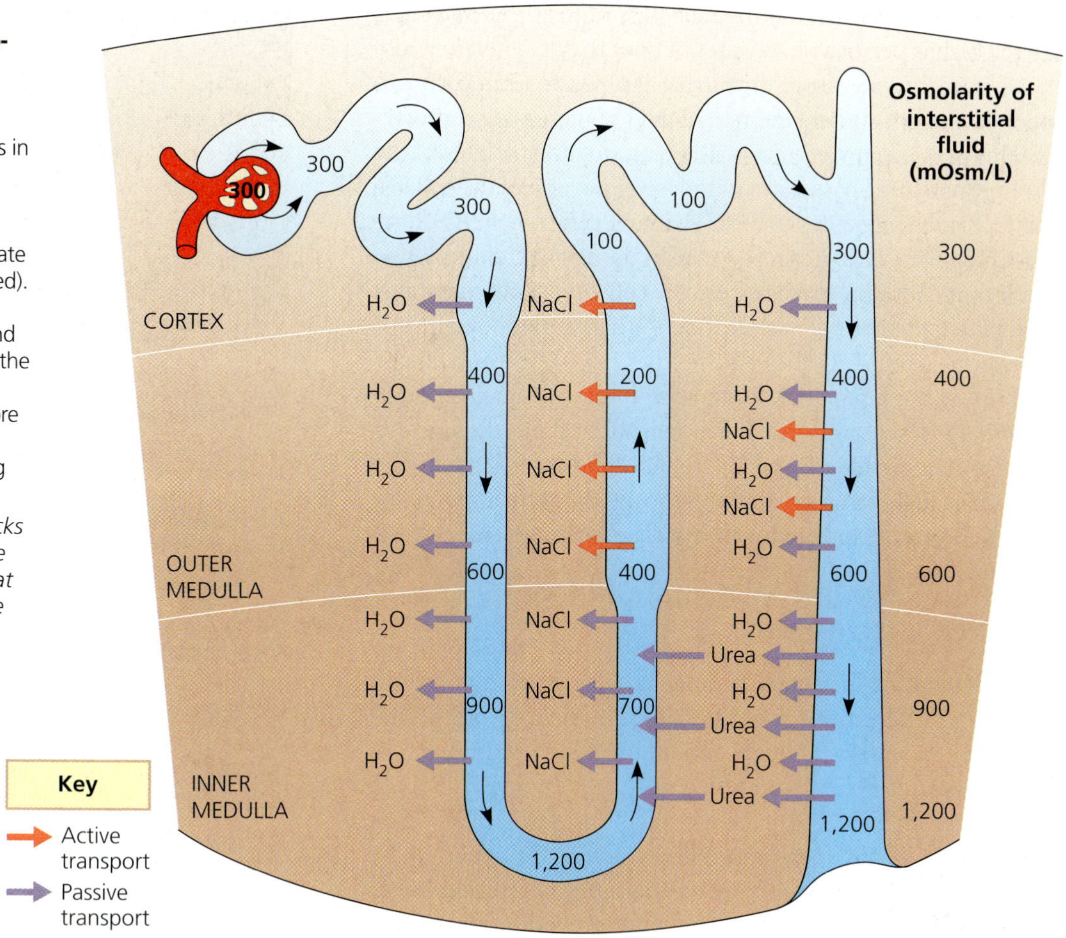

▶ **Figure 44.16 How the human kidney concentrates urine: the two-solute model.** Two solutes contribute to the osmolarity of the interstitial fluid: NaCl and urea. The loop of Henle maintains the interstitial gradient of NaCl, which increases in the descending limb and decreases in the ascending limb. Urea diffuses into the interstitial fluid of the medulla from the collecting duct (most of the urea in the filtrate remains in the collecting duct and is excreted). The filtrate makes three trips between the cortex and medulla: first down, then up, and then down again in the collecting duct. As the filtrate flows in the collecting duct past interstitial fluid of increasing osmolarity, more water moves out of the duct by osmosis, thereby concentrating the solutes, including urea, that are left behind in the filtrate.

WHAT IF? *The drug furosemide blocks the cotransporters for Na^+ and Cl^- in the ascending limb of the loop of Henle. What effect would you expect this drug to have on urine volume?*

Henle. This maximizes the diffusion of salt out of the tubule as the filtrate rounds the curve and enters the ascending limb, which is permeable to salt but not to water. NaCl diffusing from the ascending limb helps maintain a high osmolarity in the interstitial fluid of the renal medulla.

Notice that the loop of Henle has several qualities of a countercurrent system, such as those mechanisms that maximize oxygen absorption by fish gills (see Figure 42.22) or reduce heat loss in endotherms (see Figure 40.12). In those cases, the countercurrent mechanisms involve passive movement along either an oxygen concentration gradient or a heat gradient. In contrast, the countercurrent system involving the loop of Henle expends energy to actively transport NaCl from the filtrate in the upper part of the ascending limb of the loop. Such countercurrent systems, which expend energy to create concentration gradients, are called **countercurrent multiplier systems**. The countercurrent multiplier system involving the loop of Henle maintains a high salt concentration in the interior of the kidney, enabling the kidney to form concentrated urine.

What prevents the capillaries of the vasa recta from dissipating the gradient by carrying away the high concentration of NaCl in the medulla's interstitial fluid? As we noted earlier (see Figure 44.14d), the descending and ascending vessels of the vasa recta carry blood in opposite directions through the kidney's osmolarity gradient. As the descending vessel conveys blood toward the inner medulla, water is lost from the blood and NaCl is gained by diffusion. These fluxes are reversed as blood flows back toward the cortex in the ascending vessel, with water reentering the blood and salt diffusing out. Thus, the vasa recta can supply the kidney with nutrients and other important substances carried by the blood without interfering with the osmolarity gradient that makes it possible for the kidney to excrete hyperosmotic urine.

The countercurrent-like characteristics of the loop of Henle and the vasa recta help to generate the steep osmotic gradient between the medulla and cortex. However, diffusion will eventually eliminate any osmotic gradient within animal tissue unless gradient formation is supported by an expenditure of energy. In the kidney, this expenditure largely occurs in the thick segment of the ascending limb of the loop of Henle, where NaCl is actively transported out of the tubule. Even with the benefits of countercurrent exchange, this process—along with other renal active transport systems—consumes considerable ATP. Thus, for its size, the kidney has one of the highest metabolic rates of any organ.

As a result of active transport of NaCl out of the thick segment of the ascending limb, the filtrate is actually hypoosmotic to body fluids by the time it reaches the distal tubule. Now the filtrate descends again toward the medulla, this time in the collecting duct, which is permeable to water but not to salt. Therefore, osmosis extracts water from the filtrate as it passes from cortex to medulla and encounters interstitial fluid of increasing osmolarity. This process concentrates salt, urea, and other solutes in the filtrate. Some urea passes out of the lower portion of the collecting duct and contributes to the high interstitial osmolarity of the inner medulla. (This urea is recycled by diffusion into the loop of Henle, but continual leakage from the collecting duct maintains a high interstitial urea concentration.) When the kidney concentrates urine maximally, the urine reaches 1,200 mOsm/L, the osmolarity of the interstitial fluid in the inner medulla. Although *isoosmotic* to the inner medulla's interstitial fluid, the urine is *hyperosmotic* to blood and interstitial fluid elsewhere in the body. This high osmolarity allows the solutes remaining in the urine to be excreted from the body with minimal water loss.

Adaptations of the Vertebrate Kidney to Diverse Environments

Vertebrate animals occupy habitats ranging from rain forests to deserts and from some of the saltiest bodies of water to the nearly pure waters of high mountain lakes. Variations in nephron structure and function equip the kidneys of different vertebrates for osmoregulation in their various habitats. The adaptations of the vertebrate kidney are made apparent by comparing species that inhabit a wide range of environments or by comparing the responses of different vertebrate groups to similar environmental conditions.

Mammals

The juxtamedullary nephron, with its urine-concentrating features, is a key adaptation to terrestrial life, enabling mammals to get rid of salts and nitrogenous wastes without squandering water. As we have seen, the remarkable ability of the mammalian kidney to produce hyperosmotic urine depends on the precise arrangement of the tubules and collecting ducts in the renal cortex and medulla. In this respect, the kidney is one of the clearest examples of how the function of an organ is inseparably linked to its structure.

Mammals that excrete the most hyperosmotic urine, such as Australian hopping mice, North American kangaroo rats, and other desert mammals, have loops of Henle that extend deep into the medulla. Long loops maintain steep osmotic gradients in the kidney, resulting in urine becoming very concentrated as it passes from cortex to medulla in the collecting ducts.

In contrast, beavers, muskrats, and other aquatic mammals that spend much of their time in fresh water and rarely face problems of dehydration have nephrons with relatively short loops, resulting in a much lower ability to concentrate urine. Terrestrial mammals living in moist conditions have loops of Henle of intermediate length and the capacity to produce urine intermediate in concentration to that produced by freshwater and desert mammals.

▲ **Figure 44.17 The roadrunner (*Geococcyx californianus*), an animal well adapted for conserving water.**

Birds and Other Reptiles

Most birds, including the albatross (see Figure 44.1) and the roadrunner **(Figure 44.17)**, live in environments that are dehydrating. Like mammals, birds have kidneys with juxtamedullary nephrons that specialize in conserving water. However, the nephrons of birds have loops of Henle that extend less far into the medulla than those of mammals. Thus, bird kidneys cannot concentrate urine to the high osmolarities achieved by mammalian kidneys. Although birds can produce hyperosmotic urine, their main water conservation adaptation is having uric acid as the nitrogen waste molecule. Since uric acid can be excreted as a paste, it reduces urine volume.

The kidneys of other reptiles, having only cortical nephrons, produce urine that is isoosmotic or hypoosmotic to body fluids. However, the epithelium of the chamber called the cloaca helps conserve fluid by reabsorbing some of the water present in urine and feces. Also like birds, most other reptiles excrete their nitrogenous wastes as uric acid.

Freshwater Fishes and Amphibians

Freshwater fishes are hyperosmotic to their surroundings, so they must excrete excess water continuously. In contrast to mammals and birds, freshwater fishes produce large volumes of very dilute urine. Their kidneys, which contain many nephrons, produce filtrate at a high rate. Freshwater fishes conserve salts by reabsorbing ions from the filtrate in their distal tubules, leaving water behind.

Amphibian kidneys function much like those of freshwater fishes. When in fresh water, the kidneys of frogs excrete dilute urine while the skin accumulates certain salts from the water by active transport. On land, where dehydration is the most pressing problem of osmoregulation, frogs conserve body fluid by reabsorbing water across the epithelium of the urinary bladder.

Marine Bony Fishes

The tissues of marine bony fishes gain excess salts from their surroundings and lose water. These environmental challenges are opposite to those faced by their freshwater relatives. Compared with freshwater fishes, marine fishes have fewer and smaller nephrons, and their nephrons lack a distal tubule. In addition, their kidneys have small glomeruli, and some lack glomeruli entirely. In keeping with these features, filtration rates are low and very little urine is excreted.

The main function of kidneys in marine bony fishes is to get rid of divalent ions (those with a charge of 2+ or 2−) such as calcium (Ca^{2+}), magnesium (Mg^{2+}), and sulfate ($SO_4{}^{2-}$). Marine fishes take in divalent ions by incessantly drinking seawater. They rid themselves of these ions by secreting them into the proximal tubules of the nephrons and excreting them in urine. Secretion by the gills maintains proper levels of monovalent ions (charge of 1+ or 1−) such as Na^+ and Cl^-.

CONCEPT CHECK 44.4

1. What do the number and length of nephrons indicate about the habitat of fishes? How do these features correlate with rates of urine production?
2. Many medications make the epithelium of the collecting duct less permeable to water. How would taking such a drug affect kidney output?
3. **WHAT IF?** If blood pressure in the afferent arteriole leading to a glomerulus decreased, how would the rate of blood filtration within Bowman's capsule be affected? Explain.

For suggested answers, see Appendix A.

CONCEPT **44.5**

Hormonal circuits link kidney function, water balance, and blood pressure

In mammals, both the volume and osmolarity of urine are adjusted according to an animal's water and salt balance and its rate of urea production. In situations of high salt intake and low water availability, a mammal can excrete urea and salt in small volumes of hyperosmotic urine with minimal water loss. If salt is scarce and fluid intake is high, the kidney can instead get rid of the excess water with little salt loss by producing large volumes of hypoosmotic urine. At such times, the urine can be as dilute as 70 mOsm/L, compared with an osmolarity of 300 mOsm/L for human blood.

The South American vampire bat shown in **Figure 44.18** illustrates the versatility of the mammalian kidney. Bats of this species feed at night on the blood of large birds and mammals. The bats use their sharp teeth to make a small incision in the prey's skin and then lap up blood from the wound (the prey animal is typically not seriously harmed). Anticoagulants in the bat's saliva prevent the blood from clotting. Because vampire bats often search for hours and fly long distances to locate a suitable victim, they benefit from consuming as much blood as possible when they do find prey—so much that after feeding, a bat could be too heavy to fly. However, the bat's kidneys offload much of the water absorbed from a blood meal by excreting large volumes of dilute urine as it feeds, up to 24% of body mass per hour. Having lost enough weight to take off, the bat can fly back to its roost in a cave or hollow tree, where it spends the day.

▲ **Figure 44.18 A vampire bat (*Desmodus rotundas*), a mammal with a unique excretory situation.**

In the roost, the bat faces a different regulatory problem. Most of the nutrition it derives from blood comes in the form of protein. Digesting proteins generates large quantities of urea, but roosting bats lack access to the drinking water necessary to dilute it. Instead, their kidneys shift to producing small quantities of highly concentrated urine (up to 4,600 mOsm/L), an adjustment that disposes of the urea load while conserving as much water as possible. The vampire bat's ability to alternate rapidly between producing large amounts of dilute urine and small amounts of very hyperosmotic urine is an essential part of its adaptation to an unusual food source.

Antidiuretic Hormone

A combination of nervous and hormonal controls manages the osmoregulatory function of the mammalian kidney. One key hormone in this regulatory circuitry is **antidiuretic hormone (ADH)**, also called *vasopressin*. ADH is produced in the hypothalamus of the brain and stored in the posterior pituitary gland, located just below the hypothalamus. Osmoreceptor cells in the hypothalamus monitor the osmolarity of blood and regulate release of ADH from the posterior pituitary.

To understand the role of ADH, let's consider what occurs when blood osmolarity rises, such as after ingesting salty food or losing water through sweating. In response to an increase in osmolarity above the set point of 300 mOsm/L, more ADH is released into the bloodstream **(Figure 44.19a)**. When ADH reaches the kidney, its main targets are the distal tubules and collecting ducts. There, ADH brings about changes that make the epithelium more permeable to water. The resulting increase in water reabsorption concentrates urine, reduces urine volume, and lowers blood osmolarity back toward the set point. (Only the gain of additional water in food and drink can bring osmolarity all the way back to 300 mOsm/L.) As the osmolarity of the blood subsides, a negative-feedback mechanism reduces the activity of osmoreceptor cells in the hypothalamus, and ADH secretion is reduced.

A reduction in blood osmolarity below the set point has the opposite set of effects. For example, intake of a large volume of water leads to a decrease in ADH secretion to a very low level. The resulting decrease in permeability of the distal tubules and collecting ducts reduces water reabsorption, resulting in discharge of large volumes of dilute urine. (Diuresis refers to increased urination, and ADH is called *anti*diuretic hormone because it opposes this state.)

ADH influences water uptake in the kidney by regulating the water-selective channels formed by aquaporins. Binding of ADH to receptor molecules leads to a temporary increase in the number of aquaporin molecules in the membranes of collecting duct cells **(Figure 44.19b)**. Additional channels recapture more water, reducing urine volume.

Mutations that prevent ADH production or that inactivate the ADH receptor gene block the increase in channel number and thus the ADH response. The resulting disorder can cause severe dehydration and solute imbalance due to production of urine that is abnormally large in volume and very dilute. These symptoms give the condition its name: *diabetes insipidus* (from the Greek for "to pass through" and "having no flavor").

Dutch researcher Bernard van Oost and his colleagues wondered whether mutations in an aquaporin gene itself might also cause diabetes insipidus. Having found aquaporin gene mutations in a patient, they set out to determine whether the alterations led to nonfunctional water channels **(Figure 44.20)**.

Taken together with previous studies, the experiments of the Dutch researchers demonstrate that a wide variety of genetic defects can disrupt ADH regulation of water balance in the body. Even in the absence of such genetic changes, certain substances can alter the regulation of osmolarity. For example, alcohol can disturb water balance by inhibiting ADH release, leading to excessive urinary water loss and dehydration (which may cause some of the symptoms of a hangover). Normally, blood osmo-

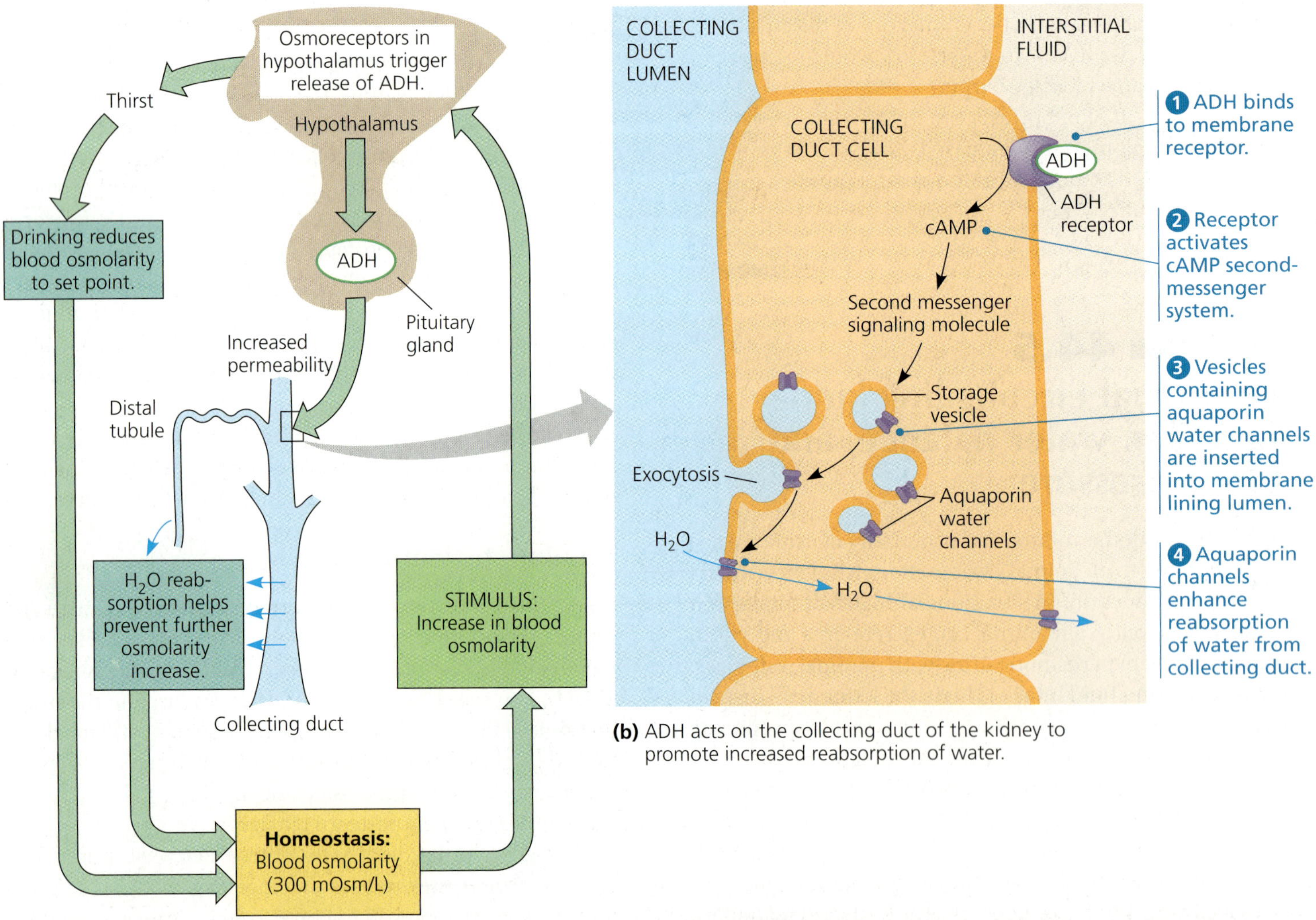

(a) The hypothalamus contributes to homeostasis for blood osmolarity by triggering thirst and ADH release.

(b) ADH acts on the collecting duct of the kidney to promote increased reabsorption of water.

▲ **Figure 44.19 Regulation of fluid retention by antidiuretic hormone (ADH).**

▼ Figure 44.20 Inquiry

Can aquaporin mutations cause diabetes insipidus?

EXPERIMENT Bernard van Oost and colleagues at the University of Nijmegen, in the Netherlands, were studying a patient who had diabetes insipidus, but whose ADH receptor gene was normal. Sequencing of the patient's DNA revealed two different mutations, one in each copy of an aquaporin gene. To determine whether each mutation blocked channel formation, they studied the mutant proteins in a cell that could be manipulated and studied outside the body. The cell they chose was the frog oocyte, which can be collected in large numbers from an adult female and will express foreign genes. The researchers synthesized messenger RNA from clones of the wild-type and mutant aquaporin genes and injected the synthetic RNA into oocytes. Within the oocytes, the cellular machinery translated the RNA into aquaporin proteins. To determine if the mutant aquaporin proteins made functional water channels, the investigators transferred the oocytes from a 200-mOsm to a 10-mOsm solution. They then measured swelling by light microscopy and calculated the permeability of the oocytes to water.

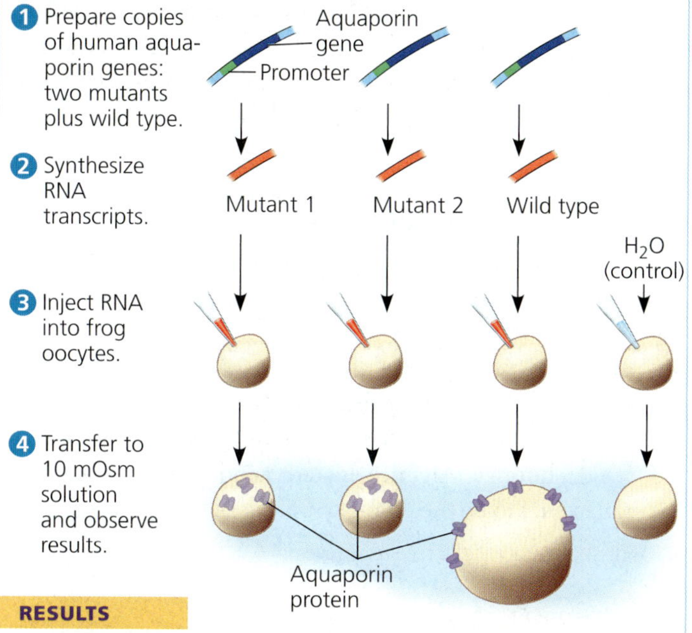

RESULTS

Injected RNA	Permeability (μm/s)
Wild-type aquaporin	196
None	20
Aquaporin mutant 1	17
Aquaporin mutant 2	18

CONCLUSION Because each mutation inactivates aquaporin as a water channel, the patient's disorder can be attributed to these mutations.

SOURCE P. M. T. Deen et al., Requirement of human renal water channel aquaporin-2 for vasopressin-dependent concentration of urine, *Science* 264:92–95 (1994).

WHAT IF? If you measured ADH levels in patients with ADH receptor mutations and in patients with aquaporin mutations, what would you expect to find, compared with wild-type subjects?

larity, ADH release, and water reabsorption in the kidney are all linked in a feedback loop that contributes to homeostasis.

The Renin-Angiotensin-Aldosterone System

A second regulatory mechanism that helps to maintain homeostasis is the **renin-angiotensin-aldosterone system (RAAS)**. The RAAS involves a specialized tissue called the **juxtaglomerular apparatus (JGA)**, located near the afferent arteriole that supplies blood to the glomerulus **(Figure 44.21)**. When blood pressure or blood volume in the afferent arteriole drops (for instance, as a result of blood loss or reduced intake of salt), the JGA releases the enzyme renin. Renin initiates chemical reactions that cleave a plasma protein called angiotensinogen, yielding a peptide called **angiotensin II**.

Functioning as a hormone, angiotensin II raises blood pressure by constricting arterioles, which decreases blood flow to many capillaries, including those of the kidney. Angiotensin II also stimulates the adrenal glands to release a hormone called **aldosterone**. This hormone acts on the nephrons' distal

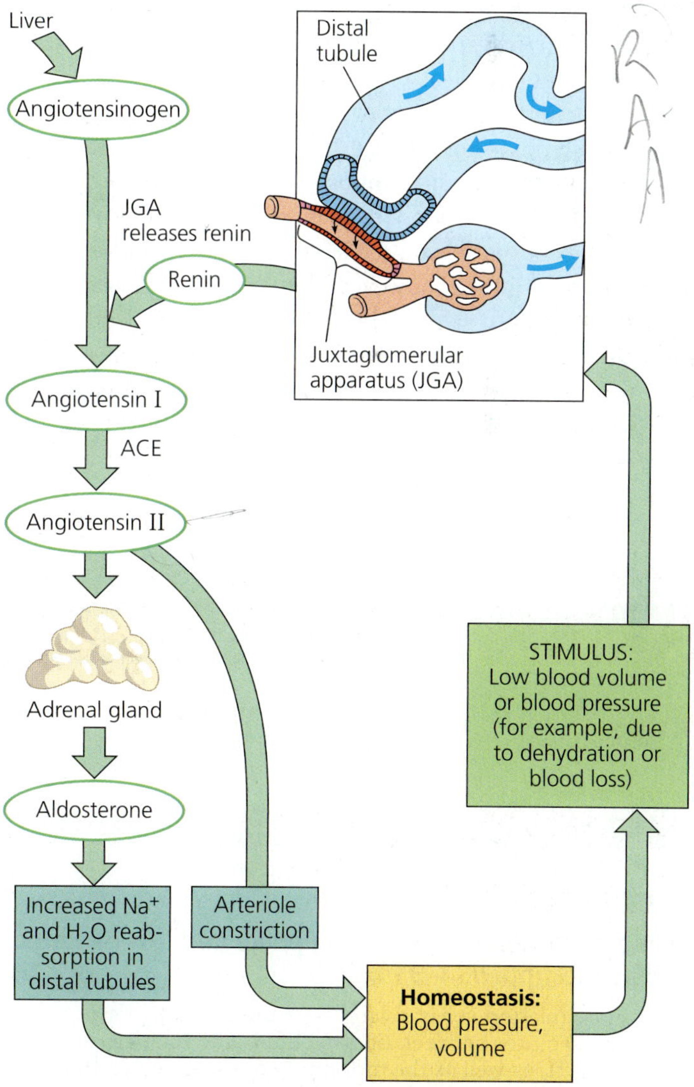

▲ **Figure 44.21 Regulation of blood volume and pressure by the renin-angiotensin-aldosterone system (RAAS).**

tubules, making them reabsorb more sodium (Na^+) and water and increasing blood volume and pressure.

Because angiotensin II acts in several ways that increase blood pressure, drugs that block angiotensin II production are widely used to treat hypertension (chronic high blood pressure). Many of these drugs are specific inhibitors of angiotensin converting enzyme (ACE), which catalyzes the second step in the production of an angiotensin II. As shown in Figure 44.21, renin released from the JGA acts on a circulating substrate, angiotensinogen, forming angiotensin I. ACE in vascular endothelium, particularly in the lungs, then splits off two amino acids from angiotensin I, forming active angiotensin II. Blocking ACE activity with drugs prevents angiotensin II production and thereby often lowers blood pressure into the normal range.

Homeostatic Regulation of the Kidney

The renin-angiotensin-aldosterone system operates as part of a complex feedback circuit that results in homeostasis. A drop in blood pressure and blood volume triggers renin release from the JGA. In turn, the rise in blood pressure and volume resulting from the various actions of angiotensin II and aldosterone reduces the release of renin.

The functions of ADH and the RAAS may seem to be redundant, but this is not the case. Both increase water reabsorption, but they counter different osmoregulatory problems. The release of ADH is a response to an increase in blood osmolarity, as when the body is dehydrated from excessive water loss or inadequate water intake. However, a situation that causes an excessive loss of both salt and body fluids—a major wound, for example, or severe diarrhea—will reduce blood volume *without* increasing osmolarity. This will not affect ADH release, but the RAAS will respond to the drop in blood volume and pressure by increasing water and Na^+ reabsorption. Thus, ADH and the RAAS are partners in homeostasis. ADH alone would lower blood Na^+ concentration by stimulating water reabsorption in the kidney, but the RAAS helps maintain the osmolarity of body fluids at the set point by stimulating Na^+ reabsorption.

Another hormone, **atrial natriuretic peptide (ANP)**, opposes the RAAS. The walls of the atria of the heart release ANP in response to an increase in blood volume and pressure. ANP inhibits the release of renin from the JGA, inhibits NaCl reabsorption by the collecting ducts, and reduces aldosterone release from the adrenal glands. These actions lower blood volume and pressure. Thus, ADH, the RAAS, and ANP provide an elaborate system of checks and balances that regulate the kidney's ability to control the osmolarity, salt concentration, volume, and pressure of blood. The precise regulatory role of ANP is an area of active research.

In all animals, certain of the intricate physiological machines we call organs work continuously in maintaining solute and water balance and excreting nitrogenous wastes. The details that we have reviewed in this chapter only hint at the great complexity of the neural and hormonal mechanisms involved in regulating these homeostatic processes.

CONCEPT CHECK 44.5

1. How does alcohol affect regulation of water balance in the body?
2. Why could it be dangerous to drink a very large amount of water in a short period of time?
3. **WHAT IF?** Conn's syndrome is a condition caused by tumors of the adrenal cortex that secrete high amounts of aldosterone in an unregulated manner. What would you expect to be the major symptom of this disorder?

For suggested answers, see Appendix A.

Chapter 44 Review

MEDIA Go to the Study Area at **www.masteringbio.com** for BioFlix 3-D Animations, MP3 Tutors, Videos, Practice Tests, an eBook, and more.

SUMMARY OF KEY CONCEPTS

CONCEPT 44.1

Osmoregulation balances the uptake and loss of water and solutes (pp. 954–959)

- Osmoregulation is based largely on the controlled movement of solutes between internal fluids and the external environment, as well as the movement of water, which follows by osmosis.
- **Osmosis and Osmolarity** Cells require a balance between osmotic gain and loss of water. Water uptake and loss are balanced by various mechanisms of osmoregulation in different environments.
- **Osmotic Challenges** Osmoconformers, all of which are marine animals, are isoosmotic with their surroundings and do not regulate their osmolarity. Among marine animals, most invertebrates are osmoconformers.
- **Energetics of Osmoregulation** Osmoregulators expend energy to control water uptake and loss in a hypoosmotic or hyperosmotic environment, respectively. Sharks have an osmolarity slightly higher than seawater because they retain urea. Terrestrial animals combat desiccation through behavioral adaptations, water-conserving excretory organs, and drinking and eating food with high water content. Animals in temporary waters may be anhydrobiotic.

Animal	Inflow/Outflow	Urine
Freshwater fish. Lives in water less concentrated than body fluids; fish tends to gain water, lose salt	Does not drink water Salt in (active transport by gills) H_2O in  Salt out	▶ Large volume of urine ▶ Urine is less concentrated than body fluids
Marine bony fish. Lives in water more concentrated than body fluids; fish tends to lose water, gain salt	Drinks water Salt in H_2O out  Salt out (active transport by gills)	▶ Small volume of urine ▶ Urine is slightly less concentrated than body fluids
Terrestrial vertebrate. Terrestrial environment; tends to lose body water to air	Drinks water Salt in (by mouth)  H_2O and salt out	▶ Moderate volume of urine ▶ Urine is more concentrated than body fluids

▶ **Transport Epithelia in Osmoregulation** Water balance and waste disposal depend on transport epithelia, layers of specialized epithelial cells that regulate the solute movements required for waste disposal and for tempering changes in body fluids.

CONCEPT 44.2

An animal's nitrogenous wastes reflect its phylogeny and habitat (pp. 959–960)

▶ **Forms of Nitrogenous Waste** Protein and nucleic acid metabolism generates ammonia, a toxic waste product. Most aquatic animals excrete ammonia across the body surface or gill epithelia into the surrounding water. The liver of mammals and most adult amphibians converts ammonia to the less toxic urea, which is carried to the kidneys, concentrated, and excreted with a minimal loss of water. Uric acid is a slightly soluble nitrogenous waste excreted in the paste-like urine of land snails, insects, and many reptiles, including birds.

▶ **The Influence of Evolution and Environment on Nitrogenous Wastes** The kind of nitrogenous waste excreted depends on an animal's evolutionary history and habitat. The amount of nitrogenous waste produced is coupled to the animal's energy budget and amount of dietary protein.

CONCEPT 44.3

Diverse excretory systems are variations on a tubular theme (pp. 960–964)

▶ **Excretory Processes** Most excretory systems produce urine by refining a filtrate derived from body fluids. Key functions of most excretory systems are filtration (pressure filtering of body fluids, producing a filtrate); production of urine from the filtrate by selective reabsorption (reclaiming valuable solutes from the filtrate); and secretion (addition of toxins and other solutes from the body fluids to the filtrate).

▶ **Survey of Excretory Systems** Extracellular fluid is filtered into the protonephridia of the flame bulb system in flatworms; these tubules excrete a dilute fluid and may also function in osmoregulation. Each segment of an earthworm has a pair of open-ended metanephridia that collect coelomic fluid and produce dilute urine. In insects, Malpighian tubules function in osmoregulation and removal of nitrogenous wastes from the hemolymph. Insects produce a relatively dry waste matter, an important adaptation to terrestrial life. Kidneys, the excretory organs of vertebrates, function in both excretion and osmoregulation.

▶ **Structure of the Mammalian Excretory System** Excretory tubules (consisting of nephrons and collecting ducts) and associated blood vessels pack the kidney. Filtration occurs as blood pressure forces fluid from the blood in the glomerulus into the lumen of Bowman's capsule. Filtration of small molecules is nonselective, and the filtrate initially contains a mixture of small molecules that mirrors the concentrations of these substances in blood plasma. Fluid from several nephrons flows into a collecting duct. The ureter conveys urine from the renal pelvis to the urinary bladder.

MEDIA

Activity Structure of the Human Excretory System

CONCEPT 44.4

The nephron is organized for stepwise processing of blood filtrate (pp. 964–969)

▶ **From Blood Filtrate to Urine: *A Closer Look*** Nephrons control the composition of the blood by filtration, secretion, and reabsorption. Secretion and reabsorption in the proximal tubule substantially alter the volume and composition of filtrate. The descending limb of the loop of Henle is permeable to water but not to salt; water moves by osmosis into the hyperosmotic interstitial fluid. The ascending limb is permeable to salt, but not to water, with salt leaving as the filtrate ascends first by diffusion and then by active transport. The distal tubule and collecting duct play key roles in regulating the K^+ and NaCl concentration of body fluids. The collecting duct carries the filtrate through the medulla to the renal pelvis and can respond to hormonal signals to reabsorb water.

▶ **Solute Gradients and Water Conservation** In a mammalian kidney, the cooperative action of the loops of Henle and the collecting ducts is largely responsible for the osmotic gradient that concentrates the urine. A countercurrent multiplier system involving the loop of Henle maintains the gradient of salt concentration in the interior of the kidney, which enables the kidney to form concentrated urine. The urine can be further concentrated by water exiting the filtrate by osmosis in the collecting duct. Urea, which diffuses out of the collecting duct as it traverses the inner medulla, contributes to the osmotic gradient of the kidney.

▶ **Adaptations of the Vertebrate Kidney to Diverse Environments** The form and function of nephrons in various vertebrates are related primarily to the requirements for osmoregulation in the animal's habitat. Desert mammals, which excrete the most hyperosmotic urine, have loops of Henle that extend deep into the kidney medulla, whereas mammals living in moist or aquatic habitats have shorter loops and excrete less concentrated urine. Although birds can produce a hyperosmotic urine, the main water conservation adaptation of birds is removal of nitrogen as uric acid, which can be excreted as a paste. Most other terrestrial reptiles excrete uric acid. Freshwater fishes and amphibians produce large volumes of very dilute urine. The kidneys of marine bony fishes have low filtration rates and excrete very little urine.

MEDIA

Activity Nephron Function

CONCEPT **44.5**

Hormonal circuits link kidney function, water balance, and blood pressure (pp. 969–972)

- **Antidiuretic Hormone** ADH is released from the posterior pituitary gland when the osmolarity of blood rises above a set point. ADH increases epithelial permeability to water in the distal tubules and collecting ducts of the kidney. The permeability increase in the collecting duct results from an increase in the number of water channels in the membrane.
- **The Renin-Angiotensin-Aldosterone System** When blood pressure or blood volume in the afferent arteriole drops, renin released from the juxtaglomerular apparatus (JGA) initiates conversion of angiotensinogen to angiotensin II. Functioning as a hormone, angiotensin II raises blood pressure by constricting arterioles and triggering release of the hormone aldosterone. The rise in blood pressure and volume in turn reduces the release of renin.
- **Homeostatic Regulation of the Kidney** ADH and the RAAS have overlapping but distinct functions. Atrial natriuretic peptide (ANP) opposes the action of the RAAS.

MEDIA

Activity Control of Water Reabsorption
Investigation What Affects Urine Production?

TESTING YOUR KNOWLEDGE

SELF-QUIZ

1. *Unlike* an earthworm's metanephridia, a mammalian nephron
   a. is intimately associated with a capillary network.
   b. forms urine by changing fluid composition inside a tubule.
   c. functions in both osmoregulation and excretion.
   d. receives filtrate from blood instead of coelomic fluid.
   e. has a transport epithelium.

2. Which of the following is *not* a normal response to increased blood osmolarity in humans?
   a. increased permeability of the collecting duct to water
   b. production of more dilute urine
   c. release of ADH by the pituitary gland
   d. increased thirst
   e. reduced urine production

3. The high osmolarity of the renal medulla is maintained by all of the following *except*
   a. diffusion of salt from the thin segment of the ascending limb of the loop of Henle.
   b. active transport of salt from the upper region of the ascending limb.
   c. the spatial arrangement of juxtamedullary nephrons.
   d. diffusion of urea from the collecting duct.
   e. diffusion of salt from the descending limb of the loop of Henle.

4. Natural selection should favor the highest proportion of juxtamedullary nephrons in which of the following species?
   a. a river otter
   b. a mouse species living in a tropical rain forest
   c. a mouse species living in a temperate broadleaf forest
   d. a mouse species living in a desert
   e. a beaver

5. Which process in the nephron is *least* selective?
   a. filtration
   b. reabsorption
   c. active transport
   d. secretion
   e. salt pumping by the loop of Henle

6. Which of the following animals generally has the lowest volume of urine production?
   a. a marine shark
   b. a salmon in freshwater
   c. a marine bony fish
   d. a freshwater bony fish
   e. a shark inhabiting freshwater Lake Nicaragua

7. African lungfish, which are often found in small stagnant pools of fresh water, produce urea as a nitrogenous waste. What is the advantage of this adaptation?
   a. Urea takes less energy to synthesize than ammonia.
   b. Small stagnant pools do not provide enough water to dilute the toxic ammonia.
   c. The highly toxic urea makes the pool uninhabitable to potential competitors.
   d. Urea forms an insoluble precipitate.
   e. Urea makes lungfish tissue hypoosmotic to the pool.

8. **DRAW IT** Using Figure 44.4 as an example, sketch the exchange of salt (NaCl) and water between a shark and its marine environment.

For Self-Quiz answers, see Appendix A.

MEDIA Visit the Study Area at **www.masteringbio.com** for a Practice Test.

EVOLUTION CONNECTION

9. Merriam's kangaroo rats (*Dipodomys merriami*) live in North American habitats ranging from moist, cool woodlands to hot deserts. Assuming that natural selection has resulted in differences in water conservation between *D. merriami* populations, propose a hypothesis concerning the relative rates of evaporative water loss by populations that live in moist versus dry environments. Using a humidity sensor to detect evaporative water loss by kangaroo rats, how could you test your hypothesis?

SCIENTIFIC INQUIRY

10. You are exploring kidney function in kangaroo rats. You measure urine volume and osmolarity, as well as the amount of chloride (Cl^-) and urea in the urine. If the water source provided to the animals were switched from tap water to a 2% NaCl solution, what change in urine osmolarity would you expect? How would you determine if this change was more likely due to a change in the excretion of Cl^- or urea?

45 Hormones and the Endocrine System

▲ **Figure 45.1 What role do hormones play in transforming a caterpillar (below) into a butterfly?**

KEY CONCEPTS

45.1 Hormones and other signaling molecules bind to target receptors, triggering specific response pathways

45.2 Negative feedback and antagonistic hormone pairs are common features of the endocrine system

45.3 The endocrine and nervous systems act individually and together in regulating animal physiology

45.4 Endocrine glands respond to diverse stimuli in regulating metabolism, homeostasis, development, and behavior

OVERVIEW

The Body's Long-Distance Regulators

In becoming an adult, a butterfly like the anise swallowtail (*Papilio zelicaon*) in **Figure 45.1** is dramatically transformed. The plump, crawling caterpillar that encases itself in a cocoon bears little resemblance to the delicate free-flying butterfly that emerges days later. Within the cocoon, specialized groups of cells assemble into the adult tissues and organs while most other tissues of the caterpillar break down.

A caterpillar's complete change of body form, called *metamorphosis*, is one of many biological processes controlled by hormones. In animals, a **hormone** (from the Greek *horman*, to excite) is a molecule that is secreted into the extracellular fluid, circulates in the blood or hemolymph, and communicates regulatory messages throughout the body. In the case of the caterpillar, communication by hormones regulates the timing of metamorphosis and ensures that different parts of the insect's adult body develop in unison.

Although the circulatory system allows a hormone to reach all cells of the body, only its target cells have the receptors that enable a response. A hormone elicits a specific response—such as a change in metabolism—from its target cells, whereas cells lacking a receptor for that particular hormone are unaffected.

Chemical signaling by hormones is the function of the **endocrine system**, one of the two basic systems for communication and regulation throughout the body. Hormones secreted by endocrine cells regulate reproduction, development, energy metabolism, growth, and behavior. The other major communication and control system is the **nervous system**, a network of specialized cells—neurons—that transmit signals along dedicated pathways. These signals in turn regulate other cells, including neurons, muscle cells, and endocrine cells. Because signaling by neurons can regulate the release of hormones, the nervous and endocrine systems often overlap in function.

In this chapter, we'll begin with an overview of the different types of chemical signaling in animals. We will then explore how hormones regulate target cells, how hormone secretion is regulated, and how hormones help maintain homeostasis. We will also look at how the activities of the endocrine and nervous systems are coordinated. We'll conclude by examining the role of hormones in regulating growth, development, and reproduction, topics we'll return to in Chapters 46 and 47.

CONCEPT 45.1

Hormones and other signaling molecules bind to target receptors, triggering specific response pathways

Hormones, the focus of this chapter, are one of several types of secreted chemicals that transmit information between animal cells. Let's consider the similarities and differences in the functions of these signaling molecules.

Types of Secreted Signaling Molecules

Hormones and other signaling molecules trigger responses by binding to specific receptor proteins in or on target cells. Only cells that have receptors for a particular secreted molecule are target cells; other cells are unresponsive to that molecule. Molecules used in signaling are often classified by the type of secreting cell and the route taken by the signal in reaching its target.

Hormones

As illustrated in **Figure 45.2a**, hormones secreted into extracellular fluids by endocrine cells reach target cells via the bloodstream (or hemolymph). Some endocrine system cells are found in organs that are part of other organ systems. For example, within the digestive and excretory systems, the stomach and kidney both contain endocrine cells. Other endocrine cells are grouped in ductless organs called **endocrine glands**.

Like isolated endocrine cells, endocrine glands secrete hormones directly into the surrounding fluid. Endocrine glands thus contrast with *exocrine glands*, such as salivary glands, which have ducts that carry secreted substances onto body surfaces or into body cavities. This distinction is reflected in their names: The Greek *endo* (within) and *exo* (out of) reflect secretion into or out of body fluids, while *crine* (from the Greek for "separate") reflects movement away from the secreting cell.

Hormones serve a range of functions in the body. They maintain homeostasis; mediate responses to environmental stimuli; and regulate growth, development, and reproduction. For example, hormones coordinate the body's responses to stress, dehydration, or low blood glucose. They also control the appearance of characteristics that distinguish a juvenile animal from an adult.

Local Regulators

Many types of cells produce **local regulators**, secreted molecules that act over short distances and reach their target cells solely by diffusion. In Chapter 43, we saw how immune cells communicate with each other by local regulators called cytokines (see Figures 43.17 and 43.19). As we will discuss shortly, local regulators play roles in many other processes, including blood pressure regulation, nervous system function, and reproduction.

Local regulators function in paracrine and autocrine signaling. In **paracrine** signaling (from the Greek *para*, to one side of), target cells lie near the secreting cell **(Figure 45.2b)**. In **autocrine** signaling (from the Greek *auto*, self), the secreted molecules act on the secreting cell itself **(Figure 45.2c)**. Some secreted molecules have both paracrine and autocrine activity. Although the definition of hormones can be broadened to include local regulators, in this chapter we use *hormone* to refer to chemicals that reach target cells through the bloodstream.

Neurotransmitters and Neurohormones

Secreted molecules also have a critical role in the transmission of information by neurons. Neurons communicate with target cells, such as other neurons and muscle cells, at specialized junctions known as synapses. At many synapses, neurons secrete molecules called **neurotransmitters** that diffuse a very short distance to bind receptors on the target cells **(Figure 45.2d)**. Neurotransmitters are central to sensation, memory, cognition, and movement, as we will explore in Chapters 48–50.

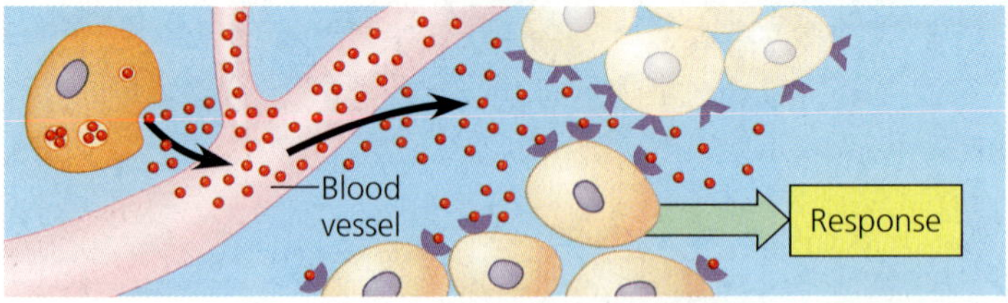

(a) In **endocrine signaling**, secreted molecules diffuse into the bloodstream and trigger responses in target cells anywhere in the body.

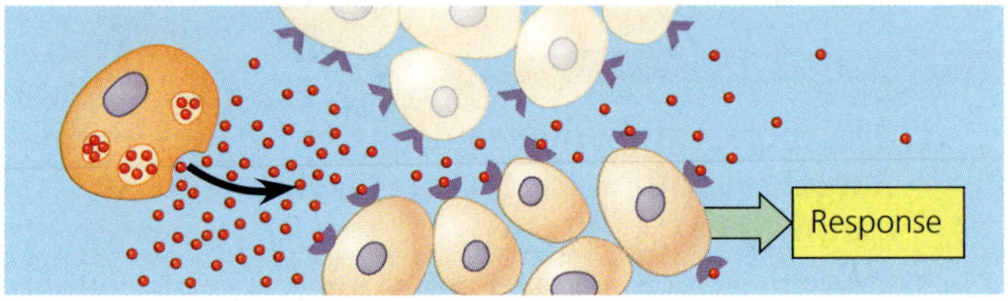

(b) In **paracrine signaling**, secreted molecules diffuse locally and trigger a response in neighboring cells.

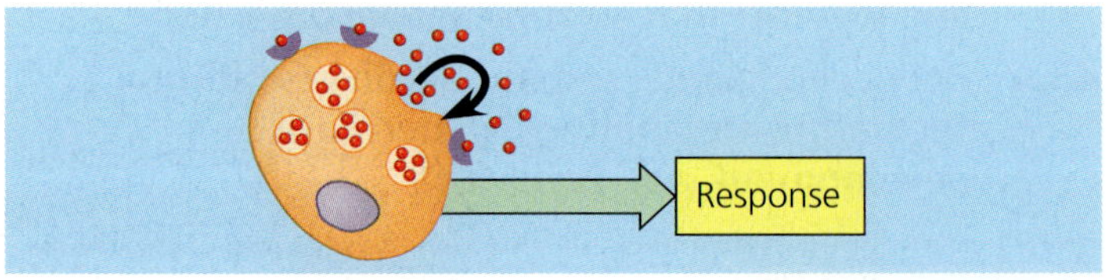

(c) In **autocrine signaling**, secreted molecules diffuse locally and trigger a response in the cells that secrete them.

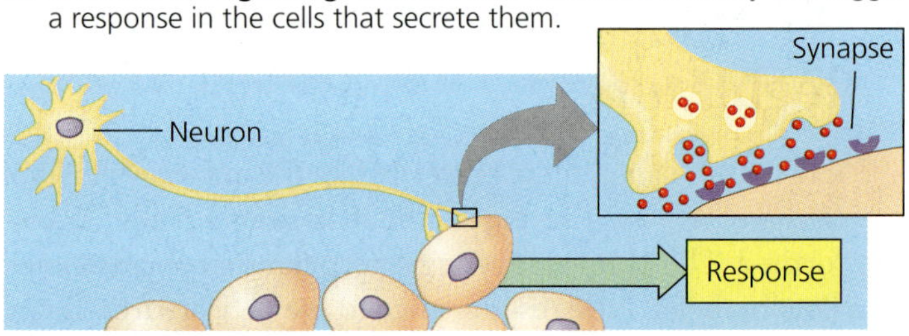

(d) In **synaptic signaling**, neurotransmitters diffuse across synapses and trigger responses in cells of target tissues (neurons, muscles, or glands).

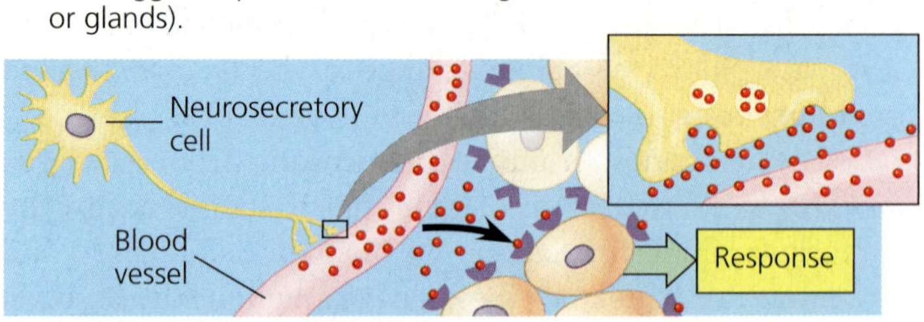

(e) In **neuroendocrine signaling**, neurohormones diffuse into the bloodstream and trigger responses in target cells anywhere in the body.

▲ **Figure 45.2 Intercellular communication by secreted molecules.** In each type of signaling, secreted molecules bind to a specific receptor protein expressed by target cells. Receptors are sometimes located inside cells, but for simplicity all are drawn here on the cell surface.

In neuroendocrine signaling, *neurosecretory cells*, specialized neurons typically found in the brain, secrete molecules that diffuse from nerve cell endings into the bloodstream **(Figure 45.2e)**. These molecules, which travel through the bloodstream to reach target cells, are a class of hormones called **neurohormones**. One example is ADH (vasopressin), a hormone critical to kidney function and water balance (see Chapter 44).

Pheromones

Not all secreted signaling molecules act within the body. Members of the same animal species sometimes communicate with **pheromones**, chemicals that are released into the external environment. Pheromones serve many functions, including marking trails leading to food, defining territories, warning of predators, and attracting potential mates.

Chemical Classes of Hormones

Having distinguished hormones from other secreted signaling molecules based on the type and location of cells involved, we turn now to the chemical composition of hormones. Based on their structure and pathway for synthesis, hormones are often divided into three groups: polypeptides (proteins and peptides), amines, and steroids.

Figure 45.3 displays examples of each major hormone class. The polypeptide hormone insulin is made up of two polypeptide chains. Like most hormones in this group, insulin is formed by cleavage of a longer protein chain. Epinephrine and thyroxine are amine hormones, which are synthesized from a single amino acid, either tyrosine or tryptophan. Steroid hormones, such as cortisol, are lipids that contain four fused carbon rings. All are derived from the steroid cholesterol (see Figure 5.15).

As Figure 45.3 also indicates, hormones vary in their solubility in aqueous and lipid-rich environments. Polypeptides and many amine hormones are water-soluble. Being insoluble in lipids, these hormones cannot pass through the plasma membranes of cells. In contrast, steroid hormones, as well as other largely nonpolar hormones, such as thyroxine, are lipid-soluble and can pass through cell membranes readily. As we will discuss next, whether or not a hormone is able to cross cell membranes correlates with a difference in the location of receptors in target cells.

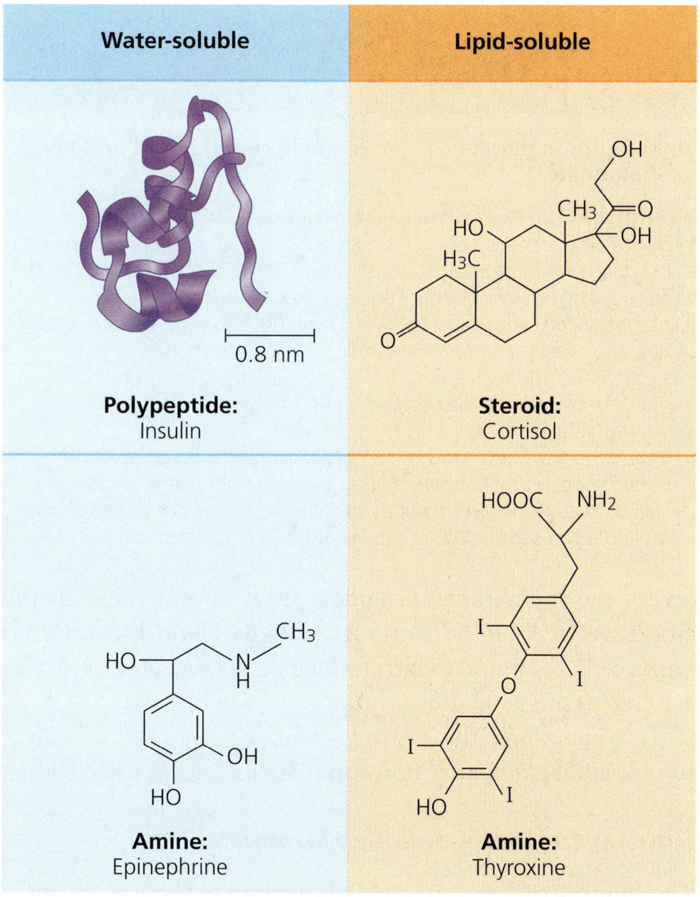

▲ **Figure 45.3 Hormones differ in form and solubility.** Structures of insulin, a polypeptide hormone; epinephrine and thyroxine, amine hormones; and cortisol, a steroid hormone. Insulin and epinephrine are water-soluble; thyroxine and cortisol are lipid-soluble.

Hormone Receptor Location: *Scientific Inquiry*

In studying hormone receptors, biologists needed to find out where they are located and where they functionally interact with hormones. To learn how they answered these questions, let's review some of the critical experiments.

Evidence that receptors for steroid hormones are located inside target cells came from studying the vertebrate hormone estradiol, a form of estrogen. For most mammals, including humans, estrogens are necessary for the normal development and function of the female reproductive system. In experiments conducted in the early 1960s, female rats were treated with radioactive forms of estradiol. When the researchers examined cells from the rats' reproductive systems, they found that the hormone had accumulated within the nuclei. In contrast, estradiol failed to accumulate in the cells of tissues that are not responsive to estrogens.

When scientists later identified the receptors for estrogens, they confirmed that the receptor molecules were located inside cells. Other steroid hormones and lipid-soluble hormones such as thyroxine also had intracellular receptors. But what about water-soluble hormones? Because these hormones cannot diffuse across a lipid bilayer, researchers hypothesized that their receptors would be located on the cell surface. Studies demonstrating that radioactive hormones bind to isolated cell membranes supported this model. Nevertheless, some biologists wondered whether water-soluble hormones could also initiate signaling from within cells.

In the 1970s, John Horowitz and colleagues at the University of California, Davis, investigated whether receptors for a water-soluble hormone are exclusively on the cell surface. In frogs, melanocyte-stimulating hormone (MSH) controls the location of pigment granules in skin cells. To determine where the hormone is active, the investigators used microinjection, a

▼ Figure 45.4 **Inquiry**

Where in the cell is the receptor for melanocyte-stimulating hormone?

EXPERIMENT John Horowitz and colleagues at the University of California, Davis, were studying how melanocyte-stimulating hormone (MSH), a peptide hormone, triggers changes in the skin color of frogs. Skin cells called melanocytes contain the dark brown pigment melanin in cytoplasmic organelles called melanosomes. The skin appears light when melanosomes cluster tightly around the melanocyte nuclei. When a frog encounters a dark environment, increased production of MSH causes melanosomes to disperse throughout the cytoplasm, darkening the skin and making the frog less visible to predators. To identify the location of the receptors that control melanosome clustering, the researchers microinjected MSH into the melanocytes or into the surrounding interstitial fluid.

RESULTS Microinjecting MSH into individual melanocytes did not induce melanosome dispersion. However, microinjection into the interstitial fluid (blue) surrounding the melanocytes caused the melanosomes to disperse.

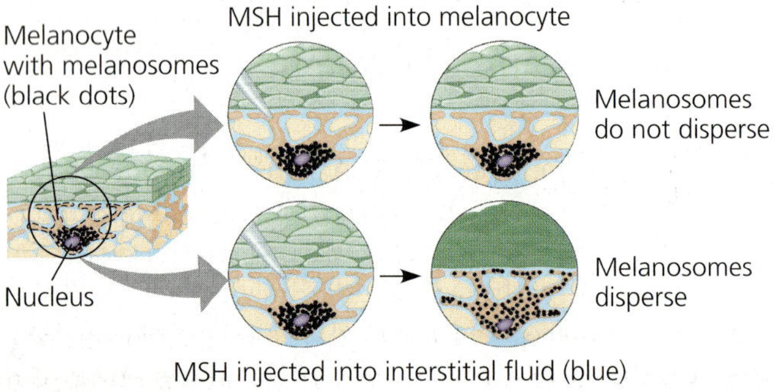

CONCLUSION These results provided evidence that MSH interacts with a receptor on the outside surface of the cell to induce a response.

SOURCE J. Horowitz et al., The response of single melanophores to extracellular and intracellular iontophoretic injection of melanocyte-stimulating hormone, *Endocrinology* 106:770–777 (1980).

WHAT IF? What result would you expect if you carried out the same experiments with a lipid-soluble hormone that had a receptor in the nucleus? Explain.

technique that can introduce tiny amounts of a substance into a cell or surrounding fluid **(Figure 45.4)**. Their experiments revealed that MSH triggered a response only if it was injected into the interstitial fluid, allowing it to bind to cell-surface receptors.

Cellular Response Pathways

Receptor location is one of several differences between the response pathways for water-soluble and lipid-soluble hormones **(Figure 45.5)**. Water-soluble hormones are secreted by exocytosis, travel freely in the bloodstream, and bind to cell-surface signal receptors. Binding of such hormones to receptors induces changes in cytoplasmic molecules and sometimes alters gene transcription (synthesis of messenger RNA molecules). In contrast, lipid-soluble hormones diffuse out

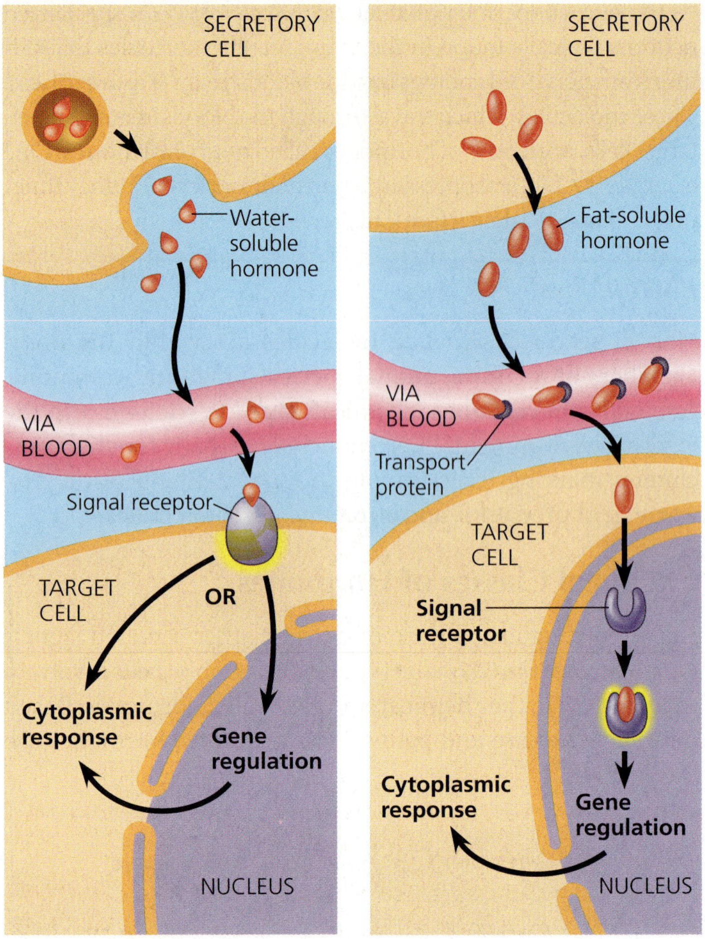

(a) Receptor in plasma membrane **(b) Receptor in cell nucleus**

▲ **Figure 45.5 Receptor location varies with hormone type. (a)** A water-soluble hormone binds to a signal receptor protein on the surface of a target cell. This interaction triggers events that lead to either a change in cytoplasmic function or a change in gene transcription in the nucleus. **(b)** A lipid-soluble hormone penetrates the target cell's plasma membrane and binds to an intracellular signal receptor, either in the cytoplasm or in the nucleus (shown here). The hormone-receptor complex acts as a transcription factor, typically activating gene expression.

? *Suppose you were studying a cell's response to a particular hormone, and you observed that the cell continued to respond to the hormone even when treated with a chemical that blocks transcription. What could you surmise about the hormone and its receptor?*

across the membranes of endocrine cells and travel in the bloodstream bound to transport proteins. Upon diffusing into target cells, they bind to intracellular signal receptors and trigger changes in gene transcription.

To understand the distinct cellular responses to water-soluble and lipid-soluble hormones, we'll examine each further.

Pathway for Water-Soluble Hormones

The binding of a water-soluble hormone to a signal receptor protein triggers events at the plasma membrane that result in a cellular response. The response may be the activation of an enzyme, a change in the uptake or secretion of specific molecules, or a rearrangement of the cytoskeleton. In addition,

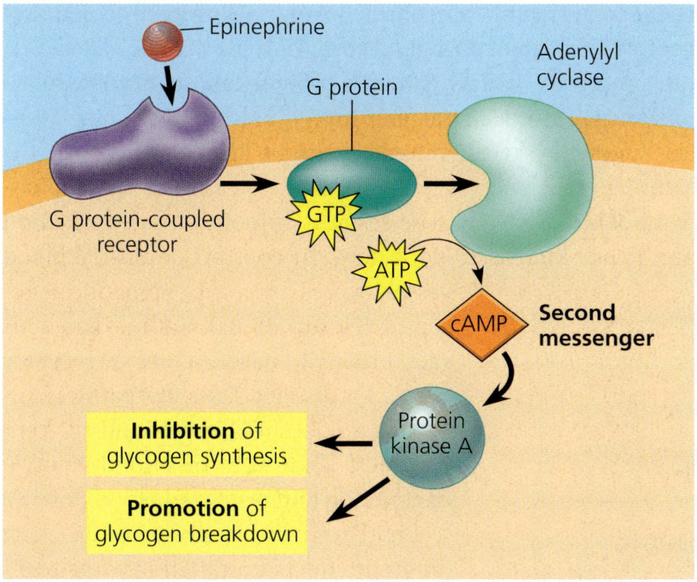

▲ **Figure 45.6 Cell-surface hormone receptors trigger signal transduction.**

some cell-surface receptors cause proteins in the cytoplasm to move into the nucleus and alter transcription of specific genes.

The series of changes in cellular proteins that converts the extracellular chemical signal to a specific intracellular response is called **signal transduction**. As described in Chapter 11, a signal transduction pathway typically involves multiple steps, each involving specific molecular interactions.

To explore how signal transduction contributes to hormone signaling, let's consider one response to short-term stress. When you find yourself in a stressful situation, perhaps running to catch a bus, your adrenal glands secrete **epinephrine**. When epinephrine reaches liver cells, it binds to a G protein-coupled receptor in the plasma membrane, as discussed in Chapter 11 and reviewed in **Figure 45.6**. The binding of hormone to receptor triggers a cascade of events involving synthesis of cyclic AMP (cAMP) as a short-lived *second messenger*. Activation of protein kinase A by cAMP leads to activation of an enzyme required for glycogen breakdown and inactivation of an enzyme necessary for glycogen synthesis. The net result is that the liver releases glucose into the bloodstream, providing the fuel you need to chase the departing bus.

Pathway for Lipid-Soluble Hormones

Intracellular receptors usually perform the entire task of transducing a signal within a target cell. The hormone activates the receptor, which then directly triggers the cell's response. In most cases, the response to a lipid-soluble hormone is a change in gene expression.

Steroid hormone receptors are located in the cytosol prior to binding to a hormone. When a steroid hormone binds to its cytosolic receptor, a hormone-receptor complex forms, which moves into the nucleus. There, the receptor portion of the complex interacts with DNA or with a DNA-binding protein, stimulating transcription of specific genes. For example, estradiol has a specific receptor in the liver cells of female birds and frogs. Binding of estradiol to this receptor activates transcription of the gene for the protein vitellogenin **(Figure 45.7)**. Following translation of the messenger RNA, vitellogenin is secreted and transported in the blood to the reproductive system, where it is used to produce egg yolk.

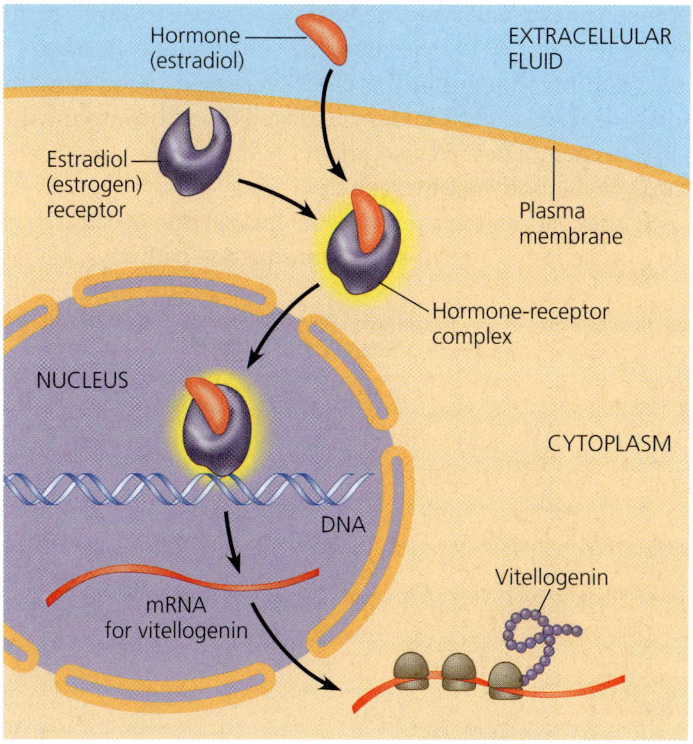

▲ **Figure 45.7 Steroid hormone receptors directly regulate gene expression.**

Thyroxine, vitamin D, and other lipid-soluble hormones that are not steroid hormones have receptors that are typically located in the nucleus. These receptors bind hormone molecules that diffuse from the bloodstream across both the plasma membrane and nuclear envelope. Once bound by a hormone, the receptor binds to specific sites in the cell's DNA and stimulates the transcription of specific genes.

Recent experiments indicate that lipid-soluble hormones can sometimes trigger responses at the cell surface without first entering the nucleus. How and when these responses arise are currently the subjects of active investigation.

Multiple Effects of Hormones

Many hormones elicit more than one type of response in the body. The effects brought about by a particular hormone can vary if target cells differ in the molecules that receive or produce the response to that hormone. Consider the effects of epinephrine in mediating the body's response to short-term stress **(Figure 45.8)**. Epinephrine simultaneously triggers glycogen breakdown in the liver, increased blood flow to major skeletal muscles, and decreased blood flow to the digestive tract. These varied effects enhance the rapid reactions of the body in emergencies.

Tissues vary in their response to epinephrine because they vary in their receptors or signal transduction pathways. Target cell recognition of epinephrine involves G protein-coupled receptors. The epinephrine receptor of a liver cell is called a β-type receptor. It acts through protein kinase A to regulate enzymes in glycogen metabolism **(Figure 45.8a)**. In blood vessels supplying skeletal muscle, the same kinase activated by the same epinephrine receptor inactivates a muscle-specific enzyme **(Figure 45.8b)**. The result is smooth muscle relaxation and hence increased blood flow. In contrast, intestinal blood vessels express an α-type epinephrine receptor **(Figure 45.8c)**. Rather than activate protein kinase A, the α receptor triggers a distinct signaling pathway involving a different G protein and different enzymes. The result is smooth muscle contraction and restricted blood flow.

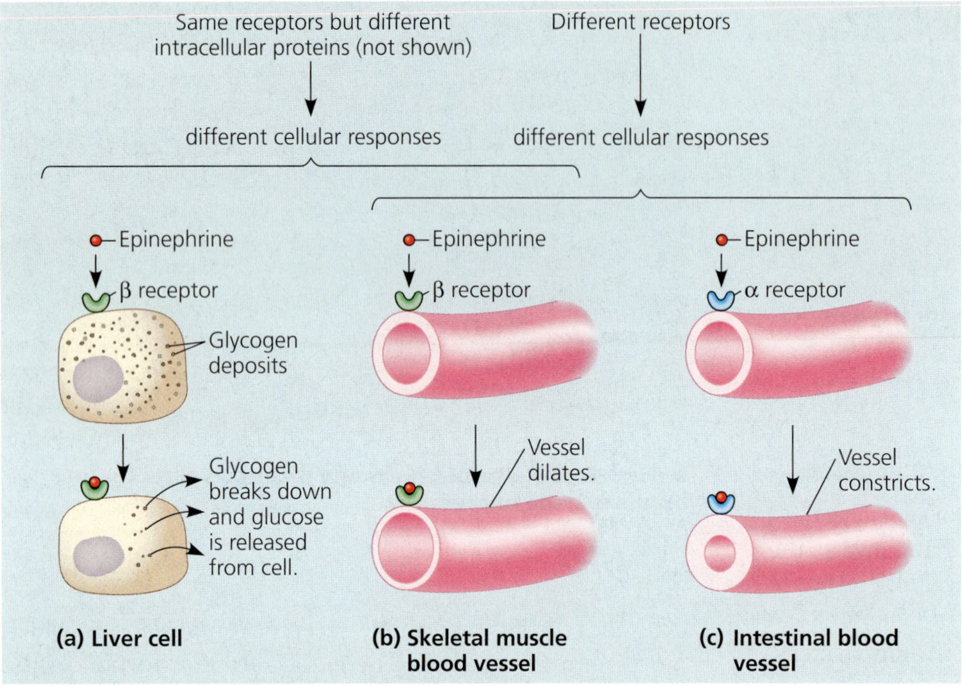

▲ **Figure 45.8 One hormone, different effects.** Epinephrine, the primary "fight-or-flight" hormone, produces different responses in different target cells. Target cells with the same receptor exhibit different responses if they have different signal transduction pathways and/or effector proteins [compare (a) with (b)]. Responses of target cells may also differ if they have different receptors for the hormone [compare (b) with (c)].

Lipid-soluble hormones often exert different effects on different target cells as well. For example, the estrogen that stimulates a bird's liver to synthesize the yolk protein vitellogenin also stimulates its reproductive system to synthesize proteins that form the egg white.

In some cases, a given hormone has different effects in different *species*. For instance, thyroxine produced by the thyroid gland regulates metabolism in frogs, humans, and other vertebrates. However, thyroxine has an additional and distinct effect in frogs, stimulating resorption of the tadpole's tail in its metamorphosis into an adult **(Figure 45.9)**.

▲ **Figure 45.9 Specialized role of a hormone in frog metamorphosis.** The hormone thyroxine is responsible for the resorption of the tadpole's tail (a) as the frog develops into its adult form (b).

Signaling by Local Regulators

Recall that local regulators are secreted molecules that link neighboring cells (paracrine signaling) or that provide feedback to the secreting cell (autocrine signaling). Once secreted, local regulators act on their target cells within seconds or even milliseconds, eliciting responses more quickly than do hormones. Nevertheless, the pathways by which local regulators trigger responses are the same as those activated by hormones.

Several types of chemical compounds function as local regulators. Polypeptide local regulators include **cytokines**, which play a role in immune responses (see Chapter 43), and most **growth factors**, which stimulate cell proliferation and differentiation. Many types of cells grow, divide, and develop normally only when growth factors are present in their extracellular environment.

The gas **nitric oxide (NO)**, which consists of nitrogen double-bonded to oxygen, serves in the body as both a neurotransmitter and a local regulator. When the level of oxygen (O_2) in the blood falls, endothelial cells in blood vessel walls synthesize and release NO. Nitric oxide activates an enzyme that relaxes the neighboring smooth muscle cells, resulting in vasodilation, which improves blood flow to tissues. In human males, the ability of NO to promote vasodilation enables sexual function by increasing blood flow into the penis, producing an erection. Highly reactive and potentially toxic, NO usually triggers changes in a target cell within a few seconds of contact and then breaks down. The drug Viagra (sildenafil citrate), a treatment for male erectile dysfunction, sustains an erection by interfering with this breakdown of NO.

A group of local regulators called **prostaglandins** are modified fatty acids. They are so named because they were first discovered in prostate gland secretions that contribute to semen. Prostaglandins are produced by many cell types and have varied activities. In semen that reaches the reproductive tract of a female, prostaglandins stimulate the smooth muscles of the female's uterine wall to contract, helping sperm reach an egg. At the onset of childbirth, prostaglandin-secreting cells of the placenta cause the nearby muscles of the uterus to become more excitable, helping to induce labor (see Figure 46.18).

In the immune system, prostaglandins promote fever and inflammation and also intensify the sensation of pain. The anti-inflammatory and pain-relieving effects of aspirin and ibuprofen are due to the inhibition of prostaglandin synthesis by these drugs. Prostaglandins also help regulate the aggregation of platelets, one step in the formation of blood clots. Because blood clots can cause a heart attack by blocking blood flow in vessels that supply the heart (see Chapter 42), some physicians recommend that people at risk for a heart attack take aspirin on a regular basis. However, because prostaglandins also help maintain a protective lining in the stomach, long-term aspirin therapy can cause debilitating stomach irritation.

CONCEPT CHECK 45.1

1. How do the mechanisms that induce responses in target cells differ for water-soluble hormones and lipid-soluble hormones?
2. In what way does one activity described for prostaglandins resemble that of a pheromone?
3. **WHAT IF?** Which explanation of the distinct effects of epinephrine in different tissues might best account for the distinct effects of hormones in different species? Explain your answer.

For suggested answers, see Appendix A.

CONCEPT **45.2**

Negative feedback and antagonistic hormone pairs are common features of the endocrine system

So far, we have explored the chemical nature of hormones and other signaling molecules and gained a basic understanding of their activities in cells. We turn now to considering how regulatory pathways that control hormone secretion are organized. For these and later examples taken from the human endocrine system, **Figure 45.10** provides a useful point of reference for locating endocrine glands and tissues.

Simple Hormone Pathways

In response to an internal or environmental stimulus, endocrine cells secrete a particular hormone. The hormone travels in the bloodstream to target cells, where it interacts with its specific receptors. Signal transduction within target cells brings about a physiological response. Finally, the response leads to a reduction in the stimulus and the pathway shuts off.

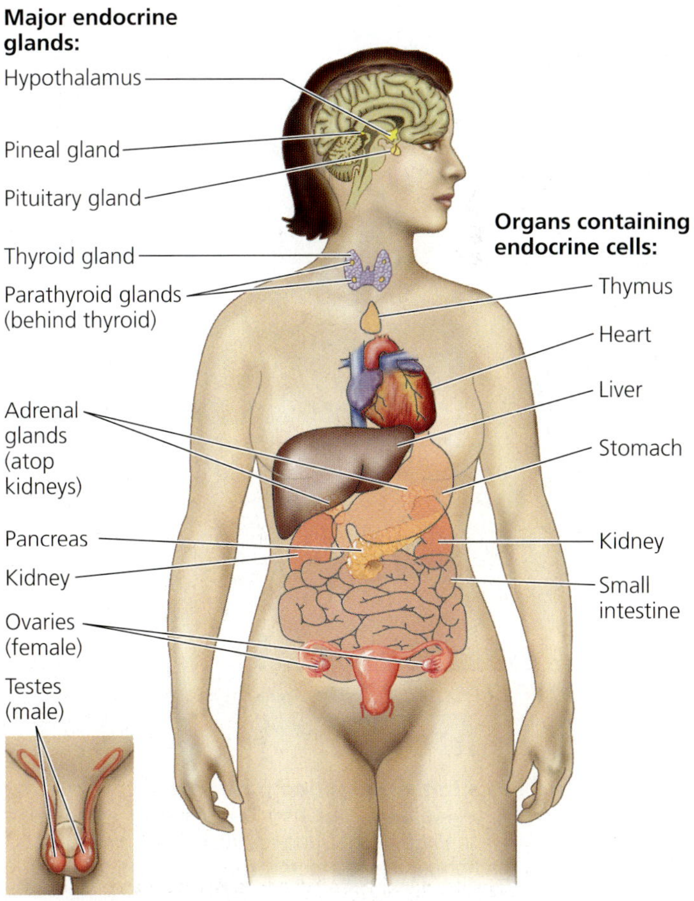

▲ **Figure 45.10 Major human endocrine glands.**

In the example shown in **Figure 45.11**, acidic stomach contents released into the duodenum (the first part of the small intestine) serve as the stimulus. Low pH in the small intestine stimulates certain endocrine cells of the duodenum, called S cells, to secrete the hormone *secretin*. Secretin enters the bloodstream and reaches target cells in the **pancreas**, a gland located behind the stomach (see Figure 45.10), causing them to release bicarbonate, which raises the pH in the duodenum. The pathway is self-limiting because the response to secretin (bicarbonate release) reduces the stimulus (low pH).

A feedback loop connecting the response to the initial stimulus is characteristic of control pathways. For secretin and many other hormones, the response pathway involves **negative feedback**, a loop in which the response reduces the initial stimulus. By decreasing or abolishing hormone signaling, negative-feedback regulation prevents excessive pathway activity. Negative-feedback loops are an essential part of many hormone pathways, especially those involved in maintaining homeostasis.

Simple hormone pathways are widespread among animals. Some homeostatic control systems rely on sets of simple hormone pathways with coordinated activities. One common arrangement is a pair of pathways, each counterbalancing the other. To see how such control systems operate, we'll consider the regulation of blood glucose levels.

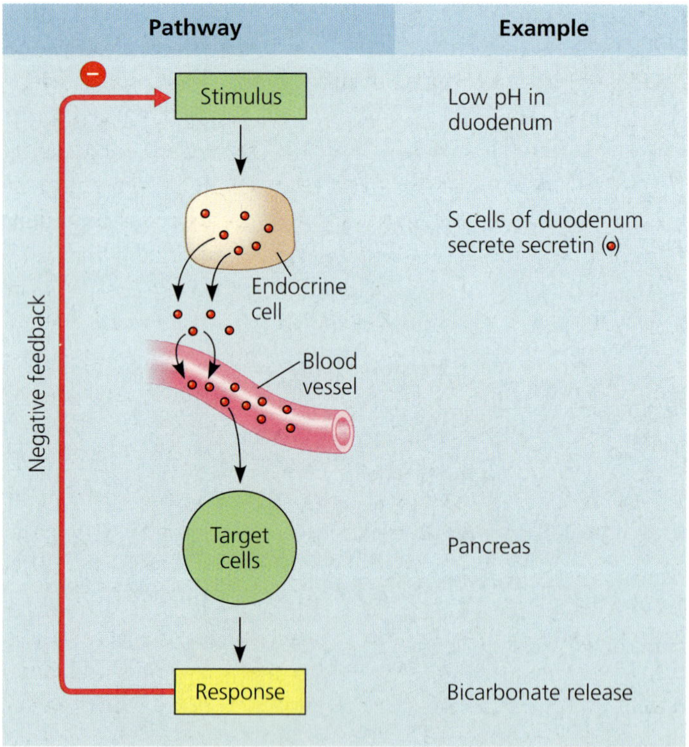

▲ **Figure 45.11 A simple endocrine pathway.** A change in some internal or external variable—the stimulus—causes the endocrine cell to secrete a hormone (red dots). Upon reaching its target cell via the bloodstream, the hormone binds to its receptor, triggering signal transduction that results in a specific response. Secretin signaling is an example of a simple endocrine pathway.

Insulin and Glucagon: Control of Blood Glucose

In humans, metabolic balance depends on a blood glucose concentration at or very near 90 mg/100 mL. Because glucose is a major fuel for cellular respiration and a key source of carbon skeletons for biosynthesis, maintaining blood glucose concentrations near this set point is a critical bioenergetic and homeostatic function.

Two antagonistic hormones, insulin and glucagon, regulate the concentration of glucose in the blood **(Figure 45.12)**. Each hormone operates in a simple endocrine pathway regulated by negative feedback. When blood glucose rises above the set point, release of **insulin** triggers uptake of glucose from the blood, decreasing the blood glucose concentration. When blood glucose drops below the set point, the release of **glucagon** promotes the release of glucose into the blood, increasing the blood glucose concentration. Because insulin and glucagon have opposing effects, the combined activity of these two hormones tightly controls the concentration of glucose in the blood.

Glucagon and insulin are produced in the pancreas. Scattered throughout the pancreas are clusters of endocrine cells known as the **islets of Langerhans**. Each islet has *alpha cells*, which make glucagon, and *beta cells*, which make insulin. Like all hormones, insulin and glucagon are secreted into the interstitial fluid and enter the circulatory system.

Overall, hormone-secreting cells make up only 1–2% of the mass of the pancreas. Other cells in the pancreas produce and secrete bicarbonate ions and digestive enzymes. These secretions are released into small ducts that empty into the pancreatic duct, which leads to the small intestine (see Figure 41.14). Thus, the pancreas is both an endocrine gland and an exocrine gland with functions in the endocrine and digestive systems.

Target Tissues for Insulin and Glucagon

Insulin lowers blood glucose levels by stimulating nearly all body cells outside the brain to take up glucose from the blood. (Brain cells can take up glucose without insulin, so the brain almost always has access to circulating fuel.) Insulin also decreases blood glucose by slowing glycogen breakdown in the liver and inhibiting the conversion of amino acids and glycerol (from fats) to glucose.

Glucagon influences blood glucose levels through its effects on target cells in the liver. The liver, skeletal muscles, and adipose tissues store large amounts of fuel. The liver and muscles store sugar as glycogen, whereas cells in adipose tissue convert sugars to fats. Of these tissues, only those in the liver are sensitive to glucagon. When the blood glucose level decreases to or below the set point (approximately 90 mg/100 mL), glucagon signals the liver cells to increase glycogen hydrolysis, convert amino acids and glycerol to glucose, and release glucose into

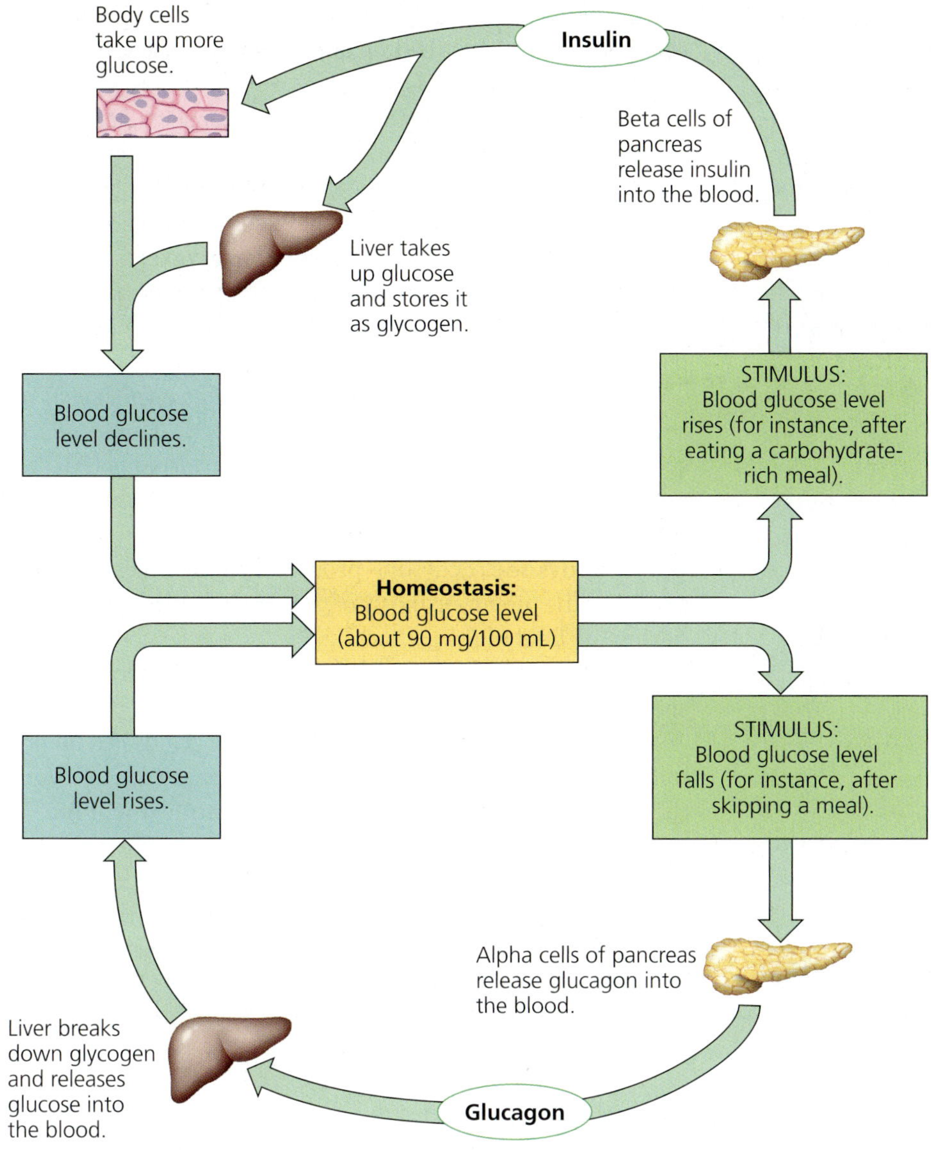

▲ **Figure 45.12 Maintenance of glucose homeostasis by insulin and glucagon.** The antagonistic effects of insulin and glucagon help maintain the blood glucose level near its set point.

the bloodstream. The net effect is to restore the blood glucose level to the set point.

The antagonistic effects of glucagon and insulin are vital to managing fuel storage and consumption by body cells. For both hormones, the liver is a critical target. As discussed in Chapter 41, nutrients absorbed by blood vessels of the small intestine are transported directly to the liver by the hepatic portal vein. Within the liver, glucagon and insulin regulate nutrient processing in ways that support glucose homeostasis. However, glucose homeostasis also relies on responses to glucagon and insulin elsewhere in the body as well as responses to other hormones—growth hormone and glucocorticoids—discussed later in this chapter.

Diabetes Mellitus

A disruption in glucose homeostasis can be quite serious, affecting the heart, blood vessels, eyes, and kidneys. One such disorder, **diabetes mellitus**, is caused by a deficiency of insulin or a decreased response to insulin in target tissues. Blood glucose levels rise, but cells are unable to take up enough glucose to meet metabolic needs. Instead, fat becomes the main substrate for cellular respiration. In severe cases, acidic metabolites formed during fat breakdown accumulate in the blood, threatening life by lowering blood pH and depleting sodium and potassium ions from the body.

In people with diabetes mellitus, the high level of glucose in blood exceeds the capacity of the kidneys to reabsorb this nutrient. Glucose that remains in the filtrate is excreted. For this reason, the presence of sugar in urine is one test for this disorder. As glucose is concentrated in the urine, more water is excreted along with it, resulting in excessive volumes of urine. *Diabetes* (from the Greek *diabainein*, to pass through) refers to this copious urination; and *mellitus* (from the Greek *meli*, honey) refers to the presence of sugar in urine. (*Diabetes insipidus*, discussed in Chapter 44, is a rare disorder of kidney function that results in large volumes of dilute urine but no major disruption in glucose metabolism.)

There are two main types of diabetes mellitus. Each is marked by high blood glucose, but with very different causes. *Type 1 diabetes*, or insulin-dependent diabetes, is an autoimmune disorder in which the immune system destroys the beta cells of the pancreas. Type 1 diabetes, which usually appears during childhood, destroys the person's ability to produce insulin. Treatment consists of insulin, typically injected several times daily. In the past, insulin was extracted from animal pancreases, but now human insulin can be obtained from genetically engineered bacteria, a relatively inexpensive source (see Figure 20.2). Stem cell research may someday provide a cure for type 1 diabetes by generating replacement beta cells that restore insulin production by the pancreas.

Type 2 diabetes, or non-insulin-dependent diabetes, is characterized by a failure of target cells to respond normally to insulin. Insulin is produced, but target cells fail to take up glucose from the blood, and blood glucose levels remain elevated. Although heredity can play a role in type 2 diabetes, excess body weight and lack of exercise significantly increase the risk. This form of diabetes generally appears after age 40, but even children who are overweight and sedentary can develop the disease. More than 90% of people with diabetes have type 2. Many can control their blood glucose levels with regular exercise and a healthy diet; some require medications. Nevertheless, type 2 diabetes is the seventh most common cause of death in the United States and a growing public health problem worldwide.

CONCEPT CHECK 45.2

1. In a glucose tolerance test, periodic measurements of blood glucose level are taken after a person drinks a glucose-rich solution. In a healthy individual, blood glucose rises moderately at first but falls to near normal within 2–3 hours. Predict the results of this test in a person with diabetes mellitus. Explain your answer.
2. What property of a stimulus might make negative feedback less important for a hormone pathway?
3. **WHAT IF?** Consider a diabetes patient who has a family history of type 2 diabetes but is active and not obese. To identify genes that might be defective in the patient, which genes would you examine first?

For suggested answers, see Appendix A.

CONCEPT **45.3**

The endocrine and nervous systems act individually and together in regulating animal physiology

Our discussion to this point has focused on the structure of hormones and the organization of hormone pathways. We'll now consider how signals from the nervous system initiate and regulate endocrine signaling. We will begin with examples from invertebrates and then turn to the vertebrate brain and endocrine system.

Coordination of Endocrine and Nervous Systems in Invertebrates

In all animals but the simplest invertebrates, the endocrine and nervous systems are integrated in the control of reproduction and development. In the sea slug *Aplysia*, for instance, specialized nerve cells secrete egg-laying hormone, which stimulates the animal to lay thousands of eggs. This neurohormone further enhances the sea slug's reproductive success by inhibiting feeding and locomotion, activities that might disrupt egg-laying.

To explore neurohormone function in insects, let's return to the example of the caterpillar in this chapter's Overview. Before hormones stimulate the metamorphosis of the caterpillar, a larva, into the adult butterfly, they regulate development of a newly hatched egg into the fully grown larva. During its development, the larva grows in stages. Because its exoskeleton cannot stretch, the larva must periodically molt, shedding the old exoskeleton and secreting a new one.

The signals that direct molting and metamorphosis in insects originate in the brain **(Figure 45.13)**. There, neurosecretory cells produce *prothoracicotropic hormone* (PTTH), a peptide neurohormone. In response to PTTH, the prothoracic glands, a pair of endocrine glands just behind the brain, release **ecdysone**. Ecdysone promotes each successive molt, as well as the metamorphosis of the caterpillar into a butterfly during the final molt.

Because ecdysone causes both molting and metamorphosis, what determines when metamorphosis takes place? The answer is found in a pair of small endocrine glands just behind the brain. Called the corpora allata (singular, *corpus allatum*), they secrete a third signaling molecule, **juvenile hormone**. As its name suggests, one of the many functions of juvenile hormone is to maintain larval (juvenile) characteristics.

Juvenile hormone influences development indirectly by modulating the activity of ecdysone. In the presence of high levels of juvenile hormone, ecdysone stimulates molting that results in a larger larva. At the end of the larval stage, the level of juvenile hormone wanes. When the juvenile hormone level is low, ecdysone-induced molting produces the cocoon, or pupal form, within which metamorphosis occurs.

Knowledge of insect neurohormone and hormone signaling has important agricultural applications. For example, synthetic versions of juvenile hormone are used as a biological pest control method to prevent insects from maturing into reproducing adults.

Coordination of Endocrine and Nervous Systems in Vertebrates

In vertebrates, the **hypothalamus** plays a central role in integrating the endocrine and nervous systems. One of several endocrine glands located in the brain **(Figure 45.14)**, the hypothalamus receives information from nerves throughout the body and from other parts of the brain. In response, it initiates endocrine signaling appropriate to environmental conditions. In many vertebrates, for example, nerve signals from the brain pass sensory information to the hypothalamus about seasonal changes and the availability of a mate. The hypothalamus, in turn, regulates the release of reproductive hormones required for breeding.

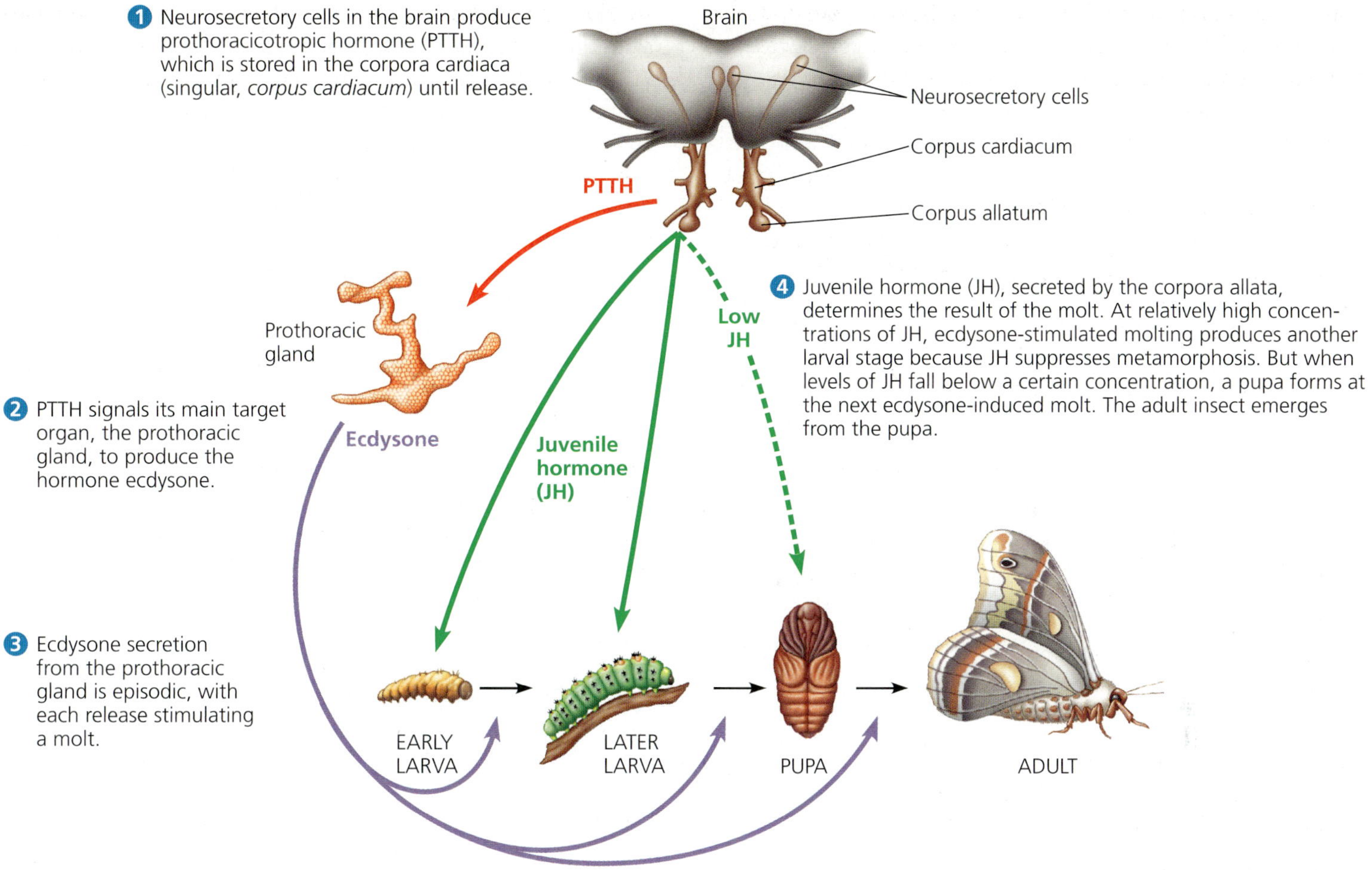

▲ **Figure 45.13 Hormonal regulation of insect development.** Most insects go through a series of larval stages, with each molt (shedding of the old exoskeleton) leading to a larger larva. Molting of the final larval stage gives rise to a pupa, in which metamorphosis produces the adult form of the insect. Hormones control the progression of stages, as shown here.

Signals from the hypothalamus travel to the **pituitary gland**, a gland located at its base. Roughly the size and shape of a lima bean, the pituitary has discrete posterior and anterior parts (lobes), which are actually two glands, the posterior pituitary and the anterior pituitary (see Figure 45.14). These glands initially develop in separate regions of the embryo. Although they fuse together later in development, their functions are distinct.

The **posterior pituitary**, or *neurohypophysis*, is an extension of the hypothalamus that grows downward toward the mouth during embryonic development. The posterior pituitary stores and secretes two hormones made by the hypothalamus.

The **anterior pituitary**, or *adenohypophysis*, develops from a fold of tissue at the roof of the embryonic mouth; this tissue grows upward toward the brain and eventually loses its connection to the mouth. Hormones released by the hypothalamus regulate secretion of hormones by the anterior pituitary.

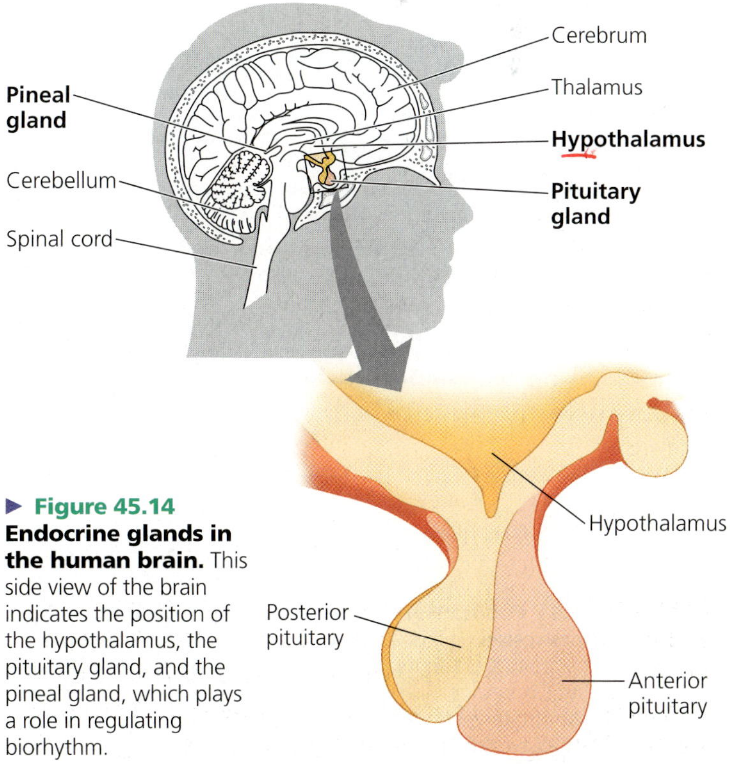

▶ **Figure 45.14 Endocrine glands in the human brain.** This side view of the brain indicates the position of the hypothalamus, the pituitary gland, and the pineal gland, which plays a role in regulating biorhythm.

Under the control of the hypothalamus, the anterior pituitary and posterior pituitary produce a set of hormones central to endocrine signaling throughout the body, as evident in **Table 45.1**. (This table will also be a useful reference later.) We'll consider the posterior pituitary, which releases just two hormones, first.

Posterior Pituitary Hormones

The posterior pituitary releases two neurohormones, oxytocin and antidiuretic hormone (ADH). Synthesized in the hypothalamus, these hormones travel along the long axons of neurosecretory cells to the posterior pituitary **(Figure 45.15)**. There they are stored, to be released as needed.

One function of **oxytocin** in mammals is to regulate milk release during nursing; this function is mediated by a simple neurohormone pathway **(Figure 45.16)**. In such pathways, a stimulus received by a sensory neuron stimulates a neurosecretory cell. The neurosecretory cell then secretes a neurohormone, which diffuses into the bloodstream and travels to target cells. In the case of the oxytocin pathway, the initial stimulus is the infant's suckling. Stimulation of sensory nerve cells in the nipples generates signals in the nervous system that reach the hypothalamus. A nerve impulse from the hypothalamus then triggers the release of oxytocin from the posterior pituitary gland. In response to circulating oxytocin, the mammary glands secrete milk.

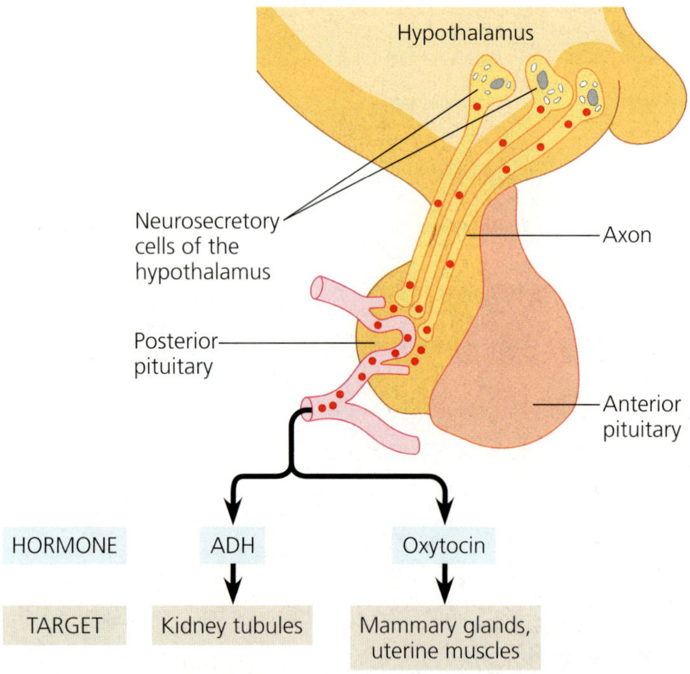

▲ **Figure 45.15 Production and release of posterior pituitary hormones.** The posterior pituitary gland is an extension of the hypothalamus. Certain neurosecretory cells in the hypothalamus make antidiuretic hormone (ADH) and oxytocin, which are transported to the posterior pituitary, where they are stored. Nerve signals from the brain trigger release of these neurohormones (red dots).

The oxytocin pathway regulating the mammary gland provides an example of a positive-feedback mechanism. Unlike negative feedback, which dampens a stimulus, **positive feedback** reinforces a stimulus, leading to an even greater response. Thus, oxytocin stimulates milk release, which leads to more suckling and therefore more stimulation. Activation of the pathway is sustained until the baby stops suckling.

Oxytocin has several additional roles related to reproduction. When mammals give birth, it induces target cells in the uterine muscles to contract. This pathway, too, is characterized by positive-feedback regulation, such that it drives the birth process to completion. Oxytocin also functions in regulating mood and sexual arousal in both males and females.

The second hormone released by the posterior pituitary, **antidiuretic hormone (ADH)**, or *vasopressin*, helps regulate blood osmolarity. As you read in Chapter 44, ADH is one of several hormones that regulate kidney function. In particular, ADH increases water retention in the kidneys, thus decreasing urine volume.

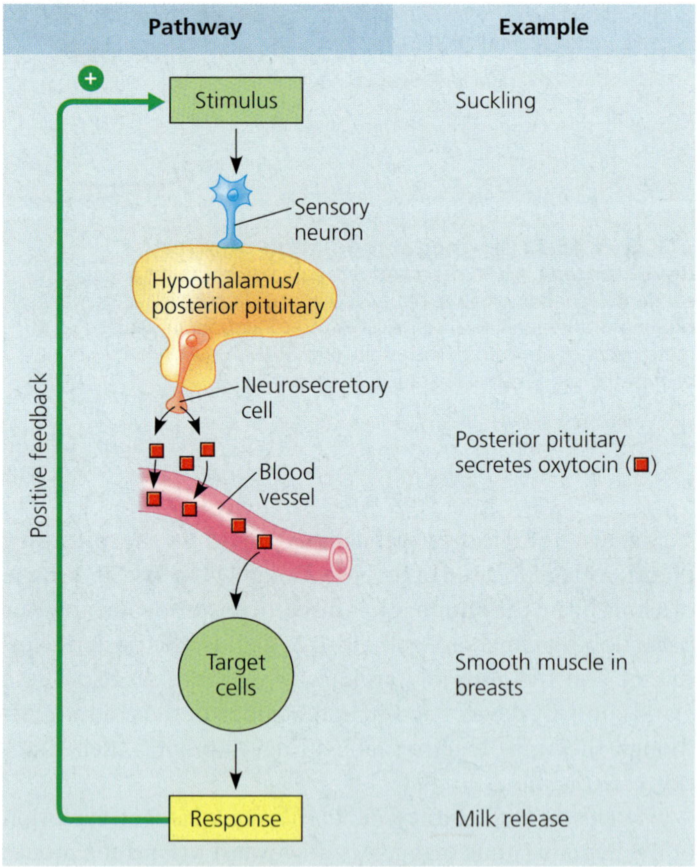

▲ **Figure 45.16 A simple neurohormone pathway.** In this example, the stimulus causes the hypothalamus to send a nerve impulse to the posterior pituitary, which responds by secreting a neurohormone (red squares). Upon reaching its target cell via the bloodstream, the neurohormone binds to its receptor, triggering signal transduction that results in a specific response. In the neurohormone pathway for oxytocin signaling, the response increases the stimulus, forming a positive-feedback loop that amplifies signaling in the pathway.

Table 45.1 Major Human Endocrine Glands and Some of Their Hormones

Gland		Hormone	Chemical Class	Representative Actions	Regulated By
Hypothalamus	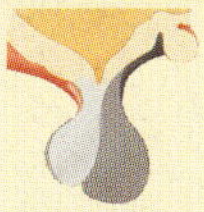	Hormones released from the posterior pituitary and hormones that regulate the anterior pituitary (see below)			
Posterior pituitary gland (releases neurohormones made in hypothalamus)		Oxytocin	Peptide	Stimulates contraction of uterus and mammary gland cells	Nervous system
		Antidiuretic hormone (ADH)	Peptide	Promotes retention of water by kidneys	Water/salt balance
Anterior pituitary gland	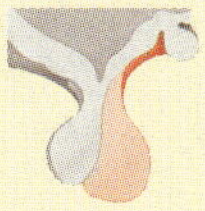	Growth hormone (GH)	Protein	Stimulates growth (especially bones) and metabolic functions	Hypothalamic hormones
		Prolactin (PRL)	Protein	Stimulates milk production and secretion	Hypothalamic hormones
		Follicle-stimulating hormone (FSH)	Glycoprotein	Stimulates production of ova and sperm	Hypothalamic hormones
		Luteinizing hormone (LH)	Glycoprotein	Stimulates ovaries and testes	Hypothalamic hormones
		Thyroid-stimulating hormone (TSH)	Glycoprotein	Stimulates thyroid gland	Hypothalamic hormones
		Adrenocorticotropic hormone (ACTH)	Peptide	Stimulates adrenal cortex to secrete glucocorticoids	Hypothalamic hormones
Thyroid gland	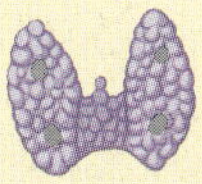	Triiodothyronine (T_3) and thyroxine (T_4)	Amine	Stimulate and maintain metabolic processes	TSH
		Calcitonin	Peptide	Lowers blood calcium level	Calcium in blood
Parathyroid glands	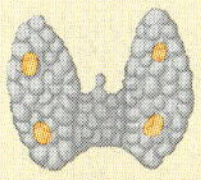	Parathyroid hormone (PTH)	Peptide	Raises blood calcium level	Calcium in blood
Pancreas		Insulin	Protein	Lowers blood glucose level	Glucose in blood
		Glucagon	Protein	Raises blood glucose level	Glucose in blood
Adrenal glands	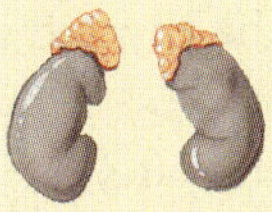				
Adrenal medulla		Epinephrine and norepinephrine	Amines	Raise blood glucose level; increase metabolic activities; constrict certain blood vessels	Nervous system
Adrenal cortex		Glucocorticoids	Steroid	Raise blood glucose level	ACTH
		Mineralocorticoids	Steroid	Promote reabsorption of Na^+ and excretion of K^+ in kidneys	K^+ in blood; angiotensin II
Gonads					
Testes	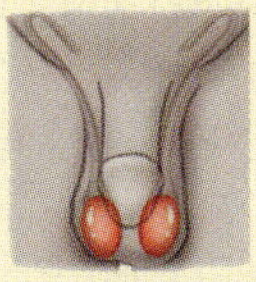	Androgens	Steroid	Support sperm formation; promote development and maintenance of male secondary sex characteristics	FSH and LH
Ovaries	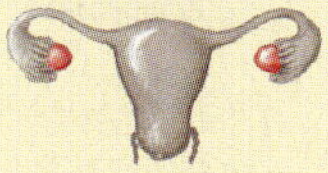	Estrogens	Steroid	Stimulate uterine lining growth; promote development and maintenance of female secondary sex characteristics	FSH and LH
		Progestins	Steroid	Promote uterine lining growth	FSH and LH
Pineal gland	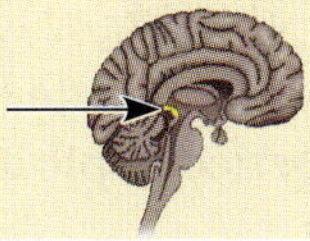	Melatonin	Amine	Involved in biological rhythms	Light/dark cycles

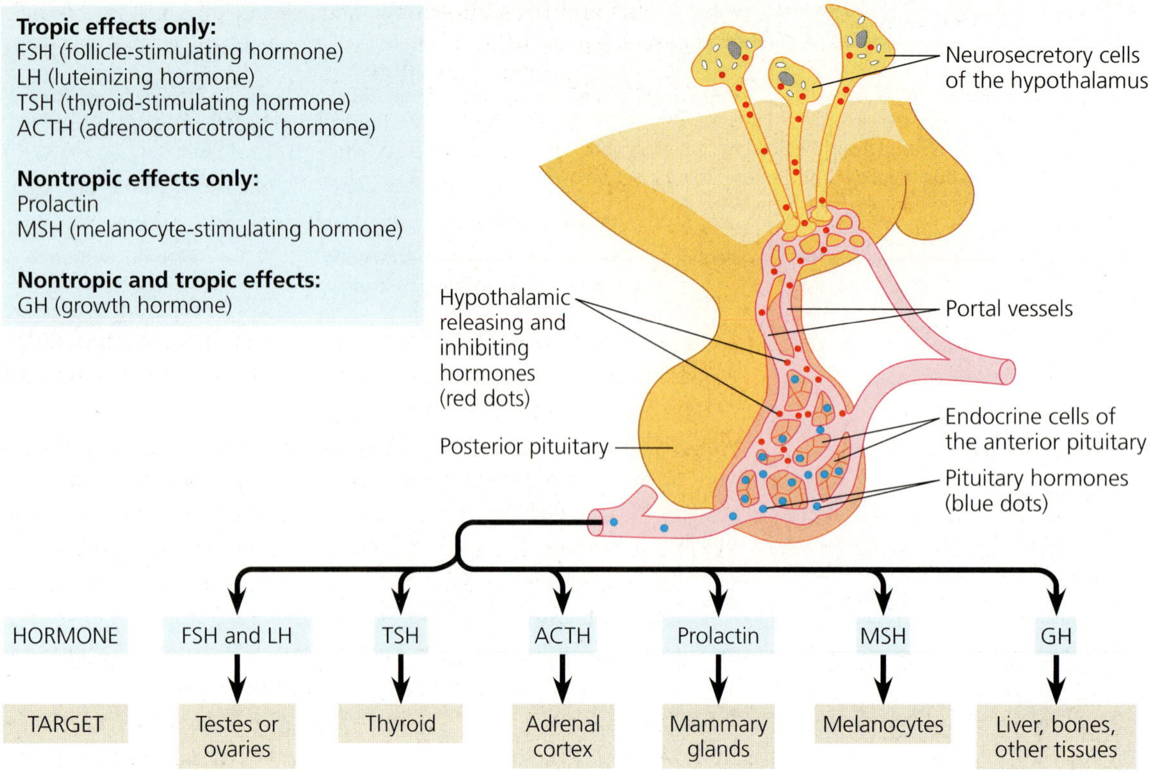

◀ **Figure 45.17 Production and release of anterior pituitary hormones.** The release of hormones synthesized in the anterior pituitary gland is controlled by hypothalamic releasing and inhibiting hormones. The hypothalamic hormones are secreted by neurosecretory cells and enter a capillary network within the hypothalamus. These capillaries drain into portal vessels that connect with a second capillary network in the anterior pituitary.

Anterior Pituitary Hormones

The anterior pituitary synthesizes and secretes many different hormones and is itself regulated by hormones secreted by the hypothalamus **(Figure 45.17)**. Each hypothalamic hormone is either a *releasing hormone* or an *inhibiting hormone*, reflecting its role in promoting or inhibiting release of one or more specific hormones by the anterior pituitary. *Thyrotropin-releasing hormone (TRH)*, for example, is a product of the hypothalamus that stimulates the anterior pituitary to secrete thyrotropin, also known as *thyroid-stimulating hormone (TSH)*. Every anterior pituitary hormone is controlled by at least one releasing hormone. Some have both a releasing hormone and an inhibiting hormone.

The hypothalamic releasing and inhibiting hormones are secreted near capillaries at the base of the hypothalamus. The capillaries drain into short blood vessels, called portal vessels, which subdivide into a second capillary bed within the anterior pituitary. In this way, the releasing and inhibiting hormones have direct access to the gland they control.

Hormone Cascade Pathways

Sets of hormones from the hypothalamus, the anterior pituitary, and a target endocrine gland are often organized into a hormone cascade pathway **(Figure 45.18)**. Signals to the brain stimulate the hypothalamus to secrete a hormone that in turn either stimulates or inhibits release of a particular anterior pituitary hormone. The anterior pituitary hormone acts on a target endocrine tissue, stimulating secretion of yet another hormone that exerts systemic metabolic or developmental effects.

To learn how a hormone cascade pathway works, let's consider activation of the thyroid gland when an infant is exposed to cold (see Figure 45.18). When a young child's body temperature drops, the hypothalamus secretes TRH. TRH targets the anterior pituitary, which responds by secreting TSH. TSH acts on the thyroid gland to stimulate release of *thyroid hormone*. As it accumulates, thyroid hormone increases metabolic rate, releasing thermal energy that raises body temperature.

Like simple hormone pathways, hormone cascade pathways typically involve negative feedback. In the case of the thyroid hormone pathway, thyroid hormone itself carries out negative feedback. Because thyroid hormone blocks TSH release from the anterior pituitary and TRH release from the hypothalamus, the negative-feedback loop prevents overproduction of thyroid hormone. Overall, the hormone cascade pathway brings about a self-limiting response to the original stimulus in the target cells.

Tropic Hormones

TSH is an example of a **tropic hormone**—a hormone that regulates the function of endocrine cells or glands. Three other anterior pituitary hormones act primarily or exclusively as tropic hormones: **follicle-stimulating hormone (FSH)**, **luteinizing hormone (LH)**, and **adrenocorticotropic hormone (ACTH)**.

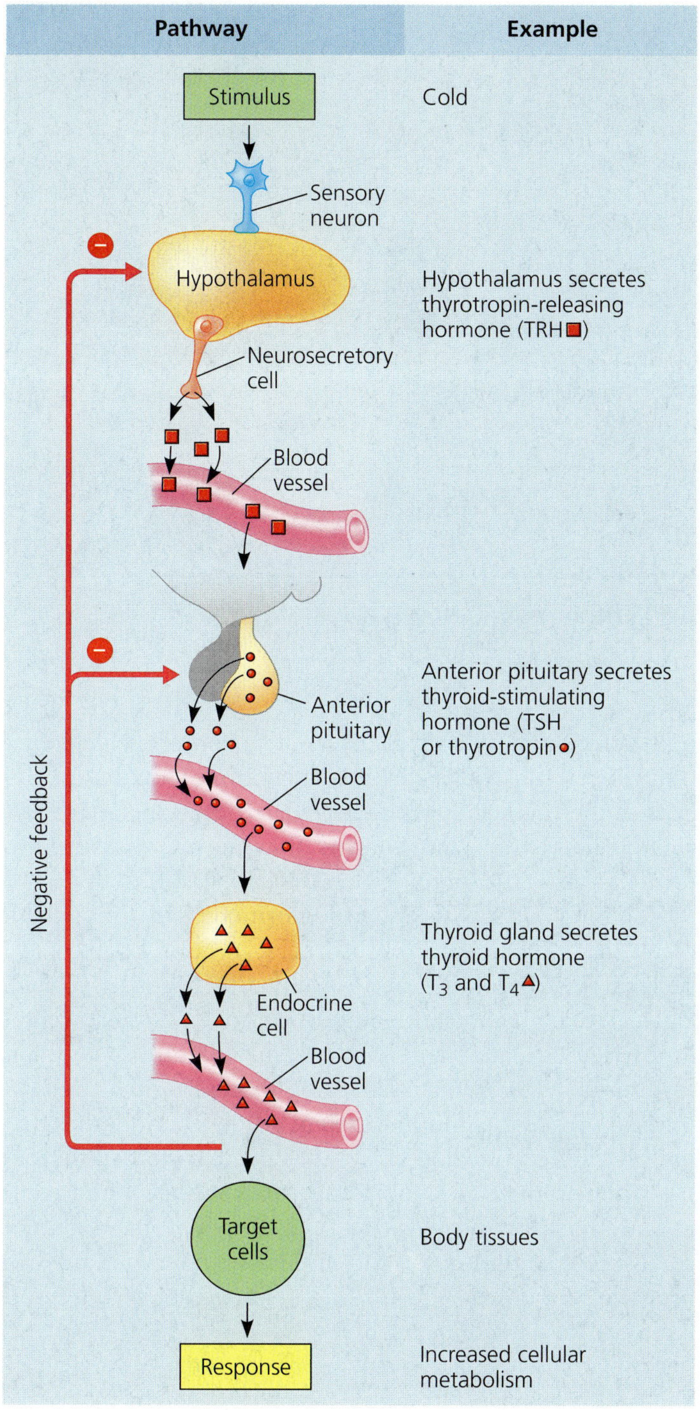

▲ **Figure 45.18 A hormone cascade pathway.** In response to the stimulus, the hypothalamus secretes a releasing hormone (red squares) that targets the anterior pituitary. The anterior pituitary responds by secreting a second tropic hormone (red dots), which travels through the bloodstream to an endocrine gland. In response to this tropic hormone, the endocrine gland secretes a hormone (red triangles) that travels to target cells, where it induces a response. In the example of thyroid hormone regulation, thyroid hormone exerts negative feedback on the hypothalamus and anterior pituitary. This feedback inhibits release of TRH and TSH, preventing overreaction to the stimulus (such as low temperature in the case of a human infant).

? *Suppose a lab test of two patients, each diagnosed with excessive thyroid hormone production, revealed elevated levels of TSH in one but not the other. Was the diagnosis of one patient necessarily incorrect? Explain.*

FSH and LH stimulate the activities of the male and female gonads, the testes and ovaries, respectively. For this reason, FSH and LH are also known as *gonadotropins*. In Chapter 46, we will discuss how these hormones regulate reproductive functions.

ACTH stimulates the production and secretion of steroid hormones by the adrenal cortex. We will take a closer look at the hormone pathway involving ACTH later in this chapter.

Nontropic Hormones

Two major hormones of the anterior pituitary target nonendocrine tissues and are thus nontropic. They are prolactin and melanocyte-stimulating hormone (MSH).

Prolactin (PRL) is remarkable for the diversity of its effects among vertebrate species. For example, prolactin stimulates mammary gland growth and milk synthesis in mammals, regulates fat metabolism and reproduction in birds, delays metamorphosis in amphibians, and regulates salt and water balance in freshwater fishes. These varied roles suggest that prolactin is an ancient hormone with functions that have diversified during the evolution of vertebrate groups.

As you saw in Figure 45.4, **melanocyte-stimulating hormone (MSH)** regulates the activity of pigment-containing cells in the skin of some amphibians (as well as fishes and reptiles). In mammals, MSH appears to act on neurons in the brain, inhibiting hunger.

Growth Hormone

Growth hormone (GH), which is secreted by the anterior pituitary, stimulates growth through tropic and nontropic effects. A major target, the liver, responds to GH by releasing *insulin-like growth factors* (*IGFs*), which circulate in the blood and directly stimulate bone and cartilage growth. (IGFs also appear to play a key role in aging in many animal species.) In the absence of GH, the skeleton of an immature animal stops growing. GH also exerts diverse metabolic effects that tend to raise blood glucose levels, thus opposing the effects of insulin.

Abnormal production of GH in humans can result in several disorders, depending on when the problem occurs and whether it involves hypersecretion (too much) or hyposecretion (too little). Hypersecretion of GH during childhood can lead to gigantism, in which the person grows unusually tall—as tall as 2.4 m (8 feet)—though body proportions remain relatively normal. Excessive GH production in adulthood stimulates bony growth in the few tissues that are still responsive to the hormone. Because remaining target cells are predominantly in the face, hands, and feet, the result is an overgrowth of the extremities called acromegaly (from the Greek *acros*, extreme, and *mega*, large).

Hyposecretion of GH in childhood retards long-bone growth and can lead to pituitary dwarfism. Individuals with this disorder are for the most part properly proportioned but generally reach a height of only about 1.2 m (4 feet). If diagnosed before puberty, pituitary dwarfism can be treated successfully with human GH.

Since the mid-1980s, scientists have produced human GH from bacteria programmed with DNA encoding the hormone (see Chapter 20). Treatment with this genetically engineered GH is now fairly routine for children with pituitary dwarfism.

CONCEPT CHECK 45.3

1. How do the two fused glands of the pituitary gland differ in function?
2. Suggest a reason why hypothalamic control of oxytocin involves only an inhibiting factor.
3. **WHAT IF?** Propose an explanation for why people with defects in specific endocrine pathways typically have defects in the final gland in the pathway rather than in the hypothalamus or pituitary.

For suggested answers, see Appendix A.

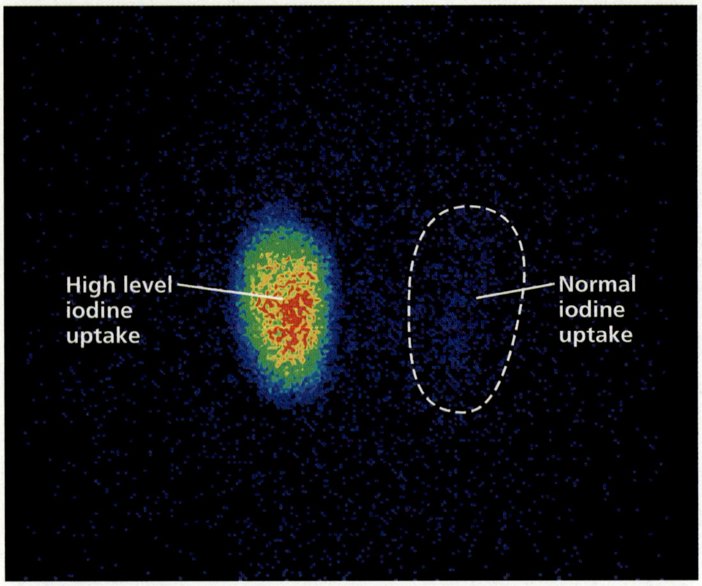

▲ **Figure 45.19 Thyroid scan.** A tumor in one lobe of the thyroid gland caused the accumulation of radioactive iodine.

CONCEPT 45.4

Endocrine glands respond to diverse stimuli in regulating metabolism, homeostasis, development, and behavior

Having seen how endocrine glands in the brain initiate hormone cascade pathways, we return here to the broader question of how endocrine signaling regulates animal physiology. We'll focus on metabolism, homeostasis, development, and behavior, leaving the topic of reproduction largely for later chapters. We will discuss more examples of hormone regulation by metabolic stimuli, by nervous system input, and by hormones of the anterior pituitary. To begin, let's explore a pathway introduced in Figure 45.18, the hormone cascade leading to thyroid hormone production.

Thyroid Hormone: Control of Metabolism and Development

Among the vertebrates, thyroid hormone, secreted by the thyroid gland, regulates both homeostasis and development. In humans and other mammals, thyroid hormone regulates bioenergetics; helps maintain normal blood pressure, heart rate, and muscle tone; and regulates digestive and reproductive functions. In these animals, the **thyroid gland** consists of two lobes on the ventral surface of the trachea (see Figure 42.24). In many other vertebrates, the two halves of the gland are separately located on the two sides of the pharynx.

The term *thyroid hormone* actually refers to a pair of very similar hormones derived from the amino acid tyrosine. **Triiodothyronine (T_3)** contains three iodine atoms, whereas tetraiodothyronine, or **thyroxine (T_4)**, contains four iodine atoms (see Figure 45.3). In mammals, the same receptor binds both hormones. The thyroid secretes mainly T_4, but target cells convert most of it to T_3 by removing one iodine atom. Because iodine in the body is dedicated to the production of thyroid hormone, radioactive forms of iodine are often used to form images of the thyroid gland **(Figure 45.19)**.

Too much or too little thyroid hormone in the blood can result in serious metabolic disorders. In humans, excessive secretion of thyroid hormone, known as hyperthyroidism, can lead to high body temperature, profuse sweating, weight loss, irritability, and high blood pressure. The most common form of hyperthyroidism is Graves' disease. In this autoimmune disorder, the immune system produces antibodies that bind to the receptor for TSH and activate sustained thyroid hormone production. Protruding eyes, caused by fluid accumulation behind the eyes, are a typical symptom. Hypothyroidism, a condition of too little thyroid function, can produce symptoms such as weight gain, lethargy, and intolerance to cold in adults.

Proper thyroid function requires dietary iodine. Although iodine is readily obtained from seafood or from iodized salt, people in many parts of the world suffer from inadequate iodine in their diet. Without sufficient iodine, the thyroid gland cannot synthesize adequate amounts of T_3 and T_4, and the resulting low blood levels of T_3 and T_4 cannot exert the usual negative feedback on the hypothalamus and anterior pituitary (see Figure 45.18). As a consequence, the pituitary continues to secrete TSH. Elevated TSH levels cause an enlargement of the thyroid that results in goiter, a characteristic swelling of the neck (see Figure 2.4).

Among the vertebrates, thyroid hormones have a variety of roles in development and maturation. A striking example is the thyroid control of the metamorphosis of a tadpole into a frog, which involves massive reorganization of many different tissues (see Figure 45.9). All vertebrates require thyroid hormones for the normal functioning of bone-forming cells and the branching of nerve cells during embryonic development of the brain. In humans, congenital hypothyroidism, an inherited condition of thyroid deficiency, results in markedly retarded skeletal growth and poor mental development. These defects can often be prevented, at least partially, if treatment with thyroid hormones begins early in life. Iodine deficiency in childhood causes the same defects, but it is fully preventable if iodized salt is used in food preparation.

Parathyroid Hormone and Vitamin D: Control of Blood Calcium

Because calcium ions (Ca^{2+}) are essential to the normal functioning of all cells, homeostatic control of blood calcium level is critical. If the blood Ca^{2+} level falls substantially, skeletal muscles begin to contract convulsively, a potentially fatal condition called tetany. If the blood Ca^{2+} level rises substantially, precipitates of calcium phosphate can form in body tissues, leading to widespread organ damage.

In mammals, the **parathyroid glands**, a set of four small structures embedded in the posterior surface of the thyroid (see Figure 45.10), play a major role in blood Ca^{2+} regulation. When blood Ca^{2+} falls below a set point of about 10 mg/100 mL, these glands release **parathyroid hormone (PTH)**.

PTH raises the level of blood Ca^{2+} by direct and indirect effects **(Figure 45.20)**. In bone, PTH causes the mineralized matrix to decompose and release Ca^{2+} into the blood. In the kidneys, PTH directly stimulates reabsorption of Ca^{2+} through the renal tubules. PTH also has an indirect effect on the kidneys, promoting the conversion of vitamin D to an active hormone. An inactive form of vitamin D, a steroid-derived molecule, is obtained from food or synthesized in the skin when exposed to sunlight. Vitamin D activation begins in the liver and is completed in the kidneys, the process stimulated by PTH. The active form of vitamin D acts directly on the intestines, stimulating the uptake of Ca^{2+} from food and thus augmenting the effect of PTH. As blood Ca^{2+} rises, a negative-feedback loop inhibits further release of PTH from the parathyroid glands (not shown in figure).

The thyroid gland can also contribute to calcium homeostasis. If blood Ca^{2+} rises above the set point, the thyroid gland releases **calcitonin**, a hormone that inhibits bone resorption and enhances Ca^{2+} release by the kidney. In fishes, rodents, and some other animals, calcitonin is required for Ca^{2+} homeostasis. In humans, however, it is apparently needed only during the extensive bone growth of childhood.

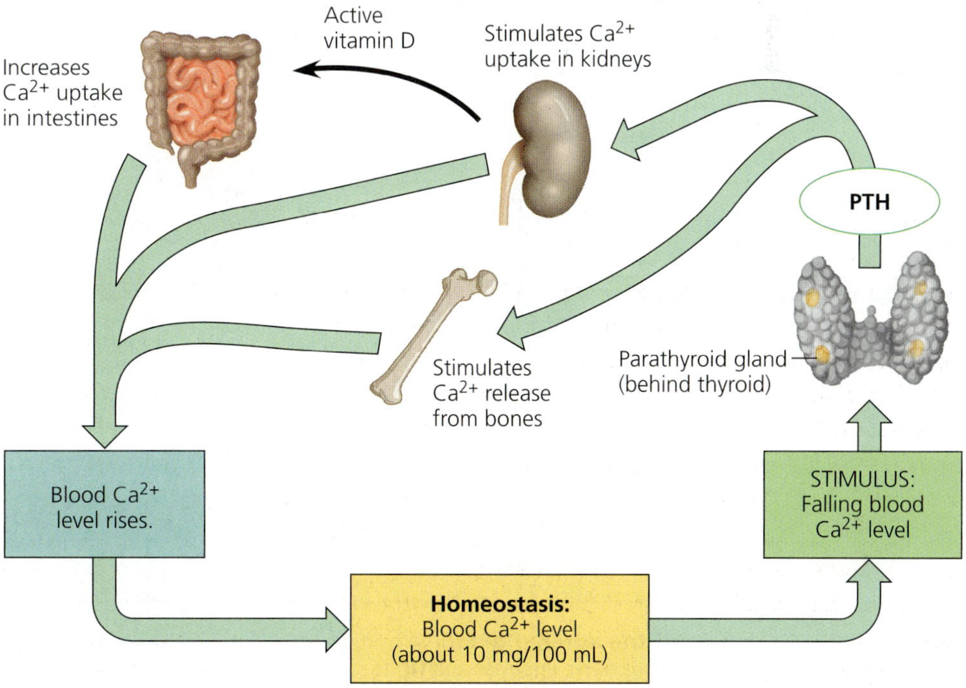

▲ **Figure 45.20 The roles of parathyroid hormone (PTH) in regulating blood calcium levels in mammals.**

Adrenal Hormones: Response to Stress

The **adrenal glands** of vertebrates are in each case associated with the kidneys (the *renal* organs). In mammals, each adrenal gland is actually made up of two glands with different cell types, functions, and embryonic origins: the *adrenal cortex*, the outer portion, and the *adrenal medulla*, the central portion. The adrenal cortex consists of true endocrine cells, whereas the secretory cells of the adrenal medulla derive from neural tissue during embryonic development. Thus, like the pituitary gland, each adrenal gland is a fused endocrine and neuroendocrine gland.

Catecholamines from the Adrenal Medulla

Imagine that while walking in the woods at night you hear a growling noise nearby. "A bear?" you wonder. Your heart beats faster, your breath quickens, your muscles tense, and your thoughts speed up. These and other rapid responses to perceived danger comprise the "fight-or-flight" response. This coordinated set of physiological changes is triggered by two hormones of the adrenal medulla, epinephrine (also known as adrenaline) and **norepinephrine** (noradrenaline). Both are **catecholamines**, a class of amine hormones synthesized from the amino acid tyrosine.

The adrenal medulla secretes epinephrine and norepinephrine in response to stress—whether extreme pleasure or life-threatening danger. A major activity of these hormones is to increase the amount of chemical energy available for immediate use. Both epinephrine and norepinephrine increase the rate of glycogen breakdown in the liver and skeletal muscles, promote glucose release by liver cells, and stimulate the release of fatty acids from fat cells. The released glucose and fatty acids circulate in the blood and can be used by body cells as fuel.

In addition to increasing the availability of energy sources, epinephrine and norepinephrine exert profound effects on the cardiovascular and respiratory systems. For example, they increase both the heart rate and stroke volume and dilate the bronchioles in the lungs, actions that raise the rate of oxygen delivery to body cells. For this reason, doctors may prescribe epinephrine as a heart stimulant or to open the airways during an asthma attack. The catecholamines also alter blood flow, causing constriction of some blood vessels and dilation of others (see Figure 45.8). The overall effect is to shunt blood away from the skin, digestive organs, and kidneys, while increasing the blood supply to the heart, brain, and skeletal muscles. Epinephrine generally has a stronger effect on heart and metabolic rates, while the primary role of norepinephrine is in modulating blood pressure.

Nerve signals carried from the brain via involuntary (autonomic) neurons regulate secretion by the adrenal medulla. In response to a stressful stimulus, nerve impulses travel to the adrenal medulla, where they trigger the release of catecholamines **(Figure 45.21a)**. Acting on target tissues, epinephrine and norepinephrine each function in a simple neurohormone pathway. As we will see in Chapter 48, epinephrine and norepinephrine also function as neurotransmitters.

Steroid Hormones from the Adrenal Cortex

Hormones from the adrenal cortex also function in the body's response to stress. But in contrast to the adrenal medulla, which reacts to nervous input, the adrenal cortex responds to endocrine signals. Stressful stimuli cause the hypothalamus to secrete a releasing hormone that stimulates the anterior pituitary to release the tropic hormone ACTH. When ACTH reaches the adrenal cortex via the bloodstream, it stimulates

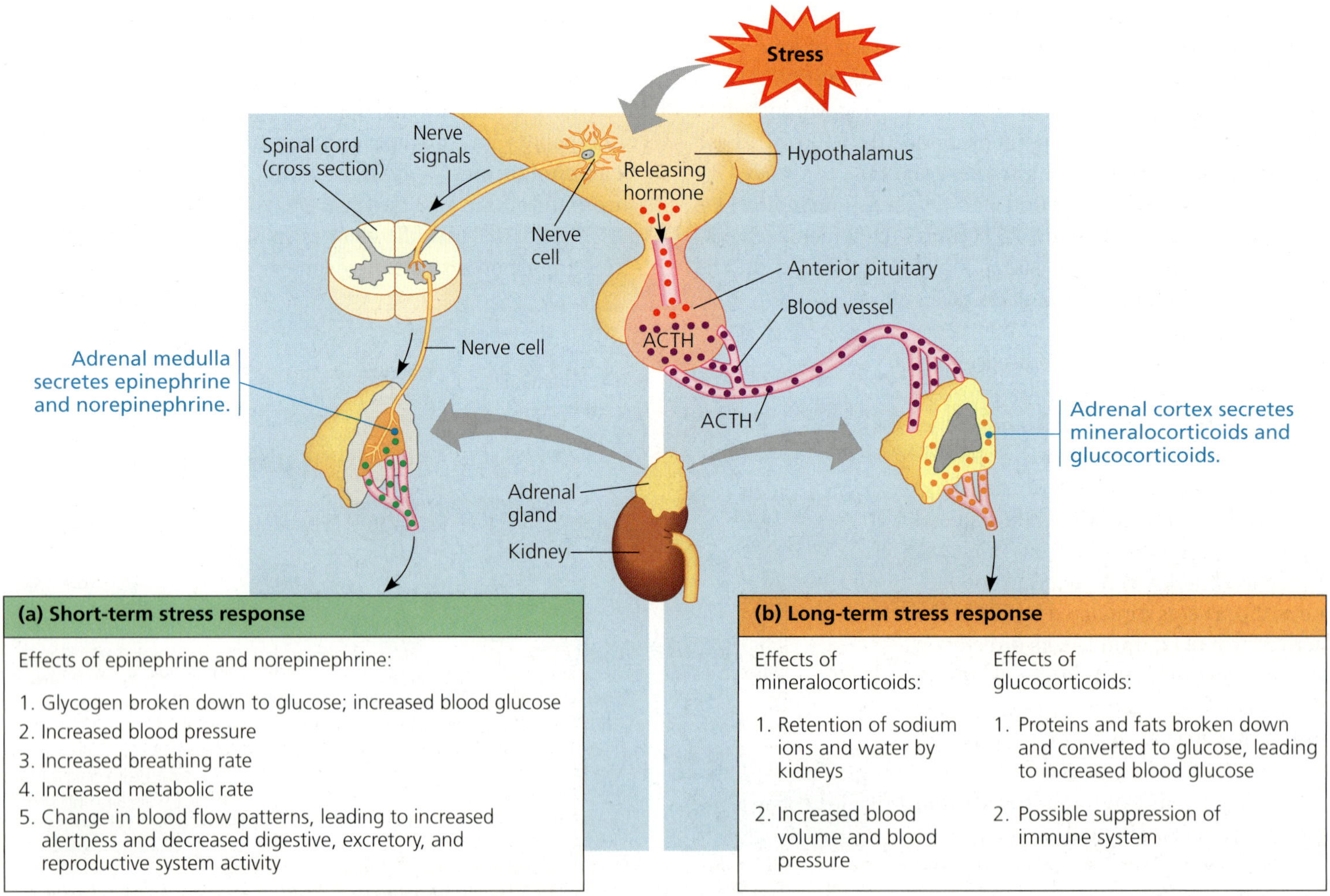

▲ **Figure 45.21 Stress and the adrenal gland.** Stressful stimuli cause the hypothalamus to activate **(a)** the adrenal medulla via nerve impulses and **(b)** the adrenal cortex via hormonal signals. The adrenal medulla mediates short-term responses to stress by secreting the catecholamine hormones epinephrine and norepinephrine. The adrenal cortex controls more prolonged responses by secreting corticosteroids.

the endocrine cells to synthesize and secrete a family of steroids called **corticosteroids** (**Figure 45.21b**). The two main types of corticosteroids in humans are *glucocorticoids* and *mineralocorticoids*.

As reflected in their name, **glucocorticoids** have a primary effect on glucose metabolism. Augmenting the fuel-mobilizing effects of glucagon from the pancreas, glucocorticoids promote glucose synthesis from noncarbohydrate sources, such as proteins, making more glucose available as fuel. Glucocorticoids, such as cortisol (see Figure 45.3), act on skeletal muscle, causing the breakdown of muscle proteins. The resulting amino acids are transported to the liver and kidneys, where they are converted to glucose and released into the blood. The synthesis of glucose from muscle proteins provides circulating fuel when the body requires more glucose than the liver can mobilize from its glycogen stores.

When glucocorticoids are introduced into the body at levels above those normally present, they suppress certain components of the body's immune system. Because of this anti-inflammatory effect, glucocorticoids are sometimes used to treat inflammatory diseases such as arthritis. However, long-term use can have serious side effects, reflecting the potent activity of glucocorticoids on metabolism. For these reasons, nonsteroidal anti-inflammatory drugs (NSAIDs), such as aspirin or ibuprofen, generally are preferred for treating chronic inflammatory conditions.

Mineralocorticoids, named for their effects on mineral metabolism, act principally in maintaining salt and water balance. For example, the mineralocorticoid *aldosterone* functions in ion and water homeostasis of the blood. Low blood volume or pressure leads to production of angiotensin II, which stimulates the secretion of aldosterone (see Figure 44.21). Aldosterone, in turn, stimulates cells in the kidneys to reabsorb sodium ions and water from filtrate, raising blood pressure and volume. Aldosterone also functions in the body's response to severe stress. In these circumstances, a rise in blood ACTH levels increases the rate at which the adrenal cortex secretes aldosterone as well as glucocorticoids.

The corticosteroid products of the adrenal cortex include small amounts of steroid hormones that function as sex hormones. All steroid hormones are synthesized from cholesterol, and their structures differ in only minor ways (see Figure 4.9). However, these small structural differences are associated with major differences in effects. The sex hormones produced by the adrenal cortex are mainly "male" hormones (androgens), with small amounts of "female" hormones (estrogens and progestins). There is evidence that adrenal androgens account for the sex drive in adult females, but otherwise the physiological roles of the adrenal sex hormones are not well understood.

Gonadal Sex Hormones

Sex hormones affect growth, development, reproductive cycles, and sexual behavior. Whereas the adrenal glands secrete small quantities of these hormones, the testes of males and ovaries of females are their principal sources. The gonads produce and secrete three major categories of steroid hormones: androgens, estrogens, and progestins. All three types are found in both males and females but in significantly different proportions.

The testes primarily synthesize **androgens**, the main one being **testosterone**. Testosterone first functions before birth, as shown in the 1940s by French researcher Alfred Jost. He was interested in how hormones determine whether an individual develops as a male or female. Working with rabbits, Jost carried out a surgical study that provided a simple and unexpected answer (**Figure 45.22**). His studies established that for mammals (but not all animals), female development is the default process in embryos.

Androgens have a major role again at human puberty, when they are responsible for the development of human male secondary sex characteristics. High concentrations of androgen lead to a low voice and male patterns of hair growth, as well as increases in muscle and bone mass. The muscle-building, or anabolic, action of testosterone and related steroids has enticed

▼ **Figure 45.22 Inquiry**

What role do hormones play in making a mammal male or female?

EXPERIMENT Alfred Jost, at the College de France in Paris, wondered whether gonadal hormones instruct an embryo to develop as male or female in accord with its chromosome set. Working with rabbit embryos still in the mother's uterus, at a stage before sex differences are observable, he surgically removed the portion of each embryo that would form the ovaries or testes. When the baby rabbits were born, Jost made note of both chromosomal sex and the sexual differentiation of the genital structures.

RESULTS

Chromosome Set	Appearance of Genitals: No surgery	Appearance of Genitals: Embryonic gonad removed
XY (male)	Male	Female
XX (female)	Female	Female

CONCLUSION In rabbits, male development requires a hormonal signal from the male gonad. In the absence of this signal, all embryos develop as female. Jost later demonstrated that embryos developed male genitals if the surgically removed gonad was replaced with a crystal of testosterone. In fact, the process of sex determination occurs in a highly similar manner in all mammals, including humans.

SOURCE A. Jost, Recherches sur la differenciation sexuelle de l'embryon de lapin (Studies on the sexual differentiation of the rabbit embryo), *Archives d'Anatomie Microscopique et de Morphologie Expérimentale* 36:271–316 (1947).

WHAT IF? What result would Jost have obtained if female development also required a signal from the gonad?

some athletes to take them as supplements, despite prohibitions against their use in nearly all sports. Use of anabolic steroids, while effective in increasing muscle mass, can cause severe acne outbreaks and liver damage. In addition, anabolic steroids have a negative-feedback effect on testosterone production, causing significant decreases in sperm count and testicular size.

Estrogens, of which the most important is **estradiol**, are responsible for the maintenance of the female reproductive system and the development of female secondary sex characteristics. In mammals, **progestins**, which include **progesterone**, are primarily involved in preparing and maintaining tissues of the uterus required to support the growth and development of an embryo.

Androgens, estrogens, and progestins are components of hormone cascade pathways. Synthesis of these hormones is controlled by gonadotropins (FSH and LH) from the anterior pituitary gland (see Figure 45.17). FSH and LH secretion is in turn controlled by a releasing hormone from the hypothalamus, GnRH (gonadotropin-releasing hormone). We will examine the feedback relationships that regulate gonadal steroid secretion in detail in Chapter 46.

Melatonin and Biorhythms

We conclude our discussion of the vertebrate endocrine system with the **pineal gland**, a small mass of tissue near the center of the mammalian brain (see Figure 45.14). The pineal gland synthesizes and secretes the hormone **melatonin**, a modified amino acid. Depending on the species, the pineal gland contains light-sensitive cells or has nervous connections from the eyes that control its secretory activity.

Melatonin regulates functions related to light and to seasons marked by changes in day length. Although melatonin affects skin pigmentation in many vertebrates, its primary functions relate to biological rhythms associated with reproduction. Melatonin is secreted at night, and the amount released depends on the length of the night. In winter, for example, when days are short and nights are long, more melatonin is secreted. Recent evidence suggests that the main target of melatonin is a group of neurons in the hypothalamus called the suprachiasmatic nucleus (SCN), which functions as a biological clock. Melatonin seems to decrease the activity of the SCN, and this effect may be related to its role in mediating rhythms. We will consider biological rhythms further in Chapter 49, where we will analyze experiments on SCN function.

In the next chapter, we will look at reproduction in both vertebrates and invertebrates. There we will see that the endocrine system is central not only to the survival of the individual, but also to the propagation of the species.

CONCEPT CHECK 45.4

1. How does the fact that two adrenal hormones act as neurotransmitters relate to the developmental origin of the adrenal gland?
2. How would a decrease in the number of corticosteroid receptors in the hypothalamus affect levels of corticosteroids in the blood?
3. **WHAT IF?** Suppose you receive an injection of cortisone, a glucocorticoid, in an inflamed joint. What aspects of glucocorticoid activity would you be exploiting? If a glucocorticoid pill were also effective at treating the inflammation, why would it still be preferable to introduce the drug locally?

For suggested answers, see Appendix A.

Chapter 45 Review

MB **MEDIA** Go to the Study Area at **www.masteringbio.com** for BioFlix 3-D Animations, MP3 Tutors, Videos, Practice Tests, an eBook, and more.

SUMMARY OF KEY CONCEPTS

CONCEPT 45.1

Hormones and other signaling molecules bind to target receptors, triggering specific response pathways (pp. 975–981)

- **Types of Secreted Signaling Molecules** Hormones are secreted into extracellular fluids by endocrine cells or ductless glands and reach target cells via the bloodstream. Local regulators act on neighboring cells in paracrine signaling, and on the secreting cell itself in autocrine signaling. Neurotransmitters also act locally, but some nerve cells secrete neurohormones that can act throughout the body. Signaling molecules called pheromones are released into the environment for communication between animals of the same species.
- **Chemical Classes of Hormones** Hormones can be polypeptides, amines, or steroids and can be water-soluble or lipid-soluble.
- **Hormone Receptor Location: *Scientific Inquiry*** Peptide/protein hormones and most hormones derived from amino acids bind to receptors embedded in the plasma membrane. Steroid hormones and thyroid hormones enter target cells and bind to specific protein receptors in the cytosol or nucleus.
- **Cellular Response Pathways** Binding of water-soluble hormones to cell-surface receptors triggers intracellular signal transduction, leading to specific responses in the cytoplasm or changes in gene expression. Complexes of a lipid-soluble hormone and its receptor act in the nucleus to regulate transcription of specific genes.

▶ **Multiple Effects of Hormones** The same hormone may have different effects on target cells that have different receptors for the hormone or different signal transduction pathways.

▶ **Signaling by Local Regulators** Local regulators include cytokines and growth factors (proteins/peptides), nitric oxide (a gas), and prostaglandins (modified fatty acids).

MEDIA

Activity Overview of Cell Signaling
Activity Peptide Hormone Action
Activity Steroid Hormone Action

CONCEPT 45.2

Negative feedback and antagonistic hormone pairs are common features of the endocrine system (pp. 981–984)

▶ **Simple Hormone Pathways**

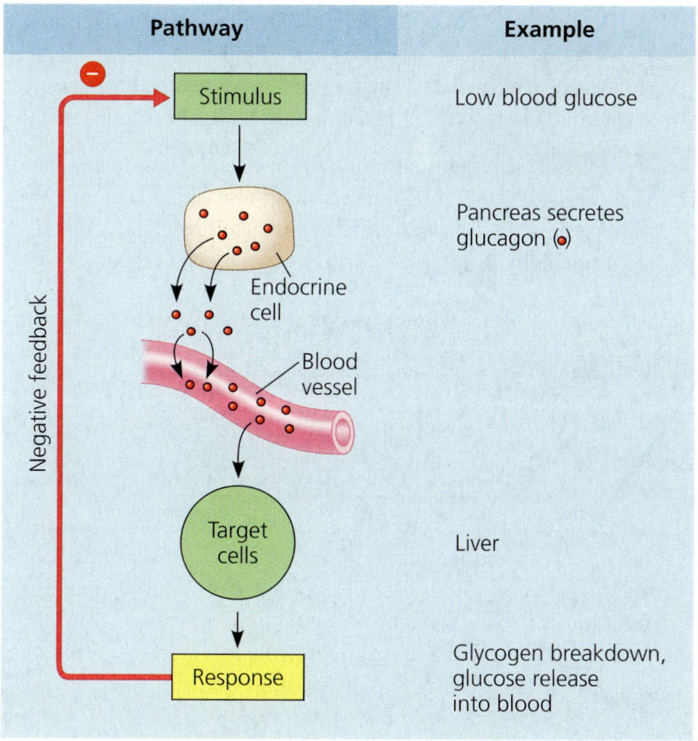

▶ **Insulin and Glucagon: Control of Blood Glucose** Insulin (from beta cells of the pancreas) reduces blood glucose levels by promoting cellular uptake of glucose, glycogen formation in the liver, protein synthesis, and fat storage. Glucagon (from alpha cells of the pancreas) increases blood glucose levels by stimulating conversion of glycogen to glucose in the liver and breakdown of fat and protein to glucose. Diabetes mellitus, which is marked by elevated blood glucose levels, results from inadequate production of insulin (type 1) or loss of responsiveness of target cells to insulin (type 2).

CONCEPT 45.3

The endocrine and nervous systems act individually and together in regulating animal physiology (pp. 984–990)

▶ The endocrine and nervous systems often function together in maintaining homeostasis, development, and reproduction.

▶ **Coordination of Endocrine and Nervous Systems in Invertebrates** Diverse hormones regulate different aspects of homeostasis in invertebrates. In insects, molting and development are controlled by prothoracicotropic hormone (PTTH), a tropic neurohormone; ecdysone, whose release is triggered by PTTH; and juvenile hormone.

▶ **Coordination of Endocrine and Nervous Systems in Vertebrates** The hypothalamus, on the underside of the brain, contains sets of neurosecretory cells. Some produce direct-acting hormones that are stored in and released from the posterior pituitary. Other hypothalamic cells produce hormones that are transported by portal blood vessels to the anterior pituitary. These hormones either promote or inhibit the release of hormones from the anterior pituitary.

▶ **Posterior Pituitary Hormones** The two hormones released from the posterior pituitary act directly on nonendocrine tissues. Oxytocin induces uterine contractions and release of milk from mammary glands, and antidiuretic hormone (ADH) enhances water reabsorption in the kidneys.

▶ **Anterior Pituitary Hormones** Hormones from the hypothalamus act as releasing or inhibiting hormones for hormone secretion by the anterior pituitary. Most anterior pituitary hormones are tropic, acting on endocrine tissues or glands to regulate hormone secretion. Often, anterior pituitary hormones act in a cascade. In the case of thyrotropin, or thyroid-stimulating hormone (TSH), TSH secretion is regulated by thyrotropin-releasing hormone (TRH), and TSH in turn regulates secretion of thyroid hormone. Like TSH, follicle-stimulating hormone (FSH), luteinizing hormone (LH), and adrenocorticotropic hormone (ACTH) are tropic. Prolactin and melanocyte-stimulating hormone (MSH) are nontropic anterior pituitary hormones. Prolactin stimulates milk production in mammals but has diverse effects in different vertebrates. MSH influences skin pigmentation in some vertebrates and fat metabolism in mammals. Growth hormone (GH) promotes growth directly and has diverse metabolic effects; it also stimulates the production of growth factors by other tissues.

CONCEPT 45.4

Endocrine glands respond to diverse stimuli in regulating metabolism, homeostasis, development, and behavior (pp. 990–994)

▶ **Thyroid Hormone: Control of Metabolism and Development** The thyroid gland produces iodine-containing hormones (T_3 and T_4) that stimulate metabolism and influence development and maturation. Secretion of T_3 and T_4 is controlled by the hypothalamus and pituitary in a hormone cascade pathway.

▶ **Parathyroid Hormone and Vitamin D: Control of Blood Calcium** Parathyroid hormone (PTH), secreted by the parathyroid glands, causes bone to release Ca^{2+} into the blood and stimulates reabsorption of Ca^{2+} in the kidneys. PTH also stimulates the kidneys to activate vitamin D, which promotes intestinal uptake of Ca^{2+} from food. Calcitonin, secreted by the thyroid, has the opposite effects in bones and kidneys as PTH. Calcitonin is important for calcium homeostasis in adults of some vertebrates, but not humans.

▶ **Adrenal Hormones: Response to Stress** Neurosecretory cells in the adrenal medulla release epinephrine and norepinephrine in response to stress-activated impulses from the nervous system. These hormones mediate various fight-or-flight responses. The adrenal cortex releases three functional classes of steroid hormones. Glucocorticoids, such as cortisol, influence glucose metabolism and the immune system; mineralocorticoids, primarily aldosterone, help regulate salt and water balance. The adrenal cortex also produces small amounts of sex hormones.

▶ **Gonadal Sex Hormones** The gonads—testes and ovaries—produce most of the body's sex hormones: androgens, estrogens, and progestins. All three types are produced in males and females but in different proportions.

▶ **Melatonin and Biorhythms** The pineal gland, located within the brain, secretes melatonin. Release of melatonin is controlled by light/dark cycles. Its primary functions appear to be related to biological rhythms associated with reproduction.

MEDIA

Activity Human Endocrine Glands and Hormones

Investigation How Do Thyroxine and TSH Affect Metabolism?

TESTING YOUR KNOWLEDGE

SELF-QUIZ

1. Which of the following is *not* an accurate statement?
   a. Hormones are chemical messengers that travel to target cells through the circulatory system.
   b. Hormones often regulate homeostasis through antagonistic functions.
   c. Hormones of the same chemical class usually have the same function.
   d. Hormones are secreted by specialized cells usually located in endocrine glands.
   e. Hormones are often regulated through feedback loops.

2. A distinctive feature of the mechanism of action of thyroid hormones and steroid hormones is that
   a. these hormones are regulated by feedback loops.
   b. target cells react more rapidly to these hormones than to local regulators.
   c. these hormones bind with specific receptor proteins on the plasma membrane of target cells.
   d. these hormones bind to receptors inside cells.
   e. these hormones affect metabolism.

3. Growth factors are local regulators that
   a. are produced by the anterior pituitary.
   b. are modified fatty acids that stimulate bone and cartilage growth.
   c. are found on the surface of cancer cells and stimulate abnormal cell division.
   d. are proteins that bind to cell-surface receptors and stimulate growth and development of target cells.
   e. convey messages between nerve cells.

4. Which hormone is *incorrectly* paired with its action?
   a. oxytocin—stimulates uterine contractions during childbirth
   b. thyroxine—stimulates metabolic processes
   c. insulin—stimulates glycogen breakdown in the liver
   d. ACTH—stimulates the release of glucocorticoids by the adrenal cortex
   e. melatonin—affects biological rhythms, seasonal reproduction

5. An example of antagonistic hormones controlling homeostasis is
   a. thyroxine and parathyroid hormone in calcium balance.
   b. insulin and glucagon in glucose metabolism.
   c. progestins and estrogens in sexual differentiation.
   d. epinephrine and norepinephrine in fight-or-flight responses.
   e. oxytocin and prolactin in milk production.

6. Which of the following is the most likely explanation for hypothyroidism in a patient whose iodine level is normal?
   a. a disproportionate production of T_3 to T_4
   b. hyposecretion of TSH
   c. hypersecretion of TSH
   d. hypersecretion of MSH
   e. a decrease in the thyroid secretion of calcitonin

7. The main target organs for tropic hormones are
   a. muscles.
   b. blood vessels.
   c. endocrine glands.
   d. kidneys.
   e. nerves.

8. The relationship between the insect hormones ecdysone and PTTH
   a. is an example of the interaction between the endocrine and nervous systems.
   b. illustrates homeostasis achieved by positive feedback.
   c. demonstrates that peptide-derived hormones have more widespread effects than steroid hormones.
   d. illustrates homeostasis maintained by antagonistic hormones.
   e. demonstrates competitive inhibition for the hormone receptor.

9. **DRAW IT** In mammals, milk production by mammary glands is controlled by prolactin and prolactin-releasing hormone. Draw a simple sketch of this pathway, including glands and tissues, hormones, routes for hormone movement, and effects.

For Self-Quiz answers, see Appendix A.

MEDIA Visit the Study Area at **www.masteringbio.com** for a Practice Test.

EVOLUTION CONNECTION

10. The intracellular receptors used by all the steroid and thyroid hormones are similar enough in structure that they are all considered members of one "superfamily" of proteins. Propose a hypothesis for how the genes encoding these receptors may have evolved. (*Hint:* See Figure 21.13.) How could you test your hypothesis using DNA sequence data?

SCIENTIFIC INQUIRY

11. Chronically high levels of glucocorticoids, called Cushing's syndrome, can result in obesity, muscle weakness, and depression. Excessive activity of either the pituitary or the adrenal gland can be the cause. To determine which gland has abnormal activity in a particular patient, doctors use the drug dexamethasone, a synthetic glucocorticoid that blocks ACTH release. Based on the graph, which gland is affected in patient X?

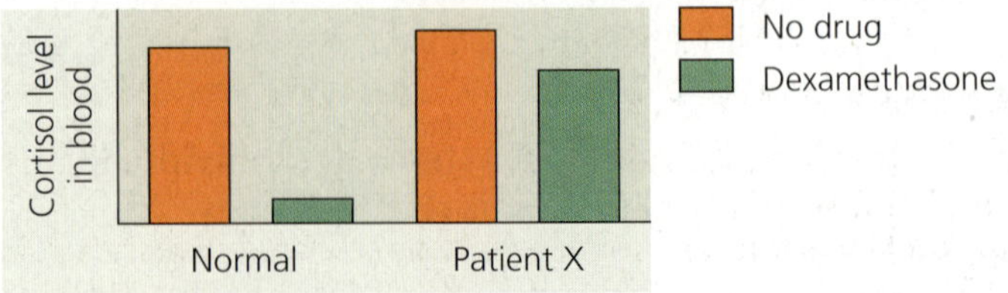

46 Animal Reproduction

▲ **Figure 46.1 How can each of these earthworms be both male and female?**

KEY CONCEPTS

46.1 Both asexual and sexual reproduction occur in the animal kingdom
46.2 Fertilization depends on mechanisms that bring together sperm and eggs of the same species
46.3 Reproductive organs produce and transport gametes
46.4 The timing and pattern of meiosis in mammals differ for males and females
46.5 The interplay of tropic and sex hormones regulates mammalian reproduction
46.6 In placental mammals, an embryo develops fully within the mother's uterus

OVERVIEW

Pairing Up for Sexual Reproduction

The two earthworms (genus *Lumbricus*) in **Figure 46.1** are mating. If not disturbed, they will remain above ground and joined like this for several hours. Sperm will be transferred, and fertilized eggs will be produced. A few weeks later, sexual reproduction will be complete. New worms will hatch, but which parent will be the mother? The answer is simple yet probably unexpected: Both will.

As humans, we tend to think of reproduction in terms of the mating of males and females and the fusion of sperm and eggs. Animal reproduction, however, takes many forms. In some species, individuals change their sex during their lifetime, while in others, such as earthworms, an individual is both male and female at the same time. There are animals that can fertilize their own eggs, as well as others that can reproduce without any form of sex. For certain species, such as honeybees, reproduction is limited to a few individuals within a large population.

The many aspects of animal form and function we have studied in earlier chapters can be viewed, in the broadest context, as adaptations contributing to reproductive success. Individuals are transient. A population transcends the finite life spans of its members only by reproduction, the generation of new individuals from existing ones. In this chapter, we will compare the diverse reproductive mechanisms that have evolved in the animal kingdom. We will then examine details of mammalian reproduction, particularly that of humans. Deferring the cellular and molecular details of embryonic development until the next chapter, we will focus here on the physiology of reproduction, mostly from the perspective of the parents.

CONCEPT 46.1

Both asexual and sexual reproduction occur in the animal kingdom

There are two principal modes of animal reproduction. In **sexual reproduction**, the fusion of haploid gametes forms a diploid cell, the **zygote**. The animal that develops from a zygote can in turn give rise to gametes by meiosis (see Figure 13.8). The female gamete, the **egg**, is a large, nonmotile cell. The male gamete, the **sperm**, is generally a much smaller, motile cell. **Asexual reproduction** is the generation of new individuals without the fusion of egg and sperm. In most asexual animals, reproduction relies entirely on mitotic cell division.

Mechanisms of Asexual Reproduction

A number of distinct forms of asexual reproduction are found among the invertebrates. Many invertebrates can reproduce asexually by **fission**, the separation of a parent organism into

▲ **Figure 46.2 Asexual reproduction of a sea anemone (*Anthopleura elegantissima*).** The individual in the center of this photograph is undergoing fission, a type of asexual reproduction. Two smaller individuals will form as the parent divides approximately in half. Each offspring will be a genetic copy of the parent.

two individuals of approximately equal size **(Figure 46.2)**. Also common among invertebrates is **budding**, in which new individuals arise from outgrowths of existing ones. For example, in certain species of coral and hydra, new individuals grow out from the parent's body (see Figure 13.2). Stony corals, which can grow to be more than 1 m across, are cnidarian colonies of several thousand connected individuals. In another form of asexual reproduction, some invertebrates, including certain sponges, release specialized groups of cells that can grow into new individuals.

A two-step process of asexual reproduction involves *fragmentation*, the breaking of the body into several pieces, followed by *regeneration*, the regrowth of lost body parts. If more than one piece grows and develops into a complete animal, the net effect is reproduction: In sea stars (starfish) of the genus *Linckia*, an arm that is broken off the body can regenerate an entire sea star. (Many other species of sea star can grow a new arm to replace a lost one, but do not create new individuals by regeneration.) Numerous sponges, cnidarians, bristle worms, and sea squirts reproduce by fragmentation and regeneration.

Parthenogenesis is a form of asexual reproduction in which an egg develops without being fertilized. The progeny of parthenogenesis can be either haploid or diploid. If haploid, the offspring develop into adults that produce eggs or sperm without meiosis. Reproduction by parthenogenesis occurs in certain species of bees, wasps, and ants. In the case of honeybees, males (drones) are fertile haploid adults that arise by parthenogenesis. In contrast, female honeybees, including both the sterile workers and the fertile queens, are diploid adults that develop from fertilized eggs. Among vertebrates, parthenogenesis is observed in roughly one in every thousand species. Recently discovered examples include the Komodo dragon and a species of hammerhead shark. In both cases, zookeepers were surprised to find offspring that had been parthenogenetically produced when females were kept apart from males of their species.

Sexual Reproduction: An Evolutionary Enigma

The vast majority of eukaryotic species reproduce sexually. Sex must enhance reproductive success or survival, because it would otherwise rapidly disappear. To see why, consider an animal population in which half the females reproduce sexually and half reproduce asexually **(Figure 46.3)**. We'll assume that the number of offspring per female is a constant, two in this case. The two offspring of an asexual female would both be daughters that are each able to give birth to more reproductive daughters. In contrast, half of a sexual female's offspring will be male. The number of offspring will remain the same at each generation, because both a male and a female are required to reproduce. Thus, the asexual condition will increase in frequency at each generation. Yet despite this "twofold cost," sex is maintained even in animal species that can also reproduce asexually.

What advantage does sex provide? The answer remains elusive. Most hypotheses focus on the unique combinations of parental genes formed during meiotic recombination and fertilization. By producing offspring of varied phenotypes, sexual reproduction may enhance the reproductive success of parents when environmental factors, such as pathogens, change relatively rapidly. In contrast, asexual reproduction is expected to be most advantageous in stable, favorable environments because it perpetuates successful genotypes faithfully and precisely.

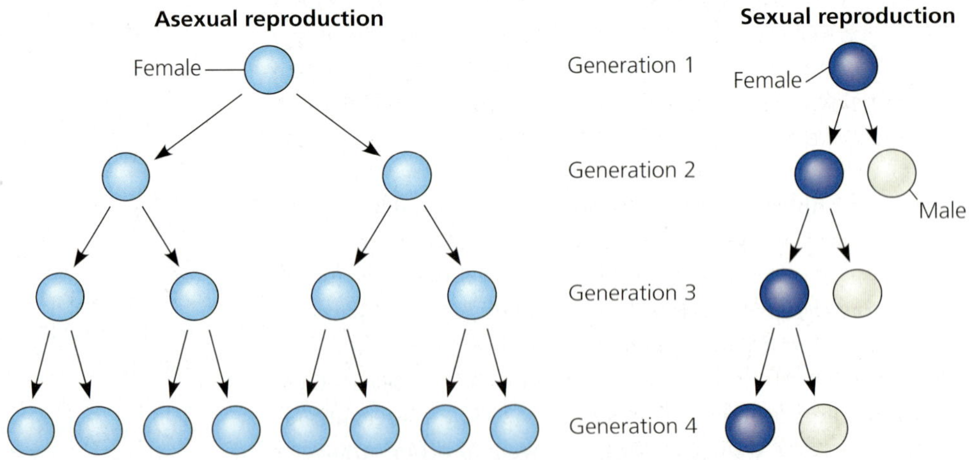

▲ **Figure 46.3 The "reproductive handicap" of sex.** These diagrams contrast the reproductive output of females (blue circles) over four generations for asexual versus sexual reproduction, assuming two surviving offspring per female. The asexual population rapidly outgrows the sexual one.

There are a number of reasons why the unique gene combinations formed during sexual reproduction might be advantageous. One is that beneficial gene combinations arising through recombination might speed up adaptation. Although this idea appears straightforward, the theoretical advantage is significant only when the rate of beneficial mutations is high and population size is small. Another idea is that the shuffling of genes during sexual reproduction might allow a population to rid itself of sets of harmful genes more readily. Experiments to test these and other hypotheses are ongoing in many laboratories.

Reproductive Cycles and Patterns

Most animals exhibit cycles in reproductive activity, often related to changing seasons. In this way, animals conserve resources, reproducing only when sufficient energy sources or stores are available and when environmental conditions favor the survival of offspring. For example, ewes (female sheep) have a reproductive cycle lasting 15–17 days. **Ovulation**, the release of mature eggs, occurs at the midpoint of each cycle. A ewe's cycles generally occur only during fall and early winter, and the length of any resulting pregnancy is five months. Thus, most lambs are born in the early spring, the time when their chances of survival are optimal. Even in such relatively unvarying habitats as the tropics or the ocean, animals generally reproduce only at certain times of the year. Reproductive cycles are controlled by hormones, which in turn are regulated by environmental cues. Common environmental cues are changes in day length, seasonal temperature, rainfall, and lunar cycles.

Animals may reproduce exclusively asexually or sexually, or they may alternate between the two modes. In aphids, rotifers, and water fleas (genus *Daphnia*), a female can produce eggs of two types. One type of egg requires fertilization to develop, but the other type does not and develops instead by parthenogenesis. In the case of *Daphnia*, the switch between sexual and asexual reproduction is often related to season. Asexual reproduction occurs when conditions are favorable, whereas sexual reproduction occurs during times of environmental stress.

Several genera of fishes, amphibians, and reptiles reproduce exclusively by a complex form of parthenogenesis that involves the doubling of chromosomes after meiosis, producing diploid offspring. For example, about 15 species of whiptail lizards in the genus *Aspidoscelis* reproduce exclusively by parthenogenesis. There are no males in these species, but the lizards carry out courtship and mating behaviors typical of sexual species of the same genus. During the breeding season, one female of each mating pair mimics a male **(Figure 46.4a)**. Each member of the pair alternates roles two or three times during the season **(Figure 46.4b)**. An individual adopts female behavior prior to ovulation, when the level of the female sex hormone estradiol is high, then switches to male-like behavior after ovulation, when the level of progesterone is highest. Ovulation is more likely to occur if the individual is mounted during the critical time of the hormone cycle; isolated lizards lay fewer eggs than those that go through the motions of sex. Apparently, these parthenogenetic lizards evolved from species having two sexes and still require certain sexual stimuli for maximum reproductive success.

Sexual reproduction that involves encounters between members of the opposite sex presents a problem for sessile (stationary) animals, such as barnacles; burrowing animals, such as clams; and some parasites, including tapeworms. One evolutionary solution to this problem is **hermaphroditism**, in which each individual has both male and female reproductive systems (the term *hermaphrodite* is derived from the names Hermes and

(a) Both lizards in this photograph are *A. uniparens* females. The one on top is playing the role of a male. Every two or three weeks during the breeding season, individuals switch sex roles.

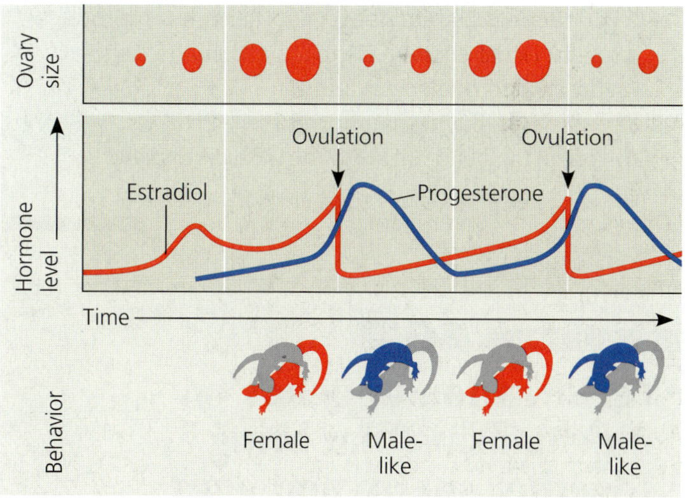

(b) The sexual behavior of *A. uniparens* is correlated with the cycle of ovulation mediated by sex hormones. As the blood level of estradiol rises, the ovaries grow, and the lizard behaves as a female. After ovulation, the estradiol level drops abruptly, and the progesterone level rises; these hormone levels correlate with male-like behavior.

▲ **Figure 46.4 Sexual behavior in parthenogenetic lizards.** The desert-grassland whiptail lizard (*Aspidoscelis uniparens*) is an all-female species. These reptiles reproduce by parthenogenesis, the development of an unfertilized egg. Nevertheless, ovulation is stimulated by mating behavior.

Aphrodite, a Greek god and goddess). Because each hermaphrodite reproduces as both a male and a female, any two individuals can mate. Each animal donates and receives sperm during mating, as the earthworms in Figure 46.1 are doing. In some species, hermaphrodites are also capable of self-fertilization.

Another reproductive pattern involves sex reversal, in which an individual changes its sex during its lifetime. The bluehead wrasse (*Thalassoma bifasciatum*), a coral reef fish, provides a well-studied example. These wrasses live in harems consisting of a single male and several females. When the male dies, the largest (and usually oldest) female in the harem becomes the new male. Within a week, the transformed individual is producing sperm instead of eggs. Because the male defends the harem against intruders, a larger size may be more important for males than females in ensuring successful reproduction.

Certain oyster species provide an example of sex reversal from male to female. By reproducing as males and then later reversing sex, these oysters become female when their size is greatest. Since the number of gametes produced generally increases with size much more for females than for males, sex reversal in this direction maximizes gamete production. The result is enhanced reproductive success: Because oysters are sedentary animals and simply release their gametes into the surrounding water, more gametes result in more offspring.

CONCEPT CHECK 46.1

1. Compare and contrast the outcomes of asexual and sexual reproduction.
2. Parthenogenesis is the most common form of asexual reproduction in animals that at other times reproduce sexually. What characteristic of parthenogenesis might explain this observation?
3. **WHAT IF?** If a hermaphrodite self-fertilizes, will the offspring be identical to the parent? Explain.

For suggested answers, see Appendix A.

CONCEPT 46.2

Fertilization depends on mechanisms that bring together sperm and eggs of the same species

Fertilization—the union of sperm and egg—can be either external or internal. In species with **external fertilization**, the female releases eggs into the environment, where the male then fertilizes them. Other species have **internal fertilization**: Sperm are deposited in or near the female reproductive tract, and fertilization occurs within the tract. (We'll discuss the cellular and molecular details of fertilization in Chapter 47.)

A moist habitat is almost always required for external fertilization, both to prevent the gametes from drying out and to allow the sperm to swim to the eggs. Many aquatic invertebrates simply shed their eggs and sperm into the surroundings, and fertilization occurs without the parents making physical contact. However, timing is crucial to ensure that mature sperm and eggs encounter one another.

Among some species with external fertilization, individuals clustered in the same area release their gametes into the water at the same time, a process known as *spawning*. In some cases, chemical signals that one individual generates in releasing gametes trigger others to release gametes. In other cases, environmental cues, such as temperature or day length, cause a whole population to release gametes at one time. For example, the palolo worm, native to coral reefs of the South Pacific, times its spawn to both the season and the lunar cycle. In October or November, when the moon is in its last quarter, palolo worms break in half, releasing tail segments engorged with sperm or eggs. These packets rise to the ocean surface and burst in such vast numbers that the sea surface turns milky with gametes. The sperm quickly fertilize the floating eggs, and within hours, the palolo's once-a-year reproductive frenzy is complete.

When external fertilization is not synchronous across a population, individuals may exhibit specific mating behaviors leading to the fertilization of the eggs of one female by one male (**Figure 46.5**). Such "courtship" behavior has two important benefits: It allows mate selection (see Chapter 23) and, by triggering the release of both sperm and eggs, increases the probability of successful fertilization.

Internal fertilization is an adaptation that enables sperm to reach an egg efficiently, even when the environment is dry. It typically requires cooperative behavior that leads to copulation,

▲ **Figure 46.5 External fertilization.** Many amphibians reproduce by external fertilization. In most species, behavioral adaptations ensure that a male is present when the female releases eggs. Here, a female frog (on bottom) has released a mass of eggs in response to being clasped by a male. The male released sperm (not visible) at the same time, and external fertilization has already occurred in the water.

as well as sophisticated and compatible reproductive systems. Male copulatory organs deliver sperm, and the female reproductive tract often has receptacles for storage and delivery of sperm to mature eggs.

No matter how fertilization occurs, the mating animals may make use of *pheromones*, chemicals released by one organism that can influence the physiology and behavior of other individuals of the same species (see Chapter 45). Pheromones are small, volatile or water-soluble molecules that disperse into the environment and, like hormones, are active in tiny amounts. Many pheromones function as mate attractants, enabling some female insects to be detected by males from as far as a mile away. (We will discuss mating behavior and pheromones further in Chapter 51.)

Ensuring the Survival of Offspring

All species generally produce more offspring than can survive to reproduce. Species with external fertilization tend to produce very large numbers of gametes, but the fraction of zygotes that survive is often quite small. Internal fertilization usually produces fewer zygotes, and is also often associated with a variety of mechanisms that provide greater protection of the embryos and parental care of the young. For example, the internally fertilized eggs of many species of terrestrial animals exhibit adaptations that protect against water loss and physical damage during their external development. In the case of birds and other reptiles, as well as monotremes (egg-laying mammals), the zygotes consist of eggs with calcium- and protein-containing shells and a series of internal membranes (see Chapter 34). In contrast, the fertilized eggs of fishes and amphibians have only a gelatinous coat and lack membranes within them.

Rather than secreting a protective eggshell, some animals retain the embryo for some portion of its development within the female's reproductive tract. Embryos of marsupial mammals, such as kangaroos and opossums, spend only a short period in the uterus; the embryos then crawl out and complete fetal development attached to a mammary gland in the mother's pouch. However, the embryos of eutherian (placental) mammals, such as humans, remain in the uterus throughout fetal development. There they are nourished by the mother's blood supply through a specialized temporary organ, the placenta. The embryos of some fishes and sharks also complete development internally, although typically the embryo and mother in such species lack any connection dedicated to nutrient exchange.

When a baby eagle hatches out of an egg or when a human is born, the newborn is not yet capable of independent existence. Instead, adult birds feed their young and mammals nurse their offspring. Parental care is in fact much more widespread than you might suspect. For example, there are many invertebrates that provide parental care **(Figure 46.6)**. Among vertebrates, the gastric brooding frogs (genus *Rheobatrachus*) of Australia provided a particularly unusual example prior to their extinction in the 1980s. During reproduction, the female frog would carry the tadpoles in her stomach until they underwent metamorphosis and hopped out of her mouth as young frogs.

▲ **Figure 46.6 Parental care in an invertebrate.** Compared with many other insects, giant water bugs of the genus *Belostoma* produce relatively few offspring, but offer much greater parental protection. Following internal fertilization, the female glues her fertilized eggs to the back of the male (shown here). The male carries them for days, frequently fanning water over them to keep the eggs moist, aerated, and free of parasites.

Gamete Production and Delivery

Sexual reproduction in animals relies on sets of cells that serve as precursors for ova and sperm. A group of cells dedicated to this purpose is often established very early in embryogenesis and remains in an inactive state while the overall body plan develops. Cycles of growth and mitosis then increase, or *amplify*, the number of cells available for making eggs or sperm.

In producing gametes from the amplified precursor cells and making them available for fertilization, animals employ a variety of reproductive systems. The simplest systems do not even include discrete **gonads**, the organs that produce gametes in most animals. The palolo and most other polychaete worms (phylum Annelida) have separate sexes but do not have distinct gonads; rather, the eggs and sperm develop from undifferentiated cells lining the coelom (body cavity). As the gametes mature, they are released from the body wall and fill the coelom. Depending on the species, mature gametes may be shed through the excretory opening, or the swelling mass of eggs may split a portion of the body open, spilling the eggs into the environment.

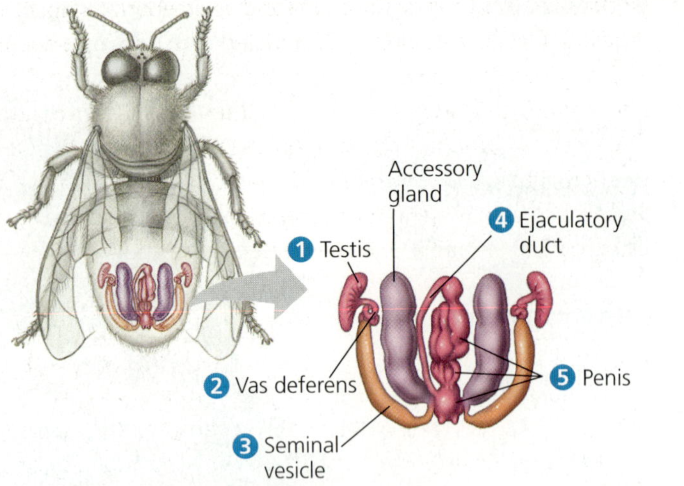

(a) Male honeybee (drone). Sperm form in the testes, pass through the sperm ducts (vas deferens), and are stored in the seminal vesicles. The male ejaculates sperm along with fluid from the accessory glands. (Males of some species of insects and other arthropods have appendages called claspers that grasp the female during copulation.)

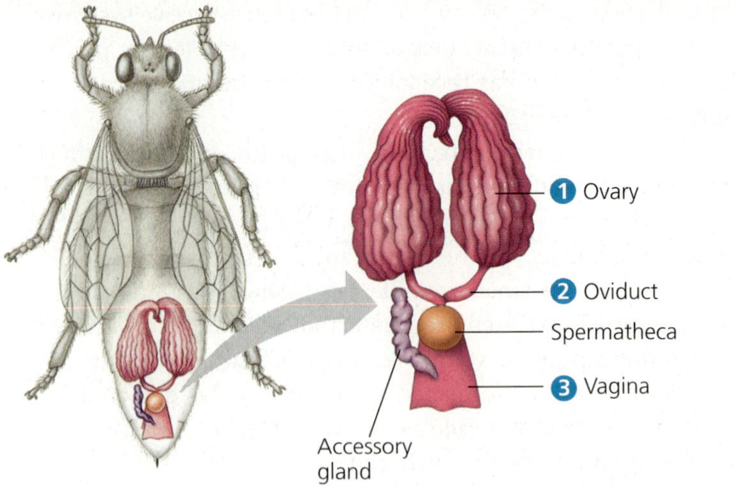

(b) Female honeybee (queen). Eggs develop in the ovaries and then pass through the oviducts and into the vagina. A pair of accessory glands (only one is shown) add protective secretions to the eggs in the vagina. After mating, sperm are stored in the spermatheca, a sac connected to the vagina by a short duct.

▲ **Figure 46.7 Insect reproductive anatomy.** Circled numbers indicate sequences of sperm and egg movement.

More elaborate reproductive systems include sets of accessory tubes and glands that carry, nourish, and protect the gametes and sometimes the developing embryos. Most insects, for example, have separate sexes with complex reproductive systems **(Figure 46.7)**. In the male, sperm develop in a pair of testes and are passed along a coiled duct to two seminal vesicles for storage. During mating, sperm are ejaculated into the female reproductive system. There, eggs develop in a pair of ovaries and are conveyed through ducts to the vagina, where fertilization occurs. In many insect species, the female reproductive system includes a **spermatheca**, a sac in which sperm may be stored for extended periods, a year or more in some species. Because the female releases male gametes from the spermatheca only in response to the appropriate stimuli, fertilization occurs under conditions likely to be well suited to embryonic development. Even more complex reproductive systems can be found in some animals whose body plans are otherwise fairly simple, such as parasitic flatworms **(Figure 46.8)**.

The basic plans of all vertebrate reproductive systems are quite similar, but there are some important variations. In many nonmammalian vertebrates, the digestive, excretory, and reproductive systems have a common opening to the outside, the **cloaca**, a structure that was probably also present in the ancestors of all vertebrates. In contrast, mammals generally lack a cloaca and have a separate opening for the digestive tract. In addition, most female mammals have separate openings for the excretory and reproductive systems. Among most vertebrates, the uterus is partly or completely divided into two chambers. However, in humans and other mammals that produce only one or a few young at a time, as well as in birds and many snakes, the uterus is a single structure. Male reproductive systems differ mainly in the copulatory organs. Many nonmammalian vertebrates lack a well-developed penis and instead ejaculate sperm by turning the cloaca inside out.

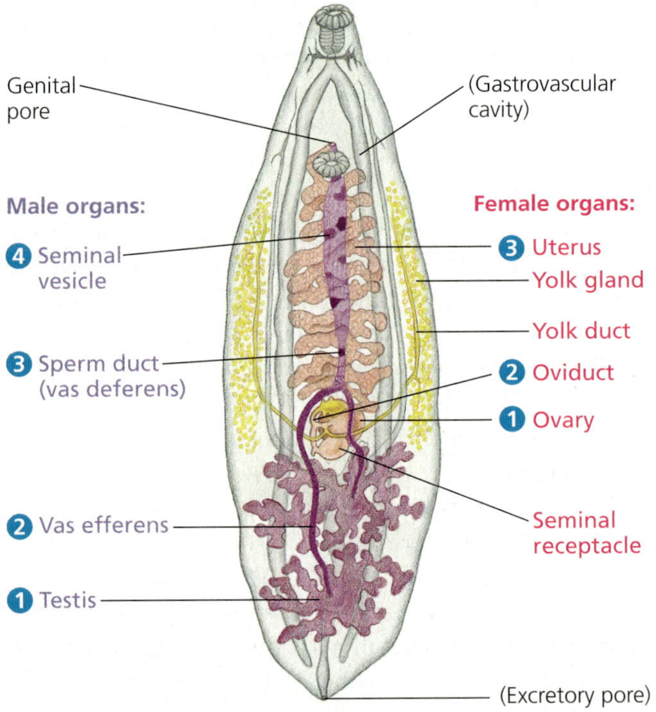

▲ **Figure 46.8 Reproductive anatomy of a hermaphrodite.** Most flatworms (phylum Platyhelminthes) are hermaphrodites. In this parasitic liver fluke, both male and female reproductive systems open to the outside via the genital pore. Sperm, made in the testis, travel as shown by the numbered sequence to the seminal vesicle, which stores them. During copulation, sperm are ejaculated into the female system (usually of another individual) and then move through the uterus to the seminal receptacle. Eggs from the ovary pass into the oviduct, where they are fertilized by sperm from the seminal receptacle and coated with yolk and shell material secreted by the yolk glands. From the oviduct, the fertilized eggs pass into the uterus and then out of the body.

Figure 46.9 Inquiry

Why is sperm usage biased when female fruit flies mate twice?

EXPERIMENT When a female fruit fly mates with two different males, 80% of the offspring result from the second mating. Some scientists had postulated that ejaculate from the second male displaces stored sperm from the first mating. To test this hypothesis, Rhonda Snook, at the University of Sheffield, and David Hosken, at the University of Zurich, took advantage of mutations that alter the male reproductive system. "No-ejaculate" males mate, but do not transfer any sperm or fluid to females. "No-sperm" males mate and ejaculate, but make no sperm. The researchers allowed females to mate twice, first with wild-type males and then with either wild-type males, no-sperm males, or no-ejaculate males. As a control, some females were mated only once. The scientists then dissected each female under a microscope and recorded whether sperm were absent from the spermatheca, the sperm storage organ.

RESULTS

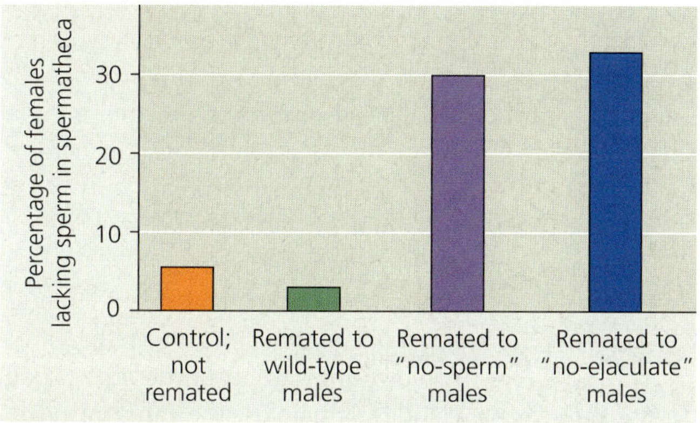

CONCLUSION Because mating reduces sperm storage when no sperm or fluids are transferred, the hypothesis that ejaculate from a second mating displaces stored sperm is incorrect. Instead, it appears that females sometimes get rid of stored sperm in response to mating. This might represent a way for females to replace stored sperm, possibly of diminished fitness, with fresh sperm.

SOURCE R. R. Snook and D. J. Hosken, Sperm death and dumping in *Drosophila*, *Nature* 428:939–941 (2004).

WHAT IF? Suppose the males in the first mating had a mutant allele for the dominant trait of reduced eye size. Predict what fraction, if any, of the females would produce some offspring with smaller eyes.

Although fertilization involves the union of a single egg and sperm, animals often mate with more than one member of the other sex. Indeed, monogamy, the sustained sexual partnership of two individuals, is relatively rare among animals, including most mammals other than humans. Mechanisms have evolved, however, that enhance the reproductive success of a male with a particular female and diminish the chance of that female mating successfully with another partner. For example, some male insects transfer secretions that make a female less receptive to courtship, reducing the likelihood of her mating again. Can females also influence the relative reproductive success of their mates? This question intrigued Rhonda Snook and David Hosken, collaborators working in the United Kingdom and Switzerland, respectively. Studying female fruit flies that copulated with one male and then another, the researchers traced the fate of sperm transferred in the first mating. As shown in **Figure 46.9**, they found that female fruit flies play a major role in determining the reproductive outcome of multiple matings. Nevertheless, the processes by which gametes and individuals compete during reproduction are only partly understood and remain a vibrant research area.

CONCEPT CHECK 46.2

1. How does internal fertilization facilitate life on land?
2. What mechanisms have evolved in animals with (a) external fertilization and (b) internal fertilization that help ensure that offspring survive to adulthood?
3. **WHAT IF?** Suppose you were analyzing chemicals found in the ejaculate of male fruit flies and discovered a peptide that kills microbes. What hypotheses might you formulate as to the function of this peptide?

For suggested answers, see Appendix A.

CONCEPT **46.3**

Reproductive organs produce and transport gametes

Having surveyed some of the general features of animal reproduction, we will focus the rest of the chapter on humans, beginning with the anatomy of the reproductive system in each sex.

Female Reproductive Anatomy

The female's external reproductive structures are the clitoris and two sets of labia, which surround the clitoris and vaginal opening. The internal organs are the gonads, which produce both eggs and reproductive hormones, and a system of ducts and chambers, which receive and carry gametes and house the embryo and fetus (**Figure 46.10** on the next page).

Ovaries

The female gonads are a pair of ovaries that flank the uterus and are held in place in the abdominal cavity by ligaments. The outer layer of each ovary is packed with **follicles**, each consisting of an **oocyte**, a partially developed egg, surrounded by a group of support cells. The surrounding cells nourish and protect the oocyte during much of **oogenesis**, the formation and development of an ovum. Although at birth the ovaries together contain about 1–2 million follicles, only about 500 follicles fully mature between puberty and menopause. During a typical 4-week menstrual cycle, one follicle matures and expels its egg, a process called ovulation. Prior to ovulation, cells of the follicle produce the primary female sex hormone, estradiol (a type of

▼ **Figure 46.10 Reproductive anatomy of the human female.** Some nonreproductive structures are labeled in parentheses for orientation purposes.

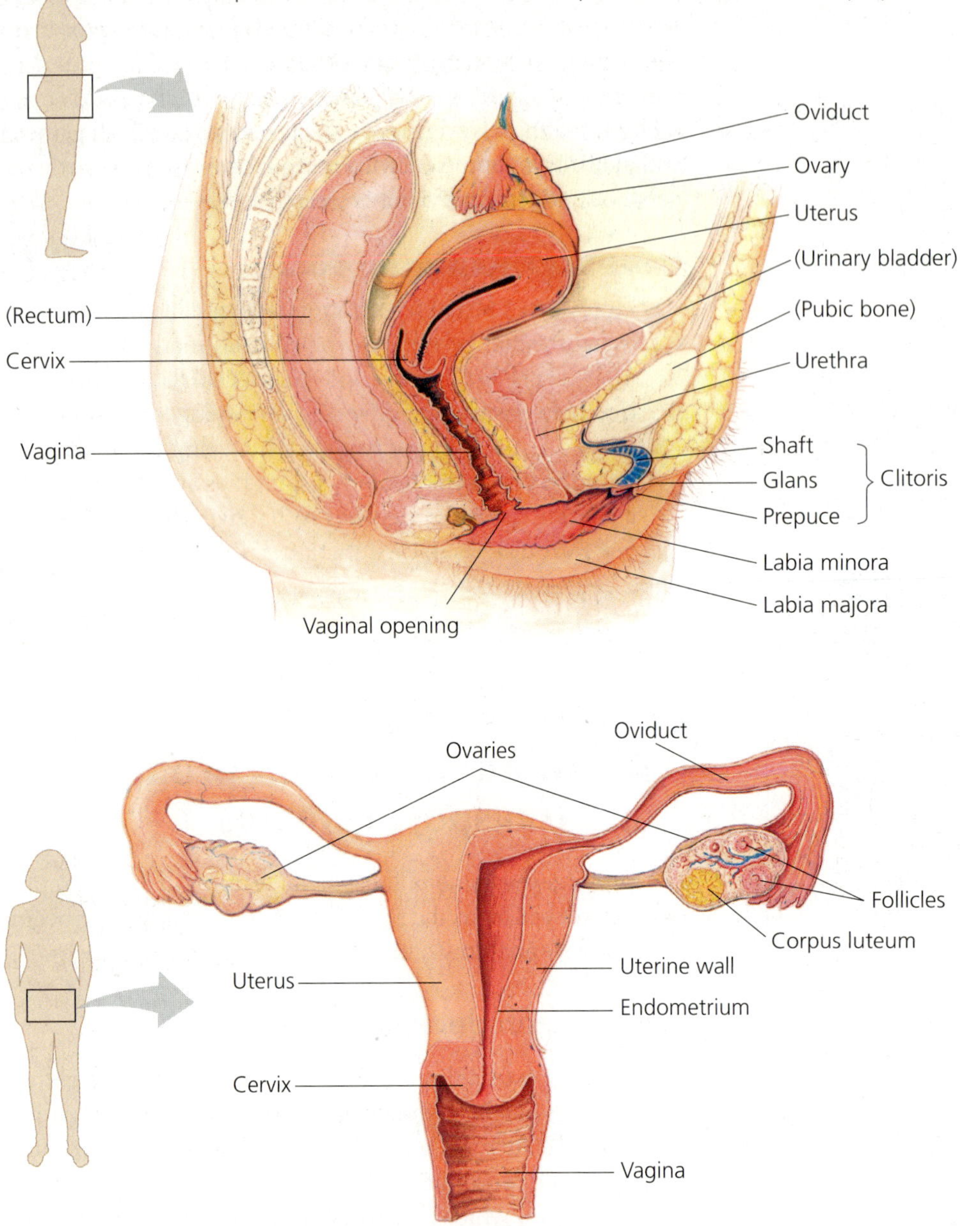

estrogen). After ovulation, the residual follicular tissue grows within the ovary, forming a mass called the **corpus luteum** ("yellow body"). The corpus luteum secretes additional estradiol, as well as progesterone, a hormone that helps maintain the uterine lining during pregnancy. If the egg cell is not fertilized, the corpus luteum degenerates, and a new follicle matures during the next cycle.

Oviducts and Uterus

An **oviduct**, or fallopian tube, extends from the uterus toward each ovary. The dimensions of this tube vary along its length, with the inside diameter near the uterus being as narrow as a human hair. At ovulation, the egg is released into the abdominal cavity near the funnel-like opening of the oviduct. Cilia on the epithelial lining of the duct help collect the egg by drawing fluid from the body cavity into the oviduct. Together with wavelike contractions of the oviduct, the cilia convey the egg down the duct to the **uterus**, also known as the womb. The uterus is a thick, muscular organ that can expand during pregnancy to accommodate a 4-kg fetus. The inner lining of the uterus, the **endometrium**, is richly supplied with blood vessels. The neck of the uterus is the **cervix**, which opens into the vagina.

Vagina and Vulva

The **vagina** is a muscular but elastic chamber that is the site for insertion of the penis and deposition of sperm during copulation. The vagina, which also serves as the birth canal through which a baby is born, opens to the outside at the **vulva**, the collective term for the external female genitals.

A pair of thick, fatty ridges, the **labia majora**, encloses and protects the rest of the vulva. The vaginal opening and the separate opening of the urethra are located within a cavity bordered by a pair of slender skin folds, the **labia minora**. A thin piece of tissue called the **hymen** partly covers the vaginal opening in humans at birth, and usually until sexual intercourse or vigorous physical activity ruptures it. Located at the upper intersection of the labia minora, the **clitoris** consists of a short shaft supporting a rounded **glans**, or head, covered by a small hood of skin, the **prepuce**. During sexual arousal, the clitoris, vagina, and labia minora all engorge with blood and enlarge; in fact, the clitoris consists largely of erectile tissue. Richly supplied with nerve endings, it is one of the most sensitive points of sexual stimulation. Sexual arousal also induces glands located near the vaginal opening to secrete lubricating mucus, thereby facilitating intercourse.

Mammary Glands

Mammary glands are present in both sexes but normally produce milk only in females. Though not part of the reproductive system, the female mammary glands are important to reproduction. Within the glands, small sacs of epithelial tissue secrete milk, which drains into a series of ducts opening at the nipple. The breasts contain connective and fatty (adipose) tissue in addition to the mammary glands. Because the low level of estradiol in males limits the development of the fat deposits, male breasts usually remain small.

Male Reproductive Anatomy

The human male's external reproductive organs are the scrotum and penis. The internal reproductive organs consist of gonads that produce both sperm and reproductive hormones, accessory glands that secrete products essential to sperm movement, and ducts that carry the sperm and glandular secretions **(Figure 46.11)**.

Testes

The male gonads, or **testes** (singular, *testis*), consist of many highly coiled tubes surrounded by several layers of connective tissue. These tubes are the **seminiferous tubules**, where sperm form. The **Leydig cells**, scattered between the seminiferous tubules, produce testosterone and other androgens (see Chapter 45).

For most mammals, sperm production occurs properly only when the testes are cooler than normal body temperature. In humans and many other mammals, the **scrotum**, a fold of the body wall, maintains testis temperature about 2°C below that in the abdominal cavity. The testes develop high in the abdominal cavity and descend into the scrotum just before birth; a testis within a scrotum is often termed a *testicle*. In many rodents, the testes are drawn back into the abdominal cavity between breeding seasons, interrupting sperm maturation. Some mammals whose body temperature is low enough to allow sperm maturation—such as monotremes, whales, and elephants—retain the testes within the abdominal cavity at all times.

Ducts

From the seminiferous tubules of a testis, the sperm pass into the coiled tubules of the **epididymis**. In humans, it takes 3 weeks for sperm to pass through the 6-m-long tubules of each epididymis. During this passage, the sperm complete their maturation and become motile, although they acquire the ability to fertilize an egg only when exposed to the chemical environment of the female reproductive system. During **ejaculation**, the sperm are propelled from each epididymis through a muscular duct, the **vas deferens**. Each vas deferens (one from each epididymis) extends around and behind the urinary bladder, where it joins a duct from the seminal vesicle, forming a short **ejaculatory duct**. The ejaculatory ducts open into the **urethra**, the outlet tube for both the excretory system and the reproductive system. The urethra runs through the penis and opens to the outside at the tip of the penis.

Accessory Glands

Three sets of accessory glands—the seminal vesicles, the prostate gland, and the bulbourethral

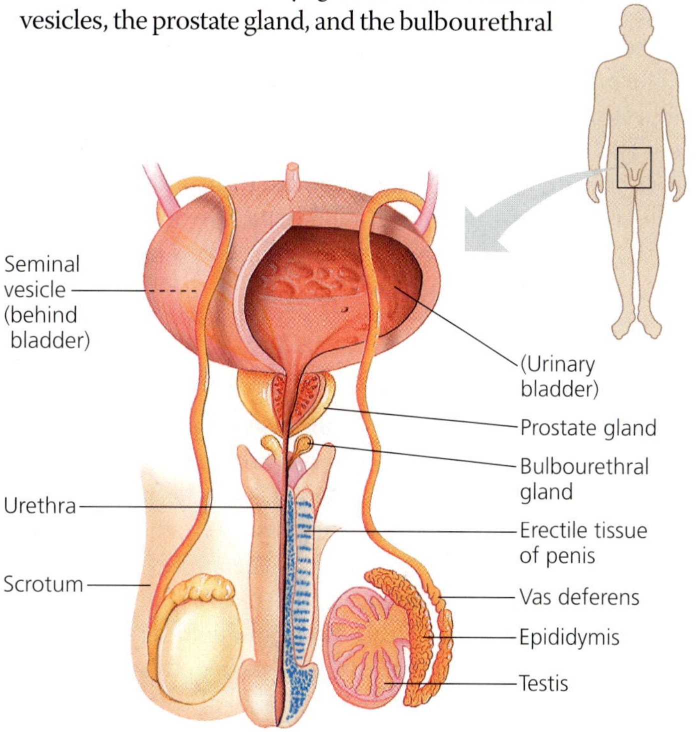

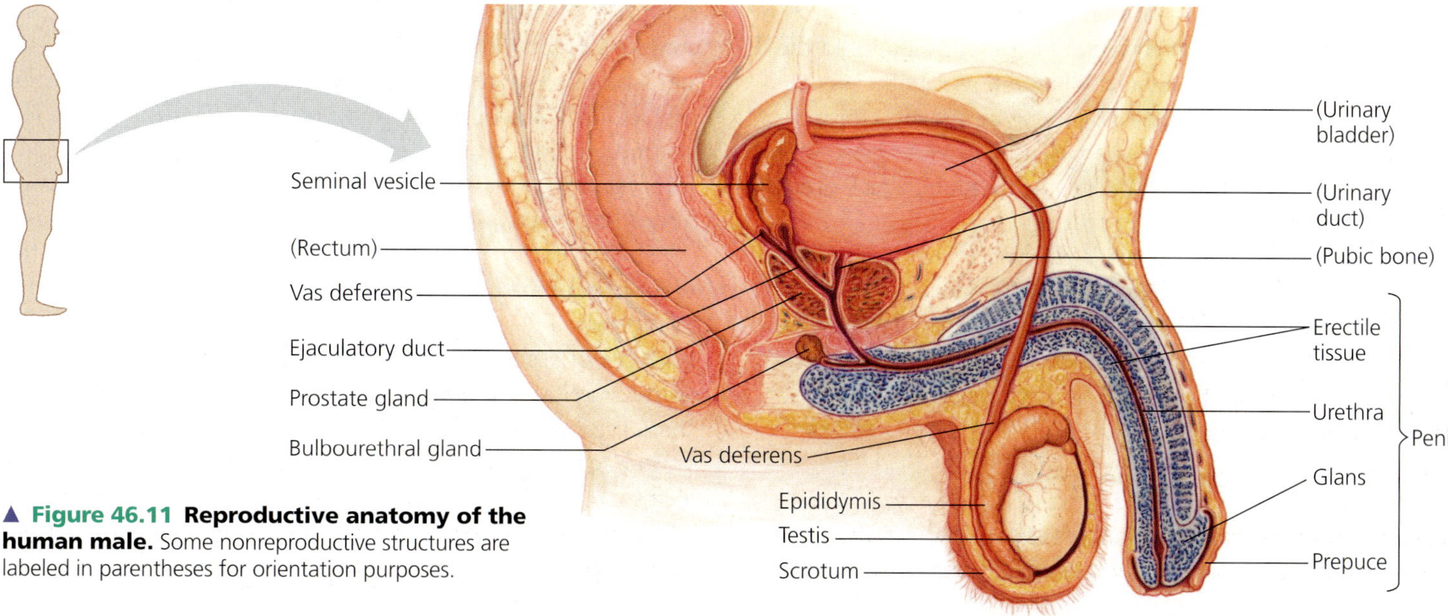

▲ **Figure 46.11 Reproductive anatomy of the human male.** Some nonreproductive structures are labeled in parentheses for orientation purposes.

glands—produce secretions that combine with sperm to form **semen**, the fluid that is ejaculated. Two **seminal vesicles** contribute about 60% of the volume of semen. The fluid from the seminal vesicles is thick, yellowish, and alkaline. It contains mucus, the sugar fructose (which provides most of the sperm's energy), a coagulating enzyme, ascorbic acid, and local regulators called prostaglandins (see Chapter 45).

The **prostate gland** secretes its products directly into the urethra through several small ducts. This fluid is thin and milky; it contains anticoagulant enzymes and citrate (a sperm nutrient). The prostate gland is the source of some of the most common medical problems of men over age 40. Benign (noncancerous) enlargement of the prostate occurs in more than half of all men in this age-group and in almost all men over 70. In addition, prostate cancer, which most often afflicts men 65 and older, is one of the most common human cancers.

The *bulbourethral glands* are a pair of small glands along the urethra below the prostate. Before ejaculation, they secrete clear mucus that neutralizes any acidic urine remaining in the urethra. Bulbourethral fluid also carries some sperm released before ejaculation, which is one reason for the high failure rate of the withdrawal method of birth control (coitus interruptus).

Penis

The human **penis** contains the urethra, as well as three cylinders of spongy erectile tissue. During sexual arousal, the erectile tissue, which is derived from modified veins and capillaries, fills with blood from the arteries. As this tissue fills, the increasing pressure seals off the veins that drain the penis, causing it to engorge with blood. The resulting erection enables the penis to be inserted into the vagina. Alcohol consumption, certain drugs, emotional issues, and aging all can cause a temporary inability to achieve an erection (erectile dysfunction). For individuals with long-term erectile dysfunction, drugs such as Viagra promote the vasodilating action of the local regulator nitric oxide (NO; see Chapter 45); the resulting relaxation of smooth muscles in the blood vessels of the penis enhances blood flow into the erectile tissues. Although all mammals rely on penile erection for mating, the penis of rodents, raccoons, walruses, whales, and several other mammals also contains a bone, the baculum, which probably further stiffens the penis for mating.

The main shaft of the penis is covered by relatively thick skin. The head, or glans, of the penis has a much thinner covering and is consequently more sensitive to stimulation. The human glans is covered by a fold of skin called the prepuce, or foreskin, which may be removed by circumcision.

Human Sexual Response

As mentioned earlier, many animals exhibit elaborate mating behavior. The arousal of sexual interest in humans is particularly complex, involving a variety of psychological as well as physical factors. Reproductive structures in the male and female that are quite different in appearance often serve similar functions, reflecting their shared developmental origin. For example, the same embryonic tissues give rise to the glans of the penis and the clitoris, the scrotum and the labia majora, and the skin on the penis and the labia minora.

The general pattern of human sexual response is similar in males and females. Two types of physiological reactions predominate in both sexes: **vasocongestion**, the filling of a tissue with blood, and **myotonia**, increased muscle tension. Both skeletal and smooth muscle may show sustained or rhythmic contractions, including those associated with orgasm.

The sexual response cycle can be divided into four phases: excitement, plateau, orgasm, and resolution. An important function of the excitement phase is to prepare the vagina and penis for **coitus** (sexual intercourse). During this phase, vasocongestion is particularly evident in erection of the penis and clitoris; enlargement of the testicles, labia, and breasts; and vaginal lubrication. Myotonia may occur, resulting in nipple erection or tension of the arms and legs.

In the plateau phase, these responses continue as a result of direct stimulation of the genitals. In females, the outer third of the vagina becomes vasocongested, while the inner two-thirds slightly expands. This change, coupled with the elevation of the uterus, forms a depression for receiving sperm at the back of the vagina. Breathing increases and heart rate rises, sometimes to 150 beats per minute—not only in response to the physical effort of sexual activity, but also as an involuntary response to stimulation of the autonomic nervous system (see Figure 49.8).

Orgasm is characterized by rhythmic, involuntary contractions of the reproductive structures in both sexes. Male orgasm has two stages. The first, emission, occurs when the glands and ducts of the reproductive tract contract, forcing semen into the urethra. Expulsion, or ejaculation, occurs when the urethra contracts and the semen is expelled. During female orgasm, the uterus and outer vagina contract, but the inner two-thirds of the vagina does not. Orgasm is the shortest phase of the sexual response cycle, usually lasting only a few seconds. In both sexes, contractions occur at about 0.8-second intervals and may also involve the anal sphincter and several abdominal muscles.

The resolution phase completes the cycle and reverses the responses of the earlier stages. Vasocongested organs return to their normal size and color, and muscles relax. Most of the changes of resolution are completed within 5 minutes, but some may take as long as an hour. Following orgasm, the male typically enters a refractory period, lasting anywhere from a few minutes to hours, during which erection and orgasm cannot be achieved. Females do not have a refractory period, making possible multiple orgasms within a short period of time.

CONCEPT CHECK 46.3

1. In the human sexual response, which organs undergo vasocongestion?
2. In theory, using a hot tub frequently might make it harder for a couple to conceive a child. Why?
3. **WHAT IF?** Suppose each vas deferens in a male was surgically sealed off. What changes would you expect in sexual response and ejaculate composition?

For suggested answers, see Appendix A.

CONCEPT **46.4**

The timing and pattern of meiosis in mammals differ for males and females

Reproduction in mammals involves two distinct types of gametes. Sperm are small and motile. In contrast, eggs, which provide the initial food stores for the embryo, are typically much larger. For embryonic development to be successful, eggs must mature in synchrony with the tissues of the female reproductive system that support the fertilized embryo. Reflecting these differences, egg and sperm development involve distinct patterns of meiotic division. We will highlight these distinctions, as well as several basic similarities, as we explore **gametogenesis**, the production of gametes.

Spermatogenesis, the formation and development of sperm, is continuous and prolific in adult males. To produce hundreds of millions of sperm each day, cell division and maturation occur throughout the seminiferous tubules coiled within the two testes. On page 1008, **Figure 46.12** details the steps and organization of spermatogenesis in humans. For a single sperm, the process takes about seven weeks from start to finish.

Oogenesis, the development of mature oocytes (eggs), is a prolonged process in the human female. Immature eggs form in the ovary of the female embryo but do not complete their development until years, and often decades, later. Page 1009 describes oogenesis in the human ovary. Be sure to study Figure 46.12 before proceeding.

Spermatogenesis differs from oogenesis in three significant ways. First, only in spermatogenesis do all four products of meiosis develop into mature gametes. In oogenesis, cytokinesis during meiosis is unequal, with almost all the cytoplasm segregated to a single daughter cell, the secondary oocyte. This large cell is destined to become the egg; the other products of meiosis, smaller cells called polar bodies, degenerate. Second, spermatogenesis, including the mitotic divisions of stem cells and differentiated spermatogonia, occurs throughout adolescence and adulthood. During oogenesis in human females, mitotic divisions are thought to be complete before birth, and the production of mature gametes ceases at about age 50. Third, spermatogenesis produces mature sperm from precursor cells in a continuous sequence, whereas oogenesis has long interruptions.

CONCEPT CHECK 46.4

1. How does the difference in size and cellular contents between sperm and eggs relate to their specific functions in reproduction?
2. Oogenesis is often described as the production of a haploid ovum, or egg, by meiosis; but in some animals, including humans, this is not an entirely accurate description. Explain.
3. **WHAT IF?** Suppose you are analyzing the DNA from the polar bodies formed during human oogenesis. If the mother has a mutation in a known human disease gene, would analyzing the polar body DNA allow you to infer whether the mutation is present in the mature oocyte? Explain.

For suggested answers, see Appendix A.

CONCEPT **46.5**

The interplay of tropic and sex hormones regulates mammalian reproduction

In both males and females, the coordinated actions of hormones from the hypothalamus, anterior pituitary, and gonads govern human reproduction. The hypothalamus secretes gonadotropin-releasing hormone (GnRH), which directs the anterior pituitary to secrete the gonadotropins, follicle-stimulating hormone (FSH) and luteinizing hormone (LH) (see Figure 45.17). These two hormones regulate gametogenesis directly, through target tissues in the gonads, as well as indirectly, by regulating sex hormone production. The principal sex hormones are steroid hormones: in males, androgens, especially testosterone; in females, estrogens, especially estradiol, and progesterone. Like the gonadotropins, the sex hormones regulate gametogenesis directly and indirectly.

Sex hormones serve many functions in addition to promoting gamete production. In many vertebrates, androgens are responsible for male vocalizations, such as the territorial songs of birds and the mating calls of frogs. During human embryogenesis, androgens promote the development of the primary sex characteristics of males, the structures directly involved in reproduction. These include the seminal vesicles and other ducts, as well as external reproductive anatomy. At puberty, sex hormones in both males and females induce formation of secondary sex characteristics, the physical and behavioral features that are not directly related to the reproductive system. In males, androgens cause the voice to deepen, facial and pubic

▼ Figure 46.12

Exploring Human Gametogenesis

Spermatogenesis

These drawings correlate the mitotic and meiotic divisions in sperm development with the microscopic structure of seminiferous tubules. The initial or *primordial* germ cells of the embryonic testes divide and differentiate into stem cells that divide mitotically to form **spermatogonia**, which in turn generate spermatocytes, also by mitosis. Each spermatocyte gives rise to four spermatids through meiotic cell divisions that reduce the chromosome number from diploid ($2n = 46$ in humans) to haploid ($n = 23$). Spermatids undergo extensive changes in cell shape and organization to differentiate into sperm.

Within the seminiferous tubules, there is a concentric organization of the steps of spermatogenesis. Stem cells are situated near the outer edge of the tubules. As spermatogenesis proceeds, cells move steadily inward as they pass through the spermatocyte and spermatid stages. In the last step, mature sperm are released into the lumen of the tubule. The sperm pass from the lumen into the epididymis, where they become motile.

The structure of a sperm cell fits its function. In humans, as in most species, a head containing the haploid nucleus is tipped with a special vesicle, the **acrosome**, which contains enzymes that help the sperm penetrate the egg. Behind the head, the sperm cell contains large numbers of mitochondria (or a single large mitochondrion in some species) that provide ATP for movement of the tail, which is a flagellum.

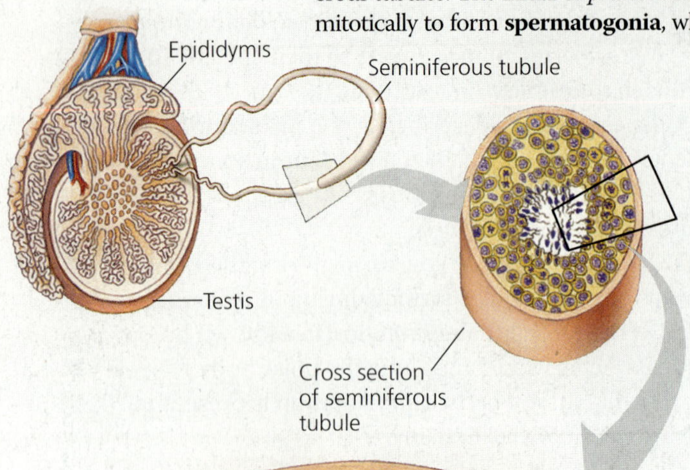

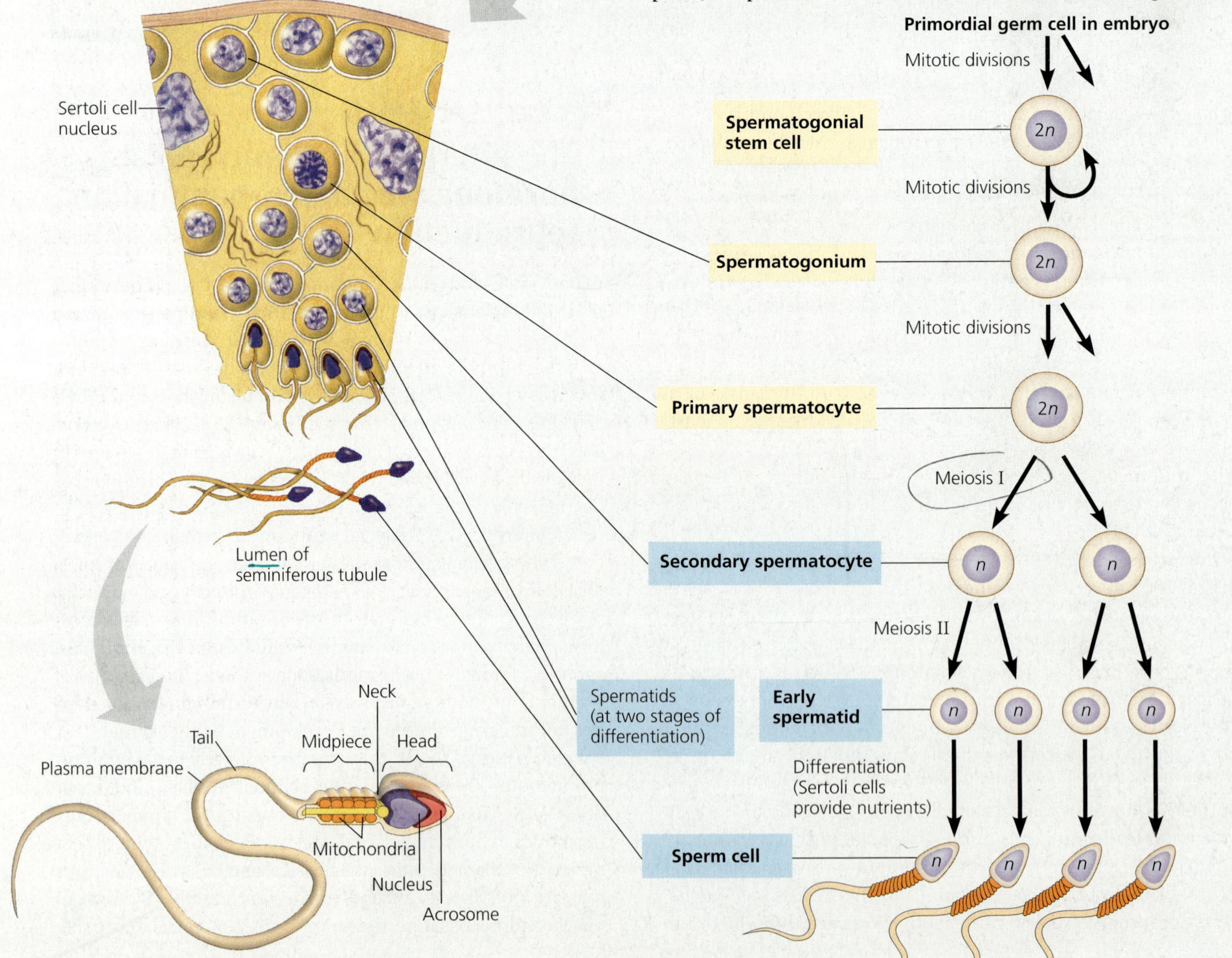

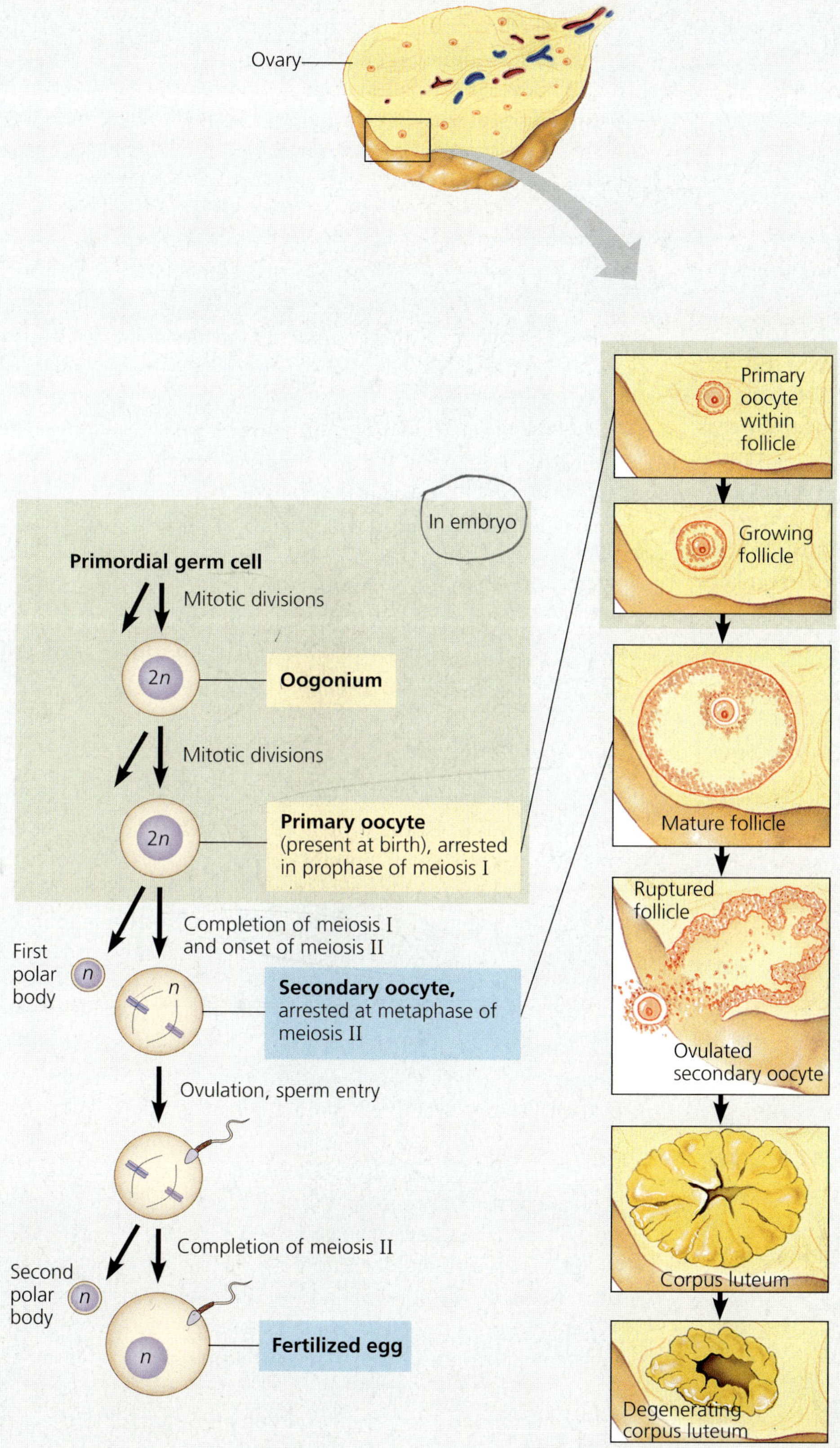

Oogenesis

Oogenesis begins in the female embryo with the production of **oogonia** from primordial germ cells. The oogonia divide mitotically to form cells that begin meiosis, but stop the process at prophase I. Contained within small follicles (cavities lined with protective cells), these **primary oocytes** arrest development before birth. Beginning at puberty, follicle-stimulating hormone (FSH) periodically stimulates a small group of follicles to resume growth and development. Typically, only one follicle fully matures each month, with its primary oocyte completing meiosis I. The second meiotic division begins, but stops at metaphase. Thus arrested in meiosis II, the **secondary oocyte** is released at ovulation, when its follicle breaks open. Only if a sperm penetrates the oocyte does meiosis II resume. (In other animal species, the sperm may enter the oocyte at the same stage, earlier, or later.) Each of the two meiotic divisions involves unequal cytokinesis, with the smaller cells becoming polar bodies that eventually degenerate (the first polar body may or may not divide again). Thus, the functional product of complete oogenesis is a single mature egg already containing a sperm head; fertilization is defined strictly as the fusion of the haploid nuclei of the sperm and secondary oocyte, although we often use it loosely to mean the entry of the sperm head into the egg.

The ruptured follicle left behind after ovulation develops into the corpus luteum. If the released oocyte is not fertilized and does not complete oogenesis, the corpus luteum degenerates.

It was long thought that women and most other female mammals are born with all the primary oocytes they will ever have. In 2004, however, researchers reported that multiplying oogonia exist in the ovaries of adult mice and can develop into oocytes. Scientists are now looking for similar cells in human ovaries. It is possible that the marked decline in fertility that occurs as women age results from a depletion of oogonia in addition to the degeneration of aging oocytes.

hair to develop, and muscles to grow (by stimulating protein synthesis). Androgens also promote specific sexual behaviors and sex drive, as well as an increase in general aggressiveness. Estrogens similarly have multiple effects in females. At puberty, estradiol stimulates breast and pubic hair development. Estradiol also influences female sexual behavior, induces fat deposition in the breasts and hips, increases water retention, and alters calcium metabolism.

Gametogenesis involves the same basic set of hormonal controls in males and females. In examining these hormonal circuits, we will begin with the simpler system found in males.

Hormonal Control of the Male Reproductive System

In males, the FSH and LH secreted in response to GnRH are both required for normal spermatogenesis. Each acts on a distinct type of cell in the testis **(Figure 46.13)**. FSH promotes the activity of Sertoli cells. Within the seminiferous tubules, these cells nourish developing sperm (see Figure 46.12). LH regulates Leydig cells, cells located in the interstitial space between the seminiferous tubules. In response to LH, Leydig cells secrete testosterone and other androgens, which promote spermatogenesis in the tubules. Both androgen secretion and spermatogenesis occur continuously from puberty onward.

Two negative-feedback mechanisms control sex hormone production in males (see Figure 46.13). Testosterone regulates blood levels of GnRH, FSH, and LH through inhibitory effects on the hypothalamus and anterior pituitary. In addition, **inhibin**, a hormone that in males is produced by Sertoli cells, acts on the anterior pituitary gland to reduce FSH secretion. Together, these negative-feedback circuits maintain androgen production at optimal levels.

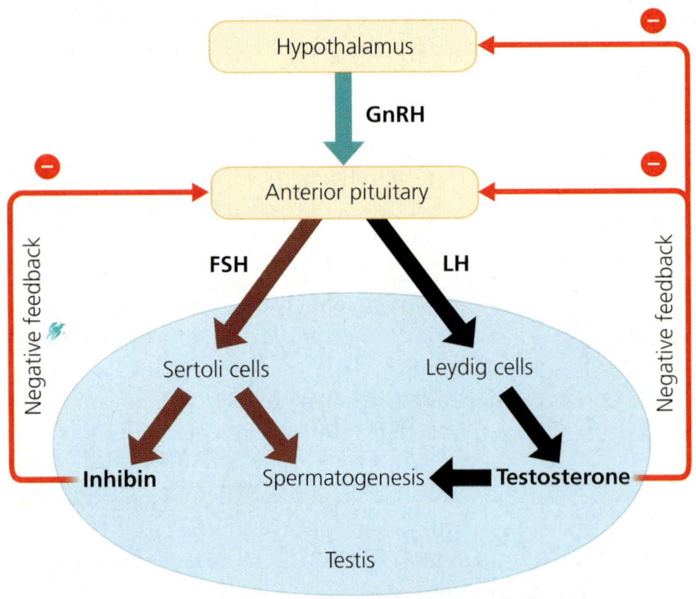

▲ **Figure 46.13 Hormonal control of the testes.** Gonadotropin-releasing hormone (GnRH) from the hypothalamus stimulates the anterior pituitary to secrete two gonadotropins, follicle-stimulating hormone (FSH) and luteinizing hormone (LH). FSH acts on Sertoli cells, which nourish developing sperm. LH acts on Leydig cells, which produce androgens, chiefly testosterone. Negative feedback by testosterone on the hypothalamus and anterior pituitary regulates blood levels of GnRH, LH, and FSH. FSH secretion is also subject to negative feedback by inhibin secreted by Sertoli cells.

The Reproductive Cycles of Females

Upon reaching sexual maturity, human males carry out gametogenesis continuously, whereas human females produce gametes in cycles. Ovulation occurs only after the endometrium (lining of the uterus) has started to thicken and develop a rich blood supply, preparing the uterus for the possible implantation of an embryo. If pregnancy does not occur, the uterine lining is sloughed off, and another cycle begins. The cyclic shedding of the endometrium from the uterus, which occurs in a flow through the cervix and vagina, is called **menstruation**.

There are two closely linked reproductive cycles in human females. The changes in the uterus define the **menstrual cycle**, also called the **uterine cycle**. Menstrual cycles average 28 days in length (although cycles vary, ranging from about 20 to 40 days). The cyclic events that occur in the ovaries define the **ovarian cycle**. Hormone activity links the two cycles, synchronizing ovarian follicle growth and ovulation with the establishment of a uterine lining that can support embryonic development.

Let's examine the reproductive cycle of the human female in more detail **(Figure 46.14)**. Although the ovaries produce inhibin, we will omit this hormone from our discussion, since its function in females is unclear. We'll begin with the series of events that occur before the egg is fertilized.

The Ovarian Cycle

The reproductive cycle begins ❶ with the release from the hypothalamus of GnRH, which ❷ stimulates the anterior pituitary to secrete small amounts of FSH and LH. ❸ Follicle-stimulating hormone (as its name implies) stimulates follicle growth, aided by LH, and ❹ the cells of the growing follicles start to make estradiol. Notice that there is a slow rise in the amount of estradiol secreted during most of the **follicular phase**, the part of the ovarian cycle during which follicles grow and oocytes mature. (Several follicles begin to grow with each cycle, but usually only one matures; the others disintegrate.) The low levels of estradiol inhibit secretion of the pituitary hormones, keeping the levels of FSH and LH relatively low. During this portion of the cycle, regulation of the hormones controlling reproduction closely parallels the regulation observed in males (see Figure 46.13).

❺ When estradiol secretion by the growing follicle begins to rise steeply, ❻ the FSH and LH levels increase markedly. Whereas a low level of estradiol inhibits the secretion of pituitary gonadotropins, a high concentration has the opposite effect: It stimulates gonadotropin secretion by acting on the hypothalamus to increase its output of GnRH. The effect is greater for LH because the high concentration of estradiol increases the GnRH sensitivity of LH-releasing cells in the pituitary. In addition, follicles respond more strongly to LH at this stage because more of their cells have receptors for this hormone.

The increase in LH concentration caused by increased estradiol secretion from the growing follicle is an example of positive feedback. The result is final maturation of the follicle. ⑦ The maturing follicle, which contains an internal fluid-filled cavity, grows very large, forming a bulge near the surface of the ovary. The follicular phase ends at ovulation, about a day after the LH surge. In response to the peak in LH levels, the follicle and adjacent wall of the ovary rupture, releasing the secondary oocyte. There is sometimes a distinctive pain in the lower abdomen at or near the time of ovulation; this pain localizes to the left or right side, corresponding to whichever ovary has matured a follicle during that cycle.

The **luteal phase** of the ovarian cycle follows ovulation. ⑧ LH stimulates the follicular tissue left behind in the ovary to transform into the corpus luteum, a glandular structure. Under continued stimulation by LH, the corpus luteum secretes progesterone and estradiol. As progesterone and estradiol levels rise, the combination of these steroid hormones exerts negative feedback on the hypothalamus and pituitary, reducing the secretion of LH and FSH to very low levels. Near the end of the luteal phase, low gonadotropin levels cause the corpus luteum to disintegrate, triggering a sharp decline in estradiol and progesterone concentrations. The decreasing levels of ovarian steroid hormones liberate the hypothalamus and pituitary from the negative-feedback effect of these hormones. The pituitary can then begin to secrete enough FSH to stimulate the growth of new follicles in the ovary, initiating the next ovarian cycle.

The Uterine (Menstrual) Cycle

Prior to ovulation, ovarian steroid hormones stimulate the uterus to prepare for support of an embryo. Estradiol se-

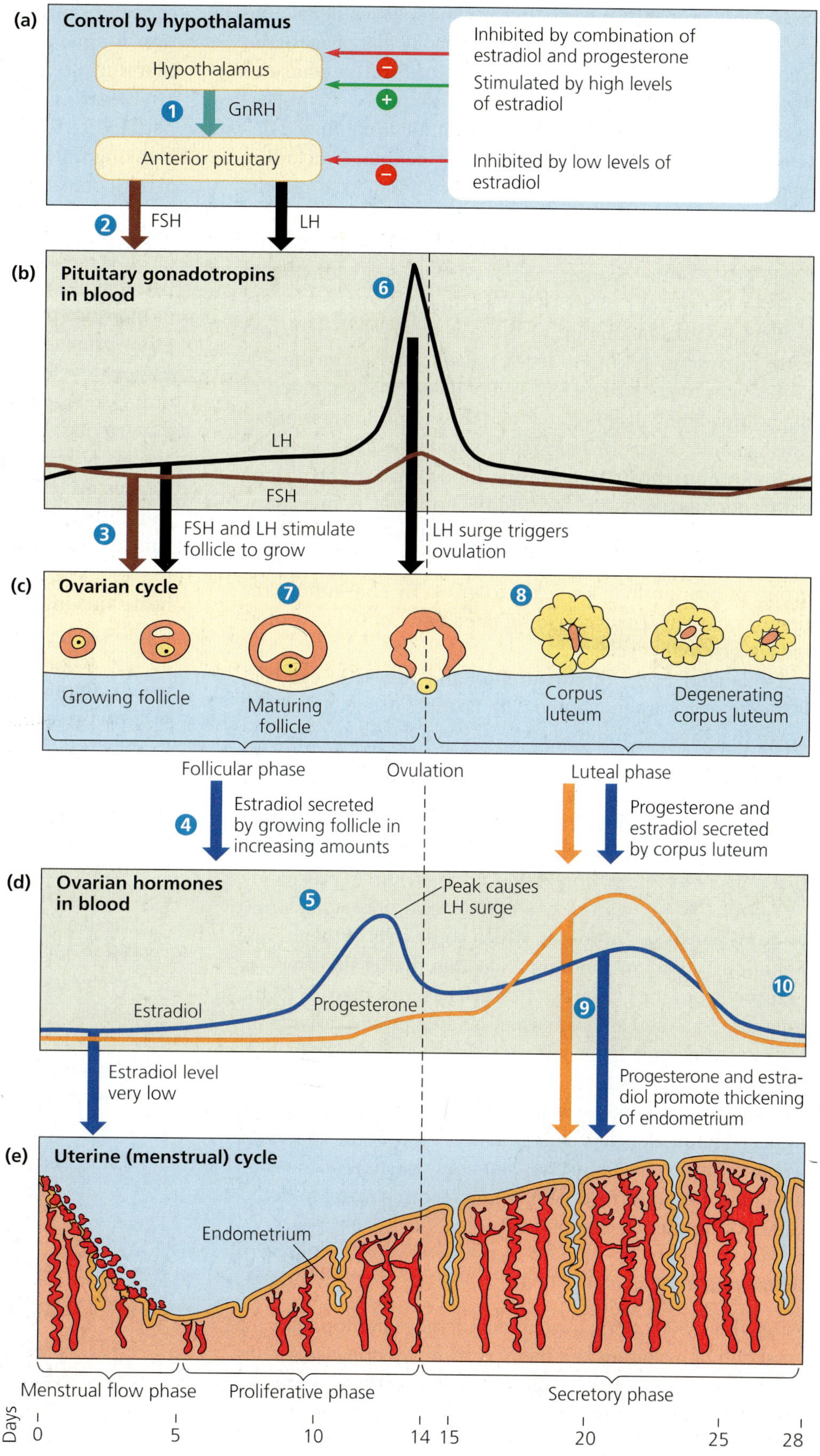

▲ **Figure 46.14 The reproductive cycle of the human female.** This figure shows how (c) the ovarian cycle and (e) the uterine (menstrual) cycle are regulated by changing hormone levels in the blood, depicted in parts (a), (b), and (d). The time scale at the bottom of the figure applies to parts (b)–(e).

creted in increasing amounts by growing follicles signals the endometrium to thicken. In this way, the follicular phase of the ovarian cycle is coordinated with the **proliferative phase** of the uterine cycle. After ovulation, 9 estradiol and progesterone secreted by the corpus luteum stimulate continued development and maintenance of the uterine lining, including enlargement of arteries and growth of endometrial glands. These glands secrete a nutrient fluid that can sustain an early embryo even before it implants in the uterine lining. Thus, the luteal phase of the ovarian cycle is coordinated with what is called the **secretory phase** of the uterine cycle.

10 Upon disintegration of the corpus luteum, the rapid drop in ovarian hormone levels causes arteries in the endometrium to constrict. Deprived of its circulation, much of the uterine lining disintegrates, and the uterus, in response to prostaglandin secretion, contracts. Small blood vessels in the endometrium constrict, releasing blood that is shed along with endometrial tissue and fluid. The result is menstruation—the **menstrual flow phase** of the uterine cycle. During menstruation, which usually persists for a few days, a new group of ovarian follicles begin to grow. By convention, the first day of menstruation is designated day 1 of the new uterine (and ovarian) cycle.

Cycle after cycle, the maturation and release of egg cells from the ovary are integrated with changes in the uterus, the organ that must accommodate an embryo if the egg cell is fertilized. If an embryo has not implanted in the endometrium by the end of the secretory phase of the uterine cycle, a new menstrual flow commences, marking the start of the next cycle. Later in the chapter, you will learn about override mechanisms that prevent disintegration of the endometrium in pregnancy.

About 7% of women of reproductive age suffer from **endometriosis**, a disorder in which some cells of the uterine lining migrate to an abdominal location that is abnormal, or **ectopic** (from the Greek *ektopos*, away from a place). Having migrated to a location such as an oviduct, ovary, or large intestine, the ectopic tissue still responds to stimulation by hormones in the bloodstream. Like the uterine endometrium, the ectopic tissue therefore swells and breaks down each ovarian cycle, resulting in pelvic pain and bleeding into the abdomen. Treatments, involving hormonal therapy or surgery, focus on lessening discomfort, while ongoing research seeks to determine why endometriosis occurs.

Menopause

After about 500 cycles, a woman undergoes **menopause**, the cessation of ovulation and menstruation. Menopause usually occurs between the ages of 46 and 54. During these years, the ovaries lose their responsiveness to FSH and LH, resulting in a decline in estradiol production by the ovary.

Menopause is an unusual phenomenon; in most other species, both females and males retain their reproductive capacity throughout life. Is there an evolutionary explanation for menopause? One intriguing hypothesis proposes that during early human evolution, undergoing menopause after bearing several children allowed a mother to provide better care for her children and grandchildren, thereby increasing the survival of individuals who share much of her genetic makeup.

Menstrual Versus Estrous Cycles

All female mammals undergo a thickening of the endometrium prior to ovulation, but only humans and certain other primates have menstrual cycles. Other mammals have **estrous cycles**, in which in the absence of a pregnancy, the uterus reabsorbs the endometrium and no extensive fluid flow occurs. Whereas human females may engage in sexual activity at any point in their menstrual cycle, mammals with estrous cycles typically copulate only during the period surrounding ovulation. This period of sexual activity, called estrus (from the Latin *oestrus*, frenzy, passion), is the only time the female is receptive to mating. Estrus is sometimes called heat, and indeed, the female's body temperature increases slightly.

The length and frequency of reproductive cycles vary widely among mammals. Bears and wolves have one estrous cycle per year; elephants have several. Rats have estrous cycles throughout the year, each lasting only 5 days.

CONCEPT CHECK 46.5

1. FSH and LH get their names from events of the female reproductive cycle, but they also function in males. How are their functions in females and males similar?
2. How does an estrous cycle differ from a menstrual cycle, and in what animals are the two types of cycles found?
3. **WHAT IF?** If a human female begins taking estradiol and progesterone immediately after the start of a new menstrual cycle, what effect on ovulation should she expect? Explain.

For suggested answers, see Appendix A.

CONCEPT **46.6**

In placental mammals, an embryo develops fully within the mother's uterus

Having surveyed the ovarian and uterine cycles of human females, we turn now to reproduction itself, beginning with the events that transform an egg into a developing embryo.

Conception, Embryonic Development, and Birth

During human copulation, 2–5 mL of semen is transferred, with 70–130 million sperm in each milliliter. The alkalinity of the semen helps neutralize the acidic environment of the vagina, protecting the sperm and increasing their motility. When first ejaculated, the semen coagulates, which may serve to keep the ejaculate in place until sperm reach the cervix. Soon after, anticoagulants liquefy the semen, and the sperm begin swimming through the uterus and oviducts.

Fertilization—also called **conception** in humans—occurs when a sperm fuses with an egg (mature oocyte) in the oviduct **(Figure 46.15a)**. About 24 hours later, the resulting zygote begins dividing, a process called **cleavage**. After another 2–3 days, the embryo typically arrives at the uterus as a ball of 16 cells. By about 1 week after fertilization, cleavage has produced an embryonic stage called the **blastocyst**, a sphere of cells surrounding a central cavity.

Several days after blastocyst formation, the embryo implants into the endometrium **(Figure 46.15b)**. Only after implantation can an embryo develop into a fetus. The implanted embryo secretes hormones that signal its presence and regulate the mother's reproductive system. One embryonic hormone, **human chorionic gonadotropin (hCG)**, acts like pituitary LH in maintaining secretion of progesterone and estrogens by the corpus luteum through the first few months of pregnancy. In the absence of this hormonal override during pregnancy, the corpus luteum would deteriorate and progesterone levels would drop, resulting in menstruation and loss of the embryo. Levels of hCG in the maternal blood are so high that some is excreted in the urine, where its presence is the basis of a common early pregnancy test.

The condition of carrying one or more embryos in the uterus is called **pregnancy**, or **gestation**. Human pregnancy averages 266 days (38 weeks) from fertilization of the egg, or 40 weeks from the start of the last menstrual cycle. Duration of pregnancy in other placental mammals correlates with body size and the maturity of the young at birth. Many rodents have gestation periods of about 21 days, whereas those of dogs are closer to 60 days. In cows, gestation averages 270 days (almost the same as in humans), while in elephants it lasts more than 600 days.

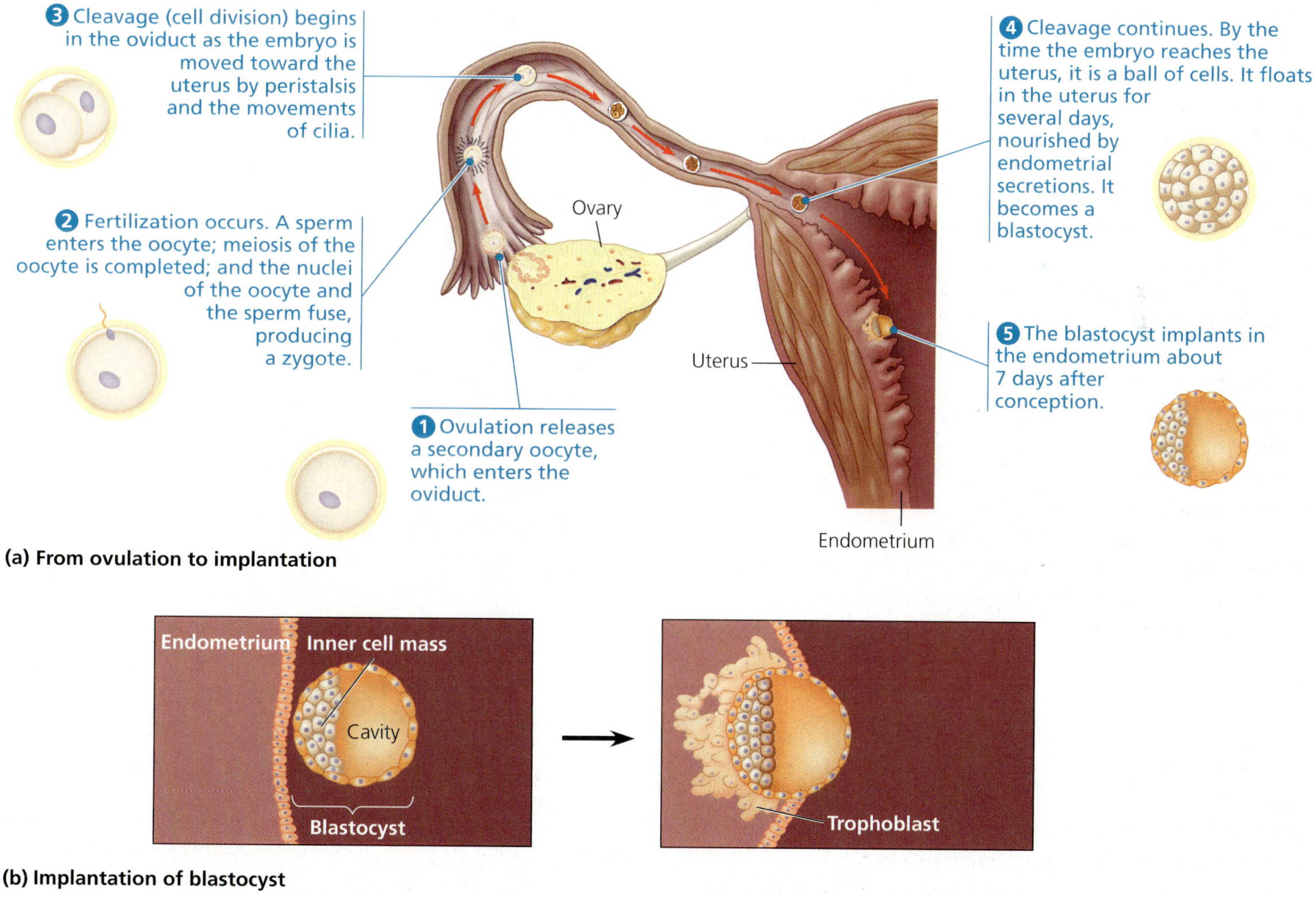

▲ **Figure 46.15 Formation of the zygote and early post-fertilization events.**

Not all fertilized eggs are capable of completing development. Many pregnancies terminate spontaneously as a result of chromosomal or developmental abnormalities. Much less often, a fertilized egg lodges in the oviduct (fallopian tube), resulting in a tubal, or ectopic, pregnancy. Such pregnancies cannot be sustained and may rupture the oviduct, resulting in serious internal bleeding. A number of conditions, including endometriosis, increase the likelihood of tubal pregnancy. Bacterial infections arising during childbirth, from medical procedures, or as a sexually transmitted disease can also scar the oviduct, making ectopic pregnancy more likely.

First Trimester

Human gestation can be divided for convenience into three **trimesters** of about three months each. The first trimester is the time of most radical change for both the mother and the embryo. Let's take up our story where we left off, at implantation. The endometrium responds to implantation by growing over the blastocyst. The embryo's body structures now begin to differentiate. (You will learn much more about embryonic development in Chapter 47.)

During its first 2–4 weeks of development, the embryo obtains nutrients directly from the endometrium. Meanwhile, the outer layer of the blastocyst, called the **trophoblast**, grows outward and mingles with the endometrium, eventually helping form the **placenta**. This disk-shaped organ, containing both embryonic and maternal blood vessels, can weigh close to 1 kg. Material diffusing between the maternal and embryonic circulatory systems supplies nutrients, provides immune protection, exchanges respiratory gases, and disposes of metabolic wastes for the embryo. Blood from the embryo travels to the placenta through the arteries of the umbilical cord and returns via the umbilical vein **(Figure 46.16)**.

Splitting of the embryo during the first month of development can result in identical, or *monozygotic* (one-egg), twins. Fraternal, or *dizygotic*, twins arise in a very different way: Two follicles mature in a single cycle, followed by independent fertilization and implantation of two genetically distinct embryos.

The first trimester is the main period of **organogenesis**, the development of the body organs **(Figure 46.17)**. It is during organogenesis that the embryo is most susceptible to damage, such as from radiation or drugs, that can lead to birth defects. At 8 weeks, all the major structures of the adult are present in rudimentary form, and the embryo is called a **fetus**. The heart begins beating by the 4th week; a heartbeat can be detected at 8–10 weeks. At the end of the first trimester, the fetus, although well differentiated, is only 5 cm long.

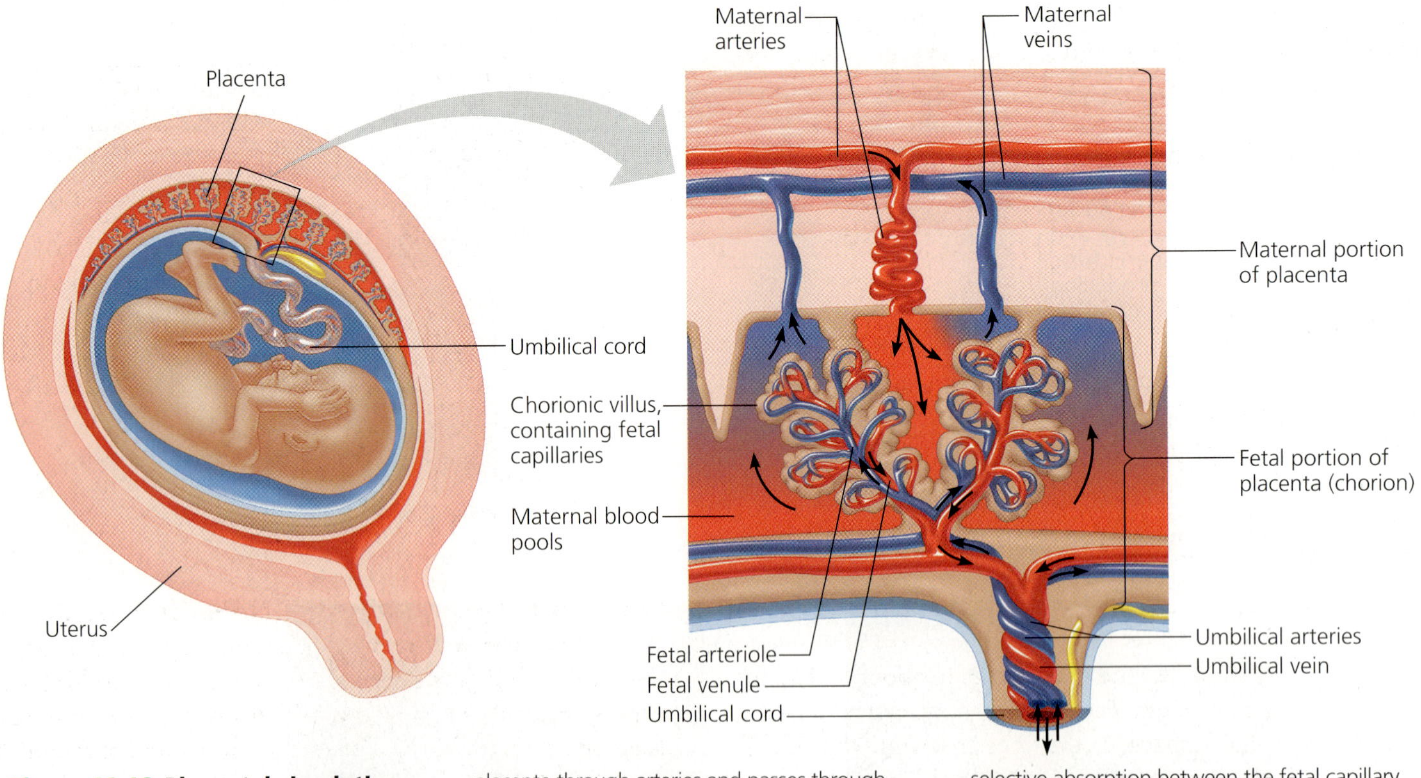

▲ **Figure 46.16 Placental circulation.** From the 4th week of development until birth, the placenta, a combination of maternal and embryonic tissues, transports nutrients, respiratory gases, and wastes between the embryo or fetus and the mother. Maternal blood enters the placenta in arteries, flows through blood pools in the endometrium, and leaves via veins. Embryonic or fetal blood, which remains in vessels, enters the placenta through arteries and passes through capillaries in fingerlike chorionic villi, where oxygen and nutrients are acquired. As indicated in the drawing, the fetal (or embryonic) capillaries and villi project into the maternal portion of the placenta. Fetal blood leaves the placenta through veins leading back to the fetus. Materials are exchanged by diffusion, active transport, and selective absorption between the fetal capillary bed and the maternal blood pools.

? *In a very rare genetic disorder, the absence of a particular enzyme leads to increased testosterone production. When the fetus has this disorder, the mother develops a male-like pattern of body hair during the pregnancy. Explain.*

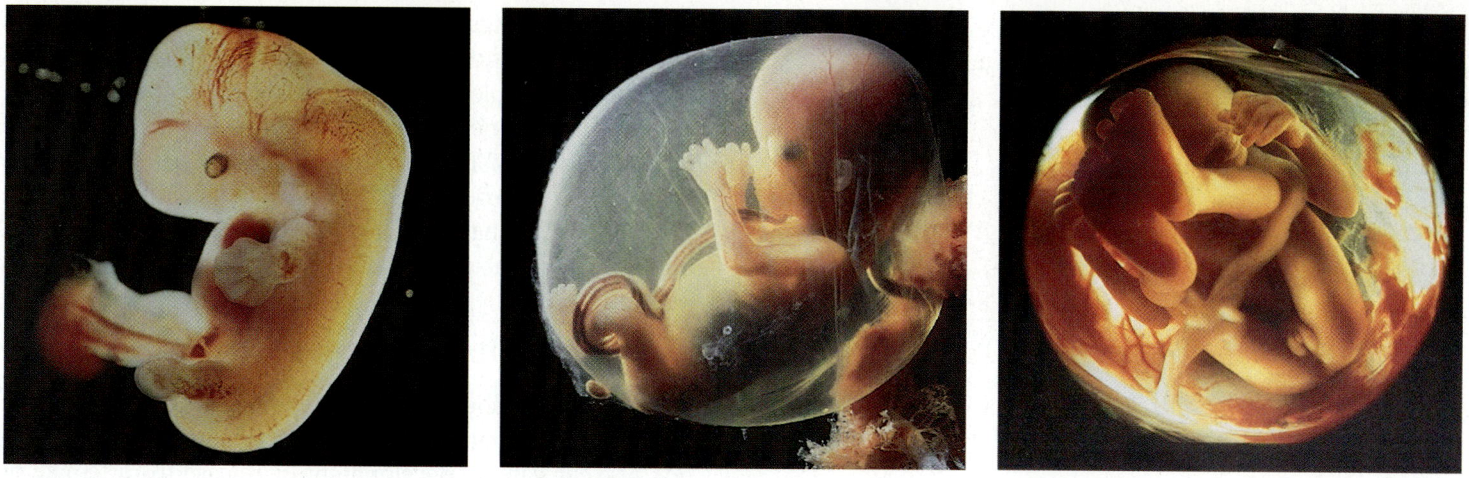

(a) 5 weeks. Limb buds, eyes, the heart, the liver, and rudiments of all other organs have started to develop in the embryo, which is only about 1 cm long.

(b) 14 weeks. Growth and development of the offspring, now called a fetus, continue during the second trimester. This fetus is about 6 cm long.

(c) 20 weeks. Growth to nearly 20 cm in length requires adoption of the fetal position (head at knees) due to the limited space available.

▲ **Figure 46.17 Human fetal development.**

Meanwhile, the mother is also undergoing rapid changes. High levels of progesterone initiate changes in her reproductive system: increased mucus in the cervix forms a plug to protect against infection, the maternal part of the placenta grows, the uterus gets larger, and (by negative feedback on the hypothalamus and pituitary) ovulation and menstrual cycling stop. The breasts also enlarge rapidly and are often quite tender. About three-fourths of all pregnant women experience nausea, misleadingly called "morning sickness," during the first trimester.

Second Trimester

During the second trimester, the uterus grows enough for the pregnancy to become obvious. The fetus itself grows to about 30 cm in length and is very active. The mother may feel fetal movements as early as one month into the second trimester; fetal activity is typically visible through the abdominal wall one to two months later. Hormone levels stabilize as hCG declines; the corpus luteum deteriorates; and the placenta completely takes over the production of progesterone, the hormone that maintains the pregnancy.

Third Trimester

During the final trimester, the fetus grows to about 3–4 kg in weight and 50 cm in length. Fetal activity may decrease as the fetus fills the available space. As the fetus grows and the uterus expands around it, the mother's abdominal organs become compressed and displaced, leading to frequent urination, digestive blockages, and strain in the back muscles.

A complex interplay of local regulators (prostaglandins) and hormones (chiefly estradiol and oxytocin) induces and regulates **labor**, the process by which childbirth occurs **(Figure 46.18)**. A series of strong, rhythmic uterine contractions during the three stages of labor bring about birth, or *parturition.* The first stage is the opening up and thinning of the cervix, ending with complete dilation. The second stage is expulsion, or delivery, of the baby. Continuous strong contractions force the fetus out of the uterus and through the vagina. The final stage of labor is delivery of the placenta. **Figure 46.19** on the next page summarizes these three stages.

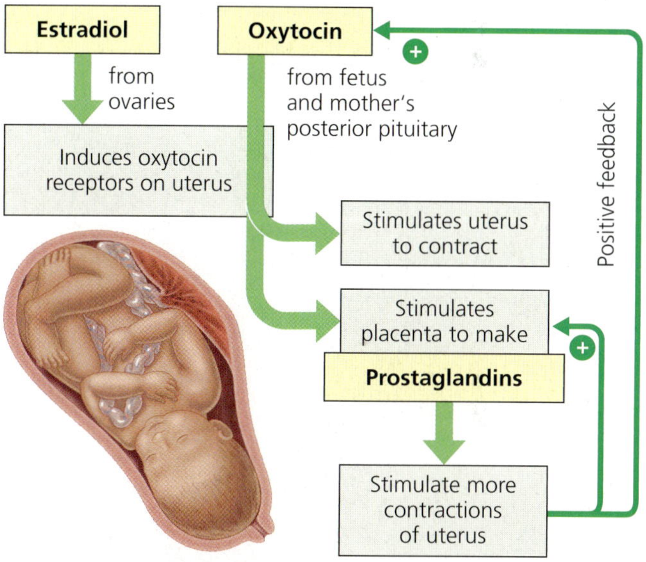

▲ **Figure 46.18 A model for the induction of labor.**

? *What would happen if a pregnant woman were given a single dose of oxytocin at the end of 39 weeks gestation?*

Lactation is an aspect of postnatal care unique to mammals. In response to suckling by the newborn, as well as changes in estradiol levels after birth, the hypothalamus signals the anterior pituitary to secrete prolactin, which stimulates the mammary glands to produce milk. Suckling also stimulates the

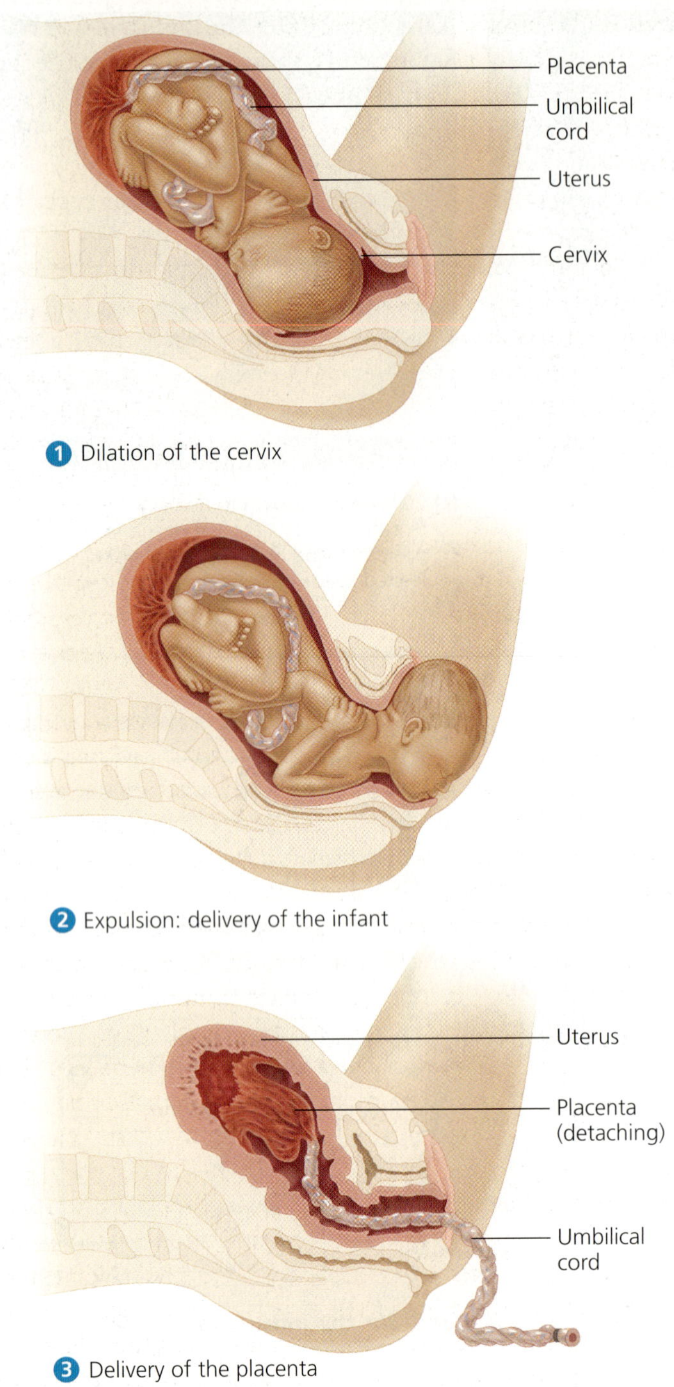

▲ **Figure 46.19 The three stages of labor.**

secretion of a posterior pituitary hormone, oxytocin, which triggers release of milk from the mammary glands (see Figure 45.15).

Maternal Immune Tolerance of the Embryo and Fetus

Pregnancy is an immunological puzzle. Half of the embryo's genes are inherited from the father; thus, many of the chemical markers present on the surface of the embryo are foreign to the mother. Why, then, does the mother not reject the embryo as a foreign body, as she would a tissue or organ graft from another person? One intriguing clue comes from the relationship between certain autoimmune disorders and pregnancy. It is known, for example, that the symptoms of rheumatoid arthritis, an autoimmune disease of the joints, become less severe during pregnancy. Thus, the overall regulation of the immune system appears to be altered by the reproductive process. Sorting out these changes and how they might protect the developing fetus is an active area of research for immunologists.

Contraception and Abortion

Contraception, the deliberate prevention of pregnancy, can be achieved in a number of ways. Some contraceptive methods prevent gamete development or release from female or male gonads; others prevent fertilization by keeping sperm and egg apart; and still others prevent implantation of an embryo **(Figure 46.20)**. The following brief introduction to the biology of the most often used methods makes no pretense of being a contraception manual. For more complete information, you should consult a health-care provider.

Fertilization can be prevented by abstinence from sexual intercourse or by any of several barriers that keep live sperm from contacting the egg. Temporary abstinence, often called the **rhythm method** of birth control or **natural family planning**, depends on refraining from intercourse when conception is most likely. Because the egg can survive in the oviduct for 24–48 hours and sperm for up to 5 days, a couple practicing temporary abstinence should not engage in intercourse for a number of days prior and subsequent to ovulation. The most effective methods for timing ovulation combine several indicators, including changes in cervical mucus and body temperature during the menstrual cycle. Thus, natural family planning requires that the couple be knowledgeable about these physiological signs. A pregnancy rate of 10–20% is typically reported for couples practicing natural family planning. (Pregnancy rate is the average number of women who become pregnant during a year for every 100 women using a particular pregnancy prevention method, expressed as a percentage.) Some couples use ovulation-timing methods to *increase* the probability of conception.

As a method of preventing fertilization, *coitus interruptus*, or withdrawal (removal of the penis from the vagina before ejaculation), is unreliable. Sperm from a previous ejaculate may be transferred in secretions that precede ejaculation. Furthermore, a split-second lapse in timing or willpower can result in tens of millions of sperm being transferred before withdrawal.

The several **barrier methods** of contraception that block the sperm from meeting the egg have pregnancy rates of less than 10%. The **condom** is a thin, latex rubber or natural membrane sheath that fits over the penis to collect the semen. For sexually active individuals, latex condoms are the only contraceptives that are highly effective in preventing the spread of sexually transmitted diseases, including AIDS. (This protection is, however, not absolute.) Another common barrier

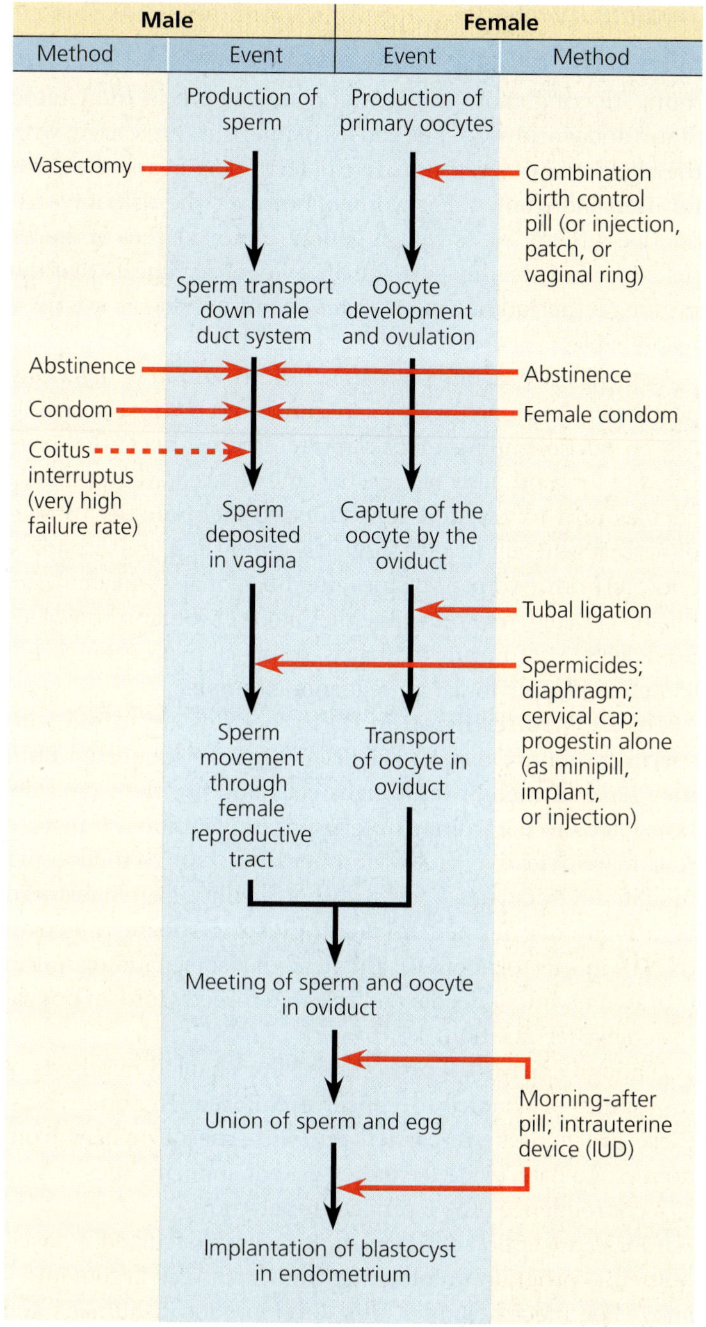

▲ **Figure 46.20 Mechanisms of several contraceptive methods.** Red arrows indicate where these methods, devices, or products interfere with events from the production of sperm and primary oocytes to an implanted, developing embryo.

device is the **diaphragm**, a dome-shaped rubber cap inserted into the upper portion of the vagina before intercourse. Both of these devices have lower pregnancy rates when used in conjunction with a spermicidal (sperm-killing) foam or jelly. Other barrier devices include the cervical cap, which fits tightly around the opening of the cervix and is held in place by suction, and the vaginal pouch, or "female condom."

Except for complete abstinence from sexual intercourse, the most effective means of birth control are sterilization, intrauterine devices (IUDs), and hormonal contraceptives. Sterilization (discussed later) is almost 100% effective. The IUD has a pregnancy rate of 1% or less and is the most commonly used reversible method of birth control outside the United States. Placed in the uterus by a doctor, the IUD interferes with fertilization and implantation. Hormonal contraceptives, most often in the form of **birth control pills**, also have pregnancy rates of 1% or less.

The most commonly prescribed birth control pills are a combination of a synthetic estrogen and a synthetic progestin (progesterone-like hormone). This combination mimics negative feedback in the ovarian cycle, stopping the release of GnRH by the hypothalamus and thus of FSH and LH by the pituitary. The prevention of LH release blocks ovulation. In addition, the inhibition of FSH secretion by the low dose of estrogens in the pills prevents follicles from developing. A similar combination of hormones is also available as an injection, in a ring inserted into the vagina, and as a skin patch. Combination birth control pills can also be used in high doses as "morning-after" pills. Taken within 3 days after unprotected intercourse, they prevent fertilization or implantation with an effectiveness of about 75%.

A different type of hormone-based contraceptive contains only progestin. Progestin causes thickening of a woman's cervical mucus so that it blocks sperm from entering the uterus. Progestin also decreases the frequency of ovulation and causes changes in the endometrium that may interfere with implantation if fertilization occurs. Progestin can be administered in several ways: time-release, match-sized capsules that are implanted under the skin and last for five years, injections that last for three months, and tablet (minipill) form taken daily. Pregnancy rates for progestin treatment are very low.

Hormone-based contraceptives have both beneficial and harmful side effects. For women taking a combination pill, cardiovascular problems are the most serious concern. Women who smoke cigarettes regularly face a three to ten times greater risk of dying from cardiovascular disease if they also use oral contraceptives. Among nonsmokers, birth control pills slightly raise a woman's risk of abnormal blood clotting, high blood pressure, heart attack, and stroke. Although oral contraceptives increase the risk for these cardiovascular disorders, they eliminate the dangers of pregnancy; women on birth control pills have mortality rates about one-half those of pregnant women. Also, the pill decreases the risk of ovarian and endometrial cancers.

One elusive research goal has been a reversible chemical contraceptive for men. Recent strategies have focused on hormone combinations that suppress gonadotropin release and thereby block spermatogenesis. Testosterone included in such combinations has two desirable effects: inhibiting reproductive functions of the hypothalamus and pituitary and maintaining secondary sex characteristics. Although there have been some promising results, hormonal male contraceptives are still in the testing stage.

Sterilization is the permanent prevention of gamete release. **Tubal ligation** in women usually involves cauterizing or tying off (ligating) a section of each oviduct to prevent eggs from traveling into the uterus. Similarly, **vasectomy** in men is the tying off or excision of a small section of each vas deferens to prevent sperm from entering the urethra. Both male and female sterilization procedures are relatively safe and free from harmful effects. Sex hormone secretion and sexual function are unaffected by both procedures, with no change in menstrual cycles in females or ejaculate volume in males. However, the procedures are difficult to reverse, so each should be considered permanent.

Abortion is the termination of a pregnancy in progress. Spontaneous abortion, or miscarriage, is very common; it occurs in as many as one-third of all pregnancies, often before the woman is even aware she is pregnant. In addition, each year about 850,000 women in the United States choose to have an abortion performed by a physician.

A drug called mifepristone, or RU486, enables a woman to terminate pregnancy nonsurgically within the first 7 weeks. RU486 blocks progesterone receptors in the uterus, thus preventing progesterone from maintaining pregnancy. It is taken with a small amount of prostaglandin to induce uterine contractions.

Modern Reproductive Technologies

Recent scientific and technological advances have made it possible to address many reproductive problems, including genetic diseases and infertility.

Detecting Disorders During Pregnancy

Many genetic diseases and developmental problems can now be diagnosed while the fetus is in the uterus. Ultrasound imaging, which generates images using sound frequencies above the normal hearing range, is commonly used to analyze the fetus's size and condition. Amniocentesis and chorionic villus sampling are techniques in which a needle is used to obtain fetal cells from fluid or tissue surrounding the embryo; these cells then provide the basis for genetic analysis (see Figure 14.18). An alternative technique for obtaining fetal tissue relies on the fact that a few fetal blood cells leak across the placenta into the mother's bloodstream. A blood sample from the mother yields fetal cells that can be identified with specific antibodies (which bind to proteins on the surface of fetal cells) and then tested for genetic disorders.

Diagnosing genetic diseases in a fetus poses ethical questions. To date, almost all detectable disorders remain untreatable in the uterus, and many cannot be corrected even after birth. Parents may be faced with difficult decisions about whether to terminate a pregnancy or to raise a child who may have profound defects and a short life expectancy. These are complex issues that demand careful, informed thought and competent genetic counseling.

Treating Infertility

Infertility—an inability to conceive offspring—is quite common, affecting about one in ten couples both in the United States and worldwide. The causes of infertility are varied, with the likelihood of a reproductive defect being nearly the same for men and women. For women, however, the risk of reproductive difficulties, as well as genetic abnormalities of the fetus, increases steadily past age 35; evidence suggests that the prolonged period of time oocytes spend in meiosis is largely responsible.

Reproductive technology can help with a number of fertility problems. Hormone therapy can sometimes increase sperm or egg production, and surgery can often correct ducts that have failed to form properly or have become blocked. Many infertile couples turn to **assisted reproductive technologies**, procedures that generally involve surgically removing eggs (secondary oocytes) from a woman's ovaries after hormonal stimulation, fertilizing the eggs, and returning them to the woman's body. Unused eggs, sperm, and embryos from such procedures are sometimes frozen for later pregnancy attempts.

For ***in vitro* fertilization (IVF)**, oocytes are mixed with sperm in culture dishes. Fertilized eggs are incubated until they have formed at least eight cells and are then typically transferred to the woman's uterus for implantation. If mature sperm are defective, of low number (less than 20 million per milliliter of ejaculate), or even absent, fertility is often restored by a technique termed **intracytoplasmic sperm injection (ICSI)**. In this form of IVF, the head of a spermatid or sperm is drawn up into a needle and injected directly into an oocyte to achieve fertilization.

Though costly, IVF procedures have enabled hundreds of thousands of couples to conceive children. In some cases, these procedures are carried out with sperm or eggs from donors. To date, evidence indicates that abnormalities arising as a consequence of IVF procedures are rare.

Once conception and implantation have occurred, a developmental program unfolds that transforms the zygote into a baby. The mechanisms of this development in humans and other animals are the subject of Chapter 47.

CONCEPT CHECK 46.6

1. Why does testing for hCG (human chorionic gonadotropin) work as a pregnancy test early in pregnancy but not late in pregnancy? What is the function of hCG in pregnancy?
2. In what ways are tubal ligation and vasectomy similar?
3. **WHAT IF?** If a spermatid nucleus were used for ICSI, what normal steps of gametogenesis and conception would be bypassed?

For suggested answers, see Appendix A.

Chapter 46 Review

MEDIA Go to the Study Area at **www.masteringbio.com** for BioFlix 3-D Animations, MP3 Tutors, Videos, Practice Tests, an eBook, and more.

SUMMARY OF KEY CONCEPTS

CONCEPT 46.1

Both asexual and sexual reproduction occur in the animal kingdom (pp. 997–1000)

- Sexual reproduction requires the fusion of male and female gametes, forming a diploid zygote. Asexual reproduction is the production of offspring without gamete fusion.
- **Mechanisms of Asexual Reproduction** Fission, budding, fragmentation with regeneration, and parthenogenesis are mechanisms of asexual reproduction in various invertebrates.
- **Sexual Reproduction: An Evolutionary Enigma** Facilitating selection for or against sets of genes may explain why sexual reproduction is widespread among animal species.
- **Reproductive Cycles and Patterns** Most animals reproduce exclusively sexually or asexually; but some alternate between the two. Variations on these two modes are made possible through parthenogenesis, hermaphroditism, and sex reversal. Hormones and environmental cues control reproductive cycles.

CONCEPT 46.2

Fertilization depends on mechanisms that bring together sperm and eggs of the same species (pp. 1000–1003)

- In external fertilization, sperm fertilize eggs shed into the external environment. In internal fertilization, egg and sperm unite within the female's body. In either case, fertilization requires coordinated timing, which may be mediated by environmental cues, pheromones, or courtship behavior. Internal fertilization requires behavioral interactions between males and females, as well as compatible copulatory organs.
- **Ensuring the Survival of Offspring** The production of relatively few offspring by internal fertilization is often associated with greater protection of embryos and parental care.
- **Gamete Production and Delivery** Reproductive systems range from undifferentiated cells in the body cavity that produce gametes to complex assemblages of male and female gonads with accessory tubes and glands that carry and protect gametes and developing embryos. Although sexual reproduction involves a partnership, it also provides an opportunity for competition between individuals and between gametes.

CONCEPT 46.3

Reproductive organs produce and transport gametes (pp. 1003–1007)

- **Female Reproductive Anatomy** Externally, the human female has the labia majora, labia minora, and clitoris, which form the vulva surrounding the openings of the vagina and urethra. Internally, the vagina is connected to the uterus, which connects to two oviducts. Two ovaries (female gonads) are stocked with follicles containing oocytes. After ovulation, the remnant of the follicle forms a corpus luteum, which secretes hormones for a variable duration, depending on whether pregnancy occurs. Although separate from the reproductive system, the mammary glands evolved in association with parental care.
- **Male Reproductive Anatomy** External reproductive structures of the human male are the scrotum and penis. The male gonads, or testes, are held in the scrotum, where they are kept at the lower temperature necessary for mammalian spermatogenesis. The testes possess hormone-producing cells and sperm-forming seminiferous tubules that successively lead into the epididymis, vas deferens, ejaculatory duct, and urethra, which exits at the tip of the penis.
- **Human Sexual Response** Both males and females experience the erection of certain body tissues due to vasocongestion and myotonia, culminating in orgasm.

MEDIA

MP3 Tutor The Female Reproductive Cycle
Activity Reproductive System of the Human Female
Activity Reproductive System of the Human Male
Investigation What Might Obstruct the Male Urethra?

CONCEPT 46.4

The timing and pattern of meiosis in mammals differ for males and females (p. 1007)

- Gametogenesis, or gamete production, consists of oogenesis in females and spermatogenesis in males. Sperm develop continuously, whereas oocyte maturation is discontinuous and cyclic. Meiosis generates one large egg in oogenesis, but four sperm in spermatogenesis.

Gametogenesis

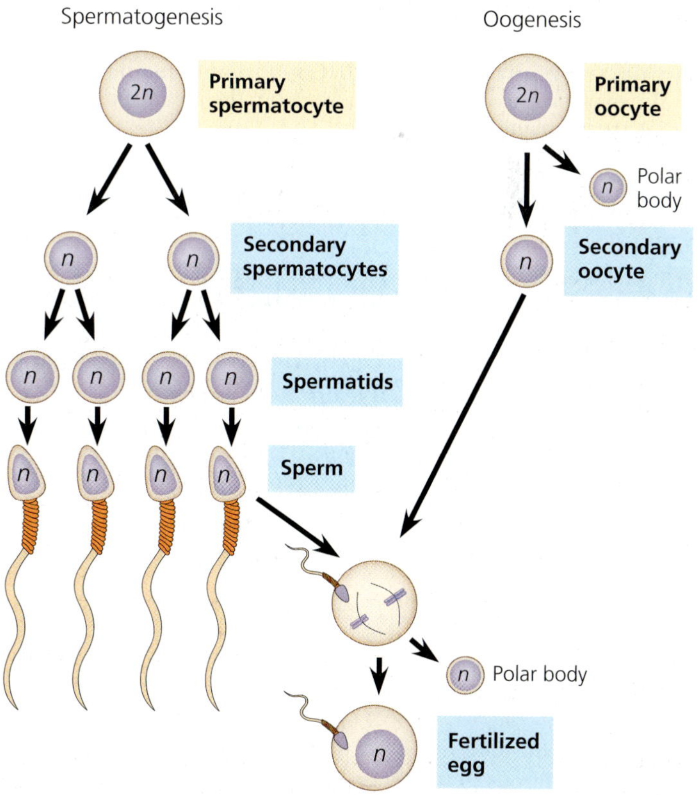

CONCEPT 46.5

The interplay of tropic and sex hormones regulates mammalian reproduction (pp. 1007–1012)

- **Hormonal Control of the Male Reproductive System** Androgens (chiefly testosterone) from the testes cause the development of primary and secondary sex characteristics in the male. Androgen secretion and sperm production are both controlled by hypothalamic and pituitary hormones.
- **The Reproductive Cycles of Females** Cyclic secretion of GnRH from the hypothalamus and of FSH and LH from the anterior pituitary orchestrate the female reproductive cycle. FSH and LH bring about changes in the ovary and uterus via estrogens, primarily estradiol, and progesterone. The developing follicle produces estradiol, and the corpus luteum secretes progesterone and estradiol. Positive and negative feedback regulate hormone levels and coordinate the cycle.

  Estrous cycles differ from menstrual cycles in that the endometrial lining is reabsorbed rather than shed and in the limitation of sexual receptivity to a heat period.

CONCEPT 46.6

In placental mammals, an embryo develops fully within the mother's uterus (pp. 1012–1018)

- **Conception, Embryonic Development, and Birth** After fertilization and the completion of meiosis in the oviduct, the zygote undergoes cleavage and develops into a blastocyst before implantation in the endometrium. Human pregnancy can be divided into three trimesters. All major organs start developing by 8 weeks. Positive feedback involving prostaglandins and the hormones estradiol and oxytocin regulates labor.
- **Maternal Immune Tolerance of the Embryo and Fetus** A pregnant woman's acceptance of her "foreign" offspring likely reflects partial suppression of the maternal immune response.
- **Contraception and Abortion** Contraceptive methods may prevent release of mature gametes from the gonads, fertilization, or implantation of the embryo.
- **Modern Reproductive Technologies** Available technologies can help detect problems before birth and assist infertile couples by hormonal methods or *in vitro* fertilization.

TESTING YOUR KNOWLEDGE

SELF-QUIZ

1. Which of the following characterizes parthenogenesis?
   a. An individual may change its sex during its lifetime.
   b. Specialized groups of cells grow into new individuals.
   c. An organism is first a male and then a female.
   d. An egg develops without being fertilized.
   e. Both mates have male and female reproductive organs.

2. In male mammals, excretory and reproductive systems share
   a. the testes.
   b. the urethra.
   c. the seminal vesicle.
   d. the vas deferens.
   e. the prostate.

3. Which of the following is *not* properly paired?
   a. seminiferous tubule—cervix
   b. Sertoli cells—follicle cells
   c. testosterone—estradiol
   d. labia majora—scrotum
   e. vas deferens—oviduct

4. Which of the following is a true statement?
   a. All mammals have menstrual cycles.
   b. The endometrial lining is shed in menstrual cycles but reabsorbed in estrous cycles.
   c. Estrous cycles occur more often than menstrual cycles.
   d. Estrous cycles are not controlled by hormones.
   e. Ovulation occurs before the endometrium thickens in estrous cycles.

5. Peaks of LH and FSH production occur during
   a. the menstrual flow phase of the uterine cycle.
   b. the beginning of the follicular phase of the ovarian cycle.
   c. the period just before ovulation.
   d. the end of the luteal phase of the ovarian cycle.
   e. the secretory phase of the menstrual cycle.

6. For which of the following is the number the same in spermatogenesis and oogenesis?
   a. interruptions in meiotic divisions
   b. functional gametes produced by meiosis
   c. meiotic divisions required to produce each gamete
   d. gametes produced in a given time period
   e. different cell types produced by meiosis

7. During human gestation, rudiments of all organs develop
   a. in the first trimester.
   b. in the second trimester.
   c. in the third trimester.
   d. while the embryo is in the oviduct.
   e. during the blastocyst stage.

8. Which statement about human reproduction is false?
   a. Fertilization occurs in the oviduct.
   b. Effective hormonal contraceptives are currently available only for females.
   c. An oocyte completes meiosis after a sperm penetrates it.
   d. The earliest stages of spermatogenesis occur closest to the lumen of the seminiferous tubules.
   e. Spermatogenesis and oogenesis require different temperatures.

9. **DRAW IT** In human spermatogenesis, mitosis of a stem cell gives rise to one cell that remains a stem cell and one cell that becomes a spermatogonium. (a) Draw four rounds of mitosis for a stem cell, and label the daughter cells. (b) For one spermatogonium, draw the cells it would produce from one round of mitosis followed by meiosis. Label the cells, and label mitosis and meiosis. (c) What would happen if stem cells divided like spermatogonia?

For Self-Quiz answers, see Appendix A.

MEDIA Visit the Study Area at **www.masteringbio.com** for a Practice Test.

EVOLUTION CONNECTION

10. Hermaphroditism is often found in animals that are fixed to a surface. Motile species are less often hermaphroditic. Why?

SCIENTIFIC INQUIRY

11. You discover a new egg-laying worm species. You dissect four adults and find both oocytes and sperm in each. Cells outside the gonad contain five chromosome pairs. Lacking genetic variants, how would you determine whether the worms can self-fertilize?

47 Animal Development

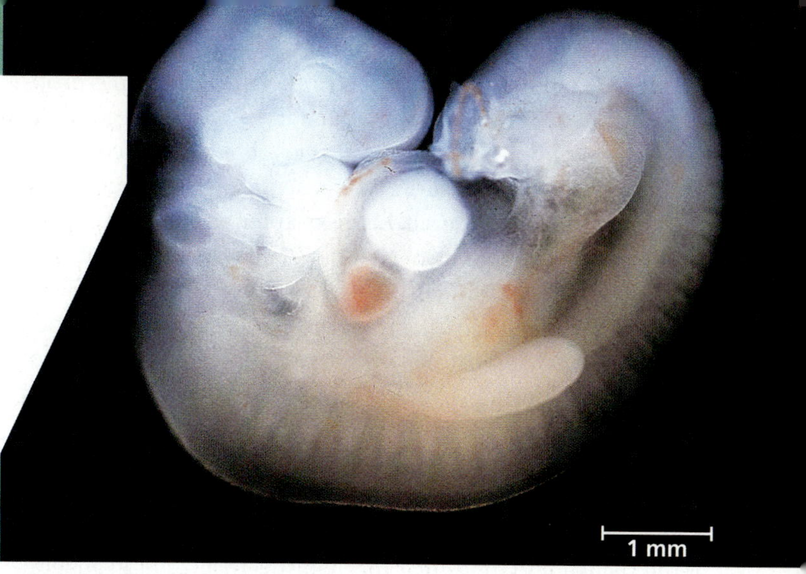

▲ **Figure 47.1 How did this complex embryo form from a single cell?**

KEY CONCEPTS

47.1 **After fertilization, embryonic development proceeds through cleavage, gastrulation, and organogenesis**

47.2 **Morphogenesis in animals involves specific changes in cell shape, position, and adhesion**

47.3 **The developmental fate of cells depends on their history and on inductive signals**

OVERVIEW

A Body-Building Plan

The 7-week-old human embryo in **Figure 47.1** has already achieved an astounding number of milestones in its development. Many of its organs are in place: Its digestive tract traverses the length of its body, and its heart (the red spot in the center) is pulsating. Its brain is forming at the upper left, and the blocks of tissue that will construct the vertebrae are lined up along its back. How did this intricately detailed embryo develop from a single-celled zygote no bigger than the period at the end of the previous sentence?

The question of how a zygote becomes an animal has intrigued scientists for centuries. In the 1700s, the prevailing notion was *preformation*: the idea that the egg or sperm contains an embryo—a preformed, miniature infant, or "homunculus"—that simply becomes larger during development **(Figure 47.2)**. The competing explanation of embryonic development was *epigenesis*: the idea that the form of an animal emerges gradually from a relatively formless egg. Epigenesis was originally proposed 2,000 years earlier by Aristotle, who had snipped open a window in the shell of a chicken egg and observed the developing embryo daily during its three-week incubation. As microscopy improved during the 1800s, biologists following in Aristotle's footsteps could see that embryos took shape in a series of progressive stages, and epigenesis displaced preformation as the favored explanation among embryologists.

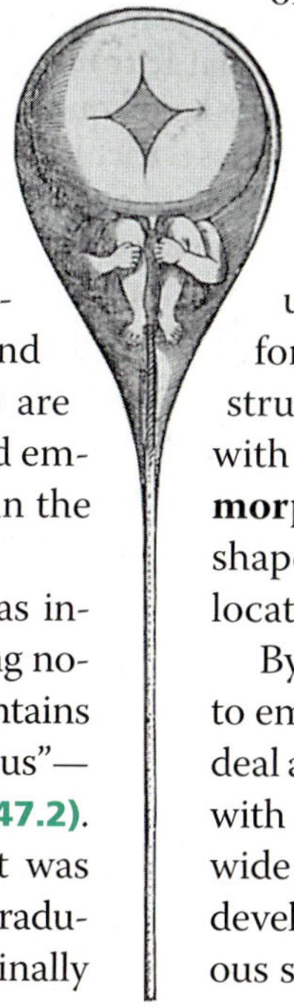

▲ **Figure 47.2 A "homunculus" inside the head of a human sperm.** This engraving was made in 1694.

An organism's development is orchestrated by a genetic program involving not only the genome of the zygote but also molecules placed into the egg by the mother. These molecules, which include proteins and RNAs, are called **cytoplasmic determinants**. As the zygote divides, differences arise between early embryonic cells due to the uneven distribution of cytoplasmic determinants and to signals from neighboring cells. These differences set the stage for distinct programs of gene expression to be carried out in each cell and its descendants. As cell division continues during embryonic development, the specific pattern of gene expression in particular cells sends them down unique paths toward their ultimate fates in the fully formed organism. This process of cell specialization in structure and function is called **cell differentiation**. Along with cell division and differentiation, development involves **morphogenesis**, the process by which an organism takes shape and the differentiated cells occupy their appropriate locations.

By combining molecular genetics with classical approaches to embryology, developmental biologists have learned a great deal about the transformation of a fertilized egg into an animal with multiple tissues and organs. Because animals display a wide variety of body plans, it is not surprising that embryonic development occurs by different schemes. Studies of numerous species, however, have revealed that animals share many basic mechanisms of development and use a common genetic toolkit.

In Chapter 18, we described the development of the fruit fly (*Drosophila melanogaster*). *Drosophila* is well suited to genetic analysis because mutants are easy to obtain in this species, so its genetic program is probably the best understood of any animal. *Drosophila* is a good example of a **model organism**, a species that lends itself to the study of a particular question, is representative of a larger group, and is easy to grow in the lab. In this chapter, we will concentrate mainly on model organisms that have been the subject of classical embryological studies as well as more recent molecular analyses: the sea urchin, the frog, the chick, and the nematode *Caenorhabditis elegans*. We will also explore some aspects of human embryonic development; even though humans are not model organisms, we are, of course, intensely interested in our own species.

We will begin with a description of the basic stages of embryonic development common to most animals. Then we will look at the cellular and molecular mechanisms that result in generation of the body form. Finally, we will consider the process by which embryonic cells travel down differentiation pathways that enable them to play their roles in a fully functional animal.

CONCEPT **47.1**

After fertilization, embryonic development proceeds through cleavage, gastrulation, and organogenesis

Important processes regulating development occur during fertilization and the three stages that begin to build the body of most animals. During the first stage, called *cleavage*, cell division creates a hollow ball of cells, the blastula, from the zygote. The second stage, *gastrulation*, rearranges the blastula into a three-layered embryo, the gastrula. During the third stage, *organogenesis*, interactions and movements of the three layers generate rudimentary organs from which adult structures grow.

In our discussion, we will focus on a few species that have been used to investigate each of these processes. For each stage of development, we first consider the species about which the most is known and then compare the same process in other species. We begin by looking at the fertilization of an egg by a sperm.

Fertilization

A complex series of developmental events in the gonads of the parents produces sperm and eggs (gametes), the highly specialized cell types that unite during fertilization (see Figure 46.12). The main function of fertilization is the combining of haploid sets of chromosomes from two individuals into a single diploid cell, the zygote. Contact of the sperm with the egg's surface also initiates metabolic reactions within the egg that trigger the onset of embryonic development, thus "activating" the egg.

Fertilization has been studied most extensively in sea urchins. Their gametes can simply be combined in seawater in the laboratory, and subsequent events are easily observed. Although sea urchins (members of phylum Echinodermata) are not vertebrates or even chordates, they share with those two groups the characteristic of deuterostome development (see Figure 32.9). Despite differences in the details, fertilization and early development in sea urchins provide good general models for similar events in vertebrates.

The Acrosomal Reaction

The eggs of sea urchins are fertilized externally after the animals release their gametes into the surrounding seawater. The jelly coat that surrounds the egg exudes soluble molecules that attract the sperm, which swim toward the egg.

When the head of a sea urchin sperm contacts the jelly coat of a sea urchin egg, molecules in the egg's coat trigger the **acrosomal reaction** in the sperm **(Figure 47.3)**. This reaction begins when a specialized vesicle at the tip of the sperm, called the **acrosome**, discharges hydrolytic enzymes. These enzymes digest the jelly coat, enabling a sperm structure called the *acrosomal process* to elongate, penetrating the coat. Molecules of a protein on the tip of the acrosomal process then adhere to specific sperm receptor proteins that extend from the egg plasma membrane through the surrounding meshwork of extracellular matrix, called the *vitelline layer*. In sea urchins and many other animals, this "lock-and-key" recognition of molecules ensures that eggs will be fertilized only by sperm of the same species. Such specificity is especially important when fertilization occurs externally in water, which may be teeming with gametes of other species.

Contact of the tip of the acrosomal process with the egg membrane leads to the fusion of sperm and egg plasma membranes. The sperm nucleus then enters the egg cytoplasm. Contact and fusion of the membranes causes ion channels to open in the egg's plasma membrane, allowing sodium ions to flow into the egg and change the membrane potential (see Chapter 7). This change in membrane potential, called depolarization, is a common feature of fertilization in animals. Occurring within about 1–3 seconds after a sperm binds to an egg, depolarization prevents additional sperm from fusing with the egg's plasma membrane. Without this **fast block to polyspermy**, multiple sperm could fertilize the egg, resulting in an aberrant number of chromosomes in the zygote.

The Cortical Reaction

The membrane depolarization lasts for only a minute or so, thus blocking polyspermy only in the short term. However, fusion of the egg and sperm plasma membranes also triggers a series of changes in the egg that cause a longer-lasting block.

Key players in the longer-lasting block are numerous vesicles lying just beneath the egg plasma membrane, in the rim of cytoplasm known as the *cortex*. Within seconds after a sperm binds to the egg, these vesicles, called **cortical granules**, fuse

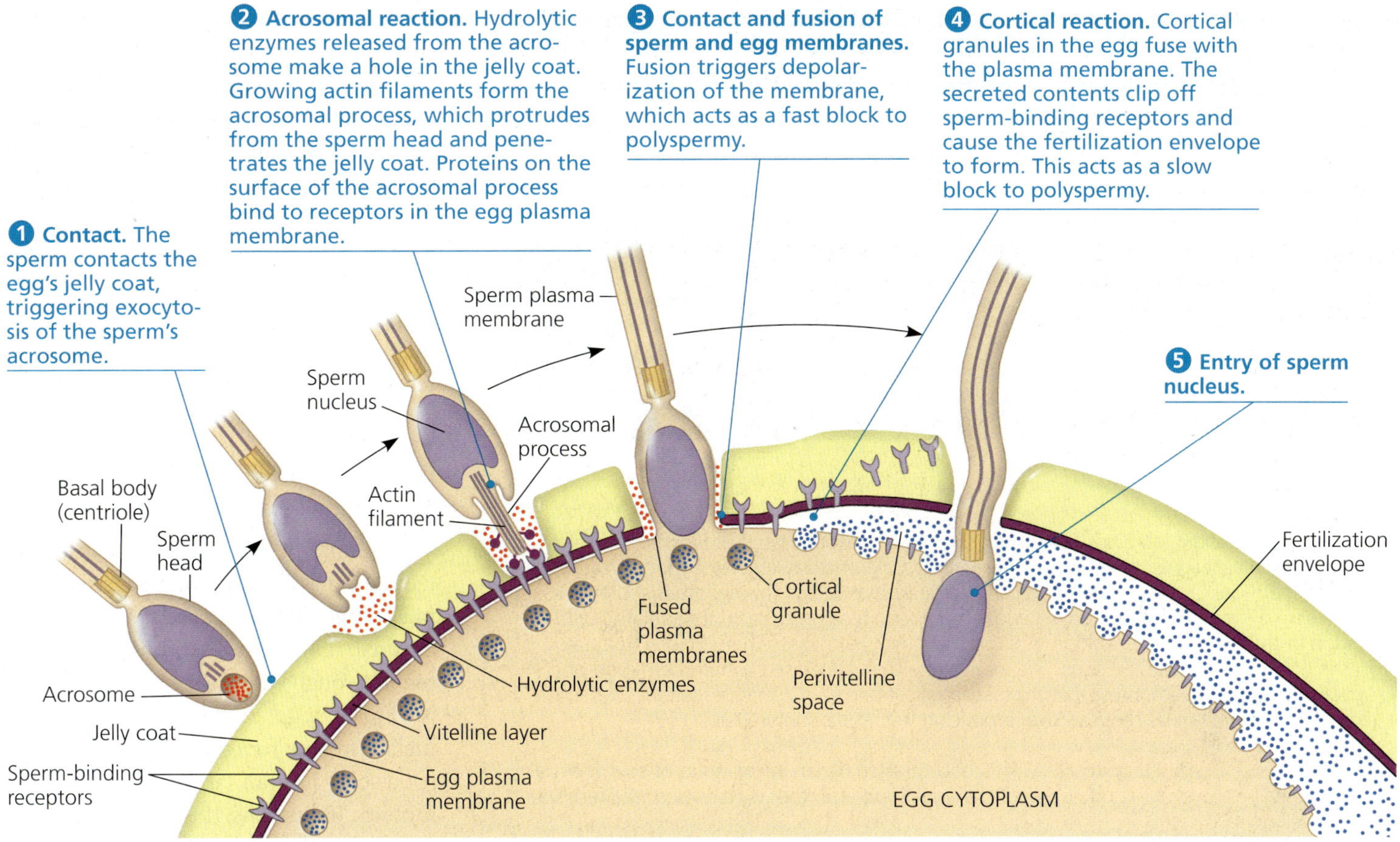

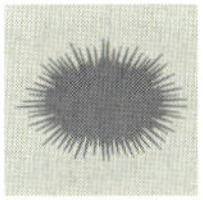

▲ **Figure 47.3 The acrosomal and cortical reactions during sea urchin fertilization.** The events following contact of a single sperm and egg ensure that the nucleus of only one sperm enters the egg cytoplasm. The icon at left is a simplified drawing of an adult sea urchin. Throughout the chapter, this and other icons of an adult frog, chicken, and human indicate the animals whose embryos are featured in certain figures.

with the egg plasma membrane, initiating the **cortical reaction** (see Figure 47.3, step 4). Cortical granules contain a treasure trove of molecules that are now secreted into the *perivitelline space,* which lies between the plasma membrane and the vitelline layer. The secreted enzymes and other macromolecules together push the vitelline layer away from the egg and harden the layer, forming a protective **fertilization envelope** that resists the entry of additional sperm nuclei. Another enzyme clips off and releases the external portions of the remaining receptor proteins, along with any attached sperm. The fertilization envelope and other changes in the egg's surface function together as a longer-term **slow block to polyspermy**.

Experimental evidence, including the results described in **Figure 47.4** on the next page, indicates that a high concentration of calcium ions (Ca^{2+}) in the egg is essential for the cortical reaction to occur. Sperm binding activates a signal transduction pathway that causes Ca^{2+} to be released from the egg's endoplasmic reticulum into the cytosol (see Figure 11.12). The elevated Ca^{2+} levels then cause cortical granules to fuse with the plasma membrane. Although understood in greatest detail in sea urchins, the cortical reaction triggered by Ca^{2+} also occurs in vertebrates such as fishes and mammals.

Activation of the Egg

Another outcome of the sharp rise in Ca^{2+} concentration in the egg's cytosol is a substantial increase in the rates of cellular respiration and protein synthesis by the egg, known as *egg activation.* Although egg activation is normally triggered by the binding and fusion of sperm, the unfertilized eggs of many species can be artificially activated by the injection of Ca^{2+} or by various mildly injurious treatments, such as temperature shock. Artificial activation switches on the metabolic responses of the egg and causes it to begin developing by parthenogenesis (without fertilization by a sperm; see Chapter 46). It is even possible to artificially activate an egg that has had its own nucleus removed. This finding shows that proteins and mRNAs present in the cytoplasm of the unfertilized egg are sufficient for egg activation.

About 20 minutes after it enters the egg, the sperm nucleus merges with the egg nucleus, creating the diploid nucleus of the zygote. DNA synthesis begins, and the first cell division occurs after about 90 minutes in the case of sea urchins and some frogs, marking the end of the fertilization stage.

Fertilization in other species shares many features with the process in sea urchins. However, the timing of events differs

▼ **Figure 47.4 Inquiry**

Is the distribution of Ca^{2+} in an egg correlated with formation of the fertilization envelope?

EXPERIMENT During fertilization, fusion of cortical granules with the egg plasma membrane causes the fertilization envelope to rise and spread around the egg from the point of sperm binding.

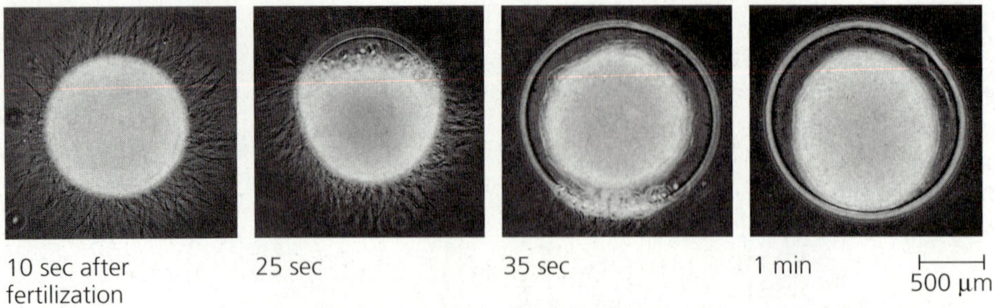

Knowing that calcium ion (Ca^{2+}) signaling is involved in exocytosis, Rick Steinhardt, Gerald Schatten, and colleagues, then at the University of California at Berkeley, hypothesized that an increase in Ca^{2+} levels triggers cortical granule fusion. To test this hypothesis, they tracked the release of free Ca^{2+} in sea urchin eggs after sperm binding to see if it correlated with formation of the fertilization envelope. A fluorescent dye that glows when it binds free Ca^{2+} was injected into unfertilized eggs. The researchers then added sea urchin sperm and observed the eggs with a fluorescence microscope. Schatten and colleagues later repeated the experiment using a more sensitive dye, producing the results shown here.

RESULTS A rise in cytosolic Ca^{2+} concentration began at the point of sperm entry and spread in a wave to the other side of the egg. Soon after the wave passed, the fertilization envelope rose.

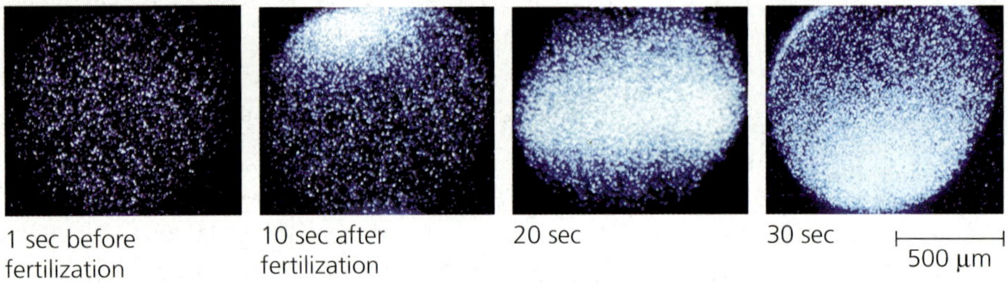

CONCLUSION The researchers concluded that Ca^{2+} release is correlated with cortical granule exocytosis and formation of the fertilization envelope, supporting their hypothesis that an increase in Ca^{2+} levels triggers cortical granule fusion.

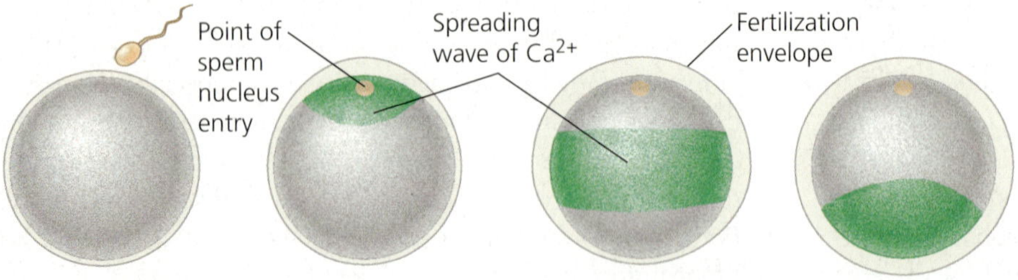

SOURCES R. Steinhardt et al., Intracellular calcium release at fertilization in the sea urchin egg, *Developmental Biology* 58:185–197 (1977). M. Hafner et al., Wave of free calcium at fertilization in the sea urchin egg visualized with Fura-2, *Cell Motility and the Cytoskeleton* 9:271–277 (1988).

WHAT IF? Suppose you were given a chemical compound that could enter the egg and bind to Ca^{2+}, blocking its function. How would you use this compound to further test the hypothesis that a rise in Ca^{2+} levels triggers exocytosis?

among species, as does the stage of meiosis the egg has reached by the time it is fertilized. When they are released from the female, sea urchin eggs have completed meiosis. In other species, the eggs are arrested at a specific stage of meiosis; upon fertilization, meiosis is quickly completed along with many of the events already described. Human eggs, for example, are arrested at metaphase of meiosis II (see Figure 46.12) until they are fertilized in the female reproductive tract.

Fertilization in Mammals

In contrast to the external fertilization of sea urchins and most other marine invertebrates, fertilization in terrestrial animals, including mammals, is generally internal. This ensures a moist environment through which the sperm can move toward the egg. Secretions in the mammalian female reproductive tract are responsible for an increase in sperm motility. In humans, this enhancement of sperm function requires about 6 hours of exposure to the female reproductive tract.

The mammalian egg is cloaked by follicle cells released along with the egg during ovulation. A sperm must travel through this layer of follicle cells before it reaches the **zona pellucida**, the extracellular matrix of the egg. One component of the zona pellucida functions as a sperm receptor. Binding of a sperm to this receptor induces an acrosomal reaction similar to that of sea urchin sperm, facilitating sperm passage through the zona pellucida to the egg and exposing a protein on the sperm that binds with the egg plasma membrane. At this point, the two cells fuse **(Figure 47.5)**.

As in sea urchin fertilization, the binding of a sperm to the egg triggers changes within the egg that lead to a cortical reaction, the release of enzymes from cortical granules to the outside of the cell via exocytosis. The released enzymes catalyze changes in the zona pellucida, which then functions as the slow block to polyspermy. (No fast block to polyspermy is known to exist in mammals.)

After the egg and sperm membranes fuse, the whole sperm, tail and all, is taken into the egg. The centriole that acted as the basal body of the sperm's flagellum ultimately generates the mitotic spindle for the first cell division. The haploid nuclei of the mammalian sperm and egg do not fuse immediately as they do in sea urchin fertilization. Instead, the envelopes of both nuclei disperse, and the two sets of chromosomes (one set from each gamete) share a common spindle apparatus during the first mitotic division of the zygote. Thus, only after this first division do the chromosomes from the two parents coexist in a true diploid nucleus with a nuclear membrane. Fertilization is much slower in mammals than in sea urchins: The first cell division occurs 12–36 hours after sperm binding in mammals, compared with about 90 minutes in sea urchins. This cell division marks the beginning of the next stage, cleavage.

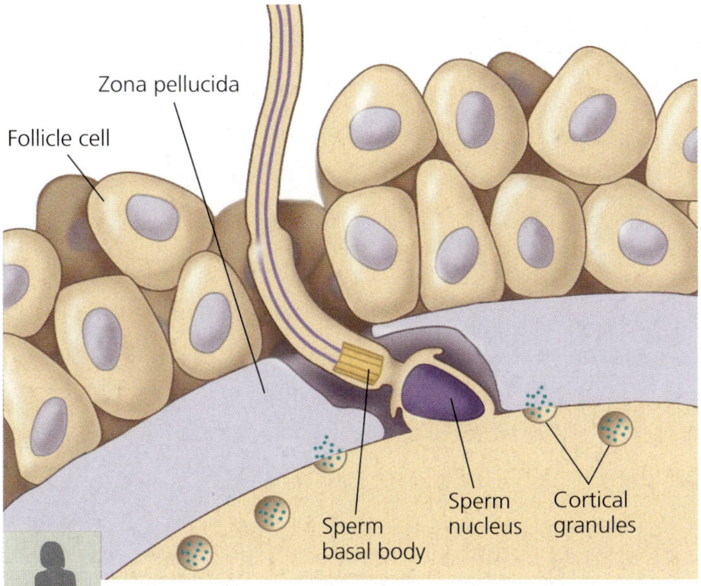

▲ **Figure 47.5 Fertilization in mammals.** The sperm shown here has traveled through the follicle cells and zona pellucida and has fused with the egg. The cortical reaction has begun, initiating events that ensure that only one sperm nucleus enters the cytoplasm of the egg.

Cleavage

Once fertilization is completed, a succession of rapid cell divisions ensues in many species. During this period, called **cleavage**, the cells carry out the S (DNA synthesis) and M (mitosis) phases of the cell cycle; however, they often virtually skip the G_1 and G_2 (gap) phases, and little or no protein synthesis occurs (see Figure 12.5 for a review of the cell cycle). As a result, the embryo does not enlarge significantly during this period of development. Cleavage simply partitions the cytoplasm of one large cell, the zygote, into many smaller cells called **blastomeres**, each with its own nucleus, as depicted for an echinoderm embryo in **Figure 47.6**.

The first five to seven divisions produce a cluster of cells, within which a fluid-filled cavity called the **blastocoel** begins to form. The blastocoel is fully formed in the **blastula** (plural, *blastulae*), which is thus a hollow ball of cells. During cleavage, different regions of cytoplasm present in the original undivided egg end up in separate blastomeres. Because the regions may contain different cytoplasmic determinants, such as specific mRNAs and proteins, in many species this partitioning sets the stage for subsequent developmental events.

The eggs and zygotes of sea urchins and other animals, with the possible exception of mammals, have a definite polarity, established as the egg developed within the mother during oogenesis. During cleavage in such organisms, the planes of division

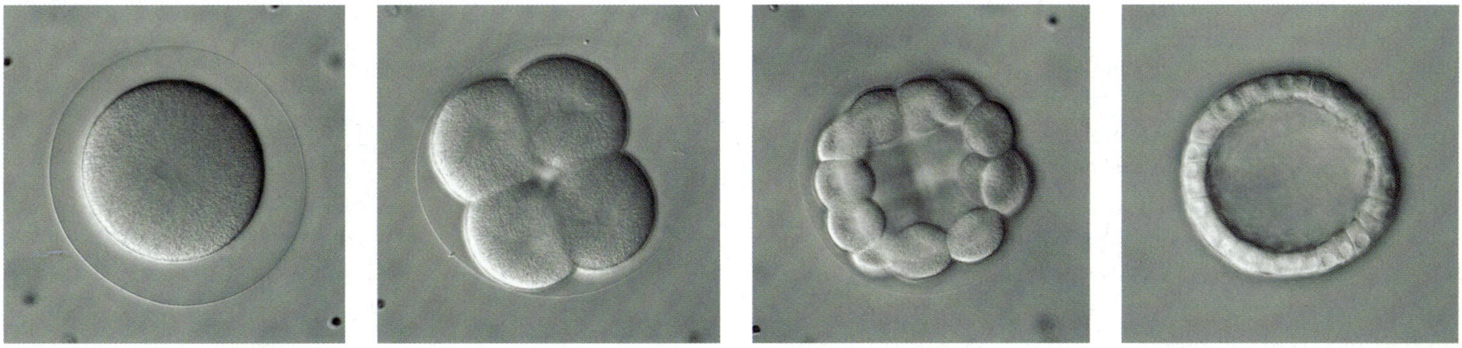

(a) Fertilized egg. Shown here is the zygote shortly before the first cleavage division, surrounded by the fertilization envelope.

(b) Four-cell stage. Remnants of the mitotic spindle can be seen between the two pairs of cells that have just completed the second cleavage division.

(c) Early blastula. After further cleavage divisions, the embryo is a multicellular ball that is still surrounded by the fertilization envelope. The blastocoel has begun to form in the center.

(d) Later blastula. A single layer of cells surrounds a large blastocoel. Although not visible here, the fertilization envelope is still present; the embryo will soon hatch from it and begin swimming.

▲ **Figure 47.6 Cleavage in an echinoderm embryo.** Cleavage is a series of mitotic cell divisions that transform the zygote into a blastula, a hollow ball composed of cells called blastomeres. These light micrographs show the embryonic stages of a sand dollar, which are virtually identical to those of a sea urchin.

follow a specific pattern relative to the poles of the zygote. The polarity is defined by the uneven distribution of substances in the cytoplasm, including not only cytoplasmic determinants but also **yolk** (stored nutrients). In frogs and many other animals, the distribution of yolk is a key factor influencing the pattern of cleavage. Yolk is often concentrated toward one pole of the egg, called the **vegetal pole**; the yolk concentration decreases significantly toward the opposite pole, the **animal pole**. The animal pole is also the site where the polar bodies of oogenesis bud from the cell (see Figure 46.12).

Establishment of the three body axes occurs early in development **(Figure 47.7a)**. This process has been well studied in particular frog species where the animal and vegetal hemispheres of the zygote, named for their respective poles, can be distinguished by color. The animal hemisphere is a deep gray because dark-colored melanin granules are embedded in the cortex in this region. The lack of melanin granules in the vegetal hemisphere allows the yellow color of the yolk to be visible.

The animal-vegetal axis of the egg determines the anterior-posterior (head-tail) axis of the embryo, so we can consider the anterior-posterior axis to be already in place in the egg. (Note, however, that these two axes are not equivalent: The head does not form where the animal pole is.) Following fusion of the egg and the sperm, rearrangement of the amphibian egg cytoplasm establishes the dorsal-ventral (back-belly) axis **(Figure 47.7b)**. The plasma membrane and associated cortex rotate with respect to the inner cytoplasm, a movement called *cortical rotation*. The animal hemisphere cortex moves toward the vegetal inner cytoplasm on the side where the sperm nucleus entered, which is always in the animal hemisphere. The vegetal hemisphere cortex across from the side of sperm nucleus entry moves toward the inner cytoplasm of the animal hemisphere.

Cortical rotation allows molecules in the unpigmented vegetal cortex on the side opposite sperm nucleus entry, placed there during oogenesis, to interact with molecules in the inner cytoplasm of the animal hemisphere. These interactions activate previously inactive proteins of the vegetal cortex. This in turn leads to the formation of cytoplasmic determinants that will later affect gene expression in the cells that inherit them, initiating development of dorsal structures. In this way, cortical rotation establishes the dorsal-ventral axis of the zygote. In some species, this rotation also exposes a light gray region of cytoplasm, the **gray crescent**, that had previously been covered by the pigmented animal cortex near the equator of the egg (see Figure 47.7b). Located on the side opposite sperm nucleus entry, the gray crescent serves as a marker for the future dorsal side of the embryo. The lighter pigment of the gray crescent can persist through many rounds of cell division.

Figure 47.8 shows the cleavage planes during the initial cell divisions in frogs. The first two divisions in frogs are meridional (vertical), resulting in four blastomeres of equal size, each extending from the animal pole to the vegetal pole. The third division is equatorial (horizontal), producing an eight-celled embryo. However, the highly uneven distribution of yolk in the frog zygote displaces the mitotic apparatus and eventual cytokinesis toward the animal end of the dividing cells in equatorial divisions. As a result, the four blastomeres in the animal hemisphere are smaller than those in the vegetal

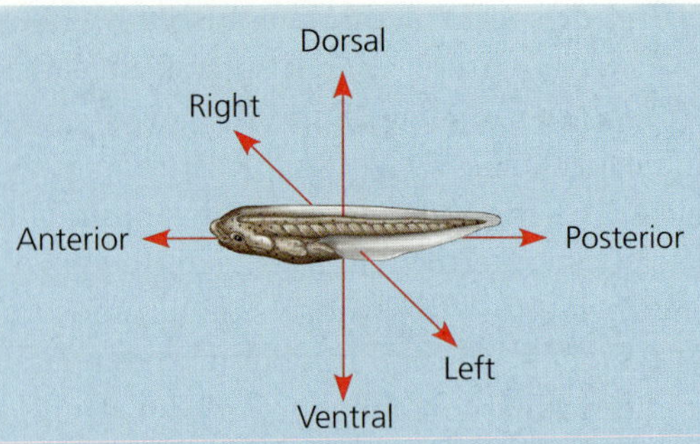

(a) The three axes of the fully developed embryo.

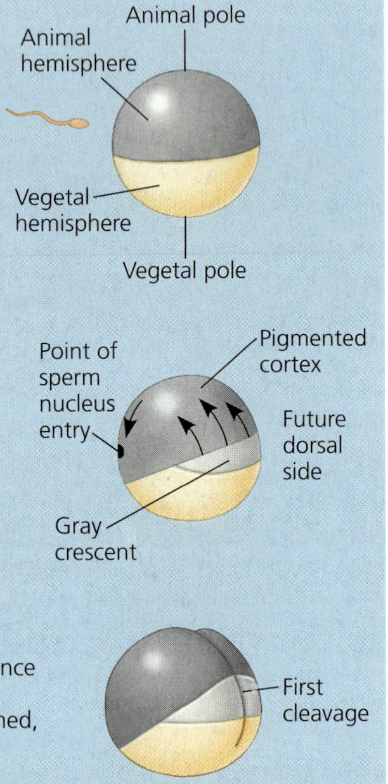

(b) Establishing the axes. The polarity of the egg and cortical rotation are critical in setting up the body axes.

▲ **Figure 47.7 The body axes and their establishment in an amphibian.** All three axes are established before the zygote begins to undergo cleavage.

? *To study axis establishment, researchers can block cortical rotation or force it to occur in a specific direction. One such study resulted in a two-headed embryo because the "back" developed on both sides. What do you think the researchers did to obtain such an embryo?*

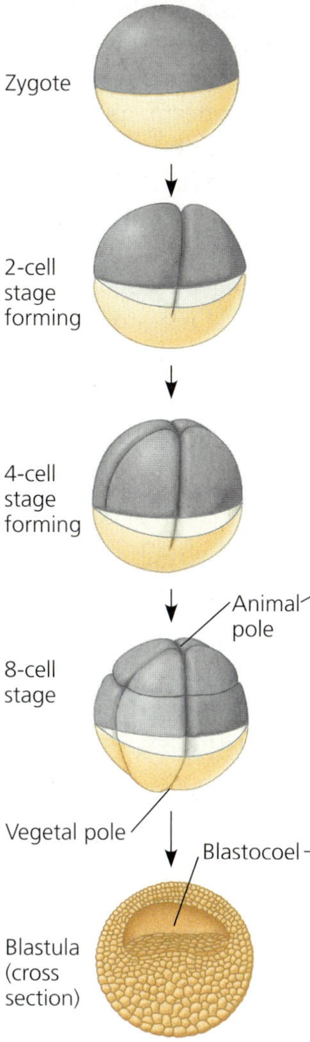

Figure 47.8 Cleavage in a frog embryo. The cleavage planes in the first and second divisions extend from the animal pole to the vegetal pole, but the third cleavage is perpendicular to the polar axis.

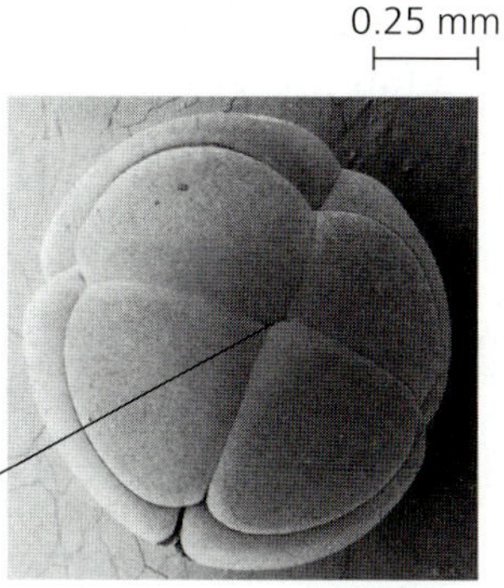

8-cell stage (viewed from the animal pole). The large amount of yolk displaces the third cleavage toward the animal pole, forming two tiers of cells. The four cells near the animal pole (closer, in this view) are smaller than the other four cells (SEM).

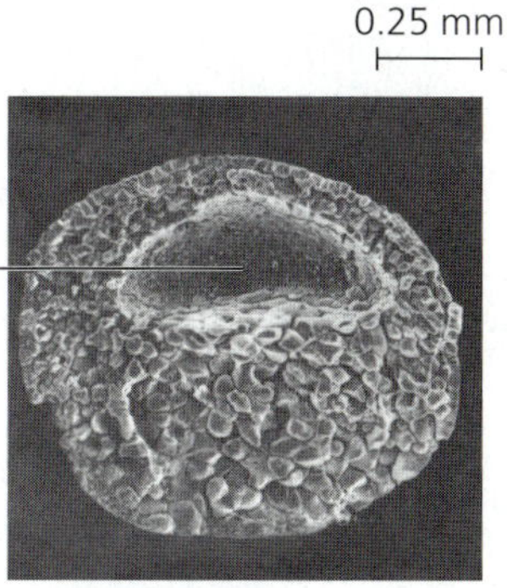

Blastula (at least 128 cells). As cleavage continues, a fluid-filled cavity, the blastocoel, forms within the embryo. Because of unequal cell division due to the large amount of yolk in the vegetal hemisphere, the blastocoel is located in the animal hemisphere. Both the drawing and the SEM show cross sections of a blastula with about 4,000 cells.

hemisphere at the eight-cell stage. The displacing effect of the yolk persists in subsequent divisions, which produce a blastula. In frogs, this unequal cell division causes the blastocoel to be located in the animal hemisphere.

Although the eggs of sea urchins and some other animals have less yolk than frog eggs, they still have an animal-vegetal axis, owing to uneven distribution of other substances. Without the restraint imposed by yolk, however, the blastomeres formed during cleavage are more likely to be of similar size, particularly during the first few divisions (see Figure 47.6). Nonetheless, the general cleavage pattern in frogs is seen in sea urchins and other echinoderms, in most chordates, and indeed in most deuterostomes. In animals whose eggs contain relatively little yolk, the blastocoel is centrally located, and the cleavage furrow passes all the way through the cells, a pattern called **holoblastic cleavage**.

Yolk is most plentiful and has its most pronounced effect on cleavage in the eggs of birds, other reptiles, many fishes, and insects. In these species, the volume of yolk is so great that cleavage furrows cannot pass through it, and only the region of the egg lacking yolk undergoes cleavage. This incomplete division of a yolk-rich egg is known as **meroblastic cleavage**.

In birds, for example, the part of the egg we commonly call the yolk is actually the entire egg cell, swollen with yolk nutrients. If you crack open a chicken egg and observe the yolk, you may see a small whitish area, which is a pool of cytoplasm located at the animal pole. Cleavage of the fertilized egg is restricted to this yolk-free cytoplasm; the dense yolk remains uncleaved. Early cleavage divisions in a bird embryo produce a cap of cells that rest on the undivided yolk and sort into upper and lower layers. The cavity between these two layers is the avian version of the blastocoel, and this embryonic stage is the avian equivalent of the blastula, although its form is different from the hollow ball of an early sea urchin or frog embryo.

In insects such as *Drosophila*, the zygote's nucleus is situated *within* a mass of yolk. Cleavage begins with the nucleus undergoing mitotic divisions that are not accompanied by cytokinesis. In other words, no cell membranes form around the early nuclei. The first several hundred nuclei are spread throughout the yolk and later migrate to the outer edge of the embryo. After several more rounds of mitosis, a plasma membrane forms around each nucleus, and the embryo, now the equivalent of a blastula, consists of a single layer of about 6,000 cells surrounding a mass of yolk.

Gastrulation

After cleavage, the rate of cell division slows dramatically. Groups of cells then undergo the morphogenetic process called **gastrulation**, taking up new locations that will allow the later formation of tissues and organs. During this process, the embryo is called a **gastrula** (plural, *gastrulae*). For organisms with a two-layered body plan, such as the cnidarian *Hydra*, this rearrangement can be fairly simple. For most animals, however, gastrulation is a dramatic rearrangement of the cells of the blastula that produces a three-layered embryo with a primitive digestive tube. Although gastrulation differs in detail from one animal group to another, the process is driven by the same general mechanisms in all species: changes in cell motility, changes in cell shape, and changes in cellular adhesion to other cells and to molecules of the extracellular matrix. The result of gastrulation is that some cells at or near the surface of the blastula move to an interior location, and three cell layers are established. The positioning of the three cell layers in the fully developed gastrula allows cells to interact with each other in new ways, leading to the generation of the body's organs.

The three layers produced by gastrulation are embryonic tissues collectively called the embryonic **germ layers**. In the late gastrula, the **ectoderm** forms the outer layer, the **endoderm** lines the embryonic digestive tract, and the **mesoderm** partly fills the space between the ectoderm and the endoderm. Eventually, these three cell layers develop into all the tissues and organs of the adult animal. Here we examine the events that occur during gastrulation in the sea urchin, frog, and chick.

Figure 47.9 outlines gastrulation in a sea urchin embryo. The sea urchin blastula consists of a single layer of cells enclosing the central blastocoel. Gastrulation begins at the vegetal pole, where individual cells detach from the blastocoel wall and enter the blastocoel as migratory cells called *mesenchyme cells*. The remaining cells near the vegetal pole flatten slightly and form a *vegetal plate* that buckles inward as a result of cell shape changes we will discuss later. This process is called **invagination**. The buckled vegetal plate then undergoes extensive rearrangement of its cells, transforming the shallow invagination into a deeper, narrower, blind-ended tube called the **archenteron**. The open end of the archenteron, which will become the anus, is called the **blastopore**. A second opening, which will become the mouth, forms when the opposite end of the archenteron touches the inside of the ectoderm and the two layers fuse, producing a rudimentary digestive tube. As you learned in Chapter 32, the developmental mode of animals can be categorized in part by whether the mouth is the first opening formed (protostome development) or the second (deuterostome development). Sea urchins and other echinoderms have deuterostome development, as do chordates like ourselves and other vertebrates.

Gastrulation in sea urchins produces an embryo with a primitive digestive tube and three germ layers, which developmental biologists commonly color-code in diagrams: blue for ectoderm, red for mesoderm, and yellow for endoderm (see Figure 47.9). This three-layered body plan is characteristic of most animal phyla and is established very early in development. In the sea urchin, the gastrula develops into a ciliated larva that drifts in ocean surface waters as zooplankton, feeding on bacteria and unicellular algae. Eventually, the larva metamorphoses into the adult form of the sea urchin, which takes up residence on the ocean floor.

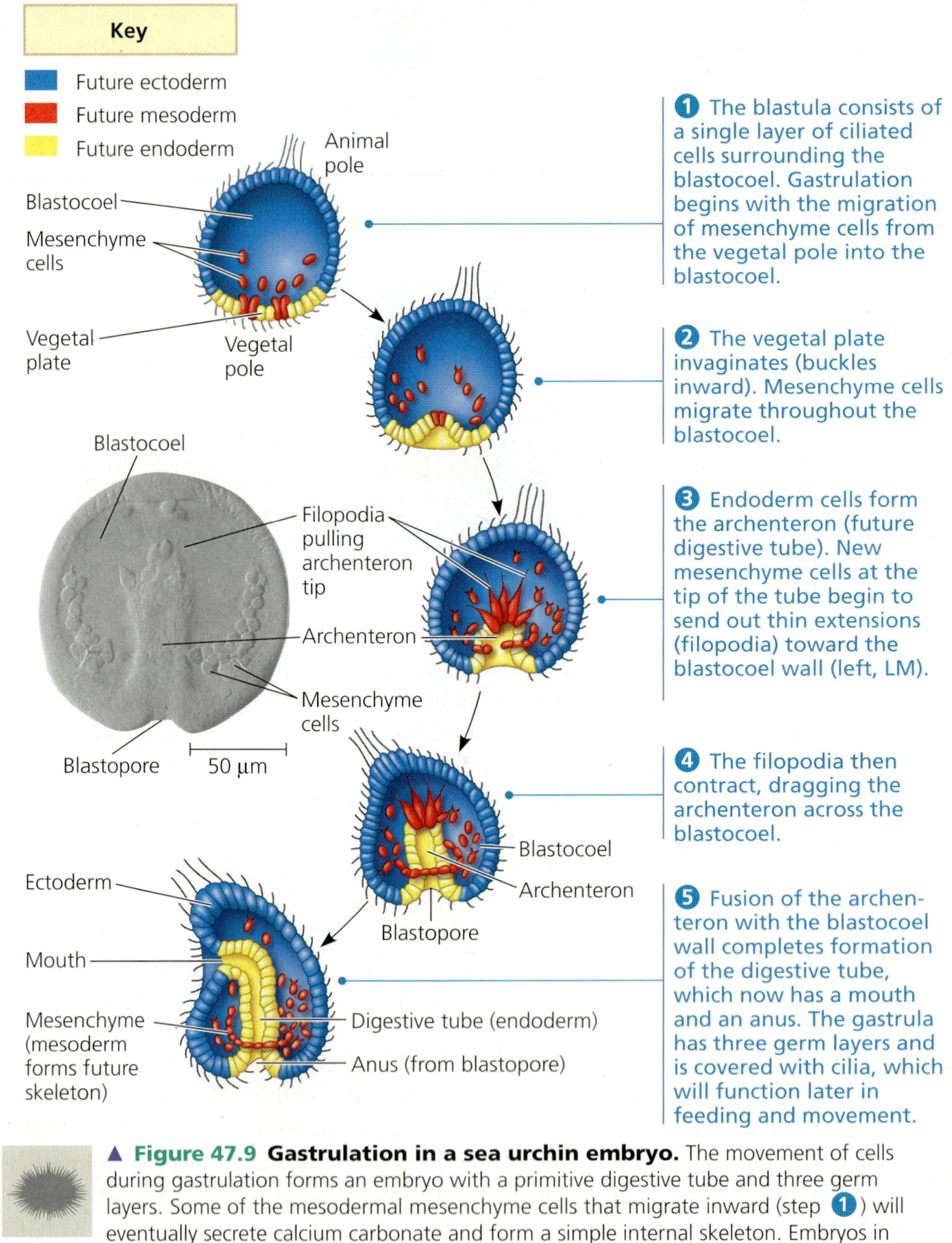

▲ **Figure 47.9 Gastrulation in a sea urchin embryo.** The movement of cells during gastrulation forms an embryo with a primitive digestive tube and three germ layers. Some of the mesodermal mesenchyme cells that migrate inward (step 1) will eventually secrete calcium carbonate and form a simple internal skeleton. Embryos in steps 1–3 are viewed from the front, those in 4 and 5 from the side.

In the frog, gastrulation also produces a three-layered embryo with an archenteron. The mechanics of gastrulation are more complicated in a frog, however, because of the large, yolk-laden cells of the vegetal hemisphere and because the wall of the blastula is more than one cell thick in most species. Gastrulation begins on the dorsal side of the blastula when a group of cells begins to invaginate—change shape and push inward—forming a crease along the region where the gray crescent formed in the zygote (see Figure 47.7). It may help to think of this crease as the site where two thin lips are pressed together. The part above this crease becomes the dorsal side of the blastopore, called the **dorsal lip** **(Figure 47.10)**. Like a slowly widening frown, the blastopore extends at each end of the crease as new cells push inward. Finally, the two ends of the blastopore meet on the ventral side. The blastopore is now a complete circle.

As the blastopore is forming, future endoderm and mesoderm cell layers on the surface of the embryo roll over the edge

1 Gastrulation begins when a small indented crease, the blastopore, appears on the dorsal side of the late blastula. The crease is formed by cells changing shape and pushing inward from the surface (invagination). Sheets of outer cells then roll inward over the dorsal lip (involution) and move into the interior (shown by the dashed arrow), where they will form endoderm and mesoderm. Meanwhile, cells at the animal pole, the future ectoderm, change shape and begin spreading over the outer surface.

2 The blastopore extends around both sides of the embryo (red arrows), as more cells invaginate. When the ends finally meet on the other side, the blastopore forms a circle that becomes smaller as ectoderm spreads downward over the surface. Internally, continued involution expands the endoderm and mesoderm, and the archenteron begins to form; as a result, the blastocoel becomes smaller.

3 Late in gastrulation, the endoderm-lined archenteron has completely replaced the blastocoel and the three germ layers are in place. The circular blastopore surrounds a plug of yolk-filled cells.

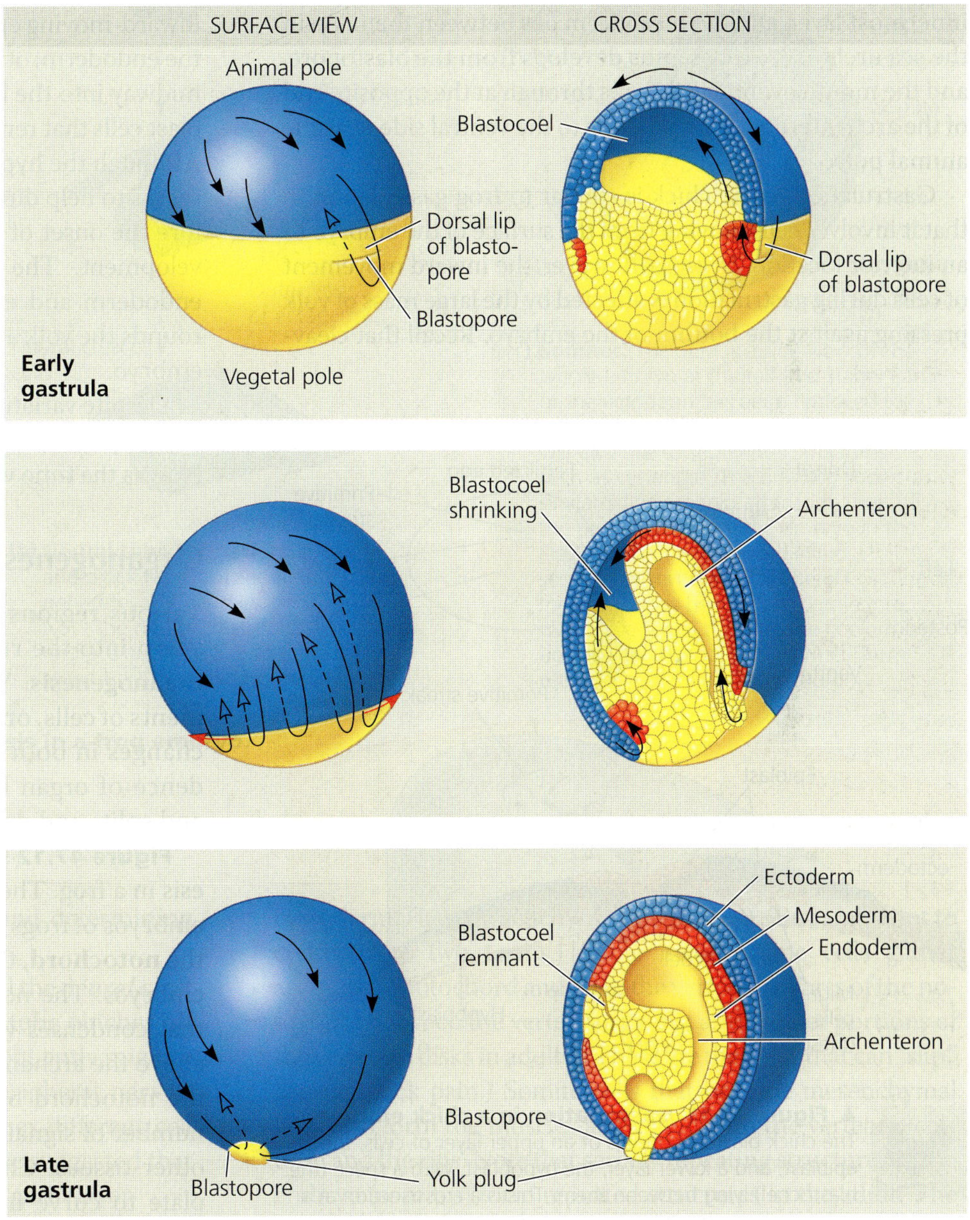

Key

- Future ectoderm
- Future mesoderm
- Future endoderm

▲ **Figure 47.10 Gastrulation in a frog embryo.**
In the frog blastula, the blastocoel is displaced toward the animal pole and is surrounded by a wall several cells thick. The cell movements that begin gastrulation occur on the dorsal side of the blastula, where the gray crescent was located in the zygote (see Figure 47.7b). Although still visible as gastrulation begins, the gray crescent is not shown here.

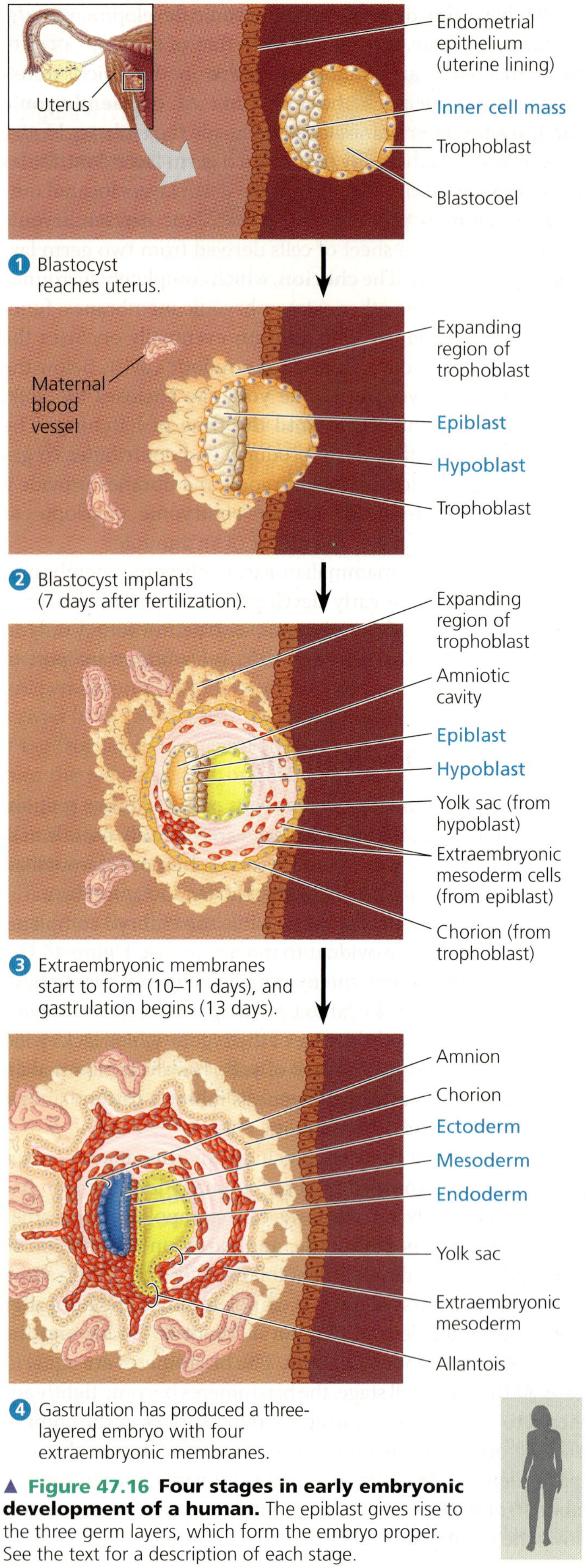

▲ **Figure 47.16 Four stages in early embryonic development of a human.** The epiblast gives rise to the three germ layers, which form the embryo proper. See the text for a description of each stage.

1 At the completion of cleavage, the embryo has more than 100 cells arranged around a central cavity and has traveled down the oviduct to the uterus. This embryonic stage, the **blastocyst**, is the mammalian version of a blastula. Clustered at one end of the blastocyst cavity is a group of cells called the **inner cell mass**, which will subsequently develop into the embryo proper and form or contribute to all the extraembryonic membranes. It is the cells of the very early blastocyst stage that are the source of embryonic stem cell lines.

2 The **trophoblast**, the outer epithelium of the blastocyst, does not contribute to the embryo itself but instead provides support services. First, it initiates implantation by secreting enzymes that break down molecules of the endometrium, the lining of the uterus. This allows the blastocyst to invade the endometrium. Then, as the trophoblast thickens through cell division, it extends fingerlike projections into the surrounding maternal tissue, which is rich in blood vessels. Invasion by the trophoblast leads to erosion of capillaries in the endometrium, causing blood to spill out and bathe trophoblast tissues. Around the time of implantation, the inner cell mass of the blastocyst forms a flat disk with an upper layer of cells, the *epiblast*, and a lower layer, the *hypoblast*, which are homologous to the epiblast and hypoblast of birds. As in birds, the human embryo develops almost entirely from epiblast cells.

3 As implantation is completed, gastrulation begins. Cells move inward from the epiblast through a primitive streak and form mesoderm and endoderm, just as in the chick (see Figure 47.11). At the same time, extraembryonic membranes begin to form. The trophoblast continues to expand into the endometrium. The invading trophoblast, mesodermal cells derived from the epiblast, and adjacent endometrial tissue all contribute to formation of the placenta (see Figure 46.16). The placenta is a vital organ that mediates exchange of nutrients, gases, and nitrogenous wastes between the embryo and the mother. The placenta also produces hormones and protects the embryo from a maternal immune response.

4 By the end of gastrulation, the embryonic germ layers have formed. The three-layered embryo is now surrounded by proliferating extraembryonic mesoderm and the four extraembryonic membranes.

The extraembryonic membranes in mammals are homologous to those of birds and other reptiles (see Figure 47.15) and develop in a similar way. Gas exchange occurs across the chorion, and the amnion cushions the developing embryo. The fluid from the amniotic cavity is the "water" expelled from the mother's vagina when the amnion breaks just prior to childbirth. Below the developing mammalian embryo, the yolk sac encloses more fluid. Although this cavity contains no yolk, the membrane that surrounds it is given the same name as the homologous membrane in birds and other reptiles. The yolk sac membrane of mammals is a site of early formation of blood cells, which later migrate into the embryo proper. The allantois in mammals is incorporated into the umbilical cord. Here it forms blood vessels that transport oxygen and nutrients from the placenta to the embryo and rid the embryo of carbon dioxide and nitrogenous wastes. Thus, the extraembryonic membranes of shelled eggs, where embryos are nourished with yolk, were conserved in mammals as they diverged from reptiles in the course of evolution, but with modifications adapted to development within the reproductive tract of the mother.

As you learned in Chapter 46, identical (monozygotic) twins can arise when embryonic cells become separated. The timing of the separation determines the nature of the twins' arrangement in the uterus with regard to their extraembryonic membranes. If the separation occurs quite early, before the trophoblast and inner cell mass become differentiated, then two embryos will grow, each with its own chorion and amnion. This is the case in about a third of twin births. In most of the remainder, the separation occurs a little later, after the chorion forms but before the amnion forms. The two embryos that develop therefore share a chorion but have separate amnions. In very rare cases, two groups of cells become separated even later, and the two embryos share a common chorion and amnion.

In this section, you have learned about the main events of embryonic development in animals. Next, we will address the cellular and molecular mechanisms by which these events occur.

CONCEPT CHECK 47.1

1. How does the fertilization envelope form in sea urchins? What is its function?
2. A frog zygote and frog blastula are nearly the same size. Explain this observation.
3. Contrast the effects of cleavage and gastrulation on development of the embryo.
4. Explain how the neural tube forms and how neural crest cells arise.
5. **WHAT IF?** Predict what would happen if you injected Ca^{2+} into an unfertilized sea urchin egg.
6. **WHAT IF?** How many chorions and amnions are present in the case of conjoined ("Siamese") twins? (These twins are always monozygotic.)

For suggested answers, see Appendix A.

CONCEPT 47.2

Morphogenesis in animals involves specific changes in cell shape, position, and adhesion

Although biologists are far from fully understanding cellular and molecular developmental mechanisms, several key principles have emerged as being fundamental to the development of all animals. Morphogenesis is a major aspect of development in both animals and plants, but only in animals does it involve the *movement* of cells. The rigid cell wall that surrounds plant cells prevents complex movements like those occurring during gastrulation. In animals, movement of parts of a cell can bring about changes in cell shape or enable a cell to migrate from one place to another within the embryo. Changes in both cell shape and cell position are involved in cleavage, gastrulation, and organogenesis. Here we consider some of the cellular components and behaviors that contribute to these events.

The Cytoskeleton, Cell Motility, and Convergent Extension

Changes in the shape of a cell usually involve reorganization of the cytoskeleton (see Table 6.1). Consider, for example, how the cells of the neural plate form the neural tube **(Figure 47.17)**. First, microtubules oriented parallel to the dorsal-ventral axis of the embryo apparently help lengthen the cells in that direction. At the dorsal end of each cell is a parallel array of microfilaments (actin filaments) oriented crosswise. These microfilaments contract, giving the cells a wedge shape that forces the ectoderm layer to

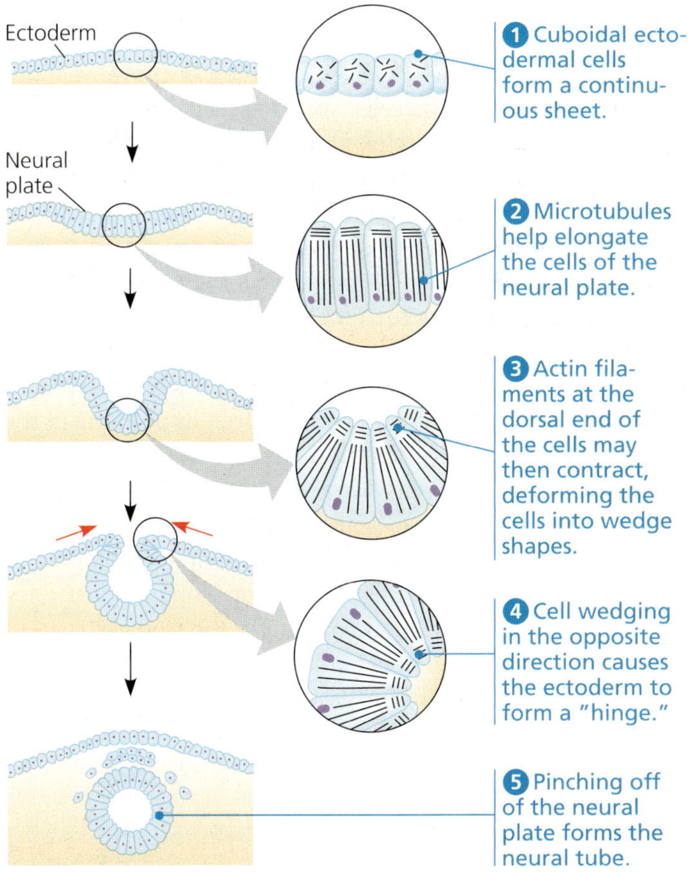

▲ **Figure 47.17 Change in cell shape during morphogenesis.** Reorganization of the cytoskeleton is associated with morphogenetic changes in embryonic tissues, as shown here for the formation of the neural tube in vertebrates.

bend inward. Similar changes in cell shape occur throughout development in other places, such as the hinge regions where the neural tube is pinching off from the ectoderm and sites where evaginations (outpocketings) of tissue layers form.

The cytoskeleton also drives cell migration, the active movement of cells from one place to another in developing animals. Cells "crawl" within the embryo by using cytoskeletal fibers to extend and retract cellular protrusions. This type of motility is akin to the amoeboid movement described in Figure 6.27b; but in contrast with the thick pseudopodia of some amoeboid cells, the cellular protrusions of migrating embryonic cells are usually flat sheets (lamellipodia) or spikes (filopodia).

During gastrulation in some organisms, invagination begins when cuboidal cells on the surface of the blastula become wedge-shaped. However, the movement of cells deeper into the embryo involves the extension of filopodia by cells at the leading edge of the migrating tissue. The cells that first move through the blastopore and up along the inside of the blastocoel wall drag others behind them, thus helping direct movement of the entire sheet of cells from the embryo's surface into appropriate locations in the blastocoel. The involuted sheet then forms the endoderm and mesoderm of the embryo (see Figure 47.10). There are also many situations in which cells migrate individually, as when the cells of a somite or the neural crest disperse to various parts of the embryo. In fact, during gastrulation in many species, the mesoderm moves into the embryo as individual cells. We have seen two such examples thus far, in the sea urchin and the chick.

Cell crawling is also involved in **convergent extension**, a type of morphogenetic movement in which the cells of a tissue layer rearrange themselves so that the sheet becomes narrower (converges) while it becomes longer (extends). It's as if a crowd of people waiting to enter a theater for a concert were told that the doors would not open until they formed a single-file line; the line would become much longer as it narrowed. In the embryo, the cells elongate, with their ends pointing in the direction they will move, and they wedge between each other into fewer columns of cells **(Figure 47.18)**. When many cells converge this way, the tissue can extend dramatically. Convergent extension is important in early embryonic development. It occurs, for example, as the archenteron elongates in the sea urchin embryo and during involution in the frog gastrula. In the latter case, convergent extension is responsible for changing the spherical shape of the gastrula to the rounded rectangular shape of the frog embryo seen in Figure 47.12c.

Role of Cell Adhesion Molecules and the Extracellular Matrix

Scientists are refining their understanding of the signaling pathways that trigger and guide cell movement and cell interactions during morphogenesis. A key group of proteins that contribute to cell migration and stable tissue structure are glycoproteins called **cell adhesion molecules (CAMs)**, transmembrane cell-surface proteins that bind to CAMs on other cells. CAMs vary in amount, chemical identity, or both from one type of cell to another. These differences help regulate morphogenetic movements and tissue building.

One important class of CAMs is the **cadherins**, which require calcium ions outside the cell for proper function. There are many different cadherins, and the gene for each cadherin is expressed in specific locations at specific times during embryonic development. Janet Heasman, Chris Wylie, and colleagues have vividly demonstrated the importance of one particular cadherin in the formation of the frog blastula **(Figure 47.19)**. Cadherins are also involved in the tight adhesion of cells in the mammalian embryo that first occurs at the eight-cell stage, when cadherin production begins.

The processes of cell migration and tissue organization also involve the extracellular matrix (ECM), the meshwork of secreted glycoproteins and other macromolecules lying outside the plasma membranes of cells (see Figure 6.30). The ECM helps to guide cells in many types of morphogenetic movements, such as migration of individual cells or shape changes of cell sheets. On the cells that undergo movement, membrane proteins act as receptors that bind specific ECM molecules. An organized array of ECM fibers may function as tracks, directing migrating cells along particular routes. Other substances in the ECM keep cells on the correct paths by *inhibiting* migration off the path. Thus, nonmigratory cells along migration pathways may promote or inhibit movement of other cells, depending on the specific molecules they secrete into the ECM.

Several kinds of extracellular glycoproteins, such as fibronectin, promote cell migration by providing specific molecular anchorage for moving cells. For example, fibronectin plays such a role at the leading edge of the involuting tissue during frog gastrulation. Fibronectin fibers line the roof of the blastocoel, and as the future mesoderm moves into the interior of the embryo, the cells at the free edge of the involuting sheet migrate along the fibers (see Figure 47.10). Researchers can prevent the attachment of cells to fibronectin by injecting embryos with antibodies against either fibronectin or the

▶ **Figure 47.18 Convergent extension of a sheet of cells.** In this simplified diagram, the cells elongate in a particular direction and crawl between each other (convergence), as the sheet becomes longer and narrower (extension).

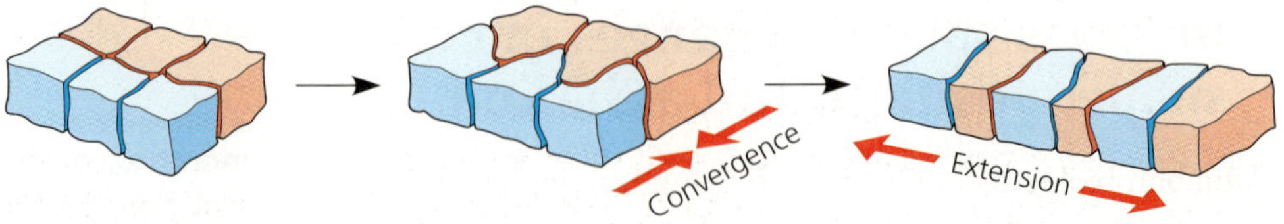

▼ Figure 47.19 Inquiry

Is cadherin required for development of the blastula?

EXPERIMENT In 1994, Janet Heasman, Chris Wylie, and colleagues, then at the Wellcome/CRC Institute in Cambridge, England, injected frog eggs with nucleic acid complementary to the mRNA encoding a cadherin known as EP cadherin. This "antisense" nucleic acid leads to destruction of EP cadherin mRNA, so no EP cadherin protein is produced. Frog sperm were then added to experimental (injected) eggs and to control (noninjected) eggs. The embryos that developed were observed with a scanning electron microscope.

RESULTS As shown in these SEMs of cut-open embryos, fertilized control eggs developed into normal blastulae, but fertilized experimental eggs did not. In the absence of EP cadherin, the blastocoel did not form properly, and the cells were arranged in a disorganized fashion.

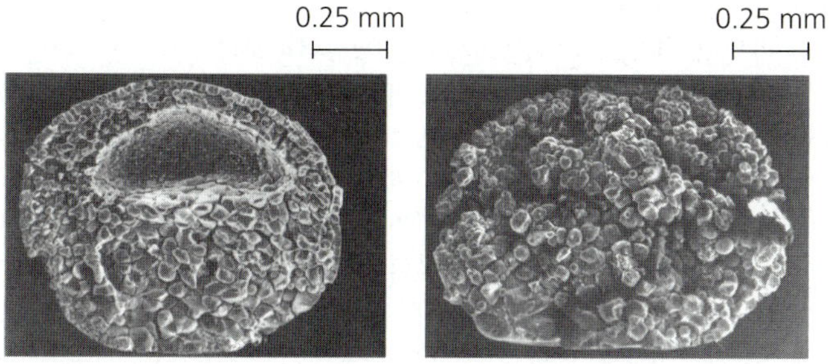

Control embryo — Embryo without EP cadherin

CONCLUSION During embryonic development in the frog, the cell adhesion molecule EP cadherin is required for proper cell organization in the blastula.

SOURCE J. Heasman et al., A functional test for maternally inherited cadherin in *Xenopus* shows its importance in cell adhesion at the blastula stage, *Development* 120:49–57 (1994).

WHAT IF? What do you predict would be the effect on embryos if you placed frog blastulae in water from which all the calcium had been removed?

receptors that bind fibronectin at the cell surface. Either treatment prevents the crawling of mesoderm.

A wealth of evidence supports the conclusion that moving cells engage in an ongoing dialogue with the ECM and other cells in the vicinity. As migrating cells move along specific paths, a variety of receptor proteins on their surfaces pick up directional cues from the immediate environment. Such signaling molecules, which may be ECM molecules or small soluble factors (see Chapter 11), can initiate intracellular signaling pathways that direct the orientation of cytoskeletal elements so that the cell moves in the proper direction. Such signaling may also affect the expression or function of other proteins involved in the migration.

Based on previous studies, Mungo Marsden and Doug DeSimone were intrigued by the possibility that cell-ECM and cell-cell binding systems might affect each other during convergent extension. **Figure 47.20** describes their initial experiments to investigate this possibility. The results of their full study support a model in which fibronectin binding to its

▼ Figure 47.20 Inquiry

Is an organized fibronectin matrix required for convergent extension?

EXPERIMENT Mungo Marsden and Doug DeSimone, at the University of Virginia, wondered whether an organized fibronectin matrix was essential for convergent extension. Into the blastocoels of frog blastulae, they injected molecules that would block the interaction of fibronectin with its receptor protein on cell surfaces, knowing from previous work that this would block organization of the fibronectin matrix. As a control, they injected a very similar molecule that did not block matrix assembly. They compared convergent extension in matrix-blocked and control embryos in a series of experiments, two of which are shown here.

Experiment 1: In whole embryos, a probe was used to detect the presence of an mRNA that marks tissues normally undergoing convergent extension.

Experiment 2: Certain tissues that normally undergo convergent extension were removed from embryos, placed between glass cover slips, allowed to develop, and observed through a microscope.

RESULTS

Experiment 1: The marked tissue in the matrix-blocked whole embryo was shorter and wider than that in the control embryo.

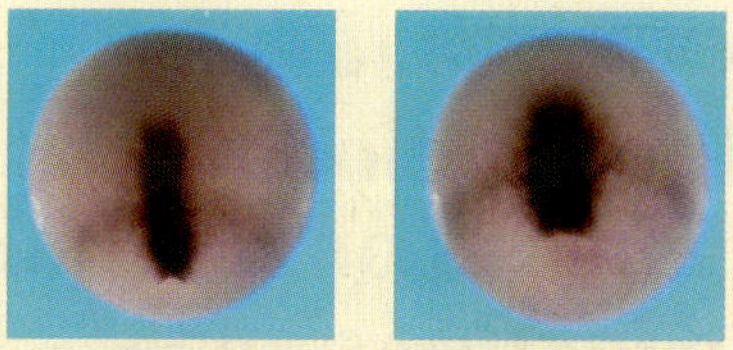

Control — Matrix blocked

Experiment 2: Cells (nuclei marked by yellow arrowheads) were tightly packed in a column in the control tissues but not in the matrix-blocked tissues. (Red arrows indicate column widths.)

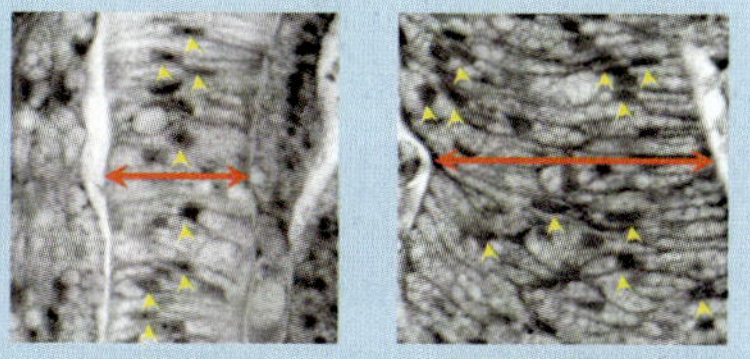

Control — Matrix blocked

CONCLUSION Fibronectin matrix assembly is crucial for the cell behaviors underlying convergent extension.

SOURCE M. Marsden and D. W. DeSimone, Integrin-ECM interactions regulate cadherin-dependent cell adhesion and are required for convergent extension in *Xenopus*, *Current Biology* 13:1182–1191 (2003).

WHAT IF? Suppose you wanted to determine if convergent extension can occur on a *preexisting* fibronectin matrix or if it requires a matrix formed *during* convergent extension. If you could make an artificial fibronectin matrix on glass cover slips, how would you design an experiment to ask this question?

receptor provides a molecular signal to the cell that ultimately affects the function of cadherins. ECM molecules and cadherins thus appear to be linked in a single pathway driving convergent extension.

As you have seen, cell behavior and the molecular mechanisms underlying it are crucial to the morphogenesis of the embryo. In the next section, you'll learn that the same basic cellular and genetic processes ensure that the various types of cells end up in the right places in each embryo.

CONCEPT CHECK 47.2

1. During formation of the neural tube, cube-shaped cells change to wedge-shaped cells. Describe the roles of microtubules and microfilaments in this process.
2. In the frog embryo, convergent extension is thought to elongate the notochord along the anterior-posterior axis. Explain how the words *convergent* and *extension* apply to this process.
3. **WHAT IF?** Predict what would happen if, just before neural tube formation, you treated embryos with a drug that blocks the function of microfilaments.

For suggested answers, see Appendix A.

CONCEPT **47.3**

The developmental fate of cells depends on their history and on inductive signals

Coupled with the morphogenetic changes that give an animal and its parts their characteristic shapes, development also requires the timely differentiation of many kinds of cells in specific locations. In Chapter 20, you learned about the principle of genomic equivalence: Virtually every cell in an organism has the same genome. However, different cell types make different sets of proteins because they end up expressing different sets of genes. Therefore, during differentiation, some mechanism must send cells down different pathways of gene expression. Two general principles integrate our current knowledge of the genetic and cellular mechanisms that underlie differentiation during embryonic development.

First, *during early cleavage divisions, embryonic cells must somehow become different from one another.* In many animal species, initial differences between cells result from the uneven distribution of cytoplasmic determinants in the unfertilized egg. By partitioning the heterogeneous cytoplasm of a polarized egg, cleavage parcels out different mRNAs, proteins, and other molecules to blastomeres in a type of asymmetrical cell division (see Figure 18.15a). These cytoplasmic determinants are in many cases transcription factors, DNA-binding proteins that activate one set of genes rather than another. Thus, the resulting differences in the cells' cytoplasmic composition help specify the body axes and influence the expression of genes that affect the cells' developmental fate. In amniotes, local environmental differences play the principal role in establishing early differences between embryonic cells. For example, cells of the inner cell mass are located internally in the early human embryo, whereas trophoblast cells are located on the outside surface of the blastocyst. The different environments of these two groups of cells appear to determine their very different fates.

Second, *once initial cell asymmetries are set up, subsequent interactions among the embryonic cells influence their fate, usually by causing changes in gene expression.* This mechanism, called **induction**, eventually brings about the differentiation of the many specialized cell types making up an animal. Induction may be mediated by diffusible signaling molecules or, if the cells are in contact, by cell-surface interactions.

It will help to keep these two principles in mind as we delve into the molecular and cellular mechanisms of differentiation and morphogenesis during embryonic development of the species we're focusing on in this chapter. But to ask questions about *how* the fate of an early embryonic cell is determined, we need to know what that fate is. So let's first look at some historic experiments that provided early researchers with information about cell fates.

Fate Mapping

Biologists have studied the early development of many species, carefully scrutinizing each cell division, in an attempt to follow the fate and trace the ancestry of each embryonic cell. These labor-intensive studies have produced extremely useful territorial diagrams of embryonic development, called **fate maps**.

In classic studies performed in the 1920s, German embryologist Walther Vogt charted fate maps for the different regions of early amphibian embryos. Vogt's results were among the earliest indications that the lineages of cells making up the three germ layers created by gastrulation are traceable to cells in the blastula, before gastrulation has begun **(Figure 47.21a)**. Later researchers developed techniques that allowed them to mark an individual blastomere during cleavage and then follow the marker as it was distributed to all the mitotic descendants of that cell **(Figure 47.21b)**.

Perhaps the ultimate approach to fate mapping has been carried out on the soil-dwelling nematode *Caenorhabditis elegans*. This worm is easily raised in the laboratory in petri dishes. It is about 1 mm long, has a simple transparent body with only a few types of cells, and grows from zygote to mature adult in only 3½ days. Most individuals are hermaphrodites, producing both eggs and sperm, which has advantages for genetic studies.

The attributes of *C. elegans* allowed Sydney Brenner, Robert Horvitz, and Jonathan Sulston to determine the complete

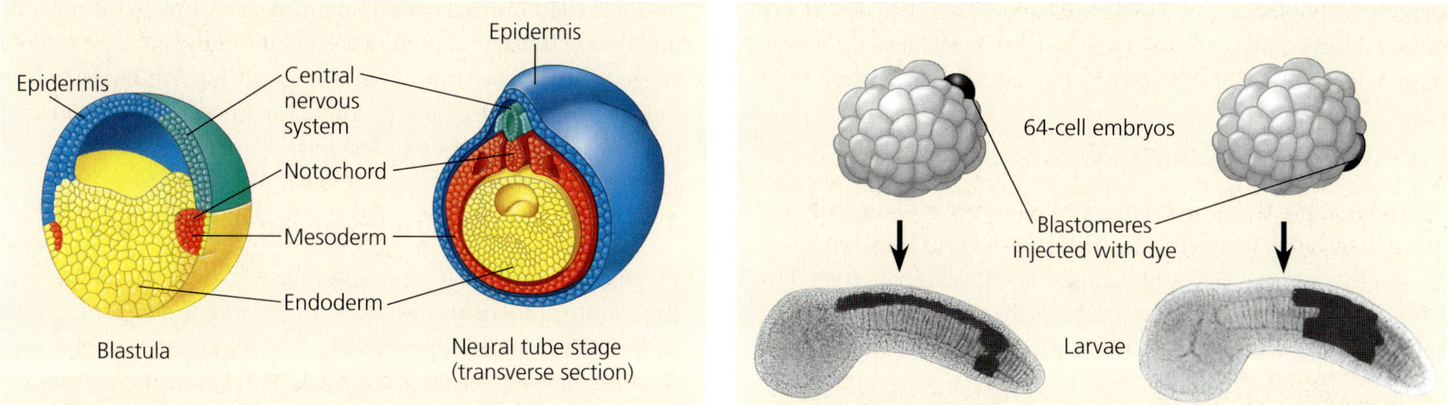

(a) Fate map of a frog embryo. The fates of groups of cells in a frog blastula (left) were determined in part by marking different regions of the blastula surface with nontoxic dyes of various colors. The embryos were sectioned at later stages of development, such as the neural tube stage shown on the right, and the locations of the dyed cells determined. The two embryonic stages shown here represent the result of numerous such experiments.

(b) Cell lineage analysis in a tunicate. In lineage analysis, an individual blastomere is injected with a dye during cleavage, as indicated in the drawings of 64-cell embryos of a tunicate, an invertebrate chordate (top). The dark regions in the light micrographs of larvae (bottom) correspond to the cells that developed from the two different blastomeres indicated in the drawings.

▲ **Figure 47.21 Fate mapping for two chordates.**

cell lineage of this organism, using a multipronged approach. Every adult hermaphrodite of the species has exactly 959 somatic cells, which arise from the zygote in virtually the same way for every individual. Careful microscopic observations during the entire period of development, coupled with experiments in which particular cells or groups of cells were destroyed by a laser beam or through mutations, resulted in the cell lineage diagram shown in **Figure 47.22**. In 2002, these researchers shared a Nobel Prize for their accomplishment, which led to *C. elegans* becoming the model organism of choice for many developmental biologists.

Developmental biologists have combined fate-mapping studies with experimental manipulation of parts of embryos to ascertain whether a cell's fate can be changed. Starting with the normal embryo's fate map, researchers can examine how the differentiation of cells is altered in experimental situations or in mutant embryos. Two important conclusions have emerged. First, in most animals, specific tissues of the older embryo are the products of certain early "founder cells" that contain unique factors as the result of asymmetrical cell divisions. Second, as development proceeds, a cell's *developmental potential*—the range of

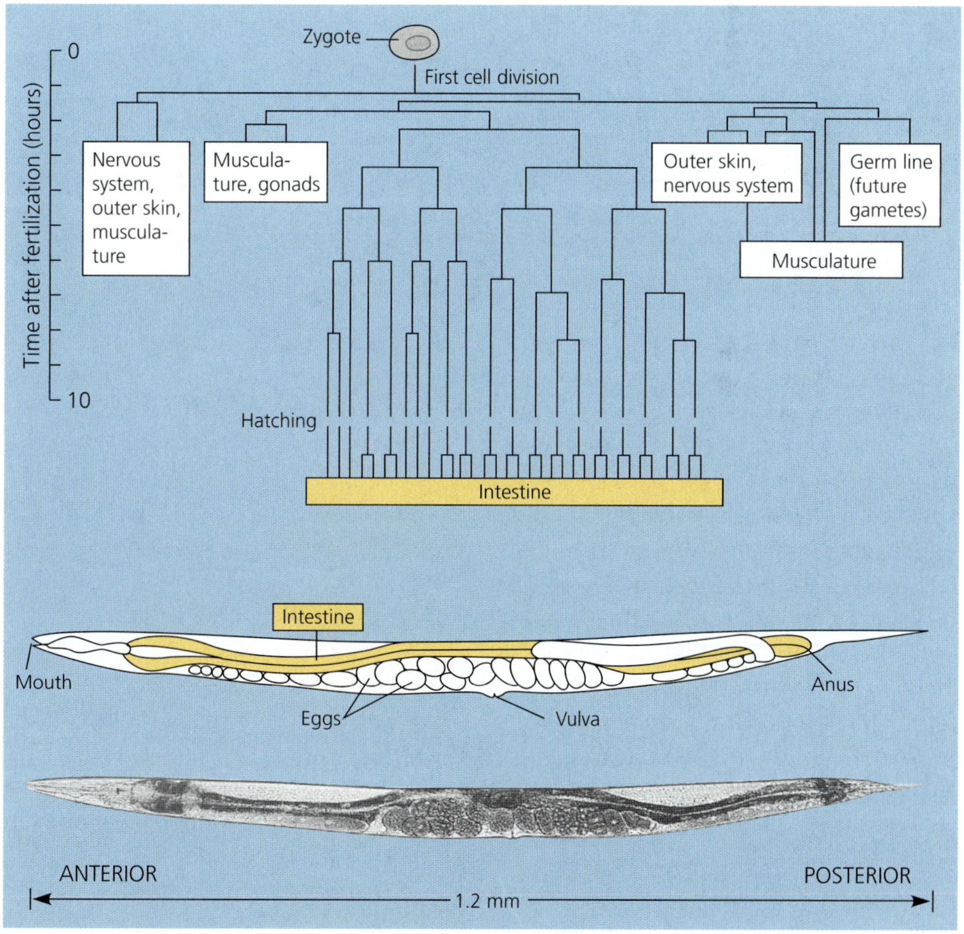

▲ **Figure 47.22 Cell lineage in *Caenorhabditis elegans*.** The *C. elegans* embryo is transparent, making it possible for researchers to trace the lineage of every cell, from the zygote to the adult worm (LM). The diagram shows a detailed lineage only for the intestine, which is derived exclusively from one of the first four cells formed from the zygote. The eggs will be fertilized internally and released through the vulva.

structures that it can give rise to—becomes restricted. Let's look more closely at these two aspects by which cell fates are determined. (For review of cell fate determination, see Chapter 18.)

Establishing Cellular Asymmetries

To understand at the molecular level how embryonic cells acquire their fates, it is helpful to think first about how the basic axes of the embryo are established. This can often be traced to a specific event in early development that sets up a particular cellular asymmetry, thus beginning to lay out the body plan.

The Axes of the Basic Body Plan

As you have learned, a bilaterally symmetrical animal has an anterior-posterior axis, a dorsal-ventral axis, and left and right sides (see Figure 47.7a). Establishing this basic body plan is the first step in morphogenesis and a prerequisite for the development of tissues and organs.

In nonamniote vertebrates, basic instructions for forming the body axes are established early, during oogenesis or fertilization. For example, in many frogs, including the species we've discussed, the locations of melanin and yolk in the unfertilized egg define the animal and vegetal hemispheres, respectively. The animal-vegetal axis indirectly determines the anterior-posterior body axis. Fertilization then triggers cortical rotation, which establishes the dorsal-ventral axis and at the same time leads to the appearance of the gray crescent, whose position marks the dorsal side (see Figure 47.7b). Once any two axes are established, the third (in this case, the left-right) axis is specified by default. (Of course, specific molecular mechanisms must then establish which side is left and which is right.)

In amniotes, the body axes are not fully established until later. In chicks, gravity is apparently involved in establishing the anterior-posterior axis as the egg travels down the hen's oviduct before being laid. Later, pH differences between the two sides of the blastoderm cells establish the dorsal-ventral axis. If the pH is artificially reversed above and below the blastoderm, the part facing the egg white will turn into the belly (ventral side) and the side facing the yolk will turn into the back (dorsal side), opposite to their normal fates. In mammals, no polarity is obvious until after cleavage. However, the results of recent experiments suggest that the orientation of the egg and sperm nuclei before they fuse influences the location of the first cleavage plane and thus may play a role in establishing the embryonic axes.

Restriction of the Developmental Potential of Cells

In many species that have cytoplasmic determinants, only the zygote is **totipotent**—that is, capable of developing into all the different cell types of that species. In these organisms, the first cleavage is asymmetrical, with the two blastomeres

▼ Figure 47.23 Inquiry

How does distribution of the gray crescent affect the developmental potential of the first two daughter cells?

EXPERIMENT Hans Spemann, at the University of Freiburg-im-Breisgau in Germany, carried out the following experiment in 1938 to test whether substances were located asymmetrically in the gray crescent.

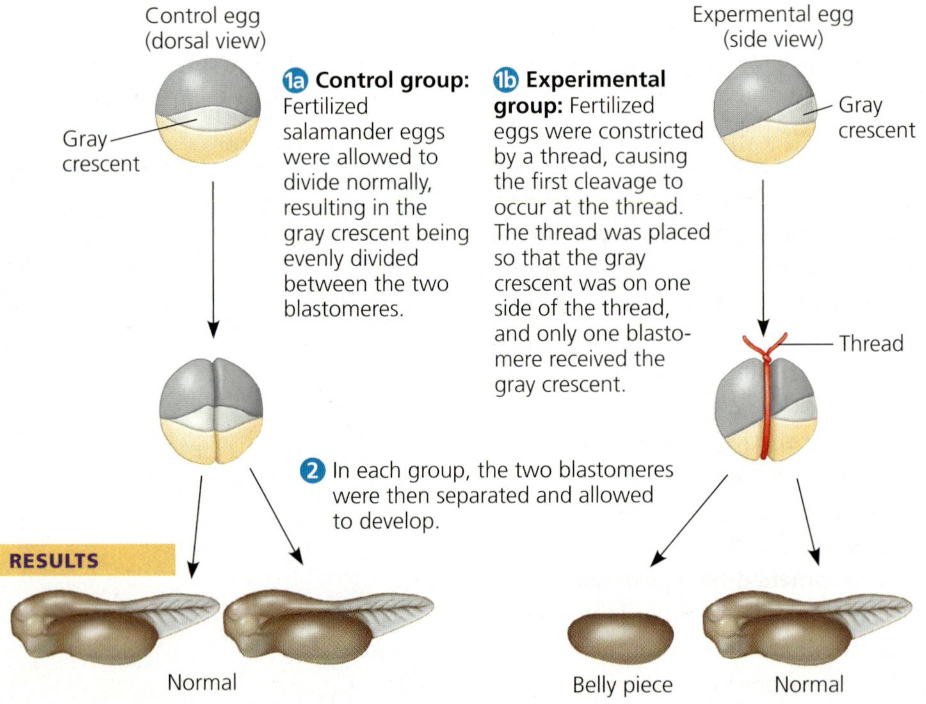

RESULTS

Blastomeres that received half or all of the material in the gray crescent developed into normal embryos, but a blastomere that received none of the gray crescent gave rise to an abnormal embryo without dorsal structures. Spemann called it a "belly piece."

CONCLUSION The developmental potential of the two blastomeres normally formed during the first cleavage division depends on their acquisition of cytoplasmic determinants localized in the gray crescent.

SOURCE H. Spemann, *Embryonic Development and Induction*, Yale University Press, New Haven (1938).

WHAT IF? In a similar experiment 40 years earlier, embryologist Hans Roux allowed the first cleavage to occur and then used a needle to kill just one blastomere. The embryo that developed from the remaining blastomere (plus remnants of the dead cell) was abnormal, resembling a half-embryo. Propose a hypothesis to explain why Roux's result differed from the control result in Spemann's experiment.

receiving different cytoplasmic determinants. However, even in species that have cytoplasmic determinants, the first cleavage may occur along an axis that produces two identical blastomeres, which then have equal developmental potential. This occurs in amphibians, for instance, as demonstrated in 1938 in an experiment by German zoologist Hans Spemann **(Figure 47.23)**. Thus, the fates of embryonic cells can be affected not only by the distribution of cytoplasmic determinants but also by how this distribution relates to the zygote's characteristic pattern of cleavage.

In contrast with the embryonic cells of many other animals, the cells of mammalian embryos remain totipotent until the 16-cell stage, when their location determines whether they will give rise to cells of the trophoblast or of the inner cell mass of the blastocyst, thus establishing their ultimate fates. Through the 8-cell stage, the blastomeres of a mammalian embryo all look alike, and each can form a complete embryo if isolated. Researchers have taken this as evidence that the early blastomeres of mammals probably receive equivalent amounts of cytoplasmic components from the egg. Recent work, however, suggests that the very early cells (even the first two) are not actually equivalent in a normal embryo, and their ability to form a complete embryo if isolated shows that they may be able to regulate their fate, depending on their environment. The jury is still out on this matter, which is an area of great interest to researchers.

Regardless of how similar or different early embryonic cells are in a particular species, the progressive restriction of developmental potential is a general feature of development in all animals. In some species, the cells of the early gastrula retain the capacity to give rise to more than one kind of cell, though they have lost their totipotency. If left alone, the dorsal ectoderm of an early amphibian gastrula will develop into a neural plate above the notochord. And if the dorsal ectoderm is experimentally replaced with ectoderm from some other location in the same gastrula, the transplanted tissue will form a neural plate. But if the same experiment is performed on a late-stage gastrula, the transplanted ectoderm will not respond to its new environment and will not form a neural plate. In general, the tissue-specific fates of cells in a late gastrula are fixed. Even when they are manipulated experimentally, these cells usually give rise to the same types of cells as in the normal embryo, indicating that their fate is already determined.

Cell Fate Determination and Pattern Formation by Inductive Signals

Once embryonic cell division creates cells that differ from each other, the cells begin to influence each other's fates by induction. At the molecular level, the response to an inductive signal is usually to switch on a set of genes that make the receiving cells differentiate into a specific tissue. Here we examine two examples of induction, an essential process in the development of many tissues in most animals.

The "Organizer" of Spemann and Mangold

The importance of induction during development of amphibians was dramatically demonstrated in transplantation experiments performed by Hans Spemann and his student Hilde Mangold in the 1920s. Based on the results of their most famous experiment, summarized in **Figure 47.24**, they concluded that

▼ Figure 47.24 Inquiry

Can the dorsal lip of the blastopore induce cells in another part of the amphibian embryo to change their developmental fate?

EXPERIMENT In 1924, Hans Spemann and Hilde Mangold, at the University of Freiburg-im-Breisgau in Germany, transplanted a piece of the dorsal lip from a pigmented newt gastrula to the ventral side of a nonpigmented newt gastrula to investigate the inductive ability of the dorsal lip. Cross sections of the gastrulae are shown here.

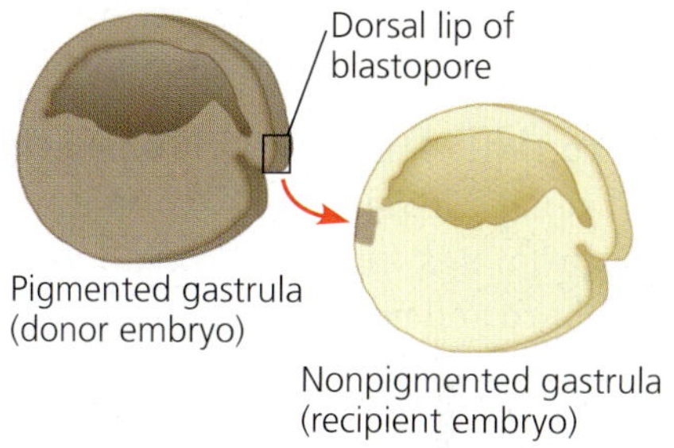

RESULTS The recipient embryo formed a second notochord and neural tube in the region of the transplant, and eventually most of a second embryo developed. Examination of the interior of the double embryo revealed that the secondary structures were formed partly, but not wholly, from recipient tissue.

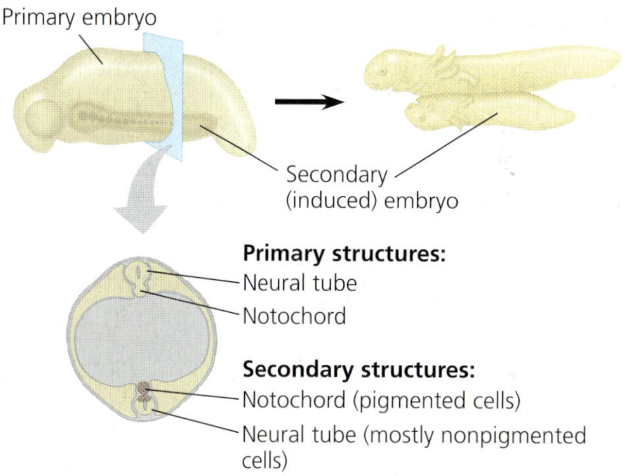

CONCLUSION The transplanted dorsal lip was able to induce cells in a different region of the recipient to form structures different from their normal fate. In effect, the transplanted dorsal lip "organized" the later development of an entire extra embryo.

SOURCE H. Spemann and H. Mangold, Induction of embryonic primordia by implantation of organizers from a different species, Trans. V. Hamburger (1924). Reprinted in *International Journal of Developmental Biology* 45:13–38 (2001).

WHAT IF? Because the transplanted dorsal lip caused the recipient tissue to become something it would not otherwise have become, a signal of some sort must have passed from the dorsal lip. If you identified a protein candidate for the signaling molecule, how could you test whether it actually functions in signaling?

the dorsal lip of the blastopore in the early gastrula functions as an "organizer" of the embryo's body plan by initiating a chain of inductions that results in the formation of the notochord, the neural tube, and other organs.

Developmental biologists are still working intensively to identify the molecular basis of induction by *Spemann's organizer* (also called the *gastrula organizer* or simply the *organizer*). An important clue has come from studies of a growth factor called bone morphogenetic protein 4 (BMP-4). (Bone morphogenetic proteins, a family of related proteins with a variety of developmental roles, derive their name from members of the family that are important in bone formation.) In amphibians, a high concentration of BMP-4 signals cells on the ventral side of the gastrula to travel down the pathway toward formation of ventral structures. One major function of the cells of the organizer seems to be to *inactivate* BMP-4 on the dorsal side of the embryo by producing proteins that bind to BMP-4, rendering it unable to signal. This inactivation, along with signaling by other molecules not yet identified, promotes formation of dorsal structures such as the notochord and neural tube. In tissues between the dorsal and ventral sides, a lower concentration of BMP-4 results in lateral structures appropriate for the specific location along the dorsal-ventral axis. The varying concentration of BMP-4 along this axis is an example of a morphogen gradient (see Chapter 18). Proteins related to BMP-4 and its inhibitors are also found in other animals, including invertebrates such as the fruit fly, where they also regulate the dorsal-ventral axis. The ubiquity of these molecules suggests that they evolved long ago and may participate in the development of many different organisms.

The induction by BMP-4 of ventral and lateral structures is only one example of many cell-cell interactions that transform the three germ layers into organ systems. Many inductions seem to involve a sequence of inductive steps from different surrounding tissues that progressively determine the fate of cells. In the eye, for example, lens formation by ectodermal cells involves precisely timed inductive signals from ectodermal, mesodermal, and endodermal cells.

Formation of the Vertebrate Limb

The action of the gastrula organizer is a classic example of induction, and we can see that the organizer induces cells to take on their fates in appropriate locations relative to each other. Thus, inductive signals play a major role in **pattern formation**—the development of an animal's spatial organization, the arrangement of organs and tissues in their characteristic places in three-dimensional space. The molecular cues that control pattern formation, called **positional information**, tell a cell where it is with respect to the animal's body axes and help to determine how the cell and its descendants will respond to molecular signaling.

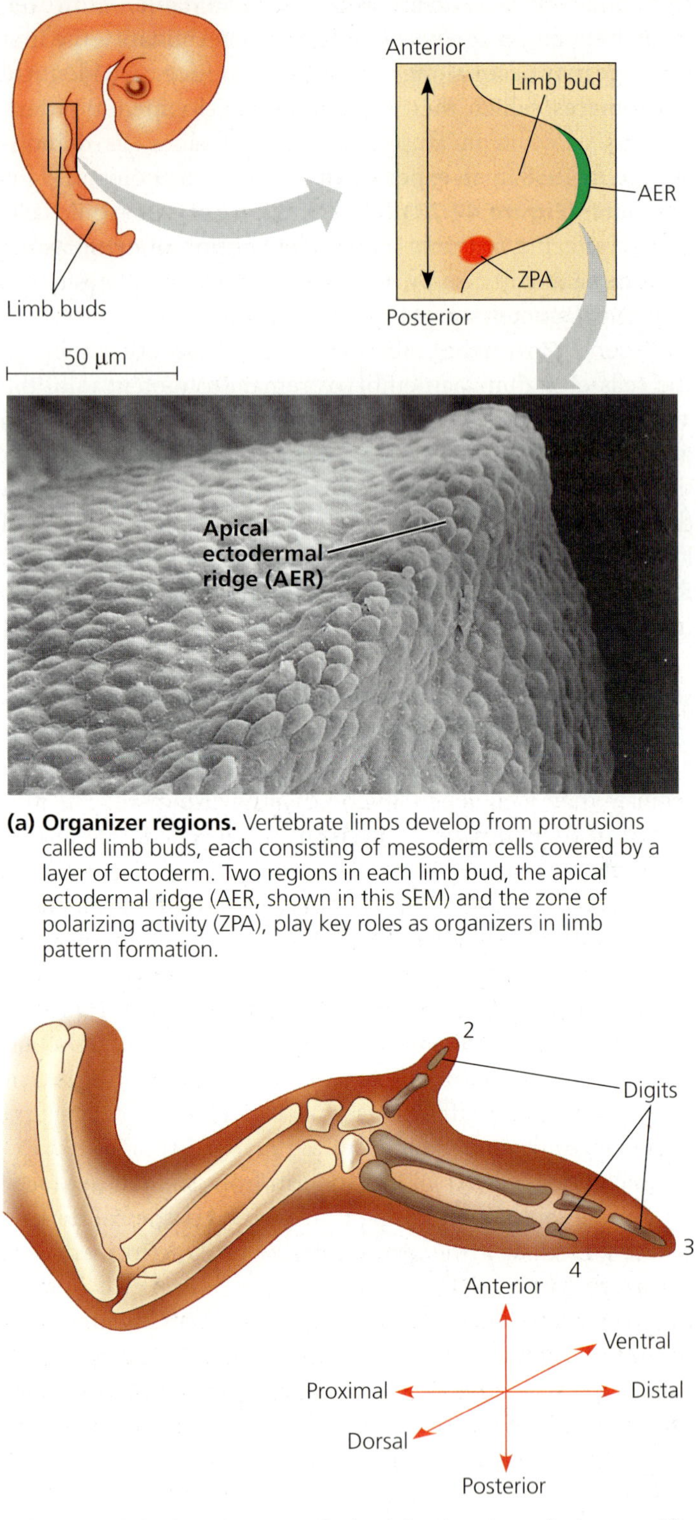

(a) Organizer regions. Vertebrate limbs develop from protrusions called limb buds, each consisting of mesoderm cells covered by a layer of ectoderm. Two regions in each limb bud, the apical ectodermal ridge (AER, shown in this SEM) and the zone of polarizing activity (ZPA), play key roles as organizers in limb pattern formation.

(b) Wing of chick embryo. As the bud develops into a limb, a specific pattern of tissues emerges. In the chick wing, for example, the digits are always present in the arrangement shown here. Pattern formation requires each embryonic cell to receive some kind of positional information indicating location along the three axes of the limb. The AER and ZPA secrete molecules that help provide this information. (Numbers are assigned to the digits based on a convention established for vertebrate limbs. The chicken wing has only four digits; the first digit points backward and is not shown in the diagram.)

▲ **Figure 47.25 Vertebrate limb development.**

In Chapter 18, we discussed pattern formation in the development of *Drosophila*. For the study of pattern formation in vertebrates, a classic model system has been limb development in the chick. The wings and legs of chicks, like all vertebrate limbs, begin as limb buds, bumps of mesodermal tissue covered by a layer of ectoderm **(Figure 47.25a)**. Each component of a chick limb, such as a specific bone or muscle, develops with a precise location and orientation relative to three axes: the proximal-distal axis (the "shoulder-to-fingertip" axis), the anterior-posterior axis (the "thumb-to-little finger" axis), and the dorsal-ventral axis (the "knuckle-to-palm" axis). The embryonic cells within a limb bud respond to positional information indicating location along these three axes **(Figure 47.25b)**.

Two critical organizer regions in a limb bud have profound effects on the limb's development. These regions are present in all vertebrate limb buds, including those that will develop into forelimbs (such as wings or arms) and those destined to become hind limbs. The cells of these regions secrete proteins that provide key positional information to the other cells of the bud.

One limb-bud organizer region is the **apical ectodermal ridge (AER)**, a thickened area of ectoderm at the tip of the bud (see Figure 47.25a). Removing the AER blocks outgrowth of the limb along the proximal-distal axis. The cells of the AER secrete several protein signals in the fibroblast growth factor (FGF) family that promote limb-bud outgrowth. If the AER is surgically removed and beads soaked with FGF are put in its place, a nearly normal limb will develop. In 2006, researchers identified an FGF-secreting AER that appears to be responsible for building a shark's unpaired (median) fins. This finding suggests that the AER may have predated the appearance of paired limbs in the vertebrate lineage, giving the AER a longer evolutionary history than previously thought.

The second major limb-bud organizer region is the **zone of polarizing activity (ZPA)**, a block of mesodermal tissue located underneath the ectoderm where the posterior side of the bud is attached to the body (see Figure 47.25a). The ZPA is necessary for proper pattern formation along the anterior-posterior axis of the limb. Cells nearest the ZPA give rise to the posterior structures, such as the most posterior of the chick's three digits (positioned like our little finger); cells farthest from the ZPA form anterior structures, including the most anterior digit (like our thumb).

The tissue transplantation experiment outlined in **Figure 47.26** supports the hypothesis that the ZPA produces an inductive signal that conveys positional information indicating "posterior." Indeed, researchers have discovered that the cells of the ZPA secrete an important protein growth factor called Sonic hedgehog.* These cells set up a gradient of Sonic hedgehog and other growth factors that Sonic hedgehog causes to be expressed. If cells genetically engineered to produce large amounts of Sonic hedgehog are implanted in the anterior region of a normal limb bud, a mirror-image limb results—just as if a ZPA had been grafted there. Studies of the mouse version of Sonic hedgehog suggest that extra toes in mice—and perhaps also in humans—can result when the wrong amounts of this protein are produced in part of the limb bud.

▼ **Figure 47.26 Inquiry**

What role does the zone of polarizing activity (ZPA) play in limb pattern formation in vertebrates?

EXPERIMENT In 1985, Dennis Summerbell and Lawrence Honig, then at the National Institute for Medical Research in Mill Hill, near London, were eager to investigate the nature of the zone of polarizing activity. They transplanted ZPA tissue from a donor chick embryo under the ectoderm in the anterior margin of a limb bud in another chick (the host).

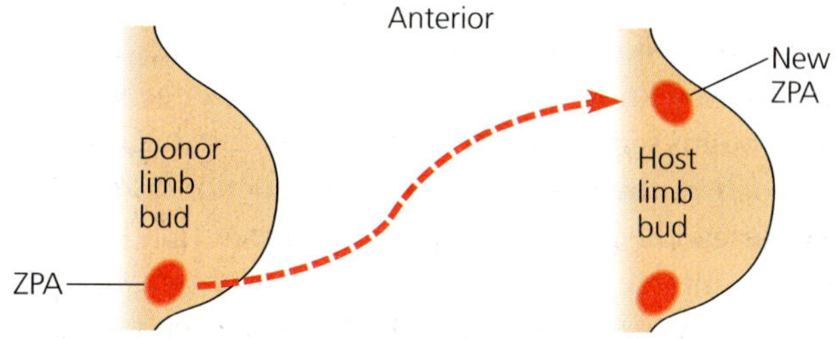

RESULTS The host limb bud developed extra digits from host tissue in a mirror-image arrangement to the normal digits, which also formed (compare with Figure 47.25b, which shows a normal chick wing).

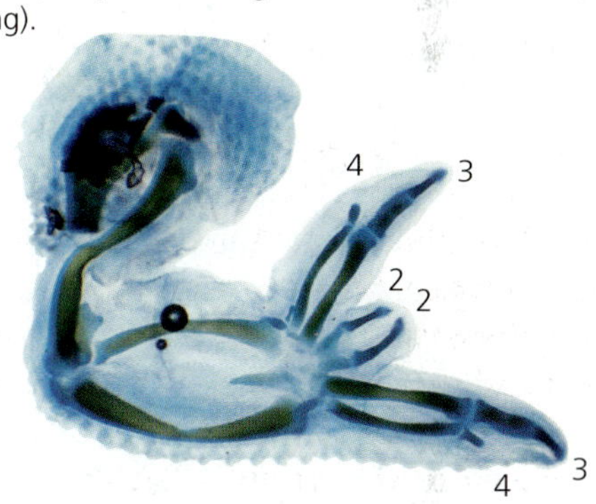

CONCLUSION The mirror-image duplication observed in this experiment suggests that ZPA cells secrete a signal that diffuses from its source and conveys positional information indicating "posterior." As the distance from the ZPA increases, the signal concentration decreases, and hence more anterior digits develop.

SOURCE L. S. Honig and D. Summerbell, Maps of strength of positional signaling activity in the developing chick wing bud, *Journal of Embryology and Experimental Morphology* 87:163–174 (1985).

WHAT IF? Suppose you learned that the ZPA forms after the AER, leading you to develop the hypothesis that the AER is necessary for formation of the ZPA. Given what you know about molecules expressed in the AER and ZPA (see the text), how could you test your hypothesis?

---

* Sonic hedgehog gets its name from two sources: its similarity to a *Drosophila* protein called Hedgehog, which is involved in segmentation of the fly embryo, and a video game character.

The *Hox* genes that you learned about in Chapter 21 also seem to play various roles at several distinct points during limb pattern formation. The importance of these genes in humans is illustrated by a condition called polysyndactyly ("many digits joined together"), which is caused by a specific mutation in a *Hox* gene named *HoxD13* **(Figure 47.27)**.

Such observations, along with experiments like those previously described, support the notion that pattern formation requires cells to receive and interpret environmental cues that vary from one location to another. These cues, acting together along three axes, often in gradients, tell cells where they are in the three-dimensional realm of a developing organ. For instance, we now know that in vertebrate limb development, specific proteins serve as some of these cues and that organizer regions such as the AER and the ZPA function as signaling centers. Researchers have recently established that these two regions also interact with each other by way of signaling molecules and signaling pathways that influence each other's developmental fates. Such mutual signaling interactions between mesoderm and ectoderm also occur during formation of the neural tube and many other tissues and organs.

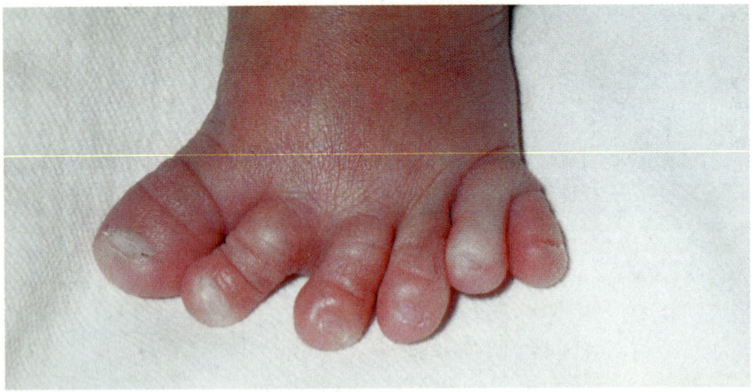

▲ **Figure 47.27 Human polysyndactyly in a baby's foot due to a homozygous mutation in a *Hox* gene.**

What determines whether a limb bud develops into a forelimb or a hind limb? The cells receiving the signals from the AER and ZPA respond according to their developmental histories. Before the AER or ZPA issues its signals, earlier developmental signaling has set up patterns of *Hox* gene expression that distinguish the future forelimbs from the future hind limbs and the different regions within a limb from each other. These differences cause cells of the forelimb and hind limb buds—and cells in different parts of each limb bud—to react differently to the same positional cues.

Thus, constructing the fully formed animal involves a sequence of events that include many steps of signaling and differentiation. Initial cell asymmetries allow different types of cells to influence each other, resulting in the expression of specific sets of genes. The products of these genes then direct cells to differentiate into specific types. Coordinated with morphogenesis, various pathways of pattern formation occur in all the different parts of the developing embryo. These processes ultimately produce a complex arrangement of multiple tissues and organs, each functioning in its appropriate location and each coordinated with the other tissues and organs of the whole organism.

CONCEPT CHECK 47.3

1. Although there are three body axes, only two must be determined during development. Why?
2. **WHAT IF?** If the ventral cells of an early frog gastrula are experimentally induced to express large amounts of a protein that inhibits BMP-4, could a second embryo develop? Explain.
3. **WHAT IF?** If you removed the ZPA from a limb bud and then placed a bead soaked in Sonic hedgehog in the middle of the limb bud, what would be the most likely result?

For suggested answers, see Appendix A.

Chapter 47 Review

MEDIA Go to the Study Area at **www.masteringbio.com** for BioFlix 3-D Animations, MP3 Tutors, Videos, Practice Tests, an eBook, and more.

SUMMARY OF KEY CONCEPTS

CONCEPT 47.1

After fertilization, embryonic development proceeds through cleavage, gastrulation, and organogenesis (pp. 1022–1035)

▶ **Fertilization** Fertilization brings together the nuclei of sperm and egg, forming a diploid zygote, and activates the egg, initiating embryonic development. The acrosomal reaction, which is triggered when the sperm meets the egg, releases hydrolytic enzymes that digest material surrounding the egg. Gamete contact and/or fusion depolarizes the egg cell membrane and sets up a fast block to polyspermy in many animals. Sperm-egg fusion also initiates the cortical reaction:

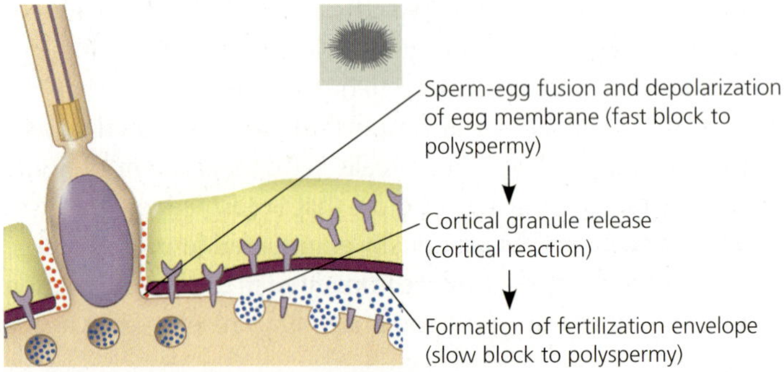

In mammalian fertilization, the cortical reaction modifies the zona pellucida as a slow block to polyspermy.

▶ **Cleavage** Fertilization is followed by cleavage, a period of rapid cell division without growth, which results in the production of a large number of cells called blastomeres. Cleavage planes usually follow a specific pattern relative to the animal and vegetal poles of the zygote. In many species, cleavage creates a multicellular ball called the blastula, which contains a fluid-filled cavity, the blastocoel. Holoblastic cleavage (division of the entire egg) occurs in species whose eggs have little or moderate amounts of yolk (as in sea urchins, frogs, and mammals). Meroblastic cleavage (incomplete division of the egg) occurs in species with yolk-rich eggs (as in birds and other reptiles).

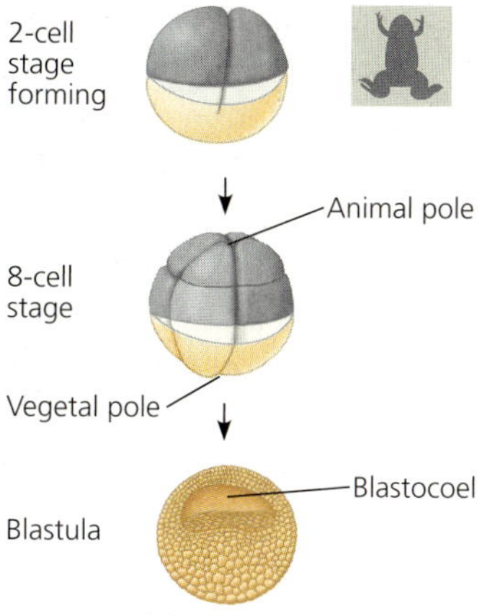

▶ **Gastrulation** Gastrulation transforms the blastula into a gastrula, which has a primitive digestive cavity (the archenteron) and three embryonic germ layers: the ectoderm (blue), mesoderm (red), and endoderm (yellow).

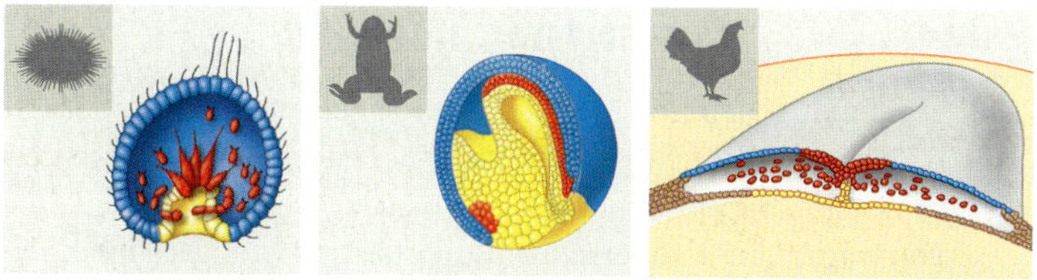

▶ **Organogenesis** The organs of the animal body develop from specific portions of the three embryonic germ layers. Early events in organogenesis in vertebrates include formation of the notochord by condensation of dorsal mesoderm, formation of the coelom from splitting of lateral mesoderm, and development of the neural tube from infolding of the ectodermal neural plate:

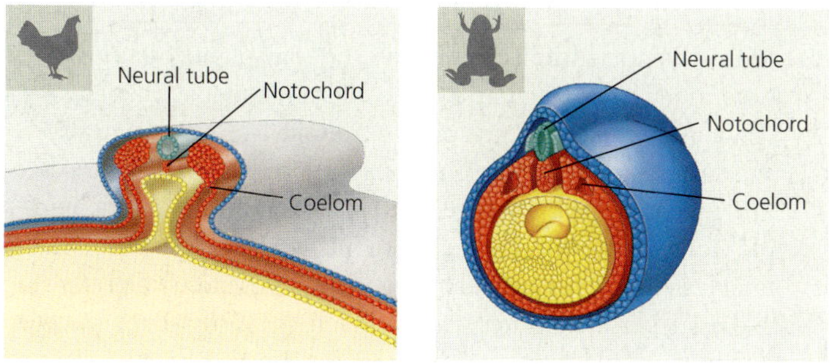

▶ **Developmental Adaptations of Amniotes** The embryos of birds, other reptiles, and mammals develop within a fluid-filled sac that is contained within a shell or the uterus. In these organisms, the three germ layers give rise not only to embryonic tissue but also to the four extraembryonic membranes: the amnion, chorion, yolk sac, and allantois.

▶ **Mammalian Development** The eggs of marsupial and eutherian mammals are small and store few nutrients. They exhibit holoblastic cleavage and show no obvious polarity. Gastrulation and organogenesis, however, resemble the processes in birds and other reptiles. After fertilization and early cleavage in the oviduct, the blastocyst implants in the uterus. The trophoblast initiates formation of the fetal portion of the placenta, and the embryo proper develops from a single layer of cells, the epiblast, within the blastocyst. Extraembryonic membranes homologous to those of birds and other reptiles function in intrauterine development.

MEDIA

Activity Sea Urchin Development
Investigation What Determines Cell Differentiation in the Sea Urchin?
Activity Frog Development

CONCEPT 47.2

Morphogenesis in animals involves specific changes in cell shape, position, and adhesion (pp. 1035–1038)

▶ **The Cytoskeleton, Cell Motility, and Convergent Extension** Cytoskeletal rearrangements are responsible for changes in both the shape and position of cells. Both kinds of changes are involved in tissue invaginations, as occurs in gastrulation, for example. In convergent extension, cell movements cause a sheet of cells to become narrower and longer.

▶ **Role of Cell Adhesion Molecules and the Extracellular Matrix** Cell adhesion molecules such as cadherins help hold cells together in tissues. Fibers of the extracellular matrix provide anchorage for cells and also help guide migrating cells toward their destinations. Fibronectin and other glycoproteins located on cell surfaces are important for cell migration and appear to affect cadherin function.

CONCEPT 47.3

The developmental fate of cells depends on their history and on inductive signals (pp. 1038–1044)

▶ **Fate Mapping** Experimentally derived fate maps of embryos have shown that specific regions of the zygote or blastula develop into specific parts of older embryos. The complete cell lineage has been worked out for *C. elegans*.

▶ **Establishing Cellular Asymmetries** In nonamniotes, unevenly distributed cytoplasmic determinants in the egg are important in establishing the body axes and in setting up differences between the blastomeres resulting from cleavage of the zygote. Cells that receive different cytoplasmic determinants undergo different fates. In amniotes, local environmental differences play the major role in establishing initial differences between cells and later the body axes. As embryonic development proceeds, the developmental potential of cells becomes progressively more limited in all species.

▶ **Cell Fate Determination and Pattern Formation by Inductive Signals** Cells in a developing embryo receive and respond to positional information that varies with location. This information is often in the form of signaling molecules secreted by cells in special "organizer" regions of the embryo, such as the dorsal lip of the blastopore in the amphibian gastrula and the AER and ZPA of the vertebrate limb bud. The signaling molecules influence gene expression in the cells that receive them, leading to differentiation and the development of particular structures.

TESTING YOUR KNOWLEDGE

SELF-QUIZ

1. The cortical reaction of sea urchin eggs functions directly in
a. the formation of a fertilization envelope.
b. the production of a fast block to polyspermy.
c. the release of hydrolytic enzymes from the sperm.
d. the generation of an electrical impulse by the egg.
e. the fusion of egg and sperm nuclei.

2. Which of the following is common to the development of both birds and mammals?
a. holoblastic cleavage
b. epiblast and hypoblast
c. trophoblast
d. yolk plug
e. gray crescent

3. The archenteron develops into
a. the mesoderm.
b. the blastocoel.
c. the endoderm.
d. the placenta.
e. the lumen of the digestive tract.

4. In a frog embryo, the blastocoel is
a. completely obliterated by yolk.
b. lined with endoderm during gastrulation.
c. located in the animal hemisphere.
d. the cavity that becomes the coelom.
e. the cavity that later forms the archenteron.

5. What structural adaptation in chickens allows them to lay their eggs in arid environments, rather than in water?
a. extraembryonic membranes
b. yolk
c. cleavage
d. gastrulation
e. development of the brain from ectoderm

6. In an amphibian embryo, a group of cells called neural crest cells
a. rolls up and forms the neural tube.
b. develops into the main sections of the brain.
c. produces cells that migrate to form teeth, skull bones, and other structures in the embryo.
d. has been shown by experiments to be the organizer region of the developing embryo.
e. induces the formation of the notochord.

7. In the early development of an amphibian embryo, Spemann's "organizer" is located in the
a. neural tube.
b. notochord.
c. archenteron roof.
d. dorsal ectoderm.
e. dorsal lip of the blastopore.

8. DRAW IT Fill in the blanks in the figure below, and draw arrows showing the movement of ectoderm, mesoderm, and endoderm.

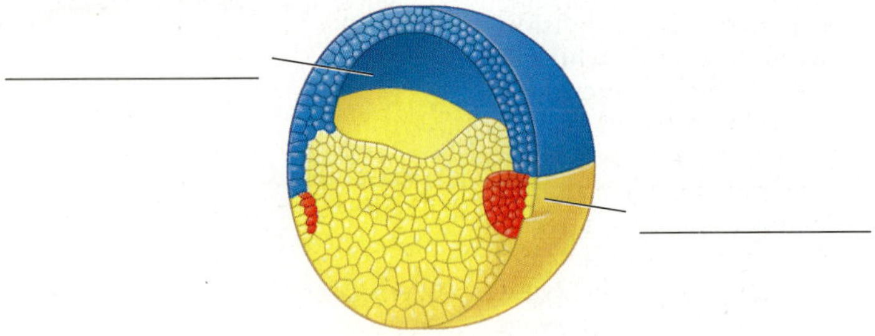

Species: ______________

Stage: ______________

For Self-Quiz answers, see Appendix A.

MEDIA Visit the Study Area at **www.masteringbio.com** for a Practice Test.

EVOLUTION CONNECTION

9. Evolution in insects and vertebrates has involved the repeated duplication of body segments, followed by fusion of some segments and specialization of their structure and function. What parts of vertebrate anatomy reflect the vertebrate segmentation pattern?

SCIENTIFIC INQUIRY

10. The "snout" of a frog tadpole bears a sucker. A salamander tadpole has a mustache-shaped structure called a balancer in the same area. Suppose that you perform an experiment in which you transplant ectoderm from the side of a young salamander embryo to the snout of a frog embryo. The tadpole that develops has a balancer. When you transplant ectoderm from the side of a slightly older salamander embryo to the snout of a frog embryo, the frog tadpole ends up with a patch of salamander skin on its snout. Suggest a hypothesis to explain these results in terms of developmental mechanisms. How might you test your hypothesis?

SCIENCE, TECHNOLOGY, AND SOCIETY

11. Many scientists think that fetal tissue transplants offer great potential for treating Parkinson's disease, epilepsy, diabetes, Alzheimer's disease, and spinal cord injuries. Why might tissues from a fetus be particularly useful for replacing diseased or damaged cells in patients with such conditions? Some people would allow only tissues from miscarriages to be used in fetal transplant research. However, most researchers prefer to use tissues from surgically aborted fetuses. Why? Explain your position on this controversial issue.

48 Neurons, Synapses, and Signaling

▲ **Figure 48.1 What makes this snail such a deadly predator?**

KEY CONCEPTS

48.1 Neuron organization and structure reflect function in information transfer

48.2 Ion pumps and ion channels maintain the resting potential of a neuron

48.3 Action potentials are the signals conducted by axons

48.4 Neurons communicate with other cells at synapses

OVERVIEW

Lines of Communication

The tropical cone snail (*Conus geographus*) in **Figure 48.1** is both beautiful and dangerous. A carnivore, this marine snail hunts, kills, and dines on fish. Injecting venom with a hollow, harpoon-like part of its mouth, the cone snail paralyzes its free-swimming prey in seconds. The cone snail's venom is so potent that a single injection has killed scuba divers unaware of the danger within its intricately patterned shell. What makes cone snail venom so fast acting and lethal? The answer is a mixture of molecules that disable **neurons**, the nerve cells that transfer information within the body. Because the venom almost instantaneously disrupts neuronal control of vital functions, such as locomotion and respiration, an animal attacked by the cone snail can neither defend itself nor escape.

Communication by neurons largely consists of two distinct types of signals: long-distance electrical signals and short-distance chemical signals. The specialized structure of neurons allows them to use pulses of electrical current to receive, transmit, and regulate the flow of information over long distances within the body. In transferring information from one cell to another, neurons often rely on chemical signals that act over very short distances. The cone snail's venom is particularly potent because it interferes with both electrical and chemical signaling by neurons.

Neurons transfer many different types of information. They transmit sensory information, control heart rate, coordinate hand and eye movement, record memories, generate dreams, and much more. All of this information is transmitted within neurons as an electrical current, consisting of the movement of ions. The connections made by a neuron specify what information is transmitted. Interpreting signals in the nervous system therefore involves sorting a complex set of neuronal paths and connections. In more complex animals, this higher-order processing is carried out largely in groups of neurons organized into a **brain** or into simpler clusters called **ganglia**.

In this chapter, we examine the structure of a neuron and explore the molecules and physical principles that govern signaling by neurons. In Chapter 49, we will look at the organization of nervous systems and at higher-order information processing in vertebrates. In Chapter 50, we will investigate systems that detect environmental stimuli and systems that carry out the body's responses to those stimuli. Finally, in Chapter 51, we will consider how these nervous system functions are integrated into the activities and interactions that make up animal behavior.

CONCEPT **48.1**

Neuron organization and structure reflect function in information transfer

Before delving into the activity of an individual neuron, let's take an overall look at how neurons function in the flow of information through the animal body. We'll use as our example the squid, an organism that has some extraordinarily large nerve cells that are well suited for physiological studies.

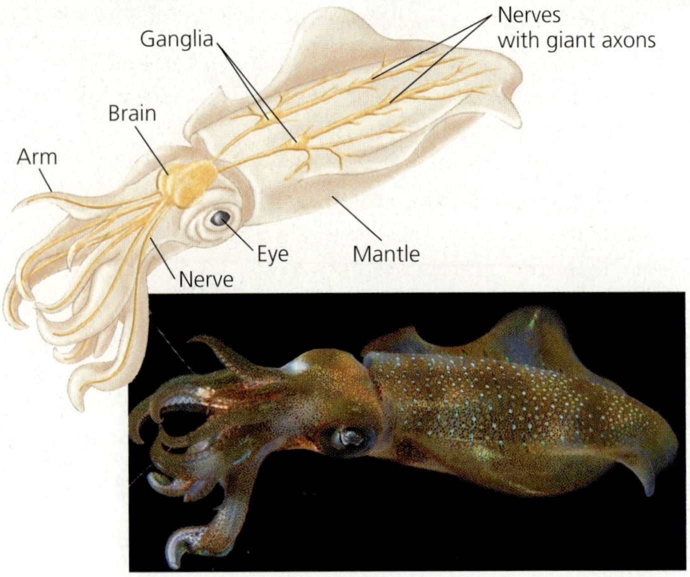

▲ **Figure 48.2 Overview of the squid nervous system.** Signals travel from the brain to the muscular mantle along *giant axons*, nerve cell extensions of unusually large diameter.

Introduction to Information Processing

Like the cone snail in Figure 48.1, the squid in **Figure 48.2** is an active predator. Using its brain to process information captured by its image-forming eyes, the squid surveys its environment. When the squid spots prey, signals traveling from its brain to neurons in its mantle cause muscle contractions that propel the squid forward.

The squid's hunting activity illustrates the three stages in information processing: sensory input, integration, and motor output. In all but the simplest animals, specialized populations of neurons handle each stage. **Sensory neurons** transmit information from eyes and other sensors that detect external stimuli (light, sound, touch, heat, smell, and taste) or internal conditions (such as blood pressure, blood carbon dioxide level, and muscle tension). This information is sent to processing centers in the brain or in ganglia. Neurons in the brain or ganglia integrate (analyze and interpret) the sensory input, taking into account the immediate context and the animal's experience. The vast majority of neurons in the brain are **interneurons**, which make only local connections. Motor output relies on neurons that extend out of the processing centers in bundles called *nerves* and generate output by triggering muscle or gland activity. For example, **motor neurons** transmit signals to muscle cells, causing them to contract.

In many animals, the neurons that carry out integration are organized in a **central nervous system (CNS)**, which includes the brain and a longitudinal nerve cord. The neurons that carry information into and out of the CNS constitute the **peripheral nervous system (PNS)**. **Figure 48.3** summarizes CNS and PNS function in information flow within the nervous system. In exploring how this transmission of information occurs, we'll begin with the unique structure of neurons.

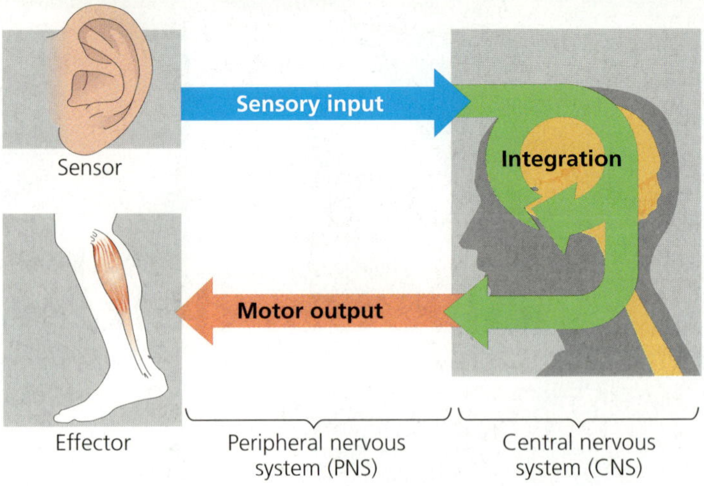

▲ **Figure 48.3 Summary of information processing.**

Neuron Structure and Function

The ability of a neuron to receive and transmit information is based on a highly specialized cellular organization **(Figure 48.4)**. Most of a neuron's organelles, including its nucleus, are located in the **cell body**. A typical neuron has numerous **dendrites** (from the Greek *dendron*, tree), highly branched extensions that *receive* signals from other neurons. A neuron also has a single **axon**, an extension that *transmits* signals to other cells. Axons are often much longer than dendrites, and some, such as those that reach from the spinal cord of a giraffe to the muscle cells in its feet, are over a meter long. The cone-shaped region of an axon where it joins the cell body is called the **axon hillock**; as we will see, this is typically the region where the signals that travel down the axon are generated. Near its other end, the axon usually divides into several branches.

Each branched end of an axon transmits information to another cell at a junction called a **synapse** (see Figure 48.4). The part of each axon branch that forms this specialized junction is a **synaptic terminal**. At most synapses, chemical messengers called **neurotransmitters** pass information from the transmitting neuron to the receiving cell. In describing a synapse, we refer to the transmitting neuron as the **presynaptic cell** and the neuron, muscle, or gland cell that receives the signal as the **postsynaptic cell**. Depending on the number of synapses a neuron has with other cells, its shape can vary from simple to quite complex **(Figure 48.5)**. Some interneurons have highly branched dendrites that take part in about 100,000 synapses. In contrast, neurons with simpler dendrites have far fewer synapses.

To function normally, the neurons of vertebrates and most invertebrates require supporting cells called glial cells, or **glia** (from a Greek word meaning "glue"). Depending on the type, glia may nourish neurons, insulate the axons of neurons, or regulate the extracellular fluid surrounding neurons. Overall, glia outnumber neurons in the mammalian brain 10- to 50-fold. We will examine functions of specific glia later in this chapter and in Chapter 49.

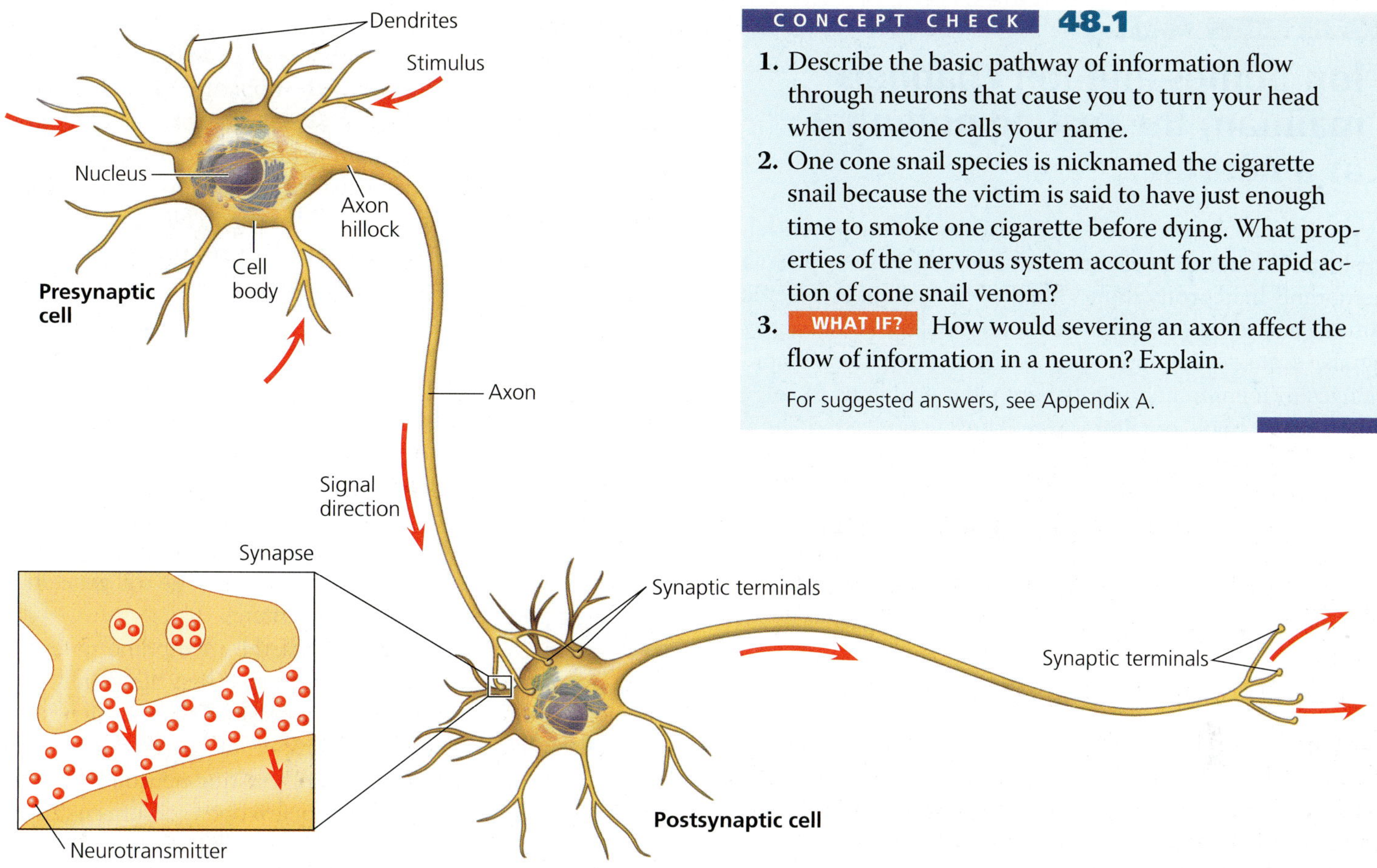

▲ **Figure 48.4 Neuron structure and organization.**

CONCEPT CHECK 48.1

1. Describe the basic pathway of information flow through neurons that cause you to turn your head when someone calls your name.
2. One cone snail species is nicknamed the cigarette snail because the victim is said to have just enough time to smoke one cigarette before dying. What properties of the nervous system account for the rapid action of cone snail venom?
3. **WHAT IF?** How would severing an axon affect the flow of information in a neuron? Explain.

For suggested answers, see Appendix A.

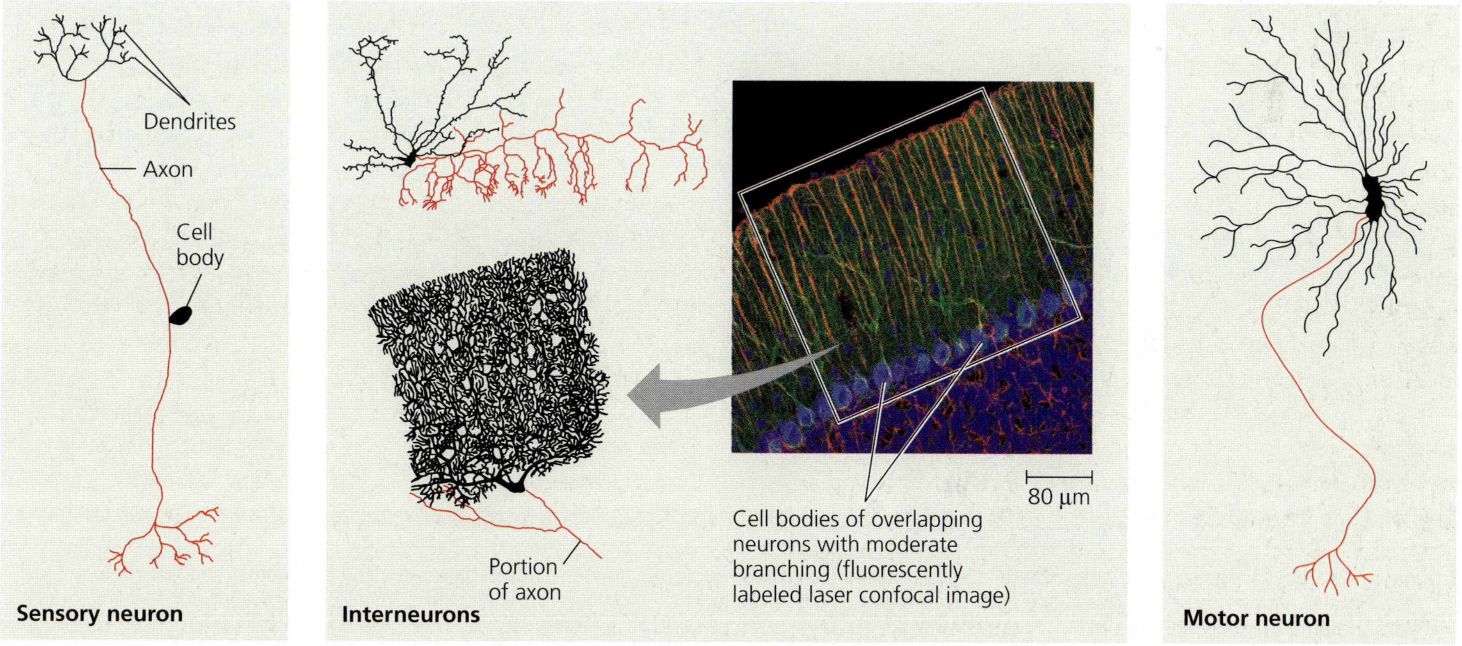

▲ **Figure 48.5 Structural diversity of neurons.** In the drawings, cell bodies and dendrites are black and axons are red. The sensory neuron, unlike the other neurons here, has a cell body located partway along the axon that conveys signals from the dendrites to the axon's terminal branches. The micrograph shows tissue from a rat brain, with interneurons labeled green, glia red, and DNA blue (revealing locations of cell nuclei). These interneurons are the same type as those in the bottom drawing.

CONCEPT 48.2

Ion pumps and ion channels maintain the resting potential of a neuron

As you read in Chapter 7, all cells have a **membrane potential**, a voltage (difference in electrical charge) across their plasma membrane. In neurons, inputs from other neurons or specific stimuli cause changes in this membrane potential that act as signals, transmitting and processing information. Rapid changes in membrane potential are what enable us to see a flower, read a book, or climb a tree. Thus, to understand how neurons function, we first need to examine how membrane potentials are formed, maintained, and altered.

The membrane potential of a resting neuron—one that is not sending signals—is its **resting potential** and is typically between −60 and −80 mV (millivolts). The minus sign indicates that the inside of a neuron at rest is negative relative to the outside.

Formation of the Resting Potential

Potassium ions (K^+) and sodium ions (Na^+) play critical roles in the formation of the resting potential. For each, there is a concentration gradient across the plasma membrane of a neuron. In the case of mammalian neurons, the concentration of K^+ is 140 millimolar (m*M*) inside the cell, but only 5 m*M* outside. The Na^+ concentration gradient is nearly the opposite: 150 m*M* outside and only 15 m*M* inside **(Figure 48.6a)**. These Na^+ and K^+ gradients are maintained by *sodium-potassium pumps* in the plasma membrane. As discussed in Chapter 7, these ion pumps use the energy of ATP hydrolysis to actively transport Na^+ out of the cell and K^+ into the cell **(Figure 48.6b)**. (There are also concentration gradients for chloride ions (Cl^-) and other anions, but we will ignore these for the moment.)

The concentration gradients of K^+ and Na^+ across the plasma membrane represent a chemical form of potential energy. Converting this chemical potential to an electrical potential involves **ion channels**, pores formed by clusters of specialized proteins that span the membrane. Ion channels allow ions to diffuse back and forth across the membrane. As ions diffuse through channels, they carry with them units of electrical charge. Any resulting *net* movement of positive or negative charge will generate a voltage, or potential, across the membrane.

The ion channels that establish the membrane potential have *selective permeability*, meaning that they allow only certain ions to pass. For example, a potassium channel allows K^+ to diffuse freely across the membrane, but not other ions, such as Na^+. As shown in Figure 48.6b, a resting neuron has many open potassium channels, but very few open sodium channels.

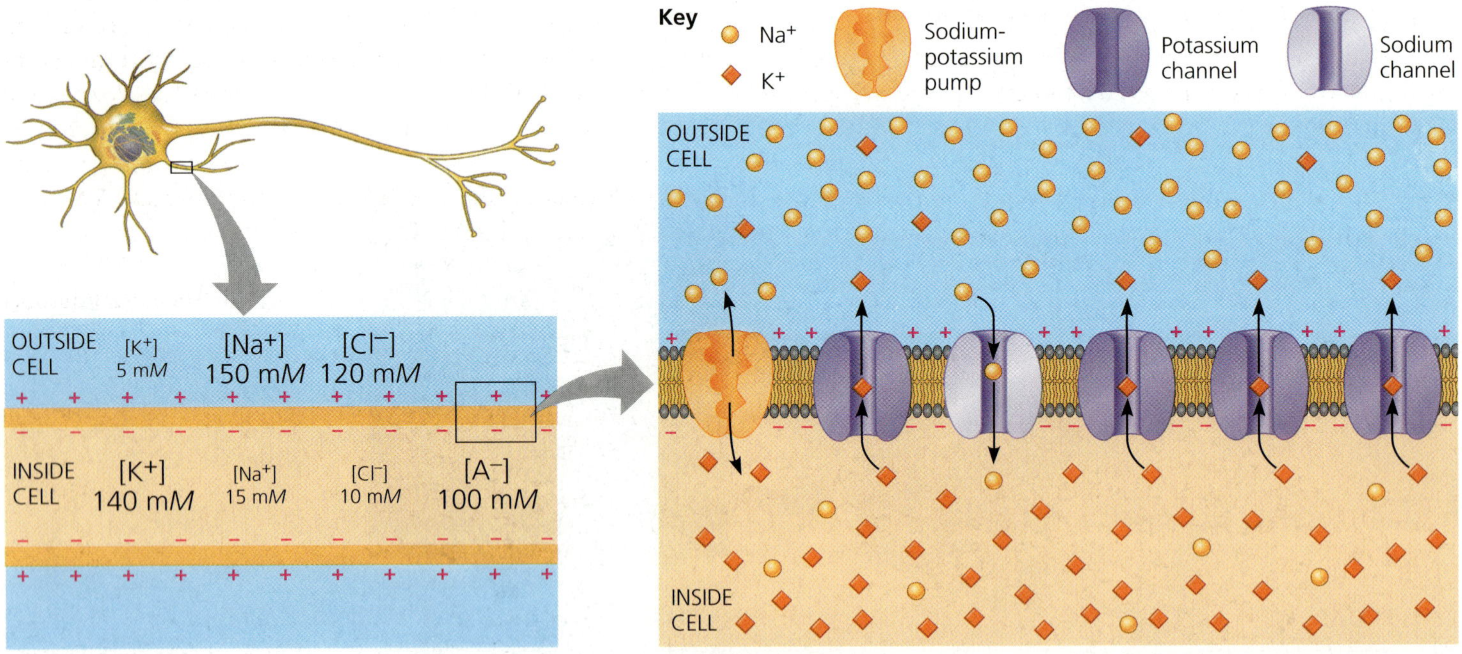

(a) The values shown represent the approximate concentrations in millimoles per liter (m*M*) for ions in the fluids within and surrounding a mammalian neuron: $[K^+]$ = potassium concentration; $[Na^+]$ = sodium concentration; $[Cl^-]$ = chloride concentration; and $[A^-]$ = other anions.

(b) The sodium-potassium pump generates and maintains the ionic gradients of Na^+ and K^+ shown in (a). The pump uses ATP to actively transport Na^+ out of the cell and K^+ into the cell. Although there is a substantial concentration gradient of sodium across the membrane, very little net diffusion of Na^+ occurs because there are very few open sodium channels. In contrast, the large number of open potassium channels allow a significant net outflow of K^+. Because the membrane is only weakly permeable to chloride and other anions, this outflow of K^+ results in a net negative charge inside the cell.

▲ **Figure 48.6 The basis of the membrane potential.**

The diffusion of K^+ through open potassium channels is critical for formation of the resting potential. In the resting mammalian neuron, these channels allow K^+ to pass in either direction across the membrane. Because the concentration of K^+ is much higher inside the cell, the chemical concentration gradient favors a net outflow of K^+. However, since the potassium channels allow only K^+ to pass, Cl^- and other anions inside the cell cannot accompany the K^+ across the membrane. As a result, the outflow of K^+ leads to an excess of negative charge inside the cell. This buildup of negative charge within the neuron is the source of the membrane potential.

What prevents the buildup of negative charge from increasing indefinitely? The answer lies in the electrical potential itself. The excess negative charges inside the cell exert an attractive force that opposes the flow of additional positively charged potassium ions out of the cell. The separation of charge (voltage) thus results in an electrical gradient that counterbalances the chemical concentration gradient of K^+.

Modeling of the Resting Potential

The net flow of K^+ out of a neuron proceeds until the chemical and electrical forces are in balance. How well do just these two forces account for the resting potential in a mammalian neuron? To answer this question, let's consider a simple model consisting of two chambers separated by an artificial membrane **(Figure 48.7a)**. To begin, imagine that the membrane contains many open ion channels, all of which allow only K^+ to diffuse across. To produce a concentration gradient for K^+ like that of a mammalian neuron, we place a solution of 140 m*M* potassium chloride (KCl) in the inner chamber and 5 m*M* KCl in the outer chamber. The potassium ions (K^+) will diffuse down their concentration gradient into the outer chamber. But because the chloride ions (Cl^-) lack a means of crossing the membrane, there will be an excess of negative charge in the inner chamber.

When our model neuron reaches equilibrium, the electrical gradient will exactly balance the chemical gradient, such that no further net diffusion of K^+ occurs across the membrane. The magnitude of the membrane voltage at equilibrium for a particular ion is called that ion's **equilibrium potential** (**E_{ion}**). For a membrane permeable to a single type of ion, E_{ion} can be calculated using a formula called the Nernst equation. At human body temperature (37°C) and for an ion with a net charge of 1+, such as K^+ or Na^+, the Nernst equation is

$$E_{ion} = 62 \text{ mV}\left(\log \frac{[\text{ion}]_{\text{outside}}}{[\text{ion}]_{\text{inside}}}\right)$$

Plugging the K^+ concentrations into the Nernst equation reveals that the equilibrium potential for K^+ (E_K) is -90 mV (see Figure 48.7a). The minus sign indicates that K^+ is at equilibrium when the inside of the membrane is 90 mV more negative than the outside.

Although the equilibrium potential for K^+ is -90 mV, the resting potential of a mammalian neuron is somewhat less negative. This difference reflects the small but steady movement of Na^+ across the few open sodium channels in a resting neuron. Because the concentration gradient of Na^+ has a direction opposite to that of K^+, Na^+ diffuses into the cell and thus makes the inside of the cell less negative. If we model a membrane in which the only open channels are selectively permeable to Na^+, we find that a tenfold higher concentration of Na^+ in the outer chamber results in an equilibrium potential (E_{Na}) of $+62$ mV **(Figure 48.7b)**. The resting potential of an actual neuron is -60 to -80 mV. The resting potential is much closer to E_K than to E_{Na} in a neuron because there are many open potassium channels but only a small number of open sodium channels.

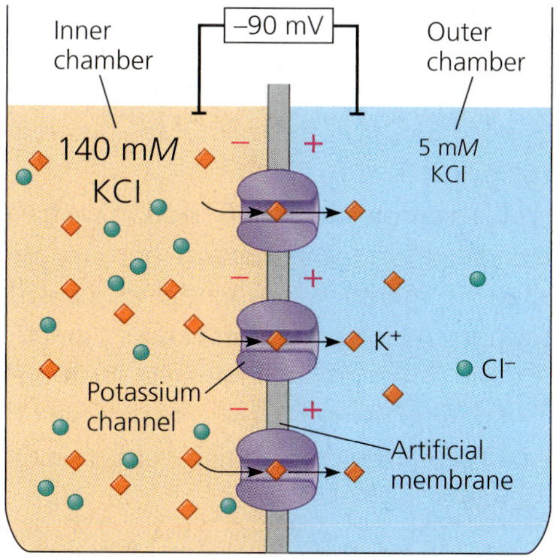

(a) Membrane selectively permeable to K^+

Nernst equation for K^+ equilibrium potential at 37°C:

$$E_K = 62 \text{ mV}\left(\log \frac{5 \text{ m}M}{140 \text{ m}M}\right) = -90 \text{ mV}$$

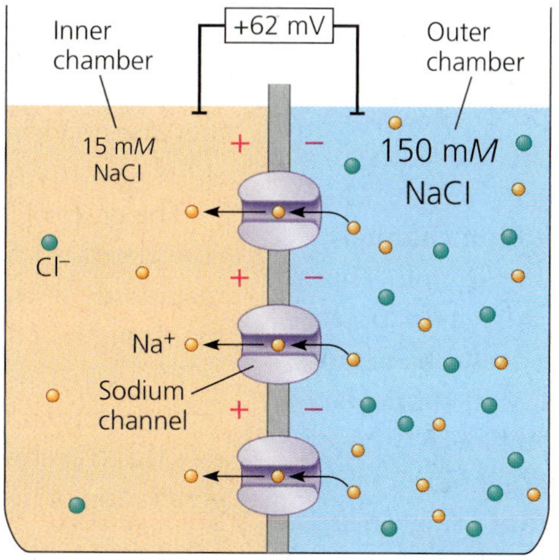

(b) Membrane selectively permeable to Na^+

Nernst equation for Na^+ equilibrium potential at 37°C:

$$E_{Na} = 62 \text{ mV}\left(\log \frac{150 \text{ m}M}{15 \text{ m}M}\right) = +62 \text{ mV}$$

◄ **Figure 48.7 Modeling a mammalian neuron.** Each container is divided into two chambers by an artificial membrane. Ion channels allow free diffusion for particular ions, resulting in the net ion flow represented by arrows. **(a)** The presence of open potassium channels makes the membrane selectively permeable to K^+, and the inner chamber contains a 28-fold higher concentration of K^+ than the outer chamber; at equilibrium, the inside of the membrane is -90 mV relative to the outside. **(b)** The membrane is selectively permeable to Na^+, and the inner chamber contains a tenfold lower concentration of Na^+ than the outer chamber; at equilibrium, the inside of the membrane is $+62$ mV relative to the outside.

WHAT IF? *Adding channels specific for one type of ion to the membrane in (b) would alter the membrane potential. Which ion passes through these channels, and in what direction would the membrane potential change?*

Because neither K^+ nor Na^+ is at equilibrium in a resting neuron, each ion has a net flow (a current) across the membrane. The resting potential remains steady, which means that the K^+ and Na^+ currents are equal and opposite. Ion concentrations on either side of the membrane also remain steady because the charge separation needed to generate the resting potential is extremely small (about 10^{-12} mole/cm^2 of membrane). This represents the movement of far fewer ions than would be required to alter the chemical concentration gradient.

Under conditions that allow Na^+ to cross the membrane more readily, the membrane potential will move toward E_{Na} and away from E_K. As we will see in the next section, this is precisely what happens during the transmission of a nerve impulse along an axon.

CONCEPT CHECK 48.2

1. Under what circumstances could ions flow through ion channels from regions of low ion concentration to regions of high ion concentration?
2. **WHAT IF?** Suppose a cell's membrane potential shifts from −70 mV to −50 mV. What changes in the cell's permeability to K^+ or Na^+ could cause such a shift?
3. **WHAT IF?** Suppose you treated a neuron with ouabain, an arrow poison and drug that specifically disables the sodium-potassium pump. What change in the resting potential would you expect to see? Explain.

For suggested answers, see Appendix A.

CONCEPT 48.3

Action potentials are the signals conducted by axons

We saw in the previous section that the resting potential results from the fact that the plasma membrane of a resting neuron contains many open potassium channels but only a few open sodium channels. However, when neurons are active, membrane permeability and membrane potential change. The changes occur because neurons contain **gated ion channels**, ion channels that open or close in response to stimuli. This gating of ion channels forms the basis of nearly all electrical signaling in the nervous system. The opening or closing of ion channels alters the membrane's permeability to particular ions, which in turn alters the membrane potential. How have scientists studied these changes? The technique of intracellular recording provides a readout of the state of a single neuron in real time **(Figure 48.8)**.

▼ **Figure 48.8 Research Method**

Intracellular Recording

APPLICATION Electrophysiologists use intracellular recording to measure the membrane potential of neurons and other cells.

TECHNIQUE A microelectrode is made from a glass capillary tube filled with an electrically conductive salt solution. One end of the tube tapers to an extremely fine tip (diameter <1 μm). While looking through a microscope, the experimenter uses a micropositioner to insert the tip of the microelectrode into a cell. A voltage recorder (usually an oscilloscope or a computer-based system) measures the voltage between the microelectrode tip inside the cell and a reference electrode placed in the solution outside the cell.

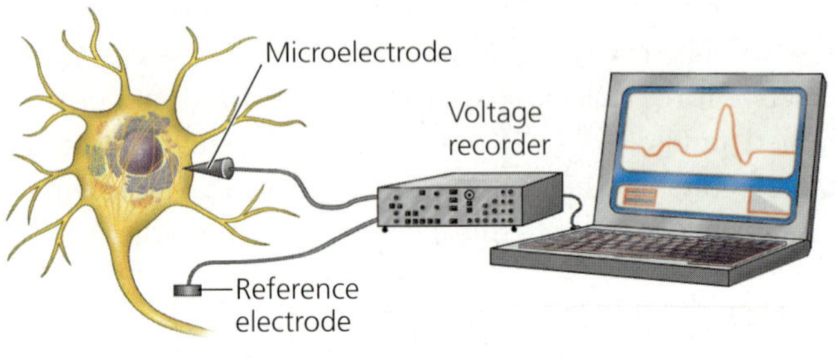

To begin exploring gated channels, let's consider what happens when gated potassium channels that are closed in a resting neuron open. Opening more potassium channels increases the membrane's permeability to K^+, increasing the net diffusion of K^+ out of the neuron. In other words, the inside of the membrane becomes more negative **(Figure 48.9a)**. As the membrane potential approaches E_K (−90 mV at 37°C), the separation of charge, or polarity, increases. Thus, the increase in the magnitude of the membrane potential is called a **hyperpolarization**. In general, hyperpolarization results from any stimulus that increases either the outflow of positive ions or the inflow of negative ions.

Although opening potassium channels causes hyperpolarization, opening some other types of ion channels has an opposite effect, making the inside of the membrane less negative **(Figure 48.9b)**. This reduction in the magnitude of the membrane potential is called a **depolarization**. Depolarization in neurons often involves gated sodium channels. If the gated sodium channels open, the membrane's permeability to Na^+ increases, causing a depolarization as the membrane potential shifts toward E_{Na} (+62 mV at 37°C).

The types of hyperpolarization and depolarization we have considered so far are called *graded potentials* because the magnitude of the change in membrane potential varies with the strength of the stimulus. A larger stimulus causes a greater change in permeability and thus a greater change in the membrane potential. Graded potentials are not the actual nerve signals that travel along axons, but they have a major effect on the generation of nerve signals.

Production of Action Potentials

Many of the gated ion channels in neurons are **voltage-gated ion channels**; that is, they open or close in response to a

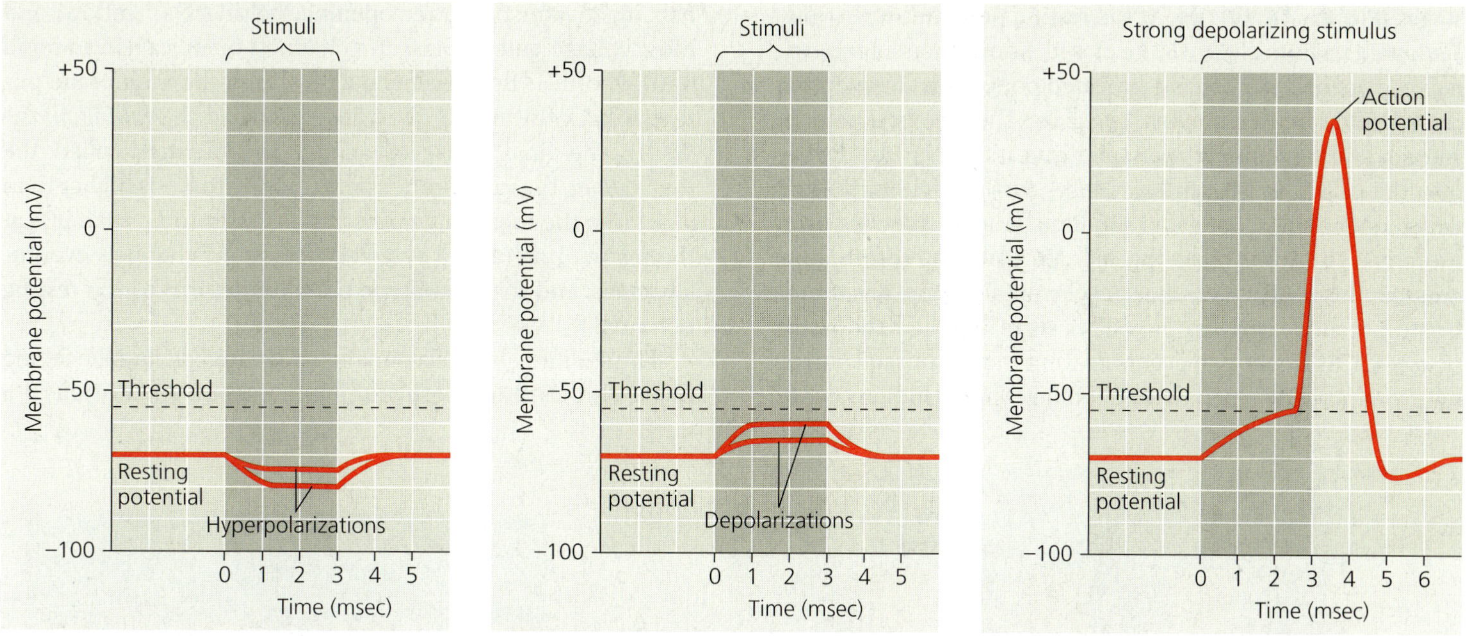

(a) Graded hyperpolarizations produced by two stimuli that increase membrane permeability to K^+. The larger stimulus produces a larger hyperpolarization.

(b) Graded depolarizations produced by two stimuli that increase membrane permeability to Na^+. The larger stimulus produces a larger depolarization.

(c) Action potential triggered by a depolarization that reaches the threshold.

▲ **Figure 48.9 Graded potentials and an action potential in a neuron.**

change in the membrane potential. If a depolarization opens voltage-gated sodium channels, the resulting flow of Na^+ into the neuron results in further depolarization. Because the sodium channels are voltage gated, an increased depolarization in turn causes more sodium channels to open, leading to an even greater flow of current. The result is a very rapid opening of all the voltage-gated sodium channels. Such a series of events triggers a massive change in membrane voltage called an **action potential** **(Figure 48.9c)**.

Action potentials are the nerve impulses, or signals, that carry information along an axon. Before we can discuss how these signals move, or propagate, along an axon, we must first understand more about the changes in membrane voltage that accompany an action potential.

Action potentials occur whenever a depolarization increases the membrane voltage to a particular value, called the **threshold**. For mammalian neurons, the threshold is a membrane potential of about −55 mV. Once initiated, the action potential has a magnitude that is independent of the strength of the triggering stimulus. Because action potentials occur fully or not at all, they represent an *all-or-none* response to stimuli. This all-or-none property reflects the fact that depolarization opens voltage-gated sodium channels, and the opening of sodium channels causes further depolarization. This positive-feedback loop of depolarization and channel opening triggers an action potential whenever the membrane potential reaches the threshold.

Generation of Action Potentials: *A Closer Look*

In most neurons, an action potential lasts only 1–2 milliseconds (msec). Because action potentials are so brief, a neuron can produce hundreds of them per second. Furthermore, the frequency with which a neuron generates action potentials can vary in response to input. Such differences in action potential frequency convey information about signal strength. In hearing, for example, louder sounds are reflected by more frequent action potentials in neurons connecting the ear to the brain.

The characteristic shape of the graph of an action potential (see Figure 48.9c) reflects the large change in membrane potential resulting from ion movement through voltage-gated sodium and potassium channels. Membrane depolarization opens both types of channels, but they respond independently and sequentially. Sodium channels open first, initiating the action potential. As the action potential proceeds, the sodium channels become inactivated: A loop of the channel protein moves, blocking ion flow through the opening. Sodium channels remain inactivated until after the membrane returns to the resting potential and the channels close. Potassium channels open more slowly than sodium channels, but remain open and functional throughout the action potential.

To understand further how voltage-gated channels shape the action potential, we'll consider the process as a series of stages **(Figure 48.10)**. ❶ At the resting potential, most voltage-gated sodium channels are closed. Some potassium channels are open, but most voltage-gated potassium channels are closed. ❷ When a stimulus depolarizes the membrane, some gated sodium channels open, allowing more Na^+ to diffuse into the cell. The Na^+ inflow causes further depolarization, which opens still more gated sodium channels, allowing even more Na^+ to diffuse into the cell. ❸ Once the threshold is crossed, this positive-feedback cycle rapidly brings the membrane potential close to E_{Na}. This stage is called the *rising phase*. ❹ However, two events prevent the membrane potential from actually reaching E_{Na}: Voltage-gated sodium channels inactivate soon after opening, halting Na^+ inflow; and most voltage-gated potassium channels open, causing a rapid outflow of K^+. Both events quickly bring the membrane potential back toward E_K. This stage is called the *falling phase*. ❺ In the final phase of an action potential, called the *undershoot*, the membrane's permeability to K^+ is higher than at rest, so the membrane potential is closer to E_K than it is at the resting potential. The gated potassium channels eventually close, and the membrane potential returns to the resting potential.

The sodium channels remain inactivated during the falling phase and the early part of the undershoot. As a result, if a

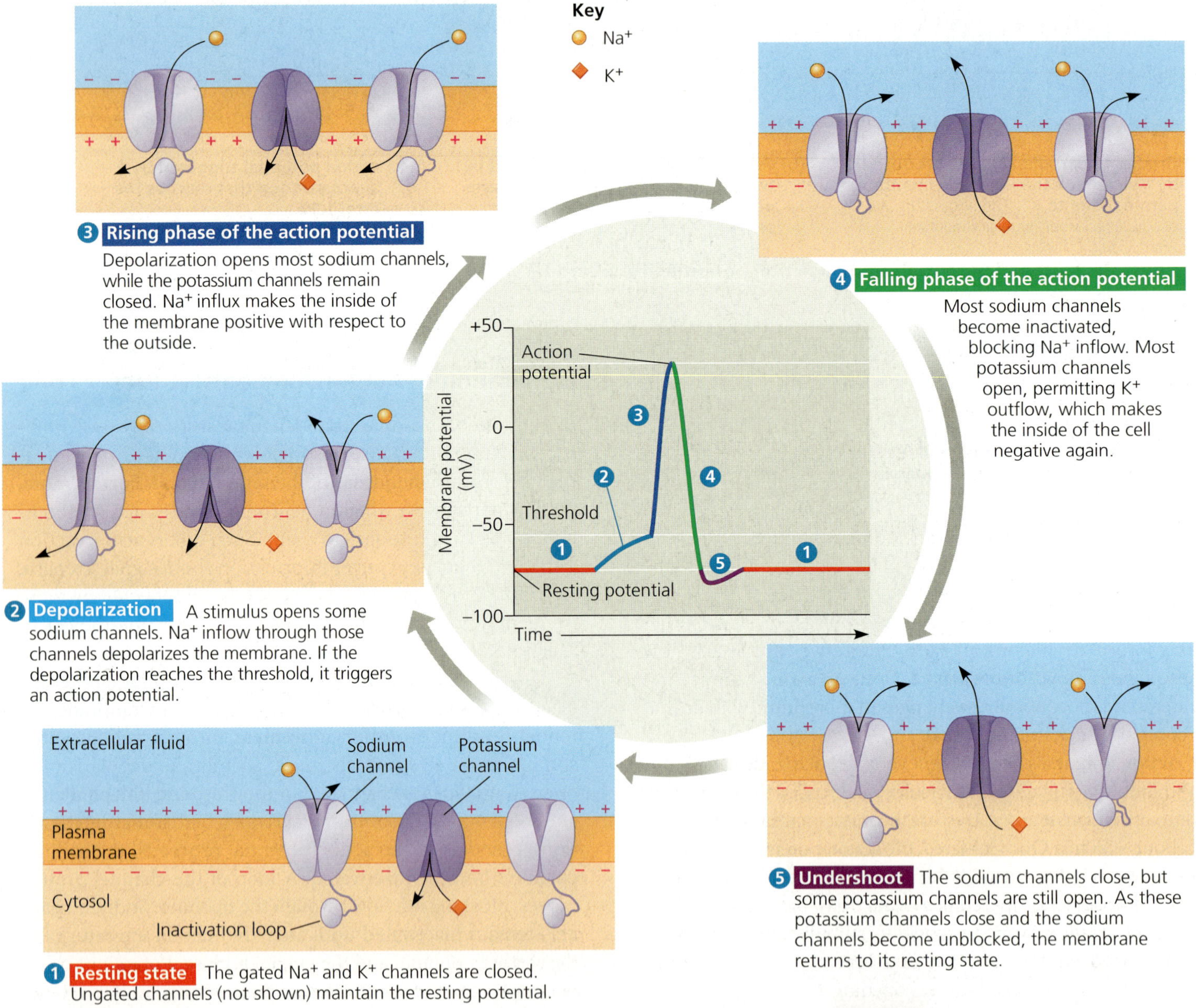

▲ **Figure 48.10 The role of voltage-gated ion channels in the generation of an action potential.** The circled numbers on the graph in the center and the colors of the action potential phases correspond to the five diagrams showing voltage-gated sodium and potassium channels in a neuron's plasma membrane. (Ungated ion channels are not illustrated.)

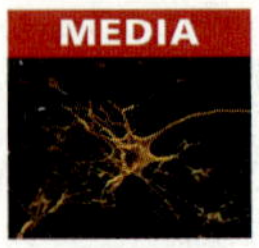

BioFlix Visit the Study Area at **www.masteringbio.com** for the BioFlix 3-D Animation on How Neurons Work.

second depolarizing stimulus occurs during this period, it will be unable to trigger an action potential. The "downtime" following an action potential when a second action potential cannot be initiated is called the **refractory period**. This interval sets a limit on the maximum frequency at which action potentials can be generated. As we will discuss shortly, the refractory period also ensures that all signals in an axon travel in one direction, from the cell body to the axon terminals.

Note that the refractory period is due to the inactivation of sodium channels, not to a change in the ion gradients across the plasma membrane. The flow of charged particles during an action potential involves far too few ions to change the concentration on either side of the plasma membrane.

Conduction of Action Potentials

An action potential functions as a long-distance signal by regenerating itself as it travels from the cell body to the synaptic terminals, much like a flame traveling along a lit fuse. At the site where an action potential is initiated (usually the axon hillock), Na^+ inflow during the rising phase creates an electrical current that depolarizes the neighboring region of the axon membrane **(Figure 48.11)**. The depolarization in the neighboring region is large enough to reach the threshold, causing the action potential to be reinitiated there. This process is repeated over and over again as the action potential travels the length of the axon. At each position along the axon, the process is identical, such that the shape and magnitude of the action potential remain constant.

Immediately behind the traveling zone of depolarization due to Na^+ inflow is a zone of repolarization due to K^+ outflow. In the repolarized zone, the sodium channels remain inactivated. Consequently, the inward current that depolarizes the axon membrane *ahead* of the action potential cannot produce another action potential *behind* it. This prevents action potentials from traveling back toward the cell body. Thus, an action potential that starts at the axon hillock moves in only one direction—toward the synaptic terminals.

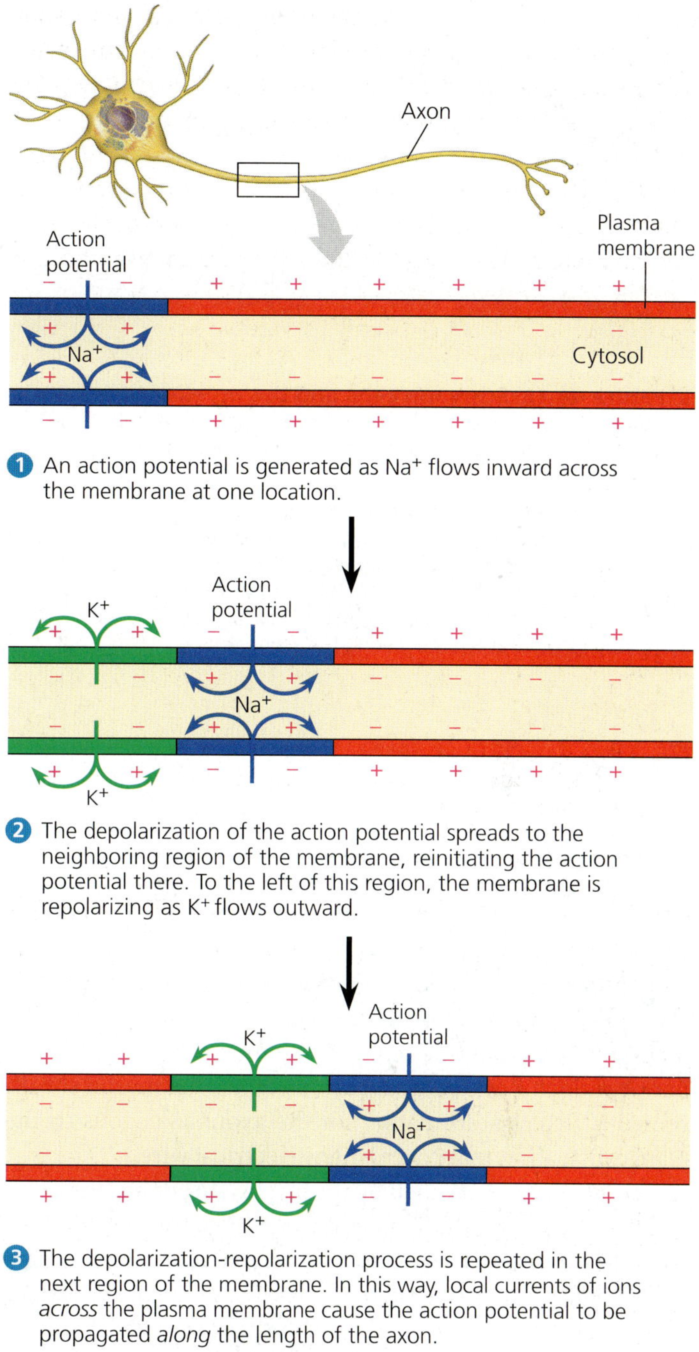

▲ **Figure 48.11 Conduction of an action potential.** The three parts of this figure show events that occur in an axon at three successive times as an action potential passes from left to right. At each point along the axon, voltage-gated ion channels go through the sequence of changes described in Figure 48.10. The colors of membrane regions shown here correspond to the action potential phases in Figure 48.10.

Conduction Speed

Several factors affect the speed at which action potentials are conducted. One is axon diameter: Wider axons conduct action potentials more rapidly than narrow ones because resistance to electrical current flow is inversely proportional to the cross-sectional area of a conductor (such as a wire or an axon). Just as a wide hose offers less resistance to the flow of water than a narrow hose does, a wide axon provides less resistance to the current associated with an action potential than a narrow axon does. Therefore, the resulting depolarization can spread farther along the interior of a wide axon, bringing more distant regions of the membrane to the threshold sooner. In invertebrates, conduction speed varies from several centimeters per second in very narrow axons to about 30 m/sec in the giant axons of some arthropods and molluscs (see Figure 48.2). These giant axons (up to 1 mm wide) function in rapid behavioral responses, such as the muscle contraction that propels a squid toward its prey.

Vertebrate axons have narrow diameters but can still conduct action potentials at high speed. How is this possible? The adaptation that enables fast conduction in narrow axons is a **myelin sheath**, a layer of electrical insulation that surrounds

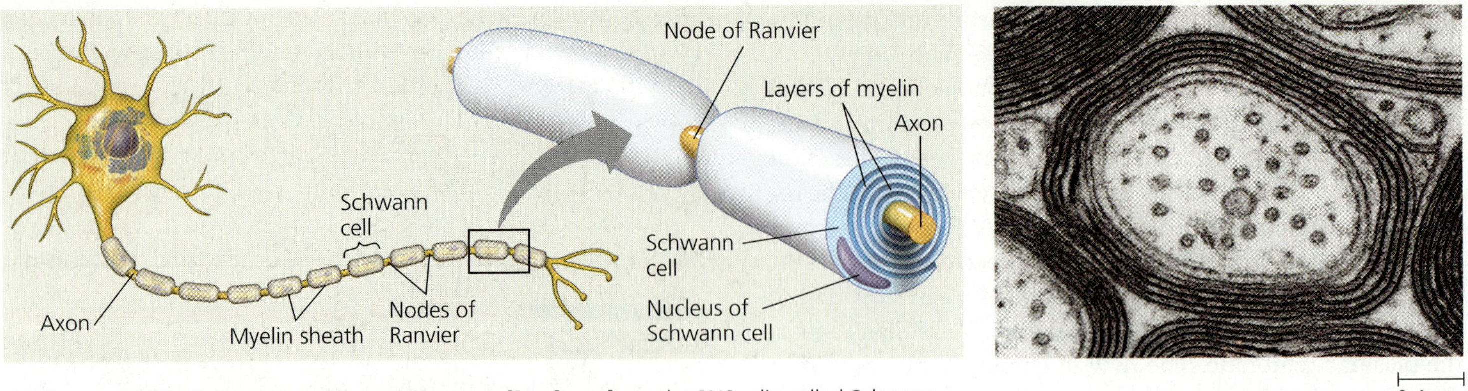

▲ **Figure 48.12 Schwann cells and the myelin sheath.** In the PNS, glia called Schwann cells wrap themselves around axons, forming layers of myelin. Gaps between adjacent Schwann cells are called nodes of Ranvier. The TEM shows a cross section through a myelinated axon.

▶ **Figure 48.13 Saltatory conduction.** In a myelinated axon, the depolarizing current during an action potential at one node of Ranvier spreads along the interior of the axon to the next node (blue arrows), where it will reinitiate itself. Thus, the action potential jumps from node to node as it travels along the axon (red arrows).

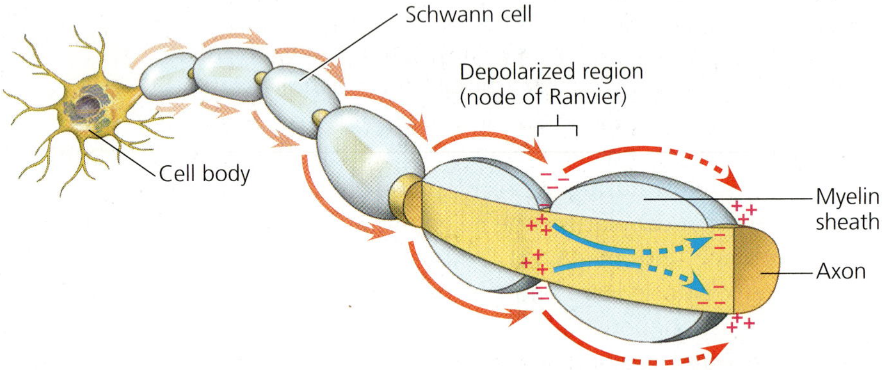

vertebrate axons **(Figure 48.12)**. Myelin sheaths are produced by two types of glia—**oligodendrocytes** in the CNS and **Schwann cells** in the PNS. During development, these specialized glia wrap axons in many layers of membrane. The membranes forming these layers are mostly lipid, which is a poor conductor of electrical current. Thus, the myelin sheath provides electrical insulation for the axon, analogous to the plastic insulation that covers many electrical wires.

The insulation provided by the myelin sheath has the same effect as increasing the axon's diameter: It causes the depolarizing current associated with an action potential to spread farther along the interior of the axon, bringing more distant regions of the membrane to the threshold sooner. The great advantage of myelination is its space efficiency. A myelinated axon 20 μm in diameter has a conduction speed faster than that of a squid giant axon that has a diameter 40 times greater. Furthermore, more than 2,000 of those myelinated axons can be packed into the space occupied by just one giant axon.

In a myelinated axon, voltage-gated sodium channels are restricted to gaps in the myelin sheath called **nodes of Ranvier** (see Figure 48.12). The extracellular fluid is in contact with the axon membrane only at the nodes. As a result, action potentials are not generated in the regions between the nodes. Rather, the inward current produced during the rising phase of the action potential at a node travels all the way to the next node, where it depolarizes the membrane and regenerates the action potential **(Figure 48.13)**. This mechanism is called **saltatory conduction** (from the Latin *saltare*, to leap) because the action potential appears to jump along the axon from node to node.

CONCEPT CHECK 48.3

1. How does an action potential differ from a graded potential?
2. In the disease multiple sclerosis (from the Greek *skleros*, hard), myelin sheaths gradually harden and deteriorate. How would this affect nervous system function?
3. **WHAT IF?** Suppose that a mutation caused gated sodium channels to remain inactivated for a longer time following an action potential. How would such a mutation affect the maximum frequency at which action potentials could be generated? Explain.

For suggested answers, see Appendix A.

CONCEPT **48.4**

Neurons communicate with other cells at synapses

In most cases, action potentials are not transmitted from neurons to other cells. However, information is transmitted, and this transmission occurs at the synapses. Some synapses, called *electrical synapses*, contain gap junctions (see Figure 6.32), which *do* allow electrical current to flow directly from one neuron to another. In both vertebrates and invertebrates, electrical synapses synchronize the activity of neurons responsible for certain rapid, unvarying behaviors. For example, electrical synapses associated with the giant axons of squids and lobsters facilitate the swift execution of escape responses. There are also many electrical synapses in the vertebrate brain.

The majority of synapses are *chemical synapses*, which involve the release of a chemical neurotransmitter by the presynaptic neuron. The cell body and dendrites of one postsynaptic neuron may receive inputs from chemical synapses with hundreds or even thousands of synaptic terminals **(Figure 48.14)**. At each terminal, the presynaptic neuron synthesizes the neurotransmitter and packages it in multiple membrane-bounded compartments called **synaptic vesicles**. The arrival of an action potential at a synaptic terminal depolarizes the plasma membrane, opening voltage-gated channels that allow Ca^{2+} to diffuse into the terminal **(Figure 48.15)**. The resulting rise in Ca^{2+} concentration in the terminal causes some of the synaptic vesicles to fuse with the terminal membrane, releasing the neurotransmitter. The neurotransmitter then diffuses across the **synaptic cleft**, the narrow gap that separates the presynaptic neuron from the postsynaptic cell.

Information transfer is much more readily modified at chemical synapses than at electrical synapses. A variety of factors can affect the amount of neurotransmitter that is released or the responsiveness of the postsynaptic cell. Such modifications underlie an animal's ability to alter its behavior in response to change and form the basis for learning and memory, as you will learn in Chapter 49.

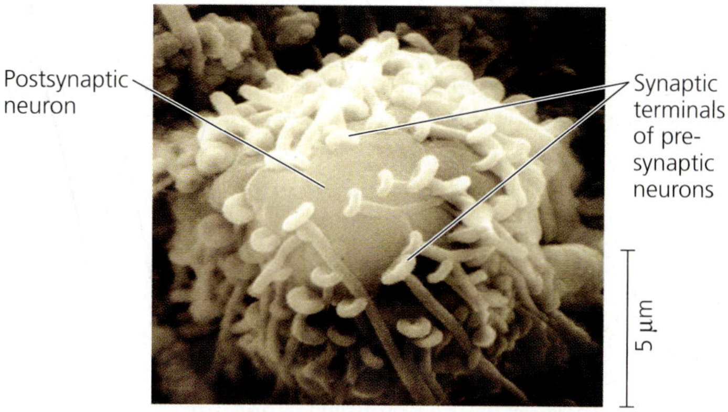

▲ **Figure 48.14 Synaptic terminals on the cell body of a postsynaptic neuron** (colorized SEM).

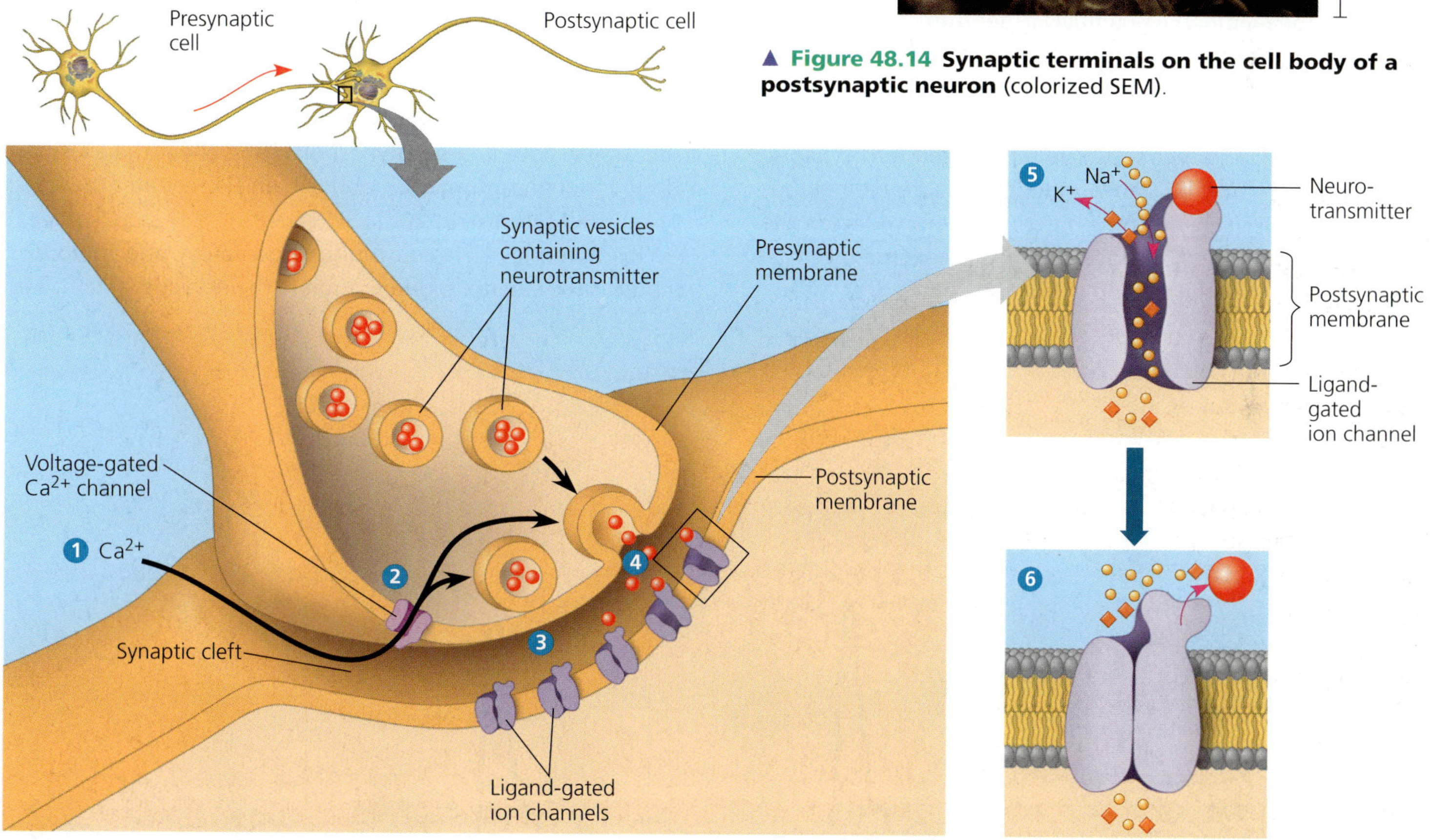

▲ **Figure 48.15 A chemical synapse.**
1 When an action potential depolarizes the plasma membrane of the synaptic terminal, it 2 opens voltage-gated calcium channels in the membrane, triggering an influx of Ca^{2+}. 3 The elevated Ca^{2+} concentration in the terminal causes synaptic vesicles to fuse with the presynaptic membrane. 4 The vesicles release neurotransmitter into the synaptic cleft. 5 The neurotransmitter binds to the receptor portion of ligand-gated ion channels in the postsynaptic membrane, opening the channels. In the synapse illustrated here, both Na^+ and K^+ can diffuse through the channels. 6 The neurotransmitter is released from the receptors, and the channels close. Synaptic transmission ends when the neurotransmitter diffuses out of the synaptic cleft, is taken up by the synaptic terminal or by another cell, or is degraded by an enzyme.

WHAT IF? *If all the Ca^{2+} in the fluid surrounding a neuron were removed, how would this affect the transmission of information within and between neurons?*

Generation of Postsynaptic Potentials

At many chemical synapses, as in Figure 48.15, *ligand-gated* ion channels capable of binding to the neurotransmitter are clustered in the membrane of the postsynaptic cell, directly opposite the synaptic terminal. Binding of the neurotransmitter to a particular part of the channel opens the channel and allows specific ions to diffuse across the postsynaptic membrane. The result is generally a *postsynaptic potential*, a change in the membrane potential of the postsynaptic cell. At synapses like the one in the figure, the neurotransmitter binds to a type of channel through which both K^+ and Na^+ can diffuse. When those channels open, the postsynaptic membrane depolarizes as the membrane potential approaches a value roughly midway between E_K and E_{Na}. Because these depolarizations bring the membrane potential toward threshold, they are called **excitatory postsynaptic potentials (EPSPs)**. At other synapses, a different neurotransmitter binds to channels that are selectively permeable for only K^+ or Cl^-. When those channels open, the postsynaptic membrane hyperpolarizes. Hyperpolarizations produced in this manner are called **inhibitory postsynaptic potentials (IPSPs)** because they move the membrane potential farther from threshold.

Various mechanisms rapidly clear neurotransmitters from the synaptic cleft, terminating their effect on postsynaptic cells. Certain neurotransmitters may be actively transported into the presynaptic neuron, to be repackaged into synaptic vesicles, or they may be transported into glia, to be metabolized as fuel. Other neurotransmitters are removed from the synaptic cleft by simple diffusion or by an enzyme that catalyzes hydrolysis of the neurotransmitter.

Summation of Postsynaptic Potentials

Unlike action potentials, which are all-or-none events, postsynaptic potentials are graded; their magnitude varies with a number of factors, including the amount of neurotransmitter released by the presynaptic neuron. Furthermore, postsynaptic potentials usually do *not* regenerate as they spread along the membrane of a cell; they become smaller with distance from the synapse. Recall that most synapses on a neuron are located on its dendrites or cell body, whereas action potentials are generally initiated at the axon hillock. Therefore, a single EPSP is usually too small to trigger an action potential in a postsynaptic neuron **(Figure 48.16a)**.

On some occasions, two EPSPs occur at a single synapse in such rapid succession that the postsynaptic neuron's membrane potential has not returned to the resting potential before the arrival of the second EPSP. When that happens, the EPSPs add together, an effect called **temporal summation** **(Figure 48.16b)**. Moreover, EPSPs produced nearly simultaneously by *different* synapses on the same postsynaptic neuron can also add together, an effect called **spatial summation** **(Figure 48.16c)**. Through spatial and temporal summation, several EPSPs can depolarize the membrane at the axon hillock to the threshold, causing the postsynaptic neuron to produce an action potential. Summation applies as well to IPSPs: Two or more IPSPs occurring nearly simultaneously or in rapid succession have a larger hyperpolarizing effect than a single IPSP. Through summation, an IPSP can also counter the effect of an EPSP **(Figure 48.16d)**.

The interplay between multiple excitatory and inhibitory inputs is the essence of integration in the nervous system. The

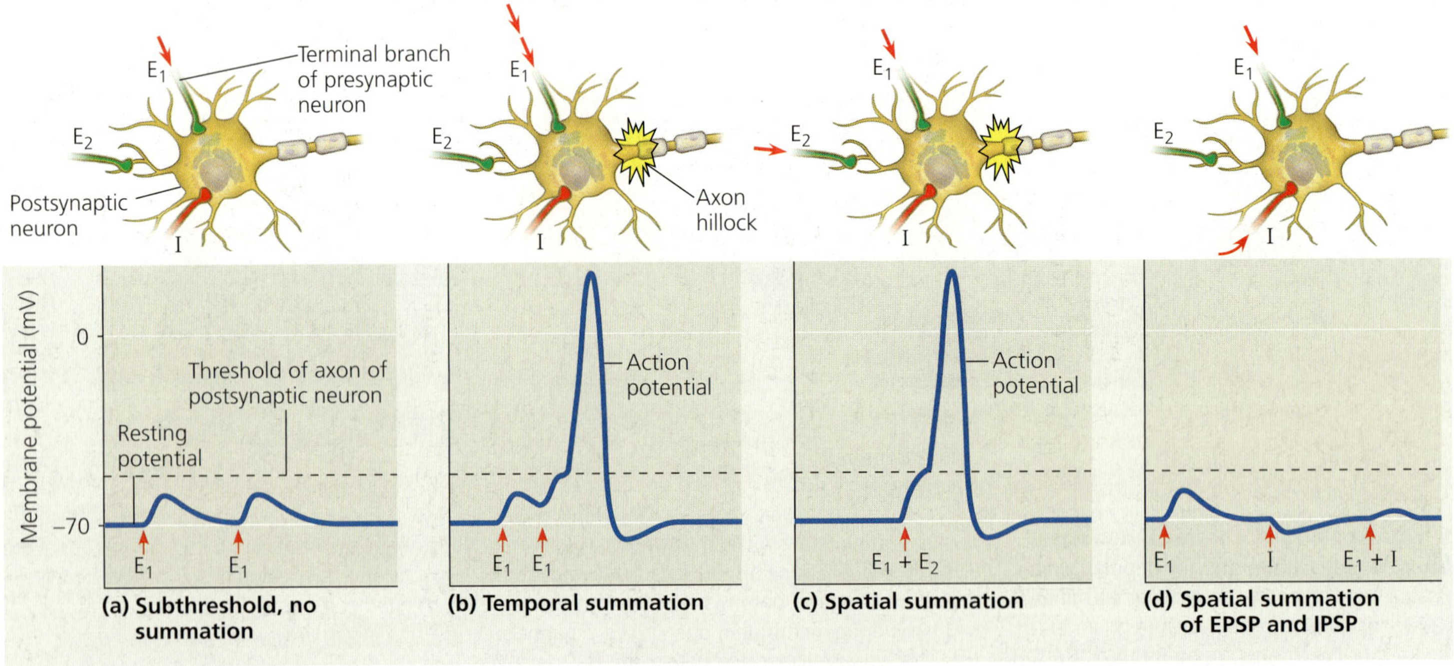

▲ **Figure 48.16 Summation of postsynaptic potentials.** These graphs trace changes in the membrane potential at a postsynaptic neuron's axon hillock. The arrows indicate times when postsynaptic potentials occur at two excitatory synapses (E_1 and E_2, green in the diagrams above the graphs) and at one inhibitory synapse (I, red). Like most EPSPs, those produced at E_1 or E_2 do not reach the threshold at the axon hillock without summation.

axon hillock is the neuron's integrating center, the region where the membrane potential at any instant represents the summed effect of all EPSPs and IPSPs. Whenever the membrane potential at the axon hillock reaches the threshold, an action potential is generated and travels along the axon to its synaptic terminals. After the refractory period, the neuron may produce another action potential, provided the membrane potential at the axon hillock once again reaches the threshold.

Modulated Synaptic Transmission

So far, we have focused on synapses containing ligand-gated ion channels, in which a neurotransmitter binds directly to an ion channel, causing the channel to open. However, there are also synapses in which the receptor for the neurotransmitter is *not* part of an ion channel. Instead, binding of the neurotransmitter to its receptor in the postsynaptic cell activates a signal transduction pathway involving a second messenger (see Chapter 11). Compared with the postsynaptic potentials produced by ligand-gated channels, the effects of these second-messenger systems have a slower onset but last longer (minutes or even hours). Second messengers modulate the responsiveness of postsynaptic neurons to inputs in diverse ways, such as by altering the number of open potassium channels.

A variety of signal transduction pathways play a role in modulating synaptic transmission. One of the best-studied pathways involves cyclic AMP (cAMP) as a second messenger. For example, when the neurotransmitter norepinephrine binds to its receptor, the neurotransmitter-receptor complex activates a G protein, which in turn activates adenylyl cyclase, the enzyme that converts ATP to cAMP (see Figure 11.11). Cyclic AMP activates protein kinase A, which phosphorylates specific channel proteins in the postsynaptic membrane, causing them to open or close. Because of the amplifying effect of the signal transduction pathway, the binding of a neurotransmitter molecule to a single receptor can open or close many channels.

Neurotransmitters

There are more than 100 known neurotransmitters. However, nearly all of these fall into one of a few groups based on chemical structure. As shown in **Table 48.1**, the major classes of

Table 48.1 Major Neurotransmitters

Neurotransmitter	Structure	Functional Class	Secretion Sites
Acetylcholine	$H_3C-C(=O)-O-CH_2-CH_2-N^+-[CH_3]_3$	Excitatory to vertebrate skeletal muscles; excitatory or inhibitory at other sites	CNS; PNS; vertebrate neuromuscular junction
Biogenic Amines			
Norepinephrine	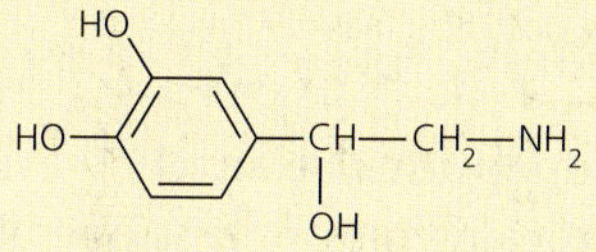	Excitatory or inhibitory	CNS; PNS
Dopamine	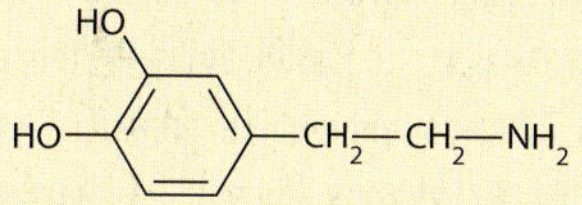	Generally excitatory; may be inhibitory at some sites	CNS; PNS
Serotonin	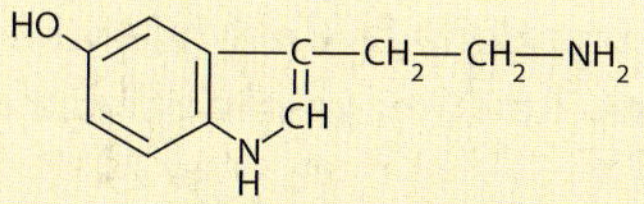	Generally inhibitory	CNS
Amino Acids			
GABA (gamma-aminobutyric acid)	$H_2N-CH_2-CH_2-CH_2-COOH$	Inhibitory	CNS; invertebrate neuromuscular junction
Glutamate	$H_2N-CH(COOH)-CH_2-CH_2-COOH$	Excitatory	CNS; invertebrate neuromuscular junction
Glycine	H_2N-CH_2-COOH	Inhibitory	CNS
Neuropeptides (a very diverse group, only two of which are shown)			
Substance P	Arg—Pro—Lys—Pro—Gln—Gln—Phe—Phe—Gly—Leu—Met	Excitatory	CNS; PNS
Met-enkephalin (an endorphin)	Tyr—Gly—Gly—Phe—Met	Generally inhibitory	CNS
Gases			
Nitric oxide	N=O	Excitatory or inhibitory	PNS

neurotransmitters are acetylcholine, biogenic amines, amino acids, neuropeptides, and gases.

A single neurotransmitter may have more than a dozen different receptors. Furthermore, the receptors for a specific neurotransmitter can vary significantly in their effects on postsynaptic cells. For this reason, many drugs used to treat nervous system diseases or affect brain function are targeted to specific receptors rather than particular neurotransmitters.

Acetylcholine

One of the most common neurotransmitters in both invertebrates and vertebrates is **acetylcholine**. Except in the heart, vertebrate neurons that form a synapse with muscle cells release acetylcholine as an excitatory transmitter. Acetylcholine binds to receptors on ligand-gated channels in the muscle cell, producing an EPSP. Nicotine, a chemical found in tobacco and tobacco smoke, binds to the same receptors, which are also found elsewhere in the PNS and in the CNS. Nicotine's effects as a physiological and psychological stimulant result from its affinity for this type of acetylcholine receptor. Acetylcholine activity is terminated by *acetylcholinesterase*, an enzyme in the synaptic cleft that hydrolyzes the neurotransmitter.

Certain bacteria produce a toxin that specifically inhibits presynaptic release of acetylcholine. This toxin is the cause of a rare but severe form of food poisoning called botulism. Untreated botulism is typically fatal because muscles required for breathing fail to contract when acetylcholine release is blocked. Recently, the same botulinum toxin has become a controversial tool in a cosmetic procedure. Injections of the toxin, known by the trade name Botox, minimize wrinkles around the eyes or mouth by blocking transmission at synapses that control particular facial muscles.

In regulating vertebrate cardiac (heart) muscle, acetylcholine has inhibitory rather than excitatory effects. In the heart, acetylcholine released by neurons activates a signal transduction pathway. The G proteins in the pathway inhibit adenylyl cyclase and open potassium channels in the muscle cell membrane. Both effects reduce the rate at which cardiac muscle cells contract.

Biogenic Amines

Biogenic amines are neurotransmitters derived from amino acids. The biogenic amine **serotonin** is synthesized from tryptophan. Several other biogenic amines, the catecholamines, are derived from tyrosine. One catecholamine, **dopamine**, acts only as a neurotransmitter. Two others—**epinephrine** and **norepinephrine**—act both as neurotransmitters and as hormones (see Chapter 45).

In the PNS of vertebrates, norepinephrine is one of two major neurotransmitters, the other being acetylcholine. Acting through a G protein-coupled receptor (see Chapter 11), norepinephrine generates EPSPs in the autonomic nervous system, a branch of the PNS discussed in Chapter 49.

In the CNS, the biogenic amines are often involved in modulating synaptic transmission. Dopamine and serotonin are released at many sites in the brain and affect sleep, mood, attention, and learning. Some psychoactive drugs, including LSD and mescaline, apparently produce their hallucinatory effects by binding to brain receptors for serotonin and dopamine.

Biogenic amines have a central role in a number of nervous system disorders and treatments (see Chapter 49). The degenerative illness Parkinson's disease is associated with a lack of dopamine in the brain. In addition, depression is often treated with drugs that increase the brain concentrations of biogenic amines. Prozac, for instance, enhances the effect of serotonin by inhibiting its reuptake after release.

Amino Acids

Two amino acids serve as the major neurotransmitters in the vertebrate CNS: **gamma-aminobutyric acid (GABA)** and **glutamate**. GABA, which appears to be the neurotransmitter at most inhibitory synapses in the brain, produces IPSPs by increasing the permeability of the postsynaptic membrane to Cl^-. In contrast, glutamate, the most common neurotransmitter in the brain, is always excitatory. A third amino acid, glycine, acts at inhibitory synapses in parts of the CNS that lie outside of the brain.

Neuropeptides

Several **neuropeptides**, relatively short chains of amino acids, serve as neurotransmitters that operate via signal transduction pathways. Such peptides are typically produced by cleavage of much larger protein precursors. The neuropeptide **substance P** is a key excitatory neurotransmitter that mediates our perception of pain, while other neuropeptides, called **endorphins**, function as natural analgesics, decreasing pain perception.

In the 1970s, Candace Pert, then a graduate student at Johns Hopkins University, and her research supervisor, Solomon Snyder, discovered endorphins as an outcome of their research on the biochemistry of behavior. Previous studies had indicated that the brain contains specific receptors for opiates, painkilling drugs such as morphine and heroin. To find these receptors, Pert and Snyder had the insight to apply existing knowledge about the activity of different drugs in the brain **(Figure 48.17)**. In a single, straightforward experiment, they provided the first demonstration that opiate receptors exist. Setting out to identify molecules normally present in the brain that could also activate these receptors, they discovered endorphins.

Endorphins are produced in the brain during times of physical or emotional stress, such as childbirth. In addition to relieving

▼ **Figure 48.17 Inquiry**

Does the brain have a specific protein receptor for opiates?

EXPERIMENT In 1973, Candace Pert and Solomon Snyder, of Johns Hopkins University, were searching for an opiate receptor in the mammalian brain. It was known that the drug naloxone antagonizes (opposes) the narcotic effect of opiates. Pert and Snyder reasoned that naloxone acts as an opiate antagonist by binding tightly to the opiate receptor without activating the receptor. They first prepared radioactive naloxone and then incubated it with a protein mixture prepared from rodent brains. If proteins that could bind naloxone were present, the radioactivity would become stably associated with the protein mixture. Furthermore, the researchers could determine whether a specific receptor was present by examining the ability of different drug molecules to interfere with the binding activity.

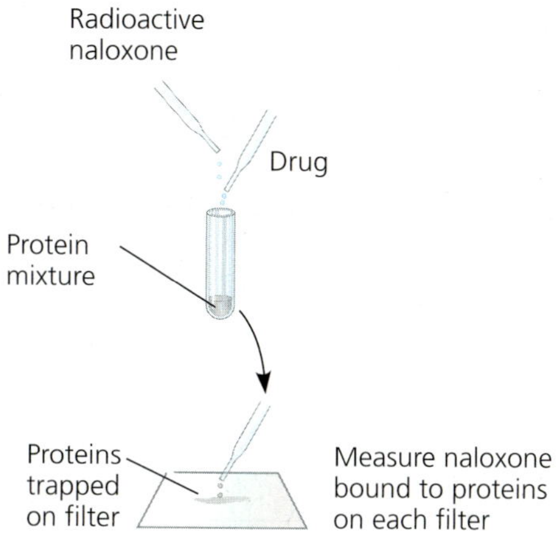

RESULTS

Drug	Opiate	Concentration That Blocked Naloxone Binding
Morphine	Yes	6×10^{-9} *M*
Methadone	Yes	2×10^{-8} *M*
Levorphanol	Yes	2×10^{-9} *M*
Phenobarbital	No	No effect at 10^{-4} *M*
Atropine	No	No effect at 10^{-4} *M*
Serotonin	No	No effect at 10^{-4} *M*

CONCLUSION Because opiates interfere with naloxone binding, but unrelated drugs do not, the binding activity had the specificity expected of the opiate receptor. Pert and Snyder also found that the binding activity was present in tissue from regions of the brain involved in the sensation of pain, but not in tissue from the cerebellum, a brain region that coordinates motor activity.

SOURCE C. B. Pert and S. H. Snyder, Opiate receptor: demonstration in nervous tissue, *Science* 179:1011–1014 (1973).

WHAT IF? How would the results have been affected if the researchers had used a radioactive opiate rather than a radioactive opiate antagonist?

pain, they decrease urine output, depress respiration, and produce euphoria, as well as other emotional effects. Because opiates bind to the same receptor proteins as endorphins, opiates mimic endorphins and produce many of the same physiological effects (see Figure 2.18).

Gases

In common with many other types of cells, some neurons in vertebrates release dissolved gases, notably nitric oxide (NO; see Chapter 45), that act as local regulators. For example, during sexual arousal, certain neurons in human males release NO into the erectile tissue of the penis. In response, smooth muscle cells in the blood vessel walls of the erectile tissue relax, which causes the blood vessels to dilate and fill the spongy erectile tissue with blood, producing an erection. As you read in Chapter 45, the erectile dysfunction drug Viagra increases the ability to achieve and maintain an erection by inhibiting an enzyme that terminates the action of NO.

Unlike most neurotransmitters, NO is not stored in cytoplasmic vesicles but is instead synthesized on demand. NO diffuses into neighboring target cells, produces a change, and is broken down—all within a few seconds. In many of its targets, including smooth muscle cells, NO works like many hormones, stimulating an enzyme to synthesize a second messenger that directly affects cellular metabolism.

Although inhaling air containing the gas carbon monoxide (CO) can be deadly, the vertebrate body produces small amounts of CO, some of which acts as a neurotransmitter. Carbon monoxide is generated by the enzyme heme oxygenase, one form of which is found in certain populations of neurons in the brain and PNS. In the brain, CO regulates the release of hypothalamic hormones. In the PNS, it acts as an inhibitory neurotransmitter that hyperpolarizes intestinal smooth muscle cells.

In the next chapter, we will consider how the cellular and biochemical mechanisms we have discussed contribute to nervous system function on the system level.

CONCEPT CHECK 48.4

1. How is it possible for a particular neurotransmitter to produce opposite effects in different tissues?
2. Organophosphate pesticides work by inhibiting acetylcholinesterase, the enzyme that breaks down the neurotransmitter acetylcholine. Explain how these toxins would affect EPSPs produced by acetylcholine.
3. **WHAT IF?** If a drug mimicked the activity of GABA in the CNS, what general effect on behavior might you expect? Explain.

For suggested answers, see Appendix A.

Chapter 48 Review

MB **MEDIA** Go to the Study Area at **www.masteringbio.com** for BioFlix 3-D Animations, MP3 Tutors, Videos, Practice Tests, an eBook, and more.

SUMMARY OF KEY CONCEPTS

CONCEPT 48.1

Neuron organization and structure reflect function in information transfer (pp. 1047–1049)

▶ **Introduction to Information Processing** Nervous systems process information in three stages: sensory input, integration, and motor output to effector cells. Nervous systems are often divided into a central nervous system (CNS) that includes the brain and nerve cord and a peripheral nervous system (PNS).

▶ **Neuron Structure and Function** Most neurons have highly branched dendrites that receive signals from other neurons. They also typically have a single axon that transmits signals to other cells at synapses. Neurons have a wide variety of shapes that reflect their input and output interactions and depend on glia for supporting functions.

MEDIA
BioFlix 3-D Animation How Neurons Work
Activity Neuron Structure

CONCEPT 48.2

Ion pumps and ion channels maintain the resting potential of a neuron (pp. 1050–1052)

▶ **Formation of the Resting Potential** Every living cell has a voltage across its plasma membrane called a membrane potential. The inside of the cell is negative relative to the outside.

▶ **Modeling of the Resting Potential** The membrane potential depends on ionic gradients across the plasma membrane: The concentration of Na^+ is higher in the extracellular fluid than in the cytosol, while the reverse is true for K^+. A neuron that is not transmitting signals contains many open potassium channels and few open sodium channels in its plasma membrane. The diffusion of K^+ and Na^+ through these channels leads to the separation of charges across the membrane, producing the resting potential.

CONCEPT 48.3

Action potentials are the signals conducted by axons (pp. 1052–1056)

▶ Neurons have gated ion channels that open or close in response to stimuli, leading to changes in membrane potential. A change in the membrane potential toward a more negative value is a hyperpolarization; a change toward a more positive value is a depolarization. Changes in membrane potential that vary with the strength of a stimulus are known as graded potentials.

▶ **Production of Action Potentials** An action potential is a brief, all-or-none depolarization of a neuron's plasma membrane. When a graded depolarization brings the membrane potential to the threshold, many voltage-gated Na^+ channels open, triggering an inflow of Na^+ that rapidly brings the membrane potential to a positive value. The membrane potential is restored to its normal resting value by the inactivation of sodium channels and by the opening of many voltage-gated potassium channels, which increases K^+ outflow.

MEDIA
Activity Nerve Signals: Action Potentials
Investigation What Triggers Nerve Impulses?

▶ **Generation of Action Potentials: *A Closer Look*** A refractory period follows the action potential, corresponding to the interval when the sodium channels are inactivated.

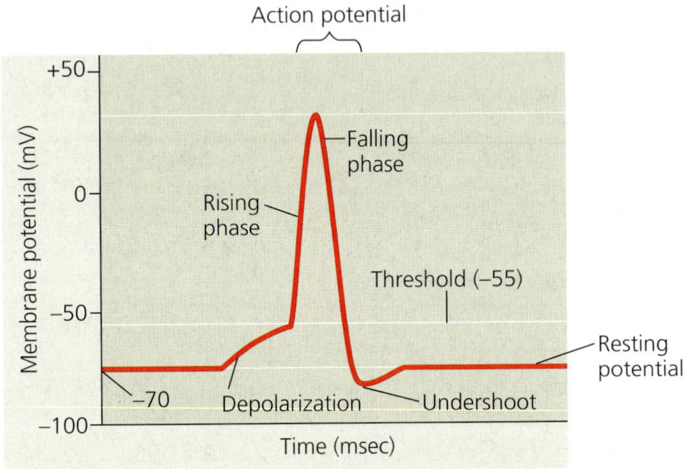

▶ **Conduction of Action Potentials** An action potential travels from the axon hillock to the synaptic terminals by regenerating itself along the axon. The speed of conduction of an action potential increases with the diameter of the axon and, in many vertebrate axons, with myelination. Action potentials in myelinated axons jump between the nodes of Ranvier, a process called saltatory conduction.

CONCEPT 48.4

Neurons communicate with other cells at synapses (pp. 1056–1061)

▶ In an electrical synapse, electrical current flows directly from one cell to another via gap junctions. In a chemical synapse, depolarization of the synaptic terminal causes synaptic vesicles to fuse with the terminal membrane and release neurotransmitter into the synaptic cleft.

▶ **Generation of Postsynaptic Potentials** At many synapses, the neurotransmitter binds to ligand-gated ion channels in the postsynaptic membrane, producing an excitatory or inhibitory postsynaptic potential (EPSP or IPSP). After release, the neurotransmitter diffuses out of the synaptic cleft, is taken up by surrounding cells, or is degraded by enzymes.

▶ **Summation of Postsynaptic Potentials** A single neuron has many synapses on its dendrites and cell body. Whether it generates an action potential depends on the temporal and spatial summation of EPSPs and IPSPs at the axon hillock.

▶ **Modulated Synaptic Transmission** The binding of neurotransmitter to some receptors activates signal transduction pathways, which produce slowly developing but long-lasting effects in the postsynaptic cell.

▶ **Neurotransmitters** The same neurotransmitter can produce different effects on different types of cells, depending on the receptor type. Major known neurotransmitters include acetylcholine; biogenic amines (serotonin, dopamine, epinephrine, and norepinephrine); the amino acids GABA, glutamate, and glycine; neuropeptides; and gases such as nitric oxide.

MEDIA

Activity Signal Transmission at a Chemical Synapse

TESTING YOUR KNOWLEDGE

SELF-QUIZ

1. What happens when a neuron's membrane depolarizes?
a. There is a net diffusion of Na^+ out of the cell.
b. The equilibrium potential for K^+ (E_K) becomes more positive.
c. The neuron's membrane voltage becomes more positive.
d. The neuron becomes less likely to generate an action potential.
e. The inside of the cell becomes more negative relative to the outside.

2. Why are action potentials usually conducted in only one direction along an axon?
a. The nodes of Ranvier can conduct potentials in only one direction.
b. The brief refractory period prevents reopening of voltage-gated Na^+ channels.
c. The axon hillock has a higher membrane potential than the terminals of the axon.
d. Ions can flow along the axon in only one direction.
e. Voltage-gated channels for both Na^+ and K^+ open in only one direction.

3. A common feature of action potentials is that they
a. cause the membrane to hyperpolarize and then depolarize.
b. can undergo temporal and spatial summation.
c. are triggered by a depolarization that reaches the threshold.
d. move at the same speed along all axons.
e. result from the diffusion of Na^+ and K^+ through ligand-gated channels.

4. Which of the following is a *direct* result of depolarizing the presynaptic membrane of an axon terminal?
a. Voltage-gated calcium channels in the membrane open.
b. Synaptic vesicles fuse with the membrane.
c. The postsynaptic cell produces an action potential.
d. Ligand-gated channels open, allowing neurotransmitters to enter the synaptic cleft.
e. An EPSP or IPSP is generated in the postsynaptic cell.

5. Where are neurotransmitter receptors located?
a. on the nuclear membrane
b. at nodes of Ranvier
c. on the postsynaptic membrane
d. on the membranes of synaptic vesicles
e. in the myelin sheath

6. Temporal summation always involves
a. both inhibitory and excitatory inputs.
b. synapses at more than one site.
c. inputs that are not simultaneous.
d. electrical synapses.
e. multiple inputs at a single synapse.

For Self-Quiz answers, see Appendix A.

MEDIA Visit the Study Area at **www.masteringbio.com** for a Practice Test.

7. **DRAW IT** Suppose a researcher inserts a pair of electrodes at two different positions along the middle of an axon dissected out of a squid. By applying a depolarizing stimulus, the researcher brings the plasma membrane at both positions to threshold. Using the drawing below as a starting point, create one or more drawings that illustrate where each action potential would terminate.

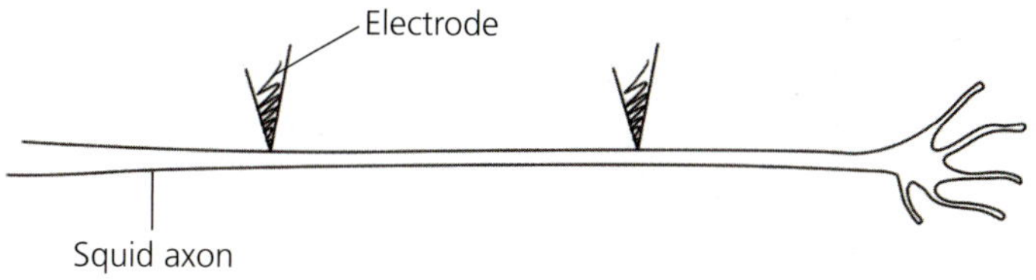

EVOLUTION CONNECTION

8. An action potential is an all-or-none event. This on/off signaling is an evolutionary adaptation of animals that must sense and act in a complex environment. It is possible to imagine a nervous system in which the action potentials are graded, with the amplitude depending on the size of the stimulus. What advantage might on/off signaling have over a graded (continuously variable) kind of signaling?

SCIENTIFIC INQUIRY

9. From what you know about action potentials and synapses, propose two or three hypotheses for how various anesthetics might prevent pain.

SCIENCE, TECHNOLOGY, AND SOCIETY

10. Nervous system damage from accidents or disease can cause pain that is sensed as a constant burning, an electrical shock, or shooting pain. Researchers are conducting studies to determine whether cone snail toxins can be used to treat these types of pain. How would you envision these toxins being used? What risks might there be for the patient? Could such toxins pose a risk for large-scale bioterrorist attacks?

49 Nervous Systems

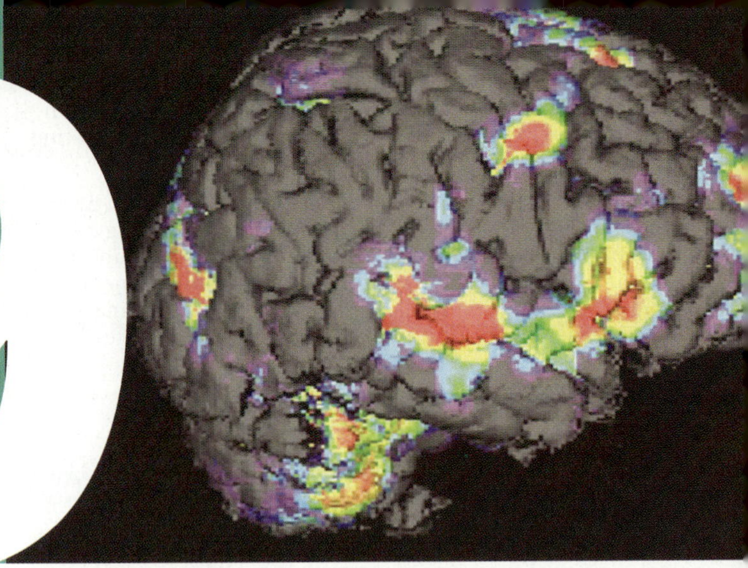

▲ **Figure 49.1 How do scientists map activity within the human brain?**

KEY CONCEPTS

49.1 Nervous systems consist of circuits of neurons and supporting cells
49.2 The vertebrate brain is regionally specialized
49.3 The cerebral cortex controls voluntary movement and cognitive functions
49.4 Changes in synaptic connections underlie memory and learning
49.5 Nervous system disorders can be explained in molecular terms

OVERVIEW

Command and Control Center

What happens in your brain when you picture something with your "mind's eye"? Until quite recently, scientists had little hope of answering that question. The human brain contains an estimated 10^{11} (100 billion) neurons. The circuits that interconnect these brain cells are more complex than those of even the most powerful supercomputers. Yet except for rare glimpses, such as during brain surgery, even the large-scale circuitry of the living human brain has been hidden from view. That's no longer the case, thanks in part to recent technologies that can record brain activity from outside a person's skull **(Figure 49.1)**.

The image in Figure 49.1 was produced by functional magnetic resonance imaging (fMRI). During an fMRI, the subject lies with his or her head in the center of a large, doughnut-shaped magnet. When the brain is scanned with electromagnetic waves, changes in blood oxygen where the brain is active generate a signal that can be recorded. A computer then uses the data to construct a three-dimensional map of the subject's brain activity, like the one shown in Figure 49.1. These recordings can be made while the subject is doing various tasks, such as speaking, moving a hand, looking at pictures, or forming a mental image of a person's face. Scientists can then look for a correlation between a particular task and activity in specific regions of the brain.

The ability to sense and react originated billions of years ago with prokaryotes that could detect changes in their environment and respond in ways that enhanced their survival and reproductive success. For example, bacteria keep moving in a particular direction as long as they encounter increasing concentrations of a food source. Later, modification of simple recognition and response processes provided multicellular organisms with a mechanism for communication between cells of the body. By the time of the Cambrian explosion more than 500 million years ago (see Chapter 32), systems of neurons allowing animals to sense and move rapidly were present in essentially their current forms.

In this chapter, we will discuss the organization and evolution of animal nervous systems, exploring how groups of neurons function in specialized circuits dedicated to specific tasks. First we'll focus on specialization in regions of the vertebrate brain. We will then turn to the ways in which brain activity makes information storage and organization possible. Finally, we'll consider several disorders of the nervous system that are the subject of intense research today.

CONCEPT 49.1

Nervous systems consist of circuits of neurons and supporting cells

In most animals with nervous systems, clusters of neurons perform specialized functions. However, such clustering is absent in the cnidarians, the simplest animals with nervous systems. Hydras, jellies, and other cnidarians have radially symmetrical bodies organized around a gastrovascular cavity (see Figure 33.5). In most cnidarians, a series of interconnected nerve cells form a diffuse **nerve net** **(Figure 49.2a)**, which controls the contraction and expansion of the gastrovascular cavity.

In more complex animals, the axons of multiple nerve cells are often bundled together, forming **nerves**. These fibrous structures channel and organize information flow along specific routes through the nervous system. For example, sea stars have a set of radial nerves connecting to a central nerve ring **(Figure 49.2b)**. Within each arm, the radial nerve is linked to a nerve net from which it receives input and to which it sends signals controlling motor activity. Such an arrangement is better suited to controlling elaborate movements than a single diffuse nerve net.

Animals with elongated, bilaterally symmetrical bodies have even more specialized nervous systems. Such animals exhibit cephalization, an evolutionary trend toward a clustering of sensory neurons and interneurons at the anterior (front) end. One or more nerve cords extending toward the posterior (back) end connect these structures with nerves elsewhere in the body. In nonsegmented worms, such as the planarian shown in **Figure 49.2c**, a small brain and longitudinal nerve cords constitute the simplest clearly defined *central nervous system (CNS)*. In some such animals, the entire nervous system is constructed from only a small number of cells, as shown by studies of another nonsegmented worm, the nematode *C. elegans*. In this species, an adult worm has exactly 302 neurons, no more and no fewer. More complex invertebrates, such as segmented worms (annelids; **Figure 49.2d**) and arthropods **(Figure 49.2e)**, have many more neurons. The behavior of such animals is regulated by more complicated brains and by ventral nerve cords containing ganglia, segmentally arranged clusters of neurons.

Within an animal group, nervous system organization often correlates with lifestyle. For example, the sessile and slow-moving molluscs, such as clams and chitons, have relatively simple sense organs and little or no cephalization **(Figure 49.2f)**. In contrast, active predatory molluscs, such as octopuses and squids **(Figure 49.2g)**, have the most sophisticated nervous systems of any invertebrates, rivaling even those of some vertebrates. With large image-forming eyes and a brain containing millions of neurons, octopuses can learn to discriminate between visual patterns and to perform complex tasks.

In vertebrates **(Figure 49.2h)**, the brain and the spinal cord form the CNS; nerves and ganglia comprise the *peripheral nervous system (PNS)*. Regional specialization is a hallmark of both systems, as we will examine further in the remainder of this chapter.

Organization of the Vertebrate Nervous System

The brain and spinal cord of the vertebrate CNS are tightly coordinated. The brain provides the integrative power that

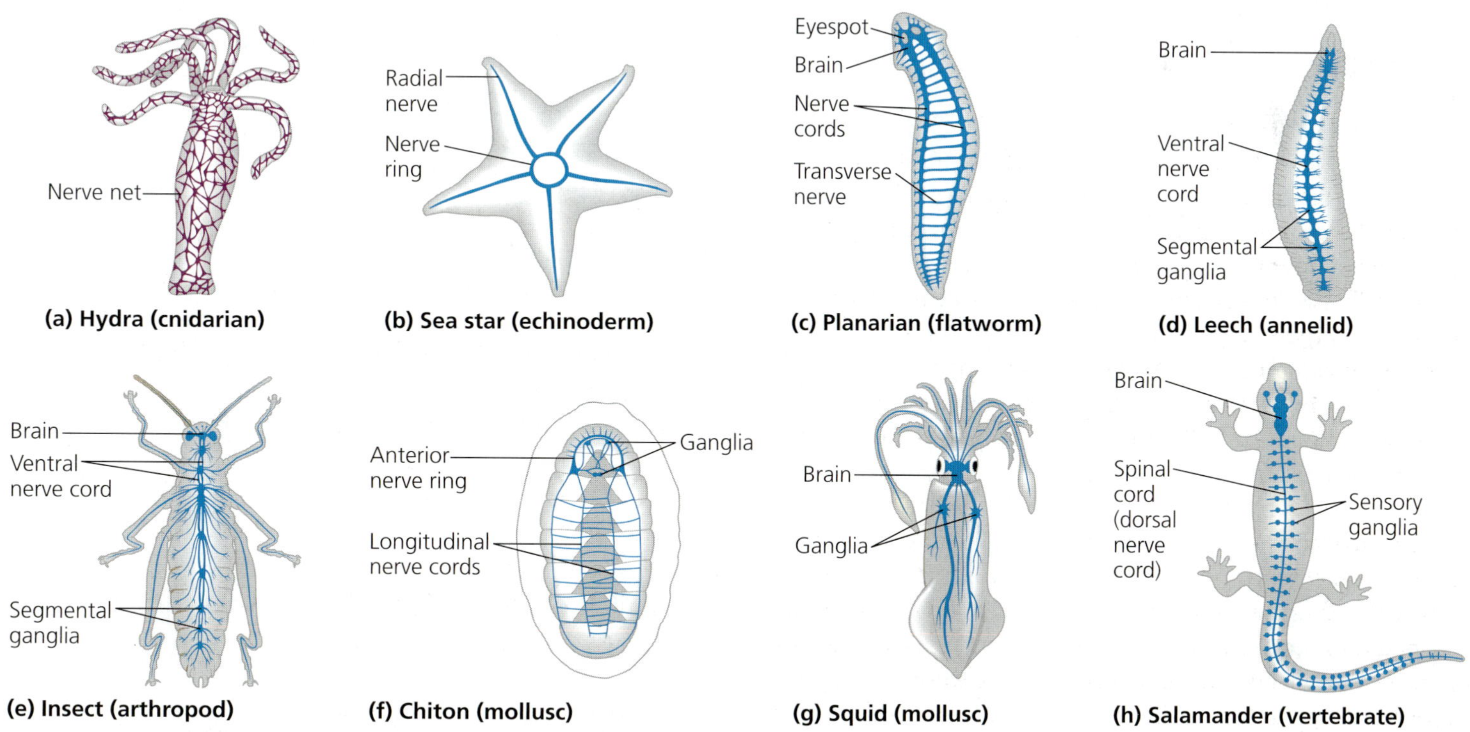

▲ **Figure 49.2 Nervous system organization. (a)** A hydra contains individual neurons (purple) organized in a diffuse nerve net. **(b–h)** Animals with more sophisticated nervous systems contain groups of neurons (blue) organized into nerves and often ganglia and a brain.

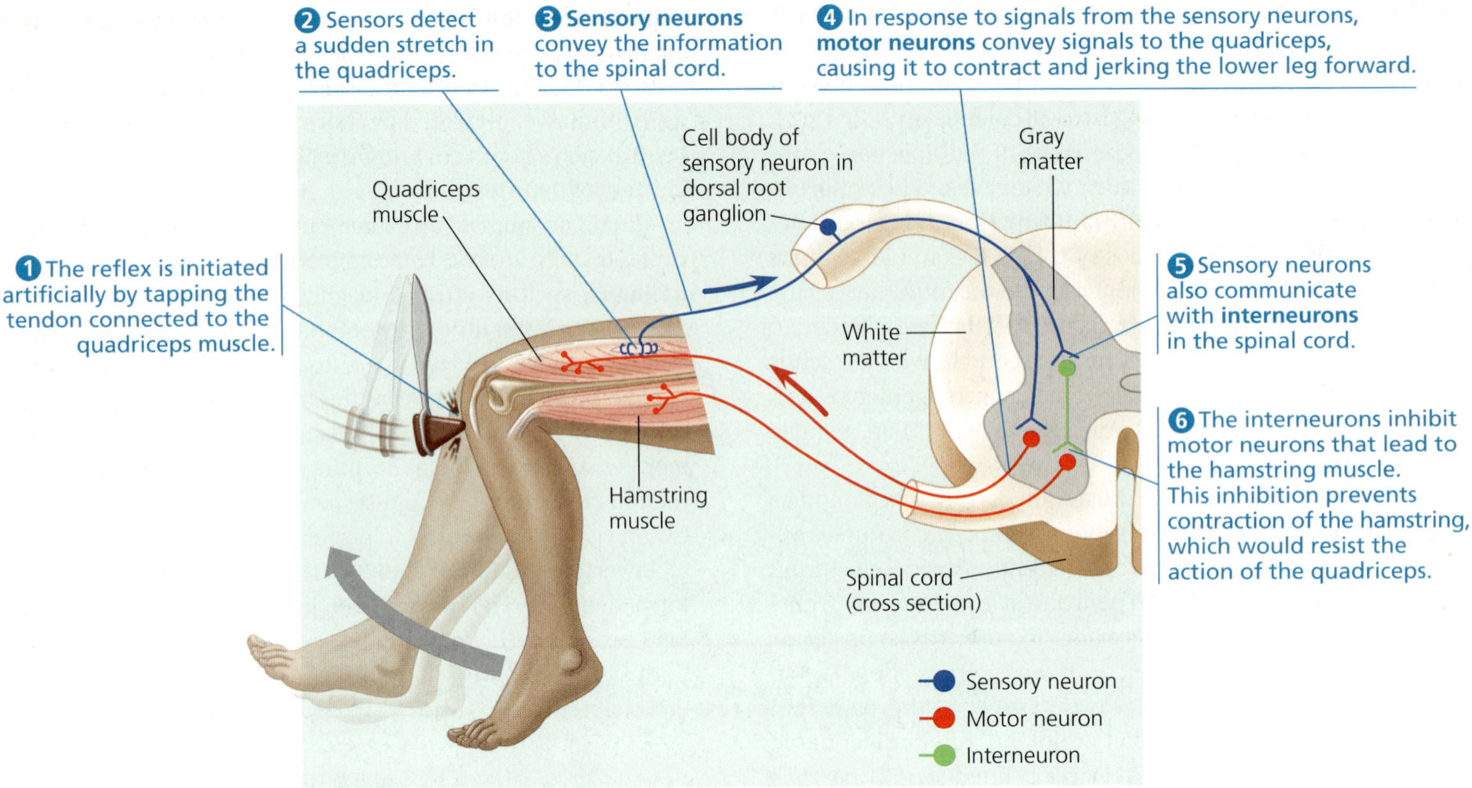

▲ **Figure 49.3 The knee-jerk reflex.** Many neurons are involved in the reflex, but for simplicity, only a few neurons are shown.

underlies the complex behavior of vertebrates. The spinal cord, which runs lengthwise inside the vertebral column (spine), conveys information to and from the brain and generates basic patterns of locomotion. The spinal cord also acts independently of the brain as part of the simple nerve circuits that produce **reflexes**, the body's automatic responses to certain stimuli.

A reflex protects the body by triggering a rapid, involuntary response to a particular stimulus. For example, if you put your hand on a hot burner, a reflex begins to pull your hand back well before the sensation of pain has been processed in your brain. Similarly, if your knees buckle when you pick up a heavy object, the tension across your knees triggers a reflex that contracts the thigh muscles, helping you stay upright and support the load. During a physical exam, your doctor may trigger this knee-jerk reflex with a mallet to help assess nervous system function **(Figure 49.3)**.

Unlike the ventral nerve cord of many invertebrates, the spinal cord of vertebrates runs along the dorsal side of the body **(Figure 49.4)**. Although the vertebrate spinal cord does not contain segmental ganglia, such ganglia are present just outside the spinal cord. Furthermore, an underlying segmental organization is apparent in the arrangement of neurons within the spinal cord.

The brain and spinal cord of vertebrates are derived from the dorsal embryonic nerve cord, which is hollow—a hallmark of chordates (see Chapter 34). During development, the

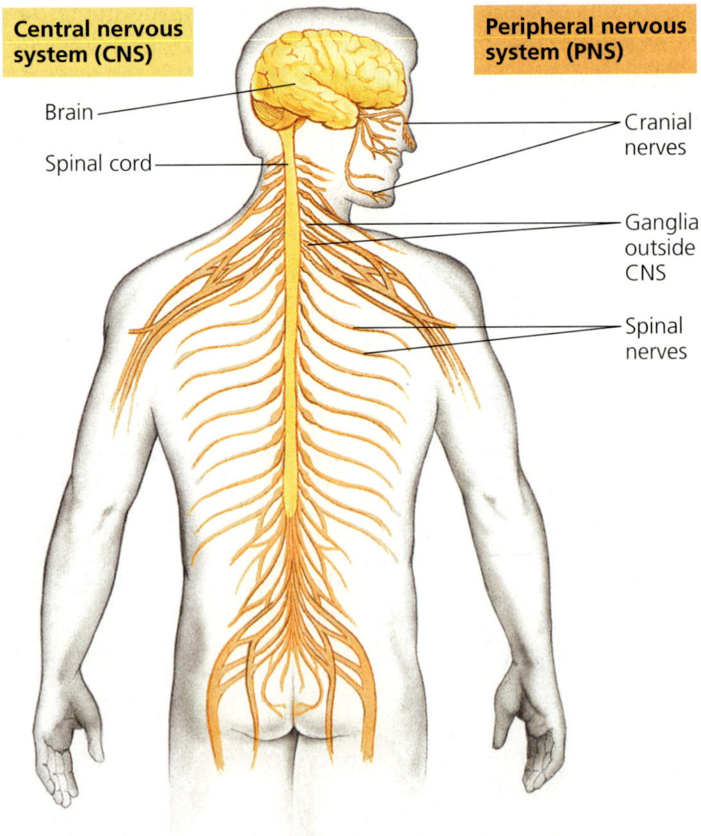

▲ **Figure 49.4 The vertebrate nervous system.** The central nervous system consists of the brain and spinal cord (yellow). Cranial nerves, spinal nerves, and ganglia outside the central nervous system make up the peripheral nervous system (dark gold).

hollow cavity of the embryonic nerve cord is transformed into the narrow **central canal** of the spinal cord and the **ventricles** of the brain **(Figure 49.5)**. Both the central canal and the four ventricles are filled with **cerebrospinal fluid**, which is formed by filtration of arterial blood in the brain. The cerebrospinal fluid circulates slowly through the central canal and ventricles and then drains into the veins, supplying different parts of the brain with nutrients and hormones and carrying away wastes. In mammals, the cerebrospinal fluid also cushions the brain and spinal cord by circulating between layers of connective tissue that surround the CNS.

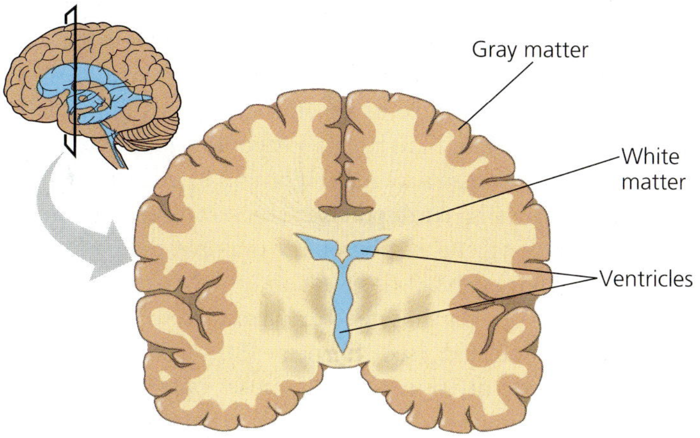

▲ **Figure 49.5 Ventricles, gray matter, and white matter.** Ventricles deep in the brain's interior contain cerebrospinal fluid. Most of the gray matter is on the surface of the brain, surrounding the white matter.

In addition to these fluid-filled spaces, the brain and the spinal cord contain gray matter and white matter. **Gray matter** consists mainly of neuron cell bodies, dendrites, and unmyelinated axons. In contrast, **white matter** consists of bundled axons that have myelin sheaths, which give the axons a whitish appearance. White matter in the spinal cord lies on the outside, consistent with its function in linking the CNS to sensory and motor neurons of the PNS. As shown in Figure 49.5, white matter in the brain is instead predominantly on the inside, reflecting the role of signaling between neurons of the brain in learning, feeling emotions, processing sensory information, and generating commands.

Glia in the CNS

The glia present throughout the vertebrate brain and spinal cord fall into a number of different categories, many of which are illustrated in **Figure 49.6**. Ependymal cells line the ventricles and have cilia that promote circulation of the cerebrospinal fluid. Microglia protect the nervous system from invading microorganisms. Oligodendrocytes function in axon myelination, a critical activity in the vertebrate nervous system (see Chapter 48). (Schwann cells perform this function in the PNS.)

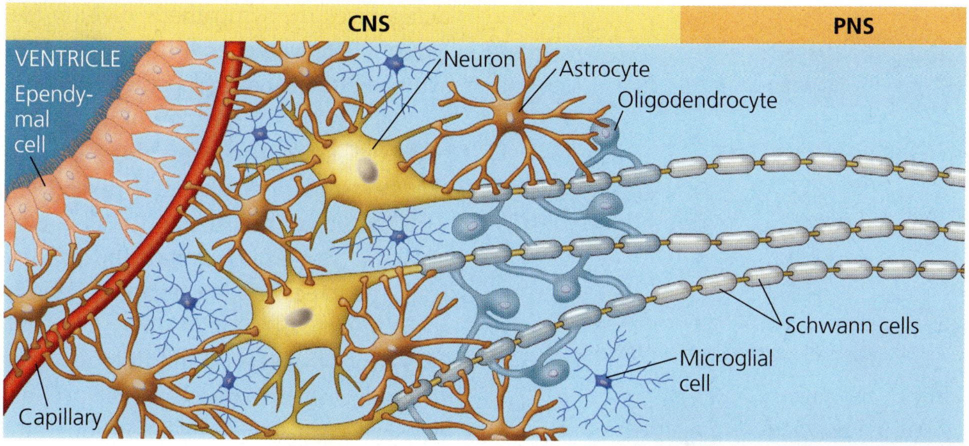

(a) The glia in vertebrates include ependymal cells, astrocytes, microglia, oligodendrocytes, and Schwann cells.

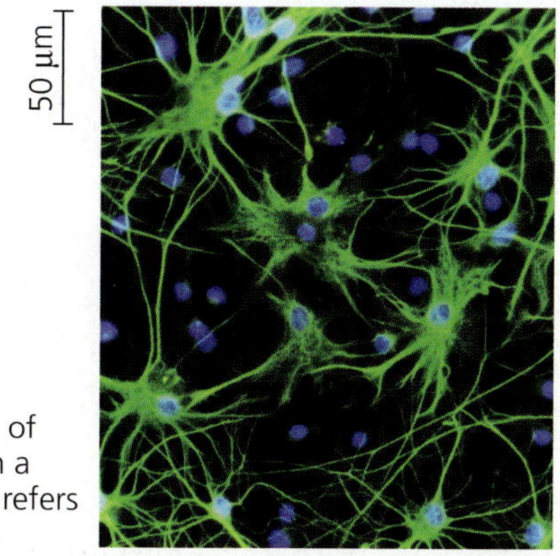

(b) In this section through a mammalian cerebral cortex, the green cells are astrocytes labeled with a fluorescent antibody. The blue dots are the nuclei of astrocytes and other cells labeled with a DNA-binding dye. The term *astrocyte* refers to the starlike shape of the cells (LM).

▲ **Figure 49.6 Glia in the vertebrate nervous system.**

Among the different types of glia, **astrocytes** appear to have the most diverse set of functions. They provide structural support for neurons and regulate the extracellular concentrations of ions and neurotransmitters. Astrocytes can respond to activity in neighboring neurons by facilitating information transfer at synapses and in some instances releasing neurotransmitters. Astrocytes adjacent to active neurons cause nearby blood vessels to dilate, increasing blood flow to the area and enabling the neurons to obtain oxygen and glucose more quickly. During development, astrocytes induce cells that line the capillaries in the CNS to form tight junctions (see Figure 6.32). The result is the **blood-brain barrier**, which restricts the passage of most substances into the CNS. The existence of this barrier permits tight control of the extracellular chemical environment of the brain and spinal cord.

Radial glia (not shown) play a critical role in development of the nervous system. In an embryo, radial glia form tracks along which newly formed neurons migrate from the neural tube, the structure that gives rise to the CNS (see Figures 47.12 and 47.13). Both radial glia and astrocytes can also act as stem cells, generating neurons and additional glia. Researchers view these multipotent precursors as a potential way to replace neurons and glia that are lost to injury or disease, a topic we'll explore further in Concept 49.5.

The Peripheral Nervous System

The PNS transmits information to and from the CNS and plays a large role in regulating an animal's movement and internal environment **(Figure 49.7)**. Sensory information reaches the CNS along PNS neurons designated as *afferent* (from the Latin, meaning "to bring toward"). Following information processing within the CNS, instructions then travel to muscles, glands, and endocrine cells along PNS neurons designated as *efferent* (from the Latin, meaning "to carry off").

Structurally, the vertebrate PNS consists of left-right pairs of cranial and spinal nerves and their associated ganglia (see Figure 49.4). The **cranial nerves** connect the brain with locations mostly in organs of the head and upper body. The **spinal nerves** run between the spinal cord and parts of the body below the head. Most of the cranial nerves and all of the spinal nerves contain both afferent and efferent neurons. A few cranial nerves are afferent only. For example, the olfactory nerve, which extends between the nose and the brain, is dedicated to conveying sensory information for *olfaction*, the sense of smell.

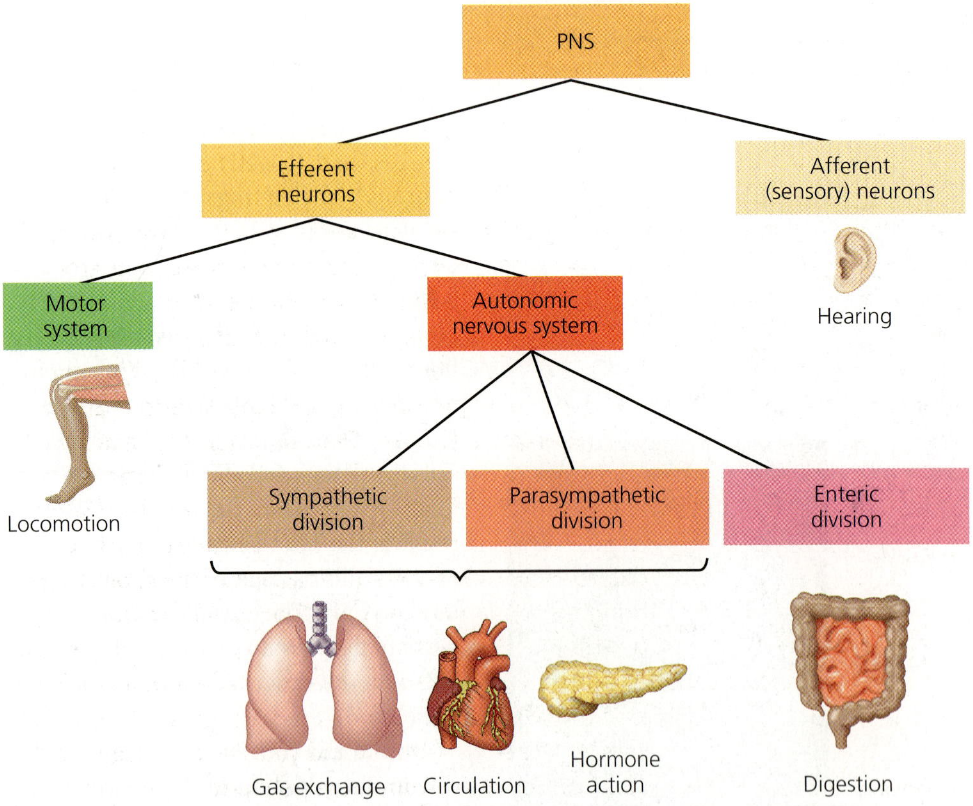

▲ **Figure 49.7 Functional hierarchy of the vertebrate peripheral nervous system.** Representative organs and activities are illustrated for each branch.

As shown in Figure 49.7, the efferent branch of the PNS consists of two functional components: the motor system and the autonomic nervous system. The **motor system** consists of neurons that carry signals to skeletal muscles, mainly in response to *external* stimuli. Although the motor system is often considered voluntary because it is subject to conscious control, much skeletal muscle activity is actually controlled by the brainstem or by reflexes mediated by the spinal cord. The **autonomic nervous system** regulates the *internal* environment by controlling smooth and cardiac muscles and the organs of the digestive, cardiovascular, excretory, and endocrine systems. This control is generally involuntary. Three divisions—sympathetic, parasympathetic, and enteric—together make up the autonomic nervous system.

The sympathetic and parasympathetic divisions of the autonomic nervous system have largely antagonistic (opposite) functions in regulating organ function **(Figure 49.8)**. Activation of the **sympathetic division** corresponds to arousal and energy generation (the "fight-or-flight" response). For example, the heart beats faster, digestion is inhibited, the liver converts glycogen to glucose, and secretion of epinephrine (adrenaline) from the adrenal medulla is stimulated (see Chapter 45). Activation of the **parasympathetic division** generally causes opposite responses that promote calming and a return to self-maintenance functions ("rest and digest"). For example, increased activity in the parasympathetic division lowers heart rate, enhances digestion, and increases glycogen production. In regulating reproductive activity, however, the parasympathetic division complements rather than antagonizes the sympathetic division (see Figure 49.8). The overall functions of the sympathetic and parasympathetic divisions are reflected in the location of neurons in each division and the neurotransmitters that these neurons release **(Table 49.1)**.

The **enteric division** of the PNS consists of networks of neurons in the digestive tract, pancreas, and gallbladder. Within these organs, neurons of the enteric division control secretion, and they also control the smooth muscles that produce peristalsis (see Chapter 41). Although the enteric division can function independently, it is normally regulated by the sympathetic and parasympathetic divisions.

The motor and autonomic nervous systems often cooperate in maintaining homeostasis. In response to a drop in body temperature, for example, the hypothalamus signals the autonomic nervous system to constrict surface blood vessels, reducing heat loss. At the same time, the hypothalamus signals the motor system to cause shivering, which increases heat production.

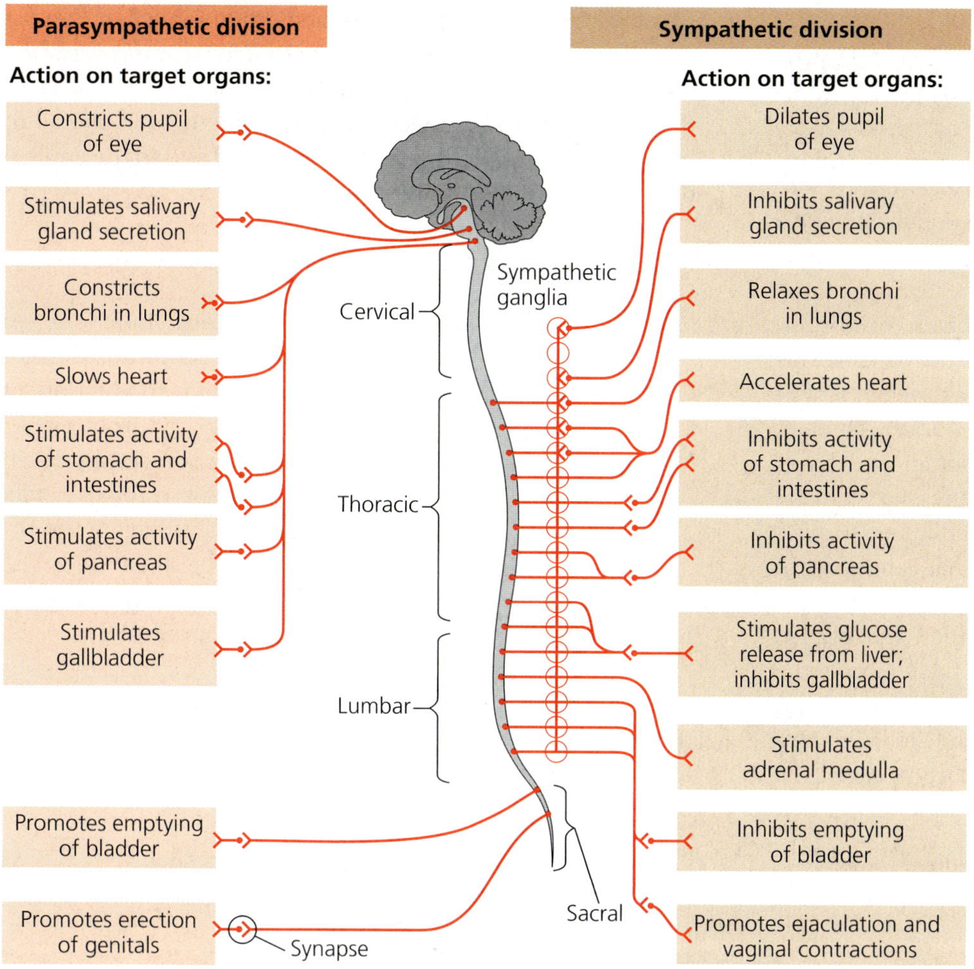

◄ **Figure 49.8 The parasympathetic and sympathetic divisions of the autonomic nervous system.** Most pathways in each division consist of preganglionic neurons (having cell bodies in the CNS) and postganglionic neurons (having cell bodies in ganglia in the PNS).

? *Most tissues regulated by the autonomic nervous system receive both sympathetic and parasympathetic input from postganglionic neurons. Responses are typically local. In contrast, the adrenal medulla receives input only from the sympathetic division and only from preganglionic neurons, yet responses are observed throughout the body. Explain.*

Table 49.1 Properties of Parasympathetic and Sympathetic Neurons

	Parasympathetic Division	Sympathetic Division
Preganglionic Neurons		
Location	Brainstem, sacral segments of spinal cord	Thoracic and lumbar segments of spinal cord
Neurotransmitter released	Acetylcholine	Acetylcholine
Postganglionic Neurons		
Location	Ganglia close to or within target organs	Ganglia close to target organs or chain of ganglia near spinal cord
Neurotransmitter released	Acetylcholine	Norepinephrine

CONCEPT CHECK 49.1

1. Which division of your autonomic nervous system would likely be activated if you learned that an exam you had forgotten about would start in 5 minutes? Explain your answer.
2. The parasympathetic and sympathetic divisions of the PNS (see Figure 49.8 and Table 49.1) use the same neurotransmitters at the axon terminals of preganglionic neurons, but different transmitters at the axon terminals of postganglionic neurons. How does this difference correlate with the function of the axons bringing signals into and out of the ganglia in the two divisions?
3. **WHAT IF?** Suppose you had an accident that severed a small nerve required to move some of the fingers of your right hand. Would you also expect an effect on sensation from those fingers?

For suggested answers, see Appendix A.

CONCEPT 49.2

The vertebrate brain is regionally specialized

Having considered the organization of the spinal cord and PNS, we turn now to the brain. In discussing brain organization, biologists often refer to subdivisions that are apparent at particular stages of embryonic development. In all vertebrates, three anterior bulges of the neural tube—the **forebrain**, **midbrain**, and **hindbrain**—become evident as the embryo develops **(Figure 49.9a)**. By the 5th week of embryonic development in humans, there are five brain regions **(Figure 49.9b)**. Three of these regions—those derived from the midbrain and hindbrain—give rise to the brainstem, a set of structures that form the lower part of the brain **(Figure 49.9c)**. The hindbrain also gives rise to a major brain center, the cerebellum, that is not part of the brainstem.

As embryogenesis proceeds, the most profound changes in the human brain occur in the *telencephalon*, the region of the forebrain that gives rise to the adult **cerebrum**. Rapid, expansive growth of the telencephalon during the 2nd and 3rd months causes the outer portion of the cerebrum, called the **cerebral cortex**, to extend over and around much of the rest of the brain. Major centers that develop from the *diencephalon* are the thalamus, hypothalamus, and epithalamus.

As we survey the function of the structures in the adult brain, we'll periodically refer to Figure 49.9 and to the embryonic history of a particular region.

The Brainstem

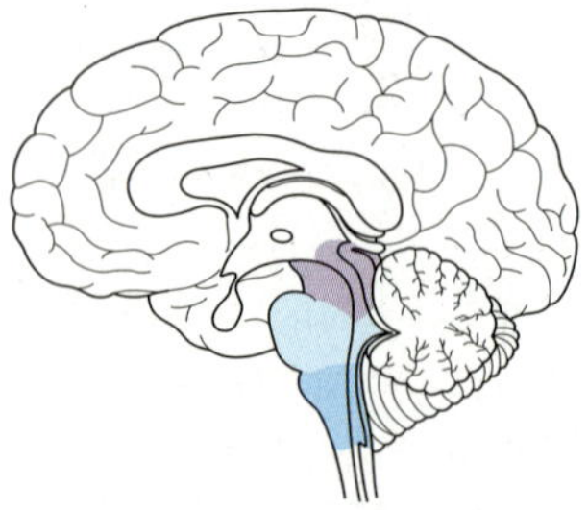

The **brainstem** functions in homeostasis, coordination of movement, and conduction of information to and from higher brain centers. Sometimes called the "lower brain," it forms a stalk with cap-like swellings at the anterior end of the spinal cord. The adult brainstem consists of the midbrain, the **pons**, and the **medulla oblongata** (commonly called the **medulla**).

The transfer of information between the PNS and the midbrain and forebrain is one of the most important functions of the medulla and pons. All axons carrying sensory information to and motor instructions from higher brain regions pass

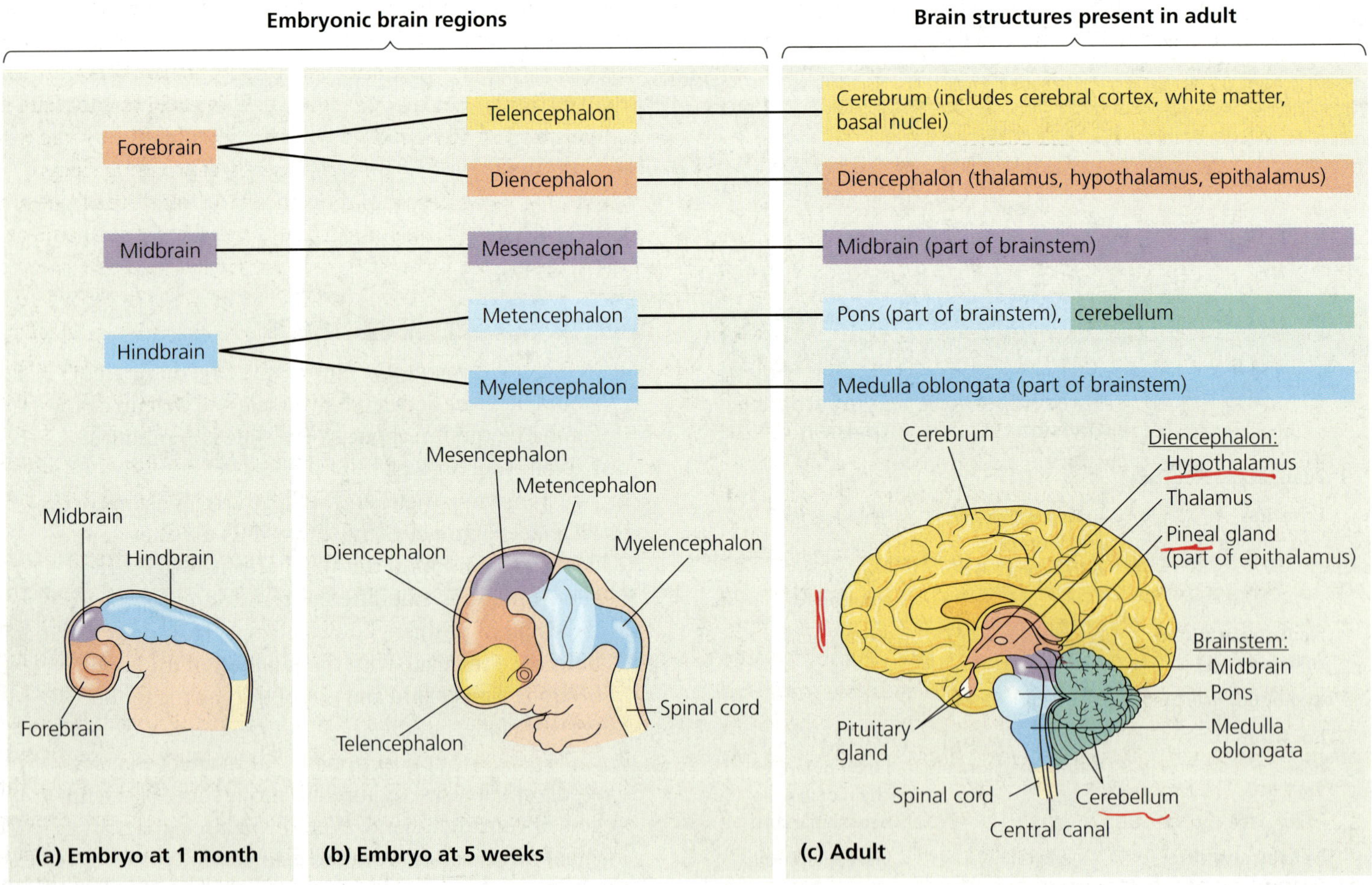

▲ **Figure 49.9 Development of the human brain.**

through the brainstem. The medulla and pons also help coordinate large-scale body movements, such as running and climbing. In carrying instructions about these movements from cell bodies in the midbrain and forebrain to synapses in the spinal cord, most axons cross in the medulla from one side of the CNS to the other. As a result, the right side of the brain controls much of the movement of the left side of the body, and vice versa.

The midbrain contains centers for receiving and integrating several types of sensory information. It also sends coded sensory information along neurons to specific regions of the forebrain. All sensory axons involved in hearing either terminate in the midbrain or pass through it on their way to the cerebrum. In nonmammalian vertebrates, portions of the midbrain form prominent optic lobes that in some cases are the animal's only visual centers. In mammals, vision is integrated in the cerebrum, not the midbrain. The midbrain instead coordinates visual reflexes, such as the peripheral vision reflex: The head turns toward an object approaching from the side without the brain having formed an image of the object.

Signals from the brainstem affect attention, alertness, appetite, and motivation. The medulla contains centers that control several automatic, homeostatic functions, including breathing, heart and blood vessel activity, swallowing, vomiting, and digestion. The pons also participates in some of these activities; for example, it regulates the breathing centers in the medulla (see Figure 42.27). These activities of the brainstem rely on axons that reach many areas of the cerebral cortex and cerebellum, releasing neurotransmitters such as norepinephrine, dopamine, serotonin, and acetylcholine.

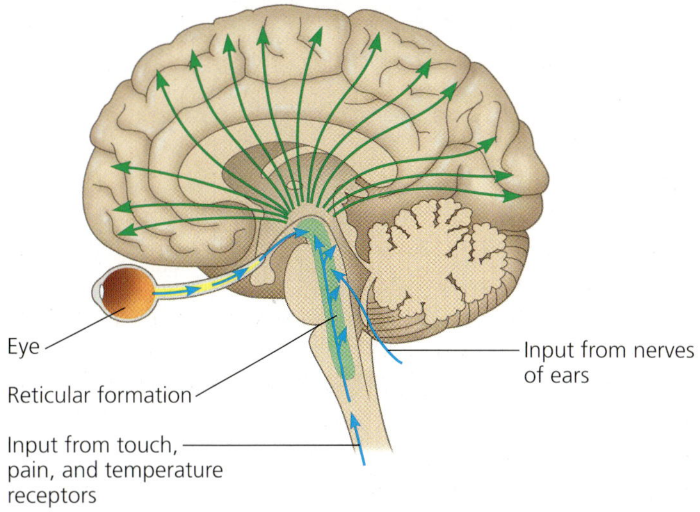

▲ **Figure 49.10 The reticular formation.** This system of neurons distributed throughout the core of the brainstem filters sensory input (blue arrows), blocking familiar and repetitive information that constantly enters the nervous system. It sends the filtered input to the cerebral cortex (green arrows).

Arousal and Sleep

As anyone who has drifted off to sleep listening to a lecture (or reading a book) knows, attentiveness and mental alertness can change rapidly. Such transitions are regulated by the brainstem and cerebrum, which control both arousal and sleep. Arousal is a state of awareness of the external world. Sleep is a state in which external stimuli are received but not consciously perceived.

The brainstem contains several centers for controlling arousal and sleep. One such regulator is the **reticular formation**, a diffuse network of neurons in the core of the brainstem **(Figure 49.10)**. Acting as a sensory filter, the reticular formation determines which incoming information reaches the cerebral cortex. The more information the cortex receives, the more alert and aware a person is, although the brain often ignores certain stimuli while actively processing other inputs. Sleep and wakefulness are also regulated by specific parts of the brainstem: The pons and medulla contain centers that cause sleep when stimulated, and the midbrain has a center that causes arousal.

All birds and mammals show characteristic sleep/wake cycles. Melatonin, a hormone produced by the pineal gland, appears to play an important role in these cycles. As you read in Chapter 45, peak melatonin secretion occurs at night. Melatonin has been promoted as a dietary supplement to treat sleep disturbances, such as those associated with jet lag, insomnia, seasonal affective disorder, and depression. Melatonin is synthesized from serotonin, which itself may be the neurotransmitter of the sleep-producing centers. Serotonin in turn is synthesized from the amino acid tryptophan. Although the protein in milk contains relatively high levels of tryptophan, it remains uncertain whether drinking milk at bedtime increases production of serotonin and melatonin, thus aiding sleep.

Although we know very little about the function of sleep, it is clear that sleep is essential for survival. Contrary to appearances, sleep is an active state, at least for the brain. By placing electrodes at multiple sites on the scalp, we can record patterns of electrical activity called brain waves in an electroencephalogram (EEG). These recordings reveal that brain wave frequencies change as the brain progresses through distinct stages of sleep. One hypothesis is that sleep and dreams are involved in consolidating learning and memory: Experiments show that regions of the brain activated during a learning task can become active again during sleep.

Some animals display evolutionary adaptations that allow for substantial activity during sleep. Bottlenose dolphins, for example, swim while sleeping, rising to the surface to breathe air on a regular basis. How do they manage this feat? A critical clue came from American physiologist John Lilly, who in 1964 observed that dolphins sleep with one eye open and one closed. As in humans and other mammals, the forebrain of dolphins is physically and functionally divided into two halves, the right and left hemispheres. Lilly suggested that a dolphin sleeping with one eye closed could mean that just one side of the brain was asleep. In 1977, Russian scientist Lev Mukhametov set out to test Lilly's hypothesis by collecting EEG recordings from each

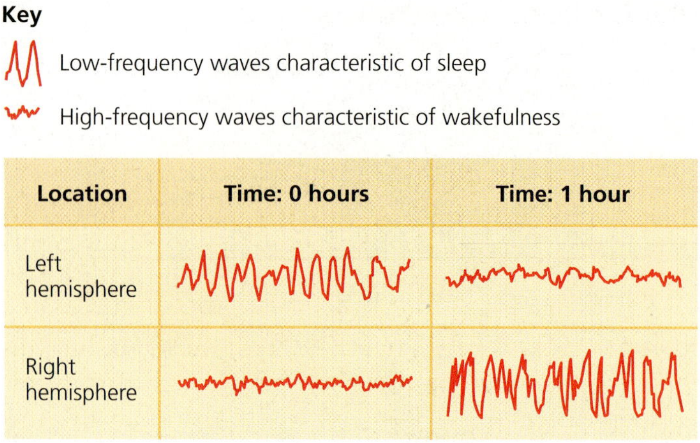

▲ **Figure 49.11 Dolphins can be asleep and awake at the same time.** EEG recordings were made separately for the two sides of a dolphin's brain. Low-frequency activity was recorded in one hemisphere while higher-frequency activity typical of being awake was recorded in the other hemisphere.

hemisphere of sleeping dolphins **(Figure 49.11)**. Mukhametov's findings demonstrate that dolphins do in fact sleep with one brain hemisphere at a time.

The Cerebellum

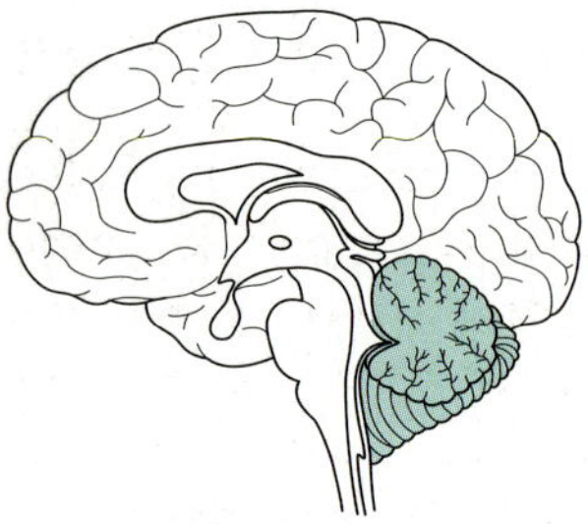

The **cerebellum**, which develops from part of the hindbrain (see Figure 49.9), coordinates movements and balance. The cerebellum receives sensory information about the position of the joints and the length of the muscles, as well as input from the auditory (hearing) and visual systems. It also monitors motor commands issued by the cerebrum. Information from the cerebrum passes first to the pons and from there to the cerebellum. The cerebellum integrates this information as it carries out coordination and error checking during motor and perceptual functions. Hand-eye coordination is an example of cerebellar control; if the cerebellum is damaged, the eyes can follow a moving object, but they will not stop at the same place as the object. Hand movement toward the object will also be erratic. The cerebellum also helps in learning and remembering motor skills.

The Diencephalon

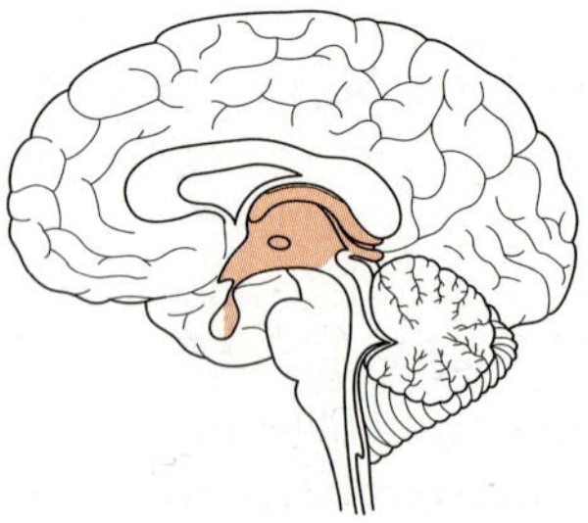

The embryonic diencephalon—the forebrain division that evolved earliest in vertebrate history—develops into three adult brain regions: the thalamus, hypothalamus, and epithalamus (see Figure 49.9). The thalamus and hypothalamus are major integrating centers that act as relay stations for information flow in the body. The *epithalamus* includes the pineal gland, the source of melatonin. It also contains one of several clusters of capillaries that generate cerebrospinal fluid from blood.

The **thalamus** is the main input center for sensory information going to the cerebrum. Incoming information from all the senses is sorted in the thalamus and sent to the appropriate cerebral centers for further processing. The thalamus also receives input from the cerebrum and other parts of the brain that regulate emotion and arousal. The thalamus is formed by two masses, each roughly the size and shape of a walnut.

Much smaller even than the thalamus, the **hypothalamus** is one of the most important brain regions for the control of homeostasis. As discussed in Chapters 40 and 45, the hypothalamus contains the body's thermostat, as well as centers for regulating hunger, thirst, and many other basic survival mechanisms. The hypothalamus is the source of posterior pituitary hormones and of releasing hormones that act on the anterior pituitary (see Figures 45.15 and 45.17). In addition, hypothalamic centers play a role in sexual and mating behaviors, the fight-or-flight response, and pleasure.

Biological Clock Regulation by the Hypothalamus

Specialized nerve cells in the hypothalamus regulate circadian rhythms, daily cycles of biological activity. Such cycles occur in organisms ranging from bacteria to fungi, plants, insects, birds, and humans (see Chapters 39 and 51). In mammals, the cycles controlled by the hypothalamus influence a number of physiological processes, including sleep, body temperature, hunger, and hormone release. As in other organisms, circadian rhythms in mammals rely on a **biological clock**, a molecular mechanism that directs periodic gene expression and cellular activity. Although biological clocks are typically synchronized to the cycles of light and dark in the environment, they can maintain a roughly 24-hour cycle even in the absence of environmental cues. For example, humans kept in a constant environment exhibit a cycle length of 24.2 hours, with very little variation among individuals.

In mammals, circadian rhythms are coordinated by a group of neurons in the hypothalamus called the **suprachiasmatic nucleus**, or **SCN**. (Certain clusters of neurons in the CNS are referred to as "nuclei.") In response to transmission of sensory information by the eyes, the SCN acts as a pacemaker, synchronizing the biological clock in cells throughout the body to the natural cycles of day length. By surgically removing the SCN from laboratory animals, scientists demonstrated that the SCN is required for circadian rhythms: Animals without an SCN lack rhythmicity in behaviors and in electrical activity of the brain. These experiments did not, however, reveal whether rhythms originate in the SCN or elsewhere. In 1990, Michael Menaker and colleagues at the University of Virginia answered this question with the aid of a mutation that changes the circadian rhythm of hamsters **(Figure 49.12)**. By transplanting brain tissue between normal and mutant hamsters, these scientists were able to show that the SCN determines the circadian rhythm of the whole animal.

▼ **Figure 49.12 Inquiry**

Which cells control the circadian rhythm in mammals?

EXPERIMENT The τ (tau) mutation alters the period of the circadian rhythm in hamsters. Whereas wild-type hamsters have a cycle lasting 24 hours in the absence of external cues, hamsters homozygous for the τ mutation have a circadian cycle lasting only about 20 hours. To determine if the SCN controls circadian rhythm, Michael Menaker and colleagues surgically removed the SCN from wild-type and τ hamsters. Several weeks later, each of these hamsters received an SCN transplanted from a hamster of the opposite genotype.

RESULTS In 80% of the hamsters in which the SCN had been destroyed, an SCN transplant restored rhythmic activity. For hamsters in which rhythm was restored, the net effect of the two procedures (SCN destruction and replacement) on circadian rhythm is graphed below. Each of the eight lines represents the change in the observed circadian cycle for an individual hamster.

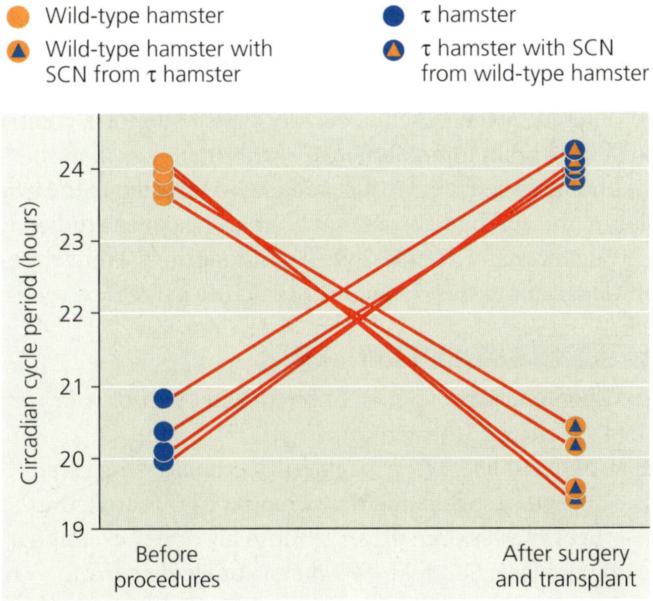

CONCLUSION Cells associated with the suprachiasmatic nucleus determine the period of circadian rhythm.

SOURCE M. R. Ralph, M. Menaker, et al., Transplanted suprachiasmatic nucleus determines circadian period, *Science* 247: 975–978 (1990).

WHAT IF? Suppose you identified a hamster mutant that lacked rhythmic activity. How might you use this mutant in transplant experiments with wild-type or τ mutant hamsters to demonstrate that the mutation affected the pacemaker function of the SCN?

The Cerebrum

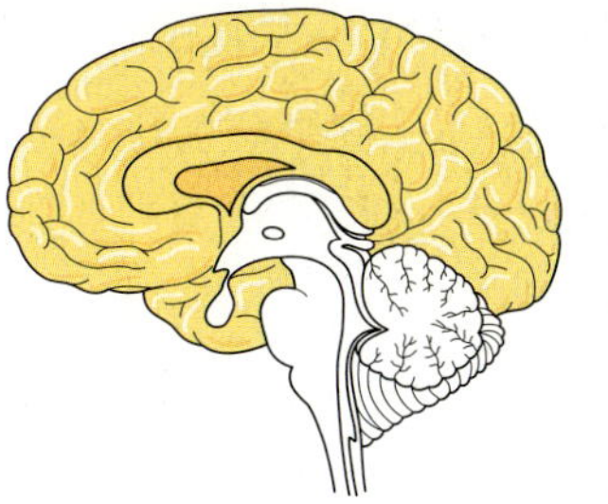

In mammals, information processing is largely centered in the cerebrum. The cerebrum develops from the embryonic telencephalon, an outgrowth of the forebrain that arose early in vertebrate evolution as a region supporting olfactory reception as well as auditory and visual processing. The cerebrum is divided into right and left **cerebral hemispheres**. Each hemisphere consists of an outer covering of gray matter, the cerebral cortex; internal white matter; and groups of neurons collectively called *basal nuclei* that are located deep within the white matter **(Figure 49.13)**. The basal nuclei are important centers for planning and learning movement sequences. Damage in this brain region during fetal development can result in cerebral palsy, a defect disrupting how motor commands are issued to the muscles.

The cerebral cortex is particularly extensive in mammals, where it is vital for perception, voluntary movement, and learning. In humans, it accounts for about 80% of total brain mass and is highly convoluted (see Figure 49.13). The convolutions allow the cerebral cortex to have a large surface area and still fit inside the skull: Less than 5 mm thick, it has a surface area of approximately 1,000 cm^2.

Like the rest of the cerebrum, the cerebral cortex is divided into right and left sides, each of which is responsible for the opposite half of the body. The left side of the cortex receives information from, and controls the movement of, the right side of the body, and vice versa. A thick band of axons known as the **corpus callosum** enables the right and left cerebral cortices to communicate (see Figure 49.13).

If damage occurs to the cerebrum early in development, the normal functions of the damaged area are frequently redirected elsewhere. A dramatic example of this phenomenon results from a treatment for the most extreme cases of epilepsy, a

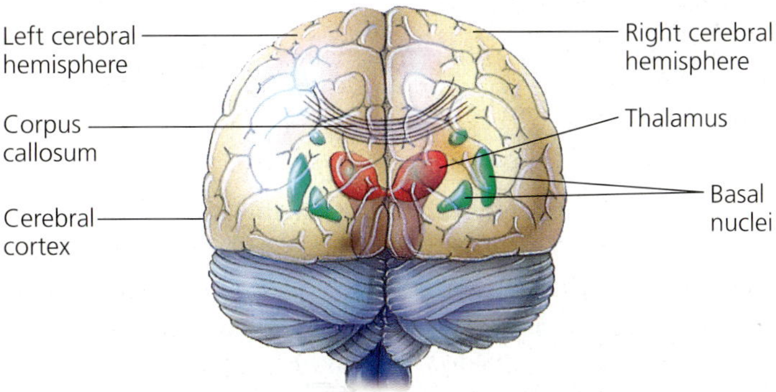

▲ **Figure 49.13 The human brain viewed from the rear.** The corpus callosum and basal nuclei are not visible from the surface because they are completely covered by the left and right cerebral hemispheres. The lighter blue structure is the cerebellum.

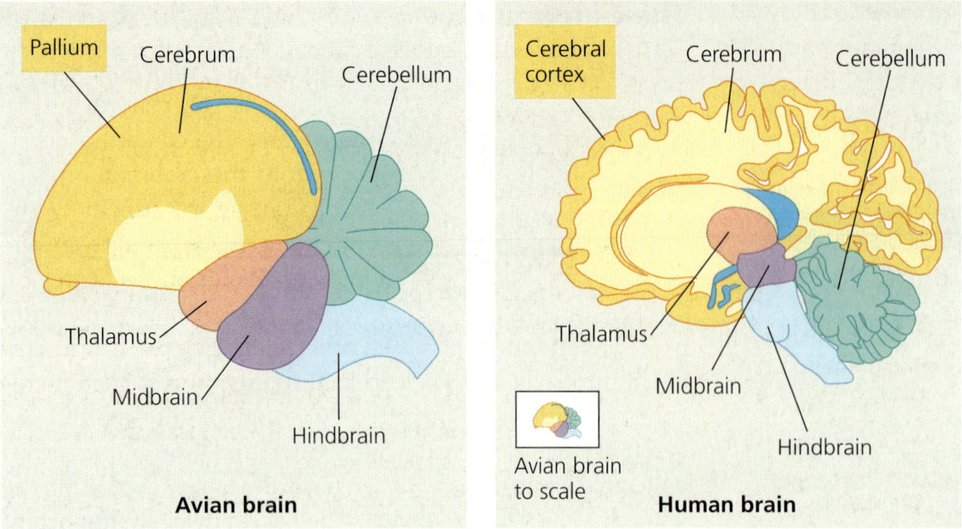

◀ **Figure 49.14 Comparison of regions for higher cognition in avian and human brains.** Although structurally different, the pallium of the avian brain (left cross section) and the cerebral cortex of the human brain (right cross section) have similar roles in higher cognitive activities and make many similar connections with other brain structures.

condition causing episodes of electrical disturbance, or seizures, in the brain. In those rare infants who are severely affected and do not respond to medication, an entire cerebral hemisphere is sometimes surgically removed. Amazingly, recovery is nearly complete. The remaining hemisphere eventually assumes most of the functions normally provided by the entire cerebrum, although one side of the body is much weaker than the other. Even in adults, damage to a portion of the cerebral cortex can trigger the development or use of new brain circuits, leading in some cases to recovery of function.

Evolution of Cognition in Vertebrates

In humans, the outermost part of the cerebral cortex forms the *neocortex*, six parallel layers of neurons arranged tangential to the brain surface. It was long thought that a large, highly convoluted neocortex was required for advanced *cognition*, the perception and reasoning that constitute knowledge. Both primates and cetaceans (whales, dolphins, and porpoises) possess an extensively convoluted neocortex. Because birds lack such a structure, they were thought to have substantially lower intellectual capacity. In recent years, however, this viewpoint has been shown to be wrong: There are now abundant examples of sophisticated information processing by birds. Western scrub jays (*Aphelocoma californica*) can remember the relative period of time that has passed since they stored and hid specific food items. New Caledonian crows (*Corvus moneduloides*) are highly skilled at making and using tools, an ability otherwise well documented only for humans and some other apes. African gray parrots (*Psittacus erithacus*) understand relational concepts that are numerical or abstract, distinguishing between "same" and "different" and grasping the concept of "none."

The sophisticated cognitive ability of birds is based on an evolutionary variation on the architecture of the *pallium*, the top or outer portion of the brain. Whereas the human pallium—the cerebral cortex—contains flat sheets of cells in six layers, the avian pallium contains neurons clustered into nuclei. It is likely that the common ancestor of birds and mammals had a pallium in which neurons were organized into nuclei, as is still found in birds. Early in mammalian evolution, this nuclear organization was transformed into a layered one. Connectivity was maintained during this transformation such that, for example, the pallium of both mammals and birds receives sensory input—sights, sounds, and touch—from the thalamus. The result was two different arrangements, each of which supports complex and flexible brain function **(Figure 49.14)**.

Although scientists are just starting to investigate the avian pallium, the cerebral cortex of mammals has been studied extensively for many decades. We'll consider the current state of knowledge about this remarkable structure in the next section.

CONCEPT CHECK 49.2

1. When you wave your right hand, what part of your brain initiates the action?
2. When a police officer stops a driver for driving erratically and suspects that the person is intoxicated, the officer may ask the driver to close his or her eyes and touch his or her nose. What can you deduce from this test about alcohol's effect on a particular part of the brain?
3. **WHAT IF?** Suppose you examine individuals with damage to the CNS that has resulted in either coma (a prolonged state of unconsciousness) or general paralysis (a loss of muscle function throughout the body). Relative to the position of the reticular formation, where would you predict the site of injury to lie in each group of patients? Explain.

For suggested answers, see Appendix A.

CONCEPT **49.3**

The cerebral cortex controls voluntary movement and cognitive functions

Each side of the cerebral cortex is customarily described as having four lobes, called the frontal, temporal, occipital, and parietal lobes (each lobe is named for a bone of the skull). Researchers have identified a number of functional areas within each lobe **(Figure 49.15)**. These include *primary sensory areas*, each of which receives and processes a specific type of sensory information, and *association areas*, which integrate the information from various parts of the brain.

During mammalian evolution, most of the increase in size of the cerebral cortex was due to an expansion of the association areas. Whereas a rat's cerebral cortex contains mainly primary sensory areas, the human cerebral cortex consists largely of association areas responsible for more complex behavior and learning.

Information Processing in the Cerebral Cortex

As you will learn further in Chapter 50, the cerebral cortex receives sensory input from two types of sources. Some input is received from dedicated sensory organs, such as the eyes and nose. Other sensory input relies on receptors in the hands, scalp, and elsewhere. These *somatosensory* receptors (from the Greek *soma*, body) provide information about touch, pain, pressure, temperature, and the position of muscles and limbs.

Most sensory information coming into the cortex is directed via the thalamus to primary sensory areas within the brain lobes. The thalamus directs different types of input to distinct locations: visual information to the occipital lobe; auditory input to the temporal lobe; and somatosensory information to the parietal lobe (see Figure 49.15). Information about taste also goes to the parietal lobe, but to a region separate from that for somatosensory input. Olfactory information is sent first to regions of the cortex that are similar in mammals and reptiles and then via the thalamus to an interior part of the frontal lobe.

Information received at the primary sensory areas is passed along to nearby association areas, which process particular features in the sensory input. In the occipital lobe, for example, some groups of neurons in the primary visual area are specifically sensitive to rays of light oriented in a particular direction. In the visual association area, information related to such features is combined in a region dedicated to recognizing complex images, such as faces.

Integrated sensory information passes to the frontal association area, which helps plan actions and movement. The cerebral cortex may then generate motor commands that cause particular behaviors—moving a limb or saying hello, for example. These commands consist of action potentials produced by neurons in the motor cortex, which lies at the rear of the frontal lobe (see Figure 49.15). The action potentials travel along axons to the brainstem and spinal cord, where they excite motor neurons, which in turn excite skeletal muscle cells.

In both the somatosensory cortex and the motor cortex, neurons are distributed in an orderly fashion according to the part of the body that generates the sensory input or receives the

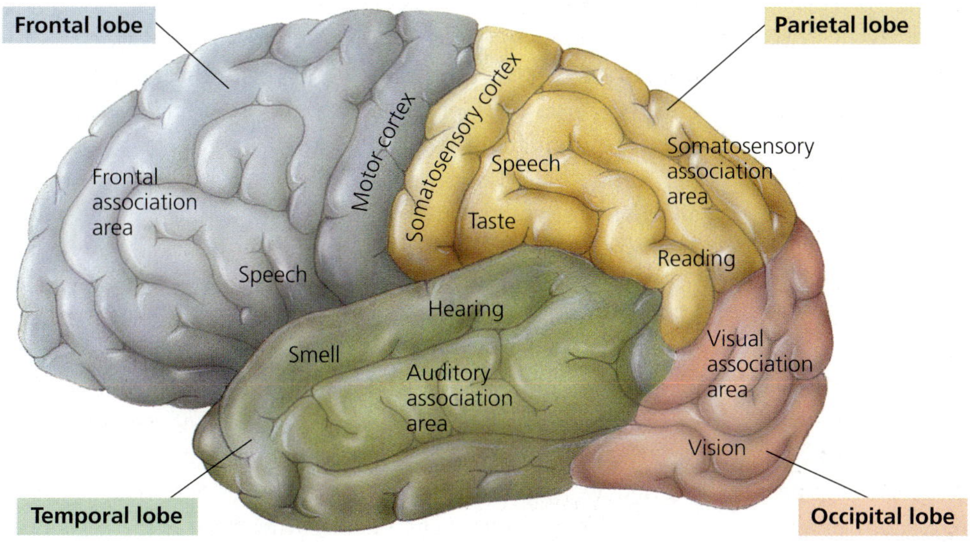

◀ **Figure 49.15 The human cerebral cortex.** Each side of the cerebral cortex is divided into four lobes, and each lobe has specialized functions. Some of the association areas on the left side of the brain (shown here) have different functions from those on the right side (not shown).

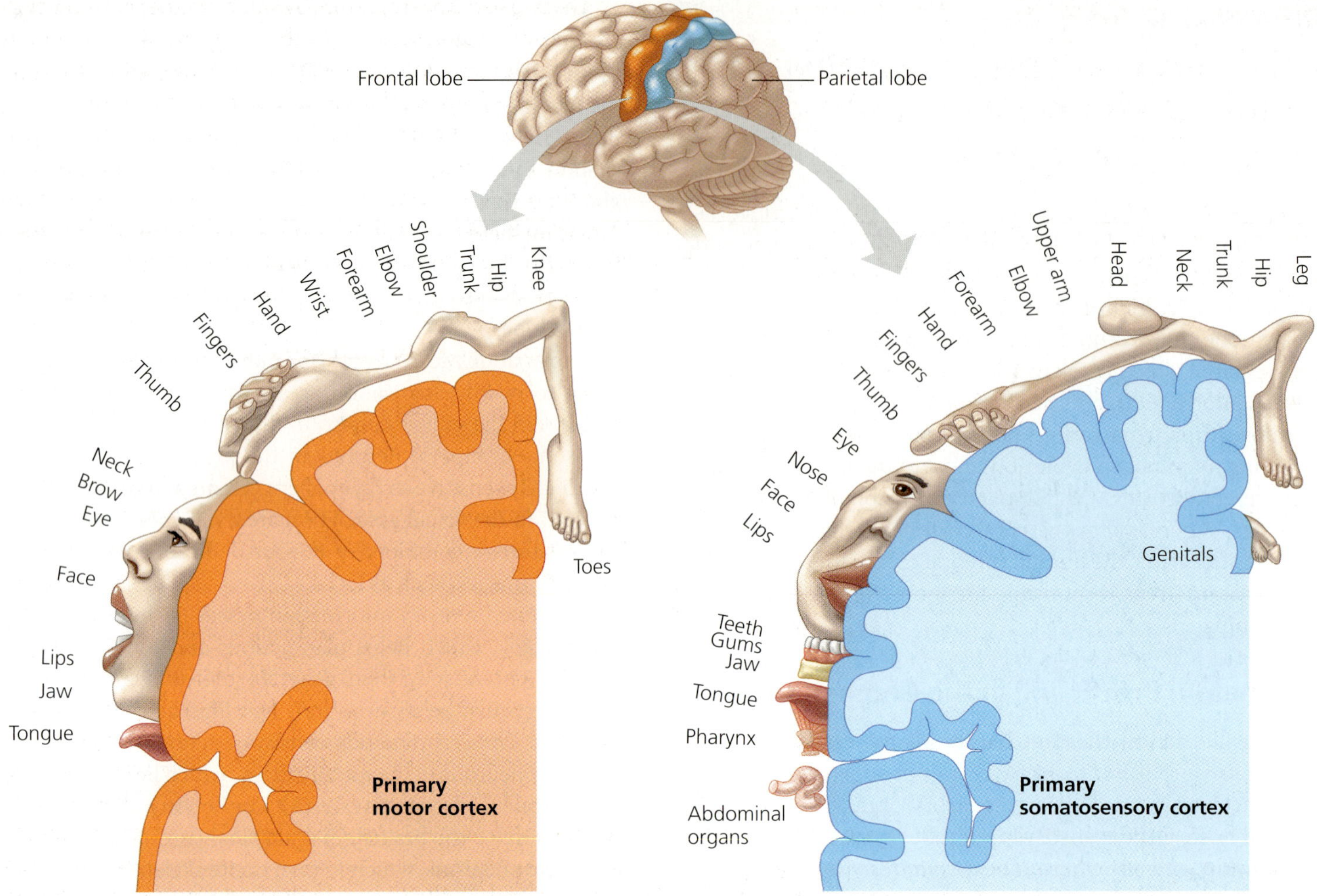

▲ **Figure 49.16 Body part representation in the primary motor and primary somatosensory cortices.** In these cross-sectional maps of the cortices, the cortical surface area devoted to each body part is represented by the relative size of that part in the cartoons.

motor commands **(Figure 49.16)**. For example, neurons that process sensory information from the legs and feet are located in the region of the somatosensory cortex that lies closest to the midline. Neurons that control muscles in the legs and feet are located in the corresponding region of the motor cortex. Notice in Figure 49.16 that the cortical surface area devoted to each body part is not proportional to the size of the part. Instead, surface area correlates with the extent of neuronal control needed for muscles in a particular body part (for the motor cortex) or with the number of sensory neurons that extend axons to that part (for the somatosensory cortex). Thus, the surface area of the motor cortex devoted to the face is much larger than that devoted to the trunk, reflecting in large part how extensively facial muscles are involved in communication.

Language and Speech

The mapping of higher cognitive functions to specific brain areas began in the 1800s when physicians learned that damage to particular regions of the cortex by injuries, strokes, or tumors can produce distinctive changes in a person's behavior. The French physician Pierre Broca conducted postmortem (after death) examinations of patients who had been able to understand language but unable to speak. He discovered that many of these patients had defects in a small region of the left frontal lobe. That region, now known as *Broca's area*, is located in front of the part of the primary motor cortex that controls muscles in the face. The German physician Karl Wernicke also conducted examinations and found that damage to a posterior portion of the left temporal lobe, now called *Wernicke's area*, abolished the ability to comprehend speech but not the ability to speak. Over a century later, studies of brain activity using fMRI and positron-emission tomography (PET; see Chapter 2) have confirmed that Broca's area is active during speech generation (**Figure 49.17**, lower left image) and Wernicke's area is active when speech is heard (Figure 49.17, upper left image).

Broca's area and Wernicke's area are part of a much larger network of brain regions involved in language. Reading a printed word without speaking activates the visual cortex (Figure 49.17, upper right image), whereas reading a printed word out loud activates both the visual cortex and Broca's area.

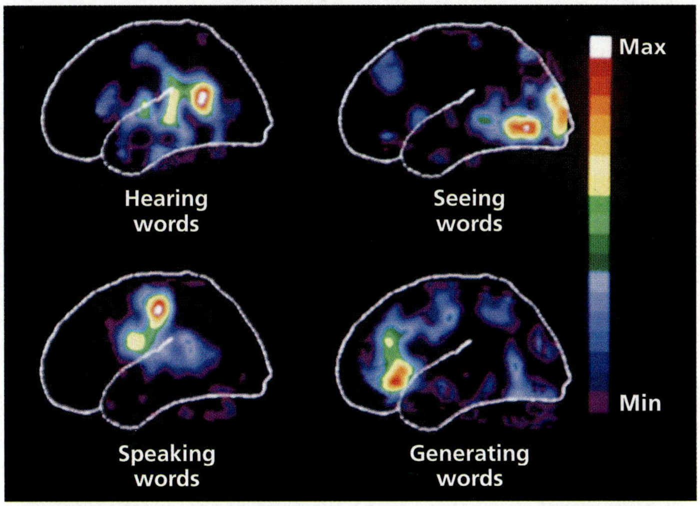

▲ **Figure 49.17 Mapping language areas in the cerebral cortex.** These PET images show regions with different activity levels in one person's brain during four activities, all related to speech.

Frontal and temporal areas become active when meaning must be attached to words, such as when a person generates verbs to go with nouns or groups related words or concepts (Figure 49.17, lower right image).

Lateralization of Cortical Function

Although each cerebral hemisphere in humans has sensory and motor connections to the opposite side of the body, the two hemispheres do not have identical functions. For example, the left side of the cerebrum has a dominant role with regard to language, as reflected in the location of both Broca's area and Wernicke's area in the left hemisphere. There are also subtler distinctions in the functions of the two hemispheres. For example, the left hemisphere is more adept at math and logical operations. In contrast, the right hemisphere appears to be dominant in the recognition of faces and patterns, spatial relations, and nonverbal thinking. The establishment of these differences in hemisphere function in humans is called **lateralization**.

At least some lateralization relates to handedness, the preference for using one hand for certain motor activities. Across human populations, roughly 90% of individuals are more skilled with their right hand than with their left hand. Studies using fMRI have revealed how language processing differs in relation to handedness. When subjects thought of words without speaking out loud, brain activity was localized to the left hemisphere in 96% of right-handed subjects but in only 76% of left-handed subjects.

The two hemispheres normally work together harmoniously, trading information back and forth through the fibers of the corpus callosum. The importance of this exchange is revealed in patients whose corpus callosum has been surgically severed. As with removal of a cerebral hemisphere, this procedure is a treatment of last resort for the most extreme forms of epilepsy. Individuals with a severed corpus callosum exhibit a "split-brain" effect. When they see a familiar word in their left field of vision, they cannot read the word: The sensory information that travels from the left field of vision to the right hemisphere cannot reach the language centers in the left hemisphere. Each hemisphere in such patients functions independently of the other.

Emotions

The generation and experience of emotions involve many regions of the brain. One such region, shown in **Figure 49.18**, contains the *limbic system* (from the Latin *limbus*, border), a group of structures surrounding the brainstem in mammals. The limbic system, which includes the amygdala, the hippocampus, and parts of the thalamus, is not dedicated to a single function. Instead, structures within the limbic system have diverse functions, including emotion, motivation, olfaction, behavior, and memory. Furthermore, parts of the brain outside the limbic system also participate in generating and experiencing emotion. For example, emotions that manifest themselves in behaviors such as laughing and crying involve an interaction of parts of the limbic system with sensory areas of the cerebrum. Structures in the forebrain also attach emotional "feelings" to basic, survival-related functions controlled by the brainstem, including aggression, feeding, and sexuality.

Emotional experiences are often stored as memories that can be recalled by similar circumstances. In the case of fear, emotional memory is stored separately from the memory system that supports explicit recall of events. The focus of emotional

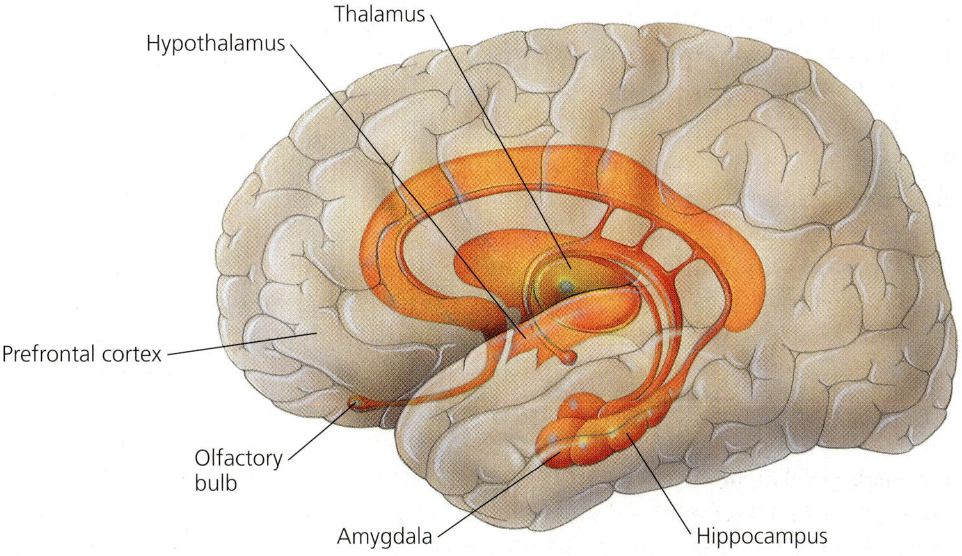

▲ **Figure 49.18 The limbic system.**

memory is the **amygdala**, which is located in the temporal lobe (see Figure 49.18). To study the function of the human amygdala, researchers sometimes present adult subjects with an image, followed by an unpleasant experience, such as a mild electrical shock. After several trials, study participants experience autonomic arousal—as measured by increased heart rate or sweating—if they see the image again. People with brain damage confined to the amygdala can recall the image, because their explicit memory is intact, but do not exhibit autonomic arousal.

The prefrontal cortex, a part of the frontal lobes critical for emotional experience, is also important in temperament and decision making. This combination of functions was discovered in 1848 from the remarkable medical case of Phineas Gage. Gage was working on a railroad construction site when an explosion drove a meter-long iron rod through his head. The rod, which was more than 3 cm in diameter at one end, entered his skull just below his left eye and exited through the top of his head, damaging large portions of his frontal lobe. Astonishingly, Gage recovered, but his personality changed dramatically. He became emotionally detached, impatient, and erratic in his behavior.

Tumors that develop in the frontal lobe sometimes cause the same combination of symptoms that Gage experienced. Intellect and memory seem intact, but decision making is flawed and emotional responses are diminished. In the 20th century, the same problems were also observed as a consequence of frontal lobotomy, a surgical procedure that severs the connection between the prefrontal cortex and the limbic system. Once a common treatment for severe behavioral disorders, frontal lobotomy later was abandoned as a medical practice. Behavioral disorders are now typically treated with medications, as discussed later in this chapter.

Consciousness

The study of human consciousness was long considered outside the province of science, more appropriate as a subject for philosophy or religion. One reason for this view is that consciousness is both broad—encompassing our awareness of ourselves and our experiences—and subjective. Over the past few decades, however, neuroscientists have begun studying consciousness using brain-imaging techniques such as fMRI and PET scans (see Figures 49.1 and 49.17). It is now possible to compare activity in the human brain during different states of consciousness—for example, before and after a person is aware of seeing an object. These imaging techniques can also be used to compare the conscious and unconscious processing of sensory information. Such studies do not pinpoint a "consciousness center" in the brain; rather, they offer an increasingly detailed picture of how neuronal activity correlates with conscious experiences.

Support is growing for the hypothesis that consciousness is an emergent property (see Chapter 1) of the brain, and that it recruits activities in many areas of the cerebral cortex. Several models postulate the existence of a sort of "scanning mechanism" that repetitively sweeps across the brain, integrating widespread activity into a unified, conscious moment. Still, a well-supported theory of consciousness may have to wait until brain-imaging technology becomes more sophisticated.

CONCEPT CHECK 49.3

1. How is the study of individuals with damage to a particular part of the brain used to provide insight into the normal function of that region?
2. Two brain areas important in the generation or perception of speech are Broca's area and Wernicke's area. How is the function of each area related to the activity of the surrounding portion of the cerebral cortex?
3. **WHAT IF?** If a woman with a severed corpus callosum viewed a photograph of a familiar face, first in the left field of vision and then in the right field, why would it be difficult for her to put a name to the face in either field?

For suggested answers, see Appendix A.

CONCEPT **49.4**

Changes in synaptic connections underlie memory and learning

During embryonic development, regulated gene expression and signal transduction establish the overall structure of the nervous system (see Chapter 47). Two processes then dominate the remaining development of the nervous system. The first is a competition among neurons for survival. Neurons compete for growth-supporting factors, which are produced in limited quantities by tissues that direct neuron growth. Cells that don't reach the proper locations fail to receive such factors and undergo programmed cell death. The competition is so severe that half of the neurons formed in the embryo are eliminated. The net effect is the preferential survival of neurons that are located properly within the nervous system.

Synapse elimination is the second major process that shapes nervous system development in the embryo. A developing neuron forms numerous synapses, more than are required for its proper function. The activity of that neuron then stabilizes some synapses and destabilizes others. By the end of embryogenesis, neurons on average have lost more than half of their initial synapses, leaving behind the connections that survive into adulthood.

Together, neuron and synapse elimination set up the network of cells and connections within the nervous system required throughout life.

Neural Plasticity

Although the basic architecture of the CNS is established during embryonic development, it can change after birth. This capacity for the nervous system to be remodeled, especially in response to its own activity, is called **neural plasticity**.

Much of the reshaping of the nervous system occurs at synapses. When activity at a synapse correlates with that of other synapses, changes may occur that reinforce that synaptic connection. Conversely, when the activity of a synapse fails to correlate with that of other synapses, the synaptic connection sometimes becomes weaker. **Figure 49.19a** illustrates how these processes can result in either the addition or loss of a synapse. If you think of signals in the nervous system as traffic on a highway, such changes are comparable to adding or removing an entrance ramp. The net effect is to increase signaling between particular pairs of neurons and decrease signaling at other sites. As shown in **Figure 49.19b**, changes can also strengthen or weaken signaling at a synapse. In our traffic analogy, this would be equivalent to widening or narrowing an entrance ramp.

Remodeling and refining of the nervous system occur in many contexts. For example, these processes are necessary steps in how we develop the ability to sense our surroundings, a topic covered in Chapter 50. They are also critical to the nervous system's limited ability to recover from injury or disease. Remodeling and refinement also underlie memory and learning, our next topic.

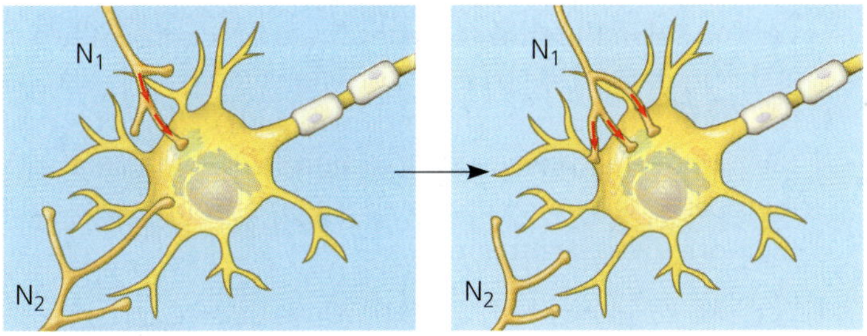

(a) Synapses are strengthened or weakened in response to activity. High-level activity at the synapse of the postsynaptic neuron with presynaptic neuron N_1 leads to recruitment of additional axon terminals from that neuron. Lack of activity at the synapse with presynaptic neuron N_2 leads to loss of functional connections with that neuron.

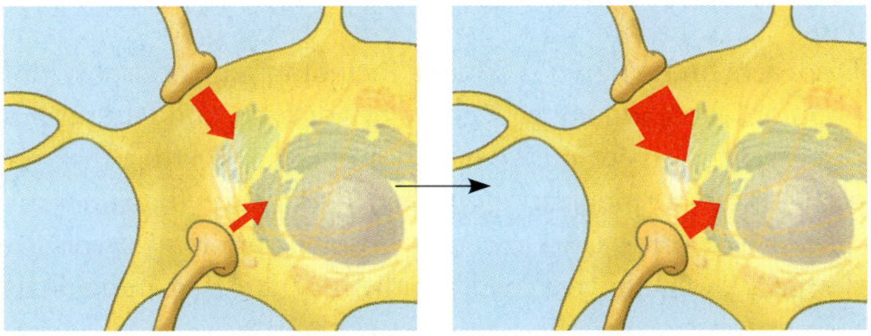

(b) If two synapses on the same postsynaptic cell are often active at the same time, the strength of the postsynaptic response may increase at both synapses.

▲ **Figure 49.19 Neural plasticity.** Synaptic connections can change over time, depending on the activity level at the synapse.

Memory and Learning

Though we may not be aware of it, we are constantly checking what is happening against what just happened a few moments ago. We hold information for a time in **short-term memory** locations and then release it if it becomes irrelevant. If we wish to retain knowledge of a name, phone number, or other fact, the mechanisms of **long-term memory** are activated. If we later need to recall the name or number, we fetch it from long-term memory and return it to short-term memory.

Scientists have long wondered where in the brain short-term and long-term memories are located. We now know that both types of memory involve the storage of information in the cerebral cortex. In short-term memory, this information is accessed via temporary links or associations formed in the hippocampus. When memories are made long-term, the links in the hippocampus are replaced by more permanent connections within the cerebral cortex itself. The hippocampus is thus essential for acquiring new long-term memories, but not for maintaining them. For this reason, people who suffer damage to the hippocampus are to some extent trapped in the past: They cannot form any new lasting memories but can freely recall events from before their injury.

What evolutionary advantage might be offered by organizing short-term and long-term memories differently? Current thinking is that the delay in forming connections in the cerebral cortex allows long-term memories to be integrated gradually into the existing store of knowledge and experience, providing a basis for more meaningful associations. Consistent with this idea, the transfer of information from short-term to long-term memory is enhanced by the association of new data with data previously learned and stored in long-term memory. For example, it's easier to learn a new card game if you already have "card sense" from playing other card games.

Motor skills, such as walking, tying your shoes, or writing, are usually learned by repetition. You can perform these skills without consciously recalling the individual steps required to do these tasks correctly. Learning skills and procedures, such as those required to ride a bicycle, appears to involve cellular mechanisms very similar to those responsible for brain growth and development. In such cases, neurons actually make new connections. In contrast, memorizing phone numbers, facts, and places—which can be very rapid and may require only one exposure to the relevant item—may rely mainly on changes in the strength of existing neuronal connections. Next we will consider one way that such changes in strength can take place.

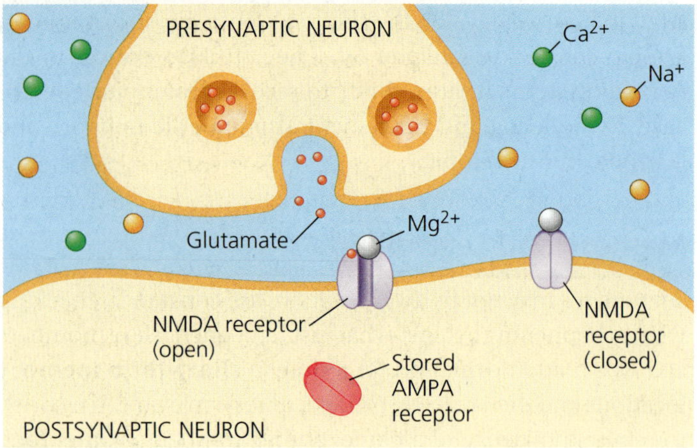

(a) Synapse prior to long-term potentiation (LTP). The NMDA glutamate receptors open in response to glutamate, but are blocked by Mg^{2+}.

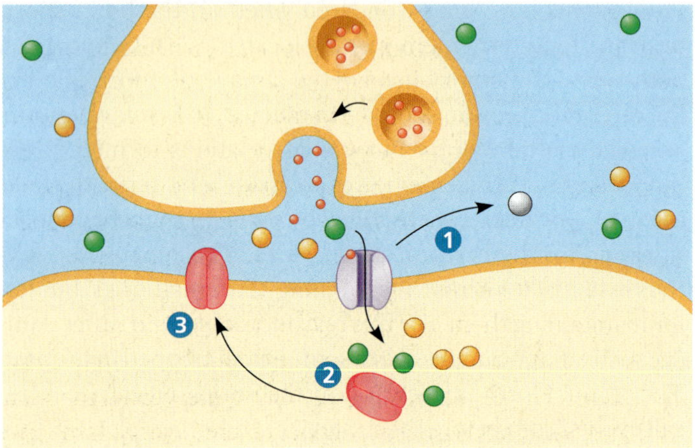

(b) Establishing LTP. Activity at nearby synapses depolarizes the postsynaptic membrane, causing Mg^{2+} release from NMDA receptors. The unblocked receptors respond to glutamate by allowing an influx of Na^+ and Ca^{2+}. The Ca^{2+} influx triggers insertion of stored AMPA glutamate receptors into the postsynaptic membrane.

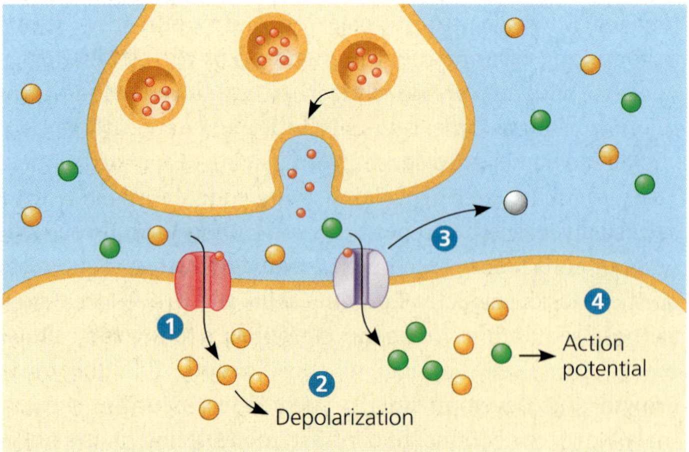

(c) Synapse exhibiting LTP. Glutamate release activates AMPA receptors that trigger depolarization, unblocking NMDA receptors. Together, the AMPA and NMDA receptors trigger postsynaptic potentials strong enough to initiate action potentials without input from other synapses. Additional mechanisms (not shown) contribute to LTP, including receptor modification by protein kinases.

▲ **Figure 49.20 Long-term potentiation in the brain.**

Long-Term Potentiation

Researchers have identified several processes that can alter a synaptic connection, making the flow of communication either more efficient or less efficient. We will focus here on **long-term potentiation (LTP)**, a lasting increase in the strength of synaptic transmission. LTP, which was first characterized in tissue slices from the hippocampus, involves a presynaptic neuron that releases the excitatory neurotransmitter glutamate. For LTP to occur, there must be a brief high-frequency series of action potentials in this presynaptic neuron. In addition, these action potentials must arrive at the synaptic terminal at the same time that the postsynaptic cell receives a depolarizing stimulus.

LTP involves two types of glutamate receptors, each named for a molecule—NMDA or AMPA—that artificially activates that particular receptor. As shown in **Figure 49.20**, the set of receptors present on the postsynaptic membranes changes in response to an active synapse and a depolarizing stimulus. The result is LTP—a stable increase in the size of the postsynaptic potentials at the synapse. Because LTP can last for days or weeks in dissected tissue, it is thought to represent one of the fundamental processes by which memories are stored and learning takes place.

CONCEPT CHECK 49.4

1. Outline two mechanisms by which the flow of information between two neurons in adults is increased.
2. Individuals with localized brain damage have been very useful in the study of many brain functions. Why is this unlikely to be true for consciousness?
3. **WHAT IF?** Suppose that a person with damage to the hippocampus is unable to acquire new long-term memories. Why might the acquisition of short-term memories also be impaired?

For suggested answers, see Appendix A.

CONCEPT 49.5

Nervous system disorders can be explained in molecular terms

Disorders of the nervous system, including schizophrenia, depression, drug addiction, Alzheimer's disease, and Parkinson's disease, are a major public health problem. Together, they result in more hospitalizations in the United States than do heart disease or cancer. Until recently, hospitalization was typically the only available treatment, and many affected individuals were institutionalized for the rest of their lives. Today, many disorders that alter mood or behavior can be treated with medications, reducing average hospital stays for these disorders to only a few weeks. At the same time, societal attitudes are changing as awareness grows that nervous system disorders often result from chemical or anatomical changes in the brain.

Many challenges remain, however, especially for Alzheimer's and other diseases that lead to nervous system degeneration.

Major research efforts are under way to identify genes that cause or contribute to disorders of the nervous system. Identifying such genes offers hope for identifying causes, predicting outcomes, and developing effective treatments. For most nervous system disorders, however, genetic contributions only partially account for which individuals are affected. The other significant contribution to disease comes from environmental factors. Unfortunately, environmental contributions are typically very difficult to identify.

To distinguish between genetic and environmental variables, scientists often carry out family studies. In such studies, researchers track how family members are related genetically, which individuals are affected, and which family members grew up in the same household. These studies are especially informative when one of the affected individuals has a genetically identical twin or an adopted sibling who is genetically unrelated. The results of family studies indicate that certain nervous system disorders, such as schizophrenia, have a very strong genetic component **(Figure 49.21)**.

Schizophrenia

About 1% of the world's population suffer from **schizophrenia**, a severe mental disturbance characterized by psychotic episodes

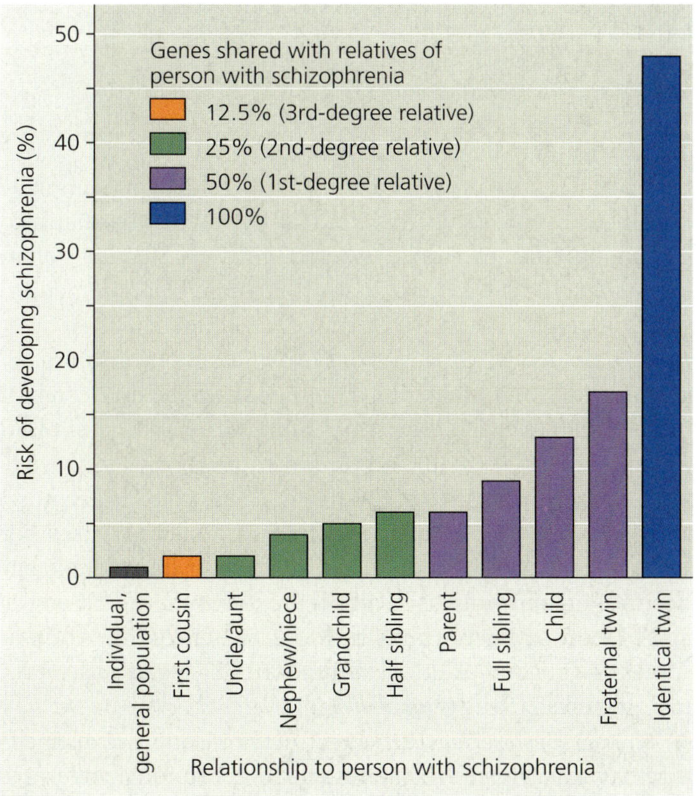

▲ **Figure 49.21 Genetic contribution to schizophrenia.** First cousins, uncles, and aunts of a person with schizophrenia have twice the risk of unrelated members of the population of developing the disease. The risks for closer relatives are many times greater.

in which patients have a distorted perception of reality. People with schizophrenia typically suffer from hallucinations (such as "voices" that only they can hear) and delusions (for example, the idea that others are plotting to harm them). Despite the commonly held notion, schizophrenia does not necessarily result in multiple personalities. Rather, the name schizophrenia (from the Greek *schizo*, split, and *phren*, mind) refers to the fragmentation of what are normally integrated brain functions.

Two lines of evidence suggest that schizophrenia affects neuronal pathways that use dopamine as a neurotransmitter. First, the drug amphetamine ("speed"), which stimulates dopamine release, can produce the same set of symptoms as schizophrenia. Second, many of the drugs that alleviate the symptoms of schizophrenia block dopamine receptors. Schizophrenia may also alter glutamate signaling, since the street drug "angel dust," or PCP, blocks glutamate receptors and induces strong schizophrenia-like symptoms.

Fortunately, medications frequently can alleviate the major symptoms of schizophrenia. Although the first treatments developed often had substantial negative side effects, newer medications are equally effective and much safer to use. Ongoing research aimed at identifying the genetic mutations responsible for schizophrenia may yield new insights about the causes of the disease and lead to even more effective therapies.

Depression

Depression is a disorder characterized by depressed mood, as well as abnormalities in sleep, appetite, and energy level. Two broad forms of depressive illness are known: major depressive disorder and bipolar disorder. Individuals affected by **major depressive disorder** undergo periods—often lasting many months—during which once enjoyable activities provide no pleasure and provoke no interest. One of the most common nervous system disorders, major depression affects about one in every seven adults at some point, and twice as many women as men. **Bipolar disorder**, or manic-depressive disorder, involves swings of mood from high to low and affects about 1% of the world's population. Like schizophrenia, bipolar disorder and major depression have genetic and environmental components.

In bipolar disorder, the manic phase is characterized by high self-esteem, increased energy, a flow of ideas, overtalkativeness, and increased risk taking. In its milder forms, this phase is sometimes associated with great creativity, and some well-known artists, musicians, and literary figures (including Vincent Van Gogh, Robert Schumann, Virginia Woolf, and Ernest Hemingway, to name a few) have had very productive periods during manic phases. The depressive phase comes with lowered ability to feel pleasure, loss of motivation, sleep disturbances, and feelings of worthlessness. These symptoms can be so severe that affected individuals attempt suicide. Nevertheless, some patients prefer to endure the depressive phase rather than take medication and risk losing the enhanced creative output of their manic phase.

Major depressive and bipolar disorders are among the nervous system disorders for which available therapies are most effective. Many drugs used to treat depressive illness, including fluoxetine (Prozac), increase the activity of biogenic amines in the brain. Depressive disorders are also sometimes treated with anticonvulsant drugs or lithium.

Drug Addiction and the Brain Reward System

Drug addiction is a disorder characterized by compulsive consumption of a drug and loss of control in limiting intake. Any of a number of drugs that vary considerably in their effects on the CNS can be addictive. For example, cocaine and amphetamine act as stimulants, whereas heroin is a pain-relieving sedative. However, all of these drugs, as well as alcohol and nicotine, are addictive for the same reason: Each increases activity of the brain's reward system, neural circuitry that normally functions in pleasure, motivation, and learning. In the absence of drug addiction, the reward system provides motivation for activities that enhance survival and reproduction, such as eating in response to hunger, drinking when thirsty, and engaging in sexual activity when aroused. In addicted individuals, "wanting" is instead directed toward further drug consumption.

Scientists have made enormous progress in learning how the brain's reward system works and how particular drugs affect its function. Laboratory animals have proved especially useful. Rats, for example, will provide themselves with cocaine, heroin, or amphetamine when given a dispensing system linked to a lever in their cage. Furthermore, they exhibit addictive behavior in such circumstances, continuing to self-administer the drug rather than seek food, even to the point of starvation. These and other studies have led to the identification of both the organization of the reward system and its key neurotransmitter, dopamine.

Inputs to the reward system are received by neurons in a region near the base of the brain called the *ventral tegmental area (VTA)*. When activated, these neurons direct action potentials along axons that synapse with neurons in specific regions of the cerebrum. There, the axon terminals release dopamine.

Addictive drugs affect the reward system in several ways. First, each drug has an immediate effect that enhances the activity of the dopamine pathway **(Figure 49.22)**. As addiction develops, there are also long-lasting changes in the reward circuitry. The result is a craving for the drug that is present independent of any pleasure associated with consumption. As scientists continue to expand their knowledge about both the reward system and addiction, there is hope that the insights will lead to more effective prevention measures and treatments.

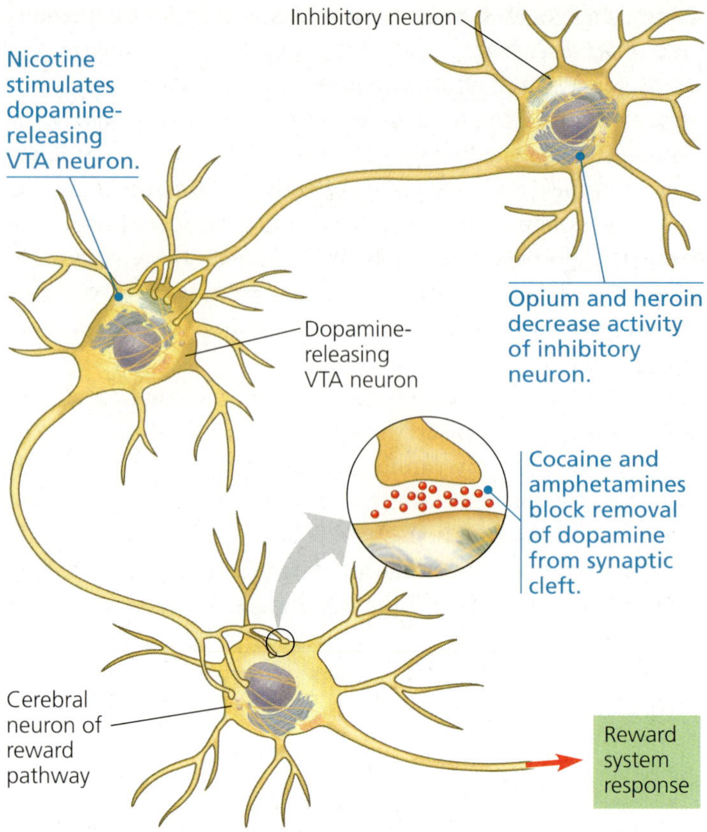

▲ **Figure 49.22 Effects of addictive drugs on the reward pathway of the mammalian brain.** Addictive drugs alter the transmission of signals in the pathway formed by neurons of the ventral tegmental area (VTA).

? *If you depolarized the cell bodies in the ventral tegmental area, what effect would you expect?*

Alzheimer's Disease

Alzheimer's disease is a mental deterioration, or dementia, characterized by confusion, memory loss, and a variety of other symptoms. Its incidence is age related, rising from about 10% at age 65 to about 35% at age 85. The disease is progressive, with patients gradually becoming less able to function and eventually needing to be dressed, bathed, and fed by others. There are also personality changes, almost always for the worse. Patients often lose their ability to recognize people, including their immediate family, and may treat them with suspicion and hostility.

Alzheimer's disease leads to the death of neurons in many areas of the brain, including the hippocampus and cerebral cortex. As a result, there is often massive shrinkage of brain tissue. Although visible with brain imaging, this shrinkage is not enough to positively identify the disease. Furthermore, many symptoms of Alzheimer's disease are shared with other forms of dementia. It is therefore difficult for doctors to diagnose Alzheimer's disease with certainty while the patient is alive. What is diagnostic is the postmortem finding of two features—amyloid plaques and neurofibrillary tangles—in remaining brain tissue **(Figure 49.23)**.

The plaques are aggregates of β-amyloid, an insoluble peptide that is cleaved from a membrane protein found in neurons. Membrane enzymes, called secretases, catalyze the cleavage, causing β-amyloid to accumulate in plaques outside the neurons. It is these plaques that appear to trigger the death of surrounding neurons.

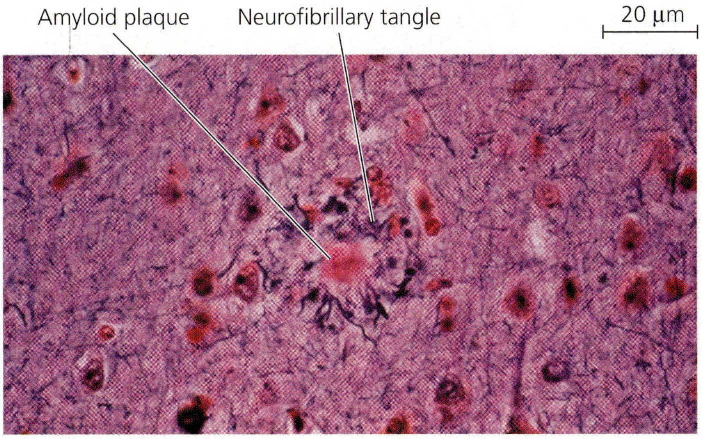

▲ **Figure 49.23 Microscopic signs of Alzheimer's disease.** A hallmark of Alzheimer's disease is the presence in brain tissue of neurofibrillary tangles surrounding plaques made of β-amyloid (LM).

The neurofibrillary tangles observed in Alzheimer's disease are primarily made up of the tau protein. (This protein is unrelated to the τ (tau) mutation that affects circadian rhythm in hamsters; see Figure 49.12.) The normal function of tau in neurons is to help regulate the movement of nutrients along microtubules. In Alzheimer's disease, tau undergoes changes that cause it to bind to itself, resulting in neurofibrillary tangles. There is evidence that changes in tau are associated with the appearance of Alzheimer's disease in relatively young individuals.

An enormous effort has led to the recent development of drugs that are partially effective in relieving the symptoms of Alzheimer's disease, but there is currently no cure.

Parkinson's Disease

A motor disorder, **Parkinson's disease** is characterized by difficulty in initiating movements, slowness of movement, and rigidity. Patients often have muscle tremors, poor balance, a flexed posture, and a shuffling gait. Their facial muscles become rigid, making them less able to vary their expressions. Like Alzheimer's disease, Parkinson's disease is a progressive brain illness and is more common with advancing age. The incidence of Parkinson's disease is about 1% at age 65 and about 5% at age 85. In the U.S. population, approximately 1 million people are afflicted.

The symptoms of Parkinson's disease result from the death of neurons in the midbrain that normally release dopamine at synapses in the basal nuclei. As with Alzheimer's disease, protein aggregates accumulate. Most cases of Parkinson's disease lack an identifiable cause; however, a rare form of the disease that appears in relatively young adults has a clear genetic basis. Molecular studies of mutations linked to this early-onset Parkinson's disease reveal disruption of genes required for certain mitochondrial functions. Researches are investigating whether mitochondrial defects also contribute to the more frequent form of the disease in older patients.

At present there is no cure for Parkinson's disease. Approaches used to manage the symptoms include brain surgery, deep-brain stimulation, and drugs such as L-dopa, a molecule that can cross the blood-brain barrier and be converted to dopamine in the CNS. One potential cure is to implant dopamine-secreting neurons, either in the midbrain or in the basal nuclei. Laboratory studies of this strategy show promise: In rats with an experimentally induced condition that mimics Parkinson's disease, implanting dopamine-secreting neurons can lead to a recovery of motor control. Whether this regenerative approach can also work in humans is one of many important questions in modern brain research.

Stem Cell-Based Therapy

A major current research effort is directed at finding ways to replace brain tissue that has ceased to function properly. Unlike the PNS, the mammalian CNS cannot fully repair itself when damaged or diseased. Surviving neurons in the brain can make new connections and sometimes compensate for damage, as in the remarkable recoveries of some stroke victims. Generally speaking, however, brain and spinal cord injuries, strokes, and disorders that destroy CNS neurons, such as Alzheimer's disease and Parkinson's disease, have devastating and irreversible effects.

The possibility of repairing a damaged or diseased brain with new nerve cells became much more plausible after a groundbreaking 1998 report that the adult human brain produces new neurons. This finding, which overturned a widely held idea, resulted from research carried out by Fred Gage at the Salk Institute in California and Peter Ericksson at the Sahlgrenska University Hospital in Sweden. The evidence that new neurons form in the brains of adults came from a group of terminally ill cancer patients who had agreed to donate their brains for research upon their death. To monitor their tumor growth, the patients were given bromodeoxyuridine (BrdU), an altered nucleotide that is incorporated into DNA during replication. DNA containing BrdU can be readily detected and thus marks cells that grow and divide after BrdU enters the body. Gage and Ericksson reasoned that BrdU would mark not only the growing tumor but also any cells in the brain that had recently divided. When the patients were examined postmortem, there was evidence of newly divided neurons in the hippocampus of each brain **(Figure 49.24)**.

The discovery of dividing neurons in the adult brain indicated the presence of stem cells. Recall from Chapters 20 and 46

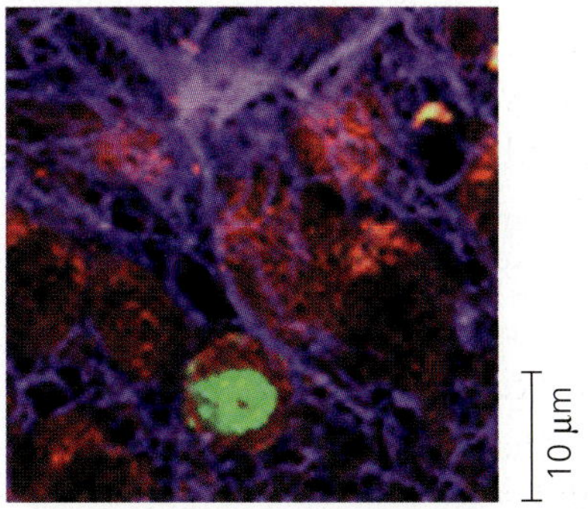

◀ **Figure 49.24 A newly born neuron in the hippocampus of a human adult.** All the red cells in this LM are neurons. The cell that is both red and green is a neuron that has incorporated BrdU, indicating that it resulted from a recent cell division.

that stem cells retain the ability to divide indefinitely. While some of their progeny remain undifferentiated, others differentiate into specialized cells. In the brain, the stem cells are called neural progenitor cells and are committed to becoming either neurons or glia. One goal of researchers is to find a way to induce the body's own neural progenitor cells to differentiate into specific types of neurons or glia when and where they are needed. Another quest is to restore function in a damaged CNS by transplantation of cultured neural progenitor cells.

Having surveyed CNS organization and function, we will examine in the next chapter how sensory systems gather the signals processed by the CNS and how the responses initiated by the CNS lead to muscle contraction and locomotion.

CONCEPT CHECK 49.5

1. Compare Alzheimer's disease and Parkinson's disease.
2. Dopamine is a key neurotransmitter of the nervous system. How is dopamine activity related to schizophrenia, addiction, and Parkinson's disease?
3. **WHAT IF?** Suppose that scientists found a way to detect Alzheimer's disease at a very early stage. Do you think they would observe the same types of changes in the brain, although less extensive, as those seen in autopsies of patients who die of this disease? Explain.

For suggested answers, see Appendix A.

Chapter 49 Review

MEDIA Go to the Study Area at **www.masteringbio.com** for BioFlix 3-D Animations, MP3 Tutors, Videos, Practice Tests, an eBook, and more.

SUMMARY OF KEY CONCEPTS

CONCEPT 49.1

Nervous systems consist of circuits of neurons and supporting cells (pp. 1064–1069)

- Invertebrate nervous systems range in complexity from simple nerve nets to highly centralized nervous systems having complicated brains and ventral nerve cords. In vertebrates, the central nervous system (CNS) consists of the brain and the spinal cord, which is located dorsally. The CNS integrates information, while the nerves of the peripheral nervous system (PNS) transmit sensory and motor signals between the CNS and the rest of the body.
- **Organization of the Vertebrate Nervous System** The simplest circuits in the vertebrate nervous system are found in reflex responses in which sensory input is linked to motor output without involvement of the brain. Neurons in vertebrates are supported by several types of glia, including astrocytes, oligodendrocytes, Schwann cells, ependymal cells, and radial glia.
- **The Peripheral Nervous System** The PNS consists of paired cranial and spinal nerves and associated ganglia. Signals reach the CNS along afferent neurons and leave the CNS via efferent neurons. The efferent neurons function in either the motor system, which carries signals to skeletal muscles, or the autonomic nervous system, which regulates the primarily automatic, visceral functions of smooth and cardiac muscles. The autonomic nervous system has three divisions: the sympathetic and parasympathetic divisions, which usually have antagonistic effects on target organs, and the enteric division, which controls the activity of the digestive tract, pancreas, and gallbladder.

MEDIA
Activity Neuron Structure

CONCEPT 49.2

The vertebrate brain is regionally specialized (pp. 1070–1074)

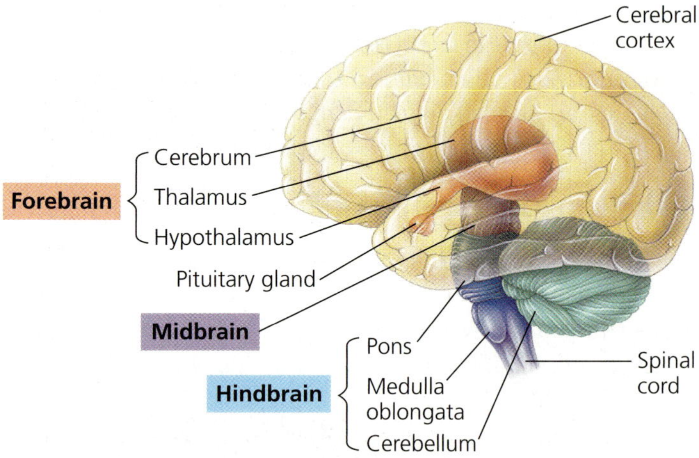

- **The Brainstem** The pons and medulla serve as relay stations for information traveling between the PNS and the higher brain. The reticular formation, a network of neurons within the brainstem, regulates sleep and arousal.
- **The Cerebellum** The cerebellum helps coordinate motor, perceptual, and cognitive functions. It also is involved in learning and remembering motor skills.
- **The Diencephalon** The thalamus is the main center through which sensory and motor information passes to the cerebrum. The hypothalamus regulates homeostasis and basic survival behaviors. In addition, the suprachiasmatic nucleus (SCN) in the hypothalamus acts as the pacemaker for circadian rhythms.
- **The Cerebrum** The cerebrum has two hemispheres, each of which consists of cortical gray matter overlying white matter and basal nuclei, which are important in planning and learning movements. In mammals, the convoluted cerebral cortex is also called the neocortex. A thick band of axons, the corpus callo-

sum, provides communication between the right and left cerebral cortices.

- **Evolution of Cognition in Vertebrates** The region of the avian brain called the pallium contains clustered nuclei that carry out functions similar to those performed by the mammalian cerebral cortex.

CONCEPT **49.3**

The cerebral cortex controls voluntary movement and cognitive functions (pp. 1075–1078)

- Each side of the cerebral cortex has four lobes—frontal, temporal, occipital, and parietal—that contain primary sensory areas and association areas.
- **Information Processing in the Cerebral Cortex** Specific types of sensory input enter the primary sensory areas. Adjacent association areas process particular features in the sensory input and integrate information from different sensory areas. In the somatosensory cortex and the motor cortex, neurons are distributed according to the part of the body that generates sensory input or receives motor commands.
- **Language and Speech** Portions of the frontal and temporal lobes, including Broca's area and Wernicke's area, are essential for generating and understanding language.
- **Lateralization of Cortical Function** The left cerebral hemisphere has a dominant role with regard to language and is often the focus of math and logic operations. The right hemisphere appears to be stronger at pattern recognition and nonverbal thinking. At least some of this lateralization of functions relates to handedness.
- **Emotions** The generation and experience of emotions involve many regions of the brain, with the amygdala playing a key role in recognizing and recalling a number of emotions.
- **Consciousness** Modern brain-imaging techniques suggest that consciousness may be an emergent property of the brain based on activity in many areas of the cortex.

CONCEPT **49.4**

Changes in synaptic connections underlie memory and learning (pp. 1078–1080)

- During development, more neurons and synapses form than are needed. The programmed death of neurons and elimination of synapses in embryos establish the basic structure of the nervous system.
- **Neural Plasticity** Reshaping of the adult nervous system often occurs at synapses. Changes can involve the loss or addition of a synapse or the strengthening or weakening of signaling at a synapse.
- **Memory and Learning** Short-term memory relies on temporary associations in the hippocampus. In long-term memory, these temporary links are replaced by connections within the cerebral cortex. This transfer of information from short-term to long-term memory is enhanced by the association of new data with that already in long-term memory.
- **Long-Term Potentiation** LTP is a lasting increase in the strength of synaptic transmission and appears to be an important process in memory storage and learning.

MEDIA

Activity Signal Transmission at a Chemical Synapse

CONCEPT **49.5**

Nervous system disorders can be explained in molecular terms (pp. 1080–1084)

- **Schizophrenia** Schizophrenia, which is characterized by hallucinations, delusions, and other symptoms, affects neuronal pathways that use dopamine as a neurotransmitter.
- **Depression** Bipolar disorder, characterized by manic (high-mood) and depressive (low-mood) phases, and major depression, in which patients have a persistent low mood, are often treated with drugs that increase the activity of biogenic amines in the brain.
- **Drug Addiction and the Brain Reward System** The compulsive drug use that characterizes addiction reflects altered activity of the brain's reward system, which normally provides motivation for actions, such as eating, that enhance survival or reproduction.
- **Alzheimer's Disease** Alzheimer's disease is an age-related dementia in which neurofibrillary tangles and amyloid plaques form in the brain.
- **Parkinson's Disease** Parkinson's disease is a motor disorder caused by the death of dopamine-secreting neurons and associated with the presence of protein aggregates.
- **Stem Cell-Based Therapy** The adult human brain contains stem cells that can differentiate into mature neurons. The induction of stem cell differentiation and the transplantation of cultured stem cells are potential methods for replacing neurons lost to trauma or disease.

TESTING YOUR KNOWLEDGE

SELF-QUIZ

1. Wakefulness is regulated by the reticular formation, which is present in the
  a. basal nuclei.
  b. cerebral cortex.
  c. brainstem.
  d. limbic system.
  e. spinal cord.

2. Which of the following structures or regions is *incorrectly* paired with its function?
  a. limbic system—motor control of speech
  b. medulla oblongata—homeostatic control
  c. cerebellum—coordination of movement and balance
  d. corpus callosum—communication between the left and right cerebral cortices
  e. hypothalamus—regulation of temperature, hunger, and thirst

3. What is the neocortex?
  a. a primitive brain region that is common to reptiles and mammals
  b. a region deep in the cortex that is associated with the formation of emotional memories
  c. a central part of the cortex that receives olfactory information

d. an additional outer layer of neurons in the cerebral cortex that is unique to mammals
e. an association area of the frontal lobe that is involved in higher cognitive functions

4. Patients with damage to Wernicke's area have difficulty
a. coordinating limb movement.
b. generating speech.
c. recognizing faces.
d. understanding language.
e. experiencing emotion.

5. The sympathetic division of the autonomic portion of the PNS does all of the following *except*
a. relaxing bronchi in lungs.
b. inhibiting bladder emptying.
c. stimulating glucose release.
d. accelerating heart rate.
e. stimulating the salivary glands.

6. The cerebral cortex plays a major role in all of the following *except*
a. short-term memory.
b. long-term memory.
c. circadian rhythm.
d. foot-tapping rhythm.
e. breath holding.

7. **DRAW IT** Draw a simple circuit for the pain withdrawal reflex that pulls your hand away when you prick your finger on a sharp object. (a) Using a circle to represent the spinal cord, label the types of neurons, the direction of information flow in each, and the locations of synapses. (b) Draw a simple diagram of the brain indicating where pain would eventually be perceived.

For Self-Quiz answers, see Appendix A.

MEDIA Visit the Study Area at **www.masteringbio.com** for a Practice Test.

EVOLUTION CONNECTION

8. Scientists often use measures of "higher-order thinking" to assess intelligence in other animals. For example, birds are judged to have sophisticated thought processes because they can use tools and make use of abstract concepts. What problems do you see in defining intelligence in these ways?

SCIENTIFIC INQUIRY

9. Consider an individual who had been fluent in American Sign Language before suffering damage to the left cerebral hemisphere. After the injury, this person could still understand signs, but could not readily generate signs that represented his thoughts. What two hypotheses might explain this finding, and how might you distinguish between them?

SCIENCE, TECHNOLOGY, AND SOCIETY

10. With increasingly sophisticated methods for scanning brain activity, scientists are rapidly developing the ability to detect an individual's particular emotions and thought processes from outside the body. What benefits and problems do you envision when such technology becomes readily available?

50 Sensory and Motor Mechanisms

▲ **Figure 50.1 Can a moth evade a bat in the dark?**

KEY CONCEPTS

50.1 **Sensory receptors transduce stimulus energy and transmit signals to the central nervous system**
50.2 **The mechanoreceptors responsible for hearing and equilibrium detect moving fluid or settling particles**
50.3 **The senses of taste and smell rely on similar sets of sensory receptors**
50.4 **Similar mechanisms underlie vision throughout the animal kingdom**
50.5 **The physical interaction of protein filaments is required for muscle function**
50.6 **Skeletal systems transform muscle contraction into locomotion**

OVERVIEW

Sensing and Acting

A flash of light reveals an instant in a nighttime confrontation **(Figure 50.1)**. A bat, patrolling the summer air in search of food, is on the verge of catching a moth. Startled from its flight, the moth has only a fraction of a second to escape death. What will happen?

Both predator and prey rely on sensation and response. The bat produces pulses of sound and uses the returning echoes to direct its flight toward the moth. At the same time, the bat's ultrasonic chirps activate vibration sensors in the abdomen of the moth. The moth most likely detects the bat at 30 m, a distance ten times that at which the bat could sense the moth. Altering the motor output to its wing muscles, the moth begins an evasive maneuver. The bat, however, flies much faster than the moth. In this encounter, the insect is unlikely to survive.

The detection and processing of sensory information and the generation of motor output provide the physiological basis for all animal activity. Although it is customary to think of behavior as a linear sequence of sensing, analyzing, and acting, this is not the case. When animals are in motion, they are constantly probing the environment, sensing changes and using the information to generate the next action. This is a continuous cycle rather than a linear sequence, with sensation directing output and action altering sensory input.

In this chapter, we will explore the processes of sensing and acting in both invertebrates and vertebrates. We will start with sensory processes that convey information about the external and internal environment to the brain. We will then consider the structure and function of muscles and skeletons that carry out movements as instructed by the brain. Finally, we will investigate various mechanisms of animal movement.

CONCEPT 50.1

Sensory receptors transduce stimulus energy and transmit signals to the central nervous system

All stimuli represent forms of energy. Sensation involves converting this energy to a change in the membrane potential of sensory receptor cells and thereby regulating the output of action potentials to the central nervous system (CNS).

Sensory Pathways

We'll begin our consideration of sensory systems with the sensory pathway controlled by the stretch receptor of a crayfish

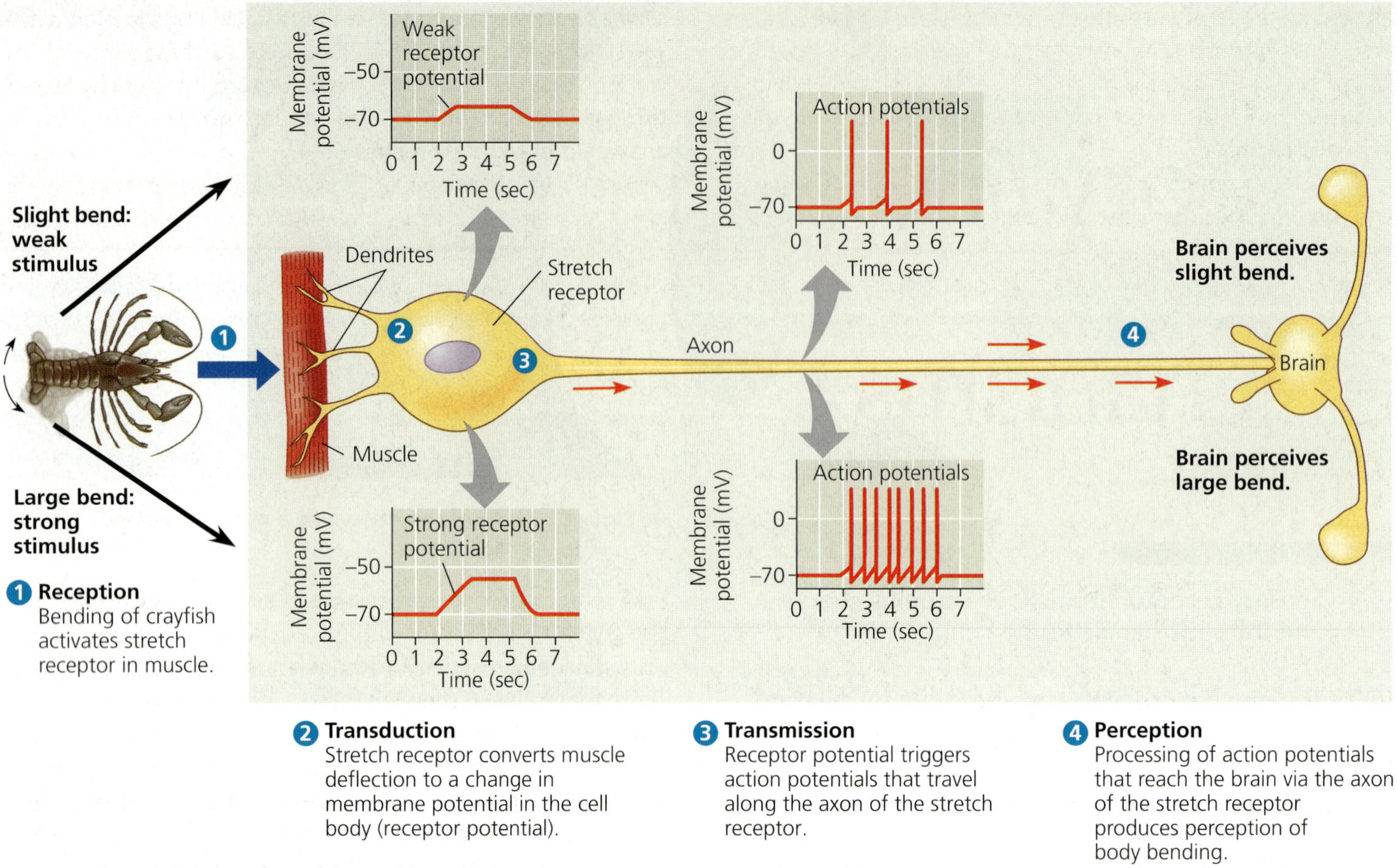

▲ **Figure 50.2 A simple sensory pathway: Response of a crayfish stretch receptor to bending.**

(Figure 50.2). This and other sensory pathways have in common four basic functions: sensory reception, transduction, transmission, and perception.

Sensory Reception and Transduction

A sensory pathway begins with **sensory reception**, the detection of a stimulus by sensory cells. Most sensory cells are specialized neurons or epithelial cells. Some exist singly; others are found collected in sensory organs, such as eyes and ears. Sensory cells and organs, as well as the structures within sensory cells that respond to specific stimuli, are called **sensory receptors**. Many sensory receptors detect stimuli from outside the body, such as heat, light, pressure, and chemicals, but there are also receptors for stimuli from within the body, such as blood pressure and body position.

In the case of the crayfish, bending of body muscle stimulates stretch-sensitive dendrites in the stretch receptor cell to open ion channels (see Figure 50.2). In other sensory receptors, channels open or close when substances outside the cell bind to proteins on the membrane or when pigments in the sensory receptor absorb light. The resulting flow of ions across the plasma membrane changes the membrane potential.

The conversion of a physical or chemical stimulus to a change in the membrane potential of a sensory receptor is called **sensory transduction**, and the change in membrane potential itself is known as a **receptor potential**. Receptor potentials are graded potentials; their magnitude varies with the strength of the stimulus (see Figure 50.2).

One remarkable feature of many sensory receptors is their extreme sensitivity: They can detect the smallest possible physical unit of stimulus. For example, most light receptors can detect a single quantum (photon) of light, and chemical receptors can detect a single molecule.

Transmission

Sensory information is transmitted through the nervous system in the form of nerve impulses, or action potentials. For many sensory receptors, transducing the energy in a stimulus into a receptor potential initiates **transmission** of action potentials to the CNS. Some sensory receptor cells, such as the crayfish stretch receptor, are neurons that produce action potentials; they have an axon that extends into the CNS (see Figure 50.2). As we will see shortly, other sensory receptor cells release neurotransmitters at synapses with sensory (afferent) neurons. At almost all such synapses, the receptor releases an excitatory neurotransmitter. (One exception is in the vertebrate visual system, discussed in Concept 50.4.)

The magnitude of a receptor potential controls the rate at which action potentials are produced by a sensory receptor. If the receptor is a sensory neuron, a larger receptor potential results in more frequent action potentials (see Figure 50.2). If the receptor is not a sensory neuron, a larger receptor potential causes more neurotransmitter to be released, which usually increases the production of action potentials by the postsynaptic neuron.

Many sensory neurons spontaneously generate action potentials at a low rate. In these neurons, a stimulus does not switch the production of action potentials on or off, but it does change how often an action potential is produced. In this manner, such neurons are also able to alert the CNS to changes in stimulus intensity.

Processing of sensory information can occur before, during, and after transmission of action potentials to the CNS. In many cases, the *integration* of sensory information begins as soon as the information is received. Receptor potentials produced by stimuli delivered to different parts of a sensory receptor cell are integrated through summation, as are postsynaptic potentials in sensory neurons that synapse with multiple receptors (see Figure 48.16). As we will discuss shortly, sensory structures such as eyes also provide higher levels of integration, and the brain further processes all incoming signals.

Perception

When action potentials reach the brain via sensory neurons, circuits of neurons process this input, generating the **perception** of the stimuli. Perceptions—such as colors, smells, sounds, and tastes—are constructions formed in the brain and do not exist outside it. If a tree falls and no animal is present to hear it, is there a sound? The fall certainly produces pressure waves in the air, but if sound is defined as a perception, then there is none unless an animal senses the waves and its brain perceives them.

Action potentials are all-or-none events (see Figure 48.9c). An action potential triggered by light striking the eye has the same properties as an action potential triggered by air vibrating in the ear. How, then, do we distinguish sights, sounds, and other stimuli? The answer lies in the connections that link sensory receptors to the brain. Action potentials from sensory receptors travel along neurons that are dedicated to a particular stimulus; these dedicated neurons synapse with particular neurons in the brain or spinal cord. As a result, the brain distinguishes sensory stimuli such as sight or sound solely by along which paths to the brain the action potentials arrive.

Amplification and Adaptation

The transduction of stimuli by sensory receptors is subject to two types of modification—amplification and adaptation. **Amplification** refers to the strengthening of stimulus energy during transduction. The effect can be considerable. For example, an action potential conducted from the eye to the human brain has about 100,000 times as much energy as the few photons of light that triggered it. Amplification that occurs in sensory receptor cells often requires signal transduction pathways involving second messengers. Because these pathways include enzyme-catalyzed reactions, they amplify signal strength through the formation of many product molecules by a single enzyme molecule. Amplification may also take place in accessory structures of a complex sense organ, as when sound waves are enhanced by a factor of more than 20 before reaching receptors in the innermost part of the ear.

Upon continued stimulation, many receptors undergo a decrease in responsiveness termed **sensory adaptation** (not to be confused with the evolutionary term *adaptation*). Without sensory adaptation, you would be constantly aware of feeling every beat of your heart and every bit of clothing on your body. Adaptation also enables you to see, hear, and smell changes in environments that vary widely in stimulus intensity.

Types of Sensory Receptors

A sensory cell typically has a single type of receptor specific for a particular stimulus, such as light or cold. Often, distinct cells and receptors are responsible for particular qualities of a sensation, such as distinguishing red from blue. Before exploring these specializations, let's consider sensory receptor function at a more basic level. We can classify sensory receptors into five categories based on the nature of the stimuli they transduce: mechanoreceptors, chemoreceptors, electromagnetic receptors, thermoreceptors, and pain receptors.

Mechanoreceptors

Mechanoreceptors sense physical deformation caused by forms of mechanical energy such as pressure, touch, stretch, motion, and sound. Mechanoreceptors typically consist of ion channels that are linked to structures that extend outside the cell, such as "hairs" (cilia), as well as internal cell structures, such as the cytoskeleton. Bending or stretching of the external structure generates tension that alters the permeability of the ion channels. This change in ion permeability alters the membrane potential, resulting in a depolarization or hyperpolarization (see Chapter 48).

The vertebrate stretch receptor, like that of the crayfish (see Figure 50.2), is a mechanoreceptor that detects muscle movement. The mechanoreceptors in this case are dendrites of sensory neurons that spiral around the middle of small skeletal muscle fibers. Groups of about 2 to 12 of these fibers, formed into a spindle shape and surrounded by connective tissue, are distributed throughout the muscle, parallel to other muscle fibers. When the muscle is stretched, the spindle fibers are stretched, depolarizing sensory neurons and triggering action potentials that are transmitted to the spinal cord. The familiar knee-jerk reflex (see Figure 49.3) relies on just this type of interaction between spindle fibers and stretch receptors.

The mammalian sense of touch also relies on mechanoreceptors that are the dendrites of sensory neurons. Touch receptors

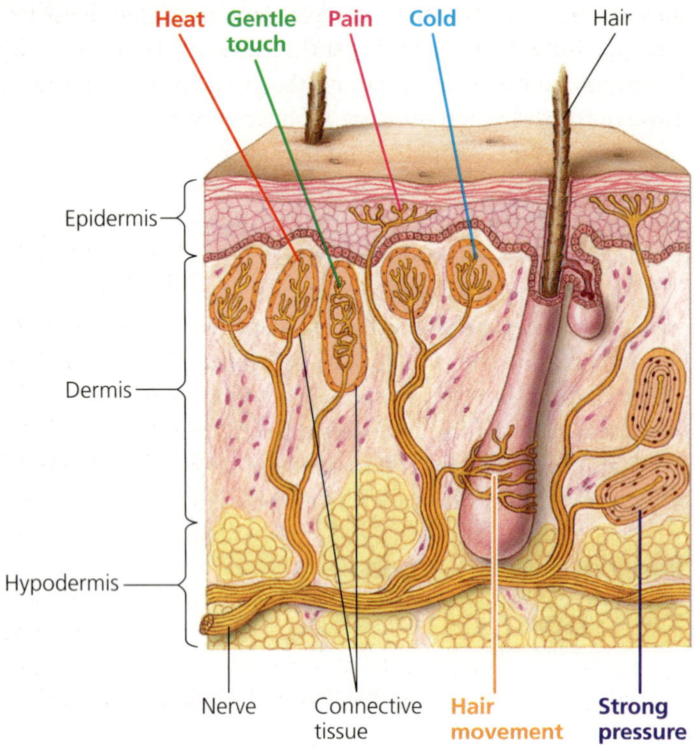

▲ **Figure 50.3 Sensory receptors in human skin.** Most receptors in the dermis are encapsulated by connective tissue. Receptors in the epidermis are naked dendrites, as are hair movement receptors that wind around the base of hairs in the dermis.

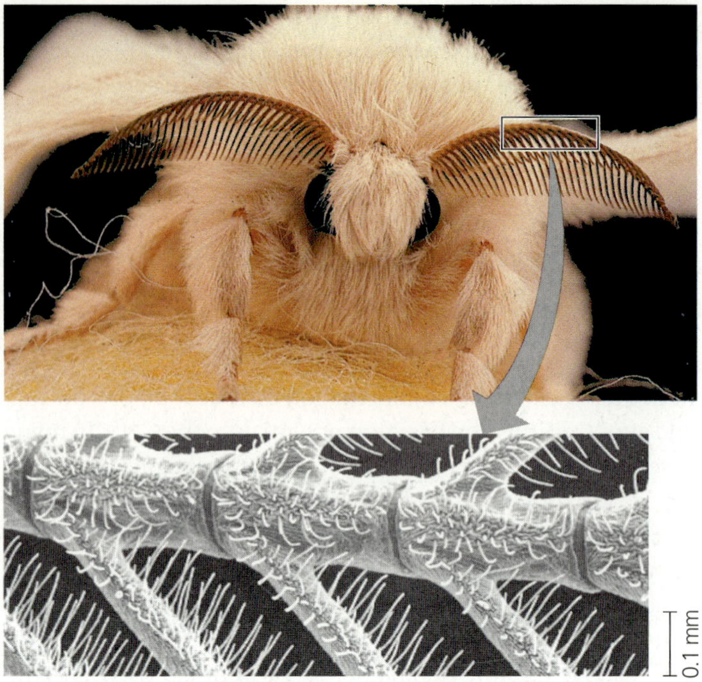

▲ **Figure 50.4 Chemoreceptors in an insect.** The antennae of the male silkworm moth *Bombyx mori* are covered with sensory hairs, visible in the SEM enlargement. The hairs have chemoreceptors that are highly sensitive to the sex pheromone released by the female.

are often embedded in layers of connective tissue. The structure of the connective tissue and the location of the receptors dramatically affect the type of mechanical energy (light touch, vibration, or strong pressure) that best stimulates them **(Figure 50.3)**. Receptors that detect a light touch or vibration are close to the surface of the skin; they transduce very slight inputs of mechanical energy into receptor potentials. Receptors that respond to stronger pressure and vibrations are in deep skin layers. Other receptors sense movement of hairs. For example, cats and many rodents have extremely sensitive mechanoreceptors at the base of their whiskers. Because deflection of different whiskers triggers action potentials that reach different cells in the brain, an animal's whiskers provide detailed information about nearby objects.

Chemoreceptors

Chemoreceptors include both general receptors—those that transmit information about total solute concentration—and specific receptors—those that respond to individual kinds of molecules. Osmoreceptors in the mammalian brain, for example, are general receptors that detect changes in the total solute concentration of the blood and stimulate thirst when osmolarity increases (see Figure 44.19). Most animals also have receptors for specific molecules, including glucose, oxygen, carbon dioxide, and amino acids. Two of the most sensitive and specific chemoreceptors known are found in the antennae of the male silkworm moth **(Figure 50.4)**; they detect the two chemical components of the female moth sex pheromone. In all these examples, the stimulus molecule binds to the specific chemoreceptor on the membrane of the sensory cell and initiates changes in ion permeability.

Electromagnetic Receptors

Electromagnetic receptors detect various forms of electromagnetic energy, such as visible light, electricity, and magnetism. Photoreceptors, electromagnetic receptors that detect energy in the form of light, are often organized into eyes. Some snakes have very sensitive infrared receptors that detect the body heat of prey **(Figure 50.5a)**. Some fishes generate electrical currents and use electroreceptors to locate objects, such as prey, that disturb those currents. The platypus, a monotreme mammal, has electroreceptors on its bill that probably detect electric fields generated by the muscles of crustaceans, frogs, small fish, and other prey. Many animals appear to use Earth's magnetic field lines to orient themselves as they migrate **(Figure 50.5b)**. The iron-containing mineral magnetite is found in the skulls of many vertebrates (including salmon, pigeons, sea turtles, and humans), in the abdomen of bees, in the teeth of some molluscs, and in certain protists and prokaryotes that orient to Earth's magnetic field. Once collected by sailors to make compasses for navigation, magnetite may be part of an orienting mechanism in many animals (see Chapter 51).

(a) This rattlesnake and other pit vipers have a pair of infrared receptors, one anterior to and just below each eye. These organs are sensitive enough to detect the infrared radiation emitted by a warm mouse a meter away. The snake moves its head from side to side until the radiation is detected equally by the two receptors, indicating that the mouse is straight ahead.

(b) Some migrating animals, such as these beluga whales, apparently sense Earth's magnetic field and use the information, along with other cues, for orientation.

▲ **Figure 50.5 Specialized electromagnetic receptors.**

Thermoreceptors

Thermoreceptors detect heat and cold. Located in the skin and in the anterior hypothalamus, thermoreceptor cells send information to the body's thermostat, located in the posterior hypothalamus. The key to understanding how sensory cells detect temperature initially came from the dinner table, not the laboratory. Jalapeno and cayenne peppers taste "hot" because they contain a natural product called capsaicin. It turns out that exposing sensory neurons to capsaicin triggers an influx of calcium ions. When scientists identified the receptor protein that opens a calcium channel upon binding capsaicin, they made a fascinating discovery: The receptor responds not only to the chemical capsaicin, but also to high temperatures (42°C or higher). In essence, we describe spicy foods as "hot" because they activate the same sensory receptors as do hot soup and coffee.

Mammals have a number of kinds of thermoreceptors, each specific for a particular temperature range. The capsaicin receptor and at least five other types of thermoreceptors belong to the TRP (transient receptor potential) family of ion channel proteins. Remarkably, the TRP-type receptor specific for temperatures below 28°C can be activated by menthol, a plant product that we perceive to have a "cool" flavor.

Pain Receptors

Extreme pressure or temperature, as well as certain chemicals, can damage animal tissues. To detect stimuli that reflect such noxious (or harmful) conditions, animals rely on **nociceptors** (from the Latin *nocere*, to hurt), also called **pain receptors**. By triggering defensive reactions, such as withdrawal from danger, the perception of pain serves an important function. Rare individuals who are born without the ability to perceive pain may die from conditions such as a ruptured appendix because they cannot feel the associated pain and are unaware of the danger.

In humans, certain naked dendrites detect noxious thermal, mechanical, or chemical stimuli (see Figure 50.3). The capsaicin receptor, which acts as a thermoreceptor, is thus also a nociceptor. Although nociceptor density is highest in skin, some pain receptors are associated with other organs.

Chemicals produced in an animal's body sometimes enhance the perception of pain. For example, damaged tissues produce prostaglandins, which act as local regulators of inflammation (see Chapter 45). Prostaglandins worsen pain by increasing nociceptor sensitivity to noxious stimuli. Aspirin and ibuprofen reduce pain by inhibiting the synthesis of prostaglandins.

CONCEPT CHECK 50.1

1. Which one of the five categories of sensory receptors is primarily dedicated to external stimuli?
2. Why does eating food containing "hot" peppers sometimes cause you to sweat?
3. **WHAT IF?** If you stimulated a sensory neuron electrically, how would that stimulation be perceived?

For suggested answers, see Appendix A.

CONCEPT **50.2**

The mechanoreceptors responsible for hearing and equilibrium detect moving fluid or settling particles

Hearing and the perception of body equilibrium, or balance, are related in most animals. For both senses, mechanoreceptor cells produce receptor potentials when settling particles or moving fluid cause deflection of cell surface structures.

Sensing of Gravity and Sound in Invertebrates

To sense gravity and maintain equilibrium, most invertebrates rely on sensory organs called **statocysts** **(Figure 50.6)**. A common type of statocyst consists of a layer of ciliated receptor cells surrounding a chamber that contains one or more **statoliths**, which are grains of sand or other dense granules. Gravity causes the statoliths to settle to the low point in the chamber, stimulating mechanoreceptors in that location. Such statocysts can be found at the fringe of jellies and at the base of antennules in lobsters and crayfish. In experiments in which statoliths were replaced with metal shavings, researchers "tricked" crayfish into swimming upside down by using magnets to pull the shavings to the upper end of the statocysts.

Many (perhaps most) insects have body hairs that vibrate in response to sound waves. Hairs of different stiffnesses and lengths vibrate at different frequencies. Often, hairs are tuned to frequencies of sounds produced by other organisms. For example, some caterpillars have vibrating body hairs that can detect the buzzing wings of predatory wasps, warning the caterpillars of the danger. Similarly, fine hairs on the antennae of a male mosquito vibrate in a specific way in response to the hum produced by the beating wings of flying females. In this way, the male mosquito can locate a potential mate. The importance of this sensory system for mosquitoes in mate attraction can be demonstrated very simply: A tuning fork vibrating at the same frequency as a that of a female's wings will by itself attract males.

Many insects also detect sound by means of "ears" consisting of a tympanic membrane (eardrum) stretched over an internal air chamber **(Figure 50.7)**. Sound waves vibrate the tympanic membrane, stimulating receptor cells attached to the inside of the membrane and resulting in nerve impulses that are transmitted to the brain. As discussed at the beginning of the chapter, this sensory system allows some moths to perceive the high-pitched sounds produced by bats, potentially helping the moth to escape. Similarly, a cockroach's ability to detect vibrations caused by a descending human foot often provides enough warning for the insect to avoid being crushed.

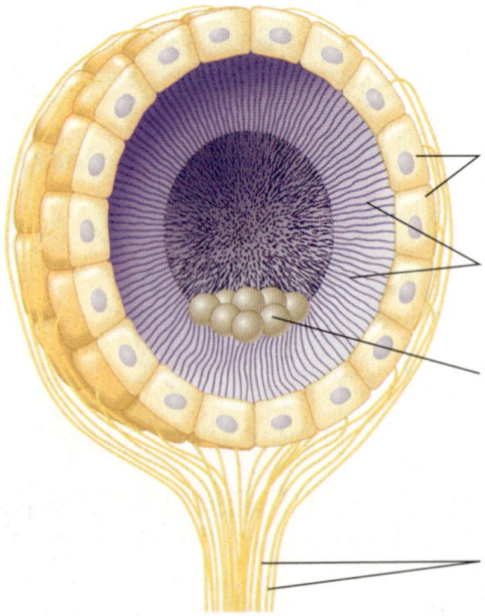

▲ **Figure 50.6 The statocyst of an invertebrate.** The settling of statoliths to the low point in the chamber bends cilia on receptor cells in that location, providing the brain with information about the orientation of the body with respect to gravity.

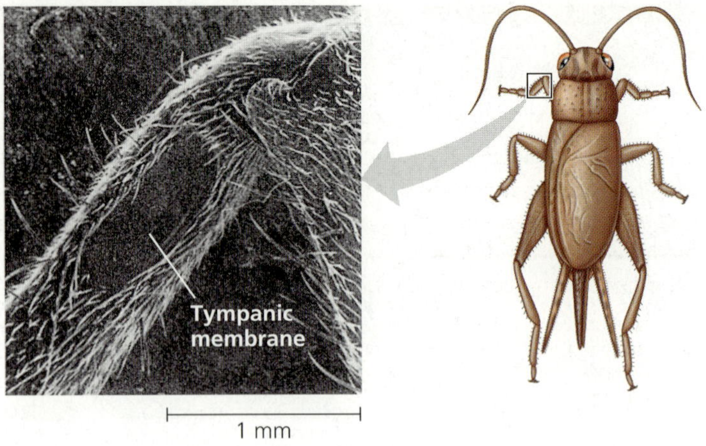

▲ **Figure 50.7 An insect's "ear"—on its leg.** The tympanic membrane, visible in this SEM of a cricket's front leg, vibrates in response to sound waves. The vibrations stimulate mechanoreceptors attached to the inside of the tympanic membrane.

Hearing and Equilibrium in Mammals

In mammals, as in most other terrestrial vertebrates, the sensory organs for hearing and equilibrium are closely associated. **Figure 50.8** explores the structure and function of these organs in the human ear.

Hearing

Vibrating objects, such as a plucked guitar string or the vocal cords of your instructor, create pressure waves in the surrounding air. In *hearing*, the ear converts the energy of these waves to nerve impulses that the brain perceives as sound. To hear music, speech, or noise in our environment, we rely on sensory receptors that are hair cells, a type of mechanoreceptor. Before the vibration waves reach the hair cells, however, they are amplified and transformed by several accessory structures.

The first steps in hearing involve structures in the ear that convert the vibrations of moving air to pressure waves in fluid. Upon reaching the outer ear, moving air causes the tympanic membrane to vibrate. The three bones of the middle ear transmit the vibrations to the oval window, a membrane on the cochlea's surface. When one of those bones, the stapes, vibrates against the oval window, it creates pressure waves in the fluid inside the cochlea.

Upon entering the vestibular canal, the fluid pressure waves push down on the cochlear duct and basilar membrane. In response, the basilar membrane and attached hair cells vibrate up and down. The hairs projecting from the moving hair cells are

▼ **Figure 50.8**

Exploring The Structure of the Human Ear

1 Overview of Ear Structure The **outer ear** consists of the external pinna and the auditory canal, which collect sound waves and channel them to the **tympanic membrane** (eardrum), separating the outer and middle ear. In the **middle ear**, three small bones—the malleus (hammer), incus (anvil), and stapes (stirrup) transmit vibrations to the **oval window**, which is a membrane beneath the stapes. The middle ear also opens into the **Eustachian tube**, which connects to the pharynx and equalizes pressure between the middle ear and the atmosphere. The **inner ear** consists of fluid-filled chambers, including the **semicircular canals**, which function in equilibrium, and the coiled **cochlea** (Latin, "snail"), which is involved in hearing.

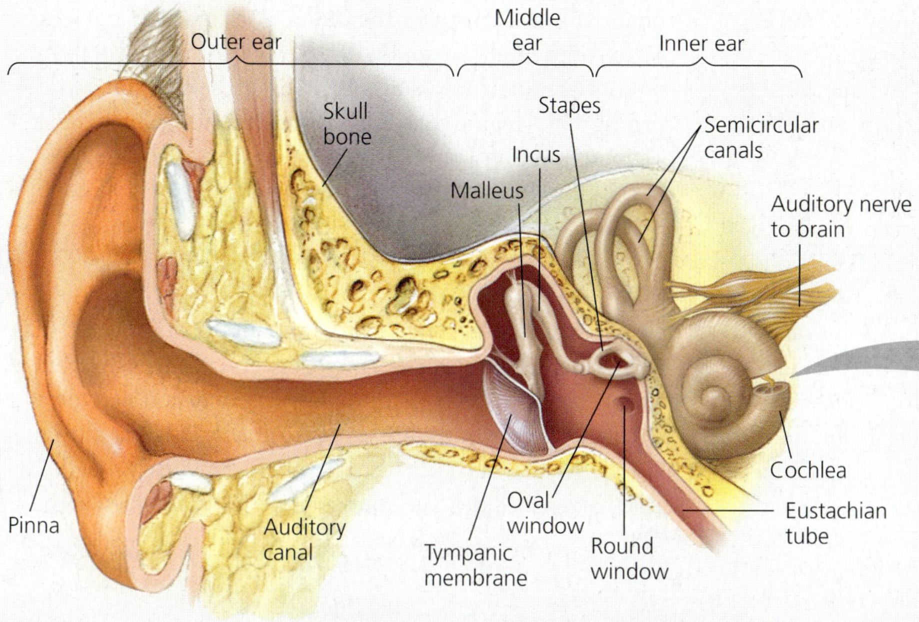

2 The Cochlea The cochlea has two large canals—an upper vestibular canal and a lower tympanic canal—separated by a smaller cochlear duct. The vestibular and tympanic canals contain a fluid called perilymph, and the cochlear duct is filled with a fluid called endolymph.

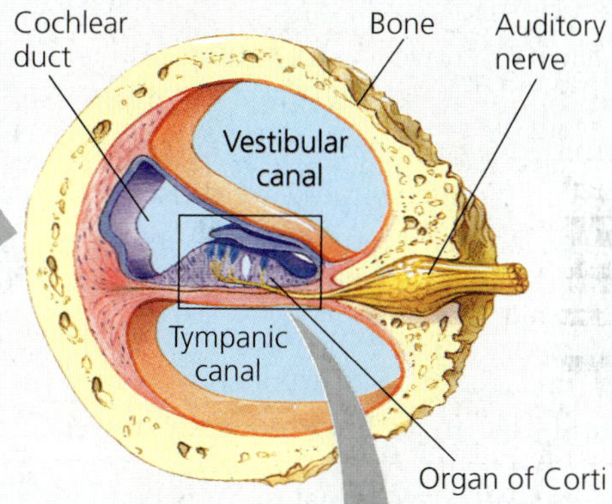

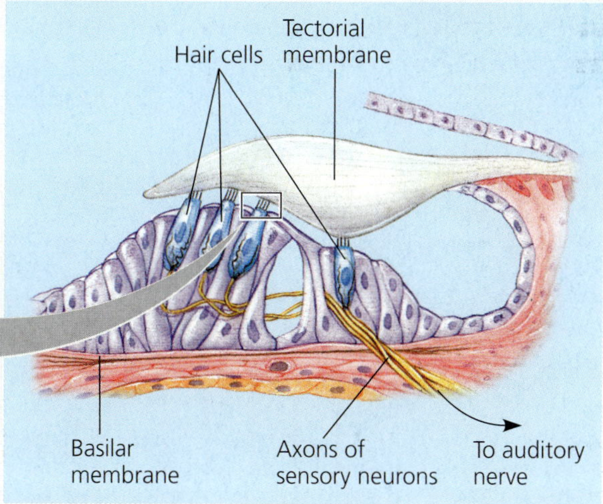

3 The Organ of Corti The floor of the cochlear duct, the basilar membrane, bears the **organ of Corti**, which contains the mechanoreceptors of the ear, hair cells with hairs projecting into the cochlear duct. Many of the hairs are attached to the tectorial membrane, which hangs over the organ of Corti like an awning. Sound waves make the basilar membrane vibrate, which results in bending of the hairs and depolarization of the hair cells.

Hair cell bundle from a bullfrog; the longest cilia shown are about 8 μm (SEM).

4 Hair Cells Projecting from each hair cell is a bundle of rod-shaped "hairs," each containing a core of actin filaments. Vibration of the basilar membrane in response to sound raises and lowers the hair cells, bending the hairs against the surrounding fluid and the tectorial membrane. Displacement of the hairs within the bundle activates mechanoreceptors, changing the hair cell membrane potential.

deflected by the tectorial membrane that lies in a fixed position immediately above (see Figure 50.8). With each vibration, the hairs projecting above the hair cells bend first in one direction and then the other. Mechanoreceptors in the hair cells respond to the bending by opening or closing ion channels in the plasma membrane. As shown in **Figure 50.9**, bending in one direction depolarizes hair cells, increasing neurotransmitter release and the frequency of action potentials directed to the brain along the auditory nerve. Bending the hairs in the other direction hyperpolarizes the hair cells, reducing neurotransmitter release and the frequency of auditory nerve sensations.

What prevents pressure waves from reverberating within the ear and causing prolonged sensation? Once pressure waves travel through the vestibular canal, they pass around the apex (tip) of the cochlea. The waves then continue through the tympanic canal, dissipating as they strike the **round window** **(Figure 50.10a)**. This damping of sound waves resets the apparatus for the next vibrations that arrive.

The ear conveys information to the brain about two important sound variables: volume and pitch. *Volume* (loudness) is determined by the amplitude, or height, of the sound wave. A large-amplitude sound wave causes more vigorous vibration of the basilar membrane, greater bending of the hairs on hair cells, and more action potentials in the sensory neurons. *Pitch* is a function of a sound wave's frequency, the number of vibrations per unit time. High-frequency waves produce high-pitched sounds, whereas low-frequency waves produce low-pitched sounds. Pitch is commonly expressed in cycles per second, or hertz (Hz). Healthy young humans can hear in the range of 20–20,000 Hz; dogs can hear sounds as high as 40,000 Hz; and bats can emit and hear clicking sounds at frequencies above 100,000 Hz, using this ability to locate objects.

The cochlea can distinguish pitch because the basilar membrane is not uniform along its length: It is relatively narrow and stiff at the base of the cochlea near the oval window and wider and more flexible at the apex. Each region of the basilar membrane is tuned to a particular vibration frequency **(Figure 50.10b)**. At any instant, the region of the membrane vibrating most vigorously triggers the highest frequency of action potentials in the neuronal pathway leading to the brain. There, within the cerebral cortex, the actual perception of pitch occurs. Axons in the auditory nerve project into auditory areas of the cerebral cortex according to the region of the basilar membrane in which the signal originated. When a particular site in our cortex is stimulated, we perceive the sound of a particular pitch.

Equilibrium

Several organs in the inner ear of humans and most other mammals detect body movement, position, and balance. Situated in a vestibule behind the oval window, the **utricle** and **saccule** allow us to perceive position with respect to gravity or linear movement **(Figure 50.11)**. Each of these chambers contains a sheet of hair cells that project into a gelatinous material. Embedded in this gel

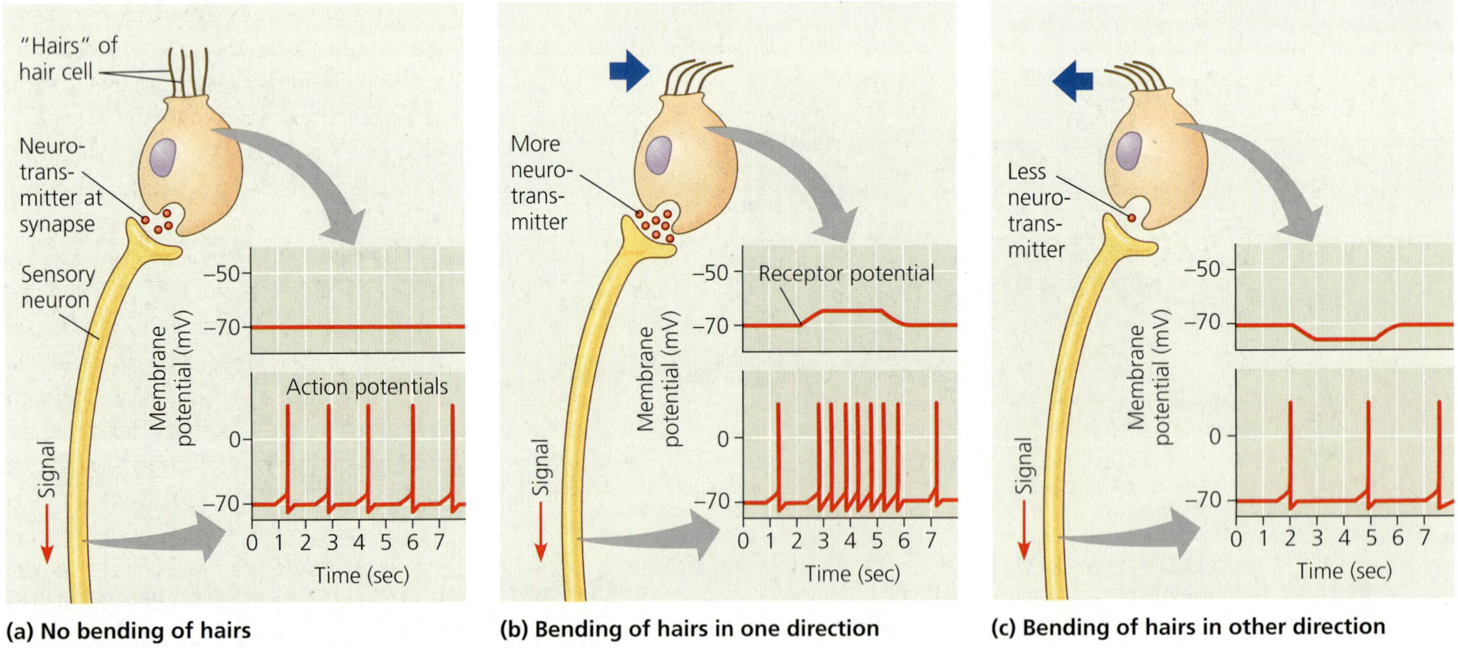

▲ **Figure 50.9 Sensory reception by hair cells.** Vertebrate hair cells required for hearing and balance have "hairs" formed into a bundle that bends when surrounding fluid moves. Each hair cell releases an excitatory neurotransmitter at a synapse with a sensory neuron, which conducts action potentials to the CNS. Bending of the bundle in one direction depolarizes the hair cell, causing it to release more neurotransmitter and increasing the frequency of action potentials in the sensory neuron. Bending in the other direction has the opposite effect.

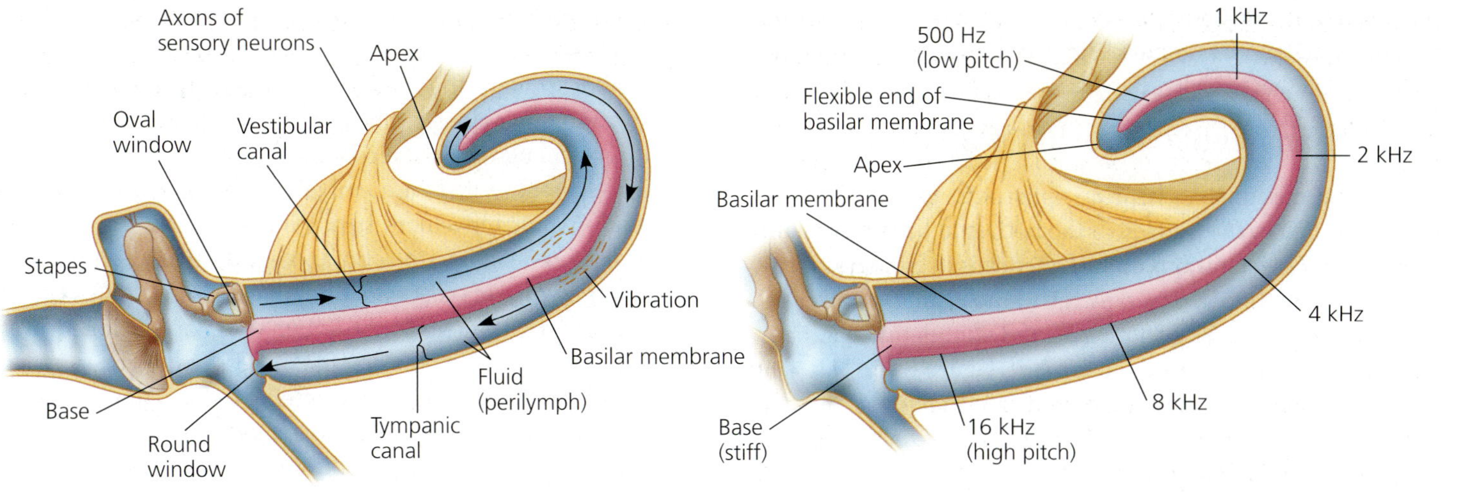

(a) For purposes of illustration, the cochlea is shown partially uncoiled. Vibrations of the stapes against the oval window produce pressure waves in the fluid (perilymph) of the cochlea. The waves (black arrows) travel to the apex of the cochlea through the vestibular canal and back toward the base through the tympanic canal. The energy in the waves causes the basilar membrane (pink) to vibrate, stimulating hair cells.

(b) Variation in the stiffness of the basilar membrane (pink) along its length "tunes" specific regions to specific frequencies. As a result, different frequencies of pressure waves in the cochlea cause different portions of the basilar membrane to vibrate, stimulating particular hair cells and sensory neurons. The selective stimulation of hair cells is perceived in the brain as sound of a certain pitch.

▲ **Figure 50.10 Transduction in the cochlea.**

? *A musical chord consists of several notes, each formed by a sound wave of different frequency. When you hear a chord, where in your body are these notes combined?*

are many small calcium carbonate particles called otoliths ("ear stones"). When you tilt your head, the otoliths press on the hairs protruding into the gel. Through the hair cell receptors, this deflection of the hairs is transformed into a change in the output of sensory neurons, signaling the brain that your head is at an angle. The otoliths are also responsible for your ability to perceive acceleration, as, for example, when a stationary car in which you are sitting pulls forward. Because the utricle is oriented horizontally and the saccule is positioned vertically, you can detect motion in either the forward-and-back or up-and-down direction.

Three semicircular canals connected to the utricle detect turning of the head and other forms of angular acceleration (see Figure 50.11). Within each canal the hair cells form a single cluster, with the hairs projecting into a gelatinous cap called the cupula. Because the three canals are arranged in the three spatial planes, they can detect angular motion of the head in any direction. For example, if you turn your head from left to right, the fluid within the horizontal canal pushes against the cupula, deflecting the hairs. The brain interprets the resulting changes in impulse production by the sensory neurons as turning of the head. If you spin in place, the fluid and canal eventually come to equilibrium and

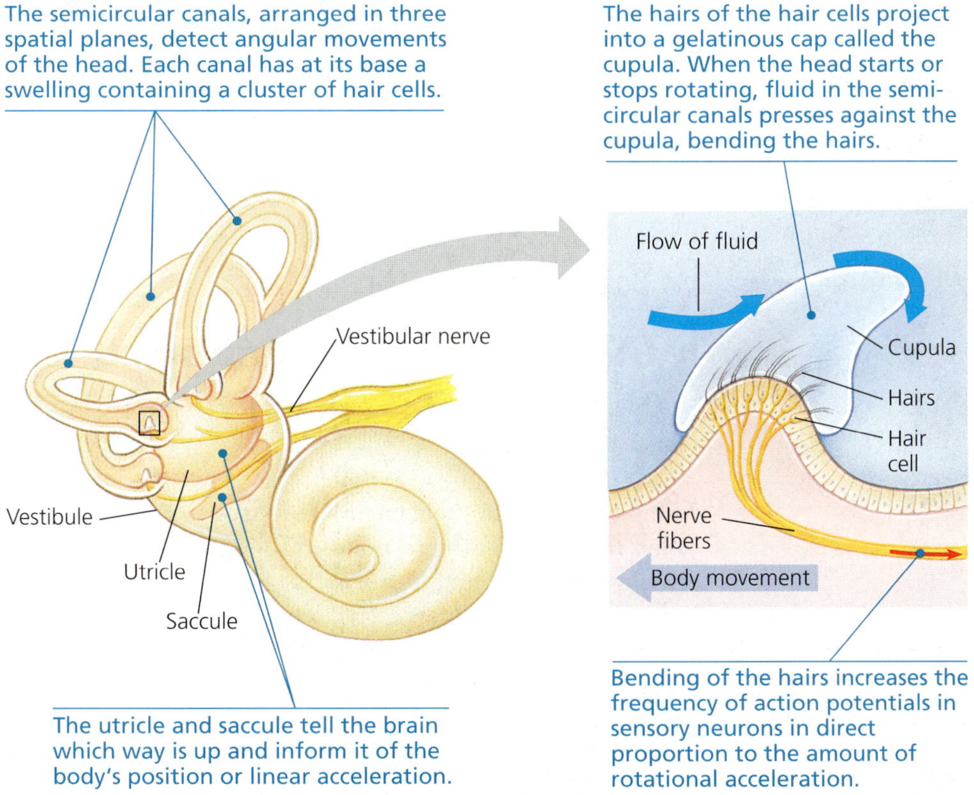

▲ **Figure 50.11 Organs of equilibrium in the inner ear.**

remain in that state until you stop. At that point the moving fluid encounters a stationary cupula, triggering the false sensation of angular motion that we call dizziness.

Hearing and Equilibrium in Other Vertebrates

Unlike the mammalian hearing apparatus, the ear of a fish does not open to the outside of the body and has no eardrum or cochlea. The vibrations of the water caused by sound waves are conducted through the skeleton of the head to a pair of inner ears, setting otoliths in motion and stimulating hair cells. The fish's air-filled swim bladder (see Figure 34.16) also vibrates in response to sound. Some fishes, including catfishes and minnows, have a series of bones that conduct vibrations from the swim bladder to the inner ear.

As discussed in Chapter 34, most fishes and aquatic amphibians also have a **lateral line system** along both sides of their body **(Figure 50.12)**. The system contains mechanoreceptors that detect low-frequency waves by a mechanism similar to that of the mammalian inner ear. Water from the animal's surroundings enters the lateral line system through numerous pores and flows along a tube past the mechanoreceptors. As in our semicircular canals, receptors are formed from a cluster of hair cells whose hairs are embedded in a gelatinous cap, the cupula. Water movement bends the cupula, depolarizing the hair cells and leading to action potentials that are transmitted along the axons of sensory neurons to the brain. In this way, the fish perceives its movement through water or the direction and velocity of water currents flowing over its body. The lateral line system also detects water movements or vibrations generated by prey, predators, and other moving objects.

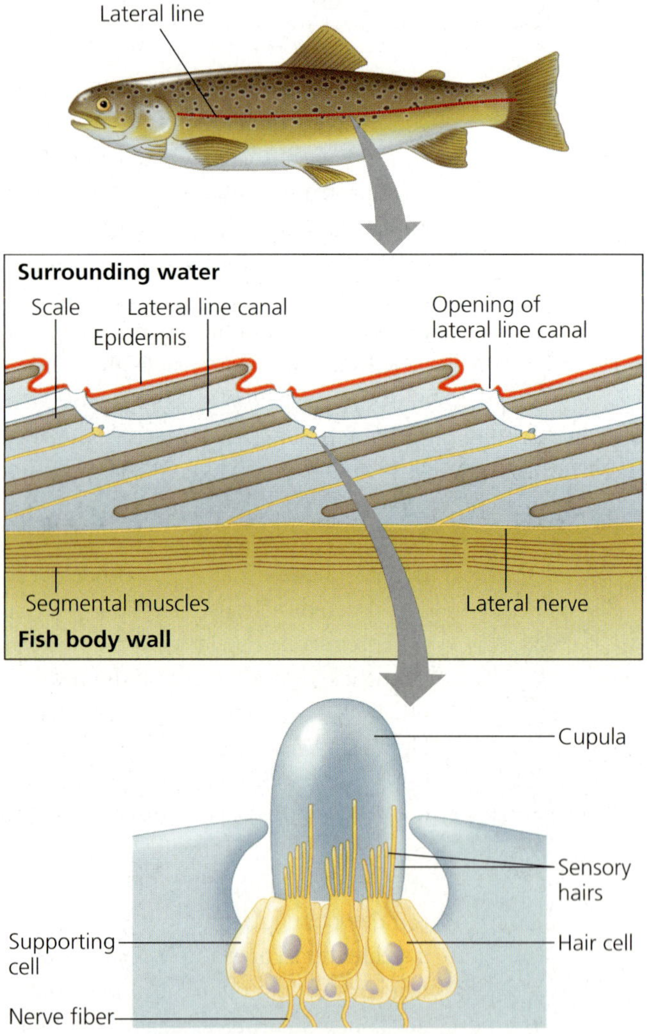

▲ **Figure 50.12 The lateral line system in a fish.** Water flowing through the system bends hair cells. The hair cells transduce the energy into receptor potentials, triggering action potentials that are conveyed to the brain. The lateral line system enables a fish to monitor water currents, pressure waves produced by moving objects, and low-frequency sounds conducted through the water.

In terrestrial vertebrates, the inner ear has evolved as the main organ of hearing and equilibrium. Some amphibians have a lateral line system as tadpoles, but not as adults living on land. In the ear of a terrestrial frog or toad, sound vibrations in the air are conducted to the inner ear by a tympanic membrane on the body surface and a single middle ear bone. Birds, like mammals, have a cochlea. However, as in amphibians, sound is conducted from the tympanic membrane to the inner ear by a single bone.

CONCEPT CHECK 50.2

1. How are statocysts adaptive for animals that burrow underground or live deep in the ocean?
2. **WHAT IF?** Suppose a series of pressure waves in your cochlea causes a vibration of the basilar membrane that moves gradually from the apex toward the base. How would your brain interpret this stimulus?
3. **WHAT IF?** If the stapes became fused to the other middle ear bones or to the oval window, how would this condition affect hearing? Explain.

For suggested answers, see Appendix A.

CONCEPT **50.3**

The senses of taste and smell rely on similar sets of sensory receptors

Many animals use their chemical senses to find mates (as when male silk moths respond to pheromones emitted by females), to recognize territory that has been marked by some chemical substance (as when dogs and cats sniff boundaries that have been staked out by their spraying neighbors), and to help navigate during migration (as when salmon use the unique scent of their streams of origin to return for breeding). Animals such as ants and bees that live in large social groups rely extensively on chemical "conversation." In all animals, chemical senses are important in feeding behavior. For example, a hydra retracts its tentacles toward its mouth when it detects the compound glutathione, which is released from prey captured by the tentacles.

The perceptions of **gustation** (taste) and **olfaction** (smell) both depend on chemoreceptors that detect specific chemicals in the environment. In the case of terrestrial animals, taste is the detection of chemicals called **tastants** that are present in a solution, and smell is the detection of **odorants** that are carried through the air. There is no distinction between taste and smell in aquatic animals.

The taste receptors of insects are located within sensory hairs called sensilla, which are located on the feet and in mouthparts. These animals use their sense of taste to select food. A tasting hair contains several chemoreceptors, each especially responsive to a particular class of tastant, such as sugar or salt. Insects are also capable of smelling airborne odorants using olfactory hairs, usually located on the antennae (see Figure 50.4).

Taste in Mammals

The receptor cells for taste in mammals are modified epithelial cells organized into **taste buds**, which are scattered in several areas of the tongue and mouth **(Figure 50.13)**. Most taste buds on the tongue are associated with nipple-shaped projections called papillae. The receptors in taste buds are responsible for recognizing five types of tastants. Four represent the familiar taste perceptions—sweet, sour, salty, and bitter. The fifth, called umami (Japanese for "delicious"), is elicited by the amino acid glutamate. Often used as a flavor enhancer, monosodium glutamate (MSG) occurs naturally in foods such as meat and aged cheese, imparting a quality sometimes described as savory. Any region of the tongue with taste buds can detect any of the five types of taste. (The frequently reproduced taste maps of the tongue are thus incorrect.)

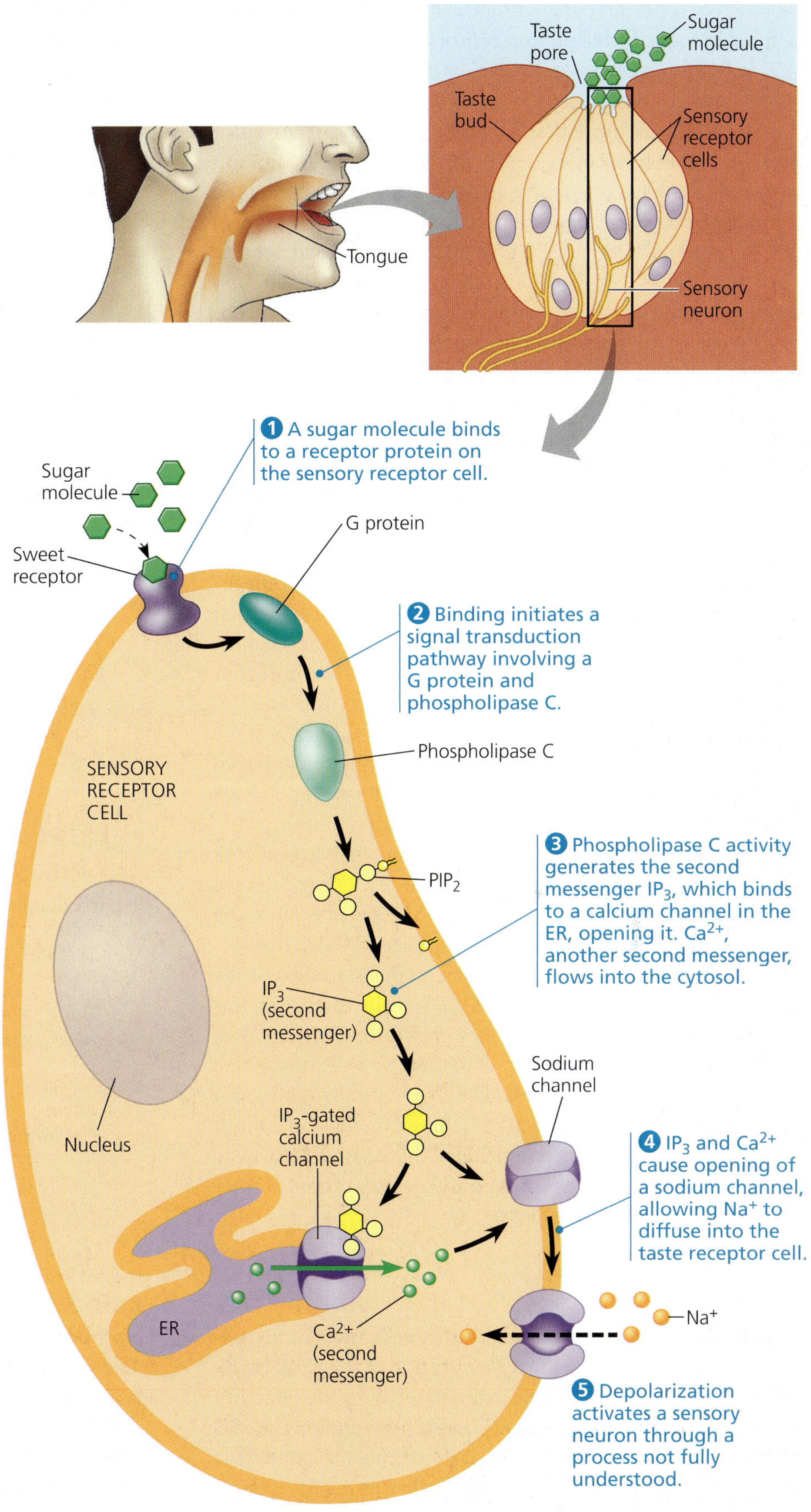

▲ **Figure 50.13 Sensory transduction by a sweet receptor.**

Researchers have identified the receptor proteins for all of the tastes except salty. The receptors fall into two categories, each evolutionarily related to receptors for other senses.

The sensation of sweet, umami, and bitter tastes requires a G protein-coupled receptor, or GPCR (see Figure 11.7). In humans, there are more than 30 different receptors for bitter taste, each able to recognize multiple bitter tastants. In contrast, humans have one type of sweet receptor and one type of umami receptor, each assembled from a different pair of GPCR proteins. Other GPCR proteins are critical for the sense of smell, as we will discuss shortly. Signal transduction to sensory neurons occurs similarly for all GPCR-type receptors; Figure 50.13 illustrates this process for the sweet receptor. Binding of the receptor to the tastant molecule—in this case, a sugar—triggers a signal transduction pathway involving a G protein, the enzyme phospholipase C and the second messengers IP_3 and Ca^{2+}. These second messengers cause opening of an ion channel, allowing an influx of Na^+ that depolarizes the membrane. Scientists are currently exploring how this depolarization leads to sensory neuron activation.

Unlike the other identified taste receptors, the receptor for sour tastants belongs to the TRP (transient receptor potential) family. Formed from a pair of TRP proteins, the sour receptor is similar to the capsaicin receptor and other thermoreceptor proteins. In taste buds, the TRP proteins of the sour receptor assemble into a channel in the plasma membrane of the taste cell. Binding of an acid or other sour-tasting substance to the receptor triggers a change in the ion channel. Depolarization occurs, resulting in activation of a sensory neuron.

For decades, many researchers assumed that a taste cell could have more than one type of receptor. An alternative idea is that each taste cell has a single receptor type, programming the cell to recognize only one of the five tastes. Which hypothesis is correct? In 2005, Ken Mueller, a graduate student at the University of California at San Diego, set out to answer this question. Working in the laboratory of Professor Charles Zuker, Mueller had identified the family of bitter taste receptors. Using a cloned bitter receptor, he was able to genetically reprogram gustation in a mouse **(Figure 50.14)**. Based on these and other experiments, the researchers concluded that an individual taste cell expresses a single receptor type and detects tastants representing only one of the five tastes.

▼ Figure 50.14 Inquiry

How do mammals detect different tastes?

EXPERIMENT To investigate the basis of mammalian taste perception, Ken Mueller, Nick Ryba, and Charles Zuker used a chemical called phenyl-β-D-glucopyranoside (PBDG). Humans find the taste of PBDG extremely bitter. Mice, however, appear to lack a receptor for PBDG. Whereas mice avoid drinking water containing other bitter tastants, they show no aversion to water that contains PBDG.

Using a molecular cloning strategy, Mueller generated mice that made the human PBDG receptor in cells that normally make either a sweet receptor or a bitter receptor. The mice were given a choice of two bottles, one filled with pure water and one filled with water containing PBDG at varying concentrations. The researchers then observed whether the mice had an attraction or an aversion to PBDG.

RESULTS

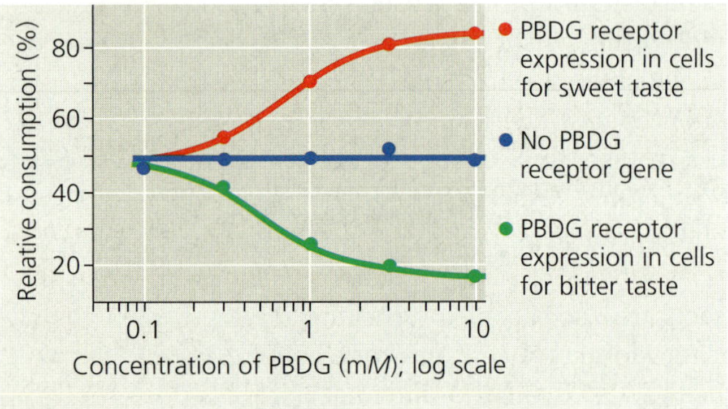

Relative consumption = (Fluid intake from bottle containing PBDG ÷ Total fluid intake) × 100%

CONCLUSION The researchers found that the presence of a bitter receptor in sweet taste cells is sufficient to cause mice to be attracted to a bitter chemical. They concluded that the mammalian brain must therefore perceive sweet or bitter taste solely on the basis of which sensory neurons are activated.

SOURCE K. L. Mueller et al., The receptors and coding logic for bitter taste, *Nature* 434:225–229 (2005).

WHAT IF? Suppose instead of the PBDG receptor the researchers had used a receptor specific for a sweetener that humans crave but mice ignore. How would the results of the experiment have differed?

Smell in Humans

In olfaction, unlike gustation, the sensory cells are neurons. Olfactory receptor cells line the upper portion of the nasal cavity and send impulses along their axons directly to the olfactory bulb of the brain **(Figure 50.15)**. The receptive ends of the cells contain cilia that extend into the layer of mucus coating the nasal cavity. When an odorant diffuses into this region, it binds to a specific GPCR protein called an odorant receptor (OR) on the plasma membrane of the olfactory cilia. These events trigger signal transduction leading to the production of cyclic AMP. In olfactory cells, cyclic AMP opens channels in the plasma membrane that are permeable to both Na^+ and Ca^{2+}. The flow of these ions into the receptor cell leads to depolarization of the membrane, generating action potentials.

Humans can distinguish thousands of different odors, each caused by a structurally distinct odorant. This level of sensory discrimination requires many different ORs. In 1991, Richard Axel and Linda Buck, working at Columbia University, discovered a family of more than 1,000 OR genes—about 3% of all human

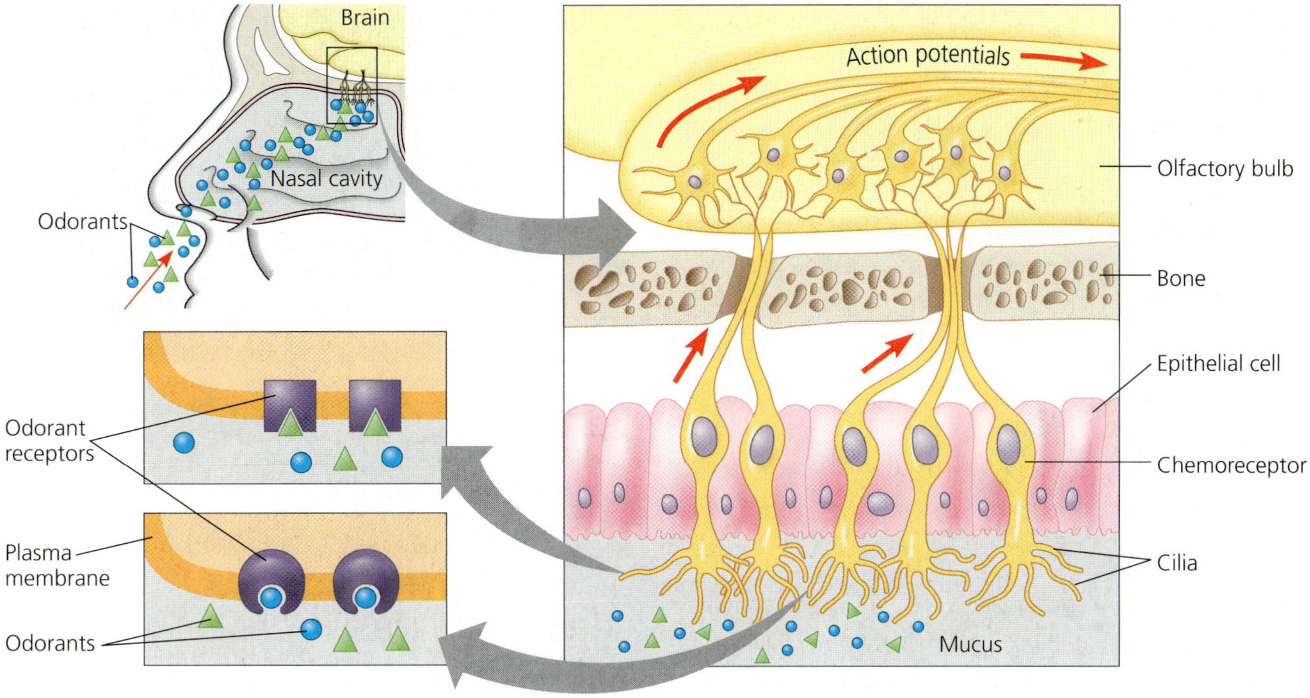

▲ **Figure 50.15 Smell in humans.** Odorant molecules bind to specific receptor proteins in the plasma membrane of olfactory receptor cells, triggering action potentials.

WHAT IF? *If you spray an "air freshener" in a musty room, would you be affecting detection, transmission, or perception of the odorants responsible for the musty smell?*

genes. Each olfactory receptor cell appears to express one OR gene. Cells with different odorant selectivities are interspersed in the nasal cavity. Those cells that express the same OR gene transmit action potentials to the same small region of the olfactory bulb. In 2004, Axel and Buck shared a Nobel Prize for their studies of the gene family and receptors that function in olfaction.

Although the receptors and brain pathways for taste and smell are independent, the two senses do interact. Indeed, much of the complex flavor we experience when eating is due to our sense of smell. If the olfactory system is blocked, as by a head cold, the perception of taste is sharply reduced.

CONCEPT CHECK 50.3

1. Explain why some taste receptor cells and all olfactory receptor cells use G protein-coupled receptors, yet only olfactory receptor cells produce action potentials.
2. Pathways involving G proteins provide an opportunity for an increase in signal strength in the course of signal transduction, a change referred to as amplification. How might this be beneficial in olfaction?
3. WHAT IF? If you discovered a mutation in mice that disrupted the ability to taste sweet, bitter, and umami, but not sour or salty, what might you predict about where this mutation acts in the signaling pathways used by these receptors?

For suggested answers, see Appendix A.

CONCEPT 50.4

Similar mechanisms underlie vision throughout the animal kingdom

Many types of light detectors have evolved in the animal kingdom, from simple clusters of cells that detect only the direction and intensity of light to complex organs that form images.

Vision in Invertebrates

Most invertebrates have some kind of light-detecting organ. One of the simplest is the ocellus (plural, *ocelli*) of planarians **(Figure 50.16)**. A pair of ocelli, which are sometimes called eyespots or eyecups, are located in the head region. The ocelli are surrounded on three sides by a layer of darkly pigmented cells that block light. Light shining on the planarian stimulates light-sensitive cells called **photoreceptors** in each ocellus only through the opening where there are no pigmented cells. Because the opening of one ocellus faces left and slightly forward and that of the other ocellus faces right and forward, light shining from one side of the planarian stimulates only the ocellus on that side. The planarian brain compares the rate of action potentials coming from the two ocelli and directs turning movements that minimize the stimulation of both ocelli. The result is that the planarian moves away from the light source

(a) The planarian's brain directs the body to turn until the sensations from the two ocelli are equal and minimal, causing the animal to move away from light.

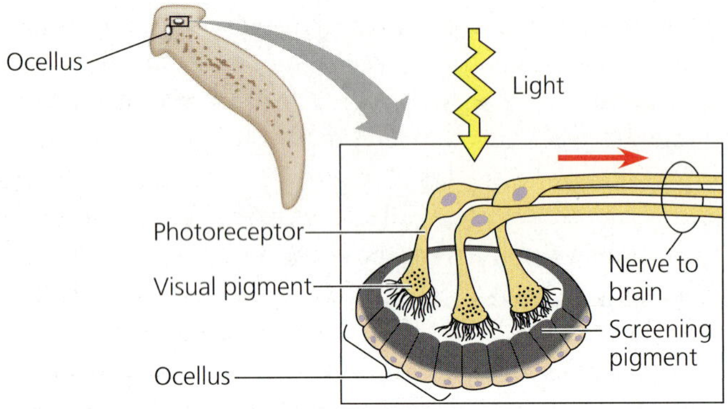

(b) Whereas light striking the front of an ocellus excites the photoreceptors, light striking the back is blocked by the screening pigment. In this way, the ocelli indicate the direction of a light source, triggering the light avoidance behavior.

▲ **Figure 50.16 Ocelli and orientation behavior of a planarian.**

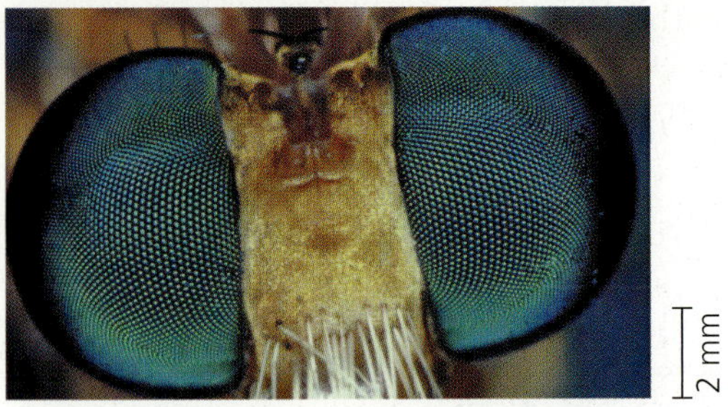

(a) The faceted eyes on the head of a fly, photographed with a stereomicroscope.

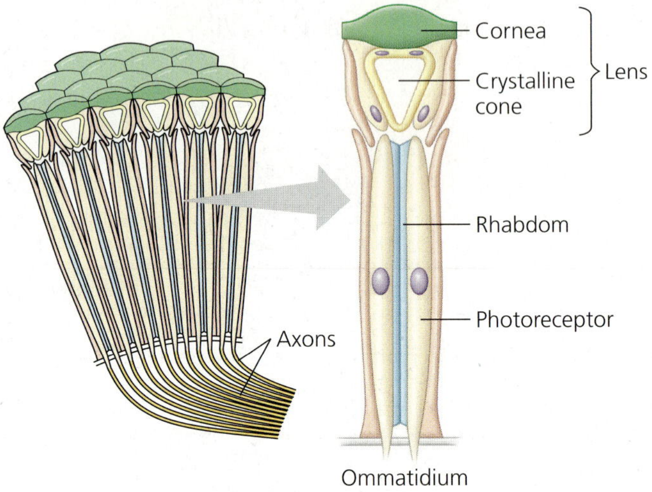

(b) The cornea and crystalline cone of each ommatidium together function as a lens that focuses light on the rhabdom, a stack of pigmented plates of microvilli extending inward from a circle of photoreceptors. The rhabdom traps light, serving as the photosensitive part of the ommatidium. Information gathered from different intensities of light entering the many ommatidia from different angles is used to form a visual image.

▲ **Figure 50.17 Compound eyes.**

until it reaches a shaded location, where a rock or other object is likely to hide the animal from predators.

Two major types of image-forming eyes have evolved in invertebrates: the compound eye and the single-lens eye. **Compound eyes** are found in insects and crustaceans (phylum Arthropoda) and in some polychaete worms (phylum Annelida). A compound eye consists of up to several thousand light detectors called **ommatidia** (the "facets" of the eye), each with its own light-focusing lens **(Figure 50.17)**. Each ommatidium detects light from a tiny portion of the visual field. A compound eye is very effective at detecting movement, an important adaptation for flying insects and small animals constantly threatened with predation. Whereas the human eye can distinguish only about 50 flashes of light per second, the compound eyes of some insects can detect flickering at six times that rate. (If they slipped into a movie theater, these insects could easily resolve each frame of the film being projected as a separate still image). Insects also have excellent color vision, and some (including bees) can see into the ultraviolet (UV) range of the electromagnetic spectrum. Because UV light is invisible to us, we miss seeing differences in the environment that bees and other insects detect. In studying animal behavior, we cannot extrapolate our sensory world to other species; different animals have different sensitivities and different brain organizations.

Among invertebrates, **single-lens eyes** are found in some jellies and polychaetes, as well as spiders and many molluscs. A single-lens eye works on a camera-like principle. The eye of an octopus or squid, for example, has a small opening, the **pupil**, through which light enters. Like a camera's adjustable aperture, the **iris** contracts or expands, changing the diameter of the pupil to let in more or less light. Behind the pupil, a single lens focuses light on a layer of photoreceptors. Similar to a camera's focusing action, muscles in an invertebrate's single-lens eye move the lens forward or backward, focusing on objects at different distances.

The Vertebrate Visual System

We turn next to the eyes of vertebrates, which differ from the single-lens eyes of invertebrates in several respects. Although the eye is the first stage in vision, remember that it is actually the brain that "sees." Thus, to understand vision, we must examine how action potentials arise in the vertebrate eye and then follow these signals to the visual centers of the brain, where images are perceived.

Structure of the Eye

The globe of the vertebrate eye, or eyeball, consists of the **sclera**, a tough white outer layer of connective tissue, and a thin, pigmented inner layer called the **choroid** **(Figure 50.18)**. At the front of the eye, the sclera becomes the transparent **cornea**, which lets light into the eye and acts as a fixed lens. Also at the front of the eye, the choroid forms the doughnut-shaped iris, which gives the eye its color. By changing size, the iris regulates the amount of light entering the pupil, the hole in the center of the iris. Just inside the choroid, the **retina** forms the innermost layer of the eyeball and contains layers of neurons and photoreceptors. Information from the photoreceptors leaves the eye at the optic disk, a spot on the lower outside of the retina where the optic nerve attaches to the eye. Because there are no photoreceptors in the optic disk, it forms a "blind spot": Light focused onto that part of the retina is not detected.

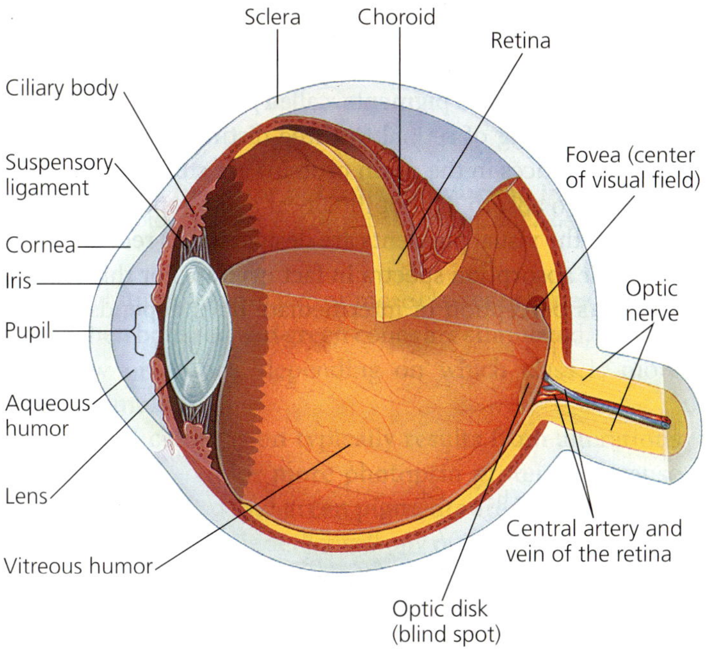

▲ **Figure 50.18 Structure of the vertebrate eye.** In this longitudinal section of the eye, the jellylike vitreous humor is illustrated only in the lower half of the eyeball. The conjunctiva, a mucous membrane that surrounds the sclera, is not shown.

The **lens** and **ciliary body** divide the eye into two cavities, an anterior cavity between the cornea and the lens and a much larger posterior cavity behind the lens. The ciliary body constantly produces the clear, watery **aqueous humor** that fills the anterior cavity. Blockage of the ducts that drain the aqueous humor can produce glaucoma, a condition in which increased pressure in the eye damages the optic nerve, causing vision loss and sometimes blindness. The posterior cavity, filled with the jellylike **vitreous humor**, constitutes most of the volume of the eye. The lens itself is a transparent disk of protein. Many fishes focus by moving the lens forward or backward, as do squids and octopuses. Humans and other mammals, however, focus by changing the shape of the lens **(Figure 50.19)**. When focusing on a close object, the lens becomes almost spherical. When viewing a distant object, the lens is flattened.

The human retina contains **rods** and **cones**, two types of photoreceptors that differ in shape and in function. Rods are more sensitive to light but do not distinguish colors; they enable us to see at night, but only in black and white. Cones provide color vision, but, being less sensitive, contribute very little to night vision. There are three types of cones. Each has a different sensitivity across the visible spectrum, providing an optimal response to red, green, or blue light.

The relative numbers of rod and cones in the retina varies among different animals, correlating to some degree with the extent to which an animal is active at night. Most fishes, amphibians, and reptiles, including birds, have strong color vision. Humans and other primates also see color well, but are among the minority of mammals with this ability. Many mammals are nocturnal, and having a high proportion of rods in the retina is an adaptation that gives these animals keen night vision. Cats, for instance, are usually most active at night; they have limited color vision and probably see a pastel world during the day.

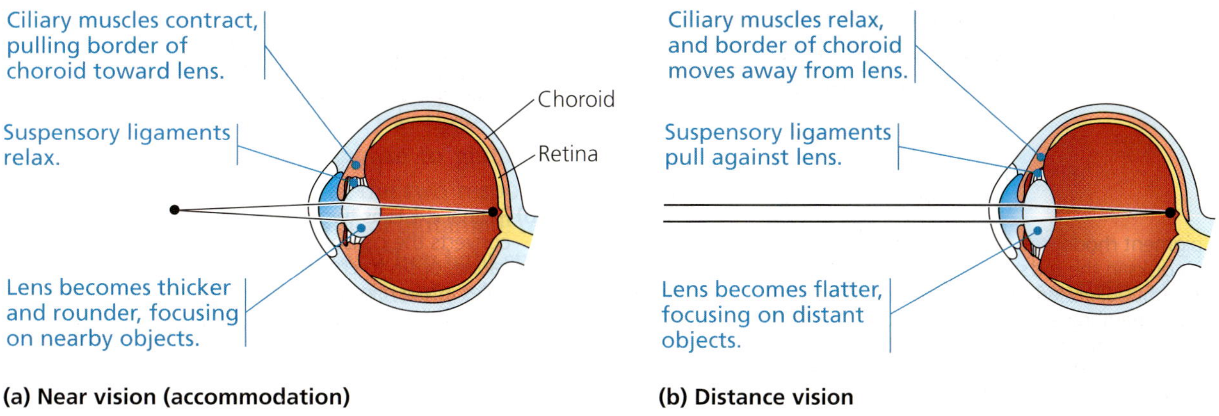

◀ **Figure 50.19 Focusing in the mammalian eye.** Ciliary muscles control the shape of the lens, which bends light and focuses it on the retina. The thicker the lens, the more sharply the light is bent.

hierarchy of smaller and smaller units **(Figure 50.25)**. Most skeletal muscles consist of a bundle of long fibers running parallel to the length of the muscle. Each fiber is a single cell with multiple nuclei, reflecting its formation by the fusion of many embryonic cells. A muscle fiber contains a bundle of smaller **myofibrils** arranged longitudinally. The myofibrils, in turn, are composed of thin filaments and thick filaments. **Thin filaments** consist of two strands of actin and two strands of a regulatory protein (not shown here) coiled around one another. **Thick filaments** are staggered arrays of myosin molecules.

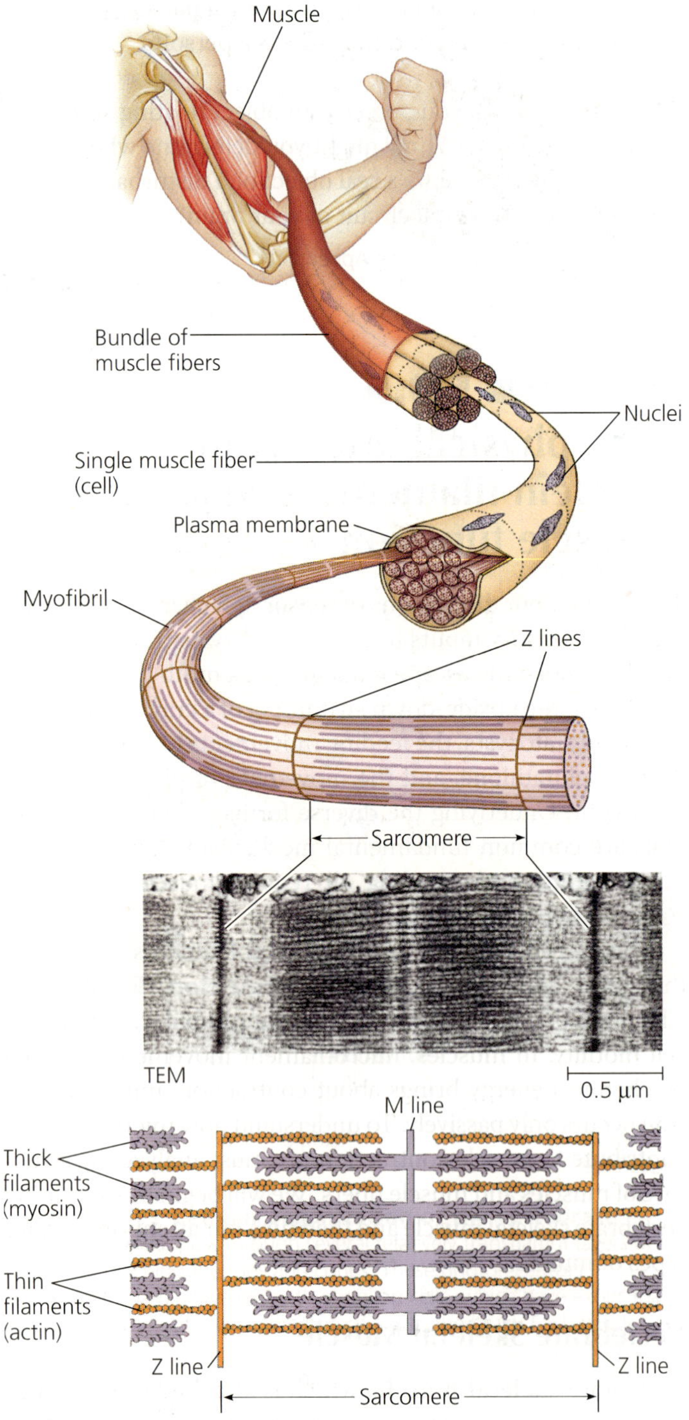

▲ **Figure 50.25 The structure of skeletal muscle.**

Skeletal muscle is also called **striated muscle** because the regular arrangement of the filaments creates a pattern of light and dark bands. Each repeating unit is a **sarcomere**, the basic contractile unit of the muscle. The borders of the sarcomere are lined up in adjacent myofibrils and contribute to the striations visible with a light microscope. Thin filaments are attached at the Z lines and project toward the center of the sarcomere, while thick filaments are attached at the M lines centered in the sarcomere. In a muscle fiber at rest, thick and thin filaments only partially overlap. Near the edge of the sarcomere are only thin filaments, whereas the zone in the center contains only thick filaments. This arrangement is the key to how the sarcomere, and hence the whole muscle, contracts.

The Sliding-Filament Model of Muscle Contraction

We can explain much of what happens during contraction of a whole muscle by focusing on a single sarcomere **(Figure 50.26)**. According to the **sliding-filament model** of muscle contraction, neither the thin filaments nor the thick filaments change in length when the sarcomere shortens; rather, the filaments slide past each other longitudinally, increasing the overlap of the thin and thick filaments.

The sliding of the filaments is based on the interaction between the myosin and actin molecules that make up the thick and thin filaments. Each myosin molecule consists of a long "tail" region and a globular "head" region extending to the side. The tail adheres to the tails of other myosin molecules that form the thick filament. The head is the center of bioenergetic reactions that power muscle contractions. It can bind ATP and hydrolyze it into ADP and inorganic phosphate. As shown in **Figure 50.27**, hydrolysis of ATP converts myosin to a high-energy form that can bind to actin, form a cross-bridge, and pull the thin filament toward the center of the sarcomere. The cross-bridge is broken when a new molecule of ATP binds to the myosin head. In a repeating cycle, the free head cleaves the new ATP and attaches to a new binding site on another actin molecule farther along the thin filament. Each of the approximately 350 heads of a thick filament forms and reforms about five cross-bridges per second, driving filaments past each other.

A typical muscle fiber at rest contains only enough ATP for a few contractions. The energy needed for repetitive contractions is stored in two other compounds: creatine phosphate and glycogen. Creatine phosphate can transfer a phosphate group to ADP to synthesize additional ATP. The resting supply of creatine phosphate is sufficient to sustain contractions for about 15 seconds. Glycogen is broken down to glucose, which can be used to generate ATP by either aerobic respiration or glycolysis (and lactic acid fermentation; see Chapter 9). Using the glucose

▶ **Figure 50.26 The sliding-filament model of muscle contraction.** The drawings on the left show that the lengths of the thick (myosin) filaments (purple) and thin (actin) filaments (orange) remain the same as a muscle fiber contracts.

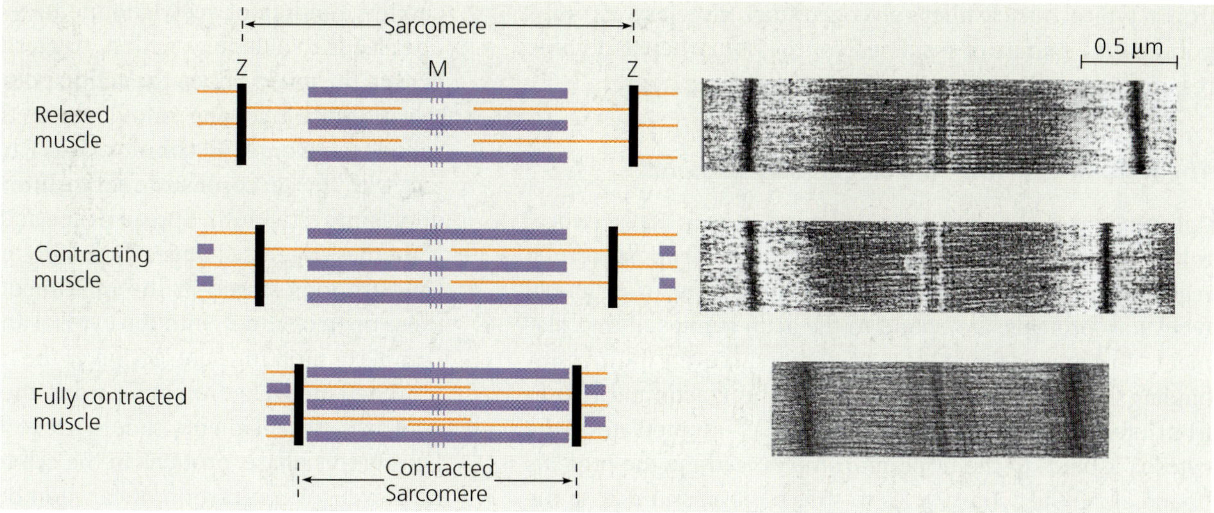

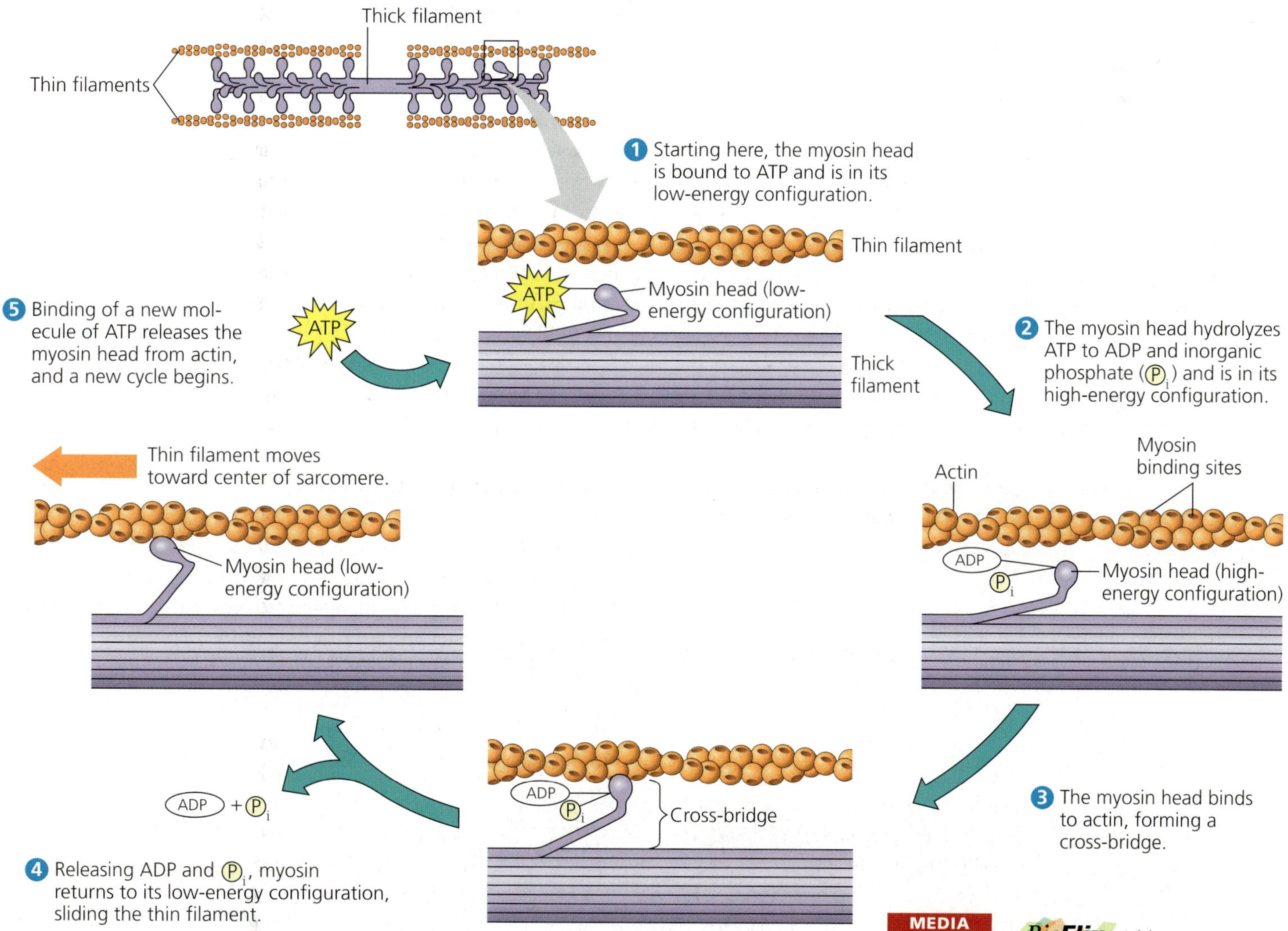

▲ **Figure 50.27 Myosin-actin interactions underlying muscle fiber contraction.**

? *When ATP binds, what prevents the filaments from sliding back into their original positions?*

MEDIA **BioFlix** Visit **www.campbellbiology.com** for the BioFlix 3-D Animation on Muscle Contraction.

from a typical muscle fiber's glycogen store, glycolysis can support about 1 minute of sustained contraction, whereas aerobic respiration can power contractions for nearly an hour.

The Role of Calcium and Regulatory Proteins

Calcium ions (Ca^{2+}) and proteins bound to actin play a critical role in muscle cell contraction and relaxation. **Tropomyosin**, a regulatory protein, and the **troponin complex**, a set of additional regulatory proteins, are bound to the actin strands of thin filaments. In a muscle fiber at rest, tropomyosin covers the myosin-binding sites along the thin filament, preventing actin and myosin from interacting **(Figure 50.28a)**. When Ca^{2+} accumulates in the cytosol, it binds to the troponin complex, causing the proteins bound along the actin strands to shift position and expose the myosin-binding sites on the thin filament **(Figure 50.28b)**. Thus, when the Ca^{2+} concentration rises in the cytosol, the thin and thick filaments slide past each other, and the muscle fiber contracts. When the Ca^{2+} concentration falls, the binding sites are covered, and contraction stops.

Motor neurons cause muscle contraction by triggering release of Ca^{2+} into the cytosol of muscle cells with which they form synapses. This regulation of Ca^{2+} concentration is a multistep process involving a network of membranes and compartments within the muscle cell. As you read the following description, refer to the overview and diagram in **Figure 50.29**.

The arrival of an action potential at the synaptic terminal of a motor neuron causes release of the neurotransmitter acetylcholine. Binding of acetylcholine to receptors on the muscle fiber leads to a depolarization, triggering an action potential. Within the muscle fiber, the action potential spreads deep into the interior, following infoldings of the plasma membrane called **transverse (T) tubules**. The T tubules make close contact with the **sarcoplasmic reticulum (SR)**, a specialized endoplasmic reticulum. Spread of the action potential along the T tubules triggers changes in the SR, opening Ca^{2+} channels. Calcium ions stored in the interior of the SR flow through these open channels into the cytosol and bind to the troponin complex, initiating contraction of the muscle fiber.

When motor neuron input stops, the muscle cell relaxes. As it relaxes, the filaments slide back to their starting position. During this phase, proteins in the cell reset the muscle for the next cycle of contraction. Relaxation begins as transport proteins in the SR pump Ca^{2+} out of the cytosol. When the Ca^{2+} concentration in the cytosol is low, the regulatory proteins bound to the thin filament shift back to their starting position, once again blocking the myosin-binding sites. At the same time, the Ca^{2+} pumped from the cytosol accumulates in the SR, providing the stores needed to respond to the next action potential.

Several diseases cause paralysis by interfering with the excitation of skeletal muscle fibers by motor neurons. In amyotrophic lateral sclerosis (ALS), also called Lou Gehrig's disease, motor neurons in the spinal cord and brainstem degenerate, and the muscle fibers with which they synapse atrophy. ALS is progressive and usually fatal within five years after symptoms appear; currently there is no cure or treatment. Myasthenia gravis is an autoimmune disease in which a person produces antibodies to the acetylcholine receptors on skeletal muscle fibers. As the number of these receptors decreases, synaptic transmission between motor neurons and muscle fibers declines. Fortunately, effective treatments are available for this disease.

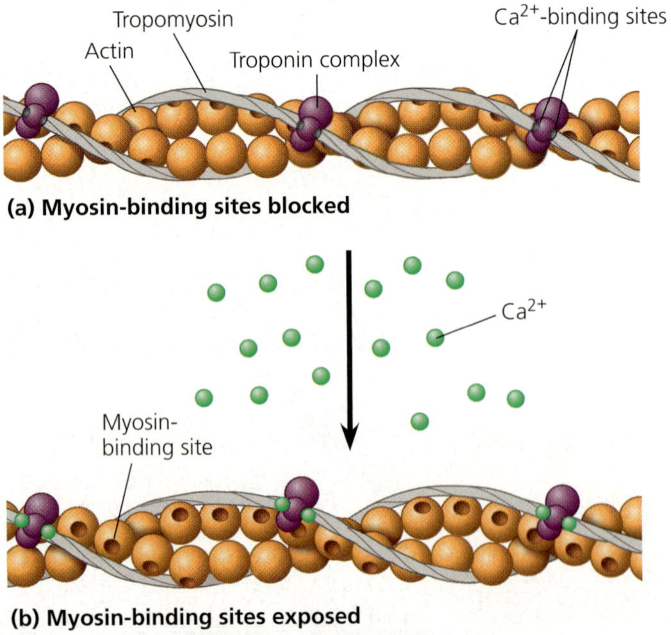

▲ **Figure 50.28 The role of regulatory proteins and calcium in muscle fiber contraction.** Each thin filament consists of two strands of actin, tropomyosin, and the troponin complex.

Nervous Control of Muscle Tension

Whereas contraction of a single skeletal muscle fiber is a brief all-or-none twitch, contraction of a whole muscle, such as the biceps in your upper arm, is graded; you can voluntarily alter the extent and strength of its contraction. There are two basic mechanisms by which the nervous system produces graded contractions of whole muscles: (1) by varying the number of muscle fibers that contract and (2) by varying the rate at which muscle fibers are stimulated. Let's consider each mechanism in turn.

In a vertebrate skeletal muscle, each muscle fiber is controlled by only one motor neuron, but each branched motor neuron may form synapses with many muscle fibers. There may be hundreds of motor neurons controlling a muscle, each with its own pool of muscle fibers scattered throughout the muscle. A **motor unit** consists of a single motor neuron and all the muscle fibers it controls. When a motor neuron produces an action potential,

▼ **Figure 50.29**

Exploring The Regulation of Skeletal Muscle Contraction

The electrical, chemical, and molecular events regulating skeletal muscle contraction are shown in a cutaway view of a muscle cell and in the enlarged diagram below. Action potentials (red arrows) triggered by the motor neuron sweep across the muscle fiber and into it along the transverse (T) tubules, initiating the movements of calcium (green dots) that regulate muscle activity.

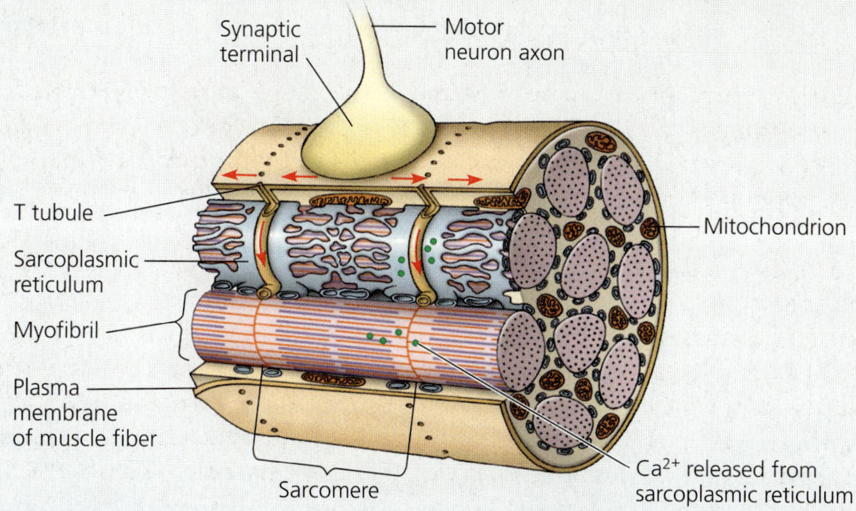

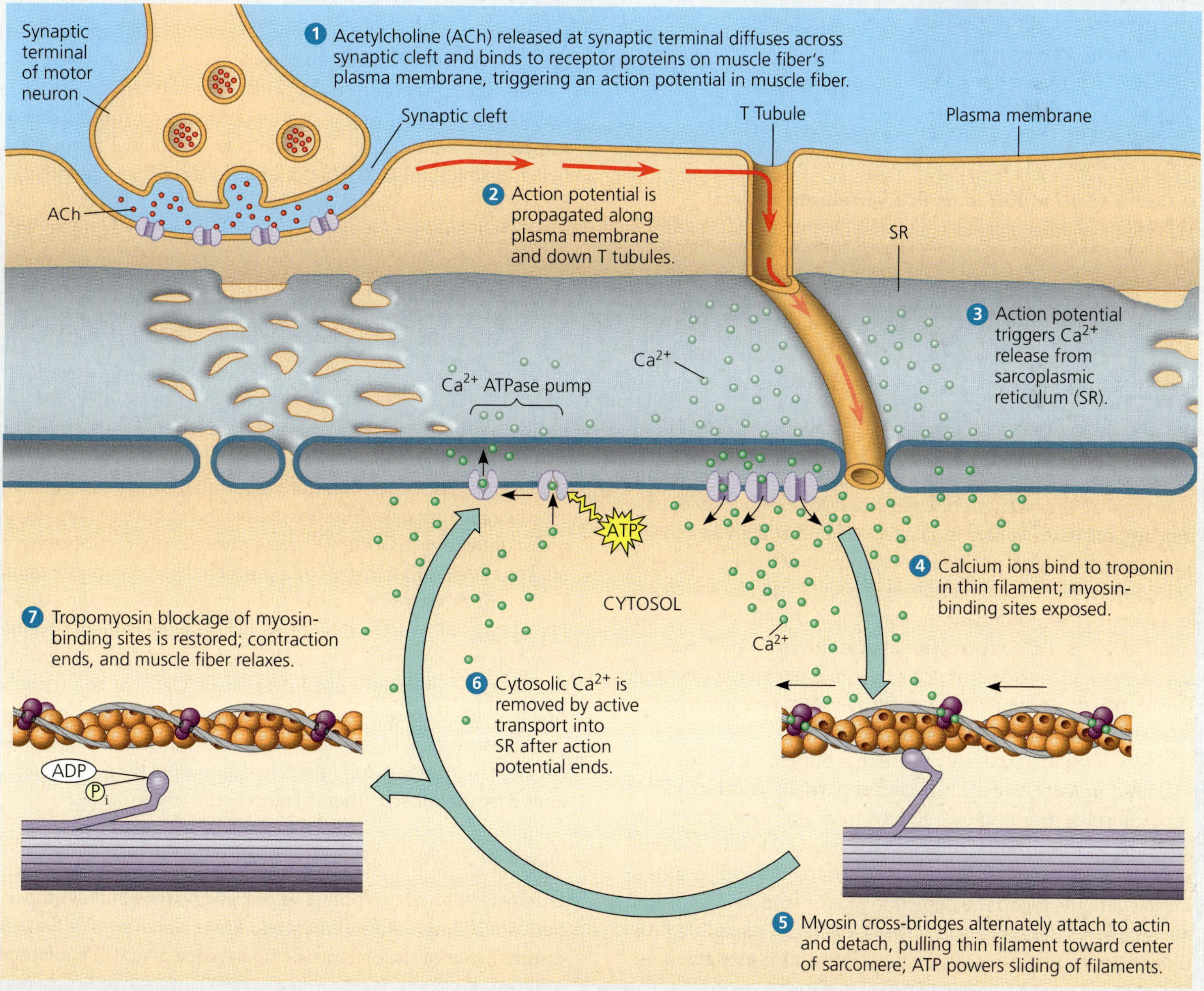

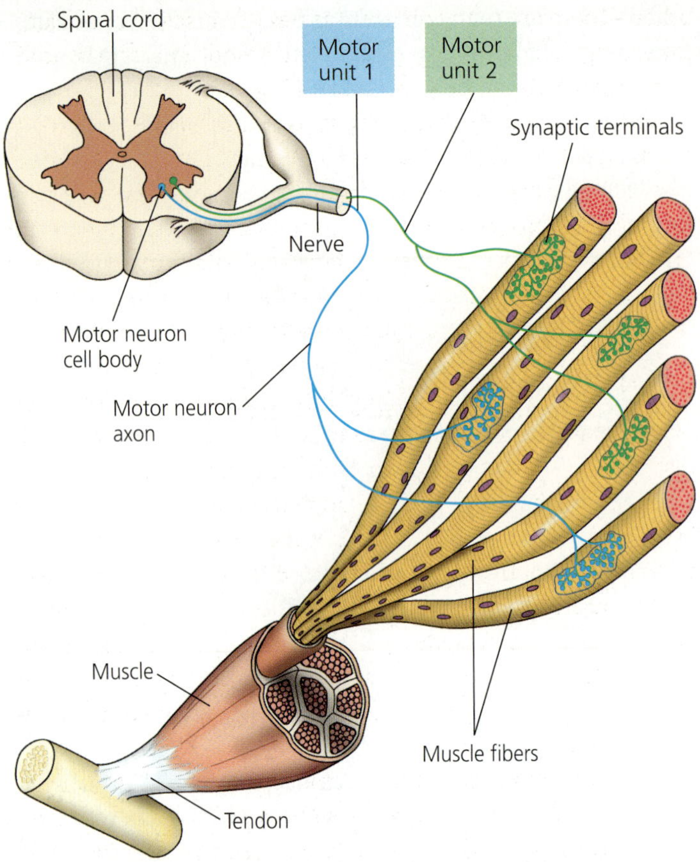

▲ **Figure 50.30 Motor units in a vertebrate skeletal muscle.** Each muscle fiber (cell) has a single synapse with one motor neuron, but each motor neuron typically synapses with many muscle fibers. A motor neuron and all the muscle fibers it controls constitute a motor unit.

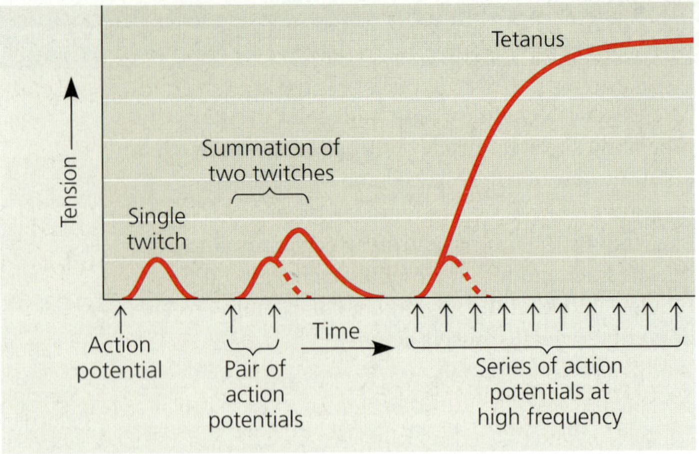

▲ **Figure 50.31 Summation of twitches.** This graph compares the tension developed in a muscle fiber in response to a single action potential in a motor neuron, a pair of action potentials, and a series of action potentials. The dashed lines show the tension that would have developed if only the first action potential had occurred.

all the muscle fibers in its motor unit contract as a group **(Figure 50.30)**. The strength of the resulting contraction depends on how many muscle fibers the motor neuron controls. In most muscles, the number of muscle fibers in different motor units ranges from a few to hundreds. The nervous system can thus regulate the strength of contraction in a muscle by determining how many motor units are activated at a given instant and by selecting large or small motor units to activate. The force (tension) developed by a muscle progressively increases as more and more of the motor neurons controlling the muscle are activated, a process called **recruitment** of motor neurons. Depending on the number of motor neurons your brain recruits and the size of their motor units, you can lift a fork or something much heavier, like your biology textbook.

Some muscles, especially those that hold up the body and maintain posture, are almost always partially contracted. In such muscles, the nervous system may alternate activation among the motor units, reducing the length of time any one set of fibers is contracted. Prolonged contraction can result in muscle fatigue due to the depletion of ATP and dissipation of ion gradients required for normal electrical signaling. Although accumulation of lactate (see Figure 9.18) may also contribute to muscle fatigue, recent research actually points to a beneficial effect of lactate on muscle function.

The second mechanism by which the nervous system produces graded whole-muscle contractions is by varying the rate of muscle fiber stimulation. A single action potential produces a twitch lasting about 100 msec or less. If a second action potential arrives before the muscle fiber has completely relaxed, the two twitches add together, resulting in greater tension **(Figure 50.31)**. Further summation occurs as the rate of stimulation increases. When the rate is high enough that the muscle fiber cannot relax at all between stimuli, the twitches fuse into one smooth, sustained contraction called **tetanus** (not to be confused with the disease of the same name). Motor neurons usually deliver their action potentials in rapid-fire volleys, and the resulting summation of tension results in the smooth contraction typical of tetanus rather than the jerky actions of individual twitches.

The increase in tension during summation and tetanus occurs because muscle fibers are connected to bones via tendons and connective tissues. When a muscle fiber contracts, it stretches these elastic structures, which then transmit tension to the bones. In a single twitch, the muscle fiber begins to relax before the elastic structures are fully stretched. During summation, however, the high-frequency action potentials maintain an elevated concentration of Ca^{2+} in the muscle fiber's cytosol, prolonging cross-bridge cycling and causing greater stretching of the elastic structures. During tetanus, the elastic structures are fully stretched, and all of the tension generated by the muscle fiber is transmitted to the bones.

Types of Skeletal Muscle Fibers

Our discussion to this point has focused on the general properties of vertebrate skeletal muscles. There are, however, several distinct types of skeletal muscle fibers, each of which is adapted to a particular set of functions. Scientists typically classify these varied fiber types either by the source of ATP used to power muscle activity or by the speed of muscle contraction. We'll consider each of the two classification schemes.

Oxidative and Glycolytic Fibers Fibers that rely mostly on aerobic respiration are called oxidative fibers. Such fibers are specialized in ways that enable them to make use of a steady energy supply: They have many mitochondria, a rich blood supply, and a large amount of an oxygen-storing protein called **myoglobin**. Myoglobin, a brownish red pigment, binds oxygen more tightly than does hemoglobin, so it can effectively extract oxygen from the blood. A second class of fibers use glycolysis as their primary source of ATP and are called glycolytic fibers. Having a larger diameter and less myoglobin than oxidative fibers, glycolytic fibers fatigue much more readily. The two fiber types are readily apparent in the muscle of poultry and fish: The light meat is composed of glycolytic fibers, and the dark meat is made up of oxidative fibers rich in myoglobin.

Fast-Twitch and Slow-Twitch Fibers Muscle fibers vary in the speed with which they contract, with **fast-twitch fibers** developing tension two to three times faster than **slow-twitch fibers**. Fast fibers are used for brief, rapid, powerful contractions. Slow fibers, often found in muscles that maintain posture, can sustain long contractions. A slow fiber has less sarcoplasmic reticulum and pumps Ca^{2+} more slowly than a fast fiber. Because Ca^{2+} remains in the cytosol longer, a muscle twitch in a slow fiber lasts about five times as long as one in a fast fiber.

The difference in contraction speed between slow-twitch and fast-twitch fibers mainly reflects the rate at which their myosin heads hydrolyze ATP. However, there isn't a one-to-one relationship between contraction speed and ATP source. Whereas all slow-twitch fibers are oxidative, fast-twitch fibers can be either glycolytic or oxidative.

Most human skeletal muscles contain both fast- and slow-twitch fibers, although the muscles of the eye and hand are exclusively fast twitch. In a muscle that has a mixture of fast and slow fibers, the relative proportions of each are genetically determined. However, if such a muscle is used repeatedly for activities requiring high endurance, some fast glycolytic fibers can develop into fast oxidative fibers. Because fast oxidative fibers fatigue more slowly than fast glycolytic fibers, the result will be a muscle that is more resistant to fatigue.

Some vertebrates have skeletal muscle fibers that twitch at rates far faster than any human muscle. For example, both the rattlesnake's rattle and the dove's coo are produced by superfast muscles that can contract and relax every 10 msec.

Other Types of Muscle

Although all muscles share the same fundamental mechanism of contraction—actin and myosin filaments sliding past each other—there are many different types of muscle. Vertebrates, for example, have cardiac muscle and smooth muscle in addition to skeletal muscle (see Figure 40.5).

Vertebrate **cardiac muscle** is found in only one place—the heart. Like skeletal muscle, cardiac muscle is striated. However, structural differences between skeletal and cardiac muscle fibers result in differences in their electrical and membrane properties. Whereas skeletal muscle fibers do not produce action potentials unless stimulated by a motor neuron, cardiac muscle cells have ion channels in their plasma membrane that cause rhythmic depolarizations, triggering action potentials without input from the nervous system. Action potentials of cardiac muscle cells last up to 20 times longer than those of the skeletal muscle fibers. Plasma membranes of adjacent cardiac muscle cells interlock at specialized regions called **intercalated disks**, where gap junctions (see Figure 6.32) provide direct electrical coupling between the cells. Thus, the action potential generated by specialized cells in one part of the heart spreads to all other cardiac muscle cells, causing the whole heart to contract. A long refractory period prevents summation and tetanus.

Smooth muscle in vertebrates is found mainly in the walls of hollow organs, such as blood vessels and organs of the digestive tract. Smooth muscle cells lack striations because their actin and myosin filaments are not regularly arrayed along the length of the cell. Instead, the thick filaments are scattered throughout the cytoplasm, and the thin filaments are attached to structures called dense bodies, some of which are tethered to the plasma membrane. There is less myosin than in striated muscle fibers, and the myosin is not associated with specific actin strands. Some smooth muscle cells contract only when stimulated by neurons of the autonomic nervous system. Others can generate action potentials without input from neurons—they are electrically coupled to one another. Smooth muscles contract and relax more slowly than striated muscles.

Although smooth muscle contraction is regulated by Ca^{2+}, the mechanism for regulation is different from that in skeletal and cardiac muscle. Smooth muscle cells have no troponin complex or T tubules, and their sarcoplasmic reticulum is not well developed. During an action potential, Ca^{2+} enters the cytosol mainly through the plasma membrane. Calcium ions cause contraction by binding to the protein calmodulin, which activates an enzyme that phosphorylates the myosin head, enabling cross-bridge activity.

Invertebrates have muscle cells similar to vertebrate skeletal and smooth muscle cells, and arthropod skeletal muscles are nearly identical to those of vertebrates. However, the flight muscles of insects are capable of independent, rhythmic contraction, so the wings of some insects can actually beat faster than action potentials can arrive from the central nervous system. Another interesting evolutionary adaptation has been discovered in the muscles that hold a clam's shell closed. The thick filaments in these muscles contain a protein called paramyosin that enables the muscles to remain contracted for as long as a month with only a low rate of energy consumption.

CONCEPT CHECK 50.5

1. How can the nervous system cause a skeletal muscle to produce the most forceful contraction it is capable of?
2. Contrast the role of Ca^{2+} in the contraction of a skeletal muscle fiber and a smooth muscle cell.
3. **WHAT IF?** Why are the muscles of an animal that has recently died likely to be stiff?

For suggested answers, see Appendix A.

CONCEPT 50.6

Skeletal systems transform muscle contraction into locomotion

So far we have focused on muscles as effectors for nervous system output. To move an animal in part or in whole, muscles must work in concert with the skeleton. Unlike the softer tissues in an animal body, the skeleton provides a rigid structure to which muscles can attach. Because muscles exert force only during contraction, moving a body part back and forth typically requires two muscles attached to the same section of the skeleton. We can see such an arrangement of muscles in the upper portion of a human arm or grasshopper leg **(Figure 50.32)**. Although we call such muscles an antagonistic pair, their function is actually cooperative, coordinated by the nervous system. For example, when you extend your arm, motor neurons trigger your triceps muscle to contract while the absence of neuronal input allows your biceps to relax.

Skeletons function in support and protection as well as movement. Most land animals would sag from their own weight if they had no skeleton to support them. Even an animal living in water would be a formless mass without a framework to maintain its shape. In many animals, a hard skeleton also protects soft tissues. For example, the vertebrate skull protects the brain, and the ribs of terrestrial vertebrates form a cage around the heart, lungs, and other internal organs.

Types of Skeletal Systems

Although we tend to think of skeletons only as interconnected sets of bones, skeletons come in many different forms. Hardened support structures can be external (as in exoskeletons), internal (as in endoskeletons), or even absent (as in fluid-based or hydrostatic skeletons).

Hydrostatic Skeletons

A **hydrostatic skeleton** consists of fluid held under pressure in a closed body compartment. This is the main type of skeleton in most cnidarians, flatworms, nematodes, and annelids (see Chapter 33). These animals control their form and movement by using muscles to change the shape of fluid-filled compartments. Among the cnidarians, for example, a hydra elongates by closing its mouth and using contractile cells in its body wall to constrict its central gastrovascular cavity.

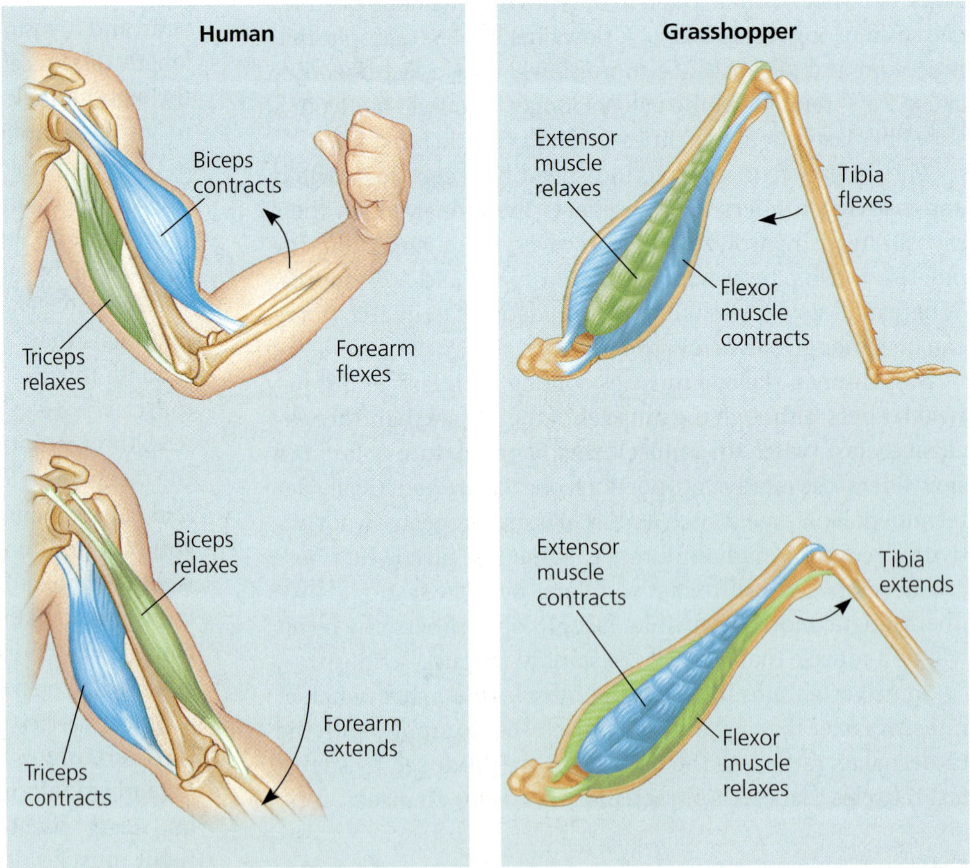

▲ **Figure 50.32 The interaction of muscles and skeletons in movement.** Back-and-forth movement of a body part is generally accomplished by antagonistic muscles. This arrangement works with either an internal skeleton, as in mammals, or an external skeleton, as in insects.

Because water cannot be compressed very much, decreasing the diameter of the cavity forces the cavity to become longer.

Worms use hydrostatic skeletons in diverse ways to move through their environment. In planarians and other flatworms, the interstitial fluid is kept under pressure and functions as the main hydrostatic skeleton. Planarian movement results mainly from muscles in the body wall exerting localized forces against the hydrostatic skeleton. Nematodes (roundworms) hold fluid in their body cavity, which is a pseudocoelom (see Figure 32.8b). Contractions of longitudinal muscles move the animal forward by undulations, or wavelike motions, of the body. In earthworms and other annelids, the coelomic fluid functions as a hydrostatic skeleton. The coelomic cavity in many annelids is divided by septa between the segments, allowing the animal to change the shape of each segment individually, using both circular and longitudinal muscles. Such annelids use their hydrostatic skeleton for **peristalsis**, a type of movement produced by rhythmic waves of muscle contractions passing from front to back **(Figure 50.33)**.

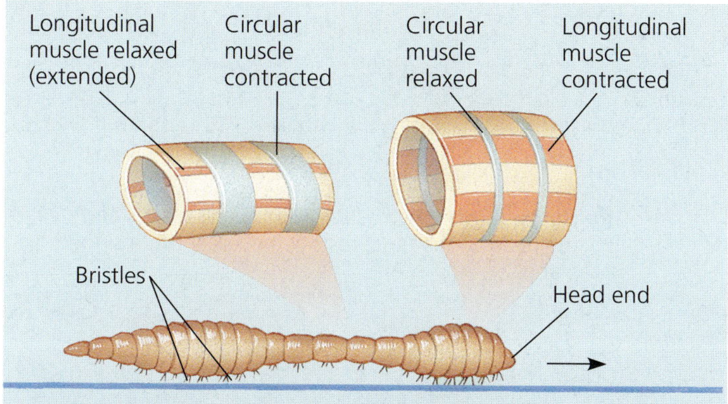

(a) At the moment depicted, body segments at the earthworm's head end and just in front of the rear end are short and thick (longitudinal muscles contracted; circular muscles relaxed) and are anchored to the ground by bristles. The other segments are thin and elongated (circular muscles contracted; longitudinal muscles relaxed).

(b) The head has moved forward because circular muscles in the head segments have contracted. Segments behind the head and at the rear are now thick and anchored, thus preventing the worm from slipping backward.

(c) The head segments are thick again and anchored in their new positions. The rear segments have released their hold on the ground and have been pulled forward.

▲ **Figure 50.33 Crawling by peristalsis.** Contraction of the longitudinal muscles thickens and shortens the earthworm; contraction of the circular muscles constricts and elongates it.

Hydrostatic skeletons are well suited for life in aquatic environments. They may also cushion internal organs from shocks and provide support for crawling and burrowing in terrestrial animals. However, a hydrostatic skeleton cannot support terrestrial activities in which an animal's body is held off the ground, such as walking or running.

Exoskeletons

An **exoskeleton** is a hard encasement deposited on an animal's surface. For example, most molluscs are enclosed in a calcium carbonate shell secreted by the mantle, a sheetlike extension of the body wall (see Figure 33.15). As the animal grows, it enlarges its shell by adding to the outer edge. Clams and other bivalves close their hinged shell using muscles attached to the inside of this exoskeleton.

The jointed exoskeleton of arthropods is a cuticle, a nonliving coat secreted by the epidermis. Muscles are attached to knobs and plates of the cuticle that extend into the interior of the body. About 30–50% of the arthropod cuticle consists of **chitin**, a polysaccharide similar to cellulose (see Figure 5.10). Fibrils of chitin are embedded in a protein matrix, forming a composite material that combines strength and flexibility. Where protection is most important, the cuticle is hardened with organic compounds that cross-link the proteins of the exoskeleton. Some crustaceans, such as lobsters, harden portions of their exoskeleton even more by adding calcium salts. In contrast, there is little cross-linking of proteins or inorganic salt deposition in places where the cuticle must be thin and flexible, such as leg joints. With each growth spurt, an arthropod must shed its exoskeleton (molt) and produce a larger one.

Endoskeletons

An **endoskeleton** consists of hard supporting elements, such as bones, buried within the soft tissues of an animal. Sponges are reinforced by hard needlelike structures of inorganic material (see Figure 33.4) or by softer fibers made of protein. Echinoderms have an endoskeleton of hard plates called ossicles beneath their skin. The ossicles are composed of magnesium carbonate and calcium carbonate crystals and are usually bound together by protein fibers. Whereas the ossicles of sea urchins are tightly bound, the ossicles of sea stars are more loosely linked, allowing a sea star to change the shape of its arms.

Chordates have an endoskeleton consisting of cartilage, bone, or some combination of these materials (see Figure 40.5). The mammalian skeleton is built from more than 200 bones,

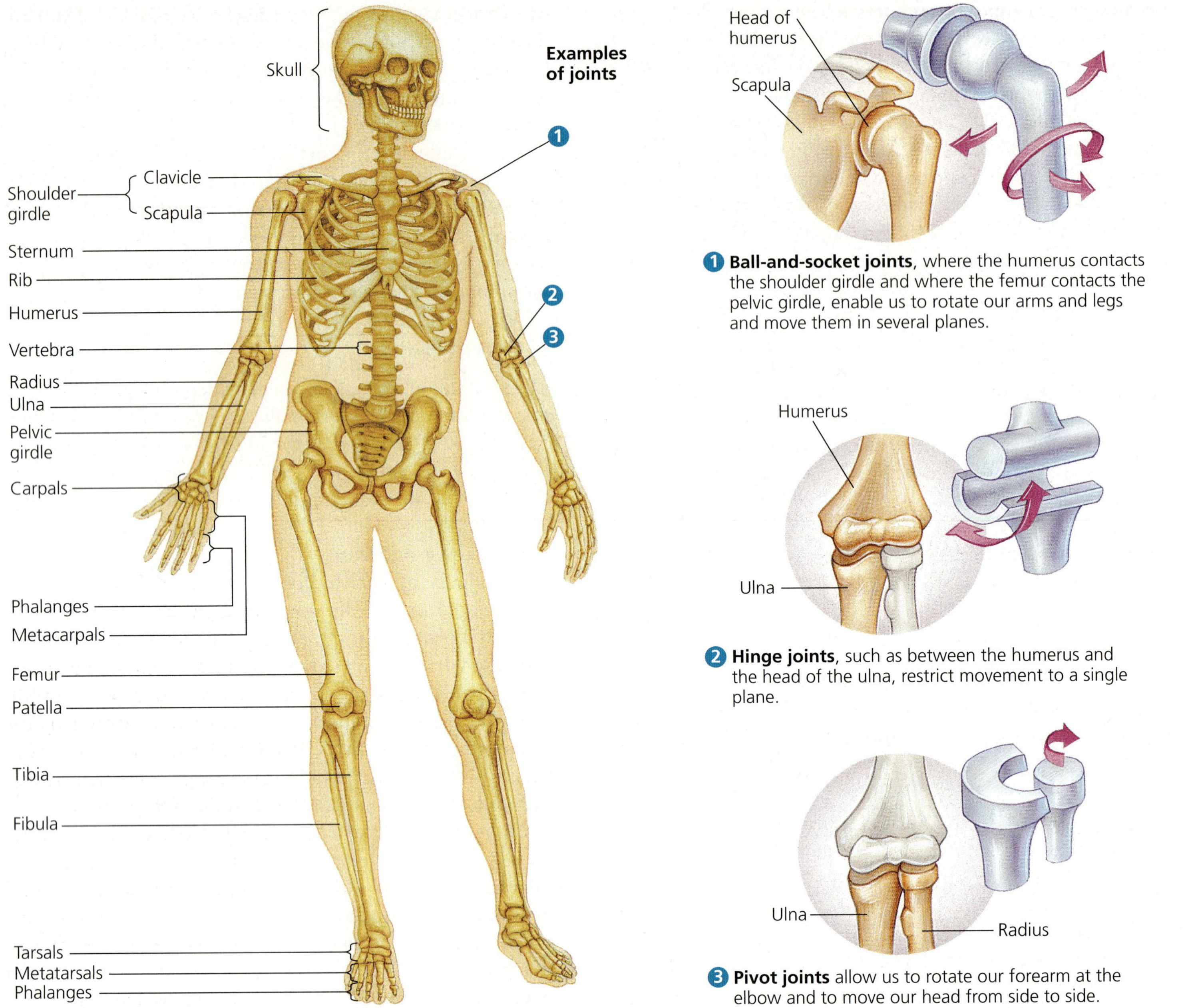

1 **Ball-and-socket joints**, where the humerus contacts the shoulder girdle and where the femur contacts the pelvic girdle, enable us to rotate our arms and legs and move them in several planes.

2 **Hinge joints**, such as between the humerus and the head of the ulna, restrict movement to a single plane.

3 **Pivot joints** allow us to rotate our forearm at the elbow and to move our head from side to side.

▲ **Figure 50.34** **Bones and joints of the human skeleton.**

some fused together and others connected at joints by ligaments that allow freedom of movement **(Figure 50.34)**.

Size and Scale of Skeletons

In analyzing the structure and function of any animal skeleton, it is useful to consider the effects of size and scale as they might apply for an engineer designing a bridge or building. For example, the strength of a building support depends on its cross-sectional area, which increases with the square of its diameter. In contrast, the strain on that support depends on the building's weight, which increases with the cube of its height or other linear dimension. In common with the structure of a bridge or building, an animal's body structure must support its size. Consequently, a large animal has very different body proportions than a small animal. If a mouse were scaled up to an elephant's size, its slender legs would buckle under its weight.

In simply applying the building analogy, we might predict that the size of an animal's leg bones should be directly proportional to the strain imposed by its body weight. However, our prediction would be inaccurate; animal bodies are complex and nonrigid, and the building analogy only partly explains the relationship between body structure and support. An animal's leg size relative to its body size is only part of the story. It turns out that body posture—the position of the legs relative to the main body—is more important in supporting body weight, at least in mammals and birds. Muscles and tendons (connective tissue that joins muscle to bone), which hold the legs of large mammals relatively straight and positioned under the body, bear most of the load.

Types of Locomotion

Movement is a hallmark of animals. Even sessile animals move their body parts: Sponges use beating flagella to generate water currents that draw and trap small food particles, and sessile cnidarians wave tentacles that capture prey (see Chapter 33). Most animals, however, are mobile and spend a considerable portion of their time and energy actively searching for food, as well as escaping from danger and looking for mates. Our focus here is **locomotion**, or active travel from place to place.

Animals have diverse modes of locomotion. Most animal phyla include species that swim. On land and in the sediments on the floor of the sea and lakes, animals crawl, walk, run, or hop. Active flight (in contrast to gliding downward from a tree or elevated ground) has evolved in only a few animal groups: insects, reptiles (including birds), and, among the mammals, bats. A group of large flying reptiles died out millions of years ago, leaving birds and bats as the only flying vertebrates.

In all its modes, locomotion requires that an animal expend energy to overcome two forces that tend to keep it stationary: friction and gravity. Exerting force requires energy-consuming cellular work.

Swimming

Because most animals are reasonably buoyant in water, overcoming gravity is less of a problem for swimming animals than for species that move on land or through the air. On the other hand, water is a much denser and more viscous medium than air, and thus drag (friction) is a major problem for aquatic animals. A sleek, fusiform (torpedo-like) shape is a common adaptation of fast swimmers (see Figure 40.2).

Animals swim in diverse ways. For instance, many insects and four-legged vertebrates use their legs as oars to push against the water. Squids, scallops, and some cnidarians are jet-propelled, taking in water and squirting it out in bursts. Sharks and bony fishes swim by moving their body and tail from side to side, while whales and dolphins move by undulating their body and tail up and down.

Locomotion on Land

In general, the problems of locomotion on land are the opposite of those in water. On land, a walking, running, hopping, or crawling animal must be able to support itself and move against gravity, but air poses relatively little resistance, at least at moderate speeds. When a land animal walks, runs, or hops, its leg muscles expend energy both to propel it and to keep it from falling down. With each step, the animal's leg muscles must overcome inertia by accelerating a leg from a standing start. For moving on land, powerful muscles and strong skeletal support are more important than a streamlined shape.

Diverse adaptations for traveling on land have evolved in various vertebrates. For example, kangaroos have large, powerful muscles in their hind legs, suitable for locomotion by hopping

▲ **Figure 50.35 Energy-efficient locomotion on land.** Members of the kangaroo family travel from place to place mainly by leaping on their large hind legs. Kinetic energy momentarily stored in tendons after each leap provides a boost for the next leap. In fact, a large kangaroo hopping at 30 km/hr uses no more energy per minute than it does at 6 km/hr. The large tail helps balance the kangaroo when it leaps as well as when it sits.

(**Figure 50.35**). As a kangaroo lands after each leap, tendons in its hind legs momentarily store energy. The farther the animal hops, the more energy the tendons store. Analogous to the energy in a compressed spring, the energy stored in the tendons is available for the next jump and reduces the total amount of energy the animal must expend to travel. The legs of an insect, a dog, or a human also retain some energy during walking or running, although a considerably smaller share than do those of a kangaroo.

Maintaining balance is another prerequisite for walking, running, or hopping. A kangaroo's large tail helps balance its body during leaps and also forms a stable tripod with its hind legs when the animal sits or moves slowly. Illustrating the same principle, a walking cat, dog, or horse keeps three feet on the ground. Bipedal animals, such as humans and birds, keep part of at least one foot on the ground when walking. When an animal runs, all four feet (or both feet for bipeds) may be off the ground briefly, but at running speeds it is momentum more than foot contact that keeps the body upright.

Crawling poses a very different situation. Because much of its body is in contact with the ground, a crawling animal must exert considerable effort to overcome friction. You have read how earthworms crawl by peristalsis. Many snakes crawl by undulating their entire body from side to side. Assisted by large, movable scales on its underside, a snake's body pushes against the ground, propelling the animal forward. Boa constrictors and pythons creep straight forward, driven by muscles that lift belly scales off the ground, tilt the scales forward, and then push them backward against the ground.

Flying

Gravity poses a major problem for a flying animal because its wings must develop enough lift to overcome gravity's downward force. The key to flight is wing shape. All types of wings are airfoils—structures whose shape alters air currents in a way that helps animals or airplanes stay aloft. As for the body to which the wings attach, a fusiform shape helps reduce drag in air as it does in water.

Flying animals are relatively light, with body masses ranging from less than a gram for some insects to about 20 kg for the largest flying birds. Many flying animals have structural adaptations that contribute to low body mass. Birds, for example, have no urinary bladder or teeth and have relatively large bones with air-filled regions that help lessen the bird's weight (see Chapter 34).

Energy Costs of Locomotion

During the 1960s, three scientists at Duke University—Dick Taylor, Vance Tucker, and Knut Schmidt-Nielsen—became interested in the bioenergetics of locomotion. Physiologists typically determine an animal's rate of energy use during locomotion by measuring oxygen consumption or carbon dioxide production (see Chapter 40). To apply such a strategy to flight, Tucker trained parakeets to fly in a wind tunnel while wearing a face mask **(Figure 50.36)**. By connecting the mask to a tube that collected the air the bird exhaled as it flew, Tucker could measure rates of gas exchange and calculate energy expenditure. In the meantime, Taylor and Schmidt-Nielsen measured energy consumption at rest and during locomotion for animals of widely varying body sizes.

In 1971, Schmidt-Nielsen was invited to give a lecture at a scientific meeting in Germany. In preparation for his speech, he set out to compare the energy cost of different forms of locomotion. He decided to express energy cost as the amount of fuel it takes to transport a given amount of body weight over a set distance. By converting data from many studies of animal locomotion to this common framework, Schmidt-Nielsen drew important conclusions about energy expenditure and locomotion **(Figure 50.37)**.

Schmidt-Nielsen's calculations demonstrated that the energy cost of locomotion depends on the mode of locomotion and the environment. Running animals generally expend more energy per meter traveled than equivalently sized swimming animals, partly because running and walking require energy to overcome gravity. Swimming is the most energy-efficient mode of locomotion (assuming that an animal is specialized for swimming). And if we compare the energy consumption per minute rather than per meter, we find that flying animals use more energy than swimming or running animals with the same body mass.

The studies described in Figure 50.37 also provide insight into the relationship of size to energy expenditure during locomotion. The downward slope of each line on the graph shows that a larger animal travels more efficiently than a smaller animal specialized for the same mode of transport. For example, a 450-kg horse expends less energy *per kilogram of body mass* than a 4-kg cat running the same distance. Of course, the total amount of energy expended in locomotion is greater for the larger animal.

▲ **Figure 50.36 Measuring energy usage during flight.** The tube connected to the plastic face mask collects the gases this parakeet exhales during flight in a wind tunnel.

▼ **Figure 50.37 Inquiry**

What are the energy costs of locomotion?

EXPERIMENT Knut Schmidt-Nielsen wondered whether there were general principles governing the energy costs of different types of locomotion among diverse animal species. To answer this question, he drew on his own studies as well as the scientific literature for measurements made when animals swam in water flumes, ran on treadmills, or flew in wind tunnels. He converted all of these data to a common set of units and graphed the results.

RESULTS

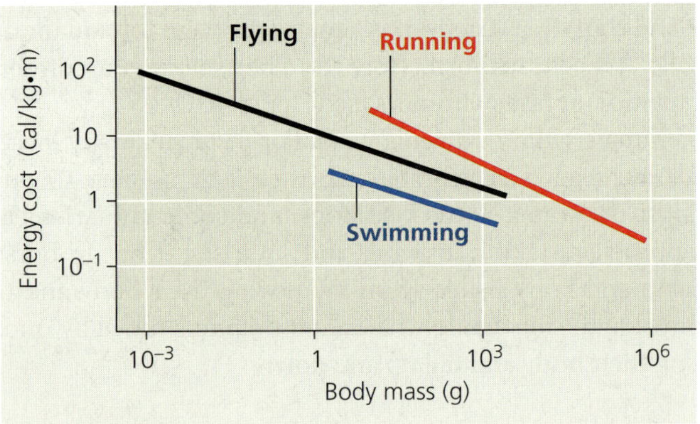

This graph plots the energy cost, in calories per kilogram of body mass per meter traveled, against body weight for animals specialized for running, flying, and swimming. Note that both axes are plotted on logarithmic scales.

CONCLUSION For most animals of a given body mass, swimming is the most energy-efficient and running the least energy-efficient mode of locomotion. In addition, a small animal typically expends more energy per kilogram of body mass than a large animal, regardless of the type of locomotion used.

SOURCE K. Schmidt-Nielsen, Locomotion: Energy cost of swimming, flying, and running, *Science* 177:222–228 (1972).

WHAT IF? If you plotted the efficiency of a duck as a swimmer on this graph, where might you expect it to fall, and why?

Energy from food that is used for locomotion is unavailable for other activities, such as growth and reproduction. Therefore, structural and behavioral adaptations that maximize the efficiency of locomotion increase the evolutionary fitness of an organism.

Although we have discussed sensory receptors and muscles separately in this chapter, they are part of a single integrated system linking together brain, body, and the external world. An animal's behavior is the product of this system. In Chapter 51, we'll discuss behavior in the context of animal form and function and also link it to ecology, the study of interactions between organisms and their environment.

CONCEPT CHECK 50.6

1. In what way are septa an important feature of the earthworm skeleton?
2. Contrast swimming and flying in terms of the main problems they pose and the adaptations that allow animals to overcome those problems.
3. **WHAT IF?** Suppose you wanted to extend your arm from the elbow by controlling your biceps muscle rather than your triceps. How could you manage this feat?

For suggested answers, see Appendix A.

Chapter 50 Review

MEDIA Go to the Study Area at **www.masteringbio.com** for BioFlix 3-D Animations, MP3 Tutors, Videos, Practice Tests, an eBook, and more.

SUMMARY OF KEY CONCEPTS

CONCEPT 50.1

Sensory receptors transduce stimulus energy and transmit signals to the central nervous system (pp. 1087–1091)

► **Sensory Pathways** Sensory receptors are usually specialized neurons or epithelial cells that detect external or internal stimuli. Sensory reception, the detection of a stimulus by sensory cells, precedes transduction, the conversion of stimulus energy to a change in the membrane potential of a sensory receptor. The resulting receptor potential controls transmission of action potentials to the CNS, where sensory information is integrated to generate perceptions. Signal transduction pathways in receptor cells often amplify the signal, which causes the receptor cell either to produce action potentials or to release neurotransmitter at a synapse with a sensory neuron.

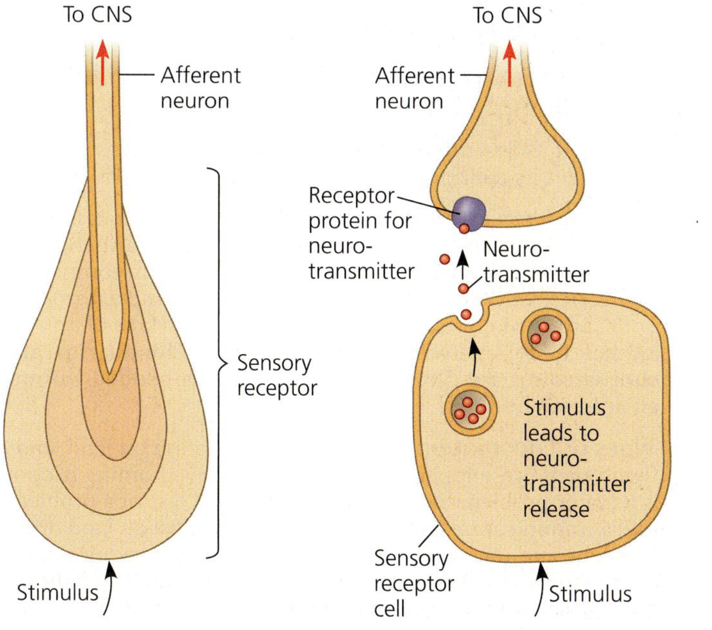

(a) Receptor *is* afferent neuron. **(b)** Receptor *regulates* afferent neuron.

► **Types of Sensory Receptors** Mechanoreceptors respond to stimuli such as pressure, touch, stretch, motion, and sound. Chemoreceptors detect either total solute concentrations or specific molecules. Electromagnetic receptors detect different forms of electromagnetic radiation. Various types of thermoreceptors signal surface and core temperatures of the body. Pain is detected by a group of diverse receptors that respond to excess heat, pressure, or specific classes of chemicals.

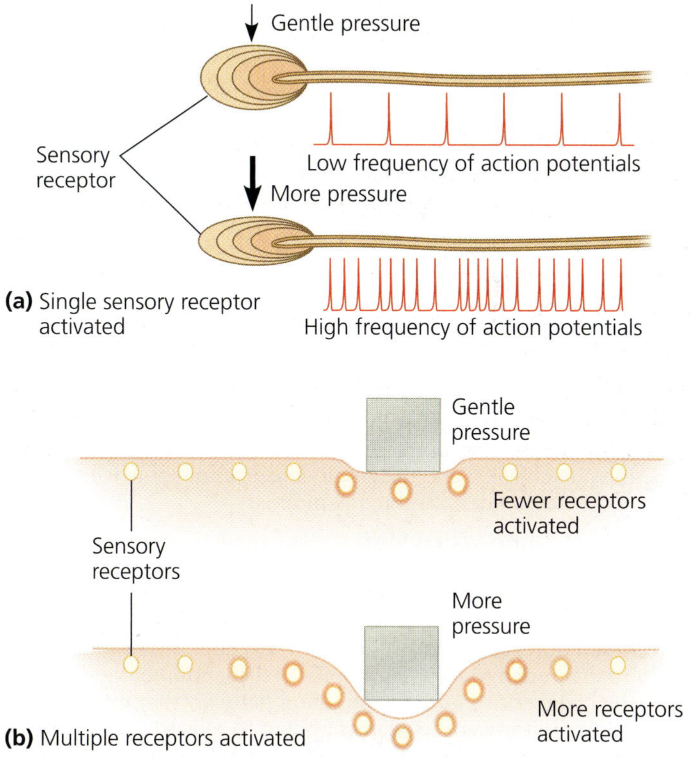

(a) Single sensory receptor activated

(b) Multiple receptors activated

CONCEPT 50.2

The mechanoreceptors responsible for hearing and equilibrium detect moving fluid or settling particles (pp. 1091–1096)

► **Sensing of Gravity and Sound in Invertebrates** Most invertebrates sense their orientation with respect to gravity by means of statocysts. Many arthropods sense sounds with body hairs that vibrate and with localized "ears," consisting of a tympanic membrane and receptor cells.

- **Hearing and Equilibrium in Mammals** The tympanic membrane (eardrum) transmits sound waves to three small bones of the middle ear, which transmit the waves through the oval window to the fluid in the coiled cochlea of the inner ear. Pressure waves in the fluid vibrate the basilar membrane, depolarizing hair cells and triggering action potentials that travel via the auditory nerve to the brain. Each region of the basilar membrane vibrates most vigorously at a particular frequency and leads to excitation of a specific auditory area of the cerebral cortex. Receptors in the saccule, utricle, and three semicircular canals of the inner ear function in balance and equilibrium.

- **Hearing and Equilibrium in Other Vertebrates** The detection of water movement in fishes and aquatic amphibians is accomplished by a lateral line system containing clustered hair cells.

CONCEPT 50.3

The senses of taste and smell rely on similar sets of sensory receptors (pp. 1096–1099)

- **Taste in Mammals** Both taste and smell depend on the stimulation of chemoreceptors by small dissolved molecules that bind to proteins on the plasma membrane. In humans, taste receptors are organized into taste buds on the tongue and in the mouth. Sensory cells within taste buds express a single receptor type specific for one of the five taste perceptions—sweet, sour, salty, bitter, and umami (elicited by glutamate).

- **Smell in Humans** Olfactory receptor cells line the upper part of the nasal cavity. Their axons extend to the olfactory bulb of the brain. More than 1,000 genes code for membrane proteins that bind to specific classes of odorants, and each receptor cell appears to express only one of those genes.

CONCEPT 50.4

Similar mechanisms underlie vision throughout the animal kingdom (pp. 1099–1105)

- **Vision in Invertebrates** The light detectors of invertebrates include the simple light-sensitive eyespots of planarians; the image-forming compound eyes of insects, crustaceans, and some polychaetes; and the single-lens eyes of some jellies, polychaetes, spiders, and many molluscs.

- **The Vertebrate Visual System** The main parts of the vertebrate eye are the sclera, which includes the cornea; the choroid, which includes the iris; the retina, which contains the photoreceptors; and the lens, which focuses light on the retina. Photoreceptors (rods and cones) contain a pigment, retinal, bonded to a protein (opsin). Absorption of light by retinal triggers a signal transduction pathway that hyperpolarizes the photoreceptors, causing them to release less neurotransmitter. Synapses transmit information from photoreceptors to bipolar cells and then to ganglion cells, whose axons in the optic nerve convey action potentials to the brain. Other neurons in the retina integrate information before it is sent to the brain. Most axons in the optic nerves go to the lateral geniculate nuclei, which relay information to the primary visual cortex.

MEDIA

Activity Structure and Function of the Eye

CONCEPT 50.5

The physical interaction of protein filaments is required for muscle function (pp. 1105–1112)

- **Vertebrate Skeletal Muscle** Vertebrate skeletal muscle consists of a bundle of muscle cells (fibers), each of which contains myofibrils composed of thin filaments of (mostly) actin and thick filaments of myosin. Myosin heads, energized by the hydrolysis of ATP, bind to the thin filaments, forming cross-bridges. Bending of the myosin heads exerts force on the thin filaments. When ATP binds to the myosin heads, they release, ready to start a new cycle. Repeated cycles cause the thick and thin filaments to slide past each other, shortening the sarcomere and contracting the muscle fiber.

  A motor neuron initiates contraction by releasing acetylcholine, which depolarizes the muscle fiber. Action potentials travel to the interior of the muscle fiber along the T tubules, stimulating the release of Ca^{2+} from the sarcoplasmic reticulum. The Ca^{2+} repositions the tropomyosin-troponin complex on the thin filaments, exposing the myosin-binding sites on actin and allowing the cross-bridge cycle to proceed. A motor unit consists of a motor neuron and the muscle fibers it controls. Recruiting multiple motor units results in stronger contractions. A twitch results from a single action potential in a motor neuron. More rapidly delivered action potentials produce a graded contraction by summation. Tetanus is a state of smooth and sustained contraction produced when motor neurons deliver a volley of action potentials. Skeletal muscle fibers can be slow-twitch oxidative, fast-twitch oxidative, or fast-twitch glycolytic.

- **Other Types of Muscle** Cardiac muscle, found only in the heart, consists of striated cells that are electrically connected by intercalated disks and that can generate action potentials without input from neurons. In smooth muscles, contractions are slow and may be initiated by the muscles themselves or by stimulation from neurons in the autonomic nervous system.

MEDIA

BioFlix 3-D Animation Muscle Contraction
Activity Skeletal Muscle Structure
Activity Muscle Contraction
Investigation How Do Electrical Stimuli Affect Muscle Contraction?

CONCEPT 50.6

Skeletal systems transform muscle contraction into locomotion (pp. 1112–1117)

- Skeletal muscles, often present in antagonistic pairs, provide movement by contracting and pulling against the skeleton.

- **Types of Skeletal Systems** A hydrostatic skeleton, found in most cnidarians, flatworms, nematodes, and annelids, consists of fluid under pressure in a closed body compartment. Exoskeletons, found in most molluscs and arthropods, are hard coverings deposited on the surface of an animal. Endoskeletons, found in sponges, echinoderms, and chordates, are rigid supporting elements embedded within an animal's body.

- **Types of Locomotion** Swimming, locomotion on land, and flying each present particular challenges. Overcoming friction is a major problem for swimmers. Gravity is less of a problem for swimming animals than for those that move on land or fly. Walking, running, hopping, or crawling on land requires an animal to support itself and to move against gravity. Flight requires that wings develop enough lift to overcome the downward force of gravity.

▶ **Energy Costs of Locomotion** Animals that are specialized for swimming expend less energy per meter traveled than equivalently sized animals specialized for flying or running. In addition, larger animals are more efficient than smaller animals specialized for the same mode of locomotion.

MEDIA

Activity Human Skeleton

TESTING YOUR KNOWLEDGE

SELF-QUIZ

1. Which of the following sensory receptors is *incorrectly* paired with its category?
a. hair cell—mechanoreceptor
b. muscle spindle—mechanoreceptor
c. taste receptor—chemoreceptor
d. rod—electromagnetic receptor
e. olfactory receptor—electromagnetic receptor

2. Some sharks close their eyes just before they bite. Although they cannot see their prey, their bites are on target. Researchers have noted that sharks often misdirect their bites at metal objects and that sharks can find batteries buried under the sand of an aquarium. This evidence suggests that sharks keep track of their prey during the split second before they bite in the same way that
a. a rattlesnake finds a mouse in its burrow.
b. a male silkworm moth locates a mate.
c. a bat finds moths in the dark.
d. a platypus locates its prey in a muddy river.
e. a flatworm avoids light places.

3. The transduction of sound waves into action potentials takes place
a. within the tectorial membrane as it is stimulated by the hair cells.
b. when hair cells are bent against the tectorial membrane, causing them to depolarize and release neurotransmitter that stimulates sensory neurons.
c. as the basilar membrane becomes more permeable to sodium ions and depolarizes, initiating an action potential in a sensory neuron.
d. as the basilar membrane vibrates at different frequencies in response to the varying volume of sounds.
e. within the middle ear as the vibrations are amplified by the malleus, incus, and stapes.

4. Which of the following is an *incorrect* statement about the vertebrate eye?
a. The vitreous humor regulates the amount of light entering the pupil.
b. The transparent cornea is an extension of the sclera.
c. The fovea is the center of the visual field and contains only cones.
d. The ciliary muscle functions in accommodation.
e. The retina lies just inside the choroid and contains the photoreceptor cells.

5. When light strikes the rhodopsin in a rod, retinal isomerizes, initiating a signal transduction pathway that
a. depolarizes the neighboring bipolar cells and initiates an action potential in a ganglion cell.
b. depolarizes the rod, causing it to release the neurotransmitter glutamate, which excites bipolar cells.
c. hyperpolarizes the rod, reducing its release of glutamate, which excites some bipolar cells and inhibits others.
d. hyperpolarizes the rod, increasing its release of glutamate, which excites amacrine cells but inhibits horizontal cells.
e. converts cGMP to GMP, opening sodium channels and hyperpolarizing the membrane, causing the rhodopsin to become bleached.

6. During the contraction of a vertebrate skeletal muscle fiber, calcium ions
a. break cross-bridges by acting as a cofactor in the hydrolysis of ATP.
b. bind with troponin, changing its shape so that the myosin-binding sites on actin are exposed.
c. transmit action potentials from the motor neuron to the muscle fiber.
d. spread action potentials through the T tubules.
e. reestablish the polarization of the plasma membrane following an action potential.

7. DRAW IT Based on the information in the text, fill in the following graph. Use one line for rods and another line for cones.

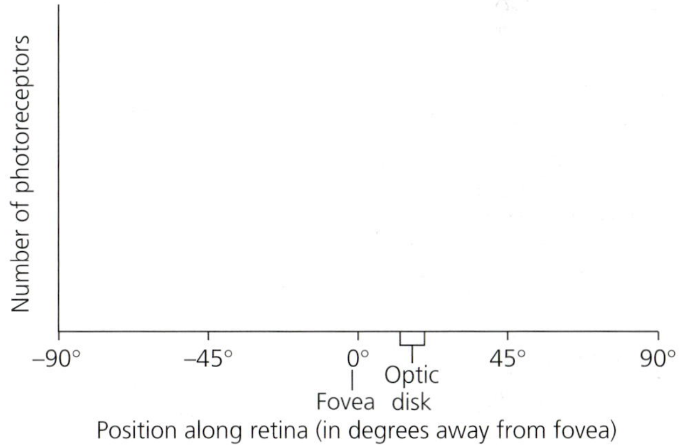

For Self-Quiz answers, see Appendix A.

MEDIA Visit the Study Area at **www.masteringbio.com** for a Practice Test.

EVOLUTION CONNECTION

8. In general, locomotion on land requires more energy than locomotion in water. By integrating what you have learned throughout these chapters on animal functions, discuss some of the evolutionary adaptations of mammals that support the high energy requirements for moving on land.

SCIENTIFIC INQUIRY

9. Although skeletal muscles generally fatigue fairly rapidly, clam shell muscles have a protein called paramyosin that allows them to sustain contraction for up to a month. From your knowledge of the cellular mechanism of contraction, propose a hypothesis to explain how paramyosin might work. How would you test your hypothesis experimentally?

51 Animal Behavior

▲ **Figure 51.1 Why do cranes dance?**

KEY CONCEPTS

51.1 Discrete sensory inputs can stimulate both simple and complex behaviors
51.2 Learning establishes specific links between experience and behavior
51.3 Both genetic makeup and environment contribute to the development of behaviors
51.4 Selection for individual survival and reproductive success can explain most behaviors
51.5 Inclusive fitness can account for the evolution of altruistic social behavior

OVERVIEW

Shall We Dance?

Red-crowned cranes (*Grus japonensis*), at one and a half meters in height, tower over the marshes and bogs of East Asia. Using their sharp eyesight, they pinpoint a variety of prey, including insects, fish, amphibians, and small rodents. Often, when the cranes gather in pairs or groups, they also prance, stretch, bow, and leap: In short, they dance **(Figure 51.1)**. How do cranes decide that it is time to dance? Moreover, why do they dance at all?

Animal behavior, be it solitary or social, fixed or variable, is based on physiological systems and processes. An individual **behavior** is an action carried out by muscles or glands under control of the nervous system in response to a stimulus. Examples of behavior include an animal using muscles in its chest and throat to produce a song, or releasing a particular scent to mark its territory. Behavior is an essential part of acquiring nutrients for digestion and of finding a partner for sexual reproduction. Behavior also contributes to homeostasis, as in honeybees huddling to produce and conserve heat (see Chapter 40). In short, all of animal physiology contributes to behavior, and animal behavior influences all of physiology.

Being essential for survival and reproduction, behavior is subject to substantial natural selection over time. Selection that acts on behavior also affects anatomy because body form and appearance contribute directly to the recognition and communication that underlie many behaviors. For example, the dance of the red-crowned crane enables males and females to form lifelong mating pairs. The birds' distinctive body shape, striking coloration, and characteristic pattern of vocalizations are adaptations that enable potential mates to recognize and communicate with each other during courtship.

In this chapter, we'll examine how behavior is controlled, how it develops during an animal's life, and how it is influenced by both genes and the environment. We'll also explore the ways in which behavior evolves over many generations. In moving from our study of an animal's inner workings to its interactions with the outside world, we also provide a transition to the broader study of ecology, the focus of Unit Eight.

CONCEPT **51.1**

Discrete sensory inputs can stimulate both simple and complex behaviors

Collectively, an animal's behavior is the sum of its responses to external and internal stimuli. Consider, for example, the male silky anole lizard (*Norops sericeus*) shown in **Figure 51.2**: He is extending his dewlap, a brightly colored skin flap beneath the throat. At various times, male anoles appear to use dewlaps to facilitate recognition by members of their own species, to establish territories, and to attract mates. Given the variety of stimuli and functions potentially associated with this and other animal behaviors, how can biologists determine how animal behaviors arose and exactly what functions they serve?

▲ **Figure 51.2 A male silky anole with dewlap extended.**

To address this question, pioneering behavioral biologists in the mid-1900s developed **ethology**, the scientific study of how animals behave, particularly in their natural environments. One early ethologist, Niko Tinbergen, of the Netherlands, suggested that understanding any behavior requires answering four questions, which can be summarized as follows:

1. What stimulus elicits the behavior, and what physiological mechanisms mediate the response?
2. How does the animal's experience during growth and development influence the response?
3. How does the behavior aid survival and reproduction?
4. What is the behavior's evolutionary history?

The first two questions ask about **proximate causation**: "how" a behavior occurs or is modified. The last two ask about **ultimate causation**: "why" a behavior occurs in the context of natural selection.

To understand the distinction between proximate and ultimate causation, let's return to the red-crowned cranes in Figure 51.1. Having formed a mating pair, the cranes breed in spring and early summer. A question about proximate causation is to ask *how* seasonal changes influence when red-crowned cranes mate. This question might lead us to examine the effect of day length on the crane's production of and responses to particular hormones. In contrast, asking *why* red-crowned cranes reproduce in spring and summer relates to ultimate causation. One hypothesis is that in those seasons parents are more likely to find food for rapidly growing offspring, which would increase reproductive success relative to breeding in other seasons.

Today, the ideas of proximate and ultimate causation underlie **behavioral ecology**, the study of the ecological and evolutionary basis for animal behavior. As we'll see shortly, Tinbergen, along with Austrian ethologists Karl von Frisch and Konrad Lorenz, not only provided a conceptual foundation for studying animal behavior but also applied these ideas to the study of specific behaviors. In recognition of their achievements, the three shared a Nobel Prize in 1973.

Let's begin by exploring behavioral responses to well-defined stimuli, starting with an example from Tinbergen's work.

Fixed Action Patterns

A type of behavior directly linked to a simple stimulus is the **fixed action pattern**, a sequence of unlearned acts that is essentially unchangeable and, once initiated, usually carried to completion. The trigger is an external cue known as a **sign stimulus**. Tinbergen studied what has become a classic example of a sign stimulus and fixed action pattern in the male three-spined stickleback fish (*Gasterosteus aculeatus*). Male sticklebacks, which have red bellies, attack other males that invade their nesting territories. Tinbergen noticed that his sticklebacks also behaved aggressively when a red truck passed in front of their tank. Inspired by this chance observation, he carried out experiments showing that the red color of an intruder's underside normally triggers the attack behavior. A male stickleback will not attack a fish lacking red coloration (note that female sticklebacks never have red bellies), but will attack even unrealistic models if they contain areas of red color **(Figure 51.3)**.

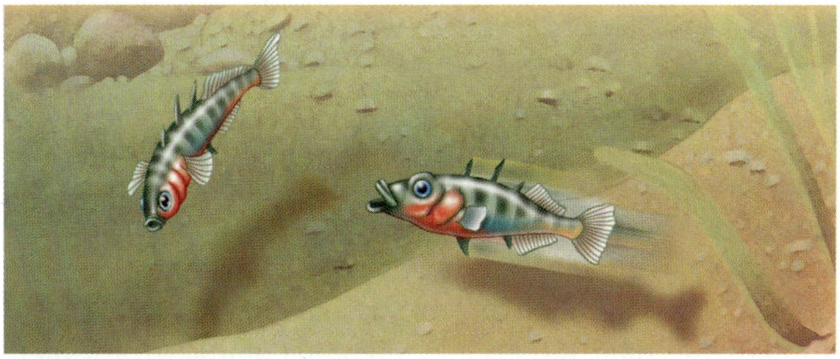

(a) A male stickleback fish attacks other male sticklebacks that invade its nesting territory. The red belly of the intruding male (left) acts as the sign stimulus that releases the aggressive behavior.

(b) The realistic model at the top, without a red underside, produces no aggressive response in a male three-spined stickleback. The other models, with red undersides, produce strong responses.

▲ **Figure 51.3 Sign stimuli in a classic fixed action pattern.**

? *Suggest an explanation for why this behavior evolved (ultimate causation).*

Oriented Movement

Environmental cues not only trigger some simple behaviors but also provide stimuli that animals use to change or orient both simple and complex movements in a particular direction.

Kinesis and Taxis

In changing locations, some animals rely on **kinesis**, a change in activity or turning rate in response to a stimulus. For example, sow bugs (genus *Oniscus*) exhibit a kinesis in response to variation in humidity. These terrestrial crustaceans become more active in dry areas and less active in humid areas. They do not move toward or away from specific conditions, but their increased movement under dry conditions makes it more likely that they will leave a dry area and encounter a moist area, where they survive better **(Figure 51.4)**.

In contrast to a kinesis, a **taxis** is an oriented movement toward (positive taxis) or away from (negative taxis) some stimulus. For example, trout and many other river fishes automatically swim or orient themselves in an upstream direction (toward the current). This taxis keeps the fish from being swept away and keeps it facing the direction from which food will come.

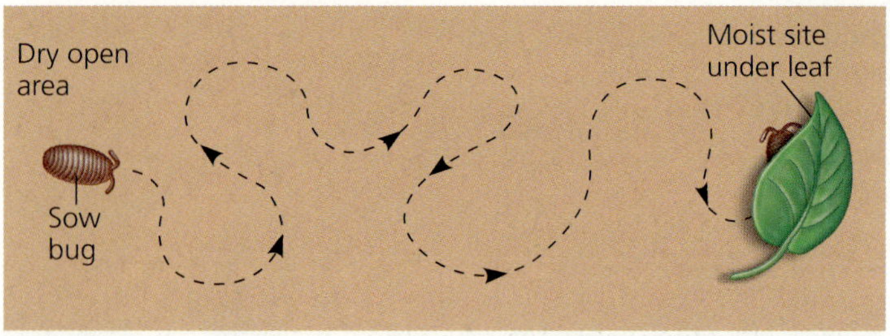

▲ **Figure 51.4 A kinesis.** Movements that vary with humidity may increase the chance that a sow bug will encounter and stay in a moist environment.

▲ **Figure 51.5 Migration.** Each spring, western sandpipers (*Calidris mauri*) migrate from their wintering grounds, which may be as far south as Peru, to their breeding grounds in Alaska. In the autumn, they return to their wintering grounds.

Migration

Migration—a regular, long-distance change in location—is observed in a wide variety of birds, fishes, and other animals **(Figure 51.5)**. In migrating, many animals pass through environments they have not previously encountered. How, then, do they find their way? Some migrating animals track their position relative to the sun, but there are problems with this approach. For one, the sun's position relative to Earth changes throughout the day. Numerous studies have demonstrated that animals adjust for these changes by means of a *circadian clock*, an internal mechanism that maintains a 24-hour activity rhythm or cycle (see Chapter 49). For example, experiments with controlled cycles of light and dark reveal that birds orient differently relative to the sun at distinct times of the day. Nocturnal animals can instead use the North Star, which has a constant position in the night sky. But there remains a second problem: Clouds can obscure both sun and stars. A simple experiment with homing pigeons demonstrates how animals can overcome this obstacle. On an overcast day, placing a small magnet on the head of a homing pigeon prevents it from returning efficiently to its roost. By sensing their position relative to Earth's magnetic field, pigeons and other animals can navigate without solar or celestial cues.

There are two competing hypotheses as to how animals detect Earth's magnetic field in navigating long-distance movements. One idea is based on the discovery of bits of magnetite, a magnetic iron mineral, in the heads of migrating fishes and birds. Some scientists hypothesize that Earth's pull on magnetite-containing structures triggers transmission of nerve impulses to the brain. The second hypothesis proposes that animals are guided by the effects of Earth's magnetic field on photoreceptors in the visual system. The idea that animals "see" the magnetic field is supported by experiments showing that birds require light of particular wavelengths in their daytime or nighttime environment to orient themselves in a magnetic field.

Behavioral Rhythms

Although the circadian clock plays a small but significant role in navigation by some migrating species, it has a major role in the daily activity of all animals. As discussed in Chapter 49, the output of the clock is a circadian rhythm, a daily cycle of rest and activity with far-reaching effects on behavioral physiology. The clock is normally synchronized with the light and dark cycles of the environment but can maintain rhythmic activity under constant environmental conditions, such as during hibernation. Having unraveled the basic molecular mechanism underlying this biological clock, scientists are now turning their attention to how signals from the clock regulate and coordinate daily behaviors.

Some behaviors, such as migration and reproduction, reflect biological rhythms with a longer cycle, or period, than the circadian rhythm. Behavioral rhythms linked to the yearly cycle of seasons are called *circannual rhythms*. Although migration and reproduction typically correlate with food availability, these behaviors are not a direct response to changes in food intake. Instead, circannual rhythms, like circadian rhythms, are influenced by the periods of daylight and darkness in the environment. For example, studies with several bird species have shown that an artificial environment with extended daylight can induce out-of-season migratory behavior.

Not all biological rhythms are linked to the light and dark cycles in the environment. Consider, for instance, the fiddler crab (genus *Uca*). Male fiddler crabs have a distinctive asymmetry: One claw grows to giant proportions, half the mass of the entire body **(Figure 51.6)**. (The name *fiddler* comes from the crab's appearance during feeding, when the smaller front claw moves to and from the mouth in front of the enlarged claw.) The adult male crabs live in burrows in mudflats or sand that are covered and uncovered by the tides. During courtship, a male positions himself at the entrance to his burrow, waving his enlarged claw to attract a potential mate. Once he lures a female to his burrow, he seals her in with mud or sand in preparation for mating. This courtship behavior is linked not to day length but to the timing of the new and full moon: Timing behavior to the lunar cycle links the crab's reproduction to the times of greatest tidal movement. The tides disperse larvae to deeper waters, where they complete early development in relative safety before returning to the tidal flats.

▲ **Figure 51.6 Male fiddler crab beckoning to potential mates.** The behavioral cycles of the fiddler crab are linked to the tides that cover and uncover its burrow.

Animal Signals and Communication

Claw waving by fiddler crabs during courtship is an example of one animal (the male crab) generating the stimulus that guides the behavior of another animal (the female crab). A stimulus transmitted from one animal to another is called a **signal**. The transmission and reception of signals constitute animal **communication**, an essential element of interactions between individuals.

As an introduction to the common modes of animal communication, let's consider the courtship behavior of the fruit fly (*Drosophila melanogaster*). Courtship in these flies constitutes a *stimulus-response chain*, in which the response to each stimulus is itself the stimulus for the next behavior.

Fruit fly courtship begins with a male identifying and orienting toward a female of the same species **(Figure 51.7a)**. When the male sees the female, he relies on *visual communication*, the flow of information to the visual system. In addition, the male's sense of smell, or olfactory system, detects chemicals released into the air by the female. This is an example of *chemical communication*, the transmission and reception of signals in the form of specific molecules. Having recognized the female, the male approaches and taps the female with a foreleg **(Figure 51.7b)**. This touching, or

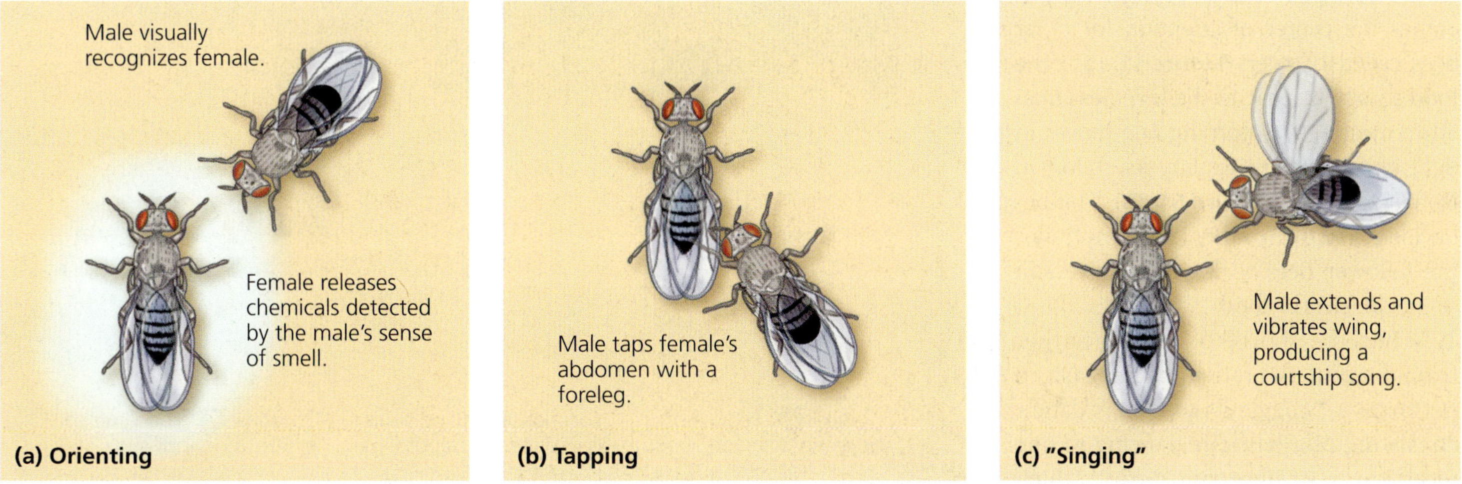

▲ **Figure 51.7 Courtship behavior of the fruit fly.** Fruit fly courtship involves a fixed set of behaviors that follow one another in fixed order.

tactile communication, alerts the female to the male's presence. In the process, chemicals on her abdomen are transferred to the male, providing further chemical confirmation of her species identity. In the third stage of courtship, the male extends and vibrates his wing, producing a specific courtship song **(Figure 51.7c)**. This singing, an example of *auditory communication,* informs the female that the male is of the same species. Only if all of these forms of communication are successful will a receptive female allow the male to attempt copulation.

The form of communication used to transmit information is closely related to an animal's lifestyle and environment. For example, most terrestrial mammals are nocturnal, which makes visual displays relatively ineffective. Instead, these species use olfactory and auditory signals, which work as well in the dark as in the light. In contrast, most birds are diurnal (active mainly in daytime) and communicate primarily by visual and auditory signals. Unlike most mammals, humans are diurnal and, like birds, use primarily visual and auditory communication. We can thus detect and appreciate the songs and bright colors used by birds to communicate but miss many chemical cues on which other mammals base their behavior.

The information content of animal communication varies considerably. One remarkable example is the symbolic language by which honeybees share information about the location of food sources. The language was discovered in the 1940s by Karl von Frisch, who watched individual European honeybees (*Apis mellifera*) as they returned to hives modified for observation. A returning bee quickly becomes the center of attention for other bees, called followers **(Figure 51.8a)**. If the food source is close to the hive (less than 50 m away), the returning bee moves in tight circles while waggling its abdomen from side to side **(Figure 51.8b)**. This behavior, called the "round dance," motivates the follower bees to leave the hive and search for nearby food.

When the source of food is farther from the nest, the returning bee instead performs a "waggle dance." This dance, consisting of a half-circle swing in one direction, a straight run during which the bee waggles its abdomen, and a half-circle swing in the other direction, communicates to the follower bees both the direction and distance of the food source from the hive **(Figure 51.8c)**. The angle of the straight run relative to the hive's vertical surface is the same as the horizontal angle of the food in relation to the sun. For example, if the returning bee runs at a 30° angle to the right of vertical, the follower bees leaving the hive fly 30° to the right of the horizontal direction of the sun. A dance with a longer straight run, and therefore more abdominal waggles per run, indicates a greater distance to the food source. As follower bees exit the hive, they fly almost directly to the area indicated by the waggle dance. By using flower odor and other clues, they locate the food source within this area.

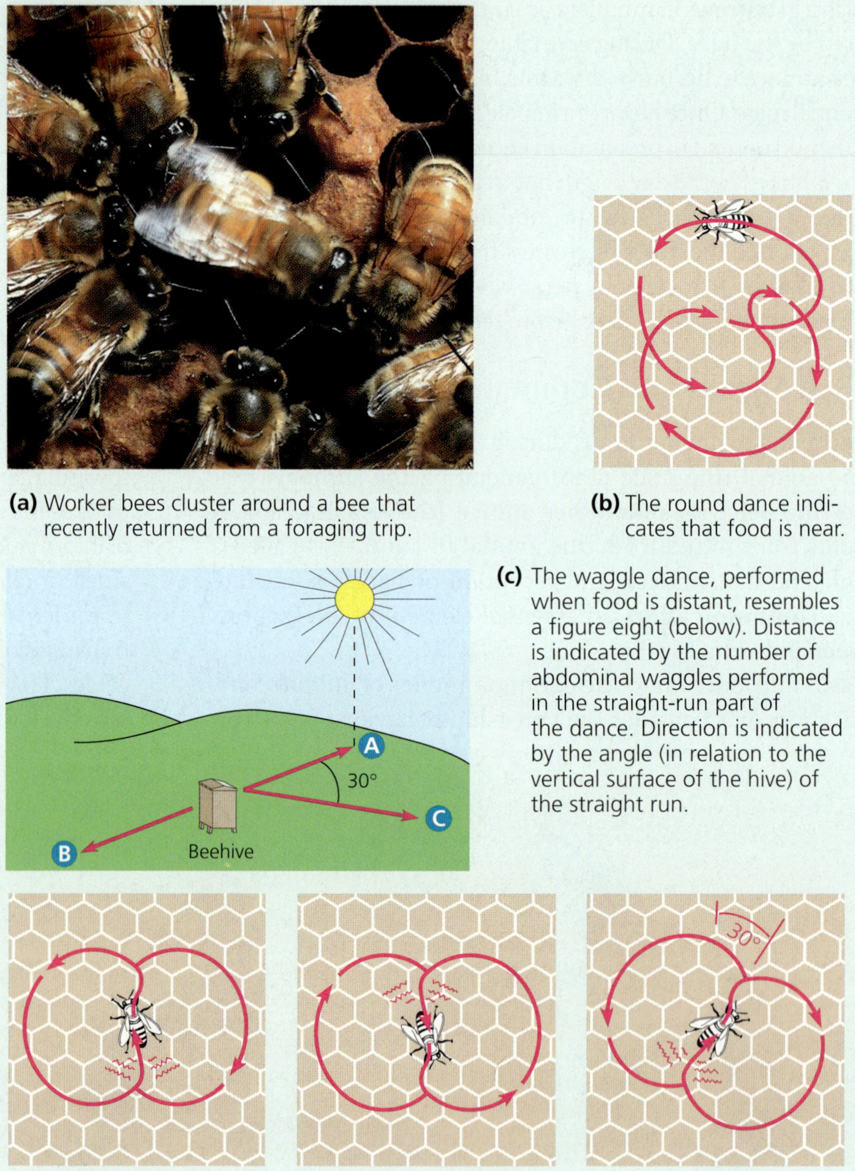

(a) Worker bees cluster around a bee that recently returned from a foraging trip.

(b) The round dance indicates that food is near.

(c) The waggle dance, performed when food is distant, resembles a figure eight (below). Distance is indicated by the number of abdominal waggles performed in the straight-run part of the dance. Direction is indicated by the angle (in relation to the vertical surface of the hive) of the straight run.

Location A: Food source is in same direction as sun.

Location B: Food source is in direction opposite sun.

Location C: Food source is 30° to right of sun.

▲ **Figure 51.8 Honeybee dance language.** Honeybees returning to the hive communicate the location of food sources through the symbolic language of a dance.

Pheromones

Many animals that communicate through odors emit chemical substances called **pheromones**. Pheromones are especially common among mammals and insects and often relate to reproductive behavior. For example, pheromones are the basis for the chemical communication in fruit fly courtship (see Figure 51.7). Pheromones are not limited to short-distance signaling, however. Researchers have shown that the pheromones from a female moth can attract a mate from several kilometers away. Once the moths are together, pheromones also trigger specific courtship behaviors.

The context of a pheromone can be as important as the chemical itself. In a honeybee colony, pheromones produced by the queen and her daughters, the workers, maintain the hive's complex social order. When male honeybees (drones) are outside the hive, where they can mate with a queen, they are attracted to her pheromone; when drones are inside the hive, they are unaffected by the queen's pheromone.

Pheromones also function in nonreproductive behavior. For example, when a minnow or catfish is injured, an alarm substance released from the fish's skin disperses in the water, inducing a fright response in other fish. These nearby fish become more vigilant and form tightly packed schools, often near the bottom, where they are safer from attack **(Figure 51.9)**. Pheromones can be very effective at remarkably low concentrations. For instance, just 1 cm^2 of skin from a fathead minnow contains sufficient alarm substance to induce a reaction in 58,000 L of water.

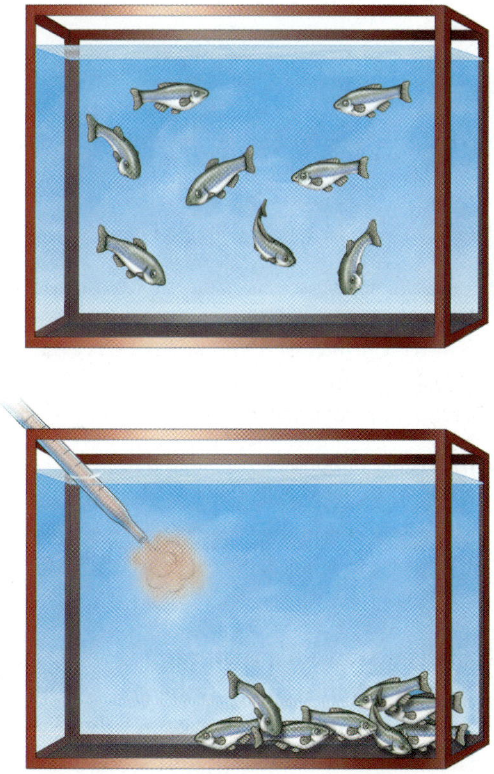

(a) Minnows are widely dispersed in an aquarium before an alarm substance is introduced.

(b) Within seconds of the alarm substance being introduced, minnows aggregate near the bottom of the aquarium and reduce their movement.

▲ **Figure 51.9 Minnows responding to the presence of an alarm substance.**

CONCEPT CHECK 51.1

1. If an egg rolls out of the nest, a mother graylag goose will retrieve it by nudging it with her beak and head. If researchers remove the egg or substitute a ball during this process, the goose continues to bob her beak and head while she moves back to the nest. What type of behavior is this? Suggest a proximate and an ultimate explanation.
2. How is migration based on circannual rhythms poorly suited for adaptation to global climate change?
3. **WHAT IF?** Suppose you exposed various fish species to the alarm substance from minnows. Suggest why some species might respond like minnows, some might increase activity, and some might show no change.

For suggested answers, see Appendix A.

CONCEPT 51.2

Learning establishes specific links between experience and behavior

For many behaviors we have discussed—such as fixed action patterns, taxis, and pheromone signaling—nearly all individuals in a population exhibit virtually the same behavior, despite internal and environmental differences during development and throughout life. Behavior that is developmentally fixed in this way is called **innate behavior**. In other cases, behavior is variable, depending on experience. One of the most powerful ways that environmental conditions can influence behavior is through **learning**, the modification of behavior based on specific experiences.

Habituation

One of the simplest forms of learning is **habituation**, a loss of responsiveness to stimuli that convey little or no new information. For example, many mammals and birds recognize alarm calls of members of their species, but eventually stop responding if these calls are not followed by an actual attack (the "cry-wolf" effect). Habituation allows an animal's nervous system to focus on stimuli that signal the presence of food, a mate, or real danger, rather than waste time or energy on stimuli that are irrelevant to the animal's survival and reproduction. In this way, habituation may increase an individual's fitness—its contribution to the gene pool of the next generation (see Chapter 23).

Imprinting

A type of behavior that includes both learned and innate components is **imprinting**, the formation at a specific stage in life of a long-lasting behavioral response to a particular individual or object. Imprinting is distinguished from other types of learning by having a **sensitive period**, also called a critical period, a limited developmental phase when certain behaviors can be learned. During the sensitive period, the young imprint on their parent and learn the basic behaviors of their species, while the parent learns to recognize its offspring. Among gulls, for instance, the sensitive period for a parent to bond with its young lasts one to two days. If bonding does not occur, the parent will not care for the infant, leading to death for the offspring and a decrease in reproductive success for the parent.

But how do the young know on whom—or what—to imprint? For example, how do young birds know that they should follow their mother? The tendency to respond is innate in the birds; the outside world provides the *imprinting stimulus*, something to which the response will be directed. Experiments with many species of waterfowl indicate that they have no innate recognition of "mother." They respond to and identify with the first object they encounter that has certain key characteristics. In classic experiments done in the 1930s, Konrad Lorenz showed that the principal imprinting stimulus in greylag geese (*Anser anser*) is a nearby object that is moving away from the young. When incubator-hatched goslings spent their first few hours with Lorenz rather than with a goose, they imprinted on him and steadfastly followed him from then on **(Figure 51.10a)**. Furthermore, they showed no recognition of their biological mother or other adults of their own species.

Cranes also imprint as hatchlings, creating both problems and opportunities in efforts to save endangered crane species. For instance, in an experiment, a group of 77 whooping cranes (*Grus americana*), which are endangered, were hatched and raised by sandhill cranes (*Grus canadensis*). Because the whooping cranes imprinted on their foster parents, none formed a mating pair-bond with another whooping crane. Therefore, captive breeding programs now isolate young cranes and expose them to the sights and sounds of members of their own species. To aid crane conservation further, young whooping cranes have been imprinted on humans in "crane suits" and taught to follow these "parents" flying ultralight aircraft along new migration routes **(Figure 51.10b)**. Importantly, these cranes still form mating pair-bonds with other whooping cranes, indicating that the crane costumes had the features required to direct "normal" imprinting.

(a) These young greylag geese imprinted on ethologist Konrad Lorenz.

(b) A pilot wearing a crane suit and flying an ultralight plane acts as a surrogate parent to direct the migration of whooping cranes.

▲ **Figure 51.10 Imprinting.** Imprinting can be altered to (a) investigate animal behavior or (b) direct animal behavior.

WHAT IF? *Suppose the geese following Lorenz were bred to each other. How might their imprinting on Lorenz affect their offspring? Explain.*

Spatial Learning

Every natural environment shows some spatial variation, such as in the locations of nest sites, hazards, food, and prospective mates. Consequently, an organism's fitness may be enhanced by the capacity for **spatial learning**, the establishment of a memory that reflects the environment's spatial structure.

Ethologist Niko Tinbergen studied spatial learning while a graduate student in 1932 in the Netherlands. Tinbergen was intrigued by the behavior of the female digger wasp (*Philanthus triangulum*), which nests in small burrows dug into sand dunes. He noticed that when a wasp left her nest to go hunting, she covered the entrance with sand. Upon her return, she flew directly to her hidden nest, despite the presence of hundreds of other burrows in the area. Tinbergen hypothesized that a wasp locates her nest by learning its position relative to visible **landmarks**, or location indicators. To test this hypothesis, Tinbergen carried out an experiment in the natural habitat of the wasps **(Figure 51.11)**. By manipulating objects around nest entrances, Tinbergen demonstrated that digger wasps engage in visual learning. This experiment was so simple and informative that it could be summarized very concisely. In fact, at 32 pages, Tinbergen's Ph.D. thesis is still the shortest ever approved at Leiden University.

Cognitive Maps

Some animals guide their activity by a **cognitive map**, a representation in the nervous system of the spatial relationships between objects in an animal's surroundings. Rather than relying solely on moving from landmark to landmark, animals using cognitive maps can navigate more flexibly and efficiently by relating landmark positions to one another.

One striking example of cognitive mapping is found in the Clark's nutcracker (*Nucifraga columbiana*). Nutcrackers are corvids, the bird family that also includes ravens, crows, and jays. In the fall, a single nutcracker stores as many as 30,000 pine seeds in thousands of hiding places called caches, distributed over an area as large as 35 km^2. During the winter, the birds relocate many of their caches. By experimentally varying the distance between landmarks, researchers demonstrated that birds can identify the halfway point between landmarks. Such behavior suggests that nutcrackers employ an abstract geometric rule, which we can approximate as "Seed caches are found halfway between particular landmarks." Such rules, a fundamental property of cognitive maps, reduce the amount of detail required to remember an object's location. As we discussed in Chapter 49, corvids also display other forms of higher nervous system function.

Associative Learning

Learning also involves making associations between experiences. Consider, for example, a white-footed mouse that bites into the brightly colored caterpillar of a monarch butterfly, only to get a mouthful of distasteful fluid. Following this experience, the mouse may avoid attacking insects of similar appearance. The ability to associate one environmental feature (such as a color) with another (such as a foul taste) is called **associative learning**.

Associative learning can be divided into two types: classical conditioning and operant conditioning. In **classical conditioning**, an arbitrary stimulus becomes associated with a particular outcome. Russian physiologist Ivan Pavlov carried out early experiments in classical conditioning, demonstrating that if he always rang a bell just before feeding a dog, the dog would eventually salivate at the bell's sound alone, in anticipation of food. In **operant conditioning**, also called trial-and-error learning, an animal learns to associate one of its own behaviors with a reward or punishment and then tends to repeat or avoid that behavior. For instance, a predator may learn to avoid certain kinds of potential prey if they are associated with painful experiences

▼ Figure 51.11 Inquiry

Does a digger wasp use landmarks to find her nest?

EXPERIMENT A female digger wasp covers the entrance to her nest while foraging for food, but finds the correct wasp nest reliably upon her return 30 minutes or more later. To test the hypothesis that a wasp learns visual landmarks that mark her nest before she leaves on hunting trips, Niko Tinbergen marked one nest with a ring of pinecones while the wasp was in the burrow. He returned two days later, shifted the ring of pinecones away from the nest, and waited to observe the wasp's behavior.

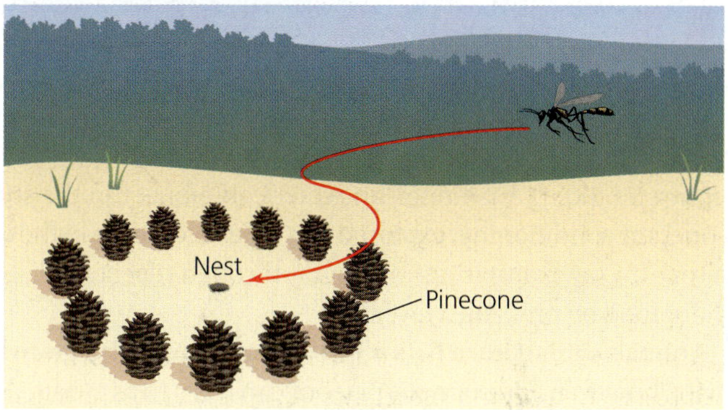

RESULTS When the wasp returned, she flew to the center of the pinecone circle instead of to the nearby nest. Repeating the experiment with many wasps, Tinbergen obtained the same results.

CONCLUSION The experiment supported the hypothesis that digger wasps use visual landmarks to keep track of their nests.

SOURCE N. Tinbergen, *The Study of Instinct*, Clarendon Press, Oxford (1951).

WHAT IF? Suppose the digger wasp had returned to her original nest site, despite the pinecones having been moved. What alternative hypotheses might you propose regarding how the wasp finds her nest and why the pinecones didn't misdirect the wasp?

▲ **Figure 51.12 Operant conditioning.** Having received a face full of quills, a young coyote has probably learned to avoid porcupines.

▲ **Figure 51.13 A young chimpanzee learning to crack oil palm nuts by observing an experienced elder.**

(Figure 51.12). B. F. Skinner, an American pioneer in the study of operant conditioning, explored this type of learning in the laboratory by, for example, training a rat through repeated trials to obtain food by pressing a lever.

Animals cannot learn to link just any stimulus with a given behavior, however. For example, pigeons can learn to associate danger with a particular sound but not with a particular color. The pigeons' inability to associate a color with danger does not reflect an inability to distinguish visual clues because pigeons *can* learn to associate a color with food. Rather, the development and organization of the pigeon nervous system apparently restrict the associations that can be formed. Such restrictions are not limited to birds. Rats, for example, can learn to avoid illness-inducing food on the basis of smells but not sights or sounds.

The associations readily formed by an animal often reflect relationships likely to occur in nature. In the case of a rat's diet, for example, a harmful food is far more likely to have a certain odor than to be associated with a particular sound. For this reason, experiments regarding associative learning need to be interpreted carefully: What we define in the laboratory as a limitation in learning may be of little or no consequence to the animal in its natural habitat.

Cognition and Problem Solving

The most complex forms of learning involve **cognition**—the process of knowing represented by awareness, reasoning, recollection, and judgment. In addition to primates, many groups of animals, including insects, appear to exhibit cognition in controlled laboratory studies. In one experiment, honeybees were shown a color and then presented with a Y-shaped maze in which one arm was the same color. If the bees flew into that arm of the maze, they were rewarded. They were then shown a black-and-white sample with either vertical or horizontal bars and tested in a maze that had vertical bars in one arm and horizontal bars in the other. They most often chose the arm with bars oriented in the same way as the sample. Another set of bees trained in the color mazes were rewarded for flying into the arm that had a *different* color than the sample. When these bees were tested in mazes with the bars, they chose the arm that differed from the sample. Honeybees thus can apparently distinguish on the basis of "same" and "different."

The information-processing ability of a nervous system can also be revealed in **problem solving**, the cognitive activity of devising a method to proceed from one state to another in the face of real or apparent obstacles. For example, if a chimpanzee is placed in a room with several boxes on the floor and a banana hung high out of reach, the chimp can "size up" the situation and stack the boxes, enabling it to reach the food. Such problem-solving behavior is highly developed in some mammals, especially primates and dolphins. Notable examples have also been observed in some bird species, especially ravens, crows, and jays. In one study, ravens were confronted with food hanging from a branch by a string. After failing to grab the food in flight, one raven flew to the branch and alternately pulled up and stepped on the string until the food was within reach. A number of other ravens eventually arrived at similar solutions. Nevertheless, some ravens failed to solve the problem, indicating that problem-solving success in this species, as in others, varies with individual experience and abilities.

Many animals learn to solve problems by observing the behavior of other individuals. Young wild chimpanzees, for example, learn how to crack oil palm nuts with two stones by copying experienced chimpanzees **(Figure 51.13)**.

Development of Learned Behaviors

Most of the acquired behaviors we have discussed involve learning that takes place over a relatively short time. Development of some other behaviors, such as singing in some bird species, occurs in distinct stages. The first stage of song learning for white-crowned sparrows takes place early in life. If a fledgling sparrow is prevented from hearing real sparrows or recordings of sparrow songs during the first 50 days of life, it fails to develop the adult song of its species. Although the young bird does not sing during the sensitive period, it memorizes the song of its species by listening to other white-crowned sparrows sing. During the sensitive period, fledglings chirp more in response to songs of their own species than to songs of other species. Thus, although young white-crowned sparrows learn the songs they will sing as adults, learning appears to be bounded by genetically controlled preferences.

The sensitive period when a white-crowned sparrow memorizes its species' song is followed by a second learning phase when the juvenile bird sings tentative notes called a subsong. The juvenile bird hears its own singing and compares it with the song memorized during the sensitive period. Once a sparrow's own song matches the one it memorized, the song "crystallizes" as the final song, and the bird sings only this adult song for the rest of its life.

There are important exceptions to the song-learning scenario seen in white-crowned sparrows. Canaries, for example, do not have a single sensitive period for song learning. A young canary begins with a subsong, but the full song the canary develops is not crystallized in the same way as it is in white-crowned sparrows. Between breeding seasons, the song becomes flexible again, and an adult male may learn new song "syllables" each year, adding to the song it already sings.

These examples of song learning illustrate how experience and genetics influence development of a behavior. We'll examine this subject more extensively in the next section, exploring how variation in environment and genetic makeup influence animal behavior.

CONCEPT CHECK 51.2

1. How might associative learning explain why unrelated distasteful or stinging insects have similar colors?
2. Clark's nutcrackers hide tens of thousands of seeds each fall, some of which they never retrieve. Why might there be an evolutionary advantage for the species if individuals forget the location of some caches?
3. **WHAT IF?** Suppose you designed a laboratory environment using just a few objects as landmarks. How might you position and manipulate the objects to determine whether an animal could use a cognitive map to remember the location of a food source?

For suggested answers, see Appendix A.

CONCEPT 51.3

Both genetic makeup and environment contribute to the development of behaviors

Animal behavior, like anatomy and physiology, is governed by complex interactions between genetic and environmental factors. Although the DNA sequence of the genome provides instructions for the development of behavior, many factors—including the environment of the fertilized egg and the animal's diet, social interactions, and surroundings—modify how these instructions are carried out. This fact contrasts sharply with the popular conception that behavior is due *either* to genes (nature) *or* to environment (nurture). In this section, we'll explore how scientists determine to what extent differences in genetic makeup and environment underlie differences in animal behavior.

Experience and Behavior

One informative approach to identifying environmental contributions to behavior is a **cross-fostering study**, in which the young of one species are placed in the care of adults from another species. The extent to which the offspring's behavior changes in such a situation is one measure of how the social and physical environment influences behavior.

The males of certain mouse species have behavioral differences that are well suited for cross-fostering experiments. Male California mice (*Peromyscus californicus*) are highly aggressive toward other mice and provide extensive parental care. In contrast, male white-footed mice (*Peromyscus leucopus*) are less aggressive and engage in little parental care. When the pups of each species were placed in the nests of the other species, the cross-fostering altered the behavior of both species **(Table 51.1)**. For instance, male California mice raised by white-footed mice were less aggressive toward intruders. Experience during development thus can have a strong influence on aggressive behavior in these rodents. However, the cross-fostering affected a wider range of behaviors for California mice than for white-footed mice.

The mouse cross-fostering experiments reveal that the influence of experience on behavior need not be confined to a single generation. When the cross-fostered California mice became parents, they spent less time retrieving their offspring than California mice raised by their own species. Thus, experience during development can modify physiology in a way

Table 51.1 Influence of Cross-Fostering on Male Mice*

Species	Aggression Toward an Intruder	Aggression in Neutral Situation	Paternal Behavior
California mice fostered by white-footed mice	Reduced	No difference	Reduced
White-footed mice fostered by California mice	No difference	Increased	No difference

*Comparisons are with mice raised by parents of their own species.

that alters parental behavior, extending the influence of environment to a subsequent generation.

For humans, the influence of genetics and environment on behavior can be explored by a **twin study**, in which researchers compare the behavior of identical twins raised apart with those raised in the same household. As discussed in Chapter 49, twin studies have been instrumental in studying human behavioral disorders, such as schizophrenia, anxiety disorders, and alcoholism. These investigations have revealed that the degree of susceptibility governed by genetic differences between individuals varies among mental disorders but is almost always greater than 20% and less than 80%. Both environment and genetics therefore contribute significantly to the behaviors that characterize these disorders in humans.

Regulatory Genes and Behavior

So far, we have talked about how experience can influence the genetic regulation of behavior. But how do genes direct behavior? As a field of research, behavioral genetics is still in its infancy. Nevertheless, we already know a great deal about some behaviors, such as courtship in certain insects.

The courtship behavior of the male fruit fly shown in Figure 51.7 involves a complex series of actions in response to multiple sensory stimuli. Nevertheless, recent evidence indicates that a single gene called *fru* controls the entire male courtship ritual. Males lacking a functional *fru* gene fail to court and mate with females. (The name *fru* is short for *fruitless*, reflecting the absence of offspring from the mutant males.) Normal male and female flies express distinct forms of the *fru* gene. When females are genetically manipulated to express the male form of *fru*, they court other females, performing the role normally played by the male. How can a single gene control so many behaviors and actions? The explanation lies in the fact that *fru* is a master regulatory gene that directs the expression and activity of many genes with narrower functions. Together, genes that are controlled by the *fru* gene bring about sex-specific development of the fly nervous system. In effect, *fru* programs the fly for male courtship behavior by overseeing a male-specific wiring of the central nervous system.

Further evidence of genetic influence on insect courtship comes from studies of the courtship song of the green lacewing. Found throughout central to northern Eurasia and North America, these insects include at least 15 species, identical in appearance but having different courtship songs. For the last three decades, Charles Henry, at the University of Connecticut, has explored the genetic basis for these differences. First, he showed that lacewings reared in isolation in the laboratory performed the song specific to their species. Thus, the courtship song must be genetically controlled. Henry then crossed different green lacewing species in the laboratory and analyzed the songs produced by the hybrid offspring **(Figure 51.14)**. These experiments demonstrated that each component or property of the courtship song is governed by a different gene. Furthermore, the

▼ Figure 51.14 Inquiry

Are the songs of green lacewing species under the control of multiple genes?

EXPERIMENT Charles Henry, Lucía Martínez, and Kent Holsinger crossed males and females of *Chrysoperla plorabunda* and *Chrysoperla johnsoni*, two morphologically identical species of lacewings that sing different courtship songs.

SOUND RECORDINGS

Chrysoperla plorabunda parent:

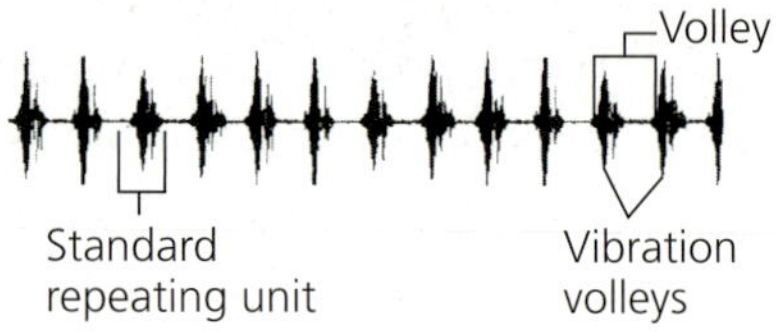

crossed with

Chrysoperla johnsoni parent:

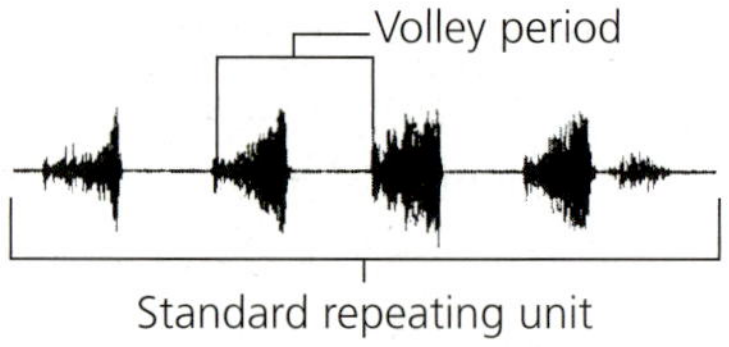

The researchers compared the songs of the male and female parents with those of the hybrid offspring that had been raised in isolation from other lacewings.

RESULTS The F_1 hybrid offspring sing a song in which the length of the standard repeating unit is similar to that sung by the *Chrysoperla plorabunda* parent, but the volley period—the interval between vibration volleys—is more similar to that of the *Chrysoperla johnsoni* parent.

F_1 hybrids, typical phenotype:

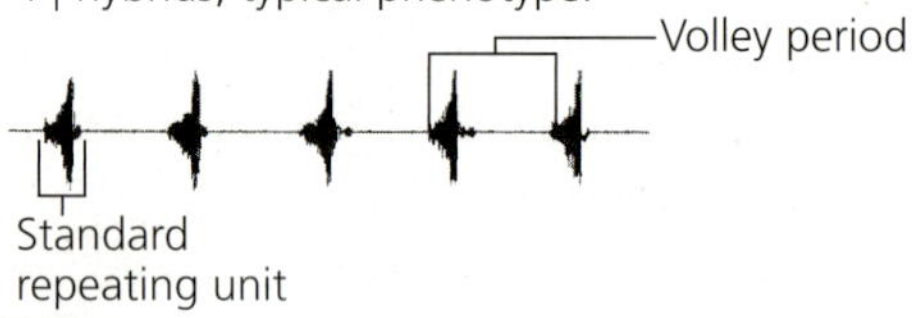

CONCLUSION Since the song of the hybrid offspring has features of the songs of both parents, the results indicate that the songs sung by *Chrysoperla plorabunda* and *Chrysoperla johnsoni* are under the control of more than one gene.

SOURCE C. S. Henry et al., The inheritance of mating songs in two cryptic, sibling lacewing species, *Genetica* 116:269–289 (2002).

WHAT IF? Suppose the hybrids generated in this experiment were fertile. Would the appearance of the hybrid song shown in the figure be likely to lead to the formation of a new species? Explain your answer.

distinct courtship song of each green lacewing species reflects genetic differences at multiple, independent loci.

Genetically Based Behavioral Variation in Natural Populations

Behavioral differences between closely related species, such as green lacewings, are common. Though often less obvious, significant differences in behavior can also be found *within* a species. When behavioral variation between populations of a species corresponds to variation in environmental conditions, it may be evidence of past evolution.

Case Study: *Variation in Migratory Patterns*

One species well suited to the study of behavioral variation is the blackcap (*Sylvia atricapilla*), a small migratory warbler. Blackcaps that breed in Germany generally migrate southwest to Spain and then south to Africa for the winter. In the 1950s, a few blackcaps began to spend their winters in Britain, and over time the population of blackcaps wintering in Britain grew to many thousands. Leg bands show that some of these birds had migrated westward from central Germany. Why were there now two patterns of migration from Germany? To answer this question, Peter Berthold, at the Max Planck Research Center in Radolfzell, Germany, devised a strategy to study migratory orientation in the laboratory **(Figure 51.15)**. The results demonstrated that the two patterns of migration reflect genetic differences between the two populations.

Berthold's study indicates that the change in migratory behavior in western European blackcaps occurred both recently and rapidly. Before 1950, there were no known westward-migrating blackcaps in Germany. By the 1990s, westward migrants made up 7–11% of the blackcap populations of Germany. Once westward migration began, it persisted and increased in frequency, perhaps due to the widespread use of winter bird feeders in Britain, as well as shorter migration distances.

Case Study: *Variation in Prey Selection*

Another well-known example of genetically based behavioral variation within a species involves prey selection by the western garter snake (*Thamnophis elegans*). The natural diet of this species differs widely across its range in California. Coastal populations feed on salamanders, frogs, and toads, but predominantly on banana slugs (*Ariolimus californicus*). Inland populations feed on frogs, leeches, and fish, but not on banana slugs. In fact, banana slugs are rare or absent in the inland habitats.

When researchers offered banana slugs to snakes from each wild population, most coastal snakes readily ate them, whereas inland snakes tended to refuse. To what extent do experience and genetics contribute to a snake's fondness for banana slugs?

▼ Figure 51.15 Inquiry

Are differences in migratory orientation within a species genetically determined?

EXPERIMENT Peter Berthold and colleagues in southern Germany raised two sets of young birds for their study. One group consisted of the offspring of blackcaps captured while wintering in Britain and then bred in Germany in an outdoor cage. The other group consisted of young birds collected from nests near the laboratory and then raised in cages. In the autumn, Berthold's team placed the blackcaps captured in Britain and the young birds raised in cages in large, glass-covered funnel cages lined with carbon-coated paper for 1.5–2 hours. When the funnels were placed outside at night, the birds moved around, making marks on the paper that indicated the direction in which they were trying to "migrate."

RESULTS The wintering adult birds captured in Britain and their laboratory-raised offspring both attempted to migrate to the west. In contrast, the young birds collected from nests in southern Germany attempted to migrate to the southwest.

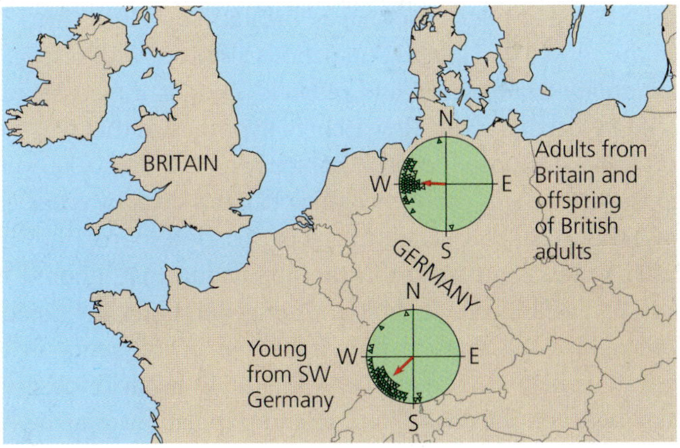

CONCLUSION The young of the British blackcaps and the young birds from Germany (the control group) were raised under similar conditions but showed very different migratory orientations, indicating that migratory orientation has a genetic basis.

SOURCE P. Berthold et al., Rapid microevolution of migratory behavior in a wild bird species, *Nature* 360:668–690 (1992).

WHAT IF? Suppose the birds had not shown a difference in orientation in these experiments. Could you conclude that the behavior was not genetically based? Explain.

▲ **Figure 51.16 Western garter snake from a coastal habitat eating a banana slug.** Experiments indicate that the preference of these snakes for banana slugs may be influenced mainly by genetics rather than by environment.

To answer this question, pregnant snakes were collected from each wild population and housed in separate cages in the laboratory. While still very young, the offspring were offered a small piece of banana slug on each of ten days. More than 60% of the young snakes from coastal mothers ate banana slugs on eight or more of the ten days. In contrast, fewer than 20% of the young snakes from inland mothers ate a piece of banana slug even once. Perhaps not surprisingly, banana slugs thus appear to be a genetically acquired taste **(Figure 51.16)**.

How did a genetically determined difference in feeding preference come to match the snakes' habitats so well? It turns out that the coastal and inland populations also vary with respect to their ability to recognize and respond to odor molecules produced by banana slugs. Researchers hypothesize that when inland snakes colonized coastal habitats more than 10,000 years ago, some of them could recognize banana slugs by scent. Because these snakes took advantage of this food source, they had higher fitness than snakes in the population that ignored the slugs. Over hundreds or thousands of generations, the capacity to recognize the slugs as prey increased in frequency in the coastal population. The marked variation in behavior observed today between the coastal and inland populations may be evidence of this past evolutionary change.

Influence of Single-Locus Variation

Many scientists think that in most cases behavior is shaped by a large number of genes that individually have small effects. This does not imply, however, that variation at a single gene locus cannot have observable effects. In some cases, differences at a single locus can cause dramatic differences in behavior, even if the behavior requires the activity of many other genes. One striking example is the behavior of two closely related species of voles, which are small, mouse-like rodents. Male meadow voles (*Microtus pennsylvanicus*) are solitary and do not form lasting relationships with mates. Following mating, they pay little attention to their pups. In contrast, male prairie voles (*Microtus ochrogaster*) form a strong attachment, or *pair-bond*, with a single female after they mate **(Figure 51.17)**. Male prairie voles hover over their young pups, licking them and carrying them, while acting aggressively toward intruders.

◄ **Figure 51.17 A pair of prairie voles (*Microtus ochrogaster*) huddling.** Male North American prairie voles associate closely with their mates, as shown here, and contribute substantially to the care of young.

Research suggested that a neurotransmitter released during mating is critical for the partnering and parental behavior of male voles. Known as vasopressin or ADH (see Chapter 44), this peptide binds to a specific receptor in the central nervous system. When male prairie voles are treated with a drug that inhibits the brain receptor for vasopressin, they fail to form pair-bonds after mating. Scientists have also observed that the vasopressin receptor gene of prairie voles is highly expressed in the brain, whereas that of meadow voles is not.

To test whether the amount of the vasopressin receptor present in the brain regulates the postmating behavior of voles, researchers inserted the vasopressin receptor gene from prairie voles into male meadow voles. The meadow voles carrying this gene not only developed brains with higher levels of the vasopressin receptor but also showed many of the same mating behaviors as male prairie voles, such as pair-bonding. Thus, although many genes influence pair-bond formation and parenting among voles, the level of the vasopressin receptor alone determines which behavioral pattern develops. When such strong single-locus effects occur, they provide an excellent opportunity to investigate behavioral evolution, as we'll see in the next section.

CONCEPT CHECK 51.3

1. Explain why geographic variation in garter snake prey choice might indicate that the behavior evolved by natural selection.
2. Why is it easier to identify mutations affecting courtship than those affecting other essential behaviors?
3. **WHAT IF?** Suppose that a pair of identical twins reared apart behave identically 80% of the time when performing a particular activity. What additional information would you need to draw a conclusion about the genetic basis of the behavior?

For suggested answers, see Appendix A.

CONCEPT **51.4**

Selection for individual survival and reproductive success can explain most behaviors

The genetic components of behavior, like all other aspects of phenotype, evolve through natural selection for traits that enhance survival and reproductive success in a population. Two behaviors that can affect fitness most directly are foraging and mate choice.

Foraging Behavior

Because adequate nutrition is essential to an animal's survival and reproductive success, we should expect natural selection to refine behaviors that enhance the efficiency of feeding. Food-obtaining behavior, or **foraging**, includes not only eating but also any activities an animal uses to search for, recognize, and capture food items.

Evolution of Foraging Behavior

The fruit fly (*Drosophila melanogaster*) has provided scientists with an opportunity to examine how genetic variation might contribute to the evolution of foraging behavior. Variation in a gene called *forager* (*for*) dictates the food search behavior of fruit fly larvae. On average, larvae carrying the for^R ("Rover") allele travel nearly twice as far while feeding as larvae with the for^s ("sitter") allele. Experiments revealed that the enzyme encoded by the *forager* locus is more active in for^R than in for^s larvae. Because this type of enzyme typically is involved in signal transduction pathways (see Chapter 45), these results indicate that changes in processing of environmental information can substantially alter behavior.

Both the for^R and for^s alleles are present in natural populations. What circumstances might favor one or the other allele? The answer became apparent in experiments when flies were kept for many generations at either low or high population densities. The larvae from the two samples clearly diverged in behavior, as measured by differences in average length of their foraging path **(Figure 51.18)**. Larvae maintained for many generations at a low density foraged over shorter distances than those kept at high density. Furthermore, genetic tests indicated that the for^s allele had increased in frequency in the low-density populations, whereas the for^R allele had increased in frequency in the high-density group. These changes make sense. At low population density, short-distance foraging yields sufficient food, while long-distance foraging would result in unnecessary energy expenditure. Under crowded conditions, however, long-distance foraging could enable larvae to move beyond areas of food depletion. In summary, there was an observable and interpretable evolutionary change in behavior in the laboratory populations.

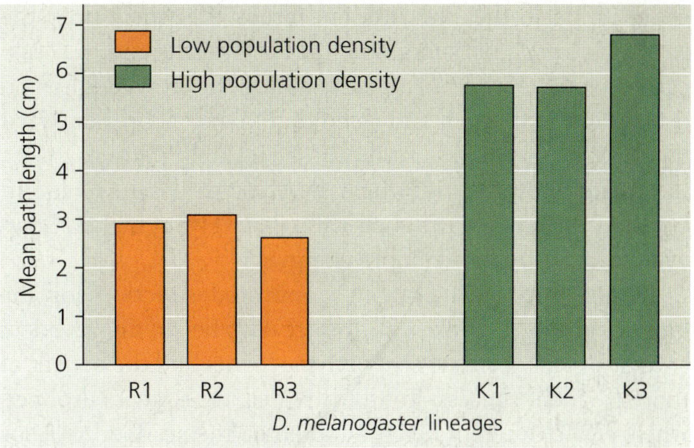

▲ **Figure 51.18 Evolution of foraging behavior by laboratory populations of *Drosophila melanogaster*.** After 74 generations of living at low population density, *D. melanogaster* larvae (populations R1–R3) followed foraging paths significantly shorter than those of *D. melanogaster* larvae that had lived at high density (populations K1–K3).

Optimal Foraging Model

To study the proximate and ultimate causation of diverse foraging strategies, behavioral ecologists sometimes apply a type of cost-benefit analysis used in economics. This idea proposes that foraging behavior is a compromise between the benefits of nutrition and the costs of obtaining food. These costs might include the energy expenditure of foraging as well as the risk of being eaten while foraging. According to this **optimal foraging model**, natural selection should favor a foraging behavior that minimizes the costs of foraging and maximizes the benefits.

As an example of how the optimal foraging model can be applied, let's consider the feeding behavior of the Northwestern crow (*Corvus caurinus*). On islands off British Columbia, these crows search rocky tide pools for gastropod molluscs called whelks. After spotting a whelk, the crow picks the whelk up in its beak, flies upward, and drops the whelk onto the rocks. If the drop is successful, the shell breaks and the crow can dine on the whelk's soft parts. If not, the crow flies up and drops the whelk again and again until the shell breaks. What determines how high the crow flies? The higher the crow flies, the greater the force with which the whelk strikes the rocks, increasing the chance the shell will break. Flying higher, however, means consuming more energy.

If energetic considerations dominated selection for the crow's foraging behavior, the average drop height might reflect a trade-off between the cost of flying higher and the benefit of more frequent success. To test this idea, researchers dropped whelks from different heights and noted the number of drops required to break a shell. For each height, they calculated the average number of drops and the average *total flight height*, the drop height times the average number of drops **(Figure 51.19)**. A drop height of about 5 m turned out to be optimal, breaking the shells with the lowest total flight height—in other words, with the least work. The actual average flight height for crows in their whelk-eating behavior is 5.23 m, very close to the prediction based on an optimal trade-off between energy gained (food) versus energy expended.

The close agreement between the predicted and actual flight heights suggests that the foraging model reflects the selective forces shaping the evolution of this behavior. However, other models could explain the findings equally well. For example, the average flight height could minimize the average *time* necessary to break open a whelk. Further experiments are needed to evaluate these possibilities.

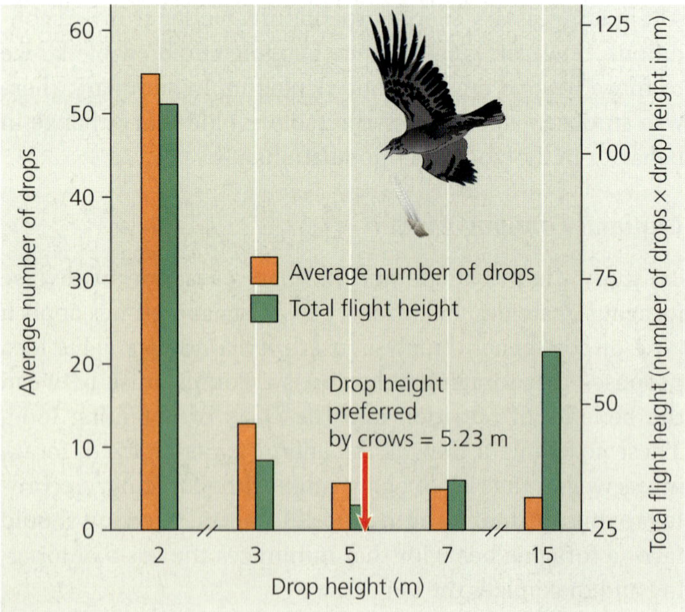

▲ **Figure 51.19 Energy costs and benefits in foraging behavior.** Experimental results indicate that dropping shells from a height of 5 m results in breakage with the least amount of work. The actual drop height preferred by crows corresponds almost exactly to the height that minimizes total flight height.

Balancing Risk and Reward

One of the most significant potential costs to a forager is risk of predation. Maximizing energy gain and minimizing energy costs are of little benefit if the behavior makes the forager a likely meal for a predator. It seems logical, therefore, that predation risk would influence foraging behavior. Such appears to be the case for the mule deer (*Odocoileus hemionus*), which lives in the mountains of western North America. Researchers found that the food available for mule deer was fairly uniform across the potential foraging areas, although somewhat lower in open, nonforested areas. In contrast, the risk of predation differed greatly; mountain lions (*Puma concolor*), the major predator, killed large numbers of mule deer at forest edges and only a small number in open areas and forest interiors.

How does mule deer foraging behavior reflect the differences in predation risk in particular areas? Mule deer feed predominantly in open areas. Thus, it appears that mule deer foraging behavior reflects the large variation in predation risk and not the smaller variation in food availability. This result underscores that behavior often reflects a compromise between competing selective pressures.

Mating Behavior and Mate Choice

Mating behavior, which includes seeking or attracting mates, choosing among potential mates, and competing for mates, is the product of a form of natural selection called sexual selection (see Chapter 23). How mating behavior enhances reproductive success varies, depending on the species' mating system.

Mating Systems and Parental Care

As we saw for voles, the mating relationship between males and females varies a great deal from species to species. In many species, mating is **promiscuous**, with no strong pair-bonds or lasting relationships. In species in which the mates remain together for a longer period, the relationship may be **monogamous** (one male mating with one female) or **polygamous** (an individual of one sex mating with several of the other). Polygamous relationships most often involve a single male and many females, a system called **polygyny**, though some species exhibit **polyandry**, in which a single female mates with several males. Among monogamous species, males and females are often so much alike morphologically that they may be difficult or impossible to distinguish based on external characteristics **(Figure 51.20a)**. Polygynous species are generally dimorphic, with males being showier and often larger than females **(Figure 51.20b)**. Polyandrous species are also dimorphic, but in this case, females are generally more ornamented and larger than males **(Figure 51.20c)**.

The needs of the young are an important factor constraining the evolution of mating systems. Most newly hatched birds, for instance, cannot care for themselves. Rather, they require a large, continuous food supply, a need that is difficult for a single

(a) In monogamous species, such as these trumpeter swans, males and females are difficult to distinguish using external characteristics only.

(b) Among polygynous species, such as elk, the male (left) is often highly ornamented.

(c) In polyandrous species, such as these Wilson's phalaropes, females (top) are generally more ornamented than males.

▲ **Figure 51.20 Relationship between mating system and male and female forms.**

parent to meet. In such cases, a male that stays with and helps a single mate may ultimately have more viable offspring than it would by going off to seek additional mates. This may explain why most birds are monogamous. In contrast, for birds with young that can feed and care for themselves almost immediately after hatching, the males derive less benefit from staying with their partner. Males of these species, such as pheasants and quail, can maximize their reproductive success by seeking other mates, and polygyny is relatively common in such birds. In the case of mammals, the lactating female is often the only food source for the young; males usually play no role in raising the young. In mammalian species where males protect the females and young, such as lions, a male or small group of males typically takes care of many females at once in a harem.

Another factor influencing mating behavior and parental care is certainty of paternity. Young born to or eggs laid by a female definitely contain that female's genes. However, even within a normally monogamous relationship, a male other than the female's usual mate may have fathered that female's offspring. The certainty of paternity is relatively low in most species with internal fertilization because the acts of mating and birth (or mating and egg laying) are separated over time. This could explain why exclusively male parental care has evolved in very few species of birds and mammals. However, the males of many species with internal fertilization engage in behaviors that appear to increase their certainty of paternity. These behaviors include guarding females, removing any sperm from the female reproductive tract before copulation, and introducing large quantities of sperm to displace the sperm of other males. Certainty of paternity is much higher when egg laying and mating occur together, as in external fertilization. This may explain why parental care in aquatic invertebrates, fishes, and amphibians, when it occurs at all, is at least as likely to be by males as by females (**Figure 51.21**; see

▲ **Figure 51.21 Paternal care by a male jawfish.** The male jawfish, which lives in tropical marine environments, holds the eggs it has fertilized in its mouth, keeping them aerated and protecting them from egg predators until the young hatch.

also Figure 46.6). Male parental care occurs in only 7% of fish and amphibian families with internal fertilization, but in 69% of families with external fertilization.

It is important to point out that *certainty of paternity* does not mean that animals are aware of those factors when they behave a certain way. Parental behavior correlated with certainty of paternity exists because it has been reinforced over generations by natural selection. Nevertheless, the relationship between certainty of paternity and male parental care remains an area of active research, enlivened by controversy.

Sexual Selection and Mate Choice

As you read in Chapter 23, the degree of sexual dimorphism within a species results from sexual selection, a form of natural selection in which differences in reproductive success among individuals are a consequence of differences in mating success. Recall from that chapter that sexual selection can take the form of *intersexual selection*, in which members of one sex choose mates on the basis of particular characteristics of the other sex, such as courtship songs, or *intrasexual selection*, which involves competition between members of one sex for mates. Let's look next at some experimental evidence for sexual selection.

Mate Choice by Females Mate preferences by females may play a central role in the evolution of male behavior and anatomy through intersexual selection. As an example, let's consider the courtship behavior of stalk-eyed flies. The eyes of these insects are at the tips of stalks, which are longer in males than in females **(Figure 51.22)**. During courtship, a male presents himself to a female, front end on. Researchers have shown that females are more likely to mate with males that have relatively long eyestalks. Why would females favor this seemingly arbitrary trait? As discussed in Chapter 23, ornaments such as long eyestalks in these flies and bright coloration in male birds correlate in general with the male's health and vitality. A female that chooses a healthy male is likely to produce more offspring that survive to reproduce.

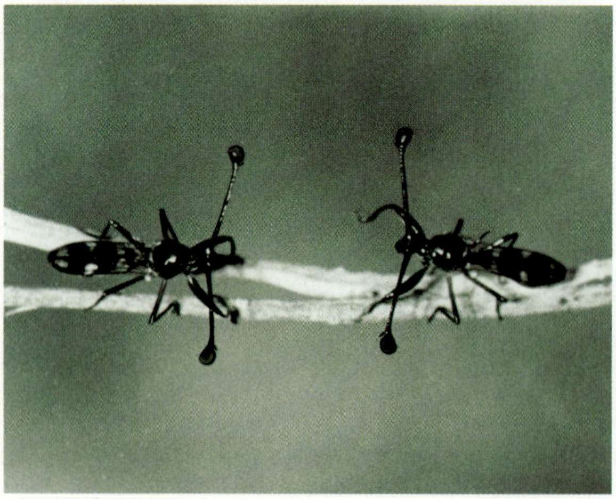

▲ **Figure 51.22 Male stalk-eyed flies.** Male eye span plays a role in ritualized contests between males, as shown here, and in mate selection by females.

▲ **Figure 51.23 Appearance of zebra finches in nature.** The male zebra finch (left) is more patterned and colorful than the female zebra finch.

Experiments carried out with zebra finches reveal that imprinting can also contribute to mate choice. Both male and female zebra finches normally lack any feather crest on their head **(Figure 51.23)**. To explore whether parental appearance affects mate preference in offspring independent of any genetic influence, researchers provided zebra finches with artificial ornamentation. A 2.5-cm-long red feather was taped to the forehead feathers of either or both zebra finch parents when their chicks were 8 days old, approximately 2 days before they opened their eyes. A control group of zebra finches were raised by unadorned parents. When the chicks matured, they were presented with prospective mates that were either artificially ornamented with a red feather or non-ornamented **(Figure 51.24)**. Males showed no preference for either ornamented or non-ornamented mating partners. Females raised by non-ornamented parents or by parents in which only the female was ornamented also showed no preference. However, females raised by parents that were both ornamented or by a pair in which the male was ornamented preferred ornamented males as their own mates. Thus, female finches apparently take cues from their fathers in choosing mates.

Male Competition for Mates The previous examples show how female choice can select for one best type of male in a given situation, resulting in low variation among males. Male competition for mates is a source of sexual selection that also can reduce variation among males. Such competition may involve **agonistic behavior**, an often ritualized contest that determines which competitor gains access to a resource, such as food or mates **(Figure 51.25)**. The outcome of such contests may be determined by strength, size, or the effective use of horns, teeth, and so forth, but the consequences may be psychological rather than physical (see Figure 51.22).

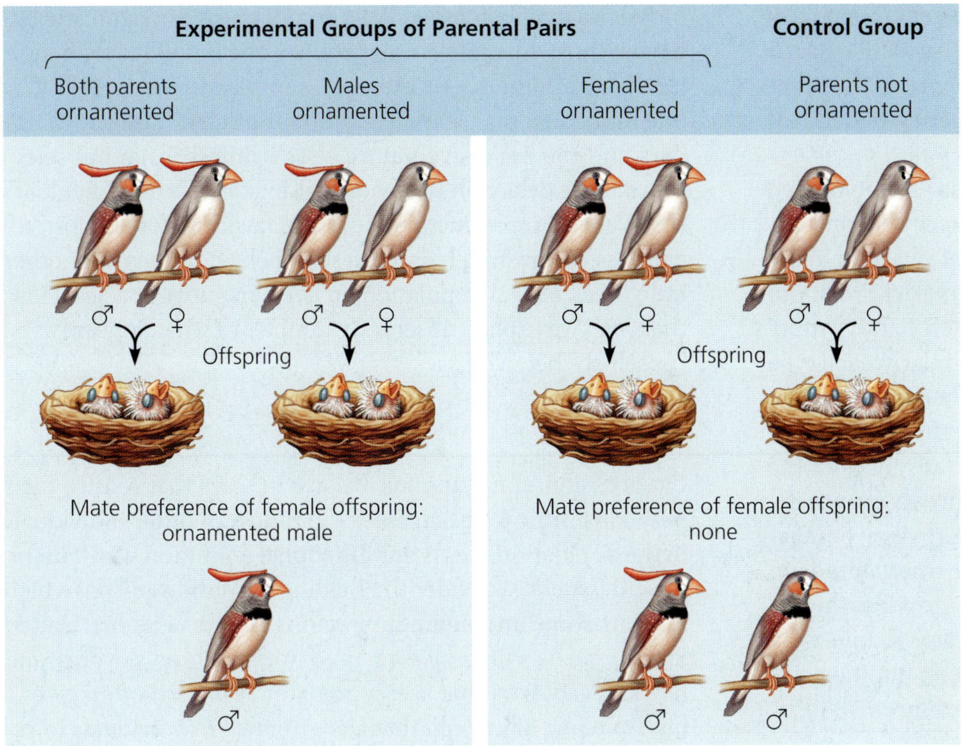

▲ **Figure 51.24 Sexual selection influenced by imprinting.** Experiments demonstrated that female zebra finch chicks that had imprinted on artificially ornamented fathers preferred ornamented males as adult mates. For all experimental groups, male offspring showed no preference for either ornamented or non-ornamented female mates.

▲ **Figure 51.25 Agonistic interaction.** Male eastern grey kangaroos (*Macropus giganteus*) often "box" in contests that determine which male is most likely to mate with an available female. Typically, one male snorts loudly before striking the other around the head and throat with his forelimbs. Further snorting and cuffing, as well as grappling, often follow. If the male under attack does not retreat, the fight may escalate, with each male balancing on his tail while attempting to kick his rival with the sharp toenails of a hind leg.

Despite the potential for male competition to select for reduced variation, behavioral and morphological variation in males is extremely high in some vertebrate species, including species of fish and deer, as well as in a wide variety of invertebrates. In some species, sexual selection has led to the evolution of alternative male mating behavior and morphology. How do scientists analyze situations where more than one mating behavior can result in successful reproduction? One approach relies on the rules that govern games.

Applying Game Theory

Often, the fitness of a particular behavioral phenotype is influenced by other behavioral phenotypes in the population. In studying such situations, behavioral ecologists use a range of tools, including game theory. Developed by American mathematician John Nash and others to model human economic behavior, **game theory** evaluates alternative strategies in situations where the outcome depends on the strategies of all the individuals involved.

As an example of applying game theory to mating behavior, let's consider the side-blotched lizard (*Uta stansburiana*) of California. Males can have orange, blue, or yellow throats **(Figure 51.26)**. Each throat color is associated with a different pattern of behavior. Orange-throat males are the most aggressive and defend large territories that contain many females. Blue-throat males are also territorial but defend smaller territories and fewer females. Yellow-throats are nonterritorial males that mimic females and use "sneaky" tactics to gain the chance to mate. Within a population, the fraction of males belonging to each genetically determined type varies over time. In one study population, the most frequent throat coloration changed over a

▲ **Figure 51.26 Male polymorphism in the side-blotched lizard (*Uta stansburiana*).** An orange-throat male, left; a blue-throat male, center; a yellow-throat male, right.

period of several years from blue to orange to yellow and back to blue. Evidence indicates that the mating success of each male type is influenced by the relative abundance of the other types in the population, an example of frequency-dependent selection.

By comparing the competition between side-blotched lizard males to the children's game of rock-paper-scissors, scientists devised an explanation for the cycles of variation in the lizard population. In the game, paper defeats rock, rock defeats scissors, and scissors defeats paper. Each hand symbol thus wins one matchup but loses the other. Similarly, each type of male lizard has an advantage over one other type, but not the other. When blue-throats are abundant, they can defend the few females in their territories from the advances of the sneaky yellow-throat males. However, blue-throats cannot defend their territories against the hyperaggressive orange-throats. Once the orange-throats become the most abundant, the larger number of females in each territory provides the opportunity for the yellow-throats to have greater mating success. The yellow-throats become more frequent, but then give way to the blue-throats, whose tactic of guarding small territories once again allows them the most success.

Game theory provides a way to think about complex evolutionary problems in which relative performance, not absolute performance, is the key to understanding the evolution of behavior. This makes game theory an important tool because the relative performance of one phenotype compared with others is a measure of Darwinian fitness.

CONCEPT CHECK 51.4

1. Why does the mode of fertilization correlate to a large degree with the presence or absence of male parental care?
2. Why was it important that the starting population for the fly-foraging experiments had both for^R and for^s alleles?
3. **WHAT IF?** Suppose a virus that infected a side-blotched lizard population killed many more males than females. How would the infection immediately affect the competition among the males for reproductive success?

For suggested answers, see Appendix A.

CONCEPT **51.5**

Inclusive fitness can account for the evolution of altruistic social behavior

Many social behaviors are selfish; that is, they benefit the individual at the expense of others, especially competitors. Even in species in which individuals do not engage in agonistic behavior, most adaptations that benefit one individual will indirectly harm others. For example, superior foraging ability by one individual may leave less food for others. It is easy to understand the pervasive nature of selfishness if natural selection shapes behavior. Behavior that maximizes an individual's survival and reproductive success is favored by selection, regardless of how much damage such behavior does to another individual, a local population, or even an entire species. How, then, can we explain observed examples of what appears to be "unselfish" behavior?

Altruism

On occasion, some animals behave in ways that reduce their individual fitness but increase the fitness of other individuals in the population; this is our functional definition of **altruism**, or selflessness. Consider the Belding's ground squirrel, which lives in some mountainous regions of the western United States and is vulnerable to predators such as coyotes and hawks. A squirrel that sees a predator approach often gives a high-pitched alarm call that alerts unaware individuals to retreat to their burrows. Note that for the squirrel that warns others, the conspicuous alarm behavior increases the risk of being killed because it brings attention to the caller's location.

Another example of altruistic behavior occurs in honeybee societies, in which the workers are sterile. The workers themselves never reproduce, but they labor on behalf of a single fertile queen. Furthermore, the workers sting intruders, a behavior that helps defend the hive but results in the death of those workers.

Altruism is also observed in naked mole rats (*Heterocephalus glaber*), highly social rodents that live in underground chambers and tunnels in southern and northeastern Africa. The naked mole rat, which is almost hairless and nearly blind, lives in colonies of 75 to 250 or more individuals (**Figure 51.27**). Each colony has only one reproducing female, the queen, who mates with one to three males, called kings. The rest of the colony consists of nonreproductive females and males who forage for underground

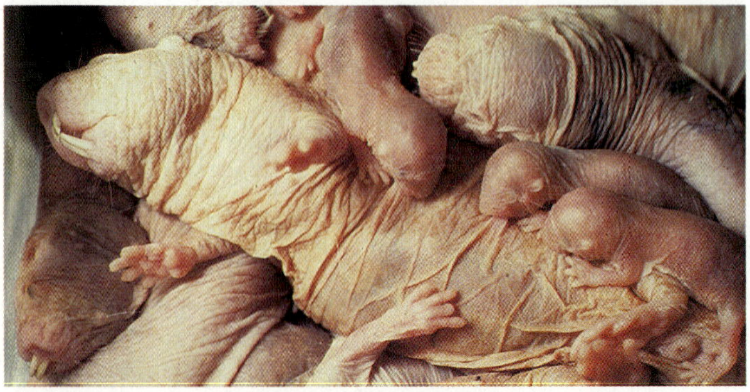

▲ **Figure 51.27 Naked mole rats, a species of colonial mammal that exhibits altruistic behavior.** Pictured here is a queen nursing offspring while surrounded by other members of the colony.

roots and tubers and care for the queen, the kings, and new offspring. The nonreproductive individuals may sacrifice their own lives in trying to protect the queen or kings from snakes or other predators that invade the colony.

Inclusive Fitness

How can a Belding's ground squirrel, a worker honeybee, or a naked mole rat enhance its fitness by aiding members of the population that may be its closest competitors? How can altruistic behavior be maintained by evolution if it does not enhance the survival and reproductive success of the self-sacrificing individuals?

The selection for altruistic behavior is most readily apparent in the act of parents sacrificing for their offspring. When parents sacrifice their own well-being to produce and aid offspring, this actually increases the fitness of the parents because it maximizes their genetic representation in the population. However, individuals sometimes help others who are not their offspring.

Biologist William Hamilton proposed that an animal could increase its genetic representation in the next generation by "altruistically" helping close relatives other than its own offspring. Like parents and offspring, full siblings have half their genes in common. Therefore, selection might also favor helping siblings or helping one's parents produce more siblings. This idea led to Hamilton's idea of **inclusive fitness**, the total effect an individual has on proliferating its genes by producing its own offspring *and* by providing aid that enables other close relatives, who share many of those genes, to produce offspring.

Hamilton's Rule and Kin Selection

According to Hamilton, the three key variables in an act of altruism are the benefit to the recipient, the cost to the altruist, and the coefficient of relatedness. The benefit, B, is the average number of *extra* offspring that the beneficiary of an altruistic act produces. The cost, C, is how many *fewer* offspring the altruist produces. The **coefficient of relatedness**, r, equals the fraction of genes that, on average, are shared. Natural selection favors altruism when the benefit to the recipient multiplied by the coefficient of relatedness exceeds the cost to the altruist—in other words, when $rB > C$. This inequality is called **Hamilton's rule.**

To better understand Hamilton's rule, let's apply it to a human population in which the average individual has two children. We'll imagine that a young man is close to drowning in heavy surf, and his brother risks his life to swim out and pull his sibling to safety. Had the young man drowned, his reproductive output would have been zero; but now, if we use the average, he can father two children. The benefit to the recipient of this altruistic act is thus two offspring ($B = 2$). Let's say that in this kind of surf an average swimmer has a 25% chance of drowning. We can then calculate the cost of the altruistic act as 0.25 times 2, the number of offspring expected if the altruist had stayed on shore: $C = 0.25 \times 2 = 0.5$. Finally, we note that full siblings who are not identical twins share half their genes on average ($r = 0.5$). One way to see this is in terms of the segregation of homologous chromosomes that occurs during meiosis of gametes (**Figure 51.28**; see also Chapter 13).

We can now use values of B, C, and r to evaluate whether natural selection would favor the altruistic act in our imaginary scenario. For our swimming brothers, $rB = 0.5 \times 2 = 1$ and $C = 0.5$. This satisfies Hamilton's rule; thus, natural selection would favor this altruistic act of one brother saving another. Averaging over many individuals and generations, any particular gene in the altruist will be passed on to more offspring if he risks the rescue than if he does not. Furthermore, among those genes propagated in this way may be some that contribute to altruistic behavior. The natural selection that favors altruistic behavior by enhancing reproductive success of relatives is called **kin selection.**

Kin selection weakens with hereditary distance. Siblings have an r of 0.5, but between an aunt and her niece, $r = 0.25$ (¼), and between first cousins, $r = 0.125$ (⅛). Notice that as the degree of relatedness decreases, the rB term in the Hamilton inequality also decreases. Would natural selection favor rescuing a cousin? Not unless the surf were less treacherous. For the original conditions, $rB = 0.125 \times 2 = 0.25$, which is only

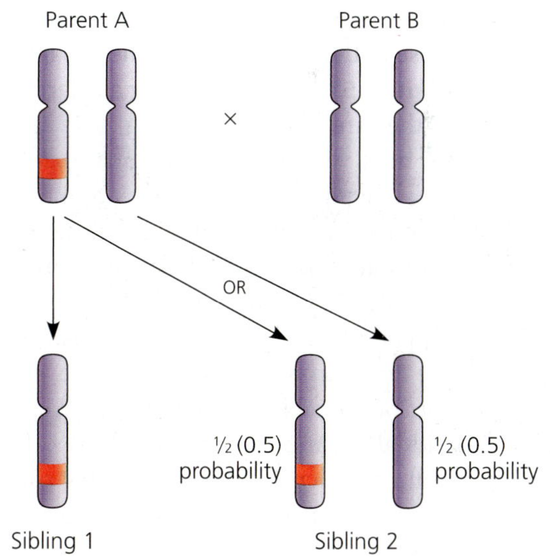

▲ **Figure 51.28 The coefficient of relatedness between siblings.** The red band indicates a particular allele (version of a gene) present on one chromosome, but not its homolog, in parent A. Sibling 1 has inherited the allele from parent A. There is a probability of ½ that sibling 2 will also inherit this allele from parent A. Any allele present on one chromosome of either parent will behave similarly. The coefficient of relatedness between the two siblings is thus ½, or 0.5.

WHAT IF? *The coefficient of relatedness of an individual to a full (nontwin) sibling or to either parent is the same, 0.5. Does this value also hold true in the cases of polyandry and polygyny?*

▶ **Figure 51.32 Both genes and culture build human nature.** Teaching of a younger generation by an older generation is one of the basic ways in which all cultures are transmitted.

species comes close to matching the social learning and cultural transmission that occurs among humans **(Figure 51.32)**.

Evolution and Human Culture

Human culture is related to evolutionary theory in the discipline of **sociobiology**. The main premise of sociobiology is that certain behavioral characteristics exist because they are expressions of genes that have been perpetuated by natural selection. In his seminal 1975 book *Sociobiology: The New Synthesis*, E. O. Wilson speculated about the evolutionary basis of certain kinds of social behavior. By including a few examples from human culture, he sparked a debate that remains heated today.

The spectrum of human social behaviors may be influenced by our genetic makeup, but this is very different from saying that genes are rigid determinants of behavior. This distinction is at the core of the debate about evolutionary perspectives on human behavior. Skeptics fear that evolutionary interpretations of human behavior could be used to justify the status quo in human society, thus rationalizing current social injustices. Evolutionary biologists argue that this is a gross oversimplification and misunderstanding of what the data tell us about human biology. Evolutionary explanations of human behavior do not reduce us to robots stamped out of rigid genetic molds. Just as individuals vary extensively in anatomical features, we should expect inherent variations in behavior as well. Environment intervenes in the pathway from genotype to phenotype for physical traits and even more so for behavioral traits. And because of our capacity for learning and our versatility, human behavior is probably more plastic than that of any other animal. Over our recent evolutionary history, we have built up a diversity of structured societies with governments, laws, cultural values, and religions that define what is acceptable behavior and what is not, even when unacceptable behavior might enhance an individual's Darwinian fitness. Perhaps it is our social and cultural institutions that make us distinct and that provide those qualities in which there is the least continuum between humans and other animals.

CONCEPT CHECK 51.5

1. What is a possible explanation for cooperative behavior among nonrelated animals?
2. **WHAT IF?** If an animal were unable to distinguish close from distant relatives, would the concept of inclusive fitness still be applicable? Explain.
3. **WHAT IF?** Suppose you applied Hamilton's logic to a situation in which one individual was past reproductive age. Could there still be a selection for an altruistic act?

For suggested answers, see Appendix A.

Chapter 51 Review

MB **MEDIA** Go to the Study Area at **www.masteringbio.com** for BioFlix 3-D Animations, MP3 Tutors, Videos, Practice Tests, an eBook, and more.

SUMMARY OF KEY CONCEPTS

CONCEPT 51.1

Discrete sensory inputs can stimulate both simple and complex behaviors (pp. 1120–1125)

▶ Behavior is the sum of responses to external and internal stimuli and includes muscular as well as nonmuscular activity. Ethology is the scientific study of animal behavior, particularly in natural environments. The mid-20th-century ethologists developed a conceptual framework defined by a set of questions that highlight the complementary nature of two perspectives. Proximate, or "how," questions focus on the environmental stimuli, if any, that trigger a behavior, as well as the genetic, physiological, and anatomical mechanisms underlying a behavioral act. Ultimate, or "why," questions address the evolutionary significance of a behavior.

▶ **Fixed Action Patterns** Fixed action patterns are largely invariant behaviors triggered by simple cues known as sign stimuli.

▶ **Oriented Movement** Animal movements in response to external stimuli include kinesis, a behavior involving a change in activity or turning rate, and taxis, an oriented movement toward or away from some stimulus. Migratory movements involve navigation, which can be based on orientation relative to the sun, the stars, or Earth's magnetic field.

- **Behavioral Rhythms** Animal behavior is sometimes synchronized to the daily, or circadian, cycle of light and dark in the environment or to the annual changes in that cycle over the seasons.
- **Animal Signals and Communication** The transmission and reception of signals constitute animal communication. Animals use visual, auditory, chemical (usually olfactory), and tactile signals. Chemical substances called pheromones are sometimes used to transmit species-specific information through the environment.

MEDIA

Activity Honeybee Waggle Dance Video

Investigation How Can Pillbug Responses to Environments Be Tested?

CONCEPT 51.2

Learning establishes specific links between experience and behavior (pp. 1125–1129)

CONCEPT 51.3

Both genetic makeup and environment contribute to the development of behaviors (pp. 1129–1133)

- Biologists study the ways both genes and the environment influence the development of behavioral phenotypes.
- **Experience and Behavior** The cross-fostering studies of California mice and white-footed mice have uncovered an influence of social environment on the aggressive and parental behaviors of these mice.
- **Regulatory Genes and Behavior** Genetic studies in insects have revealed the existence of master regulatory genes that control complex behaviors. Within the underlying hierarchy, multiple genes influence specific behaviors.
- **Genetically Based Behavioral Variation in Natural Populations** When behavioral variation within a species corresponds to variation in environmental conditions, it may be evidence of past evolution. Field and laboratory studies have documented the genetic basis for a change in migratory behavior in migratory birds over a period of a few decades. Studies with garter snakes reveal behavioral differences that correlate with geographic variation in prey availability.
- **Influence of Single-Locus Variation** Research has revealed that variation in a single gene underlies the differences in mating and parental behavior between two species of voles.

CONCEPT 51.4

Selection for individual survival and reproductive success can explain most behaviors (pp. 1133–1138)

- **Foraging Behavior** Laboratory studies of *Drosophila* populations raised in high- and low-density conditions show a clear divergence in behavior linked to specific genes. An optimal foraging model is based on the idea that natural selection should favor foraging behavior that minimizes the costs of foraging and maximizes the benefits.
- **Mating Behavior and Mate Choice** How mate choice enhances reproductive success varies, depending on the species' mating system. The mating relationship between males and females, which includes monogamous, polygynous, and polyandrous mating systems, varies a great deal from species to species. Certainty of paternity has a significant influence on mating behavior and parental care. Mate preferences by females may play a central role in the evolution of male behavior and anatomy. Male competition for mates is a source of selection that also can reduce variation among males. Sexual selection can lead to the evolution of alternative male mating behavior and morphology. Game theory provides a way of thinking about evolution in situations where the fitness of a particular behavioral phenotype is influenced by other behavioral phenotypes in the population.

CONCEPT 51.5

Inclusive fitness can account for the evolution of altruistic social behavior (pp. 1138–1142)

- **Altruism** On occasion, animals behave in altruistic ways that reduce their individual fitness but increase the fitness of the recipient of the behavior.
- **Inclusive Fitness** Altruistic behavior can be explained by the concept of inclusive fitness, the total effect an individual has on proliferating its genes by producing its own offspring *and* by providing aid that enables close relatives to produce offspring. Kin selection favors altruistic behavior by enhancing the reproductive success of relatives. Altruistic behavior toward unrelated individuals can be adaptive if the aided individual returns the favor in the future, an exchange of aid called reciprocal altruism.
- **Social Learning** Social learning forms the roots of culture, which can be defined as a system of information transfer through observation or teaching that influences the behavior of individuals in a population.
- **Evolution and Human Culture** Human behavior, like that of other species, is the result of interactions between genes and environment.

TESTING YOUR KNOWLEDGE

SELF-QUIZ

1. Which of the following is true of innate behaviors?
   a. Genes have very little influence on the expression of innate behaviors.
   b. Innate behaviors tend to vary considerably among members of a population.
   c. Innate behaviors are limited to invertebrate animals.
   d. Innate behaviors are expressed in most individuals in a population across a wide range of environmental conditions.
   e. Innate behaviors occur in invertebrates and some vertebrates but not in mammals.

2. Researchers have found that a region of the canary forebrain shrinks during the nonbreeding season and enlarges when breeding season begins. This annual enlargement of brain tissue is probably associated with the annual
   a. addition of new syllables to a canary's song repertoire.
   b. crystallization of subsong into adult songs.
   c. sensitive period in which canary parents imprint on new offspring.
   d. renewal of mating and nest-building behaviors.
   e. elimination of the memorized template for songs sung the previous year.

3. Although many chimpanzee populations live in environments containing oil palm nuts, members of only a few populations use stones to crack open the nuts. The most likely explanation for this behavioral difference between populations is that
   a. the behavioral difference is caused by genetic differences between populations.
   b. members of different populations have different nutritional requirements.
   c. the cultural tradition of using stones to crack nuts has arisen in only some populations.
   d. members of different populations differ in learning ability.
   e. members of different populations differ in manual dexterity.

4. Which of the following is *not* required for a behavioral trait to evolve by natural selection?
   a. In each individual, the form of the behavior is determined entirely by genes.
   b. The behavior varies among individuals.
   c. An individual's reproductive success depends in part on how the behavior is performed.
   d. Some component of the behavior is genetically inherited.
   e. An individual's genotype influences its behavioral phenotype.

5. Female spotted sandpipers aggressively court males and, after mating, leave the clutch of young for the male to incubate. This sequence may be repeated several times with different males until no available males remain, forcing the female to incubate her last clutch. Which of the following terms best describes this behavior?
   a. monogamy
   b. polygyny
   c. polyandry
   d. promiscuity
   e. certainty of paternity

6. According to Hamilton's rule,
   a. natural selection does not favor altruistic behavior that causes the death of the altruist.
   b. natural selection favors altruistic acts when the resulting benefit to the beneficiary, correct for relatedness, exceeds the cost to the altruist.
   c. natural selection is more likely to favor altruistic behavior that benefits an offspring than altruistic behavior that benefits a sibling.
   d. the effects of kin selection are larger than the effects of direct natural selection on individuals.
   e. altruism is always reciprocal.

7. The core idea of sociobiology is that
   a. human behavior is rigidly determined by inheritance.
   b. humans cannot choose to change their social behavior.
   c. much human behavior has evolved by natural selection.
   d. the social behavior of humans has many similarities to that of social insects such as honeybees.
   e. the environment plays a larger role than genes in shaping human behavior.

8. **DRAW IT** You are considering two optimal foraging models for the behavior of a mussel-feeding shorebird, the oystercatcher. In model A, the energetic reward increases solely with mussel size. In model B, you take into consideration that larger mussels are more difficult to open. Draw a graph of reward (energy benefit on a scale of 0–10) versus mussel length (scale of 0–70 mm) for each model. Assume that mussels under 10 mm provide no benefit and are ignored by the birds. Also assume that mussels start becoming difficult to open when they reach 40 mm in length and impossible to open when 70 mm long. Considering the graphs you have drawn, how could you distinguish between the models by observation and measurement in the oystercatcher's habitat?

For Self-Quiz answers, see Appendix A.

MEDIA Visit the Study Area at **www.masteringbio.com** for a Practice Test.

EVOLUTION CONNECTION

9. We often explain our behavior in terms of subjective feelings, motives, or reasons, but evolutionary explanations are based on reproductive fitness. What is the relationship between the two kinds of explanation? For instance, is a human explanation for behavior, such as "falling in love," incompatible with an evolutionary explanation? Does falling in love become more meaningful or less meaningful (or neither) if it has an evolutionary basis?

SCIENTIFIC INQUIRY

10. Scientists studying scrub jays found that "helpers" often assist mated pairs of birds in raising their young. The helpers lack territories and mates of their own. Instead, they help the territory owner gather food for their offspring. Propose a hypothesis to explain what advantage there might be for the helpers to engage in this behavior instead of seeking their own territories and mates. How would you test your hypothesis? If it is correct, what results would you expect your tests to yield?

Biological Inquiry: A Workbook of Investigative Cases Explore the behavior of a large gull population in a marina, and human attempts to control the population, in the case "Back to the Bay."

SCIENCE, TECHNOLOGY, AND SOCIETY

11. Researchers are very interested in studying identical twins separated at birth and raised apart. So far, the data suggest that such twins are much more alike than researchers predicted; they frequently have similar personalities, mannerisms, habits, and interests. What general question do you think researchers hope to answer by studying such twins? Why do identical twins make good subjects for this research? What are the potential pitfalls of this research? What abuses might occur if the studies are not evaluated critically and if the results are carelessly cited to support a social agenda?

UNIT 8

Ecology

AN INTERVIEW WITH

Diana H. Wall

As a past president of the Ecological Society of America and the American Institute of Biological Sciences, and in many other national and international roles, Diana Wall has made major contributions to science and the public interest. She has also distinguished herself as a researcher on carbon cycling and other ecosystem processes, focusing on the tiny roundworms called nematodes. Dr. Wall has B.A. and Ph.D. degrees from the University of Kentucky. She was a professor at the University of California, Riverside before coming to Colorado State University, where she is a professor of biology and senior research scientist at the Natural Resource Ecology Laboratory. She does much of her fieldwork in Antarctica.

How did you get started in ecology?

In graduate school, where I studied plant pathology, I focused on the interactions between two species of nematodes and the plant roots they parasitize. Later, as a post-doc at UC Riverside, I participated in the International Biological Program (IBP). My job was to go to deserts in the western U.S. and try to find out how soil nematodes contributed to the energy balance in those ecosystems.

What was the International Biological Program?

The IBP was the first truly global research project in ecology. The overall goal was to understand Earth's productivity by taking comparable measurements across different ecosystems. (Productivity is the amount of new material—biomass—that's produced in an ecosystem.) Grassland researchers from all around the world were measuring the same things, desert researchers were measuring the same things, and so forth, enabling us to combine all the data and make global comparisons. It was a jump for me from studying the interactions between two species to be asking how such interactions fit into the global scheme of things.

Why are nematodes of interest to ecologists?

Although many people know nematodes as harmful parasites of animals or plants, most nematodes are good guys, especially the free-living ones in soil. As part of my work in the desert, I got interested in free-living soil nematodes, which feed on fungi or bacteria, or sometimes on smaller animals. The "good" nematodes accelerate the turnover of organic matter by feeding on soil microbes and then releasing compounds of carbon and nitrogen to the soil. Experiments have shown that soils without nematodes have slower rates of decomposition.

Nematodes are everywhere: in soils, in streams, in ocean sediments, and in many animals and plants. It's been estimated that four out of five animals on Earth are nematodes! The geographic distribution of different species of nematodes is something we're studying. We're doing a global-scale "latitudinal gradient" experiment, where we take soil samples at different latitudes—for example, from Sweden to South Africa. We're going into places that are hotspots of biodiversity above ground—and "coldspots" as well—and looking at what's below ground. We're classifying the nematodes to see how many species there are in the soil and how species distribution differs with latitude.

What impact have modern molecular methods had on this kind of study?

They've been great for research on the diversity of all kinds of microscopic organisms. We can now go beyond asking general questions about what such organisms do in the soil and ask exactly what they are. With soil invertebrates such as nematodes and mites, it can be very difficult to tell species apart morphologically. Now we can look at DNA sequences and say, whoa, this one is really different from that one, or, hey, this one is endemic to Antarctica but it's got a really close relative hanging out in Argentina.

Why is soil biodiversity important?

From a practical perspective, soil biodiversity—the number and abundance of different species living in soils—is probably critically important for soil fertility, and soil fertility is crucial for feeding and clothing the world's people. There's still much to be learned about the role of soil biodiversity in soil fertility. Simply how soils differ over the range from a forest to a desert is still a big question. Based on climate, geologic history, and biology, there are about 13,000 kinds of soil (called "series") in the United States alone. Each is a distinct habitat where microscopic soil creatures have evolved, and so not every species is widespread. Where the species are different, can you scale up from a difference between two farms, say, or between a farm and a nearby forest, and generalize about the connections between soil biodiversity and soil fertility? How do species that are just about everywhere contribute to soil fertility? Those questions are wide open for more research.

Another important question is whether there's a correlation between biodiversity above ground and below ground. Can we predict that an area of great biodiversity above ground will have a great diversity of mites, nematodes, and so forth below ground? And will their functions in the ecosystem be predictable, too? Because I don't want to go around digging up all the soils in the world! Once we understand something about that issue, we can start to think about the relationship between diversity and soil fertility. My big push now is to persuade people that you can't think of soil biodiversity as being unrelated to what's above ground. We used to think of the ocean as a dark garbage can, and we still tend to think of the soil that way. But we found out there are a lot of organisms in the ocean that carry out processes that benefit us, even if we don't have names for all of them. I think the same is true for soils.

How did you begin doing research in Antarctica? And what do you study there?

After the IBP, I continued working in hot deserts. They're a simpler system than a forest, for example, and therefore are more suitable for working out the factors that determine different food webs in the soil. To tease out the contribution of organisms other than plants, we would compare areas with and without plants. But that's hard to do, because plant roots seem to go everywhere, even in the desert. I wanted to find an even simpler system, with fewer variables—soils where there are no plant roots. I wrote to a colleague who was in Antarctica, and he sent me some soil for analysis. It certainly didn't have plant roots, and it did have nematodes.

But when I searched the scientific literature, I read that the soils of the Antarctic Dry Valleys, where my sample had come from, were sterile, with no organisms at all, not even prokaryotes! Only in melt streams had some life been found. Researchers had looked for bacteria in the soil, but only by trying to culture them, and nothing had shown up. This was before molecular methods had been developed for identifying microorganisms from DNA alone.

We went down to Antarctica for the first time in 1989. Only 2% of Antarctica is actually soil; the rest is rock and ice. And the Dry Valleys area has no visible vegetation; when you fly in, it looks like Mars. We had enough financial support for only one field season—so only two months to find out what lived in the soil there. We adapted our hot-desert methods for this cold desert, which has precipitation the equivalent of less than 3 cm of rain per year. And as we'd hoped, we soon saw that there was an abundance of life in the soil, as much as in the Chihuahuan Desert in New Mexico. We could not believe that other people had missed it.

Our method was simple: We would take a handful of soil, about 100 g, stir it up with a sugar solution, and centrifuge it. The nematodes float in the solution, and the rock particles sink. After rinsing off the nematodes, we count them and determine their species. It was amazing to me to see these animals, knowing that they spend nine months of the year in a hard, frozen, and dark environment. It turned out that they live in water films around soil pores, and use survival mechanisms similar to those of hot-desert nematodes. When they receive certain environmental cues, such as dryness, they shrink their long bodies and curl up in a spiral, losing 99% of their water. When they're that small, they can disperse in wind. So this is a mechanism for spreading, as well as for surviving in a particular location.

These nematodes participate in very, very simple food chains, with only one to three tiers. For example, we have one chain with only two species of nematode: The one at the bottom eats bacteria, and the one above it may eat the bacteria-eater. It's remarkably simple compared with what is found in the soils up here.

In the last two years, we've been looking more closely at the different habitats. We've found that one species is almost everywhere in the valleys, *Scottnema lindsayae;* it's really tough, our "Rambo." But if there's too much salt in the soil or too much water, it's not present. We now have a model enabling us to predict where this species will be found around the valleys. In Antarctica, unlike elsewhere, I can look at individual nematode species and see that they have different niches; there's little overlap.

How is climate change affecting Antarctica?

Antarctica is the only continent that hasn't *on average* shown warming yet. The Antarctic Peninsula is warming rapidly, but the Dry Valleys are cooling, at least partly an indirect effect of ocean currents. Some people have made a big fuss about this cooling in attempts to disprove global warming. What we emphasize is that, while the continent as a whole is not warming, various regions are undergoing major changes, and there is warming and cooling occurring in different regions. In the Dry Valleys, we're seeing changes in every component of the ecosystem. For instance, we're seeing a decline in the abundance of the widespread *S. lindsayae.*

To look at this decline over a period of time, we've set up experiments in each valley basin. We've made the soil wetter in places—because if an unusual amount of melting occurs when climate warms in this region, that's going to be the biggest driver of change. We want to see what that does to the *S. lindsayae* population and to the turnover of carbon in the soil. Because it's the only nematode species in many Dry Valley areas, we can easily use a carbon-isotope tracer to see how much carbon that one species is assimilating. The nematode population has very low biomass compared to what you see in the grassland here in Colorado, but it assimilates a greater percentage of organic carbon from the soil than do all the species here together. So it's a very important player in the ecosystem.

In places where we've manipulated the environment in the past, we're looking at how long it takes the soils to return to their original states. We're also looking at the effects of human trampling because the numbers of scientists and tourists are increasing tremendously. What we see is that human movement along a path disturbs the soil enough to cause a significant decline in nematodes. Furthermore, new, potentially invasive organisms are coming in on people's shoes and and clothing.

Antarctica is not isolated from the rest of the planet. The continents are all connected by ocean and atmosphere, and there is much more movement than we once thought. So future changes are something to worry about.

What is it like doing ecological research?

It's fun. You have an idea, you come up with a hypothesis, and then you get to test it in the lab or field. But as you test the hypothesis, you learn new things, and there are unexpected challenges. You have to try to fit everything you learn into a bigger picture. The process is like gathering all the blocks in a playpen and building a structure—without having the whole thing fall over.

Fieldwork has other kinds of pleasures. When you're in the field, you get to focus on one question that really interests you—during the Antarctic summer, there's a temptation to work 24 hours a day! At the same time, you usually have colleagues with different specialties there, and it's a great opportunity for freewheeling discussion and new insights. There's a great feeling of camaraderie.

Of course, there are frustrations, too. Collecting your data may be uncomfortable or boring. And you can spend a lot of time in the field that's not very productive or even a total failure. But the result of analyzing the data from a successful field trip can be a satisfying contribution to what we know about the world.

. . . the Dry Valleys area has no visible vegetation; when you fly in, it looks like Mars.

Left to right: Diana Wall, Jane Reece, Rob Jackson

Inquiry in Action

Learn about an experiment by Diana Wall and a colleague in Inquiry Figure 54.19 on page 1210.

52 An Introduction to Ecology and the Biosphere

▲ **Figure 52.1 Why do gray whales migrate?**

KEY CONCEPTS

52.1 Ecology integrates all areas of biological research and informs environmental decision making

52.2 Interactions between organisms and the environment limit the distribution of species

52.3 Aquatic biomes are diverse and dynamic systems that cover most of Earth

52.4 The structure and distribution of terrestrial biomes are controlled by climate and disturbance

OVERVIEW

The Scope of Ecology

High in the sky, a series of satellites circle Earth. These satellites aren't relaying the chatter of cell phones. Instead, they are transmitting data on the annual migration of gray whales **(Figure 52.1)**. Leaving their calving grounds near Baja California, adult and newborn gray whales (*Eschrichtius robustus*) swim side by side on a remarkable 8,000-km journey. They are headed to the Arctic Ocean to feed on the crustaceans, tube worms, and other creatures that thrive there in summer. The satellites also help biologists track a second journey, the recovery of the gray whales from the brink of extinction. A century ago, whaling had reduced the population to only a few hundred individuals. Today, after 70 years of protection from whaling, more than 20,000 travel to the Arctic each year.

What environmental factors determine the geographic distribution of gray whales? How do variations in their food supply affect the size of the gray whale population? Questions such as these are the subject of **ecology** (from the Greek *oikos*, home, and *logos*, to study), the scientific study of the interactions between organisms and the environment. These interactions occur at a hierarchy of scales that ecologists study, from organismal to global **(Figure 52.2)**.

In addition to providing a conceptual framework for understanding the field of ecology, Figure 52.2 provides the organizational framework for our final unit. This chapter begins the unit by describing the breadth of ecology and some of the factors, both living and nonliving, that influence the distribution and abundance of organisms. The next three chapters examine population, community, and ecosystem ecology in detail. In the final chapter, we'll explore both landscape ecology and global ecology as we consider how ecologists apply biological knowledge to predict the global consequences of human activities, to conserve Earth's biodiversity, and to restore our planet's ecosystems.

CONCEPT **52.1**

Ecology integrates all areas of biological research and informs environmental decision making

Ecology's roots are in discovery science (see Chapter 1). Naturalists, including Aristotle and Darwin, have long observed organisms in nature and systematically recorded their observations. Because extraordinary insight can be gained through this descriptive approach, called *natural history,* it remains a fundamental part of the science of ecology. Present-day ecologists still observe the natural world, albeit with genes-to-globe tools that would astound Aristotle and Darwin.

Modern ecology has become a rigorous experimental science as well. Ecologists generate hypotheses, manipulate the environment, and observe the outcome. Scientists interested in the effects of climate change on tree survival, for instance, might create drought and wet conditions in experimental plots instead

▼ Figure 52.2

Exploring The Scope of Ecological Research

Ecologists work at different levels of the biological hierarchy, from individual organisms to the planet. Here we present a sample research question for each level in the biological hierarchy.

1 Organismal Ecology

Organismal ecology, which includes the subdisciplines of physiological, evolutionary, and behavioral ecology, is concerned with how an organism's structure, physiology, and (for animals) behavior meet the challenges posed by its environment.

◀ *How do hammerhead sharks select a mate?*

2 Population Ecology

A **population** is a group of individuals of the same species living in an area. **Population ecology** analyzes factors that affect population size and how and why it changes through time.

◀ *What environmental factors affect the reproductive rate of deer mice?*

3 Community Ecology

A **community** is a group of populations of different species in an area. **Community ecology** examines how interactions between species, such as predation and competition, affect community structure and organization.

◀ *What factors influence the diversity of species that make up a forest?*

4 Ecosystem Ecology

An **ecosystem** is the community of organisms in an area and the physical factors with which those organisms interact. **Ecosystem ecology** emphasizes energy flow and chemical cycling between organisms and the environment.

◀ *What factors control photosynthetic productivity in a temperate grassland ecosystem?*

5 Landscape Ecology

A **landscape** (or seascape) is a mosaic of connected ecosystems. Research in **landscape ecology** focuses on the factors controlling exchanges of energy, materials, and organisms across multiple ecosystems.

◀ *To what extent do the trees lining a river serve as corridors of dispersal for animals?*

6 Global Ecology

The **biosphere** is the global ecosystem—the sum of all the planet's ecosystems and landscapes. **Global ecology** examines how the regional exchange of energy and materials influences the functioning and distribution of organisms across the biosphere.

◀ *How does ocean circulation affect the global distribution of crustaceans?*

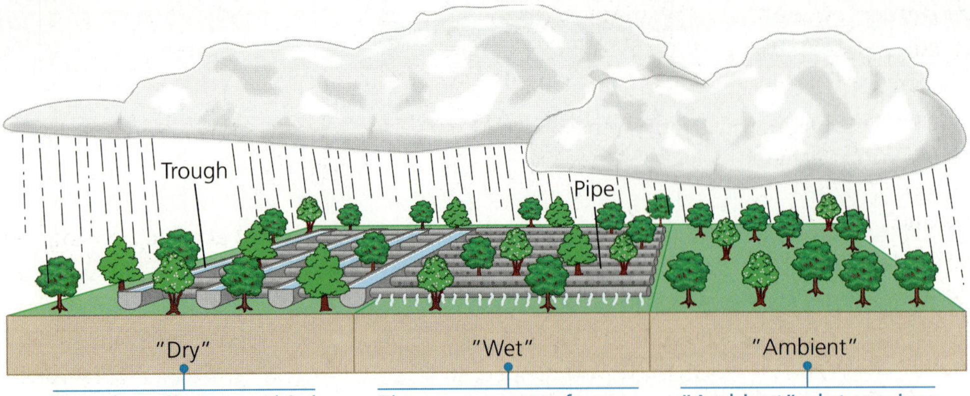

▲ **Figure 52.3 Studying how a forest responds to altered precipitation.** At the Walker Branch Watershed in Tennessee, researchers used a system of troughs and pipes to create artificial "dry" and "wet" conditions within parts of a forest.

of waiting decades for the dry or wet years that could be representative of future rainfall. Paul Hanson and colleagues, at Oak Ridge National Laboratory in Tennessee, used just such an experimental approach in a Herculean study that lasted more than ten years. In one large plot of native forest, they collected one-third of the incoming precipitation and moved it to a second plot, while leaving a third plot unchanged as a control **(Figure 52.3)**. By comparing the growth and survival of trees in each plot, the researchers found that flowering dogwoods (*Cornus florida*) were more likely to die in drought conditions than were members of any other woody species examined.

Throughout this unit, you will encounter many more examples of ecological field experiments, whose complex challenges have made ecologists innovators in the areas of experimental design and statistical inference. As these examples also demonstrate, the interpretation of ecological experiments often depends on a broad knowledge of biology.

Linking Ecology and Evolutionary Biology

As we discussed in Chapter 23, organisms adapt to their environment over many generations through the process of natural selection; this adaptation occurs over many generations—the time frame of *evolutionary time.* The differential survival and reproduction of individuals that leads to evolution occurs in *ecological time*, the minute-to-minute time frame of interactions between organisms and the environment. One example of how events in ecological time have led to evolution was the selection for beak size in Galápagos finches (see Figure 23.1). Finches with bigger beaks were better able to eat the large, hard seeds available during the drought. Smaller-beaked birds, which required smaller, softer seeds that were in short supply, were less likely to survive.

We can see the link between ecology and evolution all around us. Suppose a farmer applies a new fungicide to protect a wheat crop from a fungus. The fungicide works well at first, reducing the population size of the fungus—an ecological effect—and allowing the farmer to obtain higher yields from the crop. After a few years, however, the farmer has to apply higher and higher doses of the fungicide to obtain the same protection. The fungicide has altered the gene pool of the fungus—an evolutionary effect—by selecting for individuals that are resistant to the chemical. Eventually, the fungicide works so poorly that the farmer must find a different, more potent chemical to control the fungus.

Ecology and Environmental Issues

Ecology and evolutionary biology help us understand the emergence of pesticide-resistant organisms and many other environmental problems. Ecology also provides the scientific understanding needed to help us conserve and sustain life on Earth. Because of ecology's usefulness in conservation and environmental efforts, many people associate ecology with *environmentalism* (advocating the protection of nature).

Ecologists make an important distinction between science and advocacy. Many ecologists feel a responsibility to educate legislators and the public about environmental issues. How society uses ecological knowledge, however, depends on much more than science alone. If we know that phosphate promotes the growth of algae in lakes, for instance, policymakers may weigh the environmental benefits of limiting the use of phosphate-rich fertilizers against the costs of doing so. This distinction between knowledge and advocacy is clear in the guiding principles of the Ecological Society of America, a scientific organization that strives to "ensure the appropriate use of ecological science in environmental decision making."

An important milestone in applying ecological data to environmental problems was the publication of Rachel Carson's *Silent Spring* in 1962 **(Figure 52.4)**. In her book, which

◄ **Figure 52.4 Rachel Carson.**

was seminal to the modern environmental movement, Carson (1907–1964) had a broad message: "The 'control of nature' is a phrase conceived in arrogance, born of the Neanderthal age of biology and philosophy, when it was supposed that nature exists for the convenience of man." Recognizing the network of connections among species, Carson warned that the widespread use of pesticides such as DDT was causing population declines in many more organisms than the insects targeted for control. She applied ecological principles to recommend a less wasteful, safer use of pesticides. Through her writing and her testimony before the U.S. Congress, Carson helped promote a new environmental ethic to lawmakers and the public. Her efforts led to a ban on DDT use in the United States and more stringent controls on the use of other chemicals.

CONCEPT CHECK 52.1

1. Contrast the terms *ecology* and *environmentalism.* How does ecology relate to environmentalism?
2. How can an event that occurs on the ecological time scale affect events that occur on an evolutionary time scale?
3. **WHAT IF?** A wheat farmer tests four fungicides on small plots and finds that the wheat yield is slightly higher when all four fungicides are used together than when any one fungicide is used alone. From an evolutionary perspective, what would be the likely long-term consequence of applying all four fungicides together?

For suggested answers, see Appendix A.

CONCEPT **52.2**

Interactions between organisms and the environment limit the distribution of species

Earlier we introduced the range of scales at which ecologists work and explained how ecology can be used to understand, and make decisions about, our environment. In this section, we will examine how ecologists determine what controls the distribution of species, such as the gray whale in Figure 52.1.

In Chapter 22, we explored *biogeography*, the study of the past and present distribution of species, in the context of evolutionary theory. Ecologists have long recognized global and regional patterns in the distribution of organisms. Kangaroos, for instance, are found in Australia but nowhere else on Earth. Ecologists ask not only *where* species occur, but also *why* species occur where they do: What factors determine their distribution? In seeking to answer this question, ecologists focus on two kinds of factors: **biotic**, or living, factors—all the organisms that are part of the individual's environment—and **abiotic**, or nonliving, factors—all the chemical and physical factors, such as temperature, light, water, and nutrients, that influence the distribution and abundance of organisms.

Figure 52.5 presents an example of how both kinds of factors might affect the distribution of a species, in this case the red kangaroo (*Macropus rufus*). As the figure shows, red kangaroos are most abundant in a few areas in the interior of Australia, where precipitation is relatively sparse and variable. They are not found around most of the periphery of the continent, where

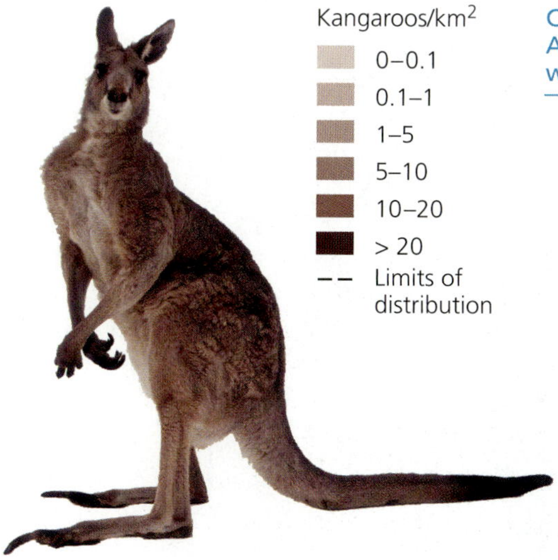

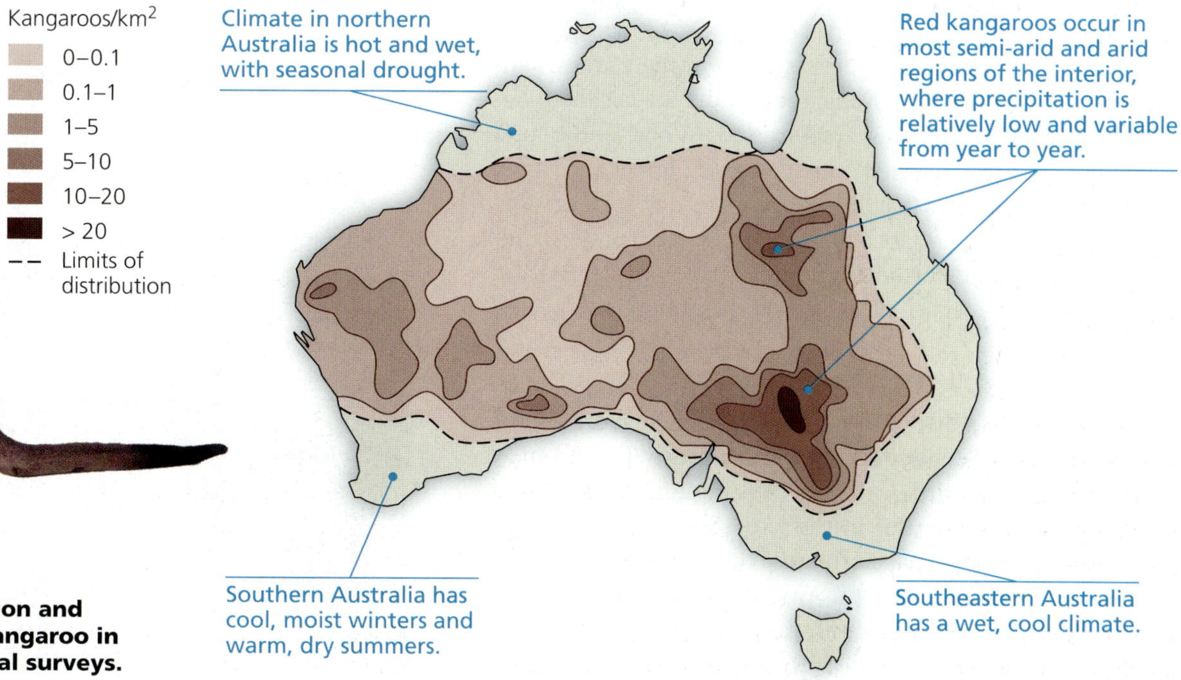

▲ **Figure 52.5 Distribution and abundance of the red kangaroo in Australia, based on aerial surveys.**

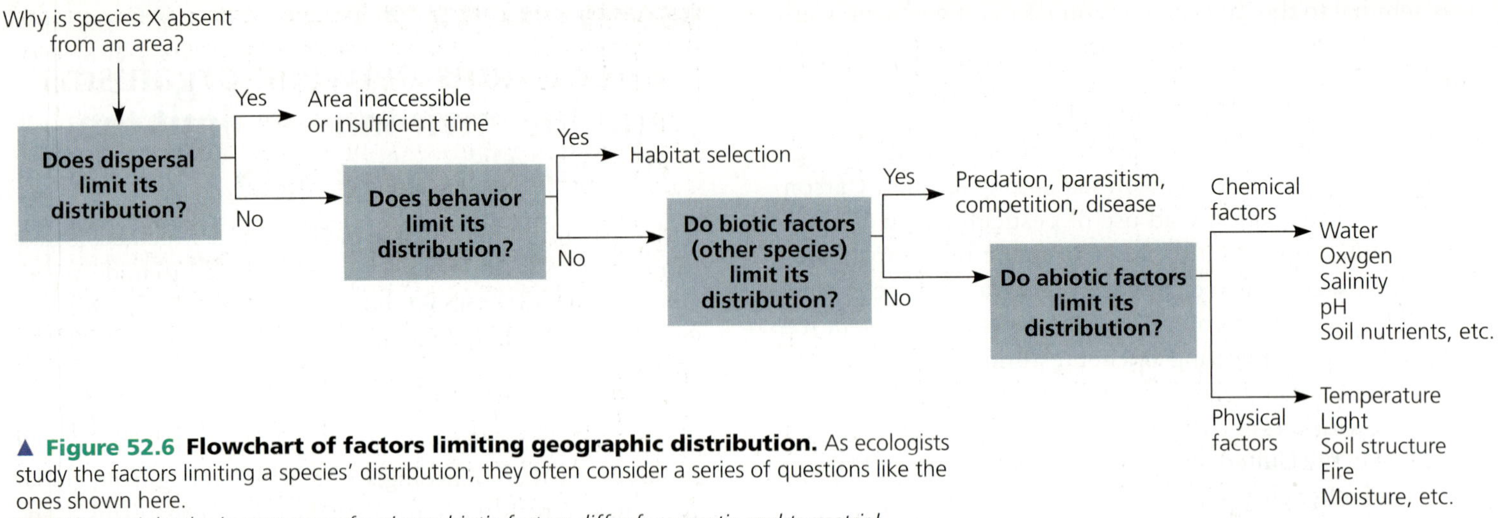

▲ **Figure 52.6 Flowchart of factors limiting geographic distribution.** As ecologists study the factors limiting a species' distribution, they often consider a series of questions like the ones shown here.

? *How might the importance of various abiotic factors differ for aquatic and terrestrial ecosystems?*

the climate ranges from moist to wet. At first glance, this distribution might suggest that an abiotic factor—the amount and variability of precipitation—directly determines where red kangaroos live. However, it is also possible that climate influences red kangaroo populations indirectly through biotic factors, such as pathogens, parasites, predators, competitors, and food availability. Ecologists generally need to consider multiple factors and alternative hypotheses when attempting to explain the distribution of species.

To see how ecologists might arrive at such an explanation, let's work our way through the series of questions in the flowchart in **Figure 52.6**.

Dispersal and Distribution

The movement of individuals away from their area of origin or from centers of high population density, called **dispersal**, contributes to the global distribution of organisms. A biogeographer might consider dispersal in hypothesizing why there are no kangaroos in North America: Kangaroos could not get there because a barrier to their dispersal existed. While land-bound kangaroos have not reached North America under their own power, other organisms that disperse more readily, such as some birds, have. The dispersal of organisms is critical to understanding both geographic isolation in evolution (see Chapter 24) and the broad patterns of current geographic distributions of species.

Natural Range Expansions

The importance of dispersal is most evident when organisms reach an area where they did not exist previously. For instance, 200 years ago, the cattle egret was found only in Africa and southwestern Europe. But in the late 1800s, some of these strong-flying birds managed to cross the Atlantic Ocean and colonize northeastern South America. From there, cattle egrets gradually spread southward and also northward through Central America and into North America, reaching Florida by 1960 **(Figure 52.7)**. Today they have breeding populations as far west as the Pacific coast of the United States and as far north as southern Canada.

Natural range expansions clearly show the influence of dispersal on distribution, but opportunities to observe such dispersal directly are rare. As a consequence, ecologists often turn to experimental methods to better understand the role of dispersal in limiting the distribution of species.

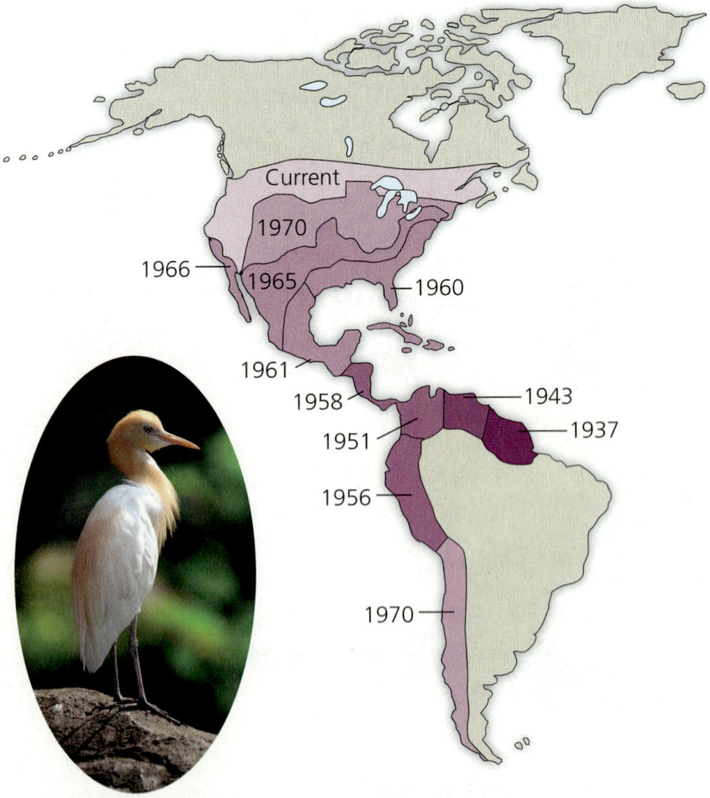

▲ **Figure 52.7 Dispersal of the cattle egret in the Americas.** Native to Africa, cattle egrets were first reported in South America in 1877.

Species Transplants

To determine if dispersal is a key factor limiting the distribution of a species, ecologists may observe the results of intentional or accidental transplants of the species to areas where it was previously absent. For a transplant to be considered successful, some of the organisms must not only survive in the new area but also reproduce there. If a transplant is successful, then we can conclude that the *potential* range of the species is larger than its *actual* range; in other words, the species *could* live in certain areas where it currently does not.

Species introduced to new geographic locations often disrupt the communities and ecosystems to which they have been introduced and spread far beyond the area of intended introduction (see Chapter 56). Consequently, ecologists rarely conduct transplant experiments across geographic regions. Instead, they document the outcome when a species has been transplanted for other purposes, such as to introduce game animals or predators of pest species, or when a species has been accidentally transplanted.

Behavior and Habitat Selection

As transplant experiments show, some organisms do not occupy all of their potential range, even though they may be physically able to disperse into the unoccupied areas. To follow our line of questioning from Figure 52.6, does behavior play a role in limiting distribution in such cases? When individuals seem to avoid certain habitats, even when the habitats are suitable, the organism's distribution may be limited by habitat selection behavior.

Although habitat selection is one of the least understood of all ecological processes, some instances in insects have been closely studied. Female insects often deposit eggs only in response to a very narrow set of stimuli, which may restrict distribution of the insects to certain host plants. Larvae of the European corn borer, for example, can feed on a wide variety of plants but are found almost exclusively on corn (maize) because egg-laying females are attracted by odors produced by the plant. Habitat selection behavior clearly restricts the plant species on which the corn borer is found.

Biotic Factors

If behavior does not limit the distribution of a species, our next question is whether biotic factors—that is, other species—are responsible (see Figure 52.6). In many cases, a species cannot complete its full life cycle if transplanted to a new area. This inability to survive and reproduce may be due to negative interactions with other organisms in the form of predation, parasitism, or competition. Alternatively, survival and reproduction may be limited by the absence of other species on which the transplanted species depends, such as pollinators for many flowering plants. Predators (organisms that kill their prey) and herbivores (organisms that eat plants or algae) are common examples of biotic factors that limit the distribution of species. Simply put, organisms that eat can limit the distribution of organisms that get eaten.

Let's examine one specific case of an herbivore limiting the distribution of a food species **(Figure 52.8)**. In certain marine ecosystems, there is often an inverse relationship between the abundance of sea urchins and seaweeds (large marine algae, such as kelp). Where sea urchins that graze on

▼ Figure 52.8 Inquiry

Does feeding by sea urchins limit seaweed distribution?

EXPERIMENT W. J. Fletcher, of the University of Sydney, Australia, reasoned that if sea urchins are a limiting biotic factor, then more seaweeds should invade an area from which sea urchins have been removed. To isolate the effect of sea urchins from that of another seaweed-eating animal, the limpet, he removed only urchins, only limpets, or both from study areas adjacent to a control site.

RESULTS Fletcher observed a large difference in seaweed growth between areas with and without sea urchins.

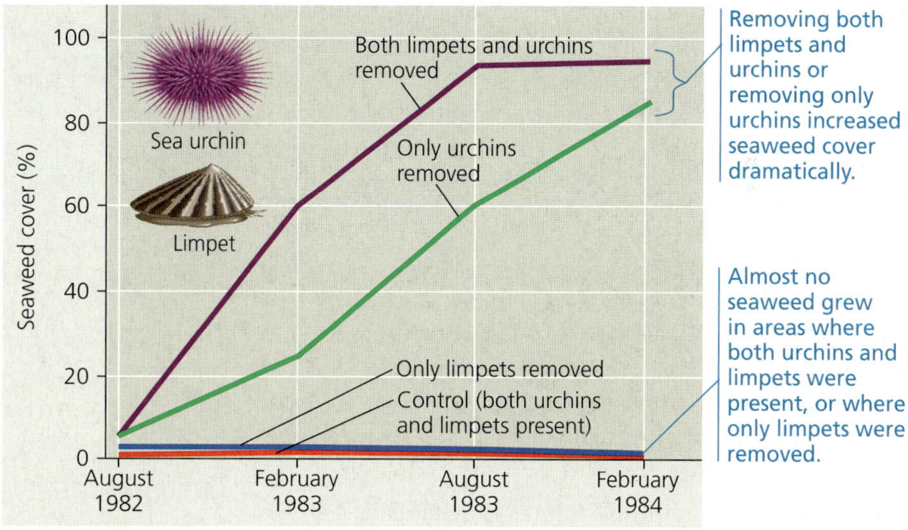

CONCLUSION Removing both limpets and urchins resulted in the greatest increase in seaweed cover, indicating that both species have some influence on seaweed distribution. But since removing only urchins greatly increased seaweed growth while removing only limpets had little effect, Fletcher concluded that sea urchins have a much greater effect than limpets in limiting seaweed distribution.

SOURCE W. J. Fletcher, Interactions among subtidal Australian sea urchins, gastropods, and algae: effects of experimental removals, *Ecological Monographs* 57:89–109 (1989).

WHAT IF? Seaweed cover increased the most when both urchins *and* limpets were removed. How might you explain this result?

seaweeds and other algae are common, large stands of seaweeds do not become established. Thus, sea urchins appear to limit the local distribution of seaweeds. This kind of interaction can be tested by "removal and addition" experiments. In studies near Sydney, Australia, W. J. Fletcher tested the hypothesis that sea urchins are a biotic factor limiting seaweed distribution. Because there are often other herbivores in the habitats where seaweeds may grow, Fletcher performed a series of manipulative field experiments to isolate the influence of sea urchins on seaweeds in his study area (see Figure 52.8). By removing sea urchins from certain plots and observing the dramatic increase in seaweed cover, he showed that urchins limited the distribution of seaweeds.

In addition to predation and herbivory, the presence or absence of food resources, parasites, pathogens, and competing organisms can act as biotic limitations on species distribution. Some of the most striking cases of limitation occur when humans accidentally or intentionally introduce exotic predators or pathogens into new areas and wipe out native species. You will encounter examples of these impacts in Chapter 56, which discusses conservation ecology.

Abiotic Factors

The last question in the flowchart in Figure 52.6 considers whether abiotic factors, such as temperature, water, salinity, sunlight, or soil, might be limiting a species' distribution. If the physical conditions at a site do not allow a species to survive and reproduce, then the species will not be found there. Throughout this discussion, keep in mind that the environment is characterized by both *spatial heterogeneity* and *temporal heterogeneity*; that is, most abiotic factors vary in space and time. Although two regions of Earth may experience different conditions at any given time, daily and annual fluctuations of abiotic factors may either blur or accentuate regional distinctions. Furthermore, organisms can avoid some stressful conditions temporarily through behaviors such as dormancy or hibernation.

Temperature

Environmental temperature is an important factor in the distribution of organisms because of its effect on biological processes. Cells may rupture if the water they contain freezes (at temperatures below 0°C), and the proteins of most organisms denature at temperatures above 45°C. In addition, few organisms can maintain an active metabolism at very low or very high temperatures, though extraordinary adaptations enable some organisms, such as thermophilic prokaryotes (see Chapter 27), to live outside the temperature range habitable by other life. Most organisms function best within a specific range of environmental temperature. Temperatures outside that range may force some animals to expend energy regulating their internal temperature, as mammals and birds do (see Chapter 40).

Water

The dramatic variation in water availability among habitats is another important factor in species distribution. Species living at the seashore or in tidal wetlands can desiccate (dry out) as the tide recedes. Terrestrial organisms face a nearly constant threat of desiccation, and the distribution of terrestrial species reflects their ability to obtain and conserve water. Desert organisms, for example, exhibit a variety of adaptations for acquiring and conserving water in dry environments, as described in Chapter 44.

Salinity

As you learned in Chapter 7, the salt concentration of water in the environment affects the water balance of organisms through osmosis. Most aquatic organisms are restricted to either freshwater or saltwater habitats by their limited ability to osmoregulate (see Chapter 44). Although many terrestrial organisms can excrete excess salts from specialized glands or in feces, salt flats and other high-salinity habitats typically have few species of plants or animals.

Sunlight

Sunlight absorbed by photosynthetic organisms provides the energy that drives most ecosystems, and too little sunlight can limit the distribution of photosynthetic species. In forests, shading by leaves in the treetops makes competition for light especially intense, particularly for seedlings growing on the forest floor. In aquatic environments, every meter of water depth selectively absorbs about 45% of the red light and about 2% of the blue light passing through it. As a result, most photosynthesis in aquatic environments occurs relatively near the surface.

Too much light can also limit the survival of organisms. The atmosphere is thinner at higher elevations, absorbing less ultraviolet radiation, so the sun's rays are more likely to damage DNA and proteins in alpine environments **(Figure 52.9)**. In other ecosystems, such as deserts, high light levels can increase temperature stress if animals are unable to avoid the light or to cool themselves through evaporation (see Chapter 40).

Rocks and Soil

The pH, mineral composition, and physical structure of rocks and soil limit the distribution of plants and thus of the animals that feed on them, contributing to the patchiness of terrestrial ecosystems. The pH of soil and water can limit the distribution of organisms directly, through extreme acidic or basic conditions, or indirectly, through the solubility of nutrients and toxins. In streams and rivers, the composition of the substrate (bottom surface) can affect water chemistry, which in turn influences the resident organisms. In freshwater and marine environments, the

▲ **Figure 52.9 Alpine tree.** Organisms living at high elevations are exposed to high levels of ultraviolet radiation. They face other challenges as well, including freezing temperatures and strong winds, which increase water loss and inhibit the growth of limbs on the windward side of trees.

structure of the substrate determines the organisms that can attach to it or burrow into it.

Now that we have surveyed some of the abiotic factors that affect the distribution of organisms, let's focus on how those factors vary with climate, as we consider the major role that climate plays in determining species distribution.

Climate

Four abiotic factors—temperature, precipitation, sunlight, and wind—are the major components of **climate**, the long-term, prevailing weather conditions in a particular area. Climatic factors, particularly temperature and water availability, have a major influence on the distribution of terrestrial organisms. We can describe climate patterns on two scales: **macroclimate**, patterns on the global, regional, and local level; and **microclimate**, very fine patterns, such as those encountered by the community of organisms that live beneath a fallen log. First let's consider Earth's macroclimate.

Global Climate Patterns

Earth's global climate patterns are determined largely by the input of solar energy and the planet's movement in space. The sun's warming effect on the atmosphere, land, and water establishes the temperature variations, cycles of air movement, and evaporation of water that are responsible for dramatic latitudinal variations in climate. **Figure 52.10**, on the next two pages, summarizes Earth's climate patterns and how they are formed.

Regional, Local, and Seasonal Effects on Climate

Proximity to bodies of water and topographic features such as mountain ranges create regional climatic variations, and smaller features of the landscape contribute to local climatic variation. Seasonal variation is another influence on climate.

Bodies of Water Ocean currents influence climate along the coasts of continents by heating or cooling overlying air masses, which may then pass across the land. Coastal regions are also generally moister than inland areas at the same latitude. The cool, misty climate produced by the cold California current that flows southward along the western United States supports a coniferous rain forest ecosystem in the Pacific Northwest and large redwood groves farther south. Similarly, the west coast of northern Europe has a mild climate because the Gulf Stream carries warm water from the equator to the North Atlantic, driven in part by the "great ocean conveyor belt" **(Figure 52.11)**. As a result, northwest Europe is warmer during winter than New England, which is farther south but is cooled by the Labrador Current flowing south from the coast of Greenland.

Because of the high specific heat of water (see Chapter 3), oceans and large lakes tend to moderate the climate of nearby land. During a hot day, when the land is warmer than the nearby body of water, air over the land heats up and

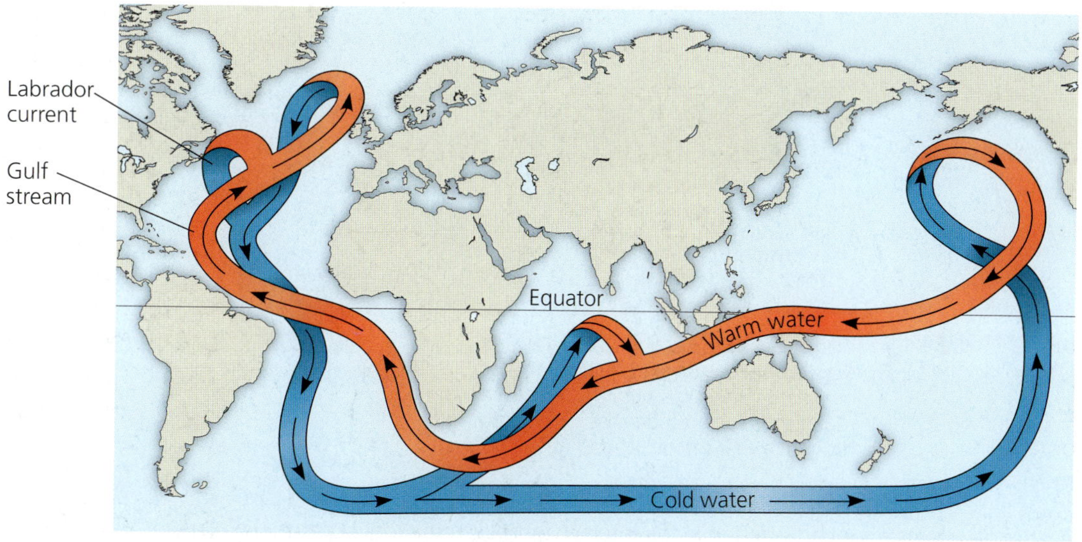

▲ **Figure 52.11 The great ocean conveyor belt.** Water is warmed at the equator and flows along the ocean surface to the North Atlantic, where it cools, becomes denser, and sinks thousands of meters. The deep, cold water may not return to the ocean surface for as long as 1,000 years.

▼ Figure 52.10

Exploring Global Climate Patterns

Latitudinal Variation in Sunlight Intensity

Earth's curved shape causes latitudinal variation in the intensity of sunlight. Because sunlight strikes the **tropics** (those regions that lie between 23.5° north latitude and 23.5° south latitude) most directly, more heat and light per unit of surface area are delivered there. At higher latitudes, sunlight strikes Earth at an oblique angle, and thus the light energy is more diffuse on Earth's surface.

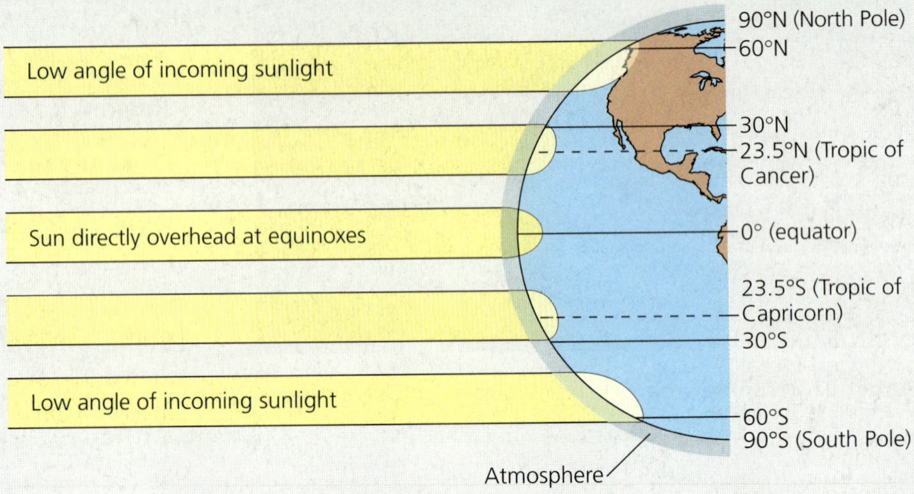

Seasonal Variation in Sunlight Intensity

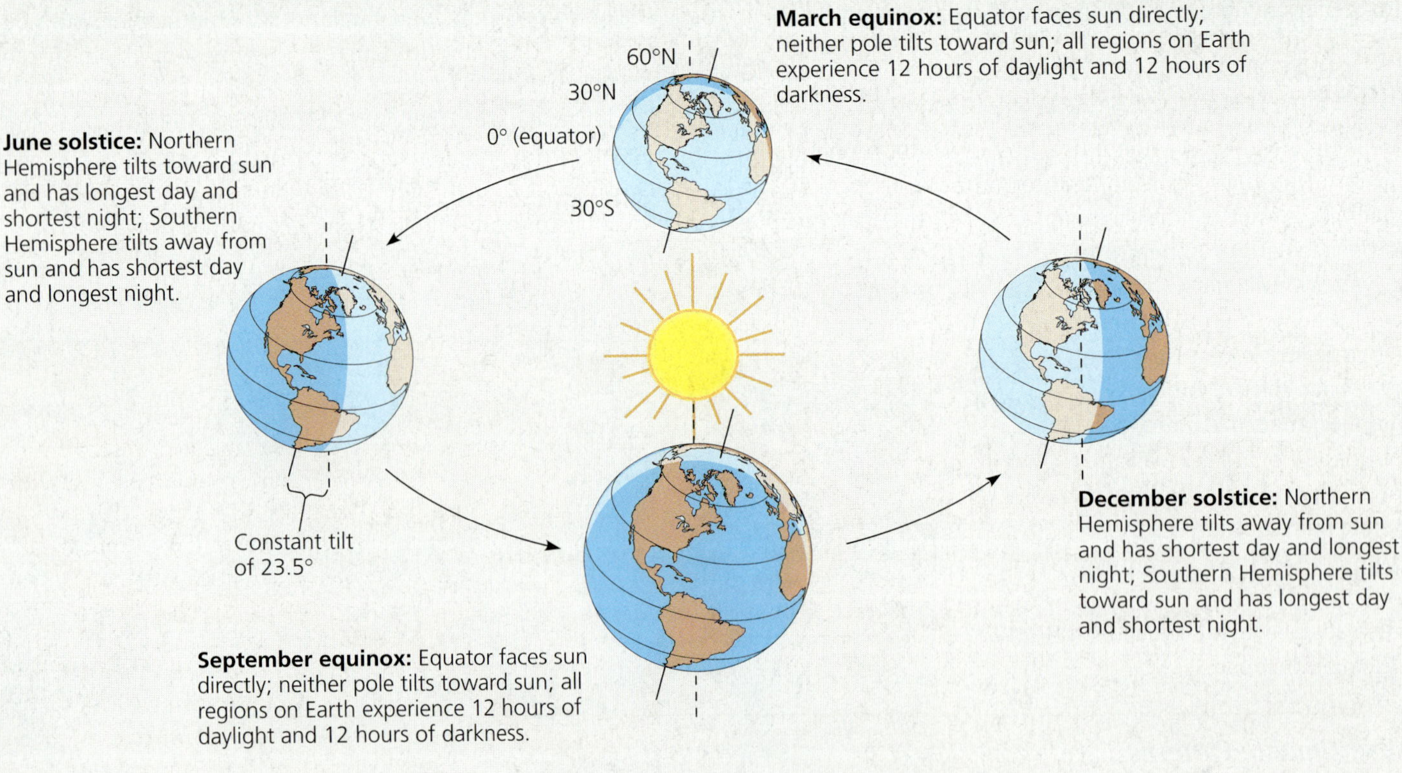

Earth's tilt causes seasonal variation in the intensity of solar radiation. Because the planet is tilted on its axis by 23.5° relative to its plane of orbit around the sun, the tropics experience the greatest annual input of solar radiation and the least seasonal variation. The seasonal variations of light and temperature increase toward the poles.

Global Air Circulation and Precipitation Patterns

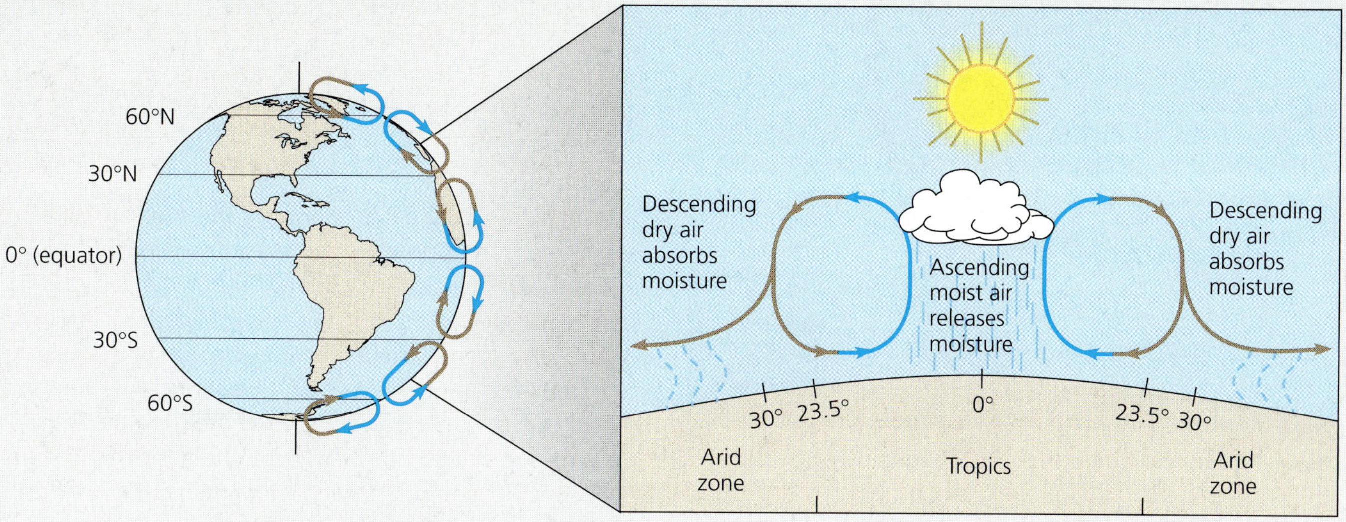

Intense solar radiation near the equator initiates a global pattern of air circulation and precipitation. High temperatures in the tropics evaporate water from Earth's surface and cause warm, wet air masses to rise (blue arrows) and flow toward the poles. The rising air masses release much of their water content, creating abundant precipitation in tropical regions. The high-altitude air masses, now dry, descend (brown arrows) toward Earth, absorbing moisture from the land and creating an arid climate conducive to the development of the deserts that are common at latitudes around 30° north and south. Some of the descending air then flows toward the poles. At latitudes around 60° north and south, the air masses again rise and release abundant precipitation (though less than in the tropics). Some of the cold, dry rising air then flows to the poles, where it descends and flows back toward the equator, absorbing moisture and creating the comparatively rainless and bitterly cold climates of the polar regions.

Global Wind Patterns

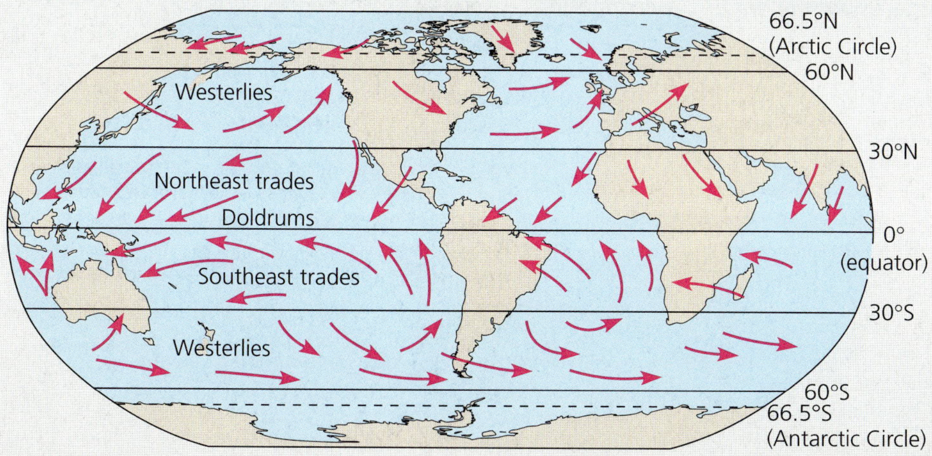

Air flowing close to Earth's surface creates predictable global wind patterns. As Earth rotates on its axis, land near the equator moves faster than that at the poles, deflecting the winds from the vertical paths shown above and creating more easterly and westerly flows. Cooling trade winds blow from east to west in the tropics; prevailing westerlies blow from west to east in the temperate zones, defined as the regions between the Tropic of Cancer and the Arctic Circle and between the Tropic of Capricorn and the Antarctic Circle.

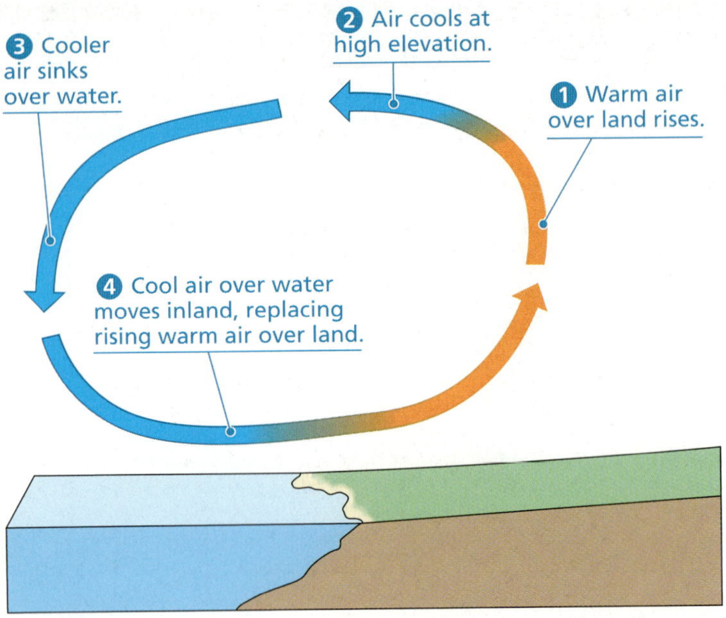

▲ **Figure 52.12 Moderating effects of a large body of water on climate.** This figure illustrates what happens on a hot summer day.

rises, drawing a cool breeze from the water across the land **(Figure 52.12)**. At night, air over the now warmer water rises, drawing cooler air from the land back out over the water, replacing it with warmer air from offshore. The moderation of climate may be limited to the coast itself, however. In certain regions, such as southern California, cool, dry ocean breezes in summer are warmed when they contact the land, absorbing moisture and creating a hot, arid climate just a few kilometers inland (see Figure 3.5). This climate pattern also occurs around the Mediterranean Sea, which gives it the name *Mediterranean climate*.

Mountains Mountains affect the amount of sunlight reaching an area and consequently the local temperature and rainfall. South-facing slopes in the Northern Hemisphere receive more sunlight than nearby north-facing slopes and are therefore warmer and drier. These abiotic differences influence species distribution; for example, in many mountains of western North America, spruce and other conifers occupy the cooler north-facing slopes, whereas shrubby, drought-resistant plants inhabit the south-facing slopes. In addition, every 1,000-m increase in elevation produces a temperature drop of approximately 6°C, equivalent to that produced by an 880-km increase in latitude. This is one reason the biological communities of mountains are similar to those at lower elevations but farther from the equator.

When warm, moist air approaches a mountain, the air rises and cools, releasing moisture on the windward side of the peak **(Figure 52.13)**. On the leeward side, cooler, dry air descends, absorbing moisture and producing a "rain shadow." Deserts commonly occur on the leeward side of mountain ranges, a phenomenon evident in the Great Basin and the Mojave Desert of western North America, the Gobi Desert of Asia, and the small deserts found in the southwest corners of some Caribbean islands.

Seasonality As described earlier, Earth's tilted axis of rotation and its annual passage around the sun cause strong seasonal cycles in middle to high latitudes (see Figure 52.10). In addition to these global changes in day length, solar radiation, and temperature, the changing angle of the sun over the course of the year affects local environments. For example, the belts of wet and dry air on either side of the equator move slightly northward and southward with the changing angle of the sun, producing marked wet and dry seasons around 20° north and 20° south latitude, where many tropical deciduous forests grow. In addition, seasonal changes in wind patterns produce variations in ocean currents, sometimes causing the upwelling of cold water from deep ocean layers. This nutrient-rich water stimulates the growth of surface-dwelling phytoplankton and the organisms that feed on them.

Microclimate

Many features in the environment influence microclimates by casting shade, affecting evaporation from soil, or changing wind patterns. For example, forest trees frequently moderate the microclimate below them. Consequently, cleared areas generally experience greater temperature extremes than the

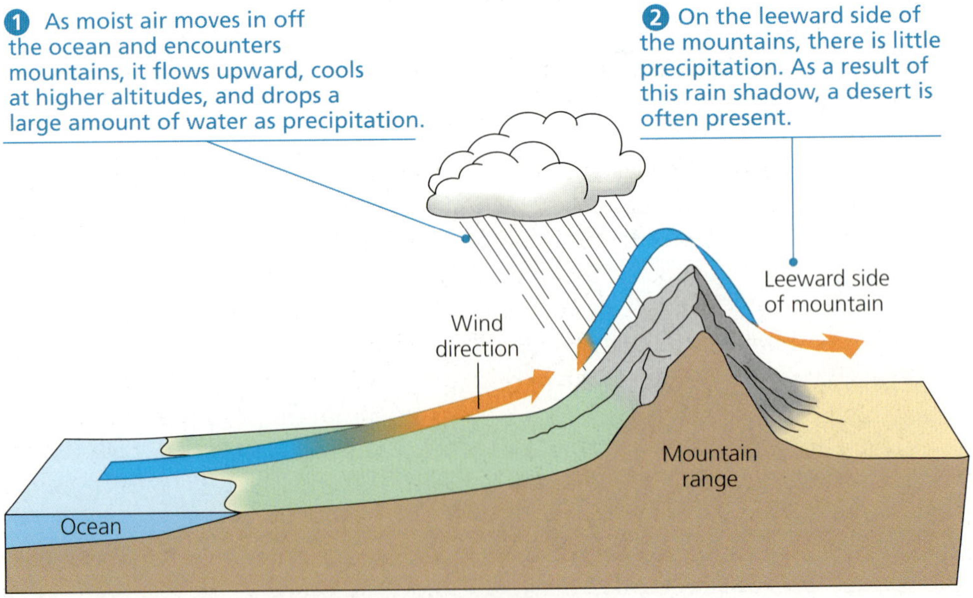

▲ **Figure 52.13 How mountains affect rainfall.**

forest interior because of greater solar radiation and wind currents that are established by the rapid heating and cooling of open land. Within a forest, low-lying ground is usually wetter than high ground and tends to be occupied by different species of trees. A log or large stone can shelter organisms such as salamanders, worms, and insects, buffering them from the extremes of temperature and moisture. Every environment on Earth is similarly characterized by a mosaic of small-scale differences in the abiotic factors that influence the local distributions of organisms.

Long-Term Climate Change

If temperature and moisture are the most important factors limiting the geographic ranges of plants and animals, then the global climate change currently under way will profoundly affect the biosphere (see Chapter 55). One way to predict the possible effects of climate change is to look back at the changes that have occurred in temperate regions since the last ice age ended.

Until about 16,000 years ago, continental glaciers covered much of North America and Eurasia. As the climate warmed and the glaciers retreated, tree distributions expanded northward. A detailed record of these migrations is captured in fossil pollen deposited in lakes and ponds. (It may seem odd to think of trees "migrating," but recall from Chapter 38 that wind and animals can disperse seeds, sometimes over great distances.) If researchers can determine the climatic limits of current geographic distributions for organisms, they can make predictions about how distributions will change with climatic warming. A major question when applying this approach to plants is whether seed dispersal is rapid enough to sustain the migration of each species as climate changes. For example, fossils suggest that the eastern hemlock was delayed nearly 2,500 years in its movement north at the end of the last ice age. This delay in seed dispersal was partly attributable to the lack of "wings" on the seeds, causing the seeds to fall close to their parent tree.

Let's look at a specific case of how the fossil record of past tree migrations can inform predictions about the biological impact of the current global warming trend. **Figure 52.14** shows the current and predicted geographic ranges of the American beech (*Fagus grandifolia*) under two different climate-change models. These models predict that the northern limit of the beech's range will move 700–900 km northward in the next century, and its southern range limit will move northward an even greater distance. If these predictions are even approximately correct, the beech must move 7–9 km per year northward to keep pace with the warming climate. However, since the end of the last ice age, the beech has migrated into its present range at a rate of only 0.2 km per year. Without human assistance in moving into new ranges where they can survive as the climate warms, species such as the American beech may have much smaller ranges and may even become extinct.

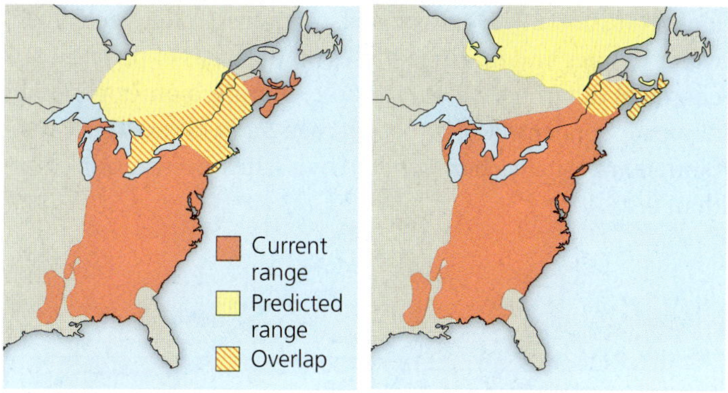

▲ **Figure 52.14 Current range and predicted range for the American beech (*Fagus grandifolia*) under two scenarios of climate change.**

? *The predicted range in each scenario is based on climate factors alone. What other factors might alter the distribution of this species?*

CONCEPT CHECK 52.2

1. Give examples of human actions that could expand a species' distribution by changing its (a) dispersal or (b) biotic interactions.
2. Explain how the sun's unequal heating of Earth's surface influences global climate patterns.
3. **WHAT IF?** You suspect that deer are restricting the distribution of a tree species by preferentially eating the seedlings of the tree. How might you test that hypothesis?

For suggested answers, see Appendix A.

CONCEPT **52.3**

Aquatic biomes are diverse and dynamic systems that cover most of Earth

We have seen how both biotic and abiotic factors influence the distribution of organisms on Earth. Combinations of these factors determine the nature of Earth's many **biomes**, major terrestrial or aquatic life zones, characterized by vegetation type in terrestrial biomes or the physical environment in aquatic biomes. We'll begin by examining Earth's aquatic biomes.

Aquatic biomes account for the largest part of the biosphere in terms of area, and all types are found around the globe **(Figure 52.15)**. Ecologists distinguish between freshwater biomes and marine biomes on the basis of physical and chemical differences. For example, marine biomes generally have salt concentrations that average 3%, whereas freshwater biomes are usually characterized by a salt concentration of less than 0.1%.

The oceans make up the largest marine biome, covering about 75% of Earth's surface. Because of their vast size, they have an enormous impact on the biosphere. The evaporation of water from the oceans provides most of the planet's rainfall, and ocean temperatures have a major effect on world climate and wind patterns. In addition, marine algae and

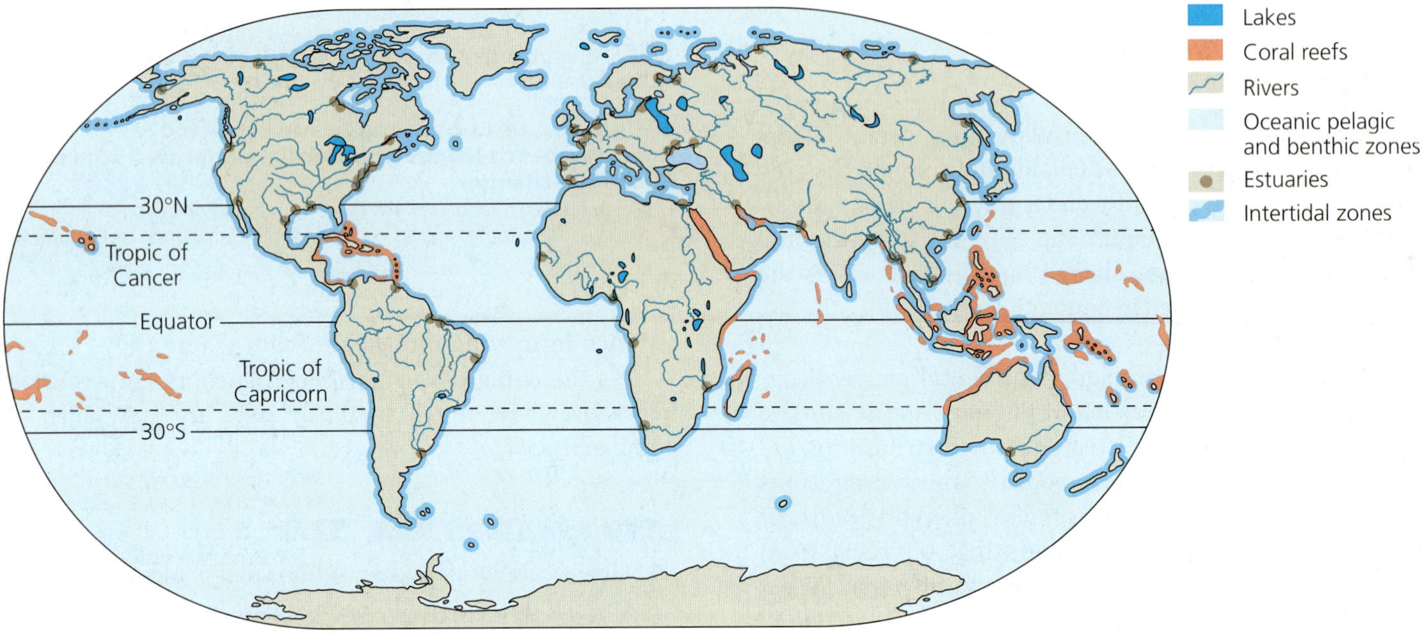

▲ **Figure 52.15 The distribution of major aquatic biomes.**

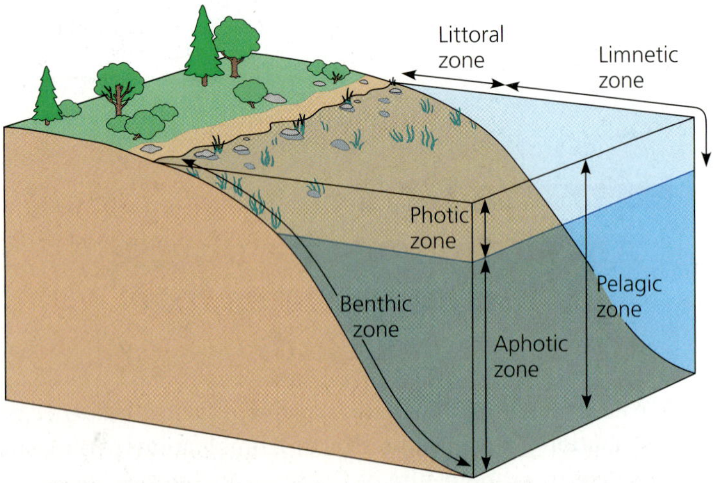

(a) Zonation in a lake. The lake environment is generally classified on the basis of three physical criteria: light penetration (photic and aphotic zones), distance from shore and water depth (littoral and limnetic zones), and whether it is open water (pelagic zone) or bottom (benthic zone).

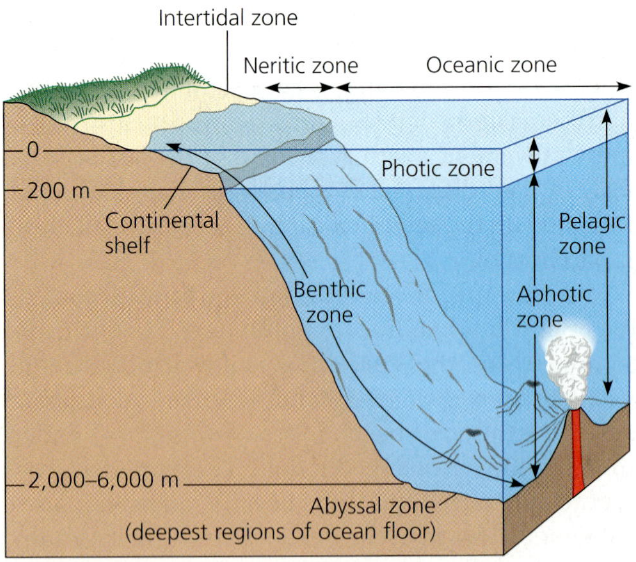

(b) Marine zonation. Like lakes, the marine environment is generally classified on the basis of light penetration (photic and aphotic zones), distance from shore and water depth (intertidal, neritic, and oceanic zones), and whether it is open water (pelagic zone) or bottom (benthic and abyssal zones).

▲ **Figure 52.16 Zonation in aquatic environments.**

photosynthetic bacteria supply a substantial portion of the world's oxygen and consume large amounts of atmospheric carbon dioxide.

Freshwater biomes are closely linked to the soils and biotic components of the terrestrial biomes through which they pass or in which they are situated. The particular characteristics of a freshwater biome are also influenced by the patterns and speed of water flow and the climate to which the biome is exposed.

Stratification of Aquatic Biomes

Many aquatic biomes are physically and chemically stratified (layered), as illustrated for both a lake and a marine environment in **Figure 52.16**, on the facing page. Light is absorbed by both the water itself and the photosynthetic organisms in it, so its intensity decreases rapidly with depth, as mentioned earlier. Ecologists distinguish between the upper **photic zone**, where there is sufficient light for photosynthesis, and the lower **aphotic zone**, where little light penetrates. At the bottom of all aquatic biomes, the substrate is called the **benthic zone**. Made up of sand and organic and inorganic sediments, the benthic zone is occupied by communities of organisms collectively called the **benthos**. A major source of food for many benthic species is dead organic matter called **detritus**, which "rains" down from the productive surface waters of the photic zone. In the ocean, the part of the benthic zone that lies between 2,000 and 6,000 m below the surface is known as the **abyssal zone**.

Thermal energy from sunlight warms surface waters to whatever depth the sunlight penetrates, but the deeper waters remain quite cold. In the ocean and in most lakes, a narrow layer of abrupt temperature change called a **thermocline** separates the more uniformly warm upper layer from more uniformly cold deeper waters. Lakes tend to be particularly layered with respect to temperature, especially during summer and winter, but many temperate lakes undergo a semiannual mixing of their waters as a result of changing temperature profiles **(Figure 52.17)**. This **turnover**, as it is called, brings oxygenated water from a lake's surface to the bottom and nutrient-rich water from the bottom to the surface in both spring and autumn. These cyclic changes in the abiotic properties of lakes are essential for the survival and growth of organisms at all levels within this ecosystem.

In both freshwater and marine environments, communities are distributed according to water depth, degree of light penetration, distance from shore, and whether they are found in open water or near the bottom. Marine communities, in particular, illustrate the limitations on species distribution that result from these abiotic factors. Plankton and many fish species occur in the relatively shallow photic zone (see Figure 52.16b). Because water absorbs light so well and the

1 In winter, the coldest water in the lake (0°C) lies just below the surface ice; water is progressively warmer at deeper levels of the lake, typically 4°C at the bottom.

2 In spring, as the sun melts the ice, the surface water warms to 4°C and sinks below the cooler layers immediately below, eliminating the thermal stratification. Spring winds mix the water to great depth, bringing oxygen to the bottom waters and nutrients to the surface.

3 In summer, the lake regains a distinctive thermal profile, with warm surface water separated from cold bottom water by a narrow vertical zone of abrupt temperature change, called a thermocline.

4 In autumn, as surface water cools rapidly, it sinks below the underlying layers, remixing the water until the surface begins to freeze and the winter temperature profile is reestablished.

▲ **Figure 52.17 Seasonal turnover in lakes with winter ice cover.** Because of the seasonal turnover shown here, lake waters are well oxygenated at all depths in spring and autumn; in winter and summer, when the lake is stratified by temperature, oxygen concentrations are lower in deeper waters and higher near the surface of the lake.

ocean is so deep, most of the ocean volume is virtually devoid of light (the aphotic zone) and harbors relatively little life, except for microorganisms and relatively sparse populations of fishes and invertebrates. Similar factors limit species distribution in deep lakes as well.

Figure 52.18, on the next four pages, surveys the major aquatic biomes.

▼ Figure 52.18

Exploring Aquatic Biomes

Lakes

Physical Environment Standing bodies of water range from ponds a few square meters in area to lakes covering thousands of square kilometers. Light decreases with depth, creating stratification (see Figure 52.16a). Temperate lakes may have a seasonal thermocline (see Figure 52.17); tropical lowland lakes have a thermocline year-round.

An oligotrophic lake in Grand Teton National Park, Wyoming

A eutrophic lake in the Okavango Delta, Botswana

Chemical Environment The salinity, oxygen concentration, and nutrient content differ greatly among lakes and can vary with season. **Oligotrophic lakes** are nutrient-poor and generally oxygen-rich; **eutrophic lakes** are nutrient-rich and often depleted of oxygen in the deepest zone in summer and if ice covered in winter. The amount of decomposable organic matter in bottom sediments is low in oligotrophic lakes and high in eutrophic lakes; high rates of decomposition in deeper layers of eutrophic lakes cause periodic oxygen depletion.

Geologic Features Oligotrophic lakes may become more eutrophic over time as runoff adds sediments and nutrients. They tend to have less surface area relative to their depth than eutrophic lakes have.

Photosynthetic Organisms Rooted and floating aquatic plants live in the **littoral zone**, the shallow, well-lighted waters close to shore. Farther from shore, where water is too deep to support rooted aquatic plants, the **limnetic zone** is inhabited by a variety of phytoplankton and cyanobacteria.

Heterotrophs In the limnetic zone, small drifting heterotrophs, or zooplankton, graze on the phytoplankton. The benthic zone is inhabited by assorted invertebrates whose species composition depends partly on oxygen levels. Fishes live in all zones with sufficient oxygen.

Human Impact Runoff from fertilized land and dumping of wastes lead to nutrient enrichment, which can produce algal blooms, oxygen depletion, and fish kills.

Wetlands

Physical Environment A **wetland** is a habitat that is inundated by water at least some of the time and that supports plants adapted to water-saturated soil. Some wetlands are inundated at all times, whereas others flood infrequently.

Chemical Environment Because of high organic production by plants and decomposition by microbes and other organisms, both the water and the soils are periodically low in dissolved oxygen. Wetlands have a high capacity to filter dissolved nutrients and chemical pollutants.

Geologic Features *Basin wetlands* develop in shallow basins, ranging from upland depressions to filled-in lakes and ponds. *Riverine wetlands* develop along shallow and periodically flooded banks of rivers and streams. *Fringe wetlands* occur along the coasts of large lakes and seas, where water flows back and forth because of rising lake levels or tidal action. Thus, fringe wetlands include both freshwater and marine biomes.

Photosynthetic Organisms Wetlands are among the most productive biomes on Earth. Their water-saturated soils favor the growth of plants such as floating pond lilies and emergent cattails, many sedges, tamarack, and black spruce, which have adaptations enabling them to grow in water or in soil that is periodically anaerobic owing to the presence of unaerated water. Woody plants dominate the vegetation of swamps, while bogs are dominated by sphagnum mosses.

Heterotrophs Wetlands are home to a diverse community of invertebrates, which in turn support a wide variety of birds. Herbivores, from crustaceans and aquatic insect larvae to muskrats, consume algae, detritus, and plants. Carnivores are also varied and may include dragonflies, otters, alligators, and owls.

Okefenokee National Wetland Reserve in Georgia

Human Impact Draining and filling have destroyed up to 90% of wetlands, which help purify water and reduce peak flooding.

Streams and Rivers

Physical Environment The most prominent physical characteristic of streams and rivers is their current. Headwater streams are generally cold, clear, turbulent, and swift. Farther downstream, where numerous tributaries may have joined, forming a river, the water is generally warmer and more turbid because of suspended sediment. Streams and rivers are stratified into vertical zones.

Chemical Environment The salt and nutrient content of streams and rivers increases from the headwaters to the mouth. Headwaters are generally rich in oxygen. Downstream water may also contain substantial oxygen, except where there has been organic enrichment. A large fraction of the organic matter in rivers consists of dissolved or highly fragmented material that is carried by the current from forested streams.

Geologic Features Headwater stream channels are often narrow, have a rocky bottom, and alternate between shallow sections and deeper pools. The downstream stretches of rivers are generally wide and meandering. River bottoms are often silty from sediments deposited over long periods of time.

Photosynthetic Organisms Headwater streams that flow through grasslands or deserts may be rich in phytoplankton or rooted aquatic plants.

Heterotrophs A great diversity of fishes and invertebrates inhabit unpolluted rivers and streams, distributed according to, and throughout, the vertical zones. In streams flowing through temperate or tropical forests, organic matter from terrestrial vegetation is the primary source of food for aquatic consumers.

Human Impact Municipal, agricultural, and industrial pollution degrade water quality and kill aquatic organisms. Damming and flood control impair the natural functioning of stream and river ecosystems and threaten migratory species such as salmon.

A headwater stream in the Great Smoky Mountains

The Mississippi River far from its headwaters

Estuaries

An estuary in a low coastal plain of Georgia

Physical Environment An **estuary** is a transition area between river and sea. Seawater flows up the estuary channel during a rising tide and flows back down during the falling tide. Often, higher-density seawater occupies the bottom of the channel and mixes little with the lower-density river water at the surface.

Chemical Environment Salinity varies spatially within estuaries, from nearly that of fresh water to that of seawater. Salinity also varies with the rise and fall of the tides. Nutrients from the river make estuaries, like wetlands, among the most productive biomes.

Geologic Features Estuarine flow patterns combined with the sediments carried by river and tidal waters create a complex network of tidal channels, islands, natural levees, and mudflats.

Photosynthetic Organisms Saltmarsh grasses and algae, including phytoplankton, are the major producers in estuaries.

Heterotrophs Estuaries support an abundance of worms, oysters, crabs, and many fish species that humans consume. Many marine invertebrates and fishes use estuaries as a breeding ground or migrate through them to freshwater habitats upstream. Estuaries are also crucial feeding areas for waterfowl and some marine mammals.

Human Impact Pollution from upstream, and also filling and dredging, have disrupted estuaries worldwide.

Continued on next page

▼ Figure 52.18 (continued)

Exploring Aquatic Biomes

Intertidal Zones

Rocky intertidal zone on the Oregon coast

Physical Environment An **intertidal zone** is periodically submerged and exposed by the tides, twice daily on most marine shores. Upper zones experience longer exposures to air and greater variations in temperature and salinity. Changes in physical conditions from the upper to the lower intertidal zones limit the distributions of many organisms to particular strata, as shown in the photograph.

Chemical Environment Oxygen and nutrient levels are generally high and are renewed with each turn of the tides.

Geologic Features The substrates of intertidal zones, which are generally either rocky or sandy, select for particular behavior and anatomy among intertidal organisms. The configuration of bays or coastlines influences the magnitude of tides and the relative exposure of intertidal organisms to wave action.

Photosynthetic Organisms A high diversity and biomass of attached marine algae inhabit rocky intertidal zones, especially in the lower zone. Sandy intertidal zones exposed to vigorous wave action generally lack attached plants or algae, while sandy intertidal zones in protected bays or lagoons often support rich beds of sea grass and algae.

Heterotrophs Many of the animals in rocky intertidal environments have structural adaptations that enable them to attach to the hard substrate. The composition, density, and diversity of animals change markedly from the upper to the lower intertidal zones. Many of the animals in sandy or muddy intertidal zones, such as worms, clams, and predatory crustaceans, bury themselves and feed as the tides bring sources of food. Other common animals are sponges, sea anemones, echinoderms, and small fishes.

Human Impact Oil pollution has disrupted many intertidal areas.

Oceanic Pelagic Zone

Physical Environment The **oceanic pelagic zone** is a vast realm of open blue water, constantly mixed by wind-driven oceanic currents. Because of higher water clarity, the photic zone extends to greater depths than in coastal marine waters.

Chemical Environment Oxygen levels are generally high. Nutrient concentrations are generally lower than in coastal waters. Because they are thermally stratified year-round, some tropical areas of the oceanic pelagic zone have lower nutrient concentrations than temperate oceans. Turnover between fall and spring renews nutrients in the photic zones of temperate and high-latitude ocean areas.

Geologic Features This biome covers approximately 70% of Earth's surface and has an average depth of nearly 4,000 m. The deepest point in the ocean is more than 10,000 m beneath the surface.

Photosynthetic Organisms The dominant photosynthetic organisms are phytoplankton, including photosynthetic bacteria, that drift with the oceanic currents. Spring turnover and renewal of nutrients in temperate oceans produces a surge of phytoplankton growth. Because of the large extent of this biome, photosynthetic plankton account for about half of the photosynthetic activity on Earth.

Heterotrophs The most abundant heterotrophs in this biome are zooplankton. These protists, worms, copepods, shrimp-like krill, jellies, and the small larvae of invertebrates and fishes graze on photosynthetic plankton. The oceanic pelagic zone also includes free-swimming animals, such as large squids, fishes, sea turtles, and marine mammals.

Human Impact Overfishing has depleted fish stocks in all Earth's oceans, which have also been polluted by waste dumping.

Open ocean off the island of Hawaii

Coral Reefs

A coral reef in the Red Sea

Physical Environment **Coral reefs** are formed largely from the calcium carbonate skeletons of corals. Shallow reef-building corals live in the photic zone of relatively stable tropical marine environments with high water clarity, primarily on islands and along the edge of some continents. They are sensitive to temperatures below about 18–20°C and above 30°C. Deep-sea coral reefs, found between 200 and 1,500 m deep, are less known than their shallow counterparts but harbor as much diversity as many shallow reefs do.

Chemical Environment Corals require high oxygen levels and are excluded by high inputs of fresh water and nutrients.

Geologic Features Corals require a solid substrate for attachment. A typical coral reef begins as a *fringing reef* on a young, high island, forming an offshore *barrier reef* later in the history of the island and becoming a *coral atoll* as the older island submerges.

Photosynthetic Organisms Unicellular algae live within the tissues of the corals, forming a mutualistic relationship that provides the corals with organic molecules. Diverse multicellular red and green algae growing on the reef also contribute substantial amounts of photosynthesis.

Heterotrophs Corals, a diverse group of cnidarians (see Chapter 33), are themselves the predominant animals on coral reefs. However, fish and invertebrate diversity is exceptionally high. Overall animal diversity on coral reefs rivals that of tropical forests.

Human Impact Collecting of coral skeletons and overfishing have reduced populations of corals and reef fishes. Global warming and pollution may be contributing to large-scale coral death. Development of coastal mangroves for aquaculture has also reduced spawning grounds for many species of reef fishes.

Marine Benthic Zone

Physical Environment The **marine benthic zone** consists of the seafloor below the surface waters of the coastal, or **neritic**, zone and the offshore, pelagic zone (see Figure 52.16b). Except for shallow, near-coastal areas, the marine benthic zone receives no sunlight. Water temperature declines with depth, while pressure increases. As a result, organisms in the very deep benthic, or **abyssal**, zone are adapted to continuous cold (about 3°C) and very high water pressure.

Chemical Environment Except in some areas of organic enrichment, oxygen is present at sufficient concentrations to support a diversity of animals.

A deep-sea hydrothermal vent community

Geologic Features Soft sediments cover most of the benthic zone. However, there are areas of rocky substrate on reefs, submarine mountains, and new oceanic crust.

Autotrophs Photosynthetic organisms, mainly seaweeds and filamentous algae, are limited to shallow benthic areas with sufficient light to support them. Unique assemblages of organisms, such as those shown in the photo, are found near **deep-sea hydrothermal vents** on mid-ocean ridges. In these dark, hot environments, the food producers are chemoautotrophic prokaryotes (see Chapter 27) that obtain energy by oxidizing H_2S formed by a reaction of the hot water with dissolved sulfate (SO_4^{2-}).

Heterotrophs Neritic benthic communities include numerous invertebrates and fishes. Beyond the photic zone, most consumers depend entirely on organic matter raining down from above. Among the animals of the deep-sea hydrothermal vent communities are giant tube worms (pictured at left), some more than 1 m long. They are nourished by chemoautotrophic prokaryotes that live as symbionts within their bodies. Many other invertebrates, including arthropods and echinoderms, are also abundant around the hydrothermal vents.

Human Impact Overfishing has decimated important benthic fish populations, such as the cod of the Grand Banks off Newfoundland. Dumping of organic wastes has created oxygen-deprived benthic areas.

CONCEPT CHECK 52.3

The first two questions refer to Figure 52.18.

1. Many organisms living in estuaries experience fresh- and saltwater conditions each day with the rising and falling of tides. What challenge does this pose for the physiology of the organisms?
2. Why are phytoplankton, and not benthic algae or rooted aquatic plants, the dominant photosynthetic organisms of the oceanic pelagic zone?
3. **WHAT IF?** Water leaving a reservoir behind a dam is often taken from deep layers of the reservoir. Would you expect fish found in a river below a dam in summer to be species that prefer colder or warmer water than fish found in an undammed river? Explain.

For suggested answers, see Appendix A.

CONCEPT **52.4**

The structure and distribution of terrestrial biomes are controlled by climate and disturbance

All the abiotic factors discussed in this chapter, but especially climate, are important in determining why a particular terrestrial biome is found in a certain area. Because there are latitudinal patterns of climate over Earth's surface (see Figure 52.10), there are also latitudinal patterns of biome distribution **(Figure 52.19)**. These biome patterns in turn are modified by **disturbance**, an event (such as a storm, fire, or human activity) that changes a community, removing organisms from it and altering resource availability. Frequent fires, for instance, can kill woody plants and keep a savanna from becoming the woodland that climate alone would otherwise support.

Climate and Terrestrial Biomes

We can see the great impact of climate on the distribution of organisms by constructing a **climograph**, a plot of the temperature and precipitation in a particular region. **Figure 52.20** is a climograph of annual mean temperature and precipitation for some of the biomes found in North America. Notice that the range of precipitation in northern coniferous forests is similar to that in temperate forests, but the temperature ranges are different. Grasslands are generally drier than either kind of forest, and deserts are drier still.

Factors other than mean temperature and precipitation also play a role in determining where biomes exist. For example, certain areas in North America with a particular combination of temperature and precipitation support a temperate broadleaf forest, but other areas with similar values for these variables support a coniferous forest. How do we explain this variation? First, remember that the climograph is based on annual *averages*. Often, however, the *pattern* of climatic variation is as important as the average climate. Some areas may receive regular precipitation throughout the year, whereas other areas with the same annual precipitation have distinct wet and dry seasons. A similar phenomenon may occur with respect to temperature. Other environmental characteristics, such as the type of bedrock in an area, may greatly affect mineral nutrient availability and soil structure, which in turn affect the kind of vegetation that can grow.

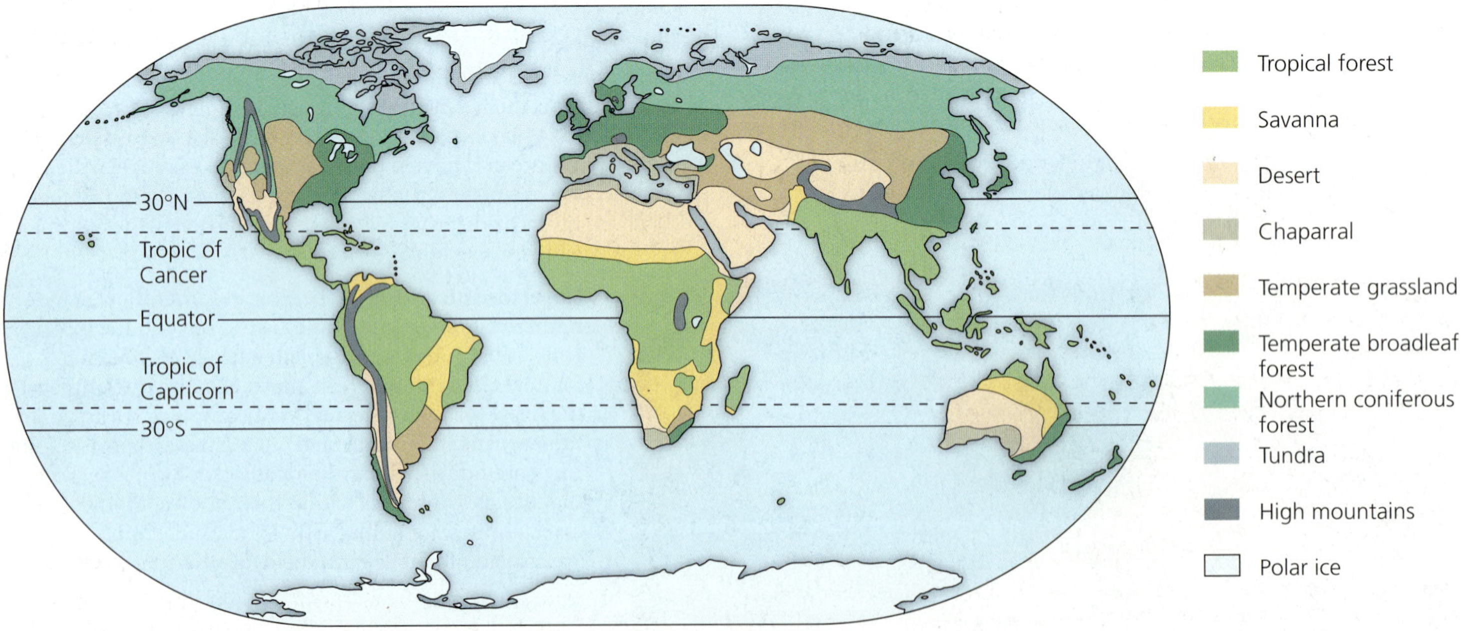

▲ **Figure 52.19 The distribution of major terrestrial biomes.** Although biomes are mapped here with sharp boundaries, biomes actually grade into one another, sometimes over large areas.

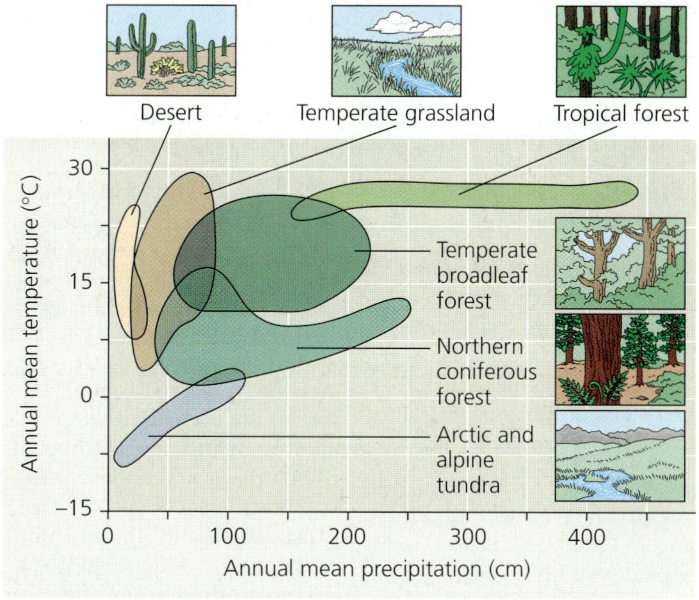

▲ **Figure 52.20 A climograph for some major types of biomes in North America.** The areas plotted here encompass the range of annual mean temperature and precipitation in the biomes.

General Features of Terrestrial Biomes and the Role of Disturbance

Most terrestrial biomes are named for major physical or climatic features and for their predominant vegetation. Temperate grasslands, for instance, are generally found in middle latitudes, where the climate is more moderate than in the tropics or polar regions, and are dominated by various grass species (see Figure 52.19). Each biome is also characterized by microorganisms, fungi, and animals adapted to that particular environment. For example, temperate grasslands are more likely than forests to be populated by large grazing mammals.

Although Figure 52.19 shows distinct boundaries between the biomes, in actuality, terrestrial biomes usually grade into each other without sharp boundaries. The area of intergradation, called an **ecotone**, may be wide or narrow.

Vertical layering is an important feature of terrestrial biomes, and the shapes and sizes of plants largely define that layering. In many forests, for example, the layers from top to bottom consist of the upper **canopy**, the low-tree layer, the shrub understory, the ground layer of herbaceous plants, the forest floor (litter layer), and the root layer. Nonforest biomes have similar, though usually less pronounced, layers. Grasslands have an herbaceous layer of grasses and forbs (small broadleaf plants), a litter layer, and a root layer. Layering of vegetation provides many different habitats for animals, which often occupy well-defined feeding groups, from the insectivorous birds and bats that feed above canopies to the small mammals, numerous worms, and arthropods that search for food in the litter and root layers.

The species composition of each kind of biome varies from one location to another. For instance, in the northern coniferous forest (taiga) of North America, red spruce is common in the east but does not occur in most other areas, where black spruce and white spruce are abundant. In an example of convergent evolution (see Figure 26.7), cacti living in North American deserts appear very similar to plants called euphorbs found in African deserts, although cacti and euphorbs belong to different evolutionary lineages.

Biomes are dynamic, and disturbance rather than stability tends to be the rule. For example, hurricanes create openings for new species in tropical and temperate forests. In northern coniferous forests, gaps are produced when old trees die and fall over or when snowfall breaks branches. These gaps allow deciduous species, such as aspen and birch, to grow. As a result, biomes usually exhibit extensive patchiness, with several different communities represented in any particular area.

In many biomes, the dominant plants depend on periodic disturbance. For example, natural wildfires are an integral component of grasslands, savannas, chaparral, and many coniferous forests. However, fires are no longer common across much of the Great Plains because tallgrass prairie ecosystems have been converted to agricultural fields that rarely burn. Before agricultural and urban development, much of the southeastern United States was dominated by a single conifer species, the longleaf pine. Without periodic burning, broadleaf trees tended to replace the pines. Forest managers now use fire as a tool to help maintain many coniferous forests.

Figure 52.21, on the next four pages, summarizes the major features of terrestrial biomes. As you read about the characteristics of each biome, remember that humans have altered much of Earth's surface, replacing original biomes with urban and agricultural ones. Most of the eastern United States, for example, is classified as temperate broadleaf forest, but little of that original forest remains.

Throughout this chapter, you have seen how the distributions of organisms and biomes depend on both abiotic and biotic factors. In the next chapter, we will begin to work our way down the hierarchy outlined in Figure 52.2, focusing on how abiotic and biotic factors influence the ecology of populations.

CONCEPT CHECK 52.4

1. Based on the climograph in Figure 52.20, what mainly differentiates dry tundra and deserts?
2. Identify the natural biome in which you live and summarize its abiotic and biotic characteristics. Do these reflect your actual surroundings? Explain.
3. **WHAT IF?** If global warming increases average temperatures on Earth by 4°C in this century, predict which biome is most likely to replace tundra in some locations as a result. Explain your answer.

For suggested answers, see Appendix A.

▼ **Figure 52.21**

Exploring Terrestrial Biomes

Tropical Forest

A tropical rain forest in Borneo

Distribution Equatorial and subequatorial regions.

Precipitation In **tropical rain forests**, rainfall is relatively constant, about 200–400 cm annually. In **tropical dry forests**, precipitation is highly seasonal, about 150–200 cm annually, with a six- to seven-month dry season.

Temperature Air temperatures are high year-round, averaging 25–29°C with little seasonal variation.

Plants Tropical forests are vertically layered, and competition for light is intense. Layers in rain forests include emergent trees that grow above a closed canopy, the canopy trees, one or two layers of subcanopy trees, and shrub and herb layers. There are generally fewer layers in tropical dry forests. Broadleaf evergreen trees are dominant in tropical rain forests, whereas tropical dry forest trees drop their leaves during the dry season. Epiphytes such as bromeliads and orchids generally cover tropical forest trees but are less abundant in dry forests. Thorny shrubs and succulent plants are common in some tropical dry forests.

Animals Earth's tropical forests are home to millions of species, including an estimated 5–30 million still undescribed species of insects, spiders, and other arthropods. In fact, animal diversity is higher in tropical forests than in any other terrestrial biome. The animals, including amphibians, birds and other reptiles, mammals, and arthropods, are adapted to the vertically layered environment and are often inconspicuous.

Human Impact Humans long ago established thriving communities in tropical forests. Rapid population growth leading to agriculture and development is now destroying some tropical forests.

Desert

A desert in the southwestern United States

Distribution **Deserts** occur in bands near 30° north and south latitude or at other latitudes in the interior of continents (for instance, the Gobi Desert of north central Asia).

Precipitation Precipitation is low and highly variable, generally less than 30 cm per year.

Temperature Temperature is variable seasonally and daily. Maximum air temperature in hot deserts may exceed 50°C; in cold deserts air temperature may fall below −30°C.

Plants Desert landscapes are dominated by low, widely scattered vegetation; the proportion of bare ground is high compared with other terrestrial biomes. The plants include succulents such as cacti, deeply rooted shrubs, and herbs that grow during the infrequent moist periods. Desert plant adaptations include heat and desiccation tolerance, water storage, and reduced leaf surface area. Physical defenses, such as spines, and chemical defenses, such as toxins in the leaves of shrubs, are common. Many of the plants exhibit C_4 or CAM photosynthesis (see Chapter 10).

Animals Common desert animals include many kinds of snakes and lizards, scorpions, ants, beetles, migratory and resident birds, and seed-eating rodents. Many species are nocturnal. Water conservation is a common adaptation, with some species surviving on water from metabolic breakdown of carbohydrates in seeds.

Human Impact Long-distance transport of water and deep groundwater wells have allowed humans to maintain substantial populations in deserts. Conversion to irrigated agriculture and urbanization have reduced the natural biodiversity of some deserts.

Savanna

Distribution Equatorial and subequatorial regions.

Precipitation Rainfall, which is seasonal, averages 30–50 cm per year. The dry season can last up to eight or nine months.

Temperature The **savanna** is warm year-round, averaging 24–29°C, but with somewhat more seasonal variation than in tropical forests.

Plants The scattered trees found at different densities in the savanna often are thorny and have small leaves, an apparent adaptation to the relatively dry conditions. Fires are common in the dry season, and the dominant plant species are fire-adapted and tolerant of seasonal drought. Grasses and forbs, which make up most of the ground cover, grow rapidly in response to seasonal rains and are tolerant of grazing by large mammals and other herbivores.

Animals Large plant-eating mammals, such as wildebeests and bison, and predators, including lions and hyenas, are common inhabitants. However, the dominant herbivores are actually insects, especially termites. During seasonal droughts, grazing mammals often migrate to parts of the savanna with more forage and scattered watering holes.

Human Impact There is evidence that the earliest humans lived in savannas. Fires set by humans may help maintain this biome. Cattle ranching and overhunting have led to declines in large-mammal populations.

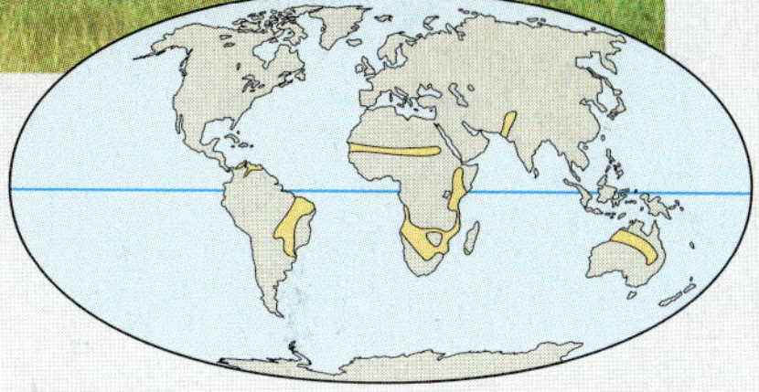

A savanna in Kenya

Chaparral

Distribution This biome occurs in midlatitude coastal regions on several continents, and its many names reflect its far-flung distribution: **chaparral** in North America, *matorral* in Spain and Chile, *garigue* and *maquis* in southern France, and *fynbos* in South Africa.

Precipitation Precipitation is highly seasonal, with rainy winters and long, dry summers. Annual precipitation generally falls within the range of 30–50 cm.

Temperature Fall, winter, and spring are cool, with average temperatures in the range of 10–12°C. Average summer temperature can reach 30°C, and daytime maximum temperature can exceed 40°C.

Plants Chaparral is dominated by shrubs and small trees, along with a many kinds of grasses and herbs. Plant diversity is high, with many species confined to a specific, relatively small geographic area. Adaptations to drought include the tough evergreen leaves of woody plants, which reduce water loss. Adaptations to fire are also prominent. Some of the shrubs produce seeds that will germinate only after a hot fire; food reserves stored in their fire-resistant roots enable them to resprout quickly and use nutrients released by the fire.

Animals Native mammals include browsers, such as deer and goats, that feed on twigs and buds of woody vegetation, and a high diversity of small mammals. Chaparral areas also support many species of amphibians, birds and other reptiles, and insects.

Human Impact Chaparral areas have been heavily settled and reduced through conversion to agriculture and urbanization. Humans contribute to the fires that sweep across the chaparral.

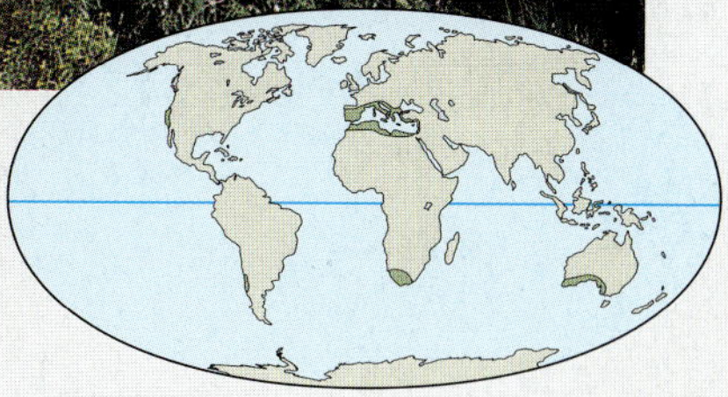

An area of chaparral in California

Continued on next page

▼ Figure 52.21 (continued)

Exploring Terrestrial Biomes

Temperate Grassland

Sheyenne National Grassland in North Dakota

Distribution The veldts of South Africa, the *puszta* of Hungary, the pampas of Argentina and Uruguay, the steppes of Russia, and the plains and prairies of central North America are all **temperate grasslands**.

Precipitation Precipitation is often highly seasonal, with relatively dry winters and wet summers. Annual precipitation generally averages between 30 and 100 cm. Periodic drought is common.

Temperature Winters are generally cold, with average temperatures frequently falling well below −10°C. Summers, with average temperatures often approaching 30°C, are hot.

Plants The dominant plants are grasses and forbs, which vary in height from a few centimeters to 2 m in tallgrass prairie. Many have adaptations that help them survive periodic, protracted droughts and fire: For example, grasses can sprout quickly following fire. Grazing by large mammals helps prevent establishment of woody shrubs and trees.

Animals Native mammals include large grazers such as bison and wild horses. Temperate grasslands are also inhabited by a wide variety of burrowing mammals, such as prairie dogs in North America.

Human Impact Deep, fertile soils make temperate grasslands ideal places for agriculture, especially for growing grains. As a consequence, most grassland in North America and much of Eurasia has been converted to farmland. In some drier grasslands, cattle and other grazers have helped change parts of the biome into desert.

Northern Coniferous Forest

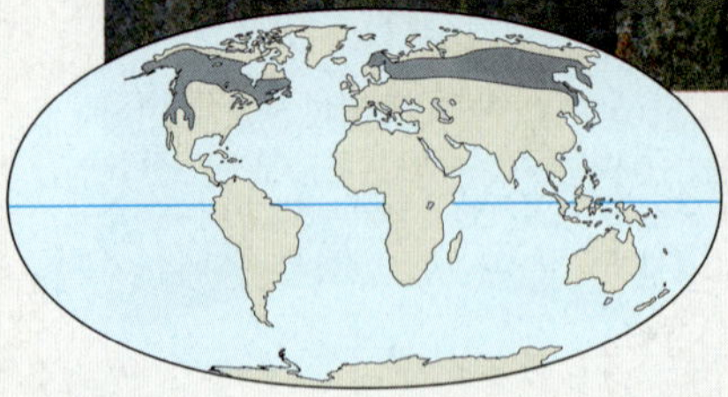

Rocky Mountain National Park in Colorado

Distribution Extending in a broad band across northern North America and Eurasia to the edge of the arctic tundra, the **northern coniferous forest**, or *taiga*, is the largest terrestrial biome on Earth.

Precipitation Annual precipitation generally ranges from 30 to 70 cm, and periodic droughts are common. However, some coastal coniferous forests of the U.S. Pacific Northwest are temperate rain forests that may receive over 300 cm of annual precipitation.

Temperature Winters are usually cold and long; summers may be hot. Some areas of coniferous forest in Siberia typically range in temperature from −50°C in winter to over 20°C in summer.

Plants Cone-bearing trees, such as pine, spruce, fir, and hemlock, dominate northern coniferous forests. The conical shape of many conifers prevents too much snow from accumulating and breaking their branches. The diversity of plants in the shrub and herb layers of these forests is lower than in temperate broadleaf forests.

Animals While many migratory birds nest in northern coniferous forests, other species reside there year-round. The mammals of this biome, which include moose, brown bears, and Siberian tigers, are diverse. Periodic outbreaks of insects that feed on the dominant trees can kill vast tracts of trees.

Human Impact Although they have not been heavily settled by human populations, northern coniferous forests are being logged at an alarming rate, and the old-growth stands of these trees may soon disappear.

Temperate Broadleaf Forest

Distribution Found mainly at midlatitudes in the Northern Hemisphere, with smaller areas in New Zealand and Australia.

Precipitation Precipitation can average from about 70 to over 200 cm annually. Significant amounts fall during all seasons, including summer rain and, in some forests, winter snow.

Temperature Winter temperatures average around 0°C. Summers, with maximum temperatures near 35°C, are hot and humid.

Plants A mature **temperate broadleaf forest** has distinct vertical layers, including a closed canopy, one or two strata of understory trees, a shrub layer, and an herbaceous stratum. There are few epiphytes. The dominant plants in the Northern Hemisphere are deciduous trees, which drop their leaves before winter, when low temperatures would reduce photosynthesis and make water uptake from frozen soil difficult. In Australia, evergreen eucalyptus dominate these forests.

Animals In the Northern Hemisphere, many mammals hibernate in winter, while many bird species migrate to warmer climates. The mammals, birds, and insects make use of all vertical layers of the forest.

Human Impact Temperate broadleaf forest has been heavily settled on all continents. Logging and land clearing for agriculture and urban development destroyed virtually all the original deciduous forests in North America. However, owing to their capacity for recovery, these forests are returning over much of their former range.

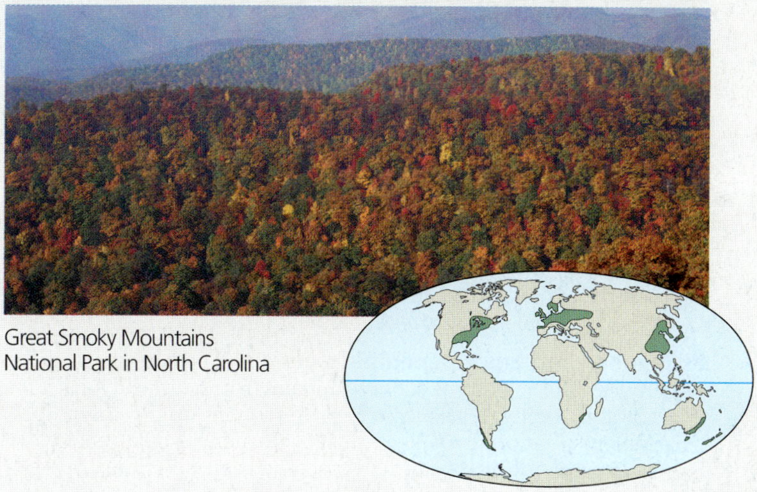

Great Smoky Mountains National Park in North Carolina

Tundra

Distribution **Tundra** covers expansive areas of the Arctic, amounting to 20% of Earth's land surface. High winds and low temperatures create similar plant communities, called *alpine tundra*, on very high mountaintops at all latitudes, including the tropics.

Precipitation Precipitation averages from 20 to 60 cm annually in arctic tundra but may exceed 100 cm in alpine tundra.

Temperature Winters are long and cold, with averages in some areas below −30°C. Summers are short with low temperatures, generally averaging less than 10°C.

Plants The vegetation of tundra is mostly herbaceous, consisting of a mixture of mosses, grasses, and forbs, along with some dwarf shrubs and trees and lichens. A permanently frozen layer of soil called **permafrost** restricts the growth of plant roots.

Animals Large grazing musk oxen are resident, while caribou and reindeer are migratory. Predators include bears, wolves, and foxes. Many bird species migrate to the tundra for summer nesting.

Human Impact Tundra is sparsely settled but has become the focus of significant mineral and oil extraction in recent years.

Denali National Park, Alaska, in autumn

Chapter 52 Review

MEDIA Go to the Study Area at **www.masteringbio.com** for BioFlix 3-D Animations, MP3 Tutors, Videos, Practice Tests, an eBook, and more.

SUMMARY OF KEY CONCEPTS

CONCEPT 52.1

Ecology integrates all areas of biological research and informs environmental decision making (pp. 1148–1151)

- **Linking Ecology and Evolutionary Biology** Events that occur in ecological time affect life in evolutionary time.
- **Ecology and Environmental Issues** Ecologists distinguish between the science of ecology and environmental advocacy. Ecology provides a scientific basis for solving environmental problems, but policymakers must also balance social, economic, and political factors in reaching their decisions.

MEDIA
Activity Science, Technology, and Society: DDT

CONCEPT 52.2

Interactions between organisms and the environment limit the distribution of species (pp. 1151–1159)

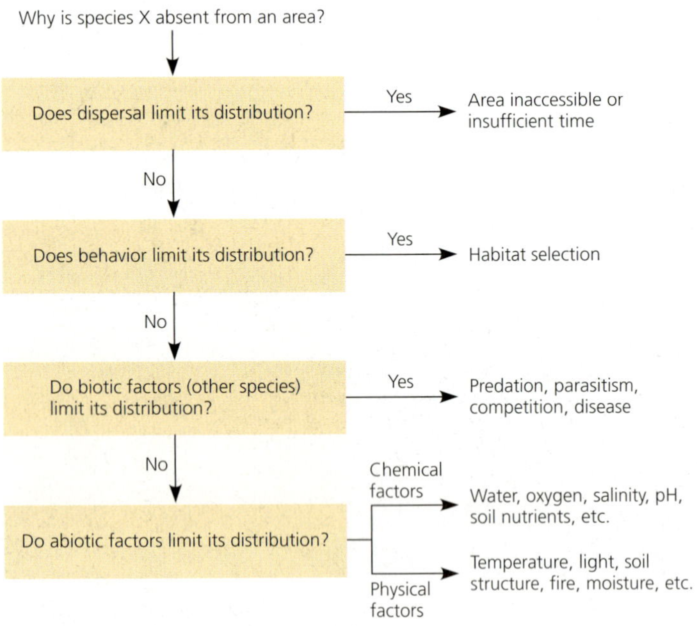

- **Climate** Global climate patterns are largely determined by the input of solar energy and Earth's revolution around the sun. Bodies of water, mountains, and the changing angle of the sun over the year exert regional, local, and seasonal effects on climate. Fine-scale differences in abiotic factors determine microclimates.

MEDIA
Activity Adaptations to Biotic and Abiotic Factors
Investigation How Do Abiotic Factors Affect Distribution of Organisms?

CONCEPT 52.3

Aquatic biomes are diverse and dynamic systems that cover most of Earth (pp. 1159–1166)

- **Stratification of Aquatic Biomes** Aquatic biomes account for the largest part of the biosphere in terms of area and are generally stratified (layered) with regard to light penetration, temperature, and community structure. Marine biomes have a higher salt concentration than freshwater biomes.

MEDIA
Activity Aquatic Biomes

CONCEPT 52.4

The structure and distribution of terrestrial biomes are controlled by climate and disturbance (pp. 1166–1171)

- **Climate and Terrestrial Biomes** Climographs show that temperature and precipitation are correlated with biomes, but because biomes overlap, other abiotic factors play a role in biome location.
- **General Features of Terrestrial Biomes and the Role of Disturbance** Terrestrial biomes are often named for major physical or climatic factors and for their predominant vegetation. Vertical layering is an important feature of terrestrial biomes. Disturbance, both natural and human induced, influences the type of vegetation found in biomes.

MEDIA
Activity Terrestrial Biomes

TESTING YOUR KNOWLEDGE

SELF-QUIZ

1. Which of the following areas of study focuses on the exchange of energy, organisms, and materials between ecosystems?
   a. population ecology
   b. organismal ecology
   c. landscape ecology
   d. ecosystem ecology
   e. community ecology

2. **WHAT IF?** If Earth's axis of rotation suddenly became perpendicular to the plane of its orbit, the most predictable effect would be
   a. no more night and day.
   b. a big change in the length of the year.
   c. a cooling of the equator.
   d. a loss of seasonal variation at high latitudes.
   e. the elimination of ocean currents.

3. When climbing a mountain, we can observe transitions in biological communities that are analogous to the changes
   a. in biomes at different latitudes.
   b. at different depths in the ocean.
   c. in a community through different seasons.
   d. in an ecosystem as it evolves over time.
   e. across the United States from east to west.

4. The oceans affect the biosphere in all of the following ways *except*
   a. producing a substantial amount of the biosphere's oxygen.
   b. removing carbon dioxide from the atmosphere.
   c. moderating the climate of terrestrial biomes.
   d. regulating the pH of freshwater biomes and terrestrial groundwater.
   e. being the source of most of Earth's rainfall.

5. Which lake zone would be absent in a very shallow lake?
   a. benthic zone
   b. aphotic zone
   c. pelagic zone
   d. littoral zone
   e. limnetic zone

6. Which of the following is true with respect to oligotrophic lakes and eutrophic lakes?
   a. Oligotrophic lakes are more subject to oxygen depletion.
   b. Rates of photosynthesis are lower in eutrophic lakes.
   c. Eutrophic lake water contains lower concentrations of nutrients.
   d. Eutrophic lakes are richer in nutrients.
   e. Sediments in oligotrophic lakes contain larger amounts of decomposable organic matter.

7. Which of the following is characteristic of most terrestrial biomes?
   a. annual average rainfall in excess of 250 cm
   b. a distribution predicted almost entirely by rock and soil patterns
   c. clear boundaries between adjacent biomes
   d. vegetation demonstrating stratification
   e. cold winter months

8. Which of the following biomes is correctly paired with the description of its climate?
   a. savanna—low temperature, precipitation uniform during the year
   b. tundra—long summers, mild winters
   c. temperate broadleaf forest—relatively short growing season, mild winters
   d. temperate grasslands—relatively warm winters, most rainfall in summer
   e. tropical forests—nearly constant day length and temperature

9. Suppose that the number of bird species is determined mainly by the number of vertical strata found in the environment. If so, in which of the following biomes would you find the greatest number of bird species?
   a. tropical rain forest
   b. savanna
   c. desert
   d. temperate broadleaf forest
   e. temperate grassland

10. **DRAW IT** After reading the experiment of W. J. Fletcher described in Figure 52.8, you decide to study feeding relationships among sea otters, sea urchins, and kelp on your own. You know that sea otters prey on sea urchins and that urchins eat kelp. At four coastal sites, you measure kelp abundance. Then you spend one day at each site and mark whether otters are present or absent every 5 minutes during daylight hours. Make a graph that shows how otter density depends on kelp abundance, using the data shown below. Then formulate a hypothesis to explain the pattern you observed.

Site	Kelp Abundance (% cover)	Otter Density (# sightings per day)
1	75	98
2	15	18
3	60	85
4	25	36

For Self-Quiz answers, see Appendix A.

MEDIA Visit the Study Area at **www.masteringbio.com** for a Practice Test.

EVOLUTION CONNECTION

11. Discuss how the concept of time applies to ecological situations and evolutionary changes. Do ecological time and evolutionary time ever overlap? If so, what are some examples?

SCIENTIFIC INQUIRY

12. Jens Clausen and colleagues, at the Carnegie Institution of Washington, studied how the size of yarrow plants (*Achillea lanulosa*) growing on the slopes of the Sierra Nevada varied with elevation. They found that plants from low elevations were generally taller than plants from high elevations, as shown below:

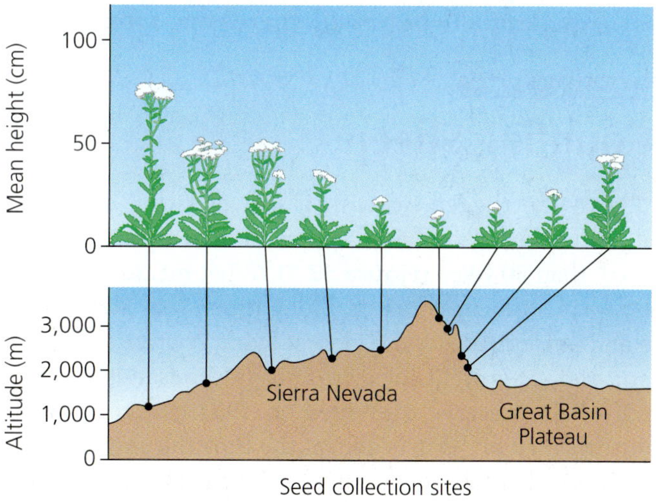

Source: J. Clausen et al., Experimental studies on the nature of species. III. Environmental responses of climatic races of *Achillea,* Carnegie Institution of Washington Publication No. 581 (1948).

Clausen and colleagues proposed two hypotheses to explain this variation within a species: (1) There are genetic differences between populations of plants found at different elevations. (2) The species has developmental flexibility and can assume tall or short growth forms, depending on local abiotic factors. If you had seeds from yarrow plants found at low and high elevations, what experiments would you perform to test these hypotheses?

53 Population Ecology

▲ **Figure 53.1 What causes a sheep population to fluctuate in size?**

KEY CONCEPTS

OVERVIEW

Counting Sheep

On the rugged Scottish island of Hirta, ecologists have been studying a population of sheep for more than 50 years **(Figure 53.1)**. What makes these animals worth studying for such a long time? Soay sheep are a rare and ancient breed, the closest living relative of the domesticated sheep that lived in Europe thousands of years ago. To help preserve the breed, in 1932 conservationists captured sheep on Soay Island, at the time the animals' only home, and released them on nearby Hirta. There, the sheep became valuable for a second reason: They provided an ideal opportunity to study how an isolated population of animals changes in size when food is plentiful and predators are absent. Surprisingly, ecologists found that the number of sheep on Hirta swung dramatically under these conditions, sometimes changing by more than 50% from one year to the next.

Why do populations of some species fluctuate greatly while populations of other species do not? To answer this question, we turn to the field of **population ecology**, the study of populations in relation to their environment. Population ecology explores how biotic and abiotic factors influence the density, distribution, size, and age structure of populations.

Our earlier study of populations in Chapter 23 emphasized the relationship between population genetics—the structure and dynamics of gene pools—and evolution. Evolution remains a central theme as we now view populations in the context of ecology. In this chapter, we will first examine some of the structural and dynamic aspects of populations. We will then explore the tools and models ecologists use to analyze populations and the factors that regulate the abundance of organisms. Finally, we will apply these basic concepts as we examine recent trends in the size and makeup of the human population.

CONCEPT **53.1**

Dynamic biological processes influence population density, dispersion, and demographics

A **population** is a group of individuals of a single species living in the same general area. Members of a population rely on the same resources, are influenced by similar environmental factors, and are likely to interact and breed with one another. Populations can evolve as natural selection acts on heritable variations among individuals and changes the frequencies of various traits over time (see Chapter 23).

Three fundamental characteristics of a population are its density, dispersion, and demographics.

Density and Dispersion

At any given moment, a population has specific boundaries and a specific size (the number of individuals living within those boundaries). Ecologists usually begin investigating a population by defining boundaries appropriate to the organism under study and to the questions being asked. A population's boundaries may be natural ones, as in the case of the sheep on Hirta Island, or they may be arbitrarily defined by an investigator—for example, the oak trees within a specific county in Minnesota. Once defined, the population can be described in terms of its density and dispersion. **Density** is the number of individuals per unit area or volume: the number of oak trees per square kilometer in the Minnesota county or the number of *Escherichia coli* bacteria per milliliter in a test tube. **Dispersion** is the pattern of spacing among individuals within the boundaries of the population.

Density: A Dynamic Perspective

In rare cases, population size and density can be determined by counting all individuals within the boundaries of the population. We could count all the Soay sheep on Hirta Island or all the sea stars in a tide pool, for example. Large mammals that live in herds, such as buffalo or elephants, can sometimes be counted accurately from airplanes. In most cases, however, it is impractical or impossible to count all individuals in a population. Instead, ecologists use a variety of sampling techniques to estimate densities and total population sizes. For example, they might count the number of oak trees in several randomly located 100 × 100 m plots (samples), calculate the average density in the samples, and then extrapolate to estimate the population size in the entire area. Such estimates are most accurate when there are many sample plots and when the habitat is fairly homogeneous. In other cases, instead of counting individual organisms, population ecologists estimate density from an index (indicator) of population size, such as the number of nests, burrows, tracks, or fecal droppings. Ecologists also use the **mark-recapture method** to estimate the size of wildlife populations **(Figure 53.2)**.

Density is not a static property but changes as individuals are added to or removed from a population **(Figure 53.3)**.

▼ Figure 53.2 Research Method

Determining Population Size Using the Mark-Recapture Method

APPLICATION Ecologists cannot count all the individuals in a population if the organisms move too quickly or are hidden from view. In such cases, researchers often use the mark-recapture method to estimate population size. Andrew Gormley and colleagues at the University of Otago applied this method to a population of endangered Hector's dolphins (*Cephalorhynchus hectori*) near Banks Peninsula, in New Zealand.

Hector's dolphins

TECHNIQUE Scientists typically begin by capturing a random sample of individuals in a population. They tag, or "mark," each individual and then release it. With some species, researchers can identify individuals without physically capturing them. For example, Gormley and colleagues identified 180 Hector's dolphins by photographing their distinctive dorsal fins from boats.

After waiting for the marked or otherwise identified individuals to mix back into the population, usually a few days or weeks, scientists capture or sample a second set of individuals. At Banks Peninsula, Gormley's team encountered 44 dolphins in their second sampling, 7 of which they had photographed before. The number of marked animals recaptured in the second sampling (x) divided by the total number of individuals recaptured (n) should equal the number of individuals marked and released in the first sampling (m) divided by the estimated population size (N):

$$\frac{x}{n} = \frac{m}{N} \qquad \text{or, solving for population size,} \qquad N = \frac{mn}{x}$$

The method assumes that marked and unmarked individuals have the same probability of being captured or sampled, that the marked organisms have mixed completely back into the population, and that no individuals are born, die, immigrate, or emigrate during the resampling interval.

RESULTS Based on these initial data, the estimated population size of Hector's dolphins at Banks Peninsula would be 180 × 44/7 = 1,131 individuals. Repeated sampling by Gormley and colleagues suggested a true population size closer to 1,100.

SOURCE A. M. Gormley et al., Capture-recapture estimates of Hector's dolphin abundance at Banks Peninsula, New Zealand, *Marine Mammal Science* 21:204–216 (2005).

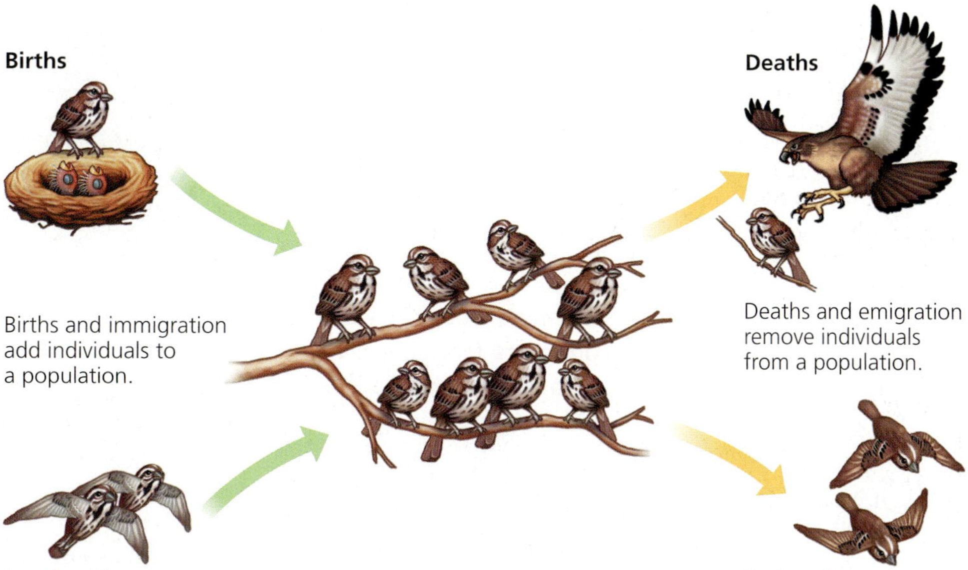

▲ Figure 53.3 Population dynamics.

Additions occur through birth (which we will define in this context to include all forms of reproduction) and **immigration**, the influx of new individuals from other areas. The factors that remove individuals from a population are death (mortality) and **emigration**, the movement of individuals out of a population.

While birth and death rates influence the density of all populations, immigration and emigration also alter the density of many populations. For example, long-term studies of Belding's ground squirrels (*Spermophilus beldingi*) in the vicinity of Tioga Pass, in the Sierra Nevada of California, show that some of the squirrels move nearly 2 km from where they are born, making them immigrants to other populations. Paul Sherman and Martin Morton, then at Cornell University and Occidental College, respectively, estimated that immigrants made up 1–8% of the males and 0.7–6% of the females in the study population. Although these immigrant percentages may seem small, they represent biologically significant exchanges between populations over time.

(a) Clumped. Many animals, such as these sea stars, group together where food is abundant.

(b) Uniform. Birds nesting on small islands, such as these king penguins on South Georgia Island in the South Atlantic Ocean, often exhibit uniform spacing, maintained by aggressive interactions between neighbors.

(c) Random. Many plants, such as these dandelions, grow from windblown seeds that land at random and later germinate.

▲ **Figure 53.4 Patterns of dispersion within a population's geographic range.**

WHAT IF? *Patterns of dispersion sometimes depend on the scale of the observation. How might the dispersion of the penguins look to you if you were flying in an airplane over the ocean?*

Patterns of Dispersion

Within a population's geographic range, local densities may vary substantially. Variations in local density are among the most important characteristics for a population ecologist to study, since they provide insight into the environmental associations and social interactions of individuals in the population. Environmental differences—even at a local level—contribute to variation in population density; some habitat patches are simply more suitable for a species than are others. Social interactions between members of the population, which may maintain patterns of spacing between individuals, can also contribute to variation in population density.

The most common pattern of dispersion is *clumped*, with the individuals aggregated in patches. Plants and fungi are often clumped where soil conditions and other environmental factors favor germination and growth. Mushrooms, for instance, may be clumped within and on top of a rotting log. Insects and salamanders may be clumped under the same log because of the higher humidity there. Clumping of animals may also be associated with mating behavior. Mayflies, which survive only a day or two as mating adults, often swarm in great numbers, a behavior that increases their chance of mating. Sea stars group together in tide pools, where food is readily available and where they can breed successfully **(Figure 53.4a)**. Forming groups may also increase the effectiveness of certain predators; for example, a wolf pack is more likely than a single wolf to subdue a moose or other large prey animal.

A *uniform*, or evenly spaced, pattern of dispersion may result from direct interactions between individuals in the population. For example, some plants secrete chemicals that inhibit the germination and growth of nearby individuals that could compete for resources. Animals often exhibit uniform dispersion as a result of antagonistic social interactions, such as **territoriality**—the defense of a bounded physical space against encroachment by other individuals **(Figure 53.4b)**. Uniform patterns are not as common in populations as clumped patterns are.

In *random* dispersion (unpredictable spacing), the position of each individual is independent of other individuals. This pattern occurs in the absence of strong attractions or repulsions among individuals of a population or where key physical or chemical factors are relatively homogeneous across the study area. For example, plants established by windblown seeds, such as dandelions, may be randomly distributed in a fairly consistent habitat (Figure 53.4c). Random patterns are not as common in nature as one might expect; most populations show at least a tendency toward a clumped distribution.

Demographics

The factors that influence population density and dispersion patterns—ecological needs of a species, structure of the environment, and interactions between individuals within the population—also influence other characteristics of populations. **Demography** is the study of the vital statistics of populations and how they change over time. Of particular interest to demographers are birth rates and how they vary among individuals (specifically among females, as you'll read shortly) and death rates. A useful way of summarizing some of the vital statistics of a population is with a life table.

Life Tables

About a century ago, when life insurance first became available, insurance companies began to estimate how long, on average, individuals of a given age could be expected to live. To do this, demographers developed **life tables**, age-specific summaries of the survival pattern of a population. Population ecologists adapted this approach to the study of nonhuman populations.

The best way to construct a life table is to follow the fate of a **cohort**, a group of individuals of the same age, from birth until all are dead. To build the life table, we need to determine the number of individuals that die in each age-group and calculate the proportion of the cohort surviving from one age to the next. Sherman and Morton's studies of the Belding's ground squirrels near Tioga Pass produced the life table in **Table 53.1**. The table reveals many things about the population. For instance, the third and eighth columns list, respectively, the proportions of females and males in the cohort that are still alive at each age. A comparison of the fifth and tenth columns reveals that males have higher death rates than females.

Survivorship Curves

A graphic method of representing the data in a life table is a **survivorship curve**, a plot of the proportion or numbers in a cohort still alive at each age. As an example, let's use the data for Belding's ground squirrels in Table 53.1 to construct a survivorship curve for this population. Generally, a survivorship curve is constructed beginning with a cohort of a specified size—say, 1,000 individuals. We can do this for the Belding's ground squirrel population by multiplying the proportion

Table 53.1 Life Table for Belding's Ground Squirrels (*Spermophilus beldingi*) at Tioga Pass, in the Sierra Nevada of California*

	FEMALES					MALES				
Age (years)	Number Alive at Start of Year	Proportion Alive at Start of Year	Number of Deaths During Year	Death Rate†	Average Additional Life Expectancy (years)	Number Alive at Start of Year	Proportion Alive at Start of Year	Number of Deaths During Year	Death Rate†	Average Additional Life Expectancy (years)
0–1	337	1.000	207	0.61	1.33	349	1.000	227	0.65	1.07
1–2	252††	0.386	125	0.50	1.56	248††	0.350	140	0.56	1.12
2–3	127	0.197	60	0.47	1.60	108	0.152	74	0.69	0.93
3–4	67	0.106	32	0.48	1.59	34	0.048	23	0.68	0.89
4–5	35	0.054	16	0.46	1.59	11	0.015	9	0.82	0.68
5–6	19	0.029	10	0.53	1.50	2	0.003	0	1.00	0.50
6–7	9	0.014	4	0.44	1.61	0				
7–8	5	0.008	1	0.20	1.50					
8–9	4	0.006	3	0.75	0.75					
9–10	1	0.002	1	1.00	0.50					

*Females and males have different mortality schedules, so they are tallied separately.
†The death rate is the proportion of individuals dying during the specific time interval.
††Includes 122 females and 126 males first captured as 1-year-olds and therefore not included in the count of squirrels age 0–1.
Source: P. W. Sherman and M. L. Morton, Demography of Belding's ground squirrel, *Ecology* 65:1617–1628 (1984).

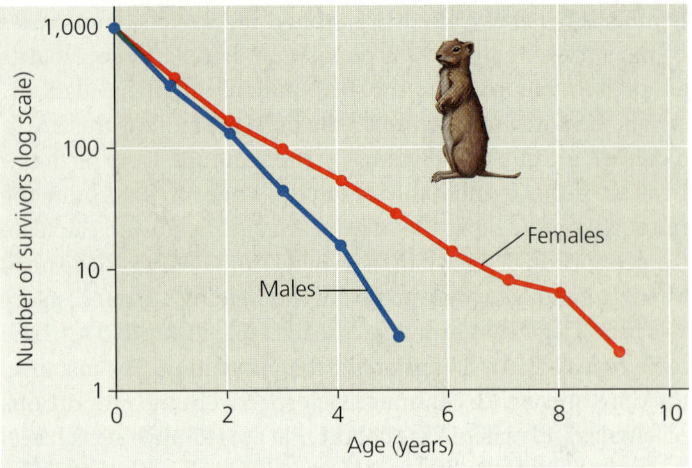

▲ **Figure 53.5 Survivorship curves for male and female Belding's ground squirrels.** The logarithmic scale on the *y*-axis allows the number of survivors to be visible across the entire range (2–1,000 individuals) on the graph.

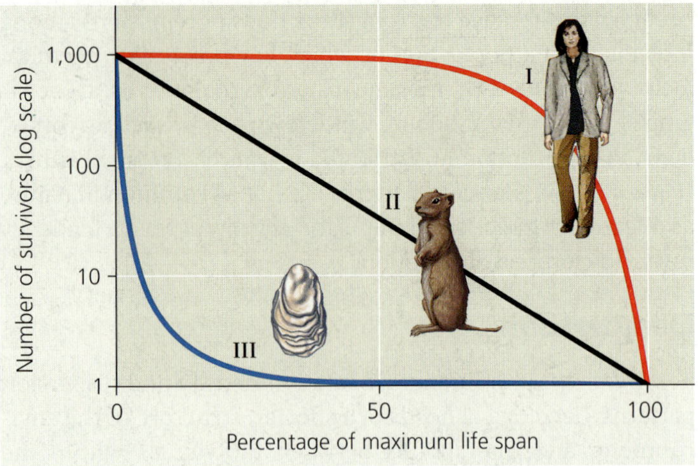

▲ **Figure 53.6 Idealized survivorship curves: Types I, II, and III.** The *y*-axis is logarithmic and the *x*-axis is on a relative scale, so that species with widely varying life spans can be presented together on the same graph.

alive at the start of each year (the third and eighth columns of Table 53.1) by 1,000 (the hypothetical beginning cohort). The result is the number alive at the start of each year. Plotting these numbers versus age for female and male Belding's ground squirrels yields **Figure 53.5.** The relatively straight lines of the plots indicate relatively constant rates of death; however, male Belding's ground squirrels have a lower survival rate overall than females have.

Figure 53.5 represents just one of many patterns of survivorship exhibited by natural populations. Though diverse, survivorship curves can be classified into three general types **(Figure 53.6)**. A Type I curve is flat at the start, reflecting low death rates during early and middle life, and then drops steeply as death rates increase among older age-groups. Many large mammals, including humans, that produce few offspring but provide them with good care exhibit this kind of curve. In contrast, a Type III curve drops sharply at the start, reflecting very high death rates for the young, but flattens out as death rates decline for those few individuals that survive the early period of die-off. This type of curve is usually associated with organisms that produce very large numbers of offspring but provide little or no care, such as long-lived plants, many fishes, and most marine invertebrates. An oyster, for example, may release millions of eggs, but most offspring die in the larval stage from predation or other causes. Those few that survive long enough to attach to a suitable substrate and begin growing a hard shell tend to survive for a relatively long time. Type II curves are intermediate, with a constant death rate over the organism's life span. This kind of survivorship occurs in Belding's ground squirrels (see Figure 53.5) and some other rodents, various invertebrates, some lizards, and some annual plants.

Many species fall somewhere between these basic types of survivorship or show more complex patterns. In birds, for example, mortality is often high among the youngest individuals (as in a Type III curve) but fairly constant among adults (as in a Type II curve). Some invertebrates, such as crabs, may show a "stair-stepped" curve, with brief periods of increased mortality during molts, followed by periods of lower mortality when their protective exoskeleton is hard.

In populations not experiencing immigration or emigration, survivorship is one of the two key factors determining changes in population size. The other key factor determining population trends in such populations is reproductive rate.

Reproductive Rates

Demographers who study sexually reproducing species generally ignore the males and concentrate on the females in a population because only females produce offspring. Therefore, demographers view populations in terms of females giving rise to new females. The simplest way to describe the reproductive pattern of a population is to ask how reproductive output varies with the ages of females.

A **reproductive table**, or fertility schedule, is an age-specific summary of the reproductive rates in a population. It is constructed by measuring the reproductive output of a cohort from birth until death. For a sexual species, the reproductive table tallies the number of female offspring produced by each age-group. **Table 53.2** illustrates a reproductive table for Belding's ground squirrels. Reproductive output for sexual organisms such as birds and mammals is the product of the proportion of females of a given age that are breeding and the number of female offspring of those breeding females. Multiplying these numbers gives the average number of female offspring for each female in a given age-group (the last column in Table 53.2). For Belding's ground squirrels, which begin to reproduce at age 1 year, reproductive output rises to a peak at 4 years of age and then falls off in older females.

Table 53.2 Reproductive Table for Belding's Ground Squirrels at Tioga Pass

Age (years)	Proportion of Females Weaning a Litter	Mean Size of Litters (Males + Females)	Mean Number of Females in a Litter	Average Number of Female Offspring*
0–1	0.00	0.00	0.00	0.00
1–2	0.65	3.30	1.65	1.07
2–3	0.92	4.05	2.03	1.87
3–4	0.90	4.90	2.45	2.21
4–5	0.95	5.45	2.73	2.59
5–6	1.00	4.15	2.08	2.08
6–7	1.00	3.40	1.70	1.70
7–8	1.00	3.85	1.93	1.93
8–9	1.00	3.85	1.93	1.93
9–10	1.00	3.15	1.58	1.58

*The average number of female offspring is the proportion weaning a litter multiplied by the mean number of females in a litter.

Source: P. W. Sherman and M. L. Morton, Demography of Belding's ground squirrel, *Ecology* 65:1617–1628 (1984).

Reproductive tables vary greatly, depending on the species. Squirrels have a litter of two to six young once a year for less than a decade, whereas oak trees drop thousands of acorns each year for tens or hundreds of years. Mussels and other invertebrates may release hundreds of thousands of eggs in a spawning cycle. Why a particular type of reproductive pattern evolves in a particular population—one of many questions at the interface of population ecology and evolutionary biology—is the subject of life history studies, the topic of the next section.

CONCEPT CHECK 53.1

1. One species of forest bird is highly territorial, while a second lives in flocks. Predict each species' likely pattern of dispersion, and explain.
2. **DRAW IT** Each female of a particular fish species produces millions of eggs per year. Draw and label the most likely survivorship curve for this species, and explain your choice.
3. **WHAT IF?** As noted in Figure 53.2, an important assumption of the mark-recapture method is that marked individuals have the same probability of being recaptured as unmarked individuals. Describe a situation where this assumption might not be valid, and explain how the estimate of population size would be affected.

For suggested answers, see Appendix A.

CONCEPT 53.2

Life history traits are products of natural selection

Natural selection favors traits that improve an organism's chances of survival and reproductive success. In every species, there are trade-offs between survival and traits such as frequency of reproduction, number of offspring produced (number of seeds produced by plants; litter or clutch size for animals), and investment in parental care. The traits that affect an organism's schedule of reproduction and survival (from birth through reproduction to death) make up its **life history**. A life history entails three basic variables: when reproduction begins (the age at first reproduction or age at maturity), how often the organism reproduces, and how many offspring are produced during each reproductive episode.

With the important exception of humans, which we will consider later in the chapter, organisms do not choose consciously when to reproduce or how many offspring to have. Rather, organisms' life history traits are evolutionary outcomes reflected in their development, physiology, and behavior.

Evolution and Life History Diversity

The fundamental idea that evolution accounts for the diversity of life is manifest in a broad range of life histories found in nature. Pacific salmon, for example, hatch in the headwaters of a stream and then migrate to the open ocean, where they require one to four years to mature. The salmon eventually return to the freshwater stream to spawn, producing thousands of eggs in a single reproductive opportunity before they die. This "one-shot" pattern of **big-bang reproduction**, or **semelparity** (from the Latin *semel*, once, and *parere*, to beget), also occurs in some plants, such as the agave, or "century plant" (**Figure 53.7**).

▶ **Figure 53.7 An agave (*Agave americana*), an example of big-bang reproduction.** The leaves of the plant are visible at the base of the giant flowering stalk, which is produced only at the end of the agave's life.

Agaves generally grow in arid climates with unpredictable rainfall and poor soils. An agave grows for years, accumulating nutrients in its tissues, until there is an unusually wet year. It then sends up a large flowering stalk, produces seeds, and dies. This life history is an adaptation to the agave's harsh desert environment.

In contrast to semelparity is **iteroparity** (from the Latin *iterare*, to repeat), or **repeated reproduction**. Some lizards, for example, produce a few large eggs during their second year of life and then reproduce annually for several years.

What factors contribute to the evolution of semelparity versus iteroparity? A current hypothesis suggests that there are two critical factors: the survival rate of the offspring and the likelihood that the adult will survive to reproduce again. Where the survival rate of offspring is low, typically in highly variable or unpredictable environments, the prediction is that big-bang reproduction (semelparity) will be favored. Adults are also less likely to survive in such environments, so producing large numbers of offspring should increase the probability that at least some of those offspring will survive. Repeated reproduction (iteroparity) may be favored in more dependable environments where adults are more likely to survive to breed again and where competition for resources may be intense. In such cases, a few relatively large, well-provisioned offspring should have a better chance of surviving until they are capable of reproducing.

Nature abounds with life histories that are intermediate between the two extremes of semelparity and iteroparity. Oak trees and sea urchins are examples of organisms that can live a long time but repeatedly produce relatively large numbers of offspring.

"Trade-offs" and Life Histories

Natural selection cannot maximize all reproductive variables simultaneously. We might imagine an organism that could produce as many offspring as a semelparous species, provision them well like an iteroparous species, and do so repeatedly, but such organisms do not exist. Time, energy, and nutrients limit the reproductive capabilities of all organisms. In the broadest sense, there is a trade-off between reproduction and survival. A study of red deer in Scotland showed that females that reproduced in a given summer were more likely to die during the next winter than females that did not reproduce. A study of European kestrels also demonstrated the survival cost to parents of caring for young **(Figure 53.8)**.

Selective pressures influence the trade-off between the number and size of offspring. Plants and animals whose young are subject to high mortality rates often produce large numbers of relatively small offspring. Plants that colonize disturbed environments, for example, usually produce many small seeds, only a few of which may reach a suitable habitat. Small size may also increase the chance of seedling establishment by enabling the seeds to be carried longer distances to a broader range of habitats **(Figure 53.9a)**. Animals that suffer high predation rates, such as quail, sardines, and mice, also tend to produce large numbers of offspring.

In other organisms, extra investment on the part of the parent greatly increases the offspring's chances of survival. Walnut trees and coconut palms both provision large seeds with energy and nutrients that help the seedlings become established **(Figure 53.9b)**. In animals, parental investment in offspring does not always end after incubation or gestation. For instance, primates generally bear only one or two offspring at a time. Parental care and an extended period of learning in the first several years of life are very important to offspring fitness in these species.

▼ Figure 53.8 Inquiry

How does caring for offspring affect parental survival in kestrels?

EXPERIMENT Cor Dijkstra and colleagues in the Netherlands studied the effects of parental caregiving in European kestrels over five years. The researchers transferred chicks among nests to produce reduced broods (three or four chicks), normal broods (five or six), and enlarged broods (seven or eight). They then measured the percentage of male and female parent birds that survived the following winter. (Both males and females provide care for chicks.)

RESULTS

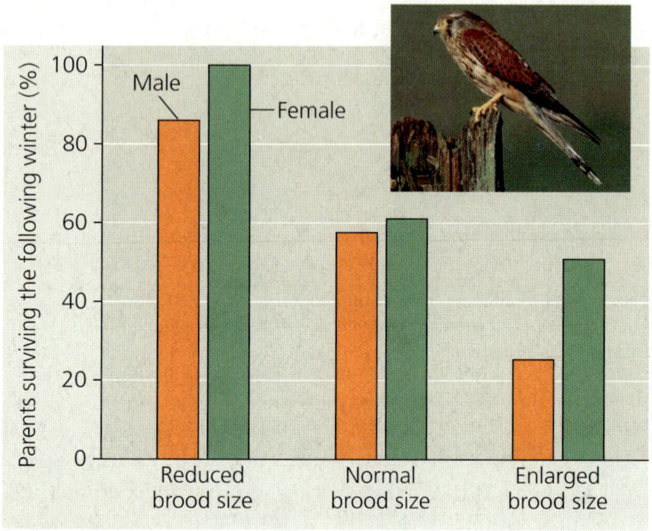

CONCLUSION The lower survival rates of kestrels with larger broods indicate that caring for more offspring negatively affects survival of the parents.

SOURCE C. Dijkstra et al., Brood size manipulations in the kestrel (*Falco tinnunculus*): effects on offspring and parent survival, *Journal of Animal Ecology* 59:269–285 (1990).

WHAT IF? The males of many bird species provide no parental care. If this were true for the European kestrel, how would the experimental results differ from those shown above?

(a) Most weedy plants, such as this dandelion, grow quickly and produce a large number of seeds, ensuring that at least some will grow into plants and eventually produce seeds themselves.

(b) Some plants, such as this coconut palm, produce a moderate number of very large seeds. Each seed's large endosperm provides nutrients for the embryo, an adaptation that helps ensure the success of a relatively large fraction of offspring.

▲ **Figure 53.9 Variation in the size of seed crops in plants.**

CONCEPT CHECK 53.2

1. Consider two rivers: One is spring fed and has a constant water volume and temperature year-round; the other drains a desert landscape and floods and dries out at unpredictable intervals. Which river would you predict is more likely to support many species of iteroparous animals? Why?
2. In the fish called the peacock wrasse (*Symphodus tinca*), females disperse some of their eggs widely and lay other eggs in a nest. Only the latter receive parental care. Explain the trade-offs in reproduction that this behavior illustrates.
3. **WHAT IF?** Mice that cannot find enough food or that experience other forms of stress will sometimes abandon their young. Explain how this behavior might have evolved in the context of reproductive trade-offs and life history.

For suggested answers, see Appendix A.

CONCEPT **53.3**

The exponential model describes population growth in an idealized, unlimited environment

Populations of all species, regardless of their life histories, have the potential to expand greatly when resources are abundant. To appreciate the potential for population increase, consider a bacterium that can reproduce by fission every 20 minutes under ideal laboratory conditions. There would be 2 bacteria after 20 minutes, 4 after 40 minutes, and 8 after 60 minutes. If reproduction continued at this rate, with no mortality, for only a day and a half, there would be enough bacteria to form a layer a foot deep over the entire globe. At the other life history extreme, an elephant may produce only 6 offspring in a 100-year life span. Still, Charles Darwin once estimated that the descendants of a single pair of mating elephants would number 19 million within only 750 years. Darwin's estimate may not have been precisely correct, but such analyses led him to recognize the tremendous capacity for growth in all populations. Although unlimited growth does not occur for long in nature, studying population growth in an idealized, unlimited environment reveals the capacity of species for increase and the conditions under which that capacity may be expressed.

Per Capita Rate of Increase

Imagine a population consisting of a few individuals living in an ideal, unlimited environment. Under these conditions, there are no restrictions on the abilities of individuals to harvest energy, grow, and reproduce, aside from the inherent biological limitations of their life history traits. The population will increase in size with every birth and with the immigration of individuals from other populations, and it will decrease in size with every death and with the emigration of individuals out of the population. We can thus define a change in population size during a fixed time interval with the following verbal equation:

$$\begin{array}{c}\text{Change in}\\ \text{population}\\ \text{size during}\\ \text{time}\\ \text{interval}\end{array} = \left(\begin{array}{c}\text{Births}\\ \text{during}\\ \text{time}\\ \text{interval}\end{array} + \begin{array}{c}\text{Immigrants}\\ \text{entering}\\ \text{population}\\ \text{during time}\\ \text{interval}\end{array}\right) - \left(\begin{array}{c}\text{Deaths}\\ \text{during}\\ \text{time}\\ \text{interval}\end{array} + \begin{array}{c}\text{Emigrants}\\ \text{leaving}\\ \text{population}\\ \text{during time}\\ \text{interval}\end{array}\right)$$

For simplicity here, we will ignore the effects of immigration and emigration, although a more complex formulation would certainly include these factors. We can also use mathematical notation to express this simplified relationship more concisely. If N represents population size and t represents time, then ΔN is the change in population size and Δt is the time interval (appropriate to the life span or generation time of the species) over which we are evaluating population growth. (The Greek letter delta, Δ, indicates change, such as change in time.) We can now rewrite the verbal equation as

$$\frac{\Delta N}{\Delta t} = B - D$$

where B is the number of births in the population during the time interval and D is the number of deaths.

Next, we can convert this simple model into one in which births and deaths are expressed as the average number of births and deaths per individual (per capita) during the specified time interval. The *per capita birth rate* is the number of offspring produced per unit time by an average member of the population. If, for example, there are 34 births per year in a population of 1,000 individuals, the annual per capita birth rate is 34/1,000, or 0.034. If we know the annual per capita birth rate (symbolized by b), we can use the formula $B = bN$ to calculate the expected number of births per year in a population of any size. For example, if the annual per capita birth rate is 0.034 and the population size is 500,

$$B = bN$$
$$B = 0.034 \times 500$$
$$B = 17 \text{ per year}$$

Similarly, the *per capita death rate* (symbolized by d) allows us to calculate the expected number of deaths per unit time in a population of any size, using the formula $D = dN$. If $d = 0.016$ per year, we would expect 16 deaths per year in a population of 1,000 individuals. For natural populations or those in the laboratory, the per capita birth and death rates can be calculated from estimates of population size and data in life tables and reproductive tables (for example, Tables 53.1 and 53.2).

Now we can revise the population growth equation again, this time using per capita birth and death rates rather than the numbers of births and deaths:

$$\frac{\Delta N}{\Delta t} = bN - dN$$

One final simplification is in order. Population ecologists are most interested in the *difference* between the per capita birth rate and per capita death rate. This difference is the *per capita rate of increase*, or r:

$$r = b - d$$

The value of r indicates whether a given population is growing ($r > 0$) or declining ($r < 0$). **Zero population growth (ZPG)** occurs when the per capita birth and death rates are equal ($r = 0$). Births and deaths still occur in such a population, of course, but they balance each other exactly.

Using the per capita rate of increase, we can now rewrite the equation for change in population size as

$$\frac{\Delta N}{\Delta t} = rN$$

Remember that this equation is for a discrete, or fixed, time interval (often one year, as in the previous example) and does not include immigration or emigration. Most ecologists prefer to use differential calculus to express population growth *instantaneously*, as growth rate at a particular instant in time:

$$\frac{dN}{dt} = r_{inst}N$$

In this case r_{inst} is simply the instantaneous per capita rate of increase. If you have not yet studied calculus, don't be intimidated by the form of the last equation; it is similar to the previous one, except that the time intervals Δt are very short and are expressed in the equation as dt. In fact, as Δt becomes shorter, the discrete r approaches the instantaneous r_{inst} in value.

Exponential Growth

Earlier we described a population whose members all have access to abundant food and are free to reproduce at their physiological capacity. Population increase under these ideal conditions is called **exponential population growth**, also known as geometric population growth. Under these conditions, the per capita rate of increase may assume the maximum rate for the species, denoted as r_{max}. The equation for exponential population growth is

$$\frac{dN}{dt} = r_{max}N$$

The size of a population that is growing exponentially increases at a constant rate, resulting eventually in a J-shaped growth curve when population size is plotted over time (**Figure 53.10**). Although the maximum *rate* of increase is constant, the population accumulates more new individuals per unit of time when it is large than when it is small; thus, the

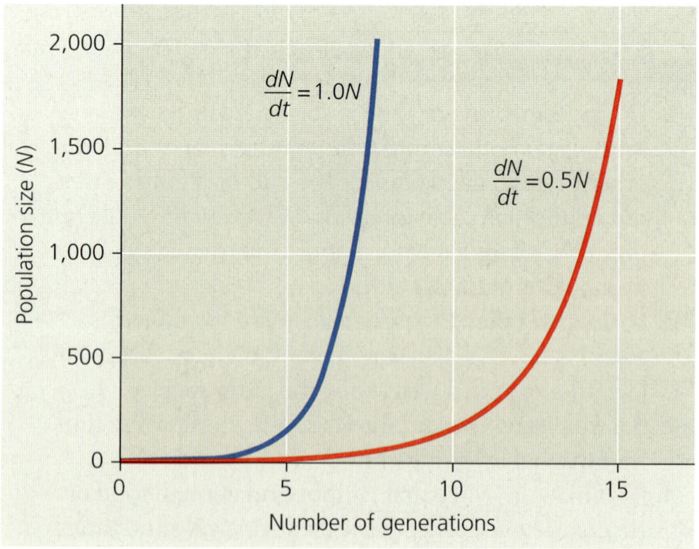

▲ **Figure 53.10 Population growth predicted by the exponential model.** This graph compares growth in two populations with different values of r_{max}. Increasing the value from 0.5 to 1.0 increases the rate of rise in population size over time, as reflected by the relative slopes of the curves at any given population size.

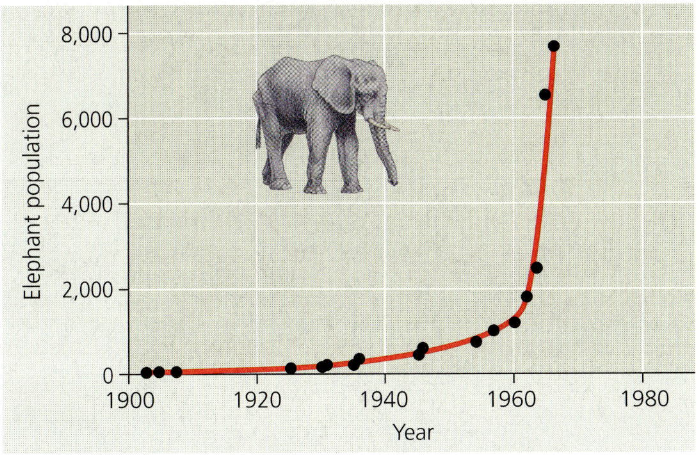

▲ **Figure 53.11 Exponential growth in the African elephant population of Kruger National Park, South Africa.**

curves in Figure 53.10 get progressively steeper over time. This occurs because population growth depends on N as well as r_{max}, and larger populations experience more births (and deaths) than small ones growing at the same per capita rate. It is also clear from Figure 53.10 that a population with a higher maximum rate of increase ($dN/dt = 1.0N$) will grow faster than one with a lower rate of increase ($dN/dt = 0.5N$).

The J-shaped curve of exponential growth is characteristic of some populations that are introduced into a new environment or whose numbers have been drastically reduced by a catastrophic event and are rebounding. For example, the population of elephants in Kruger National Park, South Africa, grew exponentially for approximately 60 years after they were first protected from hunting **(Figure 53.11)**. The increasingly large number of elephants eventually caused enough damage to vegetation in the park that a collapse in their food supply was likely. To protect other species and the park ecosystem before that happened, park managers began limiting the elephant population by using birth control and exporting elephants to other countries.

CONCEPT CHECK 53.3

1. Explain why a constant rate of increase (r_{max}) for a population produces a growth graph that is J-shaped rather than a straight line.
2. Where is exponential growth by a plant population more likely—on a newly formed volcanic island or in a mature, undisturbed rain forest? Why?
3. **WHAT IF?** In 2006, the United States had a population of about 300 million people. If there were 14 births and 8 deaths per 1,000 people, what was the country's net population growth that year (ignoring immigration and emigration, which are substantial)? Do you think the United States is currently experiencing exponential population growth? Explain.

For suggested answers, see Appendix A.

CONCEPT **53.4**

The logistic model describes how a population grows more slowly as it nears its carrying capacity

The exponential growth model assumes that resources are unlimited, which is rarely the case in the real world. As population density increases, each individual has access to fewer resources. Ultimately, there is a limit to the number of individuals that can occupy a habitat. Ecologists define **carrying capacity**, symbolized as K, as the maximum population size that a particular environment can sustain. Carrying capacity varies over space and time with the abundance of limiting resources. Energy, shelter, refuge from predators, nutrient availability, water, and suitable nesting sites can all be limiting factors. For example, the carrying capacity for bats may be high in a habitat with abundant flying insects and roosting sites, but lower where there is abundant food but fewer suitable shelters.

Crowding and resource limitation can have a profound effect on population growth rate. If individuals cannot obtain sufficient resources to reproduce, the per capita birth rate (b) will decline. If they cannot consume enough energy to maintain themselves, or if disease or parasitism increases with density, the per capita death rate (d) may increase. A decrease in b or an increase in d results in a lower per capita rate of increase (r).

The Logistic Growth Model

We can modify our mathematical model to incorporate changes in growth rate as the population size nears the carrying capacity. In the **logistic population growth** model, the per capita rate of increase approaches zero as the carrying capacity is reached.

To construct the logistic model, we start with the exponential population growth model and add an expression that reduces the per capita rate of increase as N increases. If the maximum sustainable population size (carrying capacity) is K, then $K - N$ is the number of additional individuals the environment can support, and $(K - N)/K$ is the fraction of K that is still available for population growth. By multiplying the exponential rate of increase $r_{max}N$ by $(K - N)/K$, we modify the change in population size as N increases:

$$\frac{dN}{dt} = r_{max}N\,\frac{(K-N)}{K}$$

When N is small compared to K, the term $(K - N)/K$ is large, and the per capita rate of increase, $r_{max}(K - N)/K$, is close to the maximum rate of increase. But when N is large and resources are limiting, then $(K - N)/K$ is small, and so is the per capita rate of increase. When N equals K, the population stops

Table 53.3 Logistic Growth of a Hypothetical Population (K = 1,500)

Population Size (N)	Intrinsic Rate of Increase (r_{max})	$\frac{K-N}{K}$	Per Capita Rate of Increase: $r_{max}\left(\frac{K-N}{K}\right)$	Population Growth Rate:* $r_{max}N\left(\frac{K-N}{K}\right)$
25	1.0	0.98	0.98	+25
100	1.0	0.93	0.93	+93
250	1.0	0.83	0.83	+208
500	1.0	0.67	0.67	+333
750	1.0	0.50	0.50	+375
1,000	1.0	0.33	0.33	+333
1,500	1.0	0.00	0.00	0

*Rounded to the nearest whole number.

growing. **Table 53.3** shows calculations of population growth rate for a hypothetical population growing according to the logistic model, with r_{max} = 1.0 per individual per year. Notice that the overall population growth rate is highest, +375 individuals per year, when the population size is 750, or half the carrying capacity. At a population size of 750, the per capita rate of increase remains relatively high (one-half the maximum rate), but there are more reproducing individuals (N) in the population than at lower population sizes.

The logistic model of population growth produces a sigmoid (S-shaped) growth curve when N is plotted over time (the red line in **Figure 53.12**). New individuals are added to the population most rapidly at intermediate population sizes, when there is not only a breeding population of substantial size, but also lots of available space and other resources in the environment. The population growth rate slows dramatically as N approaches K.

Note that we haven't said anything yet about *why* the population growth rate slows as N approaches K. For a population's growth rate to decrease, either the birth rate b must decrease, the death rate d must increase, or both. Later in the chapter, we will consider some of the factors affecting these rates.

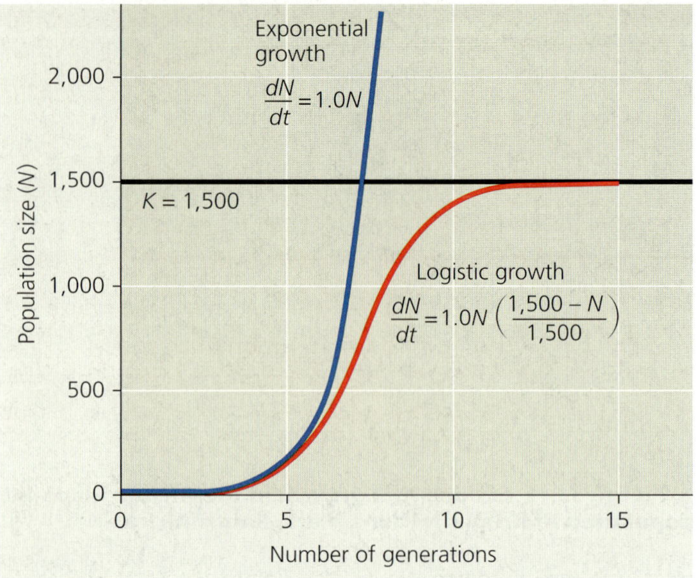

▲ **Figure 53.12 Population growth predicted by the logistic model.** The rate of population growth slows as population size (N) approaches the carrying capacity (K) of the environment. The red line shows logistic growth in a population where r_{max} = 1.0 and K = 1,500 individuals. For comparison, the blue line illustrates a population continuing to grow exponentially with the same r_{max}.

The Logistic Model and Real Populations

The growth of laboratory populations of some small animals, such as beetles and crustaceans, and of some microorganisms, such as paramecia, yeasts, and bacteria, fits an S-shaped curve fairly well under conditions of limited resources **(Figure 53.13a)**. These populations are grown in a constant environment lacking predators and competing species that may reduce growth of the populations, conditions that rarely occur in nature.

Some of the basic assumptions built into the logistic model clearly do not apply to all populations. The logistic model assumes that populations adjust instantaneously to growth and approach carrying capacity smoothly. In reality, there is often a lag time before the negative effects of an increasing population are realized. If food becomes limiting for a population, for instance, reproduction will decline eventually, but females may use their energy reserves to continue reproducing for a short time. This may cause the population to overshoot its carrying capacity temporarily, as shown for the water fleas in **Figure 53.13b.** If the population then drops below carrying capacity, there will be a delay in population growth until the increased number of offspring are actually born. Still other populations fluctuate greatly, making it difficult even to define carrying capacity. We will examine some possible reasons for such fluctuations later in the chapter.

The logistic model also incorporates the idea that regardless of population density, each individual added to a population has the same negative effect on population growth rate. However, some populations show an *Allee effect* (named after W. C. Allee, of the University of Chicago, who first described it), in which individuals may have a more difficult time surviving or reproducing if the population size is too small. For example, a single plant may be damaged by excessive wind if it is standing alone, but it would be protected in a clump of individuals.

The logistic model is a useful starting point for thinking about how populations grow and for constructing more complex models. The model is also important in conservation

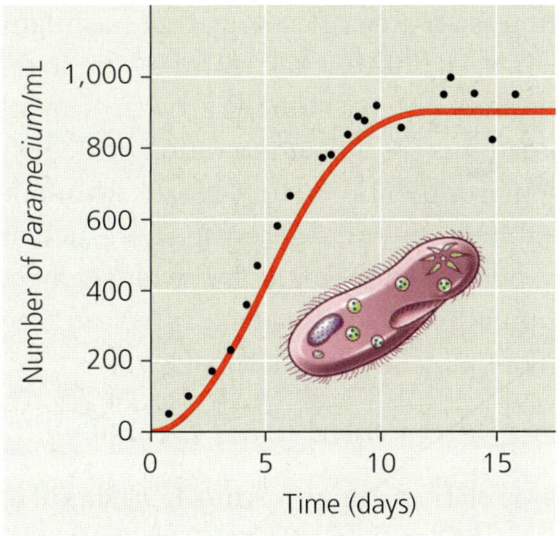

(a) A *Paramecium* population in the lab. The growth of *Paramecium aurelia* in small cultures (black dots) closely approximates logistic growth (red curve) if the researcher maintains a constant environment.

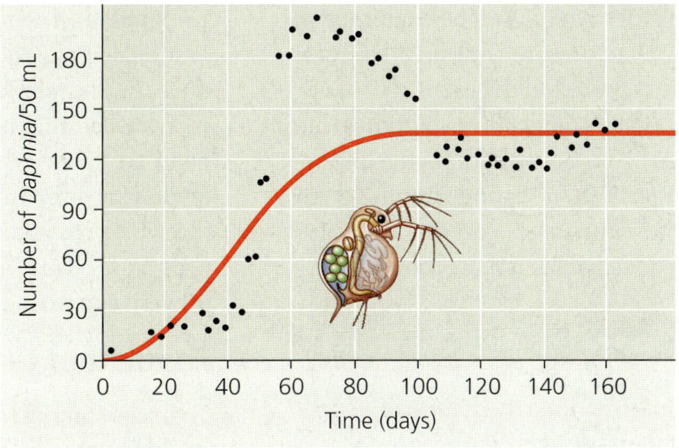

(b) A *Daphnia* population in the lab. The growth of a population of water fleas (*Daphnia*) in a small laboratory culture (black dots) does not correspond well to the logistic model (red curve). This population overshoots the carrying capacity of its artificial environment before it settles down to an approximately stable population size.

◀ **Figure 53.13 How well do these populations fit the logistic growth model?**

biology for predicting how rapidly a particular population might increase in numbers after it has been reduced to a small size and for estimating sustainable harvest rates for fish and wildlife populations. Conservation biologists can use the model to estimate the critical size below which populations of certain organisms, such as the northern subspecies of the white rhinoceros (*Ceratotherium simum*), may become extinct **(Figure 53.14)**. Like any good starting hypothesis, the logistic model has stimulated research that has led to a better understanding of the factors affecting population growth.

The Logistic Model and Life Histories

The logistic model predicts different per capita growth rates for populations of low or high density relative to the carrying capacity of the environment. At high densities, each individual has few resources available, and the population grows slowly. At low densities, per capita resources are relatively abundant, and the population grows rapidly. Different life history features are favored under each condition. At high population density, selection favors adaptations that enable organisms to survive and reproduce with few resources. Competitive ability and efficient use of resources should be favored in populations that are at or near their carrying capacity. (Note that these are the traits we associated earlier with iteroparity.) At low population density, adaptations that promote rapid reproduction, such as the production of numerous, small offspring, should be favored.

▲ **Figure 53.14 White rhinoceros mother and calf.** The two animals pictured here are members of the southern subspecies, which has a population of more than 10,000 individuals. The northern subspecies is critically endangered, with a population of fewer than 25 individuals.

Ecologists have attempted to connect these differences in favored traits at different population densities with the logistic growth model. Selection for life history traits that are sensitive to population density is known as ***K*-selection**, or density-dependent selection. In contrast, selection for life history traits that maximize reproductive success in uncrowded environments (low densities) is called ***r*-selection**, or density-independent selection. These names follow from the variables of the logistic equation. *K*-selection is said to operate in populations living at a density near the limit imposed by their resources (the carrying capacity, *K*), where competition among individuals is relatively strong. Mature trees growing in an old-growth forest are an example of *K*-selected organisms. In contrast, *r*-selection is said to maximize *r*, the per capita rate of increase, and occurs in environments in which population densities are well below carrying capacity or individuals face little competition. Such conditions are often found in disturbed habitats.

Like the concepts of semelparity and iteroparity, the concepts of *K*- and *r*-selection represent two extremes in a range of actual life histories. The framework of *K*- and *r*-selection, grounded in the idea of carrying capacity, has helped ecologists to propose alternative hypotheses of life history evolution. These alternative hypotheses, in turn, have stimulated more thorough study of how factors such as disturbance, stress, and the frequency of opportunities for successful reproduction affect the evolution of life histories. They have also forced ecologists to address the important question we alluded to earlier: Why does population growth rate decrease as population size approaches carrying capacity? Answering this question is the focus of the next section.

CONCEPT CHECK 53.4

1. Explain why a population that fits the logistic growth model increases more rapidly at intermediate size than at relatively small or large sizes.
2. When a farmer abandons a field, it is quickly colonized by fast-growing weeds. Are these species more likely to be *K*-selected or *r*-selected species? Explain.
3. **WHAT IF?** Add rows to Table 53.3 for three cases where $N > K$: $N = 1{,}600$, 1,750, and 2,000. What is the population growth rate in each case? In which portion of Figure 53.13b is the *Daphnia* population changing in a way that corresponds to the values you calculated?

For suggested answers, see Appendix A.

CONCEPT 53.5

Many factors that regulate population growth are density dependent

In this section, we will apply biology's unifying theme of *feedback regulation* (see Chapter 1) to populations. What environmental factors keep populations from growing indefinitely? Why are some populations fairly stable in size, while others, such as the Soay sheep on Hirta Island, are not (see Figure 53.1)?

Population regulation is an area of ecology that has many practical applications. In agriculture, a farmer may want to reduce the abundance of insect pests or stop the growth of an invasive weed that is spreading rapidly. Conservation ecologists need to know what environmental factors create favorable feeding or breeding habitats for endangered species, such as the white rhinoceros and the whooping crane. Management programs based on population-regulating factors have helped prevent the extinction of many endangered species.

Population Change and Population Density

To understand why a population stops growing, it is helpful to study how the rates of birth, death, immigration, and emigration change as population density rises. If immigration and emigration offset each other, then a population grows when the birth rate exceeds the death rate and declines when the death rate exceeds the birth rate.

A birth rate or death rate that does *not* change with population density is said to be **density independent**. In a classic study of population regulation, Andrew Watkinson and John Harper, of the University of Wales, found that the mortality of dune fescue grass (*Vulpia membranacea*) is mainly due to physical factors that kill similar proportions of a local population, regardless of its density. For example, drought stress that arises when the roots of the grass are uncovered by shifting sands is a density-independent factor. In contrast, a death rate that rises as population density rises is said to be **density dependent**, as is a birth rate that falls with rising density. Watkinson and Harper found that reproduction by dune fescue declines as population density increases, in part because water or nutrients become more scarce. Thus, in this grass population, the key factors regulating birth rate are density dependent, while death rate is largely regulated by density-independent factors. **Figure 53.15** models how a population may stop increasing and reach equilibrium as a result of various combinations of density-dependent and density-independent regulation.

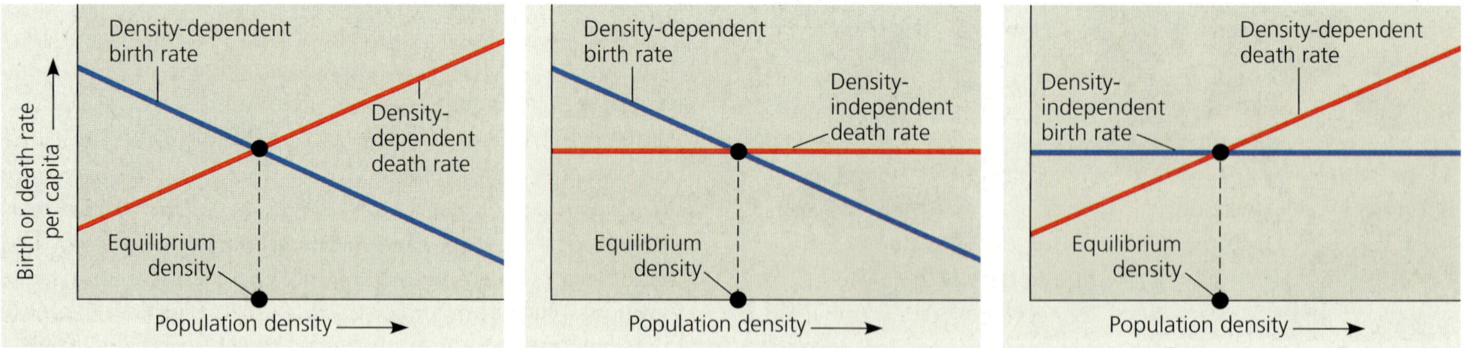

(a) Both birth rate and death rate change with population density.

(b) Birth rate changes with population density while death rate is constant.

(c) Death rate changes with population density while birth rate is constant.

▲ **Figure 53.15 Determining equilibrium for population density.** This simple model considers only birth and death rates (immigration and emigration rates are assumed to be either zero or equal).

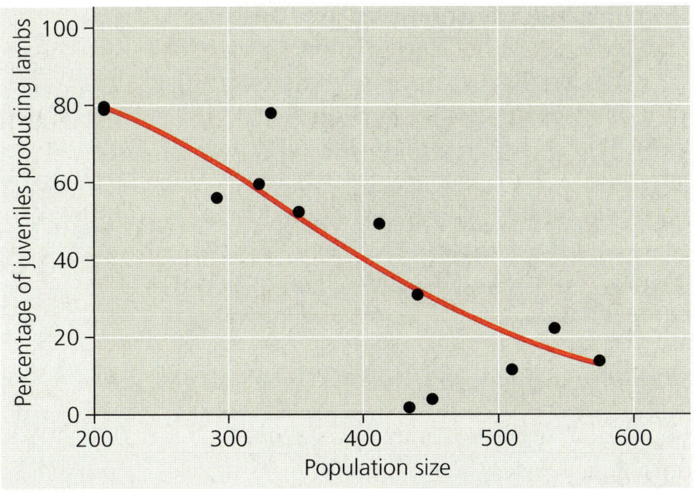

▲ **Figure 53.16 Decreased reproduction at high population densities.** Reproduction by juvenile Soay sheep on Hirta Island drops dramatically as population size increases.

(a) Cheetahs stake out their territories with a chemical marker in urine.

(b) Gannets nest virtually a peck apart and defend their territories by calling and pecking at one another.

▲ **Figure 53.17 Territoriality.** In some animals, defense of territories provides negative feedback on population density.

Density-Dependent Population Regulation

Without some type of negative feedback between population density and the vital rates of birth and death, a population would never stop growing. Density-dependent regulation provides that feedback, operating through mechanisms that help to reduce birth rates and increase death rates, halting population growth.

Competition for Resources

In a crowded population, increasing population density intensifies competition for declining nutrients and other resources, resulting in a lower birth rate. Crowding can reduce reproduction by plants, as discussed earlier for dune fescue. Many animal populations also experience internal competition for food and other resources. On Hirta Island, ecologists have closely monitored the relationship between Soay sheep density and reproduction for many years. Their results show that the effects of increasing density on birth rate are strongest for the youngest sheep that reproduce, typically 1-year-old juveniles **(Figure 53.16)**.

Territoriality

In many vertebrates and some invertebrates, territoriality can limit population density. In this case, territory space becomes the resource for which individuals compete. Cheetahs, for example, are highly territorial, using chemical communication to warn other cheetahs of their territorial boundaries **(Figure 53.17a)**. Maintaining a territory increases the likelihood that a cheetah will capture enough food to reproduce. Oceanic birds, such as gannets, often nest on rocky islands to avoid predators **(Figure 53.17b)**. Up to a certain population density, most gannets can find a suitable nest site, but beyond that threshold, few additional birds breed successfully. Birds that cannot obtain a nesting spot do not reproduce. The presence of surplus, or nonbreeding, individuals is a good indication that territoriality is restricting population growth, as it does in many bird populations.

Disease

Population density can also influence the health and thus the survival of organisms. If the transmission rate of a particular disease depends on a certain level of crowding in a population, the disease's impact may be density dependent. Among plants, the severity of infection by fungal pathogens is often greater in locations where the density of the host plant population is higher. Animals, too, can experience an increased rate of infection by pathogens at high population densities. Steven Kohler and Wade Hoiland, of the Illinois Natural History Survey, showed that in caddis flies (*Brachycentrus americanus*, a stream-dwelling insect), peaks in disease-related mortality followed years of high insect abundance, leading to cyclic fluctuations in the density of the caddis fly population. In humans, the lung disease tuberculosis, which is caused by bacteria that spread through the air when an infected person sneezes or coughs, strikes a greater percentage of people living in densely populated cities than those in rural areas.

Predation

Predation may be an important cause of density-dependent mortality if a predator encounters and captures more food as the population density of the prey increases. As a prey population builds up, predators may feed preferentially on that species, consuming a higher percentage of individuals. For example, trout may concentrate for a few days on a particular species of insect that is emerging from its aquatic larval stage and then switch to eating another insect species as it becomes more abundant.

Toxic Wastes

The accumulation of toxic wastes can contribute to density-dependent regulation of population size. In laboratory cultures of microorganisms, metabolic by-products accumulate as the populations grow, poisoning the organisms within this limited, artificial environment. For example, ethanol accumulates as a by-product of yeast fermentation. The alcohol content of wine is usually less than 13% because that is the maximum concentration of ethanol that most wine-producing yeast cells can tolerate.

Intrinsic Factors

For some animal species, intrinsic (physiological) factors, rather than the extrinsic (environmental) factors we've just discussed, appear to regulate population size. For instance, white-footed mice in a small field enclosure will multiply, but eventually their reproductive rate will decline until the population ceases to grow. This drop in reproduction is associated with aggressive interactions that increase with population density, and it occurs even when food and shelter are provided in abundance. High population densities in mice can induce a stress syndrome in which hormonal changes delay sexual maturation, cause reproductive organs to shrink, and depress the immune system. In this case, high densities cause an increase in mortality and a decrease in birth rates. Similar effects of crowding occur in other wild rodent populations.

These various examples of population regulation by negative feedback show how increased densities cause population growth rates to decline by affecting reproduction, growth, and survivorship. But although negative feedback helps explain why populations stop growing, it does not address why some populations fluctuate dramatically while others remain relatively stable. This is the topic we address next.

Population Dynamics

All populations for which we have long-term data show some fluctuation in numbers. These fluctuations from year to year or place to place influence the seasonal or annual harvest of fish and other commercially important species. They also give ecologists insight into what controls population size. The study of **population dynamics** focuses on the complex interactions between biotic and abiotic factors that cause variation in the size of populations.

Stability and Fluctuation

Populations of large mammals were once thought to remain relatively stable over time, but long-term studies have challenged that idea. The numbers of Soay sheep on Hirta Island fluctuate greatly, rising or falling by more than half from one year to the next **(Figure 53.18)**. What causes the size of this population to change so dramatically? The most important factor appears to be the weather. Harsh weather, particularly cold, wet winters, weakens the sheep and decreases food availability, leading to a decrease in the size of the population. When sheep numbers are high, other factors, such as an increase in the density of parasites, also cause the population to shrink. Conversely, when sheep numbers are low and the weather is mild, food is readily available and the population grows quickly.

Like the Soay sheep population on Hirta, the moose population on Isle Royale in Lake Superior also fluctuates over time. In the case of the moose, predation is an additional factor that regulates the population. Moose from the mainland colonized the island around 1900 by walking across the frozen lake. Wolves, which rely on moose for most of their food, followed around 1950. Because the lake has not frozen over in recent years, both populations have been isolated from immigration and emigration. Despite this isolation, the moose population

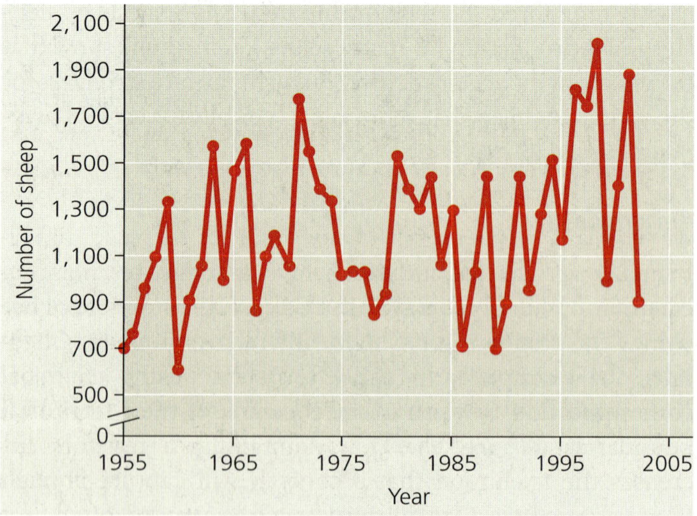

▲ **Figure 53.18 Variation in size of the Soay sheep population on Hirta Island, 1955–2002.**

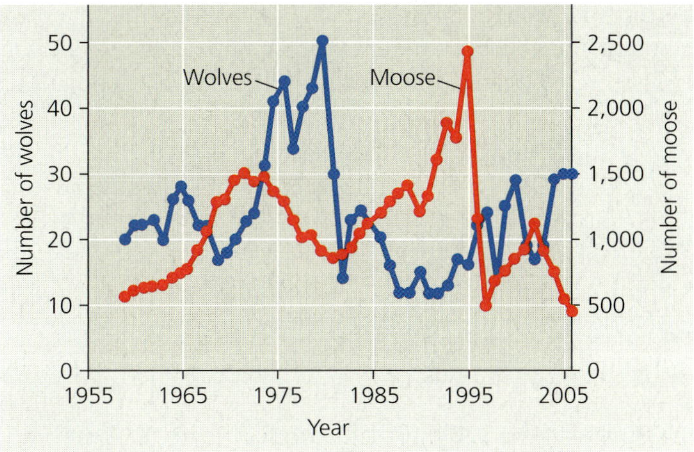

▲ **Figure 53.19 Fluctuations in moose and wolf populations on Isle Royale, 1959–2006.**

? *The first several moose reached Isle Royale in the early 1900s, and by 1925 the population on the island had grown to 2,000. Why do you think it was able to grow so quickly? What growth model best describes this initial growth?*

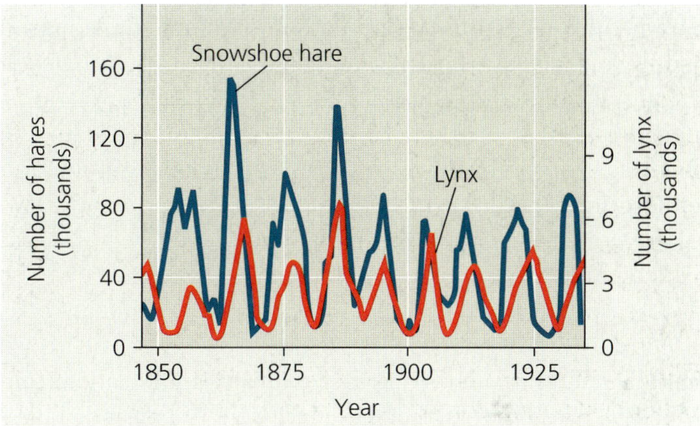

▲ **Figure 53.20 Population cycles in the snowshoe hare and lynx.** Population counts are based on the number of pelts sold by trappers to the Hudson Bay Company.

? *What do you observe about the relative timing of the peaks in lynx numbers and hare numbers? What might explain this observation?*

experienced two major increases and collapses during the last 45 years **(Figure 53.19)**. The first collapse coincided with a peak in the numbers of wolves from 1975 to 1980. The second collapse, around 1995, coincided with harsh winter weather, which increased the energy needs of the animals and made it harder for the moose to find food under the deep snow.

Population Cycles: Scientific Inquiry

While many populations fluctuate at unpredictable intervals, others undergo regular boom-and-bust cycles. Some small herbivorous mammals, such as voles and lemmings, tend to have 3- to 4-year cycles, and some birds, such as ruffed grouse and ptarmigans, have 9- to 11-year cycles.

One striking example of population cycles is the 10-year cycling of snowshoe hares (*Lepus americanus*) and lynx (*Lynx canadensis*) in the far northern forests of Canada and Alaska. Lynx are predators that specialize in preying on snowshoe hares, so it is not surprising that lynx numbers rise and fall with the numbers of hares **(Figure 53.20)**. But why do hare numbers rise and fall in 10-year cycles? Three main hypotheses have been proposed. First, the cycles may be caused by food shortage during winter. Hares eat the terminal twigs of small shrubs such as willow and birch in winter, although why this food supply might cycle in 10-year intervals is uncertain. Second, the cycles may be due to predator-prey interactions. Many predators other than lynx eat hares, and they may overexploit their prey. Third, the size of the hare population may vary with sunspot activity, which also undergoes cyclic changes. When sunspot activity is low, slightly less atmospheric ozone is produced, and slightly more UV radiation reaches Earth's surface. In response, plants produce more UV-blocking chemicals and fewer chemicals that deter herbivores, increasing the quality of the hares' food.

Let's consider the evidence for the hypotheses. If hare cycles are due to winter food shortage, then they should stop if extra food is provided to a field population. Researchers have conducted such experiments in the Yukon for 20 years—over two hare cycles. They have found that hare populations in the areas with extra food have increased about threefold in density but have continued to cycle in the same way as the unfed control populations. Thus, food supplies alone do not cause the hare cycle shown in Figure 53.20, so we can reject the first hypothesis.

Using radio collars, ecologists have tracked individual hares to determine why they died. Predators killed almost 90% of the hares in such studies, and none of the hares appeared to have died of starvation. These data support the second hypothesis. When ecologists excluded predators from one area with electric fences and excluded predators *and* provided food in another area, they found that the hare cycle is driven largely by excessive predation but that food availability also plays an important role, particularly in the winter. Perhaps better-fed hares are more likely to escape from predators.

To test the third hypothesis, ecologists compared the timing of hare cycles and sunspot activity. As predicted, periods of low sunspot activity were followed by peaks in the hare population. The results of all of these experiments suggest that both predation and sunspot activity may regulate the cycling of hare numbers and that food availability plays a less important role.

The availability of prey is the major factor influencing population changes for predators such as lynx, great-horned owls, and weasels, each of which depends heavily on a single prey species. When prey become scarce, predators often turn on one another. Coyotes kill both foxes and lynx, and great-horned owls kill smaller birds of prey as well as weasels, accelerating the collapse of the predator populations. Long-term experimental studies help to unravel the causes of such population cycles.

Immigration, Emigration, and Metapopulations

So far our discussion of population dynamics has focused mainly on the contributions of births and deaths. However, immigration and emigration also influence populations, particularly when a number of local populations are linked, forming a **metapopulation**. For example, immigration and emigration link the Belding's ground squirrel population we discussed earlier to other populations of the species, all of which make up a metapopulation.

Local populations in a metapopulation can be thought of as occupying discrete patches of suitable habitat in a sea of unsuitable habitat. The patches vary in size, quality, and isolation from other patches, factors that influence how many individuals move among the populations. Patches with many individuals, for instance, can supply more emigrants to other patches. If one population becomes extinct, the patch it occupied can be recolonized by immigrants from another population.

The Glanville fritillary (*Melitaea cinxia*) illustrates the movement of individuals between populations **(Figure 53.21)**. This butterfly is found in about 500 meadows across the Åland Islands of Finland, but its potential habitat in the islands is much larger, approximately 4,000 suitable patches. New populations of the butterfly regularly appear and existing populations become extinct, constantly shifting the locations of the 500 colonized patches. The species persists in a balance of extinctions and recolonizations.

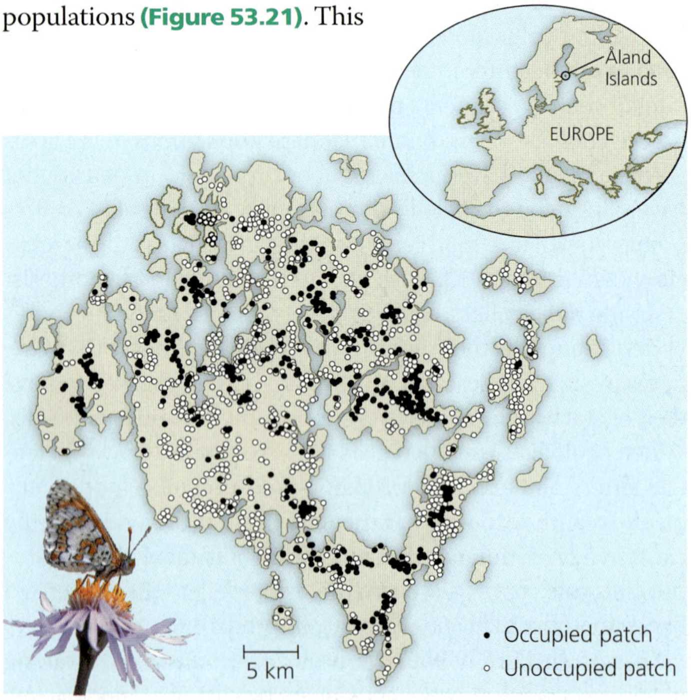

▲ **Figure 53.21 The Glanville fritillary: a metapopulation.** On the Åland Islands, local populations of this butterfly (filled circles) are found in only a fraction of the suitable habitat patches (open circles) at any given time. Individuals can move between local populations and colonize unoccupied patches.

The metapopulation concept underscores the significance of immigration and emigration in the butterfly populations. It also helps ecologists understand population dynamics and gene flow in patchy habitats, providing a framework for the conservation of species living in a network of habitat fragments and reserves.

CONCEPT CHECK 53.5

1. Identify three density-dependent factors that limit population size, and explain how each exerts negative feedback.
2. Describe three attributes of habitat patches that could affect population density and rates of immigration and emigration.
3. **WHAT IF?** If you were studying an endangered species that, like the snowshoe hare, has a 10-year population cycle, how long would you need to study the species to determine if its population size is declining? Explain.

For suggested answers, see Appendix A.

CONCEPT **53.6**

The human population is no longer growing exponentially but is still increasing rapidly

In the last few centuries, the human population has grown at an unprecedented rate, more like the elephant population in Kruger National Park (see Figure 53.11) than the fluctuating populations we considered in Concept 53.5. No population can grow indefinitely, however, and humans are no exception. In this last section of the chapter, we'll apply the concepts of population dynamics to the specific case of the human population.

The Global Human Population

The exponential growth model in Figure 53.10 approximates the human population explosion since 1650. Ours is a singular case; it is unlikely that any other population of large animals has ever sustained so much growth for so long **(Figure 53.22)**. The human population increased relatively slowly until about 1650, at which time approximately 500 million people inhabited Earth. Our population doubled to 1 billion within the next two centuries, doubled again to 2 billion between 1850 and 1930, and

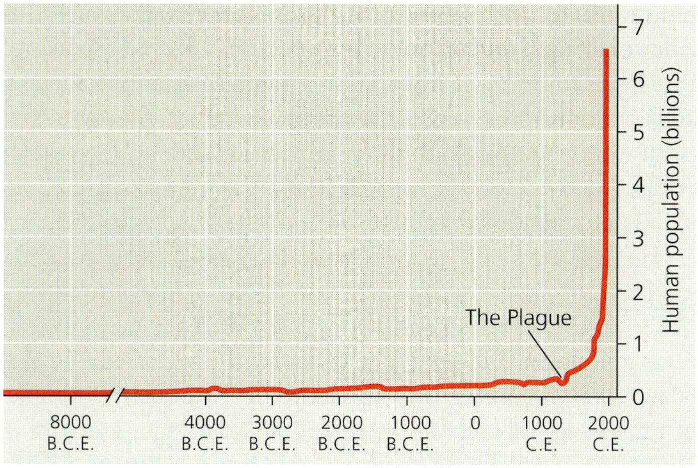

▲ **Figure 53.22 Human population growth (data as of 2006).** The global human population has grown almost continuously throughout history, but it skyrocketed after the Industrial Revolution. Though it is not apparent at this scale, the rate of population growth has slowed in recent decades, mainly as a result of decreased birth rates throughout the world.

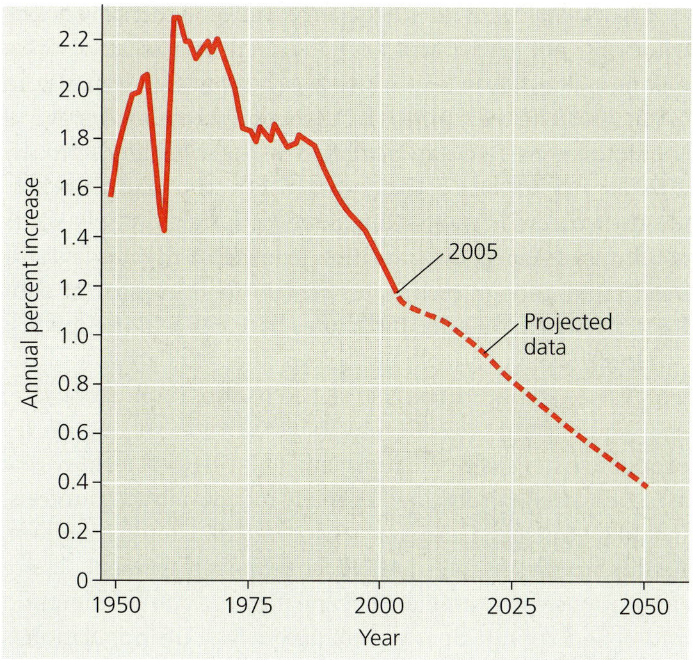

▲ **Figure 53.23 Annual percent increase in the global human population (data as of 2005).** The sharp dip in the 1960s is due mainly to a famine in China in which about 60 million people died.

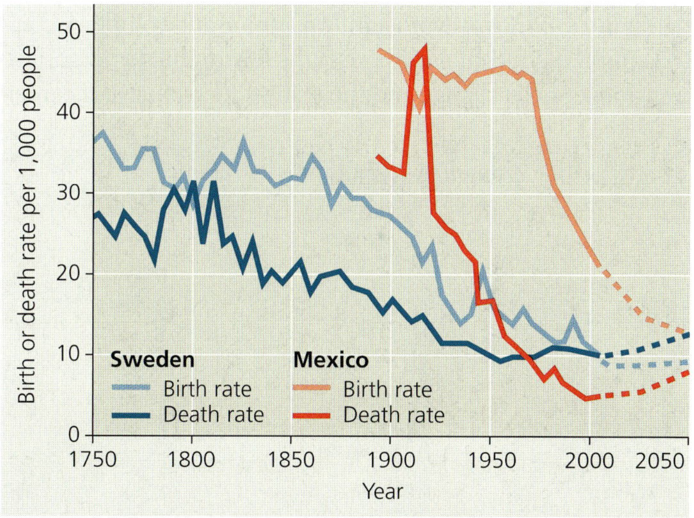

▲ **Figure 53.24 Demographic transition in Sweden and Mexico, 1750–2050 (data as of 2005).**

doubled still again by 1975 to more than 4 billion. The global population is now more than 6.6 billion people and is increasing by about 75 million each year. The population grows by approximately 200,000 people each day, the equivalent of adding a city the size of Amarillo, Texas, or Madison, Wisconsin. It takes only about four years for world population growth to add the equivalent of another United States. Population ecologists predict a population of 7.8–10.8 billion people on Earth by the year 2050.

Though the global population is still growing, the *rate* of growth began to slow during the 1960s **(Figure 53.23)**. The annual rate of increase in the global population peaked at 2.2% in 1962; by 2005, it had declined to 1.15%. Current models project a continued decline in the annual growth rate to just over 0.4% by 2050, a rate that would still add 36 million more people per year if the population climbs to a projected 9 billion. The reduction in growth rate over the past four decades shows that the human population has departed from true exponential growth, which assumes a constant rate. This departure is the result of fundamental changes in population dynamics due to diseases, including AIDS, and to voluntary population control.

Regional Patterns of Population Change

So far we have described changes in the global population, but population dynamics vary widely from region to region. In a stable regional human population, birth rate equals death rate (disregarding the effects of immigration and emigration). Two possible configurations for a stable population are

Zero population growth = High birth rate − High death rate

or

Zero population growth = Low birth rate − Low death rate

The movement toward the second configuration is called the **demographic transition. Figure 53.24** compares the demographic transition in one of the most industrialized countries, Sweden, and in a less industrialized country, Mexico. The demographic transition in Sweden took about 150 years, from 1810 to 1960, when birth rates finally approached death rates; in Mexico, the changes are projected to continue until sometime after 2050, almost the same length of time as they took in Sweden. Demographic transition is associated with an increase in the quality of health care and sanitation as well as improved access to education, especially for women.

After 1950, death rates declined rapidly in most developing countries, but birth rates have declined in a more variable manner. The fall in birth rate has been most dramatic in China. In 1970, the Chinese birth rate predicted an average of 5.9 children per woman per lifetime (total fertility rate); by 2004, largely because of the government's strict one-child policy, the expected total fertility rate was 1.7 children. In some countries of Africa, the transition to lower birth rates has also been rapid, though birth rates remain high in most of sub-Saharan Africa. In India, birth rates have fallen more slowly.

How do such variable birth rates affect the growth of the world's population? In industrialized nations, populations are near equilibrium (growth rate about 0.1% per year), with reproductive rates near the replacement level (total fertility rate = 2.1 children per female). In many industrialized countries, including Canada, Germany, Japan, and the United Kingdom, total reproductive rates are in fact *below* replacement. These populations will eventually decline if there is no immigration and if the birth rate does not change. In fact, the population is already declining in many eastern and central European countries. Most of the current global population growth (1.15% per year) is concentrated in less industrialized countries, where about 80% of the world's people now live.

A unique feature of human population growth is our potential ability to control it with family planning and voluntary contraception. Reduced family size is the key to the demographic transition. Social change and the rising educational and career aspirations of women in many cultures encourage women to delay marriage and postpone reproduction. Delayed reproduction helps to decrease population growth rates and to move a society toward zero population growth under conditions of low birth rates and low death rates. However, there is a great deal of disagreement among world leaders as to how much support should be provided for global family planning efforts.

Age Structure

One important demographic variable in present and future growth trends is a country's **age structure**, the relative number of individuals of each age in the population. Age structure is commonly graphed as "pyramids" like those in **Figure 53.25**. For Afghanistan, the pyramid is bottom-heavy, skewed toward young individuals who will grow up and may sustain the explosive growth with their own reproduction. The age structure for the United States is relatively even until the older, post-reproductive ages, except for a bulge that corresponds to the "baby boom" that lasted for about two decades after the end of World War II. Even though couples born during those years have had an average of fewer than two children, the nation's overall birth rate still exceeds the death rate because so many "boomers" and their offspring are still of reproductive age. Moreover, although the current total reproductive rate in the United States is 2.1 children per woman—approximately replacement rate—the population is projected to grow slowly

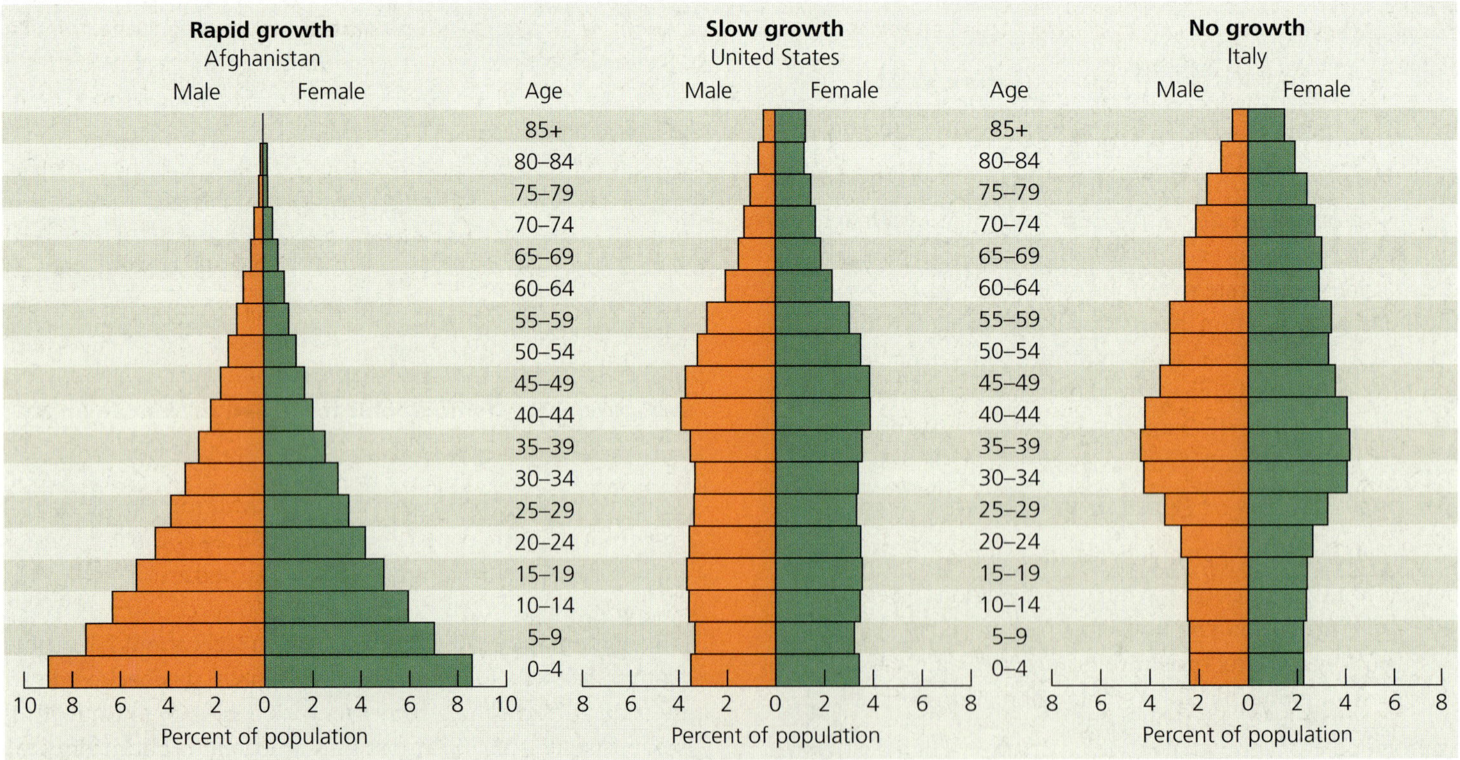

▲ **Figure 53.25 Age-structure pyramids for the human population of three countries (data as of 2005).** As of 2007, the annual rate of population growth was approximately 2.6% in Afghanistan, 0.9% in the United States, and 0.0% in Italy.

through 2050 as a result of immigration. For Italy, the pyramid has a small base, indicating that individuals younger than reproductive age are relatively underrepresented in the population. This situation contributes to the projection of a population decrease in Italy.

Age-structure diagrams not only predict a population's growth trends but can also illuminate social conditions. Based on the diagrams in Figure 53.25, we can predict, for instance, that employment and education opportunities will continue to be a significant problem for Afghanistan in the foreseeable future. The large number of young entering the Afghan population could also be a source of continuing social and political unrest, particularly if their needs and aspirations are not met. In Italy and the United States, a decreasing proportion of younger working-age people will soon be supporting an increasing population of retired "boomers." In the United States, this demographic feature has made the future of Social Security and Medicare a major political issue. Understanding age structures can help us plan for the future.

Infant Mortality and Life Expectancy

Infant mortality, the number of infant deaths per 1,000 live births, and *life expectancy at birth*, the predicted average length of life at birth, vary widely among different human populations. These differences reflect the quality of life faced by children at birth and influence the reproductive choices parents make. If infant mortality is high, then parents are likely to have more children to ensure that some of them reach adulthood. **Figure 53.26** contrasts average infant mortality and life expectancy in the industrialized and less industrialized countries of the world in 2005. While these averages are markedly different, they do not capture the broad range of the human condition. In 2005, for example, the infant mortality rate was 163 (16.3%) in Afghanistan

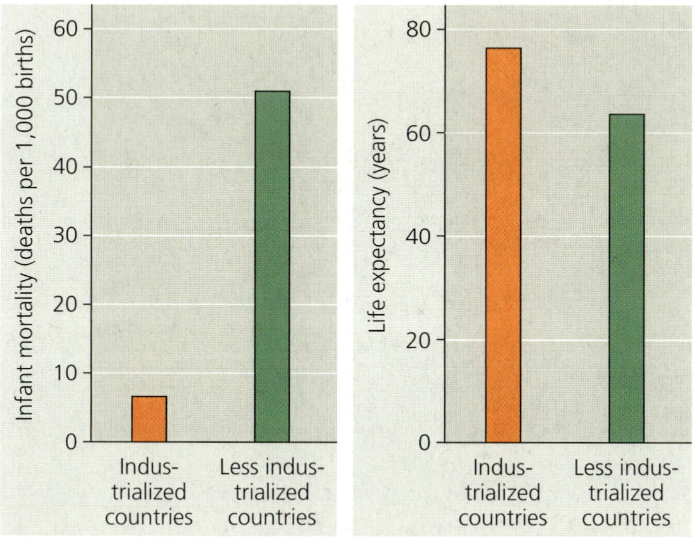

▲ **Figure 53.26 Infant mortality and life expectancy at birth in industrialized and less industrialized countries (data as of 2005).**

but only 3 (0.3%) in Japan, while life expectancy at birth was 43 years in Afghanistan and 81 years in Japan. Although global life expectancy has been increasing since about 1950, more recently it has dropped in a number of regions, including countries of the former Soviet Union and in sub-Saharan Africa. In these regions, the combination of social upheaval, decaying infrastructure, and infectious diseases such as AIDS and tuberculosis is reducing life expectancy. In the South African country of Angola, for instance, life expectancy in 2005 was approximately 39 years, about half that in Japan, Sweden, Italy, and Spain.

Global Carrying Capacity

No ecological question is more important than the future size of the human population. The projected worldwide population size depends on assumptions about future changes in birth and death rates. As we noted earlier, population ecologists project a global population of approximately 7.8–10.8 billion people in 2050. In other words, without some catastrophe, an estimated 1–4 billion people will be added to the population in the next four decades because of the momentum of population growth. But just how many humans can the biosphere support? Will the world be overpopulated in 2050? Is it *already* overpopulated?

Estimates of Carrying Capacity

For over three centuries, scientists have attempted to estimate the human carrying capacity of Earth. The first known estimate, 13.4 billion, was made in 1679 by Anton van Leeuwenhoek, the discoverer of protists (see Chapter 28). Since then, estimates have varied from less than 1 billion to more than 1,000 billion (1 trillion), with an average of 10–15 billion.

Carrying capacity is difficult to estimate, and the scientists who provide these estimates use different methods to get their answers. Some current researchers use curves like that produced by the logistic equation (see Figure 53.12) to predict the future maximum of the human population. Others generalize from existing "maximum" population density and multiply this number by the area of habitable land. Still others base their estimates on a single limiting factor, such as food, and consider many variables, including the amount of available farmland, the average yield of crops, the prevalent diet—vegetarian or meat-based—and the number of calories needed per person per day.

Limits on Human Population Size

A more comprehensive approach to estimating the carrying capacity of Earth is to recognize that humans have multiple constraints: We need food, water, fuel, building materials, and other resources, such as clothing and transportation. The **ecological footprint** concept summarizes the aggregate land and water area required by each person, city, or nation to produce all the resources it consumes and to absorb all the waste it generates.

One way to estimate the ecological footprint of the entire human population is to add up all the ecologically productive land on the planet and divide by the population. This calculation yields approximately 2 hectares (ha) per person (1 ha = 2.47 acres). Reserving some land for parks and conservation means reducing this allotment to 1.7 ha per person—the benchmark for comparing actual ecological footprints. Anyone who consumes resources that require more than 1.7 ha to produce is said to be using an unsustainable share of Earth's resources. A typical ecological footprint for a person in the United States is about 10 ha.

Ecologists sometimes calculate ecological footprints using other currencies besides land area. For instance, the amount of photosynthesis that occurs on Earth is finite, constrained by the amount of land and sea area and by the sun's radiation. Scientists recently studied the extent to which people around the world consume seven types of photosynthetic products: plant foods, wood for building and fuel, paper, fiber, meat, milk, and eggs (the last three based on estimates of how much plant material goes into their production). **Figure 53.27** shows that areas with high population densities, such as China and India, have high consumption rates. However, areas of much lower population density but higher *per capita* consumption, such as parts of the United States and Europe, have equally high rates, as much as 400 times the rate at which photosynthetic products are produced locally. The combination of population density *and* resource use per person determines our global ecological footprint.

We can only speculate about Earth's ultimate carrying capacity for the human population or about what factors will eventually limit our growth. Perhaps food will be the main factor. Malnutrition and famine are common in some regions, but they result mainly from unequal distribution of food rather than inadequate production. So far, technological improvements in agriculture have allowed food supplies to keep up with global population growth. However, the principles of energy flow through ecosystems (explained in Chapter 55) tell us that environments can support a larger number of herbivores than carnivores. If everyone ate as much meat as the wealthiest people in the world, less than half of the present world population could be fed by current food harvests.

Perhaps we humans will eventually be limited by suitable space, like the gannets on oceanic islands. Certainly, as our population grows, the conflict over how space is utilized will intensify, and agricultural land will be developed for housing. There seem to be few limits, however, on how closely humans can be crowded together, as long as adequate food and water are provided to them and space is available to dispose of their waste.

Humans could also run out of nonrenewable resources, such as certain metals and fossil fuels. The demands of many populations have already far exceeded the local and even regional supplies of one renewable resource—fresh water. More than 1 billion people do not have access to sufficient water to meet their basic sanitation needs. It is also possible that the human population will eventually be limited by the capacity of the environment to absorb its wastes. In such cases, Earth's current human occupants could lower the planet's long-term carrying capacity for future generations.

Some optimists have suggested that because of our ability to develop technology, human population growth has no practical limits. Technology has undoubtedly increased Earth's

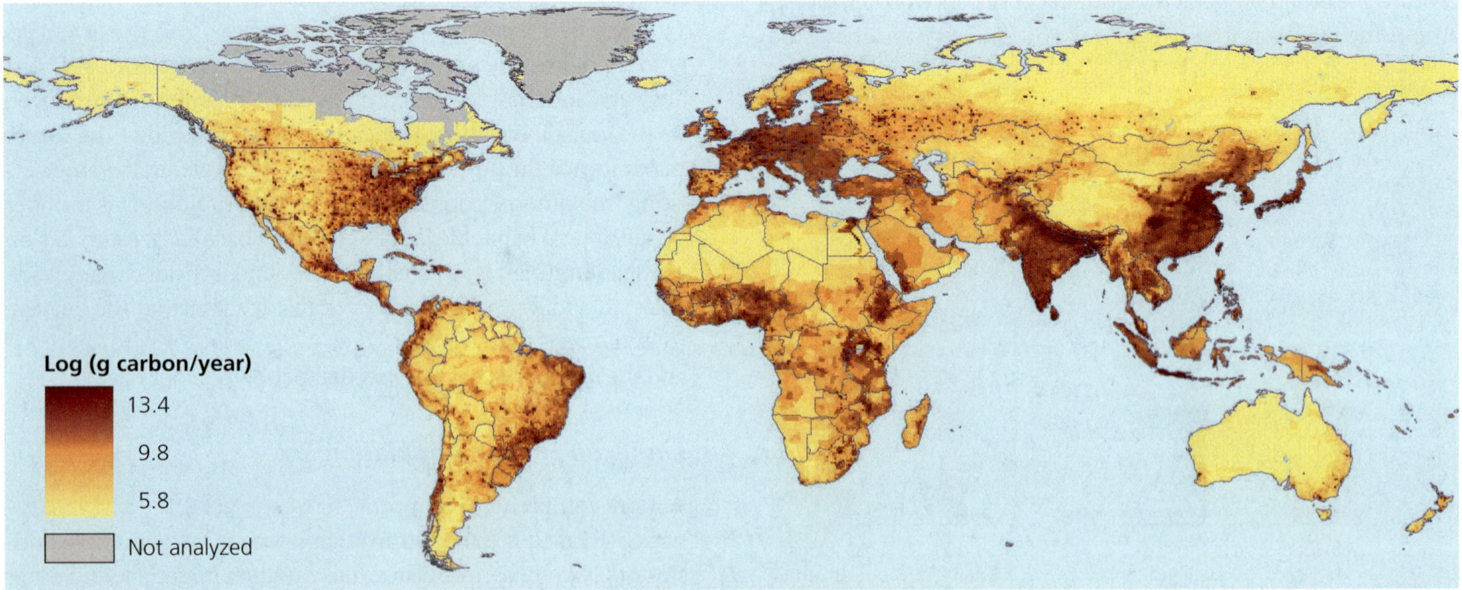

▲ **Figure 53.27 The amount of photosynthetic products that humans use around the world.** The unit of measurement is the logarithm of the number of grams of photosynthetic products consumed each year. The greatest usage is in places where population density is high or where people consume the most resources individually (high per capita consumption).

carrying capacity for humans, but as we have emphasized, no population can continue to grow indefinitely. After reading this chapter, you should realize that there is no single carrying capacity for the human population on Earth. How many people our planet can sustain depends on the quality of life each of us enjoys and the distribution of wealth across people and nations, topics of great concern and political debate. Unlike other organisms, we can decide whether zero population growth will be attained through social changes based on human choices or through increased mortality due to resource limitation, plagues, war, and environmental degradation.

CONCEPT CHECK 53.6

1. How does a human population's age structure affect its growth rate?
2. How has the growth of Earth's human population changed in recent decades? Give your answer in terms of growth rate and the number of people added each year.
3. **WHAT IF?** What choices can you make that influence your own ecological footprint?

For suggested answers, see Appendix A.

Chapter 53 Review

MEDIA Go to the Study Area at **www.masteringbio.com** for BioFlix 3-D Animations, MP3 Tutors, Videos, Practice Tests, an eBook, and more.

SUMMARY OF KEY CONCEPTS

CONCEPT 53.1

Dynamic biological processes influence population density, dispersion, and demographics (pp. 1174–1179)

- **Density and Dispersion** Population density—the number of individuals per unit area or volume—results from the interplay of births, deaths, immigration, and emigration. Environmental and social factors influence the dispersion of individuals.

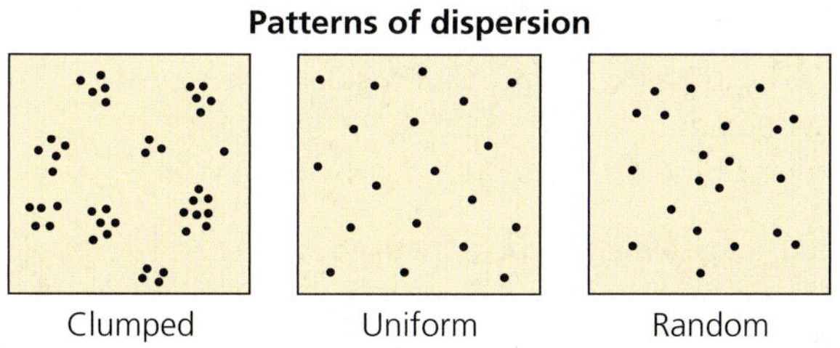

- **Demographics** Populations increase from births and immigration and decrease from deaths and emigration. Life tables, survivorship curves, and reproductive tables summarize specific demographic trends.

MEDIA
Activity Techniques for Estimating Population Density and Size
Activity Investigating Survivorship Curves

CONCEPT 53.2

Life history traits are products of natural selection (pp. 1179–1181)

- Life history traits are evolutionary outcomes reflected in the development, physiology, and behavior of an organism.
- **Evolution and Life History Diversity** Big-bang, or semelparous, organisms reproduce once and die. Iteroparous organisms produce offspring repeatedly.
- **"Trade-offs" and Life Histories** Life history traits such as brood size, age at maturity, and parental caregiving represent trade-offs between conflicting demands for time, energy, and nutrients.

CONCEPT 53.3

The exponential model describes population growth in an idealized, unlimited environment (pp. 1181–1183)

- **Per Capita Rate of Increase** If immigration and emigration are ignored, a population's growth rate (the per capita rate of increase) equals birth rate minus death rate.
- **Exponential Growth** The exponential growth equation $dN/dt = r_{max}N$ represents a population's potential growth in an unlimited environment, where r_{max} is the maximum per capita, or intrinsic, rate of increase and N is the number of individuals in the population.

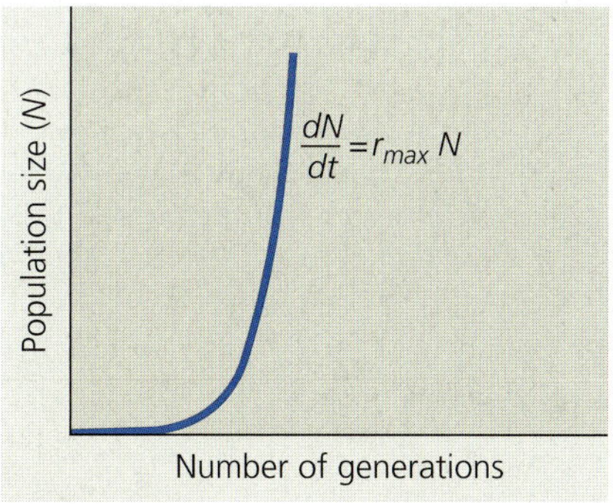

CONCEPT 53.4

The logistic model describes how a population grows more slowly as it nears its carrying capacity (pp. 1183–1186)

- Exponential growth cannot be sustained for long in any population. A more realistic population model limits growth by incorporating carrying capacity (K), the maximum population size the environment can support.

▶ **The Logistic Growth Model** According to the logistic equation $dN/dt = r_{max}N(K - N)/K$, growth levels off as population size approaches the carrying capacity.

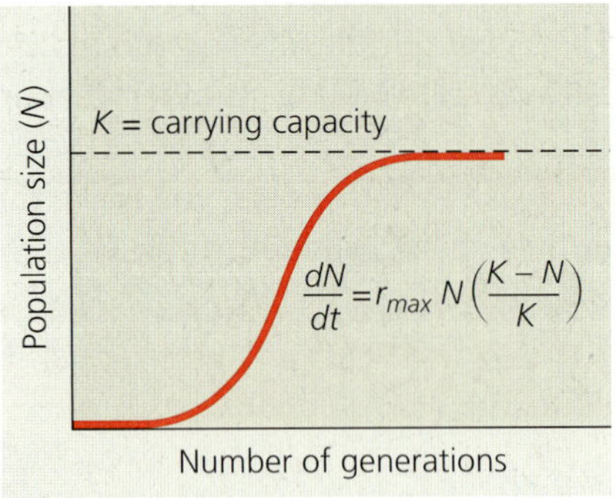

▶ **The Logistic Model and Real Populations** The logistic model fits few real populations perfectly, but it is useful for estimating possible growth.

▶ **The Logistic Model and Life Histories** Two hypothetical but controversial life history patterns are *K*-selection, or density-dependent selection, and *r*-selection, or density-independent selection.

CONCEPT 53.5

Many factors that regulate population growth are density dependent (pp. 1186–1190)

▶ **Population Change and Population Density** In density-dependent population regulation, death rates rise and birth rates fall with increasing density. In density-independent population regulation, birth and death rates do not change with increasing density.

▶ **Density-Dependent Population Regulation** Density-dependent changes in birth and death rates curb population increase through negative feedback and can eventually stabilize a population near its carrying capacity. Density-dependent limiting factors include intraspecific competition for limited food or space, increased predation, disease, stress due to crowding, and buildup of toxic substances.

▶ **Population Dynamics** Because changing environmental conditions periodically disrupt them, all populations exhibit some size fluctuations. Many populations undergo regular boom-and-bust cycles that are influenced by complex interactions between biotic and abiotic factors. A metapopulation is a group of populations linked by immigration and emigration.

MEDIA

Biology Labs On-Line PopulationEcologyLab

CONCEPT 53.6

The human population is no longer growing exponentially but is still increasing rapidly (pp. 1190–1195)

▶ **The Global Human Population** Since about 1650, the global human population has grown exponentially, but within the last 40 years, the rate of growth has fallen by nearly 50%. Differences in age structure show that while some nations' populations are growing rapidly, those of others are stable or declining in size. Infant mortality rates and life expectancy at birth differ markedly between industrialized and less industrialized countries.

▶ **Global Carrying Capacity** The carrying capacity of Earth for humans is uncertain. Ecological footprint is the aggregate land and water area needed to produce all the resources a person or group of people consume and to absorb all of their waste. It is one measure of how close we are to the carrying capacity of Earth. With a world population of more than 6.6 billion people, we are already using many resources in an unsustainable manner.

MEDIA

Activity Human Population Growth
Activity Analyzing Age-Structure Pyramids
GraphIt! Age Pyramids and Population Growth
Biology Labs On-Line DemographyLab

TESTING YOUR KNOWLEDGE

SELF-QUIZ

1. The observation that members of a population are uniformly distributed suggests that
   a. the size of the area occupied by the population is increasing.
   b. resources are distributed unevenly.
   c. the members of the population are competing for access to a resource.
   d. the members of the population are neither attracted to nor repelled by one another.
   e. the density of the population is low.

2. Population ecologists follow the fate of same-age cohorts to
   a. determine a population's carrying capacity.
   b. determine if a population is regulated by density-dependent processes.
   c. determine the birth rate and death rate of each group in a population.
   d. determine the factors that regulate the size of a population.
   e. determine if a population's growth is cyclic.

3. According to the logistic growth equation

$$\frac{dN}{dt} = r_{max}N\,\frac{(K-N)}{K}$$

   a. the number of individuals added per unit time is greatest when N is close to zero.
   b. the per capita growth rate (r) increases as N approaches K.
   c. population growth is zero when N equals K.
   d. the population grows exponentially when K is small.
   e. the birth rate (b) approaches zero as N approaches K.

4. A population's carrying capacity
   a. can be accurately calculated using the logistic growth model.
   b. generally remains constant over time.
   c. increases as the per capita growth rate (r) decreases.
   d. may change as environmental conditions change.
   e. can never be exceeded.

5. Which pair of terms most accurately describes life history traits for a stable population of wolves?
   a. semelparous; r-selected
   b. semelparous; K-selected
   c. iteroparous; r-selected
   d. iteroparous; K-selected
   e. iteroparous; N-selected

6. During exponential growth, a population always
   a. grows by thousands of individuals.
   b. grows at its maximum per capita rate.
   c. quickly reaches its carrying capacity.
   d. cycles through time.
   e. loses some individuals to emigration.

7. Scientific study of the population cycles of the snowshoe hare and its predator, the lynx, has revealed that
   a. the prey population is controlled by predators alone.
   b. hares and lynx are so mutually dependent that each species cannot survive without the other.
   c. multiple biotic and abiotic factors contribute to the cycling of the hare and lynx populations.
   d. both hare and lynx populations are regulated mainly by abiotic factors.
   e. the hare population is r-selected and the lynx population is K-selected.

8. Based on current growth rates, Earth's human population in 2010 will be closest to
   a. 2 million.
   b. 3 billion.
   c. 4 billion.
   d. 7 billion.
   e. 10 billion.

9. Which of the following statements about human population in industrialized countries is *incorrect*?
   a. Average family size is relatively small.
   b. The population has undergone the demographic transition.
   c. Life history is r-selected.
   d. The survivorship curve is Type I.
   e. Age distribution is relatively uniform.

10. A recent study of ecological footprints concluded that
   a. Earth's carrying capacity for humans is about 10 billion.
   b. Earth's carrying capacity would increase if per capita meat consumption increased.
   c. current demand by industrialized countries for resources is much smaller than the ecological footprint of those countries.
   d. the ecological footprint of the United States is large because per capita resource use is high.
   e. it is not possible for technological improvements to increase Earth's carrying capacity for humans.

11. **DRAW IT** To estimate which age cohort in a population of females produces the most female offspring, you need information about the number of offspring produced per capita within that cohort and the number of individuals alive in the cohort. Make this estimate for Belding's ground squirrels by multiplying the number of females alive at the start of the year (column 2 in Table 53.1) by the average number of female offspring produced per female (column 5 in Table 53.2). Draw a bar graph with female age in years on the x-axis (0–1, 1–2, and so on) and total number of female offspring produced for each age cohort on the y-axis. Which cohort of female Belding's ground squirrels produces the most female young?

For Self-Quiz answers, see Appendix A.

MEDIA Visit the Study Area at **www.masteringbio.com** for a Practice Test.

EVOLUTION CONNECTION

12. Write a paragraph contrasting the conditions that favor the evolution of semelparous (one-time) reproduction versus iteroparous (repeated) reproduction.

SCIENTIFIC INQUIRY

13. You are testing the hypothesis that the population density of a particular plant species influences the rate at which a pathogenic fungus infects the plant. Because the fungus causes visible scars on the leaves, you can easily determine whether a plant is infected. Design an experiment to test your hypothesis. Include your experimental treatments and control, the data you will collect, and the results expected if your hypothesis is correct.

SCIENCE, TECHNOLOGY, AND SOCIETY

14. Many people regard the rapid population growth of less industrialized countries as our most serious environmental problem. Others think that the population growth in industrialized countries, though smaller, is actually a greater environmental threat. What problems result from population growth in (a) less industrialized countries and (b) industrialized nations? Which do you think is a greater threat, and why?

54 Community Ecology

▲ **Figure 54.1 How many interactions between species are occurring in this scene?**

KEY CONCEPTS

54.1 Community interactions are classified by whether they help, harm, or have no effect on the species involved

54.2 Dominant and keystone species exert strong controls on community structure

54.3 Disturbance influences species diversity and composition

54.4 Biogeographic factors affect community biodiversity

54.5 Community ecology is useful for understanding pathogen life cycles and controlling human disease

OVERVIEW

A Sense of Community

On your next walk through a park or in the woods, or even across campus, look for evidence of interactions between different species. You may observe birds using trees as nesting sites, bees pollinating flowers, spiders trapping insects in their webs, or ferns growing in shade provided by trees—a tiny sample of the many interactions between species that exist in any ecological theater.

Some ecological interactions are more obvious than others. At first glance, **Figure 54.1** depicts a simple interaction between an herbivore, a hornworm caterpillar, and its preferred food, a tomato plant. But the white objects on the caterpillar's back are telltale signs of an interaction between the caterpillar and a third species, a parasitic wasp. The wasp lays its eggs inside the caterpillar, and the larvae that emerge from the eggs feed on the caterpillar's tissues. The larvae then develop into adult wasps inside the white cocoons on their host's back. This interaction will eventually kill the caterpillar.

In Chapter 53, you learned how individuals within a population can affect other individuals of the same species. This chapter will examine ecological interactions between populations of different species. A group of populations of different species living close enough to interact is called a biological **community**. Ecologists define the boundaries of a particular community to fit their research questions: They might study the community of decomposers and other organisms living on a rotting log, the benthic community in Lake Superior, or the community of trees and shrubs in Shenandoah National Park.

We begin this chapter by exploring the kinds of interactions that occur between species in a community. We then consider several of the factors that are most significant in structuring a community—in determining how many species there are, which particular species are present, and the relative abundance of these species. Finally, we will apply some of the principles of community ecology to the study of human disease.

CONCEPT **54.1**

Community interactions are classified by whether they help, harm, or have no effect on the species involved

Some key relationships in the life of an organism are its interactions with individuals of other species in the community. These **interspecific interactions** include competition, predation, herbivory, and symbiosis (including parasitism, mutualism, and commensalism). In this section, we will define and describe each of these interactions, recognizing that ecologists do not always agree on the precise boundaries of each type of interaction.

We will use the symbols + and − to indicate how each interspecific interaction affects the survival and reproduction of the two species engaged in the interaction. For example, predation is a +/− interaction, with a positive effect on the survival and reproduction of the predator population and a negative effect on that of the prey population. Mutualism is a +/+ interaction because the survival and reproduction of each species is increased in the presence of the other. A 0 indicates that a population is not affected by the interaction in any known way.

Historically, most ecological research has focused on interactions that have a negative effect on at least one species, such as competition and predation. However, positive interactions are ubiquitous, and their contributions to community structure are the subject of considerable study today.

Competition

Interspecific competition is a −/− interaction that occurs when individuals of different species compete for a resource that limits their growth and survival. For instance, weeds growing in a garden compete with garden plants for soil nutrients and water. Grasshoppers and bison in the Great Plains compete for the grass they both eat. Lynx and foxes in the northern forests of Alaska and Canada compete for prey such as snowshoe hares. In contrast, some resources, such as oxygen, are rarely in short supply; thus, although most species use this resource, they do not usually compete for it.

Competitive Exclusion

What happens in a community over time when two species directly compete for limited resources? In 1934, the Russian ecologist G. F. Gause studied this question in laboratory experiments with two closely related species of ciliated protists, *Paramecium aurelia* and *Paramecium caudatum*. He cultured the species under stable conditions, adding a constant amount of food every day. When Gause grew the two species in separate cultures, each population grew rapidly and then leveled off at what was apparently the carrying capacity of the culture (see Figure 53.13a for an illustration of the logistic growth of *P. aurelia*). But when Gause cultured the two species together, *P. caudatum* was driven to extinction in the culture. Gause inferred that *P. aurelia* had a competitive edge in obtaining food, and he concluded that two species competing for the same limiting resources cannot coexist in the same place. In the absence of disturbance, one species will use the resources more efficiently and thus reproduce more rapidly than the other. Even a slight reproductive advantage will eventually lead to local elimination of the inferior competitor, an outcome called **competitive exclusion**.

Ecological Niches

The sum of a species' use of the biotic and abiotic resources in its environment is called the species' **ecological niche**. American ecologist Eugene Odum used the following analogy to explain the niche concept: If an organism's habitat is its "address," the niche is the organism's "profession." Put another way, an organism's niche is its ecological role—how it "fits into" an ecosystem. For example, the niche of a tropical tree lizard consists of, among many components, the temperature range it tolerates, the size of branches on which it perches, the time of day when it is active, and the sizes and kinds of insects it eats.

We can use the niche concept to restate the principle of competitive exclusion: Two species cannot coexist permanently in a community if their niches are identical. However, ecologically similar species *can* coexist in a community if there are one or more significant differences in their niches. When competition between species with identical niches does not lead to local extinction of either species, it is generally because one species' niche becomes modified. In other words, evolution by natural selection can result in one of the species using a different set of resources. The differentiation of niches that enables similar species to coexist in a community is called **resource partitioning** (**Figure 54.2**). You can think of resource partitioning in a community as "the ghost of competition past"—the indirect evidence of earlier interspecific competition resolved by the evolution of niche differentiation.

As a result of competition, a species' *fundamental niche*, which is the niche potentially occupied by that species, is often different from its *realized niche*, the portion of its fundamental niche that it actually occupies in a particular environment.

▲ **Figure 54.2 Resource partitioning among Dominican Republic lizards.** Seven species of *Anolis* lizards live in close proximity, and all feed on insects and other small arthropods. However, competition for food is reduced because each lizard species has a different preferred perch, thus occupying a distinct niche.

Ecologists can identify the fundamental niche of a species by testing the range of conditions in which it grows and reproduces in the absence of competitors. They can also test whether a potential competitor limits a species' realized niche by removing the competitor and seeing if the first species expands into the newly available space **(Figure 54.3)**. The classic experiment depicted in the figure clearly showed that competition from one barnacle species kept a second barnacle species from occupying part of its fundamental niche.

▼ Figure 54.3 Inquiry

Can a species' niche be influenced by interspecific competition?

EXPERIMENT Ecologist Joseph Connell studied two barnacle species— *Chthamalus stellatus* and *Balanus balanoides*—that have a stratified distribution on rocks along the coast of Scotland. *Chthamalus* is usually found higher on the rocks than *Balanus*. To determine whether the distribution of *Chthamalus* is the result of interspecific competition with *Balanus*, Connell removed *Balanus* from the rocks at several sites.

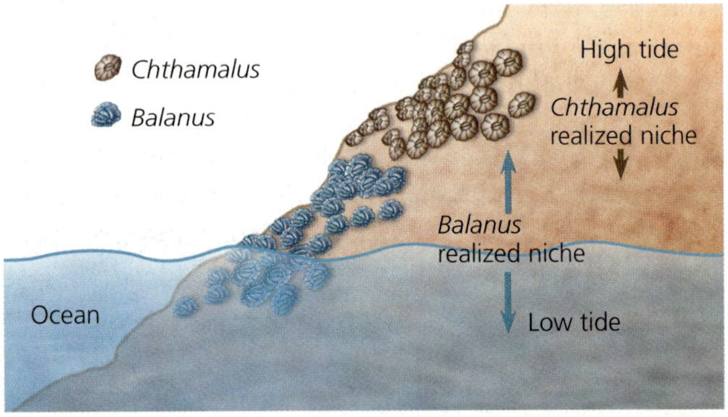

RESULTS *Chthamalus* spread into the region formerly occupied by *Balanus*.

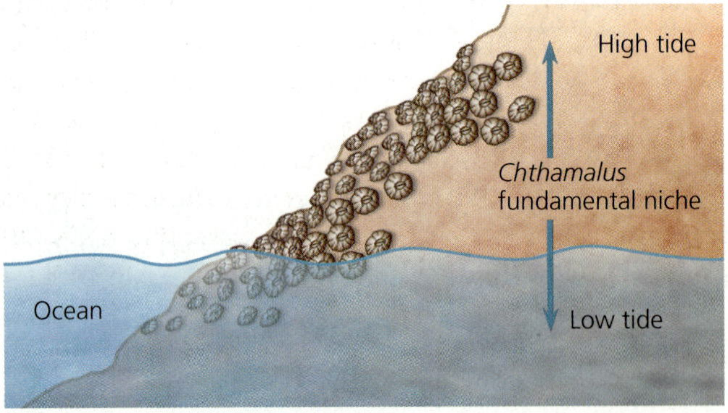

CONCLUSION Interspecific competition makes the realized niche of *Chthamalus* much smaller than its fundamental niche.

SOURCE J. H. Connell, The influence of interspecific competition and other factors on the distribution of the barnacle *Chthamalus stellatus*, *Ecology* 42:710–723 (1961).

WHAT IF? Other observations showed that *Balanus* cannot survive high on the rocks because it dries out during low tides. How would *Balanus*'s realized niche compare with its fundamental niche?

Character Displacement

Closely related species whose populations are sometimes allopatric (geographically separate; see Chapter 24) and sometimes sympatric (geographically overlapping) provide more evidence for the importance of competition in structuring communities. In some cases, the allopatric populations of such species are morphologically similar and use similar resources. By contrast, sympatric populations, which would potentially compete for resources, show differences in body structures and in the resources they use. This tendency for characteristics to diverge more in sympatric populations of two species than in allopatric populations of the same two species is called **character displacement**. An example of character displacement is the variation in beak size between different populations of the Galápagos finches *Geospiza fuliginosa* and *Geospiza fortis* **(Figure 54.4)**.

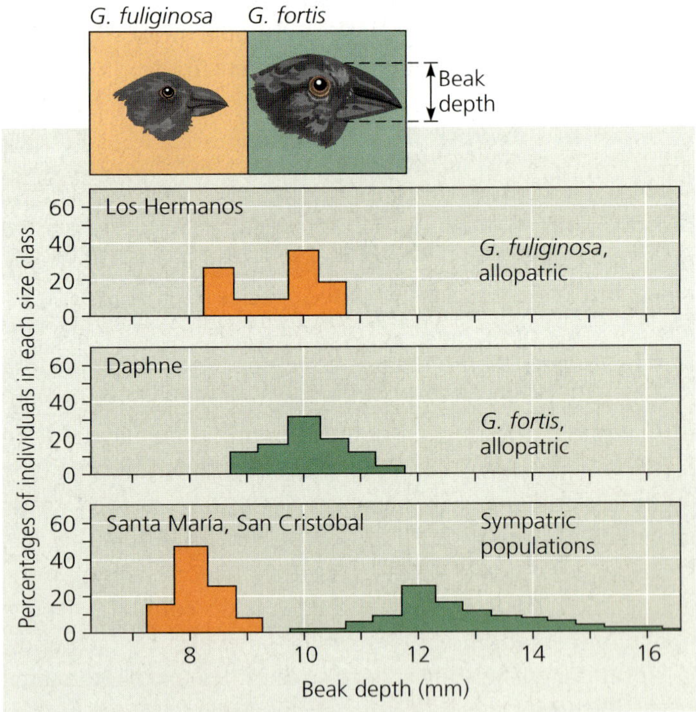

▲ **Figure 54.4 Character displacement: indirect evidence of past competition.** Allopatric populations of *Geospiza fuliginosa* and *Geospiza fortis* on Los Hermanos and Daphne Islands have similar beak morphologies (top two graphs) and presumably eat similarly sized seeds. However, where the two species are sympatric on Santa María and San Cristóbal, *G. fuliginosa* has a shallower, smaller beak and *G. fortis* a deeper, larger one (bottom graph), adaptations that favor eating different sizes of seeds.

? *Suppose that the sympatric populations of both finch species colonized a new island that contained seeds of only one size. What would you expect to happen to the differences in beak size over time? Explain your reasoning.*

Predation

Predation refers to a +/− interaction between species in which one species, the predator, kills and eats the other, the prey. Though the term *predation* generally elicits such images as a lion attacking and eating an antelope, it applies to a wide range of interactions. An animal that kills a plant by eating the plant's tissues can also be considered a predator. Because eating and avoiding being eaten are prerequisite to reproductive success, the adaptations of both predators and prey tend to be refined through natural selection.

Many important feeding adaptations of predators are both obvious and familiar. Most predators have acute senses that enable them to locate and identify potential prey. In addition, many predators have adaptations such as claws, teeth, fangs, stingers, or poison that help them catch and subdue the organisms on which they feed. Rattlesnakes and other pit vipers, for example, find their prey with a pair of heat-sensing organs located between their eyes and nostrils (see Figure 50.5a), and they kill small birds and mammals by injecting them with toxins through their fangs. Predators that pursue their prey are generally fast and agile, whereas those that lie in ambush are often disguised in their environments.

Just as predators possess adaptations for capturing prey, prey animals have adaptations that help them avoid being eaten. Some common behavioral defenses are hiding, fleeing, and forming herds or schools. Active self-defense is less common, though some large grazing mammals vigorously defend their young from predators such as lions. Other behavioral defenses include alarm calls that summon many individuals of the prey species, which then mob the predator.

Animals also display a variety of morphological and physiological defensive adaptations. For example, **cryptic coloration**, or camouflage, makes prey difficult to spot **(Figure 54.5a)**. Other animals have mechanical or chemical defenses. For example, most predators are strongly discouraged by the familiar defenses of porcupines and skunks. Some animals, such as the European fire salamander, can synthesize toxins, whereas others passively acquire a chemical defense by accumulating toxins from the plants they eat. Animals with effective chemical defenses often exhibit bright **aposematic coloration**, or warning coloration, such as that of the poison dart frog **(Figure 54.5b)**. Aposematic coloration seems to be adaptive: There is evidence that predators are particularly cautious in dealing with potential prey having bright color patterns (see Chapter 1).

Some prey species gain significant protection by mimicking the appearance of other species. In **Batesian mimicry**, a palatable or harmless species mimics an unpalatable or harmful model. For example, the larva of the hawkmoth *Hemeroplanes ornatus* puffs up its head and thorax when disturbed, looking like the head of a small poisonous snake **(Figure 54.5c)**. In this case, the mimicry even involves behavior; the larva weaves its head back and forth and hisses like a snake. In **Müllerian mimicry**, two or more unpalatable species, such as the cuckoo bee and yellow jacket, resemble each other **(Figure 54.5d)**. Presumably, each species gains an additional

▼ **Figure 54.5 Examples of defensive coloration in animals.**

(a) Cryptic coloration

▶ Canyon tree frog

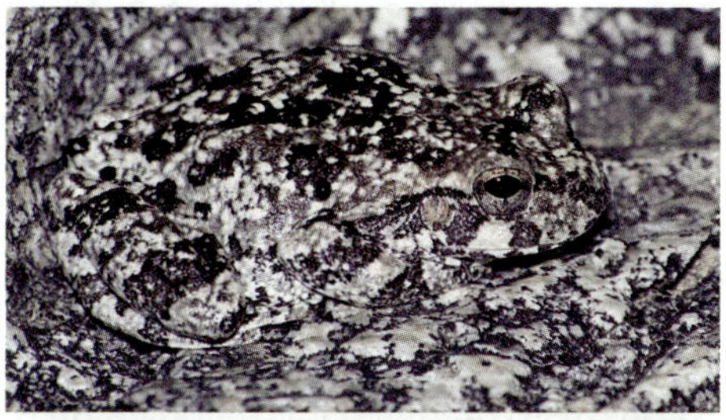

(b) Aposematic coloration

▶ Poison dart frog

(c) Batesian mimicry: A harmless species mimics a harmful one.

◀ Hawkmoth larva

▼ Green parrot snake

(d) Müllerian mimicry: Two unpalatable species mimic each other.

◀ Cuckoo bee

▼ Yellow jacket

advantage because the more unpalatable prey there are, the more quickly and effectively predators adapt, avoiding any prey with that particular appearance. The shared appearance thus becomes a kind of aposematic coloration. In an example of convergent evolution, unpalatable animals in several different taxa have similar patterns of coloration: Black and yellow or red stripes characterize unpalatable animals as diverse as yellow jackets and coral snakes (see Figure 1.25).

Predators also use mimicry. For example, some snapping turtles have tongues that resemble a wriggling worm, thus luring small fish. Any fish that tries to eat the "bait" is itself quickly consumed as the turtle's strong jaws snap closed. Anglerfish also lure prey with their own bait, in this case a modified bone of the dorsal fin that luminesces in some species.

Herbivory

Ecologists use the term **herbivory** to refer to a +/− interaction in which an organism eats parts of a plant or alga. While large mammalian herbivores such as cattle, sheep, and water buffalo may be most familiar, most herbivores are actually invertebrates, such as grasshoppers and beetles. In the ocean, herbivores include snails, sea urchins, some tropical fishes, and certain mammals, such as the manatee **(Figure 54.6)**.

Like predators, herbivores have many specialized adaptations. Many herbivorous insects have chemical sensors on their feet that enable them to distinguish between toxic and nontoxic plants as well as between more nutritious and less nutritious plants. Some mammalian herbivores, such as goats, use their sense of smell to examine plants, rejecting some and eating others. They may also eat just a specific part of a plant, such as the flowers. Many herbivores also have specialized teeth or digestive systems adapted for processing vegetation (see Chapter 41).

Unlike prey animals, plants cannot run away to avoid being eaten. Instead, a plant's arsenal against herbivores may feature chemical toxins or structures such as spines and thorns. Among the plant compounds that serve as chemical weapons are the poison strychnine, produced by the tropical vine *Strychnos toxifera*; nicotine, from the tobacco plant; and tannins, from a variety of plant species. Plants in the genus *Astragalus* accumulate selenium toxins; they are known as "locoweeds" because the cattle and sheep that eat them wander aimlessly in circles and may even die. Compounds that are not toxic to humans but may be distasteful to many herbivores are responsible for the familiar flavors of cinnamon, cloves, and peppermint. Certain plants produce chemicals that cause abnormal development in some insects that eat them.

▲ **Figure 54.6 A West Indies manatee (*Trichechus manatus*) in Florida.** The animal in this photo is feeding on water hyacinth, an introduced species.

Symbiosis

When individuals of two or more species live in direct and intimate contact with one another, their relationship is called **symbiosis**. This text adopts a general definition of symbiosis that includes all such interactions, whether harmful, helpful, or neutral. Some biologists define symbiosis more narrowly as a synonym for mutualism, in which both species benefit.

Parasitism

Parasitism is a +/− symbiotic interaction in which one organism, the **parasite**, derives its nourishment from another organism, its **host**, which is harmed in the process. Parasites that live within the body of their host, such as tapeworms, are called **endoparasites**; parasites that feed on the external surface of a host, such as ticks and lice, are called **ectoparasites**. In one particular type of parasitism, parasitoid insects—usually small wasps—lay eggs on or in living hosts (see Figure 54.1). The larvae then feed on the body of the host, eventually killing it. Some ecologists have estimated that at least one-third of all species on Earth are parasites.

Many parasites have complex life cycles involving multiple hosts. The life cycle of the blood fluke, which currently infects approximately 200 million people around the world, involves two hosts: humans and freshwater snails (see Figure 33.11). Some parasites change the behavior of their hosts in a way that increases the probability of the parasite being transferred from one host to another. For instance, the presence of parasitic acanthocephalan (spiny-headed) worms leads their crustacean hosts to engage in a variety of atypical behaviors, including leaving protective cover and moving into the open. As a result of their modified behavior, the crustaceans have a greater chance of being eaten by the birds that are the second host in the parasitic worm's life cycle.

Parasites can significantly affect the survival, reproduction, and density of their host population, either directly or indirectly. For example, ticks that live as ectoparasites on moose weaken their hosts by withdrawing blood and causing hair breakage and loss, increasing the chance that the moose will die from cold stress or predation by wolves. Some of the declines of the moose population on Isle Royale, Michigan, have been attributed to tick outbreaks (see Figure 53.19).

Mutualism

Mutualistic symbiosis, or **mutualism**, is an interspecific interaction that benefits both species (+/+). We have described many examples of mutualism in previous chapters: nitrogen fixation by bacteria in the root nodules of legumes; the digestion of cellulose by microorganisms in the digestive systems of termites and ruminant mammals; the exchange of nutrients in mycorrhizae, associations of fungi and the roots of plants; and photosynthesis by unicellular algae in corals. The interaction between termites and the microorganisms in their digestive system is an example of *obligate mutualism*, in which at least one species has lost the ability to survive without its partner. In *facultative mutualism*, as in the acacia-ant example shown in **Figure 54.7**, both species can survive alone.

Mutualistic relationships sometimes involve the evolution of related adaptations in both species, with changes in either species likely to affect the survival and reproduction of the other. For example, most flowering plants have adaptations such as nectar or fruit that attract animals that function in pollination or seed dispersal (see Chapter 38). In turn, many animals have adaptations that help them find and consume nectar.

(a) Certain species of acacia trees in Central and South America have hollow thorns that house stinging ants of the genus *Pseudomyrmex*. The ants feed on nectar produced by the tree and on protein-rich swellings (orange in the photograph) at the tips of leaflets.

(b) The acacia benefits because the pugnacious ants, which attack anything that touches the tree, remove fungal spores, small herbivores, and debris, and clip vegetation that grows close to the acacia.

▲ **Figure 54.7 Mutualism between acacia trees and ants.**

Commensalism

An interaction between species that benefits one of the species but neither harms nor helps the other (+/0) is called **commensalism**. Commensal interactions are difficult to document in nature because any close association between species likely affects both species, even if only slightly. For instance, "hitchhiking" species, such as algae that live on the shells of aquatic turtles or barnacles that attach to whales, are sometimes considered commensal. The hitchhikers gain a place to grow while having seemingly little effect on their ride. However, the hitchhikers may in fact slightly decrease the reproductive success of their hosts by reducing the hosts' efficiency of movement in searching for food or escaping from predators. Conversely, the hitchhikers may provide a benefit in the form of camouflage.

Some associations that are possibly commensal involve one species obtaining food that is inadvertently exposed by another. For instance, cowbirds and cattle egrets feed on insects flushed out of the grass by grazing bison, cattle, horses, and other herbivores. Because the birds increase their feeding rates when following the herbivores, they clearly benefit from the association. Much of the time, the herbivores may be unaffected by the relationship **(Figure 54.8)**. However, they, too, may sometimes derive some benefit; the birds tend to be opportunistic feeders that occasionally remove and eat ticks and other ectoparasites from the herbivores. They may also give warning to the herbivores of a predator's approach.

All four types of interactions that we have discussed so far—competition, predation, herbivory, and symbiosis—strongly influence the structure of communities. You will see other examples of these interactions throughout this chapter.

▲ **Figure 54.8 A possible example of commensalism between cattle egrets and water buffalo.**

CONCEPT CHECK 54.1

1. Explain how interspecific competition, predation, and mutualism differ in their effects on the interacting populations of two species.
2. According to the principle of competitive exclusion, what outcome is expected when two species with identical niches compete for a resource? Why?
3. **WHAT IF?** Suppose you live in an agricultural area. What examples of the four types of community interactions (competition, predation, herbivory, and symbiosis) might you see in the growing or use of food?

For suggested answers, see Appendix A.

CONCEPT 54.2

Dominant and keystone species exert strong controls on community structure

Although the interactions of many species influence biological communities, sometimes a few species exert strong control on a community's structure, particularly on the composition, relative abundance, and diversity of its species. Before examining the effects of these particularly influential species, we first need to consider two fundamental features of community structure: species diversity and feeding relationships.

Species Diversity

The **species diversity** of a community—the variety of different kinds of organisms that make up the community—has two components. One is **species richness**, the number of different species in the community. The other is the **relative abundance** of the different species, the proportion each species represents of all individuals in the community. For example, imagine two small forest communities, each with 100 individuals distributed among four tree species (A, B, C, and D) as follows:

Community 1: 25A, 25B, 25C, 25D
Community 2: 80A, 5B, 5C, 10D

The species richness is the same for both communities because they both contain four species of trees, but the relative abundance is very different **(Figure 54.9)**. You would easily notice the four types of trees in community 1, but without looking carefully, you might see only the abundant species A in the second forest. Most observers would intuitively describe community 1 as the more diverse of the two communities.

Ecologists use many tools to quantitatively compare the diversity of different communities across time and space. They often calculate an index of diversity based on species richness and relative abundance. One widely used index is the **Shannon diversity** (H):

$$H = -[(p_A \ln p_A) + (p_B \ln p_B) + (p_C \ln p_C) + \ldots]$$

where A, B, C . . . are the species in the community, p is the relative abundance of each species, and ln is the natural logarithm. Let's use this equation to calculate the Shannon diversity of the two communities in Figure 54.9. For community 1, $p = 0.25$ for each community, so $H = -4 \times (0.25 \ln 0.25) = 1.39$. For community 2, $H = -[(0.8 \ln 0.8) + (0.05 \ln 0.05) + (0.05 \ln 0.05) + (0.1 \ln 0.1)] = 0.71$. These calculations confirm our intuitive description of community 1 as more diverse.

Determining the number and relative abundance of species in a community is easier said than done. Many sampling techniques can be used, but since most species in a community are relatively rare, it may be hard to obtain a sample size large enough to be representative. It is also difficult to census the highly mobile or less visible members of communities, such as mites, nematodes, and microorganisms. The small size of microorganisms makes them particularly difficult to sample, so ecologists now use molecular tools to help determine microbial diversity **(Figure 54.10)**. Although measuring species diversity is often challenging, it is essential not only for understanding community structure but for conserving biodiversity, as you will read in Chapter 56.

▲ **Figure 54.9 Which forest is more diverse?** Ecologists would say that community 1 has greater species diversity, a measure that includes both species richness and relative abundance.

▼ Figure 54.10 Research Method

Determining Microbial Diversity Using Molecular Tools

APPLICATION Ecologists are increasingly using molecular techniques, such as the analysis of restriction fragment length polymorphisms (RFLPs), to determine microbial diversity and richness in environmental samples. As used in this application, RFLP analysis produces a DNA fingerprint for microbial taxa based on sequence variations in the DNA that encodes the small subunit of ribosomal RNA. Noah Fierer and Rob Jackson, of Duke University, used this method to compare the diversity of soil bacteria in 98 habitats across North and South America to help identify environmental variables associated with high bacterial diversity.

TECHNIQUE Researchers first extract and purify DNA from the microbial community in each sample. They use the polymerase chain reaction (PCR) to amplify the ribosomal DNA and label the DNA with a fluorescent dye (see Chapter 20). Restriction enzymes then cut the amplified, labeled DNA into fragments of different lengths, which are separated by gel electrophoresis. The number and abundance of these fragments characterize the DNA fingerprint of the sample.

Based on their RFLP analysis, Fierer and Jackson calculated the Shannon diversity (H) of each sample. They then looked for a correlation between H and several environmental variables, including vegetation type, mean annual temperature and rainfall, and acidity and quality of the soil at each site.

RESULTS The diversity of bacterial communities in soils across North and South America was related almost exclusively to soil pH, with the Shannon diversity being highest in neutral soils and lowest in acidic soils. Amazonian rain forests, which have extremely high plant and animal diversity, had the most acidic soils and the lowest bacterial diversity of the samples tested.

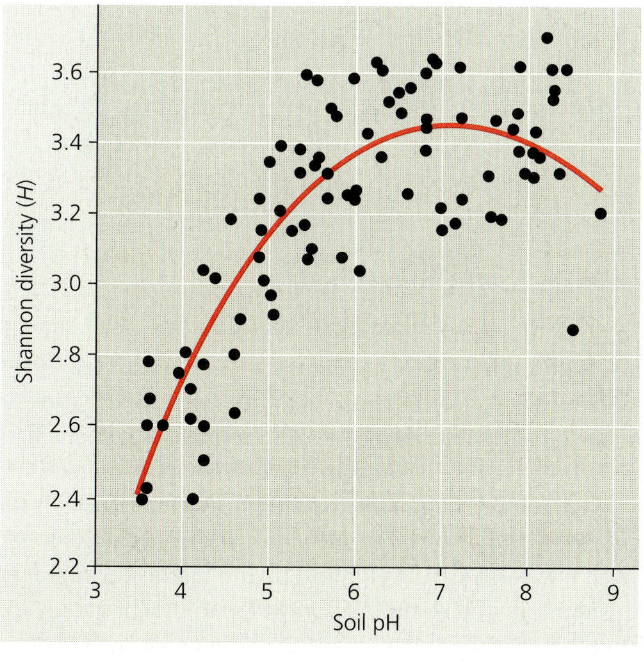

SOURCE N. Fierer and R. B. Jackson, The diversity and biogeography of soil bacterial communities, *Proceedings of the National Academy of Sciences USA* 103:626–631 (2006).

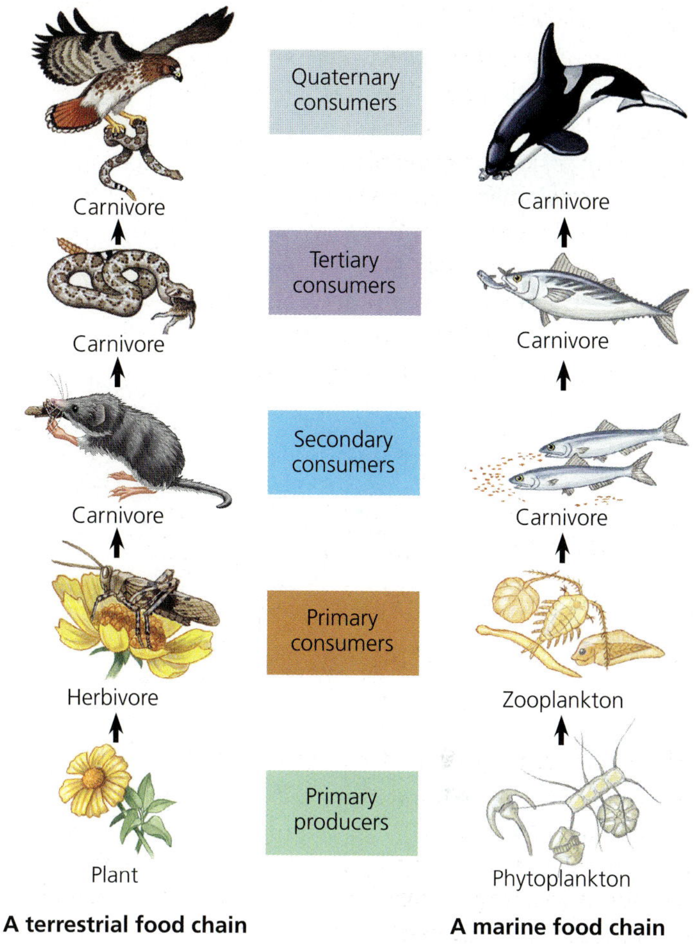

▲ **Figure 54.11 Examples of terrestrial and marine food chains.** The arrows trace energy and nutrients that pass through the trophic levels of a community when organisms feed on one another. Decomposers, which "feed" on organisms from all trophic levels, are not shown here.

Trophic Structure

The structure and dynamics of a community depend to a large extent on the feeding relationships between organisms—the **trophic structure** of the community. The transfer of food energy up the trophic levels from its source in plants and other autotrophic organisms (primary producers) through herbivores (primary consumers) to carnivores (secondary, tertiary, and quaternary consumers) and eventually to decomposers is referred to as a **food chain** **(Figure 54.11)**.

Food Webs

In the 1920s, Oxford University biologist Charles Elton recognized that food chains are not isolated units but are linked together in **food webs**. An ecologist can summarize the trophic relationships of a community by diagramming a food web with arrows linking species according to who eats whom. In an antarctic pelagic community, for example, the primary producers are phytoplankton, which serve as food for the dominant

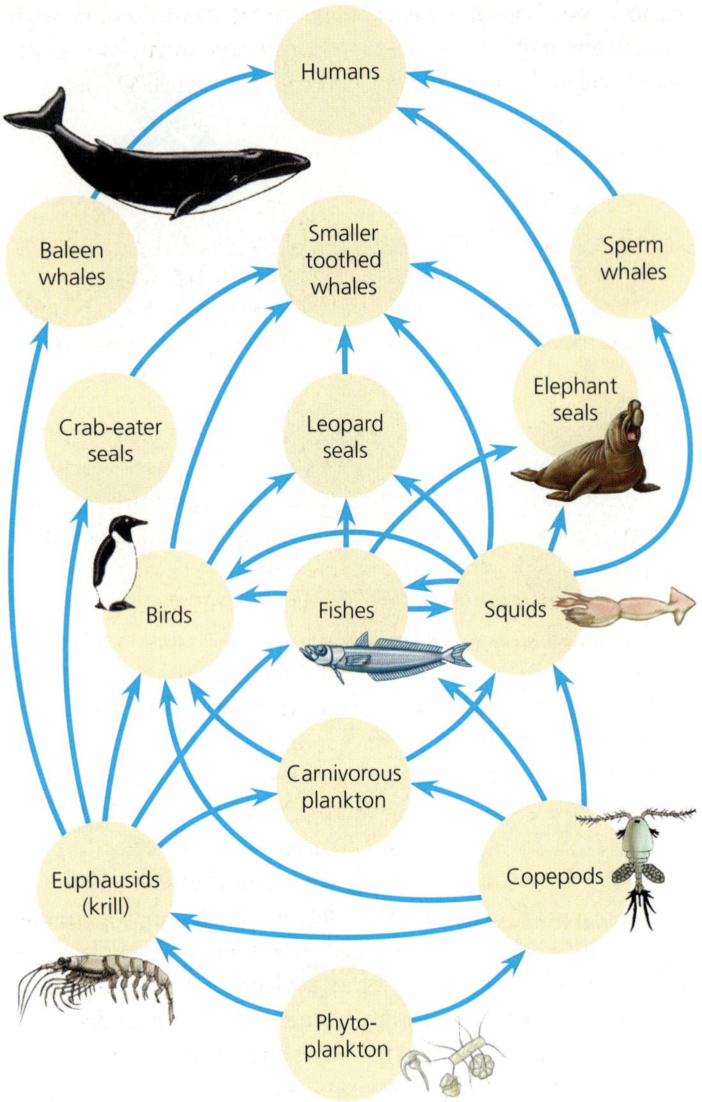

▲ **Figure 54.12 An antarctic marine food web.** Arrows follow the transfer of food from the producers (phytoplankton) up through the trophic levels. For simplicity, this diagram omits decomposers.

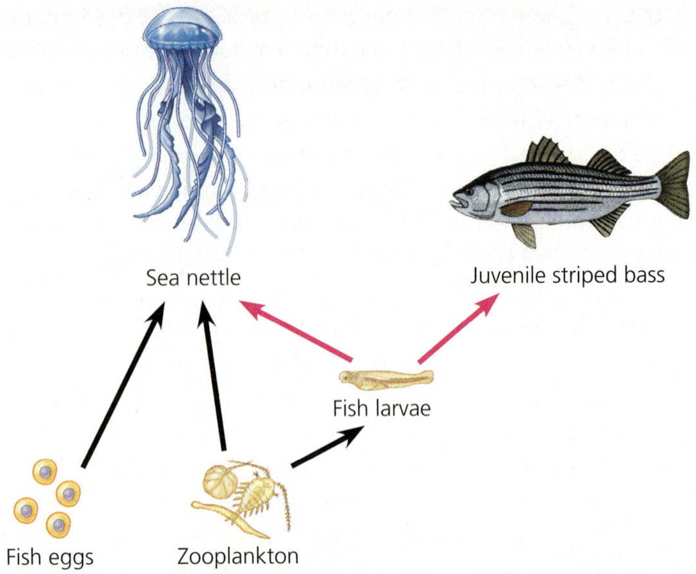

▲ **Figure 54.13 Partial food web for the Chesapeake Bay estuary on the U.S. Atlantic coast.** The sea nettle (*Chrysaora quinquecirrha*) and juvenile striped bass (*Morone saxatilis*) are the main predators of fish larvae (bay anchovy and several other species). Note that sea nettles are secondary consumers (black arrows) when they eat zooplankton, but tertiary consumers (red arrows) when they eat fish larvae, which are themselves secondary consumers of zooplankton.

grazing zooplankton, especially euphausids (krill) and copepods, both of which are crustaceans **(Figure 54.12)**. These zooplankton species are in turn eaten by various carnivores, including other plankton, penguins, seals, fishes, and baleen whales. Squids, which are carnivores that feed on fishes as well as zooplankton, are another important link in these food webs, as they are in turn eaten by seals and toothed whales. During the time when whales were commonly hunted for food, humans became the top predator in this food web. Having hunted many whale species to low numbers, humans are now harvesting at lower trophic levels, catching krill as well as fishes for food.

How are food chains linked into food webs? First, a given species may weave into the web at more than one trophic level. In the food web shown in Figure 54.12, euphausids feed on phytoplankton as well as on other grazing zooplankton, such as copepods. Such "nonexclusive" consumers are also found in terrestrial communities. For instance, foxes are omnivores whose diet includes berries and other plant materials, herbivores such as mice, and other predators, such as weasels. Humans are among the most versatile of omnivores.

Food webs can be very complicated, but we can simplify them for easier study in two ways. First, we can group species with similar trophic relationships in a given community into broad functional groups. For example, in Figure 54.12, more than 100 phytoplankton species are grouped as the primary producers in the food web. A second way to simplify a food web for closer study is to isolate a portion of the web that interacts very little with the rest of the community. **Figure 54.13** illustrates a partial food web for sea nettles (a type of cnidarian) and juvenile striped bass in Chesapeake Bay.

Limits on Food Chain Length

Each food chain within a food web is usually only a few links long. In the antarctic web of Figure 54.12, there are rarely more than seven links from the producers to any top-level predator, and most chains in this web have fewer links. In fact, most food webs studied to date have chains consisting of five or fewer links.

Why are food chains relatively short? There are two main hypotheses. One, the **energetic hypothesis**, suggests that the length of a food chain is limited by the inefficiency of energy transfer along the chain. As you will read in Chapter 55, only about 10% of the energy stored in the organic matter of each trophic level is converted to organic matter at the next trophic level. Thus, a producer level consisting of 100 kg of plant material can support about 10 kg of herbivore **biomass** (the total mass of all individuals in a population) and 1 kg of carnivore biomass. The energetic hypothesis predicts that food chains should be relatively longer in habitats of higher photosynthetic production, since the starting amount of energy is greater than in habitats with lower photosynthetic production.

A second hypothesis, the **dynamic stability hypothesis**, proposes that long food chains are less stable than short chains. Population fluctuations at lower trophic levels are magnified at higher levels, potentially causing the local extinction of top predators. In a variable environment, top predators must be able to recover from environmental shocks (such as extreme winters) that can reduce the food supply all the way up the food chain. The longer a food chain is, the more slowly top predators can recover from environmental setbacks. This hypothesis predicts that food chains should be shorter in unpredictable environments.

Most of the data available support the energetic hypothesis. For example, ecologists have used tree-hole communities in tropical forests as experimental models to test the energetic hypothesis. Many trees have small branch scars that rot, forming holes in the tree trunk. The tree holes hold water and provide a habitat for tiny communities consisting of microorganisms and insects that feed on leaf litter, as well as predatory insects. **Figure 54.14** shows the results of experiments in which researchers manipulated productivity (leaf litter falling into the tree holes). As predicted by the energetic hypothesis, holes with the most leaf litter, and hence the greatest total food supply at the producer level, supported the longest food chains.

Another factor that may limit food chain length is that carnivores in a food chain tend to be larger at successive trophic levels. The size of a carnivore and its feeding mechanism put some upper limit on the size of food it can take into its mouth. And except in a few cases, large carnivores cannot live on very small food items because they cannot procure enough food in a given time to meet their metabolic needs. Among the exceptions are baleen whales, huge suspension feeders with adaptations that enable them to consume enormous quantities of krill and other small organisms (see Figure 41.6).

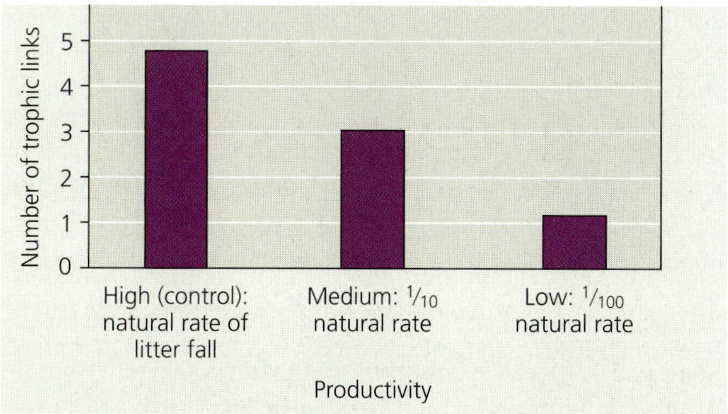

▲ **Figure 54.14 Test of the energetic hypothesis for the restriction of food chain length.** Researchers manipulated the productivity of tree-hole communities in Queensland, Australia, by providing leaf litter input at three levels. Reducing energy input reduced food chain length, a result consistent with the energetic hypothesis.

? *According to the dynamic stability hypothesis, which productivity treatment should have the most stable food chain? Explain.*

Species with a Large Impact

Certain species have an especially large impact on the structure of entire communities either because they are highly abundant or because they play a pivotal role in community dynamics. The impact of these species can occur either through their trophic interactions or through their influences on the physical environment.

Dominant Species

Dominant species are those species in a community that are the most abundant or that collectively have the highest biomass. As a result, dominant species exert a powerful control over the occurrence and distribution of other species. For example, the abundance of sugar maples, the dominant plant species in many eastern North American forest communities, has a major impact on abiotic factors such as shading and soil, which in turn affect which other species live there.

There is no single explanation for why a species becomes dominant in a community. One hypothesis suggests that dominant species are competitively superior in exploiting limited resources such as water or nutrients. Another explanation is that dominant species are most successful at avoiding predation or the impact of disease. This latter idea could explain the high biomass attained in some environments by **invasive species**, organisms (typically introduced by humans) that take hold outside their native range. Such species may not face the natural predators and agents of disease that would otherwise hold their populations in check.

One way to discover the impact of a dominant species is to remove it from the community. This type of experiment has been carried out many times by accident. The American chestnut was a dominant tree in deciduous forests of eastern North America before 1910, making up more than 40% of mature trees. Then humans accidentally introduced the fungal disease chestnut blight to New York City via nursery stock imported from Asia. Between 1910 and 1950, this fungus killed all the chestnut trees in eastern North America. In this case, removing the dominant species had a relatively small impact on some species but severe effects on others. Oaks, hickories, beeches, and red maples that were already present in the forest increased in abundance and replaced the chestnuts. No mammals or birds seemed to have been harmed by the loss of the chestnut, but seven species of moths and butterflies that fed on the tree became extinct.

The American chestnut story is only one example of a community response to the loss of a dominant species. More research is needed before we can generalize about the overall effects of such losses.

▼ **Figure 54.15 Inquiry**

Is *Pisaster ochraceus* a keystone predator?

EXPERIMENT In rocky intertidal communities of western North America, the relatively uncommon sea star *Pisaster ochraceus* preys on mussels such as *Mytilus californianus*, a dominant species and strong competitor for space. Robert Paine, of the University of Washington, removed *Pisaster* from an area in the intertidal zone and examined the effect on species richness.

RESULTS In the absence of *Pisaster*, species richness declined as mussels monopolized the rock face and eliminated most other invertebrates and algae. In a control area where *Pisaster* was not removed, species richness changed very little.

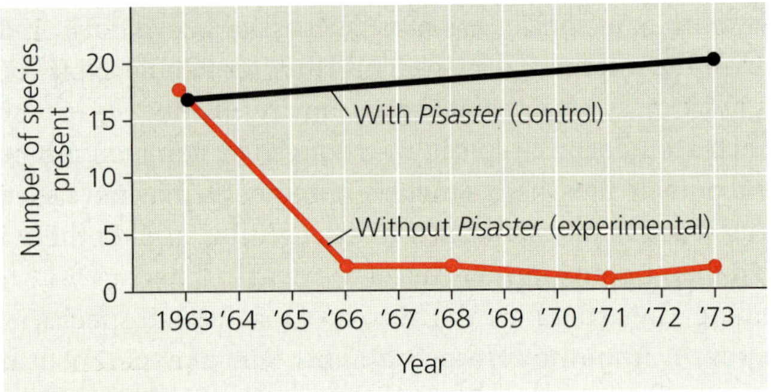

CONCLUSION *Pisaster* acts as a keystone species, exerting an influence on the community that is not reflected in its abundance.

SOURCE R. T. Paine, Food web complexity and species diversity, *American Naturalist* 100:65–75 (1966).

WHAT IF? Suppose that an invasive fungus killed most individuals of *Mytilus* at these sites. What do you think would happen to species richness if *Pisaster* were then removed?

Keystone Species

In contrast to dominant species, **keystone species** are not necessarily abundant in a community. They exert strong control on community structure not by numerical might but by their pivotal ecological roles, or niches. One way to identify keystone species is by removal experiments like the one described in **Figure 54.15**, which highlights the importance of a keystone species in maintaining the diversity of an intertidal community.

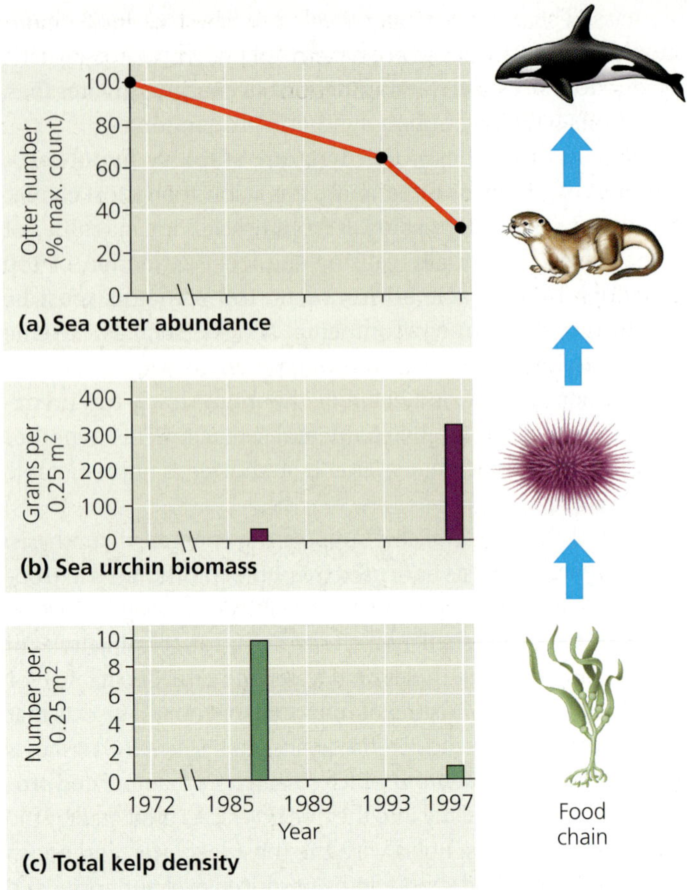

▲ **Figure 54.16 Sea otters as keystone predators in the North Pacific.** The graphs correlate changes over time in sea otter abundance **(a)** with changes in sea urchin biomass **(b)** and changes in kelp density **(c)** in kelp forests at Adak Island (part of the Aleutian Island chain). The vertical diagram on the right represents the food chain after orcas (top) entered the chain.

The sea otter, a keystone predator in the North Pacific, offers another example **(Figure 54.16)**. Sea otters feed on sea urchins, and sea urchins feed mainly on kelp. In areas where sea otters are abundant, sea urchins are rare and kelp forests are well developed. Where sea otters are rare, sea urchins are common and kelp is almost absent. Over the last 20 years, orcas have been preying on sea otters as the whales' usual prey has declined. As a result, sea otter populations have declined precipitously in large areas off the coast of western Alaska, sometimes at rates as high as 25% per year. The loss of this keystone species has allowed sea urchin populations to increase, resulting in the loss of kelp forests.

Foundation Species (Ecosystem "Engineers")

Some organisms exert their influence on a community not through their trophic interactions but by causing physical changes in the environment. Such organisms may alter the environment through their behavior or their large collective biomass.

Species that dramatically alter their physical environment on a large scale are called ecosystem "engineers" or, to avoid implying conscious intent, "foundation species." A familiar foundation species is the beaver **(Figure 54.17)**, which, through tree felling and dam building, can transform landscapes. The effects of foundation species on other species can be positive or negative, depending on the needs of the other species.

By altering the structure or dynamics of the environment, foundation species sometimes act as **facilitators**: They have positive effects on the survival and reproduction of other species in the community. For example, by modifying soils, the black rush *Juncus gerardi* increases the species richness in some zones of New England salt marshes. *Juncus* helps prevent salt buildup in the soil by shading the soil surface, which reduces evaporation **(Figure 54.18a)**. *Juncus* also prevents the salt marsh soils from becoming oxygen depleted as it transports oxygen to its belowground tissues. Sally Hacker and Mark Bertness, of Brown University, uncovered some of *Juncus*'s facilitation effects by removing *Juncus* from study plots. Their experiment suggested that without *Juncus*, the upper middle intertidal zone would support 50% fewer plant species **(Figure 54.18b)**.

▲ **Figure 54.17 Beavers as ecosystem "engineers."** By felling trees, building dams, and creating ponds, beavers can transform large areas of forest into flooded wetlands.

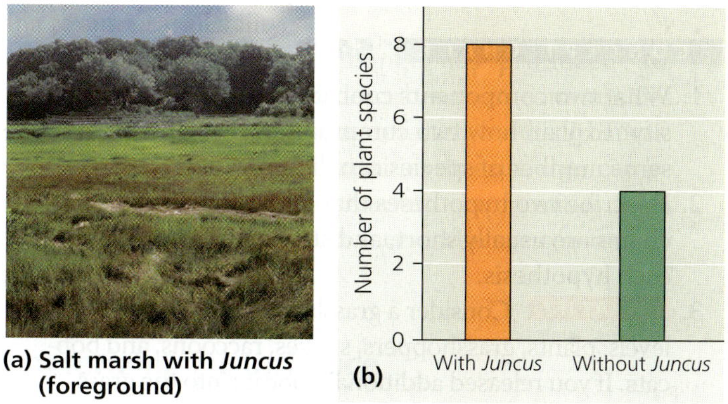

(a) Salt marsh with *Juncus* (foreground)
(b)

▲ **Figure 54.18 Facilitation by black rush (*Juncus gerardi*) in New England salt marshes.** Black rush facilitates the occupation of the middle upper zone of the marsh, which increases local plant species richness.

Bottom-Up and Top-Down Controls

Simplified models based on relationships between adjacent trophic levels are useful for discussing community organization. For example, let's consider the three possible relationships between plants (V for vegetation) and herbivores (H):

$$V \rightarrow H \qquad V \leftarrow H \qquad V \leftrightarrow H$$

The arrows indicate that a change in the biomass of one trophic level causes a change in the other trophic level. $V \rightarrow H$ means that an increase in vegetation will increase the numbers or biomass of herbivores, but not vice versa. In this situation, herbivores are limited by vegetation, but vegetation is not limited by herbivory. In contrast, $V \leftarrow H$ means that an increase in herbivore biomass will decrease the abundance of vegetation, but not vice versa. A double-headed arrow indicates that feedback flows in both directions, with each trophic level sensitive to changes in the biomass of the other.

Two models of community organization are common: the bottom-up model and the top-down model. The $V \rightarrow H$ linkage suggests a **bottom-up model**, which postulates a unidirectional influence from lower to higher trophic levels. In this case, the presence or absence of mineral nutrients (N) controls plant (V) numbers, which control herbivore (H) numbers, which in turn control predator (P) numbers. The simplified bottom-up model is thus $N \rightarrow V \rightarrow H \rightarrow P$. To change the community structure of a bottom-up community, you need to alter biomass at the lower trophic levels, allowing those changes to propagate up through the food web. For example, if you add mineral nutrients to stimulate growth of vegetation, then the higher trophic levels should also increase in biomass. If you add predators to or remove predators from a bottom-up community, however, the effect should not extend down to the lower trophic levels.

In contrast, the **top-down model** postulates the opposite: Predation mainly controls community organization because predators limit herbivores, herbivores limit plants, and plants limit nutrient levels through their uptake of nutrients during growth and reproduction. The simplified top-down model, $N \leftarrow V \leftarrow H \leftarrow P$, is also called the *trophic cascade model*. For example, in a lake community with four trophic levels, the model predicts that removing the top carnivores will increase the abundance of primary carnivores, in turn decreasing the number of herbivores, increasing phytoplankton abundance, and decreasing concentrations of mineral nutrients. If there were only three trophic levels in a lake, removing primary carnivores would increase the number of herbivores and decrease phytoplankton abundance, causing nutrient levels to rise. The effects of any manipulation thus move down the trophic structure as alternating +/− effects.

Although moderate levels of disturbance appear to maximize species diversity, small and large disturbances can have important effects on community structure. Small-scale disturbances can create patches of different habitats across a landscape, which can be a key to maintaining diversity in a community. Large-scale disturbances are also a natural part of many communities. Much of Yellowstone National Park, for example, is dominated by lodgepole pine, a tree that requires the rejuvenating influence of periodic fires. Lodgepole cones remain closed until exposed to intense heat. When a forest fire burns the trees, the cones open and the seeds are released. The new generation of lodgepole pines can then thrive on nutrients released from the burned trees and in the sunlight that is no longer blocked by taller trees.

In the summer of 1988, extensive areas of Yellowstone burned during a severe drought. By 1989, burned areas in the park were largely covered with new vegetation, suggesting that the species in this community are adapted to rapid recovery after fire **(Figure 54.21)**. In fact, large-scale fires have periodically swept through the lodgepole pine forests of Yellowstone and other northern areas for thousands of years. In contrast, more southerly pine forests were historically affected by frequent but low-intensity fires. In these forests, a century of human intervention to suppress small fires has allowed an unnatural buildup of fuels and elevated the risk of large, severe fires to which the species are not adapted.

Studies of the Yellowstone forest community and many others indicate that they are nonequilibrium communities, changing continually because of natural disturbances and the internal processes of growth and reproduction. Mounting evidence suggests that nonequilibrium conditions resulting from disturbance are in fact the norm for most communities.

Ecological Succession

Changes in the composition and structure of terrestrial communities are most apparent after some severe disturbance, such as a volcanic eruption or a glacier, strips away all the existing vegetation. The disturbed area may be colonized by a variety of species, which are gradually replaced by other species, which are in turn replaced by still other species—a process called **ecological succession**.

When this process begins in a virtually lifeless area where soil has not yet formed, such as on a new volcanic island or on the rubble (moraine) left by a retreating glacier, it is called **primary succession**. Often the only life-forms initially present are autotrophic prokaryotes and heterotrophic prokaryotes and protists. Lichens and mosses, which grow from windblown spores, are commonly the first macroscopic photosynthesizers to colonize such areas. Soil develops gradually as rocks weather and organic matter accumulates from the decomposed remains of the early colonizers. Once soil is present, the lichens and mosses are usually overgrown by grasses, shrubs, and trees that sprout from seeds blown in from nearby areas or carried in by animals. Eventually, an area is colonized by plants that become the community's prevalent form of vegetation. Producing such a community through primary succession may take hundreds or thousands of years.

Secondary succession occurs when an existing community has been cleared by some disturbance that leaves the soil intact, as in Yellowstone following the 1988 fires (see Figure 54.21). Sometimes the area begins to return to something like its original state. For instance, in a forested area that has been cleared for farming and later abandoned, the earliest plants to recolonize are often herbaceous species that grow from windblown or animal-borne seeds. If the area has not been burned or

(a) Soon after fire. The burn left a patchy landscape. Note the unburned trees in the far distance.

(b) One year after fire. The community has begun to recover. A variety of herbaceous plants, different from those in the former forest, cover the ground.

▲ **Figure 54.21 Recovery following a large-scale disturbance.** The 1988 Yellowstone National Park fires burned large areas of forests dominated by lodgepole pines.

heavily grazed, woody shrubs may in time replace most of the herbaceous species, and forest trees may eventually replace most of the shrubs.

Early arrivals and later-arriving species may be linked in one of three key processes. The early arrivals may *facilitate* the appearance of the later species by making the environment more favorable—for example, by increasing the fertility of the soil. Alternatively, the early species may *inhibit* establishment of the later species, so that successful colonization by later species occurs in spite of, rather than because of, the activities of the early species. Finally, the early species may be completely independent of the later species, which *tolerate* conditions created early in succession but are neither helped nor hindered by early species.

Let's look at how these various processes contribute to primary succession on glacial moraines. Ecologists have conducted the most extensive research on moraine succession at Glacier Bay in southeastern Alaska, where glaciers have retreated more than 100 km since 1760 **(Figure 54.22)**. By studying the communities on moraines at different distances from the mouth of the bay, ecologists can examine different stages in succession. ❶ The exposed moraine is colonized first by pioneering species that include liverworts, mosses, fireweed, scattered *Dryas* (a mat-forming shrub), willows, and cottonwood. ❷ After about three decades, *Dryas* dominates the plant community. ❸ A few decades later, the area is invaded by alder, which forms dense thickets up to 9 m tall. In the next two centuries, these alder stands are overgrown first by Sitka spruce ❹ and later by a combination of western hemlock and mountain hemlock. In areas of poor drainage, the forest floor of this spruce-hemlock forest is invaded by sphagnum moss, which holds large amounts of water and acidifies the soil, eventually killing the trees. Thus, by about 300 years after glacial retreat, the vegetation consists of sphagnum bogs on the poorly drained flat areas and spruce-hemlock forest on the well-drained slopes.

How is succession on glacial moraines related to the environmental changes caused by transitions in the vegetation? The bare soil exposed as the glacier retreats is quite basic, with a pH of 8.0–8.4 due to the carbonate compounds in the parent rocks. The soil pH falls rapidly as vegetation develops. Decomposition of acidic spruce needles in particular reduces the pH of the soil from 7.0 to approximately 4.0. The soil concentrations of mineral nutrients also change with time. Because the bare soil after glacial retreat is low in nitrogen content, almost all the pioneer plant species begin succession with poor

❶ **Pioneer stage, with fireweed dominant**

❷ ***Dryas* stage**

❸ **Alder stage**

❹ **Spruce stage**

▲ **Figure 54.22 Glacial retreat and primary succession at Glacier Bay, Alaska.** The different shades of blue on the map show retreat of the glacier since 1760, based on historical descriptions.

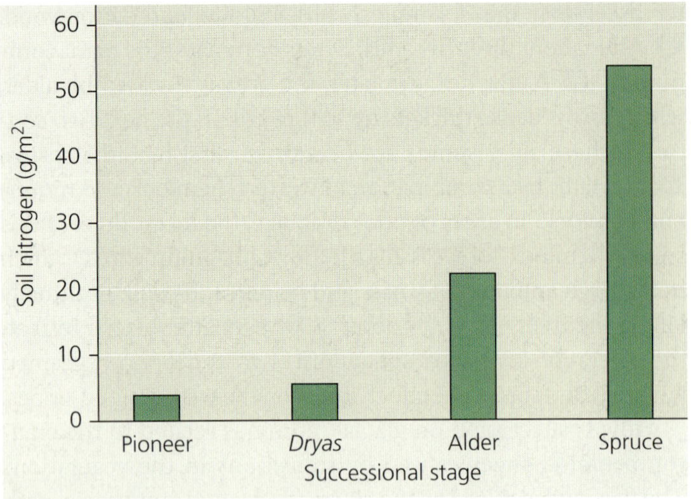

▲ **Figure 54.23 Changes in soil nitrogen content during succession at Glacier Bay.**

growth and yellow leaves due to inadequate nitrogen supply. The exceptions are *Dryas* and, particularly, alder; these species have symbiotic bacteria that fix atmospheric nitrogen (see Chapter 37). Soil nitrogen content increases rapidly during the alder stage of succession and continues to increase during the spruce stage **(Figure 54.23)**. By altering soil properties, pioneer plant species permit new plant species to grow, and the new plants in turn alter the environment in different ways, contributing to succession.

Human Disturbance

Ecological succession is a response to disturbance of the environment, and one of the strongest agents of disturbance today is human activity. Of all animals, humans have the greatest impact on biological communities worldwide. Agricultural development has disrupted what were once the vast grasslands of the North American prairie. Logging and clearing for urban development, mining, and farming have reduced large tracts of forests to small patches of disconnected woodlots in many parts of the United States and throughout Europe. After forests are clear-cut, weedy and shrubby vegetation often colonizes the area and dominates it for many years. This type of vegetation is also found in agricultural fields that are no longer under cultivation and in vacant lots and construction sites.

Human disturbance of communities is by no means limited to the United States and Europe; nor is it a recent problem. Tropical rain forests are quickly disappearing as a result of clear-cutting for lumber, cattle grazing, and farmland. Centuries of overgrazing and agricultural disturbance have contributed to famine in parts of Africa by turning seasonal grasslands into vast barren areas.

Humans disturb marine ecosystems just as extensively as terrestrial ones. The effects of ocean trawling, where boats drag weighted nets across the seafloor, are similar to those of clear-cutting a forest or plowing a field **(Figure 54.24)**. The trawls scrape and scour corals and other life on the seafloor and in its sediments. In a typical year, ships trawl 15 million km^2 of ocean floor, an area about the size of South America and 150 times larger than the area of forests that are clear-cut annually.

▲ **Figure 54.24 Disturbance of the ocean floor by trawling.** These photos show the seafloor off northwestern Australia before (top) and after (bottom) deep-sea trawlers have passed.

Because human disturbance is often severe, it reduces species diversity in many communities. In Chapter 56, we will take a closer look at how community disturbance by human activities is affecting the diversity of life.

CONCEPT CHECK 54.3

1. Why do high and low levels of disturbance usually reduce species diversity? Why does an intermediate level of disturbance promote species diversity?
2. During succession, how might the early species facilitate the arrival of other species?
3. **WHAT IF?** Most prairies experience regular fires, typically every few years. How would the species diversity of a prairie likely be affected if no burning occurred for 100 years? Explain your answer.

For suggested answers, see Appendix A.

CONCEPT 54.4

Biogeographic factors affect community biodiversity

So far we have examined relatively small-scale or local factors that influence the diversity of communities, including the effects of species interactions, dominant species, and many types of disturbances. Ecologists also recognize that large-scale biogeographic factors contribute to the tremendous range of diversity observed in biological communities. The contributions of two biogeographic factors in particular—the latitude of a community and the area it occupies—have been investigated for more than a century.

Latitudinal Gradients

In the 1850s, both Charles Darwin and Alfred Wallace pointed out that plant and animal life was generally more abundant and diverse in the tropics than in other parts of the globe. Since that time, many researchers around the world have confirmed this observation. For example, one study found that a 6.6-hectare (1 ha = 10,000 m^2) plot in tropical Malaysia contained 711 tree species, while a 2-ha plot of deciduous forest in Michigan typically contains just 10 to 15 tree species. Moreover, in all of western Europe north of the Alps there are only 50 tree species. Many groups of animals show similar latitudinal gradients. For instance, there are more than 200 species of ants in Brazil but only 7 in Alaska.

The two key factors in latitudinal gradients of species richness are probably evolutionary history and climate. Over the course of evolutionary time, species diversity may increase in a community as more speciation events occur. Tropical communities are generally older than temperate or polar communities. This age difference stems partly from the fact that the growing season is about five times as long in tropical forests as in the tundra communities of high latitudes. In effect, biological time, and hence intervals between speciation events, run about five times as fast in the tropics as near the poles. And many polar and temperate communities have repeatedly "started over" as a result of major disturbances in the form of glaciations.

Climate is likely the primary cause of the latitudinal gradient in biodiversity. In terrestrial communities, the two main climatic factors correlated with biodiversity are solar energy input and water availability, both of which are relatively high in the tropics. These factors can be considered together by measuring a community's rate of **evapotranspiration**, the evaporation of water from soil plus the transpiration of water from plants. Evapotranspiration, a function of solar radiation, temperature, and water availability, is much higher in hot areas with abundant rainfall than in areas with low temperatures or low precipitation. *Potential evapotranspiration*, a measure of potential water loss that assumes that water is readily available, is determined by the amount of solar radiation and temperature and is highest in regions where both are plentiful. The species richness of plants and animals correlates with both measures of evapotranspiration **(Figure 54.25)**.

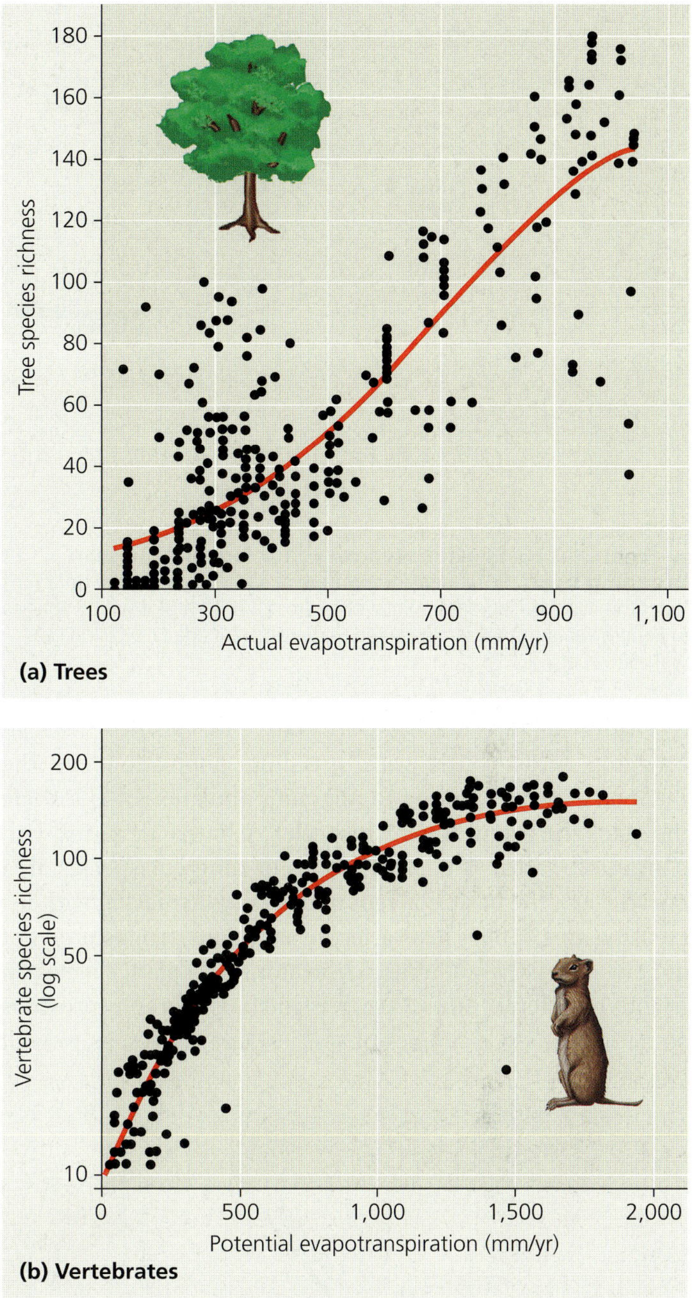

▲ **Figure 54.25 Energy, water, and species richness. (a)** Species richness of North American trees increases most predictably with actual evapotranspiration, while **(b)** vertebrate species richness in North America increases most predictably with potential evapotranspiration. Evapotranspiration values are expressed as rainfall equivalents.

Area Effects

In 1807, naturalist and explorer Alexander von Humboldt described one of the first patterns of biodiversity to be recognized, the **species-area curve**: All other factors being equal, the larger the geographic area of a community, the more species it has. The likely explanation for this pattern is that larger areas offer a greater diversity of habitats and microhabitats than smaller areas. In conservation biology, developing species-area curves for the key taxa in a community helps ecologists predict how the potential loss of a certain area of habitat is likely to affect the community's biodiversity.

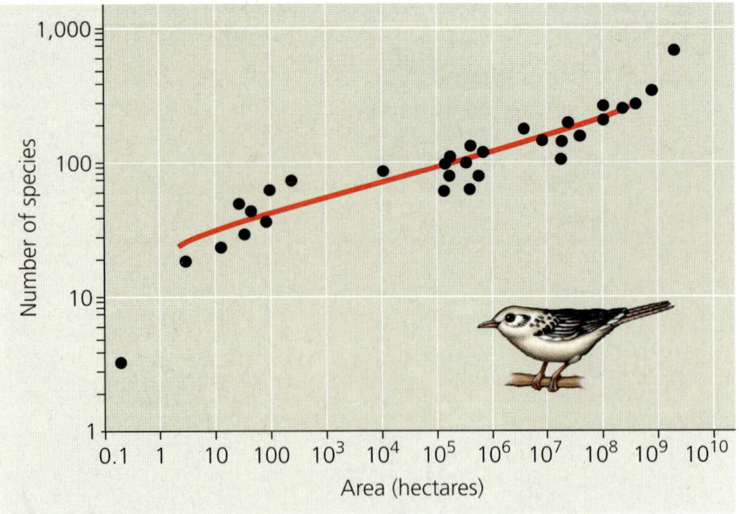

▲ **Figure 54.26 Species-area curve for North American breeding birds.** Both area and number of species are plotted on a logarithmic scale. The data points range from a 0.2-ha plot with 3 species in Pennsylvania to the whole United States and Canada (1.9 billion ha) with 625 species.

Figure 54.26 is a species-area curve for North American breeding birds (birds with breeding populations in the mapped area, as opposed to migrant populations). The slope indicates the extent to which species richness increases with community area. While the slopes of different species-area curves vary, the basic concept of diversity increasing with increasing area applies in a variety of situations, from surveys of ant diversity in New Guinea to the number of plant species on islands of different sizes. In fact, island biogeography provides some of the best examples of species-area curves, as we will discuss next.

Island Equilibrium Model

Because of their isolation and limited size, islands provide excellent opportunities for studying the biogeographic factors that affect the species diversity of communities. By "islands," we mean not only oceanic islands, but also habitat islands on land, such as lakes, mountain peaks separated by lowlands, or natural woodland fragments surrounded by areas disturbed by humans—in other words, any patch surrounded by an environment not suitable for the "island" species. In the 1960s, American ecologists Robert MacArthur and E. O. Wilson developed a general model of island biogeography identifying the key determinants of species diversity on an island with a given set of physical characteristics (**Figure 54.27**).

Consider a newly formed oceanic island that receives colonizing species from a distant mainland. Two factors that determine the number of species on the island are the rate at which new species immigrate to the island and the rate at which species become extinct on the island. At any given time, an island's immigration and extinction rates are affected by the number of species already present. As the number of species on the island increases, the immigration rate of new species decreases, because any individual reaching the island is less likely to represent a species that is not already present. At the same time, as more species inhabit an island, extinction rates on the island increase because of the greater likelihood of competitive exclusion.

Two physical features of the island further affect immigration and extinction rates: its size and its distance from the mainland. Small islands generally have lower immigration rates because potential colonizers are less likely to reach a small island. For instance, birds blown out to sea by a storm

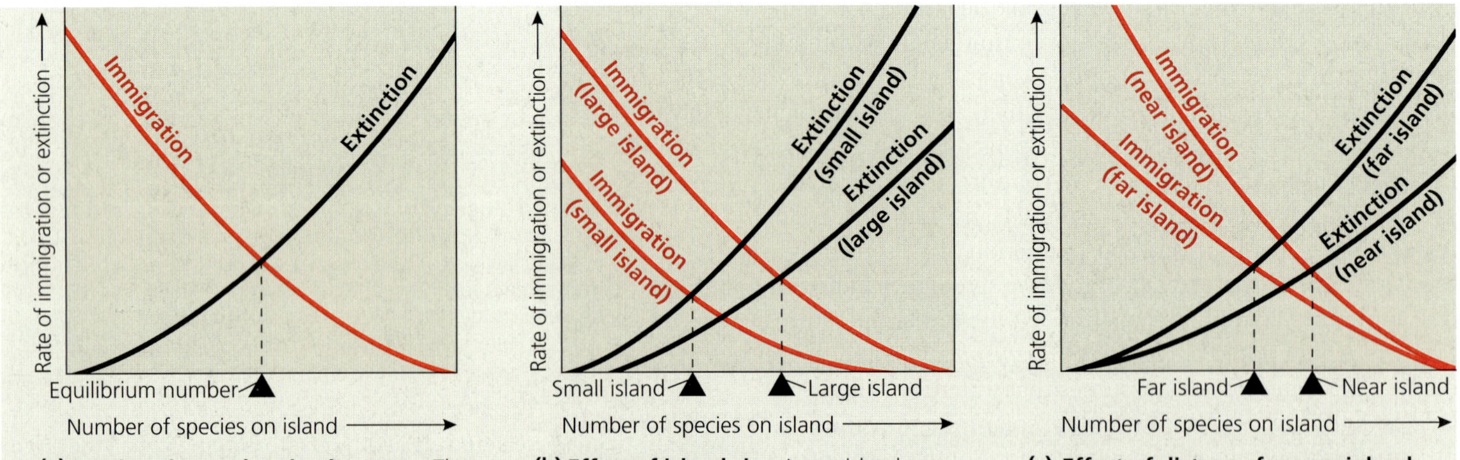

(a) Immigration and extinction rates. The equilibrium number of species on an island represents a balance between the immigration of new species and the extinction of species already there.

(b) Effect of island size. Large islands may ultimately have a larger equilibrium number of species than small islands because immigration rates tend to be higher and extinction rates lower on large islands.

(c) Effect of distance from mainland. Near islands tend to have larger equilibrium numbers of species than far islands because immigration rates to near islands are higher and extinction rates lower.

▲ **Figure 54.27 The equilibrium model of island biogeography.** Black triangles represent equilibrium numbers of species.

are more likely to land by chance on a larger island than on a small one. Small islands also have higher extinction rates, as they generally contain fewer resources and less diverse habitats for colonizing species to partition. Distance from the mainland is also important; for two islands of equal size, a closer island generally has a higher immigration rate than one farther away. Because of their higher immigration rates, closer islands also have lower extinction rates, as arriving colonists help sustain the presence of a species on a near island and prevent its extinction.

These relationships make up MacArthur and Wilson's model of island biogeography (see Figure 54.27). Immigration and extinction rates are plotted as a function of the number of species present on the island. This model is called the *island equilibrium model* because an equilibrium will eventually be reached where the rate of species immigration equals the rate of species extinction. The number of species at this equilibrium point is correlated with the island's size and distance from the mainland. Like any ecological equilibrium, this species equilibrium is dynamic; immigration and extinction continue, and the exact species composition may change over time.

MacArthur and Wilson's studies of the diversity of plants and animals on many island chains, including the Galápagos Islands, support the prediction that species richness increases with island size, in keeping with the island equilibrium model **(Figure 54.28)**. Species counts also fit the prediction that the number of species decreases with increasing remoteness of the island.

The island equilibrium model's predictions of equilibria in the species composition of communities may apply in only a limited number of cases and over relatively short periods, where colonization is the main process affecting species composition. Over longer periods, abiotic disturbances such as storms, adaptive evolutionary changes, and speciation generally alter the species composition and community structure on islands. Nonetheless, the model is widely applied in conservation biology, particularly for the design of habitat reserves and for providing a starting point for predicting the effects of habitat loss on species diversity.

CONCEPT CHECK 54.4

1. Describe two hypotheses that explain why species diversity is greater in tropical regions than in temperate and polar regions.
2. Describe how an island's size and distance from the mainland affect the island's species richness.
3. **WHAT IF?** Based on MacArthur and Wilson's model of island biogeography, how would you expect the richness of birds on islands to compare with the richness of snakes or mammals? Explain.

For suggested answers, see Appendix A.

▼ Figure 54.28 Inquiry

How does species richness relate to area?

FIELD STUDY Ecologists Robert MacArthur and E. O. Wilson studied the number of plant species on the Galápagos Islands, which vary greatly in size, in relation to the area of each island.

RESULTS

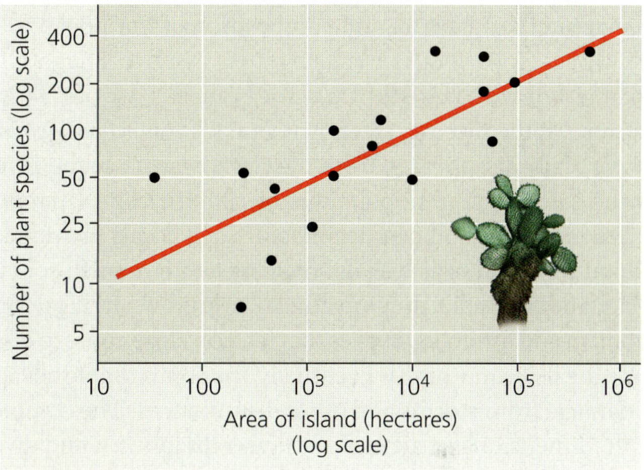

CONCLUSION Plant species richness increases with island size, supporting the island equilibrium model.

SOURCE R. H. MacArthur and E. O. Wilson, *The Theory of Island Biogeography*, Princeton University Press, Princeton, NJ (1967).

WHAT IF? Four islands in this study ranging in area from about 40 to 10,000 ha all contained about 50 plant species. What does such variation tell you about the simple assumptions of the island equilibrium model?

CONCEPT **54.5**

Community ecology is useful for understanding pathogen life cycles and controlling human disease

Now that we have examined several important factors that structure ecological communities, let's finish the chapter by examining community interactions involving **pathogens**—disease-causing microorganisms, viruses, viroids, or prions (viroids and prions are infectious RNA molecules and proteins, respectively; see Chapter 19). Scientists have recently come to appreciate how universal the effects of pathogens are in ecological communities. Pathogens can alter community structure quickly and extensively, as you saw in the discussion of chestnut blight and the fungus that causes it (see Concept 54.2). Ecologists are also applying ecological knowledge to help track and control the pathogens that cause human diseases.

Pathogens and Community Structure

In spite of the potential of pathogens to limit populations, pathogens have until recently been the subject of relatively few ecological studies. This imbalance is now being addressed as dramatic events highlight the ecological importance of disease.

Coral reef communities are increasingly susceptible to the influence of newly discovered pathogens. White-band disease, caused by an unknown pathogen, has resulted in dramatic changes in the structure and composition of Caribbean reefs. The disease kills corals by causing their tissue to slough off in a band from the base to the tip of the branches **(Figure 54.29)**. Because of the disease, staghorn coral (*Acropora cervicornis*) has virtually disappeared from the Caribbean since the 1980s. In the same region, populations of elkhorn coral (*Acropora palmata*) have also been decimated. Such corals provide key habitat for lobsters as well as snappers and other fish species. When the corals die, they are quickly overgrown by algae. Surgeonfish and other herbivores that feed on algae come to dominate the fish community. Eventually, the corals topple because of damage from storms and other disturbances. The complex, three-dimensional structure of the reef disappears, and diversity plummets.

Pathogens also influence community structure in terrestrial ecosystems. In the forests and savannas of California, trees of several species are dying from sudden oak death (SOD). This recently discovered disease is caused by the fungus-like protist *Phytophthora ramorum* (see Chapter 28). SOD was first described in California in 1995 when hikers noticed trees dying around San Francisco Bay. By 2007, it had spread more than 650 km. During that time, it killed more than a million oaks and other trees from the central California coast to southern Oregon. The loss of these oaks led to a decrease in the abundance of at least five bird species, including the acorn woodpecker and the oak titmouse, that rely on the oaks for food and habitat. Although there is currently no cure for SOD, scientists recently sequenced the genome of *P. ramorum* in hopes of finding a way to fight the pathogen.

▲ **Figure 54.29 White-band disease visible on a coral.**

One reason ecologists now study pathogens is that human activities are transporting pathogens around the world at unprecedented rates. Genetic analyses using simple sequence DNA (see Chapter 21) suggest that the fungus that causes SOD likely came from Europe through the horticulture trade. Similarly, the pathogens that cause human diseases are spread by our global economy. A person traveling by airplane can quickly introduce a pathogen to a new location; this mechanism may have been how the West Nile virus arrived in North America in 1999. Many diseases are becoming more common, and community ecology is needed to help study and combat them.

Community Ecology and Zoonotic Diseases

Three-quarters of today's emerging human diseases, including hantavirus and mad cow disease (see Chapter 19), and many historically important ones, such as malaria (see Chapter 28), are caused by **zoonotic pathogens**. Zoonotic pathogens are defined as those that are transferred from other animals to humans, either through direct contact with an infected animal or by means of an intermediate species, called a **vector**. The vectors that spread zoonotic diseases are often parasites, including ticks, lice, and mosquitoes. Community ecologists can help prevent zoonotic diseases by identifying key species interactions involving pathogens and their vectors and by tracking pathogen spread.

Understanding parasite life cycles enables scientists to devise ways to control zoonotic diseases. The disease river blindness, for instance, is caused by a nematode transmitted by blackflies. When the World Health Organization began a global fight against river blindness, doctors had no medical treatments for the disease. Scientists focused instead on controlling the blackflies that spread the pathogenic nematodes. They used airplanes to spray biodegradable insecticides (which were monitored to minimize harm to aquatic communities). Ivermectin, a drug that kills the nematodes, was developed in 1987, and since then the combination of vector control and ivermectin use has saved the sight of an estimated 300,000 people. However, research published in 2007 suggests that the nematodes are developing resistance to ivermectin, so blackfly control remains a key part of the program to fight the disease.

Ecologists also use their knowledge of community interactions to track the spread of zoonotic diseases. A timely example is ecological research on the spread of avian flu. Avian flu is caused by highly contagious viruses transmitted through the saliva and feces of birds (see Chapter 19). Most of these viruses affect wild birds mildly, but they often cause stronger symptoms in domesticated birds, the most common source of human infections. Since 2003, one particular viral strain, called H5N1, has killed hundreds of millions of poultry and more than 150 people. Millions more people are at risk of infection.

▲ **Figure 54.30 Tracking avian flu.** Graduate student Travis Booms, of the University of Alaska, Fairbanks, bands a young gyrfalcon (*Falco rusticolus*) as part of a project to monitor the spread of the disease.

Control programs that quarantine domestic birds or monitor their transport may be ineffective if avian flu spreads naturally through the movements of wild birds. From 2003 to 2006, the H5N1 strain spread rapidly from southeast Asia into Europe and Africa, but by late 2007 it had not appeared in Australia or the Americas. The most likely place for infected wild birds to enter the Americas is Alaska, the entry point for ducks, geese, and shorebirds that migrate across the Bering Sea from Asia each year. Ecologists are studying the potential spread of the virus by trapping and testing migrating and resident birds in Alaska **(Figure 54.30)**. These ecological detectives are trying to catch the first wave of the disease entering North America.

Community ecology provides the foundation for understanding the life cycles of pathogens and their interactions with hosts. Pathogen interactions are also greatly influenced by changes in the environment. To control pathogens and the diseases they cause, scientists need an ecosystem perspective—an intimate knowledge of how the pathogens interact with other species and with their environment. Ecosystems are the subject of Chapter 55.

CONCEPT CHECK 54.5

1. What are pathogens?
2. Some parasites require contact with at least two host species to complete their life cycle. Why might this characteristic be important for the spread of certain zoonotic diseases?
3. **WHAT IF?** Suppose a new zoonotic disease emerges from a tropical rain forest. Doctors have no way yet to treat the disease, so preventing infections is particularly important. As a community ecologist, how might you help prevent the spread of the disease?

For suggested answers, see Appendix A.

Chapter 54 Review

MEDIA Go to the Study Area at **www.masteringbio.com** for BioFlix 3-D Animations, MP3 Tutors, Videos, Practice Tests, an eBook, and more.

SUMMARY OF KEY CONCEPTS

CONCEPT 54.1

Community interactions are classified by whether they help, harm, or have no effect on the species involved (pp. 1198–1204)

▶ Populations are linked by interspecific interactions that affect the survival and reproduction of the species that engage in them. These interactions include competition, predation, herbivory, and symbiosis. Parasitism, mutualism, and commensalism are types of symbiotic interactions.

Interspecific Interaction	Description
Competition (−/−)	Two or more species compete for a resource that is in short supply. The competitive exclusion principle states that two species cannot coexist in the same community if their niches (ecological roles) are identical.
Predation (+/−)	One species, the predator, kills and eats the other, the prey. Predation has led to diverse adaptations, including mimicry.
Herbivory (+/−)	An herbivore eats part of a plant or alga. Plants have various chemical and mechanical defenses against herbivory, and herbivores have specialized adaptations for feeding.
Symbiosis	Individuals of two or more species live in close contact with one another. Symbiosis includes parasitism, mutualism, and commensalism.
Parasitism (+/−)	The parasite derives its nourishment from a second organism, its host, which is harmed.
Mutualism (+/+)	Both species benefit from the interaction.
Commensalism (+/0)	One species benefits from the interaction, while the other is unaffected by it.

MEDIA

Activity Interspecific Interactions
Biology Labs On-Line PopulationEcologyLab

CONCEPT 54.2

Dominant and keystone species exert strong controls on community structure (pp. 1204–1210)

- **Species Diversity** Species diversity measures the number of species in a community—its species richness—and their relative abundance. A community with similar abundances of species is more diverse than one in which one or two species are abundant and the remainder are rare.
- **Trophic Structure** Trophic structure is a key factor in community dynamics. Food chains link the trophic levels from producers to top carnivores. Branching food chains and complex trophic interactions form food webs. The energetic hypothesis suggests that the length of a food chain is limited by the inefficiency of energy transfer along the chain. The dynamic stability hypothesis proposes that long food chains are less stable than short chains.
- **Species with a Large Impact** Dominant species and keystone species exert strong controls on community structure. Dominant species are the most abundant species in a community, and their dominance is achieved by having high competitive ability. Keystone species are usually less abundant species that exert a disproportionate influence on community structure because of their ecological niche. Ecosystem "engineers," also called foundation species, exert influence on community structure through their effects on the physical environment.
- **Bottom-Up and Top-Down Controls** The bottom-up model proposes a unidirectional influence from lower to higher trophic levels, in which nutrients and other abiotic factors are the main determinants of community structure, including the abundance of primary producers. The top-down model proposes that control of each trophic level comes from the trophic level above, with the result that predators control herbivores, which in turn control primary producers.

MEDIA

Investigation How Are Impacts on Community Diversity Measured?
Activity Food Webs

CONCEPT 54.3

Disturbance influences species diversity and composition (pp. 1211–1214)

- **Characterizing Disturbance** More and more evidence suggests that disturbance and lack of equilibrium, rather than stability and equilibrium, are the norm for most communities. According to the intermediate disturbance hypothesis, moderate levels of disturbance can foster higher species diversity than can low or high levels of disturbance.
- **Ecological Succession** Ecological succession is the sequence of community and ecosystem changes after a disturbance. Primary succession occurs where no soil exists when succession begins; secondary succession begins in an area where soil remains after a disturbance. Mechanisms that produce community change during succession include facilitation and inhibition.
- **Human Disturbance** Humans are the most widespread agents of disturbance, and their effects on communities often reduce species diversity. Humans also prevent some naturally occurring disturbances, such as fire, which can be important to community structure.

MEDIA

Activity Primary Succession

CONCEPT 54.4

Biogeographic factors affect community biodiversity (pp. 1214–1217)

- **Latitudinal Gradients** Species richness generally declines along a latitudinal gradient from the tropics to the poles. The greater age of tropical environments may account for the greater species richness of the tropics. Climate also influences the biodiversity gradient through energy (heat and light) and water.
- **Area Effects** Species richness is directly related to a community's geographic size, a principle formalized in the species-area curve.
- **Island Equilibrium Model** Species richness on islands depends on island size and distance from the mainland. The island equilibrium model maintains that species richness on an ecological island reaches an equilibrium where new immigrations are balanced by extinctions. This model may not apply over long periods, during which abiotic disturbances, evolutionary changes, and speciation may alter community structure.

MEDIA

Activity Exploring Island Biogeography
GraphIt! Species-Area Effect and Island Biogeography

CONCEPT 54.5

Community ecology is useful for understanding pathogen life cycles and controlling human disease (pp. 1217–1219)

- **Pathogens and Community Structure** Recent work has highlighted the role that pathogens play in structuring terrestrial and marine communities.
- **Community Ecology and Zoonotic Diseases** Zoonotic diseases, caused by pathogens transferred from other animals to humans, are the largest class of emerging human diseases. Community ecology provides the framework for understanding the species interactions associated with such pathogens and for our ability to track and control their spread.

TESTING YOUR KNOWLEDGE

SELF-QUIZ

1. The feeding relationships among the species in a community determine the community's
   a. secondary succession.
   b. ecological niche.
   c. trophic structure.
   d. species-area curve.
   e. species richness.

2. The principle of competitive exclusion states that
   a. two species cannot coexist in the same habitat.
   b. competition between two species always causes extinction or emigration of one species.
   c. competition in a population promotes survival of the best-adapted individuals.
   d. two species that have exactly the same niche cannot coexist in a community.
   e. two species will stop reproducing until one species leaves the habitat.

3. Keystone predators can maintain species diversity in a community if they
   a. competitively exclude other predators.
   b. prey on the community's dominant species.
   c. allow immigration of other predators.
   d. reduce the number of disruptions in the community.
   e. prey only on the least abundant species in the community.

4. Food chains are sometimes short because
   a. only a single species of herbivore feeds on each plant species.
   b. local extinction of a species causes extinction of the other species in its food chain.
   c. most of the energy in a trophic level is lost as it passes to the next higher level.
   d. predator species tend to be less diverse and less abundant than prey species.
   e. most producers are inedible.

5. Based on the intermediate disturbance hypothesis, a community's species diversity is
   a. increased by frequent massive disturbance.
   b. increased by stable conditions with no disturbance.
   c. increased by moderate levels of disturbance.
   d. increased when humans intervene to eliminate disturbance.
   e. increased by intensive disturbance by humans.

6. Which of the following could qualify as a top-down control on a grassland community?
   a. limitation of plant biomass by rainfall amount
   b. influence of temperature on competition among plants
   c. influence of soil nutrients on the abundance of grasses versus wildflowers
   d. effect of grazing intensity by bison on plant species diversity
   e. effect of humidity on plant growth rates

7. The most plausible hypothesis to explain why species richness is higher in tropical than in temperate regions is that
   a. tropical communities are younger.
   b. tropical regions generally have more available water and higher levels of solar radiation.
   c. higher temperatures cause more rapid speciation.
   d. biodiversity increases as evapotranspiration decreases.
   e. tropical regions have very high rates of immigration and very low rates of extinction.

8. According to the equilibrium model of island biogeography, species richness would be greatest on an island that is
   a. small and remote.
   b. large and remote.
   c. large and close to a mainland.
   d. small and close to a mainland.
   e. environmentally homogeneous.

9. Community 1 contains 100 individuals distributed among four species (A, B, C, and D). Community 2 contains 100 individuals distributed among three species (A, B, and C).

   Community 1: 5A, 5B, 85C, 5D

   Community 2: 30A, 40B, 30C

   Calculate the Shannon diversity (*H*) for each community. Which community is more diverse?

10. **DRAW IT** Figure 54.13 presents a partial food web for the Chesapeake Bay estuary. Another important species in Chesapeake Bay is the blue crab (*Callinectes sapidus*). It is an omnivore, eating eelgrass and other primary producers as well as clams. Blue crabs are also cannibals. In turn, the crabs are a preferred food source for the endangered Kemp's Ridley sea turtle and, of course, for people. Based on this information, draw a food web that includes the blue crab. Assuming that the top-down model holds for this system, what would happen to the abundance of eelgrass if people were banned from catching crabs?

For Self-Quiz answers, see Appendix A.

MEDIA Visit the Study Area at **www.masteringbio.com** for a Practice Test.

EVOLUTION CONNECTION

11. Explain why adaptations of particular organisms to interspecific competition may not necessarily represent instances of character displacement. What would a researcher have to demonstrate about two competing species to make a convincing case for character displacement?

SCIENTIFIC INQUIRY

12. An ecologist studying plants in the desert performed the following experiment. She staked out two identical plots, each of which included a few sagebrush plants and numerous small annual wildflowers. She found the same five wildflower species in roughly equal numbers on both plots. She then enclosed one of the plots with a fence to keep out kangaroo rats, the most common grain-eaters of the area. After two years, four of the wildflower species were no longer present in the fenced plot, but one species had increased drastically. The control plot had not changed in species diversity. Using the principles of community ecology, propose a hypothesis to explain her results. What additional evidence would support your hypothesis?

SCIENCE, TECHNOLOGY, AND SOCIETY

13. By 1935, hunting and trapping had eliminated wolves from the United States except for Alaska. Because wolves have since been protected as an endangered species, they have moved south from Canada and have become reestablished in the Rocky Mountains and northern Great Lakes region. Conservationists who would like to speed up wolf recovery have reintroduced wolves into Yellowstone National Park. Local ranchers are opposed to bringing back the wolves because they fear predation on their cattle and sheep. What are some reasons for reestablishing wolves in Yellowstone National Park? What effects might the reintroduction of wolves have on the ecological communities in the region? What might be done to mitigate the conflicts between ranchers and wolves?

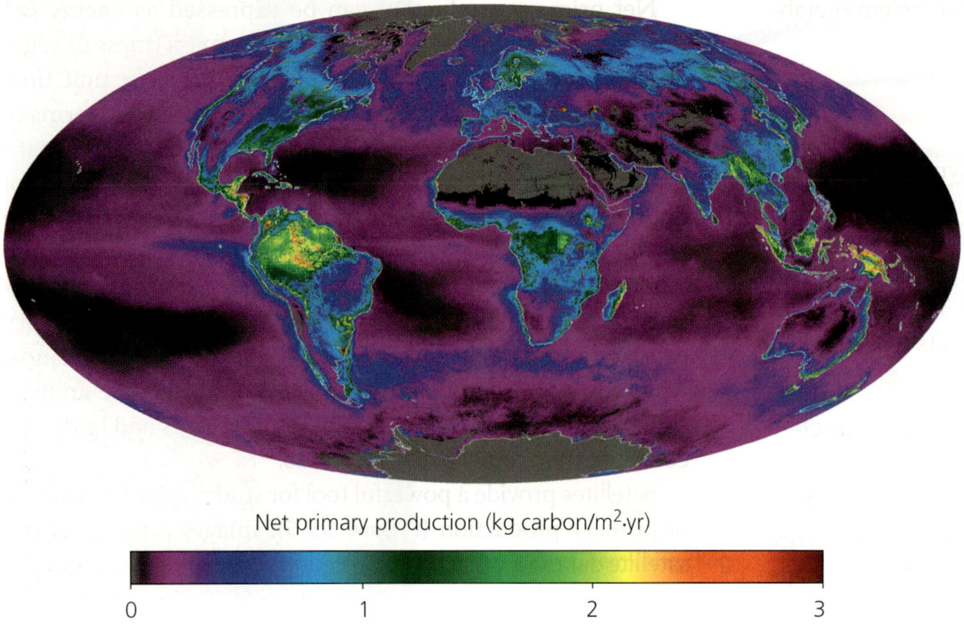

▲ **Figure 55.6 Global net primary production in 2002.** The map is based on data, such as chlorophyll activity, collected by satellites. Note that tropical areas on land have the highest rates of production (yellow and red on the map).

? *Does this global map accurately reflect the importance of some highly productive habitats, such as wetlands, coral reefs, and coastal zones? Explain.*

their net primary production **(Figure 55.6)**. Tropical rain forests are among the most productive terrestrial ecosystems and contribute a large portion of the planet's overall net primary production. Estuaries and coral reefs also have very high net primary production, but their contribution to the global total is relatively small because these ecosystems cover only about one-tenth the area covered by tropical rain forests. One striking aspect of Figure 55.6 is how unproductive the oceans are per unit area compared to tropical forests and some other ecosystems. Because of their vast size, however, the oceans altogether contribute as much global net primary production as terrestrial systems do.

What limits primary production in ecosystems? To ask this question another way, what factors could we change to increase or decrease primary production for a given ecosystem? We'll address this question first for aquatic ecosystems.

Primary Production in Aquatic Ecosystems

In aquatic (marine and freshwater) ecosystems, both light and nutrients are important in controlling primary production.

Light Limitation

Because solar radiation drives photosynthesis, you might expect that light is a key variable in controlling primary production in oceans. Indeed, the depth of light penetration affects primary production throughout the photic zone of an ocean or lake (see Figure 52.16). About half of the solar radiation is absorbed in the first 15 m of water. Even in "clear" water, only 5–10% of the radiation may reach a depth of 75 m.

If light were the main variable limiting primary production in the ocean, we would expect production to increase along a gradient from the poles toward the equator, which receives the greatest intensity of light. However, you can see in Figure 55.6 that there is no such gradient. Another factor must influence primary production in the ocean.

Nutrient Limitation

More than light, nutrients limit primary production in different geographic regions of the ocean and in lakes. A **limiting nutrient** is the element that must be added for production to increase. The nutrient most often limiting marine production is either nitrogen or phosphorus. Concentrations of these nutrients are very low in the photic zone because they are rapidly taken up by phytoplankton and because detritus tends to sink.

As detailed in **Figure 55.7**, nutrient enrichment experiments confirmed that nitrogen was limiting phytoplankton growth off the south shore of Long Island, New York. Practical applications of this work include preventing algal "blooms" caused by nitrogen pollution that fertilizes the phytoplankton. Eliminating phosphates from sewage, once thought to be the cause of the problem, will not help prevent algal blooms unless nitrogen pollution is also controlled.

Several large areas of the ocean, however, have low phytoplankton densities in spite of relatively high nitrogen concentrations. For example, the Sargasso Sea, a subtropical region of the Atlantic Ocean, has some of the clearest water in the world because of its very low density of phytoplankton. A series of nutrient enrichment experiments revealed that the availability of the micronutrient iron can limit primary production there **(Table 55.1)**. Windblown dust from the land is the main input of iron to the ocean, but relatively little windblown dust reaches the center of oceans.

The finding that iron limits production in some oceanic ecosystems encouraged marine ecologists to carry out recent large-scale experiments in the Pacific Ocean. In one study, researchers spread low concentrations of dissolved iron over 72 km^2 of ocean and then measured the change in phytoplankton density over a seven-day period. A massive phytoplankton bloom occurred, as indicated by increased chlorophyll concentration in the water. Adding iron stimulates growth of cyanobacteria that fix atmospheric nitrogen (see Chapter 27), and the extra nitrogen stimulates proliferation of phytoplankton.

Areas of upwelling, where nutrient-rich deep waters circulate to the ocean surface, have exceptionally high primary production, which supports the hypothesis that nutrient availability

▼ Figure 55.7 **Inquiry**

Which nutrient limits phytoplankton production along the coast of Long Island?

EXPERIMENT Pollution from duck farms concentrated near Moriches Bay adds both nitrogen and phosphorus to the coastal water off Long Island, New York. To determine which nutrient limits phytoplankton growth in this area, John Ryther and William Dunstan, of the Woods Hole Oceanographic Institution, cultured the phytoplankton *Nannochloris atomus* with water collected from several sites (labeled A–G on the map below). They added either ammonium (NH_4^+) or phosphate (PO_4^{3-}) to some of the cultures.

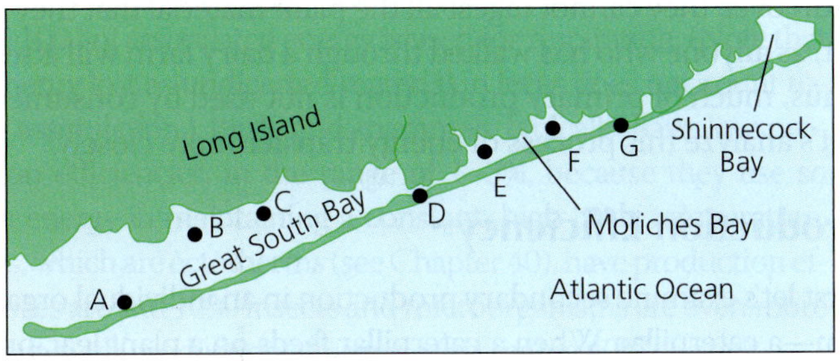

RESULTS The addition of ammonium caused heavy phytoplankton growth in the cultures, but the addition of phosphate did not.

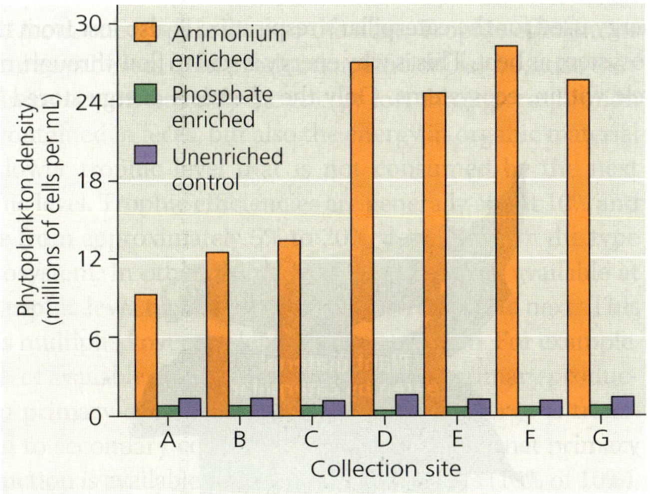

CONCLUSION Since adding phosphorus, which was already in rich supply, had no effect on *Nannochloris* growth, whereas adding nitrogen increased phytoplankton density dramatically, the researchers concluded that nitrogen is the nutrient that limits phytoplankton growth in this ecosystem.

SOURCE J. H. Ryther and W. M. Dunstan, Nitrogen, phosphorus, and eutrophication in the coastal marine environment, *Science* 171:1008–1013 (1971).

WHAT IF? How would you expect the results of this experiment to change if new duck farms substantially increased the amount of pollution in the water? Explain your reasoning.

Table 55.1 Nutrient Enrichment Experiment for Sargasso Sea Samples

Nutrients Added to Experimental Culture	Relative Uptake of ^{14}C by Cultures*
None (controls)	1.00
Nitrogen (N) + phosphorus (P) only	1.10
N + P + metals (excluding iron)	1.08
N + P + metals (including iron)	12.90
N + P + iron	12.00

*^{14}C uptake by cultures measures primary production.

Source: D. W. Menzel and J. H. Ryther, Nutrients limiting the production of phytoplankton in the Sargasso Sea, with special reference to iron, *Deep Sea Research* 7:276–281 (1961).

determines marine primary production. Because the steady supply of nutrients stimulates growth of the phytoplankton populations that form the base of marine food webs, upwelling areas are prime fishing locations. The largest areas of upwelling occur in the Southern Ocean (also called the Antarctic Ocean) and the coastal waters off Peru, California, and parts of western Africa.

Nutrient limitation is also common in freshwater lakes. During the 1970s, scientists showed that sewage and fertilizer runoff from farms and yards added large amounts of nutrients to lakes. Cyanobacteria and algae grow rapidly in response to these added nutrients, ultimately reducing the oxygen concentration and clarity of the water. This process, known as **eutrophication** (from the Greek *eutrophos*, well nourished), has many ecological impacts, including the eventual loss of all but the most tolerant fish species from the lakes (see Figure 52.18). Controlling eutrophication requires knowing which polluting nutrient is responsible; nitrogen is rarely the limiting factor for primary production in lakes. A series of whole-lake experiments conducted by ecologists showed that phosphorus availability limited cyanobacterial growth. This and other research led to the use of phosphate-free detergents and other important water quality reforms.

Primary Production in Terrestrial Ecosystems

On a large geographic scale, temperature and moisture are the main factors controlling primary production in terrestrial ecosystems. Note again in Figure 55.6 that tropical rain forests, with their warm, wet conditions that promote plant growth, are the most productive of all terrestrial ecosystems. In contrast, low-productivity terrestrial ecosystems are generally dry—for example, deserts—or cold and dry—for example, the arctic tundra. Between these extremes lie the temperate forest and grassland ecosystems, which have moderate climates and intermediate productivity. These contrasts in climate can be represented by a measure called **actual evapotranspiration**, have inverted biomass pyramids: Primary consumers outweigh the producers **(Figure 55.11b)**. Such inverted biomass pyramids occur because the producers—phytoplankton—grow, reproduce, and are consumed so quickly by the zooplankton that they never develop a large population size, or standing crop. In other words, the phytoplankton have a short **turnover time**, which means they have a small standing crop compared to their production:

$$\text{Turnover time} = \frac{\text{Standing crop (g/m}^2\text{)}}{\text{Production (g/m}^2\cdot\text{day)}}$$

Because the phytoplankton continually replace their biomass at such a rapid rate, they can support a biomass of zooplankton bigger than their own biomass. Nevertheless, because phytoplankton have much higher production than zooplankton, the pyramid of *production* for this ecosystem is still bottom-heavy, like the one in Figure 55.10.

The dynamics of energy flow through ecosystems have important implications for the human population. Eating meat is a relatively inefficient way of tapping photosynthetic production. A person obtains far more calories by eating grains directly as a primary consumer than by eating the same amount of grain fed to an animal. Worldwide agriculture could, in fact, successfully feed many more people and require less cultivated land if humans all fed more efficiently—as primary consumers, eating only plant material. Consequently, estimates of Earth's human carrying capacity (see Chapter 53) depend greatly on our diet and on the amount of resources each of us consumes.

The Green World Hypothesis

Earlier in this book, you learned why the world is green: Plants reflect more green light than red or blue light (see Figure 10.9). Land plants store approximately 70×10^{10} metric tons of carbon, and global terrestrial primary production is about 6×10^{10} metric tons per year. However, herbivores annually consume less than one-sixth the global NPP by plants **(Figure 55.12)**. Most of the rest is eventually consumed by detritivores. Thus, despite occasional outbreaks of pests, herbivores are generally only a minor nuisance to plants.

Why do herbivores consume such a small fraction of plants' net primary production? According to the **green world hypothesis**, terrestrial herbivores are held in check by a variety of factors. Plant defenses, such as spines or noxious chemicals (see Chapter 39), limit the success of herbivores. Low nutrient concentrations in plant tissues mean that large quantities of biomass are needed to support each herbivore. Other factors also limit the number of herbivores, including abiotic pressures, such as temperature and moisture extremes; intraspecific competition, including territorial behavior; and interspecific competition, particularly from predators, parasites, and pathogens (as in the top-down model of community structure, which you learned about in Chapter 54).

In the next section, we will look at how the transfer of nutrients along with energy through food webs is part of a larger picture of chemical cycling in ecosystems.

CONCEPT CHECK 55.3

1. If an insect that eats plant seeds containing 100 J of energy uses 30 J of that energy for respiration and excretes 50 J in its feces, what is the insect's net secondary production? What is its production efficiency?
2. Tobacco leaves contain nicotine, a poisonous compound that is energetically expensive for the plant to make. What advantage might the plant gain by using some of its resources to produce nicotine?
3. **WHAT IF?** As part of a new reality show on television, a group of overweight people are trying to safely lose in one month as much weight as possible. In addition to eating less, what could they do to decrease their production efficiency for the food they eat?

For suggested answers, see Appendix A.

▶ **Figure 55.12 A green ecosystem.** Most terrestrial ecosystems have large standing crops of vegetation despite the large number of resident herbivores. The green world hypothesis offers possible explanations for this observation.

CONCEPT 55.4

Biological and geochemical processes cycle nutrients between organic and inorganic parts of an ecosystem

Although most ecosystems receive an abundant supply of solar energy, chemical elements are available only in limited amounts. (The meteorites that occasionally strike Earth are the only extraterrestrial source of new matter.) Life on Earth therefore depends on the recycling of essential chemical elements. While an organism is alive, much of its chemical stock is replaced continuously as nutrients are assimilated and waste products released. When the organism dies, the atoms in its complex molecules are returned in simpler compounds to the atmosphere, water, or soil by the action of decomposers. Decomposition replenishes the pools of inorganic nutrients that plants and other autotrophs use to build new organic matter. Because nutrient cycles involve both biotic and abiotic components, they are called **biogeochemical cycles**.

Biogeochemical Cycles

An element's specific route through a biogeochemical cycle depends on the element and the trophic structure of the ecosystem. We can, however, recognize two general categories of biogeochemical cycles: global and local. Gaseous forms of carbon, oxygen, sulfur, and nitrogen occur in the atmosphere, and cycles of these elements are essentially global. For example, some of the carbon and oxygen atoms a plant acquires from the air as CO_2 may have been released into the atmosphere by the respiration of an organism in a distant locale. Other elements, including phosphorus, potassium, and calcium, are too heavy to occur as gases at Earth's surface. In terrestrial ecosystems, these elements cycle more locally, absorbed from the soil by plant roots and eventually returned to the soil by decomposers. In aquatic systems, however, they cycle more broadly as dissolved forms carried in currents.

Before examining the details of individual cycles, let's look at a general model of nutrient cycling that includes the main reservoirs of elements and the processes that transfer elements between reservoirs **(Figure 55.13)**. Each reservoir is defined by two characteristics: whether it contains organic or inorganic materials and whether or not the materials are directly available for use by organisms.

The nutrients in living organisms themselves and in detritus (reservoir A in Figure 55.13) are available to other organisms when consumers feed and when detritivores consume nonliving organic matter. Some material moved from the living organic reservoir to the fossilized organic reservoir (reservoir B) long ago, when dead organisms were converted to coal, oil, or peat (fossil fuels). Nutrients in these deposits generally cannot be assimilated directly.

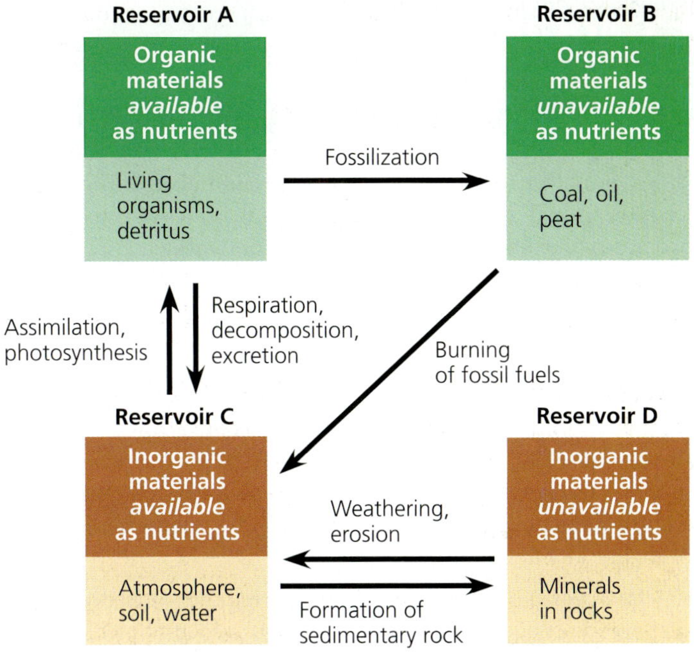

▲ **Figure 55.13 A general model of nutrient cycling.** Arrows indicate the processes that move nutrients between reservoirs.

? *Recent evidence suggests that mycorrhizal fungi can release acids that dissolve some minerals, including calcium phosphate. Where does this fungal activity fit into the model?*

Inorganic materials (elements and compounds) that are dissolved in water or present in soil or air (reservoir C) are available for use. Organisms assimilate materials from this reservoir directly and return chemicals to it through the relatively rapid processes of cellular respiration, excretion, and decomposition. Although most organisms cannot directly tap into the inorganic elements tied up in rocks (reservoir D), these nutrients may slowly become available through weathering and erosion. Similarly, unavailable organic materials move into the available reservoir of inorganic nutrients when fossil fuels are burned, releasing exhaust into the atmosphere.

How have ecologists worked out the details of chemical cycling in various ecosystems? Two common methods use isotopes—either by adding tiny amounts of radioactive isotopes of specific elements and tracking their progress or by following the movement of naturally occurring, nonradioactive isotopes through the biotic and abiotic components of an ecosystem. For example, scientists have been able to trace the flow into ecosystems of radioactive carbon (^{14}C) released into the atmosphere during atom bomb testing in the 1950s and early 1960s. This "spike" of ^{14}C can be used to date the age of bones and teeth, to measure the turnover rate of soil organic matter, and to follow changes in many other carbon pools in the environment.

Figure 55.14, on the next two pages, provides a detailed look at the cycling of water, carbon, nitrogen, and phosphorus. Examine these four biogeochemical cycles closely, considering the major reservoirs of each chemical and the processes that drive the movement of each chemical through its cycle.

▼ Figure 55.14

Exploring Nutrient Cycles

The Water Cycle

Biological importance Water is essential to all organisms (see Chapter 3), and its availability influences the rates of ecosystem processes, particularly primary production and decomposition in terrestrial ecosystems.

Forms available to life Liquid water is the primary physical phase in which water is used, though some organisms can harvest water vapor. Freezing of soil water can limit water availability to terrestrial plants.

Reservoirs The oceans contain 97% of the water in the biosphere. Approximately 2% is bound in glaciers and polar ice caps, and the remaining 1% is in lakes, rivers, and groundwater, with a negligible amount in the atmosphere.

Key processes The main processes driving the water cycle are evaporation of liquid water by solar energy, condensation of water vapor into clouds, and precipitation. Transpiration by terrestrial plants also moves significant volumes of water into the atmosphere. Surface and groundwater flow can return water to the oceans, completing the water cycle. The widths of the arrows in the diagram reflect the relative contribution of each process to the movement of water in the biosphere.

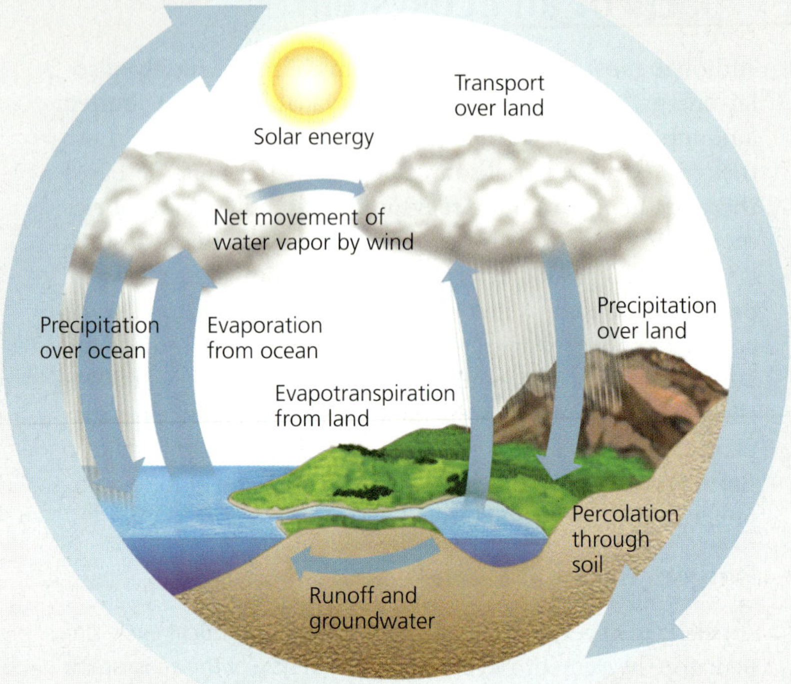

The Carbon Cycle

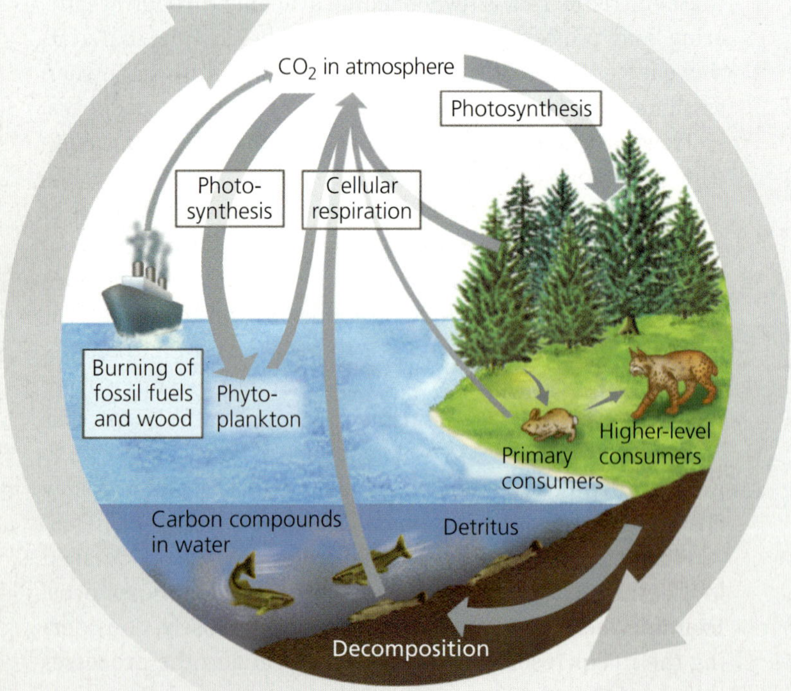

Biological importance Carbon forms the framework of the organic molecules essential to all organisms.

Forms available to life Photosynthetic organisms utilize CO_2 during photosynthesis and convert the carbon to organic forms that are used by consumers, including animals, fungi, and heterotrophic protists and prokaryotes.

Reservoirs The major reservoirs of carbon include fossil fuels, soils, the sediments of aquatic ecosystems, the oceans (dissolved carbon compounds), plant and animal biomass, and the atmosphere (CO_2). The largest reservoir is sedimentary rocks such as limestone; however, this pool turns over very slowly.

Key processes Photosynthesis by plants and phytoplankton removes substantial amounts of atmospheric CO_2 each year. This quantity is approximately equaled by CO_2 added to the atmosphere through cellular respiration by producers and consumers. Over geologic time, volcanoes are also a substantial source of CO_2. The burning of fossil fuels is adding significant amounts of additional CO_2 to the atmosphere. The widths of the arrows reflect the relative contribution of each process.

The Terrestrial Nitrogen Cycle

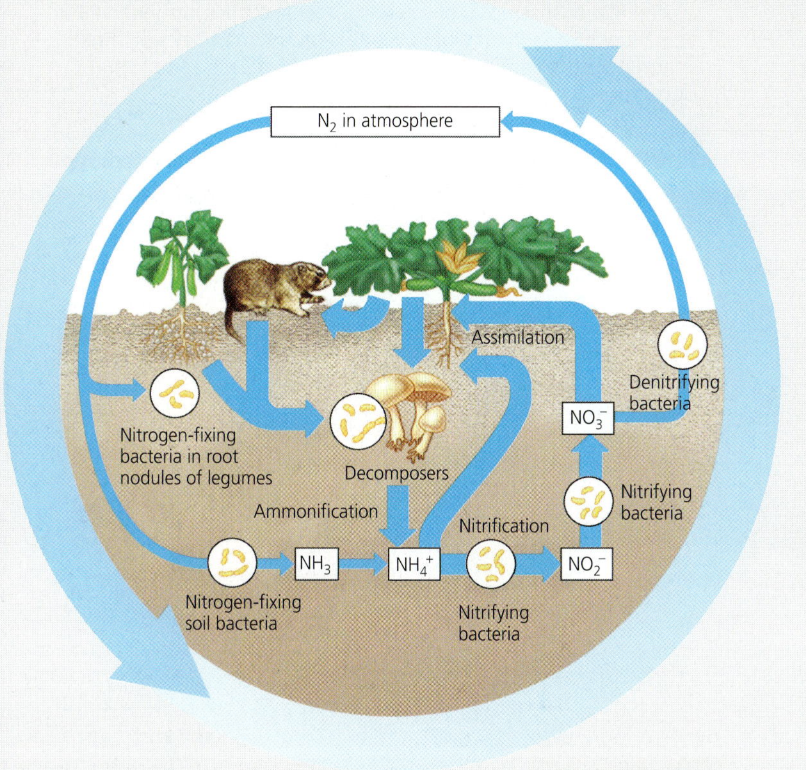

Biological importance Nitrogen is part of amino acids, proteins, and nucleic acids and is often a limiting plant nutrient.

Forms available to life Plants can use two inorganic forms of nitrogen—ammonium (NH_4^+) and nitrate (NO_3^-)—and some organic forms, such as amino acids. Various bacteria can use all of these forms as well as nitrite (NO_2^-). Animals can use only organic forms of nitrogen.

Reservoirs The main reservoir of nitrogen is the atmosphere, which is 80% nitrogen gas (N_2). The other reservoirs are soils and the sediments of lakes, rivers, and oceans (bound nitrogen); surface water and groundwater (dissolved nitrogen); and the biomass of living organisms.

Key processes The major pathway for nitrogen to enter an ecosystem is via *nitrogen fixation*, the conversion of N_2 by bacteria to forms that can be used to synthesize nitrogenous organic compounds (see Chapter 37). Some nitrogen is also fixed by lightning. Nitrogen fertilizer, precipitation, and blowing dust can also provide substantial inputs of NH_4^+ and NO_3^- to ecosystems. *Ammonification* decomposes organic nitrogen to NH_4^+. In *nitrification*, NH_4^+ is converted to NO_3^- by nitrifying bacteria. Under anaerobic conditions, denitrifying bacteria use NO_3^- in their metabolism instead of O_2, releasing N_2 in a process known as *denitrification.* The widths of the arrows reflect the relative contribution of each process.

The Phosphorus Cycle

Biological importance Organisms require phosphorus as a major constituent of nucleic acids, phospholipids, and ATP and other energy-storing molecules and as a mineral constituent of bones and teeth.

Forms available to life The most biologically important inorganic form of phosphorus is phosphate (PO_4^{3-}), which plants absorb and use in the synthesis of organic compounds.

Reservoirs The largest accumulations of phosphorus are in sedimentary rocks of marine origin. There are also large quantities of phosphorus in soils, in the oceans (in dissolved form), and in organisms. Because humus and soil particles bind phosphate, the recycling of phosphorus tends to be quite localized in ecosystems.

Key processes Weathering of rocks gradually adds PO_4^{3-} to soil; some leaches into groundwater and surface water and may eventually reach the sea. Phosphate taken up by producers and incorporated into biological molecules may be eaten by consumers and distributed through the food web. Phosphate is returned to soil or water through either decomposition of biomass or excretion by consumers. Because there are no significant phosphorus-containing gases, only relatively small amounts of phosphorus move through the atmosphere, usually in the forms of dust and sea spray. The widths of the arrows reflect the relative contribution of each process.

Decomposition and Nutrient Cycling Rates

The diagrams in Figure 55.14 illustrate the essential role that decomposers (detritivores) play in recycling carbon, nitrogen, and phosphorus. The rates at which these nutrients cycle in different ecosystems are extremely variable, mostly as a result of differences in rates of decomposition.

Decomposition is controlled by the same factors that limit primary production in aquatic and terrestrial ecosystems (see Concept 55.2). Those factors include temperature, moisture, and nutrient availability. Decomposers usually grow faster and decompose material more quickly in warmer ecosystems **(Figure 55.15)**. In tropical rain forests, for instance, most organic material decomposes in a few months to a few years, while in temperate forests, decomposition takes four to six years, on average. The difference is largely the result of the higher temperatures and more abundant precipitation in tropical rain forests.

Because decomposition in a tropical rain forest is rapid, relatively little organic material accumulates as leaf litter on the forest floor; about 75% of the nutrients in the ecosystem is present in the woody trunks of trees, and about 10% is contained in the soil. Thus, the relatively low concentrations of some nutrients in the soil of tropical rain forests result from a short cycling time, not from a lack of these elements in the ecosystem. In temperate forests, where decomposition is much slower, the soil may contain as much as 50% of all the organic material in the ecosystem. The nutrients that are present in temperate forest detritus and soil may remain there for fairly long periods before plants assimilate them.

Decomposition on land is also slower when conditions are either too dry for decomposers to thrive or too wet to supply them with enough oxygen. Ecosystems that are both cold and wet, such as peatlands, store large amounts of organic matter; decomposers grow poorly most of the year there, and net primary production greatly exceeds decomposition.

In aquatic ecosystems, decomposition in anaerobic muds can take 50 years or more. Bottom sediments are comparable to the detritus layer in terrestrial ecosystems; however, algae and aquatic plants usually assimilate nutrients directly from the water. Thus, the sediments often constitute a nutrient sink, and aquatic ecosystems are very productive only when there is interchange between the bottom layers of water and the surface (as in the upwelling regions described earlier).

Case Study: Nutrient Cycling in the Hubbard Brook Experimental Forest

In one of the longest-running ecological research experiments in North America, ecologists Herbert Bormann, Eugene Likens, and their colleagues have been studying nutrient cycling in a

▼ **Figure 55.15 Inquiry**

How does temperature affect litter decomposition in an ecosystem?

EXPERIMENT Researchers with the Canadian Forest Service placed identical samples of organic material on the ground in 21 sites across Canada (marked by letters on the map below). Three years later, they returned to see how much of each sample had decomposed.

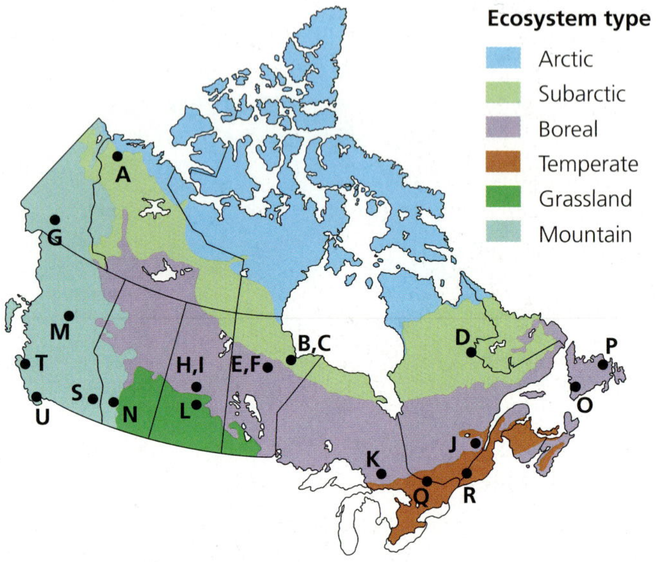

RESULTS Litter mass decreased four times faster in warmer ecosystems than in colder ones.

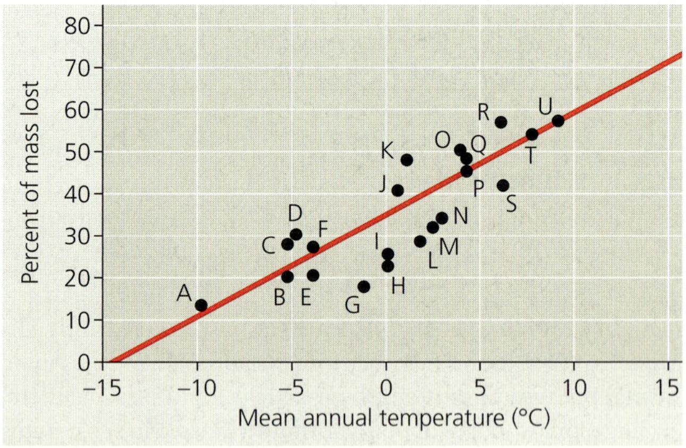

CONCLUSION Decomposition increases with temperature across much of Canada.

SOURCE T. R. Moore et al., Litter decomposition rates in Canadian forests, *Global Change Biology* 5:75–82 (1999).

WHAT IF? What factors other than temperature might also have varied across these 21 sites? How might this variation have affected the interpretation of the results?

forest ecosystem since 1963. Their study site, the Hubbard Brook Experimental Forest in the White Mountains of New Hampshire, is a deciduous forest with several valleys, each drained by a small creek that is a tributary of Hubbard Brook. Bedrock impenetrable to water is close to the surface of the soil, and each valley constitutes a watershed that can drain only through its creek.

The research team first determined the mineral budget for each of six valleys by measuring the input and outflow of several key nutrients. They collected rainfall at several sites to measure the amount of water and dissolved minerals added to the ecosystem. To monitor the loss of water and minerals, they constructed a small concrete dam with a V-shaped spillway across the creek at the bottom of each valley **(Figure 55.16a)**. About 60% of the water added to the ecosystem as rainfall and snow exits through the stream, and the remaining 40% is lost by evapotranspiration.

Preliminary studies confirmed that internal cycling within a terrestrial ecosystem conserves most of the mineral nutrients. For example, only about 0.3% more calcium (Ca^{2+}) left a valley via its creek than was added by rainwater, and this small net loss was probably replaced by chemical decomposition of the bedrock. During most years, the forest actually registered small net gains of a few mineral nutrients, including nitrogen.

In one experiment, the trees in one valley were cut down and then the valley was sprayed with herbicides for three years to prevent regrowth of plants **(Figure 55.16b)**. All the original plant material was left in place to decompose. The inflow and outflow of water and minerals in this experimentally altered watershed were compared with those in a control watershed. Over the three years, water runoff from the altered watershed increased by 30–40%, apparently because there were no plants to absorb and transpire water from the soil. Net losses of minerals from the altered watershed were huge. The concentration of Ca^{2+} in the creek increased 4-fold, for example, and the concentration of K^+ increased by a factor of 15. Most remarkable was the loss of nitrate, whose concentration in the creek increased 60-fold, reaching levels considered unsafe for drinking water **(Figure 55.16c)**.

This study demonstrated that the amount of nutrients leaving an intact forest ecosystem is controlled mainly by the plants. The effects of deforestation occur within a few months and continue as long as living plants are absent.

The 45 years of data from Hubbard Brook reveal some other trends. For instance, in the last half century, acid rain and snow have dissolved most of the Ca^{2+} in the forest soil, and the streams have carried it away. By the 1990s, the forest biomass at Hubbard Brook had stopped increasing, apparently because of a lack of Ca^{2+}. To test this idea, ecologists at Hubbard Brook began a massive experiment in 1998. They first established a control and an experimental watershed, which they monitored over two years before using a helicopter to add Ca^{2+} to the experimental watershed. By 2006, sugar maple trees growing in the Ca^{2+}-enriched location had higher Ca^{2+} concentrations in their foliage, healthier crowns, and

(a) Concrete dams and weirs built across streams at the bottom of watersheds enabled researchers to monitor the outflow of water and nutrients from the ecosystem.

(b) One watershed was clear-cut to study the effects of the loss of vegetation on drainage and nutrient cycling.

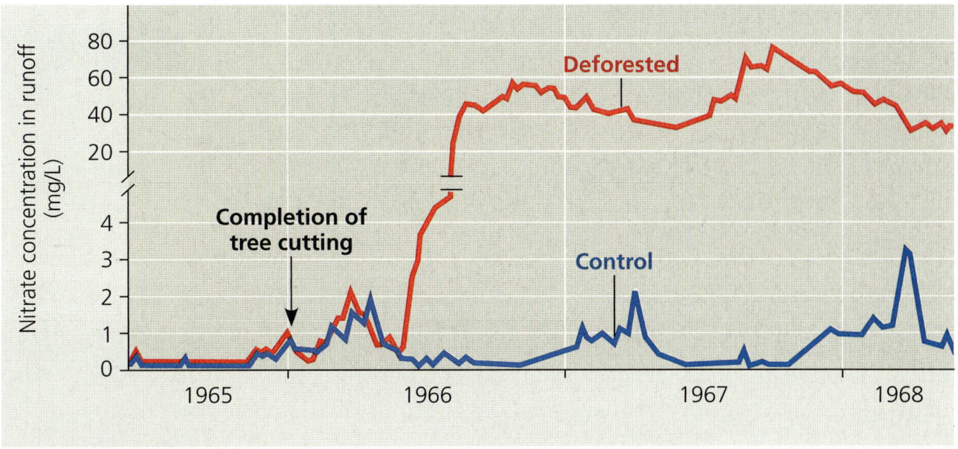

(c) The concentration of nitrate in runoff from the deforested watershed was 60 times greater than in a control (unlogged) watershed.

▲ **Figure 55.16 Nutrient cycling in the Hubbard Brook Experimental Forest: an example of long-term ecological research.**

greater seedling establishment than those growing in the control watershed. These data suggest that sugar maple declines in the northeastern United States and southern Canada are attributable at least in part to the consequences of soil acidification.

The Hubbard Brook studies, as well as many other long-term ecological research projects funded by the National Science Foundation, assess natural ecosystem processes and provide important insight into the mechanisms by which human activities affect these processes.

CONCEPT CHECK 55.4

1. **DRAW IT** For each of the four biogeochemical cycles detailed in Figure 55.14, draw a simple diagram that shows one possible path for an atom or molecule of that chemical from abiotic to biotic reservoirs and back.
2. Why does deforestation of a watershed increase the concentration of nitrates in streams draining the watershed?
3. **WHAT IF?** Why is nutrient availability in a tropical rain forest particularly vulnerable to logging?

For suggested answers, see Appendix A.

CONCEPT **55.5**

Human activities now dominate most chemical cycles on Earth

As the human population has grown rapidly in size (see Concept 53.6), our activities and technological capabilities have disrupted the trophic structure, energy flow, and chemical cycling of ecosystems. In fact, most chemical cycles are now influenced more by human activities than by natural processes.

Nutrient Enrichment

Human activity often removes nutrients from one part of the biosphere and adds them to another. On the simplest level, someone eating a piece of broccoli in Washington, DC, consumes nutrients that only days before were in the soil in California; a short time later, some of these nutrients will be in the Potomac River, having passed through the person's digestive system and a local sewage treatment facility. On a larger scale, nutrients in farm soil may run off into streams and lakes, depleting nutrients in one area, increasing them in another, and altering chemical cycles in both. Furthermore, humans have added entirely novel materials—some of them toxic—to ecosystems.

Humans have altered nutrient cycles so much that we can no longer understand any cycle without taking these effects into account. Let's examine a few specific examples of how humans are impacting the biosphere's chemical dynamics.

Agriculture and Nitrogen Cycling

After natural vegetation is cleared from an area, the existing reserve of nutrients in the soil is sufficient to grow crops for some time. In agricultural ecosystems, however, a substantial fraction of these nutrients is exported from the area in crop biomass. The "free" period for crop production—when there is no need to add nutrients to the soil—varies greatly. When some of the early North American prairie lands were first tilled, good crops could be produced for decades because the large store of organic materials in the soil continued to decompose and provide nutrients. By contrast, some cleared land in the tropics can be farmed for only one or two years because so little of the ecosystems' nutrient load is contained in the soil. Despite such variations, in any area under intensive agriculture, the natural store of nutrients eventually becomes exhausted.

Nitrogen is the main nutrient lost through agriculture; thus, agriculture has a great impact on the nitrogen cycle. Plowing mixes the soil and speeds up decomposition of organic matter, releasing nitrogen that is then removed when crops are harvested. Applied fertilizers make up for the loss of usable nitrogen from agricultural ecosystems **(Figure 55.17)**. In addition, as we saw in the case of Hubbard Brook, without plants to take up nitrates from the soil, the nitrates are likely to be leached from the ecosystem.

Recent studies indicate that human activities have more than doubled Earth's supply of fixed nitrogen available to primary producers. Industrial fertilizers provide the largest additional nitrogen source. Fossil fuel combustion also releases nitrogen oxides, which enter the atmosphere and dissolve in rainwater; the nitrogen ultimately enters ecosystems as nitrate. Increased cultivation of legumes, with their nitrogen-fixing symbionts, is a third way in which humans increase the amount of fixed nitrogen in the soil.

▲ **Figure 55.17 Fertilization of a corn (maize) crop.** To replace the nutrients removed in crops, farmers must apply fertilizers—either organic, such as manure or mulch, or synthetic, as shown here.

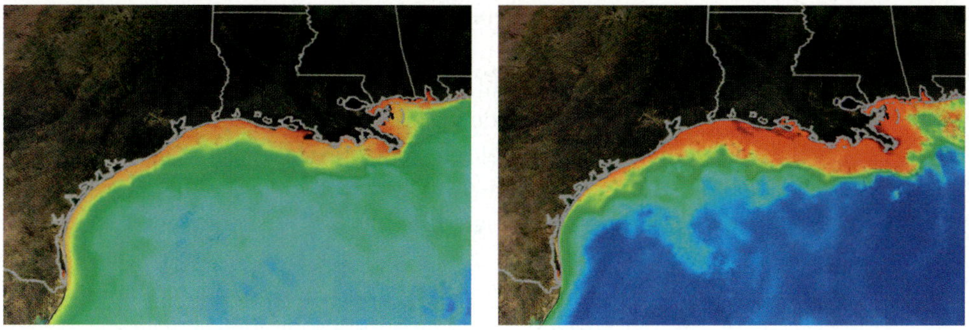

◀ **Figure 55.18 The dead zone arising from nitrogen pollution in the Mississippi basin.** In these satellite images from 2004, red and orange represent high concentrations of phytoplankton and river sediment in the Gulf of Mexico. This dead zone extends much farther from land in summer than in winter.

Contamination of Aquatic Ecosystems

The key problem with excess nutrients is the **critical load**, the amount of added nutrient, usually nitrogen or phosphorus, that can be absorbed by plants without damaging ecosystem integrity. For example, nitrogenous minerals in the soil that exceed the critical load eventually leach into groundwater or run off into freshwater and marine ecosystems, contaminating water supplies and killing fish. Nitrate concentrations in groundwater are increasing in most agricultural regions, sometimes exceeding safe levels for drinking.

Many rivers contaminated with nitrates and ammonium from agricultural runoff and sewage drain into the Atlantic Ocean, with the highest inputs coming from northern Europe and the central United States. The Mississippi River carries nitrogen pollution to the Gulf of Mexico, fueling a phytoplankton bloom each summer. When the phytoplankton die, their decomposition creates an extensive "dead zone" of low oxygen availability along the coast **(Figure 55.18)**. Fish, shrimp, and other marine animals disappear from some of the most economically important waters in the country. To reduce the size of the dead zone, farmers have begun using fertilizers more efficiently, and managers are restoring wetlands in the Mississippi watershed, two changes stimulated by the results of ecosystem experiments.

Nutrient runoff can also lead to the eutrophication of lakes, as you learned in Concept 55.2. The bloom and subsequent die-off of algae and cyanobacteria and the ensuing depletion of oxygen are similar to what occurs in a marine dead zone. Such conditions threaten the survival of organisms. For example, eutrophication of Lake Erie coupled with overfishing wiped out commercially important fishes such as blue pike, whitefish, and lake trout by the 1960s. Since then, tighter regulations on waste dumping into the lake have enabled some fish populations to rebound, but many native species of fishes and invertebrates have not recovered.

Acid Precipitation

The burning of wood and of fossil fuels, including coal and oil, releases oxides of sulfur and nitrogen that react with water in the atmosphere, forming sulfuric and nitric acid, respectively. The acids eventually fall to Earth's surface as acid precipitation—rain, snow, sleet, or fog that has a pH less than 5.2. Acid precipitation lowers the pH of streams and lakes and affects soil chemistry and nutrient availability. Although acid precipitation has been occurring since the Industrial Revolution, the emissions that cause it have increased during the past century, mainly from ore smelters and electrical generating plants.

Acid precipitation is a regional problem arising from local emissions. Smelters and generating plants are built with exhaust stacks more than 300 m high that reduce pollution at ground level but export it far downwind. Sulfur and nitrogen pollutants may drift hundreds of kilometers before falling as acid precipitation.

In the 1960s, ecologists determined that lake-dwelling organisms in eastern Canada were dying because of air pollution from factories in the midwestern United States. Lakes and streams in southern Norway and Sweden were losing fish because of acid rain from pollutants generated in Great Britain and central Europe. By 1980, the pH of precipitation in large areas of North America and Europe averaged 4.0–4.5 and occasionally dropped as low as 3.0.

In terrestrial ecosystems, such as the deciduous forests of New England, the change in soil pH due to acid precipitation causes calcium and other nutrients to leach from the soil (see the Hubbard Brook studies in Concept 55.4). The nutrient deficiencies affect the health of plants and limit their growth. Acid precipitation can also damage plants directly, mainly by leaching nutrients from leaves.

Freshwater ecosystems are particularly sensitive to acid precipitation. The lakes in North America and northern Europe that are most readily damaged by acid precipitation are those that have a low concentration of bicarbonate, an important buffer (see Chapter 3). Fish populations have declined in thousands of such lakes in Norway and Sweden, where the pH of the water has dropped below 5.0. In Canada, newly hatched lake trout, a keystone predator, die when the pH drops below 5.4. When the trout are replaced by acid-tolerant fish, the dynamics of food webs change dramatically.

Several large ecosystem experiments have been carried out to test the feasibility of reversing the effects of acid precipitation. One is the Ca^{2+} addition experiment at Hubbard Brook discussed earlier in this chapter. Another is a 17-year experiment

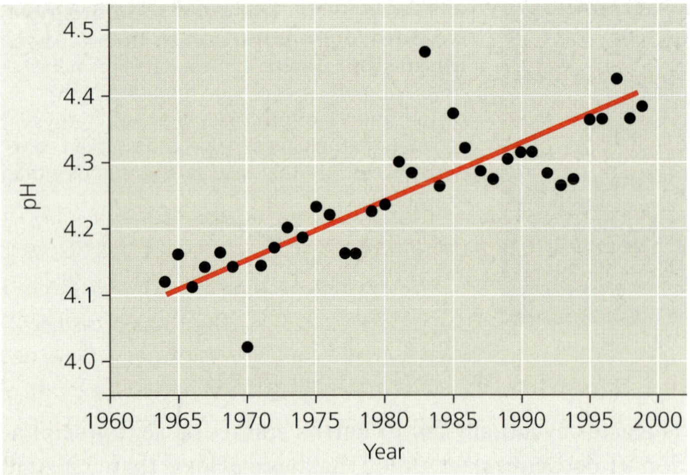

▲ **Figure 55.19 Changes in the pH of precipitation at Hubbard Brook.** Although still very acidic, the precipitation in this northeastern U.S. forest has been increasing in pH for more than three decades.

in Norway in which scientists built a glass roof over a forest and then showered the forest with precipitation from which acids had been removed. This "clean" precipitation quickly increased the pH and decreased the nitrate, ammonium, and sulfate concentrations in stream water in the forest. Results from this and other experiments helped convince leaders of more than 40 European nations to sign a treaty to reduce air pollution.

Environmental regulations and new industrial technologies have enabled many developed countries to reduce sulfur dioxide emissions during the past 40 years. In the United States, for example, sulfur dioxide emissions decreased 31% between 1993 and 2002. As a result, precipitation in the northeastern United States is gradually becoming less acidic **(Figure 55.19)**. However, ecologists estimate that it will take decades for aquatic ecosystems in this region to recover, even if sulfur dioxide emissions continue to decrease. Meanwhile, emissions of nitrogen oxides are increasing in the United States, and emissions of sulfur dioxide and acid precipitation continue to damage forests in central and eastern Europe.

Toxins in the Environment

Humans release an immense variety of toxic chemicals, including thousands of synthetic compounds previously unknown in nature, with little regard for the ecological consequences. Organisms acquire toxic substances from the environment along with nutrients and water. Some of the poisons are metabolized and excreted, but others accumulate in specific tissues, especially fat. One of the reasons accumulated toxins are particularly harmful is that they become more concentrated in successive trophic levels of a food web, a process called **biological magnification**. Magnification occurs because the biomass at any given trophic level is produced from a much larger biomass ingested from the level below (see Concept 55.3). Thus, top-level carnivores tend to be the organisms most severely affected by toxic compounds in the environment.

One class of industrially synthesized compounds that have demonstrated biological magnification are the chlorinated hydrocarbons, which include the industrial chemicals called PCBs (polychlorinated biphenyls) and many pesticides, such as DDT. Current research implicates many of these compounds in endocrine system disruption in a large number of animal species, including humans. Biological magnification of PCBs has been found in the food web of the Great Lakes, where the concentration of PCBs in herring gull eggs, at the top of the food web, is nearly 5,000 times that in phytoplankton, at the base of the food web **(Figure 55.20)**.

An infamous case of biological magnification that harmed top-level carnivores involved DDT, a chemical used to control insects such as mosquitoes and agricultural pests. In the decade after World War II, the use of DDT grew rapidly; its ecological consequences were not yet fully understood. By the 1950s, scientists were learning that DDT persists in the environment and is transported by water to areas far from where it is applied. One of the first signs that DDT was a serious en-

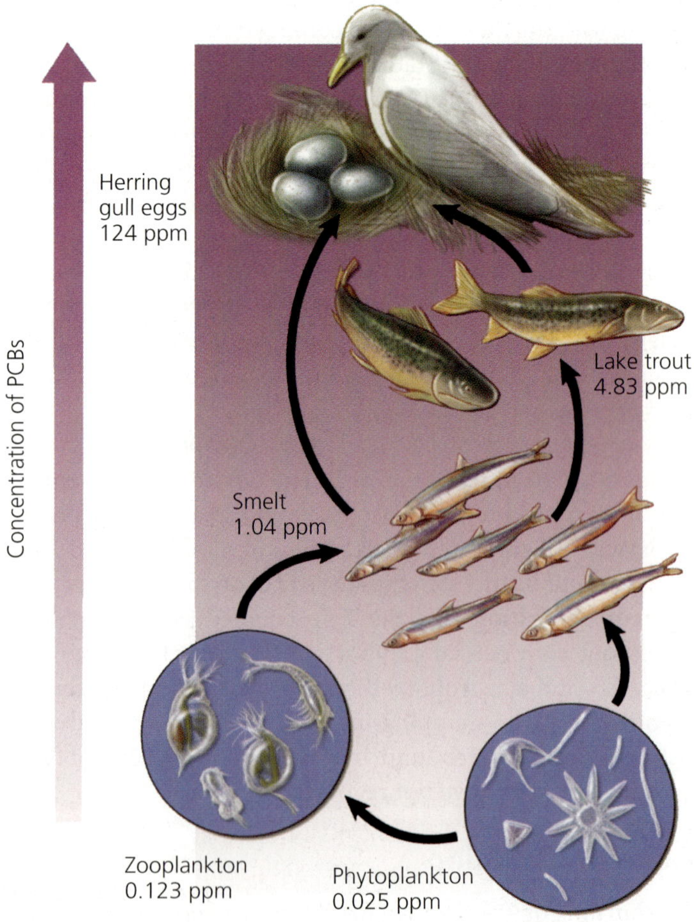

▲ **Figure 55.20 Biological magnification of PCBs in a Great Lakes food web.**

vironmental problem was a decline in the populations of pelicans, ospreys, and eagles, birds that feed at the top of food webs. The accumulation of DDT (and DDE, a product of its breakdown) in the tissues of these birds interfered with the deposition of calcium in their eggshells. When the birds tried to incubate their eggs, the weight of the parents broke the shells of affected eggs, resulting in catastrophic declines in the birds' reproduction rates. Rachel Carson's book *Silent Spring* helped bring the problem to public attention in the 1960s (see Chapter 52), and DDT was banned in the United States in 1971. A dramatic recovery in populations of the affected bird species followed.

In much of the tropics, DDT is still used to control the mosquitoes that spread malaria and other diseases. Societies there face a trade-off between saving human lives and protecting other species. The best approach seems to be to apply DDT sparingly and to couple its use with mosquito netting and other low-technology solutions. The complicated history of DDT illustrates the importance of understanding the ecological connections between diseases and communities (see Concept 54.5).

Many toxins cannot be degraded by microorganisms and persist in the environment for years or even decades. In other cases, chemicals released into the environment may be relatively harmless but are converted to more toxic products by reaction with other substances, by exposure to light, or by the metabolism of microorganisms. For example, mercury, a by-product of plastic production and coal-fired power generation, has been routinely expelled into rivers and the sea in an insoluble form. Bacteria in the bottom mud convert the waste to methylmercury (CH_3Hg^+), an extremely toxic soluble compound that accumulates in the tissues of organisms, including humans who consume fish from the contaminated waters.

Greenhouse Gases and Global Warming

Human activities release a variety of gaseous waste products. People once thought that the vast atmosphere could absorb these materials indefinitely, but we now know that such additions can cause fundamental changes to the atmosphere and to its interactions with the rest of the biosphere. In this section, we will examine how increasing atmospheric carbon dioxide concentration and global warming affect ecosystems. Although global warming will likely bring some benefits to people, it will also bring enormous costs to humans and to many other species on Earth.

Rising Atmospheric CO_2 Levels

Since the Industrial Revolution, the concentration of CO_2 in the atmosphere has been increasing as a result of the burning of fossil fuels and deforestation. Scientists estimate that the average CO_2 concentration in the atmosphere before 1850 was about 274 ppm. In 1958, a monitoring station began taking very accurate measurements on Hawaii's Mauna Loa peak, a location far from cities and high enough for the atmosphere to be well mixed. At that time, the CO_2 concentration was 316 ppm **(Figure 55.21)**. Today, it exceeds 380 ppm, an increase of about 40% since the mid-19th century. If CO_2 emissions continue to increase at the present rate, by the year 2075 the atmospheric concentration of this gas will be more than double what it was at the start of the Industrial Revolution.

Increased productivity by plants is one predictable consequence of increasing CO_2 levels. In fact, when CO_2 concentrations are raised in experimental chambers such as greenhouses, most plants grow faster. Because C_3 plants are more limited than C_4 plants by CO_2 availability (see Chapter 10), one effect of

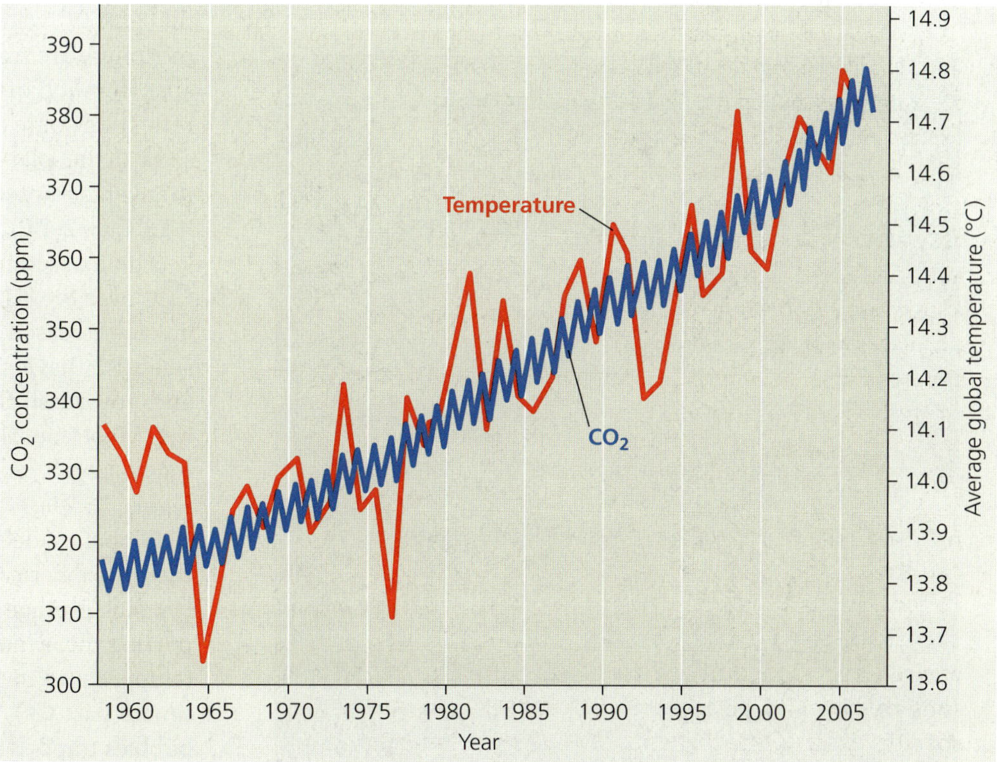

▲ **Figure 55.21 Increase in atmospheric carbon dioxide concentration at Mauna Loa, Hawaii, and average global temperatures.** Aside from normal seasonal fluctuations, the CO_2 concentration (blue curve) has increased steadily from 1958 to 2007. Though average global temperatures (red curve) fluctuated a great deal over the same period, there is a clear warming trend.

increasing global CO_2 concentration may be the spread of C_3 species into terrestrial habitats that currently favor C_4 plants. Such changes could influence whether corn (maize), a C_4 plant and the most important grain crop in the United States, will be replaced by wheat and soybeans, C_3 crops that could outproduce corn in a CO_2-enriched environment. To predict the gradual and complex effects of rising CO_2 levels on productivity and species composition, scientists are turning to long-term field experiments.

How Elevated CO_2 Levels Affect Forest Ecology: The FACTS-I Experiment

To assess how the increasing atmospheric concentration of CO_2 might affect temperate forests, scientists at Duke University began the Forest-Atmosphere Carbon Transfer and Storage (FACTS-I) experiment in 1995. The researchers are manipulating the concentration of CO_2 to which trees are exposed. The FACTS-I experiment includes six plots in an 80-hectare (200-acre) tract of loblolly pine within the university's experimental forest. Each plot consists of a circular area, approximately 30 m in diameter, ringed by 16 towers **(Figure 55.22)**. In three of the six plots, the towers produce air containing about 1½ times present-day CO_2 concentrations. Instruments on a tall tower in the center of each plot measure the direction and speed of the wind, adjusting the distribution of CO_2 to maintain a stable CO_2 concentration. All other factors, such as temperature, precipitation, and wind speed and direction, vary normally for both experimental plots and adjacent control plots exposed to atmospheric CO_2.

The FACTS-I study is testing how elevated CO_2 levels influence tree growth, carbon concentration in soils, insect populations, soil moisture, the growth of plants in the forest understory, and other factors. After ten years, trees in the experimental plots produced about 15% more wood each year than those in the control plots. This increased growth is important for timber production and carbon storage but is far lower than predicted from the results of greenhouse experiments. The availability of nitrogen and other nutrients apparently limits the ability of the trees to use the extra CO_2. Researchers at FACTS-I began removing this limitation in 2005 by fertilizing half of each plot with ammonium nitrate.

In most of the world's ecosystems, nutrients limit ecosystem productivity and fertilizers are unavailable. The results of FACTS-I and other experiments suggest that increased atmospheric CO_2 levels will increase plant production somewhat, but far less than scientists predicted even a decade ago.

▲ **Figure 55.22 Large-scale experiment on the effects of elevated CO_2 concentration.** Rings of towers in the Duke University Experimental Forest emit enough carbon dioxide to raise and maintain CO_2 levels 200 ppm above present-day concentrations in half of the experimental plots.

The Greenhouse Effect and Climate

Rising concentrations of long-lived greenhouse gases such as CO_2 are also changing Earth's heat budget. Much of the solar radiation that strikes the planet is reflected back into space. Although CO_2, water vapor, and other greenhouse gases in the atmosphere are transparent to visible light, they intercept and absorb much of the infrared radiation the Earth emits, re-reflecting some of it back toward Earth. This process retains some of the solar heat. If it were not for this **greenhouse effect**, the average air temperature at Earth's surface would be a frigid −18°C (−2.4°F), and most life as we know it could not exist.

The marked increase in the concentration of atmospheric CO_2 over the last 150 years concerns scientists because of its link to increased global temperature. For more than a century, scientists have studied how greenhouse gases warm Earth and how fossil fuel burning could contribute to the warming. Most scientists are convinced that such warming has already begun and will increase rapidly this century (see Figure 55.21).

Global models predict that by the end of the 21st century, the atmospheric CO_2 concentration will more than double, increasing average global temperature by about 3°C (5°F). Supporting these models is a correlation between CO_2 levels and temperatures in prehistoric times. One way climatologists estimate past CO_2 concentrations is to measure CO_2 levels in bubbles trapped in glacial ice, some of which are half a million years old. Prehistoric temperatures are inferred by several methods, including analysis of past vegetation based on fossils and the chemical isotopes in sediments and corals. An increase of only 1.3°C would make the world warmer than at any time in the past 100,000 years.

The ecosystems where the largest warming has *already* occurred are those in the far north, particularly northern coniferous forests and tundra. As snow and ice melt and uncover darker, more absorptive surfaces, these systems reflect less radiation back to the atmosphere and warm further. Arctic sea ice in the summer of 2007 covered the smallest area on record. Climate models suggest that there may be no summer ice there by the end of this century, decreasing habitat for polar bears, seals, and seabirds. Higher temperatures also increase the likelihood of fires. In boreal forests of western North America and Russia, fires have burned twice the usual area in recent decades.

A warming trend would also alter the geographic distribution of precipitation, making major agricultural areas of the central United States much drier, for example. However, the various mathematical models disagree about the details of how climate in each region will be affected. By studying how past periods of global warming and cooling affected plant communities, ecologists are trying to predict the consequences of future temperature changes. Analysis of fossilized pollen indicates that plant communities change dramatically with changes in temperature. Past climate changes occurred gradually, though, and plant and animal populations had time to migrate into areas where abiotic conditions allowed them to survive. Many organisms, especially plants that cannot disperse rapidly over long distances, may not be able to survive the high rates of climate change projected to result from global warming. Furthermore, many habitats today are much more fragmented than they were in the past (see Chapter 56), further limiting the ability of many organisms to migrate.

We will need many tools to slow global warming. Quick progress can be made in using energy more efficiently and in replacing fossil fuels with renewable solar and wind power and, more controversially, with nuclear power. Today, coal, gasoline, wood, and other organic fuels remain central to industrialized societies and cannot be burned without releasing CO_2. Stabilizing CO_2 emissions will require concerted international effort and the acceptance of changes in both personal lifestyles and industrial processes. Many ecologists think that effort suffered a major setback in 2001, when the United States pulled out of the Kyoto Protocol, a 1997 pledge by industrialized nations to reduce their CO_2 output by about 5%. Such a reduction would be a first step in the journey to stabilize atmospheric CO_2 concentrations.

Depletion of Atmospheric Ozone

Life on Earth is protected from the damaging effects of ultraviolet (UV) radiation by a layer of ozone molecules (O_3) located in the stratosphere 17–25 km above Earth's surface. However, satellite studies of the atmosphere show that the ozone layer has been gradually thinning since the mid-1970s **(Figure 55.23)**. The destruction of atmospheric ozone results mainly

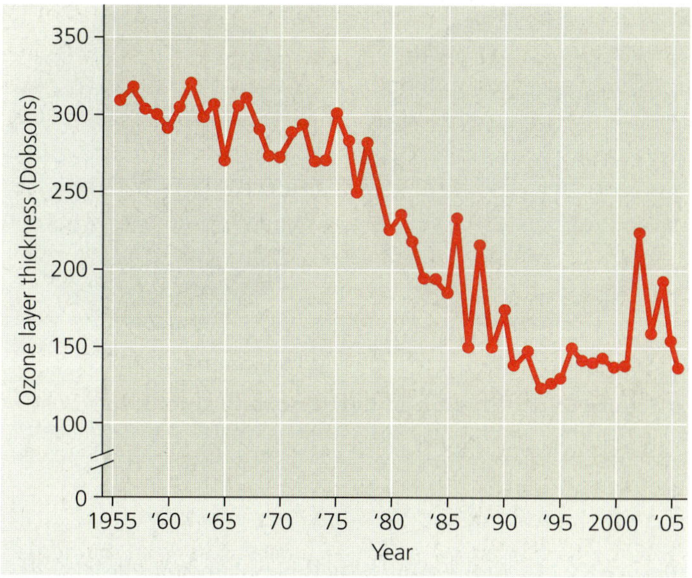

▲ **Figure 55.23 Thickness of the ozone layer over Antarctica in units called Dobsons.**

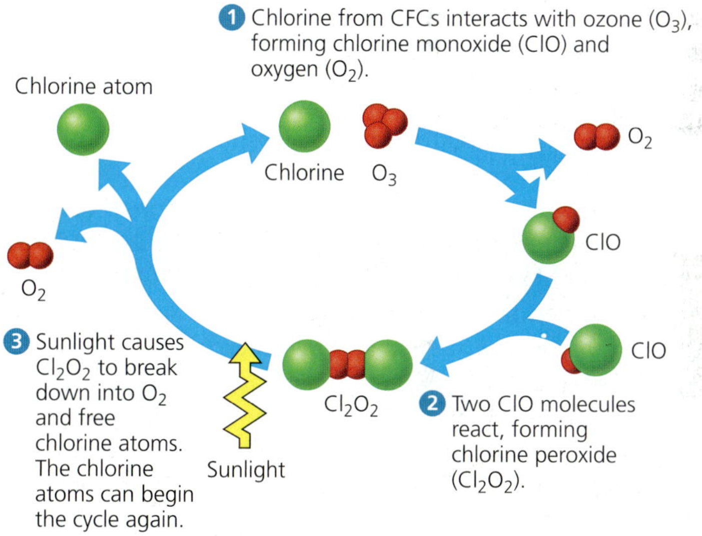

▲ **Figure 55.24 How free chlorine in the atmosphere destroys ozone.**

from the accumulation of chlorofluorocarbons (CFCs), chemicals used in refrigeration and in manufacturing. When the breakdown products from these chemicals rise to the stratosphere, the chlorine they contain reacts with ozone, reducing it to molecular O_2 **(Figure 55.24)**. Subsequent chemical reactions liberate the chlorine, allowing it to react with other ozone molecules in a catalytic chain reaction.

The thinning of the ozone layer is most apparent over Antarctica in spring, where cold, stable air allows the chain reaction to continue. The magnitude of ozone depletion and the size of the ozone hole have generally increased in recent years, and the hole sometimes extends as far as the southernmost portions of Australia, New Zealand, and South America

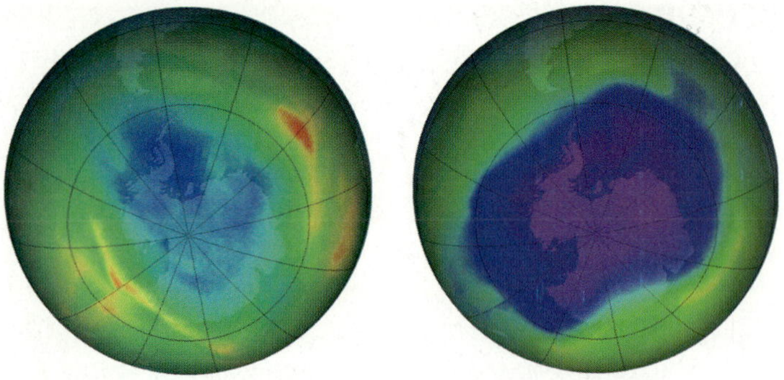

(a) September 1979 **(b) September 2006**

▲ **Figure 55.25 Erosion of Earth's ozone shield.** The ozone hole over Antarctica is visible as the dark blue patch in these images based on atmospheric data.

(Figure 55.25). At the more heavily populated middle latitudes, ozone levels have decreased 2–10% during the past 20 years.

Decreased ozone levels in the stratosphere increase the intensity of UV rays reaching Earth's surface. The consequences of ozone depletion for life on Earth may be severe for plants, animals, and microorganisms. Some scientists expect increases in both lethal and nonlethal forms of skin cancer and in cataracts among humans, as well as unpredictable effects on crops and natural communities, especially the phytoplankton that are responsible for a large proportion of Earth's primary production.

To study the consequences of ozone depletion, ecologists have conducted field experiments in which they use filters to decrease or block the UV radiation in sunlight. One such experiment, performed on a scrub ecosystem near the tip of South America, showed that when the ozone hole passed over the area, the amount of UV radiation reaching the ground increased sharply, causing more DNA damage in plants that were not protected by filters. Scientists have shown similar DNA damage and a reduction in phytoplankton growth when the ozone hole opens over the Southern Ocean each year.

The good news about the ozone hole is how quickly many countries have responded to it. Since 1987, approximately 190 nations, including the United States, have signed the Montreal Protocol, a treaty that regulates the use of ozone-depleting chemicals. Many nations, again including the United States, have ended the production of CFCs. As a consequence of these actions, chlorine concentrations in the stratosphere have stabilized and ozone depletion is slowing. Even if all CFCs were globally banned today, however, chlorine molecules that are already in the atmosphere would continue to influence stratospheric ozone levels for at least 50 years.

The partial destruction of Earth's ozone shield is one more example of how much humans have been able to disrupt the dynamics of ecosystems and the biosphere. It also highlights our ability to solve environmental problems when we set our minds to it. In this book's final chapter, we will explore how scientists in the fields of conservation biology and restoration ecology are studying the effects of human activities on Earth's biodiversity and are using ecological knowledge to reduce those effects.

CONCEPT CHECK 55.5

1. How can the addition of excess nutrients to a lake threaten its fish population?
2. In the face of biological magnification of toxins, is it healthier to feed at a lower or higher trophic level? Explain.
3. **WHAT IF?** There are vast stores of organic matter in the soils of northern coniferous forests and tundra around the world. Based on what you learned about decomposition from Figure 55.15, suggest an explanation for why scientists who study global warming are closely monitoring these stores.

For suggested answers, see Appendix A.

Chapter 55 Review

SUMMARY OF KEY CONCEPTS

CONCEPT 55.1

Physical laws govern energy flow and chemical cycling in ecosystems (pp. 1223–1224)

- **Conservation of Energy** An ecosystem consists of all the organisms in a community and all the abiotic factors with which they interact. The laws of physics and chemistry apply to ecosystems, particularly in regard to the flow of energy. Energy is conserved but degraded to heat during ecosystem processes.
- **Conservation of Mass** Ecologists study how much of a chemical element enters and leaves an ecosystem and cycles within it. Inputs and outputs are generally small compared to recycled amounts, but their balance determines whether the ecosystem gains or loses an element over time.

▶ Energy, Mass, and Trophic Levels

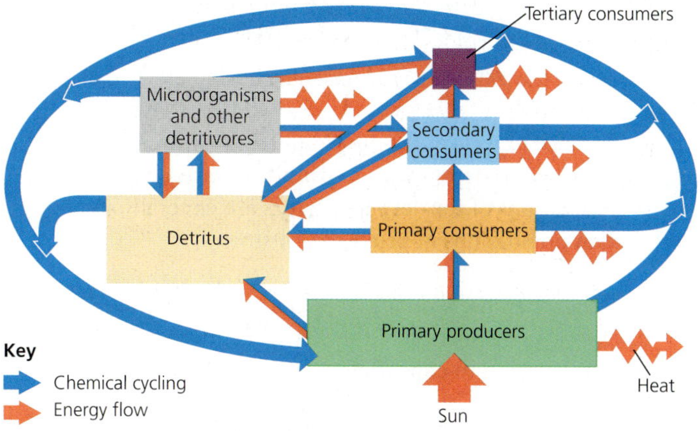

CONCEPT 55.2

Energy and other limiting factors control primary production in ecosystems (pp. 1224–1228)

▶ **Ecosystem Energy Budgets** Primary production sets the spending limit for the global energy budget. Gross primary production is the total energy assimilated by an ecosystem in a given period. Net primary production, the energy accumulated in autotroph biomass, equals gross primary production minus the energy used by the primary producers for respiration. Only net primary production is available to consumers.

▶ **Primary Production in Aquatic Ecosystems** In marine and freshwater ecosystems, light and nutrients limit primary production. Within the photic zone, the factor that most often limits primary production is a nutrient such as nitrogen, phosphorus, or iron.

▶ **Primary Production in Terrestrial Ecosystems** In terrestrial ecosystems, climatic factors such as temperature and moisture affect primary production on a large geographic scale. More locally, a soil nutrient is often the limiting factor in primary production.

MEDIA

Investigation How Do Temperature and Light Affect Primary Production?

CONCEPT 55.3

Energy transfer between trophic levels is typically only 10% efficient (pp. 1228–1230)

▶ **Production Efficiency** The amount of energy available to each trophic level is determined by the net primary production and the efficiency with which food energy is converted to biomass at each link in the food chain. The percentage of energy transferred from one trophic level to the next, called trophic efficiency, is generally 5–20%, with 10% being the typical value. Pyramids of net production and biomass reflect low trophic efficiency.

▶ **The Green World Hypothesis** According to the green world hypothesis, herbivores consume only a small percentage of vegetation because predators, pathogens, competition, nutrient limitations, and other factors keep their populations in check.

MEDIA

Activity Pyramids of Production
GraphIt! Animal Food Production Efficiency and Food Policy
MP3 Tutor Energy Flow in Ecosystems

CONCEPT 55.4

Biological and geochemical processes cycle nutrients between organic and inorganic parts of an ecosystem (pp. 1231–1236)

▶ **Biogeochemical Cycles**

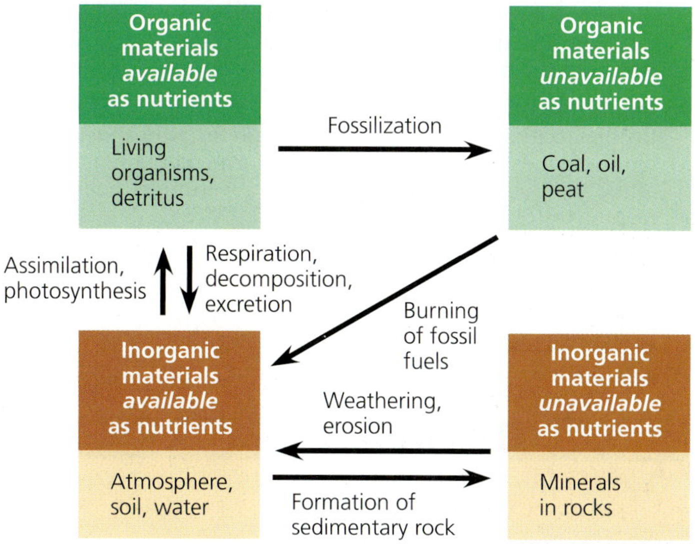

Water moves in a global cycle driven by solar energy. The carbon cycle primarily reflects the reciprocal processes of photosynthesis and cellular respiration. Nitrogen enters ecosystems through atmospheric deposition and nitrogen fixation by prokaryotes, but most of the nitrogen cycling in natural ecosystems involves local cycles between organisms and soil or water. The phosphorus cycle is relatively localized.

▶ **Decomposition and Nutrient Cycling Rates** The proportion of a nutrient in a particular form and its cycling time in that form vary among ecosystems, largely because of differences in the rate of decomposition.

▶ ***Case Study*: Nutrient Cycling in the Hubbard Brook Experimental Forest** Nutrient cycling is strongly regulated by vegetation. The Hubbard Brook study showed that logging increases water runoff and can cause large losses of minerals. It also demonstrated the importance of long-term ecological measurements in documenting the occurrence of and recovery from environmental problems.

MEDIA

Activity Energy Flow and Chemical Cycling
Activity The Carbon Cycle
Activity The Nitrogen Cycle

CONCEPT 55.5

Human activities now dominate most chemical cycles on Earth (pp. 1236–1242)

▶ **Nutrient Enrichment** Agriculture removes nutrients from ecosystems, so large supplements are usually required. The nutrients in fertilizer can pollute groundwater and surface-water aquatic ecosystems, where they can stimulate excess algal growth (eutrophication).

▶ **Acid Precipitation** Burning of fossil fuels is the main cause of acid precipitation. North American and European ecosystems downwind from industrial regions have been damaged by rain and snow containing nitric acid and sulfuric acid.

▶ **Toxins in the Environment** Toxins can become concentrated in successive trophic levels of food webs. The release of toxic wastes has polluted the environment with harmful substances that often persist for long periods and become concentrated along the food chain by biological magnification.

▶ **Greenhouse Gases and Global Warming** Because of the burning of wood and fossil fuels and other human activities, the atmospheric concentration of CO_2 has been steadily increasing. The ultimate effects include significant global warming and other climate changes.

▶ **Depletion of Atmospheric Ozone** The ozone layer reduces the penetration of UV radiation through the atmosphere. Human activities, including release of chlorine-containing pollutants, are eroding the ozone layer, but government policies are helping to solve the problem.

MEDIA

Activity Water Pollution from Nitrates
Activity The Greenhouse Effect
GraphIt! Atmospheric CO_2 and Temperature Changes
MP3 Tutor Global Warming

TESTING YOUR KNOWLEDGE

SELF-QUIZ

1. Which of the following organisms is *incorrectly* paired with its trophic level?
   a. cyanobacterium—primary producer
   b. grasshopper—primary consumer
   c. zooplankton—primary producer
   d. eagle—tertiary consumer
   e. fungus—detritivore

2. Which of these ecosystems has the *lowest* net primary production per square meter?
   a. a salt marsh
   b. an open ocean
   c. a coral reef
   d. a grassland
   e. a tropical rain forest

3. Nitrifying bacteria participate in the nitrogen cycle mainly by
   a. converting nitrogen gas to ammonia.
   b. releasing ammonium from organic compounds, thus returning it to the soil.
   c. converting ammonia to nitrogen gas, which returns to the atmosphere.
   d. converting ammonium to nitrate, which plants absorb.
   e. incorporating nitrogen into amino acids and organic compounds.

4. Which of the following has the greatest effect on the rate of chemical cycling in an ecosystem?
   a. the ecosystem's rate of primary production
   b. the production efficiency of the ecosystem's consumers
   c. the rate of decomposition in the ecosystem
   d. the trophic efficiency of the ecosystem
   e. the location of the nutrient reservoirs in the ecosystem

5. The Hubbard Brook watershed deforestation experiment yielded all of the following results *except* that
   a. most minerals were recycled within a forest ecosystem.
   b. the flow of minerals out of a natural watershed was offset by minerals flowing in.
   c. deforestation increased water runoff.
   d. the nitrate concentration in waters draining the deforested area became dangerously high.
   e. calcium levels remained high in the soil of deforested areas.

6. Which of the following is a consequence of biological magnification?
   a. Toxic chemicals in the environment pose greater risk to top-level predators than to primary consumers.
   b. Populations of top-level predators are generally smaller than populations of primary consumers.
   c. The biomass of producers in an ecosystem is generally higher than the biomass of primary consumers.
   d. Only a small portion of the energy captured by producers is transferred to consumers.
   e. The amount of biomass in the producer level of an ecosystem decreases if the producer turnover time increases.

7. The main cause of the increase in the amount of CO_2 in Earth's atmosphere over the past 150 years is
   a. increased worldwide primary production.
   b. increased worldwide standing crop.
   c. an increase in the amount of infrared radiation absorbed by the atmosphere.
   d. the burning of larger amounts of wood and fossil fuels.
   e. additional respiration by the rapidly growing human population.

8. **DRAW IT** Using Figure 55.21 as a starting point, extend the x-axis to the year 2100. Then extend the CO_2 curve, assuming that the CO_2 concentration continues to rise as fast as it did from 1974 to 2007. What will be the approximate CO_2 concentration in 2100? What ecological factors and human decisions will influence the actual rise in CO_2 concentration? How might additional scientific data help societies predict this value?

For Self-Quiz answers, see Appendix A.

MEDIA Visit the Study Area at **www.masteringbio.com** for a Practice Test.

EVOLUTION CONNECTION

9. Some biologists have suggested that ecosystems are emergent, "living" systems capable of evolving. One manifestation of this idea is environmentalist James Lovelock's Gaia hypothesis, which views Earth itself as a living, homeostatic entity—a kind of superorganism. Use the principles of evolution you have learned in this book to critique the idea that ecosystems and the biosphere can evolve. If ecosystems are capable of evolving, is this a form of Darwinian evolution? Why or why not?

SCIENTIFIC INQUIRY

10. Using two neighboring ponds in a forest as your study site, design a controlled experiment to measure the effect of falling leaves on net primary production in a pond.

Biological Inquiry: A Workbook of Investigative Cases Explore how changes to the Chesapeake affect shellfishing with the case "Back to the Bay."

56 Conservation Biology and Restoration Ecology

▲ **Figure 56.1 What will be the fate of this newly described bird species?**

KEY CONCEPTS

56.1 Human activities threaten Earth's biodiversity
56.2 Population conservation focuses on population size, genetic diversity, and critical habitat
56.3 Landscape and regional conservation aim to sustain entire biotas
56.4 Restoration ecology attempts to restore degraded ecosystems to a more natural state
56.5 Sustainable development seeks to improve the human condition while conserving biodiversity

OVERVIEW

Striking Gold

Tucking its wings, a bird lands on a branch deep inside a tropical jungle. Sensing the motion, a conservation biologist scans the branch through binoculars, a glimpse of golden orange stopping her short. Staring back is a smoky honeyeater, a species that had never been described before **(Figure 56.1)**. In 2005, a team of American, Indonesian, and Australian biologists experienced many moments like this as they spent a month cataloging the living riches hidden in a remote mountain range in Indonesia. In addition to the honeyeater, they discovered dozens of new frog, butterfly, and plant species, including five new palms.

To date, scientists have described and formally named about 1.8 million species of organisms. Some biologists think that about 10 million more species currently exist; others estimate the number to be as high as 100 million. Some of the greatest concentrations of species are found in the tropics. Unfortunately, tropical forests are being cleared at an alarming rate to make room for and support a burgeoning human population. Rates of deforestation in Indonesia are among the highest in the world **(Figure 56.2)**. What will become of the smoky honeyeater and other newly discovered species in Indonesia if such deforestation continues unchecked?

Throughout the biosphere, human activities are altering trophic structures, energy flow, chemical cycling, and natural disturbance—ecosystem processes on which we and all other species depend (see Chapter 55). We have physically altered nearly half of Earth's land surface, and we use over half of all accessible surface fresh water. In the oceans, stocks of most major fisheries are shrinking because of overharvesting. By some estimates, we are pushing more species toward extinction than the large asteroid or comet that triggered the mass extinctions at the close of the Cretaceous period 65.5 million years ago (see Figure 25.16).

Biology is the science of life. Thus, it is fitting that our final chapter focuses on two disciplines that seek to preserve life. **Conservation biology** integrates ecology, physiology, molecular biology, genetics, and evolutionary biology to conserve biological diversity at all levels. Efforts to sustain ecosystem processes and stem the loss of biodiversity also connect the life sciences with the social sciences, economics, and humanities.

▲ **Figure 56.2 Tropical deforestation in West Kalimantan, an Indonesian province.**

Restoration ecology applies ecological principles to return ecosystems that have been disturbed by human activity to a condition as similar as possible to their natural state.

In this chapter, we will take a closer look at the biodiversity crisis and examine some of the conservation and restoration strategies being adopted to slow the rate of species loss.

CONCEPT **56.1**

Human activities threaten Earth's biodiversity

Extinction is a natural phenomenon that has been occurring since life first evolved; it is the *rate* of extinction that is responsible for today's biodiversity crisis (see Chapter 25). Because we can only estimate the number of species currently existing, we cannot determine the exact rate of species loss. However, we do know for certain that the extinction rate is high and that human activities threaten Earth's biodiversity at all levels.

Three Levels of Biodiversity

Biodiversity—short for biological diversity—can be considered at three main levels: genetic diversity, species diversity, and ecosystem diversity **(Figure 56.3)**.

▲ **Figure 56.3 Three levels of biodiversity.** The oversized chromosomes in the top diagram symbolize the genetic variation within the population.

Genetic Diversity

Genetic diversity comprises not only the individual genetic variation *within* a population, but also the genetic variation *between* populations that is often associated with adaptations to local conditions (see Chapter 23). If one population becomes extinct, then a species may have lost some of the genetic diversity that makes microevolution possible. This erosion of genetic diversity in turn reduces the adaptive prospects of the species.

The loss of genetic diversity throughout the biosphere also affects human welfare. If we lose wild populations of plants closely related to agricultural species, we lose genetic resources that could be used to improve crop qualities, such as disease resistance, through plant breeding. For example, plant breeders responded to devastating outbreaks of the grassy stunt virus in rice (*Oryza sativa*) by screening 7,000 populations of this species and its close relatives for resistance to the virus. One population of a single relative, Indian rice (*Oryza nivara*), demonstrated resistance to the virus, and scientists succeeded in breeding the resistant trait into commercial rice varieties. Today, the original disease-resistant population has apparently become extinct in the wild.

Species Diversity

Public awareness of the biodiversity crisis centers on species diversity—the variety of species in an ecosystem or throughout the biosphere (see Chapter 54). As more species are lost to extinction, species diversity decreases. The U.S. Endangered Species Act (ESA) defines an **endangered species** as one that is "in danger of extinction throughout all or a significant portion of its range." Also defined for protection by the ESA, **threatened species** are those that are considered likely to become endangered in the foreseeable future. The following are just a few statistics that illustrate the problem of species loss:

- According to the International Union for Conservation of Nature and Natural Resources (IUCN), 12% of the nearly 10,000 known species of birds and at least 20% of the nearly 5,000 known species of mammals are threatened.
- A survey by the Center for Plant Conservation showed that of the nearly 20,000 known plant species in the United States, 200 have become extinct since such records have been kept, and 730 are endangered or threatened.

- About 20% of the known species of freshwater fishes in the world have either become extinct during historical times or are seriously threatened. In North America, 123 freshwater animal species have become extinct since 1900, and hundreds more species are threatened. The extinction rate for North American freshwater fauna is about five times as high as that for terrestrial animals.
- According to a 2004 report in the journal *Science* that was based on a global assessment of amphibians by more than 500 scientists, 32% of all known amphibian species are either very near extinction or endangered.

Extinction of species may be local; for example, a species may be lost in one river system but survive in an adjacent one. Global extinction of a species means that it is lost from *all* the ecosystems in which it lived, leaving them permanently impoverished **(Figure 56.4)**.

▲ **Figure 56.4 A hundred heartbeats from extinction.** These are just three members of what E. O. Wilson calls the Hundred Heartbeat Club, species with fewer than 100 individuals remaining on Earth. The Yangtze River dolphin was even thought to be extinct, but a few individuals were reportedly sighted in 2007.

? *To document that a species has actually become extinct, what spatial and temporal factors would you need to consider?*

Ecosystem Diversity

The variety of the biosphere's ecosystems is a third level of biological diversity. Because of the network of community interactions among populations of different species within an ecosystem, the local extinction of one species can have a negative impact on the overall species richness of the community (see Figure 54.15). For instance, bats called "flying foxes" are important pollinators and seed dispersers in the Pacific Islands, where they have been subject to increasing pressure from hunters, who sell them as luxury foods **(Figure 56.5)**. Conservation biologists fear that the extinction of flying foxes would also harm the native plants of the Samoan islands, where more than 79% of the trees depend on flying foxes for pollination or seed dispersal.

Some ecosystems have already been heavily impacted by humans, and others are being altered at a rapid pace. For example, since European colonization, more than 50% of wetlands in the contiguous United States have been drained and converted to other ecosystems, primarily agricultural ones. In California, Arizona, and New Mexico, approximately 90% of native riparian communities have been affected by overgrazing, flood control, water diversions, lowering of water tables, and invasion by non-native plants.

Biodiversity and Human Welfare

Why should we care about the loss of biodiversity? Perhaps the purest reason is what E. O. Wilson calls *biophilia*, our sense of connection to nature and other forms of life. The belief that other species are entitled to life is a pervasive theme of many religions and the basis of a moral argument that we should protect biodiversity. There is also a concern for future human generations: Is it fair to deprive them of Earth's species richness? Paraphrasing an old proverb, G. H. Brundtland, a former prime minister of Norway, said: "We must consider our planet to be on

▲ **Figure 56.5 The endangered Marianas "flying fox" bat (*Pteropus mariannus*), an important pollinator.**

loan from our children, rather than being a gift from our ancestors." In addition to such philosophical and moral justifications, species and genetic diversity bring us many practical benefits.

Benefits of Species and Genetic Diversity

Many species that are threatened could potentially provide crops, fibers, and medicines for human use, making biodiversity a crucial natural resource. In the United States, about 25% of the prescriptions dispensed from pharmacies contain substances originally derived from plants. In the 1970s, researchers discovered that the rosy periwinkle, which grows on the island of Madagascar, off the coast of Africa, contains alkaloids that inhibit cancer cell growth **(Figure 56.6)**. This discovery led to treatments for two deadly forms of cancer, Hodgkin's disease and a form of childhood leukemia, resulting in remission in most cases. Madagascar is also home to five other species of periwinkles, one of which is approaching extinction. The loss of these species would mean the loss of any possible medicinal benefits they might offer.

Each loss of a species means the loss of unique genes, some of which may code for enormously useful proteins. Consider the example of Taq polymerase, a DNA polymerase first extracted from the bacterium *Thermus aquaticus* in hot springs at Yellowstone National Park. This enzyme is an essential part of the polymerase chain reaction (PCR) because it is stable at the high temperatures required for PCR (see Figure 20.8). DNA from many other species of prokaryotes in a variety of environments is used in the mass production of proteins for new medicines, foods, petroleum substitutes, industrial chemicals, and other products. However, because millions of species may become extinct before we even know about them, we stand to lose irretrievably the valuable genetic potential held in their unique libraries of genes.

Ecosystem Services

The benefits that individual species provide to humans are often substantial, but saving individual species is only part of the rationale for saving ecosystems. Humans evolved in Earth's ecosystems, and we rely on these systems and their inhabitants for our survival. **Ecosystem services** encompass all the processes through which natural ecosystems help sustain human life on Earth. Ecosystems purify our air and water. They detoxify and decompose our wastes and reduce the impacts of extreme weather and flooding. The organisms in ecosystems pollinate our crops, control pests, and create and preserve our soils. Moreover, ecosystems provide all these services and countless others for free.

Perhaps because we don't attach a monetary value to the services of natural ecosystems, we generally undervalue them. In a controversial 1997 article, ecologist Robert Costanza and his colleagues estimated the value of Earth's ecosystem services at $33 trillion per year, nearly twice the gross national product of all the countries on Earth at that time ($18 trillion). It may be more realistic, and more meaningful, to do the accounting on a smaller scale. In 1996, New York City invested more than $1 billion to buy land and restore habitat in the Catskill Mountains, the source of much of the city's fresh water. This investment was spurred by increasing pollution of the water by sewage, pesticides, and fertilizers. By harnessing ecosystem services to purify its water naturally, the city saved $8 billion it would have otherwise spent to build a new filtration plant and $300 million a year to run the plant.

There is growing evidence that the functioning of ecosystems, and hence their capacity to perform services, is linked to biodiversity. As human activities reduce biodiversity, we are reducing the capacity of the planet's ecosystems to perform processes critical to our own survival.

▶ **Figure 56.6 The rosy periwinkle (*Catharanthus roseus*), a plant that saves lives.**

Three Threats to Biodiversity

Many different human activities threaten biodiversity on local, regional, and global scales. The threats posed by these activities are of three major types: habitat loss, introduced species, and overexploitation.

Habitat Loss

Human alteration of habitat is the single greatest threat to biodiversity throughout the biosphere. Habitat loss has been brought about by agriculture, urban development, forestry, mining, and pollution. Global warming is already altering habitats today and will have an even larger effect later this century (see Chapter 55). When no alternative habitat is available or a species is unable to move, habitat loss may mean extinction. The IUCN implicates destruction of physical habitat for 73% of the species that have become extinct, endangered, vulnerable, or rare in the last few hundred years.

Habitat loss and fragmentation may occur over immense regions. For instance, approximately 98% of the tropical dry forests of Central America and Mexico have been cleared (cut down). Clearing of tropical rain forest in the state of Veracruz,

▲ **Figure 56.7 Habitat fragmentation in the foothills of Los Angeles.** Development in the valleys may confine the organisms that inhabit the narrow strips of hillside.

Mexico, mostly for cattle ranching, has resulted in the loss of approximately 91% of the original forest, leaving a fragmented archipelago of small forest islands. Other natural habitats have also been fragmented by human activities **(Figure 56.7)**.

In almost all cases, habitat fragmentation leads to species loss, since the smaller populations in habitat fragments have a higher probability of local extinction. The prairies of North America are an example: Prairie covered about 800,000 hectares of southern Wisconsin when Europeans first arrived, but now occupies less than 0.1% of its original area. Plant diversity surveys of 54 Wisconsin prairie remnants were conducted in 1948–1954 and then repeated in 1987–1988. During the three decades between the surveys, the various prairie fragments lost between 8% and 60% of their plant species.

Though most studies have focused on terrestrial ecosystems, habitat loss is also a major threat to aquatic biodiversity, especially along continental coasts and around coral reefs. About 93% of coral reefs, among Earth's most species-rich aquatic communities, have been damaged by human activities. At the current rate of destruction, 40–50% of the reefs, home to one-third of marine fish species, could disappear in the next 30 to 40 years. Freshwater habitats are also being lost, often as a result of the dams, reservoirs, channel modification, and flow regulation now affecting most of the world's rivers. For example, the more than 30 dams and locks built along the Mobile River basin, in the southeastern United States, changed river depth and flow and thereby helped drive more than 40 species of endemic mussels and snails to extinction.

Introduced Species

Introduced species, also called non-native or exotic species, are those that humans move, either intentionally or accidentally, from the species' native locations to new geographic regions. Rapid human travel by ship and airplane has accelerated the transplant of species. Free from the predators, parasites, and pathogens that limit their populations in their native habitats, such transplanted species may spread very rapidly through a new region.

Some introduced species that gain a foothold disrupt their adopted community, often by preying on native organisms or outcompeting them for resources. The brown tree snake was accidentally introduced to the island of Guam as a "stowaway" in military cargo after World War II **(Figure 56.8a)**. Since then, 12 species of birds and 6 species of lizards on which the snakes prey have become extinct on Guam. The devastating zebra mussel was introduced into the Great Lakes of North America in 1988, most likely in the ballast water of ships arriving from Europe. Efficient suspension-feeding molluscs that form dense colonies, zebra mussels have extensively disrupted freshwater ecosystems, threatening native aquatic species. Zebra mussels have also clogged water intake structures, disrupting domestic and industrial water supplies and causing billions of dollars in damage.

Humans have deliberately introduced many species with good intentions but disastrous effects. For example, an Asian plant called kudzu, which the U.S. Department of Agriculture once introduced in the southern United States to help control erosion, has taken over large areas of the landscape there **(Figure 56.8b)**. The European starling, brought intentionally into New York's Central Park in 1890 by a citizens' group intent on introducing all the plants and animals mentioned in Shakespeare's plays, quickly spread across North America, increasing to a population of more than 100 million and displacing many native songbirds.

Introduced species are a worldwide problem, contributing to approximately 40% of the extinctions recorded since 1750

(a) Brown tree snake, introduced to Guam in cargo

(b) Introduced kudzu thriving in South Carolina

▲ **Figure 56.8 Two introduced species.**

and costing billions of dollars annually in damage and control efforts. There are more than 50,000 introduced species in the United States alone.

Overexploitation

The term *overexploitation* refers generally to the human harvesting of wild organisms at rates exceeding the ability of populations of those species to rebound. Species with restricted habitats, such as small islands, are particularly vulnerable to overexploitation. One such species was the great auk, a large, flightless seabird found on islands in the North Atlantic Ocean. By the 1840s, humans had hunted the great auk to extinction to satisfy demand for its feathers, eggs, and meat.

Also susceptible to overexploitation are large organisms with low intrinsic reproductive rates, such as elephants, whales, and rhinoceroses. The decline of Earth's largest extant terrestrial animals, the African elephants, is a classic example of the impact of overhunting. Largely because of the trade in ivory, elephant populations have been declining in most of Africa during the last 50 years. An international ban on the sale of new ivory resulted in increased poaching (illegal hunting), so the ban had little effect in much of central and eastern Africa. Only in South Africa, where once-decimated herds have been well protected for nearly a century, have elephant populations been stable or increasing (see Chapter 53).

Conservation biologists increasingly use the tools of molecular genetics to track the origins of tissues harvested from threatened and endangered species. For instance, Samuel Wasser and colleagues, at the University of Washington, created a DNA reference map for the African elephant using DNA isolated from elephant dung. By comparing this reference map with DNA isolated from a small sample of ivory harvested either legally or by poachers, they can determine where the elephant was killed to within a few hundred kilometers. Similarly, biologists using phylogenetic analyses of mitochondrial DNA (mtDNA) showed that some whale meat sold in Japanese fish markets came from illegally harvested species, including fin and humpback whales, which are endangered (see Figure 26.6).

Many populations of commercially important marine fishes, once thought to be inexhaustible, have been dramatically reduced by overfishing. The exploding human population's increasing demand for protein, coupled with new harvesting technologies, such as long-line fishing and modern trawlers, have reduced these fish populations to levels that cannot sustain further exploitation. The fate of the North Atlantic bluefin tuna is just one example. Until the past few decades, this big tuna was considered a sport fish of little commercial value—just a few cents per pound for cat food. Then, in the 1980s, wholesalers began airfreighting fresh, iced bluefin to Japan for sushi and sashimi. In that market, the fish now brings up to $100 per pound (**Figure 56.9**). With the increased harvesting spurred by such high prices, it took just ten years to reduce the western North Atlantic bluefin population to less than 20% of its 1980 size. The collapse of the northern cod fishery off Newfoundland in the 1990s is a more recent example of how it is possible to overharvest what was formerly a very common species.

▲ **Figure 56.9 Overexploitation.** North Atlantic bluefin tuna are auctioned in a Japanese fish market.

CONCEPT CHECK 56.1

1. Explain why it is too narrow to define the biodiversity crisis as simply a loss of species.
2. Identify the three main threats to biodiversity and explain how each damages diversity.
3. **WHAT IF?** Imagine two populations of a fish species, one in the Mediterranean Sea and one in the Caribbean Sea. Now imagine two scenarios: (1) The populations breed separately, and (2) adults of both populations migrate to the North Atlantic to interbreed. Which scenario would result in a greater loss of genetic diversity if the Mediterranean population were harvested to extinction? Explain your answer.

For suggested answers, see Appendix A.

CONCEPT 56.2

Population conservation focuses on population size, genetic diversity, and critical habitat

Biologists focusing on conservation at the population and species levels follow two main approaches: the small-population approach and the declining-population approach.

Small-Population Approach

A species is designated as endangered when its populations are very small. Small populations are particularly vulnerable to overexploitation, habitat loss, and the other threats to biodiversity that you read about in Concept 56.1. After such factors have taken their toll on population size, a population's smallness itself can drive it to extinction. Conservation biologists who adopt the small-population approach study the processes that cause extinctions once population sizes have been severely reduced.

The Extinction Vortex

A small population is prone to positive-feedback loops of inbreeding and genetic drift that draw the population down an **extinction vortex** toward smaller and smaller population size until no individuals exist **(Figure 56.10)**. One key factor driving the extinction vortex is the loss of the genetic variation necessary to enable evolutionary responses to environmental change, such as the appearance of new strains of pathogens. Both inbreeding and genetic drift can cause a loss of genetic variation (see Chapter 23), and the effects of both processes become more significant as a population shrinks. Inbreeding often reduces fitness because offspring are more likely to be homozygous for harmful recessive traits.

Not all small populations are doomed by low genetic diversity, and low genetic variability does not automatically lead to permanently small populations. For instance, overhunting of northern elephant seals in the 1890s reduced the species to only 20 individuals—clearly a bottleneck with reduced genetic variation. Since that time, however, the northern elephant seal populations have rebounded to about 150,000 individuals today, though their genetic variation remains relatively low. Furthermore, a number of plant species seem to have inherently low genetic variability. For example, many populations of cord grass (*Spartina anglica*), which thrives in salt marshes, are genetically uniform at many loci. *S. anglica* arose from a few parent plants only about a century ago by hybridization and allopolyploidy (see Figure 24.11). Having spread by cloning, this species now dominates large areas of tidal mudflats in Europe and Asia. Thus, in rare cases, low genetic diversity has not impeded population growth.

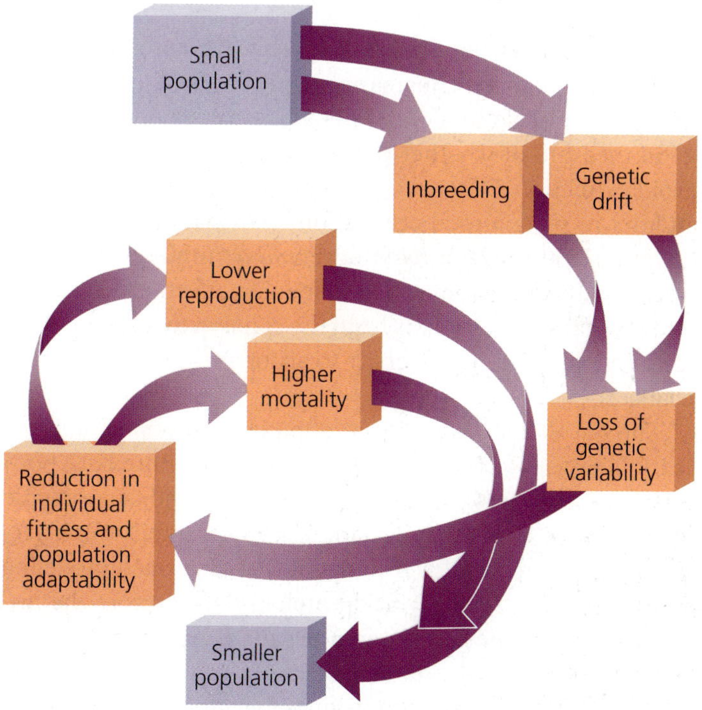

▲ **Figure 56.10 Processes culminating in an extinction vortex.**

Case Study: *The Greater Prairie Chicken and the Extinction Vortex*

When Europeans arrived in North America, the greater prairie chicken (*Tympanuchus cupido*) was common from New England to Virginia and all across the western prairies of the continent. As you read in Chapter 23, land cultivation for agriculture fragmented the populations of this species, and its abundance decreased drastically. In Illinois, there were millions of greater prairie chickens in the 19th century, but fewer than 50 were left by 1993. Researchers found that the decline in the Illinois population was associated with a decrease in fertility. As a test of the extinction vortex hypothesis, the scientists imported genetic variation by transplanting 271 birds from larger populations elsewhere (**Figure 56.11**, on the next page). The Illinois population rebounded, confirming that it had been on its way down the extinction vortex until rescued by the transfusion of genetic variation.

Minimum Viable Population Size

How small does a population have to be before it starts down an extinction vortex? The answer depends on the type of organism and other factors. For example, large predators that feed high on the food chain usually require very large individual ranges, resulting in very low population densities. Therefore, not all rare species concern conservation biologists. All populations, however, require some minimum size in order to remain viable.

The minimal population size at which a species is able to sustain its numbers and survive is known as the **minimum viable population (MVP)**. MVP is usually estimated for a given species using computer models that integrate many factors. The calculation may include, for example, an estimate of how many individuals in a small population are likely to be killed by some natural catastrophe such as a storm. Once in the extinction vortex, two or three years in a row of bad weather could finish off a population that is already below MVP.

▼ Figure 56.11 Inquiry

What caused the drastic decline of the Illinois greater prairie chicken population?

EXPERIMENT Researchers had observed that the population collapse of the greater prairie chicken was mirrored in a reduction in fertility, as measured by the hatching rate of eggs. Comparison of DNA samples from the Jasper County, Illinois, population with DNA from feathers in museum specimens showed that genetic variation had declined in the study population (see Figure 23.10). In 1992, Ronald Westemeier, Jeffrey Brawn, and colleagues began transplanting prairie chickens from Minnesota, Kansas, and Nebraska in an attempt to increase genetic variation.

RESULTS After translocation (blue arrow), the viability of eggs rapidly increased, and the population rebounded.

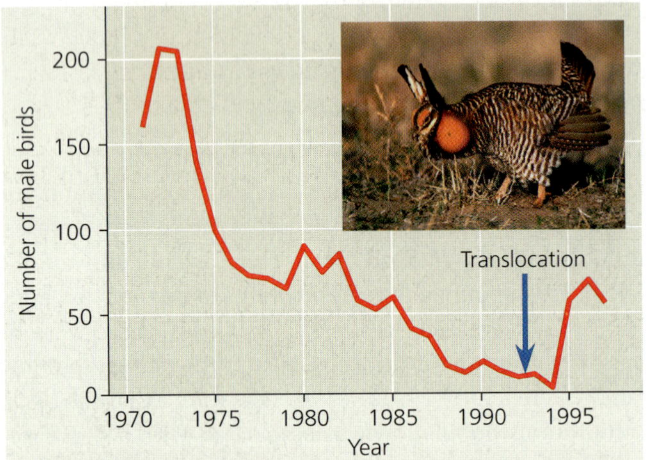

(a) Population dynamics

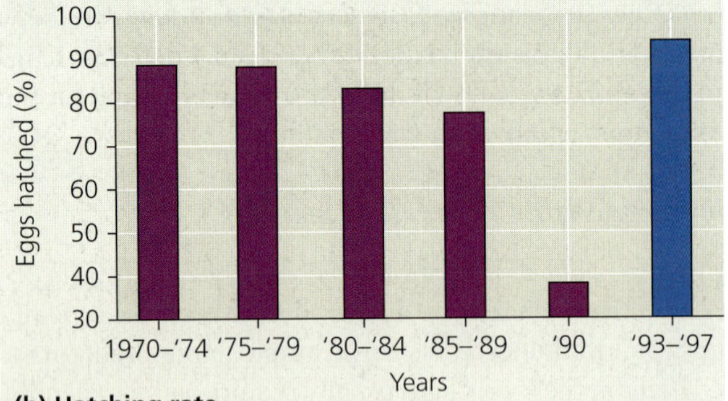

(b) Hatching rate

CONCLUSION Reduced genetic variation had started the Jasper County population of prairie chickens down the extinction vortex.

SOURCE R. L. Westemeier et al., Tracking the long-term decline and recovery of an isolated population, *Science* 282:1695–1698 (1998).

Inquiry in Action Read and analyze the original paper in *Inquiry in Action: Interpreting Scientific Papers.*

WHAT IF? Given the success of using transplanted birds as a tool for increasing the percentage of hatched eggs in Illinois, why wouldn't you transplant *additional* birds immediately to Illinois?

Effective Population Size

Genetic variation is the key issue in the small-population approach. The *total* size of a population may be misleading because only certain members of the population breed successfully and pass their alleles on to offspring. Therefore, a meaningful estimate of MVP requires the researcher to determine the **effective population size**, which is based on the breeding potential of the population.

The following formula incorporates the sex ratio of breeding individuals into the estimate of effective population size, abbreviated N_e:

$$N_e = \frac{4N_f N_m}{N_f + N_m}$$

where N_f and N_m are, respectively, the number of females and the number of males that successfully breed. If we apply this formula to an idealized population whose total size is 1,000 individuals, N_e will also be 1,000 if every individual breeds and the sex ratio is 500 females to 500 males. In this case, $N_e = (4 \times 500 \times 500)/(500 + 500) = 1{,}000$. Any deviation from these conditions (not all individuals breed or there is not a 1:1 sex ratio) reduces N_e. For instance, if the total population size is 1,000 but only 400 females and 400 males breed, then $N_e = (4 \times 400 \times 400)/(400 + 400) = 800$, or 80% of the total population size. Numerous life history traits can influence N_e, and alternative formulas for estimating N_e take into account family size, age at maturation, genetic relatedness among population members, the effects of gene flow between geographically separated populations, and population fluctuations.

In actual study populations, N_e is always some fraction of the total population. Thus, simply determining the total number of individuals in a small population does not provide a good measure of whether the population is large enough to avoid extinction. Whenever possible, conservation programs attempt to sustain total population sizes that include at least the minimum viable number of *reproductively active* individuals. The conservation goal of sustaining effective population size (N_e) above MVP stems from the concern that populations retain enough genetic diversity to adapt as their environment changes.

The MVP of a population is often used in population viability analysis. The objective of this analysis is to predict a population's chances for survival, usually expressed as a specific probability of survival (for example, a 95% chance) over a particular time interval (for instance, 100 years). Such modeling approaches allow conservation biologists to explore the potential consequences of alternative management plans. Because modeling depends on reliable information about the populations under study, conservation biology is most robust when theoretical modeling is combined with field studies of the managed populations.

Case Study: *Analysis of Grizzly Bear Populations*

One of the first population viability analyses was conducted in 1978 by Mark Shaffer, of Duke University, as part of a long-term study of grizzly bears in Yellowstone National Park and its surrounding areas **(Figure 56.12)**. A threatened species in the United States, the grizzly bear (*Ursus arctos horribilis*) is currently found in only 4 of the 48 contiguous states. Its populations in those states have been drastically reduced and fragmented: In 1800, an estimated 100,000 grizzlies ranged over about 500 million hectares of mostly continuous habitat, while today only about 1,000 individuals in six relatively isolated populations range over less than 5 million hectares.

Shaffer attempted to determine viable sizes for the Yellowstone grizzly populations. Using life history data obtained for individual Yellowstone bears over a 12-year period, he simulated the effects of environmental factors on survival and reproduction. His models predicted that, given a suitable habitat, a Yellowstone grizzly bear population of 70 to 90 individuals would have about a 95% chance of surviving for 100 years, whereas a population of 100 bears would have a 95% chance of surviving for twice as long, about 200 years.

How does the actual size of the Yellowstone grizzly population compare with Shaffer's estimates of MVP? A current estimate puts the total grizzly bear population in the greater Yellowstone ecosystem at about 400 individuals. The relationship of this estimate to the effective population size, N_e, depends on several factors. Usually, only a few dominant males breed, and it may be difficult for them to locate females, since individuals inhabit such extensive areas. Moreover, females may reproduce only when there is abundant food. As a result, N_e is only about 25% of the total population size, or about 100 bears.

Because small populations tend to lose genetic variation over time, a number of research teams have analyzed proteins, mtDNA, and short tandem repeats (see Chapter 21) to assess genetic variability in the Yellowstone grizzly bear population. All results to date indicate that the Yellowstone population has less genetic variability than other grizzly bear populations in North America. However, the isolation and decline in genetic variability in the Yellowstone grizzly bear population were gradual during the 20th century and not as severe as feared: Museum specimens collected in the early 1900s demonstrate that genetic variability among the Yellowstone grizzly bears was low even then.

How might conservation biologists increase the effective size and genetic variation of the Yellowstone grizzly bear population? Migration between isolated populations of grizzlies could increase both effective and total population sizes. Computer models predict that introducing only two unrelated bears each decade into a population of 100 individuals would reduce the loss of genetic variation by about half. For the grizzly bear, and probably for many other species whose populations are very small, finding ways to promote dispersal among populations may be one of the most urgent conservation needs.

This case study and that of the greater prairie chicken bridge small-population models to practical applications in conservation. Next, we look at an alternative approach to understanding the biology of extinction.

▲ **Figure 56.12 Long-term monitoring of a grizzly bear population.** The ecologist is fitting this tranquilized bear with a radio collar so that the bear's movements can be compared with those of other individuals in the Yellowstone National Park population.

Declining-Population Approach

The declining-population approach focuses on threatened and endangered populations that show a downward trend, even if the population is far above MVP. The distinction between a declining population (which is not always small) and a small population (which is not always declining) is less important than the different priorities of the two basic conservation approaches. The small-population approach emphasizes smallness itself as an ultimate cause of a population's extinction, especially through loss of genetic diversity. In contrast, the declining-population approach emphasizes the environmental factors that caused a population decline in the first place. If, for example, an area is deforested, then species that depend on trees will decline in number and become locally extinct, whether or not they retain genetic variation.

Steps for Analysis and Intervention

The declining-population approach requires that population declines be evaluated on a case-by-case basis, with researchers carefully dissecting the causes of a decline before taking steps to correct it. If, for example, the biological magnification of a toxic pollutant is harming some top-level consumer such as a predatory bird (see Chapter 55), then managers need to reduce or eliminate the pollutant in the environment to restore vulnerable populations of the bird. Although most situations are species use more than one kind of ecosystem, and many live on the borders between ecosystems.

Fragmentation and Edges

The boundaries, or *edges*, between ecosystems—such as between a lake and the surrounding forest or between cropland and suburban housing tracts—are defining features of landscapes **(Figure 56.14)**. An edge has its own set of physical conditions, which differ from those on either side of it. The soil surface of an edge between a forest patch and a burned area receives more sunlight and is usually hotter and drier than the forest interior, but it is cooler and wetter than the soil surface in the burned area.

(a) Natural edges. Grasslands give way to forest ecosystems in Yellowstone National Park.

(b) Edges created by human activity. Pronounced edges (roads) surround clear-cuts in this photograph of a heavily logged rain forest in Malaysia.

▲ **Figure 56.14 Edges between ecosystems.**

Some organisms thrive in edge communities because they gain resources from both adjacent areas. The ruffed grouse (*Bonasa umbellatus*) is a bird that needs forest habitat for nesting, winter food, and shelter, but it also needs forest openings with dense shrubs and herbs for summer food. White-tailed deer also thrive in edge habitats, where they can browse on woody shrubs; deer populations often expand when forests are logged and more edges are exposed.

The proliferation of edge species can have positive or negative effects on biodiversity. A 1997 study in Cameroon comparing edge and interior populations of the little greenbul (a tropical rain forest bird) suggested that forest edges may be important sites of speciation. On the other hand, communities in which edges arise from human alterations often have reduced biodiversity because the relatively large percentage of edge habitat leads to a preponderance of edge-adapted species. For example, the brown-headed cowbird (*Molothrus ater*) is an edge-adapted species that lays its eggs in the nests of other birds, particularly migratory songbirds. Cowbirds need forests, where they can parasitize the nests of other birds, and also open fields, where they forage on insects. Thus, their populations are growing where forests are being cut and fragmented, creating more edge habitat and open land. Increasing cowbird parasitism and loss of habitat are correlated with declining populations of several of the cowbird's host species.

The influence of fragmentation on the structure of communities has been explored since 1979 in the long-term Biological Dynamics of Forest Fragments Project. Located in the heart of the Amazon River basin, the study area consists of isolated fragments of forest separated from surrounding continuous tropical rain forest by distances of 80–1,000 m **(Figure 56.15)**. Researchers from all over the world have clearly documented

▲ **Figure 56.15 Amazon rain forest fragments created as part of the Biological Dynamics of Forest Fragments Project.**

the physical and biological effects of this fragmentation in organisms ranging from bryophytes to beetles to birds. They have consistently found that species adapted to forest interiors show the greatest declines in the smallest fragments, suggesting that landscapes dominated by small fragments will support fewer species, mainly due to loss of interior-adapted species.

Corridors That Connect Habitat Fragments

In fragmented habitats, the presence of a **movement corridor**, a narrow strip or series of small clumps of habitat connecting otherwise isolated patches, can be extremely important for conserving biodiversity. Streamside habitats often serve as corridors, and in some nations, government policy prohibits altering these riparian areas. In areas of heavy human use, artificial corridors are sometimes constructed. Bridges or tunnels, for instance, can reduce the number of animals killed trying to cross highways **(Figure 56.16)**.

Movement corridors also can promote dispersal and reduce inbreeding in declining populations. Corridors have been shown to increase the exchange of individuals in many organisms, including butterflies, voles, and aquatic plants. Corridors are especially important to species that migrate between different habitats seasonally. However, a corridor can also be harmful—as, for example, in the spread of disease. In a 2003 study, Agustin Estrada-Peña, of the University of Zaragoza, Spain, showed that habitat corridors facilitate the movement of disease-carrying ticks among forest patches in northern Spain. All the effects of corridors are not yet understood, and their impact is an area of active research in conservation biology and restoration ecology.

▲ **Figure 56.16 An artificial corridor.** This bridge in Banff National Park, Canada, helps animals cross a human-created barrier.

Establishing Protected Areas

Conservation biologists are applying their understanding of community, ecosystem, and landscape dynamics in establishing protected areas to slow biodiversity loss. Currently, governments have set aside about 7% of the world's land in various forms of reserves. Choosing where to place and how to design nature reserves poses many challenges. Should the reserve be managed to minimize the risks of fire and predation to a threatened species? Or should the reserve be left as natural as possible, with such processes as fires ignited by lightning allowed to play out on their own? This is just one of the debates that arise among people who share an interest in the health of national parks and other protected areas. In deciding which areas are of highest conservation priority, biologists often focus on hot spots of biological diversity.

Finding Biodiversity Hot Spots

A **biodiversity hot spot** is a relatively small area with an exceptional concentration of endemic species and a large number of endangered and threatened species **(Figure 56.17)**. Nearly 30% of all bird species are confined to only about 2% of Earth's land area. Approximately 50,000 plant species, or about one-sixth of all known plant species, inhabit just 18 hot

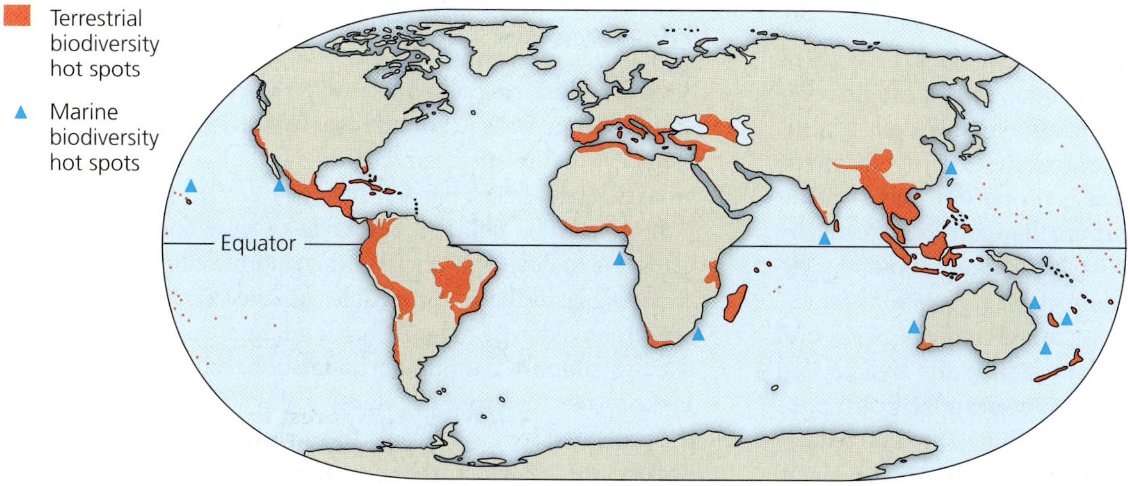

◀ **Figure 56.17 Earth's terrestrial and marine biodiversity hot spots.**

spots covering 0.5% of the global land surface. Together, the "hottest" of the terrestrial biodiversity hot spots total less than 1.5% of Earth's land but are home to more than a third of all species of plants, amphibians, reptiles (including birds), and mammals. Hot spots also include aquatic ecosystems, such as coral reefs and certain river systems.

Biodiversity hot spots are obviously good choices for nature reserves, but identifying them is not always simple. One problem is that a hot spot for one taxonomic group, such as butterflies, may not be a hot spot for some other taxonomic group, such as birds. Designating an area as a biodiversity hot spot is often biased toward saving vertebrates and plants, with less attention paid to invertebrates and microorganisms. Some biologists are also concerned that the hot-spot strategy places too much emphasis on such a small fraction of Earth's surface.

Philosophy of Nature Reserves

Nature reserves are biodiversity islands in a sea of habitat degraded to varying degrees by human activity. Protected "islands" are not isolated from their surroundings, however, and the nonequilibrium model we described in Chapter 54 applies to nature reserves as well as to the larger landscapes in which they are embedded.

An earlier policy—that protected areas should be set aside to remain unchanged forever—was based on the concept that ecosystems are balanced, self-regulating units. As we saw in Chapter 54, however, disturbance is a functional component of all ecosystems, and management policies that ignore natural disturbances or attempt to prevent them have generally failed. For instance, setting aside an area of a fire-dependent community, such as a portion of a tallgrass prairie, chaparral, or dry pine forest, with the intention of saving it is unrealistic if periodic burning is excluded. Without the dominant disturbance, the fire-adapted species are usually outcompeted and biodiversity is reduced.

Because human disturbance and fragmentation are increasingly common landscape features, the dynamics of disturbances, populations, edges, and corridors are all important for designing and managing protected areas. An important conservation question is whether to create fewer large reserves or more numerous small reserves. One argument for extensive reserves is that large, far-ranging animals with low-density populations, such as the grizzly bear, require extensive habitats. More extensive areas also have proportionately smaller perimeters than smaller areas and are therefore less affected by edges. As conservation biologists learn more about the requirements for achieving minimum viable populations for endangered species, they realize that most national parks and other reserves are far too small. For example, the area needed for the long-term survival of the Yellowstone grizzly bear population is more than ten times the combined area of Yellowstone and Grand Teton National Parks (**Figure 56.18**). Given political and economic realities, many existing parks will not be enlarged, and most newly created reserves will also be too small. Areas of private and public land surrounding reserves will likely have to contribute to biodiversity conservation. On the other side of the argument, smaller, unconnected reserves may slow the spread of disease throughout a population.

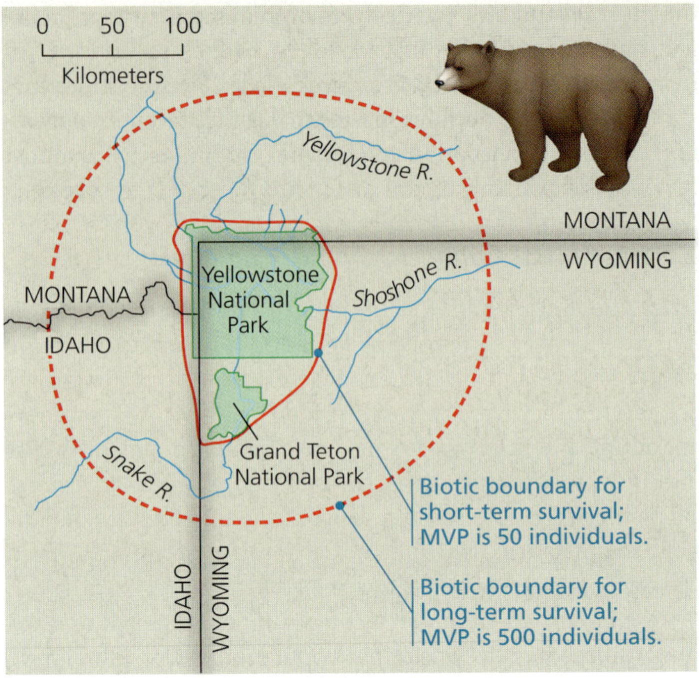

▲ **Figure 56.18 Biotic boundaries for grizzly bears in Yellowstone and Grand Teton National Parks.** The biotic boundaries (solid and dashed red lines) surround the areas needed to support minimum viable populations of 50 and 500 bears. Even the smaller of these areas is larger than the two parks.

In practical terms, land use by humans may outweigh all other considerations and ultimately dictate the size and shape of protected areas. Much of the land left for conservation efforts is useless for exploitation by agriculture or forestry. But in some cases, as when reserve land is surrounded by commercially viable property, the use of land for agriculture or forestry must be integrated into conservation strategies.

Zoned Reserves

Several nations have adopted a zoned reserve approach to landscape management. A **zoned reserve** is an extensive region that includes areas relatively undisturbed by humans surrounded by areas that have been changed by human activity and are used for economic gain. The key challenge of the zoned reserve approach is to develop a social and economic climate in the surrounding lands that is compatible with the long-term viability of the protected core. These surrounding areas continue to be used to support the human population, but with regulations that prevent the types of extensive alterations likely to impact the protected area. As a result, the surrounding habitats serve as buffer zones against further intrusion into the undisturbed area.

The small Central American nation of Costa Rica has become a world leader in establishing zoned reserves **(Figure 56.19)**. An agreement initiated in 1987 reduced Costa Rica's international debt in return for land preservation there. The agreement resulted in eight zoned reserves, called "conservation areas," that contain designated national park land. Costa Rica is making progress toward managing its zoned reserves, and the buffer zones provide a steady, lasting supply of forest products, water, and hydroelectric power and also support sustainable agriculture and tourism. An important goal is providing a stable economic base for people living there. As University of Pennsylvania ecologist Daniel Janzen, a leader in tropical conservation, has said, "The likelihood of long-term survival of a conserved wildland area is directly proportional to the economic health and stability of the society in which that wildland is embedded."

(a) Boundaries of the zoned reserves are indicated by black outlines.

(b) Local schoolchildren marvel at the diversity of life in one of Costa Rica's reserves.

▲ **Figure 56.19 Zoned reserves in Costa Rica.**

Destructive practices that are not compatible with long-term ecosystem conservation and from which there is often little local profit, such as massive logging, large-scale single-crop agriculture, and extensive mining, are ideally confined to the outermost fringes of the buffer zones and are gradually being discouraged.

Costa Rica relies on its zoned reserve system to maintain at least 80% of its native species, but the system is not without problems. A 2003 analysis of land cover change between 1960 and 1997 showed negligible deforestation within Costa Rica's national parks and a gain in forest cover in the 1-km buffer around the parks. However, significant losses in forest cover were discovered in the 10-km buffer zones around all national parks, which threaten to turn the parks into isolated habitat islands.

Although marine ecosystems have also been heavily impacted by human exploitation, reserves in the ocean are far less common than reserves on land. Many fish populations around the world have collapsed as increasingly sophisticated equipment puts nearly all potential fishing grounds within human reach. In response, Fiona Gell and Callum Roberts, of the University of York, England, have proposed establishing marine reserves around the world that would be off limits to fishing. Gell and Roberts present strong evidence that a patchwork of marine reserves can serve as a means of both increasing fish populations within the reserves and improving fishing success in nearby areas. Their proposed system is a modern application of a centuries-old practice in the Fiji Islands in which some areas have historically remained closed to fishing—a traditional example of the zoned reserve concept.

The United States adopted such a system in establishing the Florida Keys National Marine Sanctuary in 1990 **(Figure 56.20)**. Populations of marine organisms, including fishes and lobsters, recovered quickly after harvests were banned in the 9,500-km^2 reserve. Larger and more abundant fish now produce larvae that

▲ **Figure 56.20 A diver measuring coral in the Florida Keys National Marine Sanctuary.**

help repopulate reefs and improve fishing outside the sanctuary. The increased marine life within the sanctuary also makes it a favorite for recreational divers, increasing the economic value of this zoned reserve.

CONCEPT CHECK 56.3

1. What is a biodiversity hot spot?
2. How do zoned reserves provide economic incentives for long-term conservation of protected areas?
3. **WHAT IF?** Suppose a developer proposes to clear-cut a forest that serves as a corridor between two parks. To compensate, the developer also proposes to add the same area of forest to one of the parks. As a professional ecologist, how might you argue for retaining the corridor?

For suggested answers, see Appendix A.

CONCEPT **56.4**

Restoration ecology attempts to restore degraded ecosystems to a more natural state

Given enough time, biological communities can recover naturally from most disturbances through the stages of ecological succession that we discussed in Chapter 54. Sometimes that recovery takes centuries, though, particularly when humans degrade the environment. Degraded habitats are increasing in area because the natural rate of recovery by successional processes is often slower than the rate of degradation by human activities. The soils of many tropical areas quickly become unproductive and are soon abandoned after being cleared for farming. Mining activities may last for several decades, but the lands are then abandoned in a degraded state. Many ecosystems are also damaged inadvertently by the dumping of toxic chemicals or such mishaps as oil spills.

Restoration ecology seeks to initiate or speed up the recovery of degraded ecosystems. One of its basic assumptions is that environmental damage is at least partly reversible. This optimistic view must be balanced by a second assumption—that ecosystems are not infinitely resilient. Restoration ecologists therefore work to identify and manipulate the processes that most limit the speed of recovery of ecosystems from disturbances. Where disturbance is so severe that restoring all of a habitat is impractical, ecologists try to reclaim as much of a habitat or ecological process as possible, within the limits of the time and money available to them.

In extreme cases, the structure of a site may first need to be restored before biological restoration can occur. If a stream was straightened to channel water quickly through a suburb, restoration ecologists may reconstruct a meandering channel to slow down the flow of water eroding the stream bank. To restore an open-pit mine, engineers may first grade the site with heavy equipment to reestablish a gentle slope, spreading topsoil when the slope is in place **(Figure 56.21)**. Once such physical reconstruction is complete—or when it is not needed—biological restoration is the next step.

Two key strategies in restoration ecology are bioremediation and biological augmentation.

Bioremediation

The use of organisms, usually prokaryotes, fungi, or plants, to detoxify polluted ecosystems is known as **bioremediation** (see Chapter 27). Some plants adapted to soils containing heavy metals can accumulate high concentrations of potentially toxic metals such as zinc, nickel, lead, and cadmium in

(a) In 1991, before restoration

(b) In 2000, near the completion of restoration

▲ **Figure 56.21 A gravel and clay mine site in New Jersey before and after restoration.**

(a) Wastes containing uranium were dumped in these four unlined pits for more than 30 years, contaminating soils and groundwater.

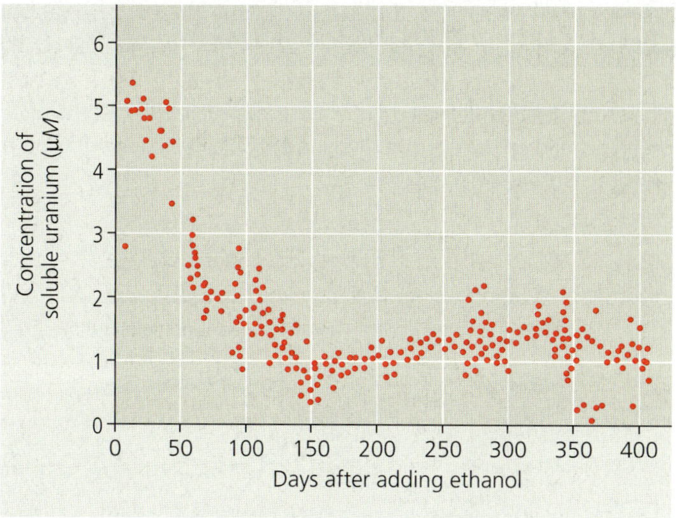

(b) After ethanol was added, microbial activity decreased the concentration of soluble uranium in groundwater near the pits.

▲ **Figure 56.22 Bioremediation of groundwater contaminated with uranium at Oak Ridge National Laboratory, Tennessee.**

their tissues. Restoration ecologists can use such plants to revegetate sites polluted by mining and other human activities and then harvest the plants to remove the metals from the ecosystem. Researchers in the United Kingdom discovered a lichen species that grows on soil polluted with uranium dust left over from mining. The lichen concentrates uranium in a dark pigment, making it useful as a biological monitor and potentially as a remediator.

Ecologists are examining the abilities of many prokaryotes to carry out bioremediation of soils and water. Scientists have sequenced the genomes of at least seven prokaryotic species specifically for their bioremediation potential. One of the species, the bacterium *Shewanella oneidensis*, appears particularly promising. It can metabolize more than ten elements under aerobic and anaerobic conditions to generate its energy. For instance, it converts soluble uranium, chromium, and nitrogen to insoluble forms that are less likely to leach into streams or groundwater. Wei-Min Wu and colleagues, at Oak Ridge National Laboratory, in Tennessee, stimulated the growth of *Shewanella* and other uranium-reducing bacteria by adding ethanol to groundwater contaminated with uranium; over five months, the concentration of soluble uranium dropped by 80% **(Figure 56.22)**. In the future, genetic engineering may become increasingly useful as a tool for improving the performance of prokaryotes and other organisms as bioremediators.

Biological Augmentation

In contrast to bioremediation, which is a strategy for removing harmful substances, **biological augmentation** uses organisms to add essential materials to a degraded ecosystem. Augmenting ecosystem processes requires determining what factors, such as chemical nutrients, have been removed from an area and thus limit its rate of recovery. Encouraging the growth of plants that thrive in nutrient-poor soils often speeds up the rate of successional changes that can lead to recovery of damaged sites. In alpine ecosystems of the western United States, nitrogen-fixing herbs such as lupines are often planted to bolster nitrogen concentrations in soils disturbed by mining and other uses. Once these nitrogen-fixing plants become established, other native species are better able to obtain enough nitrogen from the soil to survive. In other systems where the soil has been severely disturbed or where topsoil is missing entirely, plant roots may lack the mycorrhizal symbionts that help them meet their nutritional needs (see Chapter 31). Ecologists restoring a tallgrass prairie in Minnesota recognized this limitation and significantly accelerated the recovery of native species by adding mycorrhizal symbionts to the soil they seeded.

Exploring Restoration

Because restoration ecology is a relatively new discipline and because ecosystems are complex, restoration ecologists generally learn as they go. Many restoration ecologists advocate adaptive management: experimenting with several promising types of management to learn what works best.

The long-term objective of restoration is to speed the reestablishment of an ecosystem as similar as possible to the predisturbance ecosystem. **Figure 56.23**, on the next two pages, identifies several ambitious and successful restoration projects around the world. The great number of such projects, the dedication of the people engaged in them, and the successes that have been achieved suggest that restoration ecology will continue to grow as a discipline for many years.

▼ Figure 56.23

Exploring Restoration Ecology Worldwide

The examples highlighted on these pages are just a few of the many restoration ecology projects taking place around the world. The color-coded dots on the map indicate the locations of the projects.

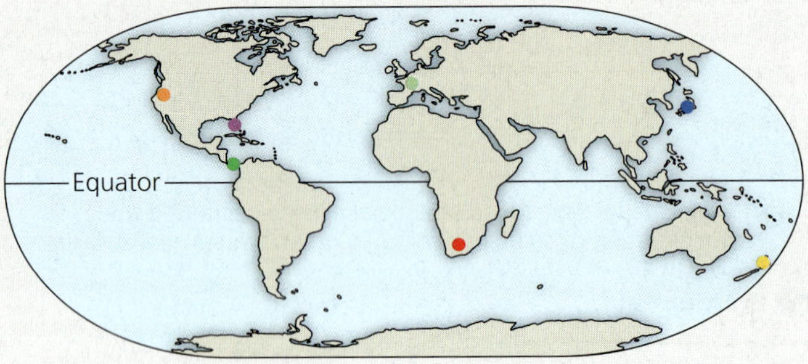

● **Truckee River, Nevada.** Damming and water diversions during the 20th century reduced flow in the Truckee River, Nevada, leading to declines in riparian forests. Restoration ecologists worked with water managers to ensure that sufficient water would be released during the short season of seed release by the native cottonwood and willow trees for seedlings to become established. Nine years of controlled-flow release led to the result shown here: a dramatic recovery of cottonwood-willow riparian forest.

● **Kissimmee River, Florida.** The Kissimmee River was converted from a meandering river to a 90-km canal, threatening many fish and wetland bird populations. Kissimmee River restoration has filled 12 km of drainage canal and reestablished 24 km of the original 167 km of natural river channel. Pictured here is a section of the Kissimmee canal that has been plugged (wide, light strip on the right side of the photo), diverting flow into remnant river channels in the center of the photo. The project will also restore the natural flow regime, which will foster self-sustaining populations of wetland birds and fishes.

● **Tropical dry forest, Costa Rica.** Clearing for agriculture, mainly for livestock grazing, eliminated approximately 98% of tropical dry forest in Central America and Mexico. Reversing this trend, tropical dry forest restoration in Costa Rica has used domestic livestock to disperse the seeds of native trees into open grasslands. The photo shows one of the first trees (right center), dispersed as seed by livestock, to colonize former pastureland. This project is a model for joining restoration ecology with the local economy and educational institutions.

Rhine River, Europe. Centuries of dredging and channeling for navigation (see the barges in the wide, main channel on the right side of the photo) have straightened the once-meandering Rhine River and disconnected it from its floodplain and associated wetlands. The countries along the Rhine, particularly France, Germany, Luxembourg, the Netherlands, and Switzerland, are cooperating to reconnect the river to side channels, such as the one shown on the left side of the photo. Such side channels increase the diversity of habitats available to aquatic biota, improve water quality, and provide flood protection.

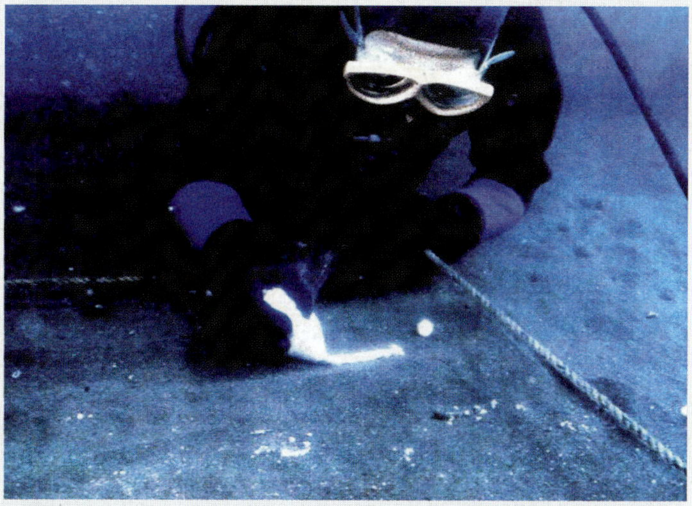

Coastal Japan. Seaweed and seagrass beds are important nursery grounds for a wide variety of fishes and shellfish. Once extensive but now reduced by development, these beds are being restored in the coastal areas of Japan. Techniques include constructing suitable seafloor habitat, transplanting from natural beds using artificial substrates, and hand seeding (shown in this photograph).

Succulent Karoo, South Africa. In this desert region of southern Africa, as in many arid regions, overgrazing by livestock has damaged vast areas. Reversing this trend, private landowners and government agencies in South Africa are restoring large areas of this unique region, revegetating the land and employing more sustainable resource management. The photo shows a small sample of the exceptional plant diversity of the Succulent Karoo; its 5,000 plant species include the highest diversity of succulent plants in the world.

Maungatautari, New Zealand. Weasels, rats, pigs, and other introduced species pose a serious threat to New Zealand's native plants and animals, including the kiwi, a flightless, ground-dwelling bird. The goal of the Maungatautari restoration project is to exclude all exotic mammals from a 3,400-ha reserve located on a forested volcanic cone. A specialized fence around the reserve eliminates the need to continue setting traps and using poisons that can harm native wildlife. In 2006, a pair of critically endangered takahe (a species of flightless rail) were released into the reserve in hopes of reestablishing a breeding population of this colorful bird on New Zealand's north island.

CONCEPT CHECK 56.4

1. Identify the main goal of restoration ecology.
2. How do bioremediation and biological augmentation differ?
3. WHAT IF? In what way is the Kissimmee River project a more complete ecological restoration than the Maungatautari project (see Figure 56.23)?

For suggested answers, see Appendix A.

CONCEPT 56.5

Sustainable development seeks to improve the human condition while conserving biodiversity

With the increasing loss and fragmentation of habitats, we face difficult trade-offs in how to manage Earth's resources. Preserving all habitat patches isn't feasible, so biologists must help societies set conservation priorities by identifying which habitat patches are most crucial. Ideally, implementing these priorities should also improve the quality of life for local people. Ecologists use the concept of *sustainability* as a tool to establish long-term conservation priorities.

Sustainable Biosphere Initiative

We must understand the complex interconnections of the biosphere to protect species from extinction and to improve the quality of human life. To this end, many nations, scientific societies, and other groups have embraced the concept of **sustainable development**, development that meets the needs of people today without limiting the ability of future generations to meet their needs. The forward-looking Ecological Society of America, the world's largest organization of professional ecologists, endorses a research agenda called the Sustainable Biosphere Initiative. The goal of this initiative is to define and acquire the basic ecological information needed to develop, manage, and conserve Earth's resources as responsibly as possible. The research agenda includes studies of global change, including interactions between climate and ecological processes; biological diversity and its role in maintaining ecological processes; and the ways in which the productivity of natural and artificial ecosystems can be sustained. This initiative requires a strong commitment of human and economic resources.

Achieving sustainable development is an ambitious goal. To sustain ecosystem processes and stem the loss of biodiversity, we must connect life science with the social sciences, economics, and humanities. We must also reassess our personal values. Those of us living in wealthier nations have a larger ecological footprint than do people living in developing nations (see Chapter 53). By reducing our orientation toward short-term gain, we can learn to value the natural processes that sustain us. The following case study illustrates how the combination of scientific and personal efforts can make a significant difference in creating a truly sustainable world.

Case Study: Sustainable Development in Costa Rica

The success of conservation in Costa Rica that we discussed in Concept 56.3 has involved an essential partnership between the national government, nongovernment organizations (NGOs), and private citizens. Many nature reserves established by individuals have been recognized by the government as national wildlife reserves and given significant tax benefits. However, conservation and restoration of biodiversity make up only one facet of sustainable development; the other key facet is improving the human condition.

How have the living conditions of the Costa Rican people changed as the country has pursued its conservation goals? As we discussed in Chapter 53, two of the most fundamental indicators of living conditions are infant mortality rate and life expectancy. From 1930 to 2007, the infant mortality rate in Costa Rica declined from 170 to 9 per 1,000 live births; over the same period, life expectancy increased from about 43 years to 77 years **(Figure 56.24)**. Another indicator of living conditions is literacy rate. The 2004 literacy rate in Costa Rica was 96%, compared to 97% in the United States. Such statistics show that living conditions in Costa Rica have improved greatly over the period in which the country has dedicated itself to conservation and restoration. While this result does not prove that conservation *causes* an increase in human welfare, we can say with certainty that development in Costa Rica has attended to both nature *and* people.

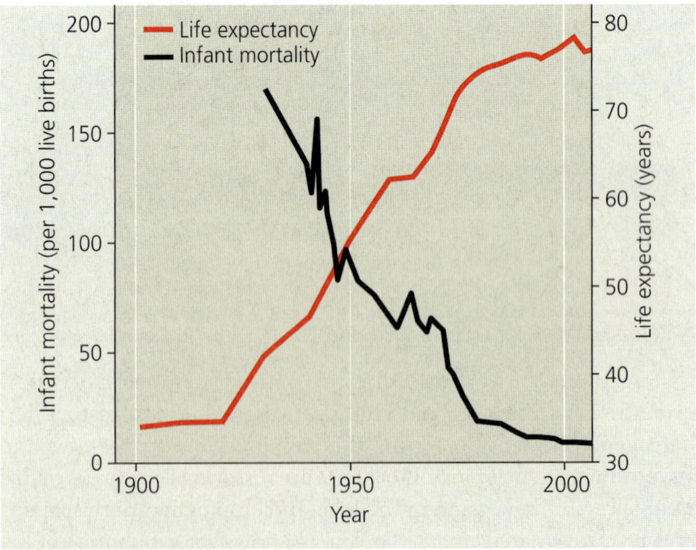

▲ **Figure 56.24 Infant mortality and life expectancy at birth in Costa Rica.**

Despite the successes in Costa Rica, many problems remain. One of the challenges that the country faces is maintaining its commitment to conservation while its population grows. Costa Rica is in the middle of a rapid demographic transition (see Chapter 53), and even though birth rates are dropping rapidly, its population is growing at about 1.5% annually (compared to 0.9% growth in the United States). Costa Rica's population, which is currently about 4 million, is predicted to continue to grow until the middle of this century, when it is projected to level off at approximately 6 million. If recent success is any guide, the people of Costa Rica will overcome the challenge of population growth in their quest for sustainable development.

The Future of the Biosphere

Our modern lives are very different from those of early humans, who hunted and gathered to survive. Their reverence for the natural world is evident in the early murals of wildlife they painted on cave walls **(Figure 56.25a)** and in the stylized visions of life they sculpted from bone and ivory **(Figure 56.25b)**.

Our lives reflect remnants of our ancestral attachment to nature and the diversity of life—the concept of *biophilia* that we introduced early in this chapter. We evolved in natural environments rich in biodiversity, and we still have an affinity for such settings **(Figure 56.25c)**. E. O. Wilson makes the case that our biophilia is innate, an evolutionary product of natural selection acting on a brainy species whose survival depended on a close connection to the environment and a practical appreciation of plants and animals.

Our appreciation of life guides the field of biology today. We celebrate life by deciphering the genetic code that makes each species unique. We embrace life by using fossils and DNA to chronicle the march of evolution through time. We preserve life through our efforts to classify and protect the millions of species on Earth. We respect life by using nature responsibly and reverently to improve human welfare.

Biology is the scientific expression of our desire to know nature. We are most likely to protect what we appreciate, and we are most likely to appreciate what we understand. By learning about the processes and diversity of life, we also become more aware of ourselves and our place in the biosphere. We hope this book serves you well in this lifelong adventure.

CONCEPT CHECK 56.5

1. What is meant by the term *sustainable development*?
2. How might biophilia influence us to conserve species and restore ecosystems?
3. **WHAT IF?** Suppose a new fishery is discovered, and you are put in charge of developing it sustainably. What ecological data might you want on the fish population? What criteria would you apply for the fishery's development?

For suggested answers, see Appendix A.

(a) Detail of animals in a 36,000-year-old cave painting, Lascaux, France

(b) A 30,000-year-old ivory carving of a water bird, found in Germany

(c) Biologist Carlos Rivera Gonzales examining a tiny tree frog in Peru

▲ **Figure 56.25 Biophilia, past and present.**

Chapter 56 Review

MEDIA Go to the Study Area at **www.masteringbio.com** for BioFlix 3-D Animations, MP3 Tutors, Videos, Practice Tests, an eBook, and more.

SUMMARY OF KEY CONCEPTS

CONCEPT 56.1

Human activities threaten Earth's biodiversity (pp. 1246–1250)

▶ **Three Levels of Biodiversity**

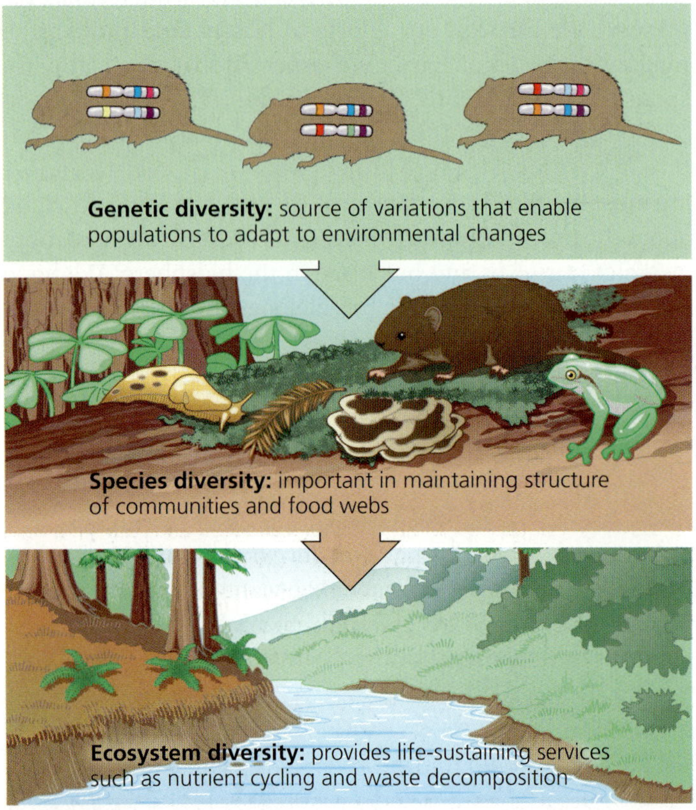

▶ **Biodiversity and Human Welfare** Our biophilia enables us to recognize the value of biodiversity for its own sake. Other species also provide humans with food, fiber, medicines, and ecosystem services.

▶ **Three Threats to Biodiversity** Three major threats to biodiversity are habitat loss, introduced species, and overexploitation.

MEDIA
Activity Madagascar and the Biodiversity Crisis
Activity Introduced Species: Fire Ants
GraphIt! Forestation Changes
GraphIt! Global Fisheries and Overfishing
GraphIt! Municipal Solid Waste Trends in the U.S.

CONCEPT 56.2

Population conservation focuses on population size, genetic diversity, and critical habitat (pp. 1250–1255)

▶ **Small-Population Approach** When a population drops below a minimum viable population (MVP) size, its loss of genetic variation due to nonrandom mating and genetic drift can trap it in an extinction vortex.

▶ **Declining-Population Approach** The declining-population approach focuses on the environmental factors that cause decline, regardless of absolute population size. It follows a step-by-step proactive conservation strategy.

▶ **Weighing Conflicting Demands** Conserving species often requires resolving conflicts between the habitat needs of endangered species and human demands.

CONCEPT 56.3

Landscape and regional conservation aim to sustain entire biotas (pp. 1255–1260)

▶ **Landscape Structure and Biodiversity** The structure of a landscape can strongly influence biodiversity. As habitat fragmentation increases and edges become more extensive, biodiversity tends to decrease. Movement corridors can promote dispersal and help sustain populations.

▶ **Establishing Protected Areas** Biodiversity hot spots are also hot spots of extinction and thus prime candidates for protection. Sustaining biodiversity in parks and reserves requires management to ensure that human activities in the surrounding landscape do not harm the protected habitats. The zoned reserve model recognizes that conservation efforts often involve working in landscapes that are greatly affected by human activity.

CONCEPT 56.4

Restoration ecology attempts to restore degraded ecosystems to a more natural state (pp. 1260–1264)

▶ **Bioremediation** Restoration ecologists harness organisms to detoxify polluted ecosystems.

▶ **Biological Augmentation** Ecologists also use organisms to add essential materials to ecosystems.

▶ **Exploring Restoration** The newness and complexity of restoration ecology require scientists to consider alternative solutions and adjust approaches based on experience.

MEDIA
Investigation How Are Potential Prairie Restoration Sites Analyzed?

CONCEPT 56.5

Sustainable development seeks to improve the human condition while conserving biodiversity (pp. 1264–1265)

▶ **Sustainable Biosphere Initiative** The goal of the Sustainable Biosphere Initiative is to acquire the ecological information needed for the development, management, and conservation of Earth's resources.

▶ ***Case Study:* Sustainable Development in Costa Rica** Costa Rica's success in conserving tropical biodiversity has involved partnerships between the government, other organizations, and private citizens. Human living conditions in Costa Rica have improved along with ecological conservation.

▶ **The Future of the Biosphere** By learning about biological processes and the diversity of life, we become more aware of our close connection to the environment and the value of other organisms in it.

MEDIA

Activity Conservation Biology Review
GraphIt! Global Freshwater Resources
GraphIt! Prospects for Renewable Energy

TESTING YOUR KNOWLEDGE

SELF-QUIZ

1. Ecologists conclude there is a biodiversity crisis because
a. biophilia causes humans to feel ethically responsible for protecting other species.
b. scientists have at last discovered and counted most of Earth's species and can now accurately calculate the current extinction rate.
c. current extinction rates are very high and many species are threatened or endangered.
d. many potential life-saving medicines are being lost as species evolve.
e. there are too few biodiversity hot spots.

2. Which of the following would be considered an example of bioremediation?
a. adding nitrogen-fixing microorganisms to a degraded ecosystem to increase nitrogen availability
b. using a bulldozer to regrade a strip mine
c. identifying a new biodiversity hot spot
d. reconfiguring the channel of a river
e. adding seeds of a chromium-accumulating plant to soil contaminated by chromium

3. What is the effective population size (N_e) of a population of 50 strictly monogamous swans (40 males and 10 females) if every female breeds successfully?
a. 50 b. 40 c. 30 d. 20 e. 10

4. One characteristic that distinguishes a population in an extinction vortex from most other populations is that
a. its habitat is fragmented.
b. it is a rare, top-level predator.
c. its effective population size is much lower than its total population size.
d. its genetic diversity is very low.
e. it is not well adapted to edge conditions.

5. The discipline that applies ecological principles to returning degraded ecosystems to more natural states is known as
a. population viability analysis.
b. landscape ecology.
c. conservation ecology.
d. restoration ecology.
e. resource conservation.

6. What is the single greatest threat to biodiversity?
a. overexploitation of commercially important species
b. introduced species that compete with or prey on native species
c. pollution of Earth's air, water, and soil
d. disruption of trophic relationships as more and more prey species become extinct
e. habitat alteration, fragmentation, and destruction

7. Which of the following strategies would most rapidly increase the genetic diversity of a population in an extinction vortex?
a. Capture all remaining individuals in the population for captive breeding followed by reintroduction to the wild.
b. Establish a reserve that protects the population's habitat.
c. Introduce new individuals transported from other populations of the same species.
d. Sterilize the least fit individuals in the population.
e. Control populations of the endangered population's predators and competitors.

8. Of the following statements about protected areas that have been established to preserve biodiversity, which one is *not* correct?
a. About 25% of Earth's land area is now protected.
b. National parks are one of many types of protected areas.
c. Most protected areas are too small to protect species.
d. Management of a protected area should be coordinated with management of the land surrounding the area.
e. It is especially important to protect biodiversity hot spots.

For Self-Quiz answers, see Appendix A.

MEDIA Visit the Study Area at **www.masteringbio.com** for a Practice Test.

EVOLUTION CONNECTION

9. One factor favoring rapid population growth by an introduced species is the absence of the predators, parasites, and pathogens that controlled its population in the region where it evolved. Over the long term, how should evolution by natural selection influence the rate at which the native predators, parasites, and pathogens in a region of introduction attack an introduced species?

SCIENTIFIC INQUIRY

10. **DRAW IT** Suppose that you are in charge of planning a forest reserve, and one of your goals is to help sustain local populations of woodland birds suffering from parasitism by the brown-headed cowbird. Reading research reports, you note that female cowbirds are usually reluctant to penetrate more than about 100 m into a forest and that nest parasitism is reduced for woodland birds nesting in denser, more central forest regions. The forested area you have to work with extends about 6,000 m from east to west and 1,000 m from north to south. Intact forest surrounds the reserve everywhere but on the west side, where the reserve borders deforested pastureland, and in the southwest corner, where it borders an agricultural field for 500 m. Your plan must include space for a small maintenance building, which you estimate to take up about 100 m^2. It will also be necessary to build a road, 10 m by 1,000 m, from the north to the south side of the reserve. Draw a map of the reserve, showing where you would construct the road and the building to minimize cowbird intrusion along edges. Explain your reasoning.

APPENDIX A Answers

CHAPTER 1

Figure Questions

Figure 1.3 Of the properties shown in this figure, the lawn mower shows only order, regulation, and energy processing. **Figure 1.6** The arrangement of fingers and opposable thumb in the human hand, combined with fingernails and a complex system of nerves and muscles, allows the hand to grasp and manipulate objects with great dexterity. **Figure 1.13** Substance B would be made continuously and would accumulate in large amounts. Neither C nor D would be made. **Figure 1.27** The percentage of brown artificial snakes attacked would probably be higher than the percentage of artificial kingsnakes attacked in all areas (whether or not inhabited by coral snakes). **Figure 1.28** The hole would allow some mixing of blood between the two ventricles. As a result, some of the blood pumped from the left ventricle to the body would not have received oxygen in the lungs, and some of the blood pumped to the lungs would already carry oxygen.

Concept Check 1.1

1. Examples: A molecule consists of *atoms* bonded together. Each organelle has an orderly arrangement of *molecules*. Photosynthetic plant cells contain *organelles* called chloroplasts. A tissue consists of a group of similar *cells*. Organs such as the heart are constructed from several *tissues*. A complex multicellular organism, such as a plant, has several types of *organs*, such as leaves and roots. A population is a set of *organisms* of the same species. A community consists of *populations* of the various species inhabiting a specific area. An ecosystem consists of a biological *community* along with the nonliving factors important to life, such as air, soil, and water. The biosphere is made up of all of Earth's *ecosystems*. **2.** (a) Structure and function are correlated. (b) Cells are an organism's basic units, *and* the continuity of life is based on heritable information in the form of DNA. (c) Organisms interact with their environments, exchanging matter and energy. **3.** Some possible answers: *Evolution:* All plants have chloroplasts, indicating their descent from a common ancestor. *Emergent properties:* The ability of a human heart to pump blood requires an intact heart; it is not a capability of any of the heart's tissues or cells working alone. *Exchange of matter and energy with the environment:* A mouse eats food, then uses the nutrients for growth and the generation of energy for its activities; some of the food material is expelled in urine and feces, and some of the energy returns to the environment as heat. *Structure and function:* The strong, sharp teeth of a wolf are well suited to grasping and dismembering its prey. *Cells:* The digestion of food is made possible by chemicals (chiefly enzymes) made by cells of the digestive tract. *DNA:* Human eye color is determined by the combination of genes inherited from the two parents. *Feedback regulation:* When your stomach is full, it signals your brain to decrease your appetite.

Concept Check 1.2

1. An address pinpoints a location by tracking from broader to narrower categories—a state, city, zip, street, and building number. This is analogous to the groups-subordinate-to-groups structure of biological taxonomy. **2.** Natural selection starts with the naturally occurring heritable variation in a population and then "edits" the population as individuals with heritable traits better suited to the environment survive and reproduce more successfully than others.

3.

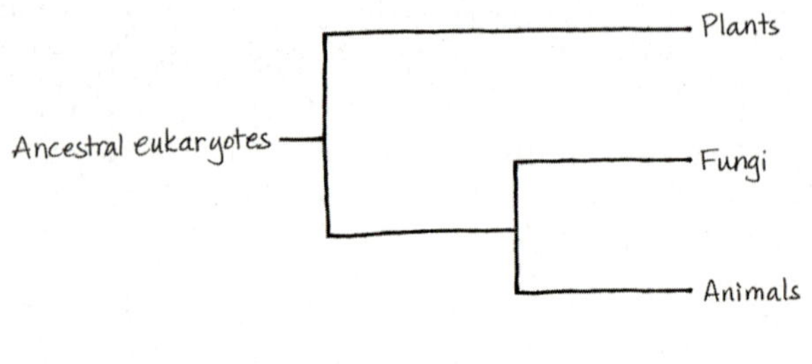

Concept Check 1.3

1. Inductive reasoning derives generalizations from specific cases; deductive reasoning predicts specific outcomes from general premises. **2.** Compared to a hypothesis, a scientific theory is usually more general and substantiated by a much greater amount of evidence. Natural selection is an explanatory idea that applies to all kinds of organisms and is supported by vast amounts of evidence of various kinds. **3.** Based on the results shown in Figure 1.27, you might predict that the colorful artificial snakes would be attacked more often than the brown ones, simply because they are easier to see. This prediction assumes that the area in Virginia where you are working has predators that attack snakes but no poisonous snakes that resemble the colorful artificial snakes.

Self-Quiz

1. b **2.** d **3.** a **4.** c **5.** c **6.** c **7.** c **8.** d **9.** b **10.** c
11. Your figure should show: (1) For the biosphere, the Earth with an arrow coming out of a tropical ocean; (2) for the ecosystem, a distant view of a coral reef; (3) for the community, a collection of reef animals and algae, with corals, fish, some seaweed, and any other organisms you can think of; (4) for the population, a group of fish of the same species; (5) for the organism, one fish from your population; (6) for the organ, the fish's stomach, and for the organ system, the whole digestive tract (see Chapter 41 for help); (7) for a tissue, a group of similar cells from the stomach; (8) for a cell, one cell from the tissue, showing its nucleus and a few other organelles; (9) for an organelle, the nucleus, where most of the cell's DNA is located; and (10) for a molecule, a DNA double helix. Your sketches can be very rough!

CHAPTER 2

Figure Questions

Figure 2.2 The most significant difference in the results would be that the two *Cedrela* saplings inside each garden would show similar amounts of dying leaf tissue because a poisonous chemical released from the *Duroia* trees would presumably reach the saplings via the air or soil and would not be blocked by the insect barrier. The *Cedrela* saplings planted outside the gardens would not show damage unless *Duroia* trees were nearby. Also, any ants present on the unprotected *Cedrela* saplings inside the gardens would probably not be observed making injections into the leaves. However, formic acid would likely still be found in the ants' glands, as for most species of ants. **Figure 2.9** Atomic number = 12; 12 protons, 12 electrons; three electron shells; 2 electrons in the valence shell
Figure 2.16

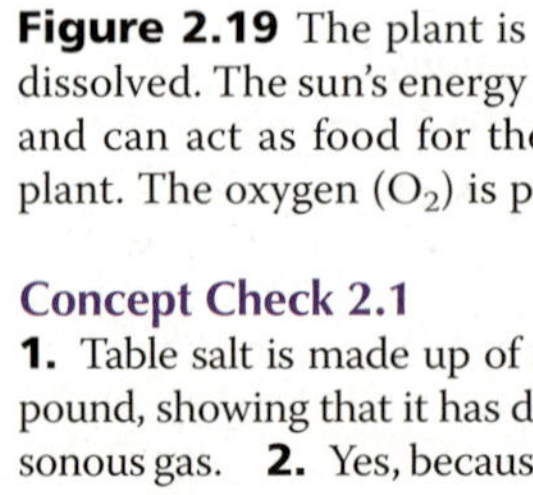

Figure 2.19 The plant is submerged in water (H_2O), in which the CO_2 is dissolved. The sun's energy is used to make sugar, which is found in the plant and can act as food for the plant itself, as well as for animals that eat the plant. The oxygen (O_2) is present in the bubbles.

Concept Check 2.1

1. Table salt is made up of sodium and chlorine. We are able to eat the compound, showing that it has different properties from those of a metal and a poisonous gas. **2.** Yes, because an organism requires trace elements, even though only in small amounts. **3.** A person with an iron deficiency will probably show effects of low oxygen in the blood, such as fatigue. (The condition is called anemia and can also result from too few red blood cells or abnormal hemoglobin.)

Concept Check 2.2

1. 7 **2.** $^{15}_{7}N$ **3.** 9 electrons; two electron shells; 1*s*, 2*s*, 2*p* (three orbitals); 1 electron is needed to fill the valence shell. **4.** The elements in a row all have the same number of electron shells. In a column, all the elements have the same number of electrons in their valence shells.

Concept Check 2.3

1. Each carbon atom has only three covalent bonds instead of the required four. **2.** The attractions between oppositely charged ions form ionic bonds. **3.** If researchers can synthesize molecules that mimic these shapes, they may be able to treat diseases or conditions caused by the inability of affected individuals to synthesize such molecules.

Concept Check 2.4

1.

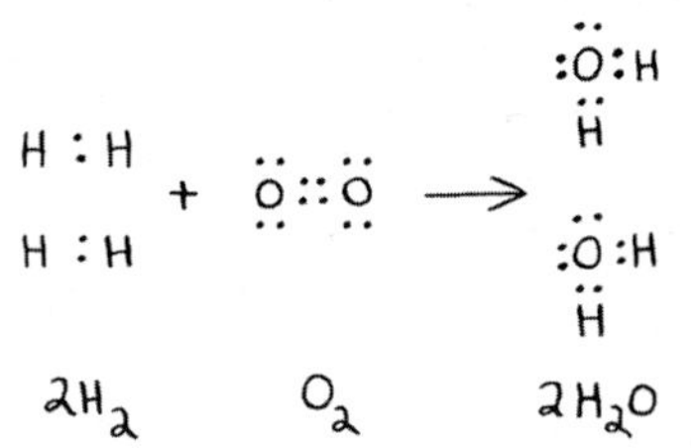

2. At equilibrium, the forward and reverse reactions occur at the same rate. **3.** $C_6H_{12}O_6 + 6\,O_2 \rightarrow 6\,CO_2 + 6\,H_2O$ + Energy. Glucose and oxygen react to form carbon dioxide, water, and energy. We breathe in oxygen because we need it for this reaction to occur, and we breathe out carbon dioxide because it is a by-product of this reaction. By the way, this reaction is called cellular respiration, and you will learn more about it in Chapter 9.

Self-Quiz

1. a **2.** b **3.** b **4.** c **5.** b **6.** a **7.** b **8.** b

9.

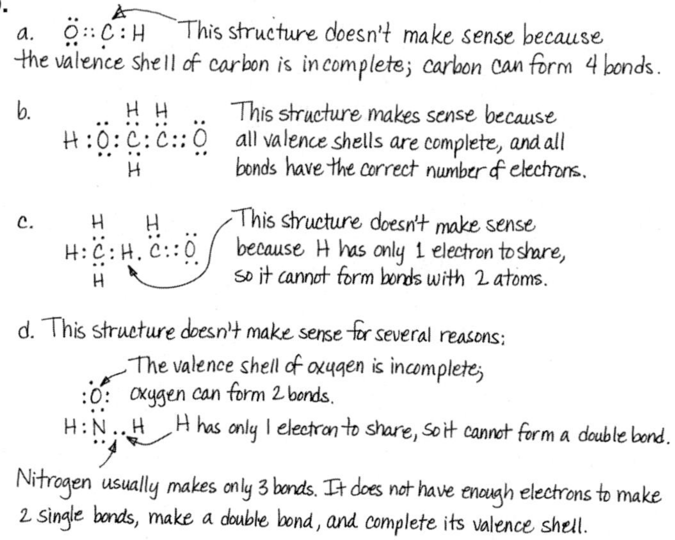

CHAPTER 3

Figure Questions

Figure 3.6 Without hydrogen bonds, water would behave like other small molecules, and the solid phase (ice) would be denser than liquid water. The ice would sink to the bottom, and because it would no longer insulate the whole body of water, it could freeze. Freezing would take a longer time because the Antarctic is an ocean (the Southern Ocean), not a pond or lake, but the average annual temperature at the South Pole is −50°C, so eventually it would freeze. The krill could not survive. **Figure 3.7** Heating the solution would cause the water to evaporate faster than it is evaporating at room temperature. At a certain point, there wouldn't be enough water molecules to solubilize the salt ions. The salt would start coming out of solution and re-forming crystals. Eventually, all the water would evaporate, leaving behind a pile of salt like the original pile. **Figure 3.11** Given that Ca^{2+} and $CO_3^{\,2-}$ must interact to form $CaCO_3$, you would predict that $[Ca^{2+}]$ would also have an effect on the calcification rate, and this result is observed in the current study. Under natural conditions in the oceans, the $[Ca^{2+}]$ remains relatively constant, so the $[CO_3^{\,2-}]$ has a much more important effect on calcification rate.

Concept Check 3.1

1. Electronegativity is the attraction of an atom for the electrons of a covalent bond. Because oxygen is more electronegative than hydrogen, the oxygen atom in H_2O pulls electrons toward itself, resulting in a partial negative charge on the oxygen atom and partial positive charges on the hydrogen atoms. Oppositely charged ends of water molecules are attracted to each other, forming a hydrogen bond. **2.** The hydrogen atoms of one molecule, with their partial positive charges, would repel the hydrogen atoms of the adjacent molecule. **3.** Water molecules would not be polar, and they would not form hydrogen bonds with each other.

Concept Check 3.2

1. Hydrogen bonds hold neighboring water molecules together. This cohesion helps the molecules resist gravity. Adhesion between water molecules and the walls of water-conducting cells also counters gravity. As water evaporates from leaves, the chain of water molecules in water-conducting cells moves upward. **2.** High humidity hampers cooling by suppressing the evaporation of sweat. **3.** As water freezes, it expands because water molecules move farther apart in forming ice crystals. When there is water in a crevice of a boulder, expansion due to freezing may crack the rock. **4.** The molecular mass of NaCl is 58.5 daltons. A mole would have a mass of 58.5 g, so you would measure out 0.5 mol, or 29.3 g, of NaCl and gradually add water, stirring until it is dissolved. You would add water to bring the final volume to 1 L. **5.** The hydrophobic substance repels water, perhaps helping to keep the ends of the legs from becoming coated with water and breaking through the surface. If the legs were coated with a hydrophilic substance, water would be drawn up them, possibly making it more difficult for the water strider to walk on water.

Concept Check 3.3

1. 10^5, or 100,000 **2.** $[H^+] = 0.01\ M = 10^{-2}\ M$, so pH = 2 **3.** $CH_3COOH \rightleftharpoons CH_3COO^- + H^+$. CH_3COOH is the acid (the H^+ donor) and CH_3COO^- is the base (the H^+ acceptor). **4.** The pH of the water should go from 7 to about 2; the pH of the acetic acid solution will only decrease a small amount, because the reaction shown for question 3 will shift to the left, with CH_3COO^- accepting the influx of H^+ and becoming CH_3COOH molecules.

Self-Quiz

1. d **2.** c **3.** b **4.** c **5.** c **6.** d **7.** c **8.** c

9.

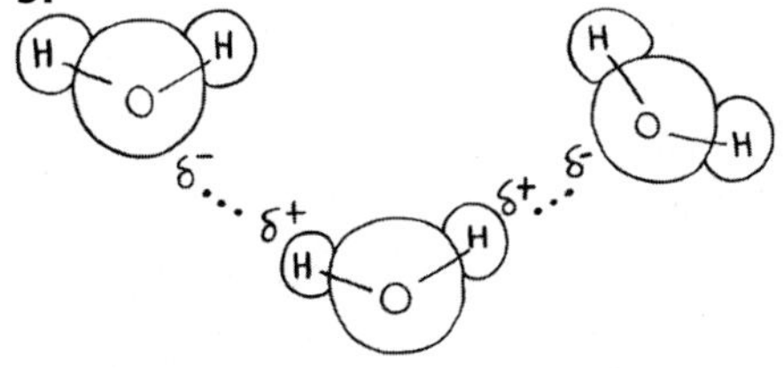

CHAPTER 4

Figure Questions

Figure 4.2 Because the concentration of the reactants influences the equilibrium (as discussed in Chapter 2), there might be more HCN relative to CH_2O, since there would be a higher concentration of the reactant gas that contains nitrogen.

Figure 4.4

Figure 4.7

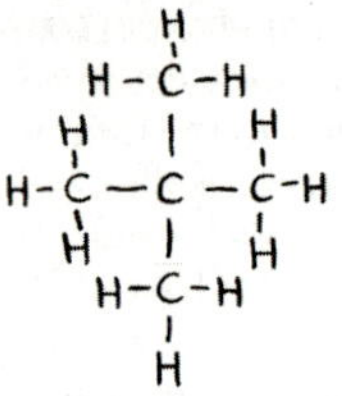

Figure 4.10 Molecule b, because there are not only the two electronegative oxygens of the carboxyl group, but also an oxygen on the next (carbonyl) carbon. All of these oxygens help make the bond between the O and H of the —OH group more polar, thus making the dissociation of H^+ more likely.

Concept Check 4.1

1. Amino acids are essential molecules for living organisms. Their synthesis from gases of the primitive atmosphere on Earth demonstrated that life's molecules could initially have been synthesized from nonliving molecules. **2.** The spark provides energy needed for the inorganic molecules in the atmosphere to react with each other. (You'll learn more about energy and chemical reactions in Chapter 8.)

Concept Check 4.2

1.

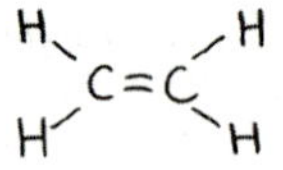

2. The forms of C_4H_{10} in (b) are structural isomers, as are the butenes in (c). **3.** Both consist largely of hydrocarbon chains. **4.** No. There is not enough diversity in the atoms. It can't form structural isomers because there is only one way for three carbons to attach to each other (in a line). There are no double bonds, so geometric isomers are not possible. Each carbon has at least two hydrogens attached to it, so the molecule is symmetrical and cannot have enantiomeric isomers.

Concept Check 4.3

1. It has both an amino group (—NH_2), which makes it an amine, and a carboxyl group (—COOH), which makes it a carboxylic acid. **2.** The ATP molecule loses a phosphate, becoming ADP.

3.

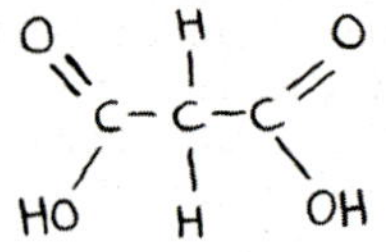

A chemical group that can act as a base has been replaced with a group that can act as an acid, increasing the acidic properties of the molecule. The shape of the molecule would also change, likely changing the molecules with which it can interact.

Self-Quiz

1. b **2.** d **3.** a **4.** b **5.** b **6.** a **7.** d

8.

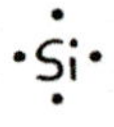

Si has four valence electrons, the same number as carbon. Therefore, silicon would be able to form long chains, including branches, that could act as skeletons for organic molecules. It would clearly do this much better than neon (with no valence electrons) or aluminum (with three valence electrons).

CHAPTER 5

Figure Questions

Figure 5.4

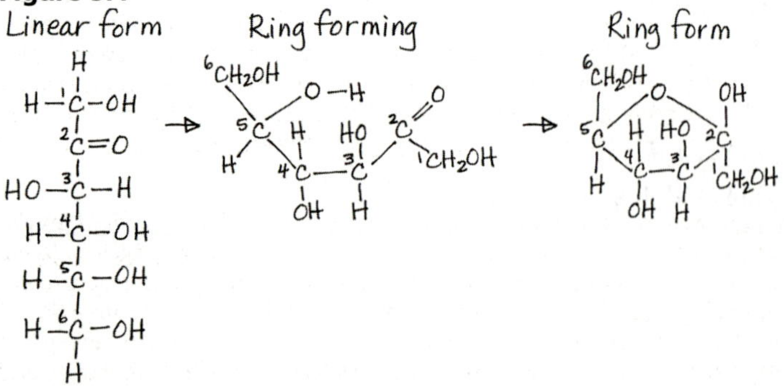

Four carbons are in the fructose ring, and two are not. (The latter two carbons are hanging off carbons 2 and 5, which are in the ring.) This form differs from glucose, which has five carbons in the ring and one that is not. (Note that the orientation of this fructose molecule is flipped relative to the one in Figure 5.5b.)

Figure 5.18

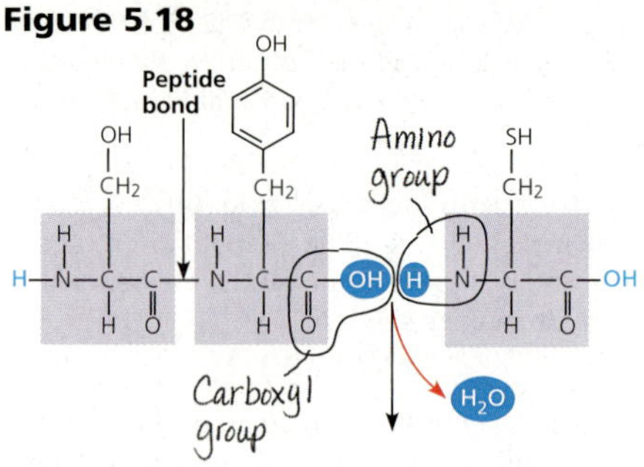

Figure 5.25 The green spiral is an α helix.

Concept Check 5.1

1. Proteins, carbohydrates, lipids, and nucleic acids **2.** Nine, with one water required to hydrolyze each connected pair of monomers **3.** The amino acids in the green bean protein are released in hydrolysis reactions and incorporated into other proteins in dehydration reactions.

Concept Check 5.2

1. $C_3H_6O_3$ **2.** $C_{12}H_{22}O_{11}$ **3.** The absence of these prokaryotes would hamper the cow's ability to obtain energy from food and could lead to weight loss and possibly death.

Concept Check 5.3

1. Both have a glycerol molecule attached to fatty acids. The glycerol of a fat has three fatty acids attached, whereas the glycerol of a phospholipid is attached to two fatty acids and one phosphate group. **2.** Human sex hormones are steroids, a type of hydrophobic compound. **3.** The oil droplet membrane could consist of a single layer of phospholipids rather than a bilayer, because an arrangement in which the hydrophobic tails of the membrane phospholipids were in contact with the hydrocarbon regions of the oil molecules would be more stable.

Concept Check 5.4

1. The function of a protein is a consequence of its specific shape, which is lost when a protein becomes denatured. **2.** Secondary structure involves hydrogen bonds between atoms of the polypeptide backbone. Tertiary structure involves bonding between atoms of the R groups of the amino acid subunits. **3.** Primary structure, the amino acid sequence, affects the secondary structure, which affects the tertiary structure, which affects the quaternary structure (if any). In short, the amino acid sequence affects the shape of the protein. Because the function of a protein depends on its shape, a change in primary structure can destroy a protein's function.

Concept Check 5.5

1.

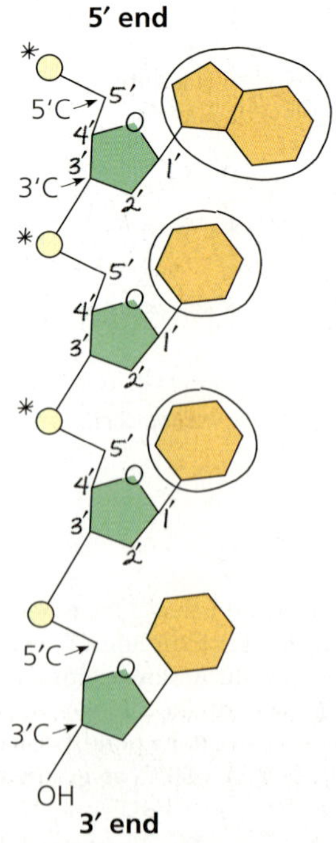

2. 5′-TAGGCCT–3′
3′–ATCCGGA–5′

3. (a)

Mismatch

5′–T A A G C C T–3′
3′–A T C C G G A–5′

(b)

3′–A T T C G G A–5′

Self-Quiz

1. d **2.** c **3.** a **4.** b **5.** a **6.** d **7.** b

8.

	Monomers or Components	Polymer or larger molecule	Type of linkage
Sugars	Monosaccharides	Polysaccharides	Glycosidic linkages
Lipids	Fatty acids	Triacylglycerols	Ester linkages
Proteins	Amino acids	Polypeptides	Peptide bonds
Nucleic acids	Nucleotides	Polynucleotides	Phosphodiester linkages

9.

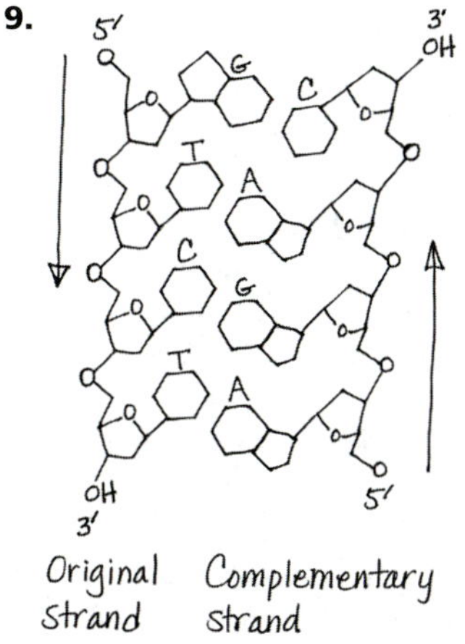

CHAPTER 6

Figure Questions

Figure 6.7 A phospholipid is a lipid, consisting of a glycerol molecule joined to two fatty acids and one phosphate group. Together, the glycerol and phosphate end of the phospholipid form is the "head," which is hydrophilic, while the hydrocarbon chains on the fatty acids form hydrophobic "tails." The presence in a single molecule of both a hydrophilic and a hydrophobic region makes the molecule ideal as the main building block of a membrane. **Figure 6.22** Each centriole has 9 sets of 3 microtubules, so the entire centrosome has 54. Each microtubule consists of a helical array of tubulin dimers (as shown in Table 6.1).

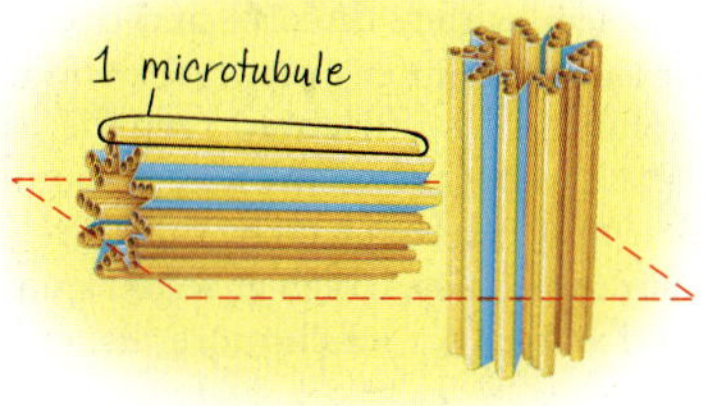

Figure 6.29 The microtubules would reorient, and based on the earlier results, the cellulose synthase proteins would also change their path, orienting along the repositioned microtubules. (This is, in fact, what was observed.)

Concept Check 6.1

1. Stains used for light microscopy are colored molecules that bind to cell components, affecting the light passing through, while stains used for electron microscopy involve heavy metals that affect the beams of electrons passing through. **2.** (a) Light microscope, (b) scanning electron microscope, (c) transmission electron microscope

Concept Check 6.2

1. See Figure 6.9.

2.

This cell would have the same volume as the cells in columns 2 and 3 but proportionally more surface area than that in column 2 and less than that in column 3. Thus, the surface-to-volume ratio should be greater than 1.2 but less than 6. To obtain the surface area, you'd have to add the area of the six sides (the top, bottom, sides, and ends): $125 + 125 + 125 + 125 + 1 + 1 = 502$. The surface-to-volume ratio equals 502 divided by a volume of 125, or 4.0.

Concept Check 6.3

1. Ribosomes in the cytoplasm translate the genetic message, carried from the DNA in the nucleus by mRNA, into a polypeptide chain. **2.** Nucleoli consist of DNA and the ribosomal RNA (rRNA) made according to its instructions, as well as proteins imported from the cytoplasm. Together, the rRNA and proteins are assembled into large and small ribosomal subunits. (These are exported through nuclear pores to the cytoplasm, where they will participate in polypeptide synthesis.) **3.** The information in a gene (on a chromosome in the nucleus) is used to synthesize an mRNA that is then transported through a nuclear pore to the cytoplasm. There it is translated into protein, which is transported back through a nuclear pore into the nucleus, where it joins other proteins and DNA, forming chromatin.

Concept Check 6.4

1. The primary distinction between rough and smooth ER is the presence of bound ribosomes on the rough ER. While both types of ER make phospholipids, membrane proteins and secretory proteins are all produced on the ribosomes of the rough ER. The smooth ER also functions in detoxification, carbohydrate metabolism, and storage of calcium ions. **2.** Transport vesicles move membranes and substances they enclose between other components of the endomembrane system. **3.** The mRNA is synthesized in the nucleus and then passes out through a nuclear pore to be translated on a bound ribosome, attached to the rough ER. The protein is synthesized into the lumen of the ER and perhaps modified there. A transport vesicle carries the protein to the Golgi apparatus. After further modification in the Golgi, another transport vesicle carries it back to the ER, where it will perform its cellular function.

Concept Check 6.5

1. Both organelles are involved in energy transformation, mitochondria in cellular respiration and chloroplasts in photosynthesis. They both have multiple membranes that separate their interiors into compartments. In both organelles, the innermost membranes—cristae, or infoldings of the inner membrane, in mitochondria, and the thylakoid membranes in chloroplasts—have large surface areas with embedded enzymes that carry out their main functions. **2.** Mitochondria, chloroplasts, and peroxisomes are not derived from the ER, nor are they connected physically or via transport vesicles to organelles of the endomembrane system. Mitochondria and chloroplasts are structurally quite different from vesicles derived from the ER, which are bounded by a single membrane.

Concept Check 6.6

1. Both systems of movement involve long filaments that are moved in relation to each other by motor proteins that grip, release, and grip again adjacent polymers. **2.** Dynein arms, powered by ATP, move neighboring doublets of microtubules relative to one another. Because they are anchored within the organelle and with respect to each other, the doublets bend instead of sliding past one another. **3.** Such individuals have defects in the microtubule-based movement of cilia and flagella. Thus, the sperm can't move because of malfunctioning flagella; the airways are compromised; and signaling events during embryogenesis do not occur correctly due to malfunctioning cilia.

Concept Check 6.7

1. The most obvious difference is the presence of direct cytoplasmic connections between cells of plants (plasmodesmata) and animals (gap junctions). These connections result in the cytoplasm being continuous between adjacent cells. **2.** The cell would not be able to function properly and would probably soon die, as the cell wall or ECM must be permeable to allow the exchange of matter between the cell and its external environment. Molecules involved with energy production and use must be allowed entry, as well as those that provide information about the cell's environment. Other molecules, such as products synthesized by the cell for export and the by-products of cellular respiration, must be allowed to exit.

Self-Quiz

1. c **2.** b **3.** d **4.** d **5.** b **6.** c **7.** e **8.** a
9. See Figure 6.9.

CHAPTER 7

Figure Questions

Figure 7.6 You couldn't rule out movement of proteins within the cell membrane of the same species. You might speculate that the membrane lipids and proteins from one species weren't able to mingle with those from the other species because of some incompatibility. **Figure 7.9** A transmembrane protein like the integrin dimer in (f) might change its shape upon binding to a particular ECM molecule. The new shape might enable the interior portion of the protein to bind to a second, cytoplasmic protein that would relay the message to the inside of the cell, as shown in (c). **Figure 7.12** The orange solute would be evenly distributed throughout the solution on both sides of the membrane. The solution levels would not be affected because the orange solute can diffuse through the membrane and equalize its concentration. Thus, no additional osmosis of water would take place in either direction.

Concept Check 7.1

1. They are on the inner side of the transport vesicle membrane. **2.** Plants adapted to cold environments would be expected to have more unsaturated fatty acids in their membranes because those remain fluid at lower temperatures. Plants adapted to hot environments would be expected to have more saturated fatty acids, which would allow the fatty acids to "stack" more closely, making the membranes less fluid and therefore helping them to stay intact at higher temperatures.

Concept Check 7.2

1. O_2 and CO_2 are both small nonpolar molecules that can easily pass through the hydrophobic core of a membrane. **2.** Water is a polar molecule, so it cannot pass very rapidly through the hydrophobic region in the middle of a phospholipid bilayer. **3.** The hydronium ion is charged, while glycerol is not. Charge is probably more significant than size as a basis for exclusion by the aquaporin channel.

Concept Check 7.3

1. CO_2 is a small nonpolar molecule that can diffuse through the plasma membrane. As long as it diffuses away so the concentration remains low outside the cell, it will continue to exit the cell in this way. (This is the opposite of the case for O_2, described in this section.) **2.** The water is hypotonic to the plant cells, so they take up water and the cells of the vegetable remain turgid, rather than plasmolyzing. The vegetable (for example, lettuce or spinach) remains crisp and not wilted. **3.** The activity of the *Paramecium's* contractile vacuole will decrease. The vacuole pumps out excess water that flows into the cell; this flow occurs only in a hypotonic environment.

Concept Check 7.4

1. The pump uses ATP. To establish a voltage, ions have to be pumped against their gradients, which requires energy. **2.** Each ion is being transported against its electrochemical gradient. If either ion were flowing down its electrochemical gradient, this *would* be considered cotransport. **3.** Even if proton pumps were still using ATP and moving protons, no proton gradient would become established. This would have serious consequences for the cells, because processes like the cotransport of sucrose (as well as synthesis of ATP) depend on establishment of a proton gradient.

Concept Check 7.5

1. Exocytosis. When a transport vesicle fuses with the plasma membrane, the vesicle membrane becomes part of the plasma membrane. **2.** Receptor-mediated endocytosis. In this case, one specific kind of molecule needs to be taken up at a particular time; pinocytosis takes up substances in a nonspecific manner.

Self-Quiz

1. b **2.** c **3.** a **4.** d **5.** b
6. a.

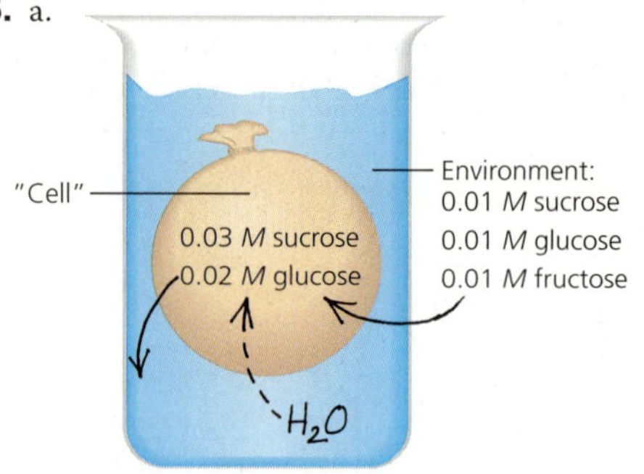

b. The solution outside is hypotonic. It has less sucrose, which is a nonpenetrating solute.
c. See answer for (a).
d. The artificial cell will become more turgid.
e. Eventually, the two solutions will have the same solute concentrations. Even though sucrose can't move through the membrane, water flow (osmosis) will lead to isotonic conditions.

CHAPTER 8

Figure Questions

Figure 8.14

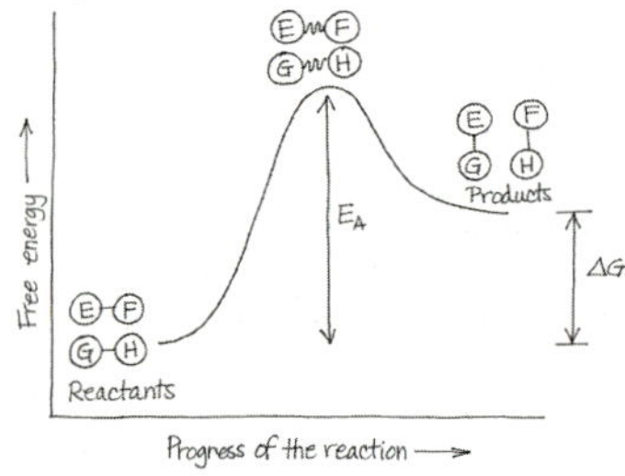

Figure 8.18

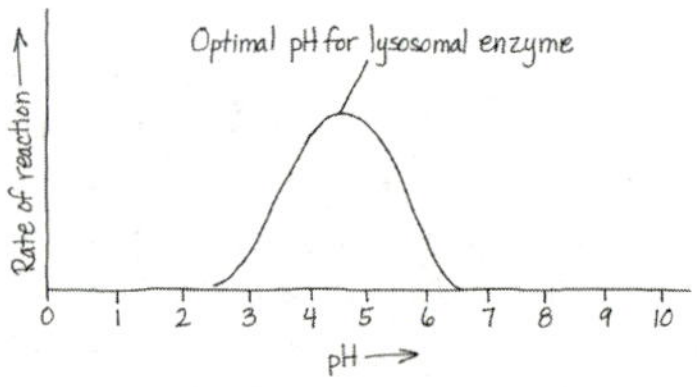

Figure 8.21 Because the affinity of the caspase for the inhibitor is very low (as is expected of an allosterically inhibited enzyme), the inhibitor is likely to diffuse away. Because no additional source of the inhibitory compound is present (the concentration of inhibitor is very low), the inhibitor is unlikely to bind again to the enzyme once the covalent linkage is broken. Thus, normal activity of the enzyme would most likely not be affected. (This test was performed by the researchers, and enzyme activity was observed to be normal upon release of the inhibitor.)

Concept Check 8.1

1. The second law is the trend toward randomness. Equal concentrations of a substance on both sides of a membrane is a more random distribution than unequal concentrations. Diffusion of a substance to a region where it is initially less concentrated increases entropy, as described by the second law. **2.** The apple has potential energy in its position hanging on the tree, and the sugars and other nutrients it contains have chemical energy. The apple has kinetic energy as it falls from the tree to the ground. Finally, when the apple is digested and its molecules broken down, some of the chemical energy is used to do work, and the rest is lost as thermal energy. **3.** The sugar crystals become less ordered (entropy increases) as they dissolve and become randomly spread out in the water. Over time, the water evaporates, and the crystals form again because the water volume is insufficient to keep them in solution. While the reappearance of sugar crystals may represent a "spontaneous" increase in order (decrease in entropy), it is balanced by the decrease in order (increase in entropy) of the water molecules, which changed from a relatively compact arrangement in liquid water to a much more dispersed and disordered form in water vapor.

Concept Check 8.2

1. Cellular respiration is a spontaneous and exergonic process. The energy released from glucose is used to do work in the cell or is lost as heat. **2.** Hydrogen ions can perform work only if their concentrations on each side of a membrane differ. When the H^+ concentrations are the same, the system is at equilibrium and can do no work. **3.** The reaction is exergonic because it releases energy—in this case, in the form of light. (This is a chemical version of the bioluminescence seen in Figure 8.1.)

Concept Check 8.3

1. ATP transfers energy to endergonic processes by phosphorylating (adding phosphate groups to) other molecules. (Exergonic processes phosphorylate ADP to regenerate ATP.) **2.** A set of coupled reactions can transform the first combination into the second. Since, overall, this is an exergonic process, ΔG is negative and the first group must have more free energy. (See Figure 8.10.)

Concept Check 8.4

1. A spontaneous reaction is a reaction that is exergonic. However, if it has a high activation energy that is rarely attained, the rate of the reaction may be low. **2.** Only the specific substrate(s) will fit properly into the active site of an enzyme, the part of the enzyme that carries out catalysis. **3.** Increase the concentration of the normal substrate (succinate) and see whether the rate of reaction increases. If it does, malonate is a competitive inhibitor.

Concept Check 8.5

1. The activator binds in such a way that it stabilizes the active form of an enzyme, whereas the inhibitor stabilizes the inactive form. **2.** You might choose to screen chemical compounds that bind allosterically to the enzyme, because allosteric regulatory sites are less likely to share similarity between different enzymes.

Self-Quiz

1. b **2.** c **3.** b **4.** a **5.** e **6.** c **7.** c

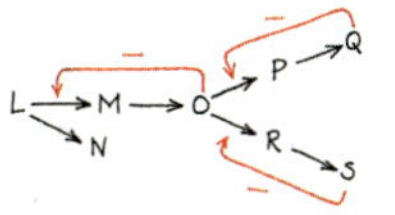

Scientific Inquiry

9.

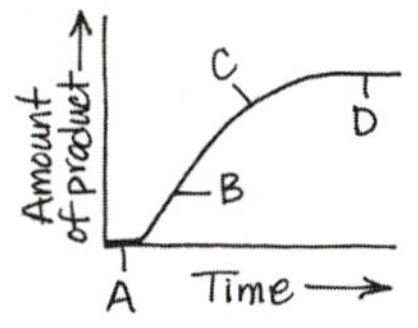

A: The substrate molecules are entering the cells, so no product is made yet.
B: There is sufficient substrate, so the reaction is proceeding at a maximum rate.
C: As the substrate is used up, the rate falls.
D: The line is flat because no new substrate remains and thus no new product appears.

CHAPTER 9

Figure Questions

Figure 9.7 Because an enzyme is catalyzing this reaction and there is no external source of energy, it must be exergonic, and the reactants must be at a higher energy level than the products. **Figure 9.9** It would probably stop glycolysis, or at least slow it down, since this would tend to push the equilibrium for this step toward the left. If less (or no) glyceraldehyde-3-phosphate were made, step 6 would slow down (or be unable to occur). **Figure 9.15** Rotation in the opposite direction (blue bars) would be expected to hydrolyze some of the ATP present, lowering ATP concentration below the background level. Thus, the blue bars would be expected to be lower than the gray bars, which is not what the researchers observed. (A possible explanation: In the article, the researchers explained that when they enclosed ATP synthases in a chamber for this assay, a number of the complexes adhered to the chamber ceiling instead of the nickel plate. The enzymes adhering to the chamber ceiling would be expected to spin in an opposite direction to those on the nickel plate on the floor. When the floor-based enzymes produce ATP during a particular spin (yellow bars), those on the ceiling would be expected to consume ATP, which would make the yellow bars lower than they would have been if all enzymes were floor-based. The opposite is also true: When the floor-based enzymes hydrolyze ATP (blue bars), the ceiling-based enzymes would be synthesizing ATP, which would make the blue bars higher than if all enzymes were floor-based. Evidence of this phenomenon is shown in the graph: The spins expected to hydrolyze ATP (blue bars) result in higher ATP levels than those with no rotation (gray bars), suggesting that there are probably some "upside-down" ceiling-based complexes generating ATP while the rest are floor-based and are hydrolyzing ATP.) **Figure 9.16** At first, some ATP could be made, since electron transport could proceed as far as complex III, and a small H^+ gradient could be built up. Soon, however, no more electrons could be passed to complex III because it could not be reoxidized by passing its electrons to complex IV.

Concept Check 9.1

1. Both processes include glycolysis, the citric acid cycle, and oxidative phosphorylation. In aerobic respiration, the final electron acceptor is molecular oxygen (O_2), whereas in anaerobic respiration, the final electron acceptor is a different substance. **2.** $C_4H_6O_5$ would be oxidized and NAD^+ would be reduced.

Concept Check 9.2

1. NAD^+ acts as the oxidizing agent in step 6, accepting electrons from glyceraldehyde-3-phosphate, which thus acts as the reducing agent. **2.** Since the overall process of glycolysis results in net production of ATP, it would make sense for the process to slow down when ATP levels have increased substantially. Thus we would expect ATP to allosterically inhibit phosphofructokinase.

Concept Check 9.3

1. NADH and $FADH_2$; they will donate electrons to the electron transport chain. **2.** CO_2 is released from the pyruvate that is formed during glycolysis, and CO_2 is also released during the citric acid cycle. **3.** In both cases, the precursor molecule loses a CO_2 molecule and then donates electrons to an electron carrier in an oxidation step. Also, the product has been activated due to the attachment of a CoA group.

Concept Check 9.4

1. Oxidative phosphorylation would stop entirely, resulting in no ATP production by this process. Without oxygen to "pull" electrons down the electron transport chain, H^+ would not be pumped into the mitochondrion's intermembrane space and chemiosmosis would not occur. **2.** Decreasing the pH is the addition of H^+. It would establish a proton gradient even without the function of the electron transport chain, and we would expect ATP synthase to function and synthesize ATP. (In fact, it was experiments like this that provided support for chemiosmosis as an energy-coupling mechanism.)

Concept Check 9.5

1. A derivative of pyruvate—such as acetaldehyde during alcohol fermentation—or pyruvate itself during lactic acid fermentation; oxygen. **2.** The cell would need to consume glucose at a rate about 19 times the consumption rate in the aerobic environment (2 ATP are generated by fermentation versus up to 38 ATP by cellular respiration).

Concept Check 9.6

1. The fat is much more reduced; it has many $—CH_2—$ units, and in all these bonds the electrons are equally shared. The electrons present in a carbohydrate molecule are already somewhat oxidized (shared unequally in bonds), as quite a few of them are bound to oxygen. **2.** When we consume more food than necessary for metabolic processes, our body synthesizes fat as a way of storing energy for later use. **3.** AMP will accumulate, stimulating phosphofructokinase, which increases the rate of glycolysis. Since oxygen is not present, the cell will convert pyruvate to lactate in lactic acid fermentation, providing a supply of ATP.

Self-Quiz

1. b **2.** d **3.** c **4.** c **5.** a **6.** a **7.** d **8.** b **9.** b

10.

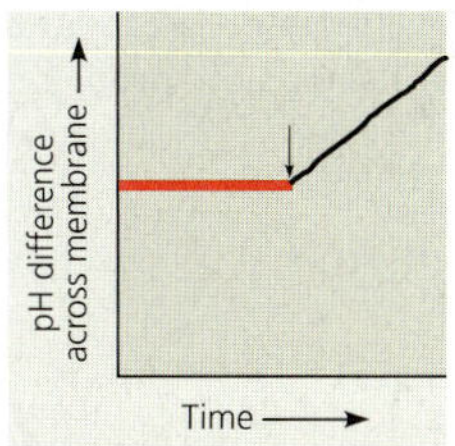

CHAPTER 10

Figure Questions

Figure 10.9 Red, but not violet-blue, wavelengths would pass through the filter, so the bacteria would not congregate where the violet-blue light normally comes through. Therefore, the left "peak" of bacteria would not be present, but the right peak would be observed because the red wavelengths passing through the filter would be used for photosynthesis. **Figure 10.11** In the leaf, most of the chlorophyll electrons excited by photon absorption are used to power the reactions of photosynthesis.

Figure 10.18

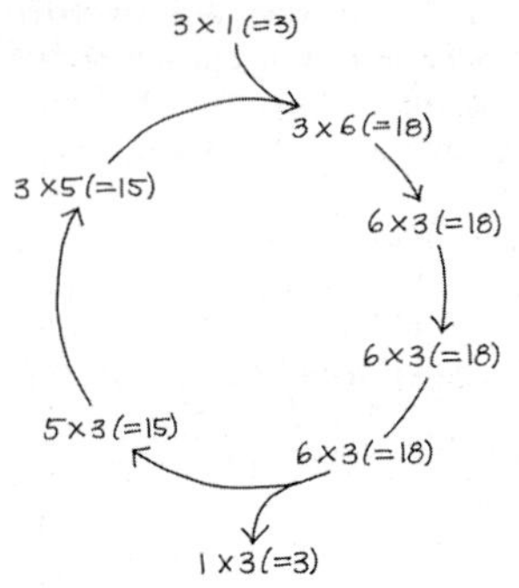

Three carbon atoms enter the cycle, one by one, as individual CO_2 molecules, and leave the cycle in one three-carbon molecule (G3P) per three turns of the cycle.

Concept Check 10.1

1. CO_2 enters leaves via stomata, and water enters via roots and is carried to leaves through veins. **2.** Using ^{18}O, a heavy isotope of oxygen, as a label, van Niel was able to show that the oxygen produced during photosynthesis originates in water, not in carbon dioxide. **3.** The light reactions could *not* keep producing NADPH and ATP without the $NADP^+$, ADP, and Ⓟ$_i$ that the Calvin cycle generates. The two cycles are interdependent.

Concept Check 10.2

1. Green, because green light is mostly transmitted and reflected—not absorbed—by photosynthetic pigments **2.** In chloroplasts, light-excited electrons are trapped by a primary electron acceptor, which prevents them from dropping back to the ground state. In isolated chlorophyll, there is no electron acceptor, so the photoexcited electrons immediately drop back down to the ground state, with the emission of light and heat. **3.** Water (H_2O) is the initial electron donor; $NADP^+$ accepts electrons at the end of the electron transport chain, becoming reduced to NADPH. **4.** In this experiment, the rate of ATP synthesis would slow and eventually stop. Because the added compound would not allow a proton gradient to build up across the membrane, ATP synthase could not catalyze ATP production.

Concept Check 10.3

1. 6, 18, 12 **2.** The more potential energy a molecule stores, the more energy and reducing power is required for the formation of that molecule. Glucose is a valuable energy source because it is highly reduced, storing lots of potential energy in its electrons. To reduce CO_2 to glucose, much energy and reducing power are required in the form of large numbers of ATP and NADPH molecules, respectively. **3.** The light reactions require ADP and $NADP^+$, which would not be formed in sufficient quantities from ATP and NADPH if the Calvin cycle stopped.

Concept Check 10.4

1. Photorespiration decreases photosynthetic output by adding oxygen, instead of carbon dioxide, to the Calvin cycle. As a result, no sugar is generated (no carbon is fixed), and O_2 is used rather than generated. **2.** Without PS II, no O_2 is generated in bundle-sheath cells. This avoids the problem of O_2 competing with CO_2 for binding to rubisco in these cells. **3.** C_4 and CAM species would replace many of the C_3 species.

Self-Quiz

1. d **2.** b **3.** b **4.** c **5.** d **6.** d **7.** c

Scientific Inquiry

9.

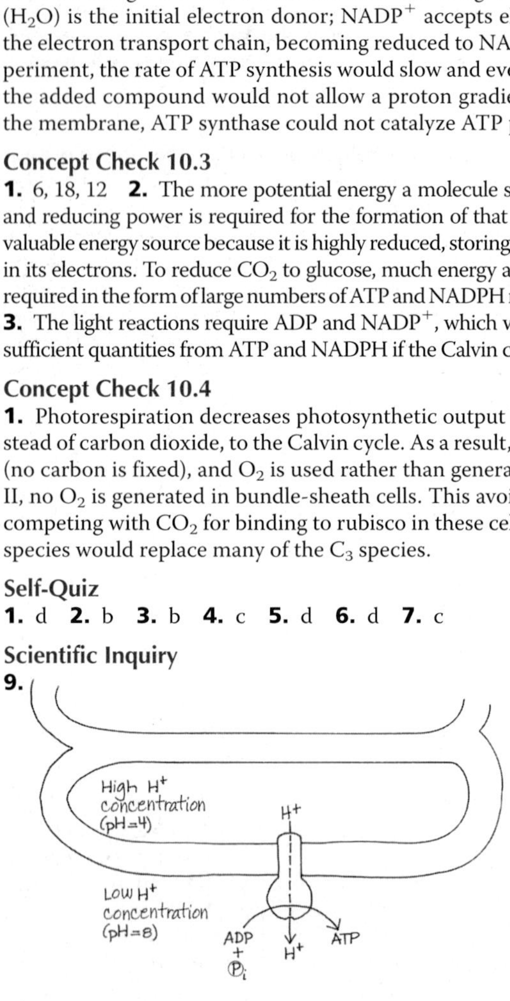

The ATP would end up outside the thylakoid. The chloroplasts were able to make ATP in the dark because the researchers set up an artificial proton concentration gradient across the thylakoid membrane; thus, the light reactions were not necessary to establish the H^+ gradient required for ATP synthesis by ATP synthase.

CHAPTER 11

Figure Questions

Figure 11.6 Epinephrine is a signaling molecule; presumably it binds to a cell-surface receptor protein. **Figure 11.8** The testosterone molecule is hydrophobic and can therefore pass directly through the lipid bilayer of the plasma membrane into the cell. (Hydrophilic molecules cannot do this.) **Figure 11.9** The active form of protein kinase 2 **Figure 11.10** The signaling molecule (cAMP) would remain in its active form and would continue to signal. **Figure 11.16** In the model, the directionality of growth is determined by the association of Fus3 with the membrane near the site of receptor activation. Thus, the development of shmoos would be severely compromised, and the affected cell would likely resemble the ΔFus3 and Δformin cells.

Concept Check 11.1

1. The two cells of opposite mating type (**a** and **α**) each secrete a certain signaling molecule, which can only be bound by receptors carried on cells of the opposite mating type. Thus, the **a** mating factor cannot bind to another **a** cell and cause it to grow toward the first **a** cell. Only an **α** cell can "receive" the signaling molecule and respond by directed growth (see Figure 11.16 for more information). **2.** The secretion of neurotransmitter molecules at a synapse is an example of local signaling. The electrical signal that travels along a very long nerve cell and is passed to the next nerve cell can be considered an example of long-distance signaling. (Note, however, that local signaling at the synapse between two cells is necessary for the signal to pass from one cell to the next.) **3.** Glucose-1-phosphate is not generated, because the activation of the enzyme requires an intact cell, with an intact receptor in the membrane and an intact signal transduction pathway. The enzyme cannot be activated directly by interaction with the signaling molecule in the test tube. **4.** Glycogen phosphorylase acts in the third stage, the response to epinephrine signaling.

Concept Check 11.2

1. The water-soluble NGF molecule cannot pass through the lipid membrane to reach intracellular receptors, as steroid hormones can. Therefore, you'd expect the NGF receptor to be in the plasma membrane—which is, in fact, the case. **2.** The cell with the faulty receptor would not be able to respond appropriately to the signaling molecule when it was present. This would most likely have dire consequences for the cell, since regulation of the cell's activities by this receptor would not occur appropriately.

Concept Check 11.3

1. A protein kinase is an enzyme that transfers a phosphate group from ATP to a protein, usually activating that protein (often a second type of protein kinase). Many signal transduction pathways include a series of such interactions, in which each phosphorylated protein kinase in turn phosphorylates the next protein kinase in the series. Such phosphorylation cascades carry a signal from outside the cell to the cellular protein(s) that will carry out the response. **2.** Protein phosphatases reverse the effects of the kinases. **3.** Information is transduced by way of sequential protein-protein interactions that change protein shapes, causing them to function in a way that passes the signal along. **4.** The IP_3-gated channel opens, allowing calcium ions to flow out of the ER, which raises the cytosolic Ca^{2+} concentration.

Concept Check 11.4

1. At each step in a cascade of sequential activations, one molecule or ion may activate numerous molecules functioning in the next step. **2.** Scaffolding proteins hold molecular components of signaling pathways in a complex with each other. Different scaffolding proteins would assemble different collections of proteins, leading to different cellular responses in the two cells.

Concept Check 11.5

1. In formation of the hand or paw in mammals, cells in the regions between the digits are programmed to undergo apoptosis. This serves to shape the digits of the hand or paw so that they are not webbed. **2.** If a receptor protein for a death-signaling molecule was defective so that it was activated for signaling even in the absence of the death signal, this would lead to apoptosis when it wouldn't normally occur. Similar defects in any of the proteins in the signaling pathway, which would activate these relay or response proteins in the absence of interaction with the previous protein or second messenger in the pathway, would have the same effect. Conversely, if any protein in the pathway were defective in its ability to respond to an interaction with an early protein or other molecule or ion, apoptosis would not occur when it normally should. For example, a receptor protein for a death-signaling ligand might not be able to be activated, even when ligand was bound. This would stop the signal from being transduced into the cell.

Self-Quiz

1. c **2.** d **3.** a **4.** c **5.** c **6.** b **7.** a **8.** d
9. This is one possible drawing of the pathway. (Similar drawings would also be correct.)

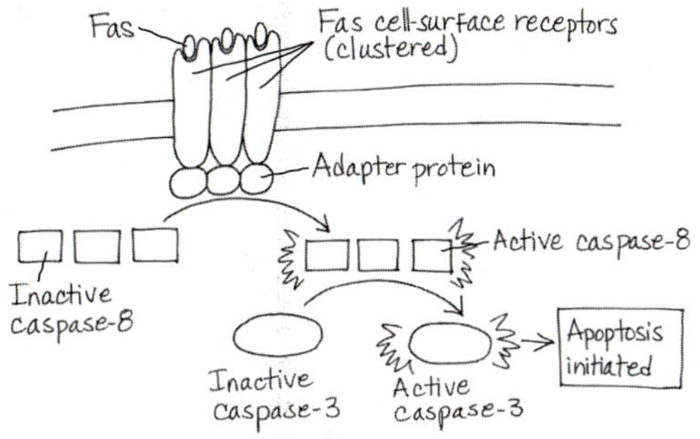

CHAPTER 12

Figure Questions

Figure 12.4

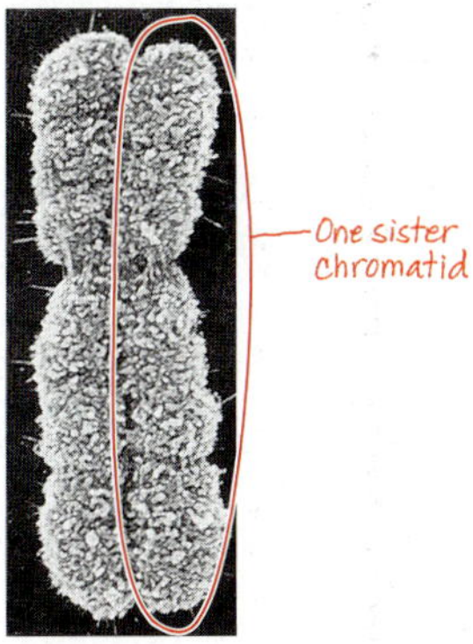

Circling the other chromatid instead would also be correct. The chromosome has four arms. **Figure 12.6** 12; 2; 2; 1

Figure 12.7

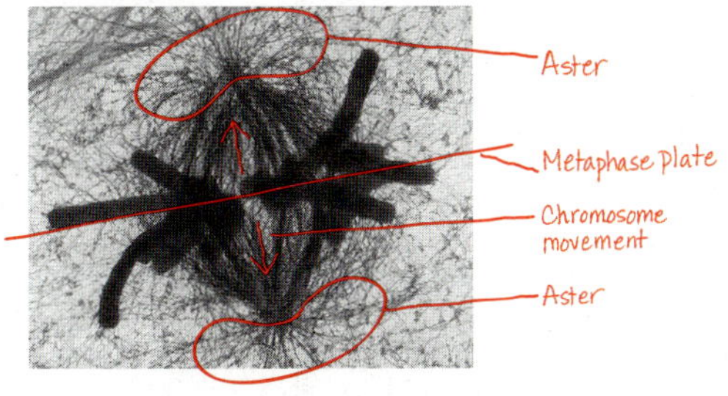

Figure 12.8 The mark would have moved toward the nearer pole. The lengths of fluorescent microtubules between that pole and the mark would have decreased, while the lengths between the chromosomes and the mark would have remained the same. **Figure 12.13** In both cases, the G_1 nucleus would have remained in G_1 until the time it normally would have entered the S phase. Chromosome condensation and spindle formation would not have occurred until the S and G_2 phases had been completed. **Figure 12.15** The cell would divide under conditions where it was inappropriate to do so. If the daughter cells and their descendants also ignored the checkpoint and divided, there would soon be an abnormal mass of cells. (This type of inappropriate cell division can contribute to the development of cancer.) **Figure 12.16** Given that control experiments showed that the *cdc2* protein kinase was the primary source of kinase activity detected in this experiment, there would be virtually no kinase activity. The percentage of cells dividing would be zero because the cells would be unable to undergo mitosis without the *cdc2* kinase. **Figure 12.18** The cells in the vessel with PDGF would not be able to respond to the growth factor signal and thus would not divide. The culture would resemble that without the added PDGF.

Concept Check 12.1

1. 32 cells **2.** 2 **3.** 39; 39; 78

Concept Check 12.2

1. 6; 12 **2.** Cytokinesis results in two genetically identical daughter cells in both plant cells and animal cells, but the mechanism of dividing the cytoplasm is different in animals and plants. In an animal cell, cytokinesis occurs by cleavage, which divides the parent cell in two with a contractile ring of actin filaments. In a plant cell, a cell plate forms in the middle of the cell and grows until its membrane fuses with the plasma membrane of the parent cell. A new cell wall grows inside the cell plate. **3.** They elongate the cell during anaphase. **4.** Sample answer: Each type of chromosome consists of a single molecule of DNA with attached proteins. If stretched out, the molecules of DNA would be many times longer than the cells in which they reside. During cell division, the two copies of each type of chromosome actively move apart, and one copy ends up in each of the two daughter cells. Chromosome movement in both types of cells may involve similar cytoskeletal proteins. **5.** During eukaryotic cell division, tubulin is involved in spindle formation and chromosome movement, while actin functions during cytokinesis. In bacterial binary fission, it's the opposite: Tubulin-like molecules are thought to act in daughter cell separation, and actin-like molecules are thought to move the daughter bacterial chromosomes to opposite ends of the cell. **6.** From the end of S phase in interphase through the end of metaphase in mitosis

Concept Check 12.3

1. The nucleus on the right was originally in the G_1 phase; therefore, it had not yet duplicated its chromosome. The nucleus on the left was in the M phase, so it had already duplicated its chromosome. **2.** A sufficient amount of MPF has to build up for a cell to pass the G_2 checkpoint. **3.** Most body cells are in a nondividing state called G_0. **4.** Both types of tumors consist of abnormal cells. A benign tumor stays at the original site and can usually be surgically removed. Cancer cells from a malignant tumor spread from the original site by metastasis and may impair the functions of one or more organs. **5.** The cells might divide even in the absence of PDGF, in which case they would not stop when the surface of the culture vessel was covered; they would continue to divide, piling on top of one another.

Self-Quiz

1. b **2.** a **3.** a **4.** c **5.** c **6.** e **7.** a **8.** b
9. See Figure 12.6 for a description of major events.

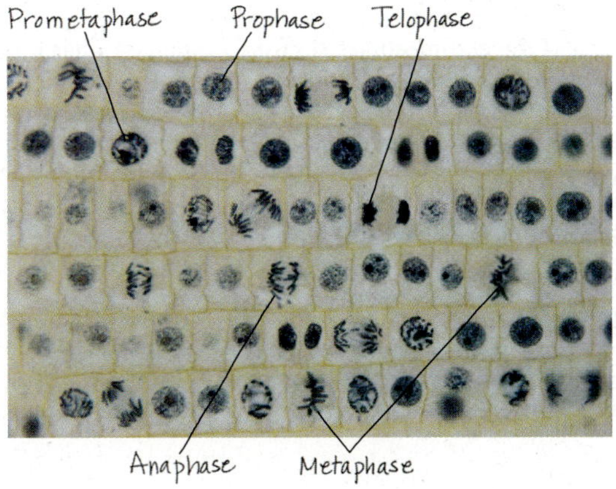

10.

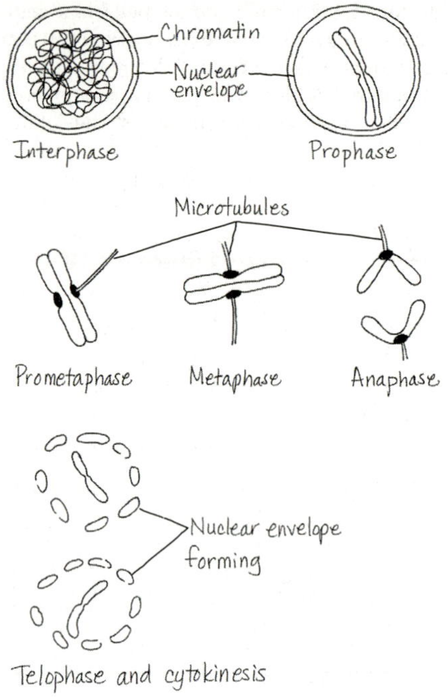

CHAPTER 13

Figure Questions

Figure 13.4 The haploid number, *n*, is 3. A set is always haploid. **Figure 13.7** A short strand of DNA is shown here for simplicity, but each chromosome or chromatid contains a very long coiled and folded DNA molecule.

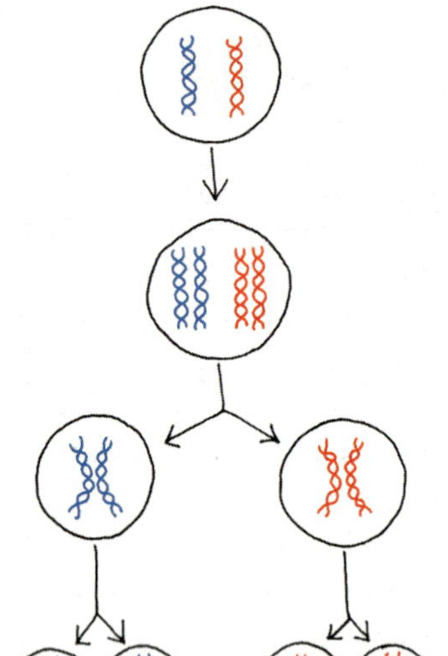

Figure 13.9 Yes. Each of the chromosomes shown in telophase I has one nonrecombinant chromatid and one recombinant chromatid. Therefore, eight possible sets of chromosomes can be generated for the cell on the left and eight for the cell on the right. **Figure 13.10** The chromosomes arising from chromatids of the unlabeled chromosome would be expected to behave exactly like those of the labeled chromosome. Therefore, the graph would look identical to the one shown in the figure.

Concept Check 13.1

1. Parents pass genes to their offspring; the genes program cells to make specific enzymes and other proteins, whose cumulative action produces an individual's inherited traits. **2.** Such organisms reproduce by mitosis, which generates offspring whose genomes are exact copies of the parent's genome (in the absence of mutation). **3.** She should clone it. Breeding it would generate offspring that have additional variation, which she no longer desires now that she has obtained her ideal orchid.

Concept Check 13.2

1. A female has two X chromosomes; a male has an X and a Y. **2.** In meiosis, the chromosome count is reduced from diploid to haploid; the union of two haploid gametes in fertilization restores the diploid chromosome count. **3.** The haploid number (n) is 7; the diploid number ($2n$) is 14. **4.** This organism has the life cycle shown in Figure 13.6c. Therefore, it must be a fungus or a protist, perhaps an alga.

Concept Check 13.3

1. The chromosomes are similar in that each is composed of two sister chromatids, and the individual chromosomes are positioned similarly on the metaphase plate. The chromosomes differ in that in a mitotically dividing cell, sister chromatids of each chromosome are genetically identical, but in a meiotically dividing cell, sister chromatids are genetically distinct because of crossing over in meiosis I. Moreover, the chromosomes in metaphase of mitosis can be a diploid set or a haploid set, but the chromosomes in metaphase of meiosis II always consist of a haploid set. **2.** If crossing over did not occur, the two homologs would not be associated in any way. This might result in incorrect arrangement of homologs during metaphase I and ultimately in formation of gametes with an abnormal number of chromosomes.

Concept Check 13.4

1. Mutations in a gene lead to the different versions (alleles) of that gene. **2.** Without crossing over, independent assortment of chromosomes during meiosis I theoretically can generate 2^n possible haploid gametes, and random fertilization can produce $2^n \times 2^n$ possible diploid zygotes. Because the haploid number (n) of grasshoppers is 23 and that of fruit flies is 4, two grasshoppers would be expected to produce a greater variety of zygotes than would two fruit flies. **3.** If the segments of the maternal and paternal chromatids that undergo crossing over are genetically identical and thus have the same two alleles for every gene, then the recombinant chromosomes will be genetically equivalent to the parental chromosomes. Crossing over contributes to genetic variation only when it involves the rearrangement of different alleles.

Self-Quiz

1. a **2.** d **3.** b **4.** a **5.** d **6.** c **7.** d **8.** This cell must be undergoing meiosis because homologous chromosomes are associated with each other; this does not occur in mitosis. **9.** Metaphase I
10.

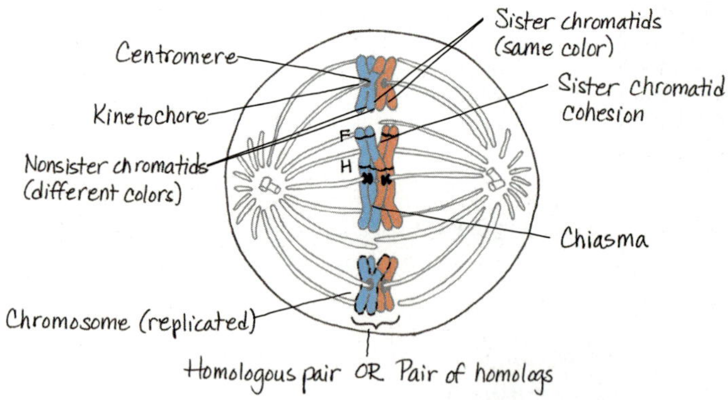

The chromosomes of one color make up a haploid set.
All red and blue chromosomes together make up a diploid set.

CHAPTER 14

Figure Questions

Figure 14.3 All offspring would have purple flowers. (The ratio would be one purple to zero white.) The P generation plants are true-breeding, so mating two purple-flowered plants produces the same result as self-pollination: All the offspring have the same trait.

Figure 14.8

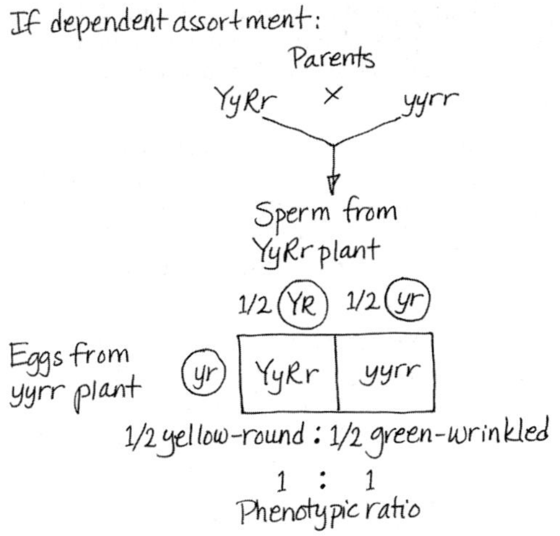

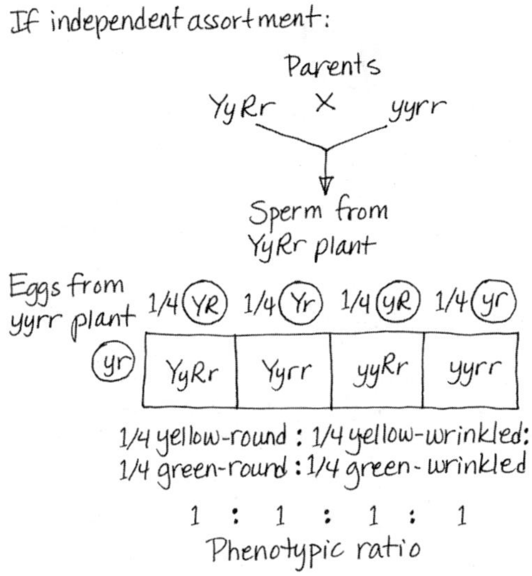

Yes, this cross would also have allowed Mendel to make different predictions for the two hypotheses, thereby allowing him to distinguish the correct one. **Figure 14.10** Your classmate would probably point out that the F_1 generation hybrids show an intermediate phenotype between those of the homozygous parents, which supports the blending hypothesis. You could respond that crossing the F_1 hybrids results in the reappearance of the white phenotype, rather than identical pink offspring, which fails to support the idea of blending traits during inheritance. **Figure 14.11** Both the I^A and I^B alleles are dominant to the *i* allele, which results in no attached carbohydrate. The I^A and I^B alleles are codominant; both are expressed in the phenotype of $I^A I^B$ heterozygotes, who have type AB blood.

Figure 14.13

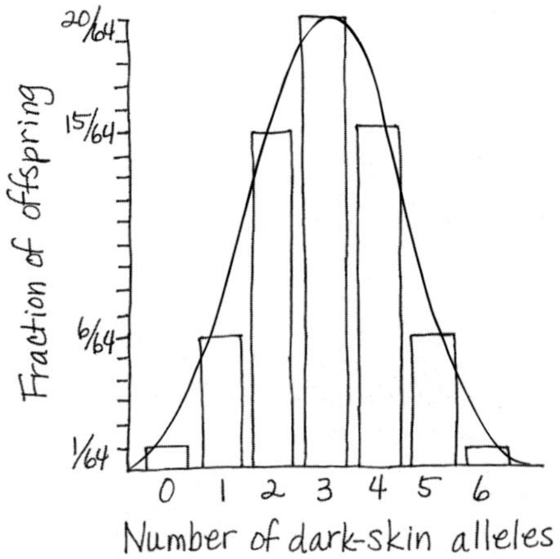

The majority of individuals have intermediate phenotypes (skin color in the middle range), while fewer individuals have phenotypes at either end (very dark or very light skin). (As you may know, this is called a "bell curve" and represents a "normal distribution.") **Figure 14.16** In the Punnett square, two of the three individuals with normal coloration are carriers, so the probability is ⅔.

Concept Check 14.1

1. A cross of *Ii* × *ii* would yield offspring with a genotypic ratio of 1 *Ii* : 1 *ii* (2:2 is an equivalent answer) and a phenotypic ratio of 1 inflated : 1 constricted (2:2 is equivalent).

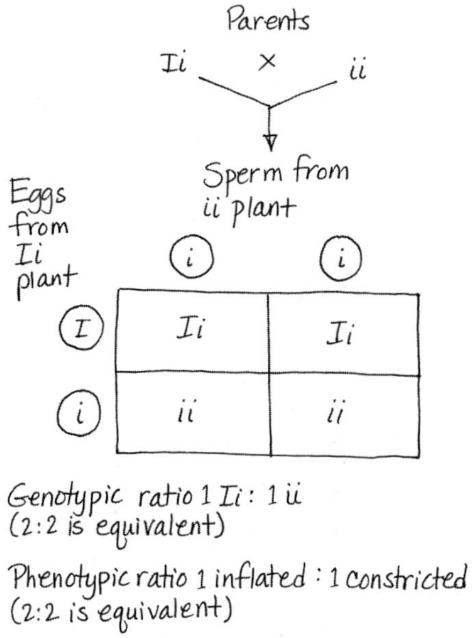

2. According to the law of independent assortment, 25 plants (1⁄16 of the offspring) are predicted to be *aatt*, or recessive for both characters. The actual result is likely to differ slightly from this value.

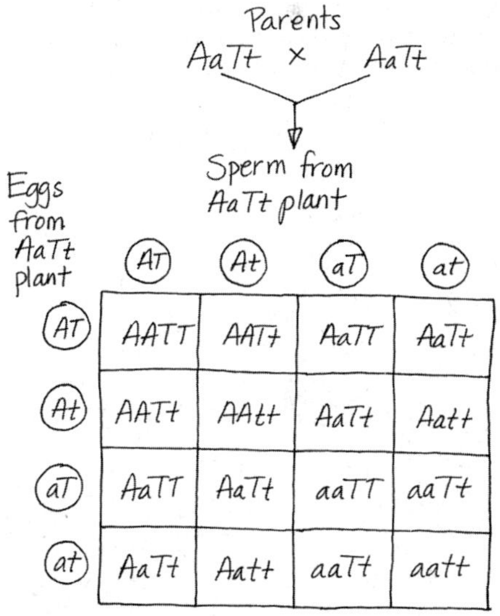

3. The plant could make eight different gametes (*YRI, YRi, YrI, Yri, yRI, yRi, yrI,* and *yri*). To fit all the possible gametes in a self-pollination, a Punnett square would need 8 rows and 8 columns. It would have spaces for the 64 possible unions of gametes in the offspring.

Concept Check 14.2

1. ½ homozygous dominant (*CC*), 0 homozygous recessive (*cc*), and ½ heterozygous (*Cc*) **2.** ¼ *BBDD*; ¼ *BbDD*; ¼ *BBDd*; ¼ *BbDd* **3.** The genotypes that fulfill this condition are *ppyyIi, ppYyii, Ppyyii, ppYYii,* and *ppyyii*. Use the multiplication rule to find the probability of getting each genotype, and then use the addition rule to find the overall probability of meeting the conditions of this problem:

ppyyIi ½ (probability of *pp*) × ¼ (*yy*) × ½ (*Ii*) $= \frac{1}{16}$
ppYyii ½ (*pp*) × ½ (*Yy*) × ½ (*ii*) $= \frac{2}{16}$
Ppyyii ½ (*Pp*) × ¼ (*yy*) × ½ (*ii*) $= \frac{1}{16}$
ppYYii ½ (*pp*) × ¼ (*YY*) × ½ (*ii*) $= \frac{1}{16}$
ppyyii ½ (*pp*) × ¼ (*yy*) × ½ (*ii*) $= \frac{1}{16}$

Fraction predicted to have at least two recessive traits $= \frac{6}{16}$ or 3/8

Concept Check 14.3

1. Incomplete dominance describes the relationship between two alleles of a single gene, whereas epistasis relates to the genetic relationship between two genes (and the respective alleles of each). **2.** Half of the children would be expected to have type A blood and half type B blood. **3.** The black and white alleles are incompletely dominant, with heterozygotes being gray in color. A cross between a gray rooster and a black hen should yield approximately equal numbers of gray and black offspring.

Concept Check 14.4

1. $^1/_9$ (Since cystic fibrosis is caused by a recessive allele, Beth and Tom's siblings who have CF must be homozygous recessive. Therefore, each parent must be a carrier of the recessive allele. Since neither Beth nor Tom has CF, this means they each have a $^2/_3$ chance of being a carrier. If they are both carriers, there is a $^1/_4$ chance that they will have a child with CF. $^2/_3 \times {}^2/_3 \times {}^1/_4 = {}^1/_9$); 0 (Both Beth and Tom would have to be carriers to produce a child with the disease.) **2.** Joan's genotype is *Dd*. Because the allele for polydactyly (*D*) is dominant to the allele for five digits per appendage (*d*), the trait is expressed in people with either the *DD* or *Dd* genotype. But because Joan's father does not have polydactyly, his genotype must be *dd*, which means Joan inherited a *d* allele from him. Therefore Joan, who does have the trait, must be heterozygous. **3.** Since polydactyly is a dominant trait, one of the parents of an affected individual should show the trait. Therefore, this must be an extremely rare case of a mutation that occurred during formation of one of the gametes involved in the fertilization that created Peter.

Genetics Problems

1. Gene, l. Allele, e. Character, g. Trait, b. Dominant allele, j. Recessive allele, a. Genotype, k. Phenotype, h. Homozygous, c. Heterozygous, f. Testcross, i. Monohybrid cross, d.

2.

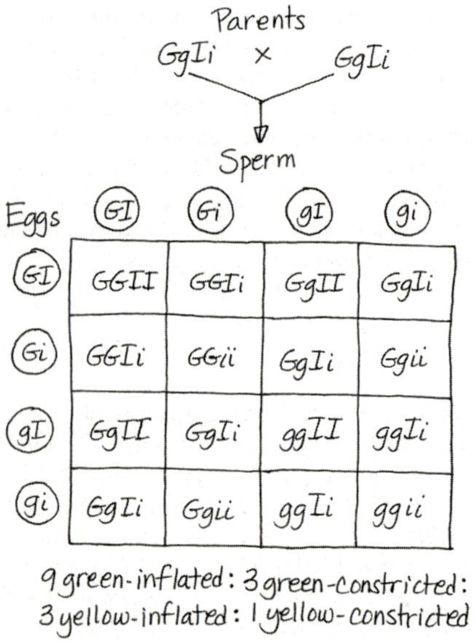

3. Parental cross is $AAC^RC^R \times aaC^WC^W$. F_1 genotype is $AaC^R C^W$, phenotype is all axial-pink. F_2 genotypes are 1 AAC^RC^R : 2 AAC^RC^W : 1 AAC^WC^W : 2 AaC^RC^R : 4 AaC^RC^W : 2 AaC^WC^W : 1 aaC^RC^R : 2 aaC^RC^W : 1 aaC^WC^W. F_2 phenotypes are 3 axial-red : 6 axial-pink : 3 axial-white : 1 terminal-red : 2 terminal-pink : 1 terminal-white.

4.
a. $^1/_{64}$
b. $^1/_{64}$
c. $^1/_8$
d. $^1/_{32}$

5. Albino (*b*) is a recessive trait; black (*B*) is dominant. First cross: parents *BB* × *bb*; gametes *B* and *b*; offspring all *Bb* (black coat). Second cross: parents *Bb* × *bb*; gametes ½ *B* and ½ *b* (heterozygous parent) and *b*; offspring ½ *Bb* and ½ *bb*.

6.
a. *PPLl* × *PPLl*, *PPLl* × *PpLl*, or *PPLl* × *ppLl*.
b. *ppLl* × *ppLl*.
c. *PPLL* × any of the 9 possible genotypes or *PPll* × *ppLL*.
d. *PpLl* × *Ppll*.
e. *PpLl* × *PpLl*.

7. Man I^Ai; woman I^Bi; child *ii*. Other genotypes for children are ¼ I^AI^B, ¼ I^Ai, ¼ I^Bi.

8.
a. ¾ × ¾ × ¾ = $^{27}/_{64}$
b. 1 − $^{27}/_{64}$ = $^{37}/_{64}$
c. ¼ × ¼ × ¼ = $^1/_{64}$
d. 1 − $^1/_{64}$ = $^{63}/_{64}$

9.
a. $^1/_{256}$
b. $^1/_{16}$
c. $^1/_{256}$
d. $^1/_{64}$
e. $^1/_{128}$

10.
a. 1
b. $^1/_{32}$
c. $^1/_8$
d. $^1/_2$

11. $^1/_9$

12. Matings of the original mutant cat with true-breeding noncurl cats will produce both curl and noncurl F_1 offspring if the curl allele is dominant, but only noncurl offspring if the curl allele is recessive. You would obtain some true-breeding offspring homozygous for the curl allele from matings between the F_1 cats resulting from the original curl × noncurl crosses whether the curl trait is dominant or recessive. You know that cats are true-breeding when curl × curl matings produce only curl offspring. As it turns out, the allele that causes curled ears is dominant. **13.** $^1/_{16}$ **14.** 25% will be cross-eyed; all of the cross-eyed offspring will also be white. **15.** The dominant allele *I* is epistatic to the *P/p* locus, and thus the genotypic ratio for the F_1 generation will be 9 *I_P_* (colorless) : 3 *I_pp* (colorless) : 3 *iiP_* (purple) : 1 *iipp* (red). Overall, the phenotypic ratio is 12 colorless : 3 purple : 1 red. **16.** Recessive. All affected individuals (Arlene, Tom, Wilma, and Carla) are homozygous recessive *aa*. George is *Aa*, since some of his children with Arlene are affected. Sam, Ann, Daniel, and Alan are each *Aa*, since they are all unaffected children with one affected parent. Michael also is *Aa*, since he has an affected child (Carla) with his heterozygous wife Ann. Sandra, Tina, and Christopher can each have the *AA* or *Aa* genotype. **17.** $^1/_2$ **18.** $^1/_6$ **19.** 9 *B_A_* (agouti) : 3 *B_aa* (black) : 3 *bbA_* (white) : 1 *bbaa* (white). Overall, 9 agouti : 3 black : 4 white.

CHAPTER 15

Figure Questions

Figure 15.2 The ratio would be 1 yellow-round : 1 green-round : 1 yellow-wrinkled : 1 green-wrinkled. **Figure 15.4** About ¾ of the F_2 offspring would have red eyes and about ¼ would have white eyes. About half of the white-eyed flies would be female and half would be male; about half of the red-eyed flies would be female. **Figure 15.7** All the males would be color-blind, and all the females would be carriers. **Figure 15.9** The two largest classes would still be the parental-type offspring, but now they would be gray-vestigial and black-normal because those were the specific allele combinations in the P generation. **Figure 15.10** The two chromosomes below, left are like the two chromosomes inherited by the F_1 female, one from each P generation fly. They are passed by the F_1 female intact to the offspring and thus could be called "parental" chromosomes. The other two chromosomes result from crossing over during meiosis in the F_1 female. Because they have combinations of alleles not seen in either of the F_1 female's chromosomes, they can be called "recombinant" chromosomes.

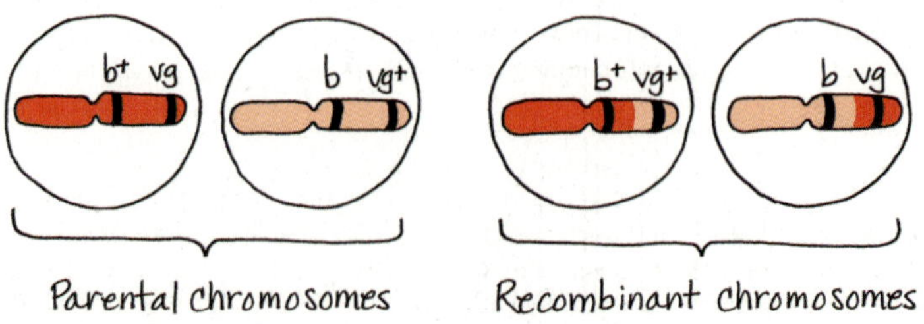

Concept Check 15.1

1. The law of segregation relates to the inheritance of alleles for a single character. The law of independent assortment of alleles relates to the inheritance of alleles for two characters. **2.** The physical basis for the law of segregation is the separation of homologs in anaphase I. The physical basis for the law of independent assortment is the alternative arrangements of homologous chromosome pairs in metaphase I. **3.** To show the mutant phenotype, a male needs to possess only one mutant allele. If this gene had been on a pair of autosomes, *two* mutant alleles would have had to be present for an individual to show the mutant phenotype, a much less probable situation.

Concept Check 15.2

1. Because the gene for this eye-color character is located on the X chromosome, all female offspring will be red-eyed and heterozygous ($X^{w+}X^{w}$); all male offspring will inherit a Y chromosome from the father and be white-eyed ($X^{w}Y$). **2.** ¼; ½ chance that the child will inherit a Y chromosome from the father and be male × ½ chance that he will inherit the X carrying the disease allele from his mother. If the child is a boy, there is a ½ chance he will have the disease; a female would have zero chance (but ½ chance of being a carrier). **3.** The cells in the eye responsible for color vision must come from multiple cells in the early embryo. The descendants of half of those cells express the allele for normal color vision and half the allele for color blindness. Having half the number of mature eye cells expressing the normal allele must be sufficient for normal color vision.

Concept Check 15.3

1. Crossing over during meiosis I in the heterozygous parent produces some gametes with recombinant genotypes for the two genes. Offspring with a recombinant phenotype arise from fertilization of the recombinant gametes by homozygous recessive gametes from the double-mutant parent. **2.** In each case, the alleles contributed by the female parent determine the phenotype of the offspring because the male contributes only recessive alleles in this cross. **3.** No. The order could be *A-C-B* or *C-A-B*. To determine which possibility is correct, you need to know the recombination frequency between *B* and *C*.

Concept Check 15.4

1. At some point during development, one of the embryo's cells may have failed to carry out mitosis after duplicating its chromosomes. Subsequent normal cell cycles would produce genetic copies of this tetraploid cell. **2.** In meiosis, a combined 14-21 chromosome will behave as one chromosome. If a gamete receives the combined 14-21 chromosome and a normal copy of chromosome 21, trisomy 21 will result when this gamete combines with a normal gamete during fertilization. **3.** No. The child can be either I^AI^Ai or I^Aii. A sperm of genotype I^AI^A could result from nondisjunction in the father during meiosis II, while an egg with the genotype *ii* could result from nondisjunction in the mother during either meiosis I or meiosis II.

Concept Check 15.5

1. Inactivation of an X chromosome in females and genomic imprinting. Because of X inactivation, the effective dose of genes on the X chromosome is the same in males and females. As a result of genomic imprinting, only one allele of certain genes is phenotypically expressed. **2.** The genes for leaf coloration are located in plastids within the cytoplasm. Normally, only the maternal parent transmits plastid genes to offspring. Since variegated offspring are produced only when the female parent is of the B variety, we can conclude that variety B contains both the wild-type and mutant alleles of pigment genes, producing variegated leaves. **3.** The situation is similar to that for chloroplasts. Each cell contains numerous mitochondria, and in affected individuals, most cells contain a variable mixture of normal and mutant mitochondria. The normal mitochondria carry out enough cellular respiration for survival.

Genetics Problems

1. 0; ½, $\frac{1}{16}$ **2.** Recessive; if the disorder were dominant, it would affect at least one parent of a child born with the disorder. The disorder's inheritance is sex-linked because it is seen only in boys. For a girl to have the disorder, she would have to inherit recessive alleles from *both* parents. This would be very rare, since males with the recessive allele on their X chromosome die in their early teens. **3.** ¼ for each daughter (½ chance that child will be female × ½ chance of a homozygous recessive genotype); ½ for first son. **4.** 17% **5.** 6%. Wild type (heterozygous for normal wings and red eyes) × recessive homozygote with vestigial wings and purple eyes

6.

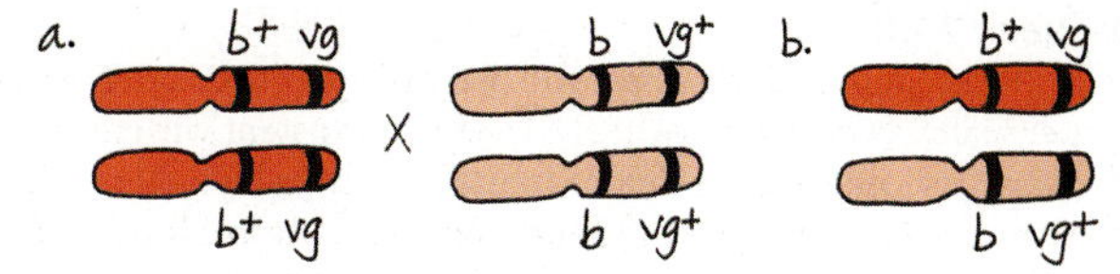

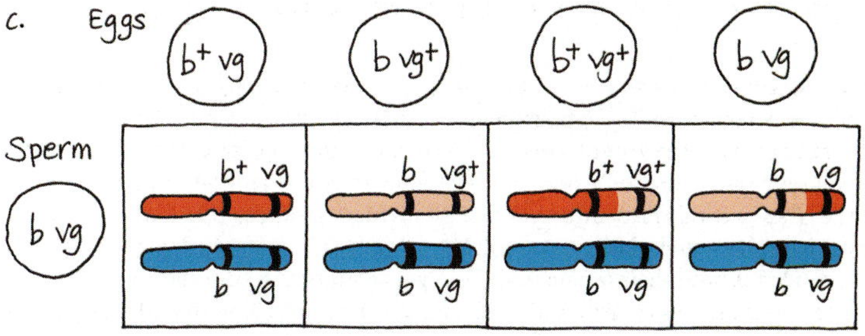

d. 41.5% gray body, vestigial wings
41.5% black body, normal wings
8.5% gray body, normal wings
8.5% black body, vestigial wings

7. The disorder would always be inherited from the mother. **8.** The inactivation of two X chromosomes in XXX women would leave them with one genetically active X, as in women with the normal number of chromosomes. Microscopy should reveal two Barr bodies in XXX women. **9.** *D–A–B–C* **10.** Fifty percent of the offspring would show phenotypes that resulted from crossovers. These results would be the same as those from a cross where *A* and *B* were not linked. Further crosses involving other genes on the same chromosome would reveal the linkage and map distances. **11.** Between *T* and *A*, 12%; between *A* and *S*, 5% **12.** Between *T* and *S*, 18%; sequence of genes is *T-A-S* **13.** 450 each of blue-oval and white-round (parentals) and 50 each of blue-round and white-oval (recombinants) **14.** About one-third of the distance from the vestigial-wing locus to the brown-eye locus **15.** Because bananas are triploid, homologous pairs cannot line up during meiosis. Therefore, it is not possible to generate gametes that can fuse to produce a zygote with the triploid number of chromosomes.

CHAPTER 16

Figure Questions

Figure 16.2 The living S cells found in the blood sample were able to reproduce to yield more S cells, indicating that the S trait is a permanent, heritable change, rather than just a one-time use of the dead S cells' capsules. **Figure 16.4** The radioactivity would have been found in the pellet when proteins were labeled (batch 1) because proteins would have had to enter the bacterial cells to program them with genetic instructions. It's hard for us to imagine now, but the DNA might have played a structural role that allowed some of the proteins to be injected while it remained outside the bacterial cell (thus no radioactivity in the pellet in batch 2). **Figure 16.11** The tube from the first replication would look the same, with a middle band of hybrid ^{15}N-^{14}N DNA, but the second tube would not have the upper band of two light blue strands. Instead it would have a bottom band of two dark blue strands, like the bottom band in the result predicted after one replication in the conservative model. **Figure 16.12** In the bubble at the top in (b), arrows should be drawn pointing left and right to indicate the two replication forks. **Figure 16.14** Looking at any of the DNA strands, we see that one end is called the 5′ end and the other the 3′ end. If we proceed from the 5′ end to the 3′ end on the left-most strand, for example, we list the components in this order: phosphate group → 5′ C of the sugar → 3′ C → phosphate → 5′ C → 3′ C. Going in the opposite direction on the same strand, the components proceed in the reverse order: 3′ C → 5′ C → phosphate. Thus, the two directions are distinguishable, which is what we mean when we say that the strands have directionality. (Review Figure 16.5 if necessary.) **Figure 16.22** The cells in the mutant would probably have the same defects in meiosis that were seen in this experiment, such as the failure of condensin to be concentrated in a small region in the nucleus. The defect in the two mutants is essentially the same: In the mutant described in the experiment, the kinase doesn't function properly; in the newly discovered mutant, the kinase could not phosphorylate the correct amino acid because that amino acid is missing.

Concept Check 16.1

1. Chargaff's rules state that in DNA, the percentages of A and T and of G and C are essentially the same, and the fly data are consistent with those rules. (Slight variations are most likely due to limitations of analytical technique.) **2.** In the Watson-Crick model, each A hydrogen-bonds to a T, so in a DNA double helix, their numbers are equal; the same is true for G and C. **3.** The mouse injected with the mixture of heat-killed S cells and living R cells would have survived, since neither type of cell alone could have killed the mouse.

Concept Check 16.2

1. Complementary base pairing ensures that the two daughter molecules are exact copies of the parent molecule. When the two strands of the parent molecule separate, each serves as a template on which nucleotides are arranged, by the base-pairing rules, into new complementary strands. **2.** DNA pol III covalently adds nucleotides to new DNA strands and proofreads each added nucleotide for correct base pairing. **3.** Synthesis of the leading strand is initiated by an RNA primer, which must be removed and replaced with DNA, a task that could not be performed if the cell's DNA pol I were nonfunctional. In the overview box in Figure 16.17, just to the left of the top origin of replication, a functional DNA pol I would replace the RNA primer of the leading strand (shown in red) with DNA nucleotides (blue).

Concept Check 16.3

1. A nucleosome is made up of eight histone proteins, two each of four different types, around which DNA is wound. Linker DNA runs from one nucleosome to the next. **2.** Euchromatin is chromatin that becomes less compacted during interphase and is accessible to the cellular machinery responsible for gene activity. Heterochromatin, on the other hand, remains quite condensed during interphase and contains genes that are largely inaccessible to this machinery. **3.** Like histones, the *E. coli* proteins would be expected to contain many basic (positively charged) amino acids, such as lysine and arginine, which can form weak bonds with the negatively charged phosphate groups on the sugar-phosphate backbone of the DNA molecule.

Self-Quiz

1. c **2.** d **3.** b **4.** c **5.** b **6.** d **7.** a **8.** c

10.

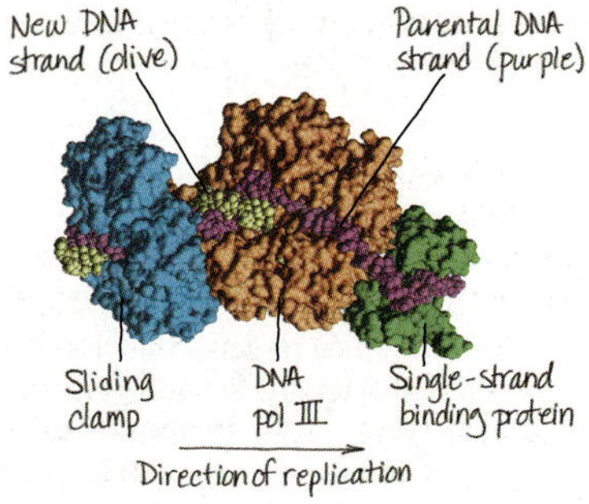

CHAPTER 17

Figure Questions

Figure 17.2 The previously presumed pathway would have been wrong. The new results would support this pathway: precursor → citrulline → ornithine → arginine. They would also indicate that class I mutants have a defect in the second step and class II mutants have a defect in the first step. **Figure 17.8** The RNA polymerase would bind directly to the promoter, rather than depending on the previous binding of other factors. **Figure 17.24** The mRNA on the right (the longest one) started transcription first. The ribosome at the top, closest to the DNA, started translating first and thus has the longest polypeptide.

Concept Check 17.1

1. A polypeptide made up of 10 Gly (glycine) amino acids

2.

Template sequence (from problem):	3′-TTCAGTCGT-5′
Nontemplate sequence:	5′-AAGTCAGCA-3′
mRNA sequence:	5′-AAGUCAGCA-3′

The nontemplate and mRNA base sequences are the same, except there is T in the nontemplate strand of DNA wherever there is U in the mRNA.

3.

"Template sequence" (from nontemplate sequence in problem, written 3′ → 5′):	3′-ACGACTGAA-5′
mRNA sequence:	5′-UGCUGACUU-3′
Translated:	Cys-STOP-Leu

(Remember that the mRNA is antiparallel to the DNA strand.) A protein translated from the nontemplate sequence would have a completely different amino acid sequence and would surely be nonfunctional. (It would also be shorter because of the stop signal shown in the mRNA sequence above—and possibly others earlier in the mRNA sequence.)

Concept Check 17.2

1. Both assemble nucleic acid chains from monomer nucleotides whose order is determined by complementary base pairing to a template strand. Both synthesize in the 5′ → 3′ direction, antiparallel to the template. DNA polymerase requires a primer, but RNA polymerase can start a nucleotide chain from scratch. DNA polymerase uses nucleotides with the sugar deoxyribose and the base T, whereas RNA polymerase uses nucleotides with the sugar ribose and the base U. **2.** The promoter is the region of DNA to which RNA polymerase binds to begin transcription, and it is at the upstream end of the gene (transcription unit). **3.** In a bacterial cell, RNA polymerase recognizes the gene's promoter and binds to it. In a eukaryotic cell, transcription factors mediate the binding of RNA polymerase to the promoter. **4.** The transcription factor that recognizes the TATA sequence would be unable to bind, so RNA polymerase could not bind and transcription of that gene probably would not occur.

Concept Check 17.3

1. The 5′ cap and poly-A tail facilitate mRNA export from the nucleus, prevent the mRNA from being degraded by hydrolytic enzymes, and facilitate ribosome attachment. **2.** In editing a video, segments are cut out and discarded (like introns), and the remaining segments are joined together (like exons) so that the regions of joining ("splicing") are not noticeable. **3.** Six different forms could be made because alternative splicing could generate six different mRNAs (two possibilities for exon 4 × three possibilities for exon 7).

Concept Check 17.4

1. First, each aminoacyl-tRNA synthetase specifically recognizes a single amino acid and attaches it only to an appropriate tRNA. Second, a tRNA charged with its specific amino acid binds only to an mRNA codon for that amino acid. **2.** Polyribosomes enable the cell to produce multiple copies of a polypeptide very quickly. **3.** A signal peptide on the leading end of the polypeptide being synthesized is recognized by a signal-recognition particle that brings the ribosome to the ER membrane. There the ribosome attaches and continues to synthesize the polypeptide, depositing it in the ER lumen. **4.** The structure and function of the ribosome seem to depend more on the rRNAs than on the ribosomal proteins. Because it is single-stranded, an RNA molecule can hydrogen-bond with itself and with other RNA molecules. RNA molecules make up the interface between the two ribosomal subunits, so presumably RNA-RNA binding helps hold the ribosome together. The binding site for mRNA in the ribosome could include rRNA that can bind the mRNA. (In fact, this turns out to be the case.) Also, complementary bonding within an RNA molecule allows it to assume a particular three-dimensional shape, and, along with the RNA's functional groups, presumably enables rRNA to catalyze peptide bond formation during translation.

Concept Check 17.5

1. In the mRNA, the reading frame downstream from the deletion is shifted, leading to a long string of incorrect amino acids in the polypeptide and, in most cases, a stop codon will arise, leading to premature termination. The polypeptide will most likely be nonfunctional.

2. Normal DNA sequence (template strand is on top): 3′-TACTTGTCCGATATC-5′
5′-ATGAACAGGCTATAG-3′

mRNA sequence: 5′-AUGAACAGGCUAUAG-3′

Amino acid sequence: Met-Asn-Arg-Leu-STOP

Mutated DNA sequence (template strand is on top): 3′-TACTTGTCCAATATC-5′
5′-ATGAACAGGTTATAG-3′

mRNA sequence: 5′-AUGAACAGGUUAUAG-3′

Amino acid sequence: Met-Asn-Arg-Leu-STOP

The amino acid sequence is Met-Asn-Arg-Leu both before and after the mutation because the mRNA codons 5′-CUA-3′ and 5′-UUA-3′ both code for Leu. (The fifth codon is a stop codon.)

Concept Check 17.6

1. No, transcription and translation are separated in space and time in a eukaryotic cell, a result of the eukaryotic cell's nuclear compartment. **2.** When one ribosome terminates translation and dissociates, the two subunits would be very close to the cap. This could facilitate their rebinding and initiating synthesis of a new polypeptide, thus increasing the efficiency of translation.

Self-Quiz

1. b **2.** d **3.** a **4.** a **5.** d **6.** e **7.** b

8.

Type of RNA	Functions
Messenger RNA (mRNA)	Carries information specifying amino acid sequences of proteins from DNA to ribosomes.
Transfer RNA (tRNA)	Serves as adapter molecule in protein synthesis; translates mRNA codons into amino acids.
Ribosomal RNA (rRNA)	Plays catalytic (ribozyme) roles and structural roles in ribosomes.
Primary transcript	Is a precursor to mRNA, rRNA, or tRNA, before being processed. Some intron RNA acts as a ribozyme, catalyzing its own splicing.
Small nuclear RNA (snRNA)	Plays structural and catalytic roles in spliceosomes, the complexes of protein and RNA that splice pre-mRNA.

CHAPTER 18

Figure Questions

Figure 18.3 As the concentration of tryptophan in the cell falls, eventually there will be none bound to repressor molecules. These will then take on their inactive shapes and dissociate from the operator, allowing transcription of the operon to resume. The enzymes for tryptophan synthesis will be made, and they will begin to synthesize tryptophan again in the cell. **Figure 18.10** The albumin gene enhancer has the three control elements colored yellow, gray, and red. The sequences in the two cells would be identical, since the cells are in the same organism. **Figure 18.16** Even if the mutant MyoD protein couldn't activate the *myoD* gene, it could still turn on genes for the other proteins in the pathway (other transcription factors, which would turn on the genes for muscle-specific proteins, for example). Therefore, some differentiation would occur. But unless there were other activators that could compensate for the loss of the MyoD protein's activation of the *myoD* gene, the cell would not be able to maintain its differentiated state. **Figure 18.19** Normal Bicoid protein would be made in the anterior end and compensate for the presence of mutant *bicoid* mRNA put into the egg by the mother. Development should be normal, with a head present. **Figure 18.21** The mutation is likely to be recessive because it is more likely to have an effect if both copies of the gene are mutated and code for nonfunctional proteins. If one normal copy of the gene is present, its product could inhibit the cell cycle. (However, there are also known cases of dominant *p53* mutations.)

Concept Check 18.1

1. Binding by the *trp* corepressor (tryptophan) activates the *trp* repressor, shutting off transcription of the *trp* operon; binding by the *lac* inducer (allolactose) inactivates the *lac* repressor, leading to transcription of the *lac* operon. **2.** The cell would continuously produce β-galactosidase and the two other enzymes for lactose utilization, even in the absence of lactose, thus wasting cell resources. **3.** With glucose scarce, cAMP would be bound to CAP and CAP would be bound to the promoter, favoring the binding of RNA polymerase. However, in the absence of lactose, the repressor would be bound to the operator, blocking RNA polymerase binding to the promoter. The operon genes would therefore not be transcribed. If another sugar were present and the genes encoding enzymes for its breakdown were in an operon regulated like the *lac* operon, we might expect to find active transcription of those genes.

Concept Check 18.2

1. Histone acetylation is generally associated with gene expression, while DNA methylation is generally associated with lack of expression. **2.** General transcription factors function in assembling the transcription initiation complex at the promoters for all genes. Specific transcription factors bind to control elements associated with a particular gene and, once bound, either increase (activators) or decrease (repressors) transcription of that gene. **3.** The three genes should have some similar or identical sequences in the control elements of their enhancers. Because of this similarity, the same specific transcription factors could bind to the enhancers of all three genes and stimulate their expression coordinately. **4.** Degradation of the mRNA, regulation of translation, activation of the protein (by chemical modification, for example), and protein degradation **5.** Expression of the gene encoding the yellow activator (YA) must be regulated at one of the steps shown in Figure 18.6. The YA gene might be transcribed only in liver cells because the necessary activators for the enhancer of the YA gene are found only in liver cells.

Concept Check 18.3

1. Both miRNAs and siRNAs are small, single-stranded RNAs that associate with a complex of proteins and then can base-pair with mRNAs that have a complementary sequence. This base pairing leads to either degradation of the mRNA or blockage of its translation. Some siRNAs, in association with other proteins, can bind back to the chromatin in a certain region, causing chromatin changes that affect transcription. Both miRNAs and siRNAs are processed from double-stranded RNA precursors by the enzyme Dicer. However, miRNAs are encoded by genes in the cell's genome, and the single transcript folds back on itself to form one or more double-stranded hairpins, each of which is processed into an miRNA. In contrast, siRNAs arise from a longer stretch of double-stranded RNA, which may be introduced into the cell by a virus or an experimenter. In some cases, a cellular gene codes for one RNA strand of the precursor molecule, and an enzyme then synthesizes the complementary strand. **2.** The mRNA would persist and be translated into the cell division–promoting protein, and the cell would probably divide. If the intact miRNA is necessary for inhibition of cell division, then division of this cell might be inappropriate. Uncontrolled cell division could lead to formation of a mass of cells (tumor) that prevents proper functioning of the organism.

Concept Check 18.4

1. Cells undergo differentiation during embryonic development, becoming different from each other; in the adult organism, there are many highly specialized cell types. **2.** By binding to a receptor on the receiving cell's surface and triggering a signal transduction pathway that affects gene expression **3.** Because their products, made and deposited into the egg by the mother, determine the head and tail ends, as well as the back and belly, of the embryo (and eventually the adult fly) **4.** The lower cell is synthesizing signaling molecules because the gene encoding them is activated, meaning that the appropriate specific transcription factors are binding to the gene's enhancer. The genes encoding these specific transcription factors are also being expressed in this cell because the transcriptional activators that can turn them on were expressed in the precursor to this cell. A similar explanation also applies to the cells expressing the receptor proteins. This scenario began with specific cytoplasmic determinants localized in specific regions of the egg. These cytoplasmic determinants were distributed unevenly to daughter cells, resulting in cells going down different developmental pathways.

Concept Check 18.5

1. The protein product of a proto-oncogene is usually involved in a pathway that stimulates cell division. The protein product of a tumor-suppressor gene is usually involved in a pathway that inhibits cell division. **2.** When an individual has inherited an oncogene or a mutant allele of a tumor-suppressor gene **3.** A cancer-causing mutation in a proto-oncogene usually makes the gene product overactive, whereas a cancer-causing mutation in a tumor-suppressor gene usually makes the gene product nonfunctional.

Self-Quiz

1. d **2.** a **3.** d **4.** a **5.** c **6.** e **7.** a **8.** c **9.** b **10.** b

11. a.

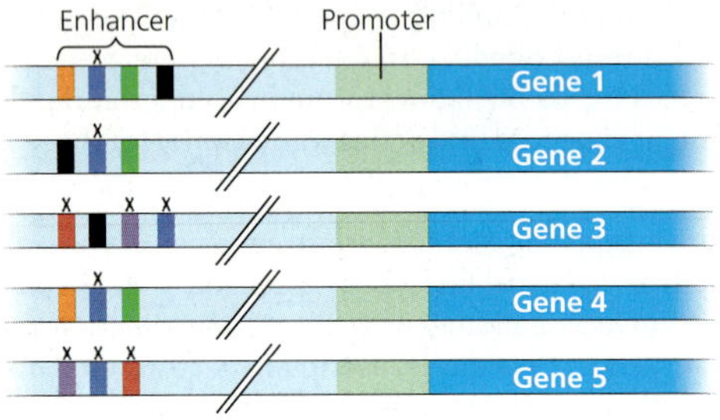

The purple, blue, and red activator proteins would be present.

b.

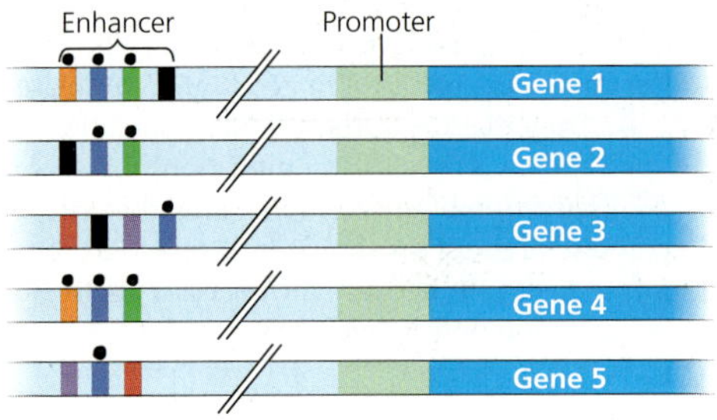

Only gene 4 would be transcribed.

c. In nerve cells, the orange, blue, green, and black activators would have to be present, thus activating transcription of genes 1, 2, and 4. In skin cells, the red, black, purple, and blue activators would have to be present, thus activating genes 3 and 5.

CHAPTER 19

Figure Questions

Figure 19.2 Beijerinck might have concluded that the agent was a toxin produced by the plant that was able to pass through a filter but that became more and more dilute. In this case, he would have concluded that the infectious agent could not reproduce. **Figure 19.4** Top vertical arrow: Infection. Left upper arrow: Replication. Right upper arrow: Transcription. Right middle arrow: Translation. Lower left and right arrows: Self-assembly. Bottom middle arrow: Exit. **Figure 19.7** Any class V virus, including the viruses that cause influenza (flu), measles, and mumps.

Concept Check 19.1

1. TMV consists of one molecule of RNA surrounded by a helical array of proteins. The influenza virus has eight molecules of RNA, each surrounded by a helical array of proteins, similar to the arrangement of the single RNA molecule in TMV. Another difference is that the influenza virus has an outer envelope. **2.** One of the arguments for regarding viruses as nonliving is that they cannot perform any activity characteristic of living organisms unless they are inside a host cell. This virus challenges that generalization because the virus can change its shape without having access to host cell proteins. (Further analysis suggested that the projections contain proteins related to intermediate filaments that may polymerize spontaneously under certain conditions.)

Concept Check 19.2

1. Lytic phages can only carry out lysis of the host cell, whereas lysogenic phages may either lyse the host cell or integrate into the host chromosome. In the latter case, the viral DNA (prophage) is simply replicated along with the host chromosome. Under certain conditions, a prophage may exit the host chromosome and initiate a lytic cycle. **2.** The genetic material of these viruses is RNA, which is replicated inside the infected cell by enzymes encoded by the virus. The viral genome (or a complementary copy of it) serves as mRNA for the synthesis of viral proteins. **3.** Because it synthesizes DNA from its RNA genome. This is the reverse ("retro") of the usual DNA → RNA information flow. **4.** There are many steps that could be interfered with: binding of the virus to the cell, reverse transcriptase function, integration into the host cell chromosome, genome synthesis (in this case, transcription of RNA from the integrated provirus), assembly of the virus inside the cell, and budding of the virus. (Many, if not all, of these are targets of actual medical strategies to block progress of the infection in HIV-infected people.)

Concept Check 19.3

1. Mutations can lead to a new strain of a virus that can no longer be effectively fought by the immune system, even if an animal had been exposed to the original strain; a virus can jump from one species to a new host; and a rare virus can spread if a host population becomes less isolated. **2.** In horizontal transmission, a plant is infected from an external source of virus, which could enter through a break in the plant's epidermis due to damage by herbivores. In vertical transmission, a plant inherits viruses from its parent either via infected seeds (sexual reproduction) or via an infected cutting (asexual reproduction). **3.** Humans are not within the host range of TMV, so they can't be infected by the virus. **4.** It is unlikely that human air travel could have spread the virus, since existing strains of the virus do not seem to be transmissible from human to human. It is conceivable but unlikely that an infected human traveling from Asia passed the virus to birds in Africa and Europe. It is possible that domestic birds carried the virus, perhaps in shipments of poultry. The likeliest scenario of all may be that migratory wild birds carried the virus during their migrations and passed it to domestic and wild birds in the new locations. To test these latter hypotheses, the timing of the outbreaks should be analyzed to see if they correlate with recent poultry shipments or known wild bird migrations. Any such migratory birds should be tested for the presence of the African or European strain of the virus, based on the nucleotide sequences of their genomes.

Self-Quiz

1. d **2.** b **3.** c **4.** d **5.** c

6. As shown below, the viral genome would be translated into capsid proteins and envelope glycoproteins directly, rather than after a complementary RNA copy was made. A complementary RNA strand would still be made, however, that could be used as a template for many new copies of the viral genome.

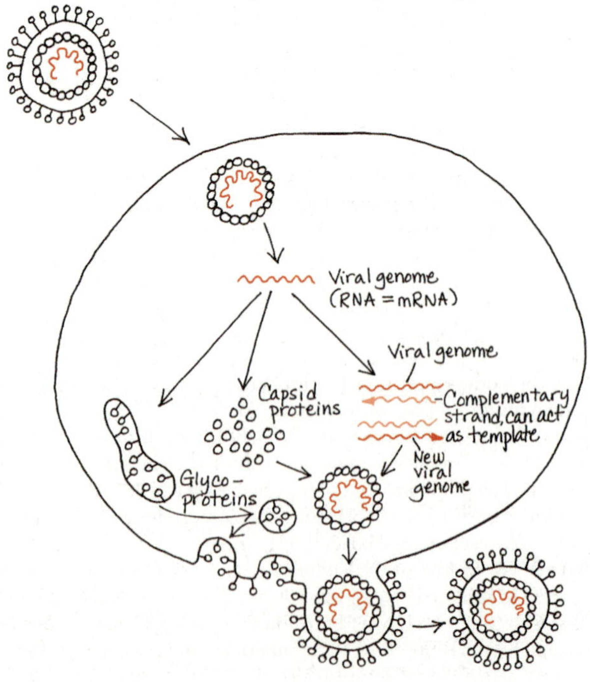

CHAPTER 20

Figure Questions

Figure 20.3

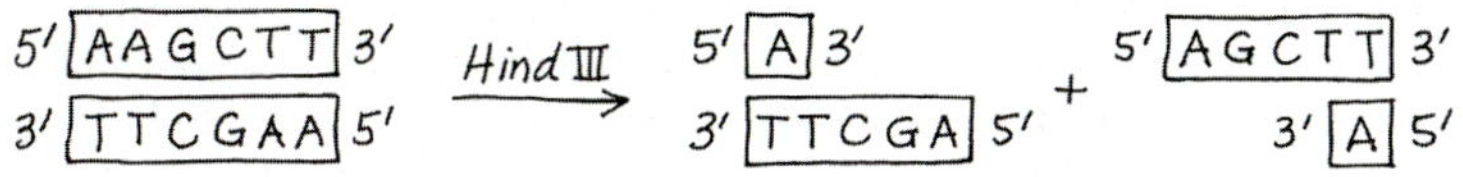

Figure 20.4 Cells containing no plasmid at all would be able to grow; these colonies would be white because they would lack functional *lacZ* genes. **Figure 20.10** Grow each clone of cells in culture. Isolate the plasmids from each and cut them with the restriction enzyme originally used to make the clone (see Figure 20.4). Run each sample on an electrophoretic gel, and recover the DNA of the insert from the gel band. **Figure 20.16** The researchers might have concluded that differentiated cells are irreversibly changed so that they can make only one type of tissue in the plant. (This result would support the idea that cloning isn't possible.) **Figure 20.17** None of the eggs with the transplanted nuclei would have developed into a tadpole. Also, the result might include only some of the tissues of a tadpole which might differ depending on which nucleus was transplanted. (This assumes that there was some way to tell the four cells apart, as one can in some frog species.)

Concept Check 20.1

1. The covalent sugar-phosphate bonds of the DNA strands **2.** Yes, *Pvu*I will cut the molecule

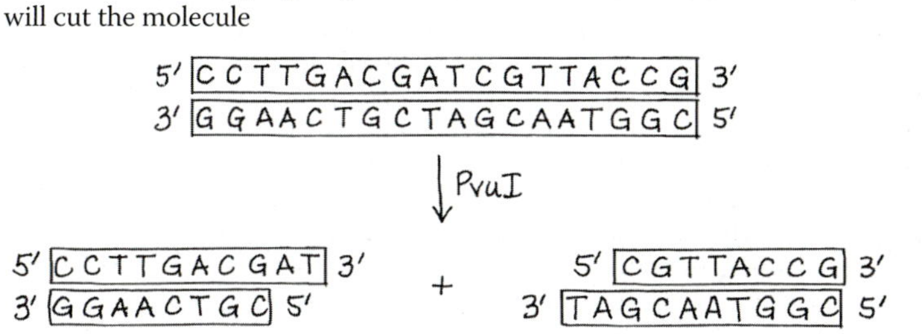

3. Some human genes are too large to be incorporated into bacterial plasmids. Bacterial cells lack the means to process RNA transcripts into mRNA, and even if the need for RNA processing is avoided by using cDNA, bacteria lack enzymes to catalyze the post-translational processing that many human proteins require to function properly. **4.** 5′-CGGT-3′ and 5′-CCTT-3′

Concept Check 20.2

1. Any restriction enzyme will cut genomic DNA in many places, generating such a large number of fragments that they would appear as a smear rather than distinct bands when the gel is stained after electrophoresis. **2.** In Southern blotting, Northern blotting, and microarray analysis, the labeled probe binds only to the specific target sequence owing to complementary nucleic acid hybridization (DNA-DNA hybridization in Southern blotting and microarray analysis, DNA-RNA hybridization in Northern blotting). In DNA sequencing, primers base-pair to the template, allowing DNA synthesis to start. In RT-PCR, the primers must base-pair with their target sequences in the DNA mixture. **3.** If a spot is green, the gene represented on that spot is expressed only in normal tissue. If red, the gene is expressed only in cancerous tissue. If yellow, the gene is expressed in both. And if black, the gene is expressed in neither type of tissue. As a researcher interested in cancer development, you would want to study genes represented by spots that are green or red because these are genes for which the expression level differs between the two types of tissues. Some of these genes may be expressed differently as a result of cancer, but others might play a role in causing cancer.

Concept Check 20.3

1. No, primarily because of subtle (and perhaps not so subtle) differences in their environments **2.** The state of chromatin modification in the nucleus from the intestinal cell was undoubtedly less similar to that of a nucleus from a fertilized egg, explaining why many fewer of these nuclei were able to be reprogrammed. In contrast, the chromatin in a nucleus from a cell at the four-cell stage would have been much more like that of a nucleus in a fertilized egg and therefore much more easily programmed to direct development. **3.** A technique would have to be worked out for turning a human iPS cell into a pancreatic cell (probably by inducing expression of pancreas-specific regulatory genes in the cell).

Concept Check 20.4

1. Stem cells continue to reproduce themselves. **2.** Herbicide resistance, pest resistance, disease resistance, salinity resistance, delayed ripening, and improved nutritional value **3.** Because hepatitis A is an RNA virus, you could isolate RNA from the blood and try to detect copies of hepatitis A RNA by one of three methods. First, you could run the RNA on a gel and then do a Northern blot using probes complementary to hepatitis A genome sequences. A second approach would be to use reverse transcriptase to make cDNA from the RNA in the blood, run the cDNA on a gel, and do a Southern blot using the same probe. However, neither of these methods would be as sensitive as RT-PCR, in which you would reverse transcribe the blood RNA into cDNA and then use PCR to amplify the cDNA, using primers specific to hepatitis A sequences. If you then ran the products on an electrophoretic gel, the presence of a band would support your hypothesis.

Self-Quiz

1. b **2.** b **3.** c **4.** b **5.** a **6.** c **7.** c **8.** d
9.

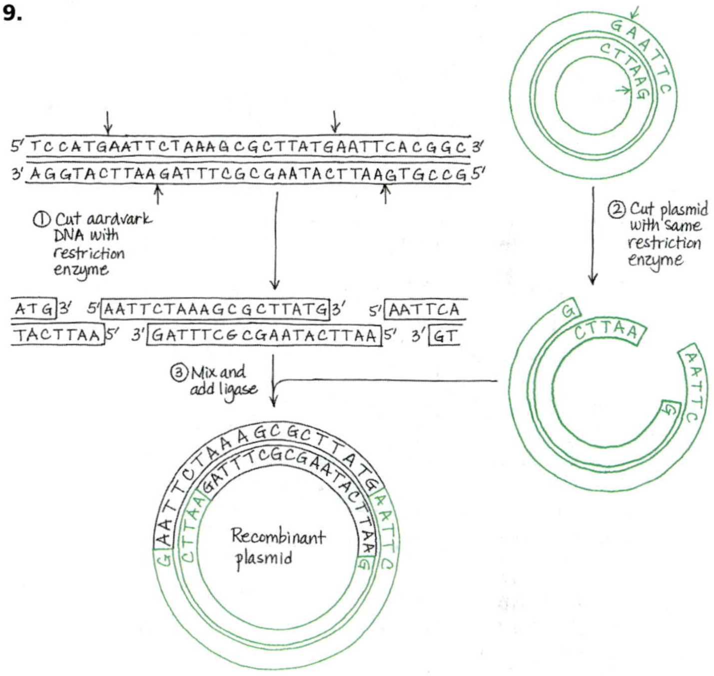

10. A cDNA library, made using mRNA from human lens cells, which would be expected to contain many copies of crystallin mRNAs

CHAPTER 21

Figure Questions

Figure 21.3 The fragments in stage 2 of this figure are like those in stage 2 of Figure 21.2, but in this figure their order relative to each other is not known and will be determined later by computer. The order of the fragments in Figure 21.2 is completely known before sequencing begins. (Determining the order takes longer but makes the eventual sequence assembly much easier.) **Figure 21.9** The transposon would be cut out of the DNA at the original site rather than copied, so part (a) would show the original stretch of DNA without the transposon after the mobile transposon had been cut out. **Figure 21.10** The RNA transcripts extending from the DNA in each transcription unit are shorter on the left and longer on the right. This means that RNA polymerase must be starting on the left end of the unit and moving toward the right. **Figure 21.13** Pseudogenes are nonfunctional. They could have arisen by any mutations in the second copy that made the gene product unable to function. Examples would be base changes that introduce stop codons in the sequence, alter amino acids, or change a region of the gene promoter so that the gene can no longer be expressed. **Figure 21.14** Let's say a transposable element (TE) existed in the intron to the left of the indicated EGF exon in the *EGF* gene, and the same TE was present in the intron to the left of the indicated F exon in the fibronectin gene. During meiotic recombination, these TEs could cause nonsister chromatids on the same chromosome to pair up incorrectly, as seen in Figure 21.12. One gene might end up with an F exon next to an EGF exon. Further mistakes in pairing over many generations might result in these two exons being separated from the rest of the gene and placed next to a single or duplicated K exon. In general, the presence of repeated sequences in introns and between genes facilitates these processes because it allows incorrect pairing of nonsister chromatids, leading to novel exon combinations. **Figure 21.16** Since you know that chimpanzees do not speak but humans do, you'd probably want to know how many amino acid differences there are between the human wild-type FOXP2 protein and that of the chimpanzee and whether these changes affect the function of the protein. (As we explain later in the text, there are two amino acid differences.) You know that humans with mutations in this gene have severe language impairment. You would want to learn more about the human mutations by checking whether they affect the same amino acids in the gene product that the chimpanzee sequence differences affect. If so, those amino acids might play an important role in the function of the protein in language. Going further, you could analyze the differences between the chimpanzee and mouse FOXP2 proteins. You might ask: Are they more similar than the chimpanzee and human proteins? (It turns out that the chimpanzee and mouse proteins have only one amino acid difference and thus are more similar than the chimpanzee and human proteins, which have two differences, and than the human and mouse proteins, which have three differences.)

Concept Check 21.1

1. In a linkage map, genes and other markers are ordered with respect to each other, but only the relative distances between them are known. In a physical map, the actual distances between markers, expressed in base pairs, are known. **2.** The three-stage approach employed in the Human Genome Project involves linkage mapping, physical mapping, and then sequencing of short, overlapping fragments that previously have been ordered relative to each other (see Figure 21.2). The whole-genome shotgun approach eliminates the linkage mapping and physical mapping stages; instead, short fragments generated by multiple restriction enzymes are sequenced and then ordered by computer programs that identify overlapping regions (see Figure 21.3). **3.** Because the two mouse species are very closely related, their genome sequences are expected to be very similar. This means that the field mouse genome fragments could be compared with the assembled lab mouse genome, providing valuable information to use in placing the field mouse genome fragments in the correct order. In a sense, the lab mouse genome could be used as a rough map for the field mouse genome, removing the necessity to carry out complete genetic and physical mapping for the field mouse.

Concept Check 21.2

1. The Internet allows centralization of databases such as GenBank and software resources such as BLAST, making them freely accessible. Having all the data in a central database, easily accessible on the Internet, minimizes the possibility of errors and of researchers working with different data. It streamlines the process of science, since all researchers are able to use the same software programs, rather than each having to obtain their own software. It speeds up dissemination of data and ensures as much as possible that errors are corrected in a timely fashion. These are just a few answers; you can probably think of more. **2.** Cancer is a disease caused by multiple factors. To focus on a single gene or a single defect would ignore other factors that may influence the cancer and even the behavior of the single gene being studied. The systems approach, because it takes into account many factors at the same time, is more likely to lead to an understanding of the causes and most useful treatments for cancer. **3.** The DNA would first be sequenced and analyzed for whether the mutation is in the coding region for a gene or in a promoter or enhancer, affecting the expression of a gene. In either case, the nature of the gene product could be explored by searching the protein database for similar proteins. If similar proteins have known functions, that would provide a clue about the function of your protein. Otherwise, biochemical and other methods could provide some ideas about possible function. Software could be used to compare what is known about your protein and similar proteins.

Concept Check 21.3

1. Alternative splicing of RNA transcripts from a gene and post-translational processing of polypeptides **2.** The total number of completed genomes is found by clicking on "Published Complete Genomes." Add the figures for bacterial, archaeal, and eukaryotic "ongoing genomes" to get the number "in progress." Finally, look at the top of the Published Complete Genomes page to get numbers of completed genomes for each domain. (*Note:* You can click on the "Size" column and the table will be re-sorted by genome size. Scroll down to get an idea of relative sizes of genomes in the three domains. Remember, though, that most of the sequenced genomes are bacterial.) **3.** Prokaryotes are generally smaller cells than eukaryotic cells, and they reproduce by binary fission. The evolutionary process involved is natural selection for more quickly reproducing cells: The faster they can replicate their DNA and divide, the more likely they will be able to dominate a population of prokaryotes. The less DNA they have to replicate, then, the faster they will reproduce.

Concept Check 21.4

1. The number of genes is higher in mammals, and the amount of noncoding DNA is greater. Also, the presence of introns in mammalian genes makes them longer, on average, than prokaryotic genes. **2.** Introns are interspersed within the coding sequences of genes. Many copies of each transposable element are scattered throughout the genome. Simple sequence DNA is concentrated at the centromeres and telomeres and is clustered in other locations. **3.** In the rRNA gene family, identical transcription units for the three different RNA products are present in long, tandemly repeated arrays. The large number of copies of the rRNA genes enable organisms to produce the rRNA for enough ribosomes to carry out active protein synthesis, and the single transcription unit ensures that the relative amounts of the different rRNA molecules produced are correct. Each globin gene family consists of a relatively small number of nonidentical genes. The differences in the globin proteins encoded by these genes result in production of hemoglobin molecules adapted to particular developmental stages of the organism. **4.** First, you could check the sequence by translating it into a predicted amino acid sequence and see if there are multiple stop codons. If there aren't, the next step would be to see whether the gene is expressed, probably by carrying out a Northern blot or *in situ* hybridization to look for the mRNA in the cells that express the gene.

Concept Check 21.5

1. If meiosis is faulty, two copies of the entire genome can end up in a single cell. Errors in crossing over during meiosis can lead to one segment being duplicated while another is deleted. During DNA replication, slippage backward along the template strand can result in a duplication. **2.** For either gene, a mistake in crossing over during meiosis could have occurred between the two copies of that gene, such that one ended up with a duplicated exon. This could have happened several times, resulting in the multiple copies of a particular exon in each gene. **3.** Homologous transposable elements scattered throughout the genome provide sites where recombination can occur between different chromosomes. Movement of these elements into coding or regulatory sequences may change expression of genes. Transposable elements also can carry genes with them, leading to dispersion of genes and in some cases different patterns of expression. Transport of an exon during transposition and its insertion into a gene may add a new functional domain to the originally encoded protein, a type of exon shuffling. **4.** Because more offspring are born to women who have this inversion, it must provide some advantage. It would be expected to persist and spread in the population. (In fact, evidence in the study allowed the researchers to conclude that it has been increasing in proportion in the population. You'll learn more about population genetics in the next unit.)

Concept Check 21.6

1. Because both humans and macaques are primates, their genomes are expected to be more similar than the macaque and mouse genomes are. The mouse lineage diverged from the primate lineage before the human and macaque lineages diverged. **2.** Homeotic genes differ in their *non*homeobox sequences, which determine the interactions of homeotic gene products with other transcription factors and hence which genes are regulated by the homeotic genes. These nonhomeobox sequences differ in the two organisms, as do the expression patterns of the homeobox genes. **3.** *Alu* elements must have undergone transposition more actively in the human genome for some reason. Their increased numbers may have then allowed more recombination errors in the human genome, resulting in more or different duplications. The divergence of the organization and content of the two genomes presumably accelerated divergence of the two species by making matings less and less likely to result in fertile offspring.

Self-Quiz

1. c **2.** e **3.** a **4.** e **5.** c **6.** a

7.
1. ATETI... PKSSD... TSSTT... NARRD
2. ATETI... PKSSE... TSSTT... NARRD
3. ATETI... PKSSD... TSSTT... NARRD
4. ATETI... PKSSD... TSSNT... SARRD
5. ATETI... PKSSD... TSSTT... NARRD
6. VTETI... PKSSD... TSSTT... NARRD

a. Lines 1, 3, and 5 are the C, G, R species.
b. Line 4 is the human sequence.
c. Line 6 is the orangutan sequence.
d. There is one amino acid difference between the mouse (line 2) and the C, G, R species; there are three amino acid differences between the mouse and the human.
e. Because only one amino acid difference arose during the 60–100 million years since the mouse and C, G, R species diverged, it is somewhat surprising that two additional amino acid differences resulted during the 6 million years since chimpanzees and humans diverged. This indicates that the *FOXP2* gene has been evolving faster in the human lineage than in the lineages of other primates.

CHAPTER 22

Figure Questions

Figure 22.8 More than 5.5 million years ago. **Figure 22.13** The original pool of the transplanted guppy population contains pike-cichlids, a potent predator of adult guppies. Brightly colored adult males would be at a disadvantage in this pool. Thus, it is likely that color patterns in the guppy population would become more drab if they were returned to their original pool. **Figure 22.19** Based on this evolutionary tree, crocodiles are more closely related to birds than to lizards because they share a more recent common ancestor with birds (ancestor 5) than with lizards (ancestor 4).

Concept Check 22.1

1. Hutton and Lyell proposed that events in the past were caused by the same processes operating today. This principle suggested that Earth must be much older than a few thousand years, the age that was widely accepted at that time. Hutton and Lyell also thought that geologic change occurs gradually, stimulating Darwin to reason that the slow accumulation of small changes could ultimately produce the profound changes documented in the fossil record. In this context, the age of Earth was important to Darwin, because unless Earth was very old, he could not envision how there would have been enough time for evolution to occur. **2.** By these criteria, Cuvier's explanation of the fossil record and Lamarck's hypothesis of evolution are both scientific. Cuvier suggested that catastrophes and the resulting extinctions were usually confined to local regions, and that such regions were later repopulated by a different set of species that immigrated from other areas. These assertions can be tested against the fossil record (they have been found to be false). With respect to Lamarck, his principle of use and disuse can be used to make testable predictions for fossils of groups such as whale ancestors as they adapt to a new habitat. Lamarck's principle of the inheritance of acquired characteristics can be tested directly in living organisms (it has been found to be false).

Concept Check 22.2

1. Organisms share characteristics (the unity of life) because they share common ancestors; the great diversity of life occurs because new species have repeatedly formed when descendant organisms gradually adapted to different environments, becoming different from their ancestors. **2.** All species have the potential to produce more offspring (overreproduce) than can be supported by the environment. This ensures there will be what Darwin called a "struggle for existence" in which many of the offspring are eaten, starved, diseased, or unable to reproduce for a variety of other reasons. Members of a population exhibit a range of heritable variations, some of which make it likely that their bearers will leave more offspring than other individuals (for example, the bearer may escape predators more effectively or be more tolerant of the physical conditions of the environment). Over time, natural selection imposed by factors such as predators, lack of food, or the physical conditions of the environment can increase the proportion of individuals with favorable traits in a population (evolutionary adaptation). **3.** The fossil mammal species (or its ancestors) would most likely have colonized the Andes from within South America, whereas ancestors of mammals currently found in African mountains would most likely have colonized those mountains from other parts of Africa. As a result, the Andes fossil species would share a more recent common ancestor with South American mammals than with mammals in Africa. Thus, for many of its traits, the fossil mammal species would probably more closely resemble mammals that live in South American jungles than mammals that live on African mountains.

Concept Check 22.3

1. An environmental factor such as a drug does not create new traits such as drug resistance, but rather selects for traits among those that are already present in the population. **2.** (a) Despite their different functions, the forelimbs of different mammals are structurally similar because they all represent modifications of a structure found in the common ancestor. (b) Convergent evolution: The similarities between the sugar glider and flying squirrel indicate that similar environments selected for similar adaptations despite different ancestry.
3. At the time that dinosaurs originated, Earth's landmasses formed a single large continent, Pangaea. Because many dinosaurs were large and mobile, it is likely that early members of these groups lived on many different parts of Pangaea. When Pangaea broke apart, fossils of these organisms would have moved with the rocks in which they were deposited. As a result, we would predict that fossils of early dinosaurs would have a broad geographic distribution (this prediction has been upheld).

Self-Quiz

1. b **2.** c **3.** d **4.** d **5.** a **6.** d
8. (a)

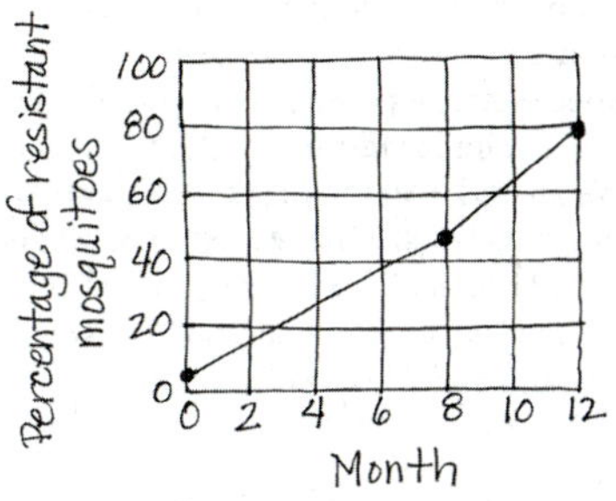

(b) The rapid rise in the percentage of mosquitoes resistant to DDT was most likely caused by natural selection in which mosquitoes resistant to DDT could survive and reproduce while other mosquitoes could not. (c) In India—where DDT resistance first appeared—natural selection would have caused the frequency of resistant mosquitoes to increase over time. If resistant mosquitoes then migrated from India (for example, transported by wind or in planes, trains, or ships) to other parts of the world, the frequency of DDT resistance would increase there as well.

CHAPTER 23

Figure Questions

Figure 23.7 The predicted frequencies are 36% C^RC^R, 48% C^RC^W, and 16% C^WC^W. **Figure 23.12** Because such a shift in prevailing winds would increase the transfer of alleles (gene flow) from plants living on mine soils to plants living at the location marked by the arrow, the change would probably lead to an increase in the index of copper tolerance of plants at that location. **Figure 23.16** Crossing a single female's eggs with both an SC and an LC male's sperm allowed the researchers to directly compare the effects of the males' contribution to the next generation, since both batches of offspring had the same maternal contribution. This isolation of the male's impact enabled researchers to draw conclusions about differences in genetic "quality" between the SC and LC males. **Figure 23.18** The researchers measured the percentages of successfully reproducing adults out of the breeding adult population that had each phenotype. This approach of determining which phenotype was favored by selection assumes that reproduction was a sufficient indicator of relative fitness (as opposed to counting the number of eggs laid or offspring hatched, for example) and that mouth phenotype was the driving factor determining the fishes' ability to reproduce.

Concept Check 23.1

1. (a) Within a population, genetic differences among individuals provide the raw material on which natural selection and other mechanisms can act. Without such differences, allele frequencies could not change over time—and hence the population could not evolve. (b) Genetic variation among populations can arise by natural selection if selection favors different alleles in different populations; this might occur, for example, if the different populations experienced different environmental conditions. Genetic variation among populations can also arise by genetic drift when the genetic differences between populations are selectively neutral. **2.** Many mutations occur in somatic cells that do not produce gametes and so are lost when the organism dies. Of mutations that do occur in cell lines that produce gametes, many do not have a phenotypic effect on which natural selection can act. Others have a harmful effect and are thus unlikely to increase in frequency because they decrease the reproductive success of their bearers. **3.** Its genetic variation (whether measured at the level of the gene or at the level of nucleotide sequences) would probably drop over time. During meiosis, crossing over and the independent assortment of chromosomes produce many new combinations of alleles. In addition, a population contains a vast number of possible mating combinations, and fertilization brings together the gametes of individuals with different genetic backgrounds. Thus, via crossing over, independent assortment of chromosomes, and fertilization, sexual reproduction reshuffles alleles into fresh combinations each generation. Without sexual reproduction, new sources of genetic variation would be reduced, causing the overall amount of genetic variation to drop.

Concept Check 23.2

1. 750. Half the loci (250) are fixed, meaning only one allele exists for each locus: $250 \times 1 = 250$. There are two alleles each for the other loci: $250 \times 2 = 500$. $250 + 500 = 750$. **2.** $p^2 + 2pq$; p^2 represents homozygotes with two *A* alleles, and $2pq$ represents heterozygotes with one *A* allele. **3.** There are 120 individuals in the population, so there are 240 alleles. Of these, there are 124 *A* alleles—32 from the 16 *AA* individuals and 92 from the 92 *Aa* individuals. Thus, the frequency of the *A* allele is $p = 124/240 = 0.52$; hence, the frequency of the *a* allele is $q = 0.48$. Based on the Hardy-Weinberg equation, if the population were not evolving, the frequency of genotype *AA* should be $p^2 = 0.52 \times 0.52 = 0.27$; the frequency of genotype *Aa* should be $2pq = 2 \times 0.52 \times 0.48 = 0.5$; and the frequency of genotype *aa* should be $q^2 = 0.48 \times 0.48 = 0.23$. In a population of 120 individuals, these expected genotype frequencies lead us to predict that there would be 32 *AA* individuals (0.27×120), 60 *Aa* individuals (0.5×120), and 28 *aa* individuals (0.23×120). The actual numbers for the population (16 *AA*, 92 *Aa*, 12 *aa*) deviate from these expectations (fewer homozygotes and more heterozygotes than expected). This suggests that the population is not in Hardy-Weinberg equilibrium and hence is evolving.

Concept Check 23.3

1. Natural selection is more "predictable" in that it alters allele frequencies in a nonrandom way: It tends to increase the frequency of alleles that increase the organism's reproductive success in its environment and decrease the frequency of alleles that decrease the organism's reproductive success. Alleles subject to genetic drift increase or decrease in frequency by chance alone, whether or not they are advantageous. **2.** Genetic drift results from chance events that cause allele frequencies to fluctuate at random from generation to generation; within a population, this process tends to decrease genetic variation over time. Gene flow is the exchange of alleles between populations; a process that can introduce new alleles to a population and hence may increase its genetic variation (albeit slightly, since rates of gene flow are often low). **3.** Selection is not important at this locus; furthermore, the populations are reasonably large, and hence the effects of genetic drift should not be pronounced. Gene flow is occurring via the movement of pollen and seeds. Thus, allele and genotype frequencies in these populations should become more similar over time as a result of gene flow.

Concept Check 23.4

1. Zero, because fitness includes reproductive contribution to the next generation, and a sterile mule cannot produce offspring. **2.** Although both gene flow and genetic drift can increase the frequency of advantageous alleles in a population, they can also decrease the frequency of advantageous alleles or increase the frequency of harmful alleles. Only natural selection *consistently* results in an increase in the frequency of alleles that enhance survival or reproduction. Thus, natural selection is the only mechanism that consistently causes adaptive evolution. **3.** The three modes of natural selection (directional, stabilizing, and disruptive) are defined in terms of the selective advantage of different *phenotypes*, not different genotypes. Thus, the type of selection represented by heterozygote advantage depends on the phenotype of the heterozygotes. In this question, because heterozygous individuals have a more extreme phenotype than either homozygote, heterozygote advantage represents directional selection.

Self-Quiz

1. d **2.** a **3.** e
4. b **5.** b
7. The frequency of the lap^{94} allele forms a cline, decreasing as one moves from southwest to northeast across Long Island Sound.

Site	1	2	3	4	5	6
lap^{94} %	13	16	16	25	36	37

Site	7	8	9	10	11
lap^{94} %	39	55	59	59	59

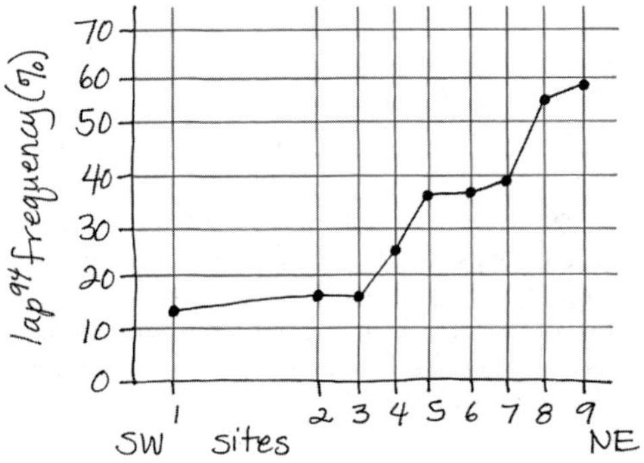

A hypothesis that explains the cline and accounts for the observations stated in the question is that the cline is maintained by an interaction between selection and gene flow. Under this hypothesis, in the southwest portion of the Sound, salinity is relatively low, and selection against the lap^{94} allele is strong. Moving toward the northeast and into the open ocean, where salinity is relatively high, selection favors a high frequency of the lap^{94} allele. However, because mussel larvae disperse long distances, gene flow prevents the lap^{94} allele from becoming fixed in the open ocean or from declining to zero in the southwestern portion of Long Island Sound.

CHAPTER 24

Figure Questions

Figure 24.3 Allele 1 (found in some birds in Population B) is more closely related to alleles found in Population A than to other alleles found in Population B. This implies that the ancestral allele from which allele 1 descended existed in Population A. Hence, the direction of gene flow was from Population A to Population B. **Figure 24.9** This change would have the effect of increasing gene flow between the populations, which would make the evolution of reproductive isolation more difficult. **Figure 24.12** Such results would suggest that mate choice based on coloration does not provide a reproductive barrier between these two cichlid species. **Figure 24.14** Because the populations had only just begun to diverge from one another at this point in the process, it is likely that any existing barriers to reproduction would weaken over time. **Figure 24.20** The presence of *M. cardinalis* plants that carry the *M. lewisii yup* allele would make it more likely that bumblebees would transfer pollen between the two monkey flower species. As a result, we would expect the number of hybrid offspring to increase.

Concept Check 24.1

1. (a) All except the biological species concept can be applied to both asexual and sexual species because they define species on the basis of characteristics other than ability to reproduce. In contrast, the biological species concept can be applied only to sexual species. (b) The easiest species concept to apply in the field would be the morphological species concept because it is based only on the appearance of the organism. Additional information about its ecological habits, evolutionary history, and reproduction are not required. **2.** Because these birds live in fairly similar environments and can breed successfully in captivity, the reproductive barrier in nature is probably prezygotic; given the species differences in habitat preference, this barrier could result from habitat isolation.

Concept Check 24.2

1. In allopatric speciation, a new species forms while in geographic isolation from its parent species; in sympatric speciation, a new species forms in the absence of geographic isolation. Geographic isolation greatly reduces gene flow between populations, whereas ongoing gene flow is more likely in sympatry. As a result, sympatric speciation is less common than allopatric speciation. **2.** Gene flow between subsets of a population that live in the same area can be reduced in a variety of ways. In some species—especially plants—changes in chromosome number can block gene flow and establish reproductive isolation in a single generation. Gene flow can also be reduced in sympatric populations by habitat differentiation (as seen in the apple maggot fly, *Rhagoletis*) and sexual selection (as seen in Lake Victoria cichlids). **3.** Allopatric speciation would be less likely to occur on a nearby island than on an isolated island of the same size. The reason we expect this result is that continued gene flow between mainland populations and those on a nearby island reduces the chance that enough genetic divergence will take place for allopatric speciation to occur.

Concept Check 24.3

1. Hybrid zones are regions in which members of different species meet and mate, producing some offspring of mixed ancestry. Such regions are "natural laboratories" in which to study speciation because scientists can directly observe factors that cause (or fail to cause) reproductive isolation. **2.** (a) If hybrids consistently survive and reproduce poorly compared to the offspring of intraspecific matings, it is possible that reinforcement would occur. If it did, natural selection would cause prezygotic barriers to reproduction between the parent species to strengthen over time, decreasing the production of unfit hybrids and leading to a completion of the speciation process. (b) If hybrid offspring survive and reproduce as well as the offspring of intraspecific matings, indiscriminate mating between the parent species would lead to the production of large numbers of hybrid offspring. As these hybrids mated with each other and with members of both parent species, the gene pools of the parent species could fuse over time, reversing the speciation process.

Concept Check 24.4

1. The time between speciation events includes (1) the length of time that it takes for populations of a newly formed species to begin diverging reproductively from one another and (2) the time it takes for speciation to be complete once this divergence begins. Although speciation can occur rapidly once populations have begun to diverge from one another, it may take millions of years for that divergence to begin. **2.** Investigators transferred alleles at the *yup* locus (which influences flower color) from each parent species to the other. *M. lewisii* plants with an *M. cardinalis yup* allele received many more visits from hummingbirds than usual; hummingbirds usually pollinate *M. cardinalis* but avoid *M. lewisii*. Similarly, *M. cardinalis* plants with an *M. lewisii yup* allele received many more visits from bumblebees than usual; bumblebees usually pollinate *M. lewisii* and avoid *M. cardinalis*. Thus, alleles at the *yup* locus can influence pollinator choice, which in these species provides the primary barrier to interspecific mating. Nevertheless, the experiment does not prove that the *yup* locus alone controls barriers to reproduction between *M. lewisii* and *M. cardinalis*; other genes might enhance the effect of the *yup* locus (by modifying flower color) or cause entirely different barriers to reproduction (for example, gametic isolation or a postzygotic barrier).

Self-Quiz

1. b **2.** a **3.** c **4.** e **5.** d **6.** c
8. One possible process is

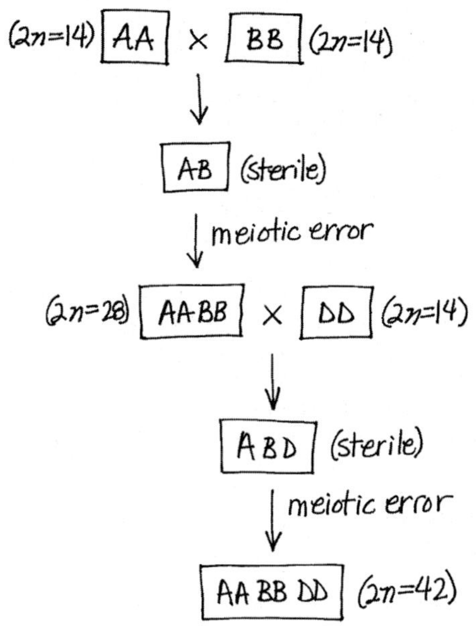

CHAPTER 25

Figure Questions

Figure 25.5 Because uranium-238 has a half-life of 4.5 billion years, the *x*-axis would be relabeled (in billions of years) as: 4.5, 9, 13.5, and 18. **Figure 25.23** The coding sequence of the *Pitx1* gene would differ between the marine and lake populations, but patterns of gene expression would not.

Concept Check 25.1

1. The hypothesis that conditions on early Earth could have permitted the synthesis of organic molecules from inorganic ingredients **2.** In contrast to random mingling of molecules in an open solution, segregation of molecular systems by membranes could concentrate organic molecules, assisting biochemical reactions. **3.** No. Such a result would only show that life *could* have begun as in the experiment.

Concept Check 25.2

1. 22,920 years (four half-lives: $5{,}730 \times 4$) **2.** The fossil record shows that different groups of organisms dominated life on Earth at different points in time and that many organisms once alive are now extinct; specific examples of these points can be found in Figure 25.4. The fossil record also indicates that new groups of organisms can arise via the gradual modification of previously existing organisms, as illustrated by fossils that document the origin of mammals from cynodont ancestors. **3.** The discovery of such a (hypothetical) fossil organism would indicate that aspects of our current understanding of the origin of mammals are not correct because mammals are thought to have originated much more recently (see Figure 25.6). For example, such a discovery could suggest that the dates of previous fossil discoveries are not correct or that the lineages shown in Figure 25.6 shared features with mammals but were not their direct ancestors. Such a discovery would also suggest that radical changes in multiple aspects of the skeletal structure of organisms could arise suddenly—an idea that is not supported by the known fossil record.

Concept Check 25.3

1. Free oxygen attacks chemical bonds and can inhibit enzymes and damage cells. **2.** All eukaryotes have mitochondria or remnants of these organelles, but not all eukaryotes have plastids. **3.** A fossil record of life today would include many organisms with hard body parts (such as vertebrates and many marine invertebrates), but might not include some species we are very familiar with, such as those that have small geographic ranges and/or small population sizes (for example, all five rhinoceros species).

Concept Check 25.4

1. Continental drift alters the physical geography and climate of Earth, as well as the extent to which organisms are geographically isolated. Because these factors affect extinction and speciation rates, continental drift has a major impact on life on Earth. **2.** Mass extinctions; major evolutionary innovations; the diversification of another group of organisms (which can provide new sources of food); migration to new locations where few competitor species exist **3.** Their fossils should be present right up to the time of the catastrophic event, then disappear. Reality is a bit more complicated because the fossil record is not perfect. So the most recent fossil for a species might be a million years before the mass extinction, even if the species did not become extinct until the mass extinction.

Concept Check 25.5

1. Heterochrony can cause a variety of morphological changes. For example, if the onset of sexual maturity changes, a retention of juvenile characteristics (paedomorphosis) may result. Paedomorphosis can be caused by small genetic changes that result in large changes in morphology, as seen in the axolotl salamander. **2.** In animal embryos, *Hox* genes influence the development of structures such as limbs or feeding appendages. As a result, changes in these genes—or in the regulation of these genes—are likely to have major effects on morphology. **3.** From genetics, we know that gene regulation is altered by how well transcription factors bind to noncoding DNA sequences called control elements. Thus, if changes in morphology are often caused by changes in gene regulation, portions of noncoding DNA that contain control elements are likely to be strongly affected by natural selection.

Concept Check 25.6

1. Complex structures do not evolve all at once, but in increments, with natural selection selecting for adaptive variants of the earlier versions. **2.** Although the myxoma virus is highly lethal, initially some of the rabbits are resistant (0.2% of infected rabbits are not killed). Thus, assuming resistance is an inherited trait, we would expect the rabbit population to show a trend for increased resistance to the virus. We would also expect the virus to show an evolutionary trend toward reduced lethality. We would expect this trend because a rabbit infected with a less lethal virus would be more likely to live long enough for a mosquito to bite it and hence potentially transmit the virus to another rabbit. (A virus that kills its rabbit host before a mosquito transmits it to another rabbit dies with its host.)

Self-Quiz

1. c **2.** a **3.** e **4.** b **5.** c **6.** d **7.** b

8.

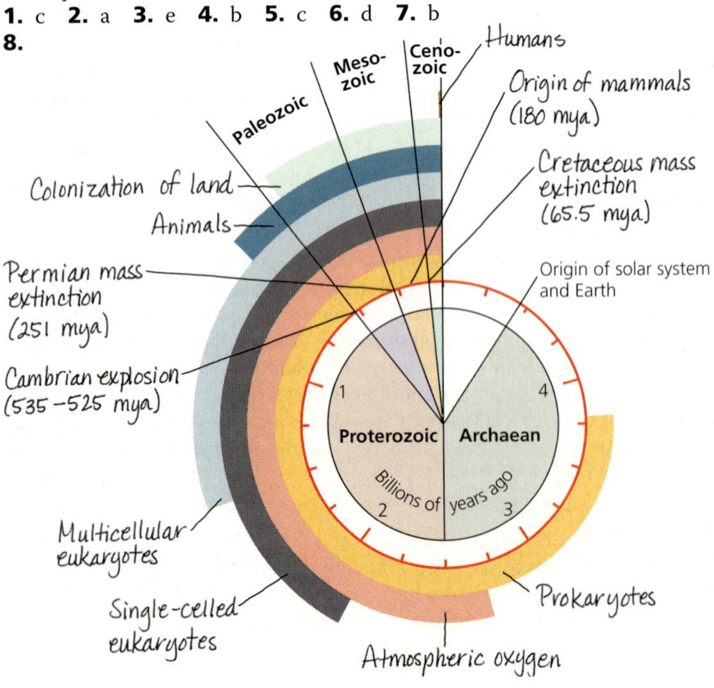

CHAPTER 26

Figure Questions

Figure 26.5 This new version does not alter any of the evolutionary relationships shown in Figure 26.5. For example, B and C remain sister taxa, taxon A is still as closely related to taxon B as it is to taxon C, and so on.

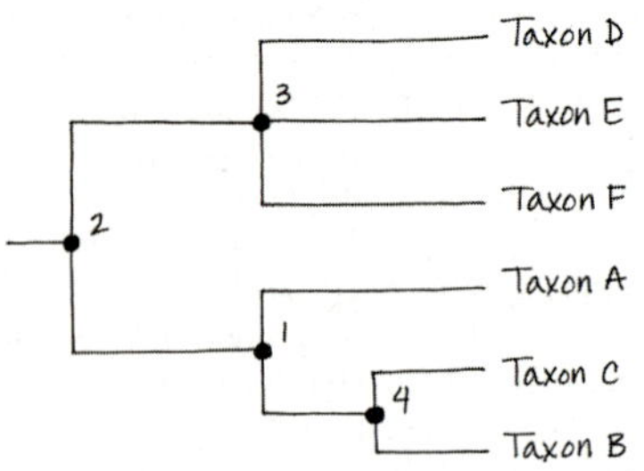

Figure 26.6 Mistakes can occur while performing the experiment (such as errors in DNA sequencing) and analyzing the results (such as misaligning the DNA sequences of different species). But an erroneous conclusion—such as concluding that a sample was from a humpback whale when in fact it came from a gray whale—could be reached even if no such errors were made. A particular humpback whale might, for example, happen to have a DNA sequence that was rare for its species, yet common for another species. To reduce the chance that such events could lead to an erroneous conclusion, gene trees could be constructed for multiple genes; if similar results emerged from all of these gene trees, there would be little reason to doubt the conclusions. **Figure 26.9** There are four possible bases (A, C, G, T) at each nucleotide position. If the base at each position depends on chance, not common descent, we would expect roughly one out of four (25%) of them to be the same. **Figure 26.12** The zebrafish lineage; of the five vertebrate lineages shown, its branch length is the longest. **Figure 26.19** The molecular clock indicates that the divergence time is roughly 45–50 million years. **Figure 26.21** Bacteria was the first to emerge. Archaea is the sister domain to Eukarya.

Concept Check 26.1

1. We are classified the same down to the class level; both the leopard and human are mammals. Leopards belong to order Carnivora, whereas humans do not. **2.** The branching pattern of the tree indicates that the badger and the wolf share a common ancestor that is more recent than the ancestor that these two animals share with the leopard. **3.** The tree in (c) shows a different pattern of evolutionary relationships. In (c), C and B are sister taxa, whereas C and D are sister taxa in (a) and (b).

4.

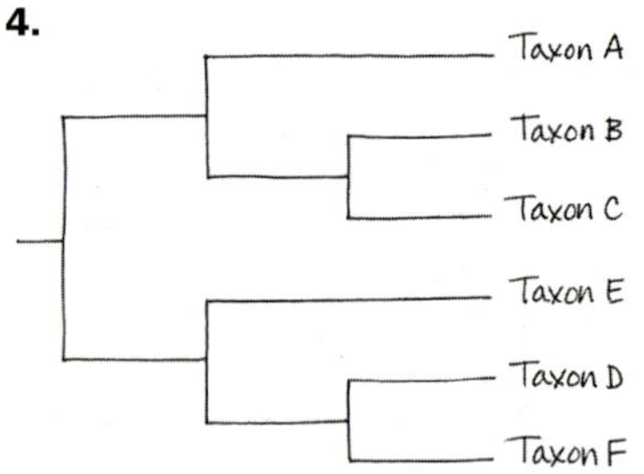

Concept Check 26.2

1. (a) Analogy, since porcupines and cacti are not closely related and since most other animals and plants do not have similar structures; (b) homology, since cats and humans are both mammals and have homologous forelimbs, of which the hand and paw are the lower part; (c) analogy, since owls and hornets are not closely related and since the structure of their wings is very different. **2.** Species 2 and 3 are more likely to be closely related. Small genetic changes (as between species 2 and 3) can produce divergent physical appearances, whereas if genes have diverged greatly (as in species 1 and 2), that suggests that the lineages have been separate for a long time.

Concept Check 26.3

1. No; hair is a shared ancestral character common to all mammals and thus is not helpful in distinguishing different mammalian subgroups. **2.** The principle of maximum parsimony states that the hypothesis about nature we investigate first should be the simplest explanation found to be consistent with the facts. Actual evolutionary relationships may differ from those inferred by parsimony owing to complicating factors such as convergent evolution. **3.** The traditional classification provides a poor match to evolutionary history, thus violating the basic principle of cladistics—that classification should be based on common descent. Both birds and mammals originated from groups traditionally designated as reptiles, making reptiles as traditionally delineated a paraphyletic group. These problems can be addressed by removing *Dimetrodon* and cynodonts from the reptiles, and by considering birds as a group of reptiles (specifically, as a group of dinosaurs).

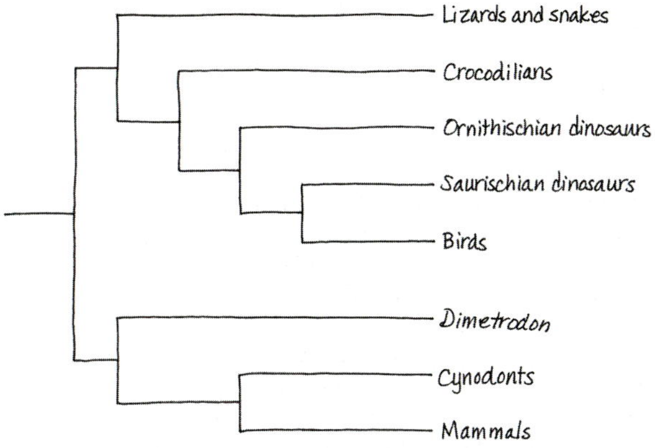

Concept Check 26.4

1. Proteins are gene products. Their amino acid sequences are determined by the nucleotide sequences of the DNA that codes for them. Thus, differences between comparable proteins in two species reflect underlying genetic differences. **2.** These observations suggest that the evolutionary lineages leading to species 1 and species 2 diverged from one another before a gene duplication event in species 1 produced gene B from gene A.

Concept Check 26.5

1. A molecular clock is a method of estimating the actual time of evolutionary events based on numbers of base changes in orthologous genes. It is based on the assumption that the regions of genomes being compared evolve at constant rates. **2.** There are many portions of the genome that do not code for genes; many base changes in these regions could accumulate through drift without affecting an organism's fitness. Even in coding regions of the genome, some mutations may not have a critical effect on genes or proteins. **3.** The gene (or genes) used for the molecular clock may have evolved more slowly in these two taxa than in the species used to calibrate the clock; as a result, the clock would underestimate the time at which the taxa diverged from one another.

Concept Check 26.6

1. The kingdom Monera included bacteria and archaea, but we now know that these organisms are in separate domains. Kingdoms are subsets of domains, so a single kingdom (like Monera) that includes taxa from different domains is not valid (it is polyphyletic). **2.** Because of horizontal gene transfer, some genes in eukaryotes are more closely related to bacteria, while others are more closely related to archaea; thus, depending on which genes are used, phylogenetic trees constructed from DNA data can yield conflicting results.
3.

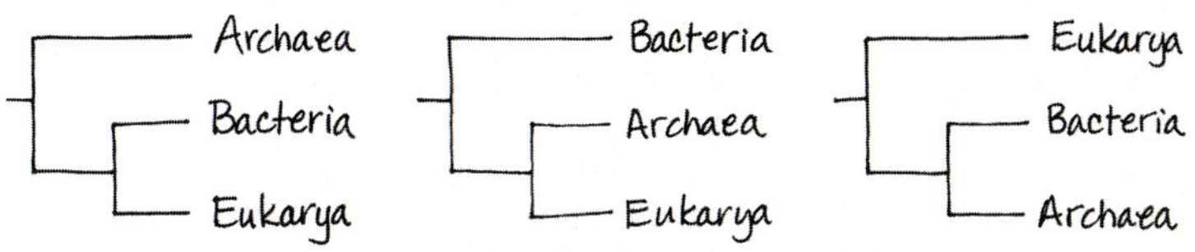

The third tree, in which the eukaryotic lineage diverged first, is not likely to receive support from genetic data because the fossil record shows that prokaryotes originated long before eukaryotes.

Self-Quiz

1. b **2.** d **3.** a **4.** d **5.** c **6.** d **7.** d

9.

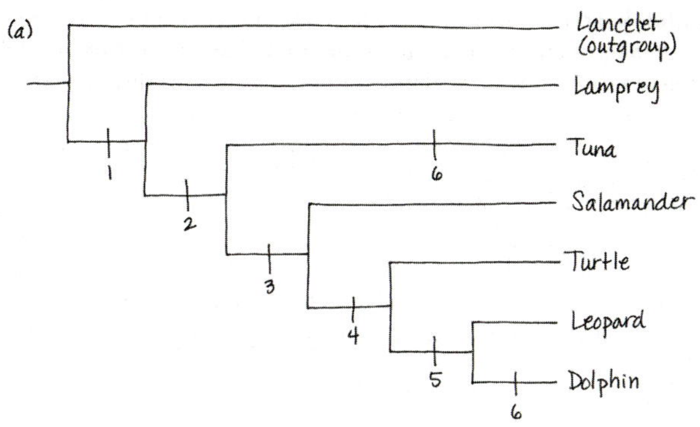

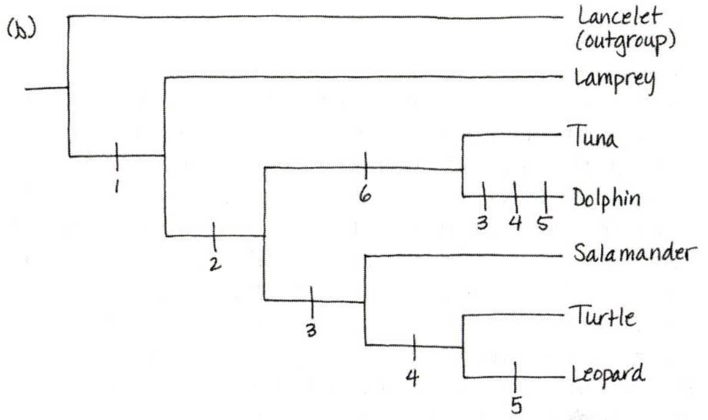

(c) The tree in (a) requires seven evolutionary changes, while the tree in (b) requires nine evolutionary changes. Thus, the tree in (a) is the most parsimonious, since it requires fewer evolutionary changes.

CHAPTER 27

Figure Questions

Figure 27.10 It is likely that the expression or sequence of genes that affect glucose metabolism may have changed; genes for metabolic processes no longer needed by the cell also may have changed. **Figure 27.12** The population that included individuals capable of conjugation would probably be more successful, since some of its members could form recombinant cells whose new gene combinations might be advantageous in a novel environment. **Figure 27.17** Thermophiles live in very hot environments, so it is likely that their enzymes can continue to function normally at much higher temperatures than do the enzymes of other organisms. At low temperatures, however, the enzymes of thermophiles may not function as well as the enzymes of other organisms. **Figure 27.19** From the graph, plant uptake can be estimated as 0.7, 0.6, and 0.95 (mg K) for strains 1, 2, and 3, respectively. These values average to 0.75 mg K. If bacteria had no effect, the average plant uptake of potassium for strains 1, 2, and 3 should be close to 0.5 mg K, the value observed for plants grown in bacteria-free soil.

Concept Check 27.1

1. Adaptations include the capsule (shields prokaryotes from host's immune system) and endospores (enable cells to survive harsh conditions and to revive when the environment becomes favorable). **2.** Prokaryotic cells generally lack the internal compartmentalization of eukaryotic cells. Prokaryotic genomes have much less DNA than eukaryotic genomes, and most of this DNA is contained in a single ring-shaped chromosome located in the nucleoid rather than within a true membrane-bounded nucleus. In addition, many prokaryotes also have plasmids, small ring-shaped DNA molecules containing a few genes. **3.** Because prokaryotic populations evolve rapidly in response to their environment, it is likely that bacteria from endospores that formed 40 years ago would already be adapted to the polluted conditions. Hence, at least initially, these bacteria would probably grow better than bacteria from endospores that formed 150 years ago, when the lake was not polluted.

and eggs) that we actually have. The multicellular haploid stages would produce gametes and reproduce sexually. An individual at the multicellular haploid stage of the human life cycle might look like us, or it might look completely different.

Concept Check 29.2

1. Bryophytes do not have an extensive vascular transport system, and their life cycle is dominated by gametophytes rather than sporophytes. **2.** Answers may include the following: Large surface area of protonema enhances absorption of water and minerals; the vase-shaped archegonia protect eggs during fertilization and transport nutrients to the embryos via placental transfer cells; the stalk-like seta conducts nutrients from the gametophyte to the capsule, where spores are produced; the peristome enables gradual spore discharge; stomata enable CO_2/O_2 exchange while minimizing water loss; lightweight spores are readily dispersed by wind.
3.

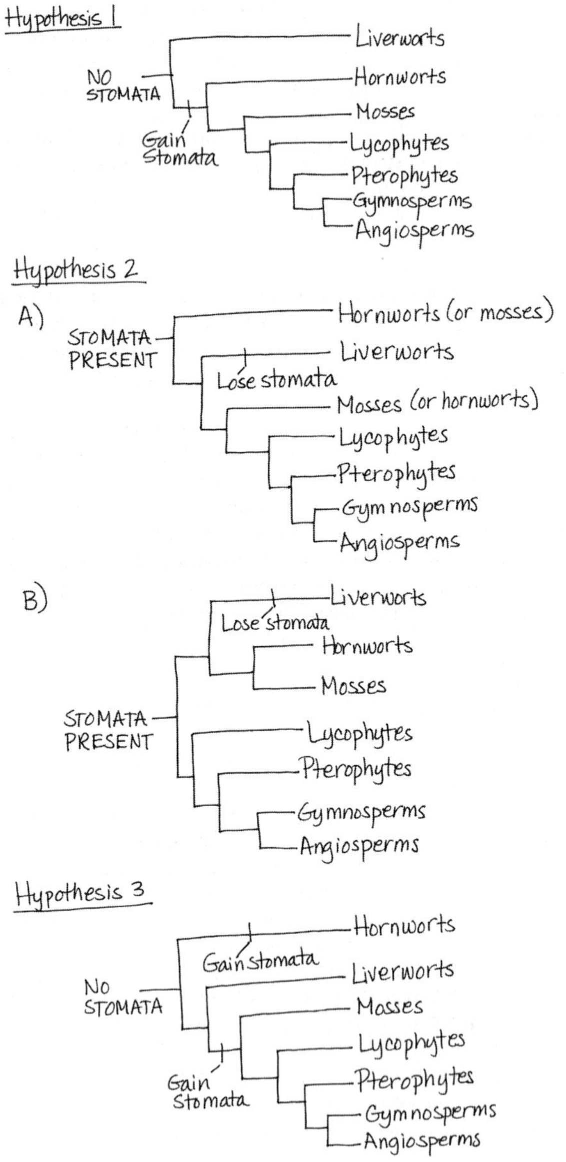

Concept Check 29.3

1. Lycophytes have microphylls, whereas seed plants and pterophytes (ferns and their relatives) have megaphylls. Pterophytes and seed plants also share other traits not found in lycophytes, such as overtopping growth and the initiation of new root branches at various points along the length of an existing root. **2.** Both seedless vascular plants and bryophytes have flagellated sperm that require moisture for fertilization; this shared similarity poses challenges for these species in arid regions. With respect to key differences, seedless vascular plants have lignified, well-developed vascular tissue, a trait that enables the sporophyte to grow tall and that has transformed life on Earth (via the formation of forests). Seedless vascular plants also have true leaves and roots, which, when compared to bryophytes, provides increased surface area for photosynthesis and improves their ability to extract nutrients from soil. **3.** If lycophytes and pterophytes formed a clade, the traits shared by pterophytes and seed plants might have been present in the common ancestor of all vascular plants, but lost in the lycophytes. Alternatively, the common ancestor of all vascular plants may have lacked the traits shared by pterophytes and seed plants; in this case, pterophytes and seed plants would share these traits as a result of convergent evolution.

Self-Quiz

1. b **2.** e **3.** a **4.** d **5.** c **6.** b **7.** c
8. a. diploid; b. haploid; c. haploid; d. diploid; e. haploid
9. Based on our current understanding of the evolution of major plant groups, the phylogeny has the four branch points shown here:

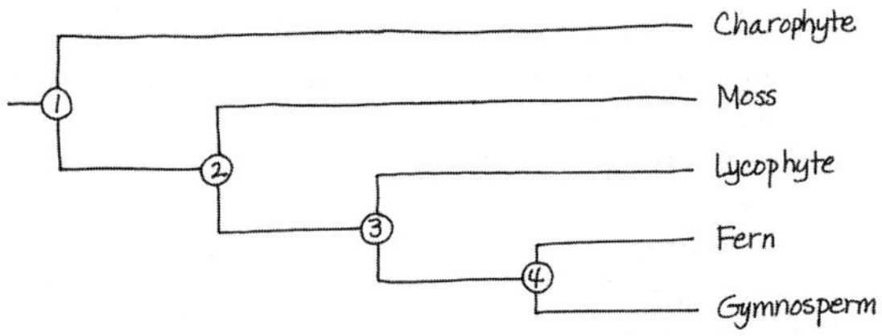

Derived characters unique to the charophyte and land plant clade (indicated by branch point 1) include rosette cellulose-synthesizing complexes, peroxisome enzymes, flagellated sperm structure, and a phragmoplast. Derived characters unique to the land plant clade (branch point 2) include apical meristems, alternation of generations, walled spores produced in sporangia, and multicellular gametangia. Derived characters unique to the vascular plant clade (branch point 3) include life cycles with dominant sporophytes, complex vascular systems (xylem and phloem), and well-developed roots and leaves. Derived characters unique to the pterophyte and seed plant clade (branch point 4) include megaphylls and overtopping growth.

CHAPTER 30

Figure Questions

Figure 30.3 Three: (1) the current sporophyte (cells of ploidy $2n$, found in the integument, or seed coat); (2) the female gametophyte (cells of ploidy n, found in the food supply); and (3) the sporophyte of the next generation (cells of ploidy $2n$, found in the embryo). **Figure 30.12** No. The branching order shown could still be correct if *Amborella* and other early angiosperms had originated prior to 150 million years ago but angiosperm fossils of that age had not yet been discovered. In such a situation, the 140-million-year-old date for the origin of the angiosperms shown on the phylogeny would be incorrect. **Figure 30.14** This study establishes a correlation between the type of floral symmetry and the rate of plant speciation—but it is possible that floral symmetry is correlated with another factor that was the actual cause of the observed results. Note, however, that floral symmetry was associated with increased speciation rates in a variety of different plant lineages. This suggests—but does not establish—that differences in floral symmetry cause differences in speciation rates. In general, strong evidence for causation can come from controlled, manipulative experiments, but such experiments are usually not possible for studies of past evolutionary events.

Concept Check 30.1

1. To have any chance of reaching the eggs, the flagellated sperm of seedless vascular plants must swim through a film of water, usually over a distance of no more than a few centimeters. In contrast, the sperm of seed plants do not require water because they are produced within pollen grains that can be transported long distances by wind or by animal pollinators. Although flagellated in some species, the sperm of seed plants do not require mobility because pollen tubes convey them from the point at which the pollen grain is deposited (near the ovules) directly to the eggs. **2.** The reduced gametophytes of seed plants are nurtured by sporophytes and protected from stress, such as drought conditions and UV radiation. Pollen grains have tough protective walls. Seeds have one or two layers of protective tissue, the seed coat, that improve survival by providing more protection from environmental stresses than do the walls of spores. Seeds also contain a stored supply of food, which enables seeds to live longer than spores and provides developing embryos with nourishment for growth. **3.** If seed plants were homosporous, only one type of spore would be produced—as opposed to the actual situation in which microspores give rise to sperm cells within pollen grains, and megaspores give rise to eggs within ovules. Thus, if structures like pollen grains and seeds were produced, they would arise in a very different way from how they now are formed.

Concept Check 30.2

1. Although gymnosperms are similar in not having their seeds enclosed in ovaries and fruits, their seed-bearing structures vary greatly. For instance, cycads have large cones, whereas some gymnosperms, such as *Ginkgo* and *Gnetum*, have small cones that look somewhat like berries, even though they are not fruits. Leaf shape also varies greatly, from the needles of many conifers to the palmlike leaves of cycads to *Gnetum* leaves that look like those of flowering plants. **2.** The life cycle illustrates heterospory, as ovulate cones produce megaspores and pollen cones produce microspores. The reduced gametophytes are evident in the form of the microscopic pollen grains and the microscopic female gametophyte within the megaspore. The egg is shown developing within an ovule, and a pollen tube is shown conveying the sperm. The figure also shows the protective and nutritive features of a seed. **3.** No. Fossil evidence indicates that gymnosperms originated at least 305 million years ago, but this does not mean that angiosperms are that old—only that the most recent common ancestor of gymnosperms and angiosperms must be that old.

Concept Check 30.3

1. In the oak's life cycle, the tree (the sporophyte) produces flowers, which contain gametophytes in pollen grains and ovules; the eggs in ovules are fertilized; the mature ovaries develop into dry fruits called acorns. We can view the oak's life cycle as starting when the acorn seeds germinate, resulting in embryos giving rise to seedlings and finally to mature trees, which produce flowers—and then more acorns. **2.** Pine cones and flowers both have sporophylls, modified leaves that produce spores. Pine trees have separate pollen cones (with pollen grains) and ovulate cones (with ovules inside cone scales). In flowers, pollen grains are produced by the anthers of stamens, and ovules are within the ovaries of carpels. Unlike pine cones, many flowers produce both pollen and ovules. **3.** Such a discovery would remove support for the idea, based on 125-million-year-old *Archaefructus sinensis* fossils, that the earliest angiosperms may have been herbaceous, aquatic plants.

Concept Check 30.4

1. Because extinction is irreversible, it decreases the total diversity of plants, many of which may have brought important benefits to humans. **2.** A detailed phylogeny of the seed plants would identify many different monophyletic groups of seed plants. Using this phylogeny, researchers could look for clades that contained species in which medicinally useful compounds had already been discovered. Identification of such clades would allow researchers to concentrate their search for new medicinal compounds among clade members—as opposed to searching for new compounds in species that were selected at random from the more than 250,000 existing species of seed plants.

Self-Quiz

1. d **2.** a **3.** b **4.** a **5.** d

6.

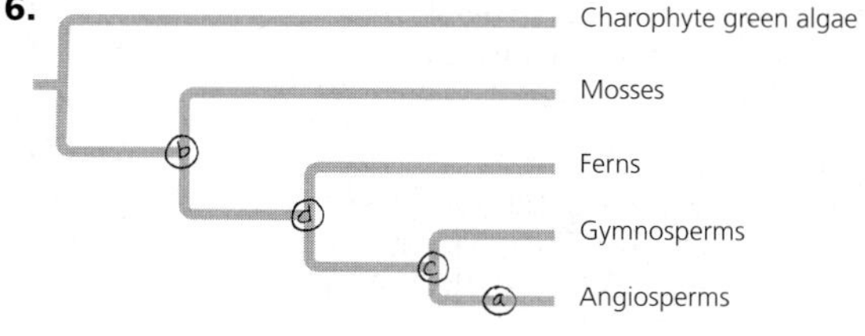

8. (a)

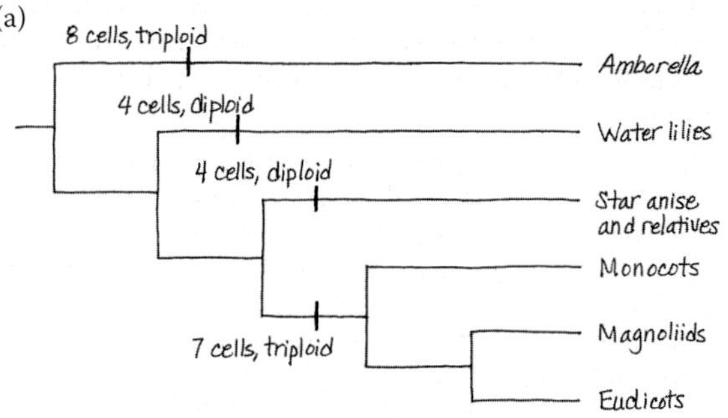

(b) The phylogeny indicates that basal angiosperms differed from other angiosperms in terms of the number of cells in female gametophytes and the ploidy of the endosperm. The ancestral state of the angiosperms cannot be determined from these data alone. It is possible that the common ancestor of angiosperms had seven-celled female gametophytes and triploid endosperm and hence that the eight-celled and four-celled conditions found in basal angiosperms represent derived traits for those lineages. Alternatively, either the eight-celled or four-celled condition may represent the ancestral state.

CHAPTER 31

Figure Questions

Figure 31.2 DNA from each of these mushrooms would be identical if each mushroom is part of a single hyphal network, as is likely. **Figure 31.16** One or both of the following would apply to each species: DNA analyses would reveal that it is a member of the ascomycetes clade, or aspects of its sexual life cycle would indicate that it is an ascomycete (for example, it would produce asci and ascospores). **Figure 31.21** Two possible controls would be E−P− and E+P−. Results from an E−P− control could be compared with results from the E−P+ experiment, and results from an E+P− control could be compared with results from the E+P+ experiment; together, these two comparisons would indicate whether the addition of the pathogen causes an increase in leaf mortality. Results from an E−P− experiment could also be compared with results from the second control (E+P−) to determine whether adding the endophytes has a negative effect on the plant.

Concept Check 31.1

1. Both a fungus and a human are heterotrophs. Many fungi digest their food externally by secreting enzymes into the food and then absorbing the small molecules that result from digestion. Other fungi absorb such small molecules directly from their environment. In contrast, humans (and most other animals) ingest relatively large pieces of food and digest the food within their bodies. **2.** The ancestors of such a mutualist most likely secreted powerful enzymes to digest the body of their insect host. Since such enzymes would harm a living host, it is likely that the mutualist would not produce such enzymes or would restrict their secretion and use.

Concept Check 31.2

1. The majority of the fungal life cycle is spent in the haploid stage, whereas the majority of the human life cycle is spent in the diploid stage. **2.** The two mushrooms might be reproductive structures of the same mycelium (the same organism). Or they might be parts of two separate organisms that have arisen from a single parent organism through asexual reproduction and thus carry the same genetic information.

Concept Check 31.3

1. DNA evidence indicates that fungi, animals, and their protistan relatives form a clade, the opisthokonts. Furthermore, an early-diverging fungal lineage, the chytrids, have posterior flagella, as do most other opisthokonts. This suggests that other fungal lineages lost their flagella after diverging from chytrids. **2.** This indicates that fungi had already established mutualistic relationships with plants by the date the fossils of the earliest vascular plants had formed. **3.** Fungi are heterotrophs. Prior to the colonization of land by plants, terrestrial fungi could have lived only where other organisms (or their remains) were present and provided a source of food. Thus, if fungi had colonized land before plants, they could have fed on any prokaryotes or protists that lived on land or by the water's edge—but not on the plants or animals on which many fungi feed today.

Concept Check 31.4

1. Flagellated spores **2.** Possible answers include the following: In zygomycetes, the sturdy, thick-walled zygosporangium can withstand harsh conditions and then undergo karyogamy and meiosis when the environment is favorable for reproduction. In glomeromycetes, the hyphae have a specialized morphology that enables the fungi to form arbuscular mycorrhizae with plant roots. In ascomycetes, the asexual spores (conidia) are often produced in chains or clusters at the tips of conidiophores, where they are easily dispersed by wind. The often cup-shaped ascocarps house the sexual spore-forming asci. In basidiomycetes, the basidiocarp supports and protects a large surface area of basidia, from which spores are dispersed. **3.** Such a change to the life cycle of an ascomycete would reduce the number and genetic diversity of ascospores that result from a mating event. Ascospore number would drop because a mating event would lead to the formation of only one ascus. Ascospore genetic diversity would also drop because in ascomycetes, one mating event leads to the formation of asci by many different dikaryotic cells. As a result, genetic recombination and meiosis occurs independently many different times—which could not happen if only a single ascus was formed. It is also likely that if such an ascomycete formed an ascocarp, the shape of the ascocarp would differ considerably from that found in its close relatives.

Concept Check 31.5

1. A suitable environment for growth, retention of water and minerals, protection from intense sunlight, and protection from being eaten **2.** A hardy spore stage enables dispersal to host organisms through a variety of mechanisms; their ability to grow rapidly in a favorable new environment enables them to capitalize on the host's resources. **3.** Many different outcomes might have occurred. Organisms that currently form mutualisms with fungi might have gained the ability to perform the tasks currently done by their fungal partners, or they might have formed similar mutualisms with other organisms (such as bacteria). Alternatively, organisms that currently form mutualisms with fungi might be less effective at living in their present environments. For example, the colonization of land by plants might have been more difficult. And if plants did eventually colonize land without fungal mutualists, natural selection might have favored plants that formed more highly divided and extensive root systems (in part replacing mycorrhizae).

Self-Quiz

1. b **2.** c **3.** d **4.** e **5.** b **6.** a

8.

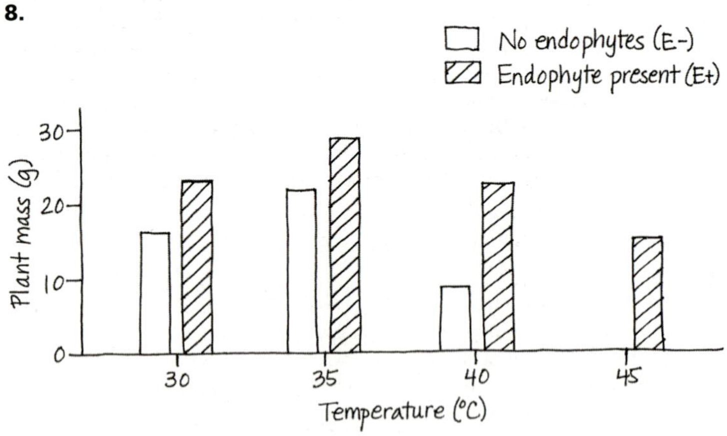

As indicated by the raw data and bar graph, grass plants with endophytes (E+) produced more new shoots and had greater biomass than did grass plants that lacked endophytes (E−). These differences were especially pronounced at the highest soil temperature, where E− grass plants produced no new shoots and had a biomass of zero (indicating they were dead).

CHAPTER 32

Figure Questions

Figure 32.3 As described in ① and ②, choanoflagellates and a broad range of animals have collar cells. Since collar cells have never been observed in plants, fungi, or non-choanoflagellate protists, this suggests that choanoflagellates may be more closely related to animals than to other eukaryotes. If choanoflagellates are more closely related to animals than is any other group of eukaryotes, choanoflagellates and animals should share other traits that are not found in other eukaryotes. The data described in ③ are consistent with this prediction. **Figure 32.6** The sea anemone embryos could be infused with a protein that can bind to β-catenin's DNA-binding site, thereby limiting the extent to which β-catenin activates the transcription of genes necessary for gastrulation. Such an experiment would provide an independent check of the results shown in step 4. **Figure 32.10** Ctenophora is the sister phylum in this figure, while Cnidaria is the sister phylum in Figure 32.11.

Concept Check 32.1

1. In most animals, the zygote undergoes cleavage, which leads to the formation of a blastula. Next, in gastrulation, one end of the embryo folds inward, producing layers of embryonic tissue. As the cells of these layers differentiate, a wide variety of animal forms result. Despite the diversity of animal forms, animal development is controlled by a similar set of *Hox* genes across a broad range of taxa. **2.** The imaginary plant would require tissues composed of cells that were analogous to the muscle and nerve cells found in animals: "muscle" tissue would be necessary for the plant to chase prey, and "nerve" tissue would be required for the plant to coordinate its movements when chasing prey. To digest captured prey, the plant would need to either secrete enzymes into one or more digestive cavities (which could be modified leaves, as in a Venus' flytrap), or secrete enzymes outside of its body and feed by absorption. To extract nutrients from the soil—yet be able to chase prey—the plant would need something other than fixed roots, perhaps retractable "roots" or a way to ingest soil. To conduct photosynthesis, the plant would require chloroplasts. Overall, such an imaginary plant would be very similar to an animal that had chloroplasts and retractable roots.

Concept Check 32.2

1. c, b, a, d **2.** We cannot infer whether animals originated before or after fungi. If correct, the date provided for the most recent common ancestor of fungi and animals would indicate that animals originated some time within the last billion years. The fossil record indicates that animals originated at least 565 million years ago. Thus, we could conclude only that animals originated some time between 565 million years ago and 1 billion years ago.

Concept Check 32.3

1. Grade-level characteristics are those that multiple lineages share regardless of evolutionary history. Some grade-level characteristics may have evolved multiple times independently. Features that unite clades are derived characteristics that originated in a common ancestor and were passed on to the various descendants. **2.** A snail has a spiral and determinate cleavage pattern; a human has radial, indeterminate cleavage. In a snail, the coelomic cavity is formed by splitting of mesoderm masses; in a human, the coelom forms from folds of archenteron. In a snail, the mouth forms from the blastopore; in a human, the anus develops from the blastopore. **3.** Most coelomate triploblasts have two openings to their digestive tract, a mouth and an anus. As such, their bodies have a structure that is analogous to that of a doughnut: The digestive tract (the hole of the doughnut) runs from the mouth to the anus and is surrounded by various tissues (the solid part of the doughnut). The doughnut analogy is most obvious at early stages of development (see Figure 32.9c).

Concept Check 32.4

1. Cnidarians possess true tissues, while sponges do not. Also unlike sponges, cnidarians exhibit body symmetry, though it is radial and not bilateral as in other animal phyla. **2.** The morphology-based tree divides Bilateria into two major clades: Deuterostomia and Protostomia. The molecular-based tree recognizes three major clades: Deuterostomia, Ecdysozoa, and Lophotrochozoa. **3.** Both statements could be correct. Figure 32.11 shows that the lineage leading to Deuterostomia was the first to diverge from the other two main bilaterian lineages (those leading to Lophotrochozoa and Ecdysozoa). By itself, however, this information does not indicate whether the most recent common ancestor of the Deuterostomia lived before or after the first arthropods. For example, the ancestors of Deuterostomia could have diverged from the ancestors of Lophotrochozoa and Ecdysozoa 570 million years ago; it could have then taken 35 million years for the clade Deuterostomia to originate, but only 10 million years for first Ecdysozoa and then the arthropod clades to originate.

Self-Quiz

1. a **2.** d **3.** b **4.** e **5.** c **6.** e

Answers

8.

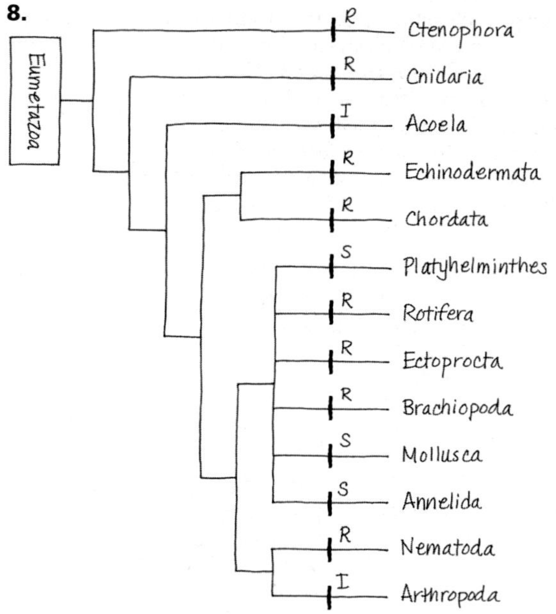

From the phylogeny, it appears that radial cleavage is the ancestral condition for eumetazoans. However, because relationships within Lophotrochozoa are not resolved, we cannot estimate the precise number of times that cleavage patterns have changed over the course of evolution. If, for example, Platyhelminthes, Mollusca, and Annelida form a clade, it would be reasonable to infer three cleavage pattern changes (one in Acoela, one in the ancestor of this hypothetical clade, and one in Arthropoda). Various other possible relationships among lophotrochozoans lead to other estimates.

CHAPTER 33

Figure Questions

Figure 33.8 Within a reproductive polyp, a cell that gives rise to a medusa would have to divide by meiosis. A resulting haploid cell would then divide repeatedly (by mitosis), forming a haploid medusa. Later, cells in the medusa's gonads would divide by mitosis, forming the haploid eggs and sperm. **Figure 33.11** Adding fertilizer to the water supply would probably increase the abundance of algae. This, in turn, might increase the abundance of both snails (which eat algae) and blood flukes (which require snails as an intermediate host). As a result, the occurrence of schistosomiasis might increase. **Figure 33.28** Such a result would be consistent with the *Ubx* and *abd-A Hox* genes having played a major role in the evolution of increased body segment diversity in arthropods. However, by itself, such a result would simply show that the presence of the *Ubx* and *abd-A Hox* genes was *correlated with* an increase in body segment diversity in arthropods; it would not provide direct experimental evidence that the acquisition of the *Ubx* and *adb-A* genes *caused* an increase in arthropod body segment diversity.

Concept Check 33.1

1. The flagella of choanocytes draw water through their collars, which trap food particles. The particles are engulfed by phagocytosis and digested, either by choanocytes or by amoebocytes. **2.** The collar cells of sponges (and other animals—see Chapter 32) bear a striking resemblance to a choanoflagellate cell. This suggests that the last common ancestor of animals and their protist sister group may have resembled a choanoflagellate. Nevertheless, mesomycetozoans could still be the sister group of animals. If this is the case, the lack of collar cells in mesomycetozoans would indicate that over time their structure evolved in ways that caused it to no longer resemble a choanoflagellate cell.

Concept Check 33.2

1. Both the polyp and the medusa are composed of an outer epidermis and an inner gastrodermis separated by a gelatinous layer, the mesoglea. The polyp is a cylindrical form that adheres to the substrate by its aboral end; the medusa is a flattened, mouth-down form that moves freely in the water. **2.** Cnidarian stinging cells (cnidocytes) function in defense and prey capture. They contain capsule-like organelles (cnidae), which in turn contain coiled threads. The threads either inject poison or stick to and entangle small prey. **3.** This would suggest that the life cycle of basal cnidarians was probably dominated by the medusa stage. Over time, the polyp stage came to be increasingly important in some groups, such as Hydrozoa, which alternate between medusa and polyp stages, and Anthozoa, which lack the medusa stage entirely.

Concept Check 33.3

1. Tapeworms can absorb food from their environment and release ammonia into their environment through their body surface because their body is very flat, due in part to the lack of a coelom. **2.** The function of the foot reflects the locomotion required in each class. Gastropods use their foot as a holdfast or to move slowly on the substrate. In cephalopods, the foot functions as a siphon and tentacles. **3.** The inner tube is the alimentary canal, which runs the length of the body. The outer tube is the body wall. The two tubes are separated by the coelom. **4.** Many lophotrochozoans lack skeletons or other structures that could support their soft bodies against the force of gravity, making it difficult for them to live above the surface of the soil. Some species, such as ectoprocts (bryozoans), have a sturdy exoskeleton, but they are stationary and so would find it difficult to capture food on land. (Note that those lophotrochozoans that do live above the soil surface, such as slugs, have some form of hydrostatic skeleton.)

Concept Check 33.4

1. Nematodes lack body segments and a true coelom; annelids have both. **2.** Arthropod mouthparts are modified appendages, which are bilaterally paired. **3.** The arthropod exoskeleton, which had already evolved in the ocean, allowed terrestrial species to retain water and support their bodies on land. Wings allowed them to disperse quickly to new habitats and to find food and mates. The tracheal system allows for efficient gas exchange despite the presence of an exoskeleton. **4.** Yes. Under the traditional hypothesis, we would expect body segmentation to be controlled by similar *Hox* genes in annelids and arthropods. However, if annelids are in Lophotrochozoa and arthropods are in Ecdysozoa, body segmentation may have evolved independently in these two groups. In such a case, we might expect that different *Hox* genes would control the development of body segmentation in the two clades.

Concept Check 33.5

1. Each tube foot consists of an ampulla and a podium. When the ampulla squeezes, it forces water into the podium, which causes the podium to expand and contact the substrate. Adhesive chemicals are then secreted from the base of the podium, thereby attaching the podium to the substrate. **2.** These two organisms look very different from one another, but they share features found in all echinoderms, such as a water vascular system and tube feet. Hence, their shared characteristics probably result from homology, not analogy. **3.** Both insects and nematodes are members of Ecdysozoa, one of the three major clades of bilaterians. Therefore, a characteristic shared by *Drosophila* and *Caenorhabditis* may be informative for other members of their clade—but not necessarily for members of Deuterostomia. Instead, Figure 33.2 suggests that a species within Echinodermata or Chordata might be a more appropriate invertebrate model organism from which to draw inferences about humans and other vertebrates.

Self-Quiz

1. c **2.** a **3.** d **4.** e **5.** b **6.** e
7.

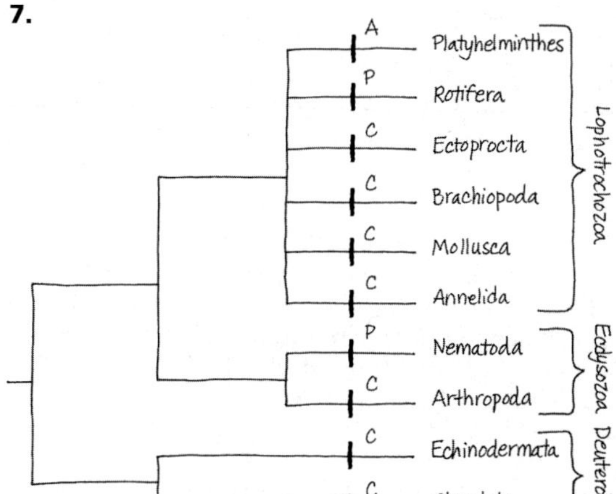

(a) Both phyla in Deuterostomia are coelomates, suggesting that their most recent common ancestor had a true coelom. Lophotrochozoa contains one phylum of acoelomates (Platyhelminthes), one phylum of pseudocoelomates (Rotifera), and four phyla of coelomates (Ectoprocta, Brachiopoda, Mollusca, Annelida); thus, we cannot from this information alone infer the condition of the most recent common ancestor shared by these phyla. Similarly, since Ecdysozoa contains one phylum of pseudocoelomates (Nematoda) and one phylum of coelomates (Arthropoda), we cannot infer whether their most recent common ancestor had a true coelom or not. (b) Depending on whether or not the last common ancestor of Bilateria had a true coelom, the presence of a true coelom has either been lost or gained multiple times during the evolutionary history of bilaterians. Thus, the presence of a true coelom appears to change over the course of evolution.

CHAPTER 34

Figure Questions

Figure 34.20 Amphibians must have originated some time between the date that the most recent common ancestor of *Hynerpeton* and later tetropods originated (380 mya) and the date of the earliest known fossils of amphibians (shown in the figure as 340 mya). **Figure 34.37** The phylogeny shows humans as the sister group to the genus *Pan*. This relationship is consistent with humans being placed in *Pan* along with its two living members, chimpanzees and bonobos. **Figure 34.43** It is not likely that these two sources of error significantly influenced the results. We can conclude this in part because the results were reproducible: similar sequences were found for mtDNA obtained from two different Neanderthal fossils and sequenced by two different research teams. In addition, the close relationship of the two Neanderthal mtDNA sequences to each other would not be expected if the fossil DNA had broken down considerably. Similarly, the fact that Europeans and other living humans formed a sister group to the Neanderthals, and that chimpanzees formed a sister group to the human/Neanderthal clade also would not be expected had the DNA broken down greatly—nor would these results be expected if the fossil DNA sequences were contaminated (for example, by DNA from microorganisms or from living humans).

Concept Check 34.1

1. As water passes through the slits, food particles are filtered from the water and transported to the digestive system. **2.** In humans, these characters are present only in the embryo. The notochord becomes disks between the vertebrae, the tail is almost completely lost, and the pharyngeal clefts develop into various adult structures. **3.** Not necessarily. It would be possible that the chordate common ancestor had this gene, which was then lost in the lancelet lineage and retained in other chordates. However, it would also be possible that the chordate common ancestor lacked this gene—this could occur if the gene originated after lancelets diverged from other chordates yet before tunicates diverged from other chordates.

Concept Check 34.2

1. Hagfishes have a head and skull made of cartilage, plus a small brain, sensory organs, and tooth-like structures. They have a neural crest, gill slits, and more extensive organ systems. In addition, hagfishes have slime glands that ward off predators and may repel competing scavengers. **2.** *Myllokunmingia*. Fossils of this organism provide evidence of ear capsules and eye capsules; these structures are part of the skull. Thus, *Myllokunmingia* is considered a craniate, as are humans. *Haikouella* did not have a skull. **3.** Such a finding suggests that early organisms with a head were favored by natural selection in several different evolutionary lineages. However, while a logical argument can be made that having a head was advantageous, fossils alone do not constitute proof.

Concept Check 34.3

1. Lampreys have a round, rasping mouth, which they use to attach to fish. Conodonts had two sets of mineralized dental elements, which may have been used to impale prey and cut it into smaller pieces. **2.** In armored jawless vertebrates, bone served as external armor that may have provided protection from predators. Some species also had mineralized mouthparts, which could be used for either predation or scavenging. Still others had mineralized fin rays, which may have enabled them to swim more rapidly and with greater steering control.

Concept Check 34.4

1. Both are gnathostomes and have jaws, four clusters of *Hox* genes, enlarged forebrains, and lateral line systems. Shark skeletons consist mainly of cartilage, whereas tuna have bony skeletons. Sharks also have a spiral valve. Tuna have an operculum and a swim bladder, as well as flexible rays supporting their fins. **2.** Aquatic gnathostomes have jaws (an adaptation for feeding) and paired fins and a tail (adaptations for swimming). Aquatic gnathostomes also typically have streamlined bodies for efficient swimming and swim bladders or other mechanisms (such as oil storage in sharks) for buoyancy. **3.** Yes, that could have happened. The paired appendages of aquatic gnathostomes other than the lobe-fins could have served as a starting point for the evolution of limbs. The colonization of land by aquatic gnathostomes other than the lobe-fins might have been facilitated in lineages that possessed lungs, as that would have enabled those organisms to breathe air.

Concept Check 34.5

1. Tetrapods are thought to have originated about 360 million years ago when the fins of some lobe-fins evolved into the limbs of tetrapods. In addition to their four limbs—a key derived trait for which the group is named—other derived traits of tetrapods include a neck (consisting of vertebrae that separate the head from the rest of the body), a pelvic girdle that is fused to the backbone, and a lack of gill slits. **2.** Some fully aquatic species are paedomorphic, retaining larval features for life in water as adults. Species that live in dry environments may avoid dehydration by burrowing or living under moist leaves, and they protect their eggs with foam nests, viviparity, and other adaptations. **3.** Many amphibians spend part of their life cycle in aquatic environments and part on land. Thus, they may be exposed to a wide range of environmental problems, including water and air pollution and the loss or degradation of aquatic and/or terrestrial habitats. In addition, amphibians have highly permeable skin, providing relatively little protection from external conditions, and their eggs do not have a protective shell.

Concept Check 34.6

1. The amniotic egg provides protection to the embryo and allows the embryo to develop on land, eliminating the necessity of a watery environment for reproduction. Another key adaptation is rib cage ventilation, which improves the efficiency of air intake and may have allowed early amniotes to dispense with breathing through their skin. And not breathing through their skin allowed amniotes to develop relatively impermeable skin, thereby conserving water. **2.** Birds have weight-saving modifications, including the absence of teeth, a urinary bladder, and a second ovary in females. The wings and feathers are adaptations that facilitate flight, and so are efficient respiratory and circulatory systems that support a high metabolic rate.

3.

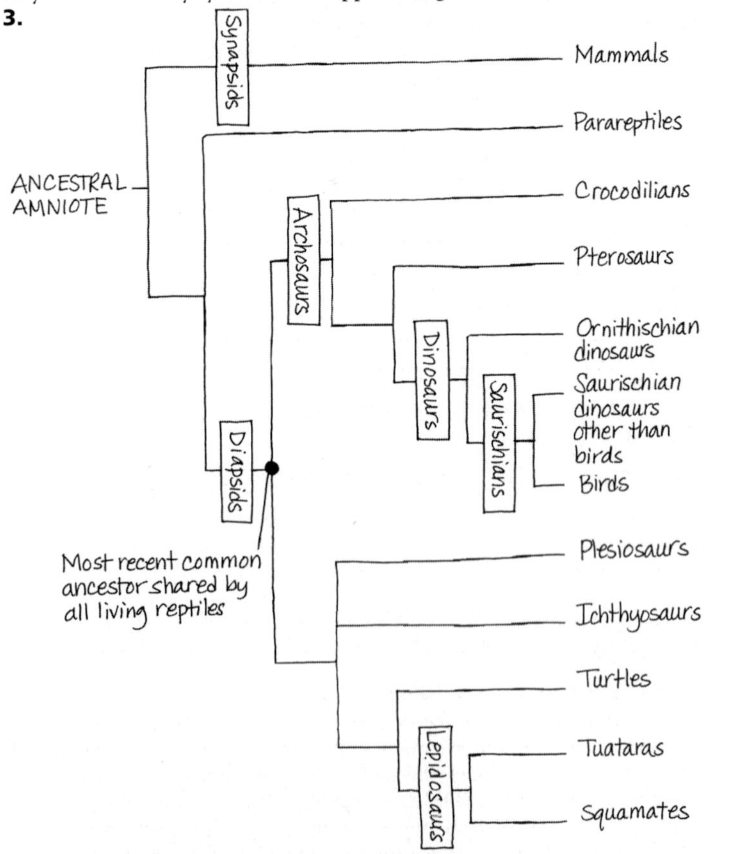

Under this convention, the reptiles would consist of all groups in Figure 34.24 except parareptiles and mammals.

Concept Check 34.7

1. Monotremes lay eggs. Marsupials give birth to very small live young that attach to a nipple in the mother's pouch, where they complete development. Eutherians give birth to more developed live young. **2.** Hands and feet adapted for grasping, flat nails, large brain, forward-looking eyes on a flat face, parental care, moveable big toe and thumb. **3.** Mammals are endothermic, enabling them to live in a wide range of habitats. Milk provides young with a balanced set of nutrients, and hair and a layer of fat under the skin help mammals retain heat. Mammals have differentiated teeth, enabling them to eat many different kinds of food. Mammals also have relatively large brains, and many species are capable learners. Following the mass extinction at the end of the Cretaceous period, the absence of large terrestrial dinosaurs may have opened many new ecological niches to mammals, promoting their adaptive radiation. Continental drift also isolated many groups of mammals from one another, promoting the formation of many new species.

Concept Check 34.8

1. Hominins are a clade within the ape clade that includes humans and all species more closely related to humans than other apes. The derived characters of hominins include bipedal locomotion and relatively larger brains. **2.** In hominins, bipedal locomotion evolved long before large brain size. *Homo ergaster*, for example, was fully upright, bipedal, and as tall as modern humans, but its brain was significantly smaller than that of modern humans. **3.** Yes, both can be correct. *Homo sapiens* may have established populations outside of Africa as early as 115,000 years ago, as indicated by the fossil record. However, those populations may have left few or no descendants today. Instead, all living humans may have descended from Africans that spread from Africa roughly 50,000 years ago, as indicated by genetic data.

Self-Quiz

1. e **2.** c **3.** a **4.** d **5.** b **6.** c **7.** c
9. (a) Because brain size tends to increase consistently in such lineages, we can conclude that natural selection favored the evolution of larger brains and hence that the benefits outweighed the costs. (b) As long as the benefits of brains that are large relative to body size are greater than the costs, large brains can evolve. Natural selection might favor the evolution of brains that are large relative to body size because such brains confer an advantage in obtaining mates and/or an advantage in survival.

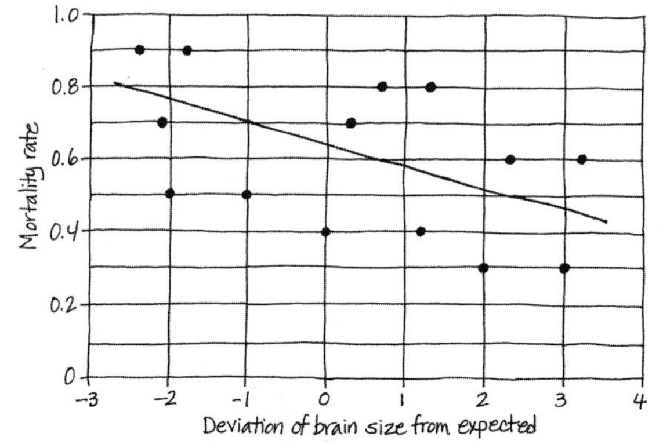

(c) Adult mortality tends to be lower in birds with larger brains.

CHAPTER 35

Figure Questions

Figure 35.9 The finding might suggest that the tawny-colored trichomes deter the beetles by some means other than physically obstructing the beetles. Perhaps they contain a chemical that is harmful or distasteful to the beetles, or their color is a deterrent. **Figure 35.17** Pith and cortex are defined, respectively, as ground tissue that is internal and external to vascular tissue. Since vascular bundles of monocot stems are scattered throughout the ground tissue, there is no clear distinction between internal and external relative to the vascular tissue. **Figure 35.19** The vascular cambium produces growth that increases the diameter of a stem or root. The tissues that are exterior to the vascular cambium cannot keep pace with the growth because their cells no longer divide. As a result, these tissues rupture. **Figure 35.31** Every root epidermal cell would develop a root hair.

Concept Check 35.1

1. The vascular tissue system connects leaves and roots, allowing sugars to move from leaves to roots in the phloem and allowing water and minerals to move to the leaves in the xylem. **2.** (a) large axillary buds; (b) petioles; (c) storage leaves; (d) storage roots **3.** The dermal tissue system is the leaf's protective covering. The vascular tissue system consists of the transport tissues xylem and phloem. The ground tissue system performs metabolic functions such as photosynthesis. **4.** Here are a few examples: The tubular, hollow structures of the tracheids and vessel elements of the xylem and the sieve plates in the sieve-tube elements of the phloem facilitate transport. Root hairs aid in absorption of water and nutrients. The cuticle in leaves and stems protects these structures from desiccation and pathogens. Leaf trichomes protect from herbivores and pathogens. Collenchyma and sclerenchyma cells have thick walls that provide support for plants. **5.** To get sufficient energy from photosynthesis, we would need lots of surface area exposed to the sun. This large surface-to-volume ratio, however, would create a new problem—evaporative water loss. We would have to be permanently connected to a water source—the soil, also our source of minerals. In short, we would probably look and behave very much like plants.

Concept Check 35.2

1. Primary growth arises from apical meristems and involves production and elongation of organs. Secondary growth arises from lateral meristems and adds to the girth of roots and stems. **2.** Your dividing cells are normally limited in the types of cells they can form. In contrast, the products of cell division in a plant meristem can differentiate into all the types of plant cells. **3.** The largest, oldest leaves would be lowest on the shoot. Since they would probably be heavily shaded, they would not photosynthesize much regardless of their size. **4.** No, the radish roots will probably be smaller at the end of the second year because the food stored in the root will be used to produce flowers, fruits, and seeds.

Concept Check 35.3

1. Lateral roots emerge from the root's interior (from the pericycle), pushing through cortical and epidermal cells. In contrast, shoot branches arise on the exterior of a shoot (from axillary buds). **2.** In roots, primary growth occurs in three successive stages, moving away from the tip of the root: the zones of cell division, elongation, and differentiation. In shoots, it occurs at the tip of apical buds, with leaf primordia arising along the sides of an apical meristem. Most growth in length occurs in older internodes below the shoot tip. **3.** Grazing animals that crop plants close to the ground have more of a detrimental effect on eudicots than on monocots because the removal of the lowest axillary buds prevents the eudicot from recovering. In contrast, the underground stems of grasses and the intercalary meristems of their leaves are less affected by grazing. Thus, the presence of grazing animals selects for the survival of grasses. **4.** No. Because vertically oriented leaves can capture light equally on both sides of the leaf, you would expect them to have mesophyll cells that are not differentiated into palisade and spongy layers. This is typically the case. Also, vertical leaves usually have stomata on both leaf surfaces.

Concept Check 35.4

1. The sign will still be 2 m above the ground because this part of the tree is no longer growing in length (primary growth); it is now growing only in thickness (secondary growth). **2.** Stomata must be able to close because evaporation is much more intensive from leaves than from the trunks of woody trees as a result of the higher surface-to-volume ratio in leaves. **3.** The growth rings of a tree from the tropics would be difficult to discern unless the tree came from an area that had pronounced wet and dry seasons. **4.** Girdling removes an entire ring of secondary phloem (part of the bark), completely preventing transport of sugars and starches from the shoots to the roots.

Concept Check 35.5

1. *Arabidopsis* is a small, easy-to-grow plant with a small genome and a short generation time. **2.** Differential gene expression **3.** In *fass* mutants, the arrangement of microtubules is disrupted so that the preprophase band does not form. This results in random planes of cell division, rather than the ordered planes of division that normally occur. Disruption of microtubule organization also prevents the alignment of cellulose microfibrils that sets the plane of cell elongation. Because of this randomness, directional growth is disrupted, and the plant becomes stubby. **4.** In theory, tepals could arise if *B* gene activity was present in all three of the outer whorls of the flower.

Self-Quiz

1. d **2.** c **3.** c **4.** d **5.** a **6.** e **7.** d **8.** d **9.** b **10.** b
11.

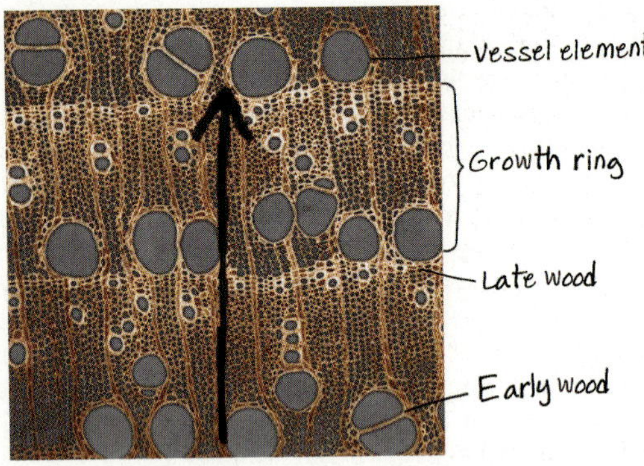

CHAPTER 36

Figure Questions

Figure 36.3 The leaves are being produced in a counterclockwise spiral. **Figure 36.4** A higher leaf area index will not necessarily increase photosynthesis because of upper leaves shading lower leaves. **Figure 36.12** The Casparian strip blocks water and minerals from moving between endodermal cells or moving around an endodermal cell via the cell's wall. Therefore, water and minerals must pass through an endodermal cell's plasma membrane. **Figure 36.21** Because the xylem is under negative pressure (tension), an isolated stylet inserted into a tracheid or vessel element would probably introduce air into the cell. No xylem sap would exude unless pressure was predominant. **Figure 36.22** Such a finding (although not considered likely) would cast doubts on the interpretation of the experiment. If the small fluorescent molecule was cleaved off the larger molecular probe, this small molecule could move through the plasmodesmata without them being dilated.

Concept Check 36.1

1. Vascular plants must transport minerals and water absorbed by the root to all the other parts of the plant. They must also transport sugars from sites of production to sites of use. **2.** Many features of plant architecture affect self-shading, including leaf arrangement, leaf orientation, and leaf area index. **3.** The fungicide may kill the mycorrhizal fungi that help the plants absorb phosphate and other minerals. **4.** Increased stem elongation would raise the plant's upper leaves. Erect leaves and reduced lateral branching would make the plant less subject to shading by the encroaching neighbors. **5.** As described in Chapter 35, pruning the shoot tips will end their apical dominance, allowing axillary buds to grow into lateral shoots (branches). This branching will produce a bushier plant with a higher leaf area index.

Concept Check 36.2

1. The cell's ψ_P is 0.7 MPa. In a solution with a ψ of -0.4 MPa, the cell's ψ_P at equilibrium would be 0.3 MPa. **2.** The cells would still adjust to changes in their osmotic environment, but their responses would be slower. Although aquaporins do not affect the water potential gradient across membranes, they allow for more rapid osmotic adjustments. **3.** If tracheids and vessel elements were living cells, their cytoplasm would impede water movement, preventing rapid long-distance transport. **4.** The protoplasts would burst. Because the cytoplasm has many dissolved solutes, water would enter the protoplast continuously without reaching equilibrium. (When present, the cell wall prevents rupturing by excessive expansion of the protoplast.)

Concept Check 36.3

1. Because water-conducting xylem cells are dead at maturity and form essentially hollow tubes, they offer little resistance to water flow, and their thick walls prevent the cells from collapsing from the negative pressure inside. **2.** At dawn, a drop is exuded because the xylem is under positive pressure due to root pressure. At noon, the xylem is under negative pressure potential due to transpiration and the root pressure cannot keep pace with the increased rate of transpiration. **3.** The endodermis regulates the passage of water-soluble solutes by requiring all such molecules to cross a selectively permeable membrane. Presumably the inhibitor never reaches the plant's photosynthetic cells. **4.** Perhaps greater root mass helps compensate for the lower water permeability of the plasma membranes.

Concept Check 36.4

1. Stomatal aperture is controlled by drought, light, CO_2 concentrations, a circadian rhythm, and the plant hormone abscisic acid. **2.** The activation of the proton pump of stomatal cells would cause the guard cells to take up K^+. The increased turgor of the guard cells would lock the stomata open and lead to extreme evaporation from the leaf. **3.** After the flowers are cut, transpiration from any leaves and from the petals (which are modified leaves) will continue to draw water up the xylem. If cut flowers are transferred directly to a vase, air pockets in xylem vessels prevent delivery of water from the vase to the flowers. Cutting stems again underwater, a few centimeters from the original cut, will sever the xylem above the air pocket. The water droplets prevent another air pocket from forming while placing the flowers in a vase.

Concept Check 36.5

1. In both cases, the long-distance transport is a bulk flow driven by a pressure difference at opposite ends of tubes. Pressure is generated at the source end of a sieve tube by the loading of sugar and resulting osmotic flow of water into the phloem, and this pressure *pushes* sap from the source end to the sink end of the tube. In contrast, transpiration generates a negative pressure potential (tension) as a force that *pulls* the ascent of xylem sap. **2.** The main sources are fully grown leaves (by photosynthesis) and fully developed storage organs (by breakdown of starch). Roots, buds, stems, expanding leaves, and fruits are powerful sinks because they are actively growing. A storage organ may be a sink in the summer when accumulating carbohydrates, but a source in the spring when breaking down starch into sugar for growing shoot tips. **3.** Positive pressure, whether it be in the xylem when root pressure predominates, or in the sieve-tube elements of the phloem, requires active transport. Most long-distance transport in the xylem depends on bulk flow driven by negative pressure potential generated ultimately by the evaporation of water from the leaf and does not require living cells. **4.** The spiral slash prevents optimal bulk flow of the phloem sap to the root sinks. Therefore, more phloem sap can move from the source leaves to the fruit sinks, making them sweeter.

Concept Check 36.6

1. Voltage between cells, cytoplasmic pH, cytoplasmic calcium, and movement proteins all affect symplastic communication, as do developmental changes in plasmodesmatal number. **2.** Plasmodesmata, unlike gap junctions, have the ability to pass RNA, proteins, and viruses from cell to cell. **3.** Although this strategy would eliminate the systemic spread of viral infections, it would also severely impact the development of the plants.

Self-Quiz

1. d **2.** e **3.** c **4.** b **5.** a **6.** d **7.** c **8.** c **9.** b **10.** c
11.

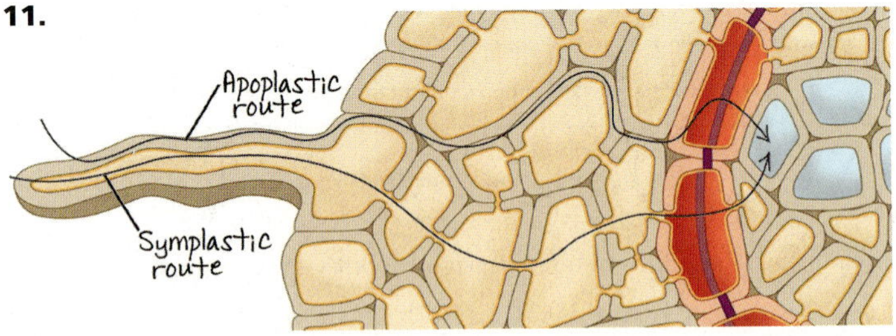

CHAPTER 37

Figure Questions

Figure 37.3 Anions. Because cations are bound to soil particles, they are less likely to be lost from the soil following heavy rains. **Figure 37.10** The legume plants benefit because the bacteria fix nitrogen that is absorbed by their roots. The bacteria benefit because they acquire photosynthetic products from the plants. **Figure 37.11** All three plant tissue systems are affected. Root hairs (dermal tissue) are modified to allow rhizobial penetration. The cortex (ground tissue) and pericycle (vascular tissue) proliferate during nodule formation. The vascular tissue of the nodule links up with the vascular cylinder of the root to allow for efficient nutrient exchange. **Figure 37.13** If phosphate were the only limiting mineral, then native tree growth would be less severely impacted by the reduction in mycorrhizal associations in soils invaded by garlic mustard.

Concept Check 37.1

1. Overwatering deprives roots of oxygen. Overfertilizing is wasteful and can lead to soil salinization and water pollution. **2.** As lawn clippings decompose, they restore mineral nutrients to the soil. If they are removed, the minerals lost from the soil must be replaced by fertilization. **3.** Because of their small size and negative charge, clay particles would increase the number of binding sites for cations and water molecules and would therefore increase cation exchange and water retention in the soil.

Concept Check 37.2

1. Table 37.1 shows that CO_2 is the source of 90% of a plant's dry weight, supporting Hales's view that plants are nourished mostly by air. **2.** No, because even though macronutrients are required in greater amounts, all essential elements are necessary for the plant to complete its life cycle. **3.** No. Most plants can complete their life cycles in the absence of silicon. Therefore, by definition, it is not an essential nutrient.

Concept Check 37.3

1. The rhizosphere is a narrow zone in the soil immediately adjacent to living roots. This zone is especially rich in both organic and inorganic nutrients and has a microbial population that is many times greater than the bulk of the soil. **2.** Soil bacteria and mycorrhizae enhance plant nutrition by making certain minerals more available for plants. For example, many types of soil bacteria are involved in the nitrogen cycle, whereas the hyphae of mycorrhizae provide a large surface area for the absorption of nutrients, particularly phosphate ions. **3.** Saturating rainfall may deplete the soil of oxygen. A lack of soil oxygen would inhibit nitrogen fixation by the peanut root nodules and decrease the nitrogen available to the plant. Alternatively, heavy rain may leach nitrate from the soil. A symptom of nitrogen deficiency is yellowing of older leaves.

Self-Quiz

1. b **2.** b **3.** c **4.** b **5.** b **6.** c **7.** d **8.** a **9.** d **10.** b
11.

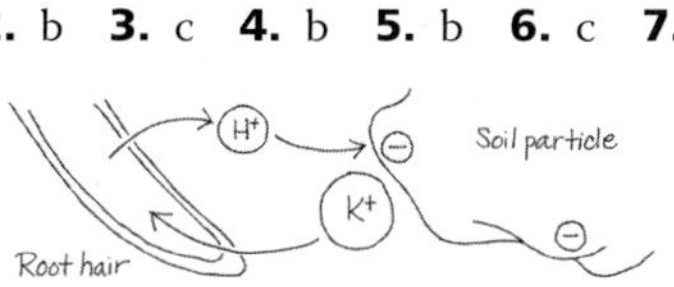

CHAPTER 38

Figure Questions

Figure 38.4 Having a specific pollinator is more efficient because less pollen gets delivered to flowers of the wrong species. However, it is also a risky strategy: If the pollinator population suffers to an unusual degree from predation, disease, or climate change, then the plant may not be able to produce seeds. **Figure 38.6** An inability to produce GABA would also prevent the establishment of a GABA gradient to help direct pollen tube growth. Thus, these mutants would be sterile also. **Figure 38.9** Beans use a hypocotyl hook to push through the soil. The delicate leaves and shoot apical meristem are also protected by being sandwiched between two large cotyledons. The coleoptile of maize seedlings helps protect the emerging leaves.

Concept Check 38.1

1. In angiosperms, pollination is the transfer of pollen from an anther to a stigma. Fertilization is the fusion of the egg and sperm to form the zygote; it cannot occur until after the growth of the pollen tube from the pollen grain. **2.** Seed dormancy prevents the premature germination of seeds. A seed will germinate only when the environmental conditions are optimal for the survival of its embryo as a young seedling. **3.** The fruit types are not completely separate categories because the term *accessory fruit* applies to any fruit that develops not only from one or more carpels but also from additional floral parts. Therefore, a simple, aggregate, or multiple fruit can also be an accessory fruit. The terms *simple, aggregate,* and *multiple* refer only to the number of carpels and flowers from which the fruit develops. **4.** Long styles help to weed out pollen grains that are genetically inferior and not capable of successfully growing long pollen tubes.

Concept Check 38.2

1. Sexual reproduction produces genetic variety, which may be advantageous in an unstable environment. The likelihood is better that at least one offspring of sexual reproduction will survive in a changed environment. Asexual reproduction can be advantageous in a stable environment because individual plants that are well suited to that environment pass on all their genes to offspring. Asexual reproduction also generally results in offspring that are less fragile than the seedlings produced by sexual reproduction. However, sexual reproduction offers the advantage of dispersal of tough seeds. **2.** Asexually propagated crops lack genetic diversity. Genetically diverse populations are less likely to become extinct in the face of an epidemic because there is a greater likelihood that a few individuals in the population are resistant. **3.** In the short term, selfing may be advantageous in a population that is so dispersed and sparse that pollen delivery is unreliable. In the long term, however, selfing is an evolutionary dead end because it leads to a loss of genetic diversity that may preclude adaptive evolution. **4.** This might be possible, but satisfactory results would be very unlikely. Both tubers and fruits are tremendous energy sinks. Each plant has only a finite amount of energy to divide between sexual and asexual reproduction. Although a tomato-potato hybrid could, in theory, produce an offspring that makes fruits and tubers equally, these fruits and tubers would be of inferior quality or low yielding.

Concept Check 38.3

1. Traditional breeding and genetic engineering both involve artificial selection for desired traits. However, genetic engineering techniques facilitate faster gene transfer and are not limited to transferring genes between closely related varieties or species. **2.** GM crops may be more nutritious and less susceptible to insect damage or pathogens that invade insect-damaged plants. They also may not require as much chemical spraying. However, unknown risks may include adverse effects on human health and nontarget organisms and the possibility of transgene escape. **3.** *Bt* maize suffers less insect damage; therefore, *Bt* maize plants are less likely to be infected by fumonisin-producing fungi that infect plants through wounds. **4.** In such species, engineering the transgene into the chloroplast DNA would not prevent its escape in pollen; such a method requires that the chloroplast DNA be found only in the egg. An entirely different method of preventing transgene escape would therefore be needed, such as male sterility, apomixis, or self-pollinating closed flowers.

Self-Quiz

1. d **2.** c **3.** a **4.** c **5.** d **6.** c **7.** e **8.** a **9.** c **10.** e
11.

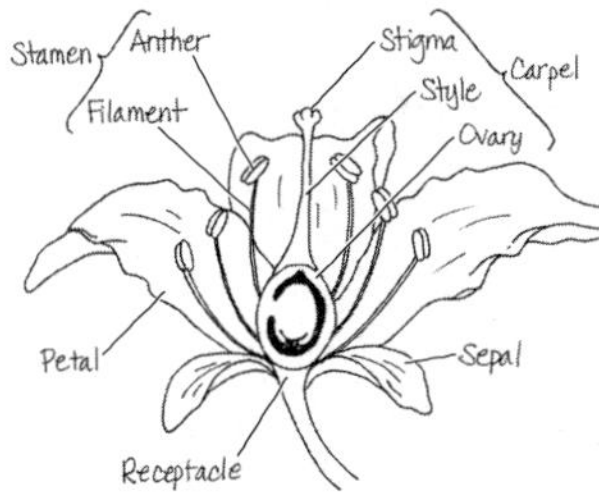

CHAPTER 39

Figure Questions

Figure 39.5 To determine which wavelengths of light are most effective in phototropism, one could use a glass prism to split white light into its component colors and see which colors cause the quickest bending (the answer is blue; see Figure 39.16). **Figure 39.6** The coleoptile would bend toward the side with the TIBA-containing agar bead. **Figure 39.7** No. Polar auxin transport depends on the polar distribution of auxin transport proteins. **Figure 39.17** Yes. The white light, which contains red light, would stimulate seed germination in all treatments. **Figure 39.22** The short-day plant would not flower. The long-day plant would flower. **Figure 39.23** If this were true, florigen would be an inhibitor of flowering, not an inducer.

Concept Check 39.1

1. Dark-grown seedlings have long stems, underdeveloped root systems, and unexpanded leaves, and their shoots lack chlorophyll. **2.** Etiolated growth is beneficial to seeds sprouting under the dark conditions they would encounter underground. By devoting more energy to stem elongation and less to leaf expansion and root growth, a plant increases the likelihood that the shoot will reach the sunlight before its stored foods run out. **3.** Cycloheximide should inhibit de-etiolation by preventing the synthesis of new proteins necessary for de-etiolation. **4.** No. Applying Viagra, like injecting cyclic GMP as described in the text, should cause only a partial de-etiolation response. Full de-etiolation would require activation of the calcium branch of the signal transduction pathway.

Concept Check 39.2

1. The release of ethylene by the damaged apple stimulates ripening in the other apples. **2.** Because cytokinins delay leaf senescence and floral parts are modified leaves, cytokinins also delay the senescence of cut flowers. **3.** Fusicoccin's ability to cause an increase in plasma H^+ pump activity is similar to an effect of auxin and leads to an auxin-like effect, a promotion of stem cell elongation. **4.** The plant will exhibit a constitutive triple response. Because the kinase that normally prevents the triple response is dysfunctional, the plant will undergo the triple response regardless of whether ethylene is present or the ethylene receptor is functional.

Concept Check 39.3

1. Not necessarily. Many environmental factors, such as temperature and light, change over a 24-hour period in the field. To determine whether the enzyme is under circadian control, the scientist would have to demonstrate that its activity oscillates even when environmental conditions are held constant. **2.** Flowering of the species may have been day-neutral or required multiple exposures to short nights. **3.** You might determine which wavelengths of light are most effective and plot an action spectrum. If the action spectrum indicates phytochrome, you could do further experiments to test for red/far-red photosensitivity. **4.** It is impossible to say. To establish that this species is a short-day plant, it would be necessary to establish the critical night length for flowering and that this species only flowers when the night is longer than the critical night length.

Concept Check 39.4

1. A plant that overproduces ABA would undergo less evaporative cooling because its stomata would not open as widely. **2.** Plants close to the aisles may be more subject to mechanical stresses caused by passing workers and air currents. The plants nearer to the center of the bench may also be taller as a result of shading and less evaporative stress. **3.** Like drought stress, freezing leads to cellular dehydration. Any process that helps mitigate drought stress will tend also to reduce freezing stress. **4.** No. Because root caps are involved in sensing gravity, roots that have their root caps removed are almost completely insensitive to gravity.

Concept Check 39.5

1. Some insects increase plants' productivity by eating harmful insects or aiding in pollination. **2.** Mechanical damage breaches a plant's first line of defense against infection, its protective dermal tissue. **3.** No. Pathogens that kill their hosts would soon run out of victims and might themselves go extinct. **4.** Perhaps the breeze dilutes the local concentration of a volatile defense compound that the plants produce.

Self-Quiz

1. a **2.** c **3.** d **4.** b **5.** e **6.** b **7.** b **8.** c **9.** e **10.** b
11.

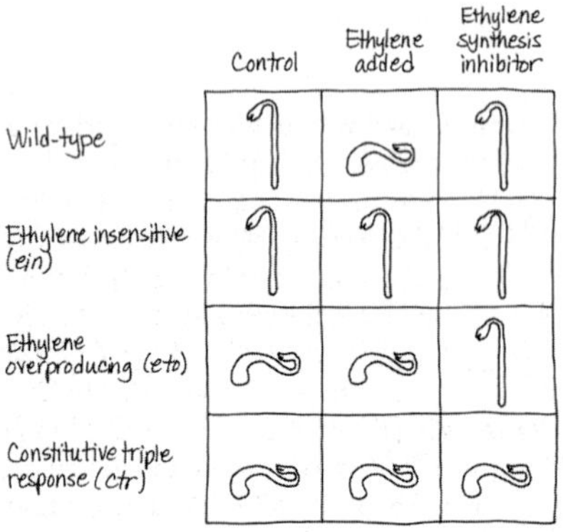

CHAPTER 40

Figure Questions

Figure 40.4 Such exchange surfaces are internal in the sense that they are inside the body. However, they are also continuous with openings on the external body surface that contact the environment. **Figure 40.8** The air conditioner would form a second negative-feedback loop, cooling the house when air temperature exceeded the set point. Such opposing, or antagonistic, pairs of negative-feedback loops increase the effectiveness of a homeostatic mechanism. **Figure 40.14** When a female Burmese python is not incubating eggs, her oxygen consumption will decrease with decreasing temperature, as for any other ectotherm. **Figure 40.21** If falling temperatures triggered hibernation, you would predict hibernation would begin earlier than normal. If another seasonal change, such as day length, controlled hibernation, its timing should be unaffected. By controlling these environmental variables in the laboratory, scientists have shown that lowering temperature without a change in day length is sufficient to induce ground squirrel hibernation.

Concept Check 40.1

1. Epithelial cells line a surface, are tightly packed, are situated on top of a basal lamina, and form an active and protective interface with the external environment. **2.** By flattening its ears along its body, the jackrabbit can reduce the total surface area of its body and hence the amount of heat absorbed when environmental temperatures are high, or the amount of heat lost when environmental temperatures are low. **3.** You need the nervous system to perceive the danger and provoke a split-second muscular response to keep from falling. The nervous system, however, does not make a direct connection with blood vessels or liver cells. Instead, the nervous system triggers the release of a hormone (called epinephrine or adrenaline) by the endocrine system, bringing about a change in these tissues in just a few seconds.

Concept Check 40.2

1. No; even though an animal regulates some aspects of its internal environment, the internal environment fluctuates slightly around set points. Homeostasis is a dynamic state. Furthermore, there are sometimes programmed changes in set points, such as those resulting in radical increases in hormone levels at particular times in development. **2.** In negative feedback, a change triggers control mechanisms that counteract further change in that direction. In positive feedback, a change triggers mechanisms that amplify the change. **3.** You would want to locate a thermostat close to where you would be spending time, protected from environmental perturbations, such as direct sunshine, and not right in the path of the output of the heating system. Similarly, the sensors for homeostasis located in the human brain are separated from environmental influences and can monitor conditions in a vital and sensitive tissue.

Concept Check 40.3

1. "Wind chill" involves heat loss through convection. **2.** The hummingbird, being a very small endotherm, has a very high metabolic rate. If by absorbing sunlight certain flowers warm their nectar, a hummingbird feeding on these flowers is saved the metabolic expense of warming the nectar to its body temperature. **3.** The ice water would cool tissues in your head, including blood that would then circulate throughout the body. This effect would accelerate the return to a normal body temperature. If, however, the ice water reached the eardrum and cooled the hypothalamic thermostat, the perceived drop in temperature would inhibit sweating and blood vessel dilation, slowing cooling elsewhere in the body.

Concept Check 40.4

1. The mouse would consume oxygen at a higher rate because it is an endotherm and therefore its basal metabolic rate is higher than the ectothermic lizard's standard metabolic rate. **2.** The house cat; the smaller an animal is, the higher its metabolic rate and its demand for food per unit of body mass are. **3.** Although penguins do not grow as adults, they increase and decrease in size as they repeatedly form and use energy stores. A significant amount of energy might be stored in fat during part of the year but be missing from the pie chart because it is used later in the year.

Self-Quiz

1. b **2.** e **3.** c **4.** e **5.** a **6.** d

7.

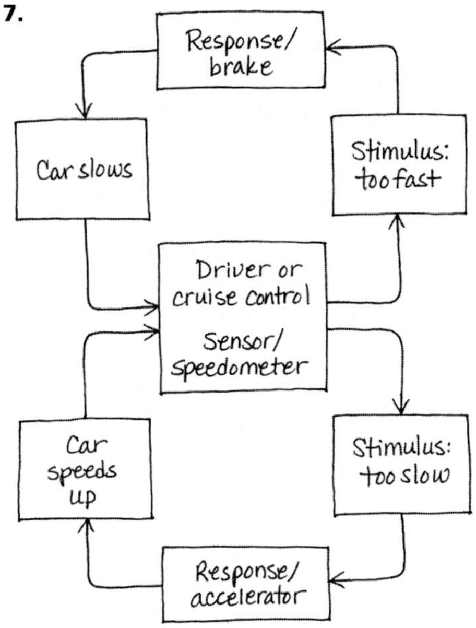

CHAPTER 41

Figure Questions

Figure 41.5 As in the described study, they needed a sample size large enough that they could expect a significant number of neural tube defects in the control group. The information needed to determine the appropriate sample size was the frequency of neural tube defects in first-time pregnancies in the general population. **Figure 41.13** Since enzymes are proteins, and proteins are hydrolyzed in the small intestine, the digestive enzymes in that compartment need to be resistant to cleavage by proteases other than the cleavage required for enzyme activation. **Figure 41.15** None. Since digestion is completed in the small intestine, tapeworms simply absorb predigested nutrients through their large body surface area. **Figure 41.24** The *db* mouse would have higher leptin levels. The wild-type mouse produces leptin after a meal. As the mouse depletes its fat stores, leptin production drops. The mouse eventually regains its appetite, eats another meal, and makes another burst of leptin. Because the *db* mouse cannot respond to leptin, its fat stores are constantly replenished through excessive consumption. As a result, leptin is produced continuously and builds up to a high concentration in the blood.

Concept Check 41.1

1. The only essential amino acids are those that an animal can't synthesize from other molecules containing carbon and nitrogen. **2.** Carbohydrates are needed throughout the body as a source of energy and carbon in the biosynthesis of cellular components, whereas vitamins typically serve as reusable enzyme cofactors or as raw materials for certain specialized cell structures. **3.** To identify the essential nutrient missing from an animal's diet, a researcher could supplement the diet with particular nutrients and determine which nutrient eliminates the signs of malnutrition.

Concept Check 41.2

1. A gastrovascular cavity is a digestive sac with a single opening that functions in both ingestion and elimination; an alimentary canal is a digestive tube with a separate mouth and anus at opposite ends. **2.** As long as nutrients are within the cavity of the alimentary canal, they are in a compartment that is continuous with the outside environment via the mouth and anus and have not yet crossed a membrane to enter the body. **3.** Just as food remains outside the body in a digestive tract, gasoline moves from the fuel tank to the engine and the exhaust without ever entering the passenger compartment of the car. In addition, gasoline, like food, is broken down in a specialized compartment, so that the rest of the body is protected from disassembly. In both cases, high-energy fuels are consumed and waste products are eliminated.

Concept Check 41.3

1. By peristalsis, which can squeeze food through the esophagus even without the help of gravity. **2.** Fats can cross the membranes of epithelial cells by diffusion, whereas proteins and sugars, which are not lipid-soluble, require transport or exchange proteins. **3.** Proteins would be denatured and digested into peptides. Further digestion, to individual amino acids, would require enzymatic secretions found in the small intestine.

Concept Check 41.4

1. The increased time for transit allows for more extensive processing, and the increased surface area provides greater opportunity for absorption. **2.** Mutualistic microbes in the intestines of vertebrates have an environment that is protected against other microbes by saliva and gastric juice, that is held at a constant temperature conducive to enzyme action, and that provides a steady source of nutrients. **3.** For the yogurt treatment to be effective, the bacteria from yogurt would have to establish a mutualistic relationship with the small intestine, where disaccharides are broken down and sugars are absorbed. Conditions in the small intestine are likely to be very different than in a yogurt culture. The bacteria might be killed before they reach the small intestine, or they might not be able to grow there in sufficient numbers to aid in digestion.

Concept Check 41.5

1. Over the long term, the body converts excess calories to fat, whether those calories are consumed as fat, carbohydrate, or protein. **2.** Both hormones have appetite-suppressing effects on the brain's satiety center. During the course of a day, PYY, secreted by the intestine, suppresses appetite after meals. Over the longer term, leptin, produced by adipose tissue, normally reduces appetite as fat storage increases. **3.** In normal individuals, leptin levels decline during fasting. The group with low levels of leptin are likely to be defective in leptin production, so leptin levels would remain low regardless of food intake. The group with high leptin levels are likely to be defective in responding to leptin, but they still should shut off leptin production as fat stores are used up.

Self-Quiz

1. e **2.** a **3.** c **4.** c **5.** c **6.** d **7.** e **8.** b

9.

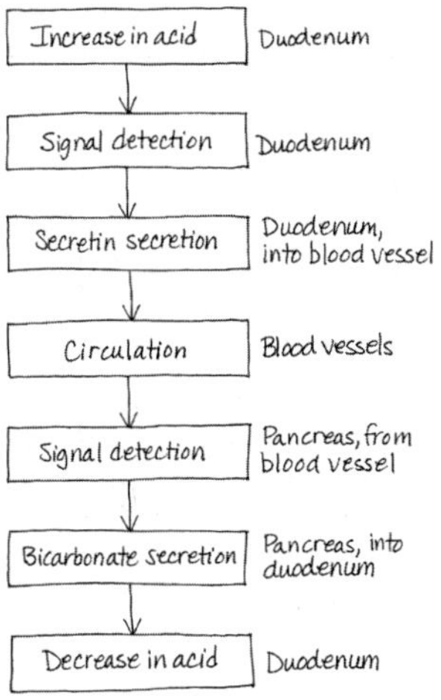

CHAPTER 42

Figure Questions

Figure 42.2 As the name indicates, a gastrovascular cavity functions in both digestion and circulation. Although gas exchange might be improved by a steady, one-way flow of fluid, there would likely be inadequate time for food to be digested and nutrients absorbed if fluids flowed through the cavity in this manner. **Figure 42.12** Because endothelin regulates the smooth muscle cells in blood vessels, you would expect it to be secreted from the basal surface of endothelial cells, a prediction that has been confirmed experimentally. **Figure 42.28** The resulting increase in tidal volume would enhance ventilation within the lungs, increasing P_{O_2} in the alveoli. **Figure 42.30** Some CO_2 is dissolved in plasma, some is bound to hemoglobin, and some is converted to bicarbonate ion (HCO_3^-), which is dissolved in plasma. **Figure 42.31** You might find some fast runners in those with the highest V_{O_2} max, but you might also find some sloths. There are two principal factors that contribute to V_{O_2} max, genetics and exercise. Elite athletes have a very high V_{O_2} max, reflecting not only the strengthening of their cardiovascular system through training but also the genetic circumstance of their having a particular combination of alleles.

Concept Check 42.1

1. In both an open circulatory system and a fountain, fluid is pumped through a tube and then returns to the pump after collecting in a pool. **2.** The ability to shut off blood supply to the lungs when the animal is submerged **3.** The O_2 content would be abnormally low because some oxygen-depleted blood returned to the right ventricle from the systemic circuit would mix with the oxygen-rich blood in the left ventricle.

Concept Check 42.2

1. The pulmonary veins carry blood that has just passed through capillary beds in the lungs, where it accumulated O_2. The venae cavae carry blood that has just passed through capillary beds in the rest of the body, where it lost O_2 to the tissues. **2.** The delay allows the atria to empty completely, filling ventricles fully before they contract. **3.** The heart, like any other muscle, becomes stronger through regular exercise. You would expect a stronger heart to have a greater stroke volume, which would allow for the decrease in heart rate.

Concept Check 42.3

1. The large total cross-sectional area of the capillaries **2.** An increase in blood pressure and cardiac output combined with the diversion of more blood to the skeletal muscles would increase the capacity for action by increasing the rate of blood circulation and delivering more O_2 and nutrients to the skeletal muscles. **3.** Additional hearts could be used to improve blood return from the legs. However, it might be difficult to coordinate the activity of multiple hearts and to maintain adequate blood flow to hearts far from the gas exchange organs.

Concept Check 42.4

1. An increase in the number of white blood cells (leukocytes) may indicate that the person is combating an infection. **2.** Clotting factors do not initiate clotting but are essential steps in the clotting process. Also, the clots that form a thrombus typically result from an inflammatory response to an atherosclerotic plaque, not from clotting at a wound site. **3.** The chest pain results from inadequate blood flow in coronary arteries. Vasodilation promoted by nitric oxide from nitroglycerin increases blood flow, providing the heart muscle with additional oxygen and thus relieving the pain.

Concept Check 42.5

1. Their interior position helps them stay moist. If the respiratory surfaces of lungs extended out into the terrestrial environment, they would quickly dry out, and diffusion of O_2 and CO_2 across these surfaces would stop. **2.** Earthworms need to keep their skin moist for gas exchange, but they need air outside this moist layer. If they stay in their waterlogged tunnels after a heavy rain, they will suffocate because they cannot get as much O_2 from water as from air. **3.** Since exhalation is largely passive, the recoil of the elastic fibers in alveoli helps force air out of the lungs. When alveoli lose their elasticity, as occurs in the disease emphysema, the volume of each breath decreases, lowering the efficiency of gas exchange.

Concept Check 42.6

1. An increase in blood CO_2 concentration causes an increase in the rate of CO_2 diffusion into the cerebrospinal fluid, where the CO_2 combines with water to form carbonic acid. Dissociation of carbonic acid releases hydrogen ions, decreasing the pH of the cerebrospinal fluid. **2.** Increased heart rate increases the rate at which CO_2-rich blood is delivered to the lungs, where CO_2 is removed. **3.** A hole would allow air to enter the space between the inner and outer layers of the double membrane, resulting in a condition called a pneumothorax. The two layers would no longer stick together, and the lung on the side with the hole would collapse and cease functioning.

Concept Check 42.7

1. Differences in partial pressure; gases diffuse from a region of higher partial pressure to a region of lower partial pressure. **2.** The Bohr shift causes hemoglobin to release more O_2 at a lower pH, such as found in the vicinity of tissues with high rates of cellular respiration and CO_2 release. **3.** The doctor is assuming that the rapid breathing is the body's response to low blood pH. Metabolic acidosis, the lowering of blood pH, can have many causes, including complications of certain types of diabetes, shock (extremely low blood pressure), and poisoning.

Self-Quiz

1. c **2.** b **3.** d **4.** e **5.** b **6.** c **7.** a **8.** a

9.

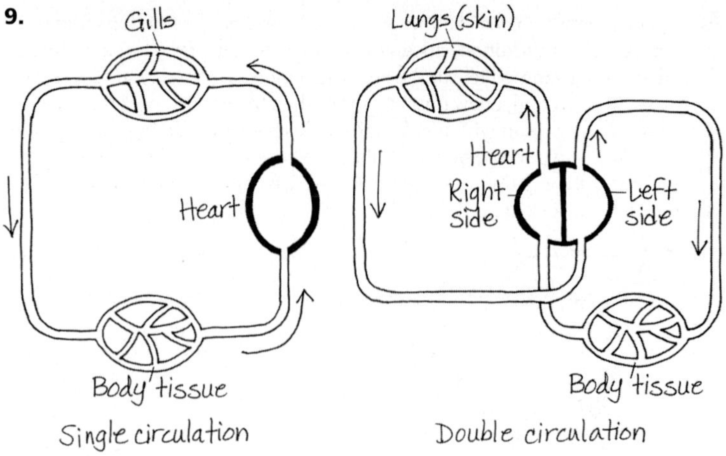

CHAPTER 43

Figure Questions

Figure 43.5 The seemingly inactive peptides might offer protection against pathogens other than those studied. Also, some antimicrobial peptides might work best in combination. **Figure 43.6** Cell surface TLRs recognize pathogens identifiable by surface molecules, whereas TLRs in vesicles recognize pathogens identifiable by internal molecules after the pathogens are broken down. **Figure 43.16** Primary response: arrows extending from Antigen (1st exposure), Antigen-presenting cell, Helper T cell, B cell, Plasma cells, Cytotoxic T cell, and Active Cytotoxic T cells; secondary response: arrows extending from Antigen (2nd exposure), Memory Helper T cells, Memory B cells, and Memory Cytotoxic T cells. **Figure 43.19** Before mounting a secondary immune response, memory cells must become activated by displaying antigen on the cell surface to a helper T cell.

Concept Check 43.1

1. A physical barrier often provides a very effective defense against infection. However, it is necessarily incomplete because animals need openings in their bodies for exchange with the environment. **2.** Because pus contains white blood cells, fluid, and cell debris, it indicates an active and at least partially successful inflammatory response against invading microbes. **3.** A microbe that grew optimally at low pH would be able to colonize the skin or stomach more readily. At the same time, it would not be well adapted to growth in other parts of the body.

Concept Check 43.2

1. See Figure 43.9a. All of the functions shared among receptors map to C regions, whereas the antigen-binding site maps to the V regions. **2.** Generating memory cells ensures both that a receptor specific for a particular epitope will be present and that there will be more lymphocytes with this specificity than in a host that had never encountered the antigen. **3.** If each B cell produced two different light and heavy chains for its antigen receptor, different combinations would make four different receptors. If any one was self-reactive, the lymphocyte would be eliminated in the generation of self-tolerance. For this reason, many more B cells would be eliminated, and those that could respond to a foreign antigen would be less effective at doing so due to the variety of receptors (and antibodies) they express.

Concept Check 43.3

1. A child lacking a thymus would have no functional T cells. Without helper T cells to help activate B cells, the child would be unable to produce antibodies against extracellular bacteria. Furthermore, without cytotoxic T cells or helper T cells, the child's immune system would be unable to kill virus-infected cells. **2.** Since the antigen-binding site is intact, the antibody fragments could neutralize viruses and opsonize bacteria. **3.** If the handler developed immunity to proteins in the antivenin, another injection could provoke a severe immune response. The handler's immune system might also now produce antibodies that could neutralize the venom.

Concept Check 43.4

1. Myasthenia gravis is considered an autoimmune disease because the immune system produces antibodies against self molecules (acetylcholine receptors).

2. A person with a cold is likely to produce oral and nasal secretions that facilitate viral transfer. In addition, since sickness can cause incapacitation or death, a virus that is programmed to exit the host when there is a physiological stress has the opportunity to find a new host at a time when the current host may cease to function. **3.** A person with a macrophage deficiency would have frequent infections. The causes would be poor innate responses, due to diminished phagocytosis and inflammation, and poor acquired responses, due to the lack of macrophages to present antigens to helper T cells.

Self-Quiz

1. b **2.** d **3.** c **4.** b **5.** c **6.** d **7.** b
8. One possible answer:

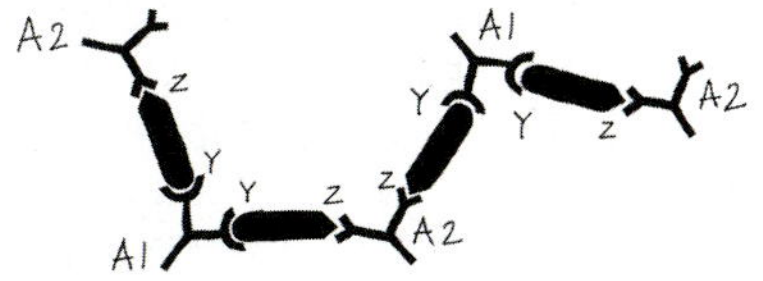

CHAPTER 44

Figure Questions

Figure 44.7 The body fluids of osmoconformers, such as most marine invertebrates, have the same salt concentration as sea water. Any such animals in the diet of the bird would add to the salt load to be eliminated. In contrast, marine fishes that osmoregulate maintain body fluids that have a much lower salt concentration than the surrounding ocean. By eating such fish, marine birds can obtain nutrients and water without adding as much to their salt load. **Figure 44.15** Tubule cells in the medulla are in contact with extracellular fluid of very high osmolarity. By producing solutes that keep intracellular osmolarity high, these cells achieve homeostasis with regard to volume. **Figure 44.16** Furosemide increases urine volume. The absence of ion transport in the ascending limb leaves the filtrate too concentrated for substantial volume reduction in the distal tubule and collecting duct. **Figure 44.20** The ADH levels would likely be elevated in both sets of patients with mutations because either defect prevents the recapture of water that restores blood osmolarity to normal levels.

Concept Check 44.1

1. Because the salt is moved against its concentration gradient, from low concentration (freshwater) to high concentration (blood) **2.** A freshwater osmoconformer would have body fluids too dilute to carry out life's processes. **3.** Without a layer of insulating fur, the camel must use the cooling effect of evaporative water loss to maintain body temperature, thus linking thermoregulation and osmoregulation.

Concept Check 44.2

1. Because uric acid is largely insoluble in water, it can be excreted as a semisolid paste, thereby reducing an animal's water loss. **2.** Humans produce uric acid from purine breakdown, and reducing purines in the diet often lessens the severity of gout. Birds, however, produce uric acid as a waste product of general nitrogen metabolism. They would therefore need a diet low in all nitrogen-containing compounds, not just purines.

Concept Check 44.3

1. In flatworms, ciliated cells draw interstitial fluids containing waste products into protonephridia. In earthworms, waste products pass from interstitial fluids into the coelom. From there they enter metanephridia by beating of cilia in a funnel surrounding an internal opening. In insects, the Malphigian tubules pump fluids from the hemolymph, which receives waste products during exchange with interstitial fluids in the course of circulation. **2.** Filtration produces a fluid for exchange processes that is free of cells and large molecules which are of benefit to the animal and could not readily be reabsorbed. **3.** The presence of Na^+ and other ions (electrolytes) in the dialysate would limit the extent to which they would be removed from the filtrate during dialysis. Adjusting the electrolytes in the starting dialysate can thus lead to the restoration of proper electrolyte concentrations in the plasma. Similarly, the absence of urea and other waste products in the starting dialysate results in their efficient removal from the filtrate.

Concept Check 44.4

1. The numerous nephrons and well-developed glomeruli of freshwater fishes produce urine at a high rate, while the small numbers of nephrons and smaller glomeruli of marine fishes produce urine at a low rate. **2.** The kidney medulla would absorb less water and thus the drug would increase the amount of water lost in the urine. **3.** A decline in blood pressure in the afferent arteriole would reduce the rate of filtration by moving less material through the vessels.

Concept Check 44.5

1. Alcohol inhibits the release of ADH, causing an increase in urinary water loss and increasing the chance of dehydration. **2.** The consumption of a large amount of water in a very short period of time, coupled with an absence of solute intake, can reduce sodium levels in the blood below tolerable levels. This condition, called hyponatremia, leads to disorientation and, sometimes, respiratory distress. It has been seen in marathon runners who drink water rather than sports drinks. (It has also caused the death of a fraternity pledge as a consequence of a water hazing ritual and the death of a contestant in a water-drinking competition.) **3.** High blood pressure

Self-Quiz

1. d **2.** b **3.** e **4.** d **5.** a **6.** c **7.** b
8.

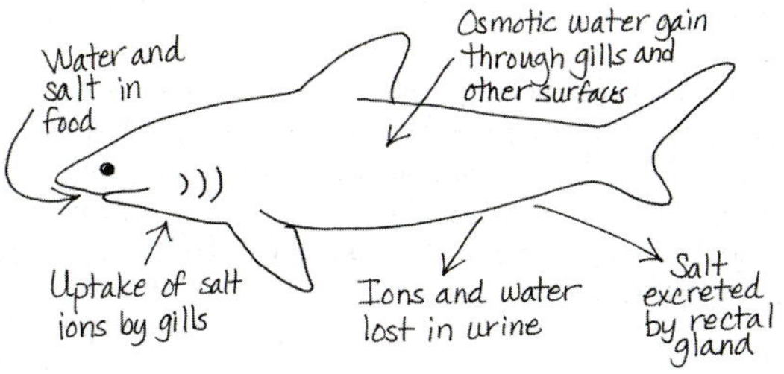

CHAPTER 45

Figure Questions

Figure 45.4 Because lipid-soluble hormones can freely diffuse across the lipid bilayers of cell membranes, you would expect to see biological activity after microinjection either into cells or into the interstitial space. **Figure 45.5** The hormone is water-soluble and has a cell-surface receptor. Such receptors, unlike those for lipid-soluble hormones, can cause observable changes in cells without hormone-dependent gene transcription. **Figure 45.18** Both diagnoses could be correct. In one case, the thyroid gland may produce excess thyroid hormone despite normal hormonal input from the hypothalamus and anterior pituitary. In the other, abnormally elevated hormonal input may be the cause of the overactive thyroid gland. **Figure 45.22** The result of the surgery would have been the same for both sexes—an absence of sexual differentiation in the genitals.

Concept Check 45.1

1. Water-soluble hormones, which cannot penetrate the plasma membrane, bind to cell-surface receptors. This interaction triggers an intracellular signal transduction pathway that ultimately alters the activity of a preexisting cytoplasmic protein and/or changes transcription of specific genes in the nucleus. Steroid hormones are lipid-soluble and can cross the plasma membrane into the cell interior, where they bind to receptors located in the cytosol or nucleus. The hormone-receptor complex then functions directly as a transcription factor that binds to the cell's DNA and activates or inhibits transcription of specific genes. **2.** Prostaglandins in semen that induce contractions in the uterus are aiding reproduction as signaling molecules that are transferred from one individual to another of the same species, like pheromones. **3.** Whether in different tissues or species, a particular hormone may cause diverse responses in target cells having different receptors for the hormone, different signal transduction pathways, and/or different proteins for carrying out the response.

Concept Check 45.2

1. In a healthy person, insulin released in response to the initial rise in blood glucose stimulates uptake of glucose by body cells. In a person with diabetes, however, inadequate production of insulin or nonresponsiveness of target cells decreases the body's ability to clear excess glucose from the blood. The initial increase in blood glucose is therefore greater in a person with diabetes, and it remains high for a prolonged period. **2.** A pathway governed by a short-lived stimulus would be less dependent on negative feedback. **3.** Since patients with type 2 diabetes produce insulin but fail to maintain normal glucose levels, you might predict that there could be mutations in the genes for the insulin receptor or the signal transduction pathway it activates. Such mutations have in fact been found in type 2 patients.

Concept Check 45.3

1. The posterior pituitary, an extension of the hypothalamus that contains the axons of neurosecretory cells, is the storage and release site for two neurohormones, oxytocin and antidiuretic hormone (ADH). The anterior pituitary, derived from tissues of the embryonic mouth, contains endocrine cells that make at least six different hormones. Secretion of anterior pituitary hormones is controlled by hypothalamic hormones that travel via portal vessels to the anterior pituitary. **2.** Because oxytocin responses involve positive feedback from suckling, the pathway does not require a sustained hormonal input stimulus. **3.** The hypothalamus and pituitary glands function in many different endocrine pathways. Many defects in these glands, such as those affecting growth or organization, would therefore disrupt many hormone pathways. Only a very specific defect, such as a mutation affecting a particular hormone receptor, would alter just one endocrine pathway. The situation is quite different for the final gland in a pathway, such as the thyroid gland. In this case, a wide range of defects that disrupt gland function would disrupt only the one pathway or small set of pathways in which that gland functions.

Concept Check 45.4

1. The adrenal medulla is derived from neural tissue during development. Reflecting this origin, it is an endocrine organ that produces two molecules—epinephrine and norepinephrine—that act both as hormones and as neurotransmitters. **2.** The levels of these hormones in the blood would become very high. This would be due to the diminished negative feedback on the hypothalamic neurons that secrete the releasing hormone that stimulates the secretion of ACTH by the anterior pituitary. **3.** By applying glucocorticoids to tissue by local injection, you in principle exploit their anti-inflammatory activity. Local injection avoids the effects on glucose metabolism that would occur if glucocorticoids were taken orally and transported throughout the body in the bloodstream.

Self-Quiz

1. c **2.** d **3.** d **4.** c **5.** b **6.** b **7.** c **8.** a
9.

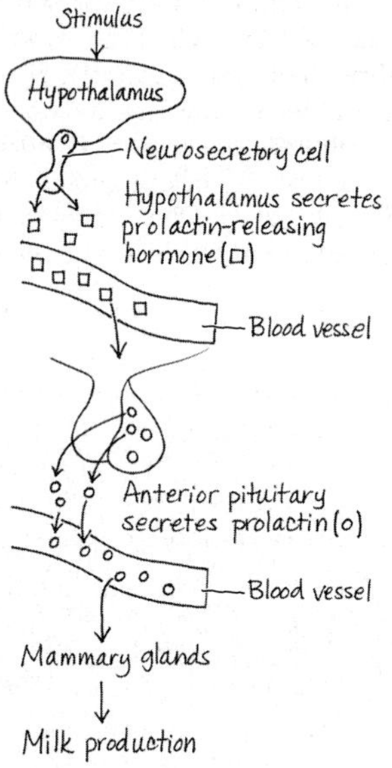

CHAPTER 46

Figure Questions

Figure 46.9 According to the graph, about one-third of the females rid themselves of all sperm from the first mating. Thus, two-thirds retain some sperm from the first mating. We would therefore predict that two-thirds of the females would have some offspring exhibiting the small eye phenotype of the dominant mutation carried by the males with which the females mated first. **Figure 46.16** Testosterone can pass from fetal blood to maternal blood via the placental circulation, temporarily upsetting the hormonal balance in the mother. **Figure 46.18** Oxytocin would most likely induce labor and start a positive-feedback loop that would direct labor to completion. Synthetic oxytocin is in fact frequently used to induce labor when prolonged pregnancy might endanger the mother or fetus.

Concept Check 46.1

1. The offspring of sexual reproduction are more genetically diverse. However, asexual reproduction can produce more offspring over multiple generations. **2.** Unlike other forms of asexual reproduction, parthenogenesis involves gamete production. By controlling whether or not haploid eggs are fertilized, species such as honeybees can readily switch between asexual and sexual reproduction. **3.** No. Owing to random assortment of chromosomes during meiosis, the offspring may receive the same copy or different copies of a particular parental chromosome from the sperm and the egg. Furthermore, genetic recombination during meiosis will result in reassortment of genes between pairs of parental chromosomes.

Concept Check 46.2

1. Internal fertilization allows the sperm to reach the egg without either gamete drying out. **2.** (a) Animals with external fertilization tend to release many gametes at once, resulting in the production of enormous numbers of zygotes. This increases the chances that some will survive to adulthood. (b) Animals with internal fertilization produce fewer offspring but generally exhibit greater care of the embryos and the young. **3.** The antimicrobial peptide might serve to protect the sperm before mating, the females with which the male mates, or the eggs those females produce. In all three cases, the reproductive success of the male would be enhanced, providing a mechanism for selection for peptide production over the course of evolution. You might want to think about how you might determine which function is most critical.

Concept Check 46.3

1. Primarily the penis and clitoris, but also the testes, labia, breasts, and outer third of the vagina **2.** Spermatogenesis occurs normally only when the testicles are cooler than normal body temperature. Extensive use of a hot tub (or of very tight-fitting underwear) can cause a decrease in sperm quality and number. **3.** The only effect of sealing off each vas deferens is an absence of sperm in the ejaculate. Sexual response and ejaculate volume are unchanged. The cutting and sealing off of these ducts, a *vasectomy*, is a common surgical procedure for men who do not wish to produce any (more) offspring.

Concept Check 46.4

1. The small size and lack of cytoplasm characteristic of a sperm are adaptations well suited to its function as a delivery vehicle for DNA. The large size and rich cytoplasmic contents of eggs support the growth and development of the embryo. **2.** In humans, the secondary oocyte combines with a sperm before it finishes the second meiotic division. Thus, oogenesis is completed after, not before, fertilization. **3.** The analysis would be informative because the polar bodies contain all of the maternal chromosomes that don't end up in the mature egg. For example, finding two copies of the disease gene in the polar bodies would indicate its absence in the egg. This method of genetic testing is sometimes carried out when oocytes collected from a female are fertilized with sperm in a laboratory dish.

Concept Check 46.5

1. In the testis, FSH stimulates the Sertoli cells, which nourish developing sperm. LH stimulates the production of androgens (mainly testosterone), which in turn stimulate sperm production. In both females and males, FSH encourages the growth of cells that support and nourish developing gametes (follicle cells in females and Sertoli cells in males), and LH stimulates the production of sex hormones that promote gametogenesis (estrogens, primarily estradiol, in females and androgens, especially testosterone, in males). **2.** In estrous cycles, which occur in most female mammals, the endometrium is reabsorbed (rather than shed) if fertilization does not occur. Estrous cycles often occur just one or a few times a year, and the female is usually receptive to copulation only during the period around ovulation. Menstrual cycles are found only in humans and some other primates. **3.** The combination of estradiol and progesterone would have a negative-feedback effect on the hypothalamus, blocking release of GnRH. This would interfere with LH secretion by the pituitary, thus preventing ovulation. This is in fact one basis of action of the most common hormonal contraceptives.

Concept Check 46.6

1. hCG secreted by the early embryo stimulates the corpus luteum to make progesterone, which helps maintain the pregnancy. During the second trimester, however, hCG production drops, the corpus luteum disintegrates, and the placenta completely takes over progesterone production. **2.** Both tubal ligation and vasectomy block the movement of gametes from the gonads to a site where fertilization could take place. **3.** By introducing a spermatid nucleus directly into an oocyte, ICSI bypasses the sperm's acquisition of motility in the epididymis, its swimming to meet the egg in the oviduct, and its fusion with the egg.

Self-Quiz

1. d **2.** b **3.** a **4.** b **5.** c **6.** c **7.** a **8.** d
9.

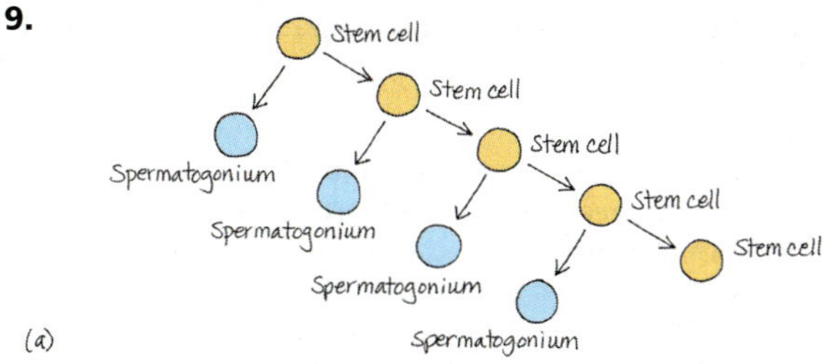

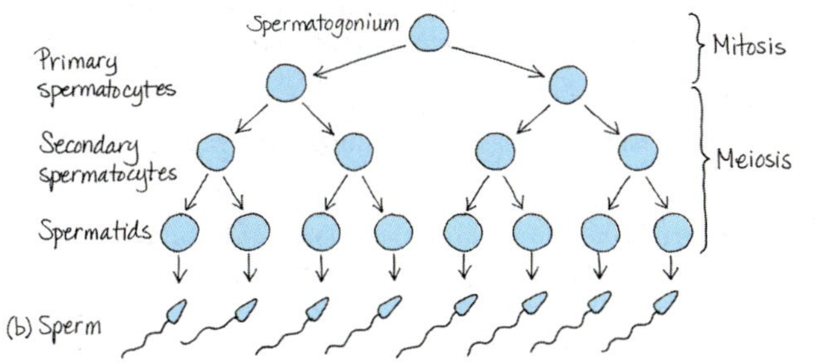

(c) The supply of stem cells would be used up and spermatogenesis would not be able to continue.

CHAPTER 47

Figure Questions

Figure 47.4 You could inject the compound into an unfertilized egg, expose the egg to sperm, and see whether the fertilization envelope forms. **Figure 47.7** The researchers allowed normal cortical rotation to occur, resulting in activation of the "back-forming" determinants. Then they forced the opposite rotation to occur, which established the back on the opposite side as well. Because the molecules on the normal side were already activated, forcing the opposite rotation apparently did not "cancel out" the establishment of the back side by the first rotation. **Figure 47.14** Given that these regions form from ectoderm but are just inside the body, you might propose that they form by an inpocketing of the ectoderm that then meets and fuses with the endoderm. And you would be right! **Figure 47.19** Cadherin is required to hold the cells of the blastula together, and extracellular calcium is required for cadherin function, so in the absence of calcium in the water, you'd expect to see a disorganized embryo like the one shown in the experimental SEM. **Figure 47.20** You could cut out the same tissues from control and injected embryos as was done in experiment 2 and place them between cover slips coated with the artificial fibronectin (FN) matrix. If convergent extension occurred in the tissues from both injected and control embryos, that would support the hypothesis that convergent extension can occur on a preexisting FN matrix in the embryo. **Figure 47.23** In Spemann's control, the two blastomeres were physically separated, and each grew into a whole embryo. In Roux's experiment, remnants of the dead blastomere were still contacting the live blastomere, which developed into a half-embryo. Therefore, molecules present in the dead cell's remnants may have been signaling to the live cell, inhibiting it from making all the embryonic structures. **Figure 47.24** You could inject the isolated protein or an mRNA encoding it into ventral cells of an earlier gastrula. If dorsal structures formed on the ventral side, that would support the idea that the protein is the signaling molecule secreted or presented by the dorsal lip. You should also do a control experiment to make sure the injection process alone did not cause dorsal structures to form. **Figure 47.26** You could remove the AER and look for Sonic hedgehog mRNA or protein as a marker of the ZPA. If either was absent, that would support your hypothesis. You could also block FGF function and see whether the ZPA formed (by looking for Sonic hedgehog).

Concept Check 47.1

1. The fertilization envelope forms after cortical granules release their contents outside the egg, causing the vitelline membrane to rise and harden. The fertilization envelope serves as a barrier to fertilization by more than one sperm. **2.** During cleavage in frogs and many other animals, the cell cycle is modified so that it virtually skips G_1 and G_2, the growth phases. As a result, the early cleavage divisions divide the zygote's cytoplasm into smaller and smaller cells as the embryo's size remains nearly the same. **3.** Cleavage transforms the single-celled zygote into an embryo consisting of many cells; cleavage does not involve cell or tissue movement. During gastrulation, the cells and tissues of a blastula are extensively rearranged, so that by the late gastrula stage there are three tissue layers positioned in new relationships to each other. **4.** The neural tube forms when a band of ectodermal tissue on the dorsal side along the anterior-posterior axis, called the neural plate, rolls into a tube and pinches off from the rest of the ectoderm. Neural crest cells arise as groups of cells in the regions between the edges of the neural tube and the surrounding ectoderm migrate away from the neural tube. **5.** The increased Ca^{2+} concentration in the egg would cause the cortical granules to fuse with the plasma membrane, releasing their contents and causing a fertilization envelope to form, even though no sperm had entered. This would prevent fertilization. **6.** Conjoined twins develop from monozygotic twins that separate quite late, after part of the embryo has already formed. (This part is shared by the twins.) By this time, both the chorion and amnion have formed, so there is only one of each.

Concept Check 47.2

1. Microtubules elongate, lengthening the cell along one axis, while microfilaments oriented crosswise at one end of the cell contract, making that end smaller and the whole cell wedge-shaped. **2.** The cells of the notochord migrate toward the midline of the embryo (converge), rearranging themselves so there are fewer cells across the notochord, which thus becomes longer overall (extends; see Figure 47.18). **3.** Because microfilaments would not be able to contract and decrease the size of one end of the cell, both the inward bending in the middle of the neural tube and the outward bending of the hinge regions at the edges would be blocked. Therefore, the neural tube probably would not form.

Concept Check 47.3

1. Once the first two axes are specified, the third one is automatically determined. (Think of your own body: If you know where your anterior and posterior ends are and where your left and right sides are, you automatically know which sides are your front and back.) Of course, there still must be a mechanism for determining where asymmetrically placed organs must go, such as the vertebrate stomach or appendix. **2.** Yes, a second embryo could develop because inhibiting BMP-4 activity would have the same effect as transplanting an organizer. **3.** The limb that developed probably would have a mirror-image duplication, with the most posterior digits in the middle and the most anterior digits at either end.

Self-Quiz

1. a **2.** b **3.** e **4.** c **5.** a **6.** c **7.** e
8.

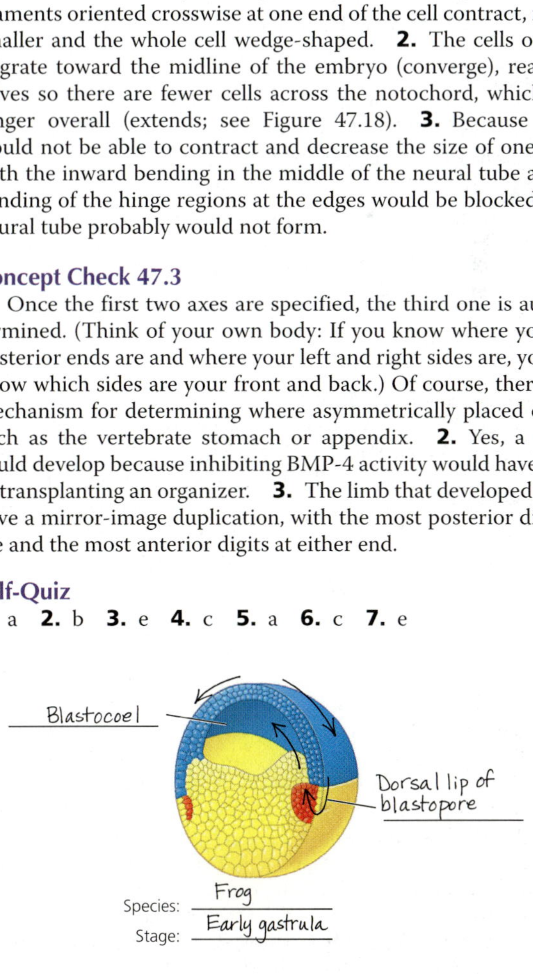

CHAPTER 48

Figure Questions

Figure 48.7 Adding chloride channels makes the membrane potential less negative. Adding sodium or potassium channels would have no effect, because sodium movement is already at equilibrium and there are no potassium ions present. **Figure 48.15** The production and transmission of action potentials would be unaffected. However, action potentials arriving at chemical synapses would be unable to trigger release of neurotransmitter. Signaling at such synapses would thus be blocked. **Figure 48.17** In theory, the results would be similar because the binding studies indicate that both opiates and naloxone, an opiate antagonist, bind directly to the receptor.

Concept Check 48.1

1. Sensors in your ear transmit information to your brain. There the activity of interneurons in processing centers enables you to recognize your name. In response, signals transmitted via motor neurons cause contraction of muscles that turn your neck. **2.** The nervous system is required for control of vital functions, such as circulation and gas exchange, and the transmission of information occurs on a very short time scale. **3.** It would prevent information from being transmitted away from the cell body along the axon.

Concept Check 48.2

1. Ions can flow against a chemical concentration gradient if there is an opposing electrical gradient of greater magnitude. **2.** A decrease in permeability to K^+, an increase in permeability to Na^+, or both. **3.** The activity of the sodium-potassium pump is essential to maintain the resting potential. With the pump inactivated, the sodium and potassium concentration gradients would gradually disappear, and so would the resting potential.

Concept Check 48.3

1. A graded potential has a magnitude that varies with stimulus strength, whereas an action potential has an all-or-none magnitude that is independent of stimulus strength. **2.** Loss of the insulation provided by myelin sheaths leads to a disruption of action potential propagation along axons. Voltage-gated sodium channels are restricted to the nodes of Ranvier, and without the insulating effect of myelin, the inward current produced at one node during an action potential cannot depolarize the membrane to the threshold at the next node. **3.** The maximum frequency would decrease because the refractory period would be extended.

Concept Check 48.4

1. It can bind to different types of receptors, each triggering a specific response in postsynaptic cells. **2.** These toxins would prolong the EPSPs that acetylcholine produces because the neurotransmitter would remain longer in the synaptic cleft. **3.** Such a drug might act as a sedative, decreasing the general level of activity in the brain and hence in the person.

Self-Quiz

1. c **2.** b **3.** c **4.** a **5.** c **6.** e

7. As shown in this pair of drawings, a pair of action potentials would move outward in both directions from each electrode. (Action potentials are unidirectional only if they begin at one end of an axon.) However, because of the refractory period, the two action potentials between the electrodes both stop where they meet. Thus, only one action potential reaches the synaptic terminals.

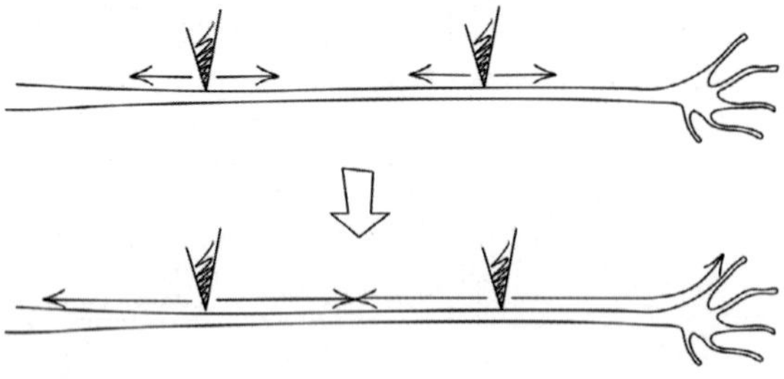

CHAPTER 49

Figure Questions

Figure 49.8 Neurosecretory cells of the adrenal medulla secrete epinephrine in response to preganglionic input from sympathetic neurons. Epinephrine travels in the circulation to reach target tissues throughout the body. Thus, the rapid changes in body tissues required for the "fight-or-flight" response rely on direct input from the nervous system as well as indirect input via neurohormone products of the adrenal medulla. **Figure 49.12** If the new mutation disrupted only pacemaker function, you should be able to restore rhythmic activity by removing the SCN and replacing it with an SCN transplant from either a wild-type or τ mutant hamster. Using the new mutant as the donor would not be as informative, since both failed transplants and successful ones would result in a lack of rhythmic activity. **Figure 49.22** The depolarization should mimic natural stimulation of the brain reward system, resulting in positive and perhaps pleasurable sensations.

Concept Check 49.1

1. The sympathetic division, which mediates the "fight-or-flight" response in stressful situations **2.** The preganglionic neurons use the same neurotransmitter and function similarly in each division (to activate postganglionic neurons). The postganglionic neurons generally have opposing functions and use different neurotransmitters. **3.** Nerves contain bundles of axons, some of which belong to motor neurons that send signals outward from the CNS, and some that belong to sensory neurons that bring signals into the CNS. Therefore, you would expect effects on both motor control and sensation.

Concept Check 49.2

1. The cerebral cortex on the left side of the brain control initiates voluntary movement of the right side of the body. **2.** Alcohol diminishes function of the cerebellum. **3.** Paralysis reflects an inability to carry out motor functions transmitted from the cerebrum to the spinal cord. You would expect these patients to have injuries below the reticular formation. A coma reflects a disruption in the cycles of sleep and arousal regulated by communication between the reticular formation and the cerebrum. You would expect these patients to have injuries at or above the reticular formation.

Concept Check 49.3

1. Brain lesions that disrupt behavior, cognition, memory, or other functions provide evidence that the portion of the brain affected by the damage is important for the normal activity that is blocked or altered. **2.** Broca's area, which is active during the generation of speech, is located near the part of the primary motor cortex that controls muscles in the face. Wernicke's area, which is active when speech is heard, is located near the part of the temporal lobe that is involved in hearing. **3.** Each cerebral hemisphere is specialized for different parts of this task—the right for face recognition and the left for language. Without an intact corpus callosum, neither hemisphere can take advantage of the other's processing abilities.

Concept Check 49.4

1. There can be an increase in the number of synapses between the neurons or an increase in the strength of existing synaptic connections. **2.** If consciousness is an emergent property resulting from the interaction of many different regions of the brain, then it is unlikely that localized brain damage will have a discrete effect on consciousness. **3.** The hippocampus is responsible for organizing newly acquired information. Without hippocampal function, the links necessary to retrieve information from the neocortex will be lacking and no functional memory, short- or long-term, will be formed.

Concept Check 49.5

1. Both are progressive brain diseases whose risk increases with advancing age. Both result from the death of brain neurons and are associated with the accumulation of peptide or protein aggregates. **2.** The symptoms of schizophrenia can be mimicked by a drug that stimulates dopamine-releasing neurons. The brain reward system, which is involved in addiction, is comprised of dopamine-releasing neurons that connect the ventral tegmental area to regions in the cerebrum. Parkinson's disease results from the death of dopamine-releasing neurons. **3.** Not necessarily. It might be that the plaques, tangles, and missing regions of the brain seen at death reflect secondary effects, the consequence of other unseen changes that are actually responsible for the alterations in brain function.

Self-Quiz

1. c **2.** a **3.** d **4.** d **5.** e **6.** c

7. 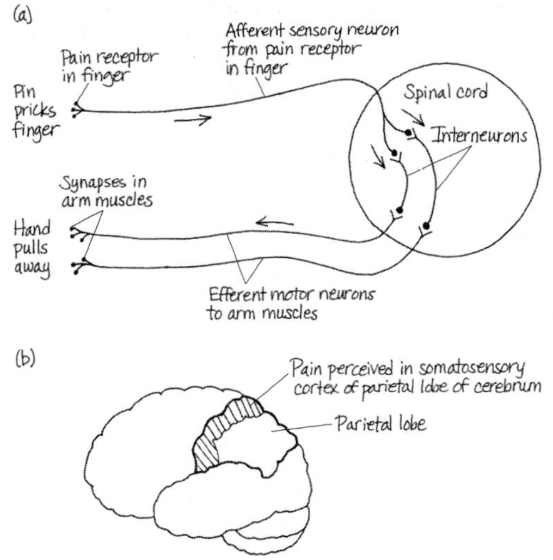

CHAPTER 50

Figure Questions

Figure 50.10 In the brain. Each note is detected separately in the ear, with each causing vibration of the basilar membrane and deflection of hair cells in a distinct location. Sensory neurons in each location provide output in the form of action potentials that travel along distinct axons in the auditory nerve. It is not until the information reaches the brain that the individual notes are detected and the perception of the chord is generated. **Figure 50.14** The results of the experiment would have been identical. What matters is the activation of particular sets of neurons, not the manner in which they are activated. Any signal from a bitter cell will be interpreted by the brain as a bitter taste, regardless of the nature of the compound and the receptor involved. **Figure 50.15** Only perception. Binding of an odorant to its receptor will cause action potentials to be sent to the brain. Although an excess of that odorant might cause a diminished response through adaptation, another odorant can mask the first only at the level of perception in the brain. **Figure 50.22** Each of the three types of cones is most sensitive to a distinct wavelength of light. A cone might be fully depolarized when there is light present if the light is of a wavelength far from its optimum. **Figure 50.27** Hundreds of myosin heads participate in sliding each pair of thick and thin filaments past each other. Because cross-bridge formation and breakdown are not synchronized, many myosin heads are exerting force on the thin filaments at all times during muscle contraction. **Figure 50.37** Since a duck is more specialized for flying than for swimming, you might expect that it would consume more energy per unit body mass and distance in swimming than would, for example, a fish. (In fact, if the value for a 10^3 g swimming duck were plotted on this graph, it would appear well above the line for swimmers and just above the line for runners.)

Concept Check 50.1

1. Electromagnetic receptors in general detect only external stimuli. Nonelectromagnetic receptors, such as chemoreceptors or mechanoreceptors, can act as either internal or external sensors. **2.** The capsaicin present in the spice mix activates the thermoreceptor for high temperatures. In response to the perceived high temperature, the nervous system triggers sweating to achieve evaporative cooling. **3.** You would perceive the electrical stimulus as if the sensory receptors that regulate that neuron had been activated. For example, electrical stimulation of the sensory neuron controlled by the thermoreceptor activated by menthol would likely be perceived as a local cooling.

Concept Check 50.2

1. Statocysts detect the animal's orientation with respect to gravity, providing information that is essential in environments such as these, where light cues are absent. **2.** As a sound that changes gradually from a very low to a very high pitch **3.** The stapes and the other middle ear bones transmit vibrations from the tympanic membrane to the oval window. Fusion of these bones, as occurs in otosclerosis, would block this transmission and result in hearing loss.

Concept Check 50.3

1. Both taste cells and olfactory cells have receptor proteins in their plasma membrane that bind certain substances, leading to membrane depolarization through a signal transduction pathway involving a G protein. However, olfactory cells are sensory neurons, whereas taste cells are not. **2.** Since animals rely on chemical signals for behaviors that include finding mates, marking territories, and avoiding dangerous substances, it is adaptive for the olfactory system to have a robust response to a very small number of molecules of a particular odorant. **3.** Because the sweet, bitter, and umami tastes involve GPCR proteins but the sour taste does not, you might predict that the mutation is in a molecule that acts in the signal transduction pathway common to the different GPCR receptors.

Concept Check 50.4

1. Planarians have ocelli that cannot form images but can sense the intensity and direction of light, providing enough information to enable the animals to find protection in shaded places. Flies have compound eyes that form images and excel at detecting movement. **2.** The person can focus on distant objects but not close objects (without glasses) because close focusing requires the lens to become almost spherical. This problem is common after age 50. **3.** Close each eye in turn. An object floating on the surface of an eyeball will appear only when that eye is open.

Concept Check 50.5

1. By causing all of the motor neurons that control the muscle to generate action potentials at a rate high enough to produce tetanus in all of the muscle fibers **2.** In a skeletal muscle fiber, Ca^{2+} binds to the troponin complex, which moves tropomyosin away from the myosin-binding sites on actin and allows cross-bridges to form. In a smooth muscle cell, Ca^{2+} binds to calmodulin, which activates an enzyme that phosphorylates the myosin head and thus enables cross-bridge formation. **3.** *Rigor mortis*, a Latin phrase meaning "stiffness of death," results from the complete depletion of ATP in skeletal muscle. Since ATP is required for release of myosin from actin and to pump Ca^{2+} out of the cytosol, muscles become chronically contracted beginning about 3 or 4 hours after death.

Concept Check 50.6

1. Septa provide the divisions of the coelom that allow for peristalsis, a form of locomotion requiring independent control of different body segments. **2.** The main problem in swimming is drag; a fusiform body minimizes drag. The main problem in flying is overcoming gravity; wings shaped like airfoils provide lift, and adaptations such as air-filled bones reduce body mass. **3.** You could start by standing with your upper arm against your side and your lower arm extended out at a ninety degree angle from your hip. You could then slowly lower your hand toward the ground. Because you are holding the weight of your hand and lower arm against gravity, you need to maintain tetanus in the biceps muscle. As you lower your hand, you are gradually decreasing the number of motor units in the biceps that are contracted. The triceps is not involved because gravity is providing the force for arm extension.

Self Quiz

1. e **2.** d **3.** b **4.** a **5.** c **6.** b
7.

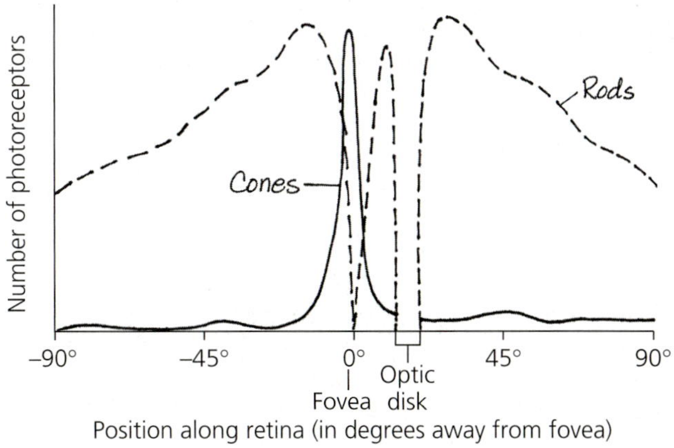

The answer shows the actual distribution of rods and cones in the human eye. Your graph may differ but should have the following properties: Only cones at the fovea; fewer cones and more rods at both ends of the x-axis; no photoreceptors in the optic disk.

CHAPTER 51

Figure Questions

Figure 51.3 The fixed action pattern based on the sign stimulus of a red belly ensures that the male will chase away any invading males of his species. By chasing away such males, the defender decreases the chance that eggs laid in his nesting territory will be fertilized by another male. **Figure 51.10** There should be no effect. Imprinting is an innate behavior that is carried out anew in each generation. Assuming the nest was not disturbed, the offspring of the Lorenz followers would imprint on the mother goose. **Figure 51.11** Perhaps the wasp doesn't use visual cues. It might also be that wasps recognize objects native to their environment, but not foreign objects, such as the pinecones. Tinbergen addressed these ideas before carrying out the pinecone study. When he swept away the pebbles and sticks around the nest, the wasps could no longer find their nests. If he shifted the natural objects in their natural arrangement, the shift in the landmarks caused a shift in the site to which the wasps returned. Finally, if the natural objects around the nest site were replaced with pinecones while the wasp was in the burrow, the wasp nevertheless found her way back to the nest site. **Figure 51.14** Courtship song generation must be coupled to courtship song recognition. Unless the genes that control generation of particular song elements also control recognition, the hybrids might be unlikely to find mating partners, depending on what aspects of the songs are important for mate recognition and acceptance. **Figure 51.15** It might be that the birds require stimuli during flight to exhibit their migratory preference. If this were true, the birds would show the same orientation in the funnel experiment despite their distinct genetic programming. **Figure 51.28** It holds true for some, but not all individuals. If a parent has more than one reproductive partner, the offspring of different partners will have a coefficient of relatedness less than 0.5.

Concept Check 51.1

1. It is an example of a fixed action pattern. The proximate explanation might be that nudging and rolling are released by the sign stimulus of an object outside the nest, and the behavior is carried to completion once initiated. The ultimate explanation might be that ensuring that eggs remain in the nest increases the chance of producing healthy offspring. **2.** Circannual rhythms are typically based on the cycles of light and dark in the environment. As the global climate changes, animals that migrate in response to these rhythms may shift to a location before or after local environmental conditions are optimal for reproduction and survival. **3.** There might be selective pressure for other prey fish to detect an injured fish because the source of the injury might threaten them as well. There might be selection for predators to be attracted to the alarm substance because they would be more likely to encounter crippled prey than would be predators that can't respond. Fish with adequate defenses might show no change because they have a selective advantage if they do not waste energy responding to the alarm substance.

Concept Check 51.2

1. Natural selection would tend to favor convergence in color pattern because a predator learning to associate a pattern with a sting or bad taste would avoid all other individuals with that same color pattern, regardless of species. **2.** Forgetting the location of some caches, which consist of pine seeds buried in the ground, might benefit the nutcracker by increasing the number of pines growing in its habitat. This example points out one of the difficulties in making simplistic assumptions about the purpose of a behavior. **3.** You might move objects around to establish an abstract rule, such as "past landmark A, the same distance as A is from the starting point," while maintaining a minimum of fixed metric relationships, that is, avoiding having the food directly adjacent to or a set distance from a landmark. As you might surmise, designing an informative experiment of this kind is not easy.

Concept Check 51.3

1. Because this geographic variation corresponds to differences in prey availability between two garter snake habitats, it seems likely that snakes with characteristics enabling them to feed on the abundant prey in their locale would have had increased survival and reproductive success, and thus natural selection would have resulted in the divergent foraging behaviors. **2.** Courtship is easier to study because it is essential for reproduction, but not for growth, development, and survival. Mutations disrupting many other behaviors would be lethal. **3.** You would need to know the percentage of time that unrelated individuals behave identically when performing this behavior.

Concept Check 51.4

1. Certainty of paternity is higher with external fertilization. **2.** Natural selection acts on genetic variation in the population. **3.** Because females would now be present in much larger numbers than males, all three types of males should have some reproductive success. Nevertheless, since the advantage that the blue-throats rely on—a limited number of females in their territory—will be absent, the yellow-throats are likely to increase in frequency in the short term.

Concept Check 51.5

1. Reciprocal altruism, the exchange of helpful behaviors for future similar behaviors, can explain cooperative behaviors between unrelated animals, though often the behavior has some potential benefit to the benefactor as well. **2.** Yes. Kin selection does not require any recognition or awareness of relatedness. **3.** The older individual cannot be the beneficiary because he or she cannot have extra offspring. However, the cost is low for an older individual performing the altruistic act because that person has already reproduced (but perhaps is still caring for a child or grandchild). There can therefore be selection for an altruistic act by a postreproductive individual that benefits a young relative.

Self-Quiz

1. d **2.** a **3.** c **4.** a **5.** c **6.** b **7.** c

8.

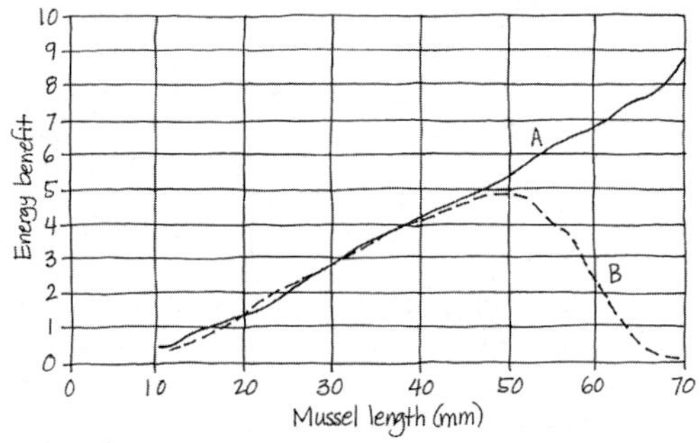

You could measure the size of mussels that oystercatchers successfully open and compare that with the size distribution in the habitat.

CHAPTER 52

Figure Questions

Figure 52.6 Some factors, such as fire, are relevant only for terrestrial systems. At first glance, water availability is primarily a terrestrial factor, too. However, species living along the intertidal zone of oceans or along the edge of lakes suffer desiccation as well. Salinity stress is important for species in some aquatic and terrestrial systems. Oxygen availability is an important factor primarily for species in some aquatic systems and in soils and sediments. **Figure 52.8** When only urchins were removed, limpets may have increased in abundance and reduced seaweed cover somewhat (the difference between the purple and blue lines on the graph). **Figure 52.14** Dispersal limitations, the activities of people (such as a broad-scale conversion of forests to agriculture or selective harvesting), or other factors listed in Figure 52.6

Concept Check 52.1

1. *Ecology* is the scientific study of the interactions between organisms and their environment; *environmentalism* is advocacy for the environment. Ecology provides scientific understanding that can inform decision making about environmental issues. **2.** Interactions in ecological time that affect the survival or reproduction of organisms can result in changes to the population's gene pool and ultimately result in a change in the population on an evolutionary time scale. **3.** If the fungicides are used together, fungi will likely evolve resistance to all four much more quickly than if the fungicides are used individually at different times.

Concept Check 52.2

1. a. Humans could transplant a species to a new area that it could not previously reach because of a geographic barrier (dispersal change). b. Humans could change a species' biotic interactions by eliminating a predator or herbivore species, such as sea urchins, from an area. **2.** The sun's unequal heating of Earth's surface produces temperature variations between the warmer tropics and colder polar regions, and it influences the movement of air masses and thus the distribution of moisture at different latitudes. **3.** One test would be to build a fence around a plot of land in an area that has trees of that species, excluding all deer from the plot. You could then compare the abundance of tree seedlings inside and outside the fenced plot over time.

Concept Check 52.3

1. Rapid changes in salinity can cause salt stress in many organisms. **2.** In the oceanic pelagic zone, the ocean bottom lies below the photic zone, so there is too little light to support benthic algae or rooted plants. **3.** In a river below a dam, the fish are more likely to be species that prefer colder water. In summer, the deep layers of a reservoir are colder than the surface layers, so a river below a dam will be colder than an undammed river.

Concept Check 52.4

1. Higher average temperature in deserts **2.** Answers will vary by location but should be based on the information and maps in Figure 52.21. How much your local area has been altered from its natural state will influence how much it reflects the expected characteristics of your biome, particularly the expected plants and animals. **3.** Northern coniferous forest is likely to replace tundra along the boundary between these biomes. To see why, note that northern coniferous forest is adjacent to tundra throughout North America, northern Europe, and Asia (see Figure 52.19) and that the temperature range for northern coniferous forest is just above that for tundra (see Figure 52.20).

Self-Quiz

1. c **2.** d **3.** a **4.** d **5.** b **6.** d **7.** d **8.** e **9.** a
10.

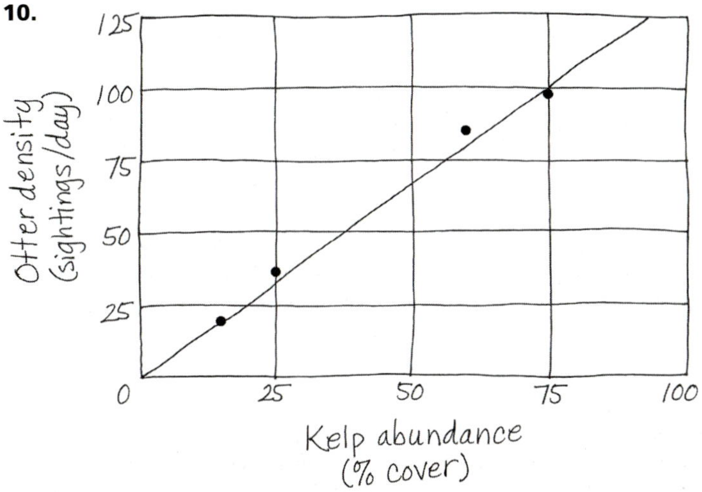

Based on what you learned from Figure 52.8 and on the positive relationship you observed in the field between kelp abundance and otter density, you could hypothesize that otters lower sea urchin density, reducing feeding of the urchins on kelp.

CHAPTER 53

Figure Questions

Figure 53.4 The dispersion of the penguins would likely appear clumped as you flew over densely populated islands and sparsely populated ocean. **Figure 53.8** If male European kestrels provided no parental care, brood size should not affect their survival. Therefore, the three bars representing male survival in Figure 53.8 should have similar heights. In contrast, female survival should still decline with increasing brood size, as shown in the current figure. **Figure 53.19** The moose population grew quickly because food was abundant and predators were absent. During this period, the population experienced exponential growth. **Figure 53.20** Hare numbers typically peaked slightly before lynx numbers did. The lynx depend on the hares for food, but there is a delay between increased food availability and increased reproduction by the lynx.

Concept Check 53.1

1. The territorial species likely has a uniform pattern of dispersion, since the interactions between individuals will maintain constant space between them. The flocking species is probably clumped, since most individuals probably live in one of the clumps (flocks).
2.

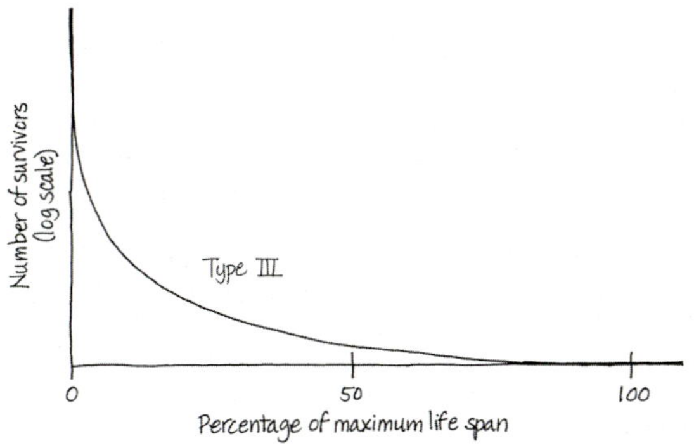

A type III survivorship curve is most likely because very few of the young probably survive. **3.** If an animal is captured by attracting it with food, it may be more likely to be recaptured if it seeks the same food. The number of marked animals recaptured (x) would be an overestimate, and because the population size $(N) = mn/x$, N would be an underestimate. Alternatively, if an animal has a negative experience during capture and learns from that experience, it may be less likely to be recaptured. In this case, x would be an underestimate and N would be an overestimate.

Concept Check 53.2

1. The constant, spring-fed stream. In more constant physical conditions, where populations are more stable and competition for resources is more likely, larger well-provisioned young, which are more typical of iteroparous species, have a better chance of surviving. **2.** By preferentially investing in the eggs it lays in the nest, the peacock wrasse increases their probability of survival. The eggs it disperses widely and does not provide care for are less likely to survive, at least some of the time, but require a lower investment by the adults. (In this sense, the adults avoid the risk of placing all their eggs in one basket.) **3.** If a parent's survival is compromised greatly by bearing young during times of stress, the animal's fitness may increase if it abandons its current young and survives to produce healthier young at a later time.

Concept Check 53.3

1. Though r_{max} is constant, N, the population size, is increasing. As r_{max} is applied to an increasingly large N, population growth ($r_{max}N$) accelerates, producing the J-shaped curve. **2.** On the new island. The first plants that found suitable habitat on the island would encounter an abundance of space, nutrients, and light. In the rain forest, competition among plants for these resources is intense. **3.** The net population growth is $\Delta N/\Delta t = bN - dN$. The annual per capita birth rate, b, equals 14/1,000, or 0.014, and the per capita death rate, d, equals 8/1,000, or 0.008. Therefore, the net population growth in 2006 is

$$\frac{\Delta N}{\Delta t} = (0.014 \times 300{,}000{,}000) - (0.008 \times 300{,}000{,}000)$$

or 1.8 million people. A population is growing exponentially only if its per capita rate of increase equals its maximum rate. That is not the case for the United States currently.

Concept Check 53.4

1. When N (population size) is small, there are relatively few individuals producing offspring. When N is large, near the carrying capacity, per capita growth is relatively small because it is limited by available resources. The steepest part of the logistic growth curve corresponds to a population with a number of reproducing individuals that is substantial but not yet near carrying capacity. **2.** r-selected. Weeds that colonize an abandoned field face little competition, and their initial populations are well below carrying capacity. These are characteristics of environments that favor r-selected species. **3.** Using a population size of 1,600 as an example,

$$\frac{dN}{dt} = r_{max}N\frac{(K-N)}{K} = \frac{1(1{,}600)(1{,}500 - 1{,}600)}{1{,}500}$$

and the population "growth" rate is −107 individuals per year. The population shrinks even faster when N is farther from the carrying capacity; when N equals 1,750 and 2,000 individuals, the population shrinks by 292 and 667 individuals per year, respectively. These negative growth rates correspond most closely to the time when the *Daphnia* population has overshot its carrying capacity and is shrinking, about days 65–100 in Figure 53.13b.

Concept Check 53.5

1. Competition for resources and space can negatively impact population growth by limiting reproductive output. Diseases that are transmitted more easily in crowded populations can exert negative feedback on increasing population size. Some predators feed preferentially on species at higher population densities, since those prey are easier to find than are prey in less dense populations. In crowded populations, toxic metabolic wastes can build up and poison the organisms. **2.** Three attributes are the size, quality, and isolation of patches. A patch that is larger or of higher quality is more likely to attract individuals and to be a source of individuals for other patches. A patch that is relatively isolated will undergo less exchange of individuals with other patches. **3.** You would need to study the population for more than one cycle (longer than 10 years and probably at least 20) before having sufficient data to examine changes through time. Otherwise, it would be impossible to know whether an observed decrease in the population size reflected a long-term trend or was part of the normal cycle.

Concept Check 53.6

1. A bottom-heavy age structure, with a disproportionate number of young people, portends continuing growth of the population as these young people begin reproducing. In contrast, a more evenly distributed age structure predicts a more stable population size. **2.** The growth rate of Earth's human population has dropped by half since the 1960s, from 2.2% in 1962 to 1.15% today. Nonetheless, growth has not slowed much because the smaller growth rate is counterbalanced by increased population size; the number of extra people on Earth each year remains enormous—approximately 75 million. **3.** Each of us influences our ecological footprint by how we live—what we eat, how much energy we use, and the amount of waste we generate—as well as by how many children we have. Making choices that reduce our demand for resources makes our ecological footprint smaller.

Self-Quiz

1. c **2.** c **3.** c **4.** d **5.** d **6.** b **7.** c **8.** d **9.** c **10.** d

11.

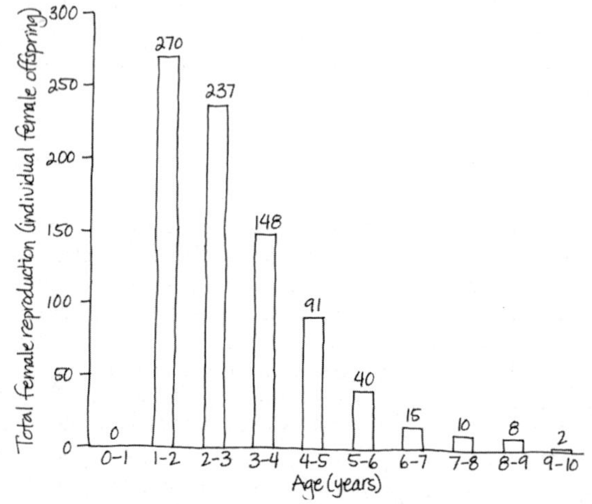

The total number of female offspring produced is greatest in females 1–2 years of age. Sample calculation for females of this age group: 252 indiv. × 1.07 female offspring/indiv. = 270 female offspring.

CHAPTER 54

Figure Questions

Figure 54.3 Its realized and fundamental niches would be similar. **Figure 54.4** If both species were feeding on seeds of the same size, you would expect differences in beak size to disappear over evolutionary time. The species could not specialize on seeds of different sizes. **Figure 54.14** The low-productivity treatment had the shortest food chain, so that food chain should be the most stable. **Figure 54.15** The death of individuals of *Mytilus*, a dominant species, should open up space for other species and increase species richness even in the absence of *Pisaster*. **Figure 54.19** Because the abundance of the second predatory species is unaffected by soil warming, there would be a less dramatic decrease in total predator numbers. Therefore, if the top-down model applies in this community, you would expect a smaller increase in *S. lindsayae* density than was actually observed. **Figure 54.28** Other factors not included in the model must contribute to the unexplained variation in the results.

Concept Check 54.1

1. Interspecific competition has negative effects on both species (−/−). In predation, the predator population benefits at the expense of the prey population (+/−). Mutualism is a symbiosis in which both species benefit (+/+). **2.** One of the competing species will become locally extinct because of the greater reproductive success of the more efficient competitor. **3.** Examples of relevant interactions include competition between weeds and food crops; predation by humans on herbivores, such as cattle; herbivory by humans on leafy vegetables, such as lettuce or spinach; and the planting of symbiotic nitrogen-fixing plants, such as beans or peas.

Concept Check 54.2

1. Species richness, the number of species in the community, and relative abundance, the proportions of the community represented by the various species, both contribute to species diversity. Compared to a community with a very high proportion of one species, one with a more even proportion of species is considered to be more diverse. **2.** The energetic hypothesis suggests that the length of a food chain is limited by the inefficiency of energy transfer along the chain, while the dynamic stability hypothesis proposes that long food chains are less stable than short chains. The energetic hypothesis predicts that food chains will be longer in habitats with higher primary productivity. The dynamic stability hypothesis predicts that food chains will be longer in more predictable environments. **3.** According to the bottom-up model, adding extra predators would have little effect on lower trophic levels, particularly vegetation. If the top-down model applied, increased bobcat numbers would decrease raccoon numbers, increase snake numbers, decrease grasshopper numbers, and increase plant biomass.

Concept Check 54.3

1. High levels of disturbance are generally so disruptive that they eliminate many species from communities, leaving the community dominated by a few tolerant species. Low levels of disturbance permit competitively dominant species to exclude other species from the community. In contrast, moderate levels of disturbance can facilitate coexistence of a greater number of species in a community by preventing competitively dominant species from becoming abundant enough to eliminate other species from the community. **2.** Early successional species can facilitate the arrival of other species in many ways, including increasing the fertility or water-holding capacity of soils or providing shelter to seedlings from wind and intense sunlight. **3.** The absence of fire for 100 years would represent a change to a low level of disturbance. According to the intermediate disturbance hypothesis, this change should cause diversity to decline as competitively dominant species gain sufficient time to exclude less competitive species.

Concept Check 54.4

1. Ecologists propose that the greater species richness of tropical regions is the result of their longer evolutionary history and the greater solar energy input and water availability in tropical regions. **2.** Immigration of species to islands declines with distance from the mainland and increases with island area. Extinction of species is lower on larger islands and on less isolated islands. Since the number of species on islands is largely determined by the difference between rates of immigration and extinction, the number of species will be highest on large islands near the mainland and lowest on small islands far from the mainland. **3.** Because of their greater mobility, birds disperse to islands more often than snakes or mammals, so birds should have greater richness.

Concept Check 54.5

1. Pathogens are microorganisms, viruses, viroids, or prions that cause disease. **2.** If the parasite requires contact with a human and another animal, the parasite might be an especially likely vector for the pathogens that cause zoonotic diseases. **3.** If you can identify the host or hosts of the disease as well as any intermediate vectors, such as mosquitoes or fleas, you can reduce the rate of infection by decreasing the abundance of the host and vector or by reducing their contact with people.

Self-Quiz

1. c **2.** d **3.** b **4.** c **5.** c **6.** d **7.** b **8.** c
9. Community 1: $H = -[(0.05)(\ln 0.05) + (0.05)(\ln 0.05) + (0.85)(\ln 0.85) + (0.05)(\ln 0.05)] = 0.59$. Community 2: $H = -[(0.30)(\ln 0.30) + (0.40)(\ln 0.40) + (0.30)(\ln 0.30)] = 1.1$. Community 2 is more diverse.
10.

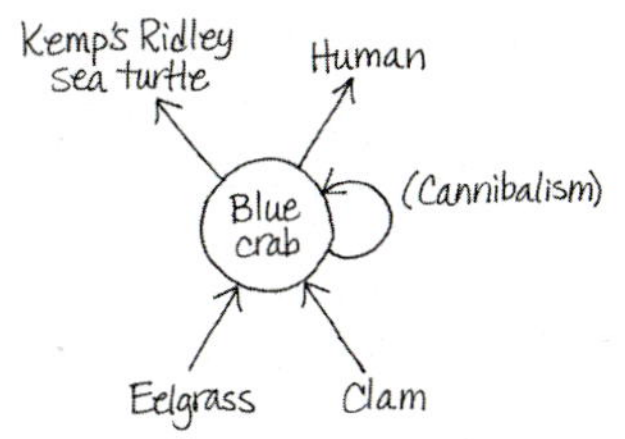

Crab numbers should increase, reducing the abundance of eelgrass.

CHAPTER 55

Figure Questions

Figure 55.6 Wetlands, coral reefs, and coastal zones cover areas too small to show up clearly on global maps. **Figure 55.7** If the new duck farms made nitrogen available in rich supply, as phosphorus already is, then adding extra nitrogen in the experiment would not increase phytoplankton density. **Figure 55.13** By dissolving minerals, the fungi move nutrients from reservoir D (inorganic materials unavailable as nutrients) to reservoir C (inorganic materials available as nutrients). **Figure 55.15** Water availability is probably another factor that varied across the sites. Such factors not included in the experimental design could make the results more difficult to interpret. Multiple factors can also covary in nature, so ecologists must be careful that the factor they are studying is actually causing the observed response and is not just correlated with it.

Concept Check 55.1

1. Energy passes through an ecosystem, entering as sunlight and leaving as heat. It is not recycled within the ecosystem. **2.** The second law states that in any energy transfer or transformation, some of the energy is dissipated to the surroundings as heat. This "escape" of energy from an ecosystem is offset by the continuous influx of solar radiation. **3.** You would need to know how much biomass the wildebeests ate from your plot and how much nitrogen was contained in that biomass. You would also need to know how much nitrogen they deposited in urine or feces.

Concept Check 55.2

1. Only a fraction of solar radiation strikes plants or algae, only a portion of that fraction is of wavelengths suitable for photosynthesis, and much energy is lost as a result of reflection or heating of plant tissue. **2.** By manipulating the level of the factors of interest, such as phosphorus availability or soil moisture, and measuring responses by primary producers **3.** The student is missing the plant biomass eaten by herbivores and the production allocated to plant roots and other belowground tissues.

Concept Check 55.3

1. 20 J; 40% **2.** Nicotine protects the plant from herbivores. **3.** There are many things they could do to reduce their production efficiency. For example, exercising vigorously will use energy that might otherwise go to biomass, and keeping the house cool will force their bodies to use energy to stay warm.

Concept Check 55.4

1. For example, for the carbon cycle:

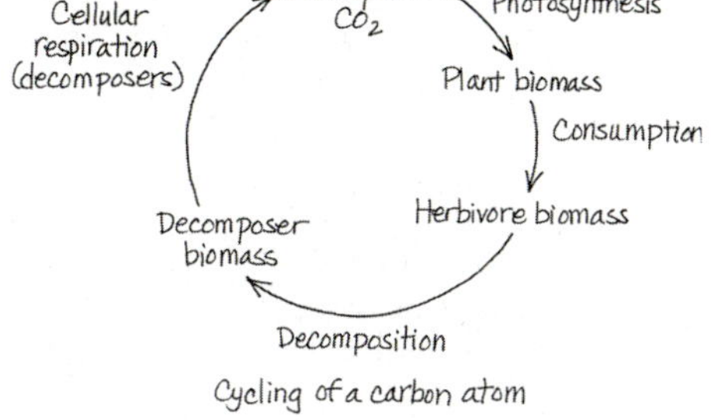

2. Removal of the trees stops nitrogen uptake from the soil, allowing nitrate to accumulate there. The nitrate is washed away by precipitation and enters the streams. **3.** Most of the nutrients in a tropical rain forest are contained in the trees, so removing the trees by logging rapidly depletes nutrients from the ecosystem. The nutrients that remain in the soil are quickly carried away into streams and groundwater by the abundant precipitation.

Concept Check 55.5

1. Adding nutrients causes population explosions of algae and the organisms that feed on them. Increased respiration by algae and consumers, including detritivores, depletes the lake's oxygen, which the fish require. **2.** At a lower trophic level, because biological magnification increases the concentration of toxins up the food chain **3.** Because higher temperatures lead to faster decomposition, organic matter in these soils could be quickly decomposed to CO_2, speeding up global warming.

Self-Quiz

1. c **2.** b **3.** d **4.** c **5.** e **6.** a **7.** d
8.

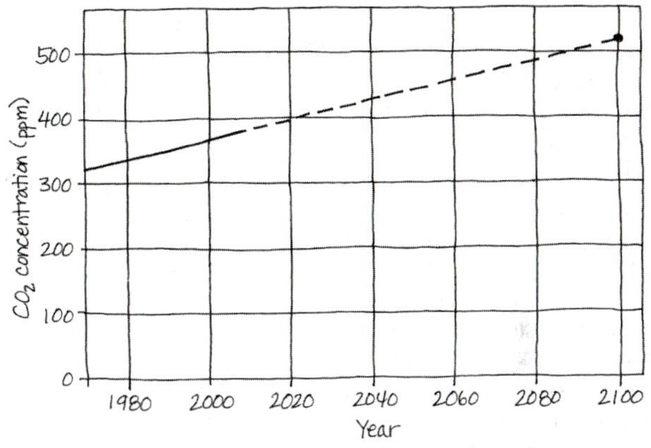

Between 1974 and 2007, Earth's atmospheric CO_2 concentration increased from approximately 330 ppm to 385 ppm. If this rate of increase of 1.7 ppm/yr continues, the concentration in 2100 will be about 540 ppm. The actual rise in CO_2 concentration could be larger or smaller, depending on Earth's human population, per capita energy use, and the extent to which societies take steps to reduce CO_2 emissions, including replacing fossil fuels with renewable or nuclear fuels. Additional scientific data will be important for many reasons, including determining how quickly greenhouse gases such as CO_2 are removed from the atmosphere by the biosphere.

CHAPTER 56

Figure Questions

Figure 56.4 You would need to know the complete range of the species and that it is missing across all of that range. You would also need to be certain that the species isn't hidden, as might be the case for an animal that is hibernating underground or a plant that is present in the form of seeds or spores. **Figure 56.11** Because the population of Illinois birds has a different genetic makeup than birds in other regions, you would want to maintain to the greatest extent possible the frequency of beneficial genes or alleles found only in that population. In restoration, preserving genetic diversity in a species is as important as increasing organism numbers. **Figure 56.13** The natural disturbance regime in this habitat included frequent fires that cleared undergrowth but did not kill mature pine trees. Without these fires, the undergrowth quickly fills in and the habitat becomes unsuitable for red-cockaded woodpeckers.

Concept Check 56.1

1. In addition to species loss, the biodiversity crisis includes the loss of genetic diversity within populations and species and the degradation of entire ecosystems. **2.** Habitat destruction, such as deforestation, channelizing of rivers, or conversion of natural ecosystems to agriculture or cities, deprives species of places to live. Introduced species, which are transported by humans to regions outside their native range, where they are not controlled by their natural pathogens or predators, often reduce the population sizes of native species through competition or predation. Overexploitation has reduced populations of plants and animals or driven them to extinction. **3.** If both populations breed separately, then gene flow between the populations would not occur and genetic differences between them would be greater. As a result, the loss of genetic diversity would be greater than if the populations interbreed.

Concept Check 56.2

1. Reduced genetic variation decreases the capacity of a population to evolve in the face of change. **2.** The effective population size, N_e, is $4(35 \times 10)/(35 + 10) = 31$ birds. **3.** Because millions of people use the greater Yellowstone ecosystem each year, it would be impossible to eliminate all contact between people and bears. Instead, you might try to reduce the kinds of encounters where bears are killed. You might recommend lower speed limits on roads in the park, adjust the timing or location of hunting seasons (where hunting is allowed outside the park) to minimize contact with mother bears and cubs, and provide financial incentives for livestock owners to try alternative means (such as guard dogs) of protecting livestock.

Concept Check 56.3

1. A small area supporting an exceptionally large number of endemic species as well as a disproportionate number of endangered and threatened species **2.** Zoned reserves may provide sustained supplies of forest products, water, hydroelectric power, educational opportunities, and income from ecotourism. **3.** Habitat corridors can increase the rate of movement or dispersal of organisms between habitat patches and thus the rate of gene flow between subpopulations. They thus help prevent a decrease in fitness attributable to inbreeding. They can also minimize interactions between organisms and humans as the organisms disperse; in cases involving potential predators, such as bears or large cats, minimizing such interactions is desirable.

Concept Check 56.4

1. The main goal is to restore degraded ecosystems to a more natural state. **2.** Bioremediation uses organisms, generally prokaryotes, fungi, or plants, to detoxify or remove pollutants from ecosystems. Biological augmentation uses organisms, such as nitrogen-fixing plants, to add essential materials to degraded ecosystems. **3.** The Kissimmee River project returns the flow of water to the original channel and restores natural flow, a self-sustaining outcome. Ecologists at the Maungatautari reserve will need to maintain the integrity of the fence indefinitely, an outcome that is not self-sustaining in the long term.

Concept Check 56.5

1. Sustainable development is an approach to development that works toward the long-term prosperity of human societies and the ecosystems that support them, which requires linking the biological sciences with the social sciences, economics, and humanities. **2.** Biophilia, our sense of connection to nature and other forms of life, may act as a significant motivation for the development of an environmental ethic that resolves not to allow species to become extinct or ecosystems to be destroyed. Such an ethic is necessary if we are to become more attentive and effective custodians of the environment. **3.** At a minimum, you would want to know the size of the population and the average reproductive rate of individuals in it. To develop the fishery sustainably, you would seek a harvest rate that maintains the population near its original size and maximizes its harvest in the long term rather than the short term.

Self-Quiz

1. c **2.** e **3.** d **4.** d **5.** d **6.** e **7.** c **8.** a
10.

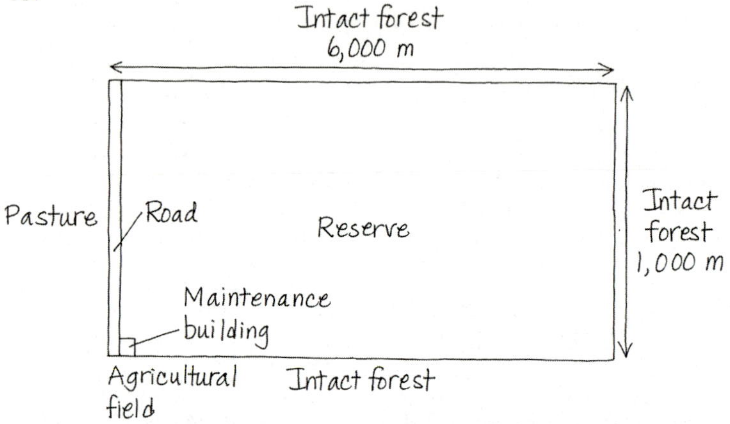

To minimize the area of forest into which the cowbirds penetrate, you should locate the road along one edge of the reserve. Any other location would increase the area of affected habitat. Similarly, the maintenance building should be in a corner of the reserve to minimize the area susceptible to cowbirds.

Answers

B Periodic Table of the Elements

Representative elements | Transition elements

Alkali metals (Group 1A) · Alkaline earth metals (Group 2A) · Halogens (Group 7A) · Noble gases (Group 8A)

Period number	1 Group 1A	2 Group 2A	3 3B	4 4B	5 5B	6 6B	7 7B	8 8B	9 8B	10 8B	11 1B	12 2B	13 Group 3A	14 Group 4A	15 Group 5A	16 Group 6A	17 Group 7A	18 Group 8A
1	1 H 1.008																	2 He 4.003
2	3 Li 6.941	4 Be 9.012											5 B 10.81	6 C 12.01	7 N 14.01	8 O 16.00	9 F 19.00	10 Ne 20.18
3	11 Na 22.99	12 Mg 24.31											13 Al 26.98	14 Si 28.09	15 P 30.97	16 S 32.07	17 Cl 35.45	18 Ar 39.95
4	19 K 39.10	20 Ca 40.08	21 Sc 44.96	22 Ti 47.87	23 V 50.94	24 Cr 52.00	25 Mn 54.94	26 Fe 55.85	27 Co 58.93	28 Ni 58.69	29 Cu 63.55	30 Zn 65.41	31 Ga 69.72	32 Ge 72.64	33 As 74.92	34 Se 78.96	35 Br 79.90	36 Kr 83.80
5	37 Rb 85.47	38 Sr 87.62	39 Y 88.91	40 Zr 91.22	41 Nb 92.91	42 Mo 95.94	43 Tc (98)	44 Ru 101.1	45 Rh 102.9	46 Pd 106.4	47 Ag 107.9	48 Cd 112.4	49 In 114.8	50 Sn 118.7	51 Sb 121.8	52 Te 127.6	53 I 126.9	54 Xe 131.3
6	55 Cs 132.9	56 Ba 137.3	57* La 138.9	72 Hf 178.5	73 Ta 180.9	74 W 183.8	75 Re 186.2	76 Os 190.2	77 Ir 192.2	78 Pt 195.1	79 Au 197.0	80 Hg 200.6	81 Tl 204.4	82 Pb 207.2	83 Bi 209.0	84 Po (209)	85 At (210)	86 Rn (222)
7	87 Fr (223)	88 Ra (226)	89† Ac (227)	104 Rf (261)	105 Db (262)	106 Sg (266)	107 Bh (264)	108 Hs (269)	109 Mt (268)	110 Ds (271)	111 — (272)	112 — (285)	113 — (284)	114 — (289)	115 — (288)			

*Lanthanides	58 Ce 140.1	59 Pr 140.9	60 Nd 144.2	61 Pm (145)	62 Sm 150.4	63 Eu 152.0	64 Gd 157.3	65 Tb 158.9	66 Dy 162.5	67 Ho 164.9	68 Er 167.3	69 Tm 168.9	70 Yb 173.0	71 Lu 175.0
†Actinides	90 Th 232.0	91 Pa 231.0	92 U 238.0	93 Np (237)	94 Pu (244)	95 Am (243)	96 Cm (247)	97 Bk (247)	98 Cf (251)	99 Es 252	100 Fm 257	101 Md 258	102 No 259	103 Lr 260

Metals · Metalloids · Nonmetals

Name (Symbol)	Atomic Number
Actinium (Ac)	89
Aluminum (Al)	13
Americium (Am)	95
Antimony (Sb)	51
Argon (Ar)	18
Arsenic (As)	33
Astatine (At)	85
Barium (Ba)	56
Berkelium (Bk)	97
Beryllium (Be)	4
Bismuth (Bi)	83
Bohrium (Bh)	107
Boron (B)	5
Bromine (Br)	35
Cadmium (Cd)	48
Calcium (Ca)	20
Californium (Cf)	98
Carbon (C)	6
Cerium (Ce)	58
Cesium (Cs)	55
Chlorine (Cl)	17
Chromium (Cr)	24
Cobalt (Co)	27
Copper (Cu)	29
Curium (Cm)	96
Darmstadtium (Ds)	110
Dubnium (Db)	105
Dysprosium (Dy)	66
Einsteinium (Es)	99
Erbium (Er)	68
Europium (Eu)	63
Fermium (Fm)	100
Fluorine (F)	9
Francium (Fr)	87
Gadolinium (Gd)	64
Gallium (Ga)	31
Germanium (Ge)	32
Gold (Au)	79
Hafnium (Hf)	72
Hassium (Hs)	108
Helium (He)	2
Holmium (Ho)	67
Hydrogen (H)	1
Indium (In)	49
Iodine (I)	53
Iridium (Ir)	77
Iron (Fe)	26
Krypton (Kr)	36
Lanthanum (La)	57
Lawrencium (Lr)	103
Lead (Pb)	82
Lithium (Li)	3
Lutetium (Lu)	71
Magnesium (Mg)	12
Manganese (Mn)	25
Meitnerium (Mt)	109
Mendelevium (Md)	101
Mercury (Hg)	80
Molybdenum (Mo)	42
Neodymium (Nd)	60
Neon (Ne)	10
Neptunium (Np)	93
Nickel (Ni)	28
Niobium (Nb)	41
Nitrogen (N)	7
Nobelium (No)	102
Osmium (Os)	76
Oxygen (O)	8
Palladium (Pd)	46
Phosphorus (P)	15
Platinum (Pt)	78
Plutonium (Pu)	94
Polonium (Po)	84
Potassium (K)	19
Praseodymium (Pr)	59
Promethium (Pm)	61
Protactinium (Pa)	91
Radium (Ra)	88
Radon (Rn)	86
Rhenium (Re)	75
Rhodium (Rh)	45
Rubidium (Rb)	37
Ruthenium (Ru)	44
Rutherfordium (Rf)	104
Samarium (Sm)	62
Scandium (Sc)	21
Seaborgium (Sg)	106
Selenium (Se)	34
Silicon (Si)	14
Silver (Ag)	47
Sodium (Na)	11
Strontium (Sr)	38
Sulfur (S)	16
Tantalum (Ta)	73
Technetium (Tc)	43
Tellurium (Te)	52
Terbium (Tb)	65
Thallium (Tl)	81
Thorium (Th)	90
Thulium (Tm)	69
Tin (Sn)	50
Titanium (Ti)	22
Tungsten (W)	74
Uranium (U)	92
Vanadium (V)	23
Xenon (Xe)	54
Ytterbium (Yb)	70
Yttrium (Y)	39
Zinc (Zn)	30
Zirconium (Zr)	40

APPENDIX

C The Metric System

Measurement	Unit and Abbreviation	Metric Equivalent	Metric-to-English Conversion Factor	English-to-Metric Conversion Factor
Length	1 kilometer (km)	= 1000 (10^3) meters	1 km = 0.62 mile	1 mile = 1.61 km
	1 meter (m)	= 100 (10^2) centimeters	1 m = 1.09 yards	1 yard = 0.914 m
		= 1000 millimeters	1 m = 3.28 feet	1 foot = 0.305 m
			1 m = 39.37 inches	
	1 centimeter (cm)	= 0.01 (10^{-2}) meter	1 cm = 0.394 inch	1 foot = 30.5 cm
				1 inch = 2.54 cm
	1 millimeter (mm)	= 0.001 (10^{-3}) meter	1 mm = 0.039 inch	
	1 micrometer (μm) (formerly micron, μ)	= 10^{-6} meter (10^{-3} mm)		
	1 nanometer (nm) (formerly millimicron, mμ)	= 10^{-9} meter (10^{-3} μm)		
	1 angstrom (Å)	= 10^{-10} meter (10^{-4} μm)		
Area	1 hectare (ha)	= 10,000 square meters	1 ha = 2.47 acres	1 acre = 0.405 ha
	1 square meter (m^2)	= 10,000 square centimeters	1 m^2 = 1.196 square yards	1 square yard = 0.8361 m^2
			1 m^2 = 10.764 square feet	1 square foot = 0.0929 m^2
	1 square centimeter (cm^2)	= 100 square millimeters	1 cm^2 = 0.155 square inch	1 square inch = 6.4516 cm^2
Mass	1 metric ton (t)	= 1000 kilograms	1 t = 1.103 tons	1 ton = 0.907 t
	1 kilogram (kg)	= 1000 grams	1 kg = 2.205 pounds	1 pound = 0.4536 kg
	1 gram (g)	= 1000 milligrams	1 g = 0.0353 ounce	1 ounce = 28.35 g
			1 g = 15.432 grains	
	1 milligram (mg)	= 10^{-3} gram	1 mg = approx. 0.015 grain	
	1 microgram (μg)	= 10^{-6} gram		
Volume (solids)	1 cubic meter (m^3)	= 1,000,000 cubic centimeters	1 m^3 = 1.308 cubic yards	1 cubic yard = 0.7646 m^3
			1 m^3 = 35.315 cubic feet	1 cubic foot = 0.0283 m^3
	1 cubic centimeter (cm^3 or cc)	= 10^{-6} cubic meter	1 cm^3 = 0.061 cubic inch	1 cubic inch = 16.387 cm^3
	1 cubic millimeter (mm^3)	= 10^{-9} cubic meter (10^{-3} cubic centimeter)		
Volume (liquids and gases)	1 kiloliter (kl or kL)	= 1000 liters	1 kL = 264.17 gallons	1 gallon = 3.785 L
	1 liter (l or L)	= 1000 milliliters	1 L = 0.264 gallons	1 quart = 0.946 L
			1 L = 1.057 quarts	
	1 milliliter (ml or mL)	= 10^{-3} liter	1 mL = 0.034 fluid ounce	1 quart = 946 mL
		= 1 cubic centimeter	1 mL = approx. 1/4 teaspoon	1 pint = 473 mL
				1 fluid ounce = 29.57 mL
			1 mL = approx. 15-16 drops (gtt.)	1 teaspoon = approx. 5 mL
	1 microliter (μl or μL)	= 10^{-6} liter (10^{-3} milliliters)		
Time	1 second (s)	= 1/60 minute		
	1 millisecond (ms)	= 10^{-3} second		
Temperature	Degrees Celsius (°C) (Absolute zero, when all molecular motion ceases, is − 273°C. The Kelvin [K] scale, which has the same size degrees as Celsius, has its zero point at absolute zero. Thus, 0°K = −273°C.)		°F = 9/5°C + 32	°C = 5/9 (°F − 32)

APPENDIX **D**

A Comparison of the Light Microscope and the Electron Microscope

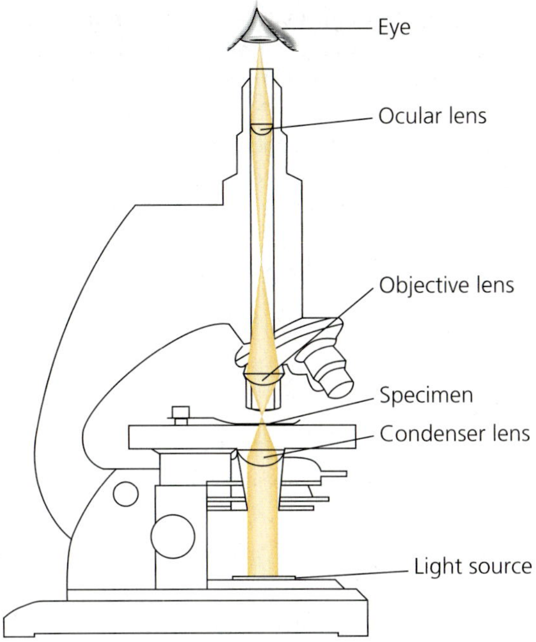

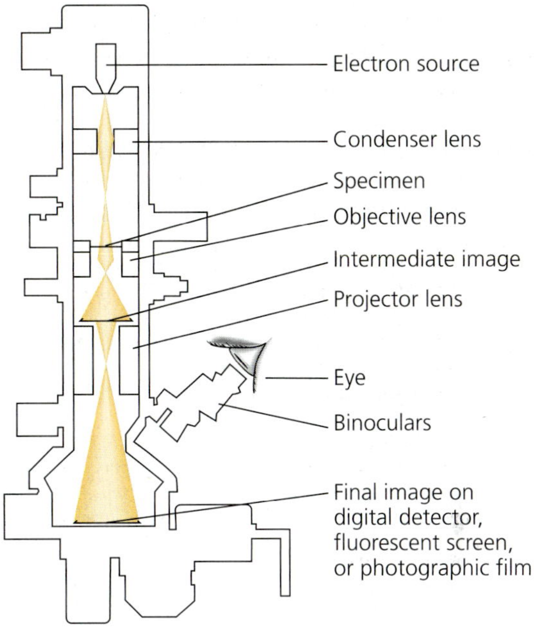

Light Microscope

In light microscopy, light is focused on a specimen by a glass condenser lens; the image is then magnified by an objective lens and an ocular lens, for projection on the eye, digital camera, digital video camera, or photographic film.

Electron Microscope

In electron microscopy, a beam of electrons (top of the microscope) is used instead of light, and electromagnets are used instead of glass lenses. The electron beam is focused on the specimen by a condenser lens; the image is magnified by an objective lens and a projector lens for projection on a digital detector, fluorescent screen, or photographic film.

APPENDIX E Classification of Life

This appendix presents a taxonomic classification for the major extant groups of organisms discussed in this text; not all phyla are included. The classification presented here is based on the three-domain system, which assigns the two major groups of prokaryotes, bacteria and archaea, to separate domains (with eukaryotes making up the third domain). This classification contrasts with the traditional five-kingdom system, which groups all prokaryotes in a single kingdom, Monera. Systematists no longer recognize the kingdom Monera because it would have members in two different domains (see Chapter 26).

Various alternative classification schemes are discussed in Unit Five of the text. The taxonomic turmoil includes debates about the number and boundaries of kingdoms and about the alignment of the Linnaean classification hierarchy with the findings of modern cladistic analysis. In this review, asterisks (*) indicate currently recognized phyla thought by some systematists to be paraphyletic.

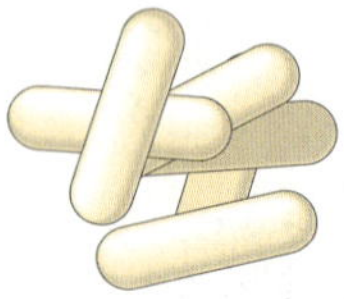

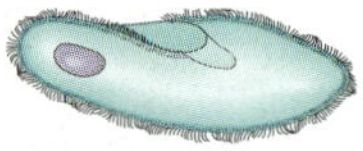

DOMAIN BACTERIA

- **Proteobacteria**
- **Chlamydia**
- **Spirochetes**
- **Gram-positive Bacteria**
- **Cyanobacteria**

DOMAIN ARCHAEA

- **Korarchaeota**
- **Euryarchaeota**
- **Crenarchaeota**
- **Nanoarchaeota**

DOMAIN EUKARYA

In the phylogenetic hypothesis we present in Chapter 28, major clades of eukaryotes are grouped together in the five "supergroups" listed below in bold type. The traditional five-kingdom classification scheme united all the eukaryotes generally called protists in a single kingdom, Protista. However, advances in systematics have made it clear that Protista is in fact polyphyletic: Some protists are more closely related to plants, fungi, or animals than they are to other protists. As a result, the kingdom Protista has been abandoned. In contrast, the kingdoms Plantae (land plants), Fungi, and Animalia (animals) have survived from the five-kingdom system.

Excavata

- Diplomonadida (diplomonads)
- Parabasala (parabasalids)
- Euglenozoa (euglenozoans)
    - Euglenophyta (euglenids)
    - Kinetoplastida (kinetoplastids)

Chromalveolata

- Alveolata (alveolates)
    - Dinoflagellata (dinoflagellates)
    - Apicomplexa (apicomplexans)
    - Ciliophora (ciliates)
- Stramenopila (stramenopiles)
    - Bacillariophyta (diatoms)
    - Chrysophyta (golden algae)
    - Phaeophyta (brown algae)
    - Oomycota (water molds)

Archaeplastida

- Rhodophyta (red algae)
- Chlorophyta (green algae: chlorophytes)
- Charophyceae (green algae: charophyceans)
- Plantae

Phylum Hepatophyta (liverworts) Phylum Anthocerophyta (hornworts) Phylum Bryophyta (mosses)	Bryophytes (nonvascular plants)	
Phylum Lycophyta (lycophytes) Phylum Pterophyta (ferns, horsetails, whisk ferns)	Seedless vascular plants	
Phylum Ginkgophyta (ginkgo) Phylum Cycadophyta (cycads) Phylum Gnetophyta (gnetophytes) Phylum Coniferophyta (conifers)	Gymnosperms	Seed plants
Phylum Anthophyta (flowering plants)	Angiosperms	Seed plants

Rhizaria

- ► Chlorarachniophyta (chlorarachniophytes)
- ► Foraminifera (forams)
- ► Radiolaria (radiolarians)

Unikonta

- ► Amoebozoa (amoebozoans)
  - Myxogastrida (plasmodial slime molds)
  - Dictyostelida (cellular slime molds)
  - Gymnamoeba (gymnamoebas)
  - Entamoeba (entamoebas)
  - Nucleariida (nucleariids)

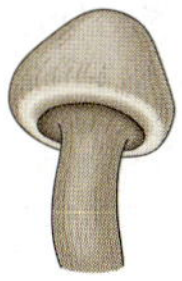

- ► Fungi
  - *Phylum Chytridiomycota (chytrids)
  - Phylum Zygomycota (zygomycetes)
  - Phylum Glomeromycota (glomeromycetes)
  - Phylum Ascomycota (sac fungi)
  - Phylum Basidiomycota (club fungi)
- ► Choanoflagellata (choanoflagellates)

- ► Animalia
  - Phylum Calcarea } (sponges)
  - Phylum Silicea } (sponges)
  - Phylum Cnidaria (cnidarians)
    - Class Hydrozoa (hydrozoans)
    - Class Scyphozoa (jellies)
    - Class Cubozoa (box jellies and sea wasps)
    - Class Anthozoa (sea anemones and most corals)
  - Phylum Ctenophora (comb jellies)
  - Phylum Acoela (acoel flatworms)
  - Lophotrochozoa (lophotrochozoans)
    - Phylum Placozoa (placozoans)
    - Phylum Kinorhyncha (kinorhynchs)
    - Phylum Platyhelminthes (flatworms)
      - Class Turbellaria (free-living flatworms)
      - Class Trematoda (flukes)
      - Class Monogenea (monogeneans)
      - Class Cestoda (tapeworms)
    - Phylum Nemertea (proboscis worms)
    - Phylum Ectoprocta (ectoprocts)
    - Phylum Phoronida (phoronids)
    - Phylum Brachiopoda (brachiopods)
    - Phylum Rotifera (rotifers)
    - Phylum Cycliophora (cycliophorans)
    - Phylum Mollusca (molluscs)
      - Class Polyplacophora (chitons)
      - Class Gastropoda (gastropods)
      - Class Bivalvia (bivalves)
      - Class Cephalopoda (cephalopods)
  - Ecdysozoa (ecdysozoans)
    - Phylum Annelida (segmented worms)
      - Class Oligochaeta (oligochaetes)
      - Class Polychaeta (polychaetes)
      - Class Hirudinea (leeches)
    - Phylum Acanthocephala (spiny-headed worms)
    - Phylum Loricifera (loriciferans)
    - Phylum Priapula (priapulans)
    - Phylum Nematoda (roundworms)
    - Phylum Arthropoda (This survey groups arthropods into a single phylum, but some zoologists now split the arthropods into multiple phyla.)
      - Subphylum Cheliceriformes (horseshoe crabs, arachnids)
      - Subphylum Myriapoda (millipedes, centipedes)
      - Subphylum Hexapoda (insects, springtails)
      - Subphylum Crustacea (crustaceans)
    - Phylum Tardigrada (tardigrades)
    - Phylum Onychophora (velvet worms)
  - Deuterostomia (deuterostomes)
    - Phylum Hemichordata (hemichordates)
    - Phylum Echinodermata (echinoderms)
      - Class Asteroidea (sea stars)
      - Class Ophiuroidea (brittle stars)
      - Class Echinoidea (sea urchins and sand dollars)
      - Class Crinoidea (see lilies)
      - Class Concentricycloidea (sea daisies)
      - Class Holothuroidea (sea cucumbers)
    - Phylum Chordata (chordates)
      - Subphylum Cephalochordata (cephalochordates: lancelets)
      - Subphylum Urochrodata (urochordates: tunicates)
      - Subphylum Craniata (craniates)
        - Class Myxini (hagfishes)
        - Vertebrates:
          - Class Cephalaspidomorphi (lampreys)
          - Class Chondrichthyes (sharks, rays, chimaeras)
          - Class Acinopterygii (ray-finned fishes)
          - Class Actinistia (coelacanths)
          - Class Dipnoi (lungfishes)
          - Class Amphibia (amphibians)
          - Class Reptilia (tuataras, lizards, snakes, turtles, crocodilians, birds)
          - Class Mammalia (mammals)

Credits

Credits

PHOTO CREDITS

Cover Image Chris Fox/Corbis

Unit Opening Interviews **Unit One** Stuart Brinin; **Unit Two** Zach Veilleux, Rockefeller University; **Unit Three** Maria Nemchuk; **Unit Four** Justin Ide; **Unit Five** Brent Nicastro; **Unit Six** Noah Berger Photography; **Unit Seven** Skeeter Hagler; **Unit Eight** William A. Cotton, Colorado State University.

Detailed Contents **Unit One** David A. Bushnell. **Unit Two** Albert Tousson, High Resolution Imaging Facility, University of Alabama at Birmingham. **Unit Three** Kosman D, Mizutani CM, Lemons D, Cox WG, McGinnis W, Bier E. Multiplex detection of RNA expression in Drosophila embryos. Science. 2004 Aug 6;305(5685):846; Fig 1. **Unit Four** Olivier Grunewald. **Unit Five** Ray Watson, canadianphotography.ca. **Unit Six** Pierre-Michel Blais, orchidees.provence.free.fr. **Unit Seven** Michael Nichols/National Geographic/Getty Images. **Unit Eight** Galen Rowell/Corbis.

Chapter 1 **1.1** Chris Fox/Corbis; **1.2** Henri and Käthi Oertli; **1.3.1** Fred Bavendam/Minden Pictures; **1.3.2** Kim Taylor and Jane Burton/Dorling Kindersley; **1.3.3** Frans Lanting/Minden Pictures; **1.3.4** Frans Lanting/Minden Pictures; **1.3.5** Michael & Patricia Fogden/Corbis; **1.3.6** Joe McDonald/Corbis; **1.3.7** ImageState/International Stock Photography Ltd.; **1.4.1** WorldSat International/Photo Researchers, Inc.; **1.4.2** Bill Brooks/Alamy; **1.4.3** Mark Raycroft/Minden Pictures, and Dave McShaffrey, Marietta College, Ohio; **1.4.4** Michael Orton/Photographer's Choice/Getty Images; **1.4.5** Ross M. Horowitz/Iconica/Getty Images; **1.4.6** Photodisc/Getty Images; **1.4.7** Jeremy Burgess/SPL/Photo Researchers; **1.4.8** Manfred Kage/Peter Arnold, Inc.; **1.4.9** E.H. Newcomb & W.P. Wergin/Biological Photo Service; **1.5** Shin Yoshino/Minden Pictures; **1.6a** PhotoLink/Photodisc/Getty Images; **1.6b** Janice Sheldon; **1.6c** T. D. Parsons, D. Kleinfeld, F. Raccuia-Behling and B. Salzberg. Biophysical Journal, July 1989. Photo courtesy of Brian Salzberg; **1.7** Conly L. Rieder, Ph.D.; **1.8.1** S. C. Holt/Biological Photo Service; **1.8.2** Visuals Unlimited; **1.9** Camille Tokerud/Stone/Getty Images; **1.10a** Photodisc/Getty Images; **1.11** Roy Kaltschmidt, Lawrence Berkeley National Laboratory; **1.12** Giot L, Bader JS, Brouwer C, Chaudhuri A, Kuang B, Li Y, Hao YL, Ooi CE, Godwin B, Vitols E, Vijayadamodar G, Pochart P, Machineni H, Welsh M, Kong Y, Zerhusen B, Malcolm R, Varrone Z, Collis A, Minto M, Burgess S, McDaniel L, Stimpson E, Spriggs F, Williams J, Neurath K, Ioime N, Agee M, Voss E, Furtak K, Renzulli R, Aanensen N, Carrolla S, Bickelhaupt E, Lazovatsky Y, DaSilva A, Zhong J, Stanyon CA, Finley RL Jr, White KP, Braverman M, Jarvie T, Gold S, Leach M, Knight J, Shimkets RA, McKenna MP, Chant J, Rothberg JM. A protein interaction map of Drosophila melanogaster. Science. 2003 Dec 5; 302 (5651): 1727-36; Fig. 4b. Image supplied by Joel S. Bader; **1.15a** Oliver Meckes/Nicole Ottawa/Photo Researchers; **1.15b** Ralph Robinson/Visuals Unlimited; **1.15c left to right** D. P. Wilson/Photo Researchers; Peter Lilja/Taxi/Getty Images; Kunst & Scheidulin/AGE Fotostock; Anup Shah/Nature Picture Library; **1.16.1** VVG/SPL/Photo Researchers; **1.16.2** Omikron/Photo Researchers; **1.16.3** W. L. Dentler, University of Kansas/Biological Photo Services; **1.17** Mike Hettwer/Project Exploration; **1.18** Archiv/Photo Researchers; **1.19.1** Michael P. Fogden/Bruce Coleman Inc./Alamy; **1.19.2** Michael & Patricia Fogden/Minden Pictures **1.19.3** Hal Horwitz/Corbis; **1.21** Frank Greenaway/Dorling Kindersley; **1.23.1** Karl Ammann/Corbis; **1.23.2** Tim Ridley/Dorling Kindersley; **1.25.1** Breck P. Kent; **1.25.2** E R Degginger; **1.26** David Pfennig; **1.29** Gloria M. Coruzzi, Professor of Biology, New York University; **1.30** Stone/Getty Images. **Chapter 2** **2.1** Martin Dohrn/BBC Natural History Unit; **2.2** Martin Dohrn/BBC Natural History Unit; **2.3** Chip Clark; **2.4a** Grant Heilman/Grant Heilman Photography; **2.4b** Ivan Polunin/Bruce Coleman Inc.; **2.6** Clayton T Hamilton, Stanford University; **2.7** CTI Molecular Imaging, Inc.; **p. 41** Jerry Young/Dorling Kindersley; **2.19** Runk/Schoenberg/Grant Heilman, Inc.; **p. 45** E. R. Degginger/Color-Pic, Inc. **Chapter 3** **3.1** NASA/Johnson Space Center; **3.3** R. Kessel-Shih/Visuals Unlimited; **3.4** Charles S. Lewallen; **3.6** Flip Nicklin/Minden Pictures; **3.10** Oliver Strewe/Stone Allstock/Getty Images; **3.11** Raena M. Cota; **inset** DeLois Galleciez; **p. 57** Kargel JS. Planetary science. Proof for water, hints of life? Science. 2004 Dec 3; 306(5702):1689-91; Fig. E and O. **Chapter 4** **4.1** Mark Moffett/Minden Pictures; **4.6a** Manfred Kage/Peter Arnold, Inc. **Chapter 5** **5.1** Lester Lefkowitz/Corbis; **5.6a** John N. A. Lott/Biological Photo Service; **5.6b** H. Shio and P. B. Lazarow; **5.8.1** Photodisc/Getty Images; **5.8.2** Manfred Kage/Peter Arnold, Inc.; **5.8.3** J. Litray/Visuals Unlimited; **5.9.1** Photodisc/Getty Images **5.9.2** T. J. Beveridge/Visuals Unlimited; **5.10b** F. Collet/Photo Researchers; **5.10c** Corbis; **5.12a** Dorling Kindersley; **5.12b** Corbis; **5.20** Tulip WR, Varghese JN, Laver WG, Webster RG, Colman PM. Refined crystal structure of the influenza virus N9 neuraminidase-NC41 Fab complex. J Mol Biol. 1992 Sep 5;227(1):122-48; **5.21** Wolfgang Kaehler; **5.22** Eye of Science/Photo Researchers; **5.24** Reprinted by permission from Nature. P. B. Sigler from Z. Xu, A. L. Horwich, and P. B. Sigler. 388:741-750 Copyright (c) 1997 Macmillan Magazines Limited; **5.25.1** Cramer P, Bushnell DA, Fu J, Gnatt AL, Maier-Davis B, Thompson NE, Burgess RR, Edwards AM, David PR, Kornberg RD. Architecture of RNA polymerase II and implications for the transcription mechanism.Science. 2000 Apr 28;288(5466):640-9; Fig. 3. Image supplied by David Bushnell; **5.25.2** David A. Bushnell. **Chapter 6** **6.1** Albert Tousson, High Resolution Imaging Facility, University of Alabama at Birmingham; **6.3.1** Biophoto Associates/Photo Researchers; **6.3.2** Ed Reschke; **6.3.3** David M. Phillips/Visuals Unlimited; **6.3.4** David M. Phillips/Visuals Unlimited; **6.3.5** Molecular Probes, Inc.; **6.3.6** Karl Garsha; **6.3.7** Karl Garsha; **6.4** William Dentler/Biological Photo Service; **6.6b** S. C. Holt, University of Texas Health Center/Biological Photo Service; **6.7a** Daniel S. Friend; **6.10.1** Reproduced by permission from L.Orci and A.Perelet, Freeze-Etch Histology. (Heidelberg: Springer-Veerlag, 1975). Copyright (c)1975 by Springer-Verlag GmbH & Co KG; **6.10.2** Reproduced by permission from A. C. Faberge, Cell Tiss. Res. 151 Copyright (c) 1974 by Springer-Verlag GmbH & Co KG; **6.10.3** Reprinted by permission from Nature 323. U. Aebi et al. Copyright (c) 1996: 560-564, figure 1a. Used with permission. Macmillan Magazines Limited; **6.11** D. W. Fawcett/Photo Researchers; **6.12** R. Bolender, D. Fawcett/Photo Researchers; **6.13** Don Fawcett/Visuals Unlimited; **6.14** Daniel S. Friend; **6.15** E. H. Newcomb; **6.17** Daniel S. Friend; **6.18** E.H. Newcomb & W.P. Wergin/Biological Photo Service; **6.19** From S. E. Fredrick and E. H. Newcomb, The Journal of Cell Biology 43 (1969): 343; **6.20** John E. Heuser, M.D., Washington University School of Medicine, St. Louis, Missouri; **6.21b** B. J. Schapp et al., 1985, Cell 40:455; p. 113 **left to right** Dr. Mary Osborn, Dr. Frank Solomon, Mark S. Ladinsky, and J. Richard McIntosh, University of Colorado; **6.22** Kent L. McDonald; **6.23a** Biophoto Associates/Photo Researchers; **6.23b** Meckes/Ottawa/Eye of Science/Photo Researchers, Inc.; **6.24.1** Omikron/Science Source/Photo Researchers; **6.24.2** W. L. Dentler/Biological Photo Service; **6.24.3** Linck RW, Stephens RE. Functional protofilament numbering of ciliary, flagellar, and centriolar microtubules. Cell Motil Cytoskeleton. 2007 Jul;64(7):489-95; cover. Micrograph by D. Woodrum Hensley; **6.26** From Hirokawa Nobutaka, The Journal of Cell Biology 94 (1982): 425. Fig.1. Reproduced by copyright permission of The Rockefeller University Press; **6.28** G. F. Leedale/Photo Researchers; **6.29** Paredez AR, Somerville CR, Ehrhardt DW. Visualization of Cellulose Synthase Demonstrates Functional Association with Microtubules. Science. 2006 Jun 9; 312 (5779): 1491-5; Fig. 2; **6.31** Micrograph by W. P. Wergin, provided by E. H. Newcomb; **6.32.1** From Douglas J. Kelly, The Journal of Cell Biology 28 (1966): 51. Fig.17. Reproduced by copyright permission of The Rockefeller University Press; **6.32.2** Reproduced by permission from L. Orci and A. Perrelet, Freeze-Etch Histology. (Heidelberg: Springer-Verlag). Copyright (c) 1975 by Springer-Verlag GmbH & Co KG; **6.32.3** From C. Peracchia and A. F. Dulhunty, The Journal of Cell Biology 70 (1976): 419. Fig. 6 Reproduced by copyright permission of The Rockefeller University Press; **6.33** Lennart Nilsson/Albert Bonniers Forlag; **p 123** E. H. Newcomb; p. 123 From S. E. Fredrick and E. H. Newcomb, The Journal of Cell Biology 43 (1969): 343. **Chapter 7** **7.1** Long SB, Campbell EB, Mackinnon R. Crystal structure of a mammalian voltage-dependent Shaker family K^+ channel. Science. 2005 Aug 5;309 (5736):897-903; cover; **7.4** D. W. Fawcett/Photo Researchers, Inc.; **7.14** Cabisco/Visuals Unlimited; **7.20.1** H. S. Pankratz, T.C. Beaman & P. Gerhardt/Biological Photo Service; **7.20.2** D. W. Fawcett/Photo Researchers, Inc.; **7.20.3** M. M. Perry & A. B. Gilbert, J. Cell Science 39(1979):257 (c) 1979 by the Company of Biologists Ltd; **7.20.4** M. M. Perry & A. B. Gilbert, J. Cell Science 39 (1979):257 (c) 1979 by the Company of Biologists Ltd. **Chapter 8** **8.1** Jean-Marie Bassot/Photo Researchers, Inc.; **8.2** David W. Hamilton/Getty Images, Inc.; **8.3a** Joe McDonald/Corbis; **8.3b** Manoj Shah/Getty Images, Inc.; **8.4** Brian Capon; **8.16** Thomas A. Steitz, Yale University; **8.21** Scheer JM, Romanowski MJ, Wells JA. A common allosteric site and mechanism in caspases. Proc Natl Acad Sci U S A. 2006 May 16;103(20): 7595-600; Fig. 4a; **8.23** Nicolae Simionescu. **Chapter 9** **9.1** Frans Lanting/Minden Pictures. **Chapter 10** **10.1** Bob Rowan, Progressive Image/Corbis;

10.2a Jim Brandenburg/Minden Pictures; **10.2b** Bob Evans/Peter Arnold, Inc.; **10.2c** Michael Abbey/Visuals Unlimited; **10.2d** Susan M. Barns, Ph.D.; **10.2e** National Library of Medicine; **10.3.1** M. Eichelberger/Visuals Unlimited; **10.3.2** Courtesy of W.P. Wergin and E.H. Newcomb, University of Wisconsin/BPS; **10.11** Christine Case, Skyline College; **10.20a** David Muench/Corbis; **10.20b** Dave Bartruff/Corbis. **Chapter 11** **11.1** CrystalGenomics, Inc.; **11.3.1** Dale Kaiser; **11.3.2** Kuner JM, Kaiser D. Fruiting body morphogenesis in submerged cultures of Myxococcus xanthus. J Bacteriol. 1982 Jul;151(1):458-61. By permission of ASM; **11.16** Matheos D, Metodiev M, Muller E, Stone D, Rose MD.Pheromone-induced polarization is dependent on the Fus3p MAPK acting through the formin Bni1p. J Cell Biol. 2004 Apr;165(1):99-109; Fig. 9; **11.19** Dr. Gopal Murti/Visuals Unlimited; **11.21** Development 127, 5245-5252 (2000). Mesenchymal cells engulf and clear apoptotic footplate cells in macrophageless PU. 1 null mouse embryos. William Wood, Mark Turmaine, Roberta Weber, Victoria Camp, Richard A. Maki, Scott R. McKercher and Paul Martin. **Chapter 12** **12.1** Jan-Michael Peters/Silke Hauf; **12.2a** Biophoto Associates/Photo Researchers, Inc.; **12.2b** C.R. Wyttenback/Biological Photo Service; **12.2c** Biophoto/Science Source/Photo Researchers, Inc.; **12.3** John Murray; **12.4** Biophoto/Photo Researchers, Inc.; **12.6** Conly L. Rieder; **12.7.1** J. Richard McIntosh, University of Colorado at Boulder; **12.7.2** Reproduced by permission from Matthew Schibler, from Protoplasma 137. Copyright (c) 1987: 29-44 by Springer-Verlag GmbH & Co KG; **12.9a** David M. Phillips/Visuals Unlimited; **12.9b** B. A. Palevitz, Courtesy of E. H. Newcomb, University of Wisconsin; **12.10** Carolina Biological Supply/Phototake NYC; **12.18** Guenter Albrecht-Buehler, Ph.D.; **12.19** Lan Bo Chen; p. 245 Carolina Biological Supply/Phototake NYC. **Chapter 13** **13.1** Steve Granitz/WireImage; **13.2a** Roland Birke/OKAPIA/ Photo Researchers; **13.2b** Robert Nessler; **13.3.1** Veronique Burger/Phanie Agency/Photo Researchers; **13.3.2** CNRI/Photo Researchers; **13.12** Petronczki M, Siomos MF, Nasmyth K. Un menage a quatre: the molecular biology of chromosome segregation in meiosis. Cell. 2003 Feb 21;112(4):423-40; Fig. 5a. **Chapter 14** **14.1** Mendel Museum, Augustinian Abbey, Brno; **14.14.1** altrendo nature/Getty Images; **14.14.2** Corbis; **14.15 top** Photodisc/Getty Images; **14.15 bottom** Anthony Loveday; **14.16** Rick Guidotti for Positive Exposure; **14.17** Dick Zimmerman/Shooting Star; **p 285** Norma Jubinville. **Chapter 15** **15.1** Peter Lichter and David Ward, Science 247 (1990). Copyright 1990 American Association for the Advancemcent of Science; **15.3** Cabisco/Visuals Unlimited; **15.5** Andrew Syred/Photo Researchers; **15.8** Dave King/Dorling Kindersley; **15.14** Milton H. Gallardo; **15.16.1** Lauren Shear/SPL/Photo Researchers; **15.16.2** CNRI/SPL/Photo Researchers; **p 301** Koichi Kamoshida/Getty Images; **15.19** Ken Wagner/Phototake NYC. **p 304** James K. Adams, Biology, Dalton State College, Dalton, Georgia. **Chapter 16** **16.1** National Institute of Health; **16.3** Oliver Meckes/Photo Researchers; **16.6a** Courtesy of the Library of Congress; **16.6b** From the Double Helix: by James D. Watson, Atheneum Press, N. Y., 1968, p. 215. (c) 1968. Courtesy CSHL Archive; **16.7c** Richard Wagner; **16.12a** Jerome Vinograd; **16.12b** From D. J. Burks and P. J. Stambrook, The Journal of Cell Biology 77 (1978). 762, fig.6 by copyright permission of The Rockefeller University Press. Photo provided by P. J. Stambrook; **16.20** Peter Lansdorp/Terry Fox Laboratory; **16.21.1** S. C. Holt. University of Texas, Health Science Center, San Antonio/Biological Photo Service; **16.21.2** Dr. Victoria E. Foe; **16.21.3** Barbara Hamkalo; **16.21.4** From J. R. Paulsen and U. K. Laemmli, Cell 12 (1977):817-828; **16.21.5** National Museum of Health and Medicine/Armed Forces Institute of Pathology; **16.22** Ivanovska I, Khandan T, Ito K and Orr-Weaver TL. A histone code in meiosis: the histone kinase, NHK-1, is required for proper chromosomal architecture in Drosophila oocytes. Genes & Development. 2005; 192571-2582; **p 324** Courtesy of J. Wang and T. A. Steitz, modified from J. Wang et al., Cell (1997) 89:1087-1099. (c)Cell Press. **Chapter 17** **17.1** DDP; **17.6a** Keith V. Wood, University of California, San Diego; **17.6b** Associated Press; **17.15** M. A. Rould, J.J. Perona, P. Vogt, and T.A. Steitz, Science 246 (1 December 1989): cover. Copyright 1989 by the American Association for the Advancement of Science. Thomas A. Steitz, Yale University; **17.16a** Joachim Frank; **17.20** B. Hamkalo and O. Miller, Jr; **17.24** Reproduced with permission from O. L. Miller, Jr., B. A. Hamkalo, and C. A. Thomas, Jr., Science 169 (1970): 392. Copyright (c)1970 American Association for the Advancement of Science. Fig# 3. **Chapter 18** **18.1** Cook O, Biehs B, Bier E. Brinker and optomotor-blind act coordinately to initiate development of the L5 wing vein primordium in Drosophila. Development. 2004 May;131(9):2113-24; **18.14a** Carolina Biological/ Visuals Unlimited; **18.14b** Hans Pfletschinger/Peter Arnold, Inc.; **18.18** F. Rudolf Turner, Indiana University; **18.19.1** Wolfgang Driever, University of Freiburg, Freiburg, Germany; **18.19.2** Wolfgang Driever, University of Freiburg, Freiburg, Germany; **18.19.3** Dr. Ruth Lahmann, The Whitehead Institution; **18.19.4** Dr. Ruth Lahmann, The Whitehead Institution; **18.23** University of Washington. **Chapter 19** **19.1** Science Photo Library/Photo Researchers; **19.2** Peter von Sengbusch/Botanik; **19.3.1** Robley C. Williams/Biological Photo Service; **19.3.2** R.C. Valentine and H.G. Pereira, J. Mol. Biol/Biological Photo Service; **19.3.3** K.G. Murti/Visuals Unlimited; **19.3.4** Robley C. Williams/Biological Photo Service; **19.8** C. Dauguet/Institute Pasteur/Photo Researchers; **19.9.1** National Museum of Health and Medicine, Armed Forces Institute of Pathology, Washington, DC (NCP 1603); **19.9.2** Eye of Science/Photo Researchers, Inc.; **19.9.3** Ryan Pyle/Corbis; **19.10.1** Thomas A. Zitter; **19.10.2** Dennis E. Mayhew; **19.10.3** Science VU/Wayside/Visuals Unlimited. **Chapter 20** **20.1** Reproduced with permission from R.F. Service, Science (1998) 282:396-3999. Copyright 1998 American Association for the Advancement of Science. Incyte Pharmaceuticals, Inc., Palo Alto, CA; **20.5c** L. Brent Selinger, Department of Biological Sciences, University of Lethbridge, Alberta, Canada; **20.9** Repligen Corporation; **20.14** Kosman D, Mizutani CM, Lemons D, Cox WG, McGinnis W, Bier E. Multiplex detection of RNA expression in Drosophila embryos. Science. 2004 Aug 6;305(5685):846; Fig 1; **20.15** Reproduced with permission from R.F. Service, Science (1998) 282:396-3999. Copyright 1998 American Association for the Advancement of Science. Incyte Pharmaceuticals, Inc., Palo Alto, CA; **20.19** Pat Sullivan/Associated Press; **20.23** Brad DeCecco; **20.24a** Steve Helber/ Associated Press. **Chapter 21** **21.1** Yann Arthus-Bertrand/Corbis; **21.5** Giot L, Bader JS, Brouwer C, Chaudhuri A, Kuang B, Li Y, Hao YL, Ooi CE, Godwin B, Vitols E, Vijayadamodar G, Pochart P, Machineni H, Welsh M, Kong Y, Zerhusen B, Malcolm R, Varrone Z, Collis A, Minto M, Burgess S, McDaniel L, Stimpson E, Spriggs F, Williams J, Neurath K, Ioime N, Agee M, Voss E, Furtak K, Renzulli R, Aanensen N, Carrolla S, Bickelhaupt E, Lazovatsky Y, DaSilva A, Zhong J, Stanyon CA, Finley RL Jr, White KP, Braverman M, Jarvie T, Gold S, Leach M, Knight J, Shimkets RA, McKenna MP, Chant J, Rothberg JM. A protein interaction map of Drosophila melanogaster. Science. 2003 Dec 5; 302 (5651): 1727-36, Fig. 4b. Image supplied by Joel S. Bader; **21.6** Affymetrix; **21.8.1** AP Wide World Photos; **21.8.2** Courtesy of Virginia Walbot, Stanford University; **21.10a** Courtesy of O. L. Miller Jr., Dept. of Biology, University of Virginia; **21.16** Shu W, Cho JY, Jiang Y, Zhang M, Weisz D, Elder GA, Schmeidler J, De Gasperi R, Sosa MA, Rabidou D, Santucci AC, Perl D, Morrisey E, Buxbaum JD. Altered ultrasonic vocalization in mice with a disruption in the Foxp2 gene. : Proc Natl Acad Sci U S A. 2005 Jul 5;102(27):9643-8; Fig. 3. Image supplied by Joseph Buxbaum. **Chapter 22** **22.1** Olivier Grunewald; **22.4** Michael S. Yamashita/Corbis; **22.5.1** Archiv/Photo Researchers; **22.5.2** National Maritime Museum Picture Library, London, England; **22.6 all** Tui De Roy/Minden Pictures; **22.7** Darwin's Tree of life sketch, MS.DAR.121:p.36. Reproduced with the permission of the Cambridge University Library; **22.9** Jack Wilburn/Animals Animals/Earth Scenes; **22.10** Wil Meinderts/FOTO NATURA/Minden Pictures; **22.11** Richard Packwood/Oxfor Scientific/Jupiter Images; **22.12a** Edward S. Ross, California Academy of Sciences; **22.12b** Michael & Patricia Fogden/Minden Pictures; **22.15** Mark Webster, Department of the Geophysical Sciences. University of Chicago; **22.18.1** Dwight R. Kuhn Photography; **22.18.2** Lennart Nilsson/Albert Bonniers Forlag AB. **Chapter 23** **23.1** Grant PR, Grant BR. Evolution of character displacement in Darwin's finches. Science. 2006 Jul 14;313(5784):224-6; Fig. 1a; **23.2a** Greene, E. A diet-induced developmental polymorphism in a caterpillar. Science. 1989. 243:643-646. Photo by Erick Greene; **23.2b** Erick Greene; **23.3a** Steve Gorton/Dorling Kindersley; **23.3b** Janice Britton-Davidian, ISEM, UMR 5554 CNRS, Universite Montpellier II. Reprinted by permission from Nature, Vol.403, 13 January 2000, p. 158 Copyright (c) 2000 Macmillan Magazines Limited; **23.4** New York State Department of Environmental Conservation; **23.5.1** Michio Hosino/Minden Pictures; **23.5.2** James L. Davis/ProWildlife; **23.10a** William Ervin/Photo Researchers, Inc.; **23.11** 1993 Time Magazine cover/TimePix; **23.12** J. Antonovics/Visuals Unlimited; **23.14a** Fred Bavendam/Minden Pictures; **23.14b** John Visser/Bruce Coleman USA; **23.15** Frans Lanting/Minden Pictures; **23.16a** Allison M. Welch, College of Charleston, South Carolina; **23.18** Dr. Michio Hori, Kyoto University; **23.19** Merlin D. Tuttle, Bat Conservation International. **Chapter 24** **24.1** George Harrison/Grant Heilman Photography, Inc.; **24.2a1** John Shaw/Tom Stack & Associates, Inc.; **24.2a2** Don & Pat Valenti/Tom Stack & Associates, Inc.; **24.2b1** Zefa/Corbis; **24.2b2** Photodisc/Getty Images; **24.2b3** Photodisc/Getty Images; **24.2b4** Photodisc/Getty Images; **24.2b5** Photodisc/Getty Images; **24.2b6** Masterfile; **24.3** Graeme Chapman; **24.4a** Joe McDonald/Bruce Coleman Inc.; **24.4b** Joe McDonald/Corbis; **24.4c** USDA/APHIS/Animal and Plant Health Inspection Service; **24.4d** Stephen Krasemann/Photo Researchers; **24.4e** Barbara Gerlach/Tom Stack & Associates, Inc.; **24.4f** Ueshima R, Asami T. Evolution: single-gene speciation by left-right reversal. Nature. 2003 Oct 16;425(6959):679; Fig. 1; **24.4g** William E. Ferguson; **24.4h** Charles W. Brown; **24.4i** Photodisc/Getty Images; **24.4j** Ralph A. Reinhold/Animals Animals/Earth Scenes; **24.4k** Grant Heilman/Grant Heilman Photography, Inc.; **24.4l** Kazutoshi Okuno; **24.6.1** Corbis; **24.6.2** John Shaw/Bruce Coleman, Inc.; **24.6.3** Michael Fogden/Bruce Coleman, Inc.; **24.12** Ole Seehausen; **24.13.1** Stephen Dalton/ Animals Animals - Earth Scenes; **24.13.2** ChristopheCorteau/naturepl.com; **24.15.1** Juan Martín Simón; **24.15.2** Melvin Grey/NHPA; **24.16** Ole Seehausen; **24.18a** Jason Rick; **24.19** Ueshima R, Asami T. Evolution: single-gene speciation by left-right reversal. Nature. 2003 Oct 16;425(6959):679; Fig. 1 **24.20** Bradshaw HD, Schemske DW. Allele substitution at a flower colour locus produces a pollinator shift in monkeyflowers. Nature. 2003 Nov 13;426(6963):176-8. **Chapter 25** **25.1** Gerhard Boeggemann; **p 507** William R. Hammer and

ReBecca Hunt, Department of Geology, Augustana College, Rock Island, Illinois; **25.2** George Luther, University of Delaware Graduate College of Marine Studies; **25.3a** Courtesy of F. M. Menger and Kurt Gabrielson, Emory University; **25.4.1a** Mitsuaki Iwago/Minden Pictures; **25.4.1b** S. M. Awramik/Biological Photo Service; **25.4.2** Andrew H. Knoll; **25.4.3** Lisa-Ann Gershwin/University of California-Berkeley, Museum of Paleontology; **25.4.4** Chip Clark, National Museum of Natural History, Smithsonian Institution; **25.4.5** http://www.fossils.eu.com; **25.4.6** Chip Clark; **25.4.7** Seelevel.com; **25.4.8** Specimen No. 12478, Markus Moser, Staatliches Museum für Naturkunde Stuttgart; **25.8** Theodore J. Bornhorst, Michigan Technological University; **25.11** Shuhai Xiao, Tulane University; **25.18.1** Gerald D. Carr;**25.18.2** Gerald D. Carr; **25.18.3** Gerald D. Carr; **25.18.4** Gerald D. Carr; **25.18.5** Gerald D. Carr; **25.18.6** Bruce G. Baldwin; **25.20** Stephen Dalton/Minden Pictures; **25.23** Shapiro MD, Marks ME, Peichel CL, Blackman BK, Nereng KS, Jonsson B, Schluter D, Kingsley DM. Genetic and developmental basis of evolutionary pelvic reduction in threespine sticklebacks.Nature. Erratum. 2006 Feb 23;439(7079):1014; Fig. 1. **Chapter 26** **26.1** Michael & Patricia Fogden/Minden Pictures; **26.2.1** Ryan McVay/Photodisc/Getty Images; **26.2.2** Neil Fletcher/Dorling Kindersley; **26.2.3** Dorling Kindersley; **26.17a** Courtesy Dept. of Library Services, American Museum of Natural History; **26.17b** EdHeck.com; **26.20** John W. Karapelou, CMI/Phototake. **Chapter 27** **27.1** Wayne P. Armstrong; **27.2a** Dr. Dennis Kunkel/Visuals Unlimited; **27.2b** Dr. Dennis Kunkel/Visuals Unlimited; **27.2c** Stem Jems/Photo Researchers; **27.3** Jack Bostrack/Visuals Unlimited; **27.4** Dr. Immo Rantala/SPL/Photo Researchers; **27.5** Fran Heyl Associates; **27.6** Julius Adler; **27.7a** S. W. Watson. ©Journal of Bacteriology, American Society of Microbiology; **27.7b** N.J. Lang/Biological Photo Service; **27.8** Huntington Potter, Byrd Alzheimer's Institute and University of South Florida and David Dressler, Oxford University and Balliol College; **27.9** H.S. Pankratz, T.C. Beaman/Biological Photo Service; **27.12** Dennis Kunkel/Phototake NYC; **27.14** Susan M. Barns, Ph.D.; **27.15** Dr. Tony Brain/Science Photo Library/Photo Researchers; **27.17** Jack Dykinga/Stone/Getty Images; **27.18.1** L. Evans/Biological Photo Service; **27.18.2** Yuichi Suwa; **27.18.3** National Library of Medicine; **27.18.4** Phototake NYC; **27.18.5** Alfred Pasieka/Peter Arnold, Inc.; **27.18.6** Photo Researchers; **27.18.7** Moredon Animal Health/SPL/Photo Researchers; **27.18.8** CNRI/SPL/Photo Researchers; **27.18.9** T.E. Adams/Visuals Unlimited; **27.18.10** Frederick P. Mertz/Visuals Unlimited; **27.18.11** David M. Phillips/Visuals Unlimited; **27.19** Pascale Frey-Klett, Tree-Microbes Interaction Joint Unit, Centre INRA de Nancy; **27.20** Ken Lucas/Biological Photo Service; **27.21.1** Scott Camazine/Photo Researchers; **27.21.2** David M. Phillips/Photo Researchers; **27.21.3** James Marshall/The Image Works; **27.22.1** Seelevel.com; **27.22.2** Mirel™ natural plastics/Metabolix; **27.22.3** Courtesy of Exxon Mobil Corporation. **Chapter 28** **28.1** Moreira D, López-García P. The molecular ecology of microbial eukaryotes unveils a hidden world. Trends Microbiol. 2002 Jan;10(1):31-8; Fig. 4. Photo by Brian S. Leander; **28.3a** Jerome Paulin/Visuals Unlimited; **28.3b** Eric Condliffe/Visuals Unlimited; **28.3c1** Manfred Kage/Peter Arnold, Inc.; **28.3c2** Visuals Unlimited; **28.3d1** Manfred Kage/Peter Arnold, Inc.; **28.3d2** David J. Patterson/microscope; **28.3e** Wim van Egmond/Getty Images; **28.4** David M. Phillips/Visuals Unlimited; **28.5** David J. Patterson; **28.6** Meckes/Ottawa/Photo Researchers, Inc.; **28.7** Michael Abbey/Visuals Unlimited; **28.8** Guy Brugerolle, Universitad Clearmont Ferrand; **28.9** Virginia Institute of Marine Science; **28.10** Masamichi Aikawa, Tokai University School of Medicine, Japan; **28.11** Mike Abbey/Visuals Unlimited; **28.12** Centers for Disease Control & Prevention; **28.13** Eric Condliffe/Visuals Unlimited; **28.14** Stephen Durr; **28.15** Colin Bates, http://www.coastalimageworks.com; **28.16** J.R. Waaland/Biological Photo Service; **28.17** Fred Rhoades; **28.18** Robert Brons/Biological Photo Service; **28.19.1** D. P. Wilson, Eric & David Hosking/Photo Researchers, Inc.; **28.19.2** Michael D. Guiry; **28.19.3** Biophoto Associates/Photo Researchers, Inc.; **28.19.4** Michael Yamashita/IPN/Aurora & Quanta Productions Inc; **28.19.5** David Murray/Dorling Kindersley; **28.20** Gerald and Buff Corsi/Visuals Unlimited; **28.21.1** Laurie Campbell/NHPA; **28.21.2** David L. Ballantine, Department of Marine Sciences, University of Puerto Rico; **28.22** William L. Dentler; **28.24.1** George Barron; **28.24.2** R. Calentine/Visuals Unlimited; **28.25** Robert Kay, MRC Cambridge; **28.26** Kevin Carpenter and Patrick Keeling. **Chapter 29** **29.1** Martin Rugner/AGE Fotostock America, Inc.; **29.2** S. C. Mueller and R. M. Brown, Jr.; **29.3a** Natural Visions; **29.3b** Linda Graham, University of Wisconsin-Madison; **29.5.1** Linda Graham, University of Wisconsin-Madison; **29.5.2** Photo courtesy Karen S. Renzaglia; **29.5.3** Alan S. Heilman; **29.5.4** Michael Clayton; **29.5.5** Barry Runk/Stan/Grant Heilman Photography, Inc.; **29.5.6** Ed Reschke; **29.5.7** Centers for Disease Control & Prevention; **29.6** Charles H. Wellman; **29.8** R. Kessel-Shih/Visuals Unlimited; **29.9.1** Runk/Schoenberger/Grant Heilman Photography, Inc.; **29.9.2** Linda Graham, University of Wisconsin-Madison; **29.9.3** Hidden Forest; **29.9.4** Hidden Forest; **29.9.5** Tony Wharton, Frank Lane Picture Agency/Corbis; **29.11a** Brian Lightfoot/AGE Fotostock America, Inc.; **29.11b** Chris Lisle/Corbis; **29.15.1** Jane Grushow/Grant Heilman Photography, Inc.; **29.15.2** Murray Fagg, Australian National Botanic Gardens; **29.15.3** Helga & Kurt Rasbach; **29.15.4** Barry Runk/Stan/Grant Heilman Photography, Inc.; **29.15.5** Milton Rand/Tom Stack & Associates, Inc.; **29.15.6** Michael Viard/Peter Arnold, Inc.; **29.16** The Open University. **Chapter 30** **30.1** National Museum of Natural History, Smithsonian Institution; **30.5.1** George Louin/Visuals Unlimited; **30.5.3** Grant Heilman Photography, Inc.; **30.5.4** Michael and Patricia Fogden/Minden Pictures; **30.5.5** Thomas Schoepke; **30.5.6** Michael Clayton; **30.5.7** Doug Sokell/Visuals Unlimited; **30.5.8** Raymond Gehman/Corbis; **30.5.9** Adam Jones/Getty Images, Inc.; **30.5.10** David Muench/Corbis; **30.5.11** Gunter Marx, Photography/Corbis; **30.5.12** Jaime Plaza/Wildlight Photo Agency; **30.5.13** Royal Botanic Gardens Sydney; **30.5.14** Kent, Breck P./Animals Animals/Earth Scenes; **30.8.1** Dave King/Dorling Kindersley; **30.8.2** Andy Crawford/Dorling Kindersley; **30.8.3** Dave King/Dorling Kindersley; **30.8.4** Bill Steele/Stone/Getty Images Inc.; **30.8.5** Roger Phillips/Dorling Kindersley; **30.9.1** C. P. George/Visuals Unlimited; **30.9.2** Hans Doeter Brandl, Frank Lane Picture Agency/Corbis; **30.9.3** Scott Camazine/Photo Researchers, Inc.; **30.9.4** Derek Hall/Dorling Kindersley; **30.11a** David L. Dilcher; **30.13.1** Howard Rice/Dorling Kindersley; **30.13.2** Bob & Ann Simpson/Visuals Unlimited; **30.13.3** Stephen McCabe; **30.13.4** Andrew Butler/Dorling Kindersley; **30.13.5** Eric Crichton/Dorling Kindersley; **30.13.6** John Dransfield; **30.13.7** Dorling Kindersley; **30.13.8** Terry W. Eggers/Corbis; **30.13.9** Ed Reschke/Peter Arnold, Inc.; **30.13.10** Matthew Ward/Dorling Kindersley; **30.13.11** Tony Wharton, Frank Lane Picture Agency/Corbis; **30.13.12** Howard Rice/Dorling Kindersley; **30.13.13** Dr. Gerald D. Carr, PhD; **p 633** Dorling Kindersley. **Chapter 31** **31.1** Georg Müller/www.pilzepilze.de; **31.2.1** Hans Reinhard/Taxi/Getty Images; **31.2.2** Fred Rhoades/Mycena Consulting; **31.2.3** Elmer Koneman/Visuals Unlimited; **31.4a** N. Allin & G.L. Barron, University of Guelph/Biological Photo Service; **31.6.1** Jack M. Bostack/Visuals Unlimited; **31.6.2** David Scharf/Peter Arnold, Inc.; **31.7** Stephen J. Kron; **31.9** Dirk Redecker, Robin Kodner, and Linda E. Graham. Glomalean Fungi from the Ordovician. Science 15. September 2000; 289:1920-1921; **31.10** Centers for Disease Control & Prevention; **31.11.1** John Taylor; **31.11.2** Ray Watson, anadianphotography.ca; **31.11.3** Kiers ET, van der Heijden MG. Mutualistic stability in the arbuscular mycorrhizal symbiosis: exploring hypotheses of evolutionary cooperation. Ecology. 2006 Jul;87(7):1627-36; Fig. 1a. Image by Marcel van der Heijden, Swiss Federal Research Station for Agroecology and Agriculture; **31.11.4** Frank Young/Papilio/Corbis; **31.11.5** Phil Dotson/Photo Researchers, Inc.; **31.12** William E. Barstow; **31.13.1** Barry Runk/Stan/Grant Heilman Photography, Inc.; **31.13.2** Barry Runk/Stan/Grant Heilman Photography, Inc.; **31.13.3** Ed Reschke/Peter Arnold, Inc.; **31.13.4** George Barron; **31.14** G.L. Barron, University of Guelph/Biological Photo Service; **31.15** M. F. Brown/Biological Photo Service; **31.16.1** David M. Dennis/Animals Animals/Earth Scenes; **31.16.2** Viard/Jacana/Photo Researchers, Inc.; **31.16c** Matt Springer; **31.17** Fred Spiegel; **31.18.1** Fletcher and Baylis/Photo Researchers, Inc.; **31.18.2** Michael Fogden/DRK Photo; **31.18.3** Konrad Wothe/Minden Pictures; **31.19** Biophoto Associates/Photo Researchers, Inc.; **31.20** Rob Simpson/Visuals Unlimited; **31.22** Mark Moffett/Minden Pictures; **31.23.1** Gerald & Buff Corsi/Visuals Unlimited; **31.23.2** Fritz Polking/Visuals Unlimited; **31.23.3** David Sieren/Visuals Unlimited; **31.24** V. Ahmadijian/Visuals Unlimited; **31.25a** Brad Mogen/Visuals Unlimited; **31.25b** Peter Chadwick/Dorling Kindersley; **31.25c** Robert Calentine/Visuals Unlimited; **31.26** Christine Case/Skyline College. **Chapter 32** **32.1** Jeff Hunter/Image Bank/Getty Images; **32.4a** Dennis Rice, South Australian Museum; **32.4b** James G. Gehling, South Australian Museum; **32.5** J Sibbick, The Natural History Museum, London; **32.6** Wikramanayake AH, Hong M, Lee PN, Pang K, Byrum CA, Bince JM, Xu R, Martindale MQ. An ancient role for nuclear beta-catenin in the evolution of axial polarity and germ layer segregation. Nature. 2003 Nov 27;426(6965): 446-50; Fig. 2, 3 and 4; **32.12** Kent Wood/Photo Researchers, Inc.; **32.13a** Carolina Biological/Visuals Unlimited. **Chapter 33** **33.1** C. Wolcott Henry III/National Geographic/Getty Images; **33.3.1** Andrew J. Martinez/Photo Researchers, Inc.; **33.3.2** Robert Brons/Biological Photo Service; **33.3.3** Stephen Dellaporta; **33.3.4** Gregory G. Dimijian/Photo Researchers, Inc.; **33.3.5** Ed Robinson/Pacific Stock/Photolibrary; **33.3.6** W. I. Walker/Photo Researchers, Inc.; **33.3.7** Colin Milkins/Oxford Scientific Films/Animals Animals/Earth Scenes; **33.3.8** Fred Bavendam/Peter Arnold, Inc.; **33.3.9** Lauritz Jensen/Visuals Unlimited; **33.3.10** Peter Funch; **33.3.11** Erling Svensen/UWPhoto ANS; **33.3.12** Robert Pickett/Papilio/Alamy Images; **33.3.13** Peter Batson/Image Quest Marine; **33.3.14** Reinhart Mobjerg Kristensen; **33.3.15** Erling Svensen/UWPhoto ANS; **33.3.16** Andrew Syred/Photo Researchers, Inc.; **33.3.17** Thomas Stromberg; **33.3.18** Reproduced with permission from A. Eizinger and R. Sommer, Max Planck Institut fur entwicklungsbiologie, Tubingen. Copyright 2000 American Association for the Advancement of Science. Cover 278(5337) 17 Oct 97; **33.3.19** Tim Flach/Stone/Getty Images; **33.3.20** Heather Angel/Natural Visions; **33.3.21** Robert Harding World Imagery/Alamy Images; **33.3.22** Robert Brons/Biological Photo Service; **33.3.23** Wim van Egmond/Visuals Unlimited; **33.4** Andrew J. Martinez/Photo Researchers, Inc.; **33.7a** Andrew J. Martinez/Photo Researchers, Inc.; **33.7b** Robert Brons/Biological Photo Service; **33.7c** Great Barrier Reef Marine Park Authority; **33.7d** Neil G. McDaniel/Photo Researchers, Inc.; **33.8** Robert Brons/Biological Photo Service; **33.9** Ed Robinson/Pacific Stock/Photolibrary;

33.11 Centers for Disease Control and Prevention (CDC); **33.12** Stanley Fleger/Visuals Unlimited; **33.13** W. I. Walker/Photo Researchers, Inc.; **33.14a** Colin Milkins, Oxford Scientific Films/Animals Animals/Earth Scenes; **33.14b** Fred Bavendam/Peter Arnold, Inc.; **33.16** Jeff Foott/Tom Stack & Associates, Inc.; **33.17a** Gerry Ellis/Minden Pictures; **33.17b** Corbis; **33.19** Harold W. Pratt/Biological Photo Service; **33.21a** Robert Pickett/Papilio/Alamy Images; **33.21b** Mark Conlin/Image Quest Marine; **33.21c** Jonathan Blair/Corbis; **33.22** A.N.T./Photoshot/NHPA Limited; **33.23** Peter Batson/Image Quest Marine; **33.24** Astrid & Hanns-Frieder Michler/Photo Researchers, Inc.; **33.25** Reproduced with permission from A. Eizinger and R. Sommer, Max Planck Institut fur entwicklungsbiologie, Tubingen. Copyright 2000 American Association for the Advancement of Science. Cover 278(5337) 17 Oct 97; **33.26** Science Photo Library/Photo Researchers, Inc.; **33.27** Dan Cooper, http://www.isotelus.com; **33.28** Grenier JK, Garber TL, Warren R, Whitington PM, Carroll S. Evolution of the entire arthropod Hox gene set predated the origin and radiation of the onychophoran/arthropod clade. Curr Biol. 1997 Aug 1;7(8):547-53; Fig. 3c; **33.30** Milton Tierney, Jr./Visuals Unlimited; **33.31.1** Tim Flach/Stone/Getty Images; **33.31.2** Andrew Syred/Photo Researchers, Inc.; **33.31.3** Peter Arnold/Peter Arnold, Inc.; **33.33** Premaphotos/Nature Picture Library; **33.34** Tom McHugh/Photo Researchers, Inc.; **33.36 all** John Shaw/Tom Stack & Associates, Inc.; **33.38a** Maximilian Weinzierl/Alamy Images; **33.38b** Peter Herring/Image Quest Marine; **33.38c** Peter Parks/Image Quest Marine; **33.40a** Fred Bavendam/Minden Pictures; **33.40b** Jeff Rotman/Photo Researchers, Inc.; **33.40c** Robert Harding World Imagery/Alamy Images; **33.40d** Jurgen Freund/Nature Picture Library; **33.40e** Hal Beral/Corbis; **33.40f** Daniel Janies. **Chapter 34** **34.1** Xian-guang H, Aldridge RJ, Siveter DJ, Siveter DJ, Xiang-hong F. New evidence on the anatomy and phylogeny of the earliest vertebrates. Proceedings of the Royal Society of London-B-Biological Sciences, Sept. 22, 2002; 269 (1503) 1865-1869; Fig. 1c; **34.4** Runk/Schoenberger/Grant Heilman Photography, Inc.; **34.5a** Robert Bron/Biological Photo Service; **34.8** Nanjing Institute of Geology and Palaeontology; **34.9** Tom McHugh/Photo Researchers, Inc.; **34.10** Breck P. Kent/Animals Animals/Earth Scenes; **34.11** Mark A. Purnell, Department of Geology, University of Leicester, UK; **34.14** The Field Museum; **34.15a** Carlos Villoch/Image Quest Marine; **34.15b** Masa Ushioda/Image Quest Marine; **34.15c** Jeff Mondragon/Mondragon Photo; **34.17a** James D. Watt/Image Quest Marine; **34.17b** Fred Bavendam/Minden Pictures; **34.17c** Marevision/AGE Fotostock America, Inc.; **34.17d** Fred McConnaughey/Photo Researchers, Inc.; **34.18** Arnaz Mehta; **34.21a** Alberto Fernandez/AGE Fotostock America, Inc.; **34.21b** Michael Fogden/Bruce Coleman Inc.; **34.21c** Michael Fogden/Bruce Coleman Inc.; **34.22a** John Cancalosi/Peter Arnold, Inc.; **34.22b** Stephen Dalton/Photo Researchers, Inc.; **34.22c** Hans Pfletschinger/Peter Arnold, Inc.; **34.23** Michael & Patricia Fogden/Minden Pictures; **34.26** Michael & Patricia Fogden/Minden Pictures; **34.27a** Doug Wechsler; **34.27b** Matt T. Lee; **34.27c** Michael & Patricia Fogden/Minden Pictures; **34.27d** Medford Taylor/National Geographic Image Collection; **34.27e** Carl & Ann Purcell/Corbis; **34.28a** Stephen J. Kraseman/DRK Photo; **34.28b** Janice Sheldon; **34.30a** Russell Mountford/Alamy Images; **34.30b** Corbis; **34.30c** Frans Lanting/Minden Pictures; **34.30d** franzfoto.com/Alamy Images; **34.32.1** D. Parer and E. Parer Cook/Auscape International Proprietary Ltd.; **34.32.2** Mervyn Griffiths/Commonwealth Scientific and Industrial Research Organization; **34.33a** ARDEA/Retna Ltd.; **34.33b** Fritz Prenzel/Animals Animals/Earth Scenes; **34.36** Frans Lanting/Minden Pictures; **34.38a** Kevin Schafer/AGE Fotostock America, Inc.; **34.38b** Frans Lanting/Minden Pictures; **34.39a** Morales/AGE Fotostock America, Inc.; **34.39b** Anup Shah/Image State/Alamy Images; **34.39c** T. J. Rick/Nature Picture Library; **34.39d** E. A. Janes/AGE Fotostock America, Inc.; **34.39e** Frans Lanting/Minden Pictures; **34.41a** The Cleveland Museum of Natural History; **34.41b** John Reader/SPL/Photo Researchers, Inc.; **34.41c** John Gurche Studios; **34.42.1** Alan Walker @ National Museums of Kenya. Printed with permission; **34.42.2** J.H. Matternes; **34.44** David L. Brill/Brill Atlanta; **34.45** C. Henshilwood & F. d'Errico. **Chapter 35** **35.3** Robert & Linda Mitchell/Robert & Linda Mitchell Photography; **35.4.1** James Strawser/Grant Heilman Photography, Inc.; **35.4.2** Rob Walls/Alamy; **35.4.3** Drew Weiner; **35.4.4** Robert Holmes/Corbis; **35.4.5** Geoff Tompkinson/Science Photo Library/Photo Researchers, Inc.; **35.5.1** Lee W. Wilcox; **35.5.2** Gusto Production/Science Photo Library/Photo Researchers, Inc.; **35.5.3** Dorling Kindersley; **35.5.4** Barry Runk/Stan/Grant Heilman Photography, Inc.; **35.7.1** Scott Camazine/Photo Researchers, Inc.; **35.7.2** Fritz Polking/Visuals Unlimited; **35.7.3** Mike Zens/Corbis; **35.7.4** Jerome Wexler/Photo Researchers, Inc.; **35.7.5** James Strawser/Grant Heilman Photography, Inc.; **35.9** Purdue Extension Entomology; **35.10.1** Brian Capon; **35.10.2** Ed Reschke/Peter Arnold, Inc.; **35.10.3** Graham Kent, Benjamin Cummings; **35.10.4** Graham Kent, Benjamin Cummings; **35.10.5** Richard Kessel and Gene Shih/Visuals Unlimited; **35.10.6** Reproduced with permission from Plant Cell Biology on CD, by B E S Gunning, http://www.plantcellbiologyonCD.com; **35.10.7** Ray F. Evert; **35.10.8** Dr. Richard Kessel & Dr. Gene Shih/Visuals Unlimited; **35.13** Carolina Biological Supply/Phototake NYC; **35.14a1** Ed Reschke; **35.14a2** Carolina Biological Supply/Phototake NYC; **35.14b** Ed Reschke; **35.15** Michael Clayton; **35.16** Michael Clayton; **35.17** Ed Reschke; **35.18** Ed Reschke; **35.19b1** Michael Clayton; **35.19b2** Alison W. Roberts; **35.21** Edward Cook, Lamont-Doherty Earth Observatory, Columbia University, Palisades, NY; **35.23** California Historical Society Collection (CHS-1177), University of Southern California on behalf of the USC Specialized Libraries and Archival Collections; **35.24** Reproduced by permission from Janet Braam, Cell 60 (9 February 1990): Cover. Copyright (c)1990 Cell Press. Image courtesy of Elsevier Sciences Ltd; **35.26** Susan Wick, University of Minnesota; **35.27** B. Wells and K. Roberts; **35.28a-b** From figure 1 in B. Scheres et al, Development 121:53. (c) 1995 The Company of Biologists Ltd; **35.28c** From figure 6c in R. Torres Ruiz and G. Jurgens, Development 120:2967-2978. (c) 1994 The Company of Biologists Ltd; **35.29** From figure 1a in U. Mayer et al, Development 117 (1): 149-162. (c) 1993 The Company of Biologists Ltd; **35.30** Reproduced by permission from figure 1 in D. Hareven et al, Cell 84 (5): 735-744. Copyright (c) 1996. by Elsevier Science Ltd; **35.31** Reproduced by permission from Figure 2g in Hung et al, Plant Physiology 117:73-84. Copyright (c) 1998 by the American Society of Plant Biologists. Image courtesy of John Schiefelbein/Univesity of Michigan; **35.32** Dr. Gerald D. Carr, PhD; **35.33** Dr. E. M. Meyerowitz and John Bowman, Development 112 1991:1-231.2, Division of Biology, California Institute of Technology; **p 763** Kitin PB, Fujii T, Abe H and Funada R. Anatomy of the vessel network within and between tree rings of Fraxinus lanuginosa (Oleaceae). American Journal of Botany. 2004;91:779-788; Fig. 1. **Chapter 36** **36.1** Peggy Heard/FLPA/Alamy Images; **36.3** Rolf Rutishauser; **36.5** Dana Richter/Visuals Unlimited; **36.10** Nigel Cattlin/Holt Studios International/Photo Researchers, Inc.; **36.13** Scott Camazine/Photo Researchers, Inc.; **36.16** Jeremy Burgess /Science Photo Library/Photo Researchers, Inc.; **36.18.1** C. C. Lockwood/Animals Animals - Earth Scenes; **36.18.2** Kate Shane; **36.18.3** Frans Lanting/Minden Pictures; **36.18.4** John D. Cunningham/Visuals Unlimited; **36.18.5** Andrew de Lory/Dorling Kindersley; **36.18.6** Maddie Thornhill/Garden World Images Ltd/Alamy; **36.21** M. H. Zimmermann, courtesy of Professor P. B. Tomlinson, Harvard University; **36.22** Kim I, Hempel FD, Sha K, Pfluger J, Zambryski PC. Identification of a developmental transition in plasmodesmatal function during embryogenesis in Arabidopsis thaliana. Development. 2002 Mar;129(5):1261-72; Fig. 3g, 6f, 8b and 8c. Images supplied by Patricia Zambryski. **Chapter 37** 37.1 NOAA Photo Library, Historic NWS collection; **37.2** Agricultural Research Service/USDA; **37.4.1** U.S. Geological Survey, Denver; **37.4.2** USGS/Menlo Park; **37.5** Kevin Horan/Stone/Getty Images Inc.; **37.7** Maurice Reece. From the Country Gentleman, courtesy of the Curtis Publishing Co.; **37.8** White et al, Plant Physiology, June 2003; **37.10a** Breck P. Kent/Animals Animals/Earth Scenes; **37.10b** E. H. Newcomb and S. R. Tandon/Biological Photo Service; **37.12a** Gerald Van Dyke/Visuals Unlimited; **37.12b** Carolina Biological Supply/Phototake NYC; **37.13** Elizabeth J. Czarapata; **37.14.1** Wolfgang Kaehler/Corbis; **37.14.2** James Strawser/Grant Heilman Photography, Inc.; **37.14.3** Kevin Schafer/Corbis; **37.14.4** Andrew Syred/Science Photo Library/Photo Researchers, Inc.; **37.14.5** Gary W. Carter/Corbis; **37.14.6** Kim Taylor and Jane Burton/Dorling Kindersley; **37.14.7** Biophoto Associates/Photo Researchers, Inc.; **37.14.8** Philip Blenkinsop/Dorling Kindersley; **37.14.9** Dr. Paul A. Zahl/Photo Researchers, Inc.; **37.14.10** Fritz Polking, Frank Lane Picture Agency/Corbis; **37.15** R. Ronacordi/Visuals Unlimited. **Chapter 38** **38.1** Pierre-Michel Blais, orchidees.provence.free.fr; **38.2.1** Craig Lovell/Corbis; **38.2.2** John Cancalosi/Nature Picture Library; **38.3.1** Ed Reschke; **38.3.2** David Scharf/Peter Arnold, Inc.; **38.3.3** Ed Reschke; **38.4.1** Marianne Wiora, gartenspaziergang.de; **38.4.2** Stephen Dalton/NHPA; **38.4.3** Bjørn Rørslett, naturfotograf.com; **38.4.4** Doug Backlund; **38.4.5** Martin Heigan, anti-matter-3d.com; **38.4.6** Michael & Patricia Fogden/Minden Pictures; **38.4.7** Merlin D. Tuttle, Bat Conservation International; **38.6** Palanivelu R, Brass L, Edlund AF, Preuss D. Pollen tube growth and guidance is regulated by POP2, an Arabidopsis gene that controls GABA levels. Cell. 2003 Jul 11; 114(1):47-59; Fig. 5ab; **38.11.1** BIOS Klein & Hubert/Peter Arnold, Inc.; **38.11.2** Satoshi Kuribayashi/Nature Production; **38.11.3** Brian Gordon Green/National Geographic Image Collection; **38.11.4** Steve Bloom Images/Alamy; **38.11.5** Aaron McCoy/Botanica/Photolibrary; **38.11.6** California Department of Food and Agriculture's Plant Health and Pest Prevention Services; **38.11.7** Steve Shattuck/CSIRO Division Entomology; **38.11.8** Kim A. Cabrera, http://www.beartracker.com; **38.11.9** Alan Williams/Alamy; **38.12** David Cavagnaro/DRK Photo; **38.13.1** Marcel E. Dorken; **38.13.2** Marcel E. Dorken; **38.13.3** Nobumitsu Kawakubo, Gifu University, Japan; **38.14** Bruce Iverson, Photomicrography; **38.15** Sinclair Stammers/Photo Researchers, Inc.; **38.16** Andrew McRobb/Dorling Kindersley; **38.17** Richard M. Manshardt; **38.18.1** Peter Berger; **38.18.2** Adrian Arbib/Peter Arnold, Inc. **Chapter 39** **39.1** Plant Physiol. 1999 Jul;120(3): Cover. By permission of the American Society of Plant Physiologists. Illustration by Niemeyer MI and Fernandez MC; **39.2** Natalie B. Bronstein, Mercy College, Dobbs Ferry, New York; **39.7** Regulation of Polar Auxin transport ATPIN1 in Arabidopsis Vascular Tissue," by Leo Galweiler, et al) Science 18 DEC 1998, vol. 282; **39.9** Malcolm B. Wilkins, University of Glasgow, Glasgow, Scotland, U.K.; **39.10a** Mark Doyle/Department of Biochemistry, University of Wisconsin, Madison; **39.10b** Fred Jensen; **39.12.1** Mia Molvray, http://www.molvray.com; **39.12.2** Karen E. Koch; **39.14a** Kurt Stepnitz, DOE Plant Research Laboratory, Michigan State University; **39.14b** Joe Kieber, University of North Carolina; **39.15** Ed Reschke; **39.16** Malcolm B. Wilkins, University of Glasgow, Glasgow, Scotland, U.K.; **39.17** Malcolm B. Wilkins, University of Glasgow, Glasgow, Scotland, U.K.; **39.20** Malcolm B. Wilkins, University of Glasgow, Glasgow, Scotland, U.K.; **39.24** Michael Evans, Ohio State University; **39.25** Reproduced by permission from Janet Braam, Cell 60 (9 February 1990: Cover. Copyright (c)1990 Cell Press. Image courtesy of Elesevier Sciences Ltd; **39.26a-b** David Sieren/Visuals Unlimited; **39.26c** From K. Esau. Anatomy of Seed Plants, 2nd ed. (New York: John Wiley and sons, 1977), fig. 19.4, p.358; **39.27** J. L. Basq and M. C. Drew. **Chapter 40** **40.1** Joe McDonald/ McDonald Wildlife Photography; **40.2a** Flip Nicklin/Minden Pictures; **40.2b** Tui De Roy/Minden Pictures; **40.2c** Norbert Wu/Minden Pictures; **40.4.1** G. Shih-R. Kessel/Visuals Unlimited; **40.4.2** D. M. Phillips/Visuals Unlimited; **40.4.3** Visuals Unlimited; **40.5.1** CNRI/SPL/Photo Researchers; **40.5.3** Chuck Brown/ Photo Researchers; **40.5.4** Science VU/Visuals Unlimited; **40.5.5** Nina Zanetti; **40.5.6** Nina Zanetti; **40.5.7** Dr. Gopal Murti/SPL/Photo Researchers; **40.5.8** Nina Zanetti; **40.5.9** Manfred Kage/Peter Arnold, Inc.; **40.5.10** Gladden Willis, M. D./Visuals Unlimited; **40.5.11** Thomas Deerinck/National Center for Microscopy and Imaging Research, University of California, San Diego; **40.5.12** Ulrich Gärtner, Paul Flechsig Institute for Brain Research, Dept. Neuroanatomy, Universität Leipzig, Germany; **40.9a** Patricio Robles Gil/naturepl.com; **40.9b** Jim Brandenburg/Minden Pictures; **40.13** Robert Ganz; **40.18** Stan Lindstedt; **40.21** John Gerlach/Visuals Unlimited. **Chapter 41** **41.1** Michael deYoung/ Corbis; **41.2** Corbis; **41.3** Roland Seitre/Peter Arnold, Inc.; **41.4** Thomas Mangelsen/Minden Pictures; **41.6.1** Brandon Cole; **41.6.2** Thomas Eisner; **41.6.3** Photo Lennart Nilsson/Albert Bonniers Forlag AB; **41.6.4** Gunter Ziesler/Peter Arnold, Inc.; **41.12** Fred E. Hossler/Visuals Unlimited; **41.17** Centers for Disease Control & Prevention; **41.19.1** Photodisc/Getty Images; **41.19.2** EyeWire Collection/Photodisc/Getty Images; **41.22** Susumu Nishinaga/ SPL/Photo Researchers; **41.24** Photo courtesy of The Jackson Laboratory, Bar Harbor, Maine; **41.25** Wolfgang Kaehler/Corbis. **Chapter 42** **42.1** Jane Burton/Bruce Coleman USA; **42.2a** © 2002 Norbert Wu /www.norbertwu.com; **42.2b** Dr. John D. Cunningham/Visuals Unlimited; **42.10.1** Dr. Richard Kessel & Dr. Randy Kardon/Visuals Unlimited; **42.10.2** Photo Lennart Nilsson/Albert Bonniers Forlag; **42.17** Nina Zanetti; **42.18** Science Source/Photo Researchers; **42.19** Nina Zanetti; **42.20a** Ed Reschke; **42.20b** W. Ober/Visuals Unlimited; **42.21a** Peter Batson/Image Quest 3-D; **42.21b** Dave Haas/The Image Finders; **42.21c** Frans Lanting/Minden Pictures; **42.23** Prepared by Dr. Hong Y. Yan, University of Kentcky and Dr. Peng Chai, University of Texas; **42.24.1** Dr. Richard Kessel & Dr. Randy Kardon/Visuals Unlimited; **42.24.2** CNRI/SPL/ Photo Researchers; **42.26** Hans-Rainer Duncker, University of Giessen, Germany. **Chapter 43** **43.1** Biology Media/Science Source/Photo Researchers; **43.4** Ferrandon D, Jung AC, Criqui M, Lemaitre B, Uttenweiler-Joseph S, Michaut L, Reichhart J, Hoffmann JA. A drosomycin-GFP reporter transgene reveals a local immune response in Drosophila that is not dependent on the Toll pathway. EMBO J. 1998 Aug 10;17(5):1217-27; Fig. 1a; **43.17** David Scharf/Peter Arnold, Inc.; **43.19** Gopal Murti/Phototake NYC; **43.22** Alamy Images; **43.24** Alain Pol/ISM/PhototakeUSA. **Chapter 44** **44.1** Felix Heintzenberg, Biofokus Nature Photography; **44.3** Brandon Cole; **44.5** Dr. John Crowe, University of California, Davis; **44.14b** Lise Bankir; **44.14d** Visuals Unlimited; **44.17** Gerry Ellis/Minden Pictures; **44.18** Michael & Patricia Fodgen/Minden Pictures. **Chapter 45** **45.1.1** Ralph A. Clevenger/Corbis; **45.1.2** Stuart Wilson/Photo Researchers, Inc.; **45.9.1** Breck P. Kent/Animals Animals - Earth Scenes; **45.9.2** Leonard Rue Enterprises/Animals Animals - Earth Scenes; **45.19** ISM/Phototake. **Chapter 46** **46.1** Robin Chittenden/Corbis; **46.2** David Wrobel; **46.4a** P. de Vries, courtesy of David Crews; **46.5** Dwight Kuhn/Dwight R. Kuhn Photography **46.6** William E. Ferguson; **46.17** Photo Lennart Nilsson/Albert Bonniers Forlag AB. A Child is Born, Dell Publishing. **Chapter 47** **47.1** Photo Lennart Nilsson/Albert Bonniers Forlag AB. Gunilla Hedesund; **47.2** Historical Collections, College of Physicians; **47.4** Exp Vacquier VD, Payne JE. Methods for quantitating sea urchin sperm-egg binding. Exp Cell Res. 1973 Nov; 82(1):227-35; **47.4** Res Hafner, M., Petzelt, C., Nobiling, R., Pawley, J., Kramp, D. and G. Schatten. Wave of Free Calcium at Fertilization in the Sea Urchin Egg Visualized with Fura-2 Cell Motil. Cytoskel., 9:271-277 (1988); **47.6** George von Dassow; **47.8** R. Kessel & G. Shih/Visuals Unlimited; **47.9** Charles A. Ettensohn; **47.12a** P. Huw Williams and Jim Smith, The Wellcome Trust/Cancer Research UK Gurdon Institute; **47.12c** Thomas Poole, SUNY Health Science Center; **47.13b** Carolina Biological Supply/Phototake; **47.19** Dr. Janet Heasman; **47.20** Marsden M, DeSimone DW. Integrin-ECM interactions regulate cadherin-dependent cell adhesion and are required for convergent extension in Xenopus. Curr Biol. 2003 Jul 15;13(14):1182-91; **47.21** Hiroki Nishida, Developmental Biology 121 (1987): 526. Reprinted by permission of Academic Press; **47.22** J. E. Sulston and H. R. Horvitz, Dev. Biol. 56 (1977):110-156; **47.25** Kathryn W. Tosney, University of Michigan; **47.26** Dennis Summerbell; **47.27** CNRI/Photo Researchers, Inc. **Chapter 48** **48.1** Marine Themes Pty Ltd, marinethemes.com; **48.2** David Fleetham/Alamy; **48.5b** Thomas Deerinck/National Center for Microscopy and Imaging Research, University of California, San Diego; **48.12** Bear, Connors, and Paradiso, Neuroscience: Exploring the Brain (c) 1996, p. 43; **48.14** Edwin R. Lewis, University of California at Berkeley. **Chapter 49** **49.1** G. Fesl MD, Dep. of Neuroradiology, LMU Munich, Germany; **49.6b** N. Kedersha/Photo Researchers, Inc.; **49.17** Marcus E. Raichle, M.D., Washington University Medical Center; **49.23** Martin M. Rotker/Photo Researchers, Inc.; **49.24** Fred H. Gage, The Salk Institute, Laboratory of Genetics. **Chapter 50** **50.1** Stephen Dalton/Photoshot/NHPA Limited; **50.4.1** OSF/Animals Animals/Earth Scenes; **50.4.2** R. A. Steinbrecht; **50.5a** Joe McDonald/Animals Animals/Earth Scenes; **50.5b** Flip Nicklin/Minden Pictures; **50.7** From Richard Elzinga, Fundamentals of Entomology 3 ed. (c)1987, p. 185. Reprinted by permission of Prentice-Hall, Upper Saddle River, NJ; **50.8** Peter Gillespie; **50.17a** USDA/APHIS Animal And Plant Health Inspection Service; **50.25** Clara Franzini-Armstrong, University of Pennsylvania; **50.26** Courtesy of Dr. H. E. Huxley; **50.35** Dave Watts/NHPA/Photo Researchers, Inc.; **50.36** Vance A. Tucker. **Chapter 51** **51.1** Steve Kaufman/ Corbis; **51.2** Michael & Patricia Fogden/Minden Pictures; **51.5** Michael Quinton/Minden Pictures; **51.6** Michael Nichols/National Geographic/Getty Images; **51.8** Kenneth Lorenzen, UC Davis; **51.10a** Thomas McAvoy/Life Magazine/Getty Images; **51.10b** Operation Migration Inc.; **51.12** Harry Engels/Animals Animals/Earth Scenes; **51.13** Clive Bromhall/OSF/Animals Animals/Earth Scenes; **51.14** Robert Pickett/Corbis; **51.16** Rory Doolin; **51.17** Lowell L. Getz and Lisa Davis; **51.20a** Thomas Mangelsen/Minden Pictures; **51.20b** Robinson, James H./Animals Animals/Earth Scenes; **51.20c** Bill Schomoker; **51.21** Fred Bavendam/Minden Pictures; **51.22** Courtesy of Gerald S. Wilkinson; from G.S. Wilkinson and G. N. Dodson, in J. Choe and B. Crespi (eds)., The Evolution of Mating Systems in Insects and Arachnids, Cambridge University Press, Cambridge (1997), pp. 310-328; **51.23** Cyril Laubscher/Dorling Kindersley; **51.25** Mitsuaki Iwago/Minden Pictures; **51.26** Erik Svensson, Lund University, Sweden; **51.27** Jennifer Jarvis; **51.29** Stephen J. Krasemann/Peter Arnold, Inc.; **51.31.1** Richard Wrangham; **51.31.2** Alissa Crandall/Corbis; **51.32** Ulf Wallin/Riser/Getty Images. **Chapter 52** **52.1** Flip Nicklin/Minden Pictures; **52.2.1** Science Faction/Getty Images; **52.2.2** Joe McDonald/Corbis; **52.2.3** Tom Bean/Corbis; **52.2.4** B. Tharp/Photo Researchers, Inc.; **52.2.5** Yann Arthus-Bertrand/Corbis; **52.2.6** Reto Stöckli, Alan Nelson, Fritz Hasler, Laboratory for Atmospheres, Goddard Space Flight Center, NASA; **52.4** Erich Hartmann/ Magnum Photos; **52.5** Geoff Dann/Dorling Kindersley; **52.7** Peter Llewellyn/ Alamy; **52.9** Tim Fitzharris/Minden Pictures; **52.18.1** Allen Russell/Index Stock Imagery, Inc.; **52.18.2** Gerry Ellis/Minden Pictures; **52.18.3** David Muench/ Corbis; **52.18.4** Ron Watts/Corbis; **52.18.5** Charles McDowell/Grant Heilman Photography, Inc.; **52.18.6** James Randklev/Image Bank/Getty Images; **52.18.7** Stuart Westmorland/Corbis; **52.18.8** Stuart Westmorland/Corbis; **52.18.9** Digital Vision/Getty Images; **52.18.10** William Lange/Woods Hole Oceanographic Institution; **52.21.1** Frans Lanting/Minden Pictures; **52.21.2** Gordon Whitten/ Corbis; **52.21.3** Wolfgang Kaehler/Corbis; **52.21.4** John D. Cunningham/Visuals Unlimited; **52.21.5** Tom Bean/Image Bank/Getty Images; **52.21.6** Bill Ross/Corbis; **52.21.7** Kennan Ward/Corbis; **52.21.8** Darrell Gulin/Corbis; **Chapter 53** **53.1** David Tipling/Nature Picture Library; **53.2** Brandon Cole, http://www.brandoncole.com; **53.4a** Bernard Castelein/Nature Picture Library/ Alamy; **53.4b** Frans Lanting/Minden Pictures; **53.4c** Niall Benvie/Corbis; **53.7** Tom Bean/Corbis; **53.8** H. Willcox/Wildlife Picture/Peter Arnold, Inc.; **53.9a** Jean Louis Batt/Taxi/Getty Images, Inc.; **53.9b** Christine Osborne/Corbis; **53.14** Gerry Ellis/Minden Pictures; **53.17a** Adrian Bailey/ Aurora & Quanta Productions Inc.; **53.17b** Wolfgang Kaehler/Corbis; **53.20** Joe McDonald/ Corbis; **53.21** Niclas Fritzén; **53.27** Marc L. Imhoff, Lahouari Bounoua, Taylor Ricketts, Colby Loucks, Robert Harriss and William T. Lawrence/NASA's Goddard Space Flight Center. **Chapter 54** **54.1** Phil Degginger/Alamy; **54.2.1** Kevin deQueiroz, National Museum of Natural History, Smithsonian Institution, Smithsonian Institution; **54.2.2** Joseph T. Collins/Photo Researchers, Inc.; **54.5a** C. Allan Morgan/Peter Arnold, Inc.; **54.5b** Fogden/Corbis; **54.5c1** Stephen J. Krasemann/Photo Researchers, Inc.; **54.5c2** Michael & Patricia Fodgen/Minden Pictures; **54.5d1** Edward S. Ross, California Academy of Sciences; **54.5d2** Runk/ Schoenberger/Grant Heilman Photography, Inc.; **54.6** Fred Bavendam/Minden Pictures; **54.7a** Fogden/Corbis; **54.7b** Daniel H. Janzen; **54.8** Peter Johnson/ Corbis; **54.15** Nancy Rotenberg/ Animals Animals - Earth Scenes; **54.17** Tom and Pat Leeson; **54.18** Sally D. Hacker; **54.20** Frank Gilliam; **54.21a** Michael Quinton/Minden Pictures; **54.21b** Scott T. Smith/Corbis; **54.22.1** Charles Mauzy/Corbis; **54.22.2** Tom Bean/DRK Photo; **54.22.3** Terry Donnelly, Donnelly-Austin Photography; **54.22.4** Glacier Bay National Park Photo/Glacier Bay National Park and Preserve; **54.24.1** R. Grant Gilmore, Dynamac Corporation; **54.24.2** Lance Horn, National Undersea Research Center, University of North Carolina-Wilmington; **54.29** Andy Bruckner, NOAA Fisheries; **54.30** Josh Spice, http://www.wildimages.blogspot.com. **Chapter 55** **55.1** Galen Rowell/Corbis; **55.2** Annette Summers Engel, Department of Geology and Geophysics, Louisiana State University; **55.3** Fritz Poelking/AGE Fotostock; **55.6** Earth Observatory NASA; **55.7** Reprinted with permission from

D. W. Schindler, Science 184 (24 May 1974): 897, Figure 1.49.20. Copyright 1974 American Association for the Advancement of Science; **55.9** TK; **55.12** Thomas Del Brase/Photographer's Choice/Getty Images; **55.16a** Hubbard Brook Research Foundation; **55.16b** USDA Forest Service; **55.17** Arthur C. Smith III/Grant Heilman Photography; **55.18** NASA; **55.22** Prof. William H. Schlesinger; **55.25** NASA. **Chapter 56** **56.1** Stephen J Richards; **56.2** Wayne Lawler/Ecoscene/ Corbis; **56.4a** Neil Lucas/Nature Picture Library; **56.4b** Mark Carwardine/Still Pictures/Peter Arnold, Inc.; **56.4c** Nazir Foead; **56.5** Merlin D. Tuttle, Bat Conservation International; **56.6** Scott Camazine/Photo Researchers, Inc.; **56.7** Michael Edwards/Getty Images; **56.8a** Michael Fodgen/Animals Animals/Earth Scenes; **56.8b** Robert Ginn/PhotoEdit Inc.; **56.9** Richard Vogel/Liaison/Getty Images, Inc.; **56.11** William Ervin/Photo Researchers, Inc.; **56.12** Lance Craighead/The Craighead Environmental Research Institute; **56.13a1** Tim Thompson/Corbis; **56.13a2** David Sieren/Visuals Unlimited; **56.13b** Blanche Haning/The Lamplighter; **56.14a** Yann Arthus-Bertrand/ Corbis; **56.14b** James P. Blair/National Geographic Image Collection; **56.15** R. O. Bierregaard, Jr., Biology Dept., University of North Carolina, Charlotte; **56.16** SPL/Photo Researchers, Inc.; **56.19b** Frans Lanting/Minden Pictures; **56.20** Mark Chiappone and Steven Miller, Center for Marine Science, University of North Carolina-Wilmington, Key Largo, Florida; **56.21** Princeton Hydro, LLC, Ringoes, NJ; **56.22** U.S. Department of Energy; **56.23.1** Stewart Rood, University of Lethbridge; **56.23.2** Daniel H. Janzen, University of Pennsylvania; **56.23.3** Photo provided by Kissimmee Division staff, South Florida Water Management District (WPB; **56.23.4** Tim Day, Xcluder Pest Proof Fencing Company; **56.23.5** Bert Boekhoven; **56.23.6** Jean Hall/Holt Studio/Photo Researchers, Inc.; **56.23.7** Kenji Morita/Environment Division, Tokyo Kyuei Co., Ltd; **56.25a** Serge de Sazo/Photo Researchers, Inc.; **56.25b** AP Photo/Hilde Jensen, University of Tübingen/Nature Magazine; **56.25c** Frans Lanting/Minden Pictures.

ILLUSTRATION CREDITS

The following figures are adapted from C. K. Matthews and K. E. van Holde, *Biochemistry,* 2nd ed. Copyright © 1996 Pearson Education, Inc., publishing as Pearson Benjamin Cummings: **4.6b, 9.9, 17.16b** and **c**. The following figures are adapted from W. M. Becker, J. B. Reece, and M. F. Poenie, *The World of the Cell,* 3rd ed. Copyright © 1996 Pearson Education, Inc., publishing as Pearson Benjamin Cummings: **4.7, 6.7b, 7.8, 11.7, 11.11, 17.10, 18.22, 20.8.,** and **21.9. Figures 6.9** and **6.23a** and cell organelle drawings in **6.12, 6.13, 6.14,** and **6.20** are adapted from illustrations by Tomo Narashima in E. N. Marieb, *Human Anatomy and Physiology,* 5th ed. **6.12a, 50.10,** and **50.11** are also from *Human Anatomy and Physiology,* 5th ed. Copyright © 2001 Pearson Education, Inc., publishing as Pearson Benjamin Cummings. The following figures are adapted from Gerard J. Tortora, Berdell R. Funke, and Christine L. Case. 1998. *Microbiology: An Introduction,* 6th ed. Copyright © 1998 Pearson Education, Inc., publishing as Pearson Benjamin Cummings: **27.6a** and **43.8**. The following figures are adapted from M. W. Nabors, *Introduction to Botany,* Copyright © 2004 Pearson Education, Inc., publishing as Pearson Benjamin Cummings: **30.4, 30.13j, 39.13,** and **41.2 (center)**. The following figures are adapted from L. G. Mitchell, J. A. Mutchmor, and W. D. Dolphin. *Zoology.* Copyright ©1988 Pearson Education, Inc., publishing as Pearson Benjamin Cummings: **41.8, 44.9,** and **51.11**. The following figures are adapted from E. N. Marieb, *Human Anatomy and Physiology,* 4th ed. Copyright © 1998 Pearson Education, Inc., publishing as Pearson Benjamin Cummings: **46.16, 49.8, 49.10 , 50.25,** and **50.29**. **Chapter 1** **1.12** and **21.5** From Figure 4B from L. Giot et al., "A Protein Interaction Map of *Drosophila melanogaster,*" *Science*, Dec. 5, 2003, p. 1733. Copyright © 2003 AAAS. Reprinted with permission from the American Association for the Advancement of Science; **1.25** Map provided courtesy of David W. Pfennig, University of North Carolina at Chapel Hill; **1.27** Data in bar graph based on D. W. Pfennig et al. 2001. Frequency-dependent Batesian mimicry. *Nature* 410: 323. **Chapter 2** **2.22** (bottom) Graph adapted from M.E. Frederickson et al. 'Devil's gardens' bedevilled by ants, *Nature*, 437: 495, 9/22/05. Reprinted by permission of Macmillan Publishers, Ltd. **Chapter 3** **3.8a** Adapted from *Scientific American,* Nov. 1998, p.102. **Chapter 5** **5.13** Adapted from *Biology: The Science of Life,* 4/e by Robert Wallace et al. Copyright © 1991. Reprinted by permission of Pearson Education, Inc.; **5.19** Adapted from D. W. Heinz et al. 1993. How amino-acid insertions are allowed in an alpha-helix of T4 lysozyme. *Nature* 361: 561; **5.21** Collagen and hemoglobin art: © Illustration, Irving Geis. Images from Irving Geis collection/Howard Hughes Medical Institute. Rights owned by Howard Hughes Medical Institute. Not to be reproduced without permission. **Chapter 6** **Table 6.1a** Adapted from W. M. Becker, L. J. Kleinsmith, and J. Hardin, *The World of the Cell,* 4th ed. p. 753. Copyright © 2000 Pearson Education, Inc., publishing as Pearson Benjamin Cummings. **Chapter 8** **8.21** Adapted from J. M. Scheer et al. 2006. A common allosteric site and mechanism in caspases. *Proceedings of the National Academy of Sciences of the United States of America* 103: 7595-7600. **Chapter 9** **9.5a, b** Copyright © 2002 from *Molecular Biology of the Cell,* 4th ed. by Bruce Alberts et al., fig. 2.69, p. 92. Reproduced by permission of Garland Science/Taylor & Francis Books, Inc.; **9.15** H. Itoh et al. 2004. Mechanically driven ATP synthesis by F_1-ATPase. *Nature* 427: 465-468. **Chapter 10** **10.14** Adapted from Richard and David Walker. *Energy, Plants and Man,* Fig. 4.1, p. 69. Sheffield: University of Sheffield. Oxygraphics http://www.oxygraphics.co.uk © Richard Walker. Used with permission courtesy of Richard Walker. **Chapter 11** **11.16** Adapted from D. Matheos et al. 2004. Pheromone-induced polarization is dependent on the Fus3p MAPK acting through the formin Bni1p, *Journal of Cell Biology* 165: 99-109. **Chapter 12** **12.12** Copyright © 2002 from *Molecular Biology of the Cell,* 4th ed., by Bruce Alberts et al., fig. 18.41, p. 1059. Garland Science/Taylor & Francis Books, Inc.; **12.16** Adapted from S. Moreno et al. 1989. Regulation of $p34^{cdc2}$ protein kinase during mitosis. *Cell* 58: 361-372. Copyright © 1989. Used by permission. **Chapter 13** **13.10** Adapted from T. S. Kitajima et al. 2004. The conserved kinetochore protein shugoshin protects centromeric cohesion during meiosis. *Nature* 427: 510-517, 2004. Copyright © 2004. Reprinted by permission of Macmillan Publishers, Ltd. **Chapter 17** **17.12** Adapted from L. J. Kleinsmith and V. M. Kish. 1995. *Principles of Cell and Molecular Biology,* 2nd ed. New York, NY: HarperCollins. Reprinted by permission of Addison Wesley Educational Publishers. **Chapter 18** **18.13a** Adapted from Fig. 1d in N. C. Lau et al. An abundant class of tiny RNAs with probable regulatory roles in *Caenorhabditis elegans. Science* 294: 858-862, 10/26/2001. Copyright © 2001. Reprinted with permission from AAAS. **Chapter 20** **20.10** Adapted from Peter Russell, *Genetics,* 5th ed., fig. 15.24, p. 481. Copyright © 1998 Pearson Education, Inc., publishing as Pearson Benjamin Cummings. **Chapter 21** **21.2** Adapted from a figure by Chris A. Kaiser and Erica Beade; **21.10:** Hemoglobin art: © Illustration, Irving Geis. Images from Irving Geis collection/Howard Hughes Medical Institute. Rights owned by Howard Hughes Medical Institute. Not to be reproduced without permission. **21.17** Adapted from an illustration by William McGinnis; **21.18** Adapted from M. Akam, "*Hox* genes and the evolution of diverse body plans," *Philosophical Transactions Biological Sciences,* Vol. 349, No. 1329, pp. 313-319, September 1995. Copyright © 1995 Royal Society of London. Used with permission. **Chapter 22** **22.8** © Utako Kikutani, 2007. Used with permission; **22.14** Adapted from R. Shurman et al. 1995. *Journal of Infectious Diseases* 171: 1411; **22.16a** Adapted from J. G. M. Thewissen et al. 2001. Skeletons of terrestrial cetaceans and the relationship of whales to artiodactyls. *Nature* 413: 277-281, fig. 2a; **22.16b** Adapted from P. D. Gingerich et al. 2001. Origin of whales from early artiodactyls: Hands and feet of eocene protocetidae from Pakistan. *Science* 293: 2239-2242, fig. 3; **22.16c** and **d** Adapted from C. de Muizon. 2001. Walking with whales, *Nature* 413: 259-260, fig. 1. **Chapter 23** **23.4** Graph adapted from D. A. Powers et al. 1991. Genetic mechanisms for adapting to a changing environment. *Annual Review of Genetics* 25: 629-659; **23.10a** and **b** J. L. Bouzat et al. 1998. The ghost of genetic diversity past: Historical DNA analysis of the greater prairie chicken. *The American Naturalist,* 152: 1-6; **23.12a** Adapted from D. Futuyma. 1998. *Evolutionary Biology* 3rd ed. Sinauer Associates, fig. 13.19. Copyright © 1998. Reprinted by permission of Sinauer Associates, Inc.; **23.14b** Art adapted from D Futuyma, 2005. *Evolution,* 1st ed. Sinauer. fig. 11.3; **23.16** Adapted from A. M. Welch et al.1998. Call duration as an indicator of genetic quality in male gray tree frogs. *Science* 280: 1928-1930; **23.17** Adapted from A. C. Allison. 1961. Abnormal hemoglobin and erythrocyte enzyme-deficiency traits. In *Genetic Variation in Human Populations,* ed. G.A. Harrison. Oxford: Elsevier Science; **Un 23.2** R. K. Koehn and T. J. Hilbish. 1987. The adaptive importance of genetic variation. *American Scientist* 75: 134-141. **Chapter 24** **24.3** Based on data from S. V. Edwards, 1993. Long-distance gene flow in a cooperative breeder detected in genealogies of mitochondrial DNA sequences. Proceedings of the Royal Society of London. Series B, *Biological Sciences* 252: 177-185; **24.7** Adapted from fig. 1 of F. Bossuyt and M. C. Milinkovitch. Amphibians as indicator of early tertiary "out-of-India" dispersal vertebrates. *Science* 292: 93-95, 4/6/01. Copyright © 2001. Reprinted with permission from AAAS; **24.8** Graph adapted from figure 2 in "Correspondence between sexual isolation and allozyme differentiation" *Proceedings of the National Academy of Science,* 87: 2715-2719, 1990, p. 2718. Copyright © 1990 Stephen G. Tilley, Paul A. Verrell, Steven J. Arnold. Used with permission; **24.9** Adapted from D. M. B. Dodd, 1989. Reproductive isolation as a consequence of adaptive divergence in *Drosophila pseudoobscura. Evolution* 43: 1308-1311; **24.13** Map and graphs adapted from J. M. Szymura, 1993. Analysis of hybrid zones with bombina. In *Hybrid Zone and the Evolutionary Process* by R. G. Harrison, ed. Oxford University Press, NY; **24.15** Adapted from figure 2, from G.P. Saetre et al., "A sexually selected character displacement in flycatchers reinforces premating isolation" *Nature* 387: 589-591, June 5, 1997. Copyright © 1997. Reprinted by permission of Macmillan Publishers, Ltd.; **24.18b** Adapted from figure 2 in L. H. Rieseberg et al., Role of gene interactions in hybrid speciation: Evidence from ancient and experimental hybrids. *Science* 272: 741-745, 1996. Copyright © 1996. Reprinted with permission from AAAS. **Chapter 25** **25.5** Adapted from D. J. Futuyma. 1998. *Evolutionary Biology,* 3rd ed., p. 128. Sunderland, MA: Sinauer Associates; **25.6a—d** Adapted from D. J. Futuyma. 2005. *Evolution,* 1st ed., fig. 4.10. Sunderland, MA: Sinauer Associates; **25.6e** Adapted from Luo et al. 2001. A new mammalia form from the Early

Jurassic and evolution of mammalian characteristics. *Science* 292: 1535; **25.7** Adapted from D. J. Des Marais. September 8, 2000. When did photosynthesis emerge on Earth? *Science* 289: 1703—1705; **25.10** Data from A. H. Knoll and S. B. Carroll, June 25, 1995. *Science* 284: 2129—2137; **25.12** Map adapted from http://gelology.er.usgs.gov/eastern/plates.html; **25.14** Graph created from D. M. Raup and J. J. Sepkoski, Jr. 1982. Mass extinctions in the marine fossil record. *Science.* 215: 1501-1503 and J. J. Sepkoski, Jr. 1984. A kinetic model of Phanerozoic taxonomic diversity. III. Post-Paleozoic families and mass extinctions. *Paleobiology.* Vol 10, No. 2, pp. 246-267 in D. J. Futuyma, fig. 7.3a, p. 143 and fig. 7.6, p. 145, Sunderland, MA: Sinauer Associates; **25.16** Graph from R. K. Bambach et al. 2002. Anatomical and ecological constraints on Phanerozoic animal diversity in the marien realm. *PNAS* 99: 6854-6859; **25.17** Adapted from Hickman, Roberts, and Larson.1997, *Zoology,* 10th ed, Wm. C. Brown, fig. 31.1; **25.22** Adapted from M. Ronshaugen et al. Feb. 21, 2002. Hox protein mutation and macroevolution of the insect body plan. *Nature* 415: 914-917, fig. 1a; **25.24** Adapted from M. Strickberger, 1990. *Evolution,* Boston: Jones & Bartlett. **Chapter 26 26.6** Adapted from C. S. Baker and S. R. Palumbi. 1994. Which whales are hunted? A molecular genetic approach to monitoring whaling. *Science* 265: 1538-1539, fig. 1. Copyright © 1994. Reprinted with permission from AAAS; **26.12** Adapted from S. M. Shimeld. 1999. The evolution of the hedgehog gene family in chordates: Insights from amphioxus hedgehog. *Development Genes and Evolution* 209: 40-47, fig. 3; **26.19** Adapted from J. C. Avise, 2004. *Molecular Markers, Natural History, and Evolution,* 2/e, fig. 4.3c. Copyright © Sinauer Associates, Inc. Used with permission; **26.20a** Graph adapted from B. Korber et al. Timing the ancestor of the HIV-1 pandemic strains. *Science* 288: 1789-1796. June 9, 2000. Copyright © 2000. Reprinted with permission from AAAS. **26.21** Adapted from S. L. Baldauf et al. 2004. The Tree of Life: An Overview. In *Assembling the Tree of Life* by J. Cracraft and MJ Donoghue (eds), Oxford University Press, NY; **26.22** Adapted from S. Blair Hedges. The origin and evolution of model organisms. *Nature Reviews Genetics* 3: 838-848, fig. 1, p. 840; **26.23** Adapted from M. C. Rivera and J. A. Lake. 2004. The ring of life provides evidence for a genome fusion origin of eukaryotes. *Nature* 431: 152-155, fig. 3. Copyright © 2004. Reprinted by permission of Macmillan Publishers, Ltd. **Chapter 27 27.10b** Graph adapted from V. S. Cooper and R. E. Lenski. 2000. The population genetics of ecological specialization in evolving *E. coli* populations. *Nature* 407: 736-739; **27.19** Graph created from data in C. Calvaruso et al. 2006. Root-associated bacteria contribute to mineral weathering and to mineral nutrition in trees: A budgeting analysis. *Applied and Environmental Microbiology* 72: 1258-1266. **Chapter 28 28.2** From Archibald and Keeling, "Recycled Plastids," *Trends in Genetics,* Vol. 18, No. 11, 2002. Copyright © 2002, with permission from Elsevier; **28.11** Adapted from R. W. Bauman. 2004. *Microbiology,* fig. 12.7, p. 350. Copyright © 2004 Pearson Education, Inc., publishing as Pearson Benjamin Cummings; **28.23** Data from A. Stechman and T. Cavalier-Smith. 2002. Rooting the eukaryote tree by using a derived gene fusion, *Science* 297: 89-91; **28.27** Copyright © 2004 The Nature Conservancy. Map produced by N. Law – Global Priorities Group – 08/14/2004. **Chapter 29 29.10** Source: R. D. Bowden. 1991. Inputs, outputs and accumulation of nitrogen in an early successional moss *(Polytrichum)* ecosystem. *Ecological Monographs* 61: 207-223; **29.14** Adapted from Raven et al. *Biology of Plants,* 6th ed., fig. 19.7. **Chapter 30 30.12a** Adapted from Soltis et al., 2005. *Phylogeny and Evolution of Angiosperms,* Sinauer Associates, pp. 17, fig. 1.11 from Crane 1985, which is based on Harris, 1964; **30.12b** Adapted from Soltis et al., *Phylogeny and Evolution of Angiosperms,* p. 28, fig. 2.3. Copyright © 2005. Reprinted by permission of Sinauer Associates, Inc.; **Table 30.1** Adapted from Randy Moore et al., *Botany,* 2nd ed. Dubuque, IA: Brown, 1998, Table 2.2, p. 37. **Chapter 31 31.21** Graphs adapted from A. E. Arnold et al. 2003. Fungal endophytes limit pathogen damage in a tropical tree. *PNAS* 100: 15649-15654, figs. 4 and 5. **Chapter 33 33.28a** From J. K. Grenier et al. 1997. Evolution of the entire arthropod *Hox* gene set predated the origin and radiation of the onychophoran/arthropod clade, *Current Biology* 7: 547-553, fig. 3c, p. 551. Copyright © 1997, with permission from Elsevier, Inc. **Chapter 34 34.8b** Adapted from J. Mallatt and J. Chen. 2003. Fossil sister group of craniates: Predicted and found. *Journal of Morphology* 258: 1-31, fig. 1, 5/15/03. Copyright © 2003. Reprinted with permission of Wiley-Liss, Inc., a subsidiary of John Wiley & Sons, Inc.; **34.12** Adapted from K. Kardong. 2001. *Vertebrates: Comparative Anatomy, Function, and Evolution,* 3/e. © 2001 McGraw-Hill Science/Engineering/Mathematics.; **34.19** and **34.20** From C. Zimmer. *At the Water's Edge.* Copyright © 1999 by Carl Zimmer. Reprinted by permission of Jankow & Nesbit; **34.31a** Adapted from D. J. Futuyma. 2005. *Evolution,* 1/e, fig. 4.10. Sunderland, MA: Sinauer Associates; **34.40** Drawn from photos of fossils: *O. tugenensis* photo in Michael Balter, Early hominid sows division, *ScienceNow,* Feb. 22, 2001, © 2001 American Association for the Advancement of Science. *A. ramidus kadabba* photo by Timothy White, 1999/Brill Atlanta. *A. anamensis, A. garhi,* and *H. neanderthalensis* adapted from *The Human Evolution Coloring Book. K platyops* drawn from photo in Meave Leakey et al., New hominid genus from eastern Africa shows diverse middle Pliocene lineages, *Nature,* March 22, 2001, 410: 433. *P. boisei* drawn from a photo by David Bill. *H. ergaster* drawn from a photo at www.inhandmuseum.com. *S. tchadensis* drawn from a photo in Michel Brunet et al., A new hominid from the Upper Miocene of Chad, Central Africa, *Nature,* July 11, 2002, 418: 147, fig. 1b.; **34.43a** and **b** Adapted from I. V. Ovchinnikov et al. 2000. Molecular analysis of Neanderthal DNA from the northern Caucasus. *Nature* 404: 492, fig.3a and b. **Chapter 35 35.24 (right)** Pie chart adapted from *Nature,* Dec. 14, 2000, 408: 799. New data from The Arabidopsis Information Resource (TAIR). **Chapter 39 39.16 (top)** Adapted from M. Wilkins. 1988. *Plant Watching,* Facts of File Publ.; **39.28** Reprinted with permission from Edward Farmer, 1997, *Science* 279: 912. Copyright © 1997 American Association for the Advancement of Science. **Chapter 40 40.14** Adapted from fig. 2 in V. H. Hutchinson et al. Thermoregulation in a brooding female Indian python, *Python molurus bivittatus. Science* 151: 694-695, fig. 2. Copyright © 1966. Reprinted with permission from AAAS; **40.15** Adapted with permission from B. Heinrich. 1974. Thermoregulation in endothermic insects. *Science* 185: 747-756, fig. 7. © 1974 American Association for the Advancement of Science. **Chapter 41 41.5** Source: R. W. Smithells et al. 1980. Possible prevention of neural-tube defects by periconceptual vitamins supplementation. *Lancet* 315: 339-340; **41.10** Adapted from R. A. Rhoades and R.G. Pflanzer, *Human Physiology,* 3/e, fig. 22-1, p. 666. Copyright © 1996. Reprinted by permission of Brooks/Cole, a division of Thomson Learning: www.thomsonrights.comFax 800 732-2215; **41.23** Adapted from J. Marx, "Cellular Warriors at the Battle of the Bulge," *Science,* Vol. 299, p. 846. Copyright © 2003 American Association for the Advancement of Science. Illustration: Katharine Sutliff. **Chapter 42 42.31** Adapted from S. L. Lindstedt et al. 1991. Running energetics in the pronghorn antelope. *Nature* 353: 748–750. Copyright © 1991. Reprinted by permission of Macmillan Publishers, Ltd. **Chapter 43 43.5** Adapted from Phoebe Tzou et al, "Constitutive expression of a single antimicrobial peptide can restore wild-type resistance to infection in immuno-deficient *Drosophila* mutants," *PNAS,* 99: 2152-2157, figs. 2a and 4a. Copyright © 2002 National Academy of Sciences, U.S.A. Used with permission. **Chapter 44 44.6** Kangaroo rat data adapted from K. B. Schmidt-Nielson. 1990. *Animal Physiology: Adaptation and Environment,* 4th ed., p. 339. Cambridge: Cambridge University Press; **44.7** Adapted from K. B. Schmidt-Nielsen et al. 1958. Extrarenal salt excretion in birds. *American Journal of Physiology* 193: 101-107; **44.20** Table adapted from P. M. T. Deen et al. 1994. Requirement of human renal water channel aquaporin-2 for vasopressin-dependent concentration in urine. *Science* 264: 92-95, table 1. Copyright © 1994. Reprinted with permission from AAAS; **44 EOC** (visual summary) Adapted from W. S. Beck et al. 1991. *Life: An Introduction to Biology,* p. 649. Copyright © 1991 HarperCollins. Reprinted by permission of Pearson Education. **Chapter 45 45.4** J. M. Horowitz, et al. 1980. The Response of Single Melanophores to Extracellular and Intracellular Iontophoretic Injection of Melanocyte-Stimulating Hormone. *Endocrinology* 106: 771, fig. B. © 1980 by The Endocrine Society; **45.22** A. Jost, Recherches sur la differenciation sexuelle de l'embryon de lapin (Studies on the sexual differentiation of the rabbit embryo). *Arch. Anat. Microsc. Morphol. Exp* (*Archives d'anatomie microscopique et de morphologie expérimentale*). 36: 271-316, 1947. **Chapter 46 46.9** Figure adapted from R. R. Snook and D. J. Hosken. 2004. Sperm death and dumping in *Drosophila.. Nature* 428: 939—941, fig. 2. Copyright © 2004. Reprinted by permission of Macmillan Publishers, Ltd. **Chapter 47 47.18** From Wolpert, et al. 1998. *Principles of Development,* fig. 8.25, p. 251 (right). Oxford: Oxford University Press. By permission of Oxford University Press; **47.21a** Copyright © 1989 from *Molecular Biology of the Cell,* 2nd ed. by Bruce Alberts et al. Reproduced by permission of Garland Science/Taylor & Francis Books, Inc.; **47.21b** From Hiroki Nishida, "Cell lineage analysis in ascidian embryos by intracellular injection of a tracer enzyme: III. Up to the tissue restricted stage," *Developmental Biology,* Vol. 121, p. 526, June, 1987. Copyright © 1987 with permission from Elsevier, Inc.; **47.22** Copyright © 2002 from *Molecular Biology of the Cell,* 4th ed. by Bruce Alberts et al., fig. 21.17, p. 1172. Reproduced by permission of Garland Science/Taylor & Francis Books, Inc.; **47.24 experiment** and **left side of results** From Wolpert et al. 1998. *Principles of Development,* fig. 1.10, Oxford: Oxford University Press. By permission of Oxford University Press; **47.24 right side of results** Figure 15.12, p. 604 from *Developmental Biology,* 5th ed. by Gilbert et al. Copyright © 1997 Sinauer Associates. Used with permission. **Chapter 48 48.10** Adapted from G. Matthews, 1986. *Cellular Physiology of Nerve and Muscle,* Cambridge, MA: Blackwell Scientific Publications. © 1986 Blackwell Science. Used with permission of Blackwell Science, Inc.; **48.17** Adapted from C. B. Pert and S. H. Snyder. 1973. Opiate receptor: Demonstration in nervous tissue. *Science* 179: 1011-1014, Table 1. **Chapter 49 49.11** Adapted from L. M. Mukhametov. 1984. Sleep in marine mammals. In *Sleep Mechanisms,* by A. A. Borbéley and J. L. Valatx (eds.). Munich: Springer-Verlag, pp 227-238; **49.12** Adapted from M. R. Ralph et al. 1990. Transplanted suprachiasmatic nucleus determines circadian period. *Science* 247: 975-978, fig. 2; **49.14** Adapted from E. D. Jarvis et al. 2005. Avian brains and a new understanding of vertebrate brain evolution. *Nature Reviews Neuroscience* 6: 151-159, fig. 1c. **Chapter 50 50.14** Adapted from K. L. Mueller et al. 1975. The receptors and coding logic for bitter taste. *Nature* 434: 225-229;

50.19 Adapted from Bear et al. 2001. *Neuroscience: Exploring the Brain,* 2nd ed., figs. 11.8 and 11.9, pp. 281 and 283. Hagerstown,MD: Lippincott Williams & Wilkins. © 2001 Lippincott Williams and Wilkins; **50.22** Adapted from Shepherd. 1988. *Neurobiology,* 2nd ed., fig. 11.4, p. 227. Oxford University Press. (From V. G. Dethier. 1976. *The Hungry Fly.* Cambridge, MA: Harvard University Press.); **50.23** Adapted from Bear et al. 2001, Neuroscience: Exploring the Brain, 2nd ed., fig. 8.7, p. 196. Hagerstown,MD: Lippincott Williams & Wilkins. © 2001 Lippincott Williams and Wilkins; **50.32** Grasshopper adapted from Hickman et al. 1993. *Integrated Principles of Zoology,* 9th ed., Fig. 22.6, p. 518. New York: McGraw-Hill Higher Education. © 1993 The McGraw-Hill Companies; **50.37** K. Schmidt-Nielsen. 1972. Locomotion: Energy cost of swimming, flying, and running. *Science* 177: 222-228. **Chapter 51 51.3b** Adapted from N. Tinbergen. 1951. *The Study of Instinct.* Oxford: Oxford University Press. By permission of Oxford University Press; **51.7** Adapted from M. B. Sokolowski, 2001. *Drosophila:* Genetics meets behavior. *Nature Reviews: Genetics* 2: 881, fig. 1. Copyright © 2001 McMillan Publishing. Used with permission; **51.14 (left)** Adapted from C. S. Henry et al. 2002. The inheritance of mating songs in two cryptic, sibling lacewings species (Neuroptera: Chrysopidae: *Chrysoperla). Genetica* 116: 269-289, fig. 2. Copyright © 2002. Reprinted by permission of Springer Verlag; **51.15 (top)** Adapted from a photograph by Jonathan Blair in Alcock, 2002. *Animal Behavior,* 7th ed. Sinauer Associates, Inc., Publiishers. **51.15 (bottom)** Adapted from P. Berthold et al. 1992. Rapid microevolution of migratory behaviour in a wild bird species. *Nature* 360, 12/17,/92, p. 668, fig. 1. Copyright © 1992 Nature Publishing, Inc., used with permission; **51.18** Adapted from M. B. Sokolowski et al. 1997. Evolution of foraging behavior in *Drosophila* by density-dependent selection. Proceedings of the National Academy of Sciences of the United States of America. 94: 7373-7377. Copyright © 1997 National Academy of Sciences, U.S.A.; **51.24** K. Witte and N. Sawka. 2003. Sexual imprinting on a novel trait in the dimorphic zebra finch: sexes differ. *Animal Behaviour* 65: 195-203. Art adapted from http://www.uni-bielefeld.de/biologue/vhf/KW/Forschungsprojekte2.html. **Chapter 52 52.3** Adapted from figure at http://tde.ornl.gov. Project supported by the U.S. Dept. of Energy's Office of Science (BER); **52.5** Map adapted from G. Caughly et al. 1987. *Kangaroos: Their Ecology and Management in the Sheep Rangelands of Australia,* p. 12, fig. 1.2, Cambridge: Cambridge University Press. Copyright © 1987 Cambridge University Press. Used with permission; **52.7** Map adapted from R. L. Smith. 1974. *Ecology and Field Biology,* fig. 11.19, p. 353. Harper and Row Publishers. Map updated from D. A. Sibley. 2000. National Audubon Society *The Sibley Guide to Birds,* Alfred A. Knopf: New York; **52.8** Data from W. J. Fletcher. 1987. Interactions among subtidal Australian sea urchins, gastropods and algae: effects of experimental removals. *Ecological Monographs* 57: 89–109; **52.11** Map adapted from Physicists track great ocean conveyor belt. http://www.anl.gov/Media_Center/Frontiers/2003/d8ee.html; **52.14** Adapted from L. Roberts. 1989. How fast can trees migrate? *Science* 243: 736, fig. 2. © 1989 by the American Association for the Advancement of Science; **52.19** Adapted from Heinrich Walter and Siegmar-Walter Breckle. 2003. *Walter's Vegetation of the Earth,* fig. 16, p. 36. Springer-Verlag, © 2003; **Un. 52.2** Data from J. Clausen, D. D. Keck, and W. M. Hiesey. 1948. Experimental studies on the nature of species. III. Environmental responses of climatic races of *Achillea.* Carnegie Institution of Washington Publication 581. **Chapter 53 53.5** Adapted from P. W. Sherman and M. L. Morton, "Demography of Belding's ground squirrels," *Ecology,* Vol. 65, No. 5, p. 1622, fig. 1a, 1984. Copyright © 1984 Ecological Society of America. Used by pemission. **53.15** Adapted from J. T. Enright. 1976. Climate and population regulation: The biogeographer's dilemma. *Oecologia* 24: 295-310; **53.16** and **53.18** Adapted from T. Clutton-Brock and J. Pemberton. 2004. Soay Sheep: Dynamics and selection in an island population. Cambridge University Press. Used with permission; **53.19** Data courtesy of Rolf O. Peterson, Michigan Technological University; **53.23** Data from U. S. Census Bureau International Data Base; **53.24** Data from Population Reference Bureau 2000 and U. S. Census Bureau International Data Base, 2003; **53.25** Data from U. S. Census Bureau International Data Base; **53.26** Data from U. S. Census Bureau International Data Base 2003; **53.27** Adapted from M. L. Imhoff et al. 2004. Global patterns in human consumption of net primary production. *Nature* 429: 870-873, fig. 1a; **Tables 53.1** and **53.2** Data from P. W. Sherman and M. L. Morton, "Demography of Belding's ground squirrels," *Ecology,* Vol. 65, No. 5, p. 1622, fig. 1a, 1984. Copyright © 1984 Ecological Society of America. **Chapter 54 54.2** A. S. Rand and E. E. Williams. 1969. The anoles of La Palma: Aspects of their ecological relationships. *Breviora* 327. Museum of Comparative Zoology, Harvard University. Copyright © 1969 by the President and Fellows of Harvard College. Reprinted with permission from the Museum of Comparative Zoology; **54.10** Adapted from N. Fierer and R. B. Jackson. 2006. The diversity and biogeography of soil bacterial communities. *Proceedings of the National Academy of Sciences USA* 103: 626–631 fig. 1a. Copyright © 2006 National Academy of Sciences, U.S.A. Used with permission; **54.12** Adapted from E. A, Knox. 1970. Antarctic marine ecosystems. In *Antarctic Ecology,* ed. M. W. Holdgate, 69-96. London: Academic Press; **54.13** Adapted from D. L. Breitburg et al. 1997. Varying effects of low dissolved oxygen on trophic interactions in an estuarine food web. *Ecological Monographs* 67: 490. Copyright © 1997 Ecological Society of America; **54.14** Adapted from B. Jenkins. 1992. Productivity, disturbance and food web structure at a local spatial scale in experimental container habitats. *Oikos* 65: 252. Copyright © 1992 Oikos, Sweden; **54.15** Adapted from R. T. Paine. 1966. Food web complexity and species diversity. *American Naturalist* 100: 65-75; **54.16** Adapted from J. A. Estes et al. 1998. Killer whale predation on sea otters linking oceanic and nearshore ecosystems. *Science* 282: 474. Copyright © 1998 by the American Association for the Advancement of Science. Reprinted with permission from AAAS; **54.18** Data for graph from S. D. Hacker and M. D. Bertness. 1999. Experimental evidence for factors maintaining plant species diversity in a New England salt marsh. *Ecology* 80: 2064-2073; **54.19** Data from D. Wall Freckman and R. A. Virginia 1997. Low-diversity Antarctic soil nematode communities: distribution and response to disturbance. *Ecology* 78: 363-369; **54.20** Graph adapted from A. R. Townsend et al. 1997. The intermediate disturbance hypothesis, refugia, and diversity in streams. *Limnology and Oceanography* 42: 938-949. Copyright © 1997 by the American Society of Limnology and Oceanography, Inc. Used with permission; **54.22** Adapted from R. L. Crocker and J. Major. 1955. Soil Development in relation to vegetation and surface age at Glacier Bay, Alaska. *Journal of Ecology* 43: 427-448; **54.23** Data from F. S. Chapin, III, et al. 1994. Mechanisms of primary succession following deglaciation at Glacier Bay, Alaska. *Ecological Monographs* 64: 149-175; **54.25** Adapted from D. J. Currie. 1991. Energy and large-scale patterns of animal- and plant-species richness. *American Naturalist* 137: 27-49; **54.26** Adapted from F. W. Preston. 1960. Time and space and the variation of species. *Ecology* 41: 611-627; **54.28** Adapted from F. W. Preston. 1962. The canonical distribution of commonness and rarity. *Ecology* 43: 185-215, 410-432. **Chapter 55 55.4** and **Un 55.1** Adapted from D. L. DeAngelis. 1992. *Dynamics of Nutrient Cycling and Food Webs.* New York: Chapman & Hall; **55.7** Adapted from J. H. Ryther and W. M. Dunstan. 1971. Nitrogen, phosphorus, and eutrophication in the coastal marine environment. *Science* 171: 1008-1013. Copyright © 1971. Reprinted with permission from AAAS; **55.8** Data from M. L. Rosenzweig. 1968. New primary productivity of terrestrial environments: Predictions from climatologic data, *American Naturalist* 102: 67-74; **55.14a** Adapted from R. E. Ricklefs. 1997. *The Economy of Nature,* 4th ed. © 1997 by W. H. Freeman and Company. Used with permission; **55.15** Map adapted from Moore et al. 1999. Litter decomposition rates in Canadian forests, Global Change Biology 5: 75-82. Trofymow et al. 1998. Canadian Intersite Decomposition Experiment (CIDET): Project and site establishment. Information Report BC-X-378. NRCAN CFS Victoria. 126pp. Produced under license from Her Majesty the Queen in Right of Canada, with permission of Natural Resources Canada. The Canadian Intersite Decomposition Experiment (CIDET) - http://cfs.nrcan.gc.ca/subsite/cidet; **55.21** CO_2 data from C. D. Keeling and T. P. Whorf, Scripps Institution of Oceanography. Temperature data from www.earth-policy.org/Indicators/Temp/Temp_data.htm. **55.23** Data from ozonewatch.gsfc.nasa.gov/facts/history/htmml; **Table 55.1** Data from Menzel and Ryther. 1961. *Deep Sea Ranch* 7: 276-281. **Chapter 56 56.10** Adapted from C. J. Krebs. 2001. *Ecology,* 5th ed., fig. 19.1. Copyright © 2001 Pearson Education, Inc., publishing as Pearson Benjamin Cummings; **56.11** Adapted from R. L. Westemeiier et al. 1998. Tracking the long-term decline and recovery of an isolated population. *Science* 282: 1696. © 1998 by the American Association for the Advancement of Science; **56.17** Adapted from N. Myers et al., "Biodiversity hotspots for conservation priorities," *Nature,* Vol. 403, p. 853, 2/24/2000. Copyright © 2000 Nature Publishing, Inc. Used with permission. Updated with data from C. H. Roberts et al. 2002. Marine biodiversity hotspots and conservation priorities for tropical reefs. *Science* 295: 1280-1284; **56.18** Adapted from W.D. Newmark, "Legal and biotic boundaries of western North American national parks: A problem of congruence." *Biological Conservation* 33: 199, 1985. © 1985 Elsevier, with kind permission; **56.19a** Map adapted from W. Purves and G. Orians, *Life, The Science of Biology,* 5th ed., fig. 55.23, p. 1239. © 1998 by Sinauer Associates, Inc. Used with permission; **56.22b** Graph adapted from http://news-service.standford.edu/news/2006/may24/gcriddle_ponds.jpg; **56.24** Data from Instituto Nacional de Estadistica y Censos de Costa Rica and Centro Centroamericano de Poblacion, Universidad de Costa Rica.

Glossary

Pronunciation Key

Pronounce

ā	as in	**ace**
a		**ash**
ch		**chose**
ē		**meet**
e/eh		**bet**
g		**game**
ī		**ice**
i		**hit**
ks		**box**
kw		**quick**
ng		**song**
ō		**robe**
o		**ox**
oy		**boy**
s		**say**
sh		**shell**
th		**thin**
ū		**boot**
u/uh		**up**
z		**zoo**

′ = primary accent
′ = secondary accent

5′ cap A modified form of guanine nucleotide added onto the nucleotide at the 5′ end of a pre-mRNA molecule.

A site One of a ribosome's three binding sites for tRNA during translation. The A site holds the tRNA carrying the next amino acid to be added to the polypeptide chain. (A stands for aminoacyl tRNA.)

ABC model A model of flower formation identifying three classes of organ identity genes that direct formation of the four types of floral organs.

abiotic (ā′-bī-ot′-ik) Nonliving; referring to physical and chemical properties of an environment.

abortion The termination of a pregnancy in progress.

abscisic acid (ABA) (ab-sis′-ik) A plant hormone that slows growth, often antagonizing actions of growth hormones. Two of its many effects are to promote seed dormancy and facilitate drought tolerance.

absorption The third stage of food processing in animals: the uptake of small nutrient molecules by an organism's body.

absorption spectrum The range of a pigment's ability to absorb various wavelengths of light; also a graph of such a range.

abyssal zone (uh-bis′-ul) The part of the ocean's benthic zone between 2,000 and 6,000 m deep.

acanthodian (ak′-an-thō′-dē-un) Any of a group of ancient jawed aquatic vertebrates from the Devonian period.

accessory fruit A fruit, or assemblage of fruits, in which the fleshy parts are derived largely or entirely from tissues other than the ovary.

acclimatization (uh-klī′-muh-tī-zā′-shun) Physiological adjustment to a change in an environmental factor.

acetyl CoA Acetyl coenzyme A; the entry compound for the citric acid cycle in cellular respiration, formed from a fragment of pyruvate attached to a coenzyme.

acetylcholine (as′-uh-til-kō′-lēn) One of the most common neurotransmitters; functions by binding to receptors and altering the permeability of the postsynaptic membrane to specific ions, either depolarizing or hyperpolarizing the membrane.

acid A substance that increases the hydrogen ion concentration of a solution.

acid precipitation Rain, snow, or fog that is more acidic than pH 5.2.

acoelomate (uh-sē′-lō-māt) A solid-bodied animal lacking a cavity between the gut and outer body wall.

acquired immunity A vertebrate-specific defense that is mediated by B lymphocytes (B cells) and T lymphocytes (T cells). It exhibits specificity, memory, and self-nonself recognition. Also called adaptive immunity.

acrosomal reaction (ak′-ruh-sōm′-ul) The discharge of hydrolytic enzymes from the acrosome, a vesicle in the tip of a sperm, when the sperm approaches or contacts an egg.

acrosome (ak′-ruh-sōm) A vesicle in the tip of a sperm containing hydrolytic enzymes and other proteins that help the sperm reach the egg.

actin (ak′-tin) A globular protein that links into chains, two of which twist helically about each other, forming microfilaments (actin filaments) in muscle and other kinds of cells.

action potential A rapid change in the membrane potential of an excitable cell, caused by stimulus-triggered, selective opening and closing of voltage-sensitive gates in sodium and potassium ion channels.

action spectrum A graph that profiles the relative effectiveness of different wavelengths of radiation in driving a particular process.

activation energy The amount of energy that reactants must absorb before a chemical reaction will start; also called free energy of activation.

activator A protein that binds to DNA and stimulates gene transcription. In prokaryotes, activators bind in or near the promoter; in eukaryotes, activators bind to control elements in enhancers.

active immunity Long-lasting immunity conferred by the action of B cells and T cells and the resulting B and T memory cells specific for a pathogen. Active immunity can develop as a result of natural infection or immunization.

active site The specific portion of an enzyme that binds the substrate by means of multiple weak interactions and that forms the pocket in which catalysis occurs.

active transport The movement of a substance across a cell membrane, with an expenditure of energy, against its concentration or electrochemical gradient; mediated by specific transport proteins.

actual evapotranspiration The amount of water transpired by plants and evaporated from a landscape over a given period of time, usually measured in millimeters and estimated for a year.

adaptation Inherited characteristic of an organism that enhances its survival and reproduction in specific environments.

adaptive radiation Period of evolutionary change in which groups of organisms form many new species whose adaptations allow them to fill vacant ecological roles in their communities.

adenylyl cyclase (uh-den′-uh-lil) An enzyme that converts ATP to cyclic AMP in response to a signal.

adhesion The attraction between different kinds of molecules.

adipose tissue A connective tissue that insulates the body and serves as a fuel reserve; contains fat-storing cells called adipose cells.

adrenal gland (uh-drē′-nul) One of two endocrine glands located adjacent to the kidneys in mammals. Endocrine cells in the outer portion (cortex) respond to ACTH by secreting steroid hormones that help maintain homeostasis during long-term stress. Neurosecretory cells in the central portion (medulla) secrete epinephrine and norepinephrine in response to nervous inputs triggered by short-term stress.

adrenocorticotropic hormone (ACTH) A tropic hormone that is produced and secreted by the anterior pituitary and that stimulates the production and secretion of steroid hormones by the adrenal cortex.

aerobic respiration A catabolic pathway that consumes oxygen (O_2) and organic molecules, producing ATP. This is the most efficient catabolic pathway and is carried out in most eukaryotic cells and many prokaryotic organisms.

afferent arteriole (af′-er-ent) In the kidney, the blood vessel supplying a nephron.

age structure The relative number of individuals of each age in a population.

aggregate fruit A fruit derived from a single flower that has more than one carpel.

agonistic behavior (a′-gō-nis′-tik) In animals, an often ritualized contest that determines which competitor gains access to a resource, such as food or mates.

AIDS (acquired immunodeficiency syndrome) The symptoms and signs present during the late stages of HIV infection, defined by a specified reduction in the number of T cells and the appearance of characteristic secondary infections.

alcohol fermentation Glycolysis followed by the conversion of pyruvate to carbon dioxide and ethyl alcohol.

aldosterone (al-dos′-tuh-rōn) A steroid hormone that acts on tubules of the kidney to regulate the transport of sodium ions (Na^+) and potassium ions (K^+).

alimentary canal (al′-uh-men′-tuh-rē) A digestive tract consisting of a tube running between a mouth and an anus; also called a complete digestive tract.

allantois (al-an′-tō′-is) One of four extraembryonic membranes; serves as a repository for the embryo's nitrogenous waste and functions in gas exchange.

allele (uh-lē′-ul) Any of the alternative versions of a gene that produce distinguishable phenotypic effects.

allopatric speciation (al′-uh-pat′-rik) The formation of new species in populations that are geographically isolated from one another.

allopolyploid (al′-ō-pol′-ē-ployd) A fertile individual that has more than two chromosome sets as a result of two different species interbreeding and combining their chromosomes.

allosteric regulation The binding of a regulatory molecule to a protein at one site that affects the function of the protein at a different site.

alpha (α) helix (al′-fuh hē′-liks) A spiral shape constituting one form of the secondary structure of proteins, arising from a specific pattern of hydrogen bonding.

alternation of generations A life cycle in which there is both a multicellular diploid form, the sporophyte, and a multicellular haploid form, the gametophyte; characteristic of plants and some algae.

alternative RNA splicing A type of eukaryotic gene regulation at the RNA-processing level in which different mRNA molecules are produced from the same primary transcript, depending on which RNA segments are treated as exons and which as introns.

altruism (al′-trū-iz-um) Selflessness; behavior that reduces an individual's fitness while increasing the fitness of another individual.

alveolate (al-vē′-uh-let) A protist with membrane-bounded sacs (alveoli) located just under the plasma membrane.

alveolus (al-vē′-uh-lus) (plural, **alveoli**) One of the dead-end, multilobed air sacs where gas exchange occurs in a mammalian lung.

Alzheimer's disease (alts′-hī-merz) An age-related dementia (mental deterioration) characterized by confusion, memory loss, and other symptoms.

amacrine cell (am′-uh-krin) A neuron of the retina that helps integrate information before it is sent to the brain.

amino acid (uh-mēn′-ō) An organic molecule possessing both carboxyl and amino groups. Amino acids serve as the monomers of polypeptides.

amino group A chemical group consisting of a nitrogen atom bonded to two hydrogen atoms; can act as a base in solution, accepting a hydrogen ion and acquiring a charge of 1+.

aminoacyl-tRNA synthetase An enzyme that joins each amino acid to the appropriate tRNA.

ammonia A small, very toxic molecule (NH_3) produced by nitrogen fixation or as a metabolic waste product of protein and nucleic acid metabolism.

ammonite A member of a group of shelled cephalopods that were important marine predators for hundreds of millions of years until their extinction at the end of the Cretaceous period (65.5 mya).

amniocentesis (am′-nē-ō-sen-tē′-sis) A technique of prenatal diagnosis in which amniotic fluid, obtained by aspiration from a needle inserted into the uterus, is analyzed to detect certain genetic and congenital defects in the fetus.

amnion (am′-nē-on) One of four extraembryonic membranes. It surrounds a fluid-filled cavity that cushions the embryo.

amniote (am′-nē-ōt) Member of a clade of tetrapods named for a key derived character, the amniotic egg, which contains specialized membranes, including the fluid-filled amnion, that protect the embryo. Amniotes include mammals as well as birds and other reptiles.

amniotic egg A shelled egg in which an embryo develops within a fluid-filled amniotic sac and is nourished by yolk. Produced by reptiles (including birds) and egg-laying mammals, it enables them to complete their life cycles on dry land.

amoeba (uh-mē′-buh) A protist grade characterized by the presence of pseudopodia.

amoebocyte (uh-mē′-buh-sīt′) An amoeba-like cell that moves by pseudopodia and is found in most animals. Depending on the species, it may digest and distribute food, dispose of wastes, form skeletal fibers, fight infections, and change into other cell types.

amoebozoan (uh-mē′-buh-zō′-an) A protist in a clade that includes many species with lobe- or tube-shaped pseudopodia.

amphibian Member of the tetrapod class Amphibia, including salamanders, frogs, and caecilians.

amphipathic (am′-fē-path′-ik) Having both a hydrophilic region and a hydrophobic region.

amplification The strengthening of stimulus energy during transduction.

amygdala (uh-mig′-duh-luh) A structure in the temporal lobe of the vertebrate brain that has a major role in the processing of emotions.

amylase (am′-uh-lās′) An enzyme in saliva that hydrolyzes starch (a glucose polymer from plants) and glycogen (a glucose polymer from animals) into smaller polysaccharides and the disaccharide maltose.

anabolic pathway (an′-uh-bol′-ik) A metabolic pathway that consumes energy to synthesize a complex molecule from simpler compounds.

anaerobic respiration (an-er-ō′-bik) The use of inorganic molecules other than oxygen to accept electrons at the "downhill" end of electron transport chains.

analogous Having characteristics that are similar because of convergent evolution, not homology.

analogy (an-al′-uh-jē) Similarity between two species that is due to convergent evolution rather than to descent from a common ancestor with the same trait.

anaphase The fourth stage of mitosis, in which the chromatids of each chromosome have separated and the daughter chromosomes are moving to the poles of the cell.

anatomy The structure of an organism and its study.

anchorage dependence The requirement that a cell must be attached to a substratum in order to divide.

androgen (an′-drō-jen) Any steroid hormone, such as testosterone, that stimulates the development and maintenance of the male reproductive system and secondary sex characteristics.

aneuploidy (an′-yū-ploy′-dē) A chromosomal aberration in which one or more chromosomes are present in extra copies or are deficient in number.

angiosperm (an′-jē-ō-sperm) A flowering plant, which forms seeds inside a protective chamber called an ovary.

angiotensin II A peptide hormone that stimulates constriction of precapillary arterioles and increases reabsorption of NaCl and water by the proximal tubules of the kidney, increasing blood pressure and volume.

anhydrobiosis (an-hī′-drō-bī-ō′-sis) A dormant state involving loss of almost all body water.

animal pole The point at the end of an egg in the hemisphere where the least yolk is concentrated; opposite of vegetal pole.

Animalia The kingdom that consists of multicellular eukaryotes that ingest their food.

anion (an′-ī-on) A negatively charged ion.

annual A flowering plant that completes its entire life cycle in a single year or growing season.

anterior Pertaining to the front, or head, of a bilaterally symmetrical animal.

anterior pituitary Also called the adenohypophysis; portion of the pituitary that develops from nonneural tissue; consists of endocrine cells that synthesize and secrete several tropic and nontropic hormones.

anther In an angiosperm, the terminal pollen sac of a stamen, where pollen grains containing sperm-producing male gametophytes form.

antheridium (an-thuh-rid′-ē-um) (plural, **antheridia**) In plants, the male gametangium, a moist chamber in which gametes develop.

Glossary

anthropoid (an′-thruh-poyd) Member of a primate group made up of the monkeys and the apes (gibbons, orangutans, gorillas, chimpanzees, bonobos, and humans).

antibody A protein secreted by plasma cells (differentiated B cells) that binds to a particular antigen; also called immunoglobulin. All antibody molecules have the same Y-shaped structure and in their monomer form consist of two identical heavy chains and two identical light chains.

anticodon (an′-tī-kō′-don) A nucleotide triplet at one end of a tRNA molecule that recognizes a particular complementary codon on an mRNA molecule.

antidiuretic hormone (ADH) (an′-tī-dī-yū-ret′-ik) A peptide hormone, also known as vasopressin, that promotes water retention by the kidneys. Produced in the hypothalamus and released from the posterior pituitary, ADH also has activities in the brain.

antigen (an′-ti-jen) A macromolecule that elicits an immune response by binding to receptors of B cells or T cells.

antigen presentation The process by which an MHC molecule binds to a fragment of an intracellular protein antigen and carries it to the cell surface, where it is displayed and can be recognized by a T cell.

antigen receptor The general term for a surface protein, located on B cells and T cells, that binds to antigens, initiating acquired immune responses. The antigen receptors on B cells are called B cell receptors, and the antigen receptors on T cells are called T cell receptors.

antigen-presenting cell A cell that upon ingesting pathogens or internalizing pathogen proteins generates peptide fragments that are bound by class II MHC molecules and subsequently displayed on the cell surface to T cells. Macrophages, dendritic cells, and B cells are the primary antigen-presenting cells.

antiparallel The opposite arrangement of the sugar-phosphate backbones in a DNA double helix.

aphotic zone (ā′-fō′-tik) The part of an ocean or lake beneath the photic zone, where light does not penetrate sufficiently for photosynthesis to occur.

apical bud (ā′-pik-ul) A bud at the tip of a plant stem; also called a terminal bud.

apical dominance Concentration of growth at the tip of a plant shoot, where a terminal bud partially inhibits axillary bud growth.

apical ectodermal ridge (AER) A thickened area of ectoderm at the tip of a limb bud that promotes outgrowth of the limb bud.

apical meristem (mār′-uh-stem) Embryonic plant tissue in the tips of roots and the buds of shoots. The dividing cells of an apical meristem enable the plant to grow in length.

apicomplexan (ap′-ē-kom-pleks′-un) A protist in a clade that includes many species that parasitize animals. Some apicomplexans cause human disease.

apomixis (ap′-uh-mik′-sis) The ability of some plant species to reproduce asexually through seeds without fertilization by a male gamete.

apoplast (ap′-ō-plast) In plants, the continuum of cell walls plus the extracellular spaces.

apoptosis (ā-puh-tō′-sus) A program of controlled cell suicide, which is brought about by signals that trigger the activation of a cascade of suicide proteins in the cell destined to die.

aposematic coloration (ap′-ō-si-mat′-ik) The bright coloration of animals with effective physical or chemical defenses that acts as a warning to predators.

appendix A small, finger-like extension of the vertebrate cecum; contains a mass of white blood cells that contribute to immunity.

aquaporin A channel protein in the plasma membrane of a plant, animal, or microorganism cell that specifically facilitates osmosis, the diffusion of water across the membrane.

aqueous humor Plasma-like liquid in the space between the lens and the cornea in the vertebrate eye; helps maintain the shape of the eye, supplies nutrients and oxygen to its tissues, and disposes of its wastes.

aqueous solution (ā′-kwē-us) A solution in which water is the solvent.

arachnid A member of a major arthropod group, the cheliceriforms. Arachnids include spiders, scorpions, ticks, and mites.

arbuscular mycorrhiza (ar-bus′-kyū-lur mī′-kō-rī′-zuh) Association of a fungus with a plant root system in which the fungus causes the invagination of the host (plant) cells' plasma membranes.

arbuscular mycorrhizal fungus A symbiotic fungus whose hyphae grow through the cell wall of plant roots and extend into the root cell (enclosed in tubes formed by invagination of the root cell plasma membrane).

Archaea (ar′-kē′-uh) One of two prokaryotic domains, the other being Bacteria.

archaean Member of the prokaryotic domain Archaea.

Archaeplastida (ar′-kē-plas′-tid-uh) One of five supergroups of eukaryotes proposed in a current hypothesis of the evolutionary history of eukaryotes. This monophyletic group, which includes red algae, green alage, and land plants, descended from an ancient protist ancestor that engulfed a cyanobacterium. *See also* Excavata, Chromalveolata, Rhizaria, and Unikonta.

archegonium (ar-ki-gō′-nē-um) (plural, **archegonia**) In plants, the female gametangium, a moist chamber in which gametes develop.

archenteron (ar-ken′-tuh-ron) The endoderm-lined cavity, formed during gastrulation, that develops into the digestive tract of an animal.

archosaur (ar′-kō-sōr) Member of the reptilian group that includes crocodiles, alligators, dinosaurs, and birds.

arteriole (ar-ter′-ē-ōl) A vessel that conveys blood between an artery and a capillary bed.

artery A vessel that carries blood away from the heart to organs throughout the body.

arthropod A segmented ecdysozoan with a hard exoskeleton and jointed appendages. Familiar examples include insects, spiders, millipedes, and crabs.

artificial selection The selective breeding of domesticated plants and animals to encourage the occurrence of desirable traits.

ascocarp The fruiting body of a sac fungus (ascomycete).

ascomycete (as′-kuh-mī′-sēt) Member of the fungal phylum Ascomycota, commonly called sac fungus. The name comes from the saclike structure in which the spores develop.

ascus (plural, **asci**) A saclike spore capsule located at the tip of a dikaryotic hypha of a sac fungus.

asexual reproduction The generation of offspring from a single parent that occurs without the fusion of gametes (by budding, division of a single cell, or division of the entire organism into two or more parts). In most cases, the offspring are genetically identical to the parent.

assisted reproductive technology A fertilization procedure that generally involves surgically removing eggs (secondary oocytes) from a woman's ovaries after hormonal stimulation, fertilizing the eggs, and returning them to the woman's body.

associative learning The acquired ability to associate one environmental feature (such as a color) with another (such as danger).

aster A radial array of short microtubules that extends from each centrosome toward the plasma membrane in an animal cell undergoing mitosis.

astrocyte A glial cell with diverse functions, including providing structural support for neurons, regulating the interstitial environment, facilitating synaptic transmission, and assisting in regulating the blood supply to the brain.

atherosclerosis A cardiovascular disease in which fatty deposits called plaques develop in the inner walls of the arteries, obstructing the arteries and causing them to harden.

atom The smallest unit of matter that retains the properties of an element.

atomic mass The total mass of an atom, which is the mass in grams of 1 mole of the atom.

atomic nucleus An atom's dense central core, containing protons and neutrons.

atomic number The number of protons in the nucleus of an atom, unique for each element and designated by a subscript to the left of the elemental symbol.

ATP (adenosine triphosphate) (a-den′-ō-sēn trī-fos′-fāt) An adenine-containing nucleoside triphosphate that releases free energy when its phosphate bonds are hydrolyzed. This energy is used to drive endergonic reactions in cells.

ATP synthase A complex of several membrane proteins that provide a port through which protons diffuse. This complex functions in chemiosmosis with adjacent electron transport chains, using the energy of a hydrogen ion (proton) concentration gradient to make ATP. ATP synthases are found in the inner mitochondrial membrane of eukaryotic cells and in the plasma membrane of prokaryotes.

atrial natriuretic peptide (ANP) (ā′-trē-ul na′-trē-yū-ret′-ik) A peptide hormone secreted by cells of the atria of the heart in response to high blood pressure. ANP's effects on the kidney alter ion and water movement and thereby reduce blood pressure.

atrioventricular (AV) node A region of specialized heart muscle tissue between the left and right atria where electrical impulses are delayed for about 0.1 second before spreading to both ventricles and causing them to contract.

atrioventricular (AV) valve A heart valve located between each atrium and ventricle that prevents a backflow of blood when the ventricle contracts.

atrium (ā′-trē-um) (plural, **atria**) A chamber of the vertebrate heart that receives blood from the veins and transfers blood to a ventricle.

autocrine Referring to a secreted molecule that acts on the cell that secreted it.

autoimmune disease An immunological disorder in which the immune system turns against self.

autonomic nervous system (ot′-ō-nom′-ik) An efferent branch of the vertebrate peripheral nervous system that regulates the internal environment; consists of the sympathetic, parasympathetic, and enteric divisions.

autopolyploid (ot′-ō-pol′-ē-ployd) An individual that has more than two chromosome sets that are all derived from a single species.

autosome (ot′-ō-sōm) A chromosome that is not directly involved in determining sex; not a sex chromosome.

autotroph (ot′-ō-trōf) An organism that obtains organic food molecules without eating other organisms or substances derived from other organisms. Autotrophs use energy from the sun or from the oxidation of inorganic substances to make organic molecules from inorganic ones.

auxin (ok′-sin) A term that primarily refers to indoleacetic acid (IAA), a natural plant hormone that has a variety of effects, including cell elongation, root formation, secondary growth, and fruit growth.

average heterozygosity (het′-er-ō-zī-gō′-si-tē) The percent, on average, of a population's loci that are heterozygous in members of the population.

avirulent Describing a pathogen that can only mildly harm, but not kill, the host.

axillary bud (ak′-sil-ār-ē) A structure that has the potential to form a lateral shoot, or branch. The bud appears in the angle formed between a leaf and a stem.

axon (ak′-son) A typically long extension, or process, of a neuron that carries nerve impulses away from the cell body toward target cells.

axon hillock The conical region of a neuron's axon where it joins the cell body; typically the region where nerve impulses are generated.

B cell receptor The antigen receptor on B cells: a Y-shaped, membrane-bound molecule consisting of two identical heavy chains and two identical light chains linked by disulfide bridges and containing two antigen-binding sites.

B cells The lymphocytes that complete their development in the bone marrow and become effector cells for the humoral immune response.

Bacteria One of two prokaryotic domains, the other being Archaea.

bacterial artificial chromosome (BAC) A large plasmid that acts as a bacterial chromosome and can carry inserts of 100,000 to 300,000 base pairs.

bacteriophage (bak-tēr′-ē-ō-fāj) A virus that infects bacteria; also called a phage.

bacterium Member of the prokaryotic domain Bacteria.

bacteroid A form of the bacterium *Rhizobium* contained within the vesicles formed by the root cells of a root nodule.

balancing selection Natural selection that maintains two or more phenotypic forms in a population.

bark All tissues external to the vascular cambium, consisting mainly of the secondary phloem and layers of periderm.

Barr body A dense object lying along the inside of the nuclear envelope in cells of female mammals, representing a highly condensed, inactivated X chromosome.

barrier method Contraception that relies on a physical barrier to block the passage of sperm. Examples include condoms and diaphragms.

basal angiosperm Member of a clade of three early-diverging lineages of flowering plants. Examples are *Amborella*, water lilies, and star anise and its relatives.

basal body (bā′-sul) A eukaryotic cell structure consisting of a 9 + 0 arrangement of microtubule triplets. The basal body may organize the microtubule assembly of a cilium or flagellum and is structurally very similar to a centriole.

basal metabolic rate (BMR) The metabolic rate of a resting, fasting, and nonstressed endotherm at a comfortable temperature.

base A substance that reduces the hydrogen ion concentration of a solution.

base-pair substitution A type of point mutation; the replacement of one nucleotide and its partner in the complementary DNA strand by another pair of nucleotides.

basidiocarp Elaborate fruiting body of a dikaryotic mycelium of a club fungus.

basidiomycete (buh-sid′-ē-ō-mī′-sēt) Member of the fungal phylum Basidiomycota, commonly called club fungus. The name comes from the club-like shape of the basidium.

basidium (plural, **basidia**) (buh-sid′-ē-um, buh-sid′-ē-ah) A reproductive appendage that produces sexual spores on the gills of mushrooms (club fungi).

Batesian mimicry (bāt′-zē-un mim′-uh-krē) A type of mimicry in which a harmless species looks like a species that is poisonous or otherwise harmful to predators.

behavior (in animals) Individually, an action carried out by muscles or glands under control of the nervous system in response to a stimulus; collectively, the sum of an animal's responses to external and internal stimuli.

behavioral ecology The study of the evolution of and ecological basis for animal behavior.

benign tumor A mass of abnormal cells that remains at the site of its origin.

benthic zone The bottom surface of an aquatic environment.

benthos (ben′-thōz) The communities of organisms living in the benthic zone of an aquatic biome.

beta (β) pleated sheet One form of the secondary structure of proteins in which the polypeptide chain folds back and forth. Two regions of the chain lie parallel to each other and are held together by hydrogen bonds.

beta oxidation A metabolic sequence that breaks fatty acids down to two-carbon fragments that enter the citric acid cycle as acetyl CoA.

bicoid A maternal effect gene that codes for a protein responsible for specifying the anterior end in *Drosophila*.

biennial (bī-en′-ē-ul) A flowering plant that requires two years to complete its life cycle.

big-bang reproduction Reproduction in which an organism produces all of its offspring in a single event; also known as semelparity.

bilateral symmetry Body symmetry in which a central longitudinal plane divides the body into two equal but opposite halves.

bilaterian (bī′-luh-ter′-ē-uhn) Member of a clade of animals with bilateral symmetry and three germ layers.

bile A mixture of substances that is produced in the liver but stored in the gallbladder and that enables formation of fat droplets in water as an aid in the digestion and absorption of fats.

binary fission A method of asexual reproduction by "division in half." In prokaryotes, binary fission does not involve mitosis; but in single-celled eukaryotes that undergo binary fission, mitosis is part of the process.

binomial The two-part latinized name of a species, consisting of the genus and specific epithet.

biodiversity hot spot A relatively small area with an exceptional concentration of endemic species and often a large number of endangered and threatened species.

bioenergetics (1) The overall flow and transformation of energy in an organism. (2) The study of how energy flows through organisms.

biofilm A surface-coating colony of one or more species of prokaryotes that engage in metabolic cooperation.

biofuel A fuel produced from dry organic matter or combustible oils produced by plants.

biogenic amine A neurotransmitter derived from an amino acid.

biogeochemical cycle Any of the various chemical cycles, which involve both biotic and abiotic components of ecosystems.

biogeography The study of the past and present distribution of species.

bioinformatics The use of computers, software, and mathematical models to process and integrate biological information from large data sets.

biological augmentation An approach to restoration ecology that uses organisms to add essential materials to a degraded ecosystem.

biological clock An internal timekeeper that controls an organism's biological rhythms. The biological clock marks time with or without environmental cues but often requires signals from the environment to remain tuned to an appropriate period. *See also* circadian rhythm.

biological magnification A process in which retained substances become more concentrated at each higher trophic level in a food chain.

biological species concept Definition of a species as a population or group of populations whose members have the potential to interbreed in nature and produce viable, fertile offspring, but do not produce viable, fertile offspring with members of other such groups.

biology The scientific study of life.

biomanipulation An approach that applies the top-down model of community organization to alter ecosystem characteristics. For example, ecologists can prevent algal blooms and eutrophication by altering the density of higher-level consumers in lakes instead of by using chemical treatments.

biomass The total mass of organic matter comprising a group of organisms in a particular habitat.

biome (bī′-ōm) Any of the world's major ecosystems, often classified according to the predominant vegetation and characterized by adaptations of organisms to that particular environment.

bioremediation The use of organisms to detoxify and restore polluted and degraded ecosystems.

biosphere The entire portion of Earth inhabited by life; the sum of all the planet's ecosystems.

biotechnology The manipulation of organisms or their components to produce useful products.

biotic (bī-ot′-ik) Pertaining to the living organisms in the environment.

bipolar cell A neuron that relays information between photoreceptors and ganglion cells in the retina.

bipolar disorder Depressive mental illness characterized by swings of mood from high to low; also called manic-depressive disorder.

birth control pill A chemical contraceptive that inhibits ovulation, retards follicular development, or alters a woman's cervical mucus to prevent sperm from entering the uterus.

blade (1) A leaflike structure of a seaweed that provides most of the surface area for photosynthesis. (2) The flattened portion of a typical leaf.

blastocoel (blas′-tuh-sēl) The fluid-filled cavity that forms in the center of a blastula.

blastocyst (blas′-tuh-sist) The blastula stage of mammalian embryonic development, consisting of an inner cell mass, a cavity, and an outer layer, the trophoblast. In humans, the blastocyst forms one week after fertilization.

blastomere An early embryonic cell arising during the cleavage stage of an early embryo.

blastopore (blas′-tō-pōr) In a gastrula, the opening of the archenteron that typically develops into the anus in deuterostomes and the mouth in protostomes.

blastula (blas′-tyū-luh) A hollow ball of cells that marks the end of the cleavage stage during early embryonic development in animals.

blood A connective tissue with a fluid matrix called plasma in which red blood cells, white blood cells, and cell fragments called platelets are suspended.

blood-brain barrier A specialized capillary arrangement in the brain that restricts the passage of most substances into the brain, thereby preventing dramatic fluctuations in the brain's environment.

blue-light photoreceptor A type of light receptor in plants that initiates a variety of responses, such as phototropism and slowing of hypocotyl elongation.

body cavity A fluid- or air-filled space between the digestive tract and the body wall.

body plan In animals, a set of morphological and developmental traits that are integrated into a functional whole—the living animal.

Bohr shift A lowering of the affinity of hemoglobin for oxygen, caused by a drop in pH. It facilitates the release of oxygen from hemoglobin in the vicinity of active tissues.

bolus A lubricated ball of chewed food.

bone A connective tissue consisting of living cells held in a rigid matrix of collagen fibers embedded in calcium salts.

book lung An organ of gas exchange in spiders, consisting of stacked plates contained in an internal chamber.

bottleneck effect Genetic drift that occurs when the size of a population is reduced, as by a natural disaster or human actions. Typically, the surviving population is no longer genetically representative of the original population.

bottom-up model A model of community organization in which mineral nutrients influence community organization by controlling plant or phytoplankton numbers, which in turn control herbivore numbers, which in turn control predator numbers.

Bowman's capsule (bō′-munz) A cup-shaped receptacle in the vertebrate kidney that is the initial, expanded segment of the nephron where filtrate enters from the blood.

brachiopod (bra′-kē-uh-pod′) A marine lophophorate with a shell divided into dorsal and ventral halves. Brachiopods are also called lamp shells.

brain Organ of the central nervous system where information is processed and integrated.

brainstem Collection of structures in the vertebrate brain, including the midbrain, the pons, and the medulla oblongata; functions in homeostasis, coordination of movement, and conduction of information to higher brain centers.

branch point The representation on a phylogenetic tree of the divergence of two or more taxa from a common ancestor. Most branch points are shown as dichotomies, in which a branch representing the ancestral lineage splits (at the branch point) into two branches, one for each of the two descendant taxa.

brassinosteroid A steroid hormone in plants that has a variety of effects, including cell elongation, retarding leaf abscission, and promoting xylem differentiation.

breathing Ventilation of the lungs through alternating inhalation and exhalation.

breathing control center A brain center that directs the activity of organs involved in breathing.

bronchiole (brong′-kē-ōl′) A fine branch of the bronchi that transports air to alveoli.

bronchus (brong′-kus) (plural, **bronchi**) One of a pair of breathing tubes that branch from the trachea into the lungs.

brown alga A multicellular, photosynthetic protist with a characteristic brown or olive color that results from carotenoids in its plastids. Most brown algae are marine, and some have a plantlike body (thallus).

bryophyte (brī′-uh-fīt) An informal name for a moss, liverwort, or hornwort; a nonvascular plant that lives on land but lacks some of the terrestrial adaptations of vascular plants.

budding Asexual reproduction in which outgrowths from the parent form and pinch off to live independently or else remain attached to eventually form extensive colonies.

buffer A substance that consists of acid and base forms in a solution and that minimizes changes in pH when extraneous acids or bases are added to the solution.

bulk feeder An animal that eats relatively large pieces of food.

bulk flow The movement of a fluid due to a difference in pressure between two locations.

bundle-sheath cell In C_4 plants, a type of photosynthetic cell arranged into tightly packed sheaths around the veins of a leaf.

C_3 plant A plant that uses the Calvin cycle for the initial steps that incorporate CO_2 into organic material, forming a three-carbon compound as the first stable intermediate.

C_4 plant A plant in which the Calvin cycle is preceded by reactions that incorporate CO_2 into a four-carbon compound, the end product of which supplies CO_2 for the Calvin cycle.

cadherin (kad-hēr′-in) A member of an important class of cell adhesion molecules that requires extracellular calcium ions for its function.

calcitonin (kal′-si-tō′-nin) A hormone secreted by the thyroid gland that lowers blood calcium levels by promoting calcium deposition in bone and calcium excretion from the kidneys; nonessential in adult humans.

callus A mass of dividing, undifferentiated cells at the cut end of a shoot.

calorie (cal) The amount of heat energy required to raise the temperature of 1 g of water by 1°C; also the amount of heat energy that 1 g of water releases when it cools by 1°C. The Calorie (with a capital C), usually used to indicate the energy content of food, is a kilocalorie.

Calvin cycle The second of two major stages in photosynthesis (following the light reactions), involving fixation of atmospheric CO_2 and reduction of the fixed carbon into carbohydrate.

CAM plant A plant that uses crassulacean acid metabolism, an adaptation for photosynthesis in arid conditions. In this process, carbon dioxide entering open stomata during the night is converted to organic acids, which release CO_2 for the Calvin cycle during the day, when stomata are closed.

Cambrian explosion A relatively brief time in geologic history when large, hard-bodied forms of animals with most of the major body plans known today appeared in the fossil record. This burst of evolutionary change occurred about 535–525 million years ago.

canopy The uppermost layer of vegetation in a terrestrial biome.

capillary (kap′-il-ār′-ē) A microscopic blood vessel that penetrates the tissues and consists of a single layer of endothelial cells that allows exchange between the blood and interstitial fluid.

capillary bed A network of capillaries in a tissue or organ.

capsid The protein shell that encloses a viral genome. It may be rod-shaped, polyhedral, or more complex in shape.

capsule (1) A sticky layer that surrounds the cell wall of some prokaryotes, protecting the cell surface and sometimes helping to glue the cell to surfaces. (2) The sporangium of a bryophyte (moss, liverwort, or hornwort).

carbohydrate (kar′-bō-hī′-drāt) A sugar (monosaccharide) or one of its dimers (disaccharides) or polymers (polysaccharides).

carbon fixation The initial incorporation of carbon from CO_2 into an organic compound by an autotrophic organism (a plant, another photosynthetic organism, or a chemoautotrophic prokaryote).

carbonyl group (kar′-buh-nēl′) A chemical group present in aldehydes and ketones and consisting of a carbon atom double-bonded to an oxygen atom.

carboxyl group (kar-bok′-sil) A chemical group present in organic acids and consisting of a single carbon atom double-bonded to an oxygen atom and also bonded to a hydroxyl group.

cardiac cycle (kar′-dē-ak) The alternating contractions and relaxations of the heart.

cardiac muscle A type of muscle that forms the contractile wall of the heart. Its cells are joined by intercalated disks that relay each heartbeat.

cardiac output The volume of blood pumped per minute by each ventricle of the heart.

cardiovascular system A closed circulatory system with a heart and branching network of arteries, capillaries, and veins. The system is characteristic of vertebrates.

carnivore An animal that mainly eats other animals.

carotenoid (kuh-rot′-uh-noyd′) An accessory pigment, either yellow or orange, in the chloroplasts of plants and in some prokaryotes. By absorbing wavelengths of light that chlorophyll cannot, carotenoids broaden the spectrum of colors that can drive photosynthesis.

carpel (kar′-pul) The ovule-producing reproductive organ of a flower, consisting of the stigma, style, and ovary.

carrier In genetics, an individual who is heterozygous at a given genetic locus, with one normal allele and one recessive allele. The heterozygote is phenotypically dominant for the character determined by the gene but can pass on the recessive allele to offspring.

carrying capacity The maximum population size that can be supported by the available resources, symbolized as *K*.

cartilage (kar′-til-ij) A flexible connective tissue with an abundance of collagenous fibers embedded in chondroitin sulfate.

Casparian strip (kas-pār′-ē-un) A water-impermeable ring of wax in the endodermal cells of plants that blocks the passive flow of water and solutes into the stele by way of cell walls.

catabolic pathway (kat′-uh-bol′-ik) A metabolic pathway that releases energy by breaking down complex molecules to simpler compounds.

catalyst (kat′-uh-list) A chemical agent that increases the rate of a reaction without being consumed by the reaction.

catastrophism (kuh-tas′-truh-fiz′-um) The principle that events in the past occurred suddenly and were caused by different mechanisms than those operating today. *See* uniformitarianism.

catecholamine (kat′-uh-kōl′-uh-mēn) Any of a class of neurotransmitters and hormones, including the hormones epinephrine and norepinephrine, that are synthesized from the amino acid tyrosine.

cation (cat′-ī-on) A positively charged ion.

cation exchange A process in which positively charged minerals are made available to a plant when hydrogen ions in the soil displace mineral ions from the clay particles.

CD4 A surface protein, present on most helper T cells, that binds to class II MHC molecules, enhancing the interaction between the T cell and an antigen-presenting cell.

CD8 A surface protein, present on most cytotoxic T cells, that binds to class I MHC molecules, enhancing the interaction between the T cell and a target cell.

cDNA library A gene library containing clones that carry complementary DNA (cDNA) inserts. The library includes only the genes that were transcribed in the cells whose mRNA was isolated to make the cDNA.

cecum (sē′-kum) (plural, **ceca**) The blind pouch at the beginning of the large intestine.

cell adhesion molecule (CAM) A transmembrane, cell-surface glycoprotein that binds to CAMs on other cells. The resulting cell-to-cell attachments contribute to stable tissue structure.

cell body The part of a neuron that houses the nucleus and most other organelles.

cell cycle An ordered sequence of events in the life of a cell, from its origin in the division of a parent cell until its own division into two; the eukaryotic cell cycle is composed of interphase (including G_1, S, and G_2 subphases) and M phase (including mitosis and cytokinesis).

cell cycle control system A cyclically operating set of molecules in the eukaryotic cell that both triggers and coordinates key events in the cell cycle.

cell differentiation The structural and functional divergence of cells as they become specialized during a multicellular organism's development. Cell differentiation depends on the control of gene expression.

cell division The reproduction of cells.

cell fractionation The disruption of a cell and separation of its parts by centrifugation.

cell plate A double membrane across the midline of a dividing plant cell, between which the new cell wall forms during cytokinesis.

cell wall A protective layer external to the plasma membrane in the cells of plants, prokaryotes, fungi, and some protists. Polysaccharides such as cellulose (in plants and some protists), chitin (in fungi), and peptidoglycan (in bacteria) are an important structural component of cell walls.

cell-mediated immune response The branch of acquired immunity that involves the activation of cytotoxic T cells, which defend against infected cells.

cellular respiration The catabolic pathways of aerobic and anaerobic respiration, which break down organic molecules for the production of ATP.

cellular slime mold A type of protist that has unicellular amoeboid cells and aggregated reproductive bodies in its life cycle.

cellulose (sel′-yū-lōs) A structural polysaccharide of plant cell walls, consisting of glucose monomers joined by β glycosidic linkages.

Celsius scale (sel′-sē-us) A temperature scale (°C) equal to $^5/_9$(°F – 32) that measures the freezing point of water at 0°C and the boiling point of water at 100°C.

central canal The narrow cavity in the center of the spinal cord that is continuous with the fluid-filled ventricles of the brain.

central vacuole A membranous sac in a mature plant cell with diverse roles in reproduction, growth, and development.

centriole (sen′-trē-ōl) A structure in the centrosome of an animal cell composed of a cylinder of microtubule triplets arranged in a 9 + 0 pattern. A centrosome has a pair of centrioles.

centromere (sen′-trō-mēr) The specialized region of the chromosome where two sister chromatids are most closely attached.

centrosome (sen′-trō-sōm) Structure present in the cytoplasm of animal cells, important during cell division; functions as a microtubule-organizing center. A centrosome has two centrioles.

cephalization (sef′-uh-luh-zā′-shun) An evolutionary trend toward the concentration of sensory equipment at the anterior end of the body.

cerebellum (sār′-ruh-bel′-um) Part of the vertebrate hindbrain located dorsally; functions in unconscious coordination of movement and balance.

cerebral cortex (suh-rē′-brul) The surface of the cerebrum; the largest and most complex part of the mammalian brain, containing nerve cell bodies of the cerebrum; the part of the vertebrate brain most changed through evolution.

cerebral hemisphere The right or left side of the cerebrum.

cerebrospinal fluid (suh-rē′-brō-spī′-nul) Blood-derived fluid that surrounds, protects against infection, nourishes, and cushions the brain and spinal cord.

cerebrum (suh-rē′-brum) The dorsal portion of the vertebrate forebrain, composed of right and left hemispheres; the integrating center for memory, learning, emotions, and other highly complex functions of the central nervous system.

cervix (ser′-viks) The neck of the uterus, which opens into the vagina.

chaparral A scrubland biome of dense, spiny evergreen shrubs found at midlatitudes along coasts where cold ocean currents circulate offshore; characterized by mild, rainy winters and long, hot, dry summers.

chaperonin (shap′-er-ō′-nin) A protein molecule that assists in the proper folding of other proteins.

character An observable heritable feature.

character displacement The tendency for characteristics to be more divergent in sympatric populations of two species than in allopatric populations of the same two species.

checkpoint A control point in the cell cycle where stop and go-ahead signals can regulate the cycle.

chelicera (kē-lih′-suh-ruh) (plural, **chelicerae**) One of a pair of clawlike feeding appendages characteristic of cheliceriforms.

cheliceriform (kē-lih-suh′-ri-form) An arthropod that has chelicerae and a body divided into a cephalothorax and an abdomen. Living cheliceriforms include sea spiders, horseshoe crabs, scorpions, ticks, and spiders.

chemical bond An attraction between two atoms, resulting from a sharing of outer-shell electrons or the presence of opposite charges on the atoms. The bonded atoms gain complete outer electron shells.

chemical energy Energy available in molecules for release in a chemical reaction; a form of potential energy.

chemical equilibrium In a chemical reaction, the state in which the rate of the forward reaction equals the rate of the reverse reaction, so that the relative concentrations of the reactants and products do not change with time.

chemical reaction The making and breaking of chemical bonds, leading to changes in the composition of matter.

chemiosmosis (kem′-ē-oz-mō′-sis) An energy-coupling mechanism that uses energy stored in the form of a hydrogen ion gradient across a membrane to drive cellular work, such as the synthesis of ATP. Most ATP synthesis in cells occurs by chemiosmosis.

chemoautotroph (kē′-mō-ot′-ō-trōf) An organism that needs only carbon dioxide as a carbon source but obtains energy by oxidizing inorganic substances.

chemoheterotroph (kē′-mō-het′-er-ō-trōf) An organism that must consume organic molecules for both energy and carbon.

chemoreceptor A sensory receptor that responds to a chemical stimulus, such as a solute or an odorant.

chiasma (plural, **chiasmata**) (kī-az′-muh, kī-az′-muh-tuh) The X-shaped, microscopically visible region where homologous nonsister chromatids have exchanged genetic material through crossing over during meiosis, the two homologs remaining associated due to sister chromatid cohesion.

chitin (kī′-tin) A structural polysaccharide, consisting of amino sugar monomers, found in many fungal cell walls and in the exoskeletons of all arthropods.

chlorophyll (klōr′-ō-fil) A green pigment located within the chloroplasts of plants and algae and in the membranes of certain prokaryotes. Chlorophyll *a* participates directly in the light reactions, which convert solar energy to chemical energy.

chlorophyll *a* A photosynthetic pigment that participates directly in the light reactions, which convert solar energy to chemical energy.

chlorophyll *b* An accessory photosynthetic pigment that transfers energy to chlorophyll *a*.

chloroplast (klōr′-ō-plast) An organelle found in plants and photosynthetic protists that absorbs sunlight and uses it to drive the synthesis of organic compounds from carbon dioxide and water.

choanocyte (kō-an′-uh-sīt) A flagellated feeding cell found in sponges. Also called a collar cell, it has a collar-like ring that traps food particles around the base of its flagellum.

cholesterol (kō-les′-tuh-rol) A steroid that forms an essential component of animal cell membranes and acts as a precursor molecule for the synthesis of other biologically important steroids, such as hormones.

chondrichthyan (kon-drik′-thē-an) Member of the class Chondrichthyes, vertebrates with skeletons made mostly of cartilage, such as sharks and rays.

chordate Member of the phylum Chordata, animals that at some point during their development have a notochord; a dorsal, hollow nerve cord; pharyngeal slits or clefts; and a muscular, post-anal tail.

chorion (kōr′-ē-on) The outermost of four extraembryonic membranes. It functions in gas exchange and contributes to the formation of the mammalian placenta.

chorionic villus sampling (CVS) (kōr′-ē-on′-ik vil′-us) A technique of prenatal diagnosis in which a small sample of the fetal portion of the placenta is removed and analyzed to detect certain genetic and congenital defects in the fetus.

choroid (kor′-oyd) A thin, pigmented inner layer of the vertebrate eye.

Chromalveolata One of five supergroups of eukaryotes proposed in a current hypothesis of the evolutionary history of eukaryotes. Chromalveolates may have originated by secondary endosymbiosis and include two large protist clades, the alveolates and the stramenopiles. *See also* Excavata, Rhizaria, Archaeplastida, and Unikonta.

chromatin (krō′-muh-tin) The complex of DNA and proteins that makes up a eukaryotic chromosome. When the cell is not dividing, chromatin exists in its dispersed form, as a mass of very long, thin fibers that are not visible with a light microscope.

chromosome (krō′-muh-sōm) A cellular structure carrying genetic material, found in the nucleus of eukaryotic cells. Each chromosome consists of one very long DNA molecule and associated proteins. (A bacterial chromosome usually consists of a single circular DNA molecule and associated proteins. It is found in the nucleoid region, which is not membrane bounded.) *See also* chromatin.

chromosome theory of inheritance A basic principle in biology stating that genes are located on chromosomes and that the behavior of chromosomes during meiosis accounts for inheritance patterns.

chylomicron (kī′-lō-mī′-kron) A small globule that transports lipids. Chylomicrons are composed of fats mixed with cholesterol and coated with proteins.

chyme (kīm) The mixture of partially digested food and digestive juices formed in the stomach.

chytrid (kī′-trid) Member of the fungal phylum Chytridiomycota, mostly aquatic fungi with flagellated zoospores that represent an early-diverging fungal lineage.

ciliary body A portion of the vertebrate eye associated with the lens. It produces the clear, watery aqueous humor that fills the anterior cavity of the eye.

ciliate (sil′-ē-it) A type of protist that moves by means of cilia.

cilium (sil′-ē-um) (plural, **cilia**) A short cellular appendage containing microtubules. A motile cilium is specialized for locomotion and is formed from a core of nine outer doublet microtubules and two inner single microtubules (the "9 + 2" arrangement) ensheathed in an extension of the plasma membrane. A primary cilium is usually nonmotile and plays a sensory and signaling role; it lacks the two inner microtubules (the "9 + 0" arrangement).

circadian rhythm (ser-kā′-dē-un) A physiological cycle of about 24 hours that is present in all eukaryotic organisms and that persists even in the absence of external cues.

citric acid cycle A chemical cycle involving eight steps that completes the metabolic breakdown of glucose molecules begun in glycolysis by oxidizing pyruvate to carbon dioxide; occurs within the mitochondrion in eukaryotic cells and in the cytosol of prokaryotes; the second major stage in cellular respiration.

clade (klayd) A group of species that includes an ancestral species and all its descendants.

cladistics (kluh-dis′-tiks) An approach to systematics in which organisms are placed into groups called clades based primarily on common descent.

class In classification, the taxonomic category above the level of order.

class I MHC molecule A type of MHC molecule found on the surface of nearly all nucleated cells and that functions in identification of infected cells by cytotoxic T cells.

class II MHC molecule A type of MHC molecule restricted to a few specialized immune cell types (dendritic cells, macrophages, and B cells) that serve as antigen-presenting cells.

classical conditioning A type of associative learning in which an arbitrary stimulus becomes associated with a particular outcome.

cleavage (1) The process of cytokinesis in animal cells, characterized by pinching of the plasma membrane. (2) The succession of rapid cell divisions without significant growth during early embryonic development that converts the zygote to a ball of cells.

cleavage furrow The first sign of cleavage in an animal cell; a shallow groove in the cell surface near the old metaphase plate.

climate The long-term prevailing weather conditions at a locality.

climograph A plot of the temperature and precipitation in a particular region.

cline A graded change in a character along a geographic axis.

clitoris (klit′-uh-ris) An organ at the upper intersection of the labia minora that engorges with blood and becomes erect during sexual arousal.

cloaca (klō-ā′-kuh) A common opening for the digestive, urinary, and reproductive tracts found in many nonmammalian vertebrates but in few mammals.

clonal selection The process by which an antigen selectively binds to and activates only those lymphocytes bearing receptors specific for the antigen. The selected lymphocytes proliferate and differentiate into a clone of effector cells and a clone of memory cells specific for the stimulating antigen.

clone (1) A lineage of genetically identical individuals or cells. (2) In popular usage, a single individual organism that is genetically identical to another individual. (3) As a verb, to make one or more genetic replicas of an individual or cell. *See also* gene cloning.

cloning vector In genetic engineering, a DNA molecule that can carry foreign DNA into a host cell and replicate there. Cloning vectors include plasmids that move recombinant DNA from a test tube back into a cell and viruses that transfer recombinant DNA by infection.

closed circulatory system A circulatory system in which blood is confined to vessels and is kept separate from the interstitial fluid.

club fungus *See* basidiomycete.

cnidocyte (nī′-duh-sīt) A specialized cell unique to the phylum Cnidaria; contains a capsule-like organelle housing a coiled thread that, when discharged, explodes outward and functions in prey capture or defense.

cochlea (kok′-lē-uh) The complex, coiled organ of hearing that contains the organ of Corti.

codominance The situation in which the phenotypes of both alleles are exhibited in the heterozygote because both alleles affect the phenotype in separate, distinguishable ways.

codon (kō′-don) A three-nucleotide sequence of DNA or mRNA that specifies a particular amino acid or termination signal; the basic unit of the genetic code.

coefficient of relatedness The fraction of genes that, on average, are shared by two individuals.

coelom (sē′-lōm) A body cavity lined by tissue derived only from mesoderm.

coelomate (sē′-lō-māt) An animal that possesses a true coelom (a body cavity lined by tissue completely derived from mesoderm).

coenocytic fungus (sē′-no-si′-tic) A fungus that lacks septa and hence whose body is made up of a continuous cytoplasmic mass that may contain hundreds or thousands of nuclei.

coenzyme (kō-en′-zīm) An organic molecule serving as a cofactor. Most vitamins function as coenzymes in metabolic reactions.

cofactor Any nonprotein molecule or ion that is required for the proper functioning of an enzyme. Cofactors can be permanently bound to the active site or may bind loosely with the substrate during catalysis.

cognition The process of knowing that may include awareness, reasoning, recollection, and judgment.

cognitive map A neural representation of the abstract spatial relationships between objects in an animal's surroundings.

cohesion The binding together of like molecules, often by hydrogen bonds.

cohort A group of individuals of the same age in a population.

coitus (kō′-uh-tus) The insertion of a penis into a vagina; also called sexual intercourse.

coleoptile (kō′-lē-op′-tul) The covering of the young shoot of the embryo of a grass seed.

coleorhiza (kō′-lē-uh-rī′-zuh) The covering of the young root of the embryo of a grass seed.

collagen A glycoprotein in the extracellular matrix of animal cells that forms strong fibers, found extensively in connective tissue and bone; the most abundant protein in the animal kingdom.

collecting duct The location in the kidney where processed filtrate, called urine, is collected from the renal tubules.

collenchyma cell (kō-len′-kim-uh) A flexible plant cell type that occurs in strands or cylinders that support young parts of the plant without restraining growth.

colloid A mixture made up of a liquid and particles that (because of their large size) remain suspended rather than dissolved in that liquid.

colon (kō′-len) The largest section of the vertebrate large intestine; functions in water absorption and formation of feces.

commensalism (kuh-men′-suh-lizm) A symbiotic relationship in which one organism benefits but the other is neither helped nor harmed.

communication In animal behavior, a process involving transmission of, reception of, and response to signals. The term is also used in connection with other organisms, as well as individual cells of multicellular organisms.

community All the organisms that inhabit a particular area; an assemblage of populations of different species living close enough together for potential interaction.

community ecology The study of how interactions between species affect community structure and organization.

companion cell A type of plant cell that is connected to a sieve-tube element by many plasmodesmata and whose nucleus and ribosomes may serve one or more adjacent sieve-tube elements.

competitive exclusion The concept that when populations of two similar species compete for the same limited resources, one population will use the resources more efficiently and have a reproductive advantage that will eventually lead to the elimination of the other population.

competitive inhibitor A substance that reduces the activity of an enzyme by entering the active site in place of the substrate whose structure it mimics.

complement system A group of about 30 blood proteins that may amplify the inflammatory response, enhance phagocytosis, or directly lyse extracellular pathogens.

complementary DNA (cDNA) A double-stranded DNA molecule made *in vitro* using mRNA as a template and the enzymes reverse transcriptase and DNA polymerase. A cDNA molecule corresponds to the exons of a gene.

complete digestive tract A digestive tube that runs between a mouth and an anus; also called an alimentary canal.

complete dominance The situation in which the phenotypes of the heterozygote and dominant homozygote are indistinguishable.

complete flower A flower that has all four basic floral organs: sepals, petals, stamens, and carpels.

complete metamorphosis The transformation of a larva into an adult that looks very different, and often functions very differently in its environment, than the larva.
compound A substance consisting of two or more different elements combined in a fixed ratio.
compound eye A type of multifaceted eye in insects and crustaceans consisting of up to several thousand light-detecting, focusing ommatidia; especially good at detecting movement.
concentration gradient A region along which the density of a chemical substance increases or decreases.
conception The fertilization of an egg by a sperm in humans.
condensation reaction A reaction in which two molecules become covalently bonded to each other through the loss of a small molecule, usually water, in which case it is also called a dehydration reaction.
condom A thin, latex rubber or natural membrane sheath that fits over the penis to collect semen.
conduction The direct transfer of thermal motion (heat) between molecules of objects in direct contact with each other.
cone A cone-shaped cell in the retina of the vertebrate eye, sensitive to color.
conformer An animal for which an internal condition conforms with a change in an environmental variable.
conidium (plural, **conidia**) A haploid spore produced at the tip of a specialized hypha in ascomycetes during asexual reproduction.
conifer Member of the largest gymnosperm phylum. Most conifers are cone-bearing trees, such as pines and firs.
conjugation (kon′-jū-gā′-shun) In prokaryotes, the direct transfer of DNA between two cells (of the same or different species) that are temporarily joined. In ciliates, a sexual process in which two cells exchange haploid micronuclei.
connective tissue Animal tissue that functions mainly to bind and support other tissues, having a sparse population of cells scattered through an extracellular matrix.
conodont An early, soft-bodied vertebrate with prominent eyes and dental elements.
conservation biology The integrated study of ecology, evolutionary biology, physiology, molecular biology, and genetics to sustain biological diversity at all levels.
continental drift The slow movement of the continental plates across Earth's surface.
contraception The deliberate prevention of pregnancy.
contractile vacuole A membranous sac that helps move excess water out of certain freshwater protists.
control element A segment of noncoding DNA that helps regulate transcription of a gene by binding a transcription factor. Multiple control elements are present in a eukaryotic gene's enhancer.
controlled experiment An experiment in which an experimental group is compared with a control group that varies only in the factor being tested.
convection The mass movement of warmed air or liquid to or from the surface of a body or object.
convergent evolution The evolution of similar features in independent evolutionary lineages.
convergent extension A process in which the cells of a tissue layer rearrange themselves, so that the sheet of cells becomes narrower (converges) and longer (extends).
cooperativity A kind of allosteric regulation whereby a shape change in one subunit of a protein caused by substrate binding is transmitted to all the others, facilitating binding of subsequent substrate molecules.
copepod (cō′-puh-pod) Any of a group of small crustaceans that are important members of marine and freshwater plankton communities.
coral reef Typically a warm-water, tropical ecosystem dominated by the hard skeletal structures secreted primarily by the resident cnidarians. Some reefs also exist in cold, deep waters.
corepressor A small molecule that binds to a bacterial repressor protein and changes its shape, allowing it to switch an operon off.
cork cambium (kam′-bē-um) A cylinder of meristematic tissue in woody plants that replaces the epidermis with thicker, tougher cork cells.
cornea (kor′-nē-uh) The transparent frontal portion of the sclera, which admits light into the vertebrate eye.
corpus callosum (kor′-pus kuh-lō′-sum) The thick band of nerve fibers that connects the right and left cerebral hemispheres in mammals, enabling the hemispheres to process information together.
corpus luteum (kor′-pus lū′-tē-um) A secreting tissue in the ovary that forms from the collapsed follicle after ovulation and produces progesterone.
cortex (1) The outer region of cytoplasm in a eukaryotic cell, lying just under the plasma membrane, that has a more gel-like consistency than the inner regions, due to the presence of multiple microfilaments. (2) In plants, ground tissue that is between the vascular tissue and dermal tissue in a root or eudicot stem.
cortical granule A vesicle containing enzymes and other macromolecules located in the cortex (the region just under the plasma membrane) of an egg. Cortical granules undergo exocytosis during the cortical reaction.
cortical nephron In mammals and birds, a nephron with a loop of Henle located almost entirely in the renal cortex.
cortical reaction Exocytosis of enzymes and other macromolecules from cortical granules in the egg cytoplasm during fertilization, leading to the formation of a fertilization envelope.
corticosteroid Any steroid hormone produced and secreted by the adrenal cortex.
cotransport The coupling of the "downhill" diffusion of one substance to the "uphill" transport of another against its own concentration gradient.
cotyledon (kot′-uh-lē′-dun) A seed leaf of an angiosperm embryo. Some species have one cotyledon, others two.
countercurrent exchange The exchange of a substance or heat between two fluids flowing in opposite directions. For example, blood in a fish gill flows in the opposite direction of water passing over the gill, maximizing diffusion of oxygen into and carbon dioxide out of the blood.
countercurrent multiplier system A countercurrent system in which energy is expended in active transport to facilitate exchange of materials and generate concentration gradients.
covalent bond (kō-vā′-lent) A type of strong chemical bond in which two atoms share one or more pairs of valence electrons.
cranial nerve A nerve that originates in the brain and terminates in an organ of the head or upper body.
craniate A chordate with a head.
crassulacean acid metabolism (CAM) An adaptation for photosynthesis in arid conditions, first discovered in the family Crassulaceae. In this process, a plant takes up CO_2 and incorporates it into a variety of organic acids at night; during the day, CO_2 is released from organic acids for use in the Calvin cycle.
crista (plural, **cristae**) (kris′-tuh, kris′-tē) An infolding of the inner membrane of a mitochondrion that houses electron transport chains and molecules of the enzyme catalyzing the synthesis of ATP (ATP synthase).
critical load The amount of added nutrient, usually nitrogen or phosphorus, that can be absorbed by plants without damaging ecosystem integrity.
crop rotation The practice of planting nonlegumes one year and legumes in alternating years to restore concentrations of fixed nitrogen in the soil.
cross-fostering study A behavioral study in which the young of one species are placed in the care of adults from another species.
crossing over The reciprocal exchange of genetic material between nonsister chromatids during prophase I of meiosis.
cross-pollination In angiosperms, the transfer of pollen from an anther of a flower on one plant to the stigma of a flower on another plant of the same species.
crustacean (kruh-stā′-shun) A member of a subphylum of mostly aquatic arthropods that includes lobsters, crayfishes, crabs, shrimps, and barnacles.
cryptic coloration Camouflage that makes a potential prey difficult to spot against its background.
culture A system of information transfer through social learning or teaching that influences the behavior of individuals in a population.
cuticle (kyū′-tuh-kul) (1) A waxy covering on the surface of stems and leaves that acts as an

adaptation that prevents desiccation in terrestrial plants. (2) The exoskeleton of an arthropod, consisting of layers of protein and chitin that are variously modified for different functions. (3) A tough coat that covers the body of a nematode.

cyclic AMP (cAMP) Cyclic adenosine monophosphate, a ring-shaped molecule made from ATP that is a common intracellular signaling molecule (second messenger) in eukaryotic cells. It is also a regulator of some bacterial operons.

cyclic electron flow A route of electron flow during the light reactions of photosynthesis that involves only photosystem I and that produces ATP but not NADPH or O_2.

cyclin (sī′-klin) A cellular protein that occurs in a cyclically fluctuating concentration and that plays an important role in regulating the cell cycle.

cyclin-dependent kinase (Cdk) A protein kinase that is active only when attached to a particular cyclin.

cystic fibrosis (sis′-tik fī-brō′-sis) A human genetic disorder caused by a recessive allele for a chloride channel protein; characterized by an excessive secretion of mucus and consequent vulnerability to infection; fatal if untreated.

cytochrome (sī′-tō-krōm) An iron-containing protein that is a component of electron transport chains in the mitochondria and chloroplasts of eukaryotic cells and the plasma membranes of prokaryotic cells.

cytogenetic map A chart of a chromosome that locates genes with respect to chromosomal features distinguishable in a microscope.

cytokine (sī′-tō-kīn′) Any of a group of proteins secreted by a number of cell types, including macrophages and helper T cells, that regulate the function of lymphocytes and other cells of the immune system.

cytokinesis (sī′-tō-kuh-nē′-sis) The division of the cytoplasm to form two separate daughter cells immediately after mitosis, meiosis I, or meiosis II.

cytokinin (sī′-tō-kī′-nin) Any of a class of related plant hormones that retard aging and act in concert with auxin to stimulate cell division, influence the pathway of differentiation, and control apical dominance.

cytoplasm (sī′-tō-plaz′-um) The contents of the cell, exclusive of the nucleus and bounded by the plasma membrane.

cytoplasmic determinant A maternal substance, such as a protein or RNA, placed into an egg that influences the course of early development by regulating the expression of genes that affect the developmental fate of cells.

cytoplasmic streaming A circular flow of cytoplasm, involving myosin and actin filaments, that speeds the distribution of materials within cells.

cytoskeleton A network of microtubules, microfilaments, and intermediate filaments that branch throughout the cytoplasm and serve a variety of mechanical, transport, and signaling functions.

cytosol (sī′-tō-sol) The semifluid portion of the cytoplasm.

cytotoxic T cell A type of lymphocyte that, when activated, kills infected cells as well as certain cancer cells and transplanted cells.

dalton A measure of mass for atoms and subatomic particles; the same as the atomic mass unit, or amu.

data Recorded observations.

day-neutral plant A plant in which flower formation is not controlled by photoperiod or day length.

decapod A member of the group of crustaceans that includes lobsters, crayfishes, crabs, and shrimps.

decomposer An organism that absorbs nutrients from nonliving organic material such as corpses, fallen plant material, and the wastes of living organisms and converts them to inorganic forms; a detritivore.

deductive reasoning A type of logic in which specific results are predicted from a general premise.

deep-sea hydrothermal vent A dark, hot, oxygen-deficient environment associated with volcanic activity on or near the seafloor. The producers in a vent community are chemoautotrophic prokaryotes.

de-etiolation The changes a plant shoot undergoes in response to sunlight; also known informally as greening.

dehydration reaction A chemical reaction in which two molecules covalently bond to each other with the removal of a water molecule.

deletion (1) A deficiency in a chromosome resulting from the loss of a fragment through breakage. (2) A mutational loss of one or more nucleotide pairs from a gene.

demographic transition A shift from rapid population growth in which birth rate outpaces death rate to zero population growth characterized by low birth and death rates.

demography The study of statistics relating to births and deaths in populations.

denaturation (dē-nā′-chur-ā′-shun) In proteins, a process in which a protein unravels and loses its native shape, thereby becoming biologically inactive; in DNA, the separation of the two strands of the double helix. Denaturation occurs under extreme (noncellular) conditions of pH, salt concentration, and temperature.

dendrite (den′-drīt) One of usually numerous, short, highly branched extensions of a neuron that receive signals from other neurons.

dendritic cell An antigen-presenting cell, located mainly in lymphatic tissues and skin, that is particularly efficient in presenting antigens to helper T cells, thereby initiating a primary immune response.

density The number of individuals per unit area or volume.

density dependent Referring to any characteristic that varies according to an increase in population density.

density independent Referring to any characteristic that is not affected by population density.

density-dependent inhibition The phenomenon observed in normal animal cells that causes them to stop dividing when they come into contact with one another.

deoxyribonucleic acid (DNA) (dē-ok′-sē-rī′-bō-nū-klā′-ik) A double-stranded, helical nucleic acid molecule consisting of nucleotide monomers with a deoxyribose sugar and the nitrogenous bases adenine (A), cytosine (C), guanine (G), and thymine (T); capable of replicating and determining the inherited structure of a cell's proteins.

deoxyribose (dē-ok′-si-rī′-bōs) The sugar component of DNA nucleotides, having one fewer hydroxyl group than ribose, the sugar component of RNA nucleotides.

depolarization A change in a cell's membrane potential such that the inside of the membrane is made less negative relative to the outside. For example, a neuron membrane is depolarized if a stimulus decreases its voltage from the resting potential of –70 mV in the direction of zero voltage.

dermal tissue system The outer protective covering of plants.

desert A terrestrial biome characterized by very low precipitation.

desmosome A type of intercellular junction in animal cells that functions as a rivet.

determinate cleavage A type of embryonic development in protostomes that rigidly casts the developmental fate of each embryonic cell very early.

determinate growth A type of growth characteristic of most animals and some plant organs, in which growth stops after a certain size is reached.

determination The progressive restriction of developmental potential in which the possible fate of each cell becomes more limited as an embryo develops. At the end of determination, a cell is committed to its fate.

detritivore (deh-trī′-tuh-vōr) A consumer that derives its energy and nutrients from nonliving organic material such as corpses, fallen plant material, and the wastes of living organisms; a decomposer.

detritus (di-trī′-tus) Dead organic matter.

deuteromycete (dū′-tuh-rō-mī′-sēt) Traditional classification for a fungus with no known sexual stage. When a sexual stage for a so-called deuteromycete is discovered, the species is assigned to a phylum.

deuterostome development (dū′-tuh-rō-stōm′) In animals, a developmental mode distinguished by the development of the anus from the blastopore; often also characterized by radial cleavage and by the body cavity forming as outpockets of mesodermal tissue.

diabetes mellitus (dī′-uh-bē′-tis mel′-uh-tus) An endocrine disorder marked by inability to maintain glucose homeostasis. The type 1 form results from autoimmune destruction of insulin-secreting cells; treatment usually requires daily insulin injections. The type 2 form most commonly results from reduced responsiveness of target cells to insulin; obesity and lack of exercise are risk factors.

diacylglycerol (DAG) (dī-a′-sil-glis′-er-ol) A second messenger produced by the cleavage of a certain kind of phospholipid in the plasma membrane.

diaphragm (dī′-uh-fram′) (1) A sheet of muscle that forms the bottom wall of the thoracic cavity in mammals. Contraction of the diaphragm pulls air into the lungs. (2) A dome-shaped rubber cup fitted into the upper portion of the vagina before sexual intercourse. It serves as a physical barrier to the passage of sperm into the uterus.

diapsid (dī-ap′-sid) Member of an amniote clade distinguished by a pair of holes on each side of the skull. Diapsids include the lepidosaurs and archosaurs.

diastole (dī-as′-tō-lē) The stage of the cardiac cycle in which a heart chamber is relaxed and fills with blood.

diastolic pressure Blood pressure in the arteries when the ventricles are relaxed.

diatom (dī′-uh-tom) A unicellular photosynthetic alga with a unique glassy cell wall containing silica.

dicot A term traditionally used to refer to flowering plants that have two embryonic seed leaves, or cotyledons. Recent molecular evidence indicates that dicots do not form a clade; species once classified as dicots are now grouped into eudicots, magnoliids, and several lineages of basal angiosperms.

differential gene expression The expression of different sets of genes by cells with the same genome.

diffusion The spontaneous movement of a substance down its concentration gradient, from a region where it is more concentrated to a region where it is less concentrated.

digestion The second stage of food processing in animals: the breaking down of food into molecules small enough for the body to absorb.

dihybrid (dī′-hī′-brid) An organism that is heterozygous with respect to two genes of interest. All the offspring from a cross between parents doubly homozygous for different alleles are dihybrids. For example, parents of genotypes *AABB* and *aabb* produce a dihybrid of genotype *AaBb*.

dikaryotic (dī′-kār-ē-ot′-ik) Referring to a fungal mycelium with two haploid nuclei per cell, one from each parent.

dinoflagellate (dī′-nō-flaj′-uh-let) Member of a group of mostly unicellular photosynthetic algae with two flagella situated in perpendicular grooves in cellulose plates covering the cell.

dinosaur Member of an extremely diverse clade of reptiles varying in body shape, size, and habitat. Birds are the only extant dinosaurs.

dioecious (dī-ē′-shus) In plant biology, having the male and female reproductive parts on different individuals of the same species.

diploblastic Having two germ layers.

diploid cell (dip′-loyd) A cell containing two sets of chromosomes ($2n$), one set inherited from each parent.

diplomonad A protist that has modified mitochondria, two equal-sized nuclei, and multiple flagella.

directional selection Natural selection in which individuals at one end of the phenotypic range survive or reproduce more successfully than do other individuals.

disaccharide (dī-sak′-uh-rīd) A double sugar, consisting of two monosaccharides joined by a glycosidic linkage formed during dehydration synthesis.

discovery science The process of scientific inquiry that focuses on describing nature.

dispersal The movement of individuals (or gametes) away from their parent location. This movement sometimes expands the geographic range of a population or species.

dispersion The pattern of spacing among individuals within the boundaries of the geographic population.

disruptive selection Natural selection in which individuals on both extremes of a phenotypic range survive or reproduce more successfully than do individuals with intermediate phenotypes.

distal tubule In the vertebrate kidney, the portion of a nephron that helps refine filtrate and empties it into a collecting duct.

disturbance A natural or human-caused event that changes a biological community and usually removes organisms from it. Disturbances, such as fires and storms, play a pivotal role in structuring many communities.

disulfide bridge A strong covalent bond formed when the sulfur of one cysteine monomer bonds to the sulfur of another cysteine monomer.

DNA (deoxyribonucleic acid) (dē-ok′-sē-rī′-bō-nū-klā′-ik) A double-stranded, helical nucleic acid molecule, consisting of nucleotide monomers with a deoxyribose sugar and the nitrogenous bases adenine (A), cytosine (C), guanine (G), and thymine (T); capable of being replicated and determining the inherited structure of a cell's proteins.

DNA ligase (lī′-gās) A linking enzyme essential for DNA replication; catalyzes the covalent bonding of the 3′ end of one DNA fragment (such as an Okazaki fragment) to the 5′ end of another DNA fragment (such as a growing DNA chain).

DNA microarray assay A method to detect and measure the expression of thousands of genes at one time. Tiny amounts of a large number of single-stranded DNA fragments representing different genes are fixed to a glass slide and tested for hybridization with samples of labeled cDNA.

DNA polymerase (puh-lim′-er-ās) An enzyme that catalyzes the elongation of new DNA (for example, at a replication fork) by the addition of nucleotides to the 3′ end of an existing chain. There are several different DNA polymerases; DNA polymerase III and DNA polymerase I play major roles in DNA replication in prokaryotes.

domain (1) A taxonomic category above the kingdom level. The three domains are Archaea, Bacteria, and Eukarya. (2) An independently folding part of a protein.

dominant allele An allele that is fully expressed in the phenotype of a heterozygote.

dominant species A species with substantially higher abundance or biomass than other species in a community. Dominant species exert a powerful control over the occurrence and distribution of other species.

dopamine A neurotransmitter that is a catecholamine, like epinephrine and norepinephrine.

dormancy A condition typified by extremely low metabolic rate and a suspension of growth and development.

dorsal Pertaining to the top of an animal with radial or bilateral symmetry.

dorsal lip The region above the blastopore on the dorsal side of the amphibian embryo.

double bond A double covalent bond; the sharing of two pairs of valence electrons by two atoms.

double circulation A circulatory system consisting of separate pulmonary and systemic circuits, in which blood passes through the heart after completing each circuit.

double fertilization A mechanism of fertilization in angiosperms in which two sperm cells unite with two cells in the female gametophyte (embryo sac) to form the zygote and endosperm.

double helix The form of native DNA, referring to its two adjacent antiparallel polynucleotide strands wound around an imaginary axis into a spiral shape.

Down syndrome A human genetic disease caused by the presence of an extra chromosome 21; characterized by mental retardation and heart and respiratory defects.

Duchenne muscular dystrophy (duh-shen′) A human genetic disease caused by a sex-linked recessive allele; characterized by progressive weakening and a loss of muscle tissue.

duodenum (dū′-uh-dēn′-um) The first section of the small intestine, where chyme from the stomach mixes with digestive juices from the pancreas, liver, and gallbladder as well as from gland cells of the intestinal wall.

duplication An aberration in chromosome structure due to fusion with a fragment from a homologous chromosome, such that a portion of a chromosome is duplicated.

dynamic stability hypothesis The idea that long food chains are less stable than short chains.

dynein (dī′-nē-un) In cilia and flagella, a large contractile protein extending from one microtubule doublet to the adjacent doublet. ATP hydrolysis drives changes in dynein shape that lead to bending of cilia and flagella.

E site One of a ribosome's three binding sites for tRNA during translation. The E site is the place where discharged tRNAs leave the ribosome. (E stands for exit.)

ecdysone (ek′-duh-sōn) A steroid hormone, secreted by the prothoracic glands, that triggers molting in arthropods.

ecdysozoan Member of a group of animal phyla identified as a clade by molecular evidence. Many ecdysozoans are molting animals.

echinoderm (i-kī′-nō-derm) A slow-moving or sessile marine deuterostome with a water vascular system and, in larvae, bilateral symmetry. Echinoderms include sea stars, brittle stars, sea urchins, feather stars, and sea cucumbers.

ecological footprint The aggregate land and water area required by a person, city, or nation to produce all of the resources it consumes and to absorb all of the waste it generates.

ecological niche (nich) The sum of a species' use of the biotic and abiotic resources in its environment.

ecological species concept A definition of species in terms of ecological niche, the sum of how members of the species interact with the nonliving and living parts of their environment.

ecological succession Transition in the species composition of a community following a disturbance; the establishment of a community in an area virtually barren of life.

ecology The study of how organisms interact with each other and their environment.

ecosystem All the organisms in a given area as well as the abiotic factors with which they interact; one or more communities and the physical environment around them.

ecosystem ecology The study of energy flow and the cycling of chemicals among the various biotic and abiotic components in an ecosystem.

ecosystem service A function performed by an ecosystem that directly or indirectly benefits humans.

ecotone The transition from one type of habitat or ecosystem to another, such as the transition from a forest to a grassland.

ectoderm (ek′-tō-durm) The outermost of the three primary germ layers in animal embryos; gives rise to the outer covering and, in some phyla, the nervous system, inner ear, and lens of the eye.

ectomycorrhiza (ek′-tō-mī′-kō-rī′-zuh) Association of a fungus with a plant root system in which the fungus surrounds the roots but does not cause invagination of the host (plant) cells' plasma membranes.

ectomycorrhizal fungus A symbiotic fungus that forms sheaths of hyphae over the surface of plant roots and also grows into extracellular spaces of the root cortex.

ectoparasite A parasite that feeds on the external surface of a host.

ectopic Occurring in an abnormal location.

ectoproct A sessile, colonial lophophorate commonly called a bryozoan.

ectothermic Referring to organisms for which external sources provide most of the heat for temperature regulation.

Ediacaran biota (ē′-dē-uh-keh′-run bī-ō′-tuh) An early group of soft-bodied, multicellular eukaryotes known from fossils that range in age from 565 million to 545 million years old.

effective population size An estimate of the size of a population based on the numbers of females and males that successfully breed; generally smaller than the total population.

effector cell (1) A muscle cell or gland cell that performs the body's response to stimuli as directed by signals from the brain or other processing center of the nervous system. (2) A lymphocyte that has undergone clonal selection and is capable of mediating an acquired immune response.

efferent arteriole In the kidney, the blood vessel draining a nephron.

egg The female gamete.

egg-polarity gene A gene that helps control the orientation (polarity) of the egg; also called a maternal effect gene.

ejaculation The propulsion of sperm from the epididymis through the muscular vas deferens, ejaculatory duct, and urethra.

ejaculatory duct In mammals, the short section of the ejaculatory route formed by the convergence of the vas deferens and a duct from the seminal vesicle. The ejaculatory duct transports sperm from the vas deferens to the urethra.

electrocardiogram (ECG or EKG) A record of the electrical impulses that travel through heart muscle during the cardiac cycle.

electrochemical gradient The diffusion gradient of an ion, which is affected by both the concentration difference of the ion across a membrane (a chemical force) and the ion's tendency to move relative to the membrane potential (an electrical force).

electrogenic pump An ion transport protein that generates voltage across a membrane.

electromagnetic receptor A receptor of electromagnetic energy, such as visible light, electricity, or magnetism.

electromagnetic spectrum The entire spectrum of electromagnetic radiation ranging in wavelength from less than a nanometer to more than a kilometer.

electron A subatomic particle with a single negative electrical charge and a mass about $^{1}/_{2,000}$ that of a neutron or proton. One or more electrons move around the nucleus of an atom.

electron microscope (EM) A microscope that uses magnets to focus an electron beam on or through a specimen, resulting in resolving power a thousandfold greater than that of a light microscope. A transmission electron microscope (TEM) is used to study the internal structure of thin sections of cells. A scanning electron microscope (SEM) is used to study the fine details of cell surfaces.

electron shell An energy level of electrons at a characteristic average distance from the nucleus of an atom.

electron transport chain A sequence of electron carrier molecules (membrane proteins) that shuttle electrons during the redox reactions that release energy used to make ATP.

electronegativity The attraction of a given atom for the electrons of a covalent bond.

electroporation A technique to introduce recombinant DNA into cells by applying a brief electrical pulse to a solution containing the cells. The pulse creates temporary holes in the cells' plasma membranes, through which DNA can enter.

element Any substance that cannot be broken down to any other substance by chemical reactions.

elimination The fourth and final stage of food processing in animals: the passing of undigested material out of the digestive system.

embryo sac (em′-brē-ō) The female gametophyte of angiosperms, formed from the growth and division of the megaspore into a multicellular structure that typically has eight haploid nuclei.

embryonic lethal A mutation with a phenotype leading to death of an embryo or larva.

embryophyte Alternate name for land plants that refers to their shared derived trait of multicellular, dependent embryos.

emergent properties New properties that arise with each step upward in the hierarchy of life, owing to the arrangement and interactions of parts as complexity increases.

emigration The movement of individuals out of a population.

enantiomer (en-an′-tē-ō-mer) One of two compounds that are mirror images of each other.

endangered species A species that is in danger of extinction throughout all or a significant portion of its range.

endemic (en-dem′-ik) Referring to a species that is confined to a specific, relatively small geographic area.

endergonic reaction (en′-der-gon′-ik) A nonspontaneous chemical reaction, in which free energy is absorbed from the surroundings.

endocrine gland (en′-dō-krin) A ductless gland that secretes hormones directly into the interstitial fluid, from which they diffuse into the bloodstream.

endocrine system The internal system of communication involving hormones, the ductless glands that secrete hormones, and the molecular receptors on or in target cells that respond to hormones; functions in concert with the nervous system to effect internal regulation and maintain homeostasis.

endocytosis (en′-dō-sī-tō′-sis) Cellular uptake of biological molecules and particulate matter via formation of new vesicles from the plasma membrane.

endoderm (en′-dō-durm) The innermost of the three primary germ layers in animal embryos; lines the archenteron and gives rise to the liver, pancreas, lungs, and the lining of the digestive tract in species that have these structures.

endodermis The innermost layer of the cortex in plant roots; a cylinder one cell thick that forms the boundary between the cortex and the vascular cylinder.

endomembrane system The collection of membranes inside and around a eukaryotic cell, related either through direct physical contact or by the transfer of membranous vesicles; includes the smooth and rough endoplasmic reticulum, the Golgi apparatus, lysosomes, and vacuoles.

endometriosis (en′-dō-mē-trē-ō′-sis) The condition resulting from the presence of endometrial tissue outside of the uterus.

endometrium (en′-dō-mē′-trē-um) The inner lining of the uterus, which is richly supplied with blood vessels.

endoparasite A parasite that lives within a host.

endophyte A fungus that lives inside a leaf or other plant part without causing harm to the plant.

endoplasmic reticulum (ER) (en′-dō-plaz′-mik ruh-tik′-yū-lum) An extensive membranous network in eukaryotic cells, continuous with the outer nuclear membrane and composed of ribosome-studded (rough) and ribosome-free (smooth) regions.

endorphin (en-dōr′-fin) Any of several hormones produced in the brain and anterior pituitary that inhibits pain perception.

endoskeleton A hard skeleton buried within the soft tissues of an animal, such as the spicules of sponges, the plates of echinoderms, and the bony skeletons of vertebrates.

endosperm In angiosperms, a nutrient-rich tissue formed by the union of a sperm with two polar nuclei during double fertilization. The endosperm provides nourishment to the developing embryo in angiosperm seeds.

endospore A thick-coated, resistant cell produced by a bacterial cell exposed to harsh conditions.

endosymbiosis A process in which a unicellular organism (the "host") engulfs another cell, which lives within the host cell and ultimately becomes an organelle in the host cell; also refers to the hypothesis that mitochondria and plastids were formerly small prokaryotes that began living within larger cells.

endothelin A peptide produced by a blood vessel's endothelium that causes the vessel to constrict.

endothelium (en′-dō-thē′-lē-um) The simple squamous layer of cells lining the lumen of blood vessels.

endothermic Referring to organisms with bodies that are warmed by heat generated by metabolism. This heat is usually used to maintain a relatively stable body temperature higher than that of the external environment.

endotoxin A toxic component of the outer membrane of certain gram-negative bacteria that is released only when the bacteria die.

energetic hypothesis The concept that the length of a food chain is limited by the inefficiency of energy transfer along the chain.

energy The capacity to cause change, especially to do work (to move matter against an opposing force).

energy coupling In cellular metabolism, the use of energy released from an exergonic reaction to drive an endergonic reaction.

enhancer A segment of eukaryotic DNA containing multiple control elements, usually located far from the gene whose transcription it regulates.

enteric division Networks of neurons in the digestive tract, pancreas, and gallbladder; normally regulated by the sympathetic and parasympathetic divisions of the autonomic nervous system.

entropy A measure of disorder, or randomness.

enzymatic hydrolysis The process in digestion that splits macromolecules from food by the enzymatic addition of water.

enzyme (en′-zīm) A macromolecule serving as a catalyst, a chemical agent that changes the rate of a reaction without being consumed by the reaction.

enzyme-substrate complex A temporary complex formed when an enzyme binds to its substrate molecule(s).

eosinophil (ē′-ō-sin′-ō-fil) A type of white blood cell with low phagocytic activity that is thought to play a role in defense against parasitic worms by releasing enzymes toxic to these invaders.

epicotyl (ep′-uh-kot′-ul) In an angiosperm embryo, the embryonic axis above the point of attachment of the cotyledon(s) and below the first pair of miniature leaves.

epidemic A general outbreak of a disease.

epidermis (1) The dermal tissue system of nonwoody plants, usually consisting of a single layer of tightly packed cells. (2) The outermost layer of cells in an animal.

epididymis (ep′-uh-did′-uh-mus) A coiled tubule located adjacent to the mammalian testis where sperm are stored.

epigenetic inheritance Inheritance of traits transmitted by mechanisms not directly involving the nucleotide sequence of a genome.

epinephrine (ep′-i-nef′-rin) A catecholamine that, when secreted as a hormone by the adrenal medulla, mediates "fight-or-flight" responses to short-term stresses; also released by some neurons as a neurotransmitter; also known as adrenaline.

epiphyte (ep′-uh-fīt) A plant that nourishes itself but grows on the surface of another plant for support, usually on the branches or trunks of tropical trees.

epistasis (ep′-i-stā′-sis) A type of gene interaction in which one gene alters the phenotypic effects of another gene that is independently inherited.

epithelial tissue (ep′-uh-thē′-lē-ul) Sheets of tightly packed cells that line organs and body cavities as well as external surfaces.

epithelium An epithelial tissue.

epitope A small, accessible region of an antigen to which an antigen receptor or antibody binds; also called an antigenic determinant.

EPSP *See* excitatory postsynaptic potential.

equilibrium potential (E_{ion}) The magnitude of a cell's membrane voltage at equilibrium; calculated using the Nernst equation.

erythrocyte (eh-rith′-ruh-sīt) A blood cell that contains hemoglobin, which transports oxygen; also called a red blood cell.

erythropoietin (EPO) (eh-rith′-rō-poy′-uh-tin) A hormone that stimulates the production of erythrocytes. It is secreted by the kidney when body tissues do not receive enough oxygen.

esophagus (eh-sof′-uh-gus) A channel that conducts food, by peristalsis, from the pharynx to the stomach.

essential amino acid An amino acid that an animal cannot synthesize itself and must be obtained from food in prefabricated form. Eight amino acids are essential in the human adult.

essential element In plants, a chemical element required for the plant to grow from a seed and complete its life cycle, producing another generation in the form of seeds.

essential fatty acid An unsaturated fatty acid that an animal needs but cannot make.

essential nutrient A substance that an organism must absorb in preassembled form because it cannot be synthesized from any other material. In humans, there are essential vitamins, minerals, amino acids, and fatty acids.

estradiol (es′-truh-dī′-ol) A steroid hormone that stimulates the development and maintenance of the female reproductive system and secondary sex characteristics; the major estrogen in mammals.

estrogen (es′-trō-jen) Any steroid hormone, such as estradiol, that stimulates the development and maintenance of the female reproductive system and secondary sex characteristics.

estrous cycle (es′-trus) A reproductive cycle characteristic of female mammals except humans and certain other primates, in which the nonpregnant endometrium is reabsorbed rather than shed, and sexual response occurs only during mid-cycle at estrus.

estuary The area where a freshwater stream or river merges with the ocean.

ethology The scientific study of how animals behave, particularly in their natural environments.

ethylene (eth′-uh-lēn) The only gaseous plant hormone. Among its many effects are response to mechanical stress, programmed cell death, leaf abscission, and fruit ripening.

etiolation Plant morphological adaptations for growing in darkness.

euchromatin (yū-krō′-muh-tin) The less condensed form of eukaryotic chromatin that is available for transcription.

eudicot (yū-dī′-kot) Member of a clade consisting of the vast majority of flowering plants that have two embryonic seed leaves, or cotyledons.

euglenid (yū′-glen-id) A protist, such as *Euglena* or its relatives, characterized by an anterior pocket from which one or two flagella emerge.

euglenozoan Member of a diverse clade of flagellated protists that includes predatory heterotrophs, photosynthetic autotrophs, and pathogenic parasites.

Eukarya (yū-kar′-ē-uh) The domain that includes all eukaryotic organisms.

eukaryotic cell (yū′-ker-ē-ot′-ik) A type of cell with a membrane-enclosed nucleus and membrane-enclosed organelles. Organisms with eukaryotic cells (protists, plants, fungi, and animals) are called eukaryotes.

eumetazoan (yū′-met-uh-zō′-un) Member of a clade of animals with true tissues. All animals except sponges and a few other groups are eumetazoans.

euryhaline (yur′-i-hā′-līn) Referring to organisms that tolerate substantial changes in external osmolarity.

eurypterid (yur-ip′-tuh-rid) An extinct carnivorous cheliceriform also called a water scorpion.

Eustachian tube (yū-stā′-shun) The tube that connects the middle ear to the pharynx.

eutherian (yū-thēr′-ē-un) Placental mammal; mammal whose young complete their embryonic development within the uterus, joined to the mother by the placenta.

eutrophic lake (yū-trōf′-ik) A lake that has a high rate of biological productivity supported by a high rate of nutrient cycling.

eutrophication A process by which nutrients, particularly phosphorus and nitrogen, become highly concentrated in a body of water, leading to increased growth of organisms such as algae or cyanobacteria.

evaporation The process by which a liquid changes to a gas.

evaporative cooling The process in which the surface of an object becomes cooler during evaporation, owing to a change of the molecules with the greatest kinetic energy from the liquid to the gaseous state.

evapotranspiration The total evaporation of water from an ecosystem, including evaporation from soil and the outside of plants, as well as the transpiration of water from within plants through stomata.

evo-devo Evolutionary developmental biology; a field of biology that compares developmental processes of different multicellular organisms to understand how these processes have evolved and how changes can modify existing organismal features or lead to new ones.

evolution Descent with modification; the idea that living species are descendants of ancestral species that were different from the present-day ones; also defined more narrowly as the change in the genetic composition of a population from generation to generation.

evolutionary tree A branching diagram that reflects a hypothesis about evolutionary relationships among groups of organisms.

Excavata One of five supergroups of eukaryotes proposed in a current hypothesis of the evolutionary history of eukaryotes. Excavates have unique cytoskeletal features, and some species have an "excavated" feeding groove on one side of the cell body. *See also* Chromalveolata, Rhizaria, Archaeplastida, and Unikonta.

excitatory postsynaptic potential (EPSP) An electrical change (depolarization) in the membrane of a postsynaptic cell caused by the binding of an excitatory neurotransmitter from a presynaptic cell to a postsynaptic receptor; makes it more likely for a postsynaptic cell to generate an action potential.

excretion The disposal of nitrogen-containing metabolites and other waste products.

exergonic reaction (ek′-ser-gon′-ik) A spontaneous chemical reaction, in which there is a net release of free energy.

exocytosis (ek′-sō-sī-tō′-sis) The cellular secretion of biological molecules by the fusion of vesicles containing them with the plasma membrane.

exon A sequence within a primary transcript that remains in the RNA after RNA processing; also refers to the region of DNA from which this sequence was transcribed.

exoskeleton A hard encasement on the surface of an animal, such as the shell of a mollusc or the cuticle of an arthropod, that provides protection and points of attachment for muscles.

exotoxin (ek′-sō-tok′-sin) A toxic protein that is secreted by a prokaryote or other pathogen and that produces specific symptoms, even if the pathogen is no longer present.

expansin Plant enzyme that breaks the cross-links (hydrogen bonds) between cellulose microfibrils and other cell wall constituents, loosening the wall's fabric.

exponential population growth Growth of a population in an ideal, unlimited environment, represented by a J-shaped curve when population size is plotted over time.

expression vector A cloning vector that contains the requisite bacterial promoter just upstream of a restriction site where a eukaryotic gene can be inserted, allowing the gene to be expressed in a bacterial cell.

external fertilization The fusion of gametes that parents have discharged into the environment.

extinction vortex A downward population spiral in which inbreeding and genetic drift combine to cause a small population to shrink and, unless the spiral is reversed, to become extinct.

extracellular digestion The breakdown of food in compartments that are continuous with the outside of an animal's body.

extracellular matrix (ECM) The substance in which animal cells are embedded, consisting of protein and polysaccharides synthesized and secreted by cells.

extraembryonic membrane One of four membranes (yolk sac, amnion, chorion, and allantois) located outside the embryo that support the developing embryo in reptiles and mammals.

extreme halophile An organism that lives in a highly saline environment, such as the Great Salt Lake or the Dead Sea.

extreme thermophile An organism that thrives in hot environments (often 60–80°C or hotter).

extremophile An organism that lives in an environment whose conditions are so extreme that few other species can survive there. Extremophiles include extreme halophiles and extreme thermophiles.

F factor In bacteria, the DNA segment that confers the ability to form pili for conjugation and associated functions required for the transfer of DNA from donor to recipient. The F factor may exist as a plasmid or be integrated into the bacterial chromosome.

F plasmid The plasmid form of the F factor.

F_1 generation The first filial, or hybrid, offspring in a series of genetic crosses.

F_2 generation Offspring resulting from interbreeding of the hybrid F_1 generation.

facilitated diffusion The spontaneous passage of molecules or ions across a biological membrane with the assistance of specific transmembrane transport proteins.

facilitator A species that has a positive effect on the survival and reproduction of other species in a community and that influences community structure.

facultative anaerobe (fak′-ul-tā′-tiv an′-uh-rōb) An organism that makes ATP by aerobic respiration if oxygen is present but that switches to anaerobic respiration or fermentation if oxygen is not present.

family In classification, the taxonomic category above genus.

fast block to polyspermy The depolarization of the egg plasma membrane that begins within 1–3 seconds after a sperm binds to an egg membrane protein. The depolarization lasts about 1 minute and prevents additional sperm from fusing with the egg during that time.

fast-twitch fiber A muscle fiber used for rapid, powerful contractions.

fat A lipid consisting of three fatty acids linked to one glycerol molecule; also called a triacylglycerol or triglyceride.

fate map A territorial diagram of embryonic development that displays the future derivatives of individual cells and tissues.

fatty acid A long carbon chain carboxylic acid. Fatty acids vary in length and in the number and location of double bonds; three fatty acids linked to a glycerol molecule form a fat molecule, also known as a triacylglycerol or triglyceride.

feces (fē′-sēz) The wastes of the digestive tract.

feedback inhibition A method of metabolic control in which the end product of a metabolic pathway acts as an inhibitor of an enzyme within that pathway.

fermentation A catabolic process that makes a limited amount of ATP from glucose without

Glossary

an electron transport chain and that produces a characteristic end product, such as ethyl alcohol or lactic acid.

fertilization (1) The union of haploid gametes to produce a diploid zygote. (2) The addition of mineral nutrients to the soil.

fertilization envelope The protective layer formed when the vitelline layer of an egg is pushed away from the plasma membrane and hardened after fertilization by molecules exocytosed during the cortical reaction.

fetus (fē′-tus) A developing mammal that has all the major structures of an adult. In humans, the fetal stage lasts from the 9th week of gestation until birth.

fiber A lignified cell type that reinforces the xylem of angiosperms and functions in mechanical support; a slender, tapered sclerenchyma cell that usually occurs in bundles.

fibrin (fī′-brin) The activated form of the blood-clotting protein fibrinogen. Fibrin aggregates into threads that form the fabric of the clot.

fibroblast (fī′-brō-blast) A type of cell in loose connective tissue that secretes the protein ingredients of the extracellular fibers.

fibronectin A glycoprotein that helps animal cells attach to the extracellular matrix.

filament In an angiosperm, the stalk portion of the stamen, the pollen-producing reproductive organ of a flower.

filtrate Cell-free fluid extracted from the body fluid by the excretory system.

filtration In excretory systems, the extraction of water and small solutes, including metabolic wastes, from the body fluid.

fimbria (plural, **fimbriae**) A short, hairlike appendage of a prokaryotic cell that helps it adhere to the substrate or to other cells; also known as an attachment pilus.

first law of thermodynamics The principle of conservation of energy: Energy can be transferred and transformed, but it cannot be created or destroyed.

fission The separation of an organism into two or more individuals of approximately equal size.

fixed action pattern In animal behavior, a sequence of unlearned acts that is essentially unchangeable and, once initiated, usually carried to completion.

flaccid (flas′-id) Limp. Lacking in stiffness or firmness, as in a plant cell in surroundings where there is no tendency for water to enter the cell.

flagellum (fluh-jel′-um) (plural, **flagella**) A long cellular appendage specialized for locomotion. Like motile cilia, eukaryotic flagella have a core with nine outer doublet microtubules and two inner single microtubules ensheathed in an extension of the plasma membrane. Prokaryotic flagella have a different structure.

florigen A flowering signal, not yet chemically identified, that may be a hormone or may be a change in relative concentrations of multiple hormones.

flower In an angiosperm, a short stem with up to four sets of modified leaves, bearing structures that function in sexual reproduction.

fluid feeder An animal that lives by sucking nutrient-rich fluids from another living organism.

fluid mosaic model The currently accepted model of cell membrane structure, which envisions the membrane as a mosaic of protein molecules drifting laterally in a fluid bilayer of phospholipids.

follicle (fol′-uh-kul) A microscopic structure in the ovary that contains the developing oocyte and secretes estrogens.

follicle-stimulating hormone (FSH) A tropic hormone that is produced and secreted by the anterior pituitary and that stimulates the production of eggs by the ovaries and sperm by the testes.

follicular phase That part of the ovarian cycle during which follicles are growing and oocytes maturing.

food chain The pathway along which food energy is transferred from trophic level to trophic level, beginning with producers.

food vacuole A membranous sac formed by phagocytosis of microorganisms or particles to be used as food by the cell.

food web The interconnected feeding relationships in an ecosystem.

foot (1) The portion of a bryophyte sporophyte that gathers sugars, amino acids, water, and minerals from the parent gametophyte via transfer cells. (2) One of the three main parts of a mollusc; a muscular structure usually used for movement. *See also* mantle, visceral mass.

foraging The seeking and obtaining of food.

foram (foraminiferan) An aquatic protist that secretes a hardened shell containing calcium carbonate and extends pseudopodia through pores in the shell.

foraminiferan *See* foram.

forebrain One of three ancestral and embryonic regions of the vertebrate brain; develops into the thalamus, hypothalamus, and cerebrum.

fossil A preserved remnant or impression of an organism that lived in the past.

founder effect Genetic drift that occurs when a few individuals become isolated from a larger population and form a new population whose gene pool composition is not reflective of that of the original population.

fovea (fō′-vē-uh) The place on the retina at the eye's center of focus, where cones are highly concentrated.

fragmentation A means of asexual reproduction whereby a single parent breaks into parts that regenerate into whole new individuals.

frameshift mutation A mutation occurring when the number of nucleotides inserted or deleted is not a multiple of three, resulting in the improper grouping of the subsequent nucleotides into codons.

free energy The portion of a biological system's energy that can perform work when temperature and pressure are uniform throughout the system. (The change in free energy of a system is calculated by the equation $\Delta G = \Delta H - T\Delta S$, where H is enthalpy [in biological systems, equivalent to total energy], T is absolute temperature, and S is entropy.)

frequency-dependent selection A decline in the reproductive success of individuals that have a phenotype that has become too common in a population.

fruit A mature ovary of a flower. The fruit protects dormant seeds and often aids in their dispersal.

functional group A specific configuration of atoms commonly attached to the carbon skeletons of organic molecules and usually involved in chemical reactions.

Fungi (fun′-jē) The eukaryotic kingdom that includes organisms that absorb nutrients after decomposing organic material.

G_0 phase A nondividing state occupied by cells that have left the cell cycle.

G_1 phase The first gap, or growth phase, of the cell cycle, consisting of the portion of interphase before DNA synthesis begins.

G_2 phase The second gap, or growth phase, of the cell cycle, consisting of the portion of interphase after DNA synthesis occurs.

gallbladder An organ that stores bile and releases it as needed into the small intestine.

game theory An approach to evaluating alternative strategies in situations where the outcome of a particular strategy depends on the strategies used by other individuals.

gametangium (gam′-uh-tan′-jē-um) (plural, **gametangia**) Multicellular plant structure in which gametes are formed. Female gametangia are called archegonia, and male gametangia are called antheridia.

gamete (gam′-ēt) A haploid reproductive cell, such as an egg or sperm. Gametes unite during sexual reproduction to produce a diploid zygote.

gametogenesis The process by which gametes are produced.

gametophore (guh-mē′-tō-fōr) The mature gamete-producing structure of a moss gametophyte.

gametophyte (guh-mē′-tō-fīt) In organisms (plants and some algae) that have alternation of generations, the multicellular haploid form that produces haploid gametes by mitosis. The haploid gametes unite and develop into sporophytes.

gamma-aminobutyric acid (GABA) An amino acid that functions as a CNS neurotransmitter in the central nervous system of vertebrates.

ganglion (gang′-glē-un) (plural, **ganglia**) A cluster (functional group) of nerve cell bodies in a centralized nervous system.

ganglion cell A type of neuron in the retina that synapses with bipolar cells and transmits action potentials to the brain via axons in the optic nerve.

gap junction A type of intercellular junction in animals that allows the passage of materials between cells.

gas exchange The uptake of molecular oxygen from the environment and the discharge of carbon dioxide to the environment.

gastric juice A digestive fluid secreted by the stomach.

gastrovascular cavity A central cavity with a single opening in the body of certain animals that functions in both the digestion and distribution of nutrients.

gastrula (gas′-trū-luh) An embryonic stage in animal development encompassing the formation of three layers: ectoderm, mesoderm, and endoderm.

gastrulation (gas′-trū-lā′-shun) In animal development, a series of cell and tissue movements in which the blastula-stage embryo folds inward, producing a three-layered embryo, the gastrula.

gated channel A transmembrane protein channel that opens or closes in response to a particular stimulus.

gated ion channel A gated channel for a specific ion. The opening or closing of such channels may alter the membrane potential.

gel electrophoresis (ē-lek′-trō-fōr-ē′-sis) A technique for separating nucleic acids or proteins on the basis of their size and electrical charge, both of which affect their rate of movement through an electric field in a gel.

gene A discrete unit of hereditary information consisting of a specific nucleotide sequence in DNA (or RNA, in some viruses).

gene cloning The production of multiple copies of a gene.

gene expression The process by which DNA directs the synthesis of proteins or, in some cases, just RNAs.

gene flow The transfer of alleles from one population to another, resulting from the movement of fertile individuals or their gametes.

gene pool The aggregate of all of the alleles for all of the loci in all individuals in a population. The term is also used in a more restricted sense as the aggregate of alleles for just one or a few loci in a population.

gene therapy The introduction of genes into an afflicted individual for therapeutic purposes.

gene-for-gene recognition A widespread form of plant disease resistance involving recognition of pathogen-derived molecules by the protein products of specific plant disease resistance genes.

genetic drift A process in which chance events cause unpredictable fluctuations in allele frequencies from one generation to the next. Effects of genetic drift are most pronounced in small populations.

genetic engineering The direct manipulation of genes for practical purposes.

genetic map An ordered list of genetic loci (genes or other genetic markers) along a chromosome.

genetic profile An individual's unique set of genetic markers, detected most often today by PCR or, previously, by electrophoresis and nucleic acid probes.

genetic recombination General term for the production of offspring with combinations of traits that differ from those found in either parent.

genetically modified (GM) organism An organism that has acquired one or more genes by artificial means; also known as a transgenic organism.

genetics The scientific study of heredity and hereditary variation.

genome (jē′-nōm) The genetic material of an organism or virus; the complete complement of an organism's or virus's genes along with its noncoding nucleic acid sequences.

genomic imprinting A phenomenon in which expression of an allele in offspring depends on whether the allele is inherited from the male or female parent.

genomic library A set of cell clones containing all the DNA segments from a genome, each within a plasmid, phage, or other cloning vector.

genomics (juh-nō′-miks) The study of whole sets of genes and their interactions.

genotype (jē′-nō-tīp) The genetic makeup, or set of alleles, of an organism.

genus (jē′-nus) (*plural,* **genera**) A taxonomic category above the species level, designated by the first word of a species' two-part scientific name.

geographic variation Differences between the gene pools of geographically separate populations or population subgroups.

geologic record The division of Earth's history into time periods, grouped into three eons—Archaean, Proterozoic, and Phanerozoic—and further subdivided into eras, periods, and epochs.

geometric isomer One of several compounds that have the same molecular formula and covalent arrangements but differ in the spatial arrangements of their atoms owing to the inflexibility of double bonds.

germ layer One of the three main layers in a gastrula that will form the various tissues and organs of an animal body.

gestation (jes-tā′-shun) Pregnancy; the state of carrying developing young within the female reproductive tract.

gibberellin (jib′-uh-rel′-in) Any of a class of related plant hormones that stimulate growth in the stem and leaves, trigger the germination of seeds and breaking of bud dormancy, and (with auxin) stimulate fruit development.

glans The rounded structure at the tip of the clitoris or penis that is involved in sexual arousal.

glial cells (glia) Supporting cells that are essential for the structural integrity of the nervous system and for the normal functioning of neurons.

global ecology The study of the functioning and distribution of organisms across the biosphere and how the regional exchange of energy and materials affects them.

glomeromycete (glō′-mer-ō-mī′-sēt) Member of the fungal phylum Glomeromycota, characterized by a distinct branching form of mycorrhizae (mutualistic relationships with plant roots) called arbuscular mycorrhizae.

glomerulus (glō-mār′-yū-lus) A ball of capillaries surrounded by Bowman's capsule in the nephron and serving as the site of filtration in the vertebrate kidney.

glucagon (glū′-kuh-gon) A hormone secreted by pancreatic alpha cells that raises blood glucose levels. It promotes glycogen breakdown and release of glucose by the liver.

glucocorticoid A steroid hormone that is secreted by the adrenal cortex and that influences glucose metabolism and immune function.

glutamate An amino acid that functions as a neurotransmitter in the central nervous system.

glyceraldehyde-3-phosphate (G3P) (glis′-er-al′-de-hīd) A three-carbon carbohydrate that is the direct product of the Calvin cycle; it is also an intermediate in glycolysis.

glycogen (glī′-kō-jen) An extensively branched glucose storage polysaccharide found in the liver and muscle of animals; the animal equivalent of starch.

glycolipid A lipid with covalently attached carbohydrate(s).

glycolysis (glī-kol′-uh-sis) The splitting of glucose into pyruvate. Glycolysis occurs in almost all living cells, serving as the starting point for fermentation or cellular respiration.

glycoprotein A protein with one or more carbohydrates covalently attached to it.

glycosidic linkage A covalent bond formed between two monosaccharides by a dehydration reaction.

gnathostome (na′-thu-stōm) Member of the vertebrate subgroup possessing jaws.

golden alga A biflagellated, photosynthetic protist named for its color, which results from its yellow and brown carotenoids.

Golgi apparatus (gol′-jē) An organelle in eukaryotic cells consisting of stacks of flat membranous sacs that modify, store, and route products of the endoplasmic reticulum and synthesize some products, notably noncellulose carbohydrates.

gonads (gō′-nadz) The male and female sex organs; the gamete-producing organs in most animals.

G protein A GTP-binding protein that relays signals from a plasma membrane signal receptor, known as a G protein-coupled receptor, to other signal transduction proteins inside the cell.

G protein-coupled receptor A signal receptor protein in the plasma membrane that responds to the binding of a signaling molecule by activating a G protein. Also called a G protein-linked receptor.

grade A group of organisms that share the same level of organizational complexity or share a key adaptation.

Gram stain A staining method that distinguishes between two different kinds of bacterial cell walls.

gram-negative Describing the group of bacteria that have a cell wall that is structurally more complex and contains less peptidoglycan than the cell wall of gram-positive bacteria. Gram-negative bacteria are often more toxic than gram-positive bacteria.

gram-positive Describing the group of bacteria that have a cell wall that is structurally less complex and contains more peptidoglycan than the cell wall of gram-negative bacteria. Gram-positive bacteria are usually less toxic than gram-negative bacteria.

granum (gran′-um) (plural, **grana**) A stack of membrane-bounded thylakoids in the chloroplast. Grana function in the light reactions of photosynthesis.

gravitropism (grav′-uh-trō′-pizm) A response of a plant or animal to gravity.

gray crescent A light gray, crescent-shaped region of cytoplasm that becomes exposed after cortical rotation, located near the equator of an egg on the side opposite sperm entry, marking the future dorsal side of the embryo.

gray matter Regions of dendrites and clustered neuron cell bodies within the CNS.

green alga A photosynthetic protist, named for green chloroplasts that are similar in structure and pigment composition to those of land plants. Green algae are a paraphyletic group, some of whose members are more closely related to land plants than they are to other green algae.

green world hypothesis The conjecture that terrestrial herbivores consume relatively little plant biomass because they are held in check by a variety of factors, including predators, parasites, and disease.

greenhouse effect The warming of Earth due to the atmospheric accumulation of carbon dioxide and certain other gases, which absorb reflected infrared radiation and reradiate some of it back toward Earth.

gross primary production (GPP) The total primary production of an ecosystem.

ground tissue system Plant tissues that are neither vascular nor dermal, fulfilling a variety of functions, such as storage, photosynthesis, and support.

growth factor (1) A protein that must be present in the extracellular environment (culture medium or animal body) for the growth and normal development of certain types of cells. (2) A local regulator that acts on nearby cells to stimulate cell proliferation and differentiation.

growth hormone (GH) A hormone that is produced and secreted by the anterior pituitary and that has both direct (nontropic) and tropic effects on a wide variety of tissues.

guard cells The two cells that flank the stomatal pore and regulate the opening and closing of the pore.

gustation The sense of taste.

guttation The exudation of water droplets, caused by root pressure in certain plants.

gymnosperm (jim′-nō-sperm) A vascular plant that bears naked seeds—seeds not enclosed in specialized chambers.

habituation A simple type of learning that involves a loss of responsiveness to stimuli that convey little or no new information.

half-life The amount of time it takes for 50% of a sample of a radioactive isotope to decay.

Hamilton's rule The principle that for natural selection to favor an altruistic act, the benefit to the recipient, devalued by the coefficient of relatedness, must exceed the cost to the altruist.

haploid cell (hap′-loyd) A cell containing only one set of chromosomes (*n*).

Hardy-Weinberg equilibrium The condition describing a nonevolving population (one that is in genetic equilibrium).

Hardy-Weinberg principle The principle that frequencies of alleles and genotypes in a population remain constant from generation to generation, provided that only Mendelian segregation and recombination of alleles are at work.

haustorium (plural, **haustoria**) (ho-stōr′-ē-um, ho-stōr′-ē-uh) In certain symbiotic fungi, a specialized hypha that can penetrate the tissues of host organisms.

heart A muscular pump that uses metabolic energy to elevate the hydrostatic pressure of the circulatory fluid (blood or hemolymph). The fluid then flows down a pressure gradient through the body and eventually returns to the heart.

heart attack The damage or death of cardiac muscle tissue resulting from prolonged blockage of one or more coronary arteries.

heart murmur A hissing sound that most often results from blood squirting backward through a leaky valve in the heart.

heart rate The frequency of heart contraction.

heat The total amount of kinetic energy due to the random motion of atoms or molecules in a body of matter; also called thermal energy. Heat is energy in its most random form.

heat of vaporization The quantity of heat a liquid must absorb for 1 g of it to be converted from the liquid to the gaseous state.

heat-shock protein A protein that helps protect other proteins during heat stress. Heat-shock proteins are found in plants, animals, and microorganisms.

heavy chain One of the two types of polypeptide chains that make up an antibody molecule and B cell receptor; consists of a variable region, which contributes to the antigen-binding site, and a constant region.

helicase An enzyme that untwists the double helix of DNA at the replication forks, separating the two strands and making them available as template strands.

helper T cell A type of T cell that, when activated, secretes cytokines that promote the response of B cells (humoral response) and cytotoxic T cells (cell-mediated response) to antigens.

hemoglobin (hē′-mō-glō′-bin) An iron-containing protein in red blood cells that reversibly binds oxygen.

hemolymph (hē′-mō-limf′) In invertebrates with an open circulatory system, the body fluid that bathes tissues.

hemophilia (hē′-muh-fil′-ē-uh) A human genetic disease caused by a sex-linked recessive allele resulting in the absence of one or more blood-clotting proteins; characterized by excessive bleeding following injury.

hepatic portal vein A large circulatory channel that conveys nutrient-laden blood from the small intestine to the liver, which regulates the blood's nutrient content.

herbivore (hur′-bi-vōr′) An animal that mainly eats plants or algae.

herbivory An interaction in which an organism eats parts of a plant or alga.

heredity The transmission of traits from one generation to the next.

hermaphrodite (hur-maf′-ruh-dīt′) An individual that functions as both male and female in sexual reproduction by producing both sperm and eggs.

hermaphroditism (hur-maf′-rō-dī-tizm) A condition in which an individual has both female and male gonads and functions as both a male and female in sexual reproduction by producing both sperm and eggs.

heterochromatin (het′-er-ō-krō′-muh-tin) Eukaryotic chromatin that remains highly compacted during interphase and is generally not transcribed.

heterochrony (het′-uh-rok′-ruh-nē) Evolutionary change in the timing or rate of an organism's development.

heterocyte (het′-er-ō-sīt) A specialized cell that engages in nitrogen fixation in some filamentous cyanobacteria; formerly called heterocyst.

heterokaryon (het′-er-ō-kār′-ē-un) A fungal mycelium that contains two or more haploid nuclei per cell.

heteromorphic (het′-er-ō-mōr′-fik) Referring to a condition in the life cycle of plants and certain algae in which the sporophyte and gametophyte generations differ in morphology.

heterosporous (het-er-os′-pōr-us) Referring to a plant species that has two kinds of spores: microspores, which develop into male gametophytes, and megaspores, which develop into female gametophytes.

heterotroph (het′-er-ō-trōf) An organism that obtains organic food molecules by eating other organisms or substances derived from them.

heterozygote advantage Greater reproductive success of heterozygous individuals compared with homozygotes; tends to preserve variation in a gene pool.

heterozygous (het′-er-ō-zī′-gus) Having two different alleles for a given gene.

hexapod An insect or closely related wingless, six-legged arthropod.

hibernation A physiological state in which metabolism decreases, the heart and respiratory system slow down, and body temperature is maintained at a lower level than normal.

high-density lipoprotein (HDL) A particle in the blood made up of cholesterol and other lipids surrounded by a single layer of phospholipids in which proteins are embedded. HDL carries less cholesterol than a related lipoprotein, LDL, and high HDL levels in the blood may be correlated with a decreased risk of blood vessel blockage.

hindbrain One of three ancestral and embryonic regions of the vertebrate brain; develops into the medulla oblongata, pons, and cerebellum.

histamine (his′-tuh-mēn) A substance released by mast cells that causes blood vessels to dilate and become more permeable in inflammatory and allergic responses.

histone (his′-tōn) A small protein with a high proportion of positively charged amino acids that binds to the negatively charged DNA and plays a key role in chromatin structure.

histone acetylation The attachment of acetyl groups to certain amino acids of histone proteins.

HIV (human immunodeficiency virus) The infectious agent that causes AIDS. HIV is a retrovirus.

holdfast A rootlike structure that anchors a seaweed.

holoblastic cleavage (hō′-lō-blas′-tik) A type of cleavage in which there is complete division of the egg; occurs in eggs that have little yolk (such as those of the sea urchin) or a moderate amount of yolk (such as those of the frog).

homeobox (hō′-mē-ō-boks′) A 180-nucleotide sequence within homeotic genes and some other developmental genes that is widely conserved in animals. Related sequences occur in plants and yeasts.

homeostasis (hō′-mē-ō-stā′-sis) The steady-state physiological condition of the body.

homeotic gene (ho′-mē-o′-tik) Any of the master regulatory genes that control placement and spatial organization of body parts in animals, plants, and fungi by controlling the developmental fate of groups of cells.

hominin (ho′-mi-nin) A species on the human branch of the evolutionary tree. Hominins include *Homo sapiens* and our ancestors, a group of extinct species that are more closely related to us than to chimpanzees.

homologous chromosomes (hō-mol′-uh-gus) A pair of chromosomes of the same length, centromere position, and staining pattern that possess genes for the same characters at corresponding loci. One homologous chromosome is inherited from the organism's father, the other from the mother. Also called homologs, or a homologous pair.

homologous structures Structures in different species that are similar because of common ancestry.

homology (hō-mol′-uh-jē) Similarity in characteristics resulting from a shared ancestry.

homoplasy (hō′-muh-play′-zē) Similar (analogous) structure or molecular sequence that has evolved independently in two species.

homosporous (hō-mos′-puh-rus) Referring to a plant species that has a single kind of spore, which typically develops into a bisexual gametophyte.

homozygous (hō′-mō-zī′-gus) Having two identical alleles for a given gene.

horizontal cell A neuron of the retina that helps integrate information before it is sent to the brain.

horizontal gene transfer The transfer of genes from one genome to another through mechanisms such as transposable elements, plasmid exchange, viral activity, and perhaps fusions of different organisms.

hormone In multicellular organisms, one of many types of secreted chemicals that are formed in specialized cells, travel in body fluids, and act on specific target cells in other parts of the body to change their functioning.

hornwort A small, herbaceous nonvascular plant that is a member of the phylum Anthocerophyta.

host The larger participant in a symbiotic relationship, serving as home and food source for the smaller symbiont.

host range The limited range of host cells that each type of virus can infect.

human chorionic gonadotropin (hCG) (kōr′-ē-on′-ik gō-na′-dō-trō′-pin) A hormone secreted by the chorion that maintains the corpus luteum of the ovary during the first three months of pregnancy.

Human Genome Project An international collaborative effort to map and sequence the DNA of the entire human genome.

humoral immune response (hyū′-mer-ul) The branch of acquired immunity that involves the activation of B cells and that leads to the production of antibodies, which defend against bacteria and viruses in body fluids.

humus (hyū′-mus) Decomposing organic material that is a component of topsoil.

Huntington's disease A human genetic disease caused by a dominant allele; characterized by uncontrollable body movements and degeneration of the nervous system; usually fatal 10 to 20 years after the onset of symptoms.

hybrid Offspring that results from the mating of individuals from two different species or two true-breeding varieties of the same species.

hybrid zone A geographic region in which members of different species meet and mate, producing at least some offspring of mixed ancestry.

hybridization In genetics, the mating, or crossing, of two true-breeding varieties.

hydration shell The sphere of water molecules around a dissolved ion.

hydrocarbon An organic molecule consisting only of carbon and hydrogen.

hydrogen bond A type of weak chemical bond that is formed when the slightly positive hydrogen atom of a polar covalent bond in one molecule is attracted to the slightly negative atom of a polar covalent bond in another molecule.

hydrogen ion A single proton with a charge of 1+. The dissociation of a water molecule (H_2O) leads to the generation of a hydroxide ion (OH^-) and a hydrogen ion (H^+).

hydrolysis (hī-drol′-uh-sis) A chemical process that lyses, or splits, molecules by the addition of water, functioning in disassembly of polymers to monomers.

hydronium ion A water molecule that has an extra proton bound to it; H_3O^+.

hydrophilic (hī′-drō-fil′-ik) Having an affinity for water.

hydrophobic (hī′-drō-fō′-bik) Having an aversion to water; tending to coalesce and form droplets in water.

hydrophobic interaction A type of weak chemical bond formed when molecules that do not mix with water coalesce to exclude water.

hydroponic culture A method in which plants are grown in mineral solutions rather than in soil.

hydrostatic skeleton A skeletal system composed of fluid held under pressure in a closed body compartment; the main skeleton of most cnidarians, flatworms, nematodes, and annelids.

hydroxide ion A water molecule that has lost a proton; OH^-.

hydroxyl group (hī-drok′-sil) A chemical group consisting of an oxygen atom joined to a hydrogen atom. Molecules possessing this group are soluble in water and are called alcohols.

hymen A thin membrane that partly covers the vaginal opening in the human female. The hymen is ruptured by sexual intercourse or other vigorous activity.

hyperpolarization A change in a cell's membrane potential such that the inside of the membrane becomes more negative relative to the outside. Hyperpolarization reduces the chance that a neuron will transmit a nerve impulse.

hypersensitive response A plant's localized defense response to a pathogen, involving the death of cells around the site of infection.

hypertension A disorder in which blood pressure remains abnormally high.

hypertonic Referring to a solution that, when surrounding a cell, will cause the cell to lose water.

hypha (plural, **hyphae**) (hī′-fuh, hī′-fē) One of many connected filaments that collectively make up the mycelium of a fungus.

hypocotyl (hī′-puh-cot′-ul) In an angiosperm embryo, the embryonic axis below the point of attachment of the cotyledon(s) and above the radicle.

hypothalamus (hī′-pō-thal′-uh-mus) The ventral part of the vertebrate forebrain; functions in maintaining homeostasis, especially in coordinating the endocrine and nervous systems; secretes hormones of the posterior pituitary and releasing factors that regulate the anterior pituitary.

hypothesis (hī-poth′-uh-sis) A tentative answer to a well-framed question, narrower in scope than a theory and subject to testing.

hypotonic Referring to a solution that, when surrounding a cell, will cause the cell to take up water.

imbibition The physical adsorption of water onto the internal surfaces of structures.

immigration The influx of new individuals into a population from other areas.

immune system An animal body's system of defenses against agents that cause disease.

immunization The process of generating a state of immunity by artificial means. In active immunization, also called vaccination, an inactive or weakened form of a pathogen is administered, inducing B and T cell responses and immunological memory. In passive immunization, antibodies specific for a particular microbe are administered, conferring immediate but temporary protection.

immunodeficiency A disorder in which the ability of an immune system to protect against pathogens is defective or absent.

immunoglobulin (Ig) (im′-yū-nō-glob′-yū-lin) Any of the class of proteins that function as antibodies. Immunoglobulins are divided into five major classes that differ in their distribution in the body and antigen disposal activities.

imprinting In animal behavior, the formation at a specific stage in life of a long-lasting behavioral response to a specific individual or object. (*See also* genomic imprinting.)

***in situ* hybridization** A technique used to detect the location of a specific mRNA using nucleic acid hybridization with a labeled probe in an intact organism.

***in vitro* fertilization (IVF)** (vē′-trō) Fertilization of oocytes in laboratory containers followed by artificial implantation of the early embryo in the mother's uterus.

***in vitro* mutagenesis** A technique used to discover the function of a gene by cloning it, introducing specific changes into the cloned gene's sequence, reinserting the mutated gene into a cell, and studying the phenotype of the mutant.

inclusive fitness The total effect an individual has on proliferating its genes by producing its own offspring and by providing aid that enables other close relatives to increase the production of their offspring.

incomplete dominance The situation in which the phenotype of heterozygotes is intermediate between the phenotypes of individuals homozygous for either allele.

incomplete flower A flower in which one or more of the four basic floral organs (sepals, petals, stamens, or carpels) are either absent or nonfunctional.

incomplete metamorphosis A type of development in certain insects, such as grasshoppers, in which the young (called nymphs) resemble adults but are smaller and have different body proportions. The nymph goes through a series of molts, each time looking more like an adult, until it reaches full size.

incus The second of three bones in the middle ear of mammals; also called the anvil.

indeterminate cleavage A type of embryonic development in deuterostomes in which each cell produced by early cleavage divisions retains the capacity to develop into a complete embryo.

indeterminate growth A type of growth characteristic of plants, in which the organism continues to grow as long as it lives.

induced fit Induced by entry of the substrate, the change in shape of the active site of an enzyme so that it binds more snugly to the substrate.

inducer A specific small molecule that binds to a bacterial repressor protein and changes the repressor's shape so that it cannot bind to an operator, thus switching an operon on.

induction The process in which one group of embryonic cells influences the development of another, usually by causing changes in gene expression.

inductive reasoning A type of logic in which generalizations are based on a large number of specific observations.

inflammatory response An innate immune defense triggered by physical injury or infection of tissue involving the release of substances that promote swelling, enhance the infiltration of white blood cells, and aid in tissue repair and destruction of invading pathogens.

inflorescence A group of flowers tightly clustered together.

ingestion The first stage of food processing in animals: the act of eating.

ingroup A species or group of species whose evolutionary relationships we seek to determine.

inhibin A hormone produced in the male and female gonads that functions in part by regulating the function of the anterior pituitary by negative feedback.

inhibitory postsynaptic potential (IPSP) An electrical change (usually hyperpolarization) in the membrane of a postsynaptic neuron caused by the binding of an inhibitory neurotransmitter from a presynaptic cell to a postsynaptic receptor; makes it more difficult for a postsynaptic neuron to generate an action potential.

innate behavior Animal behavior that is developmentally fixed and under strong genetic control. Innate behavior is exhibited in virtually the same form by all individuals in a population despite internal and external environmental differences during development and throughout their lifetimes.

innate immunity A form of defense common to all animals that is active immediately upon exposure to pathogens and that is the same whether or not the pathogen has been encountered previously.

inner cell mass An inner cluster of cells at one end of a mammalian blastocyst that subsequently develops into the embryo proper and some of the extraembryonic membranes.

inner ear One of three main regions of the vertebrate ear; includes the cochlea (which in turn contains the organ of Corti) and the semicircular canals.

inositol trisphosphate (IP$_3$) (in-ō′-suh-tol) A second messenger that functions as an intermediate between certain nonsteroid hormones and a third messenger, a rise in cytoplasmic Ca^{2+} concentration.

inquiry The search for information and explanation, often focused by specific questions.

insertion A mutation involving the addition of one or more nucleotide pairs to a gene.

insulin (in′-suh-lin) A hormone secreted by pancreatic beta cells that lowers blood glucose levels. It promotes the uptake of glucose by most body cells and the synthesis and storage of glycogen in the liver and also stimulates protein and fat synthesis.

integral protein Typically a transmembrane protein with hydrophobic regions that extend into and often completely span the hydrophobic interior of the membrane and with hydrophilic regions in contact with the aqueous solution on either side of the membrane (or lining the channel in the case of a channel protein).

integrin In animal cells, a transmembrane receptor protein that interconnects the extracellular matrix and the cytoskeleton.

integument (in-teg′-yū-ment) Layer of sporophyte tissue that contributes to the structure of an ovule of a seed plant.

integumentary system The outer covering of a mammal's body, including skin, hair, and nails.

intercalated disk (in-ter′-kuh-lā′-ted) A special junction between cardiac muscle cells that provides direct electrical coupling between the cells.

interferon (in′-ter-fēr′-on) A protein that has antiviral or immune regulatory functions. Interferon-α and interferon-β, secreted by virus-infected cells, help nearby cells resist viral infection; interferon-γ, secreted by T cells, helps activate macrophages.

intermediate disturbance hypothesis The concept that moderate levels of disturbance can foster greater species diversity than low or high levels of disturbance.

intermediate filament A component of the cytoskeleton that includes filaments intermediate in size between microtubules and microfilaments.

internal fertilization The fusion of eggs and sperm within the female reproductive tract. The sperm are typically deposited in or near the tract.

interneuron An association neuron; a nerve cell within the central nervous system that forms synapses with sensory and/or motor neurons and integrates sensory input and motor output.

internode A segment of a plant stem between the points where leaves are attached.

interphase The period in the cell cycle when the cell is not dividing. During interphase, cellular metabolic activity is high, chromosomes and organelles are duplicated, and cell size may increase. Interphase accounts for 90% of the cell cycle.

intersexual selection Selection whereby individuals of one sex (usually females) are choosy in selecting their mates from individuals of the other sex; also called mate choice.

interspecific competition Competition for resources between individuals of two or more species when resources are in short supply.

interspecific interaction A relationship between individuals of two or more species in a community.

interstitial fluid The fluid filling the spaces between cells in an animal.

intertidal zone The shallow zone of the ocean adjacent to land and between the high- and low-tide lines.

intracellular digestion The hydrolysis of food inside vacuoles.

intracytoplasmic sperm injection (ICSI) The fertilization of an egg in the laboratory by the direct injection of a single sperm.

intrasexual selection A direct competition among individuals of one sex (usually the males in vertebrates) for mates of the opposite sex.

introduced species A species moved by humans, either intentionally or accidentally, from its native location to a new geographic region; also called non-native or exotic species.

intron (in′-tron) A noncoding, intervening sequence within a primary transcript that is removed from the transcript during RNA processing; also refers to the region of DNA from which this sequence was transcribed.

invagination The infolding, or pushing inward, of cells due to changes in cell shape.

invasive species A species, often introduced by humans, that takes hold outside its native range.

inversion An aberration in chromosome structure resulting from reattachment of a chromosomal fragment in a reverse orientation to the chromosome from which it originated.

invertebrate An animal without a backbone. Invertebrates make up 95% of animal species.

involution The process by which sheets of cells roll over the edge of the lip of the blastopore into the interior of the embryo during gastrulation.

ion (ī′-on) An atom or group of atoms that has gained or lost one or more electrons, thus acquiring a charge.

ion channel A transmembrane protein channel that allows a specific ion to flow across the membrane down its concentration gradient.

ionic bond (ī-on′-ik) A chemical bond resulting from the attraction between oppositely charged ions.

ionic compound A compound resulting from the formation of an ionic bond; also called a salt.

IPSP *See* inhibitory postsynaptic potential.

iris The colored part of the vertebrate eye, formed by the anterior portion of the choroid.

islets of Langerhans Clusters of endocrine cells within the pancreas that produce and secrete the hormones glucagon (from alpha cells) and insulin (from beta cells).

isomer (ī′-sō-mer) One of several compounds with the same molecular formula but different structures and therefore different properties. The three types of isomers are structural isomers, geometric isomers, and enantiomers.

isomorphic Referring to alternating generations in plants and certain algae in which the sporophytes and gametophytes look alike, although they differ in chromosome number.

isopod A member of one of the largest groups of crustaceans, which includes terrestrial, freshwater, and marine species. Among the terrestrial isopods are the pill bugs, or wood lice.

isotonic (ī′-sō-ton′-ik) Referring to a solution that, when surrounding a cell, has no effect on the passage of water into or out of the cell.

isotope (ī′-sō-tōp′) One of several atomic forms of an element, each with the same number of protons but a different number of neutrons, thus differing in atomic mass.

iteroparity Reproduction in which adults produce offspring over many years; also known as repeated reproduction.

joule (J) A unit of energy: 1 J = 0.239 cal; 1 cal = 4.184 J.

juvenile hormone A hormone in arthropods, secreted by the corpora allata (a pair of glands), that promotes the retention of larval characteristics.

juxtaglomerular apparatus (JGA) (juks′-tuh-gluh-mār′-yū-ler) A specialized tissue in nephrons that releases the enzyme renin in response to a drop in blood pressure or volume.

juxtamedullary nephron In mammals and birds, a nephron with a loop of Henle that extends far into the renal medulla.

karyogamy (kār′-ē-og′-uh-mē) The fusion of two nuclei, as part of syngamy (fertilization).

karyotype (kār′-ē-ō-tīp) A display of the chromosome pairs of a cell arranged by size and shape.

keystone species A species that is not necessarily abundant in a community yet exerts strong control on community structure by the nature of its ecological role or niche.

kilocalorie (kcal) A thousand calories; the amount of heat energy required to raise the temperature of 1 kg of water by 1°C.

kin selection Natural selection that favors altruistic behavior by enhancing the reproductive success of relatives.

kinesis (kuh-nē′-sis) A change in activity or turning rate in response to a stimulus.

kinetic energy (kuh-net′-ik) The energy associated with the relative motion of objects. Moving matter can perform work by imparting motion to other matter.

kinetochore (kuh-net′-uh-kōr) A structure of proteins attached to the centromere that links each sister chromatid to the mitotic spindle.

kinetoplastid A protist, such as a trypanosome, that has a single large mitochondrion that houses an organized mass of DNA.

kingdom A taxonomic category, the second broadest after domain.

***K*-selection** Selection for life history traits that are sensitive to population density; also called density-dependent selection.

labia majora A pair of thick, fatty ridges that encloses and protects the rest of the vulva.

labia minora A pair of slender skin folds that surrounds the openings of the vagina and urethra.

labor A series of strong, rhythmic contractions of the uterus that expel a baby out of the uterus and vagina during childbirth.

lactation The continued production of milk from the mammary glands.

lacteal (lak′-tē-ul) A tiny lymph vessel extending into the core of an intestinal villus and serving as the destination for absorbed chylomicrons.

lactic acid fermentation Glycolysis followed by the conversion of pyruvate to lactate, with no release of carbon dioxide.

lagging strand A discontinuously synthesized DNA strand that elongates by means of Okazaki fragments, each synthesized in a 5′→3′ direction away from the replication fork.

lancelet Member of the subphylum Cephalochordata, small blade-shaped marine chordates that lack a backbone.

landmark A location indicator—a point of reference for orientation during navigation.

landscape An area containing several different ecosystems linked by exchanges of energy, materials, and organisms.

landscape ecology The study of how the spatial arrangement of habitat types affects the distribution and abundance of organisms and ecosystem processes.

large intestine The tubular portion of the vertebrate alimentary canal between the small intestine and the anus; functions mainly in water absorption and the formation of feces.

larva (lar′-vuh) (plural, **larvae**) A free-living, sexually immature form in some animal life cycles that may differ from the adult animal in morphology, nutrition, and habitat.

larynx (lār′-inks) The portion of the respiratory tract containing the vocal cords; also called the voice box.

lateral geniculate nucleus One of a pair of structures in the brain that are the destination for most of the ganglion cell axons that form the optic nerves.

lateral inhibition A process that sharpens the edges and enhances the contrast of a perceived image by inhibiting receptors lateral to those that have responded to light.

lateral line system A mechanoreceptor system consisting of a series of pores and receptor units along the sides of the body in fishes and aquatic amphibians; detects water movements made by the animal itself and by other moving objects.

lateral meristem (mār′-uh-stem) A meristem that thickens the roots and shoots of woody plants. The vascular cambium and cork cambium are lateral meristems.

lateral root A root that arises from the pericycle of an established root.

lateralization Segregation of functions in the cortex of the left and right hemispheres of the brain.

law of conservation of mass A physical law stating that matter can change form but cannot be created or destroyed. In a closed system, the mass of the system is constant.

law of independent assortment Mendel's second law, stating that each pair of alleles segregates, or assorts, independently of each other pair during gamete formation; applies when genes for two characters are located on different pairs of homologous chromosomes.

law of segregation Mendel's first law, stating that the two alleles in a pair segregate (separate) into different gametes during gamete formation.

leading strand The new complementary DNA strand synthesized continuously along the template strand toward the replication fork in the mandatory $5' \rightarrow 3'$ direction.

leaf The main photosynthetic organ of vascular plants.

leaf primordium A finger-like projection along the flank of a shoot apical meristem, from which a leaf arises.

learning The modification of behavior based on specific experiences.

lens The structure in an eye that focuses light rays onto the photoreceptors.

lenticel (len′-ti-sel) A small raised area in the bark of stems and roots that enables gas exchange between living cells and the outside air.

lepidosaur (leh-pid′-uh-sōr) Member of the reptilian group that includes lizards, snakes, and two species of New Zealand animals called tuataras.

leukocyte (lū′-kō-sīt′) A blood cell that functions in fighting infections; also called a white blood cell.

Leydig cell (lī′-dig) A cell that produces testosterone and other androgens and is located between the seminiferous tubules of the testes.

lichen The symbiotic collective formed by the mutualistic association between a fungus and a photosynthetic alga or cyanobacterium.

life cycle The generation-to-generation sequence of stages in the reproductive history of an organism.

life history The traits that affect an organism's schedule of reproduction and survival.

life table A table of data summarizing mortality in a population.

ligament A fibrous connective tissue that joins bones together at joints.

ligand (lig′-und) A molecule that binds specifically to another molecule, usually a larger one.

ligand-gated ion channel A protein pore in cellular membranes that opens or closes in response to a signaling chemical (its ligand), allowing or blocking the flow of specific ions.

light chain One of the two types of polypeptide chains that make up an antibody molecule and B cell receptor; consists of a variable region, which contributes to the antigen-binding site, and a constant region.

light microscope (LM) An optical instrument with lenses that refract (bend) visible light to magnify images of specimens.

light reactions The first of two major stages in photosynthesis (preceding the Calvin cycle). These reactions, which occur on the thylakoid membranes of the chloroplast or on membranes of certain prokaryotes, convert solar energy to the chemical energy of ATP and NADPH, releasing oxygen in the process.

light-harvesting complex A complex of proteins associated with pigment molecules (including chlorophyll *a*, chlorophyll *b*, and carotenoids) that captures light energy and transfers it to reaction-center pigments in a photosystem.

lignin (lig′-nin) A hard material embedded in the cellulose matrix of vascular plant cell walls that provides structural support in terrestrial species.

limiting nutrient An element that must be added for production to increase in a particular area.

limnetic zone In a lake, the well-lit, open surface waters farther from shore.

linear electron flow A route of electron flow during the light reactions of photosynthesis that involves both photosystems (I and II) and produces ATP, NADPH, and O_2. The net electron flow is from H_2O to $NADP^+$.

linkage map A genetic map based on the frequencies of recombination between markers during crossing over of homologous chromosomes.

linked genes Genes located close enough together on a chromosome that they tend to be inherited together.

lipid (lip′-id) One of a group of compounds, including fats, phospholipids, and steroids, that mix poorly, if at all, with water.

littoral zone In a lake, the shallow, well-lit waters close to shore.

liver The largest internal organ in the vertebrate body. The liver performs diverse functions, such as producing bile, preparing nitrogenous wastes for disposal, and detoxifying poisonous chemicals in the blood.

liverwort A small, herbaceous nonvascular plant that is a member of the phylum Hepatophyta.

loam The most fertile soil type, made up of roughly equal amounts of sand, silt, and clay.

lobe-fin Member of the vertebrate subgroup Sarcopterygii, osteichthyans with rod-shaped muscular fins, including coelacanths and lungfishes as well as the lineage that gave rise to tetrapods.

local regulator A secreted molecule that influences cells near where it is secreted.

locomotion Active motion from place to place.

locus (lō′-kus) (plural, **loci**) A specific place along the length of a chromosome where a given gene is located.

logistic population growth Population growth that levels off as population size approaches carrying capacity.

long-day plant A plant that flowers (usually in late spring or early summer) only when the light period is longer than a critical length.

long-term memory The ability to hold, associate, and recall information over one's lifetime.

long-term potentiation (LTP) An enhanced responsiveness to an action potential (nerve signal) by a receiving neuron.

loop of Henle The hairpin turn, with a descending and ascending limb, between the proximal and distal tubules of the vertebrate kidney; functions in water and salt reabsorption.

lophophore (lof′-uh-fōr) In some lophotrochozoan animals, including brachiopods, a crown of ciliated tentacles that surround the mouth and function in feeding.

lophotrochozoan Member of a group of animal phyla identified as a clade by molecular evidence. Lophotrochozoans include organisms that have lophophores or trochophore larvae.

low-density lipoprotein (LDL) A particle in the blood made up of cholesterol and other lipids surrounded by a single layer of phospholipids in which proteins are embedded. LDL carries more cholesterol than a related lipoprotein, HDL, and high LDL levels in the blood correlate with a tendency to develop blocked blood vessels and heart disease.

lung An infolded respiratory surface of a terrestrial vertebrate, land snail, or spider that connects to the atmosphere by narrow tubes.

luteal phase That portion of the ovarian cycle during which endocrine cells of the corpus luteum secrete female hormones.

luteinizing hormone (LH) (lū′-tē-uh-nī′-zing) A tropic hormone that is produced and secreted by the anterior pituitary and that stimulates ovulation in females and androgen production in males.

lycophyte (lī′-kuh-fīt) An informal name for a member of the phylum Lycophyta, which includes club mosses, spike mosses, and quillworts.

lymph The colorless fluid, derived from interstitial fluid, in the lymphatic system of vertebrates.

lymph node An organ located along a lymph vessel. Lymph nodes filter lymph and contain cells that attack viruses and bacteria.

lymphatic system A system of vessels and nodes, separate from the circulatory system, that returns fluid, proteins, and cells to the blood.

lymphocyte A type of white blood cell that mediates acquired immunity. The two main classes are B cells and T cells.

lysogenic cycle (lī′-sō-jen′-ik) A type of phage reproductive cycle in which the viral genome becomes incorporated into the bacterial host chromosome as a prophage and does not kill the host.

lysosome (lī′-suh-sōm) A membrane-enclosed sac of hydrolytic enzymes found in the cytoplasm of animal cells and some protists.

lysozyme (lī′-sō-zīm) An enzyme that destroys bacterial cell walls; in mammals, found in sweat, tears, and saliva.

lytic cycle (lit′-ik) A type of phage reproductive cycle resulting in the release of new phages by lysis (and death) of the host cell.

macroclimate Large-scale patterns in climate; the climate of an entire region.

macroevolution Evolutionary change above the species level, including the origin of a new group of organisms or a shift in the broad pattern of evolutionary change over a long period of time. Examples of macroevolutionary change include the appearance of major new features of organisms and the impact of mass extinctions on the diversity of life and its subsequent recovery.

macromolecule A giant molecule formed by the joining of smaller molecules, usually by a condensation reaction. Polysaccharides, proteins, and nucleic acids are macromolecules.

macronutrient A chemical substance that an organism must obtain in relatively large amounts. *See also* micronutrient.
macrophage (mak′-rō-fāj) A phagocytic cell present in many tissues that functions in innate immunity by destroying microbes and in acquired immunity as an antigen-presenting cell.
magnoliid Member of the angiosperm clade most closely related to eudicots. Extant examples are magnolias, laurels, and black pepper plants.
major depressive disorder A mood disorder characterized by feelings of sadness, lack of self-worth, emptiness, or loss of interest in nearly all things.
major histocompatibility complex (MHC) A family of genes that encode a large set of cell-surface proteins that function in antigen presentation. Foreign MHC molecules on transplanted tissue can trigger T cell responses that may lead to rejection of the transplant.
malignant tumor A cancerous tumor that is invasive enough to impair the functions of one or more organs.
malleus The first of three bones in the middle ear of mammals; also called the hammer.
malnourishment The long-term absence from the diet of one or more essential nutrients.
Malpighian tubule (mal-pig′-ē-un) A unique excretory organ of insects that empties into the digestive tract, removes nitrogenous wastes from the hemolymph, and functions in osmoregulation.
mammal Member of the class Mammalia, amniotes with mammary glands—glands that produce milk.
mammary glands Exocrine glands that secrete milk to nourish the young. These glands are characteristic of mammals.
mandible One of a pair of jaw-like feeding appendages found in myriapods, hexapods, and crustaceans.
mantle One of the three main parts of a mollusc; a fold of tissue that drapes over the mollusc's visceral mass and may secrete a shell. *See also* foot, visceral mass.
mantle cavity A water-filled chamber that houses the gills, anus, and excretory pores of a mollusc.
map unit A unit of measurement of the distance between genes. One map unit is equivalent to a 1% recombination frequency.
marine benthic zone The ocean floor.
mark-recapture method A sampling technique used to estimate the size of animal populations.
marsupial (mar-sū′-pē-ul) A mammal, such as a koala, kangaroo, or opossum, whose young complete their embryonic development inside a maternal pouch called the marsupium.
mass extinction Period of time when global environmental changes lead to the elimination of a large number of species throughout Earth.
mass number The sum of the number of protons and neutrons in an atom's nucleus.
mast cell A vertebrate body cell that produces histamine and other molecules that trigger inflammation in response to infection and in allergic reactions.
mate choice copying Behavior in which individuals in a population copy the mate choice of others, apparently as a result of social learning.
maternal effect gene A gene that, when mutant in the mother, results in a mutant phenotype in the offspring, regardless of the offspring's genotype. Maternal effect genes were first identified in *Drosophila*.
matter Anything that takes up space and has mass.
maximum likelihood As applied to systematics, a principle that states that when considering multiple phylogenetic hypotheses, one should take into account the hypothesis that reflects the most likely sequence of evolutionary events, given certain rules about how DNA changes over time.
maximum parsimony A principle that states that when considering multiple explanations for an observation, one should first investigate the simplest explanation that is consistent with the facts.
mechanoreceptor A sensory receptor that detects physical deformation in the body's environment associated with pressure, touch, stretch, motion, or sound.
medulla oblongata (meh-dul′-uh ob′-long-go′-tuh) The lowest part of the vertebrate brain, commonly called the medulla; a swelling of the hindbrain anterior to the spinal cord that controls autonomic, homeostatic functions, including breathing, heart and blood vessel activity, swallowing, digestion, and vomiting.
medusa (muh-dū′-suh) The floating, flattened, mouth-down version of the cnidarian body plan. The alternate form is the polyp.
megapascal (MPa) (meg′-uh-pas-kal′) A unit of pressure equivalent to about 10 atmospheres of pressure.
megaphyll (meh′-guh-fil) A leaf with a highly branched vascular system, characteristic of the vast majority of vascular plants.
megaspore A spore from a heterosporous plant species that develops into a female gametophyte.
meiosis (mī-ō′-sis) A modified type of cell division in sexually reproducing organisms consisting of two rounds of cell division but only one round of DNA replication. It results in cells with half the number of chromosome sets as the original cell.
meiosis I The first division of a two-stage process of cell division in sexually reproducing organisms that results in cells with half the number of chromosome sets as the original cell.
meiosis II The second division of a two-stage process of cell division in sexually reproducing organisms that results in cells with half the number of chromosome sets as the original cell.
melanocyte-stimulating hormone (MSH) A hormone produced and secreted by the anterior pituitary that regulates the activity of pigment-containing cells in the skin of some vertebrates.
melatonin A hormone secreted by the pineal gland that regulates body functions related to seasonal day length.
membrane potential The difference in electrical charge (voltage) across a cell's plasma membrane, due to the differential distribution of ions. Membrane potential affects the activity of excitable cells and the transmembrane movement of all charged substances.
memory cell One of a clone of long-lived lymphocytes, formed during the primary immune response, that remains in a lymphoid organ until activated by exposure to the same antigen that triggered its formation. Activated memory cells mount the secondary immune response.
menopause The cessation of ovulation and menstruation marking the end of a human female's reproductive years.
menstrual cycle (men′-strū-ul) In humans and certain other primates, a type of reproductive cycle in which the nonpregnant endometrium is shed through the cervix into the vagina.
menstrual flow phase That portion of the uterine (menstrual) cycle when menstrual bleeding occurs.
menstruation The shedding of portions of the endometrium during a uterine (menstrual) cycle.
meristem (mār′-uh-stem) Plant tissue that remains embryonic as long as the plant lives, allowing for indeterminate growth.
meristem identity gene A plant gene that promotes the switch from vegetative growth to flowering.
meroblastic cleavage (mār′-ō-blas′-tik) A type of cleavage in which there is incomplete division of a yolk-rich egg, characteristic of avian development.
mesoderm (mez′-ō-derm) The middle primary germ layer in an animal embryo; develops into the notochord, the lining of the coelom, muscles, skeleton, gonads, kidneys, and most of the circulatory system in species that have these structures.
mesohyl (mez′-ō-hīl) A gelatinous region between the two layers of cells of a sponge.
mesophyll (mez′-ō-fil) The ground tissue of a leaf, sandwiched between the upper and lower epidermis and specialized for photosynthesis.
mesophyll cell In C_4 plants, a type of loosely arranged photosynthetic cell located between the bundle sheath and the leaf surface.
messenger RNA (mRNA) A type of RNA, synthesized using a DNA template, that attaches to ribosomes in the cytoplasm and specifies the primary structure of a protein.
metabolic pathway A series of chemical reactions that either builds a complex molecule (anabolic pathway) or breaks down a complex molecule into simpler compounds (catabolic pathway).
metabolic rate The total amount of energy an animal uses in a unit of time.
metabolism (muh-tab′-uh-lizm) The totality of an organism's chemical reactions, consisting of catabolic and anabolic pathways, which manage the material and energy resources of the organism.

metamorphosis (met′-uh-mōr′-fuh-sis) A developmental transformation that turns an animal larva into either an adult or an adult-like stage that is not yet sexually mature.

metanephridium (met′-uh-nuh-frid′-ē-um) (plural, **metanephridia**) An excretory organ found in many invertebrates that typically consists of tubules connecting ciliated internal openings to external openings.

metaphase The third stage of mitosis, in which the spindle is complete and the chromosomes, attached to microtubules at their kinetochores, are all aligned at the metaphase plate.

metaphase plate An imaginary plane midway between the two poles of a cell in metaphase on which the centromeres of all the duplicated chromosomes are located.

metapopulation A group of spatially separated populations of one species that interact through immigration and emigration.

metastasis (muh-tas′-tuh-sis) The spread of cancer cells to locations distant from their original site.

methanogen (meth-an′-ō-jen) An organism that obtains energy by using carbon dioxide to oxidize hydrogen, producing methane as a waste product; all known methanogens are in domain Archaea.

methyl group A chemical group consisting of a carbon bonded to three hydrogen atoms. The methyl group may be attached to a carbon or to a different atom.

microclimate Very fine scale patterns of climate, such as the specific climatic conditions underneath a log.

microevolution Evolutionary change below the species level; change in the allele frequencies in a population over generations.

microfilament A cable composed of actin proteins in the cytoplasm of almost every eukaryotic cell, making up part of the cytoskeleton and acting alone or with myosin to cause cell contraction; also known as an actin filament.

micronutrient An element that an organism needs in very small amounts and that functions as a component or cofactor of enzymes. *See also* macronutrient.

microphyll (mī′-krō-fil) In lycophytes, a small leaf with a single unbranched vein.

micropyle A pore in the integument(s) of an ovule.

microRNA (miRNA) A small, single-stranded RNA molecule, generated from a hairpin structure on a precursor RNA transcribed from a particular gene. The miRNA associates with one or more proteins in a complex that can degrade or prevent translation of an mRNA with a complementary sequence.

microspore A spore from a heterosporous plant species that develops into a male gametophyte.

microtubule A hollow rod composed of tubulin proteins that make up part of the cytoskeleton in all eukaryotic cells and is found in cilia and flagella.

microvillus (plural, **microvilli**) One of many fine, finger-like projections of the epithelial cells in the lumen of the small intestine that increase its surface area.

midbrain One of three ancestral and embryonic regions of the vertebrate brain; develops into sensory integrating and relay centers that send sensory information to the cerebrum.

middle ear One of three main regions of the vertebrate ear; in mammals, a chamber containing three small bones (the malleus, incus, and stapes) that convey vibrations from the eardrum to the oval window.

middle lamella (luh-mel′-uh) In plants, a thin layer of adhesive extracellular material, primarily pectins, found between the primary walls of adjacent young cells.

migration A regular, long-distance change in location.

mineral In nutrition, a simple nutrient that is inorganic and therefore cannot be synthesized.

mineralocorticoid A steroid hormone secreted by the adrenal cortex that regulates salt and water homeostasis.

minimum viable population (MVP) The smallest population size at which a species is able to sustain its numbers and survive.

mismatch repair The cellular process that uses specific enzymes to remove and replace incorrectly paired nucleotides.

missense mutation A base-pair substitution that results in a codon that codes for a different amino acid.

mitochondrial matrix The compartment of the mitochondrion enclosed by the inner membrane and containing enzymes and substrates for the citric acid cycle.

mitochondrion (mī′-tō-kon′-drē-un) (plural, **mitochondria**) An organelle in eukaryotic cells that serves as the site of cellular respiration.

mitosis (mī-tō′-sis) A process of nuclear division in eukaryotic cells conventionally divided into five stages: prophase, prometaphase, metaphase, anaphase, and telophase. Mitosis conserves chromosome number by allocating replicated chromosomes equally to each of the daughter nuclei.

mitotic (M) phase The phase of the cell cycle that includes mitosis and cytokinesis.

mitotic spindle An assemblage of microtubules and associated proteins that is involved in the movements of chromosomes during mitosis.

mixotroph An organism that is capable of both photosynthesis and heterotrophy.

model A representation of a theory or process.

model organism A particular species chosen for research into broad biological principles because it is representative of a larger group and usually easy to grow in a lab.

molarity A common measure of solute concentration, referring to the number of moles of solute per liter of solution.

mold Informal term for a fungus that grows as a filamentous fungus, producing haploid spores by mitosis and forming a visible mycelium.

mole (mol) The number of grams of a substance that equals its molecular weight in daltons and contains Avogadro's number of molecules.

molecular clock A method for estimating the time required for a given amount of evolutionary change, based on the observation that some regions of genomes appear to evolve at constant rates.

molecular formula A type of molecular notation representing the quantity of constituent atoms, but not the nature of the bonds that join them.

molecular mass The sum of the masses of all the atoms in a molecule; sometimes called molecular weight.

molecular systematics A scientific discipline that uses nucleic acids or other molecules in different species to infer evolutionary relationships.

molecule Two or more atoms held together by covalent bonds.

molting A process in ecdysozoans in which the exoskeleton is shed at intervals, allowing growth by the production of a larger exoskeleton.

monoclonal antibody (mon′-ō-klōn′-ul) Any of a preparation of antibodies that have been produced by a single clone of cultured cells and thus are all specific for the same epitope.

monocot Member of a clade consisting of flowering plants that have one embryonic seed leaf, or cotyledon.

monogamous (muh-nog′-uh-mus) Referring to a type of relationship in which one male mates with just one female.

monohybrid An organism that is heterozygous with respect to a single gene of interest. All the offspring from a cross between parents homozygous for different alleles are monohybrids. For example, parents of genotypes *AA* and *aa* produce a monohybrid of genotype *Aa*.

monomer (mon′-uh-mer) The subunit that serves as the building block of a polymer.

monophyletic (mon′-ō-fī-let′-ik) Pertaining to a group of taxa that consists of a common ancestor and all its descendants. A monophyletic taxon is equivalent to a clade.

monosaccharide (mon′-ō-sak′-uh-rīd) The simplest carbohydrate, active alone or serving as a monomer for disaccharides and polysaccharides. Also known as simple sugars, monosaccharides have molecular formulas that are generally some multiple of CH_2O.

monosomic Referring to a cell that has only one copy of a particular chromosome instead of the normal two.

morphogen A substance, such as Bicoid protein in *Drosophila*, that provides positional information in the form of a concentration gradient along an embryonic axis.

morphogenesis (mōr′-fō-jen′-uh-sis) The development of body shape and organization.

morphological species concept A definition of species in terms of measurable anatomical criteria.

morphology An organism's external form.

moss A small, herbaceous nonvascular plant that is a member of the phylum Bryophyta.
motor neuron A nerve cell that transmits signals from the brain or spinal cord to muscles or glands.
motor protein A protein that interacts with cytoskeletal elements and other cell components, producing movement of the whole cell or parts of the cell.
motor system An efferent branch of the vertebrate peripheral nervous system composed of motor neurons that carry signals to skeletal muscles in response to external stimuli.
motor unit A single motor neuron and all the muscle fibers it controls.
movement corridor A series of small clumps or a narrow strip of quality habitat (usable by organisms) that connects otherwise isolated patches of quality habitat.
MPF Maturation-promoting factor (M-phase-promoting factor); a protein complex required for a cell to progress from late interphase to mitosis. The active form consists of cyclin and a protein kinase.
mucus A viscous and slippery mixture of glycoproteins, cells, salts, and water that moistens and protects the membranes lining body cavities that open to the exterior.
Müllerian mimicry (myū-lār′-ē-un) A mutual mimicry by two unpalatable species.
multifactorial Referring to a phenotypic character that is influenced by multiple genes and environmental factors.
multigene family A collection of genes with similar or identical sequences, presumably of common origin.
multiple fruit A fruit derived from an inflorescence, a group of flowers tightly clustered together.
muscle tissue Tissue consisting of long muscle cells that can contract, either on its own or when stimulated by nerve impulses.
mutagen (myū′-tuh-jen) A chemical or physical agent that interacts with DNA and causes a mutation.
mutation (myū-tā′-shun) A change in the nucleotide sequence of an organism's DNA, ultimately creating genetic diversity. Mutations also can occur in the DNA or RNA of a virus.
mutualism (myū′-chū-ul-izm) A symbiotic relationship in which both participants benefit.
mycelium (mī-sē′-lē-um) The densely branched network of hyphae in a fungus.
mycorrhiza (mī′-kō-rī′-zuh) (plural, **mycorrhizae**) A mutualistic association of plant roots and fungus.
mycosis (mī-kō′-sis) General term for a fungal infection.
myelin sheath (mī′-uh-lin) Around the axon of a neuron, an insulating coat of cell membranes from Schwann cells or oligodendrocytes. It is interrupted by nodes of Ranvier, where action potentials are generated.
myofibril (mī′-ō-fī′-bril) A fibril collectively arranged in longitudinal bundles in muscle cells (fibers); composed of thin filaments of actin and a regulatory protein and thick filaments of myosin.
myoglobin (mī′-uh-glō′-bin) An oxygen-storing, pigmented protein in muscle cells.
myosin (mī′-uh-sin) A type of protein filament that acts as a motor protein with actin filaments to cause cell contraction.
myotonia (mī′-uh-tō′-nī-uh) Increased muscle tension, characteristic of sexual arousal in certain human tissues.
myriapod (mir′-ē-uh-pod′) A terrestrial arthropod with many body segments and one or two pairs of legs per segment. Millipedes and centipedes comprise the two classes of living myriapods.
NAD^+ Nicotinamide adenine dinucleotide, a coenzyme that can accept an electron and acts as an electron carrier in the electron transport chain.
$NADP^+$ Nicotinamide adenine dinucleotide phosphate, an electron acceptor that, as NADPH, temporarily stores energized electrons produced during the light reactions.
natural family planning A form of contraception that relies on refraining from sexual intercourse when conception is most likely to occur; also called the rhythm method.
natural killer (NK) cell A type of white blood cell that can kill tumor cells and virus-infected cells as part of innate immunity.
natural selection A process in which organisms with certain inherited characteristics are more likely to survive and reproduce than are organisms with other characteristics.
negative feedback A primary mechanism of homeostasis, whereby a change in a physiological variable triggers a response that counteracts the initial change.
negative pressure breathing A breathing system in which air is pulled into the lungs.
nematocyst (nem′-uh-tuh-sist′) In a cnidocyte of a cnidarian, a specialized capsule-like organelle containing a coiled thread that when discharged can penetrate the body wall of the prey.
nephron (nef′-ron) The tubular excretory unit of the vertebrate kidney.
neritic zone The shallow region of the ocean overlying the continental shelf.
nerve A ropelike bundle of neuron fibers (axons) tightly wrapped in connective tissue.
nerve net A weblike system of neurons, characteristic of radially symmetrical animals, such as hydra.
nervous system The fast-acting internal system of communication involving sensory receptors, networks of nerve cells, and connections to muscles and glands that respond to nerve signals; functions in concert with the endocrine system to effect internal regulation and maintain homeostasis.
nervous tissue Tissue made up of neurons and supportive cells.
net primary production (NPP) The gross primary production of an ecosystem minus the energy used by the producers for respiration.
neural crest cells In vertebrates, groups of cells along the sides of the neural tube where it pinches off from the ectoderm. The cells migrate to various parts of the embryo and form pigment cells in the skin and parts of the skull, teeth, adrenal glands, and peripheral nervous system.
neural plasticity The capacity of a nervous system to change with experience.
neural tube A tube of infolded ectodermal cells that runs along the anterior-posterior axis of a vertebrate, just dorsal to the notochord. It will give rise to the central nervous system.
neurohormone A molecule that is secreted by a neuron, travels in body fluids, and acts on specific target cells to change their functioning.
neuron (nyūr′-on) A nerve cell; the fundamental unit of the nervous system, having structure and properties that allow it to conduct signals by taking advantage of the electrical charge across its plasma membrane.
neuropeptide A relatively short chain of amino acids that serves as a neurotransmitter.
neurotransmitter A molecule that is released from the synaptic terminal of a neuron at a chemical synapse, diffuses across the synaptic cleft, and binds to the postsynaptic cell, triggering a response.
neutral theory The hypothesis that much evolutionary change in genes and proteins has no effect on fitness and therefore is not influenced by Darwinian natural selection.
neutral variation Genetic variation that does not appear to provide a selective advantage or disadvantage.
neutron A subatomic particle having no electrical charge (electrically neutral), with a mass of about 1.7×10^{-24} g, found in the nucleus of an atom.
neutrophil The most abundant type of white blood cell. Neutrophils are phagocytic and tend to self-destruct as they destroy foreign invaders, limiting their life span to a few days.
nitric oxide (NO) A gas produced by many types of cells that functions as a local regulator and as a neurotransmitter.
nitrogen cycle The natural process by which nitrogen, either from the atmosphere or from decomposed organic material, is converted by soil bacteria to compounds that can be assimilated by plants. This incorporated nitrogen is then taken in by other organisms and subsequently released, acted on by bacteria, and made available again to the nonliving environment.
nitrogen fixation The conversion of atmospheric nitrogen (N_2) to ammonia (NH_3). Biological nitrogen fixation is carried out by certain prokaryotes, some of which have mutualistic relationships with plants.
nociceptor (nō′-si-sep′-tur) A sensory receptor that responds to noxious or painful stimuli; also called a pain receptor.
node A point along the stem of a plant at which leaves are attached.
node of Ranvier (ron′-vē-ā′) Gap in the myelin sheath of certain axons where an action potential may be generated. In saltatory conduction, an action potential is regenerated

at each node, appearing to "jump" along the axon from node to node.

nodule A swelling on the root of a legume. Nodules are composed of plant cells that contain nitrogen-fixing bacteria of the genus *Rhizobium*.

noncompetitive inhibitor A substance that reduces the activity of an enzyme by binding to a location remote from the active site, changing the enzyme's shape so that the active site no longer functions effectively.

nondisjunction An error in meiosis or mitosis in which members of a pair of homologous chromosomes or a pair of sister chromatids fail to separate properly from each other.

nonequilibrium model A model that maintains that communities change constantly after being buffeted by disturbances.

nonpolar covalent bond A type of covalent bond in which electrons are shared equally between two atoms of similar electronegativity.

nonsense mutation A mutation that changes an amino acid codon to one of the three stop codons, resulting in a shorter and usually nonfunctional protein.

norepinephrine A catecholamine that is chemically and functionally similar to epinephrine and acts as a hormone or neurotransmitter; also known as noradrenaline.

norm of reaction The range of phenotypes produced by a single genotype, due to environmental influences.

normal range An upper and lower limit of a variable.

Northern blotting A technique that enables specific nucleotide sequences to be detected in a sample of mRNA. It involves gel electrophoresis of RNA molecules and their transfer to a membrane (blotting), followed by nucleic acid hybridization with a labeled probe.

northern coniferous forest A terrestrial biome characterized by long, cold winters and dominated by cone-bearing trees.

no-till agriculture A plowing technique that involves creating furrows, resulting in minimal disturbance of the soil.

notochord (nō′-tuh-kord′) A longitudinal, flexible rod made of tightly packed mesodermal cells that runs along the anterior-posterior axis of a chordate in the dorsal part of the body.

nuclear envelope The double membrane in a eukaryotic cell that encloses the nucleus, separating it from the cytoplasm.

nuclear lamina A netlike array of protein filaments lining the inner surface of the nuclear envelope; it helps maintain the shape of the nucleus.

nucleariid Member of a group of unicellular, amoeboid protists that are more closely related to fungi than they are to other protists.

nuclease An enzyme that cuts DNA or RNA, either removing one or a few bases or hydrolyzing the DNA or RNA completely into its component nucleotides.

nucleic acid (nū-klā′-ik) A polymer (polynucleotide) consisting of many nucleotide monomers; serves as a blueprint for proteins and, through the actions of proteins, for all cellular activities. The two types are DNA and RNA.

nucleic acid hybridization The process of base pairing between a gene and a complementary sequence on another nucleic acid molecule.

nucleic acid probe In DNA technology, a labeled single-stranded nucleic acid molecule used to locate a specific nucleotide sequence in a nucleic acid sample. Molecules of the probe hydrogen-bond to the complementary sequence wherever it occurs; radioactive or other labeling of the probe allows its location to be detected.

nucleoid (nū′-klē-oyd) A dense region of DNA in a prokaryotic cell.

nucleolus (nū-klē′-ō-lus) (plural, **nucleoli**) A specialized structure in the nucleus, consisting of chromatin regions containing ribosomal RNA genes along with ribosomal proteins imported from the cytoplasmic site of rRNA synthesis and ribosomal subunit assembly. *See also* ribosome.

nucleosome (nū′-klē-ō-sōm′) The basic, bead-like unit of DNA packing in eukaryotes, consisting of a segment of DNA wound around a protein core composed of two copies of each of four types of histone.

nucleotide (nū′-klē-ō-tīd′) The building block of a nucleic acid, consisting of a five-carbon sugar covalently bonded to a nitrogenous base and a phosphate group.

nucleotide excision repair A repair system that removes and then correctly replaces a damaged segment of DNA using the undamaged strand as a guide.

nucleus (1) An atom's central core, containing protons and neutrons. (2) The chromosome-containing organelle of a eukaryotic cell. (3) A cluster of neurons.

nutrition The process by which an organism takes in and makes use of food substances.

obligate aerobe (ob′-lig-et ār′-ōb) An organism that requires oxygen for cellular respiration and cannot live without it.

obligate anaerobe (ob′-lig-et an′-uh-rōb) An organism that only carries out fermentation or anaerobic respiration. Such organisms cannot use oxygen and in fact may be poisoned by it.

oceanic pelagic zone Most of the ocean's waters far from shore, constantly mixed by ocean currents.

odorant A molecule that can be detected by sensory receptors of the olfactory system.

Okazaki fragment (ō′-kah-zah′-kē) A short segment of DNA synthesized away from the replication fork on a template strand during DNA replication, many of which are joined together to make up the lagging strand of newly synthesized DNA.

olfaction The sense of smell.

oligodendrocyte A type of glial cell that forms insulating myelin sheaths around the axons of neurons in the central nervous system.

oligotrophic lake A nutrient-poor, clear lake with few phytoplankton.

ommatidium (ōm′-uh-tid′-ē-um) (plural, **ommatidia**) One of the facets of the compound eye of arthropods and some polychaete worms.

omnivore An animal that regularly eats animals as well as plants or algae.

oncogene (on′-kō-jēn) A gene found in viral or cellular genomes that is involved in triggering molecular events that can lead to cancer.

oocyte A cell in the female reproductive system that differentiates to form an egg.

oogenesis (ō′-uh-jen′-uh-sis) The process in the ovary that results in the production of female gametes.

oogonium (ō′-uh- gō′-nē-em) A cell that divides mitotically to form oocytes.

oomycete (ō′-uh-mī′- sēt) A protist with flagellated cells, such as a water mold, white rust, or downy mildew, that acquires nutrition mainly as a decomposer or plant parasite.

open circulatory system A circulatory system in which fluid called hemolymph bathes the tissues and organs directly and there is no distinction between the circulating fluid and the interstitial fluid.

operant conditioning (op′-er-ent) A type of associative learning in which an animal learns to associate one of its own behaviors with a reward or punishment and then tends to repeat or avoid that behavior; also called trial-and-error learning.

operator In bacterial DNA, a sequence of nucleotides near the start of an operon to which an active repressor can attach. The binding of the repressor prevents RNA polymerase from attaching to the promoter and transcribing the genes of the operon.

operculum (ō-per′-kyuh-lum) In aquatic osteichthyans, a protective bony flap that covers and protects the gills.

operon (op′-er-on) A unit of genetic function found in bacteria and phages, consisting of a promoter, an operator, and a coordinately regulated cluster of genes whose products function in a common pathway.

opisthokont (uh-pis′-thuh-kont′) Member of the diverse clade Opisthokonta, organisms that descended from an ancestor with a posterior flagellum, including fungi, animals, and certain protists.

opposable thumb A thumb that can touch the ventral surface of the fingertips of all four fingers.

opsin A membrane protein bound to a light-absorbing pigment molecule.

optic chiasm The place where the two optic nerves meet and where the sensations from the left visual field of both eyes are transmitted to the right side of the brain and the sensations from the right visual field of both eyes are transmitted to the left side of the brain.

optimal foraging model The basis for analyzing behavior as a compromise between feeding costs and feeding benefits.

oral cavity The mouth of an animal.

orbital The three-dimensional space where an electron is found 90% of the time.

order In classification, the taxonomic category above the level of family.

organ A specialized center of body function composed of several different types of tissues.

organ identity gene A plant homeotic gene that uses positional information to determine which emerging leaves develop into which types of floral organs.

organ of Corti The actual hearing organ of the vertebrate ear, located in the floor of the cochlear duct in the inner ear; contains the receptor cells (hair cells) of the ear.

organ system A group of organs that work together in performing vital body functions.

organelle (ōr-guh-nel′) Any of several membrane-enclosed structures with specialized functions, suspended in the cytosol of eukaryotic cells.

organic chemistry The study of carbon compounds (organic compounds).

organismal ecology The branch of ecology concerned with the morphological, physiological, and behavioral ways in which individual organisms meet the challenges posed by their biotic and abiotic environments.

organogenesis (ōr-gan′-ō-jen′-uh-sis) The process in which organ rudiments develop from the three germ layers after gastrulation.

orgasm Rhythmic, involuntary contractions of certain reproductive structures in both sexes during the human sexual response cycle.

origin of replication Site where the replication of a DNA molecule begins, consisting of a specific sequence of nucleotides.

orthologous genes Homologous genes that are found in different species because of speciation.

osculum (os′-kyuh-lum) A large opening in a sponge that connects the spongocoel to the environment.

osmoconformer An animal that is isoosmotic with its environment.

osmolarity (oz′-mō-lār′-uh-tē) Solute concentration expressed as molarity.

osmoregulation Regulation of solute concentrations and water balance by a cell or organism.

osmoregulator An animal that controls its internal osmolarity independent of the external environment.

osmosis (oz-mō′-sis) The diffusion of water across a selectively permeable membrane.

osmotic potential A component of water potential that is proportional to the osmolarity of a solution and that measures the effect of solutes on the direction of water movement; also called solute potential, it can be either zero or negative.

osteichthyan (os′-tē-ik′-thē-an) Member of a vertebrate subgroup with jaws and mostly bony skeletons.

outer ear One of three main regions of the ear in reptiles (including birds) and mammals; made up of the auditory canal and, in many birds and mammals, the pinna.

outgroup A species or group of species from an evolutionary lineage that is known to have diverged before the lineage that contains the group of species being studied. An outgroup is selected so that its members are closely related to the group of species being studied, but not as closely related as any study-group members are to each other.

oval window In the vertebrate ear, a membrane-covered gap in the skull bone, through which sound waves pass from the middle ear to the inner ear.

ovarian cycle (ō-vār′-ē-un) The cyclic recurrence of the follicular phase, ovulation, and the luteal phase in the mammalian ovary, regulated by hormones.

ovary (ō′-vuh-rē) (1) In flowers, the portion of a carpel in which the egg-containing ovules develop. (2) In animals, the structure that produces female gametes and reproductive hormones.

overnourishment The consumption of more calories than the body needs for normal metabolism.

oviduct (ō′-vuh-duct) A tube passing from the ovary to the vagina in invertebrates or to the uterus in vertebrates, where it is also known as a fallopian tube.

oviparous (ō-vip′-uh-rus) Referring to a type of development in which young hatch from eggs laid outside the mother's body.

ovoviviparous (ō′-vō-vī-vip′-uh-rus) Referring to a type of development in which young hatch from eggs that are retained in the mother's uterus.

ovulation The release of an egg from an ovary. In humans, an ovarian follicle releases an egg during each uterine (menstrual) cycle.

ovule (o′-vyūl) A structure that develops within the ovary of a seed plant and contains the female gametophyte.

oxidation The loss of electrons from a substance involved in a redox reaction.

oxidative phosphorylation (fos′-fōr-uh-lā′-shun) The production of ATP using energy derived from the redox reactions of an electron transport chain; the third major stage of cellular respiration.

oxidizing agent The electron acceptor in a redox reaction.

oxytocin (ok′-si-tō′-sen) A hormone produced by the hypothalamus and released from the posterior pituitary. It induces contractions of the uterine muscles during labor and causes the mammary glands to eject milk during nursing.

P generation The parent individuals from which offspring are derived in studies of inheritance; P stands for "parental."

P site One of a ribosome's three binding sites for tRNA during translation. The P site holds the tRNA carrying the growing polypeptide chain. (P stands for peptidyl tRNA.)

***p53* gene** A tumor-suppressor gene that codes for a specific transcription factor that promotes the synthesis of cell cycle–inhibiting proteins.

paedomorphosis (pē′-duh-mōr′-fuh-sis) The retention in an adult organism of the juvenile features of its evolutionary ancestors.

pain receptor A sensory receptor that responds to noxious or painful stimuli; also called a nociceptor.

paleoanthropology The study of human origins and evolution.

paleontology (pā′-lē-un-tol′-ō-jē) The scientific study of fossils.

pancreas (pan′-krē-us) A gland with the following dual functions: The nonendocrine portion functions in digestion, secreting enzymes and an alkaline solution into the small intestine via a duct; the ductless endocrine portion functions in homeostasis, secreting the hormones insulin and glucagon into the blood.

pandemic A global epidemic.

Pangaea (pan-jē′-uh) The supercontinent that formed near the end of the Paleozoic era, when plate movements brought all the landmasses of Earth together.

parabasalid A protist, such as a trichomonad, with modified mitochondria.

paracrine Referring to a secreted molecule that acts on a neighboring cell.

paralogous genes Homologous genes that are found in the same genome as a result of gene duplication.

paraphyletic (pār′-uh-fī-let′-ik) Pertaining to a group of taxa that consists of a common ancestor and some, but not all, of its descendants.

parareptile First major group of reptiles to emerge, consisting mostly of large, stocky quadrupedal herbivores; died out in the late Triassic period.

parasite (pār′-uh-sīt) An organism that feeds on the cell contents, tissues, or body fluids of another species (the host) while in or on the host organism. Parasites harm but usually do not kill their host.

parasitism (pār′-uh-sit-izm) A symbiotic relationship in which one organism, the parasite, benefits at the expense of another, the host, by living either within or on the host.

parasympathetic division One of three divisions of the autonomic nervous system; generally enhances body activities that gain and conserve energy, such as digestion and reduced heart rate.

parathyroid gland Any of four small endocrine glands, embedded in the surface of the thyroid gland, that secrete parathyroid hormone.

parathyroid hormone (PTH) A hormone secreted by the parathyroid glands that raises blood calcium level by promoting calcium release from bone and calcium retention by the kidneys.

parenchyma cell (puh-ren′-ki-muh) A relatively unspecialized plant cell type that carries out most of the metabolism, synthesizes and stores organic products, and develops into a more differentiated cell type.

parental type An offspring with a phenotype that matches one of the parental phenotypes; also refers to the phenotype itself.

Parkinson's disease A progressive brain disease characterized by difficulty in initiating movements, slowness of movement, and rigidity.

parthenogenesis (par′-thuh-nō′-jen′-uh-sis) Asexual reproduction in which females produce offspring from unfertilized eggs.

partial pressure The pressure exerted by a particular gas in a mixture of gases (for instance, the pressure exerted by oxygen in air).

passive immunity Short-term immunity conferred by the transfer of antibodies, as occurs in the transfer of maternal antibodies to a fetus or nursing infant.

passive transport The diffusion of a substance across a biological membrane with no expenditure of energy.

pathogen An organism or virus that causes disease.

pattern formation The development of a multicellular organism's spatial organization, the arrangement of organs and tissues in their characteristic places in three-dimensional space.

peat Extensive deposits of partially decayed organic material formed primarily from the wetland moss *Sphagnum*.

pedigree A diagram of a family tree showing the occurrence of heritable characters in parents and offspring over multiple generations.

penis The copulatory structure of male mammals.

PEP carboxylase An enzyme that adds CO_2 to phosphoenolpyruvate (PEP) to form oxaloacetate in C_4 plants. It acts prior to photosynthesis.

pepsin An enzyme present in gastric juice that begins the hydrolysis of proteins.

pepsinogen The inactive form of pepsin that is first secreted by chief cells located in gastric pits of the stomach.

peptide bond The covalent bond between the carboxyl group on one amino acid and the amino group on another, formed by a dehydration reaction.

peptidoglycan (pep′-tid-ō-glī′-kan) A type of polymer in bacterial cell walls consisting of modified sugars cross-linked by short polypeptides.

perception The interpretation of sensory system input by the brain.

perennial (puh-ren′-ē-ul) A flowering plant that lives for many years.

pericycle The outermost layer in the vascular cylinder from which lateral roots arise.

periderm (pār′-uh-derm′) The protective coat that replaces the epidermis in woody plants during secondary growth, formed of the cork and cork cambium.

peripheral nervous system (PNS) The sensory and motor neurons that connect to the central nervous system.

peripheral protein A protein loosely bound to the surface of a membrane or to part of an integral protein and not embedded in the lipid bilayer.

peristalsis (pār′-uh-stal′-sis) (1) Alternating waves of contraction and relaxation in the smooth muscles lining the alimentary canal that push food along the canal. (2) A type of movement on land produced by rhythmic waves of muscle contractions passing from front to back, as in many annelids.

peristome A ring of interlocking, tooth-like structures on the upper part of a moss capsule (sporangium), often specialized for gradual spore discharge.

peritubular capillary One of the tiny blood vessels that form a network surrounding the proximal and distal tubules in the kidney.

permafrost A permanently frozen soil layer.

peroxisome (puh-rok′-suh-sōm′) An organelle containing enzymes that transfer hydrogen (H_2) from various substrates to oxygen (O_2), producing and then degrading hydrogen peroxide (H_2O_2).

petal A modified leaf of a flowering plant. Petals are the often colorful parts of a flower that advertise it to insects and other pollinators.

petiole (pet′-ē-ōl) The stalk of a leaf, which joins the leaf to a node of the stem.

pH A measure of hydrogen ion concentration equal to $-\log [H^+]$ and ranging in value from 0 to 14.

phage (fāj) A virus that infects bacteria; also called a bacteriophage.

phagocytosis (fag′-ō-sī-tō′-sis) A type of endocytosis in which large particulate substances are taken up by a cell. It is carried out by some protists and by certain immune cells of animals (in mammals, mainly macrophages, neutrophils, and dendritic cells).

pharyngeal cleft (fuh-rin′-jē-ul) In chordate embryos, one of the grooves that separate a series of pouches along the sides of the pharynx and may develop into a pharyngeal slit.

pharyngeal slit (fuh-rin′-jē-ul) In chordate embryos, one of the slits that form from the pharyngeal clefts and communicate to the outside, later developing into gill slits in many vertebrates.

pharynx (fār′-inks) (1) An area in the vertebrate throat where air and food passages cross. (2) In flatworms, the muscular tube that protrudes from the ventral side of the worm and ends in the mouth.

phase change A shift from one developmental phase to another.

phenotype (fē′-nō-tīp) The physical and physiological traits of an organism, which are determined by its genetic makeup.

pheromone (fār′-uh-mōn) In animals and fungi, a small molecule released into the environment that functions in communication between members of the same species. In animals, it acts much like a hormone in influencing physiology and behavior.

phloem (flō′-em) Vascular plant tissue consisting of living cells arranged into elongated tubes that transport sugar and other organic nutrients throughout the plant.

phloem sap The sugar-rich solution carried through sieve tubes.

phosphate group A chemical group consisting of a phosphorus atom bonded to four oxygen atoms; important in energy transfer.

phospholipid (fos′-fō-lip′-id) A lipid made up of glycerol joined to two fatty acids and a phosphate group. The hydrocarbon chains of the fatty acids act as nonpolar, hydrophobic tails, while the rest of the molecule acts as a polar, hydrophilic head. Phospholipids form bilayers that function as biological membranes.

phosphorylated Referring to a molecule that is covalently bonded to a phosphate group.

photic zone (fō′-tic) The narrow top layer of an ocean or lake, where light penetrates sufficiently for photosynthesis to occur.

photoautotroph (fō′-tō-ot′-ō-trōf) An organism that harnesses light energy to drive the synthesis of organic compounds from carbon dioxide.

photoheterotroph (fō′-tō-het′-er-ō-trōf) An organism that uses light to generate ATP but must obtain carbon in organic form.

photomorphogenesis Effects of light on plant morphology.

photon (fō′-ton) A quantum, or discrete quantity, of light energy that behaves as if it were a particle.

photoperiodism (fō′-tō-pēr′-ē-ō-dizm) A physiological response to photoperiod, the relative lengths of night and day. An example of photoperiodism is flowering.

photophosphorylation (fō′-tō-fos′-fōr-uh-lā′-shun) The process of generating ATP from ADP and phosphate by means of a proton-motive force generated across the thylakoid membrane of the chloroplast or the membrane of certain prokaryotes during the light reactions of photosynthesis.

photoreceptor An electromagnetic receptor that detects the radiation known as visible light.

photorespiration A metabolic pathway that consumes oxygen and ATP, releases carbon dioxide, and decreases photosynthetic output. Photorespiration generally occurs on hot, dry, bright days, when stomata close and the oxygen concentration in the leaf exceeds that of carbon dioxide.

photosynthesis (fō′-tō-sin′-thi-sis) The conversion of light energy to chemical energy that is stored in sugars or other organic compounds; occurs in plants, algae, and certain prokaryotes.

photosystem A light-capturing unit located in the thylakoid membrane of the chloroplast or in the membrane of some prokaryotes, consisting of a reaction-center complex surrounded by numerous light-harvesting complexes. There are two types of photosystems, I and II; they absorb light best at different wavelengths.

photosystem I (PS I) One of two light-capturing units in a chloroplast's thylakoid membrane or in the membrane of some prokaryotes; it has two molecules of P700 chlorophyll *a* at its reaction center.

photosystem II (PS II) One of two light-capturing units in a chloroplast's thylakoid membrane or in the membrane of some prokaryotes; it has two molecules of P680 chlorophyll *a* at its reaction center.

phototropism (fō′-tō-trō′-pizm) Growth of a plant shoot toward or away from light.
phragmoplast (frag′-mō-plast′) An alignment of cytoskeletal elements and Golgi-derived vesicles that forms across the midline of a dividing plant cell.
phyllotaxy (fil′-uh-tak′-sē) The arrangement of leaves on the shoot of a plant.
PhyloCode System of classification of organisms based on evolutionary relationships: Only groups that include a common ancestor and all of its descendents are named.
phylogenetic bracketing An approach in which features shared by two groups of organisms are predicted (by parsimony) to be present in their common ancestor and all of its descendants.
phylogenetic species concept A definition of species as the smallest group of individuals that share a common ancestor, forming one branch on the tree of life.
phylogenetic tree A branching diagram that represents a hypothesis about the evolutionary history of a group of organisms.
phylogeny (fī-loj′-uh-nē) The evolutionary history of a species or group of related species.
phylum (fī′-lum) (plural, **phyla**) In classification, the taxonomic category above class.
physical map A genetic map in which the actual physical distances between genes or other genetic markers are expressed, usually as the number of base pairs along the DNA.
physiology The processes and functions of an organism and their study.
phytochrome (fī′-tuh-krōm) A type of light receptor in plants that mostly absorbs red light and regulates many plant responses, such as seed germination and shade avoidance.
phytoremediation An emerging nondestructive biotechnology that seeks to cheaply reclaim contaminated areas by taking advantage of some plant species' ability to extract heavy metals and other pollutants from the soil and to concentrate them in easily harvested portions of the plant.
pineal gland (pī′-nē-ul) A small gland on the dorsal surface of the vertebrate forebrain that secretes the hormone melatonin.
pinocytosis (pī′-nō-sī-tō′-sis) A type of endocytosis in which the cell ingests extracellular fluid and its dissolved solutes.
pistil A single carpel or a group of fused carpels.
pith Ground tissue that is internal to the vascular tissue in a stem; in many monocot roots, parenchyma cells that form the central core of the vascular cylinder.
pituitary gland (puh-tū′-uh-tār′-ē) An endocrine gland at the base of the hypothalamus; consists of a posterior lobe (neurohypophysis), which stores and releases two hormones produced by the hypothalamus, and an anterior lobe (adenohypophysis), which produces and secretes many hormones that regulate diverse body functions.
placenta (pluh-sen′-tuh) A structure in the pregnant uterus for nourishing a viviparous fetus with the mother's blood supply; formed from the uterine lining and embryonic membranes.
placental transfer cell A plant cell that enhances the transfer of nutrients from parent to embryo.
placoderm A member of an extinct class of fishlike vertebrates that had jaws and were enclosed in a tough outer armor.
planarian A free-living flatworm found in unpolluted ponds and streams.
Plantae (plan′-tā) The kingdom that consists of multicellular eukaryotes that carry out photosynthesis.
plasma (plaz′-muh) The liquid matrix of blood in which the cells are suspended.
plasma cell The antibody-secreting effector cell of humoral immunity; arises from antigen-stimulated B cells.
plasma membrane The membrane at the boundary of every cell that acts as a selective barrier, regulating the cell's chemical composition.
plasmid (plaz′-mid) A small, circular, double-stranded DNA molecule that carries accessory genes separate from those of a bacterial chromosome. Plasmids are also found in some eukaryotes, such as yeasts.
plasmodesma (plaz′-mō-dez′-muh) (plural, **plasmodesmata**) An open channel in the cell wall of a plant through which strands of cytosol connect from an adjacent cell.
plasmodial slime mold (plaz-mō′-dē-ul) A type of protist that has amoeboid cells, flagellated cells, and a plasmodial feeding stage in its life cycle.
plasmodium A single mass of cytoplasm containing many diploid nuclei that forms during the life cycle of some slime molds.
plasmogamy (plaz-moh′-guh-mē) The fusion of the cytoplasm of cells from two individuals; occurs as one stage of syngamy (fertilization).
plasmolysis (plaz-mol′-uh-sis) A phenomenon in walled cells in which the cytoplasm shrivels and the plasma membrane pulls away from the cell wall; occurs when the cell loses water to a hypertonic environment.
plastid One of a family of closely related organelles that includes chloroplasts, chromoplasts, and amyloplasts (leucoplasts). Plastids are found in cells of photosynthetic organisms.
platelet A pinched-off cytoplasmic fragment of a specialized bone marrow cell. Platelets circulate in the blood and are important in blood clotting.
pleiotropy (plī-o′-truh-pē) The ability of a single gene to have multiple effects.
pluripotent Describing a cell that can give rise to many, but not all, parts of an organism.
point mutation A change in a gene at a single nucleotide pair.
polar covalent bond A covalent bond between atoms that differ in electronegativity. The shared electrons are pulled closer to the more electronegative atom, making it slightly negative and the other atom slightly positive.
polar molecule A molecule (such as water) with opposite charges on different ends of the molecule.
polarity A lack of symmetry; structural differences in opposite ends of an organism or structure, such as the root end and shoot end of a plant.
pollen grain In seed plants, a structure consisting of the male gametophyte enclosed within a pollen wall.
pollen tube A tube formed after germination of the pollen grain that functions in the delivery of sperm to the ovule.
pollination (pol′-uh-nā′-shun) The transfer of pollen to the part of a seed plant containing the ovules, a process required for fertilization.
poly-A tail A sequence of 50 to 250 adenine nucleotides added onto the 3′ end of a pre-mRNA molecule.
polyandry (pol′-ē-an′-drē) A polygamous mating system involving one female and many males.
polygamous Referring to a type of relationship in which an individual of one sex mates with several of the other.
polygenic inheritance (pol′-ē-jen′-ik) An additive effect of two or more genes on a single phenotypic character.
polygyny (puh-lij′-en-ē) A polygamous mating system involving one male and many females.
polymer (pol′-uh-mer) A long molecule consisting of many similar or identical monomers linked together.
polymerase chain reaction (PCR) (puh-lim′-uh-rās) A technique for amplifying DNA *in vitro* by incubating it with specific primers, a heat-resistant DNA polymerase, and nucleotides.
polynucleotide (pol′-ē-nū′-klē-ō-tīd) A polymer consisting of many nucleotide monomers in a chain; nucleotides can be those of DNA or RNA.
polyp The sessile variant of the cnidarian body plan. The alternate form is the medusa.
polypeptide (pol′-ē-pep′-tīd) A polymer (chain) of many amino acids linked together by peptide bonds.
polyphyletic (pol′-ē-fī-let′-ik) Pertaining to a group of taxa derived from two or more different ancestors.
polyploidy (pol′-ē-ploy′-dē) A chromosomal alteration in which the organism possesses more than two complete chromosome sets. It is the result of an accident of cell division.
polyribosome (polysome) (pol′-ē-rī′-bō-sōm′) A group of several ribosomes attached to, and translating, the same messenger RNA molecule.
polysaccharide (pol′-ē-sak′-uh-rīd) A polymer of many monosaccharides, formed by dehydration reactions.
polytomy (puh-lit′-uh-mē) In a phylogenetic tree, a branch point from which more than two descendant taxa emerge. A polytomy indicates that the evolutionary relationships among the descendant taxa are not yet clear.

pons Portion of the brain that participates in certain automatic, homeostatic functions, such as regulating the breathing centers in the medulla.

population A localized group of individuals of the same species that can interbreed, producing fertile offspring.

population dynamics The study of how complex interactions between biotic and abiotic factors influence variations in population size.

population ecology The study of populations in relation to their environment, including environmental influences on population density and distribution, age structure, and variations in population size.

positional information Molecular cues that control pattern formation in an animal or plant embryonic structure by indicating a cell's location relative to the organism's body axes. These cues elicit a response by genes that regulate development.

positive feedback A physiological control mechanism in which a change in a variable triggers mechanisms that amplify the change.

positive pressure breathing A breathing system in which air is forced into the lungs.

posterior Pertaining to the rear, or tail end, of a bilaterally symmetrical animal.

posterior pituitary Also called the neurohypophysis; an extension of the hypothalamus composed of nervous tissue that secretes oxytocin and antidiuretic hormone made in the hypothalamus; a temporary storage site for these hormones.

postsynaptic cell The target cell at a synapse.

postzygotic barrier (pōst′-zī-got′-ik) A reproductive barrier that prevent hybrid zygotes produced by two different species from developing into viable, fertile adults.

potential energy The energy that matter possesses as a result of its location or spatial arrangement (structure).

predation An interaction between species in which one species, the predator, eats the other, the prey.

pregnancy The condition of carrying one or more embryos in the uterus.

preprophase band Microtubules in the cortex (outer cytoplasm) of a cell that are concentrated into a ring.

prepuce (prē′-pyūs) A fold of skin covering the head of the clitoris or penis.

pressure potential (Ψ_P) A component of water potential that consists of the physical pressure on a solution, which can be positive, zero, or negative.

presynaptic cell The transmitting cell at a synapse.

prezygotic barrier (prē′-zī-got′-ik) A reproductive barrier that impedes mating between species or hinders fertilization if interspecific mating is attempted.

primary cell wall In plants, a relatively thin and flexible layer first secreted by a young cell.

primary consumer An herbivore; an organism that eats plants or other autotrophs.

primary electron acceptor In the thylakoid membrane of a chloroplast or in the membrane of some prokaryotes, a specialized molecule that shares the reaction-center complex with a pair of chlorophyll *a* molecules and that accepts an electron from them.

primary growth Growth produced by apical meristems, lengthening stems and roots.

primary immune response The initial acquired immune response to an antigen, which appears after a lag of about 10 to 17 days.

primary oocyte (ō′-uh-sīt) An oocyte prior to completion of meiosis I.

primary plant body The tissues produced by apical meristems, which lengthen stems and roots.

primary producer An autotroph, usually a photosynthetic organism. Collectively, autotrophs make up the trophic level of an ecosystem that ultimately supports all other levels.

primary production The amount of light energy converted to chemical energy (organic compounds) by autotrophs in an ecosystem during a given time period.

primary structure The level of protein structure referring to the specific sequence of amino acids.

primary succession A type of ecological succession that occurs in an area where there were originally no organisms present and where soil has not yet formed.

primary transcript An initial RNA transcript; also called pre-mRNA when transcribed from a protein-coding gene.

primary visual cortex The destination in the occipital lobe of the cerebrum for most of the axons from the lateral geniculate nuclei.

primase An enzyme that joins RNA nucleotides to make the primer using the parental DNA strand as a template.

primer A short stretch of RNA with a free 3′ end, bound by complementary base pairing to the template strand, that is elongated with DNA nucleotides during DNA replication.

primitive streak A thickening along the future anterior-posterior axis on the surface of an early avian or mammalian embryo, caused by a piling up of cells as they congregate at the midline before moving into the embryo.

prion An infectious agent that is a misfolded version of a normal cellular protein. Prions appear to increase in number by converting correctly folded versions of the protein to more prions.

problem solving The cognitive activity of devising a method to proceed from one state to another in the face of real or apparent obstacles.

producer An organism that produces organic compounds from CO_2 by harnessing light energy (in photosynthesis) or by oxidizing inorganic chemicals (in chemosynthetic reactions carried out by some prokaryotes).

product A material resulting from a chemical reaction.

production efficiency The percentage of energy stored in food that is not used for respiration or eliminated as waste.

progesterone A steroid hormone that prepares the uterus for pregnancy; the major progestin in mammals.

progestin Any steroid hormone with progesterone-like activity.

progymnosperm (prō′-jim′-nō-sperm) An extinct seedless vascular plant that may be ancestral to seed plants.

prokaryotic cell (prō′-kār′-ē-ot′-ik) A type of cell lacking a membrane-enclosed nucleus and membrane-enclosed organelles. Organisms with prokaryotic cells (bacteria and archaea) are called prokaryotes.

prolactin (PRL) A hormone produced and secreted by the anterior pituitary with a great diversity of effects in different vertebrate species. In mammals, it stimulates growth of and milk production by the mammary glands.

proliferative phase That portion of the uterine (menstrual) cycle when the endometrium regenerates and thickens.

prometaphase The second stage of mitosis, in which discrete chromosomes consisting of identical sister chromatids appear, the nuclear envelope fragments, and the spindle microtubules attach to the kinetochores of the chromosomes.

promiscuous Referring to a type of relationship in which mating occurs with no strong pair-bonds or lasting relationships.

promoter A specific nucleotide sequence in DNA that binds RNA polymerase, positioning it to start transcribing RNA at the appropriate place.

prophage (prō′-fāj) A phage genome that has been inserted into a specific site on a bacterial chromosome.

prophase The first stage of mitosis, in which the chromatin condenses, the mitotic spindle begins to form, and the nucleolus disappears, but the nucleus remains intact.

prostaglandin (PG) (pros′-tuh-glan′-din) One of a group of modified fatty acids secreted by virtually all tissues and performing a wide variety of functions as local regulators.

prostate gland (pros′-tāt) A gland in human males that secretes an acid-neutralizing component of semen.

protease An enzyme that digests proteins by hydrolysis.

proteasome A giant protein complex that recognizes and destroys proteins tagged for elimination by the small protein ubiquitin.

protein (prō′-tēn) A functional biological molecule consisting of one or more polypeptides folded and coiled into a specific three-dimensional structure.

protein kinase An enzyme that transfers phosphate groups from ATP to a protein, thus phosphorylating the protein.

protein phosphatase An enzyme that removes phosphate groups from (dephosphorylates) proteins, often functioning to reverse the effect of a protein kinase.

proteoglycan (prō′-tē-ō-glī′-kan) A glycoprotein consisting of a small core protein with many carbohydrate chains attached, found in the extracellular matrix of animal cells. A proteoglycan may consist of up to 95% carbohydrate.

proteomics (prō′-tē-ō′-miks) The systematic study of the full protein sets (proteomes) encoded by genomes.

protist An informal term applied to any eukaryote that is not a plant, animal, or fungus. Most protists are unicellular, though some are colonial or multicellular.

protobiont A collection of abiotically produced molecules surrounded by a membrane or membrane-like structure.

proton (prō′-ton) A subatomic particle with a single positive electrical charge, with a mass of about 1.7×10^{-24} g, found in the nucleus of an atom.

proton pump An active transport protein in a cell membrane that uses ATP to transport hydrogen ions out of a cell against their concentration gradient, generating a membrane potential in the process.

protonema (plural, **protonemata**) A mass of green, branched, one-cell-thick filaments produced by germinating moss spores.

protonephridia (prō′-tō-nuh-frid′-ē-uh) (singular, **protonephridium**) An excretory system, such as the flame bulb system of flatworms, consisting of a network of tubules lacking internal openings.

proton-motive force The potential energy stored in the form of an electrochemical gradient, generated by the pumping of hydrogen ions across a biological membrane during chemiosmosis.

proto-oncogene (prō′-tō-on′-kō-jēn) A normal cellular gene that has the potential to become an oncogene.

protoplast fusion The fusing of two protoplasts from different plant species that would otherwise be reproductively incompatible.

protostome development In animals, a developmental mode distinguished by the development of the mouth from the blastopore; often also characterized by spiral cleavage and by the body cavity forming when solid masses of mesoderm split.

provirus A viral genome that is permanently inserted into a host genome.

proximal tubule In the vertebrate kidney, the portion of a nephron immediately downstream from Bowman's capsule that conveys and helps refine filtrate.

proximate causation The mechanistic explanation of "how" a behavior (or other aspect of an organism's biology) occurs or is modified; that is, how a stimulus elicits a behavior, what physiological mechanisms mediate the response, and how experience influences the response.

pseudocoelomate (sū′-dō-sē′-lō-māt) An animal whose body cavity is lined by tissue derived from mesoderm and endoderm.

pseudogene (sū′-dō-jēn) A DNA segment very similar to a real gene but which does not yield a functional product; a DNA segment that formerly functioned as a gene but has become inactivated in a particular species because of mutation.

pseudopodium (sū′-dō-pō′-dē-um) (plural, **pseudopodia**) A cellular extension of amoeboid cells used in moving and feeding.

pterophyte (ter′-uh-fīt) An informal name for a member of the phylum Pterophyta, which includes ferns, horsetails, and whisk ferns and their relatives.

pterosaur Winged reptile that lived during the Mesozoic era.

pulmocutaneous circuit A branch of the circulatory system in many amphibians that supplies the lungs and skin.

pulmonary circuit The branch of the circulatory system that supplies the lungs.

pulse The rhythmic bulging of the artery walls with each heartbeat.

punctuated equilibria In the fossil record, long periods of apparent stasis, in which a species undergoes little or no morphological change, interrupted by relatively brief periods of sudden change.

Punnett square A diagram used in the study of inheritance to show the predicted results of random fertilization in genetic crosses.

pupil The opening in the iris, which admits light into the interior of the vertebrate eye. Muscles in the iris regulate its size.

purine (pyū′-rēn) One of two types of nitrogenous bases found in nucleotides, characterized by a six-membered ring fused to a five-membered ring. Adenine (A) and guanine (G) are purines.

pyrimidine (puh-rim′-uh-dēn) One of two types of nitrogenous bases found in nucleotides, characterized by a six-membered ring. Cytosine (C), thymine (T), and uracil (U) are pyrimidines.

quantitative character A heritable feature that varies continuously over a range rather than in an either-or fashion.

quaternary structure (kwot′-er-nār-ē) The particular shape of a complex, aggregate protein, defined by the characteristic three-dimensional arrangement of its constituent subunits, each a polypeptide.

R plasmid A bacterial plasmid carrying genes that confer resistance to certain antibiotics.

radial cleavage A type of embryonic development in deuterostomes in which the planes of cell division that transform the zygote into a ball of cells are either parallel or perpendicular to the vertical axis of the embryo, thereby aligning tiers of cells one above the other.

radial glia In an embryo, supporting cells that form tracks along which newly formed neurons migrate from the neural tube; can also act as stem cells that give rise to other glia and neurons.

radial symmetry Symmetry in which the body is shaped like a pie or barrel (lacking a left side and a right side) and can be divided into mirror-image halves by any plane through its central axis.

radiation The emission of electromagnetic waves by all objects warmer than absolute zero.

radicle An embryonic root of a plant.

radioactive isotope An isotope (an atomic form of a chemical element) that is unstable; the nucleus decays spontaneously, giving off detectable particles and energy.

radiolarian A protist, usually marine, with a shell generally made of silica and pseudopodia that radiate from the central body.

radiometric dating A method for determining the absolute ages of rocks and fossils, based on the half-life of radioactive isotopes.

radula A straplike rasping organ used by many molluscs during feeding.

***ras* gene** A gene that codes for Ras, a G protein that relays a growth signal from a growth factor receptor on the plasma membrane to a cascade of protein kinases, ultimately resulting in stimulation of the cell cycle.

ratite (rat′-īt) Member of the group of flightless birds.

ray-finned fish Member of the class Actinopterygii, aquatic osteichthyans with fins supported by long, flexible rays, including tuna, bass, and herring.

reabsorption In excretory systems, the recovery of solutes and water from filtrate.

reactant A starting material in a chemical reaction.

reaction-center complex A complex of proteins associated with a special pair of chlorophyll *a* molecules and a primary electron acceptor. Located centrally in a photosystem, this complex triggers the light reactions of photosynthesis. Excited by light energy, the pair of chlorophylls donates an electron to the primary electron acceptor, which passes an electron to an electron transport chain.

reading frame On an mRNA, the triplet grouping of ribonucleotides used by the translation machinery during polypeptide synthesis.

receptacle The base of a flower; the part of the stem that is the site of attachment of the floral organs.

receptor potential An initial response of a receptor cell to a stimulus, consisting of a change in voltage across the receptor membrane proportional to the stimulus strength. The intensity of the receptor potential determines the frequency of action potentials traveling to the nervous system.

receptor tyrosine kinase A receptor protein in the plasma membrane, the cytoplasmic (intracellular) part of which can catalyze the transfer of a phosphate group from ATP to a tyrosine on another protein. Receptor tyrosine kinases often respond to the binding of a signaling molecule by dimerizing and then phosphorylating a tyrosine on the cytoplasmic portion of the other receptor in the dimer. The phosphorylated tyrosines on the receptors then activate other signal transduction proteins within the cell.

receptor-mediated endocytosis (en′-dō-sī-tō′-sis) The movement of specific molecules into a cell by the inward budding of membranous vesicles containing proteins with receptor sites specific to the molecules being taken in; enables a cell to acquire bulk quantities of specific substances.

recessive allele An allele whose phenotypic effect is not observed in a heterozygote.

reciprocal altruism Altruistic behavior between unrelated individuals, whereby the altruistic individual benefits in the future when the beneficiary reciprocates.

recombinant chromosome A chromosome created when crossing over combines the DNA from two parents into a single chromosome.

recombinant DNA A DNA molecule made *in vitro* with segments from different sources.

recombinant type (recombinant) An offspring whose phenotype differs from that of the parents; also refers to the phenotype itself.

recruitment The process of progressively increasing the tension of a muscle by activating more and more of the motor neurons controlling the muscle.

rectum The terminal portion of the large intestine where the feces are stored until they are eliminated.

red alga A photosynthetic protist, named for its color, which results from a red pigment that masks the green of chlorophyll. Most red algae are multicellular and marine.

redox reaction (rē′-doks) A chemical reaction involving the complete or partial transfer of one or more electrons from one reactant to another; short for oxidation-reduction reaction.

reducing agent The electron donor in a redox reaction.

reduction The addition of electrons to a substance involved in a redox reaction.

reflex An automatic reaction to a stimulus, mediated by the spinal cord or lower brain.

refractory period (rē-frakt′-ōr-ē) The short time immediately after an action potential in which the neuron cannot respond to another stimulus, owing to the inactivation of voltage-gated sodium channels.

regulator An animal for which mechanisms of homeostasis moderate internal changes in the face of external fluctuations.

regulatory gene A gene that codes for a protein, such as a repressor, that controls the transcription of another gene or group of genes.

reinforcement A process in which natural selection strengthens prezygotic barriers to reproduction, thus reducing the chances of hybrid formation. Such a process is likely to occur only if hybrid offspring are less fit than members of the parent species.

relative abundance The proportional abundance of different species in a community.

relative fitness The contribution an individual makes to the gene pool of the next generation, relative to the contributions of other individuals in the population.

renal artery The blood vessel bringing blood to the kidney.

renal cortex The outer portion of the vertebrate kidney.

renal medulla The inner portion of the vertebrate kidney, beneath the renal cortex.

renal pelvis The funnel-shaped chamber that receives processed filtrate from the vertebrate kidney's collecting ducts and is drained by the ureter.

renal vein The blood vessel that carries blood away from the kidney.

renin-angiotensin-aldosterone system (RAAS) A hormone cascade pathway that helps regulate blood pressure and blood volume.

repeated reproduction Reproduction in which adults produce offspring over many years; also known as iteroparity.

repetitive DNA Nucleotide sequences, usually noncoding, that are present in many copies in a eukaryotic genome. The repeated units may be short and arranged tandemly (in series) or long and dispersed in the genome.

replication fork A Y-shaped region on a replicating DNA molecule where the parental strands are being unwound and new strands are growing.

repressor A protein that inhibits gene transcription. In prokaryotes, repressors bind to the DNA in or near the promoter. In eukaryotes, repressors may bind to control elements within enhancers, to activators, or to other proteins in a way that blocks activators from binding to DNA.

reproductive isolation The existence of biological factors (barriers) that impede members of two species from producing viable, fertile offspring.

reproductive table An age-specific summary of the reproductive rates in a population.

reptile Member of the clade of amniotes that includes tuataras, lizards, snakes, turtles, crocodilians, and birds.

residual volume The amount of air that remains in the lungs after forceful exhalation.

resource partitioning The division of environmental resources by coexisting species such that the niche of each species differs by one or more significant factors from the niches of all coexisting species.

respiratory pigment A protein that transports oxygen in blood or hemolymph.

response (1) In cellular communication, the change in a specific cellular activity brought about by a transduced signal from outside the cell. (2) In homeostasis, a physiological activity that helps return a variable to a set point.

resting potential The membrane potential characteristic of a nonconducting excitable cell, with the inside of the cell more negative than the outside.

restoration ecology Applying ecological principles in an effort to return ecosystems that have been disturbed by human activity to a condition as similar as possible to their natural state.

restriction enzyme An endonuclease (type of enzyme) that recognizes and cuts DNA molecules foreign to a bacterium (such as phage genomes). The enzyme cuts at specific nucleotide sequences (restriction sites).

restriction fragment A DNA segment that results from the cutting of DNA by a restriction enzyme.

restriction fragment length polymorphism (RFLP) A single nucleotide polymorphism (SNP) that exists in the restriction site for a particular enzyme, thus making the site unrecognizable by that enzyme and changing the lengths of the restriction fragments formed by digestion with that enzyme. A RFLP can be in coding or noncoding DNA.

restriction site A specific sequence on a DNA strand that is recognized and cut by a restriction enzyme.

reticular formation (re-tik′-yū-ler) A diffuse network of neurons in the core of the brainstem that filters information traveling to the cerebral cortex.

retina (ret′-i-nuh) The innermost layer of the vertebrate eye, containing photoreceptor cells (rods and cones) and neurons; transmits images formed by the lens to the brain via the optic nerve.

retinal The light-absorbing pigment in rods and cones of the vertebrate eye.

retrotransposon (re′-trō-trans-pō′-zon) A transposable element that moves within a genome by means of an RNA intermediate, a transcript of the retrotransposon DNA.

retrovirus (re′-trō-vī′-rus) An RNA virus that reproduces by transcribing its RNA into DNA and then inserting the DNA into a cellular chromosome; an important class of cancer-causing viruses.

reverse transcriptase (tran-skrip′-tās) An enzyme encoded by certain viruses (retroviruses) that uses RNA as a template for DNA synthesis.

reverse transcriptase–polymerase chain reaction (RT-PCR) A technique for determining expression of a particular gene. It uses reverse transcriptase and DNA polymerase to synthesize cDNA from all the mRNA in a sample and then subjects the cDNA to PCR amplification using primers specific for the gene of interest.

Rhizaria (rī-za′-rē-uh) One of five supergroups of eukaryotes proposed in a current hypothesis of the evolutionary history of eukaryotes; a morphologically diverse protist clade that is defined by DNA similarities. *See also* Excavata, Chromalveolata, Archaeplastida, and Unikonta.

rhizobacterium A soil bacterium whose population size is much enhanced in the rhizosphere, the soil region close to a plant's roots.

rhizoid (rī′-zoyd) A long, tubular single cell or filament of cells that anchors bryophytes to the ground. Unlike roots, rhizoids are not composed of tissues, lack specialized conducting cells, and do not play a primary role in water and mineral absorption.

rhizosphere The soil region close to plant roots and characterized by a high level of microbiological activity.

rhodopsin (rō-dop′-sin) A visual pigment consisting of retinal and opsin. When rhodopsin absorbs light, the retinal changes shape and dissociates from the opsin, after which it is converted back to its original form.

rhythm method A form of contraception that relies on refraining from sexual intercourse when conception is most likely to occur; also called natural family planning.

ribonucleic acid (RNA) (rī′-bō-nū-klā′-ik) A type of nucleic acid consisting of nucleotide monomers with a ribose sugar and the nitrogenous bases adenine (A), cytosine (C), guanine (G), and uracil (U); usually single-stranded; functions in protein synthesis, gene regulation, and as the genome of some viruses.

ribose The sugar component of RNA nucleotides.

ribosomal RNA (rRNA) (rī′-buh-sō′-mul) The most abundant type of RNA, which together with proteins makes up ribosomes.

ribosome (rī′-buh-sōm′) A complex of rRNA and protein molecules that functions as a site of protein synthesis in the cytoplasm; consists of a large and a small subunit. In eukaryotic cells, each subunit is assembled in the nucleolus. *See also* nucleolus.

ribozyme (rī′-bō-zīm) An RNA molecule that functions as an enzyme, catalyzing reactions during RNA splicing.

RNA interference (RNAi) A technique used to silence the expression of selected genes. RNAi uses synthetic double-stranded RNA molecules that match the sequence of a particular gene to trigger the breakdown of the gene's messenger RNA.

RNA polymerase An enzyme that links ribonucleotides into a growing RNA chain during transcription.

RNA processing Modification of RNA transcripts, including splicing out of introns, joining together of exons, and alteration of the 5′ and 3′ ends.

RNA splicing After synthesis of a eukaryotic primary RNA transcript, the removal of portions (introns) of the transcript that will not be included in the mRNA.

rod A rodlike cell in the retina of the vertebrate eye, sensitive to low light intensity.

root An organ in vascular plants that anchors the plant and enables it to absorb water and minerals from the soil.

root cap A cone of cells at the tip of a plant root that protects the apical meristem.

root hair A tiny extension of a root epidermal cell, growing just behind the root tip and increasing surface area for absorption of water and minerals.

root pressure The upward push of xylem sap in the vascular tissue of roots.

root system All of a plant's roots, which anchor it in the soil, absorb and transport minerals and water, and store food.

rooted Describing a phylogenetic tree that contains a branch point (typically, the one farthest to the left) representing the last common ancestor of all taxa in the tree.

rough ER That portion of the endoplasmic reticulum studded with ribosomes.

round window In the mammalian ear, the point of contact between the stapes and the cochlea, where vibrations of the stapes create a traveling series of pressure waves in the fluid of the cochlea.

***r*-selection** Selection for life history traits that maximize reproductive success in uncrowded environments; also called density-independent selection.

rubisco (rū-bis′-kō) Ribulose bisphosphate (RuBP) carboxylase, the enzyme that catalyzes the first step of the Calvin cycle (the addition of CO_2 to RuBP).

ruminant (rū′-muh-nent) An animal, such as a cow or a sheep, with an elaborate, multicompartmentalized stomach specialized for an herbivorous diet.

S phase The synthesis phase of the cell cycle; the portion of interphase during which DNA is replicated.

sac fungus *See* ascomycete.

saccule In the vertebrate ear, a chamber in the vestibule behind the oval window that participates in the sense of balance.

salicylic acid (sal′-i-sil′-ik) A signaling molecule in plants that may be partially responsible for activating systemic acquired resistance to pathogens.

salivary gland A gland associated with the oral cavity that secretes substances to lubricate food and begin the process of chemical digestion.

salt A compound resulting from the formation of an ionic bond; also called an ionic compound.

saltatory conduction (sol′-tuh-tōr′-ē) Rapid transmission of a nerve impulse along an axon, resulting from the action potential jumping from one node of Ranvier to another, skipping the myelin-sheathed regions of membrane.

sarcomere (sar′-kō-mēr) The fundamental, repeating unit of striated muscle, delimited by the Z lines.

sarcoplasmic reticulum (SR) (sar′-kō-plaz′-mik ruh-tik′-yū-lum) A specialized endoplasmic reticulum that regulates the calcium concentration in the cytosol of muscle cells.

saturated fatty acid A fatty acid in which all carbons in the hydrocarbon tail are connected by single bonds, thus maximizing the number of hydrogen atoms that are attached to the carbon skeleton.

savanna A tropical grassland biome with scattered individual trees and large herbivores and maintained by occasional fires and drought.

scaffolding protein A type of large relay protein to which several other relay proteins are simultaneously attached, increasing the efficiency of signal transduction.

scanning electron microscope (SEM) A microscope that uses an electron beam to scan the surface of a sample to study details of its topography.

schizophrenia (skit′-suh-frē′-nē-uh) Severe mental disturbance characterized by psychotic episodes in which patients lose the ability to distinguish reality from hallucination.

Schwann cell A type of glial cell that forms insulating myelin sheaths around the axons of neurons in the peripheral nervous system.

scion (sī′-un) The twig grafted onto the stock when making a graft.

sclera (sklār′-uh) A tough, white outer layer of connective tissue that forms the globe of the vertebrate eye.

sclereid (sklār′-ē-id) A short, irregular sclerenchyma cell in nutshells and seed coats. Sclereids are scattered throughout the parenchyma of some plants.

sclerenchyma cell (skluh-ren′-kim-uh) A rigid, supportive plant cell type usually lacking a protoplast and possessing thick secondary walls strengthened by lignin at maturity.

scrotum A pouch of skin outside the abdomen that houses the testes; functions in maintaining the testes at the lower temperature required for spermatogenesis.

second law of thermodynamics The principle stating that every energy transfer or transformation increases the entropy of the universe. Ordered forms of energy are at least partly converted to heat.

second messenger A small, nonprotein, water-soluble molecule or ion, such as a calcium ion (Ca^{2+}) or cyclic AMP, that relays a signal to a cell's interior in response to a signaling molecule bound by a signal receptor protein.

secondary cell wall In plants, a strong and durable matrix often deposited in several laminated layers for cell protection and support.

secondary consumer A carnivore that eats herbivores.

secondary endosymbiosis A process in eukaryotic evolution in which a heterotrophic eukaryotic cell engulfed a photosynthetic eukaryotic cell, which survived in a symbiotic relationship inside the heterotrophic cell.

secondary growth Growth produced by lateral meristems, thickening the roots and shoots of woody plants.

secondary immune response The acquired immune response elicited on second or subsequent exposures to a particular antigen. The secondary immune response is more rapid, of greater magnitude, and of longer duration than the primary immune response.

secondary oocyte (ō′-uh-sīt) An oocyte that has completed the first of the two meiotic divisions.

secondary plant body The tissues produced by the vascular cambium and cork cambium, which thicken the stems and roots of woody plants.

secondary production The amount of chemical energy in consumers' food that is converted to their own new biomass during a given time period.

secondary structure The localized, repetitive coiling or folding of the polypeptide backbone of a protein due to hydrogen bond formation between constituents of the backbone.

secondary succession A type of succession that occurs where an existing community has been cleared by some disturbance that leaves the soil or substrate intact.

secretion (1) The discharge of molecules synthesized by a cell. (2) The discharge of wastes from the body fluid into the filtrate.

secretory phase That portion of the uterine (menstrual) cycle when the endometrium continues to thicken, becomes more vascularized, and develops glands that secrete a fluid rich in glycogen.

seed An adaptation of some terrestrial plants consisting of an embryo packaged along with a store of food within a protective coat.

seed coat A tough outer covering of a seed, formed from the outer coat of an ovule. In a flowering plant, the seed coat encloses and protects the embryo and endosperm.

seedless vascular plant An informal name for a plant that has vascular tissue but lacks seeds. Seedless vascular plants form a paraphyletic group that includes the phyla Lycophyta (club mosses and their relatives) and Pterophyta (ferns and their relatives).

selective permeability A property of biological membranes that allows them to regulate the passage of substances.

self-incompatibility The ability of a seed plant to reject its own pollen and sometimes the pollen of closely related individuals.

semelparity Reproduction in which an organism produces all of its offspring in a single event; also known as big-bang reproduction.

semen (sē′-mun) The fluid that is ejaculated by the male during orgasm; contains sperm and secretions from several glands of the male reproductive tract.

semicircular canals A three-part chamber of the inner ear that functions in maintaining equilibrium.

semiconservative model Type of DNA replication in which the replicated double helix consists of one old strand, derived from the old molecule, and one newly made strand.

semilunar valve A valve located at each exit of the heart, where the aorta leaves the left ventricle and the pulmonary artery leaves the right ventricle.

seminal vesicle (sem′-i-nul ves′-i-kul) A gland in males that secretes a fluid component of semen that lubricates and nourishes sperm.

seminiferous tubule (sem′-i-nif′-er-us) A highly coiled tube in the testis in which sperm are produced.

senescence (se-nes′-ens) The growth phase in a plant or plant part (as a leaf) from full maturity to death.

sensitive period A limited phase in an individual animal's development when learning of particular behaviors can take place; also called a critical period.

sensor In homeostasis, a receptor that detects a stimulus.

sensory adaptation The tendency of sensory neurons to become less sensitive when they are stimulated repeatedly.

sensory neuron A nerve cell that receives information from the internal or external environment and transmits signals to the central nervous system.

sensory reception The detection of the energy of a stimulus by sensory cells.

sensory receptor An organ, cell, or structure within a cell that responds to specific stimuli from an organism's external or internal environment.

sensory transduction The conversion of stimulus energy to a change in the membrane potential of a sensory receptor cell.

sepal (sē′-pul) A modified leaf in angiosperms that helps enclose and protect a flower bud before it opens.

septum (plural, **septa**) One of the cross-walls that divide a fungal hypha into cells. Septa generally have pores large enough to allow ribosomes, mitochondria, and even nuclei to flow from cell to cell.

serial endosymbiosis A hypothesis for the origin of eukaryotes consisting of a sequence of endosymbiotic events in which mitochondria, chloroplasts, and perhaps other cellular structures were derived from small prokaryotes that had been engulfed by larger cells.

serotonin (ser′-uh-tō′-nin) A neurotransmitter, synthesized from the amino acid tryptophan, that functions in the central nervous system.

set point In animal bodies, a value maintained for a particular variable, such as body temperature or solute concentration, to achieve homeostasis.

seta (sē′-tuh) (plural, **setae**) The elongated stalk of a bryophyte sporophyte.

sex chromosome A chromosome responsible for determining the sex of an individual.

sex pilus (plural, **sex pili**) (pī′-lus, pī′-lī) In bacteria, a structure that links one cell to another at the start of conjugation; also known as a conjugation pilus.

sex-linked gene A gene located on a sex chromosome (usually the X chromosome), resulting in a distinctive pattern of inheritance.

sexual dimorphism (dī-mōr′-fizm) Marked differences between the secondary sex characteristics of males and females.

sexual reproduction A type of reproduction in which two parents give rise to offspring that have unique combinations of genes inherited from the gametes of the parents.

sexual selection A form of natural selection in which individuals with certain inherited characteristics are more likely than other individuals to obtain mates.

Shannon diversity An index of community diversity symbolized by H and represented by the equation $H = [(p_A \ln p_A) + (p_B \ln p_B) + (p_C \ln p_C) + \ldots]$, where A, B, C . . . are the species in the community, p is the relative abundance of each species, and ln is the natural logarithm.

shared ancestral character A character, shared by members of a particular clade, that originated in an ancestor that is not a member of that clade.

shared derived character An evolutionary novelty that is unique to a particular clade.

shoot system The aerial portion of a plant body, consisting of stems, leaves, and (in angiosperms) flowers.

short tandem repeat (STR) Simple sequence DNA containing multiple tandemly repeated units of two to five nucleotides. Variations in STRs act as genetic markers in STR analysis, used to prepare genetic profiles.

short-day plant A plant that flowers (usually in late summer, fall, or winter) only when the light period is shorter than a critical length.

short-term memory The ability to hold information, anticipations, or goals for a time and then release them if they become irrelevant.

sickle-cell disease A human genetic disease caused by a recessive allele that results in the substitution of a single amino acid in a globin polypeptide that is part of the hemoglobin protein; characterized by deformed red blood cells (due to protein aggregation) that can lead to numerous symptoms.

sieve plate An end wall in a sieve-tube element, which facilitates the flow of phloem sap in angiosperm sieve tubes.

sieve-tube element A living cell that conducts sugars and other organic nutrients in the phloem of angiosperms; also called a sieve-tube member. Connected end to end, they form sieve tubes.

sign stimulus An external sensory cue that triggers a fixed action pattern by an animal.

signal In animal behavior, transmission of a stimulus from one animal to another. The term is also used in the context of communication in other kinds of organisms and in cell-to-cell communication in all multicellular organisms.

signal peptide A sequence of about 20 amino acids at or near the leading (amino) end of a polypeptide that targets it to the endoplasmic reticulum or other organelles in a eukaryotic cell.

signal transduction The linkage of a mechanical, chemical, or electromagnetic stimulus to a specific cellular response.

signal transduction pathway A series of steps linking a mechanical or chemical stimulus to a specific cellular response.

signal-recognition particle (SRP) A protein-RNA complex that recognizes a signal peptide as it emerges from a ribosome and helps direct the ribosome to the endoplasmic reticulum (ER) by binding to a receptor protein on the ER.

simple fruit A fruit derived from a single carpel or several fused carpels.

simple sequence DNA A DNA sequence that contains many copies of tandemly repeated short sequences.

single bond A single covalent bond; the sharing of a pair of valence electrons by two atoms.

single circulation A circulatory system consisting of a single pump and circuit, in which blood passes from the sites of gas exchange to the rest of the body before returning to the heart.

single nucleotide polymorphism (SNP) A single base-pair site in a genome where nucleotide variation is found in at least 1% of the population.

single-lens eye The camera-like eye found in some jellies, polychaetes, spiders, and many molluscs.

single-strand binding protein A protein that binds to the unpaired DNA strands during DNA replication, stabilizing them and holding them apart while they serve as templates for the synthesis of complementary strands of DNA.

sinoatrial (SA) node A region in the right atrium of the heart that sets the rate and timing at which all cardiac muscle cells contract; the pacemaker.

sister chromatid Either of two copies of a duplicated chromosome attached to each other by proteins at the centromere and, sometimes, along the arms. While joined, two sister chromatids make up one chromosome; chromatids are eventually separated during mitosis or meiosis II.

sister taxa Groups of organisms that share an immediate common ancestor and hence are each other's closest relatives.

skeletal muscle Muscle that is generally responsible for the voluntary movements of the body; one type of striated muscle.

sliding-filament model The theory explaining how muscle contracts, based on change within a sarcomere, the basic unit of muscle organization. According to this model, thin (actin) filaments slide across thick (myosin) filaments, shortening the sarcomere. The shortening of all sarcomeres in a myofibril shortens the entire myofibril.

slow block to polyspermy The formation of the fertilization envelope and other changes in an egg's surface that prevent fusion of the egg with more than one sperm. The slow block begins about 1 minute after fertilization.

slow-twitch fiber A muscle fiber that can sustain long contractions.

small interfering RNA (siRNA) A small, single-stranded RNA molecule generated by cellular machinery from a long, double-stranded RNA molecule. The siRNA associates with one or more proteins in a complex that can degrade or prevent translation of an mRNA with a complementary sequence. In some cases, siRNA can also block transcription by promoting chromatin modification.

small intestine The longest section of the alimentary canal, so named because of its small diameter compared with that of the large intestine; the principal site of the enzymatic hydrolysis of food macromolecules and the absorption of nutrients.

smooth ER That portion of the endoplasmic reticulum that is free of ribosomes.

smooth muscle A type of muscle lacking the striations of skeletal and cardiac muscle because of the uniform distribution of myosin filaments in the cell; responsible for involuntary body activities.

social learning Modification of behavior through the observation of other individuals.

sociobiology The study of social behavior based on evolutionary theory.

sodium-potassium pump A transport protein in the plasma membrane of animal cells that actively transports sodium out of the cell and potassium into the cell.

soil horizon A soil layer that parallels the land surface and has physical characteristics that differ from those of the layers above and beneath.

solute (sol′-yūt) A substance that is dissolved in a solution.

solute potential (Ψ_S) A component of water potential that is proportional to the molarity of a solution and that measures the effect of solutes on the direction of water movement; also called osmotic potential, it can be either zero or negative.

solution A liquid that is a homogeneous mixture of two or more substances.

solvent The dissolving agent of a solution. Water is the most versatile solvent known.

somatic cell (sō-mat′-ik) Any cell in a multicellular organism except a sperm or egg.

somite One of a series of blocks of mesoderm that exist in pairs just lateral to the notochord in a vertebrate embryo.

soredium (plural, **soredia**) In lichens, a small cluster of fungal hyphae with embedded algae.

sorus (plural, **sori**) A cluster of sporangia on a fern sporophyll. Sori may be arranged in various patterns, such as parallel lines or dots, which are useful in fern identification.

Southern blotting A technique that enables specific nucleotide sequences to be detected in a sample of DNA. It involves gel electrophoresis of DNA molecules and their transfer to a membrane (blotting), followed by nucleic acid hybridization with a labeled probe.

spatial learning The establishment of a memory that reflects the environment's spatial structure.

spatial summation A phenomenon of neural integration in which the membrane potential of the postsynaptic cell is determined by the combined effect of EPSPs or IPSPs produced nearly simultaneously by different synapses.

speciation (spē′-sē-ā′-shun) An evolutionary process in which one species splits into two or more species.

species (spē′-sēz) A population or group of populations whose members have the potential to interbreed in nature and produce viable, fertile offspring, but do not produce viable, fertile offspring with members of other such groups.

species diversity The number and relative abundance of species in a biological community.

species richness The number of species in a biological community.

species-area curve The biodiversity pattern, first noted by Alexander von Humboldt, that shows that the larger the geographic area of a community is, the more species it has.

specific heat The amount of heat that must be absorbed or lost for 1 g of a substance to change its temperature by 1°C.

spectrophotometer An instrument that measures the proportions of light of different wavelengths absorbed and transmitted by a pigment solution.

sperm The male gamete.

spermatheca (sper′-muh-thē′-kuh) in many insects, a sac in the female reproductive system where sperm are stored.

spermatogenesis The continuous and prolific production of mature sperm cells in the testis.

spermatogonium A cell that divides mitotically to form spermatocytes.

sphincter (sfink′-ter) A ringlike valve, consisting of modified muscles in a muscular tube, that regulates passage between some compartments of the alimentary canal.

spinal nerve In the vertebrate peripheral nervous system, a nerve that carries signals to or from the spinal cord.

spiral cleavage A type of embryonic development in protostomes in which the planes of cell division that transform the zygote into a ball of cells are diagonal to the vertical axis of the embryo. As a result, the cells of each tier sit in the grooves between cells of adjacent tiers.

spliceosome (splī′-sē-ō-sōm) A large complex made up of proteins and RNA molecules that splices RNA by interacting with the ends of an RNA intron, releasing the intron and joining the two adjacent exons.

spongocoel (spon′-jō-sēl) The central cavity of a sponge.

sporangium (spōr-an′-jē-um) (plural, **sporangia**) A multicellular organ in fungi and plants in which meiosis occurs and haploid cells develop.

spore (1) In the life cycle of a plant or alga undergoing alternation of generations, a haploid cell produced in the sporophyte by meiosis. A spore can divide by mitosis to develop into a multicellular haploid individual, the gametophyte, without fusing with another cell. (2) In fungi, a haploid cell, produced either sexually or asexually, that produces a mycelium after germination.

sporocyte A diploid cell, also known as a spore mother cell, that undergoes meiosis and generates haploid spores.

sporophyll (spō′-ruh-fil) A modified leaf that bears sporangia and hence is specialized for reproduction.

sporophyte (spō-ruh-fīt′) In organisms (plants and some algae) that have alternation of generations, the multicellular diploid form that results from the union of gametes. The sporophyte produces haploid spores by meiosis that develop into gametophytes.

sporopollenin (spōr-uh-pol′-eh-nin) A durable polymer that covers exposed zygotes of charophyte algae and forms the walls of plant spores, preventing them from drying out.

stabilizing selection Natural selection in which intermediate phenotypes survive or reproduce more successfully than do extreme phenotypes.

stamen (stā′-men) The pollen-producing reproductive organ of a flower, consisting of an anther and a filament.

standard metabolic rate (SMR) The metabolic rate of a resting, fasting, and non-stressed ectotherm at a particular temperature.

stapes The third of three bones in the middle ear of mammals; also called the stirrup.

starch A storage polysaccharide in plants, consisting entirely of glucose monomers joined by α glycosidic linkages.

statocyst (stat′-uh-sist′) A type of mechanoreceptor that functions in equilibrium in invertebrates by use of statoliths, which stimulate hair cells in relation to gravity.

statolith (stat′-uh-lith′) (1) In plants, a specialized plastid that contains dense starch grains and may play a role in detecting gravity. (2) In invertebrates, a grain or other dense granule that settles in response to gravity and is found in sensory organs that function in equilibrium.

stele (stēl)The vascular tissue of a stem or root.

stem A vascular plant organ consisting of an alternating system of nodes and internodes that support the leaves and reproductive structures.

stem cell Any relatively unspecialized cell that can produce, during a single division, one identical daughter cell and one more specialized daughter cell that can undergo further differentiation.

stenohaline (sten′-ō-hā′-līn) Referring to organisms that cannot tolerate substantial changes in external osmolarity.

steroid A type of lipid characterized by a carbon skeleton consisting of four rings with various chemical groups attached.

sticky end A single-stranded end of a double-stranded restriction fragment.

stigma (plural, **stigmata**) The sticky part of a flower's carpel, which traps pollen grains.

stimulus In homeostasis, a fluctuation in a variable that triggers a return to a set point.

stipe A stemlike structure of a seaweed.

stock The plant that provides the root system when making a graft.

stoma (stō′-muh) (plural, **stomata**) A microscopic pore surrounded by guard cells in the epidermis of leaves and stems that allows gas exchange between the environment and the interior of the plant.

stomach An organ of the digestive system that stores food and performs preliminary steps of digestion.

stramenopile A protist in which a "hairy" flagellum (one covered with fine, hairlike projections) is paired with a shorter, smooth flagellum.

stratum (strah′-tum) (plural, **strata**) A rock layer formed when new layers of sediment cover older ones and compress them.

striated muscle Muscle in which the regular arrangement of filaments creates a pattern of light and dark bands.

strobilus (strō-bī′-lus) (plural, **strobili**) The technical term for a cluster of sporophylls known commonly as a cone, found in most gymnosperms and some seedless vascular plants.

stroke The death of nervous tissue in the brain, usually resulting from rupture or blockage of arteries in the head.

stroke volume The volume of blood pumped by a heart ventricle in a single contraction.

stroma (strō′-muh) Within the chloroplast, the dense fluid of the chloroplast surrounding the thylakoid membrane; involved in the synthesis of organic molecules from carbon dioxide and water.

stromatolite Layered rock that results from the activities of prokaryotes that bind thin films of sediment together.

structural formula A type of molecular notation in which the constituent atoms are joined by lines representing covalent bonds.

structural isomer One of several compounds that have the same molecular formula but differ in the covalent arrangements of their atoms.

style The stalk of a flower's carpel, with the ovary at the base and the stigma at the top.

substance P A neuropeptide that is a key excitatory neurotransmitter that mediates the perception of pain.

substrate The reactant on which an enzyme works.

substrate feeder An animal that lives in or on its food source, eating its way through the food.

substrate-level phosphorylation The formation of ATP by an enzyme directly transferring a phosphate group to ADP from an intermediate substrate in catabolism.

sugar sink A plant organ that is a net consumer or storer of sugar. Growing roots, shoot tips, stems, and fruits are sugar sinks supplied by phloem.

sugar source A plant organ in which sugar is being produced by either photosynthesis or the breakdown of starch. Mature leaves are the primary sugar sources of plants.

sulfhydryl group A chemical group consisting of a sulfur atom bonded to a hydrogen atom.

suprachiasmatic nucleus (SCN) A group of neurons in the hypothalamus of mammals that functions as a biological clock.

surface tension A measure of how difficult it is to stretch or break the surface of a liquid. Water has a high surface tension because of the hydrogen bonding of surface molecules.

surfactant A substance secreted by alveoli that decreases surface tension in the fluid that coats the alveoli.

survivorship curve A plot of the number of members of a cohort that are still alive at each age; one way to represent age-specific mortality.

suspension feeder An aquatic animal, such as a sponge, clam, or baleen whale, that feeds by sifting small food particles from the water.

sustainable agriculture Long-term productive farming methods that are environmentally safe.

sustainable development Development that meets the needs of people today without limiting the ability of future generations to meet their needs.

swim bladder In aquatic osteichthyans, an air sac that enables the animal to control its buoyancy in the water.

symbiont (sim′-bē-ont) The smaller participant in a symbiotic relationship, living in or on the host.

symbiosis An ecological relationship between organisms of two different species that live together in direct and intimate contact.

sympathetic division One of three divisions of the autonomic nervous system of vertebrates; generally increases energy expenditure and prepares the body for action.

sympatric speciation (sim-pat′-rik) The formation of new species in populations that live in the same geographic area.

symplast In plants, the continuum of cytoplasm connected by plasmodesmata between cells.

synapse (sin′-aps) The junction where one neuron communicates with another cell across a narrow gap. Neurotransmitter molecules released by the neuron diffuse across the synapse, relaying messages to the other cell.

synapsid Member of an amniote clade distinguished by a single hole on each side of the skull. Synapsids include the mammals.

synapsis (si-nap′-sis) The pairing and physical connection of replicated homologous chromosomes during prophase I of meiosis.

synaptic cleft (sin-ap′-tik) A narrow gap separating the synaptic terminal of a transmitting neuron from a receiving neuron or an effector cell.

synaptic terminal A bulb at the end of an axon in which neurotransmitter molecules are stored and from which they are released.

synaptic vesicle Membranous sac containing neurotransmitter molecules at the tip of an axon.

systematics A scientific discipline focused on classifying organisms and determining their evolutionary relationships.

systemic Occurring throughout the body and affecting many or all body systems or organs.

systemic acquired resistance A defensive response in infected plants that helps protect healthy tissue from pathogenic invasion.

systemic circuit The branch of the circulatory system that supplies all body organs except those involved in gas exchange.

systems biology An approach to studying biology that aims to model the dynamic behavior of whole biological systems.

systole (sis′-tō-lē) The stage of the cardiac cycle in which a heart chamber contracts and pumps blood.

systolic pressure Blood pressure in the arteries during contraction of the ventricles.

T cell receptor The antigen receptor on T cells; a membrane-bound molecule consisting of one α chain and one β chain linked by a disulfide bridge and containing one antigen-binding site.

T cells The class of lymphocytes that mature in the thymus and that includes both effector cells for the cell-mediated immune response and helper cells required for both branches of adaptive immunity.

taproot A main vertical root that develops from an embryonic root and gives rise to lateral (branch) roots.

tastant Any chemical that stimulates the sensory receptors in a taste bud.

taste bud A collection of modified epithelial cells on the tongue or in the mouth that are receptors for taste in mammals.

TATA box A DNA sequence in eukaryotic promoters crucial in forming the transcription initiation complex.

taxis (tak′-sis) An oriented movement toward or away from a stimulus.

taxon (plural, **taxa**) A named taxonomic unit at any given level of classification.

taxonomy (tak-son′-uh-mē) A scientific discipline concerned with naming and classifying the diverse forms of life.

Tay-Sachs disease A human genetic disease caused by a recessive allele for a dysfunctional enzyme, leading to accumulation of certain lipids in the brain. Seizures, blindness, and degeneration of motor and mental performance usually become manifest a few months after birth, followed by death within a few years.

technology The application of scientific knowledge for a specific purpose, often involving industry or commerce but also including uses in basic research.

telomerase An enzyme that catalyzes the lengthening of telomeres in eukaryotic germ cells.

telomere (tel′-uh-mēr) The tandemly repetitive DNA at the end of a eukaryotic chromosome's DNA molecule that protects the organism's genes from being eroded during successive rounds of replication. *See also* repetitive DNA.

telophase The fifth and final stage of mitosis, in which daughter nuclei are forming and cytokinesis has typically begun.

temperate broadleaf forest A biome located throughout midlatitude regions where there is sufficient moisture to support the growth of large, broadleaf deciduous trees.

temperate grassland A terrestrial biome dominated by grasses and forbs.

temperate phage A phage that is capable of reproducing by either a lytic or lysogenic cycle.

temperature A measure of the intensity of heat in degrees, reflecting the average kinetic energy of the molecules.

template strand The DNA strand that provides the pattern, or template, for ordering the sequence of nucleotides in an RNA transcript.

temporal summation A phenomenon of neural integration in which the membrane potential of the postsynaptic cell in a chemical synapse is determined by the combined effect of EPSPs or IPSPs produced in rapid succession.

tendon A fibrous connective tissue that attaches muscle to bone.

terminator In bacteria, a sequence of nucleotides in DNA that marks the end of a gene and signals RNA polymerase to release the newly made RNA molecule and detach from the DNA.

territoriality A behavior in which an animal defends a bounded physical space against encroachment by other individuals, usually of its own species.

tertiary consumer (ter′-shē-ār′-ē) A carnivore that eats other carnivores.

tertiary structure Irregular contortions of a protein molecule due to interactions of side chains involved in hydrophobic interactions, ionic bonds, hydrogen bonds, and disulfide bridges.

testcross Breeding an organism of unknown genotype with a homozygous recessive individual to determine the unknown genotype. The ratio of phenotypes in the offspring reveals the unknown genotype.

testis (plural, **testes**) The male reproductive organ, or gonad, in which sperm and reproductive hormones are produced.

testosterone A steroid hormone required for development of the male reproductive system, spermatogenesis, and male secondary sex characteristics; the major androgen in mammals.

tetanus (tet′-uh-nus) The maximal, sustained contraction of a skeletal muscle, caused by a very high frequency of action potentials elicited by continual stimulation.

tetrapod A vertebrate with two pairs of limbs. Tetrapods include mammals, amphibians, and birds and other reptiles.

thalamus (thal′-uh-mus) One of two integrating centers of the vertebrate forebrain. Neurons with cell bodies in the thalamus relay neural input to specific areas in the cerebral cortex and regulate what information goes to the cerebral cortex.

thallus (plural, **thalli**) A seaweed body that is plantlike, consisting of a holdfast, stipe, and blades, yet lacks true roots, stems, and leaves.

theory An explanation that is broad in scope, generates new hypotheses, and is supported by a large body of evidence.

thermal energy *See* heat.

thermocline A narrow stratum of rapid temperature change in the ocean and in many temperate-zone lakes.

thermodynamics (ther′-mō-dī-nam′-iks) The study of energy transformations that occur in a collection of matter. *See* first law of thermodynamics; second law of thermodynamics.

thermoreceptor A receptor stimulated by either heat or cold.

thermoregulation The maintenance of internal body temperature within a tolerable range.

theropod Member of an ancient group of dinosaurs that were bipedal carnivores.

thick filament A filament composed of staggered arrays of myosin molecules; a component of myofibrils in muscle fibers.

thigmomorphogenesis A response in plants to chronic mechanical stimulation, resulting from increased ethylene production. An example is thickening stems in response to strong winds.

thigmotropism (thig-mo′-truh-pizm) A directional growth of a plant in response to touch.

thin filament A filament consisting of two strands of actin and two strands of regulatory protein coiled around one another; a component of myofibrils in muscle fibers.

threatened species A species that is considered likely to become endangered in the foreseeable future.

threshold The potential that an excitable cell membrane must reach for an action potential to be initiated.

thrombus A fibrin-containing clot that forms in a blood vessel and blocks the flow of blood.

thylakoid (thī′-luh-koyd) A flattened membranous sac inside a chloroplast. Thylakoids exist in an interconnected system in the chloroplast and contain the molecular "machinery" used to convert light energy to chemical energy.

thymus (thī′-mus) A small organ in the thoracic cavity of vertebrates where maturation of T cells is completed.

thyroid gland An endocrine gland, located on the ventral surface of the trachea, that secretes two iodine-containing hormones, triiodothyronine (T_3) and thyroxine (T_4), as well as calcitonin.

thyroxine (T_4) One of two iodine-containing hormones that are secreted by the thyroid gland and that help regulate metabolism, development, and maturation in vertebrates.

Ti plasmid A plasmid of a tumor-inducing bacterium (the plant pathogen *Agrobacterium*) that integrates a segment of its DNA (T DNA) into a chromosome of a host plant. The Ti plasmid is frequently used as a vector for genetic engineering in plants.

tidal volume The volume of air a mammal inhales and exhales with each breath.

tight junction A type of intercellular junction in animal cells that prevents the leakage of material between cells.

tissue An integrated group of cells with a common function, structure, or both.

tissue system One or more tissues organized into a functional unit connecting the organs of a plant.

TLR Toll-like receptor. A membrane receptor on a phagocytic white blood cell that recognizes fragments of molecules common to a set of pathogens.

tonicity The ability of a solution surrounding a cell to cause that cell to gain or lose water.

top-down model A model of community organization in which predation influences community organization by controlling herbivore numbers, which in turn control plant or phytoplankton numbers, which in turn control nutrient levels; also called the trophic cascade model.

topoisomerase A protein that breaks, swivels, and rejoins DNA strands. During DNA replication, topoisomerase helps to relieve strain in the double helix ahead of the replication fork.

topsoil A mixture of particles derived from rock, living organisms, and decaying organic material (humus).

torpor A physiological state in which activity is low and metabolism decreases.

torsion In gastropods, a developmental process in which the visceral mass rotates up to 180°, causing the animal's anus and mantle cavity to be positioned above its head.

totipotent (tō′-tuh-pŏt′-ent) Describing a cell that can give rise to all parts of the embryo and adult, as well as extraembryonic membranes in species that have them.

trace element An element indispensable for life but required in extremely minute amounts.

trachea (trā′-kē-uh) The portion of the respiratory tract that passes from the larynx to the bronchi; also called the windpipe.

tracheal system In insects, a system of branched, air-filled tubes that extends throughout the body and carries oxygen directly to cells.

tracheid (trā′-kē-id) A long, tapered water-conducting cell found in the xylem of nearly all vascular plants. Functioning tracheids are no longer living.

trait Any detectable variant in a genetic character.

trans fat An unsaturated fat containing one or more *trans* double bonds.

transcription The synthesis of RNA using a DNA template.

transcription factor A regulatory protein that binds to DNA and affects transcription of specific genes.

transcription initiation complex The completed assembly of transcription factors and RNA polymerase bound to a promoter.

transcription unit A region of DNA that is transcribed into an RNA molecule.

transduction (1) A type of horizontal gene transfer in which phages (viruses) carry bacterial DNA from one host cell to another. (2) In cellular communication, the conversion of a signal from outside the cell to a form that can bring about a specific cellular response.

transfer cell In a plant, a companion cell with numerous ingrowths of its wall, which increase the cell's surface area and enhance the transfer of solutes between apoplast and symplast.

transfer RNA (tRNA) An RNA molecule that functions as an interpreter between nucleic acid and protein language by picking up specific amino acids and recognizing the appropriate codons in the mRNA.

transformation (1) The conversion of a normal animal cell to a cancerous cell. (2) A change in genotype and phenotype due to the assimilation of external DNA by a cell.

transgenic Pertaining to an organism whose genome contains a gene introduced from another organism of the same or a different species.

translation The synthesis of a polypeptide using the genetic information encoded in an mRNA molecule. There is a change of "language" from nucleotides to amino acids.

translocation (1) An aberration in chromosome structure resulting from attachment of a chromosomal fragment to a nonhomologous chromosome. (2) During protein synthesis, the third stage in the elongation cycle when the RNA carrying the growing polypeptide moves from the A site to the P site on the ribosome. (3) The transport of organic nutrients in the phloem of vascular plants.

transmission The passage of a nerve impulse along axons.

transmission electron microscope (TEM) A microscope that passes an electron beam through very thin sections and is primarily used to study the internal ultrastructure of cells.

transpiration The evaporative loss of water from a plant.

transport epithelium One or more layers of specialized epithelial cells that regulate solute movements.

transport protein A transmembrane protein that helps a certain substance or class of closely related substances to cross the membrane.

transport vesicle A tiny membranous sac in a cell's cytoplasm carrying molecules produced by the cell.

transposable element A segment of DNA that can move within the genome of a cell by means of a DNA or RNA intermediate; also called a transposable genetic element.

transposon A transposable element that moves within a genome by means of a DNA intermediate.

transverse (T) tubule An infolding of the plasma membrane of skeletal muscle cells.

triacylglycerol (trī-as′-ul-glis′-uh-rol) Three fatty acids linked to one glycerol molecule; also called a fat or a triglyceride.

triiodothyronine (T_3) (trī′-ī-ō′-dō-thī′-rō-nēn) One of two iodine-containing hormones that are secreted by the thyroid gland and that help regulate metabolism, development, and maturation in vertebrates.

trimester In human development, one of three 3-month-long periods of pregnancy.

triple response A plant growth maneuver in response to mechanical stress, involving slowing of stem elongation, a thickening of the stem, and a curvature that causes the stem to start growing horizontally.

triplet code A set of three-nucleotide-long words that specify the amino acids for polypeptide chains.

triploblastic Possessing three germ layers: the endoderm, mesoderm, and ectoderm. Most eumetazoans are triploblastic.

trisomic Referring to a diploid cell that has three copies of a particular chromosome instead of the normal two.

trochophore larva (trō′-kuh-fōr) Distinctive larval stage observed in some lophotrochozoan animals, including some annelids and molluscs.

trophic efficiency The percentage of production transferred from one trophic level to the next.

trophic structure The different feeding relationships in an ecosystem, which determine the route of energy flow and the pattern of chemical cycling.

trophoblast The outer epithelium of a mammalian blastocyst. It forms the fetal part of the placenta, supporting embryonic development but not forming part of the embryo proper.

tropic hormone A hormone that has another endocrine gland as a target.

tropical rain forest A terrestrial biome characterized by high levels of precipitation and high temperatures year-round.

tropics Latitudes between 23.5° north and south.

tropism A growth response that results in the curvature of whole plant organs toward or away from stimuli due to differential rates of cell elongation.

tropomyosin The regulatory protein that blocks the myosin-binding sites on actin molecules.

troponin complex The regulatory proteins that control the position of tropomyosin on the thin filament.

true-breeding Referring to plants that produce offspring of the same variety when they self-pollinate.

tubal ligation A means of sterilization in which a woman's two oviducts (fallopian tubes) are tied closed to prevent eggs from reaching the uterus. A segment of each oviduct is removed.

tube foot One of numerous extensions of an echinoderm's water vascular system. Tube feet function in locomotion, feeding, and gas exchange.

tumor-suppressor gene A gene whose protein product inhibits cell division, thereby preventing the uncontrolled cell growth that contributes to cancer.

tundra A terrestrial biome at the extreme limits of plant growth. At the northernmost limits, it is called arctic tundra, and at high altitudes, where plant forms are limited to low shrubby or matlike vegetation, it is called alpine tundra.

tunicate Member of the subphylum Urochordata, sessile marine chordates that lack a backbone.

turgid (ter′-jid) Swollen or distended, as in plant cells. (A walled cell becomes turgid if it has a greater solute concentration than its surroundings, resulting in entry of water.)

turgor pressure The force directed against a plant cell wall after the influx of water and swelling of the cell due to osmosis.

turnover The mixing of waters as a result of changing water-temperature profiles in a lake.

turnover time The time required to replace the standing crop of a population or group of populations (for example, of phytoplankton), calculated as the ratio of standing crop to production.

twin study A behavioral study in which researchers compare the behavior of identical twins raised apart with that of identical twins raised in the same household.

tympanic membrane Another name for the eardrum, the membrane between the outer and middle ear.

ultimate causation The evolutionary explanation of "why" a behavior (or other aspect of an organism's biology) occurs, that is, the benefit to survival and reproduction or the evolutionary significance of the behavioral act.

undernourishment A condition that results from a diet that consistently supplies less chemical energy than the body requires.

uniformitarianism The principle stating that mechanisms of change are constant over time. *See* catastrophism.

Unikonta (yū′-ni-kon′-tuh) One of five supergroups of eukaryotes proposed in a current hypothesis of the evolutionary history of eukaryotes. This clade, which is supported by studies of myosin proteins and DNA, consists of amoebozoans and opisthokonts. *See also* Excavata, Chromalveolata, Rhizaria, and Archaeplastida.

unsaturated fatty acid A fatty acid possessing one or more double bonds between the carbons in the hydrocarbon tail. Such bonding reduces the number of hydrogen atoms attached to the carbon skeleton.

urea A soluble nitrogenous waste produced in the liver by a metabolic cycle that combines ammonia with carbon dioxide.

ureter (yū-rē′-ter) A duct leading from the kidney to the urinary bladder.

urethra (yū-rē′-thruh) A tube that releases urine from the mammalian body near the vagina in females and through the penis in males; also serves in males as the exit tube for the reproductive system.

uric acid A product of protein and purine metabolism and the major nitrogenous waste product of insects, land snails, and many reptiles. Uric acid is relatively nontoxic and largely insoluble.

urinary bladder The pouch where urine is stored prior to elimination.

uterine cycle The changes that occur in the uterus during the reproductive cycle of the human female; also called the menstrual cycle.

uterus A female organ where eggs are fertilized and/or development of the young occurs.

utricle In the vertebrate ear, a chamber in the vestibule behind the oval window that opens into the three semicircular canals.

vaccination *See* immunization.

vaccine A harmless variant or derivative of a pathogen that stimulates a host's immune system to mount defenses against the pathogen.

vacuole (vak′-yū-ōl′) A membrane-bounded vesicle whose function varies in different kinds of cells.

vagina Part of the female reproductive system between the uterus and the outside opening; the birth canal in mammals. During copulation, the vagina accommodates the male's penis and receives sperm.

valence The bonding capacity of a given atom; usually equals the number of unpaired electrons required to complete the atom's outermost (valence) shell.

valence electron An electron in the outermost electron shell.

valence shell The outermost energy shell of an atom, containing the valence electrons involved in the chemical reactions of that atom.

van der Waals interactions Weak attractions between molecules or parts of molecules that result from localized charge fluctuations.

variation Differences between members of the same species.

vas deferens In mammals, the tube in the male reproductive system in which sperm travel from the epididymis to the urethra.

vasa recta The capillary system in the kidney that serves the loop of Henle.

vascular cambium A cylinder of meristematic tissue in woody plants that adds layers of secondary vascular tissue called secondary xylem (wood) and secondary phloem.

vascular plant A plant with vascular tissue. Vascular plants include all living plant species except mosses, liverworts, and hornworts.

vascular tissue Plant tissue consisting of cells joined into tubes that transport water and nutrients throughout the plant body.

vascular tissue system A transport system formed by xylem and phloem throughout a vascular plant. Xylem transports water and minerals; phloem transports sugars, the products of photosynthesis.

vasectomy The cutting and sealing of each vas deferens to prevent sperm from entering the urethra.

vasocongestion The filling of a tissue with blood, caused by increased blood flow through the arteries of that tissue.

vasoconstriction A decrease in the diameter of blood vessels caused by contraction of smooth muscles in the vessel walls.

vasodilation An increase in the diameter of blood vessels caused by relaxation of smooth muscles in the vessel walls.

vector An organism that transmits pathogens from one host to another.

vegetal pole The point at the end of an egg in the hemisphere where most yolk is concentrated; opposite of animal pole.

vegetative reproduction Cloning of plants by asexual means.

vein (1) In animals, a vessel that carries blood toward the heart. (2) In plants, a vascular bundle in a leaf.

ventilation The flow of air or water over a respiratory surface.

ventral Pertaining to the underside, or bottom, of an animal with bilateral symmetry.

ventricle (ven′-tri-kul) (1) A heart chamber that pumps blood out of the heart. (2) A space in the vertebrate brain, filled with cerebrospinal fluid.

venule (ven′-yūl) A vessel that conveys blood between a capillary bed and a vein.

vernalization The use of cold treatment to induce a plant to flower.

vertebrate A chordate animal with a backbone: the mammals, reptiles (including birds), amphibians, sharks and rays, ray-finned fishes, and lobe-fins.

vesicle (ves′-i-kul) A sac made of membrane in the cytoplasm.

vessel A continuous water-conducting micropipe found in most angiosperms and a few nonflowering vascular plants.

vessel element A short, wide water-conducting cell found in the xylem of most angiosperms and a few nonflowering vascular plants. Dead at maturity, vessel elements are aligned end to end to form micropipes called vessels.

vestigial structure A structure of marginal, if any, importance to an organism. Vestigial structures are historical remnants of structures that had important functions in ancestors.

villus (plural, **villi**) (1) A finger-like projection of the inner surface of the small intestine. (2) A finger-like projection of the chorion of the mammalian placenta. Large numbers of villi increase the surface areas of these organs.

viral envelope A membrane that cloaks the capsid that in turn encloses a viral genome.

viroid (vī′-royd) A plant pathogen consisting of a molecule of naked, circular RNA a few hundred nucleotides long.

virulent Describing a pathogen against which an organism has little specific defense.

virulent phage A phage that reproduces only by a lytic cycle.

visceral mass One of the three main parts of a mollusc; the part containing most of the internal organs. *See also* foot, mantle.

visible light That portion of the electromagnetic spectrum that can be detected as various colors by the human eye, ranging in wavelength from about 380 nm to about 750 nm.

vital capacity The maximum volume of air that a mammal can inhale and exhale with each breath.

vitamin An organic molecule required in the diet in very small amounts. Vitamins serve primarily as coenzymes or as parts of coenzymes.

vitreous humor The jellylike material that fills the posterior cavity of the vertebrate eye.

viviparous (vī-vip′-uh-rus) Referring to a type of development in which the young are born alive after having been nourished in the uterus by blood from the placenta.

vocal cord One of a pair of bands of elastic tissue in the larynx. Air rushing past the tensed vocal cords makes them vibrate, producing sounds.

voltage-gated ion channel A specialized ion channel that opens or closes in response to changes in membrane potential.

vulva Collective term for the female external genitalia.

water potential (Ψ) The physical property predicting the direction in which water will flow, governed by solute concentration and applied pressure.

water vascular system A network of hydraulic canals unique to echinoderms that branches into extensions called tube feet, which function in locomotion, feeding, and gas exchange.

wavelength The distance between crests of waves, such as those of the electromagnetic spectrum.

wetland A habitat that is inundated by water at least some of the time and that supports plants adapted to water-saturated soil.

white matter Tracts of axons within the CNS.

wild type An individual with the phenotype most commonly observed in natural populations; also refers to the phenotype itself.

wilting The drooping of leaves and stems as a result of plant cells becoming flaccid.

wobble Flexibility in the base-pairing rules in which the nucleotide at the 5′ end of a tRNA anticodon can form hydrogen bonds with more than one kind of base in the third position (3′ end) of a codon.

xerophyte A plant adapted to an arid climate.

X-ray crystallography A technique that depends on the diffraction of an X-ray beam by the individual atoms of a crystallized molecule to study the three-dimensional structure of the molecule.

xylem (zī′-lum) Vascular plant tissue consisting mainly of tubular dead cells that conduct most of the water and minerals upward from the roots to the rest of the plant.

xylem sap The dilute solution of water and dissolved minerals carried through vessels and tracheids.

yeast Single-celled fungus that reproduces asexually by binary fission or by the pinching of small buds off a parent cell; some species exhibit cell fusion between different mating types.

yeast artificial chromosome (YAC) A cloning vector that combines the essentials of a eukaryotic chromosome—an origin for DNA replication, a centromere, and two telomeres—with foreign DNA.

yolk Nutrients stored in an egg.

yolk plug A group of large, nutrient-laden endodermal cells surrounded by the completed blastopore in an amphibian gastrula. These cells will be covered by ectoderm and end up inside the embryo.

yolk sac One of four extraembryonic membranes. It encloses the yolk in reptiles and is the first site of blood cell and circulatory system function.

zero population growth (ZPG) A period of stability in population size, when the per capita birth rate and death rate are equal.

zona pellucida The extracellular matrix surrounding a mammalian egg.

zone of polarizing activity (ZPA) A block of mesoderm located just under the ectoderm where the posterior side of a limb bud is attached to the body; required for proper pattern formation along the anterior-posterior axis of the limb.

zoned reserve An extensive region that includes areas relatively undisturbed by humans surrounded by areas that have been changed by human activity and are used for economic gain.

zoonotic pathogen A disease-causing agent that is transmitted to humans from other animals.

zoospore Flagellated spore found in chytrid fungi and some protists.

zygomycete (zī′-guh-mī′-sēt) Member of the fungal phylum Zygomycota, characterized by the formation of a sturdy structure called a zygosporangium during sexual reproduction.

zygosporangium (zī′-guh-spōr-an′-jē-um) In zygomycete fungi, a sturdy multinucleate structure in which karyogamy and meiosis occur.

zygote (zī′-gōt) The diploid product of the union of haploid gametes during fertilization; a fertilized egg.

Index

NOTE: A page number in regular type indicates where a topic is discussed in text (topic may also be in a figure on that page); a **bold** page number indicates where a term is bold and defined; an *f* following a page number indicates a figure (topic may also be discussed in text on that page); a *t* following a page number indicates a table (topic may also be discussed in text on that page).

Index

Index

Index

Index

Index

Index

Index

Index

Index

F

G

Index

Index

H

Index

Index

Index

Index

M

Index

Index

Index

O

Index

P

Index

Index

S

Index

Index

T

Index

Index